D1546399

WITHDRAWN

DEMOGRAPHIC SURVEY
OF THE
BRITISH COLONIAL EMPIRE

The Royal Institute of International Affairs is an unofficial body which promotes the scientific study of international questions and does not express opinions of its own. The opinions expressed in this publication are the responsibility of the author.

DEMOGRAPHIC SURVEY
OF THE
BRITISH COLONIAL EMPIRE

BY

R. R. KUCZYNSKI

VOLUME I
WEST AFRICA

AUGUSTUS M. KELLEY · PUBLISHERS
THE HARVESTER PRESS

First published 1948

(London: Oxford University Press, 1948)

Copyright Royal Institute of International Affairs

Reprinted 1977 by

AUGUSTUS M. KELLEY · PUBLISHERS

Fairfield, New Jersey 07006

ISBN 0 678 00740 3

and

THE HARVESTER PRESS LIMITED

(Publisher: John Spiers)

2 Stanford Terrace, Hassocks

Sussex, England

ISBN 0 85527 769 6

This reprint has been authorized by the Oxford University Press.

Library of Congress Cataloging in Publication Data
Kuczynski, Robert René, 1876-1947.
  Demographic survey of the British Colonial Empire.
  "Issued under the auspices of the Royal Institute of International Affairs."
  Reprint of the 1948-1953 ed. published by Oxford University Press, London.
  Includes bibliographies and indexes.
  CONTENTS: v. 1. West Africa. — v. 2. South Africa High Commission territories, East Africa, Mauritius and Seychelles. — v. 3. West Indian and American territories.
  1. Great Britain — Colonies — Population. I. Title.
HB3584.A1K8 1975   312'.09171'241   68-26540

PRINTED IN THE UNITED STATES OF AMERICA
by SENTRY PRESS, NEW YORK, N. Y. 10013
Bound by A. HOROWITZ & SON, CLIFTON, N. J.

PREFACE

EIGHT years ago I was asked by the Population Investigation Committee to prepare a Demographic Survey of the British Colonial Empire. I had shown in a small book *Colonial Populations* (1937) the inadequacy of existing colonial censuses and vital statistics, and one object of the Survey was to suggest improvements in the censuses to be taken in 1941. But in the spring of 1940, when the major part of the Survey was ready for the printer, colonial census plans were abandoned.

I had begun the Demographic Survey somewhat along the lines of *An Economic Survey of the Colonial Empire* published periodically by the Colonial Office. I envisaged a reference book covering in its first edition the period 1919–38, to be followed by further editions published every five years, each dealing with the most recent quinquennial period. But this scheme did not prove satisfactory. Demographic data are most scanty for the largest Colonies and most ample for the smallest. Although I gave in the case of the West Indies only totals for each Colony, and included figures for Provinces or Districts in the case of the various African Dependencies, the section dealing with West Africa, i.e., with about 40 per cent. of the population of the Colonial Empire, was much shorter than the section dealing with the West Indies which comprise 4 per cent. Therefore, when the urgency for publishing the Survey at an early date had vanished I extended its scope by discussing much more fully the demographic history and present position of the larger Colonies even where the *statistical* basis for such a discussion was slender. I also abandoned the principle of uniform treatment inasmuch as I added in every case such demographic information as bears on the special problems of the various territories. In its present form the Survey is rather a series of monographs, but I hope that (with the help of the indexes) it will at the same time prove its usefulness as a reference book.

A demographer who undertakes to survey the Colonial Empire is in a peculiar position. The basic material, in many cases, is too defective to permit the drawing of final conclusions. Numerous colonial officers are, of course, aware of the inadequacy of the population and vital statistics in the area with which they are concerned. But whether or not they are aware of this state of affairs, they cannot carry on without somehow forming an idea as to whether the population is growing, whether infant mortality is excessive, whether the incidence of specific diseases is increasing, &c. They are, moreover, expected to answer such questions in their annual reports. Where statistics are not available they have to rely on limited observations and general impressions. The demographer is, therefore, confronted by thousands of reports which submit as facts what are actually reasoned guesses. He finds over and over again a consensus of opinion without any real evidence to support this opinion.

A demographer surveying the Colonial Empire must, therefore, start

'from scratch'. I show first how the various official figures based on enumerations of the population, births and deaths records, sample surveys, &c. were obtained, and what conclusions have been drawn from the figures. In many cases these conclusions appear to be perfectly sound. But in many other cases they seem to me unacceptable, either because the basic data are obviously so defective as to be meaningless, or because the interpretation of the figures is intrinsically wrong. If, for example, in an African colony the birth-rate has risen in the course of the last ten years from 10 to 20 per thousand, the conclusion that fertility has increased seems to me quite unwarranted. The only conclusion which may safely be drawn is that ten years ago only a minority of the births were registered and that registration is still incomplete. If, for example, what is quite usual in colonial reports, a low proportion of children among the total population is taken as a proof that child mortality is high, this conclusion seems to me unacceptable because, other things being equal, a country with a high child mortality is bound to have a higher ratio of children to adults than a country with a low child mortality. A considerable portion of this Survey had, therefore, to be devoted to reinterpretation of the statistical data.

Where no figures are available I can deal only with opinions. This is particularly inconvenient in a field where the opinions of even the most competent observers so frequently prove to be wrong. There are mainly two reasons for this phenomenon. (1) Many observers lack the necessary sense for figures. To quote only one of the numerous examples to be found in this Survey: A Census Commissioner, who was an outstanding Administrative Officer, and the Senior Health Officer both wrote that 90 per cent. of the children died before reaching the age of six and many thereafter, and that at the same time the population was increasing rapidly owing to a large excess of births over deaths (they evidently did not realize that to maintain a population, with 90 per cent. children dying under six, the women must have on an average ten daughters even if none of the daughters surviving the sixth year of life die before the end of the child-bearing period). (2) To form a correct opinion on demographic matters without conclusive figures is well-nigh impossible because demographic facts are not obvious. To appraise fertility, morbidity, mortality, or migrations is about as difficult in most African Dependencies as to appraise the frequency of adultery in this country. If a Medical Officer has noted numerous cases of leprosy or sleeping-sickness in a given District his opinion on the incidence of those diseases in this District may be well founded. But until thorough and comprehensive surveys, hitherto never undertaken, have been carried out, his opinion on the incidence of the disease in the whole Colony is merely a guess. My comments on estimates not based on figures are necessarily more cautious and more scanty than those on statistical data. But the full reproduction of authoritative opinions will in any case, I trust, help the reader to realize the problems and to become aware of what we know and what we do not know.

The first volume of this Survey deals with West Africa, the second

volume with South and East Africa, the third volume with Europe and Asia, and the fourth volume with America, the Atlantic, and Oceania. The fourth volume also contains a synopsis of all the birth and death registration laws now in force.

I wish to express my thanks to the Carnegie Corporation, to the Colonial Development and Welfare Fund, and to the Population Investigation Committee for their generous financial grants which were used, in part, for securing clerical assistance and defraying other expenditure connected with the preparation of this Survey, and in part for subsidizing the publication. The publication itself I owe to the untiring efforts of the Royal Institute of International Affairs under whose auspices the work is appearing.

I thank also, most sincerely, the librarians of the Colonial Office, the Royal Empire Society, the London School of Hygiene and Tropical Medicine, and Rhodes House (Oxford) for their constant helpfulness.

Finally, I should point out that this Survey was nearing completion before I was appointed Demographic Adviser to the Colonial Office, that I did not use any material that is not accessible to other students, and that I am alone responsible for the contents.

R. R. KUCZYNSKI

LONDON
December 1946

CONTENTS

FIRST PART—WEST AFRICA

WEST AFRICA

CHAPTER I

INTRODUCTION

I. CENSUS-TAKING

FROM 1871 on,[1] censuses covering the whole or part of the territory were taken every ten years up to 1931 in the Gambia, in Lagos, and in the Colony of Sierra Leone. In the Gold Coast, a partial census was taken in 1891, and thereafter every ten years up to 1931; in some districts of Nigeria (outside Lagos) in 1911, 1921, and 1931. Finally, a census was taken in St. Mary's Island (Gambia) in 1944.

The censuses of 1891 and 1901 in the Gold Coast, the censuses of 1871 and 1881 in Lagos, and the census of 1871 in Sierra Leone were taken without special legal enactment. The censuses of 1871–1944 in the Gambia, the censuses of 1911 and 1921 in the Gold Coast, the censuses of 1891 and 1901 in Lagos, and the censuses of 1881–1931 in Sierra Leone were authorized by Ordinances *ad hoc*. The census of 1931 in the Gold Coast, the census of 1911 in Southern Nigeria (including Lagos), and the censuses of 1921 and 1931 in Nigeria (including Lagos) were taken in accordance with general Census Ordinances.[2]

With a few irrelevant exceptions, the censuses have all ascertained the *de facto* population and not the resident population.

The total cost of the censuses taken in 1931 (including in some cases counts[3] and estimates) was about £10,000, or 8s. for each 1,000 inhabitants. The expenditure, of course, varied much. In the Colony of Sierra Leone, where a complete census was taken, the cost per 1,000 inhabitants was £6. 1s. 6d.; in Nigeria, where the population was mostly arrived at by estimates, it amounted to 5s. 7d.

II. TOTAL POPULATION

Native Population. The population figures for the British Dependencies in West Africa vary considerably regarding their quality. Censuses of natives were taken only in St. Mary's Island, in urban areas of the Gold Coast and Togoland, in a few scattered areas of Nigeria, and in the Colony of Sierra Leone; they cover 4 per cent. of all natives. Counts were made

---

[1] For earlier censuses in St. Mary's Island (Gambia), Lagos, and the Colony of Sierra Leone see the respective chapters.

[2] For the text of the Ordinances governing the 1931 and 1944 censuses see the respective chapters.

[3] A census is an enumeration made by entering the name and particulars of each individual on a census form; a count is an enumeration made either without any forms or with collective forms in which are entered particulars of groups (for example, the population of a village).

WEST AFRICA

in the Protectorate of the Gambia and in the rural districts of the Gold Coast; they cover about 12 per cent. of all natives. For five-sixths of the total native population the figures are estimates, based in Nigeria on the tax rolls of adult males and in Sierra Leone on house-tax lists. While the whole of the Gambia and the Gold Coast and Togoland were covered by censuses or at least counts, such methods of obtaining population figures have so far been applied only to 3 per cent. of the natives of Nigeria and to 6 per cent. of the natives of Sierra Leone. But it is doubtful whether the counts in the Gambia yielded more accurate returns than the estimates in Nigeria.

TABLE 1. *Native Population ascertained by Censuses, Counts, and Estimates, British West Africa, 1931*

Dependencies	Census	Count	Estimate	Total
Gambia	14,096	185,150	—	199,246
Gold Coast and Togoland. .	383,471	2,776,915	—	3,160,386
Nigeria and Cameroons . .	566,760	—	19,355,969	19,922,729
Sierra Leone	98,907	—	1,667,790	1,766,697
Total	1,063,234	2,962,065	21,023,759	25,049,058

The total returned at the 1931 census in Nigeria (including the Cameroons) was 19,922,729. All one can safely say is that the population was probably not under 18,500,000 and not over 22,000,000. The total returned at the 1931 census in Sierra Leone was 1,766,697. The margin of error may be put here at ±200,000. For the Gambia the total was 199,246, and it may be assumed, I think, that it was actually not less than 180,000 and not more than 230,000. The most reliable figures are those for the Gold Coast (including Togoland). The population in 1931 was found to number 3,160,386. It was probably between 2,950,000 and 3,400,000. The total native population in the four Dependencies in 1931 was probably not less than 23,300,000 and probably not more than 27,400,000.

Estimates for 1940 are 20,820,000 for Nigeria (including Cameroons), 2,000,000 for Sierra Leone, 200,000 for the Gambia, and 3,960,000 for the Gold Coast (including Togoland). They would suggest a total increase of nearly 2,000,000 since 1931. The increase has probably been overstated for the Gold Coast (including Togoland) and Sierra Leone. The total native population of the four Dependencies may be put for 1940 between 24,500,000 and 29,000,000.

Non-Native Population. Since censuses of non-natives have been taken in every Dependency our knowledge of the number of Europeans and Asiatics, at least for census years, is more accurate than that of the number of natives.

In 1871 the total number of Europeans in the British Dependencies in West Africa was about 300. It increased to 2,000 in 1901, 5,000 in 1911, 6,500 in 1921, and 8,000 in 1931. At the outbreak of the Second World War it was apparently about 12,000.

In some Dependencies the number of Europeans has fluctuated very

much. It declined between 1921 and 1931 in the Gambia[1] from 260 to 217, and in Sierra Leone from 1,042 to 651. In the Gold Coast and Togoland it increased during the same period from 1,903 to 2,428. Taking these three Dependencies together the number of Europeans appears to have been practically the same in 1921 (3,205) and 1931 (3,296). In Nigeria and the Cameroons it increased from 3,325 in 1921 to about 4,640 in 1931; it exceeded 7,000 in 1938.

The numbers of Asiatics have been much smaller still. There were less than 500 in 1911, 1,000 in 1921, and 2,400 in 1931. In 1939 the number was about 3,000.

In 1931 the number of Asiatics was given as 57 in the Gambia, 630 in the Gold Coast and Togoland, 490 in Nigeria and the Cameroons, and 1,216 in Sierra Leone. Of these 2,393 Asiatics all but 181 were Syrians.

Thus, the proportion of non-natives has been negligible all the time. In 1939 it constituted only about 0·6 per 1,000.

Population density does not differ very much in the four Dependencies. There are about 40 inhabitants to the square mile in the Gold Coast (including Togoland), about 50 in the Gambia, about 55 in Nigeria (including Cameroons), and about 70 in Sierra Leone. Sparsely settled areas are not conspicuous. In the Southern Province of the Northern Territories of the Gold Coast there are only about 8 inhabitants to the square mile.

III. Composition of Native Population

Figures concerning the total number of males and females in 1931 have been published for each Dependency. The ratio of females to 100 males was stated to be 108 in Nigeria and Sierra Leone, 96 in the Gold Coast, and 90 in the Gambia. But all data except possibly those for the Gold Coast are quite uncertain.

Data concerning the number of boys, girls, men, and women in 1931 have been published for each Dependency. But even where the natives were actually counted, the distinction between children and adults was made by many enumerators in a more or less arbitrary manner. Even for the Gold Coast the figures are, therefore, not conclusive.

Data concerning the conjugal condition in 1931 have been published only for St. Mary's Island (Gambia) and a few selected districts of Northern Nigeria. Our knowledge in this field, therefore, is practically nil for British West Africa.

IV. Composition of Non-Native Population

The census statistics for the Gambia do not distinguish between natives and non-natives. For the Gold Coast, Nigeria, and Sierra Leone the non-native population is shown by race, nationality, sex, and age, in Nigeria and Sierra Leone also by birthplace, in the Gold Coast and Sierra Leone also by conjugal condition.

---

[1] The figures for the Gambia refer only to St. Mary's Island. The census statistics do not mention any non-natives in the Protectorate, although some Europeans and some Syrians were living there.

TABLE 2. *European Population by Nationality, British West Africa, 1931*

Dependencies	British	French	German	Other	Total
Gambia	88	89	1	27	217[1]
Gold Coast and Togoland . . .	1,843	157	86	342	2,428
Nigeria and Cameroons[2] . . .	4,167	148	264	373	4,952
Sierra Leone	435	87	21	108	651
Total	6,533	481	372	850	8,248

[1] Including 12 not stated.
[2] Including 312 non-natives enumerated on ships in Lagos harbour.

TABLE 3. *Non-African Population by Sex, British West Africa, 1931[1]*

	Europeans			Asiatics		
Sex	Gold Coast and Togoland	Nigeria and Cameroons	Sierra Leone	Gold Coast and Togoland	Nigeria and Cameroons	Sierra Leone
Males . .	1,986	4,028	481	449	348	886
Females .	442	924	170	181	142	330
Females to 100 males.	22	23	35	40	41	37

[1] No figures are available for the Gambia.

TABLE 4. *European Officials, British West Africa, 31 December 1903–38[1]*

Year	Number	Year	Number	Year	Number	Year	Number	Year	Number	Year	Number
1903	1,398	1909	2,091	1915	2,794	1921	3,235	1927	3,758	1933	3,191
1904	1,461	1910	2,212	1916	2,618	1922	3,203	1928	4,150	1934	3,001
1905	1,524	1911	2,371	1917	2,634	1923	3,278	1929	4,314	1935	2,967
1906	1,586	1912	2,446	1918	2,305	1924	3,268	1930	4,266	1936	3,060
1907	1,670	1913	2,636	1919	2,467	1925	3,488	1931	3,901	1937	3,209
1908	1,932	1914	2,839	1920	2,906	1926	3,672	1932	3,367	1938	3,289

[1] See *West Africa, Vital Statistics of Non-Native Officials 1938*, p. 3.

TABLE 5. *European Officials by Sex and Age, British West Africa, 1930–38[1]*

Date 1 Jan.	20–24 Years M.	F.	25–29 Years M.	F.	30–34 Years M.	F.	35–39 Years M.	F.	40–44 Years M.	F.	45–49 Years M.	F.	50–54 Years M.	F.	55– Years M.	F.	Age unknown M.	F.	Total M.	F.
1930	224	6	819	29	945	45	831	36	692	19	433	12	182	1	38	1	24	2	4,188	151
1931	194	3	795	31	914	42	820	46	704	22	466	8	167	5	40	1	7	1	4,107	159
1932	126	2	717	26	801	35	785	45	672	24	431	9	184	7	29	—	3	—	3,748	148
1933	67	1	609	17	750	33	729	39	566	25	351	11	139	5	14	1	—	—	3,225	132
1934	45	—	522	19	728	35	682	36	557	24	354	14	128	7	15	1	—	—	3,031	136
1935	36	—	414	15	687	33	678	34	550	30	378	19	133	1	16	2	—	—	2,892	134
1936	41	—	349	16	661	29	675	32	564	36	398	19	142	1	8	1	—	—	2,838	134
1937	77	1	321	15	686	34	674	28	626	35	456	21	156	4	13	1	—	—	3,009	139
1938	97	—	351	20	649	31	699	27	654	32	441	19	171	2	16	—	—	—	3,078	131

[1] See *West Africa, Vital Statistics of Non-Native Officials 1930*, p.1, to *1938*, p.1.

Birthplace. Of the 651 Europeans enumerated in 1931 in Sierra Leone only 10 were born there; of the 1,216 Asiatics, however, 233. Of the

5,442 non-natives enumerated in Nigeria[1] only 100 were born there; they were, no doubt, mostly Asiatics.

The proportion of Europeans in the four Dependencies born in West Africa may be estimated for 1931 at about 1 per cent.

Nationality. Of the 8,248 Europeans enumerated in 1931, 6,533 or 79 per cent. were British, and 1,703 or 21 per cent. foreigners.

Sex. Among the Europeans enumerated in 1931 in the Gold Coast and Togoland, Nigeria and the Cameroons, and Sierra Leone, the ratio of females to 100 males was only 24. Among the Asiatics it was 39.

Age. The number of European children was only 10 in the Gold Coast, 40 in Nigeria and the Cameroons, and 17 in Sierra Leone. But there were 128 Asiatic children in the Gold Coast, 69 in Nigeria and the Cameroons, and 308 in Sierra Leone.

Conjugal Condition. Of the male adult non-natives enumerated in the Gold Coast (including Togoland) and Sierra Leone 51 per cent. were bachelors, 47 per cent. husbands, and 2 per cent. widowers and divorced. Of the female adult non-natives 21 per cent. were spinsters, 75 per cent. wives, and 4 per cent. widows and divorced. The ratio of wives to 100 husbands was only 41.

European Officials. Officials in the first three decades of this century constituted about one-half of the European population. After the retrenchment of the staffs in 1930–2 the proportion dropped to about 30 per cent. Figures concerning the distribution by quinquennial age groups have been published from 1930 on; the results are summarized in Table 5.

V. Birth and Death Registration

The Birth and Death Registration Ordinances enacted in the West African Dependencies provide compulsory registration of non-native births and deaths[2]. Compulsory registration of native births and deaths was introduced in the Colony of Sierra Leone in 1801, in the Colony of the Gambia in 1845, in Lagos in 1892, in a few other townships in Nigeria in 1926, and in selected towns of the Gold Coast in 1912. The area covered by compulsory registration has changed considerably in the course of time.

The 1801 Act of Sierra Leone applied to the whole Colony which then consisted of Freetown and Granville Town. But when, from 1808 on, great numbers of slaves captured at sea were imported and other villages were founded, registration was not extended to these new localities. This was done by an Act of 1832, but compulsory registration outside Freetown remained a dead letter and was abolished in 1906. It was reintroduced in 1913, and was extended in 1935 to nineteen health areas of the Protectorate, but this extension was repealed in 1942. To-day compulsory registration applies to births and deaths in the Colony only. It covers about 6 per cent. of the total population of Sierra Leone.

In the Gambia compulsory registration applied at first (1845) only to St. Mary's Island, was extended in the 1850s and 1860s to MacCarthy's

---

[1] Including 312 enumerated on ships in Lagos harbour.
[2] It was abolished, however, in 1942 in the Protectorate of Sierra Leone.

Island, Ceded Mile, and British Kombo, but was again confined in 1916 to St. Mary's Island. It covers about 7 per cent. of the total population of the Gambia.

In Nigeria compulsory registration applied at first (1892) only to the Town and Island of Lagos, but was extended in 1901 to the mainland portion of Lagos, and in 1908 to four neighbouring towns in which, however, it was not enforced. From 1926 on it has been established in a few townships outside Lagos Township. As regards non-native births and deaths registration is compulsory everywhere. Compulsory registration covers about 1 per cent. of the total population of Nigeria and the Cameroons.

In the Gold Coast compulsory registration was introduced in 1912 in 16 selected towns. By 1942 it was established in 41 towns (though statistics have been published only for 35 towns). For non-native births and deaths registration is compulsory everywhere. Compulsory registration covers about 9 per cent. of the total population of the Gold Coast and Togoland.

The Ordinance for the Gold Coast resembles in many respects the Ordinance for Nigeria, but the Ordinances for the Gambia and for Sierra Leone differ widely from those of the two larger Dependencies.

Notice of a birth has to be given to the Registrar in the Gambia by (1) the father, (2) the mother, (3) the occupier of the house in which the birth occurred; in the Gold Coast and in Nigeria by (1) the parent, (2) the person having charge of the child, and (3) the occupier of the house in which the birth occurred; in Sierra Leone by (1) the father and mother, (2) the occupier of the house in which the birth occurred, each person present at the birth, and the person having charge of the child.

The notification has to be made in the Gambia and in Sierra Leone within 14 days,[1] in the Gold Coast and in Nigeria within 21 days.

The birth registration forms in each Dependency call for date of birth, name and sex of child, names of parents, occupation of father, date of registration. The forms in all Dependencies except the Gambia ask in addition for the place of birth; the forms in the Gambia whether White, Black, or Mulatto; the forms in the Gold Coast for nationality of parents and religion of father; the forms for natives in Nigeria for the tribe of the parents and the age of the mother; the forms for non-natives in Nigeria for the nationality of the parents and the address of the father; the forms in Sierra Leone for the race of the parents.

Notice of a death has to be given to the Registrar in the Gambia by (1) the occupier of the house in which the death occurred, (2) the nearest neighbour of the deceased; in the Gold Coast and Nigeria by (1) the relatives of the deceased present at the death or in attendance during the last illness of the deceased, (2) every person present at the death, (3) the occupier of the house in which the death occurred, (4) the person causing the body of the deceased to be buried; in Sierra Leone by (1) the nearest relatives of the deceased present at the death or in attendance during the

[1] In the Gambia by the mother or the occupier of the house within one calendar month.

last illness of the deceased, (2) every other relative of the deceased dwelling or being in the same district as the deceased, (3) each person present at the death and the occupier of the house in which the death took place, (4) each inmate of such house and the person causing the body to be buried.

The notification has to be made in the Gambia within 14 days, in the Gold Coast within 24 hours, in Nigeria within 48 hours, in Sierra Leone within 3 days.

The death registration forms in each Dependency call for date of death, name, sex, age, occupation, cause of death, duration of illness, date of registration. The forms in all Dependencies except the Gambia ask in addition for the place of burial; the forms in Nigeria and Sierra Leone for name of certifying medical practitioner (if any) and place of death; the forms in the Gambia whether White, Black, or Mulatto; the forms in the Gold Coast for nationality and tribe, address, religion, residence at death, period of continuous residence in registration area, last place of residence before arrival in registration area; the forms for natives in Nigeria for nationality or tribe, place of birth, usual place of residence, period of continuous residence in registration area, last place of residence before arrival in registration area; the forms for non-natives in Nigeria for place of death, nationality, abode; the forms in Sierra Leone for abode.

The maximum penalty for failing to register a birth or death is:

£20 in the Gold Coast,

£5 in the Gambia and Sierra Leone,[1]

£2 in Nigeria.

Registration of a birth or death, if effected in due time, is free of charge in each Dependency.

Registration of European births and deaths has probably been fairly complete in each Dependency during the last two decades. As regards Asiatics, there is little evidence to show to what extent registration has been enforced. Registration of native births is apparently more or less incomplete everywhere, though the position has improved somewhat in recent times. Registration of native deaths, on the whole, is more satisfactory, but is still quite defective in a considerable number of registration districts. The Principal Registrar of the Gold Coast said in his most recent report. 'Birth and death registration are still in their infancy in the Gold Coast . . . .' In the other Dependencies they are still embryos.

I have dealt so far only with registration imposed by the British Administration. Attempts to compile current birth and death records through Native Authorities were made in the Gambia and in Nigeria. In 1907 the Chiefs and Headmen in the Protectorate of the Gambia were given books in which they were to enter all births and deaths that occurred. In the first year the records covered apparently the whole Protectorate, but in 1908 and 1909 only three of the five Provinces were included, and in 1910 only two. There is no evidence that the experiment was carried

---

[1] In Sierra Leone only the parent neglecting to register a child and the nearest relatives neglecting to register a death are liable to a penalty.

on after 1910. In Northern Nigeria registration was introduced in a few
places by Native Authorities in the first quarter of this century. From
1925 to 1930 efforts were made to expand registration over large parts of
Northern Nigeria, and to establish it also in some places in Southern
Nigeria. Statistics prepared in 1931–2 for Northern Nigeria suggest that
while many records were quite inadequate, registration was by no means
a failure everywhere. Unfortunately the administration lost interest in
these activities of the Native Authorities, and has not published any
more recent data.

Finally, Native Authority Ordinances enacted in some Dependencies
have granted to such authorities the power to prescribe the reporting of
births and deaths occurring within their jurisdiction. But only a few
Orders have been issued, and no figures whatever have been published.

Attempts to supplement the scanty registration returns by demographic
surveys have been made in the Gold Coast, Nigeria, and Sierra Leone.
These consisted mainly in asking a small number of women how many
children they had borne, and how many of these children had died. A
more elaborate 'Medical Census' was taken in 1930–2 in Nigeria, but it
covered only 1 per 1,000 of the population.

VI. NATIVE FERTILITY, MORTALITY, AND POPULATION GROWTH

Fertility. The figures of registered births indicate that fertility is fairly
high in urban areas of the Gold Coast, but not so in the few towns of the
other Dependencies for which data are available. The sample surveys
(which include rural districts) suggest that in the first quarter of this
century fertility was moderately high in the Gold Coast, but low in
Nigeria and Sierra Leone. Venereal diseases are apparently less common
in the Gold Coast. However, the available data on fertility and on the
incidence of venereal diseases are so scanty and so uncertain that it is
impossible to draw any final conclusions. It should be borne in mind,
moreover, that nothing is known concerning fertility in rural areas for
the last two decades. But in view of the numerous reports of Medical
Officers that according to their (of course very limited) observations
syphilis is a frequent cause of still-birth, and gonorrhoea a frequent cause
of sterility, and that the space between two children is rarely less than
two or three years, there would, I think, be no justification for assuming
that fertility of native women is higher than it was in England 60 years
ago, and it may well be lower.

General Mortality. Data concerning mortality are more scanty still than
those concerning fertility, as the sample surveys covered births and child
deaths but did not inquire into the mortality of adults. On the other
hand, death registration, as a rule, is more complete than birth registration.
The available figures, it seems to me, permit the drawing of the following
tentative conclusions. In Bathurst (Gambia) mortality has never been
excessive since the influenza epidemic of 1918, but has been high all the
time. In the urban areas of the Gold Coast mortality of the resident
population is not high, but is appalling among the numerous natives who

come to work in the towns. In Lagos mortality has been considerably less in the last 30 years than in the first 40 years of British occupation; plague, it is true, in the 1920s proved at least as disastrous as smallpox in the earlier period, but since 1928 mortality, as a whole, has been fairly low. In Freetown mortality has likewise declined but is apparently still high.

It might have been expected, perhaps, that mortality of natives would be lower in towns founded by Europeans, and the fight against tropical diseases was in fact carried on there more intensely than in purely native towns. But, on the other hand, Europeans, unlike natives, often selected particularly unsuitable locations for settlements, and after having discovered their mistake were afraid of the financial sacrifices involved in either improving effectively the sanitary conditions or moving the settlements to more healthy places. Bathurst and Freetown are outstanding examples. Five years after the foundation of Bathurst (1816) Major William Gray pointed out that it might 'be impossible to remedy the present evil in any other way than raising the level of the surface, a work that would be attended with considerable expense and difficulty'. After another five years the Commissioners of Inquiry into the State of Sierra Leone said:

Attempts have been made, by drainage, to overcome this evil in the immediate vicinity of the town, but the means hitherto employed have proved totally inadequate; and it is greatly to be feared that any effectual corrective must be attended with much labour and great expense. . . . It is therefore a subject of regret that Barra Point had not in the first instance been selected for the settlement, instead of St. Mary's. The advantage which the latter place possesses as a roadstead is by no means sufficient to compensate for its disadvantages in other respects, or for the poverty of the soil and badness of the water.

More than a century later the Medical Reports for the Gambia still said:

1935. Until Bathurst is raised to allow of adequate free drainage health conditions can never be good. It is useless to complete cures and return patients to an environment which means almost certainly a recurrence of their disease.

1937. No sanitary regime, no matter how well supervised, can hope to eliminate mosquito borne diseases till such time as proper drainage of the town can be provided and this cannot be done till the centre of the township is raised to a higher level than its periphery.

In rural districts mortality probably at first decreased after the establishment of British administration, owing to the abolition of slave-raids and intertribal wars. Some diseases which were imported by Europeans or which spread over wider areas as a consequence of the opening up of communications, the greater security in travelling, and the creation of new labour markets retarded progress, but the expansion of medical and sanitary services in the decade preceding the First World War rightly raised hopes that in the course of another generation mortality would be considerably reduced. That these expectations were not fulfilled was, I think, due mainly to the fact that the medical and sanitary staffs were

depleted during the First World War and have not been adequately
replenished and supplemented since. During the war hardly more than
the most urgent routine work was performed, and the fight against the
spread of smallpox and sleeping-sickness had to be abandoned. Half a
million people may have died from influenza in the autumn of 1918
without medical attendance. After the war financial considerations and
the difficulties of securing adequate personnel prevented any progress.
In 1924, when plague raged in Lagos and the most severe epidemics of
cerebrospinal meningitis and relapsing fever killed hundreds of thousands
of natives, 34 of the 92 posts for Medical Officers in Nigeria were vacant,
and economy was apparently stricter still in sanitary matters. The
position improved somewhat in the latter half of the 1920s, but a new
setback occurred during the economic crisis, and at the outbreak of the
Second World War the ratio of Medical Officers to the population was
rather smaller than 25 years earlier. This war brought again a reduction
in the medical and sanitary staffs.

In order rightly to appraise the situation it must be realized that the
number of Medical and Sanitary Officers should have increased considerably in order to prove as effective as 30 years ago. The development of
mining and other labour centres, where an ever-increasing number of
ill-nourished natives are exposed to infection and to physical exhaustion,
made it necessary to concentrate the staff at such places. Even if it had
been possible to maintain the same number of Medical Officers in the
other districts, they could not have coped with the ever-mounting
difficulties caused by returning labourers who spread diseases in their
home villages. Greater mobility necessitates, for example, more vaccinations against smallpox. With a sedentary population vaccination of one-
quarter of the people may prove of very great benefit; among a mobile
population smallpox may work havoc even if one-half are vaccinated.
A knowledge of all important sleeping-sickness foci is much more imperative to-day than it was a generation ago. Yet, owing to the lack of medical
staff, our knowledge of the spread of sleeping-sickness and other diseases,
such as leprosy, is infinitesimal in British West Africa. The expenditure
on medical services varies considerably in the various Dependencies. It
is, for example, 5d. per head per year in Nigeria (which comprises more
than three-quarters of all natives of British West Africa), and it amounts
to about 2s. per head in the Gold Coast. Medical and sanitary care in
some urban areas of the Gold Coast is fairly advanced, but in the rest of
the country conditions are probably not better than in Nigeria, and the
ignorance of the spread of, say, sleeping-sickness and leprosy is rather
greater in the Gold Coast.[1] Even serious epidemics occurring here not

---

[1] The Medical Report for 1931–2 stated concerning sleeping-sickness: 'There is no evidence that
the incidence of the disease or the severity of the type justify the diversion of funds utilised at the
moment for the control of malaria, yellow fever, diseases of the alimentary tract, and so on.' It
may seem amazing that as recently as 1932 there was no evidence of the high incidence of sleeping-
sickness in the Gold Coast. But as the Parliamentary Under-Secretary of State for the Colonies
Ormsby-Gore rightly said: 'More statistical evidence regarding the incidence of various diseases
and their relative importance in the life of peoples is urgently required. Without such data it is

far from the places where the Medical Officers are stationed escape their notice.[1]

It is very difficult, therefore, to say anything definite about the trend of mortality. The opinion of Medical Officers concerning the state of health and the incidence of diseases in the various Dependencies has become more unfavourable in the course of time. But this is no conclusive proof that morbidity and mortality have increased. Formerly most Medical Officers thought that, apart from periods of famines or acute food-shortage, the natives were on the whole adequately fed. To-day there is a consensus of opinion that the vast majority of natives are ill-nourished. It is quite possible that malnutrition has increased in the course of time. But the main cause of the change of opinion probably is that in recent years Medical Officers have paid more attention to dietetic questions. Formerly natives were believed to be practically immune against yellow fever. This belief has been shattered, but the number of authentic cases of this disease being contracted by natives in British West Africa is so small that the menace may be slighter than is now assumed. The Medical Report of the Gold Coast for 1930–1 still said: 'Judging from the incidence and death-rates during the past few years, trypanosomiasis would not appear to give cause for any anxiety in the Gold Coast.' The report for 1932–3 stated that 'a rapid increase which has taken place in the number of cases of Sleeping Sickness seen in the Northern Territories and Ashanti is causing anxiety'. New important foci were discovered in subsequent years. It may well be that part of the enormous increase in the number of cases ascertained was genuine. 'When the wholesale clearance of forest for cocoa and food farms is realised, it will be readily appreciated that conditions are becoming rapidly more favourable for the breeding of the fly vector.' But there cannot be any doubt that the rise was largely due to the more intense search for cases on the part of Medical Officers and to the growing inclination of infected natives to consult European doctors.

The following are a few quite tentative conclusions concerning the trend of the incidence of some important diseases.

Malaria, though not very frequently a direct cause of death, continues to be the most important general factor adversely affecting the health of natives in all British West African Dependencies. It is probably as common to-day as in former times.

Smallpox has caused great ravages in the Gambia and in Nigeria, while there is no evidence that in the Gold Coast or Sierra Leone it has claimed an excessive number of victims at any time. The incidence is smaller to-day than in former times both in the Gold Coast and in Southern

---

very difficult for those responsible for the direction of medical effort to make the best use of the staff and funds at their disposal.' (*Report on His Visit to West Africa during the Year 1926*, p. 71.)

[1] Even if Medical Officers are on the spot, their estimates of the numbers of cases and deaths are frequently wide of the mark. More often still their statements are so vague that it is absolutely impossible to form an opinion on the seriousness of the epidemic. Thus, the Medical Report of 1937 for the Gambia said regarding smallpox: 'An outbreak, involving practically the whole of the Protectorate, occurred during March to June. Totals of cases and deaths are not available owing to the wide spread nature of the epidemic.'

Nigeria. Whether it has decreased essentially in the other territories is doubtful.[1]

Tuberculosis is apparently increasing, and has become an important cause of death in many districts.

Sleeping-sickness has apparently been controlled in some small areas but has spread elsewhere. The incidence, on the whole, has not decreased; whether it has increased very much it is impossible to tell.

Leprosy has apparently not decreased in any Dependency, and there are reasons to assume that it has been increasing in Southern Nigeria. It is probably safe to say that more than 1 per cent. of the population of British West Africa is suffering from this disease, but it is impossible to estimate the actual proportion.[2]

Since 1939 the restrictions of medical activities (including the fight against sleeping-sickness, leprosy, and other diseases), which are due not only to the release of staff for military service but also to 'war economy', and the greater mobility and food shortages have apparently increased morbidity.

Infant Mortality. It has been believed for a very long time, and it is still taken for granted, that infant mortality is excessive in rural districts. There is no statistical evidence to support this view, and it seems safe to assume that the quite usual estimates of an infant mortality rate of 400 or more are too high. In urban areas infant mortality was likewise considered to be excessive in former times, but the enormous decrease in the ratio of registered infant deaths to registered births has led to the belief that infant mortality has decreased enormously, the main cause being intense welfare work. There cannot, however, be the least doubt that the early official infant mortality rates were defective owing to incomplete registration of births. Some improvement has certainly been achieved in a number of towns, but this improvement has been overstated considerably. Infant mortality is still high in most urban areas, but it is not excessive.

[1] Seventy-five years ago Dr. James Africanus Horton (*West African Countries*, pp. 227–8) urged 'the Necessity of Introducing by the Legislature a Strict Vaccination Act, for the Purpose of Protecting the Community against the Yearly Ravages of Small-pox'.

'The prevalence of small-pox every year in Sierra Leone, and in the other Colonies in Western Africa, should be an immediate incentive for the Government to interfere and introduce a remedy to an evil which vitally affects the public health. The prevalence of the disease is most discreditable to those who can prevent it, since it is well known that the remedy—viz., vaccination—is "specific and infallible". The protection is only temporary and limited, it is true, but during the time it lasts it completely protects the system. . . .

'In places like the Colonies of Western Africa this can only be established by a Government, who should make it compulsory on everyone to have the operation performed. I should, therefore, urge upon the authorities the appointment of properly paid vaccinators, both for vaccination and re-vaccination, as well as the appointment of inspectors of vaccination, who should make periodical inspections of the various districts, and report on the degree to which the operation has been performed, not only in districts, but also in individual cases. Every individual, parent, or guardian, who refuses to be or to have their child or ward vaccinated should be prosecuted by law.'

Unfortunately, Dr. Horton's demands have not been fulfilled in many areas of British West Africa.

[2] See in this connexion, for example, *Development and Welfare in the Gambia* (June 1943), chapter x, p. 21: 'Typical of the backward state of medical services in the Protectorate is the scanty knowledge available as to the incidence of leprosy in the Gambia.'

Population Growth. Towards the middle of the nineteenth century the question of population growth attracted much attention in the Gold Coast, but opinions were quite contradictory. The report on the *Blue Book* for 1846 expressed the belief that the population had increased very rapidly since 1830, and the report on the *Blue Book* for 1849 estimated the increase since 1846 at 5 per cent. The report for 1850 said that the population had not 'increased to the extent within the last quarter of a century which one had a right to expect', the main causes being polygamy and want of medical skill. The report for 1851 said that 'the numerical increase must be great, as there are no causes to diminish the numbers, excepting a decay of nature from old age'. The Medical Report for 1858 stated that 'the increase of population has not been in any degree commensurate with what might reasonably be expected' owing to infant mortality, polygamy, and the enormous consumption of spirits. If one may judge from the population estimates for the Gold Coast in the following decades, the population was assumed to have remained stationary.

Dr. Gouldsbury, Administrator of the Gambia, thought (1881) that 'the fact has never been sufficiently recognised that Africa, and especially the west coast of the continent, is but very meagrely populated'.

. . . in West Africa the population is not only very limited, but is, I believe, if not stationary, actually decreasing in numbers. At all events, I am convinced that there is no natural increment of increase as there is in other countries, but whether this be due to the practice of polygamy, to the frequent wars which desolate the country, or to the enormous infant mortality which undoubtedly occurs, it is not easy to decide.

The probability is that all combine in the causation of a standstill or diminishing population, but of the three factors I believe the last, viz., infant mortality, to be the most active.[1]

Shortly after the constitution of the Protectorate of Northern Nigeria (1 January 1900) the *Colonial Office List* said: 'The Protectorate includes the Foulah Empire . . . . The Hausa States of the Foulah Empire . . . are said to have the densest population of any country in the whole African Continent—estimated at 30 millions.' But Sir F. Lugard, who had taken over the administration from the Royal Niger Company, was convinced that Northern Nigeria was a country depopulated by slave-raids. He accepted Barth's estimate of from 30 to 50 millions as correct for the time when it was made (1854) and said that the population 'had by 1900 dwindled to some 9 millions'. In 1903 he expressed the opinion that as slave-raiding 'is now a thing of the past . . . the population . . . will now increase rapidly'.[2] Two years later he wrote that the population 'is no doubt increasing rapidly, both by immigration and by natural causes; but, on the other hand, the epidemics of cerebral fever and small-pox, and the severe famines of 1902–04, together with the terribly high rate of infant mortality, have counteracted the increase which might otherwise have been expected'. Epidemics of cerebrospinal meningitis and smallpox, and famines, claimed many victims also in subsequent years, and a large

[1] *Correspondence relating to the Expedition to the Upper Gambia*, p. 34.
[2] Lugard, 'Northern Nigeria', p. 18.

number of people died from influenza in 1918. In the following year Sir F. Lugard estimated the population of Northern Nigeria at 9 millions as in 1900. After another six years he said that 'there seems to be little doubt that since the partition of Tropical Africa between the European Powers the native populations in most territories have not increased and have probably decreased'.[1]

A knowledge of the causes which have led to a decrease in the population is of such great importance that local administrators should be invited to record their views and any statistics at their disposal on the following points, *inter alia*:

(*a*) Does the employment of natives on wage-labour detached from their community tend to increase mortality? If so, is this due to change of climate and unaccustomed food or to the spread of new diseases (tuberculosis, venereal, &c.) or to unaccustomed license (whether sexual or in the consumption of alcohol or otherwise), due to the absence of tribal restraints?

(*b*) If wage-labour is considered to be a contributory cause, is the demand made upon the present generation too great? In other words, does material development outrun the capacity of a primitive people to meet the strain, and how best can a solution be found?

(*c*) What other causes, apart from wage-labour, contribute to a decrease of population—such as infant mortality, lack of interest in life, freedom of intercommunication and consequent spread of disease, insufficient land, relegation to reserves, &c.?[2]

He gave as his own opinion:

The astonishing lack of inhabitants, though the races of Africa are virile and prolific, has been due in the past to intertribal warfare, slave-raiding, and the ravages of unchecked epidemics—especially sleeping-sickness and smallpox,—in more recent times to the prevalence of venereal disease, with its attendant infant mortality, and to the dissemination of diseases by freedom of communications.[3]

As regards British West Africa it should be realized first of all that it is much more densely populated than the West African countries under the administration of other European Powers. The number of inhabitants per square mile in British West Africa is about 50 as compared with about 7 in French and in Portuguese West Africa, and about 11 in Belgian West Africa. British West Africa, which covers one-tenth of the area of West Africa, comprises two-fifths of its population. There is not the least doubt that many territories in West Africa had a larger population before the advent of European slave-traders than they have now, but it is doubtful whether British West Africa as a whole had at any time many more than 50 inhabitants per square mile. The population probably remained

---

[1] Lugard, 'Economic Development of Mandated Territories in its Relation to the Well-Being of the Natives', p. 194.

[2] Ibid., pp. 196–7. It is interesting to note that exactly 100 years earlier the geographer James Macqueen wrote with regard to Sierra Leone and Jamaica: 'The cause, I believe, which occasions the decrease in both, is the same in every country, as it has been the same in every age. In settling and controlling the savage or fierce barbarian, under the sway of civilized life and manners, under whatever name the power which is to effect it is applied, the change will produce, for a considerable time, a decrease of the species. To them every yoke is slavery. Deprived of his *natural* liberty, the savage and barbarian sink into a state of torpor, indolence and decay, and generations elapse before their progeny, at first but feeble and few, become initiated into the manners of civilized life, get accustomed or inured to its labours and its industry, and become invigorated with that life and activity, which knowledge and civilization bestow.' (*Colonial Controversy*, p. 215.)

[3] Lugard, *The Dual Mandate in British Tropical Africa*, p. 66.

stationary during the first quarter of this century, but apparently increased somewhat in the course of the following 15 years. As regards the various Dependencies I have come to the following tentative conclusions:

For the Gambia there is no evidence that the population increased either before or after 1920.

For the Gold Coast and Togoland it is doubtful whether the population increased up to 1920, but it certainly has risen considerably thereafter, owing in part to natural increase, and in part to immigration.

The early population estimates for Northern Nigeria were grossly exaggerated. I doubt whether the population decreased very much in the second half of the nineteenth century. It probably did not increase in the first 25 years of British administration. From 1926 to 1940 it apparently grew somewhat, but it seems unlikely that the increase exceeded 10 per cent. In Southern Nigeria, with about 100 inhabitants per square mile, the population apparently increased considerably through immigration in the latter part of the nineteenth century, and it is now probably a little larger than at the beginning of this century.

In the Colony of Sierra Leone the population has increased through immigration. As regards the Protectorate any statement referring to the times prior to 1920 would be mere guessing. Since then the population of the Northern Provinces has apparently grown through natural increase, but the scanty available data do not suggest that the same has occurred in the Southern Provinces.

VII. Mortality of Europeans

In his first report on Northern Nigeria (1901) Sir F. Lugard said: 'Among the flood of literature which has lately been poured out on tropical diseases, the diseases of the natives seem to have been lost sight of.' This certainly is no longer true to-day. But all through the nineteenth century British literature on tropical diseases in West Africa focused on this territory as the White Man's Grave. Reports on European deaths were 'news' and often wrong news.[1] The actual number of deaths was of course always very small because the number of whites in British West Africa was always small, but the proportion of deaths was often excessive. The mortality of the 'Troops stationed at the different Settlements upon the West Coast of Africa' from 25 June 1810 to the end of 1825 was recorded as follows (see overleaf):[2]

The figures reveal an appalling mortality among European troops, though owing to the loss of records the data were incomplete. Mortality among civilians was lower, but all through the nineteenth century there occurred epidemics which in one or another Dependency carried off one-quarter or more of those who were not on leave. A yearly death-rate of

[1] The earliest example is possibly the following paragraph which appeared in *The Times*: 'Sir J— H—y stated, that in the spring of the year 1788 he had been at Sierra Leone, where he had touched in an East-India ship, and found the insalubrity of the climate such, that of one thousand seven hundred persons who had been there in the preceding year, only one remained ....' (Quoted from Hoare, *Memoirs of Granville Sharp*, p. 314.)

[2] See *Papers relating to Sierra Leone 1830*, pp. 90–3.

			Non-Commissioned Officers, Drummers, and Privates					
			Europeans			Africans		
	Officers		Joined during the year	Total number	Deaths	Joined during the year	Total number	Deaths
Year	Number	Deaths						
1810	28	1	149	657	77	—	—	—
1811	32	2	36	608	138	—	—	—
1812	34	3	741	911	330	—	90	—
1813	31	3	23	324	61	238	789	29
1814	36	4	141	417	79	216	850	50
1815	43	4	103	600	85	71	558	9
1816	45	4	8	497	114	394	556	20
1817	23	3	3	130	61	8	337	16
1818	20	2	14	81	38	—	312	7
1819	29	1	6	—	5	362	351	6
1820	25	5	—	20	—	84	349	10
1821	26	—	—	—	—	22	333	9
1822	38	4	—	—	—	296	571	16
1823	39	10	39	39	—	248	695	40
1824	41	26	283	346	303	255	496	33
1825	51	17	1,154	1,193	621	196	482	9

10 per cent. was not unusual, and a death-rate of 5 per cent. was considered favourable, although nearly all residents were between the ages of 18 and 50. The high mortality was generally attributed to unhealthy climate and to intemperance. But this explanation is quite inadequate. Excessive drinking, no doubt, was one of the reasons why deaths were more frequent among soldiers, and a number of officials and merchants undermined their strength by intemperance. But mortality was apparently not any lower among missionaries than among the rest of the community. As regards climate the Medical Report of the Gold Coast for 1917 said:

A study of the Gold Coast Annual Medical and Sanitary Reports issued during the last years of the pre-mosquito period indicate that the belief was generally held that the health of the population was largely dependent upon the meteorological conditions. . . .

It is not surprising, therefore, to find that since the diseases that were so often fatal were believed to be due to climatic conditions it became customary to describe the climate as unhealthy, nor, as it is little more than 20 years since the discovery that many of the diseases formerly believed to be climatic were insect-borne, is it to be wondered at that the climate is so spoken of by the laity of this day.[1]

It should be noted, however, that the laity was not the only one to commit this error. Official reports from Sierra Leone in 1927, as 40 years earlier, distinguished between 'climatic' and other deaths.

The excessive mortality of Europeans in the nineteenth century was, I think, mainly due to inadequate knowledge of how to prevent and how to cure tropical diseases, but an important contributing factor was the choice of entirely unsuitable locations for European settlements mentioned above. Dr. Henry Strachan, Chief Medical Officer for Lagos, when asked in 1900 by the African Trade Section of the Liverpool Chamber of Commerce to offer suggestions as to what action should be taken to improve,

[1] Gold Coast, Medical and Sanitary Report for the Year 1917, pp. 11–12.

if possible, the living conditions of Europeans in British West Africa 'in order that the terrible amount of illness and death may be reduced', submitted a paper in which he said:

... the sites of the European towns are, for the most part, far from being suitable for the erection of collections of dwellings. Speaking generally, they are to be found on a low-lying sea coast, and either on or near swamps, lagoons, or river estuaries. The houses of Europeans are, as often as not, in close proximity to the native huts, or even actually among them . . . .

No doubt the selection of these unsuitable sites for towns was forced on the pioneers of commerce by circumstances relating to trade and defence, some of which, owing to railways, and telegraph and telephone lines, have not all of their old importance; but, as that acute observer, the late Miss Kingsley, points out in one of her books on West Africa, when once the Englishman has planted himself, even if it be on the margin of some foetid swamp, nothing seems able to move him from the place,[1] even, I may add, if there is a more suitable site within a reasonable distance.

Be this as it may, the simplest and most rapid solution of most of the difficulties which now confront the sanitary reformer in many important African towns would be the removal of the latter to new sites, where good water supply and proper drainage could be secured, and where the soil could produce the fruit and vegetables so necessary for health, and could support a breed of cattle and sheep capable of yielding nourishing meat.

For of these three essentials of healthy living—pure water, good drainage, and good food supply—the first two are absent from most Coast towns, while the third is, in many, a matter of expensive importation.[2]

But the time at which Dr. Strachan wrote this paper was the turning-point in European mortality, and this sudden change came quite unexpectedly. The average death-rate of European officials in the Gold Coast in 1881–97 had been 76 per 1,000. That of non-officials had been apparently at least as high. In 1902 the death-rate of the whole European community was 31. In 1903 it dropped to 22. The Principal Medical Officer, who had considered the 1902 rate to be 'very satisfactory', was sceptical. He feared 'it is too much to hope that such a very low death rate will be maintained in all future years'. But the rate dropped in 1904 to 13, and never again reached the 'very satisfactory' level of 1902. There were, to be sure, still years in which tropical diseases claimed many victims. In 1910 the rate rose to 27, and of the 46 deaths that occurred 15 were due to malaria, 10 to blackwater fever, and 10 to yellow fever. But from 1912 on the rate exceeded 13 only in the influenza year 1918 when it jumped to nearly 31, and it has been below 10 in every year since 1923. European mortality has likewise decreased enormously in the other Dependencies.

There probably has never been in the history of mankind another case of such a gigantic reduction of mortality in so short a time. It has been generally attributed to sanitary measures against malaria and yellow fever, to improved methods of treatment of tropical diseases, and to

---

[1] It should, however, not be overlooked that the natives who died prematurely in these towns were many times as numerous as the Europeans. They went to live there either because they were forced to do so (the 'Liberated Africans') or in order to secure British protection and to gain a livelihood.

[2] Strachan, *Paper on the Health Conditions of West Africa*, p. 4.

segregation of European residential quarters. But the available data are far too scanty to permit a numerical appraisal of these and other factors which, no doubt, have contributed to the enormous change. As regards, for example, mortality from malaria it is impossible to estimate even approximately to what extent it has been lowered by a reduction of the incidence of the disease, and how much by the reduction of the proportion of fatal cases.

Considering, however, the qualitative improvements in medical care, it is probably safe to assume that mortality among Europeans has decreased more than has morbidity. The death-rate itself, low as it is compared with earlier rates and even with rates in European countries, should be treated with caution. Most white residents in West Africa are people who were declared physically fit by a doctor before embarkation; they belong to age groups with the lowest specific mortality rates; they are in a better economic position than the bulk of their countrymen in Europe; they frequently go on leave and recuperate their strength.

Table 6 shows mortality of officials including deaths occurring on leave.

TABLE 6. *Deaths and Death-rates of Non-Native Officials, British West Africa, 1903–38*[1]

Year	Deaths	Death-rate	Year	Deaths	Death-rate	Year	Deaths	Death-rate
1903	26	20·6	1915	38	13·5	1927	36	9·9
1904	39	27·3	1916	28	10·3	1928	27	6·7
1905	42	28·1	1917	38	14·4	1929	33	7·7
1906	33	21·2	1918	41	16·5	1930	23	5·3
1907	29	17·8	1919	30	12·5	1931	37	9·1
1908	32	17·7	1920	44	16·3	1932	13	3·6
1909	35	17·3	1921	37	12·0	1933	15	4·6
1910	44	20·4	1922	26	8·0	1934	20	6·5
1911	32	13·9	1923	38	11·7	1935	15	5·1
1912	30	12·4	1924	42	12·8	1936	27	9·4
1913	30	11·8	1925	41	12·1	1937	18	5·7
1914	35	12·7	1926	31	8·6	1938	29	8·9

[1] See *West Africa, Vital Statistics of Non-Native Officials 1921*, p. 3; *1938*, p. 3. Deaths exclude war casualties in 1914–18 (18, 34, 4, 95, and 41 respectively).

CHAPTER II

SIERRA LEONE[1]

I. CENSUS-TAKING

THE first census was taken in 1802.[2] It seems that the major part of the population was enumerated, but some figures were evidently obtained by estimate. On 9 March 1811 the following 'Bill to estimate the population of this Colony' was read and passed:

Whereas it is expedient, that a correct account should be taken of the Population of this Colony, all Householders, Lodgers, Tenants, and Inhabitants are hereby directed to give to the Officers who may be Appointed to take the same, a true return (when called upon) of the number of Men, Women and Children usually dwelling in their Houses, with all other particulars required by the said Officers.

And any House Keeper, Lodger, Tenant, or Inhabitant, refusing to make such a return, or giving a false Account, shall be liable to a fine not less than One shilling nor more than Six dollars, to be levied upon Conviction, before any two of His Majesty's Justices of the Peace.[3]

It is doubtful, however, whether the census taken in April 1811 covered the whole Colony. Figures have been published only for the 'Houses and Population within the Walls of Sierra Leone',[4] and even these figures evidently exclude the 'Liberated Africans' (captured slaves). Another census, again confined to Freetown and excluding the Liberated Africans, was taken in March 1817.[5] Censuses of the whole Colony were effected in 1818,[6]

---

[1] Sierra Leone consists of (1) the Peninsula of Sierra Leone, Tasso Island, Banana Islands, York Island, and the township of Bonthe in Sherbro Island, administered as strictly Colony; (2) the rest of the Colony (Sherbro Island except Bonthe township, Turtle and Plantain Islands and other small islets, the Bake Loko, Mafoki, and part of the Bure Chiefdoms in the Northern Province, the Bumpe, Kagboro-Bagru, Mano Bagru, Timdel, Bendu, Cha, Nonkoba Bullom, Messi Krim, and part of the Mano Sa Krim Chiefdoms in the Southern Province, and a strip of land varying in depth from a quarter of a mile to one mile throughout the coast line), administered as part of the Protectorate; and (3) the Protectorate. For census purposes Sierra Leone is subdivided into two areas only, the first corresponding to (1) and the second to (2) and (3). For the sake of convenience the procedure of the census has been followed here.

[2] See 'The Colony of Sierra Leone, Return of Settlers, Europeans, and Resident Strangers, in the said Colony; taken by Order of the Governor and Council, the 29th March 1802', *Report from Committee on Petition of Sierra Leone Company 1804*, p. 127. It is interesting to note that the 'Rules and Instructions from the Directors of the Sierra Leone Company to the Superintendent and Council for the Settlement' (reproduced in Evans, *An Early Constitution of Sierra Leone, pp. 13-77*), which were issued in 1791 or 1792, contained already the following Article (Evans, p. 73):

'The points on each of which we especially wish to have distinct intelligence, by the first regular communication, and on which you will not fail to write to us, are the following, and we beg you to quote each query on one side and to place your answer opposite it:

'10. What towns and what number of inhabitants in them or in villages are within our districts, and what are their occupations and descriptions severally.'

[3] Sierra Leone, *Acts 1800–27*, pp. 104–5.

[4] See *Report of Commissioners on Coast of Africa 1811*, p. 8.

[5] See *Missionary Register*, Aug. 1817, p. 355.

[6] The returns were published (1) in *The Royal Gazette and Sierra Leone Advertiser*, 27 Feb. 1819, p. 168; (2) in *Missionary Register*, Sept. 1819, p. 399, 'with a few slight corrections'; (3) in *Fourteenth Report of Directors of African Institution 1820*, Table facing p. 80; and (4) in *Accounts relating to the Duties, &c., Population, &c., of Sierra Leone*, 1825, pp. 13–15. (1), (3), and (4) are identical. In the *Missionary Register* (2) the figures entered for 'Natives, Servants or Apprentices' are those

1820[1], and 1822;[2] none of these censuses were authorized by special legislation, but the details published suggest that the enumerations were, on
the whole, fairly complete. On 17 June 1824 the House of Commons
accepted a Resolution requesting that another comprehensive census be
taken in the Colony, but the Colonial Secretary of Sierra Leone replied:

> The various duties which have occupied the attention of the Colonial Government,
> from the commencement of the present year, and particularly since the arrival of
> his Excellency General Turner, have prevented a Census being taken, which,
> however, it is the Governor's intention to have done immediately on his return
> from the Gold Coast.[3]

No further steps were taken until, in 1826, the Commissioners of Inquiry
came to the Colony.

One of the first objects to which the Commissioners directed their attention on
arriving at Sierra Leone, was, that of obtaining a correct census of the actual
population. With this view they addressed themselves to Major General Turner,
the late governor, who, although he represented the difficulties of the undertaking
with the inefficient means which he had at his disposal, readily engaged to make
the endeavour. But unfortunately the absence of the General in the Sherbro, and
his subsequent demise, retarded the undertaking, which was however commenced
by Mr. K. Macaulay, immediately upon his accession to the temporary administration of the government.

In a letter accompanying this census, the colonial secretary expresses an opinion
that the document, although faithfully copied from the several Returns, was, in
addition to its being incomplete, too incorrect in the numbers given to be relied
upon.[4] In proof of this he states, that in the Return from Leopold, the children
at school, and in that from Freetown, the liberated Africans employed in the public
works, are omitted. In addition to this, he doubts the probability of the total
number being correct, considering the increase that is known to have been made
by the captured negroes brought to the colony, as well as that supposed to have
taken place in the population (particularly in the class of strangers) since 1822,
when he thinks that the census was more correctly taken than in 1826.

If the census of 1826 be so defective as the secretary seems to think, it is doubtful
whether any of the preceding ones can be greatly relied upon; there exist, however,
no other means of forming any estimate of the increase or decrease of the population,
and therefore it has been endeavoured to complete the census of 1826 from other
documents.

The number of children at school in Leopold, and the captured negroes employed
in the works at Freetown, have been added to the other inhabitants at these places.

No statement having been received of the numbers at the village of Hastings,
these have been given from a Return furnished to the Commissioners by the superintendent of that place. The numbers for Wilberforce and Bathurst were also

entered in (1), (3), and (4) for 'Captured Negro Servants or Apprentices' and vice versa. The allocation in (1), (3), and (4) seems to me to be correct.

[1] The returns were published in (1) *General Census, 8 July 1820*, (2) in *Missionary Register*,
Sept. 1820, p. 381, and (3) in *Accounts*, 1825, pp. 16–18. (1) and (3) are identical and contain many
mistakes, both arithmetical and as regards the classification of the population. The returns as
shown in (2) seem to me to be correct.

[2] The returns were published in (1) 'Census, 1 Jan. 1822', *The Royal Gazette*, 10 Aug. 1822, p. 126,
and (2) in *Accounts*, 1825, pp. 19–21. The statements are identical.

[3] Ibid., 1825, p. 41.

[4] See also the following statement by the Colonial Secretary in the annual *Blue Book* for 1825,
p. 142: 'Population 1826. By the Census taken for the Commissioners of Enquiry in April &
May of this year, but which however I am convinced is so informal as not to be at all depended
upon, the population was as follows . . . .'

wanting, and have been supplied from the census of 1822, since which period they have probably not increased, for having both been long without superintendents, captured negroes have not latterly been sent to them.[1]

But at the same time 'the necessity of adopting the most effectual measures for the future control and instruction of the liberated Africans',[2] i.e. the numerous slaves captured at sea and settled in Sierra Leone, gave a new impetus to regular census-taking. According to Instructions issued on 16 November 1826 by the Lords Commissioners of His Majesty's Treasury,[3] quarterly accounts of Liberated Africans were to be made by the newly appointed General Superintendent of Liberated Africans. These Instructions were not carried out effectively,[4] but a new effort which aimed at an enumeration not only of the Liberated Africans but also of the rest of the population was made in 1831. In a Dispatch dated 30 July Lieutenant-Governor Findlay reported to Viscount Goderich, Principal Secretary of State for War and the Colonies:

In order to give your Lordship a correct view of the actual Numbers and State of the Liberated African Population settled in this Colony which could only be partially conveyed in the Returns suggested by the Lords Commissioners of His Majesty's Treasury, I have caused a complete Census to be again taken of every Individual present on the 30th Ult° within the several Districts under the Superintendence of the Liberated African Department, and which I have now the honor of transmitting. Those Documents having been verified upon Oath by the different local Managers of the Liberated African Department will I trust satisfy your Lordship of their accuracy.

The taking of the Census of the entire Population of Freetown and which will be the only correct one made since 1822, is now in progress, and would have accompanied this had the weather permitted the Officers appointed to that Duty to have devoted to it their constant attention; but by the next conveyance I hope to have it completed for transmission to your Lordship.[5]

Three months later, on 3 November, he transmitted 'a Copy of the Census of the Inhabitants of Freetown, taken during the last Quarter by Messrs McDonald and De Groft which they have sworn to as being correct according to the best of their knowledge and belief'.[6]

In the meantime alarming reports about the kidnapping and re-enslave-

---

[1] Report of the Commissioners of Inquiry into the State of Sierra Leone, First Part, p. 20.

[2] Dispatch from Earl Bathurst to Governor Major-General Sir Neil Campbell, 25 Nov. 1826, Papers relating to Sierra Leone 1830, p. 9.

[3] See ibid., p. 10.

[4] See ibid., pp. 35, 37. See also dispatch from Secretary Sir George Murray to Lieutenant Governor Major Ricketts, 4 July 1829 (C.O. 268, vol. xxviii, pp. 273–5):

'. . . I am surprised to find that for a long time past no quarterly Reports have been received of the State of the Liberated Africans—an omission which is so extraordinary that I can only account for it by supposing that Lieutenant Colonel Lumley was, and that you are ignorant of the Instructions which were given to Lieutenant Colonel Denham.

'I therefore transmit to you a copy of the Treasury letter of the 16 November 1826 pointing out the nature of the Quarterly Reports which as General Superintendent you consequently are bound to furnish . . . .

'The last Quarterly Report from Lieutenant Colonel Denham being dated in May 1827, it will be necessary that a connected Report should be transmitted to me without loss of time, for the purpose of being laid before Parliament early in the ensuing Session, of the subsequent transactions of the Liberated African Department, down to the present time.'

[5] C.O. 267, vol. cxi.

[6] Ibid.

ment of Liberated Africans had reached London, and on 18 January 1832 Viscount Goderich wrote to Lieutenant-Governor Findlay:

Another simple and effectual measure . . . would be, the holding of musters of all the liberated Africans in their different towns and villages, at stated intervals. Once for example in each quarter, or perhaps even more frequently. This is a regulation which might be established and enforced without any difficulty, and you will immediately take the necessary measures for carrying it into effect. The result will inevitably be, to furnish the Local Government with the most early and authentic intelligence of any diminution in the number of the liberated Africans, which may be occasioned by the operations of the Slave Traders.

An additional precaution of great importance will be found, in establishing by law a complete Annual Census of all the Inhabitants of the Colony; distinguishing of course the liberated Africans from other classes.[1]

Thereupon, at a Council held on 24 December 1832, the following Act was passed:[2]

Whereas it is expedient that a general census of the population of this colony should be taken annually, and that the same should be done at fixed periods, and that the measure should be established by law:

I. Be it therefore enacted by his Excellency the Lieutenant-Governor, by and with the advice and consent of the Council now assembled, and by the authority of the same it is hereby enacted, That all managers and superintendents of districts or parishes shall once in each and every year take an accurate estimate and account of the whole population contained in each district or parish under their charge, and according to the form contained in the Schedule (A.) hereunto annexed, keeping each district or parish distinct and separate; and shall deliver or cause to be delivered into the secretary's office all and every such estimate or estimates on or before the Thirty-first day of December in each and every year.

II. And be it further enacted by the authority aforesaid, That all such managers and superintendents do, within as short a period as possible after the passing of this Act, cause every house and hut within the district or districts under their charge to be numerically marked and distinguished.

III. And be it further enacted by the authority aforesaid, That an officer be appointed by the Governor or Lieutenant-Governor, whose duty it shall be to take an annual census, in form as aforesaid, of the whole of the population of the parish of Saint George, including Freetown; and to make up, between the First and Thirty-first days of January annually (according to the form contained in Schedule B.,) a general census of the whole population of this colony, comprising as well such officer's own return for the parish of Saint George as those of the said managers and superintendents for the several districts under their charge; and which general census he shall deliver or cause to be delivered to the clerk of the Council, together with his own particular census of the said parish of Saint George and those of the said managers for the several districts as aforesaid, on or before the First day of February in each and every year.

IV. And be it further enacted and enjoined by the authority aforesaid, That all householders, tenants, lodgers, and others, inhabitants of this colony, do give true and faithful answers to all questions touching such census as shall be put to them by the said officer; or in case such inhabitant residing out of the parish of Saint George, by the manager or superintendent of the district in which such inhabitant shall dwell, and to render him the said officer and them the said managers every assistance in their power in furtherance of the object of this Act.

[1] *Charge delivered by Chief Justice Jeffcott on the Subject of the Slave Trade, with Correspondence thereon*, pp. 39–40.
[2] 'An Act for taking an annual Census of the Population of the Colony of Sierra Leone', *Sierra Leone Acts 1811–48*; reprinted in *Ordinances of the Colony of Sierra Leone in Force 1857*, pp. 24–7.

V. And be it further enacted by the authority aforesaid, That every householder and other inhabitant of this colony who shall refuse to render such replies, or who shall wilfully answer incorrectly, or behave insolently or disrespectfully to any such officer, manager, or superintendent when engaged in taking such census, shall, upon summary conviction before any one magistrate (other than such officer, manager, or superintendent), forfeit and pay to His Majesty for every such offence any sum not exceeding forty shillings, and in default of payment thereof be committed to the common gaol or house of correction, there to be imprisoned for any period not exceeding thirty days.

VI. And be it further enacted by the authority aforesaid, That the forms contained in Schedules (A.) and (B.) hereunto annexed be printed and furnished to the said managers and to the officer aforesaid.

Schedule A was a most elaborate form. The headings were as follows:

No. of House or Lot.
Name of Principal Inhabitant.
Nation.
Names of Family: Wife, Husband, Sons, Daughters, Male Apprentices, Female Apprentices, Total Inhabitants living.
Births since last Census: Sons, Daughters, Total.
Apprentices taken since last Census: Males, Females, Total.
Ditto [Apprentices] Discharged Ditto [since last Census]: Males, Females, Total.
Deaths since last Census: Wife, Husband, Sons, Daughters, Male Apprentices, Female Apprentices, Total.
Apprentices run away or missing: Males, Females, Total.
Apprentices taken away by Superintendent: Males, Females, Total.
Remarks, Containing Causes for taking away of Apprentices and Marriage, &c. &c.

Schedule B had the following headings:

Name of principal Inhabitant.
District where residing.
Nation.
Family: Males, Females, Total.
Remarks.

Censuses were thereupon taken in nearly every year until and including 1851.[1] But the figures published suggest that, as a rule, not more than the sex and the 'nation' or colour were ascertained. The official comments on the accuracy of the censuses are not very illuminating, since there was, as usual, a tendency to consider a census as accurate when the returns were higher than at the preceding census, and to consider either the current or the preceding census as inaccurate when the reverse was true. For 1845–50 the returns were as follows:

	1845	1846	1847	1848	1849	1850
Residents . . .	43,622	41,735	45,006	45,320	43,881	44,472
Strangers . . .	1,316	1,395	655	1,191	2,528	1,000
Total . . .	44,938	43,130	45,661	46,511	46,409	45,472

The Reports on the annual Blue Books said:

1846. The census of the population of the colony for the year 1846 shows a decrease of nearly 3,000 souls compared with that for 1845.[2]

[1] No census, however, was taken in Freetown in 1837 and 1841.
[2] The decrease was actually only 1,808. Owing to an arithmetical error, the *Blue Book* for 1845 had given as total population 45,938 instead of 44,938.

I am, however, inclined to believe that there must have been some error in taking the census for 1846; for there has not been any cause during the year which would, in any way, account for so very marked a decrease.

Excepting during the years when emigration was carried on from this colony to the West Indies, I have found that the population of the colony remained pretty stationary, and that the births, on an average of years, equalled the deaths; and I think that the population of the colony may safely be stated at about 45,000 souls.

There has been no emigration from the colony during the past year, neither has there been any increase in the mortality, which would account for a decrease of 2,708 souls, on the contrary, there has been an importation of nearly 600 liberated Africans in the 'Paqueto de Rio,' . . . and the past year has been an extraordinarily healthy one. It is clear, therefore, that there must have been an error in taking the census; and that if there exists any difference in the population of the two years, it ought rather to be in favour of 1846.

It is extremely difficult to take the census here correctly. It cannot be taken, as in England, in one day. Here, it is the duty of one individual alone to be engaged between two and three months in visiting each house in the town, and taking down, as correctly as he can obtain it, the names of their occupants; and even with the greatest care errors will occur.

I shall, however, try to devise some mode, which will have the effect of rendering it less difficult than at present to take the census of the colony; and I hope to have a new plan adopted for taking that for this year (1847).[1]

1847. The total population of this colony, according to the census for 1847, is 45,006, which is an increase of about 2,000 as compared with 1846.[2] But, owing to the imperfect manner in which the Census is taken, its returns cannot be altogether depended upon.[3]

1848. I stated in my Report for 1847 that the returns of the census cannot be considered as absolutely correct. The taking of the census instead of being accomplished in a single day, as in England, occupies some weeks. I believe, however, that it gives a pretty close approximation to the number of the people.

These returns for 1848 give the following results: . . . Total population 46,511, showing an increase as compared with the returns for the preceding year of 1,505.[4]

1849–1850. The population . . . appears to have been as follows:—1849 . . . 46,369 . . . 1850 . . . 45,472, showing a decrease in the total population of the colony for the year 1850, as compared with its predecessor, of 897 souls.

That the amount of the population of the colony must fluctuate plus or minus each year is obvious; and my own experience would lead me to the conclusion that, of late years, and owing to emigration, the population here has decreased: but I do not think that so great a decrease as that shown by the foregoing figures has occurred in the two years under review, and which, I am of opinion, is owing to some clerical error in taking the census for 1849.[5]

Here, the performance of this duty is attended with difficulties unknown in civilized communities; and it is with the greatest trouble that the native population of the colony generally can be induced to give a correct return or statement to the Census Master of the numbers of which their families are composed: they cannot comprehend why the information should be required, and they are therefore ex-

[1] Governor Macdonald, 13 May 1847, State of Colonial Possessions 1846, p. 138.

[2] The Acting-Governor compared by mistake the resident population of 1847 (45,006) with the total population of 1846 (43,130). The resident population had increased by 3,271 and the total population by 2,531.

[3] Acting-Governor Pine, 27 Oct. 1848, State of Colonial Possessions 1847, p. 198.

[4] Same, 2 Nov. 1849, ibid. 1848, p. 304. The Acting-Governor compared by mistake the total population of 1848 with the resident population of 1847. The total population had increased by 850, and the resident population by 314.

[5] I see no reason to assume that such clerical error was made. The decrease in the total population was due to the fact that the number of strangers which for 1849 was returned as 2,528 was estimated for 1850 at 1,000. The resident population had increased by 591.

tremely suspicious at its being sought for, and always afford it reluctantly, and, in many instances, incorrectly. And at present, with the very imperfect means at the disposal of the local government, and the difficulties raised by the native population, it is next to an impossibility that so voluminous a return can be as perfect as the local Government are desirous it should be ; still, intrinsically, its general correctness can be relied on, although it is not so accurately correct as one would wish.

The census in the rural districts is taken by the respective managers, and in Freetown by an officer appointed annually by the Governor for that duty ; and that, for the past year, has been taken by a European, the Superintendent of Police, and according to the plan suggested to Her Majesty's Government by Major Graham, and adopted, I believe, in England: and I am apt to think it is as correct as, under existing circumstances, it is possible to make it.[1]

1851. The return of the population of the Colony for 1851, compared with that for 1850, shows the following results:— . . . 1851 . . . 44,501 . . . 1850 . . . 44,472.

The above return shows a slight increase in the population for 1851 over 1850, but so slight as not to deserve notice . . . .[2]

1853. I am not prepared to vouch for the accuracy of returns under this head, there being no adequate machinery for ascertaining the facts correctly. The population of this colony must ever be fluctuating, according to the inducements held out for trade in the neighbouring territories and rivers. Natives of Sierra Leone may be found trading from Gambia to Fernando Po, and far into the interior, and with undoubted profit to themselves.[3]

But the 'returns under this head' for 1853 were literally the same as for 1851, no new census having been taken since. Censuses were taken again in 1855, 1858, and 1860. In submitting the returns for 1860 Governor Hill wrote:

It is a proof of civilization, in no small degree established, when a census can be taken of the existing population of this colony such as I have the honour now to exhibit. For thus it becomes manifest that the inducements to seek a settled habitation have been successful; that the interests of the people, no longer to be considered transient, have been adequately provided for; whether in the encouragement afforded to them for commerce, trade, and manufacture, or the restraints of just, and therefore, useful government.[4]

No censuses were taken in 1861–7,[5] but a comprehensive census of the Colony, including British Quiah and Bulama though excluding British Sherbro, was effected in 1868.

The series of decennial censuses started in Sierra Leone, as in many other British Dependencies, in 1871. The first census of this kind covered only the peninsula, excluding British Quiah. It was not authorized by any special legal Act, and little is known about the methods used apart from the fact that the enumerators themselves filled in the schedules.

. . . in 1871 the sum of five shillings per diem was considered sufficient for the Superintending persons and two shillings and sixpence per diem to the ordinary Enumerators amongst whom were many policemen, who received one shilling and threepence per diem in addition to their ordinary pay as Police Constables.

The principle adopted . . . was for Enumerators to go out with their blank sheets for several days previously and calling at each house write down the number of

---

[1] Governor Macdonald, 18 Aug. 1851, *State of Colonial Possessions 1850*, pp. 183–4.
[2] Same, 26 June 1852, ibid. *1851*, p. 181.
[3] Governor Kennedy, 7 July 1854, ibid. *1853*, p. 177.
[4] Ibid. *1860*, Part II, p. 16.
[5] See *Blue Book 1867*, pp. 174–5: 'The last Census was taken in 1860 . . . .'

inmates and other particulars furnished by the householder or other responsible person.[1]

The Report on the Blue Books for 1881 and 1882 states that 'the Census taken in 1871 was not altogether reliable',[2] and the Superintendent of the 1881 census says:

> The general impression of persons who were good judges of the working of the Census in 1871, including the then Census Master himself, was that Freetown was imperfectly taken, and it is extremely doubtful whether the difference which is thus exposed can be taken as a reliable increase. I am inclined to think that the real increase of souls on the peninsula in the past decade should not be estimated at more than 5,000.[3]

As the increase of souls on the peninsula (excluding Quiah) indicated by the census returns was 7,482, the Superintendent of the 1881 census apparently estimated the omissions in 1871 at about 2,500. But I suspect that they were much larger. The population of Freetown was returned in 1868, 1871, and 1881 as 21,974, 14,830, and 21,931, and the population of the rest of the peninsula (excluding Quiah) as 25,681, 24,106, and 24,487. It would seem, therefore, that the omissions in Freetown exceeded 2,500 considerably.

TABLE 1. *Population of Colony of Sierra Leone, 1871–1931*[1]

Districts	1871	1881	1891	1901	1911	1921	1931
Freetown . . .	14,830	21,931	30,033	34,463	34,090	44,142	55,509
Kissy . .	4,930	4,685	4,213	3,947	3,491	3,596	4,391
Kissy (Regent) .	} 6,170	5,956	6,080	2,051	1,690	1,491	2,073
Wilberforce .				5,311	5,681	6,340	6,848
Total Freetown District	25,930	32,572	40,326	45,772	44,952	55,569	68,821
Western District . .	4,712	5,560	5,441	} 22,010	23,163	23,992	21,347
Eastern District . .	8,294	8,286	} 12,681				
Quiah . . .	2	7,444		3	3	3	3
Total Peninsula	38,936	53,862	58,448	67,782	68,115	79,561	90,168
Bonthe, York Island .	2	} 4,333[4]	4,472	5,490	5,484	4,281	5,110
Rest of Sherbro District	2		9,036	2	764[5]	2	2
Tassoh Island . .	2	828	1,040	1,079	1,209	1,321	1,295
Kaikonkah . . .	2	52	90	882	2	2	2
Factories Sierra Leone River	2	100	171[6]	2	2	2	2
Isles de Los. . .	2	1,371	1,578	1,422	7	7	7
Total Colony . .	38,936	60,546[8]	74,835[9]	76,655[10]	75,572[11]	85,163[12]	96,573[13]

[1] See *Census Report 1881*, pp. 4, 6; *1891*, pp. 3–4, 16, 22; *1901*, pp. 4–5, 20; *1911*, pp. 5–6, 21, 38; *1921*, pp. 6, 20; *1931*, pp. 22, 73.   [2] Not returned.
[3] Included in 1896 in the Protectorate.   [4] Incomplete census.   [5] Only Bendu and Mocolo.
[6] Including Back Papelle with 136 inhabitants (formerly a factory, in 1891 a Customs preventive station).   [7] Ceded to France.
[8] Including 108 White floating population, i.e. ships in harbour, &c.
[9] Including 714 in vessels, &c., in port.   [10] Including 418 in vessels, &c., in port.
[11] Including 643 in vessels, &c., in port.   [12] Including 395 in vessels, &c., in port.
[13] Including 151 on board ships in harbour.

---

[1] *Census Report 1881*, p. 2.   [2] *Colonial Possessions Reports 1881–3*, p. 171.
[3] *Census Report 1881*, pp. 4–5.

Censuses were taken thereafter every ten years up to 1931. From 1881 on, each census has been authorized by an enabling Ordinance *ad hoc*.[1] The census of 1931 was taken in accordance with the following Ordinance :[2]

1. This Ordinance may be cited as the Census Ordinance, 1931, and shall apply to the Colony and Protectorate.

2. Subject to the provisions of this Ordinance a census of the Colony and Protectorate shall be taken in the year 1931, and the Census Day shall be the 26th day of April, 1931, or such other date as may be fixed by the Governor in Council.

3. (1) It shall be lawful for the Governor to appoint a Census Officer who, subject to the control of the Governor, shall have the general supervision and management of the census, and shall appoint a sufficient number of persons duly qualified to act as enumerators for taking the census, and also any other officers necessary for the purpose of carrying this Ordinance into effect.

(2) Notice of the appointment of such census officer and enumerators and any other officers shall be published in the *Gazette*.

4. The Census Officer shall cause to be prepared and printed, for the use of the persons to be employed in taking the census, such forms and instructions as he may deem necessary and in particular schedules to be filled up with such details as the Governor may consider necessary in order to insure as far as possible, the completeness and accuracy of the census returns.

5. The enumerators and other persons employed under this Ordinance shall have authority to ask all persons all such questions as may be necessary for obtaining any of the particulars required by this Ordinance, and every person refusing to answer, or knowingly giving a false answer to any such question shall for every such refusal or false answer be liable to a penalty not exceeding five pounds.

6. Every person who—

(a) without lawful excuse refuses or neglects to fill in any schedule of details as and when he may be required by the Census Officer, or any officer acting on his behalf so to do ; or

(b) fills in any such schedule with details which he knows to be false

shall be liable to a penalty not exceeding five pounds.

7. If any enumerator duly appointed under this Ordinance refuses or neglects to perform any of the duties required of him by this Ordinance, or knowingly makes or suffers any other person to make a false entry in any return, or makes any other return than such as he ought to make from the information actually received by him, such enumerator shall be liable to a penalty not exceeding ten pounds for every offence.

8. All penalties inflicted by this Ordinance shall be recoverable upon summary conviction before the Police Magistrate or a District Commissioner.

9. Upon the completion of the census, the Census Officer shall cause an abstract of the returns to be made, and such abstract shall be printed and laid before Legislative Council before the end of December, 1931.

The 1881 census was taken on 3 April, forms being left at each house between 28 March and 2 April and 'called for on the 4th or day following'.[3] It covered the same area as the census of 1871 and in addition British Quiah and the Out-Stations. The compensation per diem paid to

[1] For 1881–1911 see Ordinance No. 1 of 1881 (1 Feb.), amended by No. 2 of 1881 (11 Mar.), reprinted in *Census Report 1881*, Appendix A and B ; No. 25 of 1890 (7 Nov.), reprinted in *Census Report 1891*, Appendix A ; No. 7 of 1901 (21 Mar.), *Sierra Leone Ordinances 1899–1903* ; No. 26 of 1910 (31 Dec.), reprinted in *Ordinances, &c., of the Colony of Sierra Leone 1910*, pp. 63–72 ; No. 20 of 1920 (29 Sept.), reprinted ibid. *1920*, pp. 52–4.

[2] Ordinance No. 1 of 1931 (1 Apr.), 'An Ordinance for taking a Census of the Colony and Protectorate', Supplement No. 1 to *The Sierra Leone Royal Gazette*, 7 Apr. 1931, pp. 1–3.

[3] See *Census Report 1881*, pp. 1–2.

the Superintending persons and the Enumerators was the same as in 1871.[1] The Colonial Secretary and Treasurer who superintended the census reported:

...I venture to say that the total of the peninsula of 1881 may be accepted as reliable.

Of the Isles De Los, Tasso and Kikonkeh equally satisfactory results have been produced.

Of British Sherbro in which were included the following places viz. Bonthe, Mocolo, Mokate, Runteh, York Island, Yelbana, Victoria, Tasso, Bendoo, and Jamaica, I regret to say the figures are quite unreliable, and I should be sorry to entertain the idea that the totals returned by the Commandant are correct, indeed Mr. Wall himself admits the number to be understated, and urges as an excuse that some maliciously disposed persons spread the report that the natives were to be enlisted for the Ashantee war, and that in consequence large numbers of them departed. To what real extent such a stupid rumour affected the numbers I am unable to say, but I am confident that it could not have made a difference so marked as the Commandant supposes. The popular belief has always been that British Sherbro, by which is meant the places which were enumerated, together with a skirting of the banks of the rivers which there form a confluence, was from 12,000 to 15,000. I consider, however, from what has been shewn, that the population of the region mentioned has been considerably over-estimated, and that 7,000 or 8,000 persons are all which Sherbro proper might be said to contain.[2]

The cost of the census, 'every item of expense being included', was 'about £478' or £7. 18s. per 1,000 enumerated persons.[3]

The 1891 census was taken on 5 April according to 'An Ordinance for taking a Census of parts of the Colony of Sierra Leone'.

Although, since the taking of the Census of 1881, the area of the Colony had been extended, it was necessary for political reasons to confine the present census to those parts only which were comprised in that of 1881 as it was apprehended that through ignorance the aborigines living in some of our newly acquired territory would mis-construe the object of the enumeration and become unnecessarily dissatisfied. In other respects the Ordinance was drafted on the same lines as those of 1881.[4]

The Colonial Report for 1891 says that 'the unenumerated portions of the Colony are supposed to contain 50,000 souls'.[5] Since the census showed a total of 74,835, it covered probably about three-fifths of the population of the Colony.[6]

The Colonial Secretary who superintended the census makes no comment on the accuracy and completeness in general, but says with regard to Sherbro, from where 13,508 persons were returned as compared with 4,333 in 1881, that 'it is satisfactory to observe that on the present occasion an accurate return has been obtained of the number of residents in those stations of this District to which the Census law extends'.[7]

The cost of the census was £524. 12s. 11d. or £7. 0s. 3d. per 1,000 enumerated persons.[8]

The 1901 census was taken on 28 April, again according to 'An Ordinance for taking a Census of parts of the Colony of Sierra Leone'.

[1] See *Census Report 1891*, p. 1.   [2] Ibid. *1881*, pp. 5–6.   [3] See ibid., p. 13.
[4] Ibid. *1891*, p. 1.   [5] *Colonial Reports, Sierra Leone 1891*, p. 16.
[6] The unenumerated portions of the Colony were incorporated in 1896 in the Protectorate.
[7] *Census Report 1891*, p. 4.   [8] See *Blue Book 1891* C, p. 8; *1892* C, p. 12.

The area included in the Peninsula in the recent census is not quite identical with that over which the census was taken 10 years ago; in 1891 the Quiah District was included in the Eastern District, part of the present Waterloo District, but since 1896 this district has been included in the Protectorate Jurisdiction and consequently is not touched by the recent census. The difference in the Out-Stations is still greater. Back Papelle and some factories in the Sierra Leone River are not included in the recent census returns; and the census taken this year for the Sherbro District has been confined to Bonthe and York Island and their adjacent fakais; whereas 10 years ago many other towns and villages were included,[1] thus considerably reducing the returns from the outstations. Consequently it is somewhat difficult to compare the general results of the whole colony for 1901 with those of 1891.[2]

The Registrar-General who was in charge of the census makes no comment on the accuracy or completeness of the census.

The cost of the census was £648. 6s. 5d. or £8. 9s. 2d. per 1,000 enumerated persons.[3]

The 1911 census was taken on 2 April, again according to 'An Ordinance for taking a Census of parts of the Colony of Sierra Leone'. Its scope, however, was wider than that of 1901 as it covered not only the native and non-native population of the Colony but also the non-native population of the Protectorate.

. . . owing to the fewness of their numbers and the consequent fact that they are well known to the Authorities, it has been possible to obtain nearly the same full particulars of them as has been obtained of the population of the Colony.[4]

The native population of the Protectorate was not counted but estimated at this census as well as in 1921 and 1931. I shall discuss later the methods and results of these estimates and shall deal here with the censuses proper.

The area covered in 1911 by the census of the Colony differed slightly from the 1901 census area.

The Port of Sherbro District comprises the area included in the jurisdiction of the Port of Sherbro Municipal Board, and is slightly larger than the similar district censused in 1901; in that year the Board's jurisdiction extended only to Bonthe and York Island whereas at the present time it includes also Bendu and Mocolo, so that the returns for this district have consequently been swelled by the inclusion of the population of these two latter places.

In 1901 a Census was taken of the Isles de Los and Kikonkeh; the former has since been ceded to France and the information was to the effect that Kikonkeh was comprised in the Protectorate, but it now turns out that it is in the Colony;[5] accordingly this place was not included in the Colony Census, as it should have been . . . .[6]

The census report does not indicate the methods used in taking the census, but they were probably the same as at the three preceding censuses. Nor does the report make any comment on the completeness of the census.

---

[1] See p. 28 above.   [2] *Census Report 1901*, p. 3.
[3] See *Blue Book 1901* C, p. 7; *1902* C, p. 7.   [4] *Census Report 1911*, p. 3.
[5] In his preliminary report to the Colonial Secretary, dated 20 July 1911, the Compiler of Census said (p. 1) that Kikonkeh 'is now comprised in the Protectorate'.
[6] *Census Report 1911*, pp. 5-6.

The cost of the census (including the non-native census of the Protectorate) was £633. 3s. 10d. or £8. 0s. 4d. per 1,000 enumerated persons.[1]

The 1921 census of the Colony and of the non-natives in the Protectorate was taken on 24 April according to 'An Ordinance for taking a Census of the Colony and Protectorate'.

The Census was conducted on lines identical with those employed in 1911 and aimed at furnishing information and statistics of a similar nature.

With regard to the non-natives of the Protectorate it has been found possible to gather almost the same information as that obtained in regard to natives of the Colony. They are few in number and are all well known to the Authorities.[2]

The division of the Colony into seven Districts for Census purposes is identical with the arrangement made in the 1911 Census, and with the exception of the Port of Sherbro District the same areas are covered by the several Districts.

The Port of Sherbro District differs in its covering area from the corresponding District in the 1911 Census in that Bendu and Mocolo, included in the District in 1911, have this year been censused under the Bonthe District of the Protectorate.[3]

The cost of the census (including the non-native census of the Protectorate) was £924. 5s. 0d. or £10. 5s. 11d. per 1,000 enumerated persons.[4]

The 1931 census was taken on the night of 26 April.

As it was decided to add to the amount of information called for at previous censuses, both as regards Colony and Protectorate, and owing to the extra amount of work this would involve, it was considered desirable to appoint a whole time Census officer. In the case of previous censuses, the work was superintended by a Government officer who was not released from his ordinary duties and could therefore only give part time to the Census.[5]

The Colony Census Districts were the same as in 1921. The remunerations paid were likewise the same.

It was approved that the same remuneration as was paid to supervisors and enumerators in 1921 should be paid on this occasion, i.e.:—

Supervisors of Districts, £1. 10s. per 1,000 persons enumerated.
Principal enumerators (Freetown only), who were in charge of sub-areas, 7s. 6d. per day and ½d. per head of population enumerated.
Enumerators, 4s. a day and ½d. per head of population enumerated.

Two days only were allowed at the rates quoted, one for delivery of Schedules on the day or evening of the Census day and one for collection the next day.[6]

The Schedule used in the Colony,[7] which was to include all persons sleeping in the house on the night of 26 April and also those absent at

[1] See *Blue Book 1911* C, p. 10; *1912* C, p. 10.   [2] *Census Report 1921*, p. 1.
[3] Ibid., p. 6.   [4] See *Blue Book 1921*, p. 37; *1922*, p. 37.
[5] *Census Report 1931*, p. 1. For the appointment of the Census Officer see General Notice No. 221, *The Sierra Leone Royal Gazette*, 16 Apr. 1931, p. 173.
[6] *Census Report 1931*, p. 2. See also ibid., p. 5: 'The Schedules left at dwelling houses on 26th April were collected, for the most part, on the 27th. Those enumerators who were Government officials or who had large areas to work were, in some cases, unable to finish collection until the morning of the 28th. Also those who had areas containing a large number of illiterates were delayed slightly.'
[7] Reprinted in *Census Report 1931*, p. 3.

work or travelling who returned on the morning of 27 April, contained the following headings:

1. *Name and Surname.* Write first the name of the head of the family followed by others showing their relationship to the head of the family such as and in the following order 'wife', 'son', 'daughter', 'nephew', &c., then the names of any visitors, lodgers, servants.

2. *Sex.* Write 'M' opposite males and 'F' opposite females.

3. *Age last Birthday.* Age of infant under one year to be stated in months, one month as the case may be.

4. *Conjugal State.* Married. Widow. Widower. Divorced.

5. *Nationality.* State whether British born or Naturalized British Subject, American, French, German, Syrian, E. Indian, Sierra Leoneans. If of mixed blood state nationality of parents.

6. *Tribe.* (Where applicable.)

7. *Birthplace.* State Colony, Protectorate, European country or any other Colony or Country.

8. *Religion.* If Christian state denomination.

9. *Occupation* or rank or means of subsistence.

10. *Literacy.* Standard of education.

11. Whether able to speak English.

12. *Infirmity.* e.g. Whether Blind, Deaf, or Dumb, or either Imbecile, or Lunatic (if from birth this should be entered accordingly). Loss of limb or limbless or any serious Infirmity.

The questions concerning 'Conjugal State', 'Tribe', 'Literacy', and 'Whether able to speak English' had not been asked at earlier censuses. The term 'Nationality' was this time substituted for 'Race'.[1]

The census report contains the following comment on the completeness and accuracy of the returns for the Colony:

It is hoped that the figures for the population, that is to say, as far as the actual number of people existing in the Colony at the time the Census was taken, are reasonably accurate. . . .

As regards such particulars as religion, age, nationality, birthplace, literacy, conjugal state, very little can be said as to the accuracy of the information; it must be accepted as given. . . .

There are, of course, certain matters against which it is impossible to guard. The Census must depend upon the truth of the answers given by the persons rendering the returns: some may, through ignorance, give incorrect answers; others may wilfully do so, and it may be impossible to question the truth of the replies.[2]

The census of the non-native population in the Protectorate 'was taken on the same lines as that in the Colony, the same schedule being used, one being served on each non-native householder'.

Non-natives included Europeans, Sierra Leoneans of the Colony, West Indians, Mulattoes, other African non-natives and Asiatics. The District Commissioner supervised the Census in each district and the Provincial Commissioners were Commissioners of Census or Supervisors for their Provinces.

Enumerators were appointed by District Commissioners for each town with a non-native population. In cases of towns containing only a few non-native residents, the District Commissioners were asked to group them where practicable and where distances were not too great to include one or more under other towns with large non-native populations and, if neither of these suggestions was workable, to have the schedules served and collected by court messengers.[3]

[1] See ibid., p. 4.   [2] Ibid., p. 6.   [3] Ibid., p. 80.

The details of expenditure for the census of the Colony and the non-native census of the Protectorate were as follows:[1]

	£	s.	d.
Remuneration of supervisors Kissy, Kissy Regent, Wilberforce and Tassoh Island,[2] at £1. 10s. per 1,000 persons.	21	0	3
Remuneration of Supervisor Freetown	40	0	0
Principal and other enumerators Freetown and enumerators rest of Colony[3]	253	13	6½
Enumerators Non-native population, Protectorate	35	15	11
Compilation clerks	215	2	5½
Expenses in connexion with fitting up of Census office (including loan of furniture)	21	12	0
Various expenses (travelling and transport) Protectorate	4	5	11
Temporary clerks, January and February, 1932	20	0	0
Total	611	10	1

The cost per 1,000 enumerated persons was £6. 1s. 3d. It was lower than at any of the five preceding censuses.

I shall now discuss the estimates of the native population of the Protectorate made in connexion with the censuses of the Colony.

The Ordinance of 1901 provided only for a census to be taken in parts of the Colony, but the Registrar-General in his report on this census said:[4]

In 1896 a Protectorate was declared by Order-in-Council over the Hinterland of the Colony.[5] This territory has been divided for Administrative purposes into five districts, over each of which is a District Commissioner.

A rough estimate has been made by the District Commissioners of the population of their districts based upon the estimated number of persons living in each house. The following table will show the population of each District:

Districts	Houses	Population	Remarks
Ronietta	40,000	400,000	10 persons to a house.
Karene .	40,000	200,000	5 persons to a house.
Bandajuma .	27,396	109,584	4 persons to a house.
Panguma	No return	183,857	—
Koinadugu .	Do.	56,386	—
Total.	—	949,827	—

The Ordinance authorizing the census of 1911 provided again only for a census to be taken in parts of the Colony, but this time much more was done in the Protectorate.

In the Protectorate two different Censuses have been taken, one confined to the relatively small class of persons, termed non-natives, i.e., persons not belonging to the aboriginal tribes of the Protectorate and the other which deals with the larger class known as the aboriginal natives.

[1] *Census Report 1931*, p. 7.

[2] In the Headquarters Judicial and the Bonthe Districts the District Commissioners functioned as Supervisors.

[3] If each of the five Principal Enumerators and the 156 Enumerators had received the regular remuneration the total would have amounted to £270. 6s. 10½d., but Enumerators who were Government officials may not have been paid the full remuneration.

[4] *Census Report 1901*, p. 21.

[5] The 'Protectorate over the territories adjacent to the Colony of Sierra Leone' was proclaimed on 31 Aug. 1896.

It was recognized that to take such a detailed Census of the aboriginal natives [as of the non-natives] of the Protectorate would be quite impracticable, owing to the native fear that a counting of the people was but a prelude to the imposition of increased taxation,[1] and accordingly it was decided that the Census should be limited to obtaining such information as could by approximation be furnished by the District Commissioners. With this end in view information was obtained under the following heads:—

(1) *Houses.* The total number of inhabited houses and their distribution.

(2) *Area.* The total area of each district and the approximate area of the country occupied by each tribe in the district.

(3) *Population.* Certain representative towns and villages were studied in detail and an estimate made of—

(a) The average number of occupants per house.

(b) The proportion of men, women and children.

(4) *Religion.* An estimate was made of the proportion of Christians, Mohammedans and Pagans in each tribe in a district.[2]

The census report gives all the details for each tribe in each District. It begins with the Koinadugu District:

Tribe	Area sq. m.	Number of houses	Average persons per house	Men	Women	Children	Total persons	Moham-medans per cent.	Pagans per cent.
Korankos	3,600	6,651	4·5	5,986	8,979	14,965	29,930	25	75
Limbas .	1,440	8,656	8·0	13,850	20,774	34,624	69,248	5	95
Yalunkas	720	2,600	6·0	3,120	4,680	7,800	15,600	50	50
Mandingos	..	1,160	6·0	1,392	2,088	3,480	6,960	95	5
Foulahs .	..	740	5·0	740	1,110	1,850	3,700	95	5

In the case of the Korankos, Limbas and Yalunkas, the figures have been arrived at by counting the population of from three to five representative villages of each tribe. It was impossible to do the same with the Mandingos and Foulahs, as these two tribes are nomadic in their way of life.[3]

In Headquarters District the population 'was ascertained by counting the inhabitants of six representative towns in each Chiefdom'. In Northern Sherbro District the population was 'based on studies of six representative towns'.[4] For the other four Districts which comprised more than three-quarters of the total population of the Protectorate the number of villages or towns which served as a basis of the estimate is not given. Concerning the Protectorate as a whole, the census report makes the following comment:

It may be taken that the computation of houses . . . is correct, as the figures are derived from the house tax rolls,[5] but the figures as to the population, based on the number of persons estimated to be living in each house in a few representative towns, must necessarily be taken as approximate only.[6]

This statement suggests that, even in the few 'representative towns' which served as a basis for the population estimates, the population, as a

[1] According to 'The Protectorate Ordinance, 1896' (No. 20, 16 Sept.), a tax was to be paid for every house from 1 Jan. 1898 on. 'The year 1898 was marked by an insurrection in the Protectorate as the result of the imposition of a house tax. The resulting military operations were brought to a successful conclusion early in the following year, and since that date the Protectorate has remained peaceful' (*Colonial Reports, Sierra Leone 1938*, p. 5).

[2] *Census Report 1911*, pp. 3–4.   [3] Ibid., p. 32.   [4] Ibid., p. 35.

[5] But see also *Colonial Reports, Sierra Leone 1907*, p. 21: '. . . in the present incomplete state of house registration in the Protectorate, it is doubtful whether the number of houses on which tax is paid represents the number of houses actually in existence.'   [6] *Census Report 1911*, p. 29.

rule, was not counted but estimated. As regards the proportion of men, women, and children, no attempt seems to have been made to ascertain the facts in the 'representative towns'. The above table shows that, for example in the Koinadugu District, the Commissioner entered for each tribe 20 per cent. as men, 30 per cent. as women, and 50 per cent. as children. The same practice was followed throughout by the Commissioner of the Karene District, and the Commissioner of the Ronietta District, who chose a different ratio of women to men, entered also for each tribe exactly 50 per cent. of the total population as children.[1] It is out of the question that in any of those tribes as many as 50 per cent. of the people should actually have been children.

The native 'census' in the Protectorate was taken in 1921 in the same manner as in 1911.

No attempt whatever was made to compile an accurate and detailed Census of the natives of the Protectorate. Apart from the fact that any such attempt would have been regarded with the utmost suspicion by the people who would have seen in it the preliminary steps towards the imposition of a Poll Tax and would in consequence have avoided compliance with the Census instructions and thus made the attempt abortive, the machinery necessary for such a detailed Census extending over such a wide area, at present (for this purpose) so inadequately provided with means of communication, was not available. An approximation was therefore made and although not strictly accurate, there is no reason to suppose that such an approximation does not give a reasonably correct estimate of the Protectorate natives.[2]

The Census Officer reports that 'representative areas in each district were subjected to a detailed count', but does not specify this claim, and says in conclusion:

Too much emphasis cannot be placed on the fact that the enumeration of Protectorate natives is an approximation only. The information is solely derived from the several District Commissioners who, although exercising the greatest care and consideration, are not prepared and cannot be expected to offer any sort of guarantee as to more than the approximate correctness of their figures. Two entries in the above Table will make this fact abundantly clear. The number of men stated to be resident in the Moyamba District is 37,761; the number of women is also stated to be 37,761; the chances of this estimation proving to be absolutely correct if a true Census were taken are infinitesimal.[3]

The Census Officer evidently was not aware of the crude technique which the District Commissioners had used in obtaining the numbers of men, women, and children. The four District Commissioners of the Northern Province had allocated in the case of each tribe 25 per cent. to men, 45 per cent. to women, and 30 per cent. to children. Three of the four District Commissioners of the Central Province had allocated 30 per cent. to men, 40 per cent. to women, and 30 per cent. to children, while one District Commissioner (Moyamba) had allocated 37·5 per cent. to men, 37·5 per cent. to women, and 25 per cent. to children. Finally, of the four District Commissioners of the Southern Province, one had allocated 30 per

[1] The Commissioner of the Northern Sherbro District had a much more refined scheme. As his table (see *Census Report 1911*, p. 35) shows, he entered for each of the seven tribes living in his district, for every 3 houses, 2·1 boys, 2·8 girls, 4·2 men, and 5·6 women.

[2] *Census Report 1921*, p. 2.   [3] Ibid., p. 31.

cent. to men, 40 per cent. to women, and 30 per cent. to children, while the three others had used other devices. In the Koinadugu and Karene Districts, for example, where in 1911 the ratio of children to women had been assumed to be in each tribe 5 to 3, it was now assumed to be in each tribe 2 to 3!

For 1931 it had been planned to take a real census of the native population in considerable portions of the Protectorate, but this plan was abandoned and the figures were again 'obtained by an estimate based, partly, on enumeration'. Greater efforts, however, were made to secure adequate data on which to base the estimates.

The scheme at first submitted for the native Census was not approved. It contained suggestions for the complete enumeration of chiefdoms ruled by literate chiefs and of part enumeration of others, the chiefs supervising the work and being responsible for the returns. It was suggested that if chiefs carried out their own chiefdom census under the eye of the District Commissioners, very reliable returns would be obtained; there would be less likelihood of evasion and suspicion as the chiefs would be able to assure their people that the Census was merely a count of heads and that no other purpose lay behind it.

The objection to this scheme was both on the grounds of expense and the length of time it would occupy, and it was therefore abandoned . . . .

As it was not found possible to have a complete enumeration of the native population, District Commissioners were again asked to furnish an estimate of the populations of the various districts. It was hoped, however, that District Commissioners would carry out as much actual enumeration as time and circumstances permitted, so that a reliable basis might be obtained on which an estimate could be formed. In order that as much data as possible might be collected, it was arranged that the Census operations should be spread over a period of from three to six months following the Census date (26th April, 1931) and that during that time as many villages as possible should be visited and counted in detail by, or under the personal supervision of, the District Commissioners. These villages were to be used as 'key' villages; the population of the remainder of each chiefdom could then be calculated, the numbers of persons per house being ascertained from these counts and the house tax lists determining the remaining population in each case.[1]

A form of schedule was prepared and sent to each District Commissioner, one of which was to be used for each chiefdom. The figures and particulars for the towns

[1] But see also *Census Report 1931*, p. 83: 'If the house tax lists are correct, a very close estimate of the existing population must have been the result. It should be mentioned, however, that house totals are probably in excess of the number of occupied houses actually existing. Houses occupied previous to the Census but actually unoccupied when the Census was taken, would still be on the house tax lists; and houses under construction but not yet occupied, would in some cases be shown by the chiefs as occupied, being in the ownership of someone. Allowances have been made by all District Commissioners for cases of this kind, and also for the slightly varying numbers of persons per house in different localities.'

The reports on the Provincial Administration furnish ample evidence of the discrepancies between the numbers of houses taxed and the actual numbers of houses. The 1924 Report of the Northern Province, for example, speaks (p. 4) of both under-assessments and over-assessments.

'. . . there is a small decrease of £156 in house tax . . . . A considerable portion of this decrease is no doubt due to a gradually increasing tendency, largely due to agricultural conditions, for families to leave the larger villages and establish small villages or single houses nearer their farms. As a preliminary measure, if the villagers have not got time to erect permanent houses, they put up what are locally known as "shimbecks" of a semi-permanent type; a portion of these shimbecks, being hidden away in remote areas of the district, evade taxation for the time being. So far, however, as the towns and villages are concerned they are, in my opinion, fully assessed for purposes of taxation. Whilst on tour, I occasionally as a test count the number of houses in a village and ask to see the headman's receipt; it is my experience that not infrequently the receipt shows that

and villages examined in detail in each chiefdom were entered by the District Commissioners in these forms and also the figures for the remainder of the chiefdom, the district population then being ascertained from these forms. This is the first time a form of any kind was used in the Protectorate for the Census of the native population and that an estimate for each separate chiefdom was made.

As well as numbers, the detail to be collected for each chiefdom included such particulars as sex, tribe, age, literacy (including ability to speak English), religion, principal occupations and infirmities.[1]

As a matter of fact actual enumeration was carried out only on a very small scale.

District	Total houses[2]	Enumeration[3]
Port Loko	22,093	'In all, 41 towns were examined in detail and 776 domiciliary counts made, of which 366 were by the District Commissioner personally or under his supervision and the result may be regarded as reasonably correct.'
Kambia	15,022	'34 villages were examined and 626 houses were visited by the District Commissioner and his agents.'
Karene	15,274	'949 houses.'
Bombali	18,348	'The District Commissioner was unable to deal with more than twelve towns, but these were thoroughly studied. These towns contained 357 houses, each of which was visited and the inhabitants enumerated.'
Koinadugu	17,381	'It is not certain how many villages were visited, but the Schedule shows that 398 domiciliary counts were made.'

one or two houses have been paid for which do not exist in the village; the explanation usually being that someone has intended to build a new house but has not done so, or else he has built a new house closer to his farm.'

The 1928 Report on the Provincial Administration said (p. 2) with regard to the Northern Province: '. . . in some parts of the country the increase in the number of houses is not commensurate with the increase in tax. In some places people paid the tax in anticipation of building, started to build, and then thought they had done enough to satisfy the Government and did not complete their houses. Others paid tax but did not build at all, evidently hoping that the old system of collecting tax on "konkos" would be reverted to and save them the trouble of building.' The same report said (p. 17) concerning the Southern Province: 'House tax increased, I think, unduly: the increase was over 12 per cent. and I reckon that about 4 per cent. would be a normal and satisfactory increase. Chiefs and people were over-optimistic about the number of houses that would be completed in 1928 . . . .' (Acting Commissioner, Southern Province.)

The 1933 Report of the Northern Province said (pp. 1–2): 'The decrease in House Tax [£557] . . . is due to the fact that the Protectorate has been over assessed in the past, and to the fact that old and demolished houses are frequently not replaced, the people taking this means to save their pockets in these times of stress when they cannot get an adequate price for their produce.'

The 1934 Report stated (p. 1): 'The house tax again shews a decrease of £153, which as explained in 1933, is due to previous over-assessment.'

The 1937 Report of the Provincial Administration said (p. 4) with regard to the Northern Province: 'The decrease of £924 in House Tax receipts is due to more careful assessing on the part of Native Authorities who were about to undergo re-organisation.' The same report stated (p. 13) concerning the Southern Province: 'House tax showed a falling off of £475 5s. 0d. as compared with 1936. . . . there has always been a tendency for the local chiefs to over-assess.'

Finally it should be noted that even when the house registers are accurate they do not necessarily convey an accurate picture of changes in population. The 1928 Report on the Provincial Administration said (p. 7): 'For many years the house tax of the whole Protectorate has shown little increase whilst there was no doubt that the population was increasing. Investigation proved that overcrowding was becoming the rule in nearly every village despite the fact that it violated a fundamental native law, was against the House Tax Ordinance, and proved to be the common cause of sickness.'

[1] Census Report 1931, p. 79. [2] See ibid., p. 83.
[3] See ibid., pp. 110, 114, 119, 123, 128, 133, 138, 142, 148, 153, 158, 164.

District	Total houses	Enumeration
Moyamba	33,745	'For administrative reasons the District Commissioner was unable to visit many villages for the purpose of collecting data. No record of the number of villages and houses is available ....'
Bonthe	22,131	'Thirty-six villages were examined in detail, 703 houses being visited ....'
Pujehun	26,780	'Thirteen towns were examined in detail, entailing 1,100 house counts.'
Bo	38,991	'One complete Chiefdom, Bagbo, containing 2,992 houses, was censused in its entirety by the Paramount Chief, a literate chief. In addition to this the District Commissioner, or his agent under supervision, visited and examined in detail 32 villages, containing 2,676 houses.'
Kenema	39,592	'The District Commissioner made a most diligent census survey of this District; he visited and personally supervised the detailed counts of his agents in thirty-one villages, containing 1,838 houses. In addition two chiefdoms of 4,534 houses were counted by the Paramount Chiefs' representatives and clerks.'
Kailahun	39,918	'In all, 144 towns were visited and this entailed the house by house enumeration of 9,748 houses by the District Commissioner and his agents.'
Kono	18,884	'In all, twenty-four towns were examined in detail and 1,324 house to house counts made by the Acting District Commissioner personally or under his supervision. In addition, the Paramount Chief's representative and clerks of the Sawo Chiefdom carried out a count, which may be accepted as fairly reliable, of two sections of that chiefdom containing 923 houses.'

The reports for the various Districts contain furthermore the following comments on the estimates made:[1]

Port Loko. The accuracy of the Census, so far as the number of persons and distribution of sex is concerned, is considered to be fairly close.

Kambia. The District Commissioner thinks that the population has been underestimated.

Karene. The District Commissioner took infinite pains to render an approximately correct return. He personally visited fifty-eight towns and thoroughly dealt with each. This involved detailed counts of 949 houses and it is considered, therefore, that the Census represents a close estimate of the actual population.

Bombali. The estimate is considered a fair one.

Koinadugu. The District Commissioner considers a very fair estimate of the population was obtained ....

Moyamba. ... it is considered that the population has been underestimated.

Bonthe. The District Commissioner considers the Census of villages actually counted was accurate within a very small degree of error. ... it is considered that a very fair basis to work on was obtained.

Pujehun. The District Commissioner considers a very close approximation of the population has been arrived at. The figures given are the result of close investigation in towns chosen in the trade areas as well as outlying parts, and a sound basis was formed for each Chiefdom.

Bo. The District Commissioner ... thinks the population has been slightly underestimated.

Kailahun. ... the estimate may be taken to be a very close approximation. Indeed, very great interest in the Census appears to have been taken by the District

[1] *Census Report 1931*, pp. 110, 114, 119, 123, 128, 133, 138, 142, 148, 158, 164.

Commissioner, who dealt very thoroughly with all points. . . . The figures for occupations, religions, literacy and infirmities are also as accurate as possible, as not only were counts made in the towns mentioned [144], but careful enquiries were made throughout the District from chiefs. The returns therefore for this District should be of value not only inasmuch as they are a correct representation of the population in the District, but serve as a useful model for comparison with other districts.

Kono. It is quite clear from the report and returns sent in to the Census Office that the greatest care and pains were taken to render as close an approximation as was reasonably possible. . . . in the Kissi portion of the District close to French Guinea he [the District Commissioner] considers it quite probable that a number of Kissi people took up temporary abode over the border, viewing with distrust and suspicion the census operations. Some allowances were made for this, but even then it is considered that the Kissi population has been under-estimated.

The Census Officer summarizes the position as follows:

This is the fourth Census of the Protectorate. At the previous censuses the population figures were also arrived at by an estimate. That for 1901 was said to have been of a very rudimentary character, but for 1911 and 1921 the estimates were based on counts carried out in various villages. As a much larger number of villages were dealt with on this occasion it is hoped that a closer estimate has been arrived at.[1]

It seems necessary, however, to distinguish between various sections of the Protectorate. In the Northern Province, which comprises nearly one-half of the total population, apparently not more than 3,106 out of 88,118 houses were visited, and it may be doubtful, therefore, whether the estimates for this Province were closer than in 1921. The Bombali District may serve as an illustration. The population here apparently increased by 64 per cent. in 1921–31.

It cannot be said that this increase is a natural one. The difference is due to the system adopted in this Census and to the discovery that the average number per house is 13·31 instead of 7 as in 1921.[2]

The report does not tell how this 'discovery' was made, but as 'the District Commissioner was unable to deal with more than 12 towns', containing 357 out of a total of 18,348 houses in the District, it may be assumed that the average number of 13·31 persons per house was found in these towns. If this assumption is correct, the estimate of 7 persons per house in 1921 may have led to a more correct total than the generalization of results ascertained in 1931 by a sample covering less than 2 per cent. of all houses.

In three of the seven Districts of the Southern Province the proportion of houses visited was also very small. In Pujehun with 26,780 houses, 'thirteen towns were examined in detail, entailing 1,100 house counts'. The returns for the various tribes were as follows:

| | 1921 | 1931 | Increase | |
			Number	Per cent.
Mendi[1]	42,218	82,449	+40,231	+95
Gallinas	24,541	19,865	− 4,676	−19
Krim	23,471	13,734	− 9,737	−41
Gola	7,043	6,731	− 312	− 4

[1] The Malen Chiefdom with 10,040 people in 1931 was transferred to the Pujehun District in 1930.

[1] *Census Report 1931*, p. 79.   [2] Ibid., p. 123.

It is seen that the Mendi figures show a large increase and the other tribes a decrease. These figures reveal that either the Mendi tribe was very much underestimated and the others overestimated in 1921 or that the reverse has taken place this Census; but in view of the careful manner in which the District Commissioner dealt with the Census on this occasion, the detailed counts and study of conditions, it is probable that the former was the case.[1]

The classification of the 20 Chiefdoms 'according to tribal territory' shows 11 Mendi, 3 Gallinas, 5 Krim, and 1 Gola. The results of the counts in 13 towns do not afford, it seems to me, a conclusive proof that in 1921 the population had been grossly underestimated in the Mendi Chiefdoms and grossly overestimated in the other Chiefdoms.

The position is somewhat different in the four other Districts of the Southern Province comprising nearly one-third of the total population of the Protectorate. The counts covered here between 12 and 25 per cent. of all houses. Owing to the changes in boundaries comparisons between the 1931 and 1921 returns is possible only for two Districts. In the Kailahun District, in which one-quarter of the houses were visited in 1931, the returns show an increase of 6·2 per cent.[2] There seems to be no reason to assume that the 1921 estimate was far off the mark. But in the Kono District, in which nearly one-eighth of the houses were counted, the returns in 1931 were 39 per cent. lower than in 1921.

A letter was addressed to the District Commissioner on these figures, who explained that the figures now furnished are a very reasonable approximation and that he was satisfied that the Census was most carefully and diligently carried out by the Acting District Commissioner; he is of opinion that the population was grossly overestimated in 1921.[3]

It will be remembered that the Census Officer in 1921 likewise claimed that 'there is no reason to suppose that such approximation does not give a reasonably correct estimate of the Protectorate natives', but I think that in those Districts where a notable proportion of houses was visited in 1931 the 1931 returns should be considered more reliable wherever there are irreconcilable differences.

As regards the question whether and how many times a native census has been taken in the Protectorate there will be, I suppose, a consensus of opinion that the Census Officer, 1931, was wrong in considering the crude guesses made in 1901 as a census. Concerning the 1911 and 1921 figures there may be a difference of opinion as to whether they were obtained by reasoned guesses or by estimates, but even the most careful estimate, though it may come nearer the truth than a census, is not a census. Finally, whether a native census was taken in 1931 or not is a controversial question. It may be argued that the population of nearly one-tenth of all houses was counted, and that if the Intensive Census in Northern Nigeria which covered only about 4 per cent. of the population is considered to be a census, a similar claim may be staked for Sierra Leone. But such a claim, it seems to me, would not be justified. In Nigeria the central authority designated the areas in which the Intensive Census was to be taken; the completed forms were sent to the Census

[1] *Census Report 1931*, p. 143.   [2] See ibid., p. 158.   [3] Ibid., p. 164.

Office; the Census Office tabulated and published the results. It was only a partial census, to be sure, but, so far as it went, it was a census. In Sierra Leone it was left entirely to the discretion of the local officers in which and in how many places they counted the population; the sole purpose of the counts was to enable the Commissioners to estimate approximately the population of their Districts; neither the completed schedules nor the results of the counts were sent to the central authority; as in 1911 and 1921, all figures published are estimates. It is therefore, I think, correct to say that no census has been taken as yet of the native population of the Protectorate, which apparently comprises over 94 per cent. of the total population of the Colony and Protectorate.

II. Early Colonization

Unlike all other British Dependencies on the African mainland the Colony of Sierra Leone is inhabited in a large measure by the descendants of people who were settled there by the British Government. Before discussing the numbers and the composition of the present population I shall therefore discuss, in chronological order, the various groups of people who went to Sierra Leone with special reference to what became of them.

1. *The First Settlers*

The colonists who in 1787 sailed from England to Sierra Leone were (*a*) over 400 destitute negroes and negresses, (*b*) about 50 or 60 white prostitutes, and (*c*) about 10 white men.

(*a*) 'In 1786, the humanity of some gentlemen was excited towards the distressed blacks, who then swarmed in London.'[1] These were either (1) domestic slaves who had been brought from America by their masters and had claimed their liberty following the famous decision of Lord Mansfield in 1772 that a slave on setting foot on the British Isles became free, or (2) slaves who had escaped from the West Indies,[2] or (3) slaves who during the American War ran away from their masters and took refuge in the English army or navy.[3] The naturalist Dr. Henry Smeathman, 'who resided in that Country near Four Years', proposed

---

[1] Wadstrom, *An Essay on Colonization*, vol. ii (1795), p. 8.

[2] Wadstrom described the position of these two groups as follows (vol. ii, pp. 227–8): 'The blacks living in London are generally profligate, because uninstructed, and vitiated by slavery: for many of them were once slaves of the most worthless description, namely the idle and superfluous domestic, and the gamblers and thieves who infest the towns in the W. Indies. There are severe laws against carrying, or enticing, slaves from the Islands, without the knowledge of their owners. Yet some of those fellows contrive to conceal themselves, or are concealed by others on board ships on the point of sailing . . . . In London, being friendless and despised, on account of their complexion, and too many of them being really incapable of any useful occupation, they sink into abject poverty, and soon become St. Giles's black-birds.'

[3] 'During the American war, many negroes entered on board the British ships of war, or repaired to the British standard, and were formed into regiments of rangers; and they generally behaved well, both by sea and land. At the peace in 1783, part of them, as well as of the white loyalists, were conveyed to the Bahama islands, part to Nova Scotia, and others to G. Britain, chiefly to London. These last, having been indigent, unemployed, despised and forlorn, soon added to the vices of common soldiers and sailors those of the numerous beggars who, notwith-

to settle in Sierra Leone those negroes who were willing to go. In a pamphlet published apparently in May 1786 he said:

And whereas many black persons, and people of Colour, Refugees from America, disbanded from His Majesty's Service by sea or land, or otherwise distinguished objects of British humanity, are at this time in the greatest distress, they are invited to avail themselves of the advantages of the plan proposed.

The Committee, appointed for the relief of the Black Poor, having represented their unhappy situation to the Right Hon. the Lord Commissioners of the Treasury, Government has agreed to furnish them, not only with a passage and provision, but also with cloathing, provisions for three months after their landing, together with all sorts of tools and implements of husbandry, necessary for the establishment of a new settlement, according to the schedules annexed.[1]

The negroes were recruited through the following handbill:[2]

It having been maturely and humanely considered, by what means a support might be given to the Blacks, who seek the protection of this government; it is found that no place is so fit and proper, as the Grain Coast of Africa; where the necessaries of life may be supplied by the force of industry and moderate labour, and life rendered very comfortable. It has been meditated to send Blacks to Nova Scotia, but this plan is laid aside, as that country is unfit and improper for the said Blacks.

The Committee for the Black Poor, accordingly recommended Henry Smeath-man, Esq who is acquainted with this part of the coast of Africa, to take charge of all the said persons, who are desirous of going with him: and to give them all fit and proper encouragement, agreeably to the humanity of the British Government.

Batson's Coffee-house,   By desire of the Committee,
17th *May,* 1786.   JONAS HANWAY, Chairman.

Those who are desirous of profiting by this opportunity, of settling in one of the most pleasant and fertile countries in the known world, may apply for further information to Mr. SMEATHMAN, the Author of the Plan, and Agent for the Settlement, at the Office for Free Africans, No. 14, Canon-Street.

Smeathman who, as agent of the Committee for the Black Poor, was to lead the emigrants to Sierra Leone, died on 1 July 1786.[3] By that time about 300 negroes had 'already entered their names'.[4]

standing the prodigious sums *levied* for maintaining the poor, disgrace the police of this capital' (ibid., p. 220).

It is very difficult to appraise the numerical importance of the three groups. In 1772 the number of negro slaves in England was estimated at 14,000 or 15,000. Many of these had died by 1786, but many others had come in the meantime. In a letter to the Archbishop of Canterbury, dated 1 Aug. 1786, Granville Sharp said: 'The present set of unfortunate Negroes that are starving in our streets, were brought here on very different occasions. Some, indeed, have been brought as servants, but chiefly by officers; others were Royalists from America; but most are seamen, who have navigated the King's ships from the East and West Indies, or have served in the war, and are thereby entitled to ample protection, and a generous requital' (Hoare, *Memoirs of Granville Sharp*, p. 263).

[1] Henry Smeathman, *Plan of a Settlement to be made near Sierra Leona, on the Grain Coast of Africa; Intended more particularly for the service and happy establishment of Blacks and People of Colour, to be shipped as freemen under the direction of the Committee for Relieving the Black Poor, and under the protection of the British Government*, pp. 16–17. 'The Government had long regarded the numerous Negroes who begged in the streets as a nuisance, and therefore readily consented to lend a helping hand to the project' (Hoare, p. 268).   [2] Smeathman, pp. 23-4.

[3] See Sharp, *Short Sketch of Temporary Regulations for the Intended Settlement* (dated 3 July 1786), p. 41; *The Gentleman's Magazine, 1786*, vol. lvi, p. 620. Some recent authors (Butt-Thompson, *Sierra Leone in History and Tradition*, 1926, p. 73; Utting, *Story of Sierra Leone*, 1931, p. 82) say erroneously that Smeathman sailed with the emigrants in 1787 and died at sea.

[4] Sharp, *Short Sketch of Temporary Regulations*, p. 64.

Granville Sharp[1] who financially, by interviewing applicants, and in many other ways had collaborated with Smeathman, now took charge of all the preparations and persuaded the Government to intensify its assistance.

> . . . provision was made for the settlers, both for transporting them, and for supplying them with necessaries during the first six or eight months of their residence in Africa; and Captain (afterwards Admiral) Thompson was appointed to accompany them in the Nautilus sloop of war, and to see the promises given by Mr. Sharp fulfilled towards them.[2]

(b) As regards the recruitment of the white women, Anna Maria Falconbridge, in a letter from Sierra Leone dated 13 May 1791, wrote:

> I always supposed these people had been transported as convicts, but some conversation I lately had with one of the women has partly undeceived me: She said, the women were mostly of that description of persons who walk the streets of London, and support themselves by the earnings of prostitution; that men were employed to collect and conduct them to Wapping, where they were intoxicated with liquor, then inveigled on board of ship, and married to *black men*, whom they had never seen before; that the morning after she was married, she really did not remember a syllable of what had happened over night, and when informed, was obliged to inquire, *who was her husband?* After this to the time of their sailing, they were amused and buoyed up by a prodigality of fair promises, and great expectations which awaited them in the country they were going to . . . .[3]

(c) Very little is known about the white men who then went to Sierra Leone. Sharp mentions an agent conductor, three surgeons, a chaplain, a land surveyor, a town-major, and a gardener.[4]

In a letter to Dr. Lettsom dated 13 October 1788 Sharp described the embarkation as follows:

> Many of the Black poor were embarked in the river Thames before Christmas 1786; but others delayed going on board till January and February 1787, being deterred by a jealousy which prevailed among them that Government intended to send them to Botany Bay, as the transports for that expedition were then waiting at Portsmouth, where the ships for Sierra Leone were ordered also. On the 20th February 1787, instead of 700 Black poor who had offered themselves to go to the proposed settlement, there were only 439 or 441 (for the accounts differ) that embarked on board the three transports appointed for them—viz. the Belisarius, Atlantic, and Vernon—which by that time were all arrived at Portsmouth. On the 22d February 1787, they sailed, under the command of Captain Thompson, of his

---

[1] 'Granville Sharp takes precedence of Clarkson and Wilberforce as the pioneer of the anti-slavery movement. He it was who in 1772 obtained from Lord Mansfield the famous decision . . . .' (Mathieson, *Great Britain and the Slave Trade 1839–1865*, p. 2.) When on 22 May 1787 a Committee was formed 'for procuring such information and evidence, and publishing the same, as may tend to the abolition of the Slave-trade', Sharp 'as the father of the cause in England, was called to the chair' (Thomas Clarkson, *History of the Abolition of the Slave-Trade*, vol. i, pp. 255–6).

[2] Hoare, pp. 268–9. Thompson was 'then a youth of twenty' (Butt-Thompson, p. 72).

[3] Falconbridge, *Two Voyages to Sierra Leone 1791–93*, p. 57. She adds (p. 58): 'Good heavens! how the relation of this tale made me shudder; I questioned its veracity, and enquired of the other women who exactly corroborated what I had heard; nevertheless, I cannot altogether reconcile myself to believe it; for it is scarcely possible that the British Government at this advanced and enlightened age, envied and admired as it is by the universe, could be capable of exercising or countenancing such a Gothic infringement on human Liberty.' See also Lascelles, *Granville Sharp*, p. 82: 'By whose orders and with what object this highly undesirable addition to the settlement was made is not clear. It need hardly be said that Granville . . . knew nothing of it.' (I suppose that the Government gave the orders, that the object was to get rid of those women, and that Sharp knew of it.)   [4] See Hoare, pp. 317, 328.

Majesty's sloop the Nautilus; but, meeting with stormy weather, they were separated, and it was the 19th March before they were all collected in Plymouth Sound. Thus the best part of the season was lost, and many of the people had been on board above three months, and were become very sickly. Unhappily, the allowance of rum, granted to them by the Government with the most benevolent intention, really proved their greatest bane: many of them drank their whole day's allowance at once, and got drunk with it: and this irregularity, together with a diet of salt provisions, and being rather too much crowded between decks, increased the sickness, and occasioned the loss of more than fifty lives, it is said, even before they reached Plymouth. Other bad consequences of the rum were disagreements and mutinous behaviour, for which twenty-four were discharged, and twenty-three ran away. Nevertheless, by an account before me, 411 settlers sailed from Plymouth on the 8th April 1787; so that they must have had some recruits, though they are not mentioned in the list.[1]

This account of Sharp, who does not mention the white prostitutes sailing with the negroes, is evidently not accurate. It seems that about 500 or 510 passengers—about 440 male and female black and about 60 or 70 male and female whites—were embarked in Portsmouth,[2] that 50 or more died,[3] 24 were discharged, and 23 ran away, and that finally 411 (black and white) sailed from Plymouth,[4] of whom 34 died at sea[5] and 377 arrived on 9 May 1787 in Sierra Leone.[6]

A 'grant of land to his Majesty from King Tom, the then neighbouring

[1] Ibid., pp. 315–16.

[2] The *Report of the Commissioners of Inquiry*, 1827, First Part, p. 8, contains the erroneous statement that 441 individuals, of whom 60 were white women, embarked, and this statement has since often been repeated (see, for example, Kennan, *Freetown 1800 to 1870*, p. 11). *Census Report 1931*, p. 8, says erroneously: 'It is not recorded whether any of the Africans were females: it is probable they were all males.' Statements concerning the number of white passengers vary a great deal. It is sometimes given as 60 (see, for example, *Report of Sierra Leone Company 1791*, p. 3; Macpherson, *Annals of Commerce*, vol. iv, p. 128), while sometimes the number of white women alone is said to have been 60 (see above). One of the women interviewed by Mrs. Falconbridge (see p. 51 below) told her that 'upwards of one hundred unfortunate women were seduced from England', while the Commissioner of Inquiry on the West Coast of Africa (*Report*, 1842, Part II, p. 246) put the number of 'white females' at 40. Butt-Thompson says (p. 72) that there 'were sent nine officials and sixty-two white women picked up from the streets of London and Portsmouth' (but he does not quote his source, and some of his statements concerning the journey are obviously incorrect).
As regards the male black who went to Sierra Leone Sharp stated that they were 'chiefly Seamen, that had served in the Royal Navy, last War, or as Rangers with the Army in the American Woods' (*Free English Territory in Africa*, pp. 9–10; see also the letter to his brother, dated Jan. 1788, Hoare, p. 260). Later reports even said that they were all men discharged from the army and navy after the American War (see, for example, *Report on the West Coast of Africa*, 1842, Part II, p. 246; Martin, *History of Colonies*, 1843, p. 531). But some recent writers say that they were mainly or exclusively negro slaves brought by their masters to England (see *Census Report 1931*, p. 8; Evans, *An Early Constitution of Sierra Leone*, 1932, p. 26). It seems, however, unlikely that many former domestic slaves should have been so adventurous, and I am inclined to think that the description by the earlier writers was correct.

[3] According to *Report of Sierra Leone Company 1791*, p. 5, 'about 50 died before they left Plymouth'. Many of the negroes and of the white women were apparently in ill health when they boarded the ships; see ibid., pp. 3–4.

[4] I see no reason to assume that any recruits were added at Plymouth. Sharp and Wadstrom (vol. ii, p. 221) made this assumption because they erroneously thought that the 411 people who sailed from Plymouth were all black. [5] See *Report of Sierra Leone Company 1791*, p. 5.

[6] According to *Report of the Commissioners of Inquiry*, 1827, First Part, p. 20, 'the original Settlers from London, in 1787' numbered 312, and according to *Ordinances of Sierra Leone 1858–1860*, p. 248, the 'North Americans' who arrived in 1787 numbered 347. The number of negroes who actually arrived was, I think, higher than 312 and lower than 347.

chief, was obtained for their use by Captain Thompson',[1] and the passengers were disembarked on 15 May.[2] A site was chosen for the town where Freetown is now,[3] and 'the lots were drawn and appropriated' on 12 June.[4] But 'the rains set in' on 28 June, and 'the huts of the colonists were neither wind nor water-tight, which increased the mortality so much that, though in June only 9 died, no fewer than 42 were carried off in July'.[5] By 16 September, when Captain Thompson sailed, altogether 86 of the 377 immigrants had died[6] while 15 had run away.[7] Thus 170 or more, that is about one-third of those originally embarked had died within about seven months, while 62 or nearly one-eighth had run away

[1] *Report of Sierra Leone Company 1791*, p. 3. See also Sharp, *Free English Territory in Africa*, p. 3: 'The District, lately purchased by Government for the new Free-Settlement at Sierra Leone, is nearly twice as large as the valuable Island of Barbadoes, being 20 Miles square, containing 256,000 Acres (and much more may be easily obtained) of Land, well watered with salubrious Springs, and situated on a fruitful Peninsula, between two noble navigable Rivers, (the great River of Sierra Leona, and the Sherbrô,) which receive the Waters of many others.' (This pamphlet was published anonymously at the beginning of 1790; its author, according to Hoare, p. 347, was Sharp.) All early sources give as area 20 miles square, or 400 square miles, or 256,000 acres. Only once—in his letter to Pitt of July 1790—did Sharp, probably by a slip of the pen, refer to the 'cession of twenty square miles of land' (Hoare, p. 355). Robert Montgomery Martin, who in his *History of the British Possessions in the Indian and Atlantic Ocean* (1837, p. 241) and in his *History of the Colonies of the British Empire* (1843, p. 531) still spoke of 'a piece of ground 20 miles square', said in *The British Colonies* (1852, vol. iv, p. 177) that the purchase comprised 'twenty square miles of territory', and this erroneous statement that the area was only 20 square miles has since been made over and over again (see, for example, Butt-Thompson, p. 74; Eveline C. Martin, *British West African Settlements 1750–1821*, pp. 105, 120; Lascelles, p. 83; *Census Report 1931*, p. 8).

The grant by King Tom (and its confirmation by King Jammy) was discussed on 30 May 1791 in the House of Commons. 'Mr. Buxton acknowledged it gave him pleasure to see that a different mode of obtaining foreign territory had taken place, in the instance of Africa, from that which had hitherto prevailed in other quarters of the globe. The mark of a King Tom or King Jamie subscribed to a grant, was to him infinitely more satisfactory, than the abominable and barbarous practice of seizing upon territory by driving inhabitants from their country.' But Mr. Stanley (Attorney-General for the Leeward Islands) ridiculed the grant, 'pronouncing it a circumstance that would render us the laughing stock of Europe' (*Parliamentary Register*, vol. xxix, pp. 581–2).

[2] See letter of 'Chief Magistrate' Weaver (a negro) to Sharp, 23 Apr. 1788, Hoare, p. 321.

[3] For details of the original location see Luke, 'Some Notes on the Creoles and their Land', p. 53. Captain Thompson named the harbour Saint George's Bay (see Sharp, *Free English Territory in Africa*, pp. 6–7). The town was named Granville Town (see Hoare, p. 344), and Sharp named the Colony 'Province of Freedom'. This name which was to show that no slave traffic was allowed in the Colony appears for the first time in a letter from Sharp 'to the worthy Inhabitants of the Province of Freedom, on the Mountains of Sierra Leone', dated 16 May 1788 (see ibid., p. 324).

[4] See letter of Sharp to Dr. Lettsom, 13 Oct. 1788, ibid., p. 317.   [5] Wadstrom, vol. ii, pp. 221–2.

[6] Sharp, in a letter to a lady in New York, dated 12 Jan. 1788 (Hoare, pp. 313–14), said that the delay of the ships 'fatally postponed their arrival on the coast till the rainy season commenced; whereby dreadful fevers and a great mortality ensued, the people not having had time to prepare sufficient shelter and accommodation for themselves at their landing. But the greatest blame of all is to be charged on the intemperance of the people themselves; for the most of them (both Whites and Blacks) became so besotted during the voyage, that they were totally unfit for business when they landed, and could hardly be prevailed on to assist in erecting their own huts. Besides, the distempers occasioned by their intemperance carried off a large proportion of them before they reached the coast; so that the climate of Africa is by no means chargeable with the mortality....' Sharp emphasized over and over again that the mortality on the coast was not attributable to the climate. See his letters to his brother Dr. J. Sharp, 22 Mar. 1788 (Hoare, p. 316), to the settlers, 16 May 1788 (ibid., p. 325), and to Dr. Lettsom, 13 Oct. 1788 (ibid., p. 316). See also in this connexion Evidence of Captain Thompson before a Committee of the House of Commons (*Minutes of Evidence on Slave-Trade 1790*, pp. 173–4); Wadstrom, vol. ii, p. 221.

In his letter to Dr. Lettsom, 13 Oct. 1788, Sharp mentions three Europeans who had died: the agent conductor (12 June 1787), the town-major, and the gardener (see Hoare, p. 317).

[7] See *Report of Sierra Leone Company 1791*, p. 5; Wadstrom, vol. ii, p. 8.

(23 in England and 15 in Sierra Leone) or been discharged (24 in England). Their number was, therefore, reduced to 276, of whom 212 were black men, 30 black women, 5 white men, and 29 white women.[1]

In the following years mortality was apparently low.

It does not appear . . . that after the first year was passed, there was any extraordinary mortality; it is even said by Green, one of the settlers now in England, who lived always with them, that during the two succeeding years he does not believe above five or six died out of near 200, who were then living in the same town.[2]

But when the chaplain of the Colony came home in March 1788 he told Sharp that just before his return the number of settlers was 'only 130 persons in all:[3] which great reduction he did not attribute to sickness, but merely to emigration; for they were too poor, it seems, to purchase live stock of the Natives, without which even the best land becomes almost useless, and affords but a scanty subsistence'.[4] Dispersion into the neighbourhood continued in the spring and 'sometimes there were not above forty persons left'.[5] In a letter to Pitt, written in June or July 1788, Sharp reported that 'all the surviving White people, the three surgeons, and the land-surveyor that was sent out last year at the expense of Government, have actually entered the service of the slave-dealers, and that the greater part also of the Black poor are gone into the same detestable service at different factories in the neighbourhood, and some even on board the slave-ships'.[6] Some of the negroes were sold themselves as slaves.[7]

[1] See ibid., p. 221. The accounts for the first two years never mention the presence of a child. However, the 'Chief Magistrate' in his letter dated Sierra Leone, 23 Apr. 1788, wrote to Sharp: 'I inform you that I was the person that went on board the Vernon at first, with my wife and child, and there continued till we arrived at Sierra Leone' (Hoare, p. 322).

[2] *Report of Sierra Leone Company 1791*, p. 5. The negro Green may not have been an accurate statistician, but as none of the many available letters complain of mortality (though they complain of many other things) it is safe to assume that it was actually not high. This would suggest that the main cause of the excessive mortality in the first rainy season was the lack of adequate shelter and that the intemperance of the settlers which has often been described as a decisive factor did not play such an important part.

[3] It should be noted, however, that this figure, which has been universally accepted as true, was possibly not correct, as the chaplain had lived far from the settlement. When Captain Thompson, on 14 May 1790, was asked by the Select Committee of the House of Commons 'Did they [the negroes] shew any attention or respect to the surgeon or clergyman that went out with them?' he answered: 'None; on the contrary, they could not be persuaded to build the clergyman a habitation, or any place of public worship, which was obliged to be performed, whilst I staid, under a large tree, frequently incommoded by rain; and at my departure the clergyman was obliged to take up his abode with the factor of Bens Island, a great distance from them up the River' (*Minutes of Evidence on Slave-Trade 1790*, p. 173). The chaplain stayed on that island all through the winter, a sick man, suffering from consumption, and called at the settlement only on his way back to England.   [4] Sharp's letter to Dr. Lettsom, 13 Oct. 1788, Hoare, p. 317.

[5] Sharp's letter to Thomas Steele (one of the principal secretaries to the Lords of the Treasury), dated 4 May 1789, ibid., p. 337. See also Sharp, *Free English Territory in Africa*, p. 10: '. . . the Community has sometimes been reduced, by desertion, to 30 or 40 Men.'

[6] Hoare, p. 328. The 'Chief Magistrate' wrote to Sharp on 23 Apr. 1788: 'Several of the people have left the place, I may safely say the chief part of them; some a trading in vessels for slaves, other at factories, doing what they can to get provision for their support, for we are very much in distress here' (ibid., p. 322). The Europeans had hardly an excuse for entering the service of the slave-traders—one of the surgeons, in a letter to Sharp, 'acknowledged his having been drawn away by the offer of a considerable salary'; see ibid., p. 328—but many negro settlers probably had no other means of earning a livelihood. (Hoare, p. 328, indicates the names of the three surgeons, but two of those thus named came actually only later to Sierra Leone.)

[7] The 'Chief in Command' Reid (a negro) wrote in Sept. 1788 to Sharp that the settlers 'got

When Sharp had learned through the chaplain of the reduction in the number of settlers he became 'apprehensive that all the rest would be obliged to disperse in like manner, unless a speedy supply of live stock, with some recruits, could be immediately sent out',[1] and on 23 April 1788 he chartered at his own expense the *Myro*, a brig of 160 tons.[2] He decided to send this time chiefly white colonists, and at first apparently accepted the applications of 60 people[3] but 'for fear of crowding the vessel too much' selected 50 of them. However, 'several of those that had been admitted deserted the vessel, just as she was ready to sail, when it was too late for me to make up the complement; whereby only thirty-nine passengers, instead of fifty (the intended number), actually set out'.[4] The *Myro* (Captain Taylor) sailed on 7 June,[5] 'touched at St. Jago, one of the Cape de Verd Islands, and did not arrive at S. Leona till the 6th of Aug.'[6] The new colonists again greatly disappointed Sharp.

Of these [39], twelve died of fevers and one by a wound, four were left at the Cape de Verd Islands, and two returned; so that only twenty remain there.[7]

All the White people whom I sent out last year, to assist in supporting the settlement, have been wicked enough to go into the service of the Slave Trade at the neighbouring factories, having been enticed away, I suppose, by high wages . . . .[8]

But in other respects the arrival of the *Myro* proved to be a success.

Great numbers of the dispersed settlers returned on the arrival of the *Myro*; and King Naimbanna, one of the most powerful chiefs in that neighbourhood, who

in a little trouble with King Tom, and he catched two of them, and sold them on board a Frenchman bound for the West Indies'. He further said that five of the settlers 'went up to Bance Island, and broke open a factory belonging to one Captain Boys, and stole a number of things; but they were detected, and Captain Boys sold the whole five of them' (ibid., p. 323; see also Sharp's letters to Thomas Steele, ibid., p. 339). Some more settlers were kidnapped in the following two or three years (see, for example, *Report of Sierra Leone Company 1794*, pp. 105–7). But most of the captured negroes were released.

   [1] Sharp's letter to the settlers, 16 May 1788, Hoare, p. 327.
   [2] See Sharp's letter to Pitt, June or July 1788, ibid., p. 328, and his letter to Dr. Lettsom, 13 Oct. 1788, ibid., p. 318.
   [3] See his letter to the settlers, 16 May 1788, ibid., p. 325.
   [4] Sharp's letter to Dr. Lettsom, 13 Oct. 1788, ibid., p. 318. In his letter to Thomas Steele, 4 May 1789, he reported that the 'thirty-nine' were 'chiefly White people' (ibid., p. 337). In his letter to John Jay (President of the Society at New York for promoting the Manumission of Slaves, &c., and protecting such of them as have been liberated), 7 Mar. 1789, he said that he had sent out 'some poor Negroes and other settlers' (ibid., p. 335). Macpherson (vol. iv, p. 175) says erroneously that the 50 people, Sharp had selected, were all negroes.
   [5] See Sharp's letter to Dr. Lettsom, Hoare, p. 318.   [6] Wadstrom, vol. ii, p. 223.
   [7] Letter to Thomas Steele, 4 May 1789, Hoare, p. 337. See also Sharp's letter to Jay, 7 Mar. 1789: 'It is but within a very few days that I have received the long-expected letters from the settlement, and the diary of Captain Taylor's proceedings.—I am sorry to inform you, that the accounts are much more unfavourable than I had reason to expect: thirteen persons out of thirty-nine, whom I sent by the Myro, are dead; and almost all the passengers had been ill. This, however, I still find, is not to be attributed altogether to the climate, but to a total neglect in clearing the under-wood near the settlement, and to the want of judgment in the settlers, who have built their houses and huts on swampy ground, near the bottom of a hill, instead of the top of it . . . . It seems, also, that too free a use of strong liquors (notwithstanding the earnest warning I gave to the passengers of the *Myro* concerning the fatal intemperance of the former settlers) is still to be reckoned among the causes of continued impediment and sickness.' (Ibid., p. 335; see also in this connexion his letter 'To the worthy Passengers on Board the Myro Brig', 20 May 1788, ibid., Appendix, p. xxviii, and Lascelles, pp. 83–4.)
   [8] Letter to the Rev. Mr. Samuel Hopkins (Newport, Rhode Island), 25 July 1789, Hoare, p. 343. See also his letter to the settlers in Sierra Leone, 11 Nov. 1789, ibid., p. 344.

before refused to sign the former deed of purchase for the land, and lately, just before the arrival of the *Myro*, had even given the settlers warning to quit the settlement, has now formed a solemn covenant with Captain Taylor in behalf of the settlers; and, in consideration of the presents received as the stipulated price of re-purchase, has signed a complete deed of resignation to the Settlers for ever, of all the land before granted by King Tom, whose successor, since his death, has also signed the deed, with some other chiefs:[1] so that my sending the Myro has really saved the settlement. . . .

When Captain Taylor left the settlement last September, the number of people was still about one hundred and thirty in all,[2] and I have no doubt they will gladly receive any free Negroes that the States of America shall be pleased to assist with passage, provisions, and necessaries for defence and establishment . . . .[3]

Many more returned to the Colony after Captain Taylor had left, and finally the settlers numbered again 'about 200 persons Men, Women and Children'.[4] But the Colony did not prosper, and on 22 or 23 July 1789 Sharp received letters from the 'Chief Magistrate', his wife 'in the name

---

[1] The treaty (reprinted in *British and Foreign State Papers 1872–3*, vol. lxiii, pp. 1091–2) contained a Declaration which began as follows: 'Know all men by these presents that I, King Nambaner, Chief of Sierra Leone, on the Grain Coast of Africa, by and with the consent of the other Kings, Princes, Chiefs, and potentates subscribing hereto, in consideration of the presents, as by a list annexed, now made me by Captain John Taylor, of His Britannic Majesty's brig *Miro*, in behalf of and for the sole benefit of the free community of settlers, their heirs and successors, lately arrived from England, and under the protection of the British Government, have granted, and by these presents do grant and for ever quit claim to a certain district of land for the settling of the said free community to be theirs, their heirs and successors, for ever; that is to say, all the land, wood, water, &c., which are now contained from the bay commonly called Frenchman's Bay, but by these presents changed to that of St. George's Bay, coastwise up the River Sierra Leone to Gambia Island, and southerly or inland from the river side, 20 miles.' The treaty was signed by Captain Taylor, three settlers, King Nambaner (Naimbanna) and four other native representatives (but not King Jammy). To it was added the following Note: 'This is to certify to all to whom these presents may come, that we whose names are hereunto subscribed make oath that the purchase of the land, &c., made by Captain Thompson was not (to our certain knowledge) valid, it having been purchased from people who had no authority to sell the same.'

It must have been very difficult indeed for the naval officers (Thompson, Taylor, Clarkson) who concluded treaties on behalf of the British Government between 1787 and 1792 to appraise correctly the respective rights of Naimbanna and 'the other Kings, Princes, Chiefs, and potentates'. The 'other kings', whose kingdom often comprised only a village of perhaps fifty huts and its immediate neighbourhood, frequently deceived the Europeans by claiming a sovereignty which they did not in fact enjoy, and this deception was the easier as their overlord often chose not to interfere immediately but to wait and see how matters would develop. Governor Clarkson, who at first also misunderstood the position (see his Journal, 28 Mar. 1792, Ingham, *Sierra Leone after a Hundred Years*, p. 33), recognized, after having attended several palavers, that 'the other kings', &c., were vassals of King Naimbanna: 'I understand the dominions of King Naimbanna extend from this river up to Rokelle and the interior country eastward, about two-and-a-half days' journey, reckoned at forty mile per day, and southward towards Sherbro, four or five days' journey. The power of King Naimbanna is absolute, though in matters of consequence he does not appear to like deciding without the concurrence of the inferior chiefs in the country; but if he grows angry with them, they will all submit to his opinion . . .' (*Diary of Clarkson*, 4 Oct. 1792, p. 72).

[2] Butt-Thompson says (p. 75): 'When the surviving twenty passengers landed they found waiting them 29 white women, 30 black and mulatto children, 5 officials, and 66 Negroes. All the rest had died.' But this statement is inaccurate. The 130 people whom Captain Taylor left in the Colony included not only the dispersed settlers who had returned after the arrival of the *Myro* but also practically all those who had come on the *Myro*. 'All the rest' had not died; many had migrated to other places. It seems, moreover, unlikely that none of the 29 white women whom Captain Thompson left there a year earlier should have died or emigrated. Finally, it is out of the question that there should have been as many as 30 children.

[3] Sharp's letter to Jay, 7 Mar. 1789, Hoare, pp. 335–6.

[4] Sharp, *Free English Territory in Africa*, p. 10; see also Sharp's letter to Hopkins, 25 July 1789, Hoare, p. 343.

of the ladies of Sierra Leone', and three other negroes, in which they required that some respectable merchants or factors might be prevailed on to settle among them.[1] Sharp, who could not afford to carry the financial burden of such an undertaking,[2] answered on 11 November 1789:

I am exerting myself as much as possible, to engage several respectable merchants and gentlemen to form a Company, in order to carry on an honourable trade with the coast of Africa; and I have at last great hopes of success.[3]

But in the meantime the settlers had become involved in a dispute between a British warship and King Jammy, the successor of King Tom, in the course of which the British burned the town of the King. After the warship had left, a palaver was called of all the surrounding Chiefs who, by a judicial sentence, ordered the town of the settlers to be burned down, giving them three days' notice to quit.

About 180 or 200 settlers, leaving their plantations, and a great quantity of poultry behind them, were then dispersed. The Agent of the [English] Slave Factory [at Bance Island] gave them protection for the first five or six weeks at Bob's Island in the neighbourhood, but they were sent away afterwards to Par Boson's Town, 12 miles up the country.[4]

The town was destroyed in November 1789,[5] but Sharp received 'the melancholy news' only in April 1790.[6] In the meantime he had succeeded in founding a Company of Merchants, the St. George's Bay Company. The first meeting was held on 17 February 1790,[7] and Sharp sent to the King a 'Memorial of Granville Sharp, Citizen of London, in Behalf of himself and Others' which 'humbly sheweth'

That the Black poor, and others, subjects of the Crown of Great Britain, who settled on the land lately purchased by your Majesty for their use at Sierra Leona, consisting, by the last account, of about two hundred persons, men, women, and children, are so extremely poor that they cannot effectually avail themselves of the extraordinary natural advantages of that fruitful and healthy district without some further aid; and therefore they have earnestly requested in their last letters, that some merchants or factors might be induced to settle among them, in order to keep up a constant communication between England and the new English territory in Africa, whereby they hope to procure the necessary aid and assistance.

That your Memorialist, in consequence of this request, has solicited and obtained promises from several respectable gentlemen and merchants of London, that they will form themselves into a Company, and advance their respective shares and proportions of money, to enable them to send proper factors and agents to St. George's Bay, the principal harbour of the new English territory, in order to promote and carry on the trade of the settlement in British manufactures with the Natives

---

[1] See Sharp's letters to Thomas Steele, 23 July, Hoare, p. 339, and to the Inhabitants of Granville Town, 11 Nov., ibid., p. 344; Sharp, *Free English Territory in Africa*, p. 10.

[2] See his letter to the settlers, 22 Jan. 1791: '. . . it was not in my power, as an individual, to send you any immediate assistance, having already sunk above 1,400 *l.* of my own private fortune in endeavouring to promote your welfare, partly in sending out settlers and farther assistance by the Myro brig in 1788, and partly in assisting poor People of Colour here, who are desirous of going to the settlement, and supporting several settlers returned from thence . . . .' (Hoare, p. 359.)

[3] Ibid., p. 347.

[4] *Report of Sierra Leone Company 1791*, pp. 6–7; see also ibid., p. 37, and *1794*, pp. 102–3.

[5] See Wadstrom, vol. ii, p. 225.

[6] See Sharp's letter to the settlers, 27 Sept. 1790, Hoare, p. 357.

[7] The Directors included Wilberforce and Thornton. See minutes of the meeting, Wadstrom, vol. ii, pp. 224–5.

of the neighbouring coast and rivers in Africa, provided your Majesty will be pleased to grant them a Charter of Incorporation.[1]

Sharp had written on 13 February to Wilberforce: 'It is of great importance to the safety of the New Settlement, that the Charter of Incorporation should be expedited as soon as possible.'[2] Yet, in spite of all his efforts, he did not obtain the desired charter.[3] But the Company worked without a charter until 1791 when it was transformed into the financially much more powerful Sierra Leone Company.[4]

Apparently in May 1790 Sharp got further news about the condition of the settlers.

. . . I have been informed that they have obtained some land from one of the African Chiefs, about nine miles above Bance Island, in the same river, with leave to build houses; that about seventy of them still persisted in keeping together, though much pains had been taken to separate them; that about eight or ten of them, being artificers, were employed at Bance Island; that several more of them were at Rohanna, a town adjoining to the settlement, under King Naimbanna, and that the rest were dispersed on the coast—so that I have no doubt of their reassembling as soon as their land can be recovered.[5]

Thereupon the St. George's Bay Company decided on 27 August to send the cutter *Lapwing* as soon as possible with a supply of clothing and provisions to Sierra Leone.[6] But this ship did not sail until December.[7] In the meantime the Company had appointed Alexander Falconbridge[8] to

[1] Hoare, p. 350. See also Sharp, *Free English Territory in Africa*, pp. 10–13.

[2] Hoare, p. 350.

[3] He had an interview with Pitt, apparently on 24 or 25 Apr., and sent him letters on 26 Apr., 10 June, in July, on 28 Aug., and possibly also in September (see Hoare, pp. 351–8). In his letter of 28 Aug. he speaks of 'the opposition of the Attorney-General to their [the Company's] very reasonable proposal of a limited Charter without any exclusive privileges'. See also in this connexion *Reasons against giving a Territorial Grant to a Company of Merchants, to Colonize and Cultivate the Peninsula of Sierra Leona, on the Coast of Africa*, p. 14: 'The present subscribers are only 100 individuals, at £.50 a piece, applying for a grant of territory on the coast of Africa equal to all the West Indies, and which would cost 70 million, before they could settle it.' (A pencil mark on the title-page of the copy of this pamphlet in the British Museum gives Mr. Campbel as author.)

See also Eveline Martin, pp. 108–9, as regards the opposition from the Company of Merchants Trading to Africa.

[4] See p. 53 below.

[5] Sharp's letter to Pitt, 10 June 1790, Hoare, p. 353.

[6] See Sharp's letter to Pitt, 28 Aug. 1790, ibid., p. 355.

[7] See postscript to Sharp's letter to the settlers (of 27 Sept.), dated 14 Dec. 1790, printed in *The Royal Gazette and Sierra Leone Advertiser*, 7 Mar. 1818, p. 57: 'Though the Lapwing Cutter, was ordered and prepared for Sailing in September last, yet so great has been the urgency and uncertainty of public affairs in the expectation of a war (which now, God be thanked, is at an end) that we could not venture to give Alexander Kennedy, his final orders for Sailing 'till this day.'

[8] Falconbridge had been to the coast of Africa as a surgeon of slave ships for four voyages, but 'had left the trade upon principle' and had settled in England, where he collaborated with Thomas Clarkson and the committee for the abolition of the slave trade (see Thomas Clarkson, vol. i, pp. 348–53, 459–60, 463). On the instance of Clarkson he 'quitted his comfortable situation at Ludway, to enlist in the present (though I fear chimerical) cause of freedom and humanity' (Falconbridge, p. 117). Unlike most other officers sent to Sierra Leone in the 1790's he was an uncompromising enemy of the slave-traders. (Zachary Macaulay, on 18 June 1793, wrote quite indignantly in his Journal: 'Falconbridge's professions and conduct indeed gave the Slave-traders great reason to believe that nothing less was intended than to ruin them by the most unfair means . . .' (Viscountess Knutsford, *Life and Letters of Zachary Macaulay*, p. 27).)

be their chief agent, and on 5 January 1791 he embarked[1] with a commission to examine and report on the state of the Colony, to collect the settlers

[1] See Falconbridge, p. 4. Hoare, p. 273, and Evans, p. 27, say that Falconbridge sailed in Sept.
1790: this is evidently a mistake. On the other hand, Sharp cannot have written to the settlers
as late as 22 Jan. 1791 (see Hoare, pp. 359–60): 'The Company have appointed Mr. Alexander
Falconbridge, the bearer of this letter . . . .' Some writers, for example Eveline Martin (p. 110),
say that Falconbridge sailed in the *Lapwing*, but he actually sailed in the *Duke of Bucleugh*, which
arrived in Sierra Leone two or three weeks after the *Lapwing* (see Falconbridge, p. 12). What the
Viscountess Knutsford tells of a simultaneous journey of her grandfather Zachary Macaulay (the
father of the historian) to Sierra Leone seems also quite inaccurate. She relates (pp. 19–22): 'It
[the *Lapwing*] was soon followed by another vessel, which carried out to Sierra Leone the Reverend
Nathaniel Gilbert . . . and Zachary Macaulay, whose mission on this voyage appears to have been
one simply of interest and observation, prompted by Thomas Babington . . . . In Macaulay's first
letter to Mr. Babington from the West coast of Africa, dated River Gambia, January 1, 1791, the
following sentence occurs: "We arrived here on the 25th after a passage of four weeks, which passed
very pleasantly in the society of Mr. Gilbert. . . ." In the spring of [1792] Macaulay returned to
England. The prudence, discretion, and firmness of character which he had evinced during his
stay in the Colony had gained the approbation of the Directors, and he received the appointment
of second Member of Council at Sierra Leone. He left England again at the end of the year, and
arrived in Africa in January 1793.' Actually Macaulay had never been in Sierra Leone before he
went there as second councillor. He therefore had no opportunity of evincing his 'prudence, discretion, and firmness of character' in the Colony before 1793. It may seem unbelievable that
Macaulay's biographer conveys such a wrong picture of his life in 1791–2, but there is ample
evidence to prove that he was not in Sierra Leone at any time during those years.

(1) When in 1804 the Committee on the Petition of the Sierra Leone Company asked Macaulay
'How long did you reside in Sierra Leone . . . ?' he answered 'I resided there from the Beginning of
January 1793 to the Month of April 1799, except about a Year that I was absent' (*Report*, p. 52).

(2) Mrs. Falconbridge, who stayed in Sierra Leone from Jan. to June 1791 and from Feb. 1792
to June 1793, wrote on 15 Jan. 1793 (Falconbridge, p. 185): 'Arrived a Cutter belonging to Bance
Island, from Isle de Loss. A Mr. M'Aulay, Member of Council, and the Reverend Mr. Gilbert,
came passengers in her.' (Macaulay's letter to Babington was evidently written on his way to
Sierra Leone on 1 Jan. 1793 and not on 1 Jan. 1791.)

(3) The chairman of the Sierra Leone Company wrote in July 1792 to Governor John Clarkson
who had been in the Colony since the beginning of March: 'We have a very capable manager of an
estate who has left Jamaica for Sierra Leone; and is now among us; he is brother in law of Mr.
Babington and possibly might be fit for more general service. His name is Macaulay.' (*Diary of
Clarkson*, pp. 28–9.)

It is obvious that if Macaulay had been in Sierra Leone in 1791–2 (1) he would have told the
Committee so, (2) Mrs. Falconbridge would not, in 1793, have spoken of him as a perfect stranger,
(3) the chairman of the Company would have mentioned the fact in his letter to the Governor.

George Otto Trevelyan called his sister's book 'a complete and excellent biography of Zachary
Macaulay' (*Life and Letters of Lord Macaulay*, p. 520), and this recommendation may have
induced recent writers to repeat the story of Zachary's journey as an observer to Sierra Leone (see
Charles Booth, *Zachary Macaulay*, 1934, p. 24; Coupland, 'The Abolition of the Slave Trade',
1940, p. 211). Trevelyan himself did not commit this mistake but said: 'Born in 1768, he was sent
out at the age of sixteen by a Scotch house of business as bookkeeper to an estate in Jamaica, of
which he soon rose to be sole manager. . . . But by the time he was four-and-twenty he . . . returned
to his native country.' (*Life and Letters*, pp. 21–3.) Zachary may have told his children, for pedago-
gical reasons, what a marvellous youngster he was at 16, but he told the Committee of the House in
1804 that he 'resided in the West Indies about Six Years; at Jamaica.' (*Report of Committee*, p. 56),
and as he returned in 1792 he went out at the age of 18—under what circumstances is anybody's
guess.—I see no reason to doubt that Zachary actually stayed about six years (1786–92) in Jamaica,
but there seems to be a consensus of opinion that whatever may have been the number of years it
was not six.

| | Macaulay in Jamaica | |
Authority	Period	Years
Knutsford (granddaughter), pp. 6, 9 .	1785–9	4
Booth (great-grandson), p. 20 .	1785–9	4
Trevelyan (grandson), pp. 21–3	1784–92	8
Dictionary of National Biography, vol. xii, p. 419	1784–92	8
The Christian Observer (ed. by Zachary 1802–16) *1839*, p. 759	1782–92	10

and—pending the grant of the Charter—to take measures for their temporary relief. He arrived in Sierra Leone apparently on 30 January.[1]

The location of the settlers at that time has been described as follows:

About 50 of them live at Pa Boson's, about 12 miles above Bance Island, and a few live and sometimes work on Bance Island. The others are scattered up and down the country. I cannot get any exact account how many there are, &c.[2]

The Court of Directors of the Sierra Leone Company published the following statement:

Mr. Falconbridge ... found forty-eight of these settlers residing at this town of Par Boson; some were living in the parts around; some had gone to the West Indies, some to England, and there was a general fear of their being all made slaves. Mr. Falconbridge brought down these forty-eight settlers to form a new settlement at Fora Bay, which is about a mile and a half further from King Jammy's ground than their former town, where he took possession of some deserted houses that were standing.[3] Sixteen settlers had joined them from other parts before he came away, and more were expected to come in.

Of the sixty-four settlers left at Fora Bay, thirty-nine were black men, nineteen black women, and six white women.[4]

Mrs. Falconbridge, who met the white women, wrote:

I never did, and God grant I never may again, witness so much misery as I was forced to be a spectator of here: Among the outcasts were seven of our country women, decrepid with disease, and so disguised with filth and dirt, that I should never have supposed they were born white; add to this, almost naked from head to foot; in short, their appearance was such as I think would extort compassion from the most callous heart; but I declare they seemed insensible to shame, or the wretchedness of their situation themselves; I begged they would get washed, and gave them what cloaths I could conveniently spare: Falconbridge had a hut appropriated as a hospital, where they were kept separate from the other settlers, and by his attention and care, they recovered in a few weeks.[5]

The 64 people collected by Falconbridge in Granville Town (Forah Bay) constituted only one-third of the settlers who had lived in the Colony before the attack by the natives, and the remainder apparently never returned.[6] Falconbridge sailed on 16 June 1791,[7] leaving the settlers in charge of a Greek who had come to Sierra Leone in the *Lapwing*.[8]

[1] See Falconbridge, p. 10.

[2] Letter from Alexander Kennedy to the St. George's Bay Company, dated Baunce Island, 9 Feb. 1791, quoted by Wadstrom, vol. ii, p. 225.

[3] See also Wadstrom, vol. ii, p. 220. 'At the palaver held on this occasion, Mr. Falconbridge, in behalf of the St. George's Bay Company repurchased from King Naimbanna, and the subordinate chiefs ... all the land which had formerly been purchased by Capt. Thompson. But it was agreed that the colonists should not build on the former spot. Mr. F. therefore took possession of a village, consisting of 15 or 16 good huts, which the natives had recently abandoned, from a notion of it's being haunted; and he rightly thought that their superstitious fears would tend to prevent their hostile attempts, especially in the night.' The village was again named Granville Town. For further details see Falconbridge, pp. 26–31, 45–56.

[4] *Report of Sierra Leone Company 1791*, pp. 7–8.

[5] Letter dated Granville Town, 13 May 1791, Falconbridge, pp. 56–7.

[6] 'Many of them turned slave dealers probably in some instances from necessity ...' (*Diary of Clarkson*, p. 9). Zachary Macaulay, referring to the native Chief of Port Logo in the Rio Pongo, who had afforded shelter to many of the original settlers at the time of their dispersion, wrote in his Journal (12 Sept. 1793): 'He has now with him two of the first Settlers, who have continued to prefer living with him to returning to Sierra Leone ...' (Knutsford, p. 49).

[7] See Falconbridge, p. 85.   [8] See ibid., p. 54.

The men appeared to be determined to defend themselves; they are warmly attached to the Society that sent them out; but having been long disused to the restraint of regular government, they seemed in general turbulent and disorderly.[1]

They continued in fact to be most turbulent and disorderly. Lieutenant Clarkson, who came from Nova Scotia to Sierra Leone in March 1792 with over a thousand negroes whom he settled in Freetown,[2] and who was a most generous man with deep sympathies for all suffering blacks, wrote on 18 April to the Chairman of the Court of Directors of the Sierra Leone Company:

There is no man for whom I have a more perfect respect than Mr Sharp, but he has allowed his goodness to be most sadly imposed upon. The black people he sent out, have, generally speaking, so bad a character, that we are afraid to trust them among us. I have once tried them, but was obliged to turn them all out of the colony, and threaten to flog the first that returned. But I have since received a petition from them, begging to be favoured with another trial, and I mean to grant it, though I shall judge it prudent to keep them for a time in suspense.[3]

On 2 August he sent the following message 'to the Freeholders of Granville Town':

As we are now ready to lay out the lots of land for the different people of Free Town, I cannot suffer them to draw their lots without giving you an opportunity of partaking of the same chance. I am ready to receive you under our protection, provided you agree to our laws, and to consider you with the same tenderness as those I brought with me from America. I am determined to forget everything that has passed, and consider you and our people as one. If you will behave well, I will do my utmost to promote your happiness, and, therefore, I hope we shall live in perfect harmony together. After this offer, and having put off the people from drawing for their lands, on purpose to give you an opportunity of joining them, I now declare, if you do not agree, you must consider this as a warning to quit your present residence, and we shall give you *eight months* to remove your property, houses, etc.[4]

Having obtained a satisfactory reply, he wrote on 4 August:

I have just received your letter, and am happy to find such a likelihood of unanimity and harmony between the Freeholders of Granville and Free Town. It gives me heartfelt satisfaction to find that we are likely to get into some kind of order, and hope we may begin, under the blessing of God, to date our happiness with that of your posterity from this hour. I shall from this day consider the inhabitants of Granville and Free Town as breathren . . . .[5]

Thus, the remnant of the first settlers became merged in the much larger body of negroes who had been transferred to the Colony from Nova Scotia,[6] and it is impossible to appraise numerically what became of them. The

---

[1] *Report of Sierra Leone Company 1791*, p. 8. See also letter of Mrs. Falconbridge, dated Granville Town, 13 May 1791: ' . . . I really think [we] have less to fear from them [the natives] than our own people, who are extremely turbulent, and so unruly at times, that 'tis with difficulty Falconbridge can assuage them, or preserve the least decorum' (Falconbridge, p. 60).

[2] See p. 66 below.   [3] Ingham, p. 58. See also ibid., pp. 35–6.
[4] Ibid., pp. 102–3.   [5] Ibid., p. 103.

[6] In their report of 1798 the Directors of the Company, writing of the settlers, made the following footnote: 'By settlers, the reader is always to understand the Nova Scotian blacks, and a few of the black poor originally sent from England; there being few or no other settlers now in the Colony' (p. 5). But even half a century later, when many thousands of other settlers were living in the Colony, the term 'settler' was used officially and unofficially to designate the descendants of the Nova Scotians (and of the original black poor).

Commissioners of Inquiry reported in 1827: 'At present there are not more than six or eight of them in the colony.'[1] I doubt very much that anyone was still living there 40 years after their arrival,[2] but the number of their descendants may well have exceeded six or eight.[3]

2. 'Nova Scotians'

Granville Sharp had found it impossible to obtain a charter for the St. George's Bay Company. Thereupon the Company withdrew their application, changed their name to the Sierra Leone Company, and put out a new Manifesto.[4] On 28 March 1791 Henry Thornton (the prominent London banker) moved in the House of Commons, 'That leave be given to bring in a bill for establishing a Company for carrying on trade between the kingdom of Great Britain and the coasts, harbours, and countries of Africa; and for enabling the said Company to hold by grant from His Majesty, his heirs, and successors, and from the native Princes of Africa, a certain district of land, commonly called the Peninsula of Sierra Leona, now vested in His Majesty, or belonging to the said Princes, for the better enabling the said Company to carry on the said trade.'[5] The Bill met again with considerable opposition on the part of Liverpool merchants and other advocates of slavery.[6] At the third reading, on 30 May, Thornton defended the Bill:

When first brought in, he said, it had been objected to as a grant of country which His Majesty had no right to give. The fact was, it granted no land whatever, but enabled His Majesty to grant such land as he should hereafter possess in consequence of purchases to be made. Another objection was, that the bill was calculated to establish a monopoly. This also had been refuted, and it had been shewn, that it was no monopoly, but that it was intended to secure a set of gentlemen, who upon public spirited motives, mixed with some speculative views of commerce, were willing to venture a certain capital, from being made answerable, with their private fortunes, for more than their respective shares in the undertaking.[7]

'At length the House divided; Ayes, 87; Noes, 9'[8] and on 6 June the Bill 'received the Royal assent by commission'.[9] The duration of the Act,[10] and consequently of the Company, was limited to 31 years from 1 July 1791.

In the election of the Company's officers, the compliment, so often paid to Mr. Sharp on other occasions, of placing him in the chair, was here omitted, as the philanthropic object of the settlement had by many been deemed so highly visionary,

[1] *Report*, First Part, p. 8.
[2] Their number had been reduced not only by deaths but also by voluntary or involuntary migration. Some, no doubt, after having committed a crime or for other reasons, took refuge among the natives. One, named Cambridge, sold 'a slave to a Dutch Sloop' and was sent back 'to England to be disposed of as the Court of directors of the Sierra Leone Company might think proper' (see *Diary of Clarkson*, pp. 9–11, 16–17).
[3] Butt-Thompson says (p. 79): 'Some of their names, Strong, Somerset, Bidwell, and Cambridge ... are still to be found in the colony.'
[4] See Butt-Thompson, p. 80.   [5] *Parliamentary Register*, vol. xxix, p. 18.
[6] See ibid., pp. 18, 316–18, 486, 575–84. See also Eveline Martin, pp. 110–11.
[7] *Parliamentary Register*, vol. xxix, p. 579.   [8] Ibid., p. 584.   [9] Ibid., vol. xxx, p. 293.
[10] 31 Geo. III, cap. 55. The Act provided among other things 'That it shall not be lawful for the said Company ... to deal or traffic in the buying or selling of Slaves, or ... to have, hold, appropriate, or employ any Person or Persons in a State of Slavery'.

that it was judged advisable to elect a chairman, whose ordinary connections with concerns of more acknowledged substantial foundation might seem to authorise the expectation of success. The person chosen was the late Henry Thornton, Esq. afterwards Governor of the Bank.[1]

In a later report the Directors of the Company stated:

When the Act of Parliament had passed for incorporating the Sierra Leone Company, and a considerable capital appeared likely to be raised for carrying on the undertaking, the Directors had an opportunity of rendering, as they conceived, a very important service to the colony, by the acquisition of an additional number of free black colonists, acquainted with the English language, and accustomed to labor in hot climates.[2]

As stated above, a number of American negroes had been brought in 1783 to Nova Scotia, where they suffered great hardship.

. . . these people were formerly slaves in America and during their servitude many of them were treated with the greatest barbarity. In consequence of the war in America and a proclamation from the British army offering freedom to any slave who would desist from his master and join the British troops, the present colonists with several others, took every opportunity of leaving their oppressors in hopes of finding a happy asylum under the protection of the British army.

At the conclusion of the war, from their fidelity and bravery, the English nation were determined to reward them for their services, and put themselves to an enormous expense in transporting them and their families from the American Provinces, to New Brunswick and Nova Scotia. Upon their arrival they were promised a certain quantity of land, and provisions for three years, with every other encouragement, such as implements of husbandry, a musket each, and various other things, for the purchase of which Government actually paid. When I tell you that upwards of three thousand people embarked for Nova Scotia, etc., you will be surprised to hear that not three hundred got their promises performed . . . .[3]

Thomas Peters . . . seems to have been selected by his fellow negroes to go to England, to lay the complaints of himself and other blacks similarly situated before the king. Shortly after his arrival he presented a memorial to the Secretary of State —then the Hon. Mr. Grenville, setting forth the grievances of himself and his friends. He stated . . . that some of the negroes would prefer to take their allotments and remain in the province. But others, and among them himself, would rather go to a warmer climate—one better suited to their constitutions.[4]

While in London Peters got into touch with the Sierra Leone Company, which apparently persuaded him that the would-be emigrants should go to the new Colony.[5]

The Directors concurred with the Delegate in applying to his Majesty's Ministers for a passage for them at the expense of government, and having obtained a favourable answer to their application,[6] they immediately availed themselves of the

---

[1] Hoare, p. 364. The Directors were elected on 13 July; 'roughly the balance seems to have been preserved between profit-seeking and philanthropy' (Eveline Martin, p. 113).

[2] *Report of Sierra Leone Company 1794*, p. 4.

[3] Instructions of Governor John Clarkson to William Dawes, 5 Oct. 1792, *Diary of Clarkson*, p. 84. See also *Report of Sierra Leone Company 1794*, pp. 63–7.

[4] Archibald, 'Story of Deportation of Negroes from Nova Scotia to Sierra Leone', p. 135.

[5] According to the Directors' report of 1794 Peters had said that many of the negroes in Nova Scotia 'were desirous of becoming colonists at the settlement which they understood was likely to be made at Sierra Leone' (pp. 4–5), but it seems improbable that they actually had heard of such a plan.

[6] The Viscountess Knutsford says (p. 21): 'The English Government, after receiving a reply from the Company accepting the negroes as Colonists, thankful to get rid of so troublesome a responsi-

services of Lieut. Clarkson, who very handsomely offered to go to Nova Scotia, in order to make the necessary proposals, and to superintend the collecting and bringing over such free blacks to Sierra Leone, as might be willing to emigrate.[1]

The Directors then decided to send to Sierra Leone Europeans as colonists and for the administration of the Colony. In their report, submitted 19 October 1791, they said:

The Directors have . . . felt themselves bound to take care, that together with their first adventure, a sufficient strength shall be sent out for security against external violence, and maintaining domestic tranquility.

They have resolved, that three or four vessels shall sail at once with a considerable number of persons who will thus be an effectual protection and accommodation to each other. The ships will sail in a few weeks, and will carry a sufficient quantity of articles, both for opening a store in the way of commerce, and for the use of the colony itself.[2]

---

bility on such easy terms, agreed to defray the whole expense of their removal.' But this statement does not do justice to the intentions of the Government. See Archibald, pp. 135–6: 'In a dispatch to Mr. Parr, then governor of Nova Scotia, dated the 3rd August, 1791, Mr. Grenville reprehends him vehemently for the neglect complained of, orders an immediate inquiry into the facts, and directs him, if he finds them as stated, to issue the promised grants in places so favorable as to make some atonement for the injustice done to the negroes. He then goes on to state what Peters had brought to his notice, in reference to the wish of some of the blacks to be sent to a warmer climate, and orders him to despatch messengers to the different places where the negroes were settled, and then to make them an offer to carry them free of expense to Sierra Leone, if they preferred that to staying where they were . . . .'

[1] *Report of Sierra Leone Company 1794*, p. 5. 'A commission was given to him under date of August 12th' (Archibald, p. 136), and he sailed on 19 Aug. (see Hoare, p. 275). It is very much to be regretted that the Journal kept by John Clarkson has not been published adequately as yet. Fragments are to be found (1) in a paper by Ex-Governor Archibald of Nova Scotia, (2) in a book by Ingham, Bishop of Sierra Leone, and (3) in *Sierra Leone Studies*, No. VIII (1927).

(1) Archibald says (p. 136): 'From the 6th of August [1791], when he volunteered till the 15th March following, he kept a journal of his proceedings . . . .' But the extracts which Archibald reproduces (pp. 137–45) are few and mostly irrelevant.

(2) Ingham gives (pp. 18–167) 'extracts from Governor Clarkson's Sierra Leone Diary and Correspondence. They have been carefully selected from two thick volumes of manuscript' (p. 16) which 'have been placed in his [Ingham's] hands by the family, for any use which he may decide to make of it' (p. vi). 'Where dates occur, it will be because they have come naturally into the extracts made. Where none are mentioned, the period referred to will be approximately apprehended' (p. 16). Actually dates are given only in the rare cases where the extract happens to be the first entry of the day. Passages which should have been dated 7 to 20 Aug. 1792 (pp. 84–91) are inserted by mistake before entries dated 20 June to 4 Aug. (pp. 91–105). Clarkson's description of a speech which he made to the Nova Scotians on 2 Sept. is reproduced as part of a letter which he received on that day from the Directors of the Company (see p. 117). The instructions which he wrote on 4 Oct. to Dubois (the man whom Mrs. Falconbridge married one month after the death of her husband) are reproduced as part of a letter which he wrote on the following day to Dawes (see pp. 135–6). Notes made during Clarkson's absence on a cruise (6 to 26 Oct.) by his secretary, Strand, are reproduced as entries by Clarkson (see pp. 136–8). As regards the size of the extracts it appears that for the period from 5 Aug. to 26 Nov. they cover about one-fifth of the original Journal, and it seems that in selecting the passages Ingham considered those showing the deep religious feelings of Clarkson to be particularly important.

(3) *Sierra Leone Studies* (No. VIII, pp. 1–114) reproduces from a manuscript, 'kindly placed at the disposal of *Sierra Leone Studies* by Governor Clarkson's grand daughter Miss Jane Maynard, its present owner' (ibid., No. IX, p. 2), the 'Diary of Lieutenant Clarkson, R.N.' from 5 Aug. to 26 Nov. 1792. This publication is excellent as far as it goes, but it covers only a short and not very eventful period.

It is interesting to note that Thomas Clarkson in a letter (which is undated) had urged John to keep a journal in which the geography, history, and agriculture of Africa would be clearly presented. 'Everyone is curious of reading histories of new countries now—this is a taste of the age—and if you get a good history of all these particulars, I will get you £500 for it, whenever you return.' See Griggs, *Thomas Clarkson*, p. 67. [2] *Report 1791*, p. 41.

The persons going out are of three descriptions.—The servants of the Company, under a regular and permanent salary, of whom the chief persons will form a small council, and in them will be vested the management and superintendence.

Secondly. Artificers and others, to whom for a limited time, a certain support will be promised.

Thirdly. Settlers on their own account, to whom grants of land will be promised . . . .[1]

The fixed servants of the Company whom it is now thought proper to send out, as far as they can be at present accurately stated, are—the Superintendent or Chief,[2] and his Secretary; a Commercial Agent,[3] a Surveyor, a Store-keeper, a Medical person, a Surgeon and assistant Surgeon, a Book-keeper and Clerk, a Clergyman, a School-master and School-mistress; the salaries of these may be reckoned at about £.2000 per annum.

Several of the officers take their wives, and some of them their children by the first ships. Many of the first settlers also propose to take their wives and children with them.[4]

In the meantime, on 19 August, Lieutenant Clarkson had sailed for Nova Scotia where he arrived on 7 October.[5] The Directors had inferred from their conversations with Peters that only 'a few hundred' were anxious to emigrate,[6] but as the terms which the Company offered to the negroes were most favourable,[7] Clarkson's recruiting officer succeeded in collecting about 1,200 people.

The number of Nova Scotians who were willing to embark for Sierra Leone, proved, to the great surprise of the Directors, to be no less than 1,196. The accession of so large a body of people could not fail to produce many important consequences, and to give, in some measure, a new character to the whole undertaking.[8]

It became necessary to increase the Company's capital[9] and to strengthen the European personnel which was to go to the Colony. While the

---

[1] *Report 1791*, pp. 46–7.

[2] 'A Mr. Dalrymple was engaged by the Directors of the Sierra Leone Company to come out as governor of this colony; but they disagreed from some trifling circumstance, and Mr. Dalrymple feeling himself offended, set on foot . . . a subscription for forming a settlement on the Island [of Bulam] . . . in opposition to the Sierra Leone Company' (Falconbridge, p. 148). Dalrymple founded on 2 Nov. 1791 'a society for the purpose of establishing a settlement upon an eligible spot on the western coast of Africa' (see Beaver, pp. 1–2). His expedition to Bulama Island was a failure. On his way back to England in Aug. 1792 he, with 152 other people, called at Sierra Leone for assistance (see *Diary of Clarkson*, pp. 3–47).

[3] Mrs. Falconbridge wrote in a letter dated 30 Sept. 1791 (six days after her and her husband's arrival in London): 'The Directors seem much pleased with Falconbridge's exertions, have appointed him commercial agent to the Company, and he is shortly to return to Sierra Leone' (p. 120). Two months later she relates that the Directors increased 'Falconbridge's salary near three times what it was' (p. 121).

[4] *Report of Sierra Leone Company 1791*, p. 48.   [5] See Archibald, pp. 136–7.

[6] See *Report of Sierra Leone Company 1794*, p. 4.

[7] The terms on which the Company engaged to receive them into the colony were contained in a printed declaration (see ibid., pp. 5–6), dated 2 Aug. 1791, which stipulated among other things that 'every free black . . . shall have a grant of not less than twenty acres of land for himself, ten for his wife, and five for every child'. It is significant that the 'Terms of the Sierra Leone Company, to all such Settlers as shall sail from England, within three months from the date thereof [3 Nov. 1791], in order to go to Sierra Leone' provided the same grant for the white settlers (see Wadstrom, vol. ii, p. 228).

[8] *Report of Sierra Leone Company 1794*, p. 7.

[9] The General Court held on 19 Oct. 1791 had resolved 'That the Capital of the Company be not less than £.100,000' (*Report of Sierra Leone Company 1791*, p. 56). The General Court held on 30 Nov. 1791 resolved that £50,000 should be added to the £100,000 capital already subscribed for (see ibid., 2nd ed., p. 20; Wadstrom, vol. ii, p. 7). 'The Directors having reported to the general

Directors had planned to send out only a dozen servants of the Company,[1] this group was considerably enlarged. The Government of the Colony was to consist of the Superintendent and seven councillors.[2] The 'artificers and others' were put on a yearly salary. Finally, the Company decided to include soldiers among the passengers.[3] Never again have such a large number of Europeans emigrated together to Sierra Leone, and I shall deal here first with their fate.

The Directors in their report of 1794 said:

The first vessel sent out by the Company from England, reached Sierra Leone in February 1792, and she was soon followed by two other vessels from hence, one of

court of Proprietors [held on 8 Feb. 1792], that the whole capital of £.150,000 . . . was already subscribed; a resolution was then proposed and adopted, with a view to it's further extension, by which a discretion was given to the Directors to enlarge the subscriptions to such amount as they should think proper, within the limit of the act of incorporation, which confines the capital to £.500,000' (*Report 1791*, 2nd ed., pp. 25–6). The capital thereupon was raised to £235,280 (see Wadstrom, vol. ii, p. 30). It seems doubtful, however, whether the Directors knew on 30 Nov. 1791 that the number of Nova Scotians willing to embark for Sierra Leone was so much larger than they had expected. Clarkson wrote his first letter from Halifax to the chairman of the Company on 19 Oct. (see Archibald, p. 138), left Halifax on 22 Oct., and travelled for several weeks over the country for recruiting purposes (see ibid., pp. 141–3). His letter informing the Directors of the number of emigrants, therefore, had probably not arrived in London by 30 Nov. (But it certainly had arrived by 3 Jan. 1792 since in a postscript of that date to their report read on 19 Oct. 1791 they speak of 'a number of Free Black Families, to the amount, it is believed, of at least 1000 souls' which 'the new colony is about to receive from America'; see *Report 1791*, 2nd ed., p. 31.)

[1] See *Report of Sierra Leone Company 1791*, p. 48.

[2] See Rules and Instructions from the Directors of the Sierra Leone Company to the Superintendent and Council for the Settlement (Evans, pp. 47–9):

'17. As our Superintendent and Council you are hereby invested with the Government of the Peninsula of Sierra Leone in all matters, civil, military, political and commercial . . . . All Acts and Orders of your Board are to run in the name of the *Superintendent and Council of Sierra Leone*, even though the Superintendent may not have been present or may have been out-voted.

'21. The Superintendent is in every respect to have the precedence in the Colony; he is to be our Representative with the native chiefs; he is to head the Military, to command the Fort, and is to take the chair in the Council, where he is to have a casting vote, that is to say where the numbers including himself are on each side equal, he is to have another vote to decide the question. . . .

'22. In the case of the death or resignation of the Superintendent, the senior Councillor on the spot [Falconbridge] is in all respects to stand in his place, until a Superintendent is appointed by the Court of Directors . . . .'

Evans, who published these Rules and Instructions in 1932, said in his Introduction: 'These regulations are undated. The date put conjecturally as about 1791 is probably correct' (p. 27). He adds that the date 'cannot be earlier' and 'cannot be much later' than 'the latter end of 1791' (p. 28). Actually there can be hardly any doubt, I think, that they were issued between 20 Dec. 1791 and 10 Jan. 1792. (1) Falconbridge sailed from Falmouth on 19 Dec. 1791, and the Rules said: '83. Mr. Falconbridge having been so long detained at Falmouth, he will probably have no opportunity of acting upon the separate instructions given to him on leaving London, and we therefore enclose another letter to him directing him to fall into his station under the general arrangements now made and to act in subordination to the voices of the Superintendent and Council' (p. 75). It seems therefore practically certain that these Rules which established the Council and appointed Falconbridge Senior Councillor were issued after he had sailed. (2) The Rules said, on the other hand: '81. We expect that a vessel from Bristol will sail in three weeks from this time . . . .' (p. 75). According to Clarkson's Journal this ship sailed in January (see Ingham, p. 73). Moreover, the Councillors who took the Rules to Sierra Leone arrived there on 13 Feb. (see Falconbridge, pp. 127, 199), and it is practically certain that the Rules were issued some time before their ship sailed.

[3] See *Report of Sierra Leone Company 1791*, 2nd ed., p. 20. See also ibid., p. 30: 'The Directors have besides engaged a Mineralogist and a Botanist, of great ability in their respective professions, who are going out to explore the Company's district, and its vicinity . . . .'

them carrying a considerable number of passengers. There went out in all, by these ships, rather more than 100 white persons, of whom about 40 were Company's servants, or artificers, at a yearly salary; 10 were settlers; 16 were soldiers; and between 30 and 40 were women and children.[1]

Some more people sailed a few months later.[2]

In all there went out in the first year one hundred and nineteen white persons . . . .[3]

According to a letter from Mrs. Falconbridge dated 10 April 1792, only 2 whites had died by that time.[4] But soon thereafter mortality became appalling.[5]

Occupation	Went out	Died
Company's Upper Servants (the Superintendent, 7 councillors, a chaplain, several medical persons, a secretary, an accountant, a botanist, a mineralogist, &c., including their families) . .	26	4
Company's Lower Servants (clerks in the store-house, overseers, a gardener, a baker, several artificers, &c., including their families)	59	29
Settlers (including their families)	18	13
Soldiers	16	11
Total	119	57

[1] *Report 1794*, p. 7. The *Harpy*, which arrived on 13 Feb., conveyed four councillors, 'a few Soldiers, and some independent Settlers' (see Falconbridge, pp. 125, 127, 199). The *Amy*, which arrived on 16 Feb., conveyed Mr. and Mrs. Falconbridge (see ibid., p. 124). The third ship was evidently the *Trusty*, which was to sail from Bristol in January with 'about eighteen or twenty Artificers' (Evans, p. 75); 'but unfortunately she met with a severe gale of wind, which damaged her considerably, and she was obliged to put into Cork to unload her cargo, and to be put into a state of repair. The directors, finding the length of time she was likely to be detained there, made an offer of ten guineas each to a number of artificers on board to cancel their agreement, and most sincerely do I hope they will all come into the measure . . . .' (Clarkson's Journal, Ingham, p. 73.) Actually few of the artificers cancelled the agreement. See *Report of Sierra Leone Company 1794*, pp. 39–40: 'They [the Directors] were so sensible also of the danger to which the artificers and their families, who formed a material part of the third class [lower servants and artificers], were exposed, (most of whom through an accident at sea were likely not to arrive till the eve of the rainy season,) that they offered to discharge a great part of them in England, not only indemnifying them for their loss of time but adding also some gratuity; a few accepted the offer, but a great part, including almost all those who had families, were bent on the prosecution of the voyage.' The *Trusty* arrived in Sierra Leone between 12 and 15 May (see Clarkson's Journal, Ingham, p. 78). In this ship 'came the store-keeper, with his wife, mother-in-law, and a large family of children; a mineralist [the Swede Nordenskiold], and several clerks and tradesmen, in all twenty-three' (Falconbridge, p. 143).

[2] They came in the *Sierra Leone Packet* which arrived shortly before the *Trusty* and conveyed among other passengers the Swedish botanist Afzelius. See Falconbridge, pp. 142–3; Minutes of Council Meeting, Freetown, 12 May (C.O. 270, vol. ii, p. 36).

[3] *Report of Sierra Leone Company 1794*, p. 37. The 119 whites included probably those who came with Clarkson from Nova Scotia. Butt-Thompson says (p. 81) that they included 30 women and 10 children.

[4] See Falconbridge, pp. 133–4. The deceased were Dr. Bell (see p. 61 below) and the *Harpy's* gunner (who could not properly be called a resident of the Colony). 'While the corpse [of Dr. Bell] moved on in solemn pace, attended by the Members of Council, and others, in procession, minute guns were fired from the Harpy; in executing this, the gunner lost his arm, of which he died very shortly.'

[5] See *Report of Sierra Leone Company 1794*, pp. 36–7. It should be noted, however, that, as usual, the number of deaths was first grossly overstated in some quarters. See *Annual Register for the Year 1792*, Chronicle, p. 33, 15 Aug.: 'A packet arrived from Sierra Leone, which brings the most melancholy accounts from this new settlement. So dreadful a mortality has prevailed, that upwards of 200 white persons have died since the last accounts were received.'

What was the decisive cause of this excessive mortality is a controversial question. At one place in their report of 1794 the Directors said:

The precautions taken by the Directors, and the early as well as liberal supply of necessaries sent out by them, unhappily were not effectual in preventing a considerable mortality during the first rainy season.[1] The rains began about the third week in May; many settlers houses were not completed, the Company's storehouse was but imperfectly built, and their servants, especially those of the lower order, were accommodated extremely ill; the soldiers also were liable, from various causes, to be much exposed, and the few settlers who went from England, were least of all prepared to meet the impending difficulties of a rainy season. Perhaps the high degree of health which almost universally prevailed at the period antecedent to the rains, by creating too much confidence in the goodness of the climate, especially among the Europeans, might occasion some slackness in making the necessary preparations.

The Directors think they ought not to conceal from the Proprietors, that a considerable degree of misunderstanding had prevailed, antecedent to this period, between the Governor and the Council, and that to their inefficiency during the first three or four most important months, a part at least of the subsequent calamity is evidently to be traced.

The office of Governor having become vacant at the time when the first ship sailed, Mr. Clarkson, who had given great satisfaction by his conduct in Nova Scotia, was requested to fill the situation till a successor should be appointed, and he had the casting vote in council.

The Directors, alarmed by the evident want of order and energy betrayed even by the first accounts, adopted the temporary expedient of throwing the whole responsibility on Mr. Clarkson, giving him permission at the same time to assume the whole power. Whether the Directors erred in dividing the authority among so many as eight persons, or whether the blame belonged more properly to the Governor and Council, it is not perhaps material now to canvas. The Directors acquit the body of acting counsellors of all wilful misconduct, with the exception indeed of one person detained in their employ, but not originally appointed by them [Falconbridge], whose knowledge of the natives and of the country made him appear a person of importance at the outset of the undertaking, but whose habits of intoxication, idleness, and irregularity, as well as want of accuracy in his information, are necessary to be mentioned as one chief cause of the first difficulties of the colony, and of the first commercial disappointments of the company. It is partly to be ascribed to the extraordinary neglect of this person (whom it was the duty of the Governor and Council to direct and control) that the colony was not supplied with any fresh provisions before the sickly season arrived. The Company's ships were not employed for this purpose as was directed to be done, and the original body of instructions to the Governor and Council, drawn up by the Court of Directors and read to the Proprietors, received little or no consideration till long after this period. Confusion in the accounts, in the stores, in the government, in the information sent home, and in the operations of every kind prevailed; and this confusion not only tended to

---

[1] In the postscript of 3 Jan. 1792 to their 1791 Report the Directors had said: 'In considering the difficulties which may be expected to occur it is easy to foresee that the chief of them must arise from the following causes; from the first transition of the settlers to a hot climate, the clearing of the country, the want of accommodations, particularly during the first rainy season, and the uncertainty of obtaining on the spot a sufficient supply of fresh provisions. These difficulties are the greater because they come together, and come at the very outset of the undertaking; it has therefore been the anxious study of the Directors to provide against them by every possible expedient; they have considered this to be eminently their duty, not only as the success of the Colony must materially depend on getting over the first obstacles, without considerable loss or hinderance, but also as an act of justice to those, who, on the faith of the Company's protection, have embarked themselves and their families in the undertaking' (*Report 1791*, 2nd ed., pp. 24–5).

aggravate in many ways the distress of the sickly season, but it ought, perhaps, to be stated as one principal cause of the extraordinary mortality.[1]

Mr. Falconbridge was an ideal scapegoat: he was dead, and when alive had been quite disagreeable whether drunk or sober. But while he no doubt was a failure as a commercial agent (and as a husband) it was not fair to make him to such an extent responsible for the high mortality among the European immigrants. At another place in their report the Directors put in fact the main blame rather on the poor accommodation and the intemperance of the Europeans themselves.

Upper servants of the Company. [They] were all well accommodated: no more than four of this class have died, and of these four deaths only two can properly be charged to the climate.

Lower servants of the Company. Many of these were often exposed to the rains, and several of them were intemperate; they were also in general uncomfortably lodged, and in consequence of the sickness prevailing among the surgeons they could have but a small share of the medical attendance.[2]

Settlers. Some of these were much addicted to liquor, and their situation was in every respect worse than that of the last-mentioned class.

Soldiers. [They] were almost universally intemperate; when it is also considered how they must have been circumstanced in other respects, it cannot excite much surprise that so many . . . should have died.[3]

The Directors repeatedly emphasized that the climate itself was not responsible for the high mortality,[4] but the Commissioners of Inquiry, in 1827, attributed it in the first place to the effects of the climate and in the second place to unavoidable privations. After having quoted the above figures of European deaths, they said:

It has been thought right to quote this statement, because the occasion is the only one upon which there arrived together, at Sierra Leone, any number of Europeans (other than Military) sufficiently considerable to afford the means of forming an estimate of the effect of climate upon their constitutions; but considerable allowance should be made for the privations and difficulties to which they were necessarily exposed.[5]

Mrs. Falconbridge, however, who was on the spot, put all the blame on the poor accommodation. In a letter of 1 July 1792, after having described the mortality in the preceding weeks, she wrote:

After reading this, methinks I hear you invectively exclaim against the country, and charging the ravages to its unhealthiness; but suspend your judgment for a moment, and give me time to paint the true state of things, when I am of opinion you will think otherwise, or at least allow the climate has not a fair tryal.

[1] *Report 1794*, pp. 8–11. See also ibid., p. 41.

[2] See also ibid., p. 11: 'In the height of the sickness, all the medical persons, with but one exception, were laid up, so that a few of the chief servants only could be properly attended. The storekeepers living in a damp storehouse, were some of the first victims; increasing difficulty and confusion in the delivery of the stores was the consequence . . . .'

[3] Ibid., p. 36.

[4] See, for example, ibid., p. 37. See also 'Statement of the Chairman and Court of Directors' submitted to the Committee on the Petition of the Sierra Leone Company (*Report 1802*, p. 15): 'The Climate of Sierra Leone has . . . proved quite as healthy as was expected. It is true that the first British Adventurers suffered greatly by Sickness, and that a large Proportion of them died. But the chief Sufferers were Men of the lower Class.'

[5] *Report*, First Part, p. 9.

This is the depth of the rainy season, our inhabitants were not covered in before it commenced, and the huts they have been able to make, are neither wind or water tight; few of them have bedsteads, but are obliged to lie on the wet ground; without medical assistance, wanting almost every comfort of life, and exposed to nauceous putrid staunches, produced by stinking provisions, scattered about the town.

Would you, under such circumstances, expect to keep your health, or even live a month in the healthiest part of the world? I fancy not; then pray do not attribute our mortality altogether, to baseness of climate.[1]

Governor Clarkson himself, who probably was the best judge in this matter, put the main blame on the lack of adequate preparations made by the Company, on their decision to entrust the government to eight councillors with ill-defined responsibilities, on the inefficiency and obstructive spirit of these councillors, and on the inexperience of the colonists.

In his letter to the chairman of the Company, dated 19 October 1791, 'he expresses his hope that Mr. Dalrymple, who was to be the governor of the new colony should be on the spot before his arrival and make preparation for the reception and protection of the emigrants'.[2] Clarkson's surprise at the conditions he found on his arrival in Sierra Leone (6 March 1792) was great.

After all Dalrymple had not come. He had declined at the last moment, and the Company had introduced a new form of government. They had appointed a council of seven. . . . Mr. Clarkson was to be the president, with a casting vote. . . .

And now he began to find out what was the style of Councillors over whom he was to preside. One of them, a Dr. Bell, had been so drunk for the week following Clarkson's arrival that he had never been seen.[3]

On 30 March he wrote in his Journal:

The council are daily seeing the dreadful confusion existing through their means with apparent indifference. I have this day again offered to take the whole executive

---

[1] Falconbridge, pp. 140-1.   [2] Archibald, p. 141.

[3] Ibid., p. 146. Dr. Bell died of delirium tremens about a month after his arrival in Sierra Leone. Wadstrom relates (vol. ii, p. 239): 'Dr. B. was a man of merit in his profession, before he contracted this fatal habit, which he had so successfully concealed, that it did not come to the knowledge of the Directors, till he had been appointed. When informed of it, they took immediate steps to prevent his sailing for S. Leona: but he had sailed, before their resolution to that effect could overtake him. The Directors, however, not only allowed his widow one year's salary, (£250) but also made up a sum, out of their private purses, sufficient to purchase her an annuity of £50, during her life.'

Dr. Bell was by no means the only drunkard among the councillors. Clarkson, on 7 Aug. 1792, wrote in his Journal: 'Mr. Falconbridge talks of making a trip to purchase stock for the Colony, but from his constant drinking, he has rendered himself incapable of being trusted, and I do all I can to amuse him, in order to keep him quiet, if he had not one of the strongest constitutions, he must have been dead long ago' (Diary of Clarkson, p. 2; see also ibid., p. 12). Three weeks later the Directors' letter dismissing Falconbridge arrived in Sierra Leone. From then on Falconbridge 'kept himself constantly intoxicated'; he died on 19 Dec. (see Falconbridge, p. 161).

But the Directors were by no means deterred by these experiences. The ship which brought the letter dismissing Falconbridge brought also his successor, whom Thornton introduced to Clarkson as follows: 'Mr. Wallace (though once in the slave trade, and I sometimes have fancied a little fond of liquor) will be more useful and more obedient than Mr. Falconbridge' (Diary of Clarkson, p. 28). A week after the arrival of Wallace, Clarkson wrote in his Journal: 'I cannot say that I feel prepossessed with the highest opinion of Mr. W—— the new commercial Agent. I am satisfied, Mr. Thornton's fears were correct . . . .' (Ibid., p. 43.) Two days later he noted: '. . . I have not a good opinion of the new Commercial Agent as an efficient character, and I am persuaded when he gets from the Colony with the entire charge of his vessel and cargo and no check upon his conduct, he will continually be in such a state as to be unfit for active and profitable business' (p. 45).

power upon myself, subjecting myself to account to them once a month in council; but they insist upon nothing being done but in council, and according to their pleasure. Thus, after commanding and countermanding each other on every subject, nothing is done.[1]

On 18 April he wrote to the chairman of the Company:

Eight gentlemen, all invested with great power, each of them acting from himself, and none of them accountable to the other, form to be sure, a system of government, as pregnant with contradictions and inconsistencies as can be imagined; in such a government there can be nothing but tardiness in council and obstruction in all its operations.[2]

Give me authority, and if it does not come too late, I will pledge myself to remedy the whole. If you do not, my resolution is fixed, I must return home . . . .[3]

You appear to have been cheated in every department—ships, stores and cargo. Very few of the things of any kind are near what they ought to be for the money they cost you.[4]

Clarkson had apprehended from the outset a high mortality. Early in April he wrote in his Journal:

If putrid fevers do not break out amongst us, unsheltered as we are from the rain, crowded, and living upon salt provisions, it will be owing to a particular interposition of Providence.[5]

A few weeks later he noted:

It is painful to observe the sickness which generally prevails in the colony, and also to notice the extreme negligence of the medical gentlemen. They are seldom or ever to be found in the afternoon; and I cannot help believing that we have lost many people, principally from mere neglect of the surgeons; though many may have sunk under their complaints, from the disordered state of the colony having prevented their being properly attended to. I have no fault to find with the

---

[1] Ingham, p. 33. He soon complained of the inefficiency of individual councillors. See, for example, ibid., p. 64: 'To him [Mr. P——] and Mr. C—— I may safely lay the whole blame of the disorders in the colony, as well as those on board the *Harpy*.' See also Mrs. Falconbridge's letter dated 10 Apr.: 'Perhaps the Directors imagine they were particularly circumspect in their choice of representatives, if so, they are grossly deceived, for never were characters worse adapted to manage any purpose of magnitude than some whom they have nominated' (Falconbridge, p. 126). Speaking of her husband she says: '. . . I should suppose it did not require any great discernment, to know that a Surgeon, unacquainted with mercantile affairs, would make but as poor a figure in that line, as a Merchant, who had not studied physic or anatomy, would make in the practice of surgery' (ibid., pp. 276–7).

[2] Ingham, pp. 53–4.   [3] Ibid., p. 57.

[4] Ibid., p. 58. Before this letter had reached London the Court of Directors sent a circular letter 'To our Superintendent and Council at Sierra Leone', dated 22 May, which arrived in July. It stipulated that 'our Superintendent, Mr. Clarkson, be invested with full power to act according to his sole direction in all such cases and emergencies as may appear to him to call for the exercise of such an authority, without or against the opinion of the Council . . . . It can hardly be necessary for us to suggest that this is meant merely as a temporary arrangement' (ibid., pp. 96–7). Another circular letter from the Court of Directors, dated 18 July, arrived on 28 Aug. The 'charge of all the affairs Civil, Military, Commercial, and Political of the Sierra Leone Company' was 'now vested in a Governor and two Counsellors—our Governor is John Clarkson Esq., the two members of the Council will be announced hereafter' (*Diary of Clarkson*, p. 26). The two members of the Council were William Dawes, who came on 4 Sept. (see ibid., p. 42), and Zachary Macaulay, who arrived, as shown above, on 15 Jan. 1793. Dawes succeeded Clarkson (who was dismissed by the Company after his return to England in Feb. 1793), and Macaulay succeeded Dawes.

At the time when the Directors appointed Clarkson as Governor they were apparently very pleased with his services. In a letter, dated 17 July 1792, in which Thomas Clarkson announced that John was to have full powers as Governor he said: '. . . the Company have presented you with a Pipe of Madeira and £300 of furniture.' See Griggs, p. 68.   [5] Ingham, p. 36.

abilities or apparent willingness on the part of the medical gentlemen to do their duty; but from the general insubordination in the colony, and every councillor giving leave to whom he pleases to be absent from the colony, arises a want of regular habits, and a listlessness in the conduct of every one highly prejudicial to the well-doing of the settlement. . . .

The people are full of complaints at the method of serving their provisions; some of them getting too much, others too little, and some nothing at all.[1]

On 9 or 10 May he wrote:

What a pity it is that the directors should have encouraged, as they appear to have done, a number of women and children coming out at the commencement of a colony![2]

Independent of the extreme misery occasioned to individuals, it has greatly added to the distresses of the colony from having so *many* people, who had never left England before, and were accustomed to the common comforts of life, experiencing all at once the difficulties, distresses, and inconveniences of a new settlement, without an effective government, with insufficient shelter from the weather, deprived of the common necessaries of life, and with their wives and children and friends dying, and no means of furnishing them with the attention they require.[3]

Regarding the soldiers he says:

11 May. A terrible noise in the military tent—all the soldiers drunk. Care has been taken to supply them with abundance of liquor.[4]

16 May. Sickness continues to increase amongst us,[5]—half of the soldiers are now confined with illness and some in danger . . . .[6]

20 August. The European soldiers are nearly all dead or useless from the effects of irregular conduct and the climate.[7]

12 September. There are only four of the soldiers left of the original party; they have applied to me to be sent home—they are emaciated and unfit for service, so that I purpose sending them to England by the first opportunity.[8]

After the rainy season had passed he wrote:

27 September. No one but those who were witnesses to our distressed situation during the severe sickness, can have the least idea of the sufferings individuals experienced from the want of many comforts which we should have had in abundance, had proper care been taken in the package of the various articles, nor the great loss the Company have sustained from damage by leakage etc., etc.[9]

[1] Ibid., p. 66. [2] Ibid., pp. 74–5. [3] Ibid., p. 75.
[4] Ibid., p. 76. [5] See also ibid., p. 82. [6] Ibid., p. 79.
[7] *Diary of Clarkson*, p. 16. In general, he did not attribute mortality to the climate. On 18 Apr. he wrote to the chairman of the Company: 'With respect to the climate, I fear nothing; it is too warm, to be sure, to be perfectly pleasant, but I see no probability of its being unhealthy, unless it be made so by the imprudence and vicious conduct of the inhabitants' (Ingham, p. 57). On 2 July he wrote in his Journal: 'We have lost many lives yet I will not pronounce the climate bad to a prudent man' (ibid., p. 94). [8] *Diary of Clarkson*, p. 47.
[9] Ibid., p. 60. The day before he had noted: 'It is astonishing the loss we have experienced from the cargoes of the different vessels not having been properly packed or put into proper casks—The complaints made to me of the state of provisions, &c., in all the ships, convinces me of the carelessness of those who ordered them as well as those who attended their being shipped . . . .' (Ibid., p. 58.) On 21 Nov. he wrote: 'This morning anchored the Felicity, with dispatches from London. . . . The Felicity's cargo does not appear to be well selected considering our wants; she has brought out an immense number of *garden watering pots*, which seem to occasion a smile from every one' (ibid., pp. 108–9).

The carelessness of the Directors in neglecting the most elementary wants of the Colony may seem incredible in view of the sufferings caused by the same carelessness to the people sent from England to Sierra Leone in the course of the five preceding years and in view of the fact that England had had two centuries of colonial experience. Yet, Viscountess Knutsford says of Thornton: 'His superior understanding and knowledge of business were invaluable for the guidance of the infant Colony . . . .' (p. 20.)

Shortly before leaving the Colony on 31 December he said:

No one can have an idea how much the impositions on the company have affected me, not only with respect to the inconvenience and disappointment it occasions us, but it gives me such a bad opinion of the management at home, which, if continued, must end in ruin.[1] Sometimes an officer will observe to me, that in all companies at their commencement irregularities and impositions will occur, and are not to be avoided. I only know that, when I had the fitting out of fifteen vessels, I not only inspected their outfit, but examined every article of provisions. I was blamed by some of my best friends at the time for being so minute, when so much was to be done. My reply was, I am going to cross the sea with a cargo of *human beings*, I am going to a country where I cannot go to a store to recruit any stock, therefore, as I am limited to three months' provisions, I am determined to see that what I take is really good, as the government pays the best price for it.[2]

He landed at Dartmouth on 10 February 1793[3] and wrote the following day to Mr. Thornton and to each of the Directors:

It gives me great pleasure to inform you, that I left the colony on the 31st December last in perfect health; I believe not one person was dangerously ill. The fine weather had commenced, and to make short, I believe all the difficulties of forming a new colony were at an end.[4]

[1] See also Mrs. Falconbridge's letter dated 18 Nov. (pp. 177-8): 'Mr. Clarkson is so convinced the Company have been sadly imposed upon, that a few weeks ago he wrote a circular letter to the gentlemen of the Colony, acquainting them with his intention of sailing for England very quickly,—requesting ... their general ideas as to the wants of the Colony, and their advice how to prevent abuses being practised on the company in future. . . . Had my opinion been asked, I should have said, "let the Directors shake off a parcel of hypocritical puritans, they have about them, who, under the cloak of religion, are sucking out the very vitals of the company; let them employ men conversant in trade, acquainted with the coast of Africa, and whose *religious tenets have never been noticed*; under this description they will find persons of sound morals, fit to be intrusted, but they will ever be subject to impositions, while they employ a pack of canting parasites, who have just cunning enough to deceive them."' Mrs. Falconbridge was certainly embittered by the dismissal of her husband, but the hostile attitude taken by the Directors towards Falconbridge and, after his death, towards herself, and other events such as the dismissal of Governor Clarkson, suggest that there was some truth in her accusations. Who prompted the dismissal of Falconbridge for incompetence a few months after his return to the Colony it is impossible to tell. Eveline Martin says quite judiciously (p. 120): 'Partly owing to misfortune and partly to his own weakness for strong waters, partly to his lack of suitable training, having been "bred to physic," and partly to lack of assistance from the Governor and Council, Falconbridge did not have much success in his duties . . . .' Clarkson himself, though complaining of 'the intemperate and then violent conduct of our commercial agent', showed him much consideration and held him in high esteem. In a letter dated 15 Dec. 1793 he said: 'I hope I speak truth, when I pronounce their late Commercial Agent an honest man, but a very unfortunate one, not in the least calculated for the station he filled, which men of discernment might have discovered at first view . . . .' (Falconbridge, p. 245.)

That the Directors of the Company, also in subsequent years, paid an extraordinary attention to the 'religious tenets' of their upper servants is confirmed by John Grant, who wrote in 1810: 'Their agents in the colony, and their servants of every description, appear to have been almost uniformly selected from a class of men, whose want of education was not compensated by liberal sentiments, and whose ignorance of the foundations of civil government and morality was ill supplied by an austere tincture of sectarian piety' (*Account of some recent Transactions in Sierra Leone*, pp. 52-3).

[2] Ingham, p. 153. [3] See ibid., p. 155.

[4] Ibid., p. 156. Clarkson could in fact be proud of his record, and Thorpe was right, on the whole, when he said: 'While Mr. John Clarkson remained, peace resided there . . .; with Messrs. Dawes and Macaulay discord commenced . . . .' (*Postscript to the Reply*, pp. 58-9.) See also Griggs, p. 68. George Otto Trevelyan, it is true, believed that his grandfather Zachary Macaulay was 'the very man' to manage 'an aggregation of negroes from Jamaica, London, and Nova Scotia, who possessed no language except an acquired jargon, and shared no associations beyond the recollections of a common servitude' (*Life and Letters of Lord Macaulay*, p. 25). Actually the first

The 62 Europeans (including women and children) who survived the first rainy season consisted of 22 Company's upper servants, 30 Company's lower servants (mainly clerks and overseers[1]), 5 settlers, and 5 soldiers.[2] 'In the second year, all the soldiers and settlers, as well as the families of the lower whites, having either died or returned to England,[3] the whites resident in the colony were reduced to about forty, of whom only four or five have died.'[4] This fact seems to support the view that the main cause of the excessive mortality in the first rainy season was the failure to provide the people with adequate shelter. In the following years mortality became more favourable still. In a statement submitted in 1802 to a Committee of the House of Commons, the Directors said:

The European Deaths at Sierra Leone will be found to have been very few, if those which happened a few Months after the first Settlement of the Place, and those which followed the Capture of the Colony by the French,[5] and those also which were occasioned by the late Attack of the Natives, are excluded from the Account.—It may be affirmed, that, generally speaking, not more than about One White Servant of the Company has died in the Colony in each Two Years, or, at

negroes from Jamaica arrived eight years later, when Macaulay was no longer in the Colony. The Nova Scotians were born in British America, had served many years in the British army, had thereafter lived together eight years in Nova Scotia, spoke English, and shared many other associations beyond the recollections of a common servitude. The negroes from London, who numbered about 50, of course, also spoke English and had been merged in the much larger body of about 1,000 Nova Scotians before Macaulay arrived.

[1] Clarkson wrote in his Journal on 20 Aug. 1792: 'The artificers from Europe are mostly dead and those remaining are useless from a variety of causes' (*Diary of Clarkson*, p. 16; see also ibid., p. 9).

[2] Mortality seems to have been particularly great among the twenty-three Europeans who came in the *Trusty* in the rainy season (though they did not include soldiers). 'Six returned to England, one left the Colony and went into the employ of Bance Island, and the remainder died in the course of three or four months' (Falconbridge, p. 143).

[3] See also *Report of Sierra Leone Company 1794*, p. 57: 'The persons in whom they [the Directors] have been the most disappointed, have been the lower overseers, of whom it was difficult to get any thorough knowledge at the time of engaging them, on account of their having resided in the West Indies: of the several individuals of this class that originally went out, none are now remaining in the Colony.'

[4] Ibid., p. 37.

[5] The French landed in Sierra Leone on 28 Sept. 1794, plundered and destroyed a great deal, left about 120 British sailors on shore whom they had captured on various ships, and sailed on 13 Oct. (see Macaulay's Journal, Knutsford, pp. 64–77). 'It appears that in about three weeks afterwards, an almost universal sickness prevailed among the whites; being evidently the consequence, in a great measure, of the exertions made by some, and the miseries endured by others, at that crisis. The difficulty of getting medical attendance, (the physician and both the surgeons being ill, one of the latter of whom died), together with the want of proper food and accommodations, materially aggravated the disorder, which, as in the instance of the first sickly season, was fatal chiefly, and almost exclusively, to the lower Europeans' (*Report of Sierra Leone Company 1795*, pp. 17–18). 'Of the 120 British sailors, who were said in the former Report to be landed by the French from captured ships, and of whom 80 were then known to have died, it has since appeared that many more than 80 were carried off; but their deaths, as well as that of two or three valuable servants of the Company, which happened about the same time, are distinctly to be traced to the hardships which they went through at that period, and to the subsequent want of medicines, as well as to the difficulty of obtaining accommodations in the Colony' (ibid., *1796*, p. 6).

It should be noted, however, that the state of health of the Europeans had been very poor before the arrival of the French. Macaulay wrote in his Journal on 23 July: 'To-day there was not a clerk in any of the offices, as all Europeans were down with fever' (Knutsford, p. 61). On 10 Aug. he noted: 'The whites are all sickly, some recovering' (ibid.).

As regards the sailors, Butt-Thompson says (p. 107) that 'all the survivors were, some six months later, "safely shipped home"'.

most, about Two Servants in Three Years, out of the 20, 25, or 30 White Servants who have been usually resident.[1]

But with the departure of the settlers and artificers in 1793 the project to establish European colonists in Sierra Leone had failed to all intents and purposes.[2] The Europeans remaining in the Colony were mostly officials of the Company,[3] who usually stayed there at best for a few years.[4]

As stated above, Lieutenant Clarkson, on his arrival in Nova Scotia in the autumn of 1791, had collected there a large number of negroes wishing to emigrate.

The whole body waited several weeks in tents at Halifax, for the collection of the shipping, during which time they were exposed to much inclemency of weather, and contracted a considerable degree of sickness . . . .[5]

The fleet consisting of fifteen vessels left Halifax on 15 January 1792 and arrived in Sierra Leone on 6 March.[6] The Directors of the Company reported the ensuing events as follows:

After two or three weeks delay, arising from a palaver (or council) of the natives which however ended favourably for the Company,[7] the scite on which the first body of blacks sent from hence had originally settled was pitched upon as the most proper spot for the intended settlement. The land on which the town was to stand was cleared in a few weeks more . . . . The town was named Freetown, in consequence of an instruction sent out to this purpose.[8]

The mortality among the Nova Scotians has been as follows. The number of these that landed in the year 1792 was eleven hundred and thirty-one, many of them being very ill through the remains of a fever which appears to have been fatal to a few of their original body in Nova Scotia, and to have carried off sixty-five of them

---

[1] *Report from Committee on Petition of Sierra Leone Company 1802*, p. 15. For further details see ibid. *1804*, p. 86, and *Report of Sierra Leone Company 1798*, p. 1.

[2] The Directors had originally planned to send more European colonists to Sierra Leone after the first rainy season. 'Persons indeed of some property and of exemplary character who wish to settle at Sierra Leone, and working people who are used to any art or trade likely to be wanted there, will probably, after the first rainy season is over, be considered as a valuable acquisition to the colony; but the Directors wish it may be considered both by the Proprietors and the Public, to be a fundamental principle of the Sierra Leone Company, that no persons whatsoever shall be permitted to go out in their ships, or to reside as settlers in their district, without obtaining a regular authority from the Directors, and before this authority is granted, they purpose always to make the same examination of character, as in the case of their own actual servants' (*Report of Sierra Leone Company 1791*, 2nd ed., pp. 21–2). But after their failure in 1792 the Company never again sent out European colonists.

[3] According to Macaulay there were on 1 Jan. 1794 23 English officials in the Colony and in Oct. 1794 altogether about 40 resident Europeans; at the end of 1797 the European community included 3 ladies. See Knutsford, pp. 58, 77, 184.

[4] The *Report from the Committee on the Petition of the Sierra Leone Company 1804* contains (p. 126) 'A List of Persons formerly in the Service of the Sierra Leone Company, who have since been engaged in the Slave Trade'. Their 'Occupations in the Company's Service' had been 1 formerly acting Governor, 1 Sheriff, 1 Mayor, 1 Secretary, 3 Surgeons, 3 Storekeepers, 1 Trader, 1 Shipwright. See also *Special Report of African Institution, 1815*, pp. 12–13, 41; Thorpe, *Reply to Special Report of African Institution*, p. 8; Walker, *Missions in Western Africa*, p. 222; Butt-Thompson, p. 85.

[5] *Report of Sierra Leone Company 1794*, pp. 67–8.

[6] See Archibald, p. 144. One ship evidently had arrived late in February; see Minutes of Council Meeting, 29 Feb. (C.O. 270, vol. ii, p. 6).

[7] This palaver with King Naimbanna and King Jammy took place on 26 and 27 Mar. See for details Clarkson's Journal, Ingham, pp. 23–9.

[8] *Report of Sierra Leone Company 1794*, pp. 7–8.

during the passage: of these eleven hundred and thirty-one persons thus landed, forty died within a few weeks after they reached Sierra Leone, evidently in consequence of the same fever: the whole body then became extremely healthy, but when the rainy season was set in, an almost universal sickness prevailed, of which ninety-eight Nova Scotians died, which was nearly one-tenth of their whole number.[1]

Governor Clarkson's Journal contains many additional interesting details. I shall confine myself to quoting a few.

27 March. Great dissatisfaction appears amongst the settlers, and many of them begin to be very troublesome. The bad example set them by the Europeans when they first landed, the unfeeling manner in which they are often addressed, the promiscuous intercourse with so many dissatisfied sailors, and the old settlers, added to the many inconveniences attending a new colony, and the general sickness which at present prevails, may in a great degree account for the irritability of temper, and peevish disposition which it is painful for me to observe amongst them.[2]

11 April. According to a general notice given to the settlers yesterday, the whole of them assembled this morning at the tent to have their names registered afresh . . . . The people were called over according to the companies formed for their embarkation. At this interview I had an opportunity of correcting and confirming the returns made to me relative to the deaths to this period. The account will stand as follows. Total number of deaths from the time we formed the people into companies at Halifax, 112. . . .

Total number of men embarked at Halifax	385
Dead to this period	55
Remains	330
Men qualified for particular trades	162
Labourers acquainted with all tropical production	127
Porters at wharfs and general labourers	41
	330

Of men qualified for particular trades there were . . . 162.
These men were also capable of cultivating the land and of general husbandry.
Births since embarkation 14.[3]

The number of negroes who sailed from Nova Scotia was reported to have been 1,196. Including the children born in the meantime the total exposed to death would have been 1,210, consisting of 385 men and 825 women and children. The number of deaths up to 11 April would have been 55 or 14 per cent. for men and 57 or only 7 per cent. for women and children

12 April. It is distressing to me to see the poor Nova Scotians (who look up to me as their best friend) in their present deplorable state, their houses not covered in, sickness generally prevailing, and many of them appearing scorbutic.[4]

[1] Ibid., pp. 37–8. See also ibid., pp. 11–12:
'The sickness was the most severe and alarming at the beginning of the rains: about 800 blacks were supposed to be laid up at one time, and very few passed through the whole of this trying season without some indisposition. The disorder, which was the fever common to hot climates, while it affected in different degrees the blacks and whites almost indiscriminately, proved much the most fatal to the Europeans . . . .
'. . . the settlers huts, which were very small, were also many of them damp, and a few were as yet unfinished.'
See also Falconbridge, p. 140.
[2] Ingham, pp. 26–7. See also, for example, Diary of Clarkson, pp. 12, 102–3.
[3] Ingham, pp. 44–6.   [4] Ibid., pp. 46–7. See also his entry of 8 Apr.; ibid., p. 38.

About end of April. In the colony, *want* makes rapid strides; the rainy season fast approaches. With hunger comes mutiny—who can convince an empty belly ? or say to the hungry man, be satisfied ?[1]

9 or 10 May. The store tent is now in horrible confusion, people dying for want of food, from the confusion and irregularity in distributing the provisions, rather than for want of little comforts, all of which, however, with proper arrangement, might have easily been remedied.[2]

About end of May. The officers are extremely unguarded in their conduct to the black settlers—I mean as to their violent and hasty behaviour to them . . . .[3]

22 September. . . . mustered the number of souls in the Colony at present (I mean the Nova Scotians) 290 men, 275 women, and 430 children—in the whole 995, subject to correction.[4]

If the number of Nova Scotians had actually been only 995, it would have been reduced between 11 April and 22 September by 103, and as no doubt births occurred in the meantime the number of deaths would have exceeded 110 and possibly even 120. Yet according to the Directors' report it was 98 (in the rainy season), and according to the following entry in Clarkson's Journal made in the second half of December it had amounted to only 54 (since 11 April).[5]

Of the Nova Scotians we lost on the voyage sixty-five, and since our arrival to this day one hundred and one, making the whole loss of Nova Scotians since we left Halifax to amount to one hundred and sixty-six, about one-seventh of the whole. With respect to the loss of the Nova Scotians, I do not consider it so great as might have been expected, from the situation in which many of them were placed, not having any effective shelter during the heavy rains, and all the medical gentlemen being so ill as not to be able to do common justice to them. Added to this, the articles sent out for their nourishment, although ample in quantity, were, from neglect in packing, and other causes, so damaged, as to be in many instances not fit for use.[6]

But Clarkson himself thought that his count of the Nova Scotians on 22 September had been incomplete. In his letter to the Court of Directors, dated Dartmouth, 11 February 1793, he wrote:

I believe (but as I have not got the exact accounts out of my trunk, I cannot speak to a certainty) that we had when I left the colony upwards of 1,025 of the Nova Scotians, including the births.[7]

Assuming that 1,196 people were embarked in Nova Scotia, that 35 births occurred between 15 January and 31 December, that 112 deaths occurred between 15 January and 11 April, that no Nova Scotians absconded, and that 1,025 were surviving on 31 December, the number of deaths between 11 April and 31 December would have amounted to 94. It is possible, of course, that the number of people embarked in Nova Scotia was somewhat smaller than 1,196[8] and that the number living in

[1] Ingham, p. 60.   [2] Ibid., p. 76.
[3] Ibid., p. 81.   [4] *Diary of Clarkson*, p. 52.
[5] Probably few deaths had occurred after 22 Sept. See *Diary of Clarkson*, pp. 67, 72, 100; Falconbridge, p. 151.
[6] Ingham, pp. 152–3.   [7] Ibid., p. 156.
[8] The published extracts from Clarkson's Journal do not state the number, but Archibald, who had access to the whole of Clarkson's Journal during his stay in Nova Scotia, put it at 1,190 (p. 144).

the Colony on 31 December was somewhat larger than 1,025, but I am inclined to think that Clarkson's account which showed only 54 deaths since 11 April understated mortality in this period.[1]

In 1793 mortality was quite low.

In the second rainy season, although some return of sickness has been experienced, yet the deaths among the Nova Scotians have been very few indeed. The account which the Directors have received does not extend to the whole year, but it appears that not more than five of them have died during three of the most unhealthy months.[2]

The Company's physician (Dr. Winterbottom) wrote to the Directors on 14 October 1793:

Although the degree of sickness since the commencement of the present year has been upon the whole comparatively small and the loss sustained by deaths trifling, yet those months which have elapsed since the beginning of the rains have proved more sickly than all the preceding. The Nova Scotians have experienced during the rains a considerable share of sickness, but in general the complaints were trifling. They appear now to be so well accustomed to the climate that there is little reason to apprehend any great mortality among them. There are but few who still suffer from the effects of last year's sickness, or whose health is precarious. Few places perhaps in England of the same size can shew a greater number of fine healthy looking children than are daily to be seen in our schools; the heat of the climate appears to have little effect upon them.[3]

Mortality among the Nova Scotians continued to be favourable.[4] In their report of 1796 the Directors said that 'the births among them are supposed to have exceeded the deaths very considerably'.[5] But in 1797 'the mortality of the Nova Scotian blacks has been greater than in any former year, the first excepted'.[6] According to the censuses

---

[1] *The Annual Register for the Year 1793*, Chronicle, pp. 4–5, 20 Jan., says:

'Advices were received at the Sierra Leone house, from that settlement, dated Oct. 20 . . . . It appears by the returns, that the mortality among them had not been so very great as was apprehended, only 98 American blacks having died, from the time of their landing to the 20th of October: the number of those remaining alive was 1026. . . .

'Information has been received, by the Harpy, of the colony's progress up to the 20th of November.

'. . . Of the 1190 free blacks embarked at Halifax in January, 1792, the following is a return of the deaths up to the 2d of September, 1792, which in the men and women have been principally old and infirm, and many of those who died on shore were landed in a diseased state. On their passage 35 men, 18 women, 7 boys, and 5 girls: total 65. Since their arrival, 28 men, 28 women, 21 boys, and 22 girls; total, 99. General total, 104.'

It is quite true that if 'of the 1,190 free blacks embarked' 164 died, 'the number of those remaining alive was 1,026'. But Clarkson said explicitly that there were upwards of 1,025, *including the births*. It seems, moreover, unlikely that the Directors of the Company, in their report submitted in 1794, should have put the number of deaths at 203 if it actually was only 164.

[2] *Report of Sierra Leone Company 1794*, p. 38.

[3] Ibid. See also letter from the Company's botanist Afzelius to Clarkson, 3 Sept. 1793, Ingham, pp. 158–9.

[4] See, for example, letter from Afzelius to the Secretary to the Swedish Embassy in London, 11 May 1794, Wadstrom, vol. ii, p. 129; *Report of Sierra Leone Company 1794*, p. 22, *1796*, pp. 6–7; Letter from Secretary of the Colony to the Chairman and Court of Directors, 3 June 1795, C.O. 268, vol. v, p. 62; Hoare, p. 295.

[5] *Report*, p. 7.

[6] *Report 1798*, p. 3. The health of the Nova Scotians was bad also in the first months of 1798; see Letter to the Chairman and Court of Directors, 5 June 1798, C.O. 268, vol. v, pp. 445–6, 458.

of 1802–26 the numbers of Nova Scotians living in the Colony were as follows:[1]

Sex and age	29 Mar. 1802[1]	Apr. 1811	31 Dec. 1818	8 July 1820	1 Jan. 1822	Apr. 1826
Men . .	} 425	188	134	177	161	113
Boys . .		} 499	159	147	182	158
Girls . .	} 479		205	166	171	161
Women . .		295	193	240	208	146
Total . .	904	982	691	730	722	578

[1] According to *Report of Commissioners of Inquiry*, Appendix A, No. 1, there were listed 913 Nova Scotians (238 men, 245 women, 198 boys, and 232 girls).

The Commissioners of Inquiry into the State of Sierra Leone, after having shown the mortality in the first rainy season according to the Directors' Report, gave the following explanation for the apparent decline in the number of Nova Scotians in the period 1793–1826:

If the foregoing extract exemplifies the effect produced upon the Nova Scotians by the climate, it may also serve in some measure to account for their very limited number at the present day, as compared with what might fairly have been expected in a country more congenial to them.[2]

It will be seen from the Statement of their present condition (Appendix A. No. 1.) as furnished by some of the most intelligent and respectable of their number, that they still neglect all those means of improving their condition which agriculture presents. A few, indeed, of those who have accumulated a little money by trade or other occupations, have small farms, or gardens of two or three acres in the vicinity of Freetown, and two or three have small coffee plantations. Little attention being given to these, the profit derived from them is inconsiderable. And no instance can be adduced of a Nova Scotian actually living upon his farm, or placing his chief dependence upon the produce of the soil. . . .

This document accounts more or less satisfactorily for 224 of the *families* which are stated to have existed in 1802, and for 24 individuals who since that period have left the colony; 15 for England, 1 for America, and 8 for different parts of Africa.

In the 224 families of 1802 here accounted for, 409 deaths and 167 births appear to have occurred; reducing the number of families at the end of 1825 to 146. . . .

The means of obtaining a correct census of the colony, are at present very inadequate. But as the Nova Scotians reside altogether in Freetown, the accuracy of that document, as far as it respects them, may in some degree be relied on. Other sources of information, however, have been consulted, and from these, as well as from the census, it is clear that their number is greatly diminished.

It has been already stated, that in March 1792, 1,131 Nova Scotians arrived at Sierra Leone. In the census of 1822, their number is stated to be 722. Great as this diminution is, it will appear inconsiderable, when compared to that which has since taken place. For in the census of 1826, their number is stated to be only 578, showing a decrease of 144, in little more than four years. . . .

It will be seen, by a reference to the same document, that this decrease cannot be accounted for by any great disproportion between the males and females, nor by an over proportion of aged people; on the contrary, there appear to have been, in 1802, 386 boys and girls, out of a total of 776; neither can it be accounted for by any considerable emigration, as of the total number in 1802, only 29 are stated to have since left the colony. There appears, therefore, no other adequate cause than climate

[1] See *Report on Petition of Sierra Leone Company 1804*, p. 127; *Report of Commissioners on Coast of Africa*, 1811, p. 8; *Accounts relating to Population, &c., of Sierra Leone*, 1825, pp. 13–21; *Report of Commissioners of Inquiry*, 1827, Appendix A, No. 38. The figures for 1811 comprise only the area 'within the Walls of Sierra Leone'.   [2] *Report*, First Part, p. 9.

to which it can be ascribed; indeed this conclusion seems justified, not only by the excess of deaths as compared with the births, but also by the fact of much sickness having prevailed amongst the Nova Scotians, even so late as the rains of 1826, a season when the *natives* of the country are generally in the enjoyment of good health. Had the decrease been confined to a few of the first years after their arrival in the colony, it might, in part, have been ascribed to the exposure and privations incidental to a new settlement; but it will be observed that the period embraced by the statement in the Appendix, commences more than 10 years after their arrival at Sierra Leone.[1]

Thus, the Commissioners claim that the number of Nova Scotians decreased between March 1792 and March 1802 from 1,131 to 776, between March 1802 and January 1822 from 776 to 722, and between January 1822 and April 1826 from 722 to 578. But the actual trend seems to have been quite different. The number of Nova Scotians had dropped to about 1,025 by the end of 1792. At the census of 29 March 1802 there were enumerated 904 Nova Scotians, according to the *Report from the Committee on the Petition of the Sierra Leone Company* (1804), and 913 Nova Scotians according to a list of all individual families used by the Commissioners. Both these figures include the original settlers and their descendants. The Commissioners say that according to a careful examination made by a Nova Scotian, Mr. Jewitt,[2] 139[3] of the 913 people were not Nova Scotians. But the original settlers and their descendants cannot have numbered more than a few dozen, and it seems safe to assume that Jewitt, in correcting in 1826 the 1802 lists, discarded as not belonging to the Nova Scotians not only the original settlers but also all those Nova Scotians whom he could not remember (perhaps because they had emigrated at an early date). I am, therefore, inclined to think that the Commissioners understated the number of Nova Scotians in 1802 by about 100, and that they decreased by not more than about 150 from the end of 1792 to March 1802. Even so the decrease was considerable, but it must not be attributed to the effects of the climate. The Nova Scotians were at first all living in Freetown (while the original settlers lived in Granville Town). The Directors reported in 1794:

It [Freetown] . . . occupies between seventy and eighty acres of land . . . . It contains near four hundred houses . . . .[4]

The nearest of the lots [of land given to the Nova Scotians] is about a third of a mile from the town, and the most distant about two miles and a quarter; they occupy in all about four square miles, or two thousand five hundred and sixty acres . . . ,[5]

Thus the area occupied by the Nova Scotians was very small;[6] they could not increase by immigration; but as most of them were most of the

---

[1] *Report*, First Part, pp. 11–12.

[2] 'The information . . . was communicated principally by Mr. Jewitt, himself a Nova Scotian; he is a respectable and intelligent man, who fills the situation of a branch pilot, and is at the same time one of the preachers of the Methodist chapel. As the great majority of his country people are connected with this institution, the latter avocation must lead to an extensive acquaintance with their circumstances' (*Report*, First Part, p. 12).   [3] 62 men, 33 women, 28 boys, and 16 girls.

[4] *Report of Sierra Leone Company 1794*, p. 51. The Directors probably overstated the number of houses.   [5] Ibid., p. 53.

[6] According to 'a Survey, in the Hand-writing of Mr. Ludlam, of the Quantity of Land in Cultivation within the Colony on the 1st of April 1800', 'there were then about 650¼ Acres in Cultivation' (see *Report from Committee on Petition of Sierra Leone Company 1804*, pp. 54, 71–2).

time thoroughly dissatisfied with the government[1] there was probably some emigration.

As early as 1793 a few had left the neighbourhood of Freetown.

Three or four Nova Scotians are said to be settled up the river, who have large plantations of rice, land having been given them gratuitously by the natives.[2]

On 20 June 1794 an insurrection broke out among the Nova Scotians which was suppressed without bloodshed, but six of the insurgents were sent to England for trial.[3]

The French attack which occurred three months after the insurrection may not have damped their spirit of independence,[4] but it shattered their belief that they were more secure near the coast than up-river.[5] The Government encouraged their removal.

As under is an Abstract of a Scheme of Premiums which on the 19 May we came to a Resolution of allowing for the encouragement of industry the ensuing Season viz:— 1st To encourage Settlers to go on & improve their distant farm Lots.— The Settler who shall be settled farthest back not less distant than 1 Mile from the

---

[1] They complained, not altogether without justification, that the promises made to them before they left Nova Scotia had not been fulfilled. See for details *Report of Commissioners of Inquiry 1827*, First Part, pp. 9–12.

[2] *Report of Sierra Leone Company 1794*, pp. 152–3. See also Macaulay's Journal, 26 July 1793, Knutsford, p. 40. See, finally, Minutes of Council Meeting, 11 Nov. 1793 (C.O. 270, vol. ii, pp. 109–12).

[3] Ibid., pp. 181–5; Hoare, p. 286; Sharp's letter to Thornton, 26 Nov. 1794, ibid., p. 376. In addition, 7 Nova Scotian settlers were sent on 4 Aug. to England as witnesses for the trial; see Macaulay's Journal, Knutsford, p. 61.

[4] Macaulay reported on 26 Nov. 1794 that 'the conduct of the Settlers . . . during the stay of the French . . . was unusually kind and even affectionate toward us. . . . But we had not been delivered two days from the fear of our enemies than . . . the Settlers minds [became] uneasy and agitated' (Knutsford, p. 83). He sent, however, more favourable reports on 31 Jan. and 8 and 11 Mar. 1795 (see C. O. 268, vol. v, pp. 16, 26, 28), and Governor Dawes and the Secretary of the Colony, in their letters of 11 Apr., 13 July, and 27 July 1795, likewise expressed satisfaction with the settlers' conduct towards the government (see ibid., pp. 44, 78, 87–8). In their report submitted on 30 Mar. 1796 the Directors, thereupon, stated: '. . . the conduct of the Nova Scotians has, ever since the æra of the French attack, been, in general, orderly and respectful towards the Government. . . . The enthusiasm that had prevailed among the Nova Scotians is thought also to have abated, their minds are said to have become more enlightened, and their morals to have improved, and the more mischievous and designing persons have sunk in the general estimation, their character having now become better known' (*Report of Sierra Leone Company 1796*, p. 12). Thereafter difficulties arose again, but until 1800 the Government succeeded in maintaining peace (see letters from Macaulay 16 May 1796, 30 July 1796, and 8 Feb. 1797, Knutsford, pp. 147, 193, 307, and other letters from the Government to the Company, 22 Jan. and 5 June 1798, ibid., pp. 420–2, 452).

[5] See *Report of Sierra Leone Company 1795*, pp. 19–20: 'The Governor and Council . . . observe that the late events have opened the eyes of the Nova Scotians of their own folly, in having contended for the ground nearest to the water side, and in having so much neglected the cultivation of the more distant and mountainous parts; they even remark that the improvement about to take place in the mountains during the ensuing dry season, seems likely to be as great and important as the detriment which has been recently done to the town. A very favourable opportunity is said to be thus afforded of dismissing from the Company's service, a number of Nova Scotians, whom the Governor and Council had been long endeavouring in vain to fix on their farms.' See also ibid. *1796*, pp. 9–10: 'The Proprietors were informed in the last report which was made to them, that many Nova Scotians had been induced, through the terror inspired into those who lived nearest the coast, by the French depredations, to retire farther into the country, and to enter upon the cultivation of many distant farm-lots, which before had been neglected. It appears by an account dated the 14th March, 1795, that . . . the cultivation of about fifty new farms had at that time been set on foot.' See finally Macaulay's Journal, 26 Nov. 1794 and 24 May 1796, Knutsford, pp. 84, 137.

Base line having a well built House on his lot & his family living there also One Acre of land in cultivation on

the 1 Septr next shall be entitled to a premium of 40 Dollars
The next farthest back not less than one Mile &c. 30 Dollars
The next   D°   D°   20 Dollars.[1]

But the response was nil.

In regard to our Scheme of Premiums—we were in hopes our liberal offers would have brought forward many Competitors for the Prizes; which would have proved highly beneficial to the Colony; & we have pleasure in your approbation of what we did; but we are sorry the result of the Scheme has not turned out according to our wishes.[2]

In 1798 the Directors reported:

The Nova Scotian settlers are still backward to go upon the Mountains; and while their neighbours permit them to cultivate an acre of land below, they prefer eating cassada, in a miserable way, to climbing the hill, where they may enrich themselves, by exertion. But this, though a frequent, is far from being an universal, case: 20 or 30 families have settled in the Mountains, and are doing well; though with more exertion they might do far better.[3]

By that time quite a few Nova Scotians had left the Colony to become slave traders or employees of slave factories.[4]

In September 1800 there was a new and most serious insurrection of the Nova Scotians which might have succeeded if at the critical moment a large number of Maroons had not landed in Sierra Leone with a military escort[5] and had rescued the Government. Two insurgents were killed in the fight, and 35 were made prisoners, of whom 3 were executed while 32 were condemned to 'remove from the Colony, and never return to it'.[6] 'Some of the Ringleaders escaped among the Natives.'[7] Finally, the Directors stated:

A large Portion of the more unprincipled Nova Scotians have lately been removed from Freetown by other Causes.[8]

[1] Governor Dawes to the Sierra Leone Company, 3 June 1795 (C.O. 268, vol. v, p. 60).
[2] Same to same, 6 Feb. 1796 (ibid., p. 99).   [3] *Report of Sierra Leone Company 1798*, p. 11.
[4] See Macaulay's Journal, 8 Aug. 1797: 'I had long suspected, and I was this day confirmed in my suspicion, that the Settlers were gradually contracting a more friendly disposition to the Slave Trade. At this moment there are two in the Rio Nunez, and three in the Rio Pongo, who are actually engaged in it; to say nothing of the number who, without carrying on a Slave Trade on their own account, are employed in the service of Slave-traders, and thus are aiding and abetting in carrying it on' (Knutsford, p. 174). See also *Special Report of African Institution 1815*, pp. 18–19: '. . . if any other mode of subsistence, requiring less bodily exertion, could be found, the pursuit of agriculture was infallibly neglected. Hence the Slave Trade presented an irresistable attraction to many of the Settlers, who quitted the Colony, and fixed themselves in slave factories.'
[5] See p. 88 below.
[6] *Report of Sierra Leone Company 1801*, p. 18. Seven were sent to Goree and 25 'were transported to the Bullom shore, which forms the north bank of the river Sierra Leone, where they were directed to form a settlement, and to cultivate lands for their subsistence'. It may be assumed that some who left were accompanied by their families.
[7] *Report from Committee on Petition of Sierra Leone Company 1802*, p. 11. The Natives attacking the Colony on 18 Nov. 1801 (see p. 79 below) were 'headed by Two of the Nova Scotian Insurgents, who had effected their Escape after the Insurrection of the former Year' (Statement by Directors, *Report from Committee on Petition of Sierra Leone Company 1802*, p. 12). The native forces making a second attack on 11 Apr. 1802 included 'eleven of the rebel settlers, who had fled from the Colony and resided among the Natives' (*Report of Sierra Leone Company 1804*, p. 40; see also *Report on Petition of Sierra Leone Company 1804*, p. 49). Hoare reports (p. 306), I suppose erroneously, that these were 'eleven of the rebel settlers who had been banished from the settlement'; the same statement is to be found in Martin, *British Colonies*, vol. iv, p. 178.
[8] *Report from Committee on Petition of Sierra Leone Company 1802*, p. 13. The Directors stated

Thus any decrease in the number of Nova Scotians between 1792 and 1802 can be easily accounted for by voluntary or forced emigration. From 1802 to 1811 the number of Nova Scotians increased,[1] and it was in the latter year again as large as at the end of 1792. But for 1811–26 the situation is quite obscure. It cannot be doubted that the number of Nova Scotians declined considerably in this period. Yet it is most unlikely that this was due to the effects of the climate. The Commissioners of Inquiry reported that in 1802–25 the deaths numbered 409 and the births 167.[2] It is possible that the deaths averaged something like 17 per year,[3] but this would not suggest a high mortality, as the average number of Nova Scotians in this period was about 800. It is obvious, on the other hand, that the actual number of births in those 24 years cannot have been as low as 167 since the numbers of children enumerated at the censuses of 1811, 1818, 1820, 1822, and 1826 were 499, 364, 313, 353, and 319, respectively! I am inclined, therefore, to think that the decrease in the number of Nova Scotians in the Colony after 1811 was due mainly to migration into neighbouring native hamlets,[4] and that their number in 1826 was larger than ascertained at the census.

No authentic figures for Nova Scotians seem to have been published for 1827–43, but their number probably did not change much in this period.[5] The censuses of 1844, 1847, and 1848 showed 597, 568, and 560 respec-

furthermore: '. . . the Male Adults among the Maroons are full as numerous as the remaining Male Adults of the other Class of Settlers'; see also ibid. *1804*, p. 50. But this was evidently a mistake. According to the Return of 29 Mar. 1802, the male Nova Scotians in the Colony numbered 425 and the male Maroons 245 (see ibid., p. 127).

[1] The increase was apparently due in part to the fact that some of those who had been exiled in 1800 had come back. See Hoare, p. 302: 'After a few years of probation, they were permitted to return to the colony.'

[2] These data were provided by Mr. Jewitt, who entered for each family enumerated in 1802 the number of births and deaths as best he could. (He omitted those families which he did not consider to be Nova Scotian.)

[3] According to a 'Return of Burials registered in the Parish of Saint George, Freetown, Sierra Leone from January 1st 1809, to December 31st 1825', furnished to the Commissioners by the rector of the parish, the burials of Nova Scotians numbered in that period 362 or 21 per year. See *Report of Commissioners*, Appendix A, No. 19.

[4] Part of the decrease may also have been due to intermarriage with Liberated Africans and Maroons. According to letters sent from Sierra Leone between December 1815 and February 1816 'many intermarriages between the Nova-Scotian and Maroon Settlers had taken place, which it was thought would result in the improvement of both' (*Tenth Report of African Institution. 1816*, p. 73).

[5] Rankin reported that 'in 1834 only three hundred survived' (*The White Man's Grave*, vol. i, p. 97), and Henry William Macaulay, in 1837, put the figure at 500 (see *Report from Select Committee on Aborigines*, 1837, Minutes of Evidence, p. 32), but these were merely estimates. Rankin (1834) added: 'I questioned that intelligent and respectable man, Prince Stober, as to the probable cause of decay amongst the Settlers. Many reasons were assigned; the departure of the young men in former times of dispute with the government, and "the desire of such as continue in Freetown to imitate the white man, who seldom marries". Pride, however, has been their worst enemy; resting upon the remembrance of what they once were, and displaying itself in contempt for the Maroons and Liberated, now in almost all respects their equals. Originally landholders, if they labour for subsistence, it must be in competition with those whom they disdain as their inferiors, and by associating with them. This they will not generally do.' See also Lieutenant Forbes, *Six Months' Service in the African Blockade, 1848*, pp. 22–3: 'The emigrants from Nova Scotia are no great addition to the colony; lazy, and exhibiting a strong taste for dress. They seldom marry, but live in concubinage, and despise the liberated Africans, who, though no blacker than themselves, are designated niggers.'

tively.[1] What became afterwards of the Nova Scotians is not clear. The censuses of 1850, 1851, and 1860 showed 49, 112, and 69 respectively,[2] but from 1850 onwards the number of Native Creoles was asked separately, and it is likely that many descendants of Nova Scotians were counted as such.[3] No figures were given for later years and recent census reports say explicitly that the descendants of the Nova Scotians were included among the Creoles (Descendants of Liberated Africans).[4]

3. Native Immigrants

In their report of 1827 the Commissioners of Inquiry into the State of Sierra Leone said:

> The Natives . . . may be classed under Three Heads:—The *Kroomen*, who repair to the colony generally with a view to be employed as labourers, sailors, or domestics, the *Mandingoes* and *Timmanees*, or other Africans, who resort to Freetown for the purposes of trade, and the *Timmanees*, who are residents in the small hamlets dispersed throughout the peninsula.[5]

This subdivision was quite appropriate in 1827 when the boundaries of the Colony were well defined, but in earlier times the Timmanees resident 'in the small hamlets dispersed throughout the peninsula' could hardly be considered to be living in the Colony. Theoretically, it is true, the area of the Colony was even larger in 1787 than in 1827 since it was said to cover 400 square miles, but until the beginning of the nineteenth century hardly more than 1 per cent. of this area was actually occupied by the settlers under British administration, and it proved impossible to maintain any serious claim to the country beyond this settlement.[6] There

---

[1] See *Reports made in 1844 and 1845 by Butts and Guppy*, pp. 38–41; *State of Colonial Possessions 1847*, p. 198; *1848*, p. 304. On 31 Dec. 1844 there were 251 males and 346 females.

[2] See *State of Colonial Possessions 1850*, p. 185; *1851*, p. 182; *1860*, Part II, p. 24.

[3] See in this connexion Luke, 'Notes on Creoles', p. 53: 'The term "Creole" . . . was originally applied exclusively to the children of the Liberated Africans; with intermarriage and the passage of time this distinction came to be ignored and the term applied generally to the settlers and their descendants.'

[4] See *Census Report 1911*, p. 11; *1921*, p. 10.   [5] *Report*, First Part, p. 16.

[6] Clarkson in his Journal describes at length the situation in 1792. Two quotations may serve as an illustration:

9 Aug. 'We continue to meet with obstacles in running our lines into the country, as in many instances we interfere with the natives' plantations, and it requires great care in settling little differences with them on this head. In fact we purchased the whole of the land as we believed to a certain distance up the river and then straight into the country; but when the chiefs sold us the country, they had not the least idea that we could want to make use of the whole, and therefore they are not prepared to part with their plots of ground hastily' (*Diary of Clarkson*, pp. 4–5).

25 Sept. 'In consequence of a complaint made to me by Mr. Pepys of his having been molested by the natives while laying out the lots of land, from his interfering with the native villages which lay scattered in many parts of the company's district, I have sent Mr. Watt in the "Ocean" to fetch King Naimbanna to settle the business, and have also informed Signor Dommingo and other chiefs in our district that a palaver will shortly be held, when I requested them to meet King Naimbanna at Free Town that the subject in dispute might be amicably discussed' (ibid., pp. 56–7).

Clarkson is somewhat vague concerning the outcome of the palaver held on 27 and 28 Sept. (see ibid., pp. 60–5, 71), and Hoare relates (p. 280) that 'the palaver closed, as before, without laying any restraint on the settlers'. But Mrs. Falconbridge writes (p. 165): 'They finished by curtailing the bounds from twenty miles square, (the quantity purchased by Captain Thompson, and afterwards confirmed to the St. George's Bay Company) to about two miles and a quarter fronting the sea, and running in a direct line back, as far as the district of Sierra Leone may be, which is generally supposed not to exceed five or six miles . . . .' Moreover, the Nova Scotians in a petition

seems to have been on the whole a tendency to exclude native settlers from the Colony, though the methods used varied[1] and though exceptions may have been made in individual cases.[2] On the other hand, the Sierra Leone Company had from the outset a strong desire to attract native labourers.[3] Such labourers had in fact already been employed by the very first settlers. Captain Thompson told a Committee of the House of Commons:

> . . . several of the natives at Sierra Leone were employed at a small expence by the black people whom I carried out, to assist them in building their habitations.[4]

to the Directors written in Mar. 1793 complained 'That Mr. Clarkson informed them before he sailed for England, the Company had been mistaken in the quantity of land they supposed themselves possessed of, and in consequence only one fifth part of what was originally promised them (the petitioners) could be at present performed . . . .' (ibid., p. 206).

The territory actually under control of the Company remained very small until the end of the century and was essentially extended only from 1801 on.

[1] See, on the one hand, the instructions of Governor Clarkson to William Dawes, 5 Oct. 1792, concerning the allocation of land to the Nova Scotians: 'If in laying off the lots of land, you should meet with any houses of the natives, you must be very circumspect in your behaviour to them, you must consider them as what they really are, very ignorant, and you must treat them as such,—I mean with gentleness, endeavouring to persuade them to relinquish their situation, and offering them if persuasion will not do a little trifling present for their loss' (Diary of Clarkson, p. 75). See, on the other hand, the statement of the Governor and Council 10 years later: 'We claim by Conquest all the Territory formerly claimed by or of Right belonging to King Firama . . . . The Conquest was made by the taking and destroying of every Town belonging to the Enemy, and the Expulsion of every Timmaneese Inhabitant' (Report from Committee on Petition of Sierra Leone Company 1804, p. 84; see also Claude George, pp. 131–2).

[2] See Diary of Clarkson, p. 91 (23 Oct. 1792): 'Some time ago, a black man who had been kidnapped on the opposite Bullam shore, made his escape hither, and now works as a grommotto [free labourer] . . . . The young man wishes to settle in our Colony.'

[3] It should be noted in this connexion that the Company also wanted native children to come into the Colony to be educated there. The Rules and Instructions to the Superintendent and Council said (Evans, pp. 60, 72–3):

'51. As it may probably be very desirable to King Naimbainna and other native chiefs to obtain for their children and other near relations the advantages of European education, we have no objection to gratify them in this circumstance.'

'78. . . . it is our purpose to provide as far as possible for the general instruction of the Colony, by appointing Schoolmasters to be sent from home, and we wish you to encourage and assist natives in general, and particularly those in your service or under your influence to learn to read and write.' (See also Report of Sierra Leone Company 1791, p. 52.)

Clarkson thereupon used every opportunity to inform the natives of 'our readiness to instruct their children to learn book, and to make them have good heads' (Diary of Clarkson, p. 6; see also ibid., pp. 62, 64). On 10 Sept. 1792 he wrote in his Journal: 'I have had several applications from the different Head men in the neighbourhood, to admit their children into our schools, but at present we have no accommodation to lodge them. My plan is, when we can do it effectually, to take the native children and lodge them with different trades people, that they may thus get an insight into the various trades and receive their education at the same time' (ibid., pp. 46–7; see also ibid., p. 93). The Minutes of a Council Meeting, held a year later, on 19 Sept. 1793, relate: 'As the number of native children sent hither for the purpose of education is encreasing; and as their progress in improvement is not so rapid, while they continue confounded with the mass of the Settlers Children—Resolved, that Mingo Jordan, be appointed School Master, with a Salary of £40 p. Ann and that his attention be wholely directed to the Instruction of Native Children' (C.O. 270, vol. ii, pp. 90–91). The Directors of the Company, in their report submitted in Mar. 1794, said (p. 153): 'The Directors understand that there are now in the schools at Freetown, about twenty native children in all, a great proportion of whom are the sons of chiefs. It has been already noticed, that more than the same number of native children are under instruction on the Bulam side of the river.' See furthermore Wadstrom, vol. ii, p. 121; Report of Sierra Leone Company 1798, p. 51; Report from Committee on Petition of Sierra Leone Company 1802, p. 28; Special Report of African Institution 1815, p. 24.

[4] Minutes of Evidence before a Committee of the House of Commons respecting African Slave Trade, 1790, pp. 167–8.

In their report of 1791 the Directors of the Sierra Leone Company announced that 'the strongest injunctions' will be laid upon the Governor and Council 'to cultivate the general friendship of the natives, among whom they trust they shall find labourers on reasonable terms'.[1] A few months later they said in their Rules and Instructions to the Superintendent and Council:

55. . . . we are on reflection strongly disposed to the utmost extension of cultivation on behalf of the Company which may consist with our engagements to the settlers . . . . On this and other grounds it will be desirable that you should procure as many labourers as possible to which end perhaps liberal encouragement should be held out to them, and in this view we think it will be expedient to promise small lots of land to such labourers as behave industriously and satisfactorily after they have worked for one year.[2]

Thus, cultivation on behalf of the Company, which, of course, presupposed a supply of native labourers, was envisaged on a large scale. The 'Rules and Instructions' said:

55. Our conviction of the utility of cultivation to all our views in Africa both respecting the Natives and the Company, and the apparent necessity of setting and encouraging example in this way, having determined us . . . to undertake an extensive plantation for this purpose, Mr. Watt whom we have nominated to a seat in Council is engaged. He is to be the Conductor of the first attempt to be made and for the present will generally superintend the cultivation undertaken for the Company. . . .[3]

But 'the soil around Freetown was not so favourable to cultivation as was expected',[4] and Governor Clarkson, on 14 November, noted in his Journal that he had sent Mr. Watt 'to examine the land on the Bullam shore, on the other side of the river; this he reports, is calculated to answer every purpose, and he speaks of the soil and his reception with rapture'.[5] On 23 November he wrote:

This evening Mr. Dawes and Mr. Watt returned from the Bullam shore, having agreed to rent a square mile of land for 100 bars per annum of the Bullam King . . . . The people there are desirous that we should settle amongst them. A house is to be built for Mr. Watt, and the King to find him as many grumettas or labourers as he may want . . . .[6]

The Directors in their report submitted in March 1794 spoke of 'the advancing state of a regular plantation of the Company, worked by native labourers, on the side of the river opposite to Freetown'.[7] But this was

---

[1] *Report 1791*, p. 50. See also ibid., 2nd ed., p. 21: 'The impossibility indeed, of finding any Europeans who can work in Africa in the sun, without the utmost prejudice to their health, has made the Directors conceive it to be their duty to discourage labourers from hence, who would go out with this view; and they trust therefore to the native labourers, or the free Americans, who . . . are expected immediately to arrive.' On 12 Dec. 1792 the Council resolved 'that the boats Crew of every Vessel in the Company's service should consist only of Gromettas' (C.O. 270, vol. ii, p. 66).

[2] Evans, pp. 62–3. The Company, therefore, at the outset, seemed ready to accept native settlers, and at the palaver of 28 Sept. 1792, Councillor Dawes told the natives that 'we should be happy if they would live in our Colony, incorporate themselves with us .. . .' (*Diary of Clarkson*, p. 64.) But this policy was not pursued.

[3] Evans, p. 62.   [4] *Report of Sierra Leone Company 1794*, p. 47.

[5] *Diary of Clarkson*, p. 102. See also ibid., pp. 107–8.

[6] Ibid., pp. 110–11. See also Lewis, *Agricultural Position of Sierra Leone*, p. 7.

[7] *Report of Sierra Leone Company 1794*, p. 19.

probably too favourable a description,[1] and four years later the Directors reported that 'cultivation on the Bullom shore, for the Company's account, has hitherto proved unprofitable'[2] and had been restricted. 'The management is now committed to a black settler [Nova Scotian] . . . and he has 4 or 5 grumettas under him.'[3] Two or three other plantations started within and outside the Colony[4] were apparently less important still, and the factory established by the Company in the river Rio Pongas,[5] about 40 miles from Freetown, was, of course, too remote to attract native labourers from the neighbourhood of this town, and it was also abandoned before long.

Nevertheless there was practically all the time a temporary migration of Natives into the Colony, and from 1792 to 1799 intercourse between the Timmanees (the original possessors of the land) and the settlement was, on the whole, friendly and lively. A few quotations may serve as an illustration.

25 August 1792. The natives daily grow more intimate with us, and are constantly bringing in fruits of different kinds . . . .[6]

22 September 1792. Many of the natives offer themselves to work for us.[7]

11 October 1792. There seems to be a general spirit for commercial pursuits, throughout the Colony, and the natives and those of the Nova Scotians who have saved a little money, appear to be dealing beyond what we could have expected.[8]

23 October 1792. . . . the natives . . . begin to be more and more friendly with us. Some days no less than 150 come into the town with various articles for trade; each of them has among our settlers one whom he calls his friend, with whom he barters his commodities.[9]

1794. . . . the natives (who continued perfectly friendly and often flocked to the settlement) appeared to view the improving state of Sierra Leone with increasing satisfaction.[10]

It has lately been discovered, that several towns adjacent to the Company's plantation are very much increased, not only by the accession of those natives who work for the Company, but also of many others.[11]

1798. At the Period now spoken of [1798], about 3 or 400 Native Labourers, called Grumettas, worked in the Settlement for Hire, chiefly on the Farms, which were increasing rapidly; some in the Service of Europeans, some in that of the Nova Scotians. These Native Labourers were Freemen, who came from neighbouring Parts—They received Monthly Wages, the whole of which was their own. It was

[1] Mrs. Falconbridge wrote:
28 Dec. 1792. '. . . much advantage may be looked for, provided no disagreement arises with the natives, and a sufficient number of steady labourers can be obtained . . .' (p. 176).
[7] 7 Jan. 1793. 'The manager of Clarkson's plantation complains that most of his gramattos or labourers have left him to attend the cry or funeral ceremony of one of their breathren . . . it is uncertain how long the cry will last' (p. 182).
[3] 3 Feb. 1793. '. . . yesterday the manager of Clarkson plantation came over from Bulam. . . . His advances in cultivation, I understand are very slow; for he is not able to keep any number of labourers together, more than a month at a time; it is customary to pay them every moon, and when they get their wages, like our English tars, they quit work while they have money' (p. 196).
[2] See in this connexion also Macaulay's letter to the Directors, 30 July 1796 (C.O. 268, vol. v, p. 196).   [3] Report of Sierra Leone Company 1798, pp. 8–9. See also Lewis, p. 10.
[4] See Falconbridge, p. 182; Wadstrom, vol. ii, p. 60; Journal of Macaulay, Knutsford, p. 209; Report of Sierra Leone Company 1798, pp. 9–10; Lewis, p. 6.
[5] See Falconbridge, p. 187; Journal of Macaulay, Knutsford, pp. 49, 121, 126, 213; Report of Sierra Leone Company 1796, p. 8, 1798, pp. 6–8; Claude George, p. 27.
[6] Falconbridge, p. 152.   [7] Diary of Clarkson, p. 52.   [8] Ibid., p. 88.
[9] Ibid., p. 91.   [10] Report of Sierra Leone Company 1794, p. 17.   [11] Ibid., p. 49.

usual for most of them to return Home after a short Time, after remaining Five or Six Months in the Colony; but the Place of those who went was always supplied by a Succession of other Labourers.

Freetown was at this Time a Place of considerable Resort. It is estimated that from One to Two Hundred Natives visited the Settlement every Day for the Sake chiefly of exchanging Articles of African Produce for British Manufactures. Many of the Natives came in Canoes, some of them from a Distance of 80 or 100 Miles.[1]

This peaceful development[2] was interrupted in 1799 when the native chiefs assumed a hostile attitude towards the Colony.

. . . the Labour of their [the Europeans'] Grumettas was interrupted, in the End of the Year 1799, by the Interference of the Native Chiefs.[3]

. . . Cultivation languished in consequence of the Native Chiefs having in the Years 1799 and 1800 drawn off their Grumettas,[4] and of the Insurrection [of the Nova Scotians] which happened towards the Close of the latter Year.[5]

On 18 November 1801 the Natives attacked the Colony, and though a truce was concluded on 31 March 1802 they made another attack on 11 April 1802. The colonists abandoned their farms and took refuge in the town.[6] In the course of 1803 cultivation was resumed, and native labourers 'returned to work for Hire as formerly on the Farms of the Settlers'.[7] But they did apparently no longer come in sufficient numbers. Dispatches from the Colony, dated 29 October 1806, said:

There are, it is true, upwards of 400 native labourers in the Colony who work for hire, but this supply falls very far below the demand.[8]

[1] Statement of Directors, *Report from Committee on Petition of Sierra Leone Company 1802*, p. 10. See also ibid., p. 28: 'Mr. Zachary Macaulay . . . observed, That the greatest Number of Grumettas or Free Labourers, whom he remembers to have been employed in the Colony at any one Time, was from Three to Four Hundred. A greater Number might have been easily obtained if a Demand for more had existed in the Colony.'

[2] See Hoare, p. 294: 'A term of four years, which succeeded the French invasion [1794], may be considered as the most prosperous period of the colony, prior to its transfer to the Crown [1808].'

[3] Statement of Directors, *Report from Committee on Petition of Sierra Leone Company 1802*, p. 19.

[4] See also ibid. *1804*, p. 5: '. . . those Natives who had repaired to the Colony for Employment, and had been in some Degree domesticated in its Territory, have been induced to fly from the Colony . . . .'

[5] 'Extract from the Report to the Court of Proprietors, 18th March 1802', ibid., p. 105.

[6] See ibid., pp. 42, 48–51, 59, 61, 100–6; *Report of Directors of Sierra Leone Company 1804*, pp. 40–1; *Special Report of African Institution 1815*, pp. 19–20.

[7] Statement of Directors, *Report from Committee on Petition of Sierra Leone Company 1804*, p. 43; see also ibid. *1807*, p. 5. At that time some native labourers seem to have settled permanently in the Colony. See statement of Captain William Day, of the Royal Navy, before the Committee on Petition of Sierra Leone Company (*Report 1804*, p. 114): 'A Part of these Labourers settled with their Families in the Colony: Some of them, after a Stay of some Months, returned Home, and sometimes have come again to the Colony.'

But the number of natives who settled permanently in the Colony was, on the whole, very small. See the Memorandum by Zachary Macaulay sent on 4 May 1808 to Governor Ludlam (Macaulay, *Letter to the Duke of Gloucester*, Appendix, p. *2):

'The question . . . which it is proposed to consider is this: By what means may the colony of Sierra Leone obtain an accession to its population of any considerable number of native Africans ?

'It may be supposed that much may be done to effect this object by inducing free natives to hire themselves to the colonists, in the capacity of labourers. But although a considerable number of such persons have usually been employed in Sierra Leone, hardly any of them have been found willing, even while the Slave Trade flourished, to reside there permanently. Their relations have lived in some native village at a distance; and to them, after acquiring a little property by their labour for eight or nine months, they have almost always chosen to return. The free native labourers, therefore, have been a shifting body . . . .'

[8] *Report from Committee on Petition of Sierra Leone Company 1807*, p. 7.

The Natives thus coming to the Colony from 1792 on were mostly Timmanees,[1] but some were Mandingoes (Mohammedans).[2] Finally, there also
came some Kroomen, who are not included in the various figures mentioned
above. The Directors, in describing the insurrection of the Nova Scotians
in September 1800, said:

... the number of loyal settlers, who chose to arm in defence of themselves and the
government, amounted only to 30, besides about twelve Europeans, and between
40 and 50 natives, from that part of the coast to leeward of Sierra Leone, called the
Crou Coast, who were employed at the time in navigating the Company's vessels,
and who seemed disposed cordially to unite in supporting their employers.[3]

The crewmen . . . formed, as the muster-rolls will shew, no inconsiderable part of
our strength, and without their accession to our side, we should have been too weak
to have secured ourselves from a nocturnal attack. . . . It is much to be lamented
that they are so attached to each others society, and to employments connected
with shipping, that there is no hope of diverting any of them to the prosecution of
labour on the farms.[4]

A year later the Directors stated:

. . . there is usually in the Settlement, a Body of Crewmen (Men coming from
a distant Part of Africa) who, though preferring Employment on the Water, might
be induced, by an Advance of Wages, to assist for a Time in cultivating the Soil.[5]

The 'Return of Settlers, Europeans, and Resident Strangers, 29 March
1802', lists:[6]

Crewmen: Supposed Average for the last year   60
          They are at present 90 in Number.

Through the abolition of the slave trade (1807) many Kroomen lost their
livelihood, and considerable numbers thereupon sought employment in
the Colony.

They have long been the exclusive intermediate merchants, or rather factors,
between the vessels trading on this part of the coast and the people of the interior;
and while the Slave Trade flourished, this employment occupied a considerable
number of hands. Since the abolition of that trade they have sought other lines of
service, and, in the year 1809 . . . the number of those who had hired themselves as

---

[1] See also Statement by Directors, *Report from Committee on Petition of Sierra Leone Company
1802*, p. 14: 'The only Natives who come into immediate Contact with the Colony, are those of the
Timmaney Nation, from whom the Lands occupied by the Company were originally purchased;
and whose Country is of small Extent, and thinly peopled.'

[2] Zachary Macaulay spoke of the Mandingoes 'who were in the Habit of frequently visiting the
Colony, sometimes to the Number of 40 or 50 at a Time . . . . The Extent of their Country is about
900 Square Miles, and the Number of its Inhabitants about 48,000, which is about Six Times the
usual Average Population of the Sea Coast of Africa in the Neighbourhood of Sierra Leone, that
being reckoned not to exceed Eight Persons to a Square Mile. This Calculation however, is
necessarily a loose one' (ibid., pp. 28–9). The 'Return of Settlers, Europeans, and Resident
Strangers' made on 29 Mar. 1802 shows 'Dalla Moodo's People: Estimated at 40' (ibid. *1804*,
p. 127).   [3] *Report of Sierra Leone Company 1801*, pp. 15–16.

[4] Ibid., pp. 19–20. According to Zachary Macaulay, 'the Croumen . . . though occasionally
employed on Shore, are chiefly occupied in Ships on the Coast, and in managing small Craft.
Their Number did not at any Time exceed Sixty. They come from the Coast between Cape Mount
and Cape Palmas, a Distance of about Three Hundred and Fifty Miles to the Southward of the
Colony' (*Report from Committee on Petition of Sierra Leone Company 1802*, p. 28). See also
Winterbottom, vol. i, p. 9: 'The Kroos, or Kroomen, are a very industrious people, and frequently
engage themselves to European vessels upon the coast, continuing on board several months, and
acting in the capacity of sailors and traders, in both which situations they shew much intelligence
and activity.'

[5] *Report from Committee on Petition of Sierra Leone Company 1802*, p. 19.   [6] Ibid. *1804*, p. 127.

labourers at Sierra Leone alone, a place distant about 350 miles from their own country, was estimated at 800.[1]

But they still came only to acquire 'such goods as are most valuable in their own country' and did not settle permanently in the Colony.

In eighteen months or two years, a sufficient stock having been collected, the Krooman returns home with his wealth.[2]

The Government was anxious to induce Kroomen to bring their wives with them, and in December 1808 the Governor and Council offered 'To each of the six Kroomen who shall first introduce their wives and families into this Colony, and shall live with them in one or more distinct houses to each family, and shall cultivate a quantity of ground not less than two acres for the space of two years, £5 5s.'[3] But apparently not one Krooman took the opportunity of earning this reward. Yet, the number of men, coming temporarily, increased still further, and on 8 November 1816 the Governor and Council passed 'An Act for purchasing and vesting in His Majesty certain Lands now belonging or said to belong to Eli Ackim of Freetown in this Colony Trader for the site of a Town for the Kroomen resorting to the Colony for Labour'.[4]

It is difficult to tell how many Kroomen migrated to the Colony at that time. In May 1816 they were estimated at 700[5] and in March 1817 at 650.[6] The censuses of 1818, 1820, and 1822 showed the following figures for the Colony:[7]

31 December 1818					8 July 1820					1 Jan. 1822		
Freetown and Suburbs		Elsewhere			Freetown and Suburbs		Elsewhere			Free-town	Else-where	Total
Men	Boys	Men	Boys	Total	Men	Boys	Men	Boys	Total			
486	55	155	50	746	553	62	89	23	727	801	146	947

But the Commissioners of Inquiry (1827), after having quoted the totals for 1817–22, say:

These estimates are understood to be exclusive of those Kroomen employed in His Majesty's ships, each of which maintains a number proportioned to her establishment. Neither are those included who are employed up the river in the timber trade, and whose number must be very considerable, upwards of 100 being so employed by Mr. M'Cormack alone.[8]

They say that since 1800 the Kroomen 'are understood to have been gradually increasing till the year 1825,[9] when they were in some measure

[1] 'An Account of a Tribe of People called Kroomen' by Ludlam, *Sixth Report of African Institution 1812*, p. 89.
[2] Ibid., p. 94.   [3] Crooks, *Short History of Sierra Leone*, p. 63.
[4] Sierra Leone, *Acts 1800–27*, pp. 163–6. See also Crooks, *History of Sierra Leone*, p. 92.
[5] See *Missionary Register 1816*, p. 401; *1817*, p. 249.
[6] See ibid., p. 355. *Report of Commissioners of Inquiry*, 1827, First Part, p. 17, says: 'In 1817, Sir Charles M'Carthy estimated their number at 560.' But this was probably a slip of the pen or a misprint.
[7] See *Accounts relating to Population*, &c., *of Sierra Leone*, 1825, pp. 13–21. 'The Kroomen are included in the Census; they cannot, however, be considered as the fixed Population, although the number is never materially reduced, those returning home being replaced by new Adventurers.'
[8] *Report*, First Part, p. 17.
[9] 'On the assumption of Sir Charles Turner their number was 1,200' (Claude George, p. 203; see also ibid., p. 267).

discouraged by the late General Turner, under the impression that the colony sustained an injury by their employment;[1] and this may probably have in some degree affected their number, although the census of 1826 does not furnish the means of determining'.[2] But the *Blue Book* for 1826 stated:

> The Kroo Men, from the Neighbourhood of Cape Palmas, who work as Laborers ashore and afloat may be estimated at 1,100.[3]

Fewer, however, apparently came in the following years. The *Blue Book* for 1827 estimated them at 900,[4] and the Colonial Surgeon to Sierra Leone, James Boyle, related in 1831 that they 'are between seven hundred and eight hundred in number'.[5] According to the census of 1840, they numbered apparently 570, excluding 300 or 400 on vessels.[6] Later censuses showed the following figures:[7]

1844	1847	1848	1850	1851	1860	1881	1891	1901	1911	1921	1931
717	730	743	560	555	363	610	1,327	1,970	1,677	4,766	4,547

[1] The Commissioners evidently referred here to 'An Act for the better regulation of Mechanics, Kroomen, Labourers, Grumettas, and other Servants' (*The Royal Gazette and Sierra Leone Advertiser*, 30 July 1825, pp. 534–5), passed on 29 July 1825, which provided among other things: 'That if any Krooman, Labourer, Grumetta, or other servant, being alien strangers resorting to this Colony for hire, shall refuse to hire him or themselves when required so to do, without being hired or engaged to some other employer, or without being able to show good cause for such refusal to the Magistrate before whom any complaint shall be brought, such Krooman, Labourer, Grumetta or servant aforesaid shall, on conviction thereof, be fined in any sum not exceeding twenty shillings, to be levied on their goods and chattels; and in default of sufficient goods and chattels to pay such fine, shall be imprisoned in the Common Gaol or House of Correction for any time not exceeding one month.' But such a provision was already contained in similar Acts passed on 26 Apr. 1820 and 8 Mar. 1822 under Governor MacCarthy (see ibid., 27 May 1820, pp. 397–9, 30 Mar. 1822, pp. 49–50). The first Act restricting the freedom of the Kroomen in the Colony was in fact passed on 6 Sept. 1816 (see Sierra Leone, *Acts 1800–27*, pp. 155–63), the Preamble of which said: 'Whereas a very considerable number of free Natives of Africa, of the various denominations of Kroomen, are now resident in this Colony, and are likely successively to come to reside therein, for the purpose of being employed as Labourers for hire, as has been Customary with the people of the Kroo Nation, from the earliest period since the Establishment of this Colony, And Whereas there is good reason to suppose that many of this very considerable number of Kroomen at present resident within this Colony, either unable to procure employment or unwilling to work, are now living in the outskirts of the Town of Freetown, at their usual place of abode, called Krootown, without any visible means of support, and can therefore subsist only by depredations committed upon the properties of the industrious, and other Inhabitants of this Town and its Vicinity . . . .'

[2] *Report of Commissioners of Inquiry*, 1827, First Part, p. 17. According to *Blue Book 1825*, p. 142, the number of Kroomen ascertained at the 1826 census was only 278.

[3] Ibid. *1826*, p. 136.   [4] See ibid. *1827*, p. 64.

[5] Boyle, p. 34. The census taken in Freetown in the third quarter of 1831 showed 504 Kroomen; see C.O. 267, vol. cxi.

[6] The statements in the *Report of the Committee on the West Coast of Africa* are somewhat contradictory. On 30 Apr. 1841 both the Superintendent Assistant of Liberated Africans at Sierra Leone and the Acting Governor at Sierra Leone (J. Carr) were asked: 'What is the number of Kroomen in this settlement?' The former answered: 'Six hundred and fifty-three on the 31st December 1840, exclusive of those employed up the river, and on board of ships of war on the coast' (*Report*, 1842, Part II, p. 325). The latter said: 'By the census for the year 1840, 570; but this does not include those residing in the factories on this river' (ibid., p. 328). The Commissioner R. R. Madden himself reported: 'The casual residents, such as Kroomen, Mandingoes, and Timmanees, are chiefly employed in Freetown . . . . Their number in Freetown and its immediate vicinity on the 31st December 1840, was said to be 653; and those employed in our merchant vessels and cruisers on the coast cannot be under 300 or 400 more' (ibid., p. 247).

[7] See *Reports made by Butts*, &c., pp. 38–41; *State of Colonial Possessions 1817*, p. 198; *1848*,

Rankin, who visited Sierra Leone in 1834, reported that 'there are no Kroo women in Sierra Leone'.[1] Referring to a conversation with a Kroo-man he said:

The Krooman who compared his tribe with the white men was not aware of the strong similarity between the two classes of voluntary colonists,—in their both being migratory; seeking it for the same purpose; leaving it on the same result.[2]

Ten years later Commissioner Guppy reported:

They never take any of their women out of Kroo country; there are but two Kroo women at Sierra Leone.[3]

In the meantime, upon the abolition of slavery in the West Indies, the British Government had tried to induce Kroomen to emigrate there with their families. At first only men embarked,[4] but a very ingenious pressure brought upon the Kroomen by the Government seemed to meet with success. On 23 September 1841 the Agent-general for Immigration, British Guiana, reported:

I had nearly forgot to mention the important fact that of the number now come, about 60 are Kroomen, several of whom have brought their wives, and many more of the same class are waiting to follow.[5]

But this was a delusion. On 3 August 1841 Lieutenant-Governor Sir Henry MacLeod, Trinidad, wrote to Lord John Russell:

. . . on the late arrival of immigrants from Sierra Leone, the Kroomen on being told previous to their embarkation, that their passages would not be paid for by the Government, unless an equal number of females accompanied them, actually persuaded women of the very lowest character and not of their own tribe, to embark with them.[6]

The number of Kroomen who actually went to the West Indies was small. It possibly did not exceed 1,000.[7]

In 1860 only 363 people were returned as Kroomen and in 1881, 610. The census report for the latter year still gives the impression that they were all men.[8] But according to the 1891 report the 1,327 'Kroomen' included 239 females,[9] and in 1901 there were 1,129 males and 841 females.[10]

Kroomen.—This tribe have increased by 643, but the increase has taken place almost entirely among the females; the males remain about the same as in 1891.[11]

p. 305; *1850*, p. 185; *1851*, p. 182; *1860*, Part II, p. 24; *Census Report 1891*, p. 5; *1901*, p. 7; *1911*, p. 10; *1931*, pp. 46, 73.   [1] Rankin, vol. i, p. 151.   [2] Ibid., pp. 168–9.
[3] *Reports made in 1844 by Butts and Guppy*, p. 7. See also the statement by Commissioner Butts, ibid., p. 33: 'The true cause of the Kroos and others not permitting the women to emigrate is, that they are the property of the family entailed . . . .'
[4] In May 1841, 16 Kroomen arrived in Trinidad and 23 in British Guiana (see *Papers relative to West Indies: Antigua, &c., 1841–2*, p. 47; *Correspondence relative to Emigration, &c., 1842*, pp. 368–9). [5] Ibid., p. 375. [6] *Papers relative to West Indies: Antigua, &c., 1841–2*, p. 59.
[7] According to *Returns showing the Number of Free Immigrants into Jamaica, &c., 1847*, p. 3, there were among the immigrants into Jamaica, British Guiana, and Trinidad from 1 July 1843 to 31 Dec. 1846, 320 'natives of the Kroo Coast'. In 1847, 108 emigrated from the Kroo Coast to British Guiana (Colonial Land and Emigration Commission, *Report 1850*, p. 131). From Jan. 1850 to Apr. 1851, 93 or 95 Kroomen emigrated to the West Indies (see ibid. *1851*, pp. 38, 128). In 1853, 273 emigrated from the Kroo Coast to British Guiana (see ibid. *1861*, p. 81). A number of Kroomen returned between 1842 and 1850 from British Guiana (see ibid. *1852*, p. 209).
[8] See *Census Report 1881*, pp. 8–9.   [9] See ibid. *1891*, p. 5.
[10] See ibid. *1901*, p. 7.   [11] Ibid., p. 8.

In 1911 the number of females (838) was practically the same as in 1901 and almost identical with the number of males (839).[1]

Kroomen show a decrease of 292, probably due to the fact that, owing to the increased shipping to which they are indispensable, more of them happened to be at sea.[2]

By 1921 the number of males had risen to 2,883 and the number of females to 1,883.[3]

The considerable increase of 3,089 among the Kroomen is due in part to the great increase in the Colony's Shipping during the War and in part to increased emigration from the Kroo Coast on account of internal troubles there.[4]

In 1931 the number of males had decreased to 2,470, while the number of females had increased to 2,077.[5]

As regards the other natives (Timmanees, Mandingoes) who were said to have exceeded 400 in 1806, the census taken in Freetown in March 1817 showed 1,009.[6] The Commissioners of Inquiry, who apparently were not aware of this census, reported in 1827:

The census of 1818 is the earliest document in which any distinct notice is taken of the several tribes of *natives* who reside in the immediate vicinity of Sierra Leone, and who occasionally resort to the colony.

This census, however, includes those only who were at the time residing in and around Freetown, without any reference to the Timmanees (the original possessors of the land) who reside in hamlets dispersed over the peninsula, but are not noticed in any census prior to that of 1820.

The *natives* resident in the colony appear, by the census made at different times, to have been as hereafter stated; but these numbers cannot be implicitly relied on, as the manners of the people and the inefficient means of enumerating them, must have presented great difficulties in the way of a correct return; the discrepancies, indeed, are very obvious.

	1818[1]	*1820*[2]	*1822*[3]	*1826*[4]
At Freetown	997	682	1,387	2,174
In liberated African villages .	..	}400	464	247
In native villages . . .	..		1,625	692

[*For notes to table see opposite*

The great majority of natives returned as resident at Freetown, are supposed to be drawn to the colony by objects in some way connected with trade; and many of them, who have acquired a knowledge of the language and customs of the place, find a lucrative occupation in acting as factors for those of their countrymen who have not the same advantages. The Mandingo's, who are the most numerous, are said to be particularly crafty and expert in this capacity. They turn their knowledge to a double account, by receiving a recompense from the merchant to whom they conduct the native traders; whilst the strangers also remunerate them for facilitating the disposal of their goods. Though their numbers appear to have considerably increased, it is believed that a very small proportion can be classed as *residents*; and they may be considered generally as resorting to the colony for purposes of trade,

[1] See *Census Report 1911*, p. 10.   [2] Ibid., p. 12.
[3] See ibid. *1921*, p. 10.   [4] Ibid., p. 12.
[5] See ibid. *1931*, pp. 46, 73.
[6] See *Missionary Register 1817*, p. 355. They were grouped as follows: 141 Native Men, 88 Native Women, 149 Native Children; 240 Men Servants, 171 Women Servants, 118 Boys Servants, 102 Girls Servants.

as much as the Kroomen do with a view to labour; with this difference, however, that the Mandingo's are accompanied by their families, which with the Kroomen is seldom the case.

This may in some measure account for the fact, that whilst, in a few instances, the former have become permanently resident, an occurrence of the kind is unknown among the latter.[1]

A part of those native Africans who have been returned as residing at Freetown, are of the Timmanee nation; but never having been distinguished from the others in any census hitherto taken, it is difficult to specify the proportion they bear to the Mandingoes, though fewer than these in number.[2]

The data for Natives inspire very little confidence, and have caused a great deal of confusion. The Commissioners of Inquiry gave figures which differed widely from the official census returns, but both sets of data indicate an enormous increase from 1820 to 1822. The *Missionary Register*, using the official census returns which showed an increase in the number of Natives from 1,046 to 3,526 (and at the same time a decrease in the number of Liberated Africans captured at sea from 8,076 to 7,969), said:

The chief increase is apparently in the class of Natives, while that of Liberated Africans seems to be somewhat diminished; but this is, in part, occasioned by a difference of arrangement in the two Returns. The large number of Natives in the Native Villages of the Peninsula, amounting in the last Return to 1,925, would have been divided, according to the arrangement in the Return of 1820—into Natives, properly so called, that is, as we conceive, the Aborigines of the Peninsula; and Liberated Africans, living in villages, but not under a Superintendent. In the Return of 1820, this distinction was made; and then the whole number, amounting to 1,468, was divided into 400 of the first class and 1,068 of the second. Both classes being

---

[1] *Report of Commissioners of Inquiry*, 1827, First Part, p. 18.   [2] Ibid., p. 19.

Notes to table opposite]

[1] Of the 997 'Natives, in Freetown and Suburbs, whether at home, Apprentices, or Servants', 376 were men, 257 women, 194 boys, and 170 girls; see *Accounts relating to Sierra Leone*, 1825, p. 15.

[2] But according to *General Census, 8 July 1820*, the numbers of 'Natives, whether at their homes, apprentices or servants' were

| | Freetown and Suburbs | | | | Elsewhere | | | | |
Men	Women	Boys	Girls	Total	Men	Women	Boys	Girls	Total
312	128	91	115	646	115	121	66	98	400

[3] But according to 'Census 1 January 1822' the 'Natives' numbered

| | Freetown | | | | Elsewhere | | | | |
Men	Women	Boys	Girls	Total	Men	Women	Boys	Girls	Total
414	268	206	199	1,087	913	709	424	393	2,439

'Of these a small part are natives of the peninsula of Sierra Leone; the remainder are natives of the surrounding and interior countries, who have, of their own accord, either settled permanently in the colony, or made it their temporary residence' (Kenneth Macaulay, *The Colony of Sierra Leone vindicated*, p. 17).

[4] But according to *Report of Commissioners*, Appendix A, No. 38, the 'Natives' numbered

| | Freetown | | | | Elsewhere | | | | |
Men	Women	Boys	Girls	Total	Men	Women	Boys	Girls	Total
810	506	404	454	2,174	471	311	166	154	1,102

called 'Natives' in the last Return, the number of Liberated Africans appears to have diminished; while it has in fact greatly increased . . . .

Still there is an increase of the class ranked as 'Natives' in the last Return, to the amount of nearly 1,000. Of these about one half are in Freetown; and the other half are chiefly resident in the Settlements of the Liberated Africans. This augmentation is derived, we conceive, from the influx of the people bordering on the Colony; and is a gratifying indication of the growth of mutual confidence between the Colony and its Neighbours.[1]

While the *Missionary Register* came to the conclusion that the number of Natives had actually increased by nearly 1,000, Macqueen claimed that the apparent rise was wholly fictitious.[2] I am inclined to think that the 1822 census returns of both Liberated Africans and Natives were fairly accurate, and that the great difference between the numbers returned as Natives in 1820 and 1822 was due (1) to incomplete enumeration of Natives in 1820, (2) to erroneous inclusion of many Natives in the number of Liberated Africans in 1820, and (3) to immigration of Natives since the census of 1820.

The 1826 data for Natives in villages were probably incomplete. For the following decades few figures only are available.[3] The numbers of Natives (excluding Kroomen) returned at the censuses of 1844, 1847, and 1848 were 2,971, 3,604, and 3,889 respectively.[4] They are likewise untrustworthy.

4. *Maroons*

Until 1800 the various societies carrying white or black settlers from Europe or America to Sierra Leone had been unfortunate in selecting the people. Either the colonists were unfit or (as in the case of the Nova Scotians) the European administrators did not succeed in establishing peaceful relations between Government and settlers. In 1800, however, there came a new group of colonists, the Maroons, who proved to be quite satisfactory, and it is interesting to note that in this case the Sierra Leone Company was most reluctant to admit them as immigrants into the Colony.

The early history of the Maroons is briefly as follows: When Jamaica was conquered by the English in 1655, most of the Spanish inhabitants retired to the island of Cuba. Of their negro slaves who altogether numbered about 1,500, some accompanied their masters, but many retreated to the

---

[1] *Missionary Register*, Dec. 1822, p. 508. See also *Sierra Leone Almanac 1822*, p. 45: 'Since the period at which the last Census was made [July 1820], the population of the Colony has greatly increased, from the influx of liberated Africans, the births of the settled colonists, and natives from the interior countries, who are continually flocking into the colony.'

[2] See Macqueen, Letters on Sierra Leone to the Earl of Liverpool, dated 12 Nov. 1824, *Colonial Controversy*, pp. 102–3: 'With regard to the apparent increase of "natives" within the space mentioned, the way the return stands, without explanation, is a complete deception. Those enrolled as "natives" are in reality captured Negroes not proceeded against, condemned and delivered over to the local authorities.' He added: 'But what must strike every one the most forcibly, my Lord, is the classes of the population here enumerated. With the exception of the few Europeans and the Kroomen, a migratory people . . . not one, I will say, not one African has come to the place from choice. . . . Not a single native has voluntarily joined the population of the place, adopted our manners, chosen our laws, sought our protection, or acknowledged our sway.' These statements are evidently absolutely wrong.

[3] Natives were sometimes included in the figures for Liberated Africans; see p. 96 below.

[4] See p. 162 below.

mountains, where they and their descendants lived for 140 years. These free negroes, called Maroons (runaway slaves), revolted in 1795 against the English but were finally forced to surrender, and about 600 out of a total of 1,400 or 1,600 were removed to Nova Scotia. They sailed from Jamaica on 6 June 1796 and the three ships which carried them arrived on 21 and 23 July in Halifax.[1]

The British Government apparently had first intended to send them to Sierra Leone. Brymner, Dominion Archivist of Canada, reports:

In 1796, before the Maroons had been sent to Nova Scotia, a correspondence had been opened by the Secretary of State with the African Company[2] on a proposal to send them to Sierra Leone. But the experience of the company with the negroes who had fled from the United States during the war ending in 1783 and taken refuge in Nova Scotia, from which they were removed in 1792, led the directors to refuse to entertain the idea of dealing with another body of negroes whose reputation could not be held to warrant such a step. The conduct of the first body of negroes had been turbulent and mutinous, causing great anxiety and expense to the company, and not unnaturally the directors dreaded that the Maroons would make common cause with their brethren in colour.[3]

The Directors of the Company do not mention these negotiations in their (printed) reports, but stated with regard to the Maroons in 1801:

The intention was to settle them permanently in Nova Scotia, but their reiterated complaints respecting the coldness of the climate, and the heavy expence of supporting them there, induced Government to determine on removing them to a warmer country. Africa having been deemed the place to which they might most conveniently be sent, application was made to the Directors on the subject. The Directors were not desirous of receiving them at Sierra Leone, but expressed their readiness to render every assistance in effecting their settlement in any other part of Africa,[4] and in afterwards superintending and instructing them, provided

---

[1] See Long, *History of Jamaica*, vol. ii, p. 338; Edwards, *History of West Indies*, 3rd ed., vol. i, pp. 522, 546, 571; Dallas, *History of the Maroons*, vol. i, pp. 22–4, vol. ii, pp. 203–5. Some recent publications convey a wrong picture of the history of the Maroons. *The Handbook of Sierra Leone* (1925), for example, says (p. 28): 'The Maroons were originally shipped from the slave station at Coromantine, near Cape Coast Castle, to Jamaica. Here they had revolted against their masters, and after having lived in the mountains for several years were induced to surrender, and were removed to Nova Scotia.' See also *Colonial Reports, Sierra Leone 1938*, p. 4.

[2] Should read 'Sierra Leone Company'.   [3] Brymner, 'The Jamaica Maroons', pp. 89–90.

[4] See also Brymner, p. 90: 'Early in 1799 the Secretary of State reopened negotiations with the African Company, which did not respond with warmth; in fact, showed a great unwillingness to undertake the charge of these people. In May [Governor] Wentworth wrote that he had heard of the negotiations, but his letter of the 23rd was very cautious. On the 24th, the following day, he gave the proposal for the removal his approval, and added, showing the changed feeling towards them after nearly three years' residence in the province, that the inhabitants had great satisfaction at their being taken away. Difficulties, however, continued to be raised by the African Company to their reception, owing to the danger apprehended from their being settled on the mainland, and the necessity of placing them on an island from which an exit would not be easy.' The readiness of the Company to assist the Government in settling the Maroons in the neighbourhood of Sierra Leone (though not in the Colony itself) may be inferred from their Dispatch to the Governor and Council at Sierra Leone dated 22 Mar. 1799 (quoted by Claude George, pp. 462–8):

'The immediate object of the present despatches is to direct you to take the earliest measures for carrying the wish of His Majesty's Government and the determination of the Court of Directors respecting the Maroons into execution . . . .

'We wish you distinctly to understand that the Government have resolved to direct that the Maroons shall be sent from Nova Scotia so as to arrive at Sierra Leone about the middle of November, even though no information of your having actually fixed on a place for their reception should arrive here antecedently to their sending the final orders.'

Government should leave to the Directors the appointment of the persons set over them, and defray every part of the expence.

Measures were accordingly taken by Government for removing the Maroons from Nova Scotia to the African coast . . . .

The Directors had previously sent Mr. George Ross, one of their servants . . . to Nova Scotia as their agent, in order to explain to the Maroons the terms on which they were to be received in Africa . . . and to accompany them to Sierra Leone river.[1]

On 30 September 1800, one day after the Nova Scotians had 'threatened to attack the pallisade defending the government house', 'a large ship appeared in the river, which proved to be the Asia transport, having on board the Maroons from Nova Scotia, in number about 550,[2] (including men, women, and children) together with a detachment of 45 soldiers under the command of Lieutenants Smith and Tolley, of his Majesty's 24th regiment'.[3] The Maroons 'made a cheerful offer of their services'[4] and helped the Government in defeating the Nova Scotians.

The Governor and Council had hoped to procure for the Maroons the island of Bananas, about 36 miles to the south of Freetown, but they appear to have been disappointed in this hope chiefly through an alarm excited by the slave traders in the minds of the natives, respecting the Company's views in placing the Maroons in the neighbourhood of the Colony. The Government then turned their thoughts to the Bullam shore . . . . When the Maroons arrived at the Colony, various circumstances concurred to induce the Governor and Council to depart from this plan. The natives on the Bullam shore had been led to entertain much fear of the Maroons . . . . The Maroons themselves were anxiously desirous of being placed under the immediate protection of the Company . . . . The favourable testimony respecting them . . . and the actual services which they had rendered to the Company in assisting to quell the insurrection, concurred in disposing the Governor and Council to grant them lands conformably to their wishes, on the same side of the river with the Company's existing settlement. . . .

Town lots were, in the month of November, 1800, marked out for them, at Granville Town, and farms near that place were soon after allotted; and it was expected

[1] *Report of Sierra Leone Company 1801*, p. 23. According to their Dispatch of 22 Mar. 1799 the Directors had expected that the Maroons would arrive in Sierra Leone in November 1799, but the embarkation was delayed for nearly a year. See Brymner, p. 90: 'Obstacles to their speedy shipment arose, too, in Nova Scotia, where transports could not be obtained, although in February, 1800, they were ready to embark at an hour's notice. When this was overcome, the agent for the African Company protested against their sailing before August, as otherwise they would arrive in the rainy season. On the 6th of August Wentworth reported that they had embarked and were ready to sail . . . .'

[2] Of the Maroons who sailed from Jamaica in June 1796, 17 died at sea (see Dallas, vol. ii, p. 204), and mortality in Nova Scotia was apparently high at first. The winter of 1796–7 'proved exceptionally severe, and there were many deaths' (Butt-Thompson, p. 127). Thus their number may have been reduced in the first nine months after they left Jamaica, but it is impossible to estimate by how much. 'The number who left Jamaica and landed at Halifax is nowhere clearly stated. "About" 600 are said to have been on board the transports on leaving Port Royal, but this can have been only an approximate estimate. The first enumeration reported is that made by the surgeon, Oxley, on 1st July, 1797, who gives the total as 526, increased 1st August to 532, and on 1st September to 543 . . .' (Brymner, p. 89). In allocating the subvention for the Maroons in Nova Scotia for the year ending 22 July 1798 the Government of Jamaica reckoned with 558 people (see Dallas, vol. ii, p. 271). In their Dispatch dated 22 Mar. 1799 the Sierra Leone Company wrote: 'We understand that about 560 Maroons in all are likely to migrate to Africa, of whom about 150 or 200 are able-bodied men.' The number of Maroons who actually embarked in August 1800 and the number of deaths at sea have not been reported.

[3] *Report of Sierra Leone Company 1801*, p. 16.

[4] Ibid., p. 17. See also Dallas, vol. ii, p. 285: '. . . they joined with alacrity in quelling the insurrection.'

that before the rains should set in, they would erect comfortable habitations, and also prepare a part of their lands to be planted with provisions.

Their progress, however, in accomplishing these objects, had been considerably retarded by the general prevalency of sickness which may be partly ascribed to their having been exposed on first landing to more heavy falls of rain, and more frequent tornadoes than were to be expected at that season. Of their number, 23 who were either very old, or very young persons, died. By the last accounts the sickness among them had subsided . . . . The medical report made to the Directors states several causes of the sickness and mortality of the Maroons, which the Court think it proper to mention, especially as it may have been reasonably expected that persons so much inured to a hot climate would not have suffered in any material degree by their migration to Sierra Leone.

1. The scanty and irregular manner in which they had been victualled on their passage from Halifax, and the consequent debility of a great number on landing. This appeared particularly in very old persons and children . . . .

2. The strong bodily exertions of the healthier part of them immediately on their arrival, as well as their exposure to the rains. . . .

3. Their perverseness in refusing to make use of bark or any other medicine by which the violence of the fever might have been abated.[1]

The Maroons stayed only a very short time at Granville Town. They had hardly completed their houses and begun farming when the attacks of the natives forced them to move to Freetown. In April 1803, after the natives had been compelled 'to evacuate that Part of the Peninsula which lies between Freetown and Cape Sierra Leone . . . Lands in this District were allotted to the Maroons'.[2]

According to the Return of 29 March 1802, the Maroons in the Colony numbered 515 (138 men, 162 women, 108 boys, and 107 girls),[3] and in April 1811 there were within the walls of Freetown alone 807 (165 men, 195 women, and 447 children).[4] This increase seems enormous,[5] but the

[1] *Report of Sierra Leone Company 1801*, pp. 23–5. This account does not convey a clear picture of the mortality among the Maroons in the first year. It is said that twenty-three persons who were either very old or very young died. But as the debility of a great number on landing, the strong bodily exertions of the healthier part of the Maroons, and the refusal to make use of proper medicines are listed as causes of mortality, there must have been in addition a considerable number of deaths among those who were neither very old nor very young. The Commissioners of Inquiry, 1827, it is true, said (*Report*, First Part, p. 13): 'The Maroons appear to have suffered from sickness immediately after their arrival, but from their having been inured to a hot climate, the amount of their loss did not bear any proportion to that of the Nova Scotians, who, besides having to contend against change of climate, were, in consequence of their being the earlier settlers, less prepared with the means of preventing or mitigating its effects.' But the Maroons who had lived in the mountains of Jamaica were probably not more 'inured to a hot climate' than the Nova Scotians, who came mostly from the Southern States, and there is no evidence that mortality of the Maroons in the first year differed essentially from that of the Nova Scotians. (Captain Benjamin Hallowell, who in January 1803 was sent out by the Admiralty to examine into the state and condition of Sierra Leone and the other British Settlements on the West Coast of Africa, told the Committee on the Petition of the Sierra Leone Company: '. . . the Maroon Chiefs . . . complained particularly of the Climate . . . . I was surprized at their complaining of the Climate, as they came from Jamaica: but they answered, that the Mountains of Jamaica were quite different to the Climate of Sierra Leone.' Governor Day, when asked by the same Committee concerning the Nova Scotians 'Did you ever hear any of them complain of the Climate ?' answered 'Never'. See *Report 1804*, pp. 46, 117.)   [2] Statement of Directors, ibid., p. 43. See also ibid., pp. 72, 103–6.
[3] See ibid., p. 127; *Report of Commissioners of Inquiry*, 1827, First Part, p. 13.
[4] See *Report of Commissioners on Coast of Africa*, 1811, p. 8. There were probably only a few, if any, outside Freetown.
[5] A large increase amongst the Maroons had already been noticed in Jamaica. Edward Long, in 1774, it is true, stated: 'These Negroes, although inhabiting more towns than at first, are

number of children listed in 1811 was about twice as large as in 1802, and this suggests that the women who came in 1800 were nearly all very young.

Shortly after the census of 1811 many Maroons left the Colony. The reports of the Directors of the African Institution[1] give the impression that all or nearly all returned within a few years.

> The Directors cannot state to the Meeting without regret, that, on account of some unpleasant misunderstanding respecting the Militia Law in the colony of Sierra Leone, many of the Maroons were, for a time, induced to withdraw themselves from that settlement; but it is now stated, by Governor Maxwell, that most of them have returned to the colony, and regained the possession of their property, and the rest were expected soon to follow.[2]

> This [Militia] law was so obnoxious to a large part of the Settlers, that they preferred abandoning their farms and houses, and quitting the Colony entirely, to submitting to its provisions. Many of them did actually abandon the Colony on this account, and left their farms to desolation.[3]

The Directors quote a letter from Robert Thorpe, Chief Justice of Sierra Leone, to Governor Maxwell, dated 31 March 1812, in which he

diminished in their number by deaths, and cohabitation with slaves on the plantations, instead of intermixing with each other' (*History of Jamaica*, vol. ii, p. 347). But Bryan Edwards in 1793 said: 'It is generally supposed, and has been very confidently asserted, that these people have decreased; but the fact is otherwise. The mistake has arisen from the circumstance that some of their towns have been deserted; which is indeed true, but the cause has been, that the negroes have only removed from one town to another' (*History of West Indies*, 1st ed., vol. i, pp. 218–19). According to Long (vol. ii, p. 350), the Maroons numbered in 1749, 664 (273 men, 211 women, 88 boys, and 92 girls). Edwards said in 1793 that in 1739 there were 'under 600. In the year 1770 they consisted of 885 men, women and children. In the year 1773 they were 1,028; and they were increased in 1788 to 1,333. ... by the last return that I have seen, [they] amount to about 1,400' (*History of West Indies*, 1st ed., vol. i, pp. 217–19). The 'return' showing 'about 1,400' was an estimate made in 1791 (see ibid., 3rd ed., vol. i, p. 284), and in his 'Account of the Maroon Negroes', first published in 1796, he said: 'The aggregate number in 1795, was about 1,600 men, women and children' (ibid., p. 530). Two witnesses heard by a Committee of the House of Commons in 1791 shared the opinion of Edwards. Lieutenant Baker Davison, who had been in Jamaica from 1771 to 1783 and had practised surgery there, said: 'They increased most certainly, as I have frequently been in all their towns, and always saw a great quantity of children, and the numbers were, when I left the island, considerably increased to what they were when I first went to it.' He was sure they did not incorporate among them runaway negro slaves 'as they had a reward and mile money for bringing them to any public gaols' (*Minutes of Evidence before a Committee on Slave-Trade, 1791*, p. 180). Mr. Mark Cook, who had been in Jamaica from 1774 to 1790, three years in the planting business, the rest of the time as clerk and schoolmaster, said: 'I believe, from what I have seen of them, they are increasing very fast' (ibid., p. 197). The increase from 664 in 1749 to 885 in 1770 may have been actually due to an excess of births over deaths. But the further rise to 1,333 in 1788 (and to 'about 1,600' in 1795) is acceptable only if one assumes that the Maroons in that period absorbed a number of runaway slaves. Lieutenant Davison denied this possibility, and the 'Articles of Pacification with the Maroons of Trelawny Town, concluded March 1, 1738', stipulated in fact: 'Ninth, That if any negroes shall hereafter run away from their masters or owners, and fall into Captain Cudjoe's hands, they shall immediately be sent back to the chief magistrate of the next parish where they are taken; and those that bring them are to be satisfied for their trouble, as the legislature shall appoint' (Dallas, vol. i, pp. 62–3; see also ibid., pp. 97–101). But it may well be that the Maroons did not send back all the (male and female) runaways who took refuge among them.

[1] The African Institution was created on 14 April 1807, three months after the Directors of the Sierra Leone Company had agreed to surrender the Colony to the Crown. Many Directors of the Sierra Leone Company, such as Sharp and Thornton, became Directors of the African Institution. Zachary Macaulay was its first secretary.

[2] *Eighth Report of the African Institution* (read 23 Mar. 1814), p. 15.

[3] *Special Report of the African Institution* (made 12 Apr. 1815), p. 118.

recommended that severe measures be taken against the Maroons, but according to the Directors the Governor did not follow this advice.

Had it not been for the moderation and forbearance of Governor Maxwell, these violent counsels might have produced the most calamitous consequences. By pursuing a more lenient course, the Settlers were reclaimed to their duty, returned to the Colony, and resumed their farms, but not until a month or two after Mr. Thorpe had quitted it.[1]

But these reports are evidently inaccurate. The Militia Act of 20 November 1811[2] provided that all males from 13 to 60 should take an oath and be enrolled, and that every person 'neglecting to attend to enrol himself, and take the said Oath, shall be considered as out of the protection of the Law'. Most of the Maroons refused to take the oath.[3] Thereupon the Governor, on 26 September 1812, published the following Royal Proclamation:

Whereas, we have hitherto forborne carrying into effect the penalty consequent to refusal of the oath prescribed by an Act . . . bearing date the 20th day of November, 1811, . . . and this forbearance . . . has . . . made erroneous impressions on many: We . . . declare, that . . . all persons coming within the limits of the aforesaid Act, or between the ages of thirteen and sixty, who by refusing to take the said Militia oath, have set an example of disaffection and insubordination to their children and apprentices . . . are . . . declared outlaws. . . . Know therefore, that as soon as the rains are well over, or on the 20th of November next ensuing, it is our will and pleasure, that every person coming within the operation of the Militia Act, and persisting in refusal to conform to this or any one other law by which our subjects are governed, shall cease to be residents in any part of the peninsula of Sierra Leone. In conformity, however, with that moderation which has guided us in every measure of the Government of this our Colony, and which by some may have been ascribed to timidity, we are pleased to declare that the Princess Charlotte, or some other of our vessels, shall convey to whatever part of the coast, in the neighbourhood they may point out, such people, with their families, as are dissatisfied with our laws.[4]

---

[1] Ibid., p. 119. Thorpe left the Colony in March 1813; see ibid., p. 5. [2] *Sierra Leone Acts 1811–48*.

[3] It seems that already the Act of 15 Oct. 1808 which provided that a Militia be formed 'of all the Male Inhabitants of this Colony from the age of twelve Years and upwards' (see *Acts of Governor and Council 1800–27*, pp. 56–60) caused a great deal of trouble. Crooks relates that the Act 'was made the pretext by a great portion of the inhabitants for resistance to the Government, and placards of the most inflammatory nature were posted in different parts of Freetown' (*Short History of Sierra Leone*, p. 62). It was, I suppose, the opposition to this Act which induced the Governor and Council to pass, on 11 Nov. 1808, another Act (see *Acts 1800–27*, pp. 69–74) which began as follows:

'*Whereas* the use of the Name of Freetown has been found to have been perverted to purposes of Insubordination and Rebellion

'Be it *Enacted* by the Governor and Council of this Colony, and it is hereby *Enacted* accordingly

'That from and after the thirty first Day of December, in the Year of Our Lord, One thousand, Eight Hundred, and Eight, it shall be lawful to call the Town, Place, or settlement heretofore called Freetown, by the name of George-Town; And that in all public and private Acts, Deeds, or other Instruments where in the Name of George-Town shall be used, shall be understood thereby to all Intents and purposes whatever the same, Town, place, or settlement heretofore called Freetown, and the whole thereof and None Other.'

The Militia Act of 1808 was to remain in force for one year. After its expiration the Governor and Council, on 15 Dec. 1809, passed another Act providing that the 'Militia shall consist of all the Male Inhabitants of this Colony, from the Age of fifteen Years to the Age of sixty Years' (see ibid., pp. 80–8). This Act was repealed by the Act of 20 Nov. 1811, which, unlike the earlier Acts, provided a heavy penalty for neglect to enrol and at the same time made it obligatory for the militia men to take an oath.

[4] Thorpe, *Reply to Special Report of Directors of African Institution* (5 Aug. 1815), pp. 91–2. Granville Sharp, then 77 years old, and six months before his death, wrote a long letter, dated 22 Dec. 1812, to Governor Maxwell, defending the attitude of the Maroons; see Hoare, pp. 377–9.

Thorpe says that this Proclamation, issued without his 'advice, consent, or even knowledge', 'drove the Maroons from the Colony; their houses and property were then seized upon in the King's name . . . .'[1] There is in fact not the least doubt that many Maroons left the Colony, that 'the Settlers' had not 'returned to the Colony and resumed their farms' by April or May 1813, and that dissatisfaction among the Maroons persisted for some years more.[2] It is not surprising, therefore, that the number of Maroons which had been 807 in 1811 was only 610 in 1818.[3] It amounted to 594 in 1820[4] and to 601 in 1822.[5] The census of 1826 showed 681 Maroons, but another statement which the Commissioners of Inquiry considered to be more trustworthy listed only 636.[6] In 1837 they were estimated at 650;[7] the census of 1844, however, showed only 470.[8] In the meantime there had been some emigration, but the reports about the amount of emigration are quite contradictory.

In a Dispatch dated 20 March 1840 (six years after the abolition of slavery in the West Indies), Governor Doherty of Sierra Leone wrote to Lord John Russell:

At this moment it . . . happens that many of the Maroon and settler populations,[9] having been informed of the encouragement given to immigration in Trinidad and others of the West Indies, express the wish and purpose of removing thither with their families: and, in my opinion, nothing ought to be done to discourage their

[1] Thorpe, *Reply*, pp. 92–3.

[2] See ibid., p. 94: '. . . there has been a deputation from the Maroons in London for three months past, whose declared object is to complain against the oppressive proceedings of Governor Maxwell, and if they are not redressed, they declare it to be their intention to abandon the colony of Sierra Leone and return to Jamaica, or to emigrate to the Boolam shore: they have also declared, that if Colonel Maxwell shall be permitted to return as Governor to Sierra Leone, they will leave the colony . . . . This is the development of what the Directors term Colonel Maxwell's "moderation, forbearance, and lenient course of conciliation" . . . .' It is interesting to note in this connexion that shortly after the arrival of the Maroons in the Colony the Directors of the Sierra Leone Company had stated: 'They universally harbour a Desire of going back at some Period of their Lives to Jamaica' (*Report from Committee on Petition of Sierra Leone Company 1802*, p. 21). That the Directors of the African Institution had misrepresented the facts is also confirmed by the following statement in the *Sierra Leone Almanac 1822*, pp. 57–8: '1814 & 15. From the wisdom of Gov. MacCarthy's policy, all the dissatisfied Maroons who had withdrawn from the colony during Gov. Maxwell's administration, returned.'

[3] See *Missionary Register*, Sept. 1819, p. 399. There were 110 men, 154 women, 171 boys, and 175 girls, all living in Freetown and suburbs. The census of March 1817 showed only 82 men, 91 women, and 248 children, or altogether 421 Maroons in Freetown (see ibid. Aug. 1817, p. 355), but this was undoubtedly an understatement.

[4] See *General Census, 8 July 1820*. There were in Freetown and suburbs 147 men, 136 women, 156 boys, and 150 girls, and elsewhere in the Colony 3 men and 2 women.

[5] See 'Census 1 Jan. 1822'. There were 114 men, 168 women, 165 boys, and 154 girls, all living in Freetown.

[6] See *Report of Commissioners of Inquiry*, 1827, First Part, pp. 13–15, 21, and Appendix A, No. 2. Of the 636 Maroons 107 were men, 161 women, 190 boys, and 178 girls, all living in Freetown.

[7] See statement by Henry William Macaulay, 20 Mar. 1837, before the Select Committee on Aborigines (*Report with Minutes of Evidence*, Minutes, p. 32). Rankin, who visited Sierra Leone in 1834 reported (vol. i, p. 115): 'A considerable number of the original emigrants, the actual insurgent warriors of Jamaica, have survived the lapse of years, and reside in Freetown at the present time.' But it seems impossible that many of the 'actual insurgent warriors' still lived in Freetown 38 years after the insurrection.

[8] See *Reports made in 1844 and 1845 by Butts*, &c., pp. 38–41. There were in Freetown 193 males and 261 females, and elsewhere in the Colony 6 males and 10 females.

[9] 'Settler population' means Nova Scotians.

departure, which if, as they conceive, it would be beneficial to themselves, would undoubtedly be not less so to the colony.[1]

Lord Russell, who wanted to include in this emigration scheme not only the Maroons and Nova Scotians but also the much more numerous 'Liberated Africans' (captured slaves) living in Sierra Leone,[2] transmitted on 9 June copies of Governor Doherty's Dispatch to the Governors of British Guiana, Jamaica, and Trinidad and asked them to explain 'the advantages which might be placed within the reach of any able-bodied natives of Africa who may be desirous of transferring their labour' to British Guiana, Jamaica, or Trinidad respectively.[3] The Lieutenant-Governor of Trinidad 'communicated on this subject with the best-informed parties in the island' and found 'a great and general desire to obtain the services of such people as these [Maroon and old] settlers'.[4] The Governor of British Guiana said likewise that emigrants from Sierra Leone would be welcome without indicating a predilection for any specific group.[5] But Governor Metcalfe of Jamaica evidently preferred Liberated Africans.

Any of them, Maroons as well as others, but liberated Africans most of all, would be very acceptable in Jamaica.

He added:

A small party, calling themselves Maroons, lately found their way to the Port of Kingston from the coast of Africa.[6]

Another party of Maroons sailed on 12 April 1841 for Jamaica. When Acting Governor Carr of Sierra Leone was asked on 30 April 1841 by the Select Committee on the West Coast of Africa 'Have they [the Maroons] expressed any desire to return to Jamaica?' he answered: 'Yes, some of them went away to Jamaica with Mr. Barclay about a month ago.'[7] But the evidence given on the same day by Colonel Jones, Superintendent Assistant of Liberated Africans, differed widely from Carr's statement.

What was the number of Maroons, originally removed from Jamaica and Nova Scotia, carried to this settlement?—Five hundred and fifty.
What is the number now living?—Seventy, exclusive of those recently gone to Jamaica.

[1] *Report from Committee on West India Colonies 1842*, p. 554.
[2] See his Dispatch to Governor Doherty, 17 June 1840, ibid.
[3] See, for example, Dispatch from Lord John Russell to Governor Metcalfe of Jamaica, 9 June 1840, *Papers relative to the West Indies 1841*, Part II, p. 100.
[4] Dispatch from Lieutenant-Governor Sir H. Macleod to Lord John Russell, 21 July 1840, *Report from Committee on West India Colonies 1842*, p. 555.
[5] See Dispatch from Governor Light to Lord John Russell, 17 July 1840, ibid., pp. 554–5.
[6] Dispatch from Governor Metcalfe to Lord John Russell, 24 July 1840, ibid., p. 554. According to the Return of the Number of Immigrants into the Island of Jamaica, between 1 Aug. 1834 and 15 Apr. 1843 (*Correspondence relative to Emigration of Labourers to the West Indies*, 1844, p. 8) no emigrant from Sierra Leone came before 1841, but according to the Return of the Number of Emigrants from the Colony of Sierra Leone from 25 Oct. 1839 to 30 Apr. 1841 (*Report from Committee on West India Colonies 1842*, p. 593), 8 emigrants sailed on 1 Jan. 1840 in the *Mary Brown* to Jamaica. It is possible that these 8 people were the 'small party calling themselves Maroons'.
[7] *Report*, Part II, p. 328. Barclay was the agent for the *Hector* which on 12 April 1841 sailed with 151 emigrants (mainly Liberated Africans) to Jamaica. It was the first ship to sail from Sierra Leone to Jamaica after 1 January 1840. See *Report from Committee on West India Colonies 1842*, p. 593.

Are these lands [originally assigned to them] still in their possession?—Being about to leave this colony, the Maroons are disposing of their lands.

Have they expressed any desire to return to Jamaica?—Yes; this desire has never forsaken them since they left Jamaica.[1]

This statement apparently carried more weight at the time than that of Carr. The Commissioner of Inquiry, R. R. Madden, in his report dated 31 July 1841, said:

. . . in April 1841, the number left in Sierra Leone, after the recent emigration to Jamaica, was 70.[2]

Finally Macgregor Laird, in a Memorandum submitted to the Committee on 11 July 1842, said:

These people took advantage of the first opportunity of returning to Jamaica; and in 1841 there were only 70 remaining in the colony.[3]

There is, however, not the least doubt that Jones, Madden, and Laird were completely mistaken and that the great bulk of the Maroons were then still in Sierra Leone.

According to a Dispatch from Governor Macdonald to Lord Stanley, a third small party of Maroons emigrated to Jamaica in the latter part of 1841. Discussing the causes of the considerable decrease in the number of African emigrants from Sierra Leone to Jamaica he wrote:

One of the principal is that several of the maroons who about a year ago emigrated on board the West Indian, have written discouraging accounts of the island.

They were always considered here an indolent part of the population, and their desire to go to Jamaica arose, not from a wish to obtain their livelihood by working, but merely from a longing to see what they looked upon as their native country.

Here they were able to obtain apprentices who worked for them, and one of their principal complaints against Jamaica, is that if they do not work themselves, they have to pay very dearly for hired labour.[4]

Whether the apparent reduction in the number of Maroons in Sierra Leone from about 650 in 1837 to 470 in 1844 can be wholly explained by emigration to Jamaica seems doubtful,[5] and there certainly was little emigration in the next following years as, according to the censuses of 1847

---

[1] *Report from Committee on West Coast of Africa 1842*, Part II, p. 325. In 1830 the Maroons, in a Memorial sent to the Secretary of State for the Colonies, apparently had asked to be removed to Jamaica; see C.O. 268, vol. xxx, p. 164.

[2] *Report from Committee on West Coast of Africa 1842*, Part II, p. 247.

[3] Ibid., Part I, p. 570.

[4] Dispatch of 28 Dec. 1842, *Correspondence relative to Emigration of Labourers to the West Indies 1844*, p. 109. See also letter of Mr. Cathcart, Sierra Leone, to Dr. Ewart, Jamaica, 26 Dec. 1842: 'The Kingston maroons have been writing letters to their relations and friends here, which have caused much mischief . . .' (ibid., p. 42). Some months later the Agent of Immigration in Spanish Town, Jamaica, complained that in Sierra Leone 'a false impression has been created by the letters of some maroon women [washers] settled in the city of Kingston, viz., that there is a deficiency of wood and water in the colony' while actually 'wood and water are in greatest abundance' though 'it is probably true that [in Kingston] they have to pay a trifle for both these necessaries of life'. (See his reports of 25 and 29 May 1843, ibid., pp. 46, 49; see also his report of 24 Oct. 1843 in which he refers to 'some instances of discontented maroons', ibid., p. 37.)

[5] I consider it likely that the estimate of 650 Maroons in 1837 was an overestimate. That the number of Maroon emigrants from Sierra Leone to the West Indies was very small may be inferred also from the following fact. In Returns prepared in 1847 by the Secretary of the Colonial Land and Emigration Office and covering the years 1834-46 the same figures are entered for total immigrants and for Immigrant Liberated Africans. A Note to the Return of Liberated

and 1848, the Maroons numbered 460 and 462 respectively.[1] But what became finally of them it is difficult to tell. The censuses of 1850, 1851, and 1860 showed only 15, 73, and 22 respectively. This, however, is no proof of large-scale emigration. It is likely that most of the Maroons were counted at these censuses as 'Native Creoles'.

5. Liberated Africans

Introduction. Three fundamental changes occurred in the position of the Colony in 1807–8. (1) On 10 July 1807 King Farima and King Tom formally ceded to the Sierra Leone Company the part of the peninsula lying to the westward of the settlement.[2] (2) On 8 August 1807 a Bill transferring the Colony to the British Government received the Royal Assent,[3] and on 1 January 1808 Sierra Leone became a Crown Colony.

Africans says: 'The Returns received from the colonies do not afford the means of furnishing this information otherwise than by assuming as liberated Africans all the Immigrants introduced from the places named in this Return. From Returns received from Sierra Leone it would, however, appear that in the number above stated to have been introduced from Africa in the period from 1 July 1843 to 31st December 1846, there were 320 natives of the Kroo Coast; about one-half of the remainder were Africans liberated immediately previous to their departure for the West Indies, the other half being residents in the colony, but probably liberated at previous periods' (*Returns showing the Number of Free Emigrants into Jamaica, &c.*, p. 3).

[1] See *State of Colonial Possessions 1847*, p. 98; *1848*, p. 304. It should be noted, however, that many writers were of the opinion that emigration to Jamaica had been very considerable. A few quotations may serve as an illustration.

Clarke (1843, p. 40): 'In April, 1841, seventy of them embarked for Jamaica; and since that period, many other families have followed their example.' (Thus, while Jones, &c. said that in April 1841 only 70 Maroons were left in the Colony, Clarke said that in April 1841 70 Maroons left the Colony.)

Forbes (1849, p. 23): 'The emigration to the West Indies having from the traditions of the ancestors of their fatherland, drawn many of them into undertaking the transatlantic voyage, a few were lucky enough to return, which they did with a hearty determination never again to quit the colony.'

Archibald (1885, p. 154): 'They spent in the African colony about the same period of time that the Israelites passed in the wilderness, and forty years after their arrival, the great bulk of them returned to Jamaica. To-day only an inconsiderable number of their descendants remain in the African settlement.'

[2] Claude George says (p. 131): 'No material acquisition of territory accrued to the Colony from this treaty. It was a treaty of peace and friendship intended to heal up the breach and create a sort of goodwill between the Sierra Leone Company and the chiefs concerned, in consequence of wars which King Tom, principally, had waged against the Colony for seven years.' The fundamental change in the position of the Colony, as I see it, consisted in the fact that by waiving their claims to the territory conquered and occupied by the Company the native kings enabled the Colony to develop this territory without the risk of further disturbances.

[3] 47 Geo. III, Sess. 2, cap. 44 (8 Aug. 1807), 'An Act for transferring to His Majesty, certain Possessions and Rights vested in the Sierra Leone Company, and for shortening the Duration of the said Company; and for preventing any dealing or trafficking in the buying or selling of Slaves in the Colony of Sierra Leone.' The Company had asked for this transfer. 'Governor Ludlam gives this general opinion of the causes of the want of success experienced by the Company in the prosecution of their design, in the following terms: "Few places have met with greater discouragement: frequently the Colony has been threatened, and twice was actually attacked by the natives. Once it was ruined by the French; twice its own people have broken out into insurrection. When extensive commerce was carried on, the French destroyed it. When cultivation flourished, the natives first drew away the labourers, and then drove the Settlers from their farms. Even when exempt from actual violence, the turbulence of the people, the want of fortifications, and the policy, more than the ill will, of the natives, kept us in a state of constant disquietude and alarm. . . ."' (*Report from Committee on Petition of Sierra Leone Company 1807*, p. 8.) 'Governor Ludlam, the last of the Company's Governors, remained in his post to become the first Governor in Sierra Leone under the Crown' (Eveline Martin, p. 141).

(3) To give full effect to the Act for the Abolition of the Slave Trade,[1] which came into force on the very day when Sierra Leone became a Crown Colony, an Order in Council of 16 March 1808 established a Vice-Admiralty Court in the Colony for the trial and adjudication of all captured slaves brought in as prizes by His Majesty's cruisers; Sierra Leone became therefore the collecting place of Liberated Africans from all parts of the West Coast.

The recognition of the extension of the Colony by the native kings in 1807 ensured ample room for the peaceful settlement of a considerable number of Liberated Africans, but it seemed at first doubtful whether the number of captured slaves would actually be large. In a Memoir sent to Governor Ludlam on 4 May 1808 Zachary Macaulay said:

> Some increase of native population may doubtless be expected at the colony, from the confiscation of slave ships, under the Act abolishing the Slave Trade. It may prove considerable, but at the same time it may, and it is to be hoped will, prove very insignificant.[2]

Actually the increase in population through the influx of liberated slaves proved to be very large. While the other resident Africans continued to comprise a few thousand people, the number of liberated slaves (and their descendants) exceeded 40,000 in the middle of the nineteenth century. The figures concerning the Liberated Africans are not all reliable,[3] but in order to convey some idea of the trend I shall summarize here—with all reserve—the principal available data (which all exclude the military).

Date	Number	Date	Number	Date	Number
July 1814	2,750[1]	1831	25,780[9]	31 Dec. 1842	36,894[14]
1 Apr. 1817	5,130[2]	30 June 1832	25,996[10]	30 June 1843	36,136[14]
31 Dec. 1818	6,406[3]	31 Dec. 1832	25,742[10]	31 Dec. 1844	36,990[15]
8 July 1820	8,076[3]	30 June 1833	26,327[10]	1847	40,026[16]
1 Jan. 1822	7,969[3]	1837	32,000[11]	1848	40,243[16]
Apr. 1826	10,716[4]	June 1838	36,700[12]	1850	41,009[16]
31 Mar. 1827	11,878[5]	31 Dec. 1839	37,276[13]	1851	41,711[16]
31 Dec. 1828	16,886[6]	30 June 1840	37,733[13]	1860	38,375[16]
31 Dec. 1829	21,205[7]	31 Dec. 1840	37,029[13]		
30 June 1830	23,888[8]	30 June 1842	36,874[14]		

[For notes to table see opposite

[1] 47 Geo. III, Session 1, cap. 36 (25 Mar. 1807).

[2] Zachary Macaulay, *Letter to the Duke of Gloucester*, Appendix, p.*5.

[3] It should be noted in particular that some figures are not all-inclusive. Those for 31 Mar. 1827, 31 Dec. 1828, and 31 Dec. 1829 include only a portion of the Liberated Africans living in Freetown (920, 1,641, and 1,865 respectively, while the censuses of 1826 and 1831 showed 2,174 and 2,997). On the other hand, some figures include people who are not Liberated Africans. The village totals for 30 June 1831 and 30 June 1832 include 419 and 430 'Natives of the country adjacent to the Colony who are bound with the Inhabitants of the District'. For 30 June 1831 the return from Waterloo includes furthermore 513 'Natives of Mahaara in the Timmanee Country who having been engaged in a war of extermination with another Tribe were conquered and forced to seek refuge in the Colony and soliciting to be allowed to remain permanently therein, they were permitted to do so on condition that they conform to the existing regulations of the Liberated African Villages'; and the return from York includes 863 'Persons, not Liberated Africans, living within this District'. It is possible that also other returns include some Natives. Discharged soldiers are excluded from the returns of 1820–6 but are included in the village returns for 30 June 1831 and 1832 and probably also in later returns.

Although the number of Liberated Africans residing in Sierra Leone increased very much, this increase was frequently considered as small in comparison with the numbers of Africans captured or landed, and the differences between the various sets of figures were discussed at great length in many official reports. But a judicious perusal of these reports is extremely difficult because both the Administration and its critics seldom realized the meaning of the figures they used in their arguments. One example may serve as an illustration. Commissioner of Inquiry R. G. Butts reported:

> The best information that I have been able to collect leads me to suppose and to state, that from the year 1812 to 1819 there were 11,278 persons emancipated by the Vice-admiralty Court; that from that period up to 31st December 1844, 68,278 were liberated by the Mixed Court;[1] making a grand total of 79,556 liberated Africans.[2]

The figure 11,278 represents

(1) according to the above statement, the number of 'persons emancipated by the Vice-admiralty Court' from 1812 to 1819;
(2) according to another statement by Butts[3] the 'number liberated by the Admiralty Court' from 1812 to 1819;

---

[1] The treaties which Great Britain concluded with various Powers for the suppression of the slave trade gave British cruisers authority to search and detain, within wide limits, the vessels of those Powers suspected of being engaged in the trade. Provision was made by these treaties for the establishment of mixed tribunals. Courts of Mixed Commission were 'established at Surinam under Treaty with the Netherlands, at Rio de Janeiro under Convention with Portugal and Brazil, at the Havana under the Treaties with Spain, and at Sierra Leone under Treaties and Conventions with all those four powers' (Bandinel, *Account of the Trade in Slaves*, p. 276). The Court at Sierra Leone was established at Freetown on 8 June 1819 (see *Sierra Leone Almanac 1822*, pp. 18, 61). The total numbers of slaves emancipated in 1819–46 by Courts of Mixed Commission in Sierra Leone, Havana, Rio de Janeiro, and Surinam were 63,928, 11,146, 3,208, and 49 respectively (see Foreign Office, *Return of Slaves captured since 1810*). The Vice-Admiralty Court dealt from June 1819 on only with captured slaves not falling under the terms of those treaties.

[2] *Reports made in 1844 and 1845 by Butts*, &c., p. 23.   [3] See ibid., p. 24.

Notes to table opposite]

[1] Estimate excluding 300 or 400 apprentices; see *Ninth Report of African Institution 1815*, pp. 56, 59.

[2] See *Missionary Register 1817*, p. 356.

[3] Census figures; see *Missionary Register 1820*, p. 381, and *Accounts relating to the Population &c. of Sierra Leone*, 1825, pp. 13–15, 19–21.

[4] Imperfect census; see *Report of Commissioners of Inquiry, 1827, First Part*, p. 21 (The detailed table ibid., Appendix A, No. 38, shows 10,714 Liberated Africans.)

[5] See *Papers relating to Sierra Leone 1830*, pp. 18–19.   [6] See ibid., pp. 44–5.

[7] See *Report from Committee on Sierra Leone and Fernando Po*, 1830, pp. 118–19.

[8] See *Charge delivered by Chief Justice Jeffcott*, 1832, p. 33.

[9] Census of Villages on 30 June, and of Freetown in third quarter; see C.O. 267, vol. cxi.

[10] See C.O. 267, vol. cxxvii.

[11] Estimate by Henry William Macaulay, 20 Mar. 1837, *Report from Committee on Aborigines*, 1837, Minutes, p. 32.

[12] See M'Queen, *Geographical Survey of Africa*, p. xxix.

[13] See *Report from Committee on West Africa*, 1842, Part II, pp. 315–16, 323.

[14] See *Correspondence relative to Emigration to the West Indies*, 1844, pp. 114, 134.

[15] Census figure; see *Reports made in 1844 and 1845 by Butts*, &c., pp. 38–41.

[16] Census figures; see *State of Colonial Possessions 1847*, p. 198; *1848*, pp. 304–5; *1850*, p. 185; *1851*, p. 182; *1860*, Part II, p. 24.

(3) according to Acting Governor Carr the total number of negroes 'emancipated by the mixed courts' prior to 1819;[1]

(4) according to Superintendent Assistant Colonel Jones the total number of negroes who 'received their freedom from the Vice Admiralty Court' prior to 1819;[2]

(5) according to Macgregor Laird the total 'number of liberated Africans located in the colony up to 1819'.[3]

The figure actually represents the number of slaves captured and condemned by the Vice-Admiralty Court from 1808 to June 1819. In addition 824 slaves captured but not condemned were landed in those years in Sierra Leone.

In order to clarify the position it will be necessary, therefore, first of all, to show the meaning of the various sets of figures appearing in the official statistics.

(1) *Captured.* The statistics, as a rule, are said to show the 'number of slaves on board at the time of capture'. They sometimes are supplemented by Notes showing the number of 'slaves put on board after capture'.[4] A few statistics show the 'number of slaves captured', including therein the slaves put on board after capture.[5] All statistics exclude, of course, the slaves deceased before the capture was actually effected,[6] and most statistics exclude the children born on board after capture.

(2) *Liberated.* The numbers of captured slaves liberated by the Sierra Leone Courts are smaller than the numbers of 'slaves captured' because (a) many slaves died at sea after capture,[7] and (b) slaves in specific cases were restored to their owners.[8]

---

[1] See *Report from Committee on West Coast of Africa*, Part II, p. 327. Carr evidently meant to say 'emancipated by the Vice-Admiralty Court'.   [2] See ibid., p. 323.   [3] See ibid., Part I, p. 570.

[4] Unfortunately the statistics, in many cases, though claiming to show the number of slaves on board at time of capture, actually include the slaves put on board after capture.

[5] The term 'number of slaves captured' is not accurate, as the slaves put on board after capture were not necessarily captured. In 1826, for example, 34 slaves were put on board after capture 'at the instance of the Captors, by the Natives of Little Elmina near Popo' (*Correspondence with British Commissioners at Sierra Leone 1826–7*, p. 3).

[6] In 1848, for example, a slave vessel 'was run on shore off Palmas by her crew, who, after removing the slaves, set fire to her, leaving however a few on board, who, with the exception of one, perished in her' (ibid. *1848–9*, p. 152). In this case only one slave was counted as captured.

[7] The increase through births at sea is negligible.

[8] According to the Convention of 28 July 1817 between Great Britain and Portugal and the Convention of 23 Sept. 1817 between Great Britain and Spain no Portuguese or Spanish 'merchantman or Slave ship shall, on any pretence whatever, be detained, which shall be found any where near the land, or on the high seas, south of the Equator, unless after a chace that shall have commenced north of the Equator'. If slaves were captured in contravention of this (or any other) clause of the respective treaties Great Britain had either to restore them to their owner or to pay an indemnification. In the latter case the slaves were 'liberated by decree of Court'. It occurred also, however, that restored slaves were voluntarily given up to the Colonial Government by the master of the vessel (see *Correspondence with British Commissioners 1835*, p. 2). In the case of at least one vessel, captured in 1834 with 423 slaves on board, only part of the restored slaves were given up to the Colonial Government. This vessel was 'restored, as being illegally captured; of the negroes, 10 were stolen at Rio, 78 died on the passage to Sierra Leone, 26 died there pending adjudication, the remaining 309 were given up to the master with his vessel; he gave 64 sick to the British Government, and took away the remainder, 245 in number' (*Returns of Vessels adjudicated at Sierra Leone 1830–41*, p. 3). Finally in one case, in 1826, restored 'slaves revolted, and landed themselves' (see *Report on Sierra Leone and Fernando Po*, pp. 126–7); these were likewise liberated (see *Correspondence with British Commissioners 1827*, p. 14).

(3) *Landed at Sierra Leone.* The numbers of captured slaves landed at Sierra Leone are smaller than the numbers of slaves liberated because many slaves were landed elsewhere.[1]

(4) *Emancipated at Sierra Leone.* The numbers of captured slaves emancipated by Sierra Leone Courts are likewise smaller than the numbers of slaves liberated because many of the slaves surviving the sea passage could, for legal reasons, not be emancipated.[2] On the other hand, many slaves landed elsewhere were emancipated by the Courts at Sierra Leone. The number of emancipated slaves, therefore, is in some years larger and in some years smaller than the number of slaves landed in Sierra Leone.

(5) *Registered at Sierra Leone.* The numbers of captured slaves registered are much smaller than the numbers of slaves emancipated because (*a*) slaves landed elsewhere but emancipated in Sierra Leone were not registered there, and (*b*) because some slaves died or absconded after emancipation before their 'description could be taken to be registered'.[3] On account of (*b*), the numbers of slaves registered are also always smaller than the numbers of slaves landed at Sierra Leone.

(6) *Landed and Located at Sierra Leone.* The numbers of captured slaves landed and located at Sierra Leone are smaller than the numbers of slaves landed at Sierra Leone because they exclude the liberated slaves who, immediately after landing, entered His Majesty's Service, or were sent out of the Colony, or returned voluntarily to their own country.

The statistics published for the period from the establishment of the Court of Vice-Admiralty (1808) until the establishment of the Courts of

---

[1] In most of these cases the slaves had been captured at a very great distance from Sierra Leone, but in 1823, for example, the slaves captured on one ship were 'landed and delivered over to the Commanding Officer at Cape-Coast-Castle . . . in consequence of their very debilitated state' (*Correspondence with British Commissioners 1826–7*, p. 5).

[2] Slaves captured in contravention of international treaties and 'liberated by decree of Court' (see footnote 8, p. 98 above) were not emancipated. To quote another example: The Court could not decree the emancipation of the slaves put on board after capture in 1826 by the natives of Little Elmina (see footnote 5, p. 98 above). 'They were, as in other cases of similar nature, delivered over to the Colonial Government' (*Correspondence with British Commissioners 1826–7*, p. 3).

It may be mentioned incidentally that in some quite exceptional cases captured slaves surviving the sea passage were pronounced neither liberated nor emancipated. 'At the adjudication of the "*Regulo*" it was proved . . . that 5 of the number captured had been landed, on account of having the small-pox, in the River Bonny. The Court did not pronounce the emancipation of the said 5 slaves, from the possibility of their being, if alive, still held in slavery by the people of the River Bonny' (*Correspondence with British Commissioners 1832*, p. 19). On the other hand, there was at least one case in which slaves were emancipated without being included in the figures of slaves captured (or put on board after capture). 'The 23 Slaves taken on board the Dutch Vessel "*De Snelheid,*" not having been considered by the Court as Dutch property were not condemned with the Vessel; they were, therefore, libelled on the 13th of February 1827, in the British and Spanish Court of Mixed Commission, and on its being clearly proved that they were purchased by the Spanish Crew, after her seizure by the Spanish armed Ship the "Atalanta," Sentence of Emancipation was decreed upon them, on the 16th of March, as Spanish property taken on board the Netherland Brigantine "*De Snelheid,*" whilst in the possession of the Spaniards, by His Majesty's Ship "Brazen," Captain George Wickens Willes' (*ibid. 1828*, p. 2).

[3] Conditionally emancipated slaves were likewise not registered. 'Two Slaves absconded from the charge of the Liberated African Department whilst awaiting adjudication, and upon whom only a conditional Decree of emancipation was made, it being uncertain if they were alive at the time of passing sentence' (*ibid. 1836*, Supplement A, p. 2). In 1820, 71 'slaves were not registered, in consequence of their having been delivered over to the Colonial Government . . . some months previous to their emancipation' (*ibid. 1832*, p. 4).

Mixed Commission (9 June 1819) are incomplete and contradictory.[1] The returns may be summarized as follows:

	A^1	B^2			C^3	D^4	E^5	
Year	Emancipated	Captured and condemned	Captured and not condemned	Captured and landed	Captured	On board	Seized or proceeded against	Delivered to Colonial Authorities
1808	..	78	—	78	..	88	..	..
1809	115	280	—	280	..	357	..	..
1810	1,139	1,087	—	1,087	594	1,546	..	..
1811	582	545	—	545	1,362		..	..
1812	2,243	2,230	—	2,230	1,185	2,204	..	..
1813	444	446	—	446	634	..	..	..
1814	1,835	1,876	27	1,903	560	..	1,950	1,945
1815	1,298	1,296	—	1,296	626	..	1,293	1,152
1816	2,278	2,545	—	2,545	2,711	..	2,817	2,701
1817	854	603	—	603	1,028	..	753	753
1818	200	292	433	725	1,643	..	23	23
1819a[6]	—	—	364	364	3,667	..	122	120
1819b[6]	—	214	97	311		..		

[1] See *Report of Commissioners of Inquiry*, 1827, Appendix A, No. 44, 'List of Vessels adjudicated in the Court of Vice Admiralty of Sierra Leone shewing the Number of Slaves Captured and Emancipated from the third day of September 1809, to the thirty first day of December 1825' (C.O. 267, vol. xci). The heading of the column is 'Number of Slaves adjudicated, condemned and emancipated'. The Commissioners stated (*Report*, First Part, p. 22): 'The Return which has been furnished by the Registrar of the Vice-Admiralty Court, of slave vessels adjudicated in that court, from its establishment in 1809 to 1826, is very defective, owing to the absence of some records, and the imperfect manner in which others have been made. . . . the number given in the Return, when added to those adjudicated by the Mixed Courts, makes a total considerably short of the number which has actually been landed in the colony, as appears from the Returns of the Liberated African department.' The Commissioners did not realize that the Registrar had, of course, included only vessels adjudicated by the Vice-Admiralty Court, and for this Court his records were apparently complete and fairly accurate.

[2] See C.O. 267, vol. cxxvii; the yearly figures for 1814–19 are published in Liberated African Department, 10 Jan. 1825, 'General return of slaves received into the colony of Sierra Leone', *Account of the Number of Slaves captured and condemned at Sierra Leone* (*Parliamentary Papers*, 1825, vol. xxv), pp. 3–6. The yearly figures of 'Captured and condemned' in 1808–18 appear also in Colonial Office, 13 May 1829, 'Return of Slaves received into the Colony of Sierra Leone, from 1808 to 1819, prior to the Establishment of the Court of Mixed Commission', *Returns, &c.* (ibid., 1829, vol. xxv), p. 3; the same figures (and 214 for 1819) are given in 'Return of the Number of Liberated Africans landed in each Year since 1808', *Report on Sierra Leone and Fernando Po* (ibid., 1830, vol. x), p. 119, but this Return is misleading as it does not indicate that the data cover only the slaves condemned.

[3] See Foreign Office, 18 Feb. 1848, *Return of the Number of Slaves captured* (P.P. 1847–8, vol. lxiv) p. 1. A 'Note' says: 'The whole of the Slaves mentioned in this Return were landed alive.'

[4] See Colonial Department, *Return of Ships condemned 1808–12* (P.P. 1813–14, vol. xii), p. 2.

[5] See Treasury Chambers, *Account of the Number of Slaves captured and condemned at Sierra Leone* (P.P. 1824, vol xxiv), p. 1. The figures in the column Seized or proceeded against 'show, in most instances, only the numbers brought alive into port, and proceeded against'.

[6] 1819a prior to June 9; 1819b from 9 June onwards. I have made this distinction (as best I could) in the cases where each ship is listed separately.

It is impossible to draw from these Returns any conclusions concerning the number of slaves captured prior to June 1819. The Return submitted

[1] The results are shown in some statistics according to the date of capture and in other statistics according to the date of adjudication, but it is obvious that this cannot explain the enormous differences between the various sets of figures.

by the Foreign Office (C) states: '. . . there were captured, from 1810 to 1819, 14,010; and Her Majesty's Government have no returns showing how or where they were disposed of, further than that, during the ten years referred to, 11,039 slaves were landed and emancipated at Sierra Leone.' Yet, according to a Note to the Table the figure 14,010 does not in fact represent the total number of captured slaves but the number of those landed alive.

According to the Return from the Liberated African Department (B) the total number of Liberated Africans landed prior to June 1819 was 12,102.[1]

The number of Liberated Africans located in Sierra Leone was very much smaller; it amounted to 9,480.

TABLE 2. *Slaves captured, emancipated, and registered by Courts of Mixed Commission, at Sierra Leone, June 1819–June 1845, according to Dispatches from British Commissioners*[1]

Year	Captured	Emancipated	Registered	Emancipated cumulative	Registered cumulative	Year	Captured	Emancipated	Registered	Emancipated cumulative	Registered cumulative
1819	96	95	95	..	..	1833	2,017	1,838	1,836	29,535	27,992
1820	455	454	382	..	..	1834	3,276	3,068	2,582	32,603	30,574
1821	1,399	1,137	1,136	1,682	1,610	1835	5,574	4,645	4,556	37,248	35,130
1822	2,753	2,066	2,065	3,716	3,644	1836	7,545	6,906	5,454	44,154	40,584
1823	670	414	231	3,915	3,660	1837	6,775	6,083	4,396	50,237	44,980
1824	1,331	1,127	1,127	5,160	4,903	1838	5,847	5,341	3,379	55,578	48,359
1825	1,752	1,599	1,564	6,759	6,467	1839	3,390	3,233	2,795	58,811	51,154
1826	4,017	2,567	2,424	9,326	9,161	1840	732	720	717	59,531	51,871
1827	3,346	2,861	2,859	12,187	12,020	1841	309	306	306	59,837	52,177
1828	4,536	3,924	3,419	16,111	15,439	1842	447	440	439	60,277	52,616
1829	5,625	4,777	4,612	20,888	20,051	1843	830	808	805	61,085	53,421
1830	3,899	3,273	3,259	24,161	23,310	1844	2,541	2,351	2,327	63,436	55,748
1831	1,849	1,701	1,532	25,996	24,842	1845	1,234	1,189	1,187	64,625	56,935
1832	1,884	1,701	1,314	27,697	26,156						

[1] The figures for 'Captured', 'Emancipated', and 'Registered', 1819–25 are computed from *Correspondence with British Commissioners 1826–7*, pp. 3–10. The figures for 'Emancipated cumulative' 1821–5 are taken from *Correspondence with British Commissioners 1822–3*, p. 14; *1825–6*, p. 4; *1827*, p. 16. The figures for 'Registered cumulative' 1821–5 are computed by deducting from the numbers of 'Emancipated cumulative' the figures given ibid. *1832*, p. 4. The cumulative figures do not always agree with the sums of the figures for the individual years. Thus, 134 were added in 1831 to 'Emancipated cumulative' because the Commissioners believed that a mistake had been made in 1823 (see ibid., p. 3). All figures for 1826–45 are taken from ibid. *1826–7*, p. 27; *1827*, pp. 14–15, 24; *1828*, pp. 7–8; *1829*, p. 7; *1830*, p. 4; *1831*, p. 3; *1832*, p. 3; *1833*, p. 7; *1834*, p. 3; *1835*, pp. 3, 11; *1836*, Supplement A, p. 6; *1837*, Further Series, p. 6; *1838–9*, Further Series, p. 157; *1840* ii, pp. 13–14; *1841*, p. 12; *1842*, p. 7; *1843*, p. 0, *1844*, p. 4; *1845*, p. 7; *1846*, p. 13.

From the establishment of the Courts of Mixed Commission onwards the statistics became more detailed and more accurate. Table 2 shows the numbers of slaves captured, and the numbers of slaves emancipated and registered by Courts of Mixed Commission, according to the Dispatches

[1] This figure is almost identical with that given in *Sierra Leone Almanac 1822*, p. 61: 'Prior to the assembling of the Courts of Mixed Commission, established under the Conventions with Foreign Powers for the prevention of illicit traffic in slaves, there were brought into this colony 12,108.' According to a Return produced by the Registrar of the Vice-Admiralty Court, the total number of Africans liberated was reported to have been 12,114 (see *Charge delivered by Chief Justice Jeffcott*, p. 9).

of the British Commissioners at Sierra Leone. It appears that, from
June 1819 to June 1845, 74,129 slaves were captured, 64,625 emancipated, and 56,935 registered. Table 3 shows the numbers of slaves

TABLE 3. *Slaves captured and landed June 1819–December 1841*
according to Foreign Office Returns[1]

Year	On board at capture	Put on board after capture	Landed at Sierra Leone	Landed elsewhere	Year	On board at capture	Put on board after capture	Registered	Landed at Sierra Leone	Landed elsewhere
1819	96	—	95	—	1830	1,059	—	1,024	1,031	—
1820	466	—	463	—	1831	1,847	2	1,533	1,571	179
1821	1,399	—	1,136	—	1832	1,884	—	1,314	1,348	385
1822	2,652	106	2,065	—	1833	2,017	—	1,836	1,854	—
1823	547	122	422	184	1834	3,696	179	2,735	2,860	485
1824	1,213	120	1,252	—	1835	5,574	—	4,555	4,689	44
1825	1,758	—	1,565	—	1836	7,549	—	5,455	5,690	1,357
1826	3,680	262	3,015	—	1837	6,774	—	4,447	4,552	1,560
1827	3,346	—	2,836	—	1838	6,187	—	3,695	3,761	1,929
1828	4,538	—	3,419	524	1839	3,396	—	2,806	2,844	413
1829	5,652	—	4,616	161	1840	732	—	717	722	—
					1841	309	—	306	306	—

[1] Computed from Returns prepared at the Foreign Office, *Report on Sierra Leone and Fernando
Po,* 1830, pp. 122–9, and *Returns of Vessels adjudicated in the Courts of Mixed Commission at
Sierra Leone 1830–41,* pp. 2–13. In both Returns the headings are 'Number of Slaves on Board
at Time of Capture' and 'Number of Slaves Landed at Sierra Leone,' and Remarks are added
showing, for example, the numbers of slaves put on board after capture, and the numbers of
slaves landed elsewhere. The second Return says: 'In this Return, as in the Return of which
this is a continuation, the Number of Slaves actually registered on Emancipation has been
taken, as affording the nearest criterion whereby to judge of the number landed; the number
landed, when stated in the despatches, being also given in the remarks.' As, however, the first
Return evidently includes, at least for some years, slaves landed at Sierra Leone but not registered there, I have entered into the column 'Registered' the figures of slaves given in the
second Return in column 'Number of Slaves Landed at Sierra Leone', and into the column
'Landed at Sierra Leone' the figures of slaves given in the first Return as 'Number of Slaves
Landed at Sierra Leone', and the figures of Slaves given in the Remarks of the second Return
as representing the actual number of slaves landed. The difference of 779 between the total of
30,423 shown for 1830–41 as 'Registered' and 31,202 as 'Landed at Sierra Leone' is due to the
fact that 713 died and 2 absconded pending adjudication, and 64 from a restored vessel were
voluntarily delivered to the British Government.
   The figures for those landed elsewhere are not satisfactory because the Returns sometimes include
those who died at sea after capture and sometimes show the actual numbers of survivors landed.

captured, put on board after capture, registered, landed at Sierra Leone,
and landed elsewhere, according to Foreign Office Returns.[1] The data
cover (though not completely) the period from June 1819 to December
1841. They are apparently less trustworthy than the figures in the

[1] There are two such Returns. (1) The 'Return of the Number of Vessels which have been
adjudicated in the Courts of Mixed Commission at Sierra Leone, from their first Establishment
in 1819, to the latest period . . . so far as can be made out at the Foreign Office' covers the period
from June 1819 to the end of 1829. (2) The 'Return (so far as it can be made out at the Foreign
Office) of the Number of Vessels which have been adjudicated in the Courts of Mixed Commission
at Sierra Leone, from the latest Date included in the Return, No. 8, of the Appendix to the Report
of the Committee on the State of that Colony, printed by Order of the House in the Year 1830,
down to the latest Period to which the same can be made up,' leaves unfortunately a gap as it
starts only on 3 Aug. 1830 and covers only about one-third of the slaves landed in 1830.

Dispatches from the British Commissioners, but they are valuable because they give details not covered by those Dispatches.

Some additional figures were published for 1819–26 which, however, do not agree with those contained in the Dispatches of the British Commissioners or in the Foreign Office Returns.

Year	A^1		B^2			C^3
	Seized or proceeded against	Delivered to Colonial Authorities	Captured and condemned	Captured and not condemned	Captured and landed	Emancipated
1819[4]	122	120	214	461	675	94
1820	430	427	251	171	422	455
1821	1,347	1,130	1,132	—	1,132	1,134
1822	3,125	2,419	2,065	783	2,848	2,034
1823	..	..	243	373	616	199
1824	..	..	..	..	..	1,245
1825	..	..	..	..	..	1,565

[1] See *Account of Slaves captured and condemned at Sierra Leone*, 1824, p. 1.
[2] See ibid., 1825, pp. 3–6. (These figures agree with those reproduced on p. 100 above.)
[3] See *Returns of the Number of Slaves brought into Sierra Leone*, 1829, p. 3.
[4] A and B include slaves dealt with by the Vice-Admiralty Court.

Some additional figures of a similar kind were likewise published for 1828–47.

Year	A^1	B^2	C^3	D^4	E^5
	On board at time of capture	On board at time of capture	Landed at Sierra Leone	Emancipated	Received into Liberated African Department	Landed and liberated
1828	..	5,582	3,309	..	..	..
1829	..	6,607	4,927	4,777	..	..
1830	..	6,509	3,439	3,273	..	..
1831	1,334	1,851	1,468	1,701	..	..
1832	3,399	3,399	2,325	1,701	..	1,701
1833	3,427	3,427	2,569	1,838	..	1,838
1834	5,472	5,761	4,020	7,277	..	3,068
1835	7,711	7,711	4,694	..	..	4,645
1836	8,930	8,930	5,609	8,225	..	6,904
1837	6,146	6,146	4,017	6,523	..	6,033
1838	..	..	..	5,341	..	5,341
1839	..		..	3,232	2,696	3,233
1840	..	..	..	720	1,255	720
1841	..	..	..	306	903	306
1842	..	..	..	440	929	440
1843	..	..	..	808	1,255	808
1844	..	..	..	..	1,831	2,351
1845	..	..	..	..	..	1,189
1846	..	..	..	..	..	—
1847	..	..	..	..	..	—

[1] See *Accounts of Vessels captured and condemned 1831–7*, p. 9.
[2] See Foreign Office, *Returns of the Number of Slaves on Board Slave Ships*, &c., 1838.
[3] See *Returns of Cases adjudged under Slave Trade Treaties*, &c., 1845, pp. 2–4.
[4] See Liberated African Department, 'Return of Africans received into this Department 1839–1844', *Reports made in 1844 and 1845 by Butts*, &c., pp. 50–1.
[5] See Admiralty, *Returns of Vessels captured*, &c., *1832–47*.

All these data are supposed to cover slaves dealt with by the Courts of Mixed Commission.[1] But on 24 August 1839 there was passed an Act authorizing British cruisers to detain all Portuguese vessels supposed to be concerned in slave trade, and also authorizing British Vice-Admiralty Courts to condemn such vessels.[2] The statistics concerning the numbers of vessels condemned by the Courts are very imperfect.[3]

Since the passing of the Act of the 2d & 3d Vict., c. 73 (1839), up to December 31, 1845, there have been emancipated . . . by the Vice-Admiralty Court at Sierra Leone, so far as the incomplete Returns show, 1,780 slaves, who have been distributed in the colony.[4]

How incomplete these Returns were may be inferred from the fact that, according to the Proceedings of British Vice-Admiralty Courts, in 1845 alone '2,032 slaves, the survivors of 2,329 captured, were emancipated by the Court of Vice-Admiralty at Sierra Leone'.[5] For 1847–55 the following figures have been published:[6]

	1847	1848	1849	1850	1851	1852	1853	1854	1855
Captured . .	3,967	5,619	1,814	2,045	818	95	—	138	149
Emancipated .	3,671	5,282	1,722	1,614	541	94	—	—	105

Mortality. The high mortality of the slaves on board after capture is of importance in this connexion, because, though probably the strongest sur-

[1] *Report of Commissioners of Inquiry*, 1827, Appendix A, No. 44, lists for 1823, 1824, and 1825 12, 4, and 393 slaves adjudicated, condemned, and emancipated by the Vice-Admiralty Court.

[2] Act 2 & 3 Vic., cap. 73. The British and Portuguese Mixed Commissioners at Sierra Leone ceased to function in 1844; see *Correspondence with British Commissioners 1844*, p. 60.

[3] James Bandinel of the Foreign Office wrote in 1841 (*Account of the Trade in Slaves*, p. 277): 'The Returns from the Vice-Admiralty Courts established in 1839, by the Act 2nd and 3rd Victoria, c. 73, for the Suppression of Portuguese Slave Trade, have not yet been completed. But from the accounts received, it appears that in the Vice-Admiralty Court at Sierra Leone 10 vessels were condemned under that Act in the year 1840, and 15 in the year 1841. That at St. Helena, up to August 24th, 1841, there had been 19 vessels condemned; at the Cape, up to December, 1840, there had been 20 vessels condemned; at Barbadoes, up to the 25th June, 1841, there had been one vessel condemned, making a total of 65 vessels; and that from these vessels 41 slaves had been emancipated at Sierra Leone, 1,172 at St. Helena, and one at Barbadoes, making a total of 2955 slaves emancipated.' In this statement the total obviously does not tally with the sum of the items.

A Parliamentary Paper, prepared by the Admiralty and dated 29 July 1842, *Further Return of Slave Vessels brought before the Courts of Mixed Commission for Adjudication, &c., between 1 January 1840 and 31 December 1841; and Return respecting Proceeds of Slave Vessels and Cargoes captured and condemned under the Act 2 & 3 Vict., c. 73* lists 2 vessels captured in 1841 and says with regard to the first: 'The date of sentence of the Vice-Admiralty Court at Sierra Leone does not appear from any document in the Registry of the Admiralty'; and with regard to the second: ' . . . it does not appear from any document in the Registry of the Admiralty whether condemned in the Mixed Commission or Vice-Admiralty Court'. It adds: 'This Return has been prepared from the best information that can be at present obtained in this country; any further information must be procured from the several Vice-Admiralty Courts abroad.'

[4] *Return of Slaves captured since 1810*. The corresponding numbers for the Vice-Admiralty Courts at St. Helena, the Cape, Jamaica, Mauritius, and Demerara 'so far as the incomplete Returns show' were 5,430, 3,176, 812, 255, and 881 respectively.

[5] *Correspondence with British Commissioners and Proceedings of British Vice-Admiralty Courts 1846*, p. 8.

[6] See ibid. *1847-8*, p. 14; *1848-9*, pp. 3, 152-3, 155-6; *1849-50*, p. 8; *1850-1*, pp. 7, 128, 130; *1851-2*, pp. 10, 166, 168; *1852-3*, pp. 58-60; *1853-4*, pp. 135, 137; *1854-5*, pp. 3, 8; *1855-6*, pp. 44-5.

vived, many of them were landed in a debilitated state and spread diseases in the Colony. It appears that according to the Returns of the Foreign Office out of 66,371 slaves captured in 1819–41 7,118 died on board, 51,363 were landed at Sierra Leone, 7,221 were landed elsewhere, and 669 were restored to the masters of vessels. But the figures of slaves landed elsewhere or restored may include in some cases slaves deceased on board. If ships from which all surviving slaves were landed elsewhere or were restored are excluded, it appears that of 59,096 captured slaves 6,853 died on board, 51,363 were landed in Sierra Leone, and 880 were landed elsewhere or restored.

Mortality during the passage from the place of capture to Sierra Leone was extraordinarily uneven. There were ships in which only few died, while in other ships epidemics claimed an enormous number of victims.[1] Sometimes, owing to accidents, nearly all slaves perished.[2] Even of those who survived a considerable number died in the harbour before disembarkation owing in part to sickness among the Judges which caused delays in adjudication.[3]

The bad health of the Judges in Sierra Leone was also apparently the primary reason which induced the British Government to consider the

[1] See, for example, Buxton, *African Slave Trade*, pp. 175–84.

[2] A few cases of excessive mortality through accidents may serve as an illustration.

1822. One vessel with 380 captured slaves 'was upset off the Mouth of this Harbour [Freetown] in a violent tornado, and all the Slaves on board, excepting . . . 12 . . . perished' (*Correspondence with British Commissioners 1826–7*, p. 4).

1825. One vessel with 197 captured slaves 'was upset in a tornado in the Bight of Benin, and only 6 Slaves were saved' (ibid., p. 6; see also *Papers relating to Slave Trade Nov. 1825–July 1827*, p. 5).

1835. The *Formidable* landed only 408 out of 712 captured slaves; 'of the 304 who died on the passage to Sierra Leone, about 150 were killed by lightning' (*Returns of Vessels adjudicated at Sierra Leone 1830–41*, p. 5).

[3] See *Report of Commissioners of Inquiry*, 1827, p. 23: 'Instances have occurred where slaves were detained on board the vessels many weeks after their arrival in harbour, which is said to have arisen, sometimes from the sickness or absence of the individuals of whom the courts are composed, and at others, from unforeseen difficulties in the cases brought for adjudication. But whatever the causes may have been, the result is greatly to be deplored; for until the cases be decided, or unless the court (as it sometimes has done) authorize their landing before adjudication, it becomes difficult in any way to alleviate their sufferings in a state so tantalizing to their feelings and destructive of their health. . . . "La Fortuné" was captured by His Majesty's ship "Brazen," 10 days after sailing from her port; and had at the time of capture, 245 slaves on board. During a passage of 21 days to Sierra Leone, 46 of the number died. The vessel is stated to have remained in harbour six weeks before she was adjudicated, in which period 77 slaves died; making a total loss of 123 out of 245, between the date of capture and the actual landing of the negroes.' See also ibid., p. 25: 'Doubts appear latterly to have been entertained as to the proper mode of proceeding in the case of slaves retained on board ship, when the liberation of the vessel had been decreed by the courts; and although in every instance their landing was ultimately effected, these doubts lead to delays which are in proportion prejudicial to the negroes, by their continued detention on board.' See finally ibid., p. 46: 'In one instance delay is known to have arisen from the simultaneous absence (for some weeks) of the governor and the acting chief justice, who held appointments in the Mixed Courts, and without whom a court could not be formed . . . .'

Conditions in this respect seem to have been better before the establishment of the Courts of Mixed Commission. See ibid., p. 26: 'Formerly, when slave vessels were "libelled" in the Vice Admiralty Court, it was customary to land the negroes the day after their arrival, when they were at once taken charge of by the Liberated African Department; but since the establishment of the Courts of Mixed Commission, they are not brought on shore (unless sick) until adjudicated, which generally causes a delay of from 12 to 15 days, or more.'

transfer of the Mixed Commission Courts from Sierra Leone to Fernando
Po. But the long distance of Sierra Leone from the main spots of capture
played also a part. In a letter to George Bosanquet, dated 31 December
1828, the Earl of Aberdeen said:

> The first idea of the plan, for removing the Mixed Commission Court from Sierra
> Leone, originated in the complaints which were made of the unhealthiness of that
> Settlement, and in the urgent Representations which were forwarded on this subject
> by the Courts of Madrid and Lisbon. . . .
> There were, moreover, other important considerations which pointed out this
> Island as peculiarly calculated for the object in view; among the chief of which were,
> its position near the Mouths of those Rivers flowing into the Bights of Benin and
> Biafra, where the Slave-trade is still supposed to be carried on with the greatest
> activity, and a humane desire to shorten the sufferings to which the unfortunate
> victims of this inhuman traffick are exposed on Ship-board, by establishing the
> Court for their adjudication as near as possible to the place of their Capture.[1]

On 13 January 1829 the Governor and Council of Sierra Leone passed
'An Act to provide for the Good Government of the British Community
residing within the Limits of the Establishment of the mixed Commission
Courts at the Island of Fernando Po',[2] and on 23 January Under-Secretary of State R. W. Hay, in a Dispatch to J. Reffell, spoke of 'the ap-

[1] *Correspondence with Foreign Powers relating to the Slave Trade 1828*, pp. 23–4. As early as
7 Nov. 1816 Sir James Lucas Yeo, commander-in-chief on the west coast of Africa, wrote to the
Admiralty:
'The present governor, Colonel McCarthy, appears a mild, benevolent, good man; but from the
small proportion which the European bears to the black population, his efforts towards civilization can make but a slow progress, particularly when we consider the great emolument which
the merchants derive from trade, which induces them to oppose, by every means in their power,
any efforts towards cultivation. Another great objection to Sierra Leone, arises from its being
at such a distance, directly to the windward of where the slave vessels are captured, which is
generally in the Bight of Benin and Beaffra; the vessels are always crowded and sickly, and the
mortality in making the passage exceeds one tenth: added to this, the climate is detestable, the
rain commencing the end of April, and continuing to the middle of October: it proves the grave
of most Europeans who go there, and even those who escape the grave, linger out a painful and
miserable existence.
'Under these circumstances I am of opinion that Sierra Leone is not so well calculated for
forming a settlement for emancipated or captured negroes as the Gold Coast, which possesses
every advantage: it is much more temperate, the sun is more obscured, and of course has less
power, and I am certain must be much more healthy' (*Papers relating to the Slave Trade*, 1817,
p. 2).
In the same letter he recommended strongly for the sake of protecting British trade on the
west coast to obtain from the Portuguese Government one island off the Cape de Verde Islands
and St. Thomas (an island south of Fernando Po). With regard to St. Thomas he said: 'It would
also be superior as a settlement for the captured negroes to Sierra Leone, not only from its
climate, and being an island, but from its being directly in the vicinity of where the Slave Trade
is carried on; whereas, as I have before stated, Sierra Leone is in every respect the most unfit,
and worst situation on the whole coast' (ibid., p. 6).
The removal of the Mixed Courts to Fernando Po was discussed soon after their establishment
in Sierra Leone; see, for example, *The Royal Gazette and Sierra Leone Advertiser*, 17 Aug. 1822,
pp. 219–20. It was also mentioned on 25 Aug. 1827 in a Dispatch from Viscount Goderich to
Governor Major-General Sir Neil Campbell (see *Papers relating to Sierra Leone 1830*, p. 21), and
on 22 Nov. 1828 Sir George Murray wrote to Major Ricketts, that 'it is in the intention of His
Majesty's Government to remove the courts of Mixed Commission to Fernando Po as soon as
circumstances will permit' (ibid., p. 31). See also *Report of Commissioners of Inquiry*, 1827,
First Part, pp. 45–6. See furthermore the controversy on this question between Kenneth Macaulay
(*The Colony of Sierra Leone vindicated*, pp. 113–20) and James M'Queen (*A Fourth Letter to
R. W. Hay*, p. 48).
[2] Sierra Leone, *Acts 1800–27* (Appendix), pp. 337–8.

proaching removal of your mixed Commission Court to Fernando Po'.[1] Finally, on 13 July 1830, the Select Committee on the Settlements of Sierra Leone and Fernando Po, after having pointed out that it was desir- able to reduce the Europeans employed on the West Coast to the smallest number possible, recommended likewise that the Court be removed from Sierra Leone. It resolved among other things:

5. That it is the opinion of this Committee, That the situation of the Mixed Commission Court at Sierra Leone, for the adjudication of captured Slaves, is highly inconvenient for that purpose, considering that the Slaves are captured chiefly at the distance of 800 or 1,200 miles to the Eastward; and that as a current constantly sets from West to East, the captured Ships are sometimes eight or nine weeks, and on an average, upwards of five weeks, on their passage from the place of capture to Sierra Leone; occasioning a loss of the captured Slaves, amounting to from one-sixth to one-half of the whole number, whilst the survivors are generally landed in a miserable state of weakness and disease.[2]

But the Courts were not removed.

Dr. Bryson, in discussing in 1847 'Diseases most prevalent among Cap- tured Slaves', said:

The diseases from which negro slaves suffer most severely on board the vessels destined for their transportation, are, dysentery, fever, small-pox, ophthalmia, and diarrhœa; the first two are by far the more generally destructive, and it not un- frequently happens that they acquire such virulence, as to carry off a fourth, or even a third of the whole cargo in the short period of a few weeks.[3]

The debilitated and sickly condition in which many captured slaves were landed in Sierra Leone[4] caused many deaths in the brief period which elapsed between emancipation and registration.[5] The numbers of such deaths were given as follows:

Year	A¹	Year	A¹	Year	A¹	B²	Year	A¹	B²	Year	A¹
1819	—	1825	35	1831	—	38	1837	67	105	1843	3
1820	1	1826	7	1832	2	34	1838	21	64	1844	24
1821	—	1827	1	1833	2	18	1839	25	38	1845	2
1822	—	1828	—	1834	11	61	1840	3	5		
1823	—	1829	4	1835	45	134	1841	—	—		
1824	2	1830	4	1836	91	235	1842	1	..		

[1] See *Correspondence with British Commissioners 1831*, p. 6; *1832*, pp. 4–5; *1833*, p. 7; *1834*, p. 3; *1835*, pp. 3, 11; *1836*, Supplement A, p. 6; *1837*, Further Series, p. 6; *1838–9*, Further Series, p. 157; *1840* ii, p. 14; *1841*, p. 12; *1842*, p. 7; *1843*, p. 6; *1844*, p. 1; *1845*, p. 1; *1846*, p. 10.
[2] See *Returns of Vessels adjudicated in the Courts of Mixed Commissions 1840–41*, pp. 2–13.

<hr/>

[1] C.O. 268, vol. xxviii, p. 211. [2] *Report*, p. 4.
[3] Bryson, *Report on the Climate and Principal Diseases of the African Station*, pp. 255–6.
[4] See Dispatch of Smart to Lieutenant-General Sir George Murray, dated 20 Sept. 1828: 'On the arrival of slave vessels in this harbour, the surgeon to the Mixed Commissions proceeds on board and reports on the state of the slaves. . . . Vast numbers are afflicted with contagious disorders, such for instance, as venereal, small pox, meazles, crawcraw, yaws, together with various other diseases, not perhaps equally dangerous in their nature as it respects contagion, but equally distressing; such as dysentery, diarrhœa, ophthalmia, &c. and a variety of others that I am not acquainted with even by name' (*Papers relating to Sierra Leone 1830*, p. 29). See also, for example, *Eleventh Report of African Institution 1817*, pp. 134–7; *Charge by Jeffcott*, 1832, pp. 7, 14; *Report from Committee on Aborigines*, 1837, Minutes of Evidence, p. 32.
[5] ' . . . the slaves are taken before the registrar (by whom their descriptions are registered),

Mortality was excessive also in the first weeks after registration. According to Kenneth Macaulay's 'General Statement of the Disposal of the captured Negroes received into the Colony of Sierra Leone', out of 5,925 Liberated Africans 283 died before they could be disposed of 'chiefly of the scurvy and dropsy, caught on board'.[1] Mortality evidently continued to be excessive until four or six months after arrival. The Principal Secretary of State for War and the Colonies Viscount Goderich, in a Dispatch to Lieutenant-Governor Findlay, dated 18 January 1832, wrote:

> . . . in the Return made by Mr. Cole, to the Assistant Superintendent of liberated Africans, I find the following passage: 'I do, however, feel confident in stating from my own experience in the department, that one-fifth of the whole number of liberated Africans settled in the Colony from 1808 to the 30th June 1830 [33,595], as shown in the subjoined statement,[2] have died; and that three-fourths of the deaths (5,039$\frac{1}{4}$) occurred within the four first months after their arrival, through the baneful diseases generated on board the slave vessels.' Mr. Cole, therefore, allows for the decrease by death, 6,719[3] . . . .

The general statements of Messrs. Cole, Savage and M'Cormack, founded on extensive knowledge and experience, and assisted by their official means of knowledge, seem to justify the conclusion that the waste of life produced amongst these people by their sufferings in the slave ships, is such as to account for the loss of a large proportion of them.[4]

Independently of positive testimony, the apparent reason of the case and all experience in similar cases warrant the same inference. Nothing is more clearly ascertained than that within the first three months from the landing of a cargo of slaves in the West Indies, before the trade was abolished there, the loss by death amounted very commonly to a very large proportion of the whole number.

Similar causes are now in operation in Sierra Leone, and must be expected to yield corresponding results; and by a return from the Hospital at Kissy, I find that of the 478 liberated Africans who were admitted into that institution during the year 1829, 271 of that number had died.[5]

and are then delivered over by the marshal of the courts to the chief superintendent. The registering of the slaves is generally performed during the first and second day after landing; it has, however, sometimes occurred that a delay of five or six days has taken place (in consequence, as it is stated, of the want of an interpreter), and the ulterior disposal of the negroes thereby retarded . . .' (*Report of Commissioners of Inquiry*, 1827, First Part, p. 26).

[1] See second Table, p. 114 below. The Commissioners of Inquiry in 1827 complained of 'the total want of any proper place for the reception of such slaves as are brought into harbour in vessels having infectious diseases or those amongst whom such diseases show themselves after their arrival' (*Report*, First Part, p. 23; see also ibid., pp. 25–6).   [2] This statement has not been printed.

[3] Cole cannot have assumed that of the 28,556 Liberated Africans located in the Colony who survived the first four months after their arrival only 1,680 altogether died up to 30 June 1830. He probably meant to say that apart from the 5,039 who died in the first four months deaths had exceeded births by 1,680.

[4] See also in this connexion *Report of Commissioners of Inquiry*, 1827, First Part, p. 24, where, however, mortality is overstated because the numbers of deaths are related to the numbers of people received in the year under consideration and not to the total numbers of people living in the respective villages. See furthermore, for example, *Missionary Register 1816*, p. 400; *1817*, pp. 254, 486; *1824*, p. 9; and *Continuation of Appendix to Second Report of Committee on African Instruction* (1824), p. 12.

[5] *Charge delivered by Jeffcott*, pp. 33–4. See also 'Quarterly Report on the state of health of the Liberated African Population' by Andrew Foulis, Surgeon Liberated African Department, 31 Mar. 1830 (C.O. 267, vol. ciii):
'When I was appointed to take charge of the Hospital at this place on 1st of April last . . . some abuses and extreme carelessness on the part of the Hospital Attendants, were found to exist. . . . The Patients in Hospital, suffered severely from the then Manager and the Surgery man being allowed to exact the highest market prices, for every Article purchased. . . .

Mortality in Kissy Hospital (the hospital attached to the Liberated African Department) was in fact atrocious also in other years.[1]

	Year 1838	Year 1839	Year 1840[1]	Year 1841	1 Apr. 1842 to 31 Mar. 1843	1 Apr. 1845 to 31 Mar. 1846	1 Apr. 1846 to 31 Mar. 1847	1 Apr. 1847 to 31 Mar. 1848	1 Apr. 1849 to 31 Mar. 1850
Admissions .	2,774	2,773	1,140	1,181	817	1,569	414	3,014	660
Deaths .	1,509	1,635	408	541	224	839	110	1,730	151

[1] Data for July and August missing.

The patients were all or mostly newly arrived captured slaves.[2] Cole's estimate that altogether 15 per cent. of the Liberated Africans landed in 1808–30 died within four months after arrival was, therefore, possibly no overstatement.

'I am at a loss to account for the excessive number of deaths that occurred in Hospital last Season, being more than one half of the total number admitted. With facts before me so positive and incontrovertible, I would feel gratified in the career of investigation, could I fix the dreadful cause of Mortality to any circumstance but to an undue supply of Medical comforts viz Wine, nourishing Soups, Sugar Arrow Root &c. &c. which the present allowance of 3d. *per diem* under the best regulated management, is inadequate to obtain.'

See also Dispatches from Lieutenant-Governor Findlay to Sir George Murray, 27 May and 28 Aug. 1830, and to R. W. Hay, 4 Oct. 1830 (ibid., vols. ciii–civ).

After the establishment of the Courts of Mixed Commission a Hospital for Liberated Africans had been opened at Leicester Mountain. When asked in 1826 by the Commissioners of Inquiry 'Is the hospital at Leicester Mountain, at present used as a receptacle for the sick from captured slave vessels, well adapted, or does its situation render it ineligible for the purpose?' Dr. Barry answered: 'The hospital at Leicester Mountain was originally a seminary for the education of boys and girls by the Church Missionary Society; in 1820 they removed their establishment to Regent Town; it has since been occupied as an hospital for liberated Africans; I consider the building very unfit for the purpose, particularly for the newly arrived negroes; the site is too high, which renders it cold and damp from the continued fogs which lodge on the mountain. A more appropriate spot for the erection of an hospital might be pointed out in the neighbourhood of Kissy, to which the sick might be brought down from the mountains, and the newly arrived conveyed to it with ease and safety. The expense and trouble in the transport of provisions and stores would be materially diminished' (*Papers relating to Sierra Leone 1830*, pp. 62, 66–7). Between 21 Dec. 1822 and 20 Dec. 1825, 2,041 Liberated Africans had been admitted to the Hospital at Leicester Mountain and 395 had died (see ibid., p. 69). But the removal of the Hospital to Kissy was not a success. See also in this connexion the statement by ex-Governor Campbell before the General Anti-Slavery Convention, 22 June 1840: 'The sick were carried by land to Kissey Hospital, a distance of three miles, when they might have been taken by water within a quarter of a mile. On the old plan many died on their transport' (*Proceedings*, p. 502).

[1] See for 1838 and 1839 Dr. Clarke, *Description of Manners and Customs of Liberated Africans*, p. 79; for 1 Jan. to 30 June 1840 *Report from Committee on West Coast of Africa*, Part II, pp. 315–16; for 1 Sept. 1840 to 31 Mar. 1843 Colonial Office, *Return of the Number of Patients received into Kissy Hospital 1835–42*, pp. 2–3; for 1845–6 to 1849–50 Horton, *Climate of the West Coast of Africa*, pp. 256–9. It should be noted, however, that an investigation made in 1839 showed that the figures in that year had been purposely overstated by the hospital accountant. (The Governor had been 'called on to sign a return for 610 gallons of Madeira for the use of the sick in that hospital, for the quarter ending the 30th of September 1839'; *Report from Committee on West Coast of Africa*, Part II, p. 314.)

[2] 'These tables only show the number of cases of diseases amongst the liberated Africans who were taken from the slave-ships and forwarded to the Kissy Hospital' (Horton, p. 260). 'The customary proceedings on the arrival of the captured negroes are the following:—They are visited immediately after their arrival by the surgeon and marshal of the Mixed Commission Court, who make their report on their state of health; and the sick are sent to Kissy Hospital, and the sound to the liberated African yard . . .' (*Report from Committee on West Coast of Africa*, Part II, p. 249). Of the 5,657 admissions in 1845–6 to 1849–50, 1,860 were for dysentery, and of the 2,830 deaths 1,406 were due to this disease.

As regards mortality among those who survived the first months after landing, the few available records of the Department of Liberated Africans[1] suggest that it was fairly high.[2]

Many Liberated Africans originated from regions with a climate quite different from that of Sierra Leone,[3] and epidemics claimed numerous victims.[4]

Fertility. It has been often stated that the birth-rate among the Liberated Africans was low owing to the great preponderance of males among the captured slaves. But the excess of men was reduced somewhat through emigration, and it appears that while the ratio of women to 100 men amongst the Liberated Africans present in Sierra Leone was as low

[1] See *Papers relating to Sierra Leone 1830*, pp. 18–19, 44–5; *Report from Committee on Sierra Leone and Fernando Po*, 1830, pp. 118–19; C.O. 267, vols. cxi, cxxvii; *Report from Committee on West Coast of Africa*, Part II, pp. 315–16; *Correspondence relative to Emigration of Labourers to the West Indies*, 1844, pp. 114, 134.

[2] The records may be summarized as follows:

Period	Mean population	Births	Deaths	Yearly birth-rate	Yearly death-rate
1 Jan. to 31 Mar. 1827 . . .	10,001	76	73	30	29
1 Jan. to 31 Dec. 1828 . . .	13,448	461	390	34	29
1 July to 31 Dec. 1829 . . .	18,486	180	351	19	38
1 Jan. to 30 June 1831 . . .	22,220	224	339	20	31
1 Jan. to 30 June 1832 . . .	21,809	249	280	23	25
1 July 1832 to 30 June 1833 . .	25,554	633	488	25	19
1 Jan. to 30 June 1840 . . .	37,505	333	548	18	29
1 July 1842 to 30 June 1843 . .	36,633	878	885	24	24

The data up to 30 June 1832 cover the people settled in the villages; they exclude those living in Freetown and suburbs, those 'employed up the River in the Timber Trade, or otherwise', those 'employed for Three first Months after their Arrival in the Colony on the Public Works', and those who upon their arrival were transferred to Kissy Hospital and were still there; the data for 1 July 1832 to 30 June 1833 exclude likewise at least those in Kissy Hospital. These figures may convey an approximate picture of conditions among the Liberated Africans who survived the first months. The data for 1840–3 are meant to be all-inclusive, but since the numbers of slaves captured in that period were very small, the figures may likewise be considered as referring almost exclusively to Liberated Africans who had stayed some time in the Colony.

[3] Major Tulloch, after having shown the high mortality among the soldiers recruited from the Liberated Africans, says that 'the climate appears to have been nearly as unfavourable to the civil as the military portion of the negro population' (*Statistical Reports on Sickness*, &c., 1840, p. 16). Dr. Ferguson, however, in his evidence before the Commissioners of Inquiry (24 Apr. 1826) stated that the climate played no part. He said with regard to the 'Liberated Africans under two years residence' that 'it may be stated generally, that they seem to be exempt from sickness in proportion to their length of residence in the colony; the diseases to which they are liable cannot, however, be attributed in any respect to climate, but rather to long confinement in the holds of slave ships, respiration of impure air, food to which they have been unaccustomed, and to the debilitating effects of that despondency of mind to which Africans are particularly liable when forcibly separated from their homes and families; this class of persons suffer much from dropsical complaints, dysentery and diarrhœa; probably eight-tenths of all that die during the first years residence, perish from either of these diseases, of which diarrhœa and dysentery are the most common, one or either of them is frequently combined with dropsy, presenting a complication of disease that too often sets medical art at defiance' (*Papers relating to Sierra Leone 1830*, pp. 77–8).

[4] See Clarke, p. 85: 'The contagious disease, small-pox, often commits great ravages amongst the Liberated Africans, who are particularly obnoxious to this complaint. In 1837 and 1839, this scourge raged with much virulence in the Colony.' Other epidemics of smallpox occurred in 1827 and 1835–6; see *Statistical Reports on Sickness*, &c., p. 17, and statement by William Henry Savage, 20 Jan. 1831, *Charge delivered by Jeffcott*, p. 12.

as sixty in some earlier years, the figures became about equal in the 1840s when emigration to the West Indies flourished, and I found no conclusive evidence that the birth-rate was actually low.[1]

Natural Increase. Chief Justice Jeffcott, in his 'charge' delivered to the Grand Jury on 2 June 1830, in which he attributed the decrease in the number of Liberated Africans to the slave-trade prevailing in Sierra Leone, referred 'to the fact, that within the last year, and that one of the most fatal known in the Colony, the proportion of births to deaths was seven to one'.[2] This statement created quite a sensation. The Principal Secretary of State for War and the Colonies Sir George Murray wrote on 26 October 1830 to Lieutenant-Governor Findlay:

I apprehend, however, that such a rate of increase is utterly at variance with the results of general experience, and with the Returns from Sierra Leone itself. There is, I conceive, no part of the globe in which, under the most favourable circumstances, the rate of increase approaches nearly to that on which Mr. Jeffcott reasons.

Thus, at the Cape of Good Hope, the Returns in this Office show the births to be in the proportion of $1\frac{5}{8}$ to 1 death per annum. At Malta, the proportion in favour of births is as $1\frac{3}{8}$ to 1 per annum. In New South Wales, the births annually exceed the deaths in the proportion of $1\frac{1}{14}$ to 1. To suppose that in a population so ill assorted as is that of Sierra Leone, in which the number of males so greatly exceed the females, and when the persons in question have been recently delivered from the holds of Slave ships, with all the wretchedness and disease incident to that situation, the population should annually increase in the ratio of 7 births to 1 death, is an assumption to which it is quite impossible to assent, and which it is difficult to understand how Mr. Jeffcott himself could have admitted.

But the Returns of births and deaths transmitted to this Department are no less opposed to Mr. Jeffcott's conclusions. The evidence they give of the fecundity of the African race is, indeed, sufficiently remarkable. In 1828, the births exceeded the deaths in the proportion of $2\frac{7}{10}$ to 1, and in 1829 in the proportion of $2\frac{6}{10}$ to 1; this, though very remote from the proportions assumed by Mr. Jeffcott, is still so opposite to all ordinary experience, that I cannot regard the Returns to which I have referred, without much distrust of their accuracy. I find that at the Gambia the births exceeded the deaths only in the proportion of $1\frac{1}{9}$ to 1 in the year 1829. I am aware of no reason which would justify the supposition that the Gambia is less congenial to African constitutions than Sierra Leone, or more unfriendly to the multiplication of Africans by natural increase.[3]

The Royal Committee of Enquiry appointed to investigate the 'charge' by Jeffcott was non-committal as regards the ratio of births to deaths. In its report dated 17 March 1831 it said:

The Committee have to regret, that they cannot, with reference to the actual and comparative rates of fecundity and mortality, procure any definite evidence; the Returns which have been presented to them being very imperfect, no records having been kept in some of the villages prior to the 1st January 1827, and even since that period being very imperfect, from circumstances detailed in the Evidence and Returns.[4]

William Henry Savage, a legal practitioner who had been in the Colony for upwards of twenty-one years, told the Committee that 'among the old residented liberated Africans, the births are far more than the deaths;

---

[1] The birth records of the Department of Liberated Africans afford no proof as they were probably incomplete.

[2] *Charge delivered by Jeffcott,* p. 5.   [3] Ibid., p. 7.   [4] Ibid., p. 9.

but among the whole liberated African population the deaths are no doubt considerably beyond the births'.[1] But John Weeks, a school teacher, 'from a three years' residence at Regent, is led to believe that the births exceed the deaths very materially, even when the deaths among the newly-imported Africans and those arising from small pox are taken into consideration'.[2] Finally, Chief Justice Jeffcott himself gave the following quite plausible explanation of how he had obtained for 1829 the ratio of 7 births to 1 death.

It was either upon the day upon which the Quarter Sessions were held, or very shortly before it, and when Deponent was much occupied by business, that he understood, either from the Governor or from Mr. Thomas Cole, the Superintendent of the Liberated African Department, that a census had been taken for the year 1829, from which it appears that the births were, to each other, in the proportion Deponent mentioned. Acting upon this impression, Deponent made the statement referred to. Deponent has, however, since found that the census alluded to was not for the year 1829, but a partial census for 1827 or 1828, in which the excess of births over deaths appears to be *seventy-one* in number, and not, as Deponent imagined, *seven* to *one* in proportion. Deponent believes the document which led him into this mistake will be found amongst the papers handed in by Mr. Thomas Cole.[3]

The document which led the Chief Justice into this mistake was evidently 'An Account of the Number of Liberated Africans under the Charge of the General Superintendent, in the Period from the 1st January to the 31st December 1828',[4] which showed 461 births and 390 deaths. However, the year 1828 was exceptionally healthy, and in the year 1829, which according to the Chief Justice was 'one of the most fatal known in the Colony', deaths greatly exceeded births. It is probably safe to assume that on the whole deaths among the Liberated Africans considerably exceeded births and that, as a rule, the excess was particularly great in years when the number of newly arrived captured slaves was very large.

Disposal of Landed. An Order of the King in Council of 16 March 1808 stipulated:

The Collector or chief officer of the Customs for the time being, in any of his Majesty's colonies being seats of Courts of Vice-Admiralty, shall receive, protect, and provide for, all such Negroes, natives of Africa, as have been or shall be condemned, either as prize of war or forfeiture to the Crown . . . and directs the Collector or chief officer to receive all such Negroes, and to provide suitably for their support and maintenance, subject to the directions of his Majesty, until such Negroes can be entered, enlisted, apprenticed, or disposed of according to the true meaning of the Acts.

On the receipt of such Negroes, the Collector, &c. is to enter in a book, to be carefully kept for that purpose, an exact list of all such Negroes, specifying the time of their delivery; the ship (if any) in which they were seized; the date of their condemnation, and by what court, and for what cause, and at whose suit; and also the following description—viz. the name of every such Negro, with the sex and apparent age . . . .

On receiving such Negroes, the Collector, &c. shall give notice to the Chief Officer of his Majesty's land forces in the colony—or, in the West Indies, to the Commander in Chief of the land forces in that part of the West Indies—of the number of male

[1] *Charge delivered by Jeffcott*, p. 12.   [2] Ibid., p. 19.   [3] Ibid., p. 29.
[4] Reprinted in *Papers relating to Sierra Leone 1830*, pp. 44–5.

Negroes fit for military service so received, to the intent that such officer or commander in chief may take any number of such Negroes, as recruits for West-Indian or African regiments, or to form new corps, or as pioneers, according to such instructions as he may from time to time receive. And in case all the Negroes capable of military service shall not be wanted as soldiers, &c. the Collector, &c. is to signify to the naval commanding officer on the station, the number remaining fit to be employed in his Majesty's sea service, and the said officer shall receive into his Majesty's naval service any number of such Negroes that the service may want, and that may be fit for the same.

Full power and authority are given to the Collector or chief officer of the Customs for the time being, to enter and enlist such Negroes as are fit for Military service, as soldiers, seamen, or marines, and to bind all such Negroes as shall not be received into his Majesty's service, as apprentices, in manner following, and subject to such other instructions as may hereafter be given by his Majesty in Council:—

1. Such Negroes, whether male or female, the Collector, &c. is to use his best endeavours to bind as apprentices to prudent and humane masters and mistresses, either in the same or other colonies, to learn such trades, handicrafts, or employments as they may seem most fit for, or most likely to gain their livelihood by, when their apprenticeship shall expire.

The Collector, &c. shall make up an Annual Report, to the 31st of December in each year, of all proceedings in execution of this order; with an accurate account, specifying the number, names, sexes, and ages, of the Negroes received by him, enlisted, apprenticed, or otherwise disposed of; and the names, descriptions, and places of abode of their masters and mistresses; and the state and condition of the apprentice: which report and account, with his observations, he is to transmit to his Majesty's principal Secretary of State for the Colonial Department, to be by him laid before his Majesty in Council.[1]

Actually, however, the mode of managing the liberated negroes changed continuously as each new Governor adopted some favourite scheme of his own.[2] Kenneth Macaulay, in 1827, summarized the position in the two preceding decades as follows:

Every Governor has been left to follow his own plans, however crude and undigested; and no two succeeding Governors have ever pursued the same course. . . . Mr. Ludlam pursued the system of apprenticing them; Mr. Thompson set that aside, and turned them loose in the colony, without any other superintendance than its general police. Captain Columbine employed them on the public works, or apprenticed them. Colonel Maxwell, after delivering over, to the persons appointed to receive them, all the men fit for his Majesty's service, apprenticed a part of the remainder, and then commenced forming villages with those who could not be disposed of. Sir Charles MacCarthy gave up apprenticing, except in particular cases, and adopted the plan of forming them into villages, under such civil superintendance and religious instruction as he could command, keeping the youths and children in schools, or making mechanics of them; neglecting perhaps too much, in his successful attempt to make them orderly and quiet citizens, the equally desirable

[1] *Abstract of Acts of Parliament for abolishing Slave Trade*, pp. 33–41.

[2] See Walker, *The Church of England Mission in Sierra Leone* (1847), p. xxx. This was due in part to the fact that the Order of the King in Council was quite defective. See *Ninth Report of the African Institution 1815*, p. 51: 'It is, however, very material to observe, that no directions are given for the treatment of those who, from any cause, might not be either enlisted or apprenticed; nor of those whose terms of apprenticeship have expired. Those regulations are also obviously defective in some other and most important particulars, and by their very silence open a wide door to abuse in our slave colonies. Even at Sierra Leone they are stated by competent judges, and have been found by experience to be, so inadequate to meet the exigencies of the case, that the Governor of the colony has been obliged to treat and dispose of them as he thought best, taking upon himself the responsibility of so doing.'

object of making them industrious agriculturists and growers of exportable produce. General Turner dissolved in a great measure, the schools and the institutions for mechanics, and threw the people more on their own resources; but did not afford, indeed he did not possess, the means of duly superintending their settlement and progress, or of directing their energies.[1]

The annual reports on the disposal of the captured slaves were apparently quite defective until 1814.[2] A Return made by the Colonial Department in 1814 reads as follows:[3]

Date of condemnation	Number of slaves on board			Dead	Deserted	Enlisted	How disposed of		Living in the Colony, &c. &c. or have left it	At Recruiting Depot	Undisposed of
	Male	Female	Total				Entered the Navy	Apprenticed			
1808	55	23	88	1	—	—	—	43	39	—	—
1809	222	135	357	6	2	—	—	8	341	—	—
1810[1]	..	..	} 1,546							—	..
1811	..	..		36	78[2]	144[3]	4	72	331	—	1
1812	1,641	563	2,204	172	14	1,055	33	118	735	48	28

[1] 'There is nothing in this Office to show the mode in which the Slaves condemned in 1810 were disposed of.'

[2] '10 of these returned to their own country by permission of the Governor.'

[3] '19 Females, wives of recruits, are included.'

The figures for 1808 are contradictory, and the group 'Living in the Colony, &c. &c. or have left it' suggests that the accounts were not kept according to the rules established in the Order in Council of 1808.

Data covering the first six years of the functioning of the Vice-Admiralty Court are contained in the following 'General Statement of the Disposal of the captured Negroes received into the Colony of Sierra Leone, to the 9th July, 1814', prepared for the Secretary of State by Kenneth Macaulay, in his capacity as Superintendent of captured Negroes and Collector of the Customs at Sierra Leone:[4]

Settled in the colony, viz. as free labourers, carpenters, sawyers, masons, blacksmiths, &c.; living in the mountains on their farms; the girls at school; the women married in the Royal African Corps, &c. 2,757
Entered into his Majesty's land service, men and boys .   .   . 1,861
Women married to soldiers at the recruiting depôt .   .   . 65
Left the colony, being chiefly natives of the surrounding Timmanee, Mandingo, Bullom, and Soosoo countries 419
Apprentices whose indentures are in force at the present time .   .   . 347
Entered into his Majesty's navy 107
Apprentices out of the colony 68
Living as servants at Goree 12
At the Lancasterian school in England 3
Stolen from the colony, two to the Havannah and one to the Kroo country 3
Died; chiefly of the scurvy and dropsy, caught on board 283

Total   5,925

[1] Macaulay, *The Colony of Sierra Leone vindicated from the Misrepresentations of Mr. Macqueen*, pp. 5–6.

[2] See in this connexion *Ninth Report of African Institution 1815*, pp. 56–7: 'For the first two years after the passing of the Abolition Act, great irregularity seems to have existed in the management of this part of the population of Sierra Leone.' See also Report of Commissioners of African Inquiry 1811, *Papers relating to African Forts*, 1816, pp. 127–8.

[3] See *Return of all Ships brought into any Port in the Colonies of Great Britain and condemned therein 1808–1812*, pp. 2–3. I am quoting only the figures for the ships condemned at Sierra Leone.

[4] *Ninth Report of African Institution 1815*, p. 63.

Robert Thorpe, Chief Justice of Sierra Leone and Judge of the Vice-Admiralty Court, declared the whole statement to be 'a delusive compound',[1] and very acrimonious polemics ensued between him and the Directors of the African Institution. There is no need to discuss here the various points of disagreement, but Thorpe was certainly right in calling the first group in the statement an 'anomalous mixture'.[2] It may be, however, that Macaulay, with the best intentions, could only give an account of 3,168 captured slaves and, therefore, lumped together the remaining 2,757 into one group.

For 1814–33 the available material is more adequate than for any other period. The principal documents are:

(1) 'General Return of Slaves received into the Colony of Sierra Leone, Distinguishing each Year, from the 5th January 1814 to the 4th January 1824; with the manner in which the same were then, and subsequently disposed of; as appears by the Register in this Office [Liberated African Department]';[3]

(2) 'General Return of Slaves received into the Colony of Sierra Leone distinguishing each Year from 1808 to 1825 with the manner in which the same were then and subsequently disposed of, as appears by the Register in the Office of the Liberated African Department';[4]

(3) 'Return shewing the Number of Liberated Africans received into the Colony of Sierra Leone specifying the Name of the Vessel from which they were landed the date of Adjudication and the manner in which the said Persons were then and subsequently disposed of as appears by the Register kept in the Office of the Liberated African Department',[5] covering the period from 1808 to 19 October 1833.

The differences between the figures given in these three documents are very slight. The figures prior to 1814 are probably dubious. Those shown in (3) may be summarized as overleaf.[6]

It appears that of about 43,050 slaves landed, about 37,800 were settled in the Colony while about 3,450 entered the Army or Navy and about 1,800 civilians left the Colony.

Number living. From 1817 onwards there are also ample data concerning the numbers of civilian Liberated Africans actually living in the Colony.[7]

The *Missionary Register* of August 1817 contains the following 'Account

---

[1] Thorpe, *Letter to Wilberforce*, p. xv, and *Postcript to a Reply*, p. 46.

[2] Thorpe, *Letter to Wilberforce*, p. xiii.

[3] *Account of Slaves captured and condemned at Sierra Leone 5 Jan. 1814 to 5 Jan. 1824 (Parliamentary Papers*, 1825, vol. xxv), pp. 3–6.

[4] *Report of Commissioners of Inquiry*, 1827, Appendix A, No. 12 (C.O. 267, vol. xci).

[5] C.O. 267, vol. cxxvii.

[6] For 1825, 1829, and 1830 the totals do not tally with the sums of the items. According to (2) 236 men placed at Freetown and employed as Labourers at the Barracks, and 40 men, 5 women, 8 boys, and 2 girls placed after landing under Quarantine regulations at Wilberforce and deceased within two months are not included in the 1825 figures concerning disposal. I found no explanation for the divergencies in 1829 and 1830.

[7] In comparing the number of civilian Liberated Africans living in the Colony on a given date with the number of captured slaves located in the Colony up to this date it must be borne in mind that the former number includes children born in the Colony but excludes people who have died or have left the Colony after having been located there.

Year	A	B	C	D	E	F	G	H	I	J	K	L	M	N	O	P	Q	R
1808	78		78	29					45		74				4			
1809	280		280	180					92		272				1	7		
1810	1,087		1,087	598					397		995			70	10	12		
1811	545		545	339					127		466			45	31	3		
1812	2,230		2,230	141	12				878	15	1,034			1,136	30	16	14	
1813	446		446	10					40	202	252			169	24	1		
1814	1,876	27	1,903	100	55				1,262		1,374			483	7	39		
1815	1,296		1,296	11	53				1,085		1,096			198		2		
1816	2,545		2,545	70	29					2,122	2,247			273	25			
1817	603		603	21	13	11				529	603							
1818	292	433	725	16						647	703	22						
1819	214	461	675	31						631	675							
1820	251	171	422	19	26					403	422							
1821	1,132		1,132	46						1,060	1,132							
1822	2,065	783	2,848	52	9					2,796	2,848							
1823	243	373	616	11	15		21	315		588	608							
1824	1,138	9	1,147	87	45					1,004	1,127		8	14	13			
1825	1,993		1,993	279			19			1,345	1,905	20	6		2			
1826	2,949	526	3,475	204				476		2,677	3,215	36		167				55
1827	2,852	6	2,858	282				935		2,161	2,443		13	402		3		
1828	3,445		3,445	230	4			329		2,565	3,271	10		147	14			
1829	4,857		4,857	516	2					3,178	4,629	200		9	15			
1830	3,274	234	3,508	236						2,705	3,270	188		3	15	30		
1831	1,722	100	1,822	339						1,387	1,726	50		46				
1832	1,543		1,543	393						425	818	652		72	1			
1833	979		979	125						416	541	421		14	3			
Total	39,935	3,123	43,058	4,365	263	11	40	2,055	3,926	26,856	37,746	1,599	27	3,248	195	113	14	55
Men	17,649	1,377	19,026	1,088	150	7	40	2,055	1,522	9,575	14,667	1,121	26	2,967	114	72	1	40
Women	7,881	520	8,401	211		4			1,039	6,736	7,990	258		91		27	6	15
Boys	8,591	677	9,268	1,645	113				898	6,170	8,826	145	1	180	81	8	1	
Girls	5,814	549	6,363	1,421					467	4,375	6,263	75		10		6	6	

A Captured and condemned.

B Captured and not condemned.

C Captured and landed (total received).

D Apprenticed or placed as Servants, for limited periods, with Persons residing in the Colony.

E] Settled in Freetown in the Colony and employed as Labourers and Artificers in the Engineer Department.

F Settled in Freetown and employed in the Liberated African Hospital.

G] Men employed at Freetown and employed as Labourers in the Stores of the Liberated African Department.

H Men placed at Freetown and employed as Labourers at the Barracks who are rationed and clothed by Government.

I Settled in the Colony without being under any immediate Superintendence except appearing for their provisions, individually once a Week, at the Stores in Freetown, and the Boys and Girls placed at School.

J Settled in the Colony, in the Country Villages formed by themselves under the immediate Superintendence of the Governor, Boys and Girls placed at School.

K Total settled in the colony.

L Sent to Sault Mary's River Gambia to be located there.

M Settled at the Isles de Loss under the Superintendance of the Rev. Mr. (& Mrs.) Klein, Chaplain at Crawfords Island.

N Entered His Majesty's Land Service as Soldiers for the West India Regiments, Royal African Corps & Royal African Colonial Corps with their Wives and Children.

O Entered His Majesty's Naval Service as Sailors on board Ships of War upon the Coast or Merchant Service.

P Returned to their country at their own request by leave of the Governor.

Q Living as Servants at Goree & Senegal.

R Sent to Ascension.

of the Captured Negroes in the Colony of Sierra Leone', dated 1 April 1817 and signed by Governor MacCarthy:[1]

	Men	Women	Boys	Girls	Total
Settled in the Colony, on Lots, & otherwise supporting themselves by their industry	1,461	—	—	—	1,461
Wives of Ditto and others, & Wives of Men in the Royal African Corps .	—	1,263	—	—	1,263
Learning the Arts of Sawyers, Carpenters, Masons, Shingle Makers, Brickmaking, Taylors &c. . . .	152	—	194	—	346
Living as Free Servants, or Apprentices	40	40	216	97	393
Attending School	—	—	493	296	789
Living with their Parents or Country People	—	—	160	129	289
Employed trading in the adjoining Rivers, and having no fixed Place of Residence	220[1]	85[1]	—	—	305[1]
Born in the Colony	—	—	136	148	284
Total	1,873	1,388	1,199	670	5,130[2]

[1] 'This is only a supposed number, there being no means of gaining a correct account of people coming under this denomination.'

[2] Including 1,438 (253 Men, 447 Women, 490 Boys, and 248 Girls) in Freetown and Neighbourhood.

The results of the censuses of 1818, 1820, and 1822, in so far as they refer to Liberated Africans, are summarized in Table 4 (see p. 118).

Enlistment in Army and Navy. According to the Order in Council of 16 March 1808, the Collector of Customs had to surrender to the military and naval authorities all captured slaves landing in the Colony whom he considered fit for service as soldiers, seamen, or marines. But the civilian authorities at first were reluctant to comply with this provision.

Orders appear to have been given to Governor Thompson to furnish his views on the matter, but he had discouraged it[2] . . . . With the assumption of office by Governor Columbine, in 1809, a fresh report was requested of his views on the fitness or unfitness of the Natives to be enlisted in His Majesty's army and navy.

Governor Columbine . . . reported favourably on the scheme, which report was supported by Lieutenant-Colonel Maxwell, in 1812.[3]

But even if the civilian authorities had favoured from the outset the enlistment of Liberated Africans, none would have been recruited into the Army in the first two years as the military authorities were not prepared to enrol negroes. However, in May 1810 'the Commander-in-Chief approved of a portion of Black Men being enlisted for the [Royal African] Corps and formed into a Company on the present establishment of the Corps'.[4] Enrolment began in 1810[5] and in 1811 'a native company was

[1] See *Missionary Register 1817*, p. 356.

[2] See also Butt-Thompson, p. 135: '"This colony wants settlers, and many of them", the new governor declared, "settlers who will live here and farm here and make the place prosperous." This explains why he discouraged recruiting amongst the Liberated Africans.'

[3] Claude George, pp. 178-9.

[4] Crooks, *Historical Records of the Royal African Corps*, p. 69.

[5] See Kenneth Macaulay, *The Colony of Sierra Leone vindicated*, p. 12: 'In 1810, the system of recruiting for the garrison on the spot, instead of sending convicts from England, commenced . . . .'

TABLE 4. *Liberated Africans in Sierra Leone 1818–22*[1]

Groups	Men	Women	Boys	Girls	Total
		31 December 1818			
Servants or Apprentices in Freetown and Suburbs	65	38	389	117	609
Others in Freetown and Suburbs . .	201	399	146	155	901
Living elsewhere under control of a Superintendent	1,273	727	800	376	3,176
Living in their own Villages under no Superintendent	609	612	256	243	1,720
Total	2,148	1,776	1,591	891	6,406
		8 July 1820			
Servants or Apprentices in Freetown and Suburbs	116	30	221	119	486
Others in Freetown and Suburbs . .	546	430	213	161	1,350
Living elsewhere under control of a Superintendent	2,216	1,207	946	725	5,094
Living in their own Villages under no Superintendent	446	528	65	107	1,146
Total	3,324	2,195	1,445	1,112	8,076
		1 January 1822			
Servants or Apprentices in Freetown and Suburbs . . . . . } Others in Freetown and Suburbs .	655	521	405	366	1,947
Living elsewhere under control of a Superintendent . . . . } Living in their own Villages under no Superintendent	2,657	1,435	1,040	890	6,022
Total	3,312	1,956	1,445	1,256	7,969

[1] See *Missionary Register*, Sept. 1820, p. 381; *Accounts relating to Sierra Leone*, 1825, pp. 13–15, 19–21.

added to the African Corps'.[1] These recruits probably stayed in the Colony, but forty-nine of the men enrolled in 1812 were sent to England for the black regiment,[2] and in the same year a recruiting establishment for West India Regiments was formed at Bance Island.

6th April, 1812.—With a view to the completion and augmentation of the West India Regiments, the authorities directed the formation of a Recruiting Depot at Sierra Leone for the voluntary enlistment of eligible captured negroes, and a Detachment belonging to the West India Regiment, being part of the Recruiting Establishment, arrived in the Colony from Barbadoes. Shortly afterwards the Depot for Recruiting was established on Bance Island, about 16 miles up the Sierra Leone River.[3]

The numbers of Liberated Africans enlisted thereupon increased considerably. They amounted in 1811 and 1812 to 129 and 1,088 respectively,

[1] *Handbook of Sierra Leone*, p. 34.

[2] 'Unfortunately, however, this selection did not prove a success, having apparently been made, without sufficient discrimination, from slaves recently recaptured; they were therefore declared unfit by Lieutenant-General Sir George Beckwith, both on account of their indifferent description and of their physical features' (Claude George, pp. 179–80).

[3] Crooks, *Historical Records of the Royal African Corps*, p. 87. See also *Papers relating to a Recruiting Depôt on the Coast of Africa*, 1812, pp. 1–5.

and in 1814–16 to 490, 198, and 298 respectively.[1] The total number enlisted up to 9 July 1814 was 1,968,[2] and up to 25 May 1816 over 2,500. But on 7 March 1816 the War Office ordered that 'in consequence of the intended reduction of the 7th and 8th West India Regiments . . . the Recruiting Establishment on the Coast of Africa should be forthwith discontinued', and on 25 May ninety of the negro soldiers then in the Depot were transferred to the Royal African Corps while the remaining 272 were transferred to the Captured Negro Establishment.[3]

The statistics since 1816 are difficult to interpret. According to the Return prepared by the Chief Superintendent of the Liberated African Department,[4] no captured slaves entered the Army and Navy in 1817–23.[5] But other reports indicate that actually enlistments took place, although not in every year.[6] The data contained in two documents published in 1830 and 1840 may be summarized as follows:[7]

Year	Joined during the year Africans	Total number Africans	Mean strength black troops	Year	Joined during the year Africans	Total number Africans	Mean strength black troops	Year	Mean strength black troops	Year	Mean strength black troops
1817	8	208	..	1822	—	317	281	1827	749	1832	329
1818	—	197	..	1823	248	452	271	1828	765	1833	500
1819	362	351	272	1824	255	496	297	1829	487	1834	471
1820	84	349	301	1825	122	265	266	1830	303	1835	578
1821	22	333	294	1826	..	..	468	1831	328	1836	621

The Report of 1840 makes the following comment:

These troops have generally been recruited from the slaves captured by our cruizers, and liberated at Sierra Leone. None of the resident native population, nor those who occasionally come from the interior show any disposition to enlist; and even the liberated slaves are but little disposed to do so, after having been a short time located in the Colony. It is only when recently landed, and ignorant of any mode of procuring a subsistence, that they can be induced to adopt a profession, of which the active duties and necessary restraints are much at variance with their habits and disposition.

There is considerable additional evidence to prove that the bulk of the soldiers entered in the above table were Liberated Africans enlisted

[1] See Tables, pp. 114 and 116 above. The figure for 1813 was probably about the same as that for 1814. According to Further Papers relating to Captured Negroes enlisted, 1814, p. 3, 237 men and 191 boys were enlisted into the Royal African Corps and the West India Regiments from Feb. to Dec. 1813; no figures apparently are available for 1813 from the Navy, and none for Jan. 1813 from the Army.   [2] See second Table, p. 114 above.

[3] See Crooks, Historical Records, p. 98.   [4] See Table, p. 116 above.

[5] The Commissioners of Inquiry, 1827, stated (see Report, First Part, p. 20) that up to 31 Dec. 1825, 2,738 Liberated Africans were not settled in the colony but 'entered His Majesty's service, returned to their country, or were otherwise provided for'. They evidently assumed likewise that no Liberated Africans had been enlisted since 1816.

[6] See also Dispatch from Governor MacCarthy to Earl Bathurst, 14 Aug. 1823 (C.O. 267, vol. lviii, No. 328): 'On the arrival of the five Companies of the 2d West India Regiment [May 1819] a considerable proportion of the Men were found unfit for duty, from age and infirmities, and long Services. I accordingly deemed it my duty to direct the Officer Commanding to recruit such Men as might be required to replace the worn out Soldiers; from among the Liberated Africans or the discharged Soldiers of the 4th West India Regiment . . . .'

[7] See Acting Major of Brigade, Robert Gregg, 'Return shewing the Number of Troops', &c., Papers relating to Sierra Leone 1830, pp. 90–3; Major Alex M. Tulloch, War Office, Statistical Reports on Sickness, Mortality, &c. among the Troops in Western Africa, &c., p. 15. The former report states that the records were incomplete.

when put on shore. Thus Henry William Macaulay, on 20 March 1837, told the Select Committee on Aborigines:

... the whole of our African corps, and a great part of the West India regiments that serve in the West Indies, are supplied from the liberated Africans at Sierra Leone. There are always depôts of the 1st and 2d West India regiments there, and the troops are sent over from time to time to the West Indies. The African corps is always supplied from the liberated Africans.[1]

According to the Order in Council of 1808 (lifelong) military service was to be compulsory for the Liberated Africans. Some writers say that efforts were made to obtain the consent to enlistment, but others deny it. Major Ellis described the method used in the early years as follows:

In former days, whenever the cargo of a captured slaver was landed at Sierra Leone, a party from the garrison used to be admitted to the Liberated African Yard for the purpose of seeking recruits amongst the slaves. Many of the latter, pleased with the brilliant uniform, and talked over by the recruiting party, who were men specially selected for this duty on account of their knowledge of African languages, offered themselves as recruits. If medically fit, they were invariably accepted, though it must have been well known that they could not possibly have had any idea of the nature of the engagement into which they were entering. Some fifteen or twenty recruits being thus obtained, they were given high-sounding names, such as Mark Antony, Scipio Africanus, etc., their own barbaric appellations being too unpronounceable, and then marched down in a body to the cathedral to be baptised. Some might be Mohammedans, and the majority certainly believers in fetish, but the form of requiring their assent to a change in their religion was never gone through; and the following Sunday they were marched into church as a matter of course, along with their Christian comrades.[2]

But Thorpe, who in 1811–13 was Chief Justice of Sierra Leone and Judge of the Vice-Admiralty Court, said:

... I could not sanction the seizure of the poor ignorant captured negro the moment he landed a freeman, nor, their driving a terrified Being to the fort, who knew not what was said to him, nor what was to become of him, and without his feelings, knowledge or consent being in the least consulted, making him a soldier for life!![3]

Colonel Denham, Superintendent of the Liberated African Department, wrote on 14 May 1828 to the Under-Secretary of State for the Colonies, R. W. Hay:

With regard to the present practice of enlistment in the Royal African corps, I have much satisfaction in being able to assure you, that it is much better conducted than you appear to imagine. The Africans are now fed for several days after landing, and comfortably clothed; and when they are a little reconciled to this new manner of treating them, soldiers or non-commissioned officers of their own country, are allowed to visit them for several days; and after the nature of the duties they will have to perform, as soldiers, have been perfectly explained to them, an officer attends, when, in my presence, those who have already mentioned to their countrymen their intention to enlist, turn out for the regiment. Since this plan has been adopted, the desertion from the regiment has been very trifling; before, I have

---

[1] *Report with Minutes of Evidence*, Minutes, p. 34. See also, for example, *Report of Committee on West Coast of Africa*, 1842, Part II, p. 363.

[2] Ellis, *History of the First West India Regiment*, p. 16.

[3] Thorpe, *Reply to the Special Report of the Directors of the African Institution* (1815), p. 84. See also Thorpe, *Letter to Wilberforce*, p. 23; Marryatt, *Thoughts on the Abolition of the Slave Trade*, pp. 12–13; Zachary Macaulay, *An Exposure of Misstatements in Mr. Marryatt 'Thoughts on the Abolition of the Slave Trade'*, p. 13; Marryatt, *More Thoughts, occasioned by 'An Exposure'*, p. 35.

known twelve or fifteen desert in one night, and the villages scoured by constables to take up these poor fellows, who received a fee for their apprehension.[1]

Yet Rankin, after his visit to Sierra Leone in 1834, wrote:

The men are inspected by a sergeant and officer when conscripts are wanted. The most muscular are drafted at once into the King's service; and are marched in a string, *nolentes volentes*, under strong escort, to the barracks, to learn regimental discipline.[2]

But this procedure was probably stopped in the same year. On 28 May Under-Secretary of State R. W. Hay wrote to Lieutenant-Governor Temple:

I have received a Communication from the Secretary to the General Commanding in Chief, enclosing a copy of a Letter addressed to him by Captain Fraser, relative to an opinion which it is stated that you had formed, as to the practicability of effecting the forcible enrolment of Liberated Africans into the Military Service. Lord Hill has expressed a decided opinion as to the propriety of abstaining from such a course, and as Mr. Stanley fully concurs with him in that view of the question, it will be advisable to avoid in future attempting any thing like constraint in procuring recruits from the Liberated Africans.[3]

A Dispatch from Governor Macdonald to Lord Stanley, dated 10 October 1843, confirms that enlistment then was voluntary.

I permitted recruiting parties from the detachments of each of the three West India regiments stationed here to enter the liberated African yard for the purpose of obtaining recruits. They succeeded in getting 130, who cheerfully marched out, accompanied by music. When a short distance from the yard, an Akkoo woman among the crowd assembled on the occasion, called out something in the Akkoo language, when more than one-half ran away and dispersed, and could not afterwards, on any account, be prevailed upon to enlist.[4]

The strength of the enlisted forces was reduced by desertion, death, and discharge.

How numerous desertions were, it is impossible to tell. But it is safe to assume that the deserters, with few exceptions, left the Colony.

Mortality, though much lower than among European soldiers, was high. Major Tulloch, in discussing the deaths of black troops in 1819–36, said:

It might have been expected that on the coast of his native continent, and with an income sufficiently ample to procure all the necessaries and even luxuries of life, the Negro soldier would be exempt from any greater degree of mortality than other troops when serving in their native country. This expectation, however, is by no means realized . . . .

. . . the mortality during the last 18 years has averaged about 30 per thousand exclusive of sudden and accidental deaths not stated in the Medical Returns,[5] and which would probably have increased the ratio to 32 per thousand annually.

---

[1] *Papers relating to Sierra Leone 1830*, p. 26.

[2] Rankin, vol. ii (1836), p. 107.   [3] C.O. 268, vol. xxx, pp. 469–70.

[4] *Correspondence relative to Emigration of Labourers*, &c., 1844, pp. 148–9.

[5] The Medical Returns show altogether 228 deaths, and it seems that they were quite incomplete. The numbers of deaths in 1825 and 1826 are given as 1 and 2 for a mean strength of 266 and 468 respectively. Major Tulloch says: 'There can be no doubt that in 1825 and 1826 several deaths took place among the Black Troops, besides those here recorded. One of the Medical Reports refers to five deaths in the former of these years; but as the diseases are not stated, and the names cannot be distinguished from those of the White Troops, we have preferred giving the numbers precisely as they are entered in the quarterly returns from which the above table is framed.' For 1820–4 the Medical Returns show only 34 deaths, while the Returns prepared by the Acting Major of the Brigade show 104; see *Papers relating to Sierra Leone 1830*, pp. 90–3.

The ratio will be found exactly the same as among the black troops employed in Jamaica and Honduras; and though less than in the Bahamas and Windward and Leeward Command, in the proportion of 32 to 41, yet as a very large proportion of the force there was of advanced ages, while in the African corps scarcely any soldier exceeded 25, the former ratio may be held to correspond very nearly with the latter; consequently, on his own native coast, even with all the advantages enjoyed by the British soldier, the Negro exhibits a liability to mortality for which it is extremely difficult to account.

There is one circumstance, however, which, independent of climate, may have in some measure contributed to this. As already stated, recruits can seldom be obtained except among the recently liberated slaves, whose constitutions have no doubt, in many instances, been deteriorated by their previous sufferings on ship-board, and though a due exercise of medical discrimination at inspection is in general sufficient to guard against the introduction of sickly or unfit persons into the service, yet even the most scrupulous care must be inadequate to detect those latent diseases of which the seeds may have been sown in the ill-ventilated holds of slave-ships, and which may prevent the recruit from ever becoming a healthy soldier. To obviate this, it was at one time proposed, that none should be enlisted till their constitutions had been tested by a residence of some months in the colony; the proposition was, however, rejected, because where the necessaries of life could be obtained so easily the liberated slave would soon succeed in earning his livelihood in some way more congenial to his habits and feelings, than submitting to the re-straints and discipline of a military life.[1]

Data concerning current discharges are apparently not available,[2] but the disbandments effected in 1817 and 1819 have been reported upon. The soldiers pensioned in these two years are generally treated as a separate addition to the population of the Colony, and soldiers pensioned in 1817–20 (and thereafter) are also dealt with as a separate group in the census statistics of 1820, 1822, and 1826, but as these soldiers were largely Liberated Africans originally landed in Sierra Leone and as their descendants were apparently merged into the bulk of Liberated Africans, it seems more appropriate to deal with them at this place.

When Senegal and Goree were restored to France the following Order, dated Horse Guards, 28 February 1817, was issued:

> The establishment of the Royal African Corps is reduced to ten Companies of 100 rank and file, and to form the four black Companies into *three*, and to reduce those who exceed that establishment, when the force to be retained at Sierra Leone will be one European and three Black Companies, and six to be sent on to the Cape of Good Hope.[3]

Thereupon, 192 or 193 black soldiers were discharged from the Royal African Corps in April 1817; many of them were settled with their families at Waterloo and Hastings.[4] Shortly thereafter it was decided to withdraw

---

[1] *Statistical Reports on the Sickness, Mortality,* &c., 1840, pp. 15–16. See also *Reports made in 1844 and 1845 by Butts,* &c., p. 26.

[2] See in this connexion *Report of Commissioners of Inquiry,* 1827, First Part, p. 16: 'The Military records in the office of the brigade major, do not specify the number of African soldiers dis-charged and settled in Sierra Leone subsequently to 1819; and no records of the commissariat department (by which the pensioners are paid and accounted for) being preserved in the colony, except those kept by the officer actually in charge; it has been found impracticable to account accurately either for the number from time to time disbanded, or for the cause of the diminution which has since occurred.'

[3] Crooks, *Historical Records,* p. 101.

[4] See ibid.; *Papers relating to Sierra Leone 1830,* p. 91; and Crooks, *Short History,* p. 72.

the remaining detachment of the Royal African Corps and to garrison the British settlements on the West Coast of Africa with troops stationed in the West Indies.

On the 23rd and 24th May, 1819, the headquarters and five Companies of the 2nd West India Regiment, composed of negroes, arrived from Jamaica to replace the African Corps in the Sierra Leone command.[1]

Upon the arrival of these troops, 'the Detachment of the Royal African Corps stationed at Sierra Leone was disbanded'. The Europeans were sent home to be discharged on their arrival in England. Of the black soldiers 65 were transferred to the 2nd West India Regiment, and 116 were discharged.[2]

Independently from the garrisoning of the African settlements there came other troops from the West Indies for the sole purpose of being disbanded and settled in Sierra Leone.[3]

April 3rd [1819]—Three large transports anchored in the harbour, having on board the 4th West-India regiment, under the command of Lieutenant Colonel Nixon, from Gibraltar. The regiment was ordered here for the purpose of being disbanded—the men to receive rations until they provide for themselves, and afterwards allowed pensions; to the infirm 8d, and to the able 5d, per day. Thus this colony has received a valuable addition to its numbers of upwards of eight hundred tried brave men. His Majesty's government having thus liberally rewarded these warriors with a little industry, they will be able to support themselves with comfort. His Excellency settled nearly three hundred of these were [men ?] under the charge of Captain Stopney, near the mouth of the Whale River, twenty miles from Freetown; the place henceforth to be called *York*, and the parish, *Frederick*: fifty men were sent to *Kent*. Another settlement, about two miles before the Gambia island, was formed under the charge of Lieutenant Gonne, named *Wellington*, parish *Arthur*, and the remainder of the corps, with the band, under the superintendance of Lieutenant Pilkington, has been settled on King's Ground, near the sawmill. The spot was selected for the purpose of enabling them to support themselves by their labour in Freetown. The men were chosen from among the best behaved of the corps; and, it is to be hoped, that they will soon superintend the Kroomen, who, coming here for the sole purpose of raising money, and never forming any matrimonial connections, keeping their country fashions, can never prove truly useful.[4]

It would seem, therefore, that about 1,100 men from the Royal African Corps and the 4th West India Regiment were discharged in Sierra Leone in 1817 and 1819. But the records in this matter are not clear. The census returns of 31 December 1818 do not show any discharged soldiers[5] and the census returns of 8 July 1820, which list 1,216 'People discharged from the late 4th West-Ind. Regt. Royal Afr. Corps and 2nd W.I. Regt.'

[1] Crooks, *Historical Records*, p. 109. The force included 341 non-commissioned officers and men who were distributed as follows: Sierra Leone 194, Gambia 106, Isles de Los 34, Banana Island 7; see Caulfeild, *History of the 2nd Batt. West India Regiment*, p. 37. (A few sergeants were Europeans; see *Statistical Reports on Sickness*, &c., 1840, p. 6.)
[2] See Return of 24 June 1819, Crooks, *Historical Records*, p. 109. The soldiers discharged in 1817 and 1819 from the Royal African Corps were no doubt, practically all, Liberated Africans.
[3] It seems safe to assume that most of them were captured slaves who had been brought from Sierra Leone to the West Indies. See also in this connexion Macqueen, *Colonial Controversy*, pp. 106, 123–4.
[4] *The Royal Gazette and Sierra Leone Advertiser*, 12 June 1819, p. 196.
[5] They were probably omitted like the soldiers on active service.

(975 men, 183 women, 24 boys, and 34 girls), are accompanied by a Note saying:

> The Increase of Population in the Peninsula since last Census, 31st December, 1818, is 2,956 Persons; which includes . . . 1,030 discharged Soldiers and Families of the 2nd and 4th West India Regiments and Royal African Corps.[1]

The meaning of the figure 1,030 is not clear. It cannot refer to the total number of people discharged from the three military units (including those discharged in 1817) since it is much smaller than the figure representing the discharged people living on census date. If, on the other hand, it represents only those discharged after the census of 1818 it would be misleading since the apparent increase of 2,956 in the population includes not only the people discharged since 1818 but also those discharged in 1817 (and apparently omitted at the 1818 census).

Other writers each tell a quite different story:

> It appears . . . from the Military Return . . . that 192 black soldiers were discharged upon the reduction of the African corps in 1817; and by the census of 1822,[2] it will be seen that in the course of 1817 and 1818,[3] 1,030 black soldiers were discharged from the 2d and 4th West India regiments, and added to the colonial population; making a total of 1,222 men and their families.[4]

> . . . on the disbandment of the 4th West India Regiment and Royal African Corps, 1,222 black soldiers and their families were, in 1819, sent to form villages on ground allotted to them in various parts of the peninsula.[5]

> In April, 1819, the 4th West India Regiment arrived in Sierra Leone from the West Indies, and the regiment was disbanded on reduction and located in the Colony. These, together with some Black soldiers, discharged from the 2nd West India Regiment, added 1,030 to the colonial population.[6]

> In April, 1819, twelve hundred and twenty-two of these men were discharged time-expired, being from the 2nd and 4th battalions (the latter coming direct from service in the West Indies), and joined the colony.[7]

It is out of the question that as many as 1,222 men were discharged from the West India Regiments. The figure 1,222 evidently represents the sum of 192 men discharged from the Royal African Corps in April 1817 and of 1,030 men, women, and children discharged at a later date. It certainly excludes the wives and children of the soldiers discharged in April 1817 from the Royal African Corps. But whether it includes all the people discharged from the two West India Regiments between April 1819 and July 1820 or only those pensioned at the disbandment of the 4th West India Regiment in April 1819, and whether it includes the people discharged from the Royal African Corps after April 1817 it is impossible to tell.

[1] *Accounts relating to Population, &c., of Sierra Leone*, 1825, p. 18.
[2] Should read 1820.
[3] Should evidently read 1819 or 1819 and 1820, as no soldier arrived from the West Indies before April 1819. A similar mistake is to be found in Macgregor Laird's Memorandum submitted to the Committee on the West Coast of Africa (see *Report*, 1842, Part I, p. 570), while Kenneth Macaulay reported erroneously: 'In 1820 and 1821 the West-India regiments arrived at Sierra Leone, and were disbanded there' (*The Colony of Sierra Leone vindicated*, p. 13).
[4] *Report of the Commissioners of Inquiry*, 1827, First Part, p. 16.
[5] Major Tulloch, *Statistical Reports on Sickness, &c.*, 1840, p. 3.
[6] Crooks, *History*, p. 96.   [7] Butt-Thompson, p. 146.

The census of 1 January 1822 showed 1,103 discharged soldiers (including families)[1] as compared with 1,216 on 8 July 1820,[2] and the Commissioners of Inquiry reported in 1827 that 'by the return which the Commissariat furnished of the number paid on the quarter ending in March 1826, the total (independent also of those at the Isles de Los) is 949'.[3]

Major Tulloch, after having pointed out that 'recruits can seldom be obtained except among the recently liberated slaves, whose constitutions have no doubt, in many instances, been deteriorated by their previous sufferings on ship-board',[4] said:

Making all due allowance, however, for this probable source of unhealthiness among the troops, there is abundant evidence that the climate is by no means favourable even to the negro race. In the years 1818 and 1819, as previously stated, 1,222 black soldiers were discharged at Sierra Leone, not in consequence of age and infirmities, but owing to the reduction of their corps. They are described as having been mostly in the prime of life, and of quiet, sober, industrious habits; each received a pension of from 6d. to 8d. per day, which, with an allotment of land and the produce of their daily labour, placed them in comparative affluence; yet, under all these favourable circumstances, at the census of April 1826 they were reduced by death to 949, making a total mortality of 273 in eight years, or in the ratio of 31 per thousand annually, which corresponds to the mortality among pensioners in this country about the age of 55, whereas these men could not have averaged above 40.[5]

But I doubt whether any conclusions concerning mortality can be drawn from the available data. The figure 1,222, as shown above, is of dubious value, and one should rather compare the 949 pensioners listed in the first quarter of 1826 with the 975 discharged men enumerated at the census of 8 July 1820. This comparison might at first sight suggest an unbelievably low mortality, but it may well be that a number of soldiers were pensioned between 1820 and 1826 and were, therefore, included in the 1826 Return.

The census taken on 30 June 1831 in the villages[6] did not reveal the total number of discharged soldiers.[7] The census taken in the third quarter of 1831 in Freetown[8] showed 259 'Discharged Soldiers and Families'. A 'General Statement of Population of Villages'[9] for 30 June 1832 showed 587 'discharged soldiers'. Apparently the only later census which recorded separately the number of military pensioners was that of 1848 which showed 291 such people.[10] It is obvious that it provides no basis of comparison with the earlier Returns.

Emigration. The term emigration as used in this section covers both forced and voluntary emigration.

[1] See *Accounts relating to Population*, &c. of Sierra Leone, 1825, pp. 19–21.
[2] Both figures excluded the small detachments on the Isles de Los.
[3] *Report*, First Part, p. 16. The total number of people 'settled in the Isles de Los' was 28; see ibid., p. 20. The census taken in April 1826 showed 328 fewer discharged soldiers than the Military Return (see ibid., p. 21), but the census was quite incomplete in many respects. *Blue Book 1826*, p. 25, said: 'There are about 1,000 pensioners discharged from the 2nd and 4th West India Regiments and Royal African Corps, residing in Freetown and in the Liberated African Villages; the Islands de Loss, and the Gambia.'   [4] See p. 122 above.
[5] *Statistical Reports on Sickness*, 1840, p. 16.   [6] See C.O. 267, vol. cxi.
[7] No data are given for Wellington, where 177 were returned a year later. The total for the other villages was 419.
[8] See C.O. 267, vol. cxi.   [9] See C.O. 267, vol. cxxvii.
[10] See *State of Colonial Possessions 1848*, pp. 304–5.

(1) A few Liberated Africans were transferred from Sierra Leone to the Gambia shortly after the establishment of this settlement,[1] and from 1829 on considerable numbers were sent there,[2] but 'when Lieutenant-Governor Mackie assumed office in 1838, he utterly condemned this system of indiscriminate immigration and refused to receive any more liberated Africans from Sierra Leone'.[3]   The total number 'transferred to the Gambia and established in this settlement' amounted to 2,914.[4]   Transfers to other settlements were quite unimportant.[5] .

(2) The other form of forced emigration occurred in connexion with the kidnapping or purchasing of Liberated Africans. Thorpe said in 1815 that many were 'kidnapped and inveigled from the Colony'.[6]   Chief Justice Jeffcott stated in a Speech to the Grand Jury at the Session held on 2 June 1830:

I have every reason to believe, that whereas there have been imported into the Colony of Sierra Leone within the last ten years, upwards of 22,000 Africans, who have obtained their liberation, and have been located here at the expense of the British Government . . . there are not now to be found in the whole Colony above 17,000 or 18,000 men! That this decrease does not arise from any disproportion in the number of births to that of deaths, I need only refer you to the fact, that within the last year, and that one of the most fatal known in the Colony, the proportion of births to deaths was as seven to one. Judging from this ratio, and making every allowance for the necessary casualties, there ought to have been at the present moment, an increase of population to the amount of at least, one-half upon the whole, instead of such a diminution as I have stated. What then is the conclusion to which I come, and to which every honest, unprejudiced, and right-thinking man must come, upon the subject ? Why, appalling as the fact may be, and incredible as it must appear to many, that the Slave-trade is either directly carried on, although of course not openly and ostensibly, or that it is aided and abetted in this Colony.[7]

Lieutenant-Governor Findlay shared Jeffcott's opinion concerning the re-enslavement of Liberated Africans and discussed it in numerous dispatches.

To Under Secretary of State R. W. Hay, 9 June. By the first opportunity I shall be able to give you an Account of the trials at the Sessions, and some very extraordinary transactions connected with Slave dealing in this colony which I believe has been carried on to a very great extent.

Circumstances have transpired which leads me to this supposition, and I apprehend there will be sufficient proof found to lead to conviction, but until then I cannot make any official report of it, I shall however give you the earliest information.[8]

To the same, 20 June. A Man of the Name of Thos Edward Cowan a liberated African has been convicted of a crime which I fear has been too prevalent here for some time back, that of kidnapping and conveying from the Colony a Boy for the purpose of being sold into Slavery. This is not the first instance of the kind which has

[1] See Table, p. 116 above.
[2] See *Papers relating to Sierra Leone 1830*, pp. 21, 35–6, and Gray, *History of the Gambia*, pp. 358–60.   [3] Ibid., p. 364.
[4] See statement by Lieutenant-Governor Huntley before Committee on West Coast of Africa, 23 May 1841, *Report*, Part II, p. 212.
[5] Up to 9 July 1814, 68 had been apprenticed out of the Colony and 12 had been brought as servants to Goree (see *Ninth Report of African Institution 1815*, p. 63). In 1826, 40 men and 15 women were sent to Ascension (see Table, p. 116 above).
[6] Thorpe, *Postscript to Reply*, p. 10.
[7] *Charge delivered by Jeffcott*, p. 5.   [8] C.O. 267, vol. ciii.

taken place here, indeed I fear it has been carried on to a very great extent altho' the persons have not yet been detected, I have been informed that Five Boys have been carried off from some of the Mountain Villages in a Night, and never heard of by any Person in the Colony afterwards. The Man Cowan who is now under Sentence of imprisonment and hard labour for Five Years was employed by the Missionaries as an under teacher in the School at Bathurst, and the Boy he conveyed to the Bullum Shore for the purpose of Selling was one of his own pupils but I apprehend there are persons in this Colony possessed of more Capital and who move in a more respectable Society than Cowan did, deeply connected with Slave dealing. . . .

P.S. I enclose to you a Copy of His Honor Chief Justice Jeffcotts Speech to the Grand Jury at the Sessions held on the 2ᵈ June which I trust will ultimately have a Good effect on the Inhabitants of this Colony.[1]

To Secretary of State Sir George Murray, 24 June. I am fully convinced from the kidnapping system which has been carried on here, were the British Government to give up the Colony to the management of the Merchants [on the same plan as Cape Coast] there would not be many liberated Africans left in it in a few years.[2]

To R. W. Hay, 17 July. I regret in having now to acquaint you for the information of the Right Honorable Sir George Murray that since the last Sessions no less than Seven men have been committed to take their trial at the ensuing Sessions for similar Offences.

I am astonished that this kidnapping system had not been detected long before this time, it has existed in the Colony for years past, and I do believe instead of Sierra Leone being a free Colony, Slavery has been carried on in it to a very great extent.[3]

To the same, 11 Aug. I have already informed you of the kidnapping system carried on here, yesterday I went to visit the Kissy Hospital with the Colonial Surgeon, I was informed by the manager, that on the previous night a man came to the constable in charge of the sick in the house at the Water side, and requested him to sell one of the boys, for which he offered nine dollars, giving it, at the same time to the constable, but finding the constable was about to procure some assistance to secure him, he made his escape and left his money, he was persued to the water side, but he got into his canoe, and then threatened to shoot the constable; I have no doubt but many of the Africans who have been missing were carried off in this way![4]

Sir George Murray, however, was not convinced. On 26 October he wrote to Findlay:

I have read with the greatest concern, and with no less surprize, the statements made in Mr. Jeffcott's Charge to the Grand Jury, respecting the prevalence of the Slave Trade in the Colony under your Government. . . . It is almost superfluous to remark, that an officer holding the high and responsible situation of Chief Justice, could not, without extreme inconvenience and impropriety, give the sanction of his name and station to public charges, affecting the character of the whole society and the reputation of every preceding Governor or Judge, upon light or doubtful grounds. I am the rather induced to make these remarks at present, because I must confess that Mr. Jeffcott's statements carry with them the appearance of much exaggeration and improbability.[5]

---

[1] Ibid. He enclosed a printed copy of Jeffcott's Charge which in the meantime had been published as a pamphlet 'at the request of the Lieutenant-Governor & Council'.

[2] C.O. 267, vol. ciii. See also his Dispatch of the same date to R. W. Hay (ibid.).　　　[3] Ibid.

[4] Ibid. See, furthermore, his Dispatches of 5 Oct., 29 Nov., and 3, 6, 20, and 25 Dec. (C.O. 267, vols. civ–cv). In his Dispatch of 20 Dec. he said: 'On the 12th Inst. His Majesty's Ship "Favorite", Captain Harrison, boarded a short distance from the mouth of the harbour, the French Brig "La Jeune Emeline" from the Sherbro, bound for Guadaloupe with 285 Slaves on board; a great number of them, speaking good English, who I have not the slightest doubt have been kidnapped from this Colony.'　　　[5] *Charge delivered by Jeffcott*, p. 6.

He then showed why he considered Jeffcott's figures and conclusions to be incorrect.[1]

I have thought it right thus to record the grounds of my present distrust of the views of the Judge, in justice to the memory of the several Officers who have formerly administered the affairs of the Colony, and who are directly implicated in the censure which the published Charge to the Jury conveys. I am, however, most anxious that every practicable method should be taken for ascertaining the truth. With that view, you will immediately constitute a Commission or Board of Inquiry, at which you will yourself preside, assisted by the Chief Justice, the Advocate-General and such of His Majesty's Commissary Judges, or Judges of Arbitration under the Treaties with Foreign Powers, as may be able to render you their assistance.

You will add to the Commission any other persons whose co-operation you may deem useful, and who may themselves be entirely exempt from every suspicion of participation or connivance in the alleged infractions of the law.[2]

But the Committee of Enquiry, in its report dated 17 March 1831, though rejecting some of Jeffcott's figures, fully supported his main conclusion.

The Committee have to submit, that they have called before them such persons of all classes, as they were of opinion could afford them most correct information; and from the evidence adduced, the Committee cannot but conclude that the nefarious system of kidnapping has prevailed in this Colony, to a much greater extent than was even alluded to in the Charge of the Chief Justice to the Grand Jury in June 1830, as will fully appear in the evidence adduced.[3]

Some quotations may serve as an illustration:[4]

Benjamin Campbell . . . saith, He is aware that the system of kidnapping has prevailed in this Colony for the last 5 (five) years, and latterly to a very great extent. . . . On his late visit to the Rio Pongas, he made many inquiries to ascertain to what extent this kidnapping system prevailed, and the result has led him to believe that if he stated the annual export from that river, during the last three years to have been 250 (two hundred and fifty) liberated Africans, the average would not be exaggerated.

Deponent is of opinion that a great number of liberated Africans are sent to the Gallinas for the purpose of being sold; and supposed the average to be about the same as he has already stated for the Rio Pongas. . . .

Deponent believes the practice of kidnapping liberated Africans to have very much increased in the Colony during the last twelve months, owing to the impunity with which it has been carried on for many years. The practice is principally carried on by the Mandingoes, and by the liberated Africans themselves.[5]

William Henry Savage (a legal practitioner in the Colony) . . . saith, That he has been in this Colony for upwards of twenty-one years. During the government of the late Sir Charles McCarthy, this Deponent was sent to the Sherbro with a civil and military force, and brought back with him 115 (one hundred and fifteen) liberated Africans, who had been sold into slavery.[6] . . .

[1] For details of this and other criticisms of Jeffcott's figures see pp. 111 and 145 of this volume.
[2] *Charge delivered by Jeffcott*, pp. 7–8.
[3] 'The Committee have further to submit, that while the actual system of kidnapping has principally prevailed among the Mandingo tribes and liberated Africans themselves (who seem, in many instances, to have but little gratitude for the favours conferred upon them by the British Government), they cannot refrain from remarking, that great facility has at the same time been afforded to the increase of the Slave-trade by the British merchants of the Colony, who have purchased vessels condemned in the Mixed Commission Court, as agents for foreigners; which vessels have afterwards been brought into the Colony and again condemned, for a repeated infraction of the Slave-trade Abolition Act' (ibid., p. 10).
[4] The witnesses were examined between 7 January and 15 March 1831.
[5] *Charge delivered by Jeffcott*, p. 11.
[6] These Liberated Africans had apparently been persuaded to go to Sherbro and were re-enslaved there.

EARLY COLONIZATION 129

Deponent is aware that a great number of liberated Africans have been kidnapped and carried away by Mandingoes; many instances came to his knowledge during the six years he held the situation of Clerk of Police. Deponent has no doubt that four or five hundred liberated Africans might be recovered by means of a secret mission to the Mandingo country, conducted by a person possessing local information, and a knowledge of the native languages. There is not a slave town in Mandingo country, in which Deponent does not believe there are some liberated Africans. . . . There are a number of idle boys, who run away from their villages, or who having been confined in gaol, do not wish to remain in their villages, who are picked up by the Mandingoes and their agents, and are carried away into the country.

Sir Charles Macarthy took great interest in recovering the liberated Africans who were kidnapped. The succeeding Governors were so short a period in office, and their local knowledge was so small, that they were not enabled to exert themselves so much as Sir Charles Macarthy.

Deponent is of opinion, that the imperfect education given to the African by the Missionaries, instead of being of use, makes them idle and proud; and that those who have received such education, sooner than work, would not scruple to commit any improper act, to gain means of ministering to their pride.

In Sir Neil Campbell's government Deponent was sent on a mission to recover (49) forty-nine men, who had been seized in the Sherbro by General Turner, but who had never been adjudicated. These people, in the absence of General Turner, were carried from the Colony. Deponent was furnished with a commission to follow them, and bring them back; they were recovered, and afterwards adjudicated.

Deponent has no doubt that a secret mission [to the Sherbro] would be the means of recovering (4 or 500) four or five hundred liberated Africans who have been kidnapped, at a very small expense.[1]

John MacCormack (a merchant and Member of Council) . . . believes the system of kidnapping has greatly increased in the Colony of late years.[2]

John Dean Lake (attached to the Courts of Mixed Commissions). Thinks, from what he has heard in these Courts [of Justice], that the Slave trade is increasing.

Deponent has reason to believe, from the evidence adduced upon the several trials, that a great number of liberated Africans are kidnapped from the Colony, and that a great number are carried down to the Sherbro.[3]

Logan Hook (Collector of Customs) . . . saith, That he has been in the Colony for thirteen years, during the whole of which period he believes the system of kidnapping has prevailed. . . . Deponent believes the Mandingoes from the opposite shore are generally the purchasers, but thinks persons residing in the Colony are the kidnappers.[4]

Frederick Campbell . . . saith, That he has been 15 (fifteen) years on this coast in the Colonial service . . . . Thinks a great many liberated Africans are kidnapped from the Colony, and taken to the Gallinas.[5]

Willlam Oolo (Commissioner of Appraisement and Sale to the Mixed Commission Court since October 1824). Deponent believes the system of kidnapping has prevailed in the Colony for the last six or seven years. Thinks this system has been carried on by the liberated Africans themselves, who as masons and mechanics were formerly employed upon the public works, by which means they were enabled to procure luxuries for themselves and families. Not being now able, from the stoppage of these works, to procure these luxuries by legitimate trade, they have been induced to turn to slave trading. The Government, in Deponent's opinion, have done every thing in their power to put a stop to this trade; but it is carried on so systematically as to defy any police. The liberated Africans are the thieves; the Mandingoes the receivers.[6]

---

[1] *Charge delivered by Jeffcott*, pp. 11–13. [2] Ibid., p. 13.
[3] Ibid., p. 14. [4] Ibid., pp. 15–16.
[5] Ibid., pp. 19–20. See also his report to Assistant Superintendent Thomas Cole, 15 July 1830 (C.O. 267, vol. ciii). [6] *Charge delivered by Jeffcott*, p. 21.

Walter William Lewis (Registrar to the Courts of Mixed Commission). Deponent only recollects two or three instances of kidnapping, of which the Government was informed previous to his departure from this Colony in 1828. When he returned in 1829, the circumstances became more common; but owing to the very severe sickness which prevailed during that year, such active measures as were necessary to investigate the several reports which reached the Government, could not be taken. The different departments, and especially the Secretary's office, were very deficient. After the sickly season, the reports relative to this system of kidnapping, became more frequent. Deponent was removed from the Colonial service at the latter end of 1829; but is aware, from private information, that there is no diminution in the extent of that system. In 1830, the cases became very notorious. The measures taken by the present Government are well known. These measures were the first serious notice taken of the very alarming and very rapidly growing evil.[1]

Maquis Smith . . . saith, That he is Clerk of the Crown in this Colony. That two persons only have been convicted of slave-trading prior to the arrival of Chief Justice Jeffcott. These persons were convicted at the Quarter Sessions, held in September 1829. Since the arrival of the Chief Justice, on the 26th April 1830, (14) fourteen have been convicted. Of these (10) ten were sentenced to hard labour in the House of Correction for five years, and (4) four were sentenced to death, of whom the punishment has been commuted to hard labour for (10) ten years, and the other three respited during pleasure.

Cases in which (26) twenty-six persons have been concerned, have been before the Police Office. Eleven of these persons were sent to trial. Forty-five (45) persons have been brought up for the offence since the month of April 1830, of whom eight (8) have not yet been tried.[2]

Michael Proctor . . . saith, That he is a resident merchant of the Isles de Loss, where he has lived nearly twelve years. Deponent has heard that the system of kidnapping liberated Africans, and carrying them to the Rio Pongas, has prevailed. Deponent has not heard of its being carried on to any great extent, until within the last twelve months.[3]

Viscount Goderich, the successor of Sir George Murray, did not concur with the Committee.

That the Slave-trade has been extensively carried on at Sierra Leone, is a fact which the evidence has unhappily placed beyond the reach of controversy; but the just indignation which every man must feel at the disclosure of such a fact, must not be permitted to supersede that calm and dispassionate inquiry, which is necessary in order to take a correct view of the evil, and to form a clear decision as to the practical measures necessary for its prevention in future.[4]

He discussed in detail the various sets of figures and came to the conclusion:

Mr. Jeffcott's Charge to the Grand Jury, therefore, when thus brought to the test of sober inquiry and calculation, must, I fear, be considered as highly exaggerated; and I cannot but fear, that, owing to his short acquaintance with the Colony, he has been induced to give his official sanction to the publication of statements which are not to be depended upon as correct.

But while I regret, as altogether exaggerated, the conclusions drawn by Mr. Jeffcott in his Charge to the Grand Jury, I have learned, with the deepest concern, that the existence of a Slave-trade, supplied by the liberated Africans, and carried on systematically, cannot admit of any reasonable doubt. It is impossible to ascertain its actual amount with any approach to accuracy. The statements of the best-informed witnesses are merely conjectural; and I shall not attempt the hopeless

[1] *Charge delivered by Jeffcott*, pp. 25–6. [2] Ibid., p. 30.
[3] Ibid., p. 31. [4] Ibid., p. 33.

and, indeed, the unnecessary task of determining a fact which they have left in much obscurity . . . .[1]

To judge from the available evidence, kidnapping of Liberated Africans within the Colony, as distinct from kidnapping of ex-slaves who had left the Colony, was not very frequent either before the 1820s or after the early 1830s.[2] But purchase of ex-slaves was apparently still quite customary in the early 1840s.

The purchase of Liberated Africans was closely connected with the system of apprenticeship. The Order-in-Council of 16 March 1808 provided, as shown above, that the Collector of the Customs should use his best endeavours to bind all such negroes as shall not be received into His Majesty's services as apprentices to prudent and humane masters and mistresses. It stipulated also that an indenture be made for each apprenticeship and that 'in all such indentures the master or mistress shall covenant . . . to produce the apprentice, when requested by him, for his inspection—under a penalty equal to double the sum at which the apprentice would be valued if to be sold for a slave'.[3] But complaints of the lack of control exercised over these apprentices became ever more frequent in the course of time. Abuses were apparently rare in the first two decades.[4] The Commissioners of Inquiry, in 1827, could still report:

> The younger apprentices, both male and female, are chiefly employed as domestics, many of them without indentures; and although no instances have come within our knowledge of their having suffered from the neglect of this precaution, it will not be denied that the omission leaves an opening to abuse, which cannot be too cautiously guarded against.[5]

Chief Justice Jeffcott, in his Charge on the Subject of the Slave Trade, did not mention specifically the sale of apprentices, and the same is true of all witnesses heard by the Committee of Enquiry which investigated his charge, except one.

> John Weeks (27 January 1831) . . . sayth, That he was formerly in charge of the school at Regent. . . . he has no doubt, that were an investigation into the number of liberated African apprentices in the villages to be instituted, it would be found that a great number of them had disappeared, and these, Deponent has no doubt, have principally been sold as slaves.[6]

---

[1] Ibid., p. 36.

[2] Surgeon Peter Leonard of the Royal Navy wrote in 1833· 'By his Majesty's brig Plumper, lately arrived from the river Pongos, I have learned that there are upwards of a hundred Africans, recently liberated and located at Sierra Leone, who have been kidnapped from the colony, now detained in the vicinity of that river, in readiness to be reshipped and again subjected to all the horrors of a slave hold' (*Records of a Voyage to the Western Coast of Africa 1830–32*, pp. 79–80). But Captain James Edward Alexander who visited the Freetown jail in October 1834 reported: '. . . thirty persons were convicted of attempting to kidnap liberated Africans. But since the execution of a negro for this offence some time since, there has been no repetition of it' (*Narrative of a Voyage of Observations*, p. 104). [3] *Abstract of Acts for abolishing the Slave Trade*, pp. 39–40.

[4] Thorpe, it is true, said in 1815 that Kenneth Macaulay entrusted Liberated Africans 'to persons who sold or placed them in slavery; that he has neglected to make suspected persons, to whom they were intrusted, account for them' (*Postscript to Reply*, pp. 10–11). 'Woodbine, the master of a vessel, to whom some were intrusted, having sold them in the adjacent Rivers, returned to the Colony and was not punished!' (ibid., p. 10).

[5] *Report*, First Part, p. 54. See also ibid., Appendix B, No. 15.

[6] *Charge delivered by Jeffcott*, pp. 18–19.

Surgeon Peter Leonard, on the basis of his experiences in 1830–2, wrote:

By an application, any person in the colony of respectable appearance may have
several liberated African children apprenticed to him for a certain number of years
on paying a trifling sum,—the price of indenture, which amounts to ten shillings,
and stipulating to feed and clothe them during the period of their apprenticeship.
These children have frequently disappeared, and no satisfactory account given of
them. It is found that they have generally been purchased from their masters by
the Mandingoes for about £5, and by them again sold to regular slave agents, who
are engaged to collect cargoes for vessels lying in the rivers adjacent to the Peninsula.[1]

Commissioner of Inquiry, R. R. Madden, reported in 1841:

The system of apprenticeship should . . . be done away with, and the children
taken from those with whom they have been, in a great many instances, most
improperly placed. . . . The very payment of the 20s. fee made by the master on
receiving a liberated African as an apprentice is looked upon as a payment made of
the purchase of the freedom of the child; and those who raised that fee from 10s. to
20s. in order to enhance the value of their services, and as they thought to secure
a better or a richer class of masters for the apprentice, committed a very great
mistake, for the more the negro masters pay for the children, the more title they
consider they have to their labour, and even to their liberty; and the instances are
by no means rare where the children have been sold to the Mandingoes, and have
been carried into slavery and again captured by our cruisers. Lieutenant Hill, of
the Saracen, is cognizant of one case of capture where an emancipated negro had
been three times captured and emancipated.[2]

(3) The Order-in-Council of 16 March 1808 contained no instructions
as to what the Collector of the Customs should do if captured slaves
expressed the wish to return to their native country. But Governor
Columbine, in a report written in 1811, said:

. . . whenever any of them have desired to return to their own country, and such
return has been deemed practicable, they have been allowed to do so; being first

---

[1] Leonard, pp. 81–2. Rankin, who visited Sierra Leone in 1834, expressed the same opinion in
much stronger terms. 'That portion of each captured cargo which consists of children under fourteen years of age, and which is distributed amongst the negro population of the colony generally,
is liable to a second exportation. As long as any negro whatever may buy a boy from the King's
Yard on payment of ten shillings, and hold possession of him without at any time being called upon
to account for the child, or even to produce him, so long will many be induced to transfer their
young wards for five pounds each to the Mandingo merchant. The whites call the child so purchased from the King's Yard an apprentice; the blacks uniformly term it a *slave*. I cannot conceive a system better adapted to favour the slave-trade than that of apprenticeship at Sierra
Leone: it is so regarded by the blacks on the spot; and was, without doubt, one of the grounds on
which the plain-spoken Foulah rogue Ali founded his assertion that, of all spots in Africa, Freetown
was most favourable to the slave-dealer' (*The White Man's Grave*, vol. ii, pp. 91–2. See also ibid.,
p. 108). See furthermore in this connexion Butt-Thompson, p. 162: 'These were called "protected"
children. But there was no register kept of such, no personal supervision by the King's Yard
officials, no periodic visitation of the homes where they lived. There were no penalties and no
punishments for those "protectors" who failed to produce their charges when the protected period
was said to end. "Run away" was accepted as sufficient explanation—and another victim handed
over.' See finally the statement by ex-Governor Campbell before the Anti-Slavery Convention,
22 June 1840: 'There was a fee of 10s. on binding the apprentice, and it went into the pocket of
the Governor; and the consequence was, without wishing to reflect on those who preceded me,
a great inducement to grant apprenticeship indentures' (*Proceedings*, p. 502).

[2] *Report of Committee on West Coast of Africa*, Part II, p. 251. See also ibid., Part I, pp. 161, 260,
271–2, 553, Part II, pp. 324, 327. See furthermore the following statement by Butts: 'In the month of
December 1844, it came to my knowledge that on board of the prizes lately made, having slaves on
board, were four men who had been previously captured and here liberated . . . the governor ordered
the depositions of these men to be taken, and warrants were issued for the apprehension of some
parties, residents of Sierra Leone, for slaving' (*Reports made in 1844 and 1845 by Butts*, &c., p. 33).

provided with a Paper under the hand and seal of the Governor, certifying that they are to be considered as his people and under his protection, which is looked upon according to the customs and law of Africa, to be a sufficient security against further molestation.[1]

A statement prepared by the Superintendent of Captured Negroes, Kenneth Macaulay[2], shows that 419 out of 5,925 slaves received up to 9 July 1814 had 'left the colony, being chiefly natives of the surrounding Timmanee, Mandingo, Bullom, and Soosoo countries'. The Directors of the African Institution, referring to this statement, say that '419 appear to have returned to their native home in the neighbouring country',[3] but Thorpe challenged this conclusion :

Then the Committee assert 'That 419 appear to have returned to their Native home', because the superintendant's Report states that 419 *left the Colony*, surely that is not a proper construction to make on such a Report, for if 419 were criminally suffered to depart from the Colony of their own accord, so far from being restored to their native home, they would have been thrown into slavery before they had advanced thirty miles . . . .[4]

But quite apart from the fact that the Administration was not in a position to know how many of those who left the Colony actually returned to their homes, the meaning of the statement that 419 Liberated Africans left the Colony is not clear. Permission to leave the Colony was apparently given in only a few cases. The Return of Ships Condemned covering the years 1808, 1809, 1811, and 1812[5] shows that 10 persons 'returned to their own country by permission of the Governor' in 1811, while 2 'deserted' in 1809, 68 in 1811, and 14 in 1812, but these figures evidently do not include all those who left the Colony. According to the Return showing the disposal of the Liberated Africans received in 1808–33,[6] only 80 persons 'returned to their country, at their own request, by leave of the Governor' in 1809–15, 3 in 1828, and 30 in 1830.[7] It is possible, on the other hand, that the total number of captured slaves who had left the Colony exceeded 419 since the Administration's accounts of what became of the Liberated Africans were quite defective.[8] Nor did these accounts improve in the following decade, as is proven by the statements made by the Chief Superintendent of the Liberated African Department, Mr. Cole, before the Commissioners of Inquiry on 28 February 1826:

Q—Is it your opinion that any considerable number of the Liberated Africans who had been Located in the Villages, have from time to time abandoned the Settle ment and removed towards the Interior ?

---

[1] *Report of Commissioners on Coast of Africa*, 1811, p. 3.
[2] See Table, p. 114 above.　　　　[3] Thorpe, *A Letter to Wilberforce*, p. xxiv.
[4] Ibid., pp. xii–xiii. See also *Reply to Special Report of African Institution*, 1815, p. 41, and *Postscript to Reply*, p. 12.　　　[5] See Table, p. 114 above.　　　[6] See Table, p. 116 above.
[7] Thorpe stated that he had only 'heard of a solitary instance of an attempt to send some Jolliffes home' (*Reply to Special Report of African Institution*, p. 41). He says, on the other hand, that owing to cruel treatment 'in Governor Columbine's administration, many captured Negroes fled from the Colony' (*Postscript to Reply*, p. 10).
[8] Thorpe said that if the Superintendent of the captured Negroes 'was forced to account for those delivered to his charge, (as he is bound to do,) hundreds would be proved missing' (ibid., p. 11). But those missing certainly included also Africans who had not left the country volun- tarily but had been kidnapped and sold to slave traders.

A—I consider that a great portion of those settled in the Mountain Villages have abandoned them, I believe a number of them have wandered into the Interior.

Q—Have you any means of stating their number?

A—I have not.

Q—Do the Village Superintendents report to you when any of the Liberated Africans remove from the Settlements without their knowledge and authority?

A—They do of those supported by Government or employed on Public Works. It frequently occurs that those who receive no support from Government leave the Villages, and live on their Farms, which frequently lay at a considerable distance from any settlement, and therefore the Superintendent has not the power of knowing what ultimately becomes of them.[1]

The Commissioners themselves reported that the scanty Village Returns at their disposal indicated a considerable emigration.

None of these Returns embraces a period of more than six years, and yet it will be seen that, during these years, 334 persons, chiefly liberated Africans, had withdrawn themselves from these six villages, in a manner of which no account could be given; of these 147 had left one village, at which the same superintendent had been constantly resident, almost from its first establishment. If this could occur in a village so circumstanced, it will be inferred that a larger proportion may, in a similar manner have left those which were frequently or long without any superintendent.[2]

Chief Justice Jeffcott, in discussing the apparently enormous decrease in the number of Liberated Africans, did not mention voluntary emigration, and the Committee of Enquiry which investigated his 'charge' was instructed to ascertain the facts concerning such emigration. But it had to report that 'the evidence relative thereto is very contradictory'.

Mr. Thomas Cole, however, from his official situation, and the nature of his duties in the Liberated African Department, is more likely to be correct in his evidence on this point, than any other person in the Colony can be . . . .[3]

Actually the evidence of the Assistant Superintendent of Liberated Africans, Thomas Cole, was not very illuminating. He testified on 9 February 1831:

That he cannot state whether the liberated Africans, from the neighbouring countries, are generally in the habit of returning to their native country or no. The Soosoo men are sometimes in the habit of returning, but Deponent does not think any great number could return without his knowledge, it being the duty of the managers to report the circumstance to him. . . . In cases where liberated Africans have applied for leave to return to their own country, or where the chiefs have applied for such leave for them, they have been allowed to return. Africans of the Cussoo Nation have rarely been brought into the Colony until within the last three or four years, and even then not in very great numbers. Within the last four years probably (800) eight hundred of this nation have been imported from the windward, and of these possibly (250) two hundred and fifty may have returned to their country.[4]

Other witnesses said:

J. MacCormack. Those liberated Africans who have been taken in the wars between the Timmanees, Sherbros, Bulloms, Soosoos, Cussoos, Loccos, Annullas and Korankas, (i.e.) in the neighbourhood of the Colony, and who have not been sold for slaves

[1] Report, Appendix B, No. 9.

[2] Report, First Part, p. 21. See also Dispatch from Major-General Turner to Earl Bathurst, 25 Jan. 1826, Papers relating to Sierra Leone 1830, p. 6.

[3] Charge delivered by Jeffcott, pp. 9–10.   [4] Ibid., p. 24.

for any crime, on their emancipation, universally voluntarily return to their native country. Of these there are great numbers. Several have returned with the sanction of the Government.

Many of the apprentices run away from their masters and mistresses, in consequence of harsh treatment, and many rather walk than go back to them; and for fear, would allow themselves to be carried to any place voluntarily, even to be made slaves of again.[1]

W. Cole. Deponent believes that almost all the Cussoos return to their own country, their habits not at all fitting them for this Colony. This people are all agriculturists, and there is not sufficient land in this Colony for them to cultivate. Deponent has known several who have returned. This remark applies equally to women and children as to males. Cannot say what number of this nation may come into this Colony annually.

In almost every native town near this Colony, liberated Africans will be found, apparently trading.[2]

W. W. Lewis. Deponent is aware, from private information, that it is the practice of slaves taken from the neighbourhood of the Colony, to return to their native country. Thinks many of the male adults return. Deponent means the inhabitants of the Sherbro, Pongas, and Nunez countries.

Deponent does not think that the women and children return. The women form connexions here, which does away with their anxious desire of returning.

Deponent recollects in 1824, a whole family who returned to their native country in the Bight of Bereira. It is Deponent's impression, that it is a fair calculation to allow that ⅓ (one-third) of the male adults taken in the neighbourhood of this Colony, do return to their native country.

Deponent thinks that the children, by the many comforts they procure in this Colony, are weaned from the love of their country so predominant among the Africans.[3]

Viscount Goderich, in a Dispatch to Lieutenant-Governor Findlay, dated 18 January 1832, suggested that 'voluntary returns of the Africans to their native country, whether from the natural love of home or to escape from ill-usage',[4] were numerous, but Henry William Macaulay, five years later, when questioned by the Committee on Aborigines, held a different view:

To what do you ascribe the preference of these Africans for remaining in the colony rather than returning to the country from which they have been carried off;

---

[1] Ibid., pp. 13–14.

[2] Ibid., p. 21. Ten years later Colonel Doherty complained that so many Liberated Africans were 'allured by the fertile lands that border on the peninsula along its eastern frontier. The proximity of the Cossoo country on that side affords a special reason for such emigration. That flat and productive region is distant from Sierra Leone not more than three days' journey, by a path which is open to it from Waterloo; and, as the large importations of captured people who are detained near the Sherbro and Gallinas consist of Cossoos chiefly, those among them who have not been slaves in their own country, generally avail themselves of this facility of returning to it, and disappear very shortly from the colony. Within six months I have known 200 Cossoos to leave the settlement from one location; nor do any means exist of checking emigration from this cause, so long as those people are located in Sierra Leone itself' (Report to Under-Secretary Hope, dated 27 Oct. 1841, *Report from Committee on West Coast of Africa*, Part II, 1842, p. 363).

[3] *Charge by Jeffcott*, p. 26. The reason why many adult males did not 'form connexions here' was, of course, the great preponderance of men among the Liberated Africans and, therefore, among the total population of the Colony. The influence of 'the disproportion existing between the sexes' upon the emigration of male Liberated Africans was apparently discussed for the first time by Colonel Doherty (see *Report from Committee on West Coast of Africa*, Part II, 1842, p. 363). See also Crooks, *History*, p. 175: 'Large numbers left the Colony and became merged in the neighbouring tribes, from whom they obtained *wives* and employment, without the trouble of cultivating ground, building houses, and starting establishments of their own.'

[4] *Charge by Jeffcott*, p. 35.

is it, do you imagine, from their preference to habits of civilization ?—I think they are fully conscious of the improvement of their situation.

From the kindness with which they have been treated ?—Yes, from the kindness with which they have been treated, and the superior comforts which they enjoy, and I may also say, from their sense of personal security.[1] Another point, I think it fair to mention, is, that I believe it to be almost universally the law throughout Africa, that a person who has been once a slave is always a slave, so that, even if they could return to their country, they would stand a great chance of being made slaves again ; for a great many of these Africans are sent into slavery on account of pretended crimes, for the benefit of the head man of the village, or the king of the country ; and their return of course would only subject them to the same treatment again. It might not be so with regard to captives in war, but I have no doubt a great majority of the cases arise from pretended crimes charged upon these people.

So that when once a man is taken from his native country, and sold as a slave, there is no inducement for him to return to it ?—None whatever.[2]

During the first thirty years most of the Liberated Africans who left the Colony voluntarily did so for the purpose of returning to their homes in neighbouring countries. Migration to more remote territories was apparently rare and, for example, the Yorubas, who were very numerous among the captured slaves,[3] remained in Sierra Leone. But in 1838 or 1839 there started an organized emigration to Nigeria, which the Government did not view with favour, and in 1841 there began emigration to the West Indies initiated by the Government. In a Dispatch to Lord John Russell, dated 20 March 1840, Governor Doherty said:

I have the honour to acquaint your Lordship, that a pretty extensive and growing disposition exists at present among the liberated African population, both of Free-town and the villages, to emigrate from the colony to their native countries to the southward and eastward. Some time ago, two small parties of 14 and 20 sailed for Badagry in the Bight of Benin ; of which the first were, at their own request, landed and left at the British settlement of Accra, while of the second no intelligence has yet been received. At this moment not fewer than 200 persons, belonging chiefly to the Houssa country and the kingdom of Yarriba, lying east and west of the Niger, having subscribed the amount of four dollars each towards the formation of a fund, have purchased with it a condemned prize-vessel, in which it was their intention to proceed to Badagry, and from thence to seek their native homes, at a distance of some hundred miles inland. But as with this party were about to embark 100 children, I have deemed it imperative to prohibit for the present their departure and that of their parents. I have allowed passports for not more than 44 men and 17 women, who are all persons without children, and of an age so mature as renders them not likely to become the prey of the slave-dealer ; and I shall wait until I am made acquainted with your Lordship's sentiments in the matter, before I permit the others to follow.

[1] But see also ex-Governor Campbell's statement at the Anti-Slavery Convention, 22 June 1840: 'The liberated Africans when located, were placed in a village with an allowance of a penny a day for three months, after which they had to provide for themselves . . . . What was the result ? When I visited the interior of the country, I found hundreds who had voluntarily left their allotments, and returned to slavery. On asking them whether they would come back, they replied in the affirmative, but added, not to sit down where they were before. On inquiring the reason, they replied, because there was no food, no wife, they had now got both, and what more could they want. The fact is, the poor liberated Africans were cast adrift to shift for themselves' (*Proceedings*, p. 503).

[2] *Report with Minutes of Evidence*, Minutes, 20 Mar. 1837, p. 39.

[3] 'About two-thirds of the Liberated Africans were Yorubas, members of a Southern Nigeria tribe' (Luke, 'Notes on the Creoles', p. 55).

I have in vain cautioned them all against the dangers to which they may expose themselves, in returning without protection to those parts of the continent, of being again made captives, and again sold into slavery. They reply, that in their own countries they are free persons, and therefore not liable to be sold there, unless taken in war; and that in travelling through other territories in large bodies they encounter no risk. They allege that in this colony they are retarded in the career of improvement, that no opportunity is afforded them of increasing their means and further ameliorating their condition; and certainly they receive little encouragement from the Maroons and settlers, or from Europeans themselves, who on all occasions prefer for employment the tribes of Kroomen and Timmanees. The villagers complain that they are without a market for their produce. And to these causes is, no doubt, to be added a restless spirit of change which appears to be natural to Africans.[1]

After having pointed out that many Maroons and Nova Scotians had expressed the wish to emigrate to the West Indies[2] he went on:

But I am desirous of knowing from your Lordship what course it would be advisable for me to pursue, in the event of any considerable number of liberated Africans being induced by their example to decide upon removing likewise to the same part of the world.[3]

Lord John Russell replied on 17 June 1840:

I think that you have done right to discourage the designs of those liberated Africans who projected to leave the colony with children; but you may very well allow emigration to Jamaica, Trinidad, and British Guiana.[4]

But it did not prove easy to stop emigration to Nigeria, though it never reached large proportions. Five vessels sailed between 25 October 1839 and 30 April 1841 to 'Badagry and the Leeward Coast' with 273 emigrants,[5] and on 30 January 1842 the Officer administering the Government of Sierra Leone reported to Lord Stanley:

Emigration, to a certain extent (not transatlantic, but from place to place along shore), commenced in the latter part of 1839, in the determination of a few liberated Africans who had saved some money to purchase a vessel for the purpose of enabling them to revisit their own countries.

The gross number of persons who have emigrated in this manner is, as near as can be ascertained, about 500.[6]

On 9 July 1844 Lieutenant-Governor Fergusson wrote to Lord Stanley:

Another circumstance to which the failure of transatlantic emigration is, in some respects, owing, is the system adopted of late years by bodies of liberated Africans of returning to their own country. This, which commenced in 1838 or 1839, has of late years grown more and more a favourite measure.

Between 600 and 800 persons, liberated Africans from Sierra Leone, are now established in the Yarriba or Aku country; and so recently as the 12th of May ultimo, some families, numbering in all 162 persons, left this for Badagry, on their return to their own country, in a vessel which they had chartered at an expense of 1,000 dollars.[7]

---

[1] *Report from Committee on West India Colonies, 1842*, pp. 553–4.   [2] See pp. 92–3 above.
[3] *Report from Committee on West India Colonies, 1842*, pp. 554.
[4] Ibid.   [5] See ibid., p. 593.   [6] Ibid., pp. 599–600.
[7] *Reports made in 1844 and 1845 by Butts*, &c., p. 131. Commissioner Butts said in his Report dated 13 Mar. 1845: 'I cannot allow that part of his Excellency's despatch regarding the emigration of people to Badagry to pass, without stating that these parties no sooner arrived in their own country than they took to slave-dealing, and that they even thought and talked of selling their own children when on board the vessel' (ibid., p. 31).

No estimate seems to have been made at any later date, but Commander C. W. Riley, Royal Navy, on 26 March 1849, told the Committee on the Slave Trade that 'a great many of the slaves who have been liberated at Sierra Leone have gone there [to Badagry] and settled'.[1]

Lord John Russell, in his Dispatch of 17 June 1840, had notified Governor Doherty that he 'may very well allow emigration to Jamaica, Trinidad and British Guiana'. Nine months later he was ready to use the strongest possible pressure upon captured slaves to emigrate to the West Indies. In a Dispatch to Governor Sir J. Jeremie, dated 20 March 1841, he wrote:

... I am entirely opposed to any plan for taking the liberated Africans to the West Indies against their will. But, on the other hand, I consider that we are not bound to maintain in the colony of Sierra Leone all the captured negroes who are sent thither, and that Africans landed there in future should, at the expiration of three months, be bound, 1st, to show that they are in a state to maintain themselves on the spot; or, 2dly, to signify their consent to emigrate to the West Indies; or, 3dly, to leave the colony.[2]

He said in the same Dispatch:

I further consider that it is time to appoint an agent, whose duty it shall be to watch over the execution of the laws and regulations affecting emigration. I enclose a sketch of the instructions which you will give to that agent.[3] ... You will perceive that I have omitted to lay down any rule as to the proportion of females who may accompany the male emigrants. Undoubtedly it would be desirable that the number of the former should equal the number of the latter; but it is obvious that the adoption of such a rule would have the effect of restricting emigration within limits so narrow as to amount to a total prohibition. I should feel satisfied, therefore, if you could apply in all cases the rule adopted by the Legislature of Jamaica, which requires that the females accompanying male emigrants should be in the proportion of one-third.[4]

[1] *First Report 1849*, p. 28.   [2] *Report from Committee on West India Colonies 1842*, p. 559.
[3] The 'Heads of Instructions for the Government Emigration Agent for Sierra Leone, resident in that Colony' (reprinted ibid., pp. 560–1) stipulated among other things:
'The emigrants should have been resident upwards of at least six weeks in the colony previously to their embarkation ... a necessary precaution to prevent slave dealers from bringing slaves to Sierra Leone to be exported as emigrants.
'Married couples of about 30 years of age should be considered as the most eligible, and no emigrant should be above the age of 45 years.'
A previous six weeks' residence was also requested in the Emigration Act of 28 Dec. 1841 (see *Sierra Leone Acts 1811–48*), but the period was reduced to four weeks in the Emigration Act of 13 Jan. 1843 (see ibid.).
[4] *Report from Committee on West India Colonies 1842*, p. 559. Governor Light of British Guiana, on 17 July 1840, had written to Lord John Russell: 'If hereafter emigrants should be obtained from Sierra Leone, the proportion should be at least one able-bodied person in three; they should on no account come without their wives and families' (ibid., p. 555). Later on, Governor Light changed his opinion. In a Dispatch to Lord Stanley dated 25 Jan. 1844, he said: 'The influx of emigrants from Sierra Leone has hitherto been on a very limited scale, and it has been very difficult to obtain even the proportion of one-third being females. In more than one letter from the agent at Sierra Leone, he has stated that more emigrants could be obtained, but as the women objected to quit the country, he was forced to refuse the offers of the men. ... I consider it would be expedient and justifiable to abandon all restrictions as to sexes; the evil of disproportion will cure itself; the great object at present to be gained is to excite a desire to emigrate to this province amongst the natives of Africa' (Colonial Land and Emigration Commission, *Report 1845*, pp. 60–1). In the meantime the Sierra Leone Emigration Act of 28 Dec. 1841 had provided that (except as regards Kroomen) 'no Ship or Vessel carrying Passengers as Emigrants shall proceed on her voyage, without having on board a proportion of adult Females amounting to not

The expectations concerning the number of Liberated Africans, willing to emigrate at once, were fantastic in certain quarters. Lieutenant Hamilton, who in February 1841 sailed from Trinidad to Sierra Leone in order to collect there emigrants and who returned with 186 passengers,[1] was examined on 24 May 1841 by the Sub-Committee of the Agricultural and Immigration Society.

What number of labourers do you think could be procured from Sierra Leone ?— Ten thousand could be immediately removed with the greatest advantage to themselves, and to those they would leave behind.

But if you think that only 10,000 labourers can be spared from Sierra Leone, this number would constitute a fraction only of the supply required by Trinidad, Guiana, and Jamaica. Are you aware of any other sources from which labourers can be procured on the coast ?—By proposing the removal of 10,000 only in the first instance, I anticipate from the rise of wages at Sierra Leone a stream of immigration from the interior, so that notwithstanding a continued and regular emigration of labourers from thence to the West Indies, I have every expectation that the population of Sierra Leone would gradually increase.[2]

At first, to be sure, it seemed as if the expectations of a mass emigration would be fulfilled.

Transatlantic emigration commenced in April 1841, and was for some months carried on with a degree of energy and success that threatened to depopulate the colony. The great advantages of the West Indies were represented in glowing language, plenty of work, wages varying from 1s. 8d. to 4s. 2d. per diem, liberal allowances of food, gratuitous medical attendance and medicine, and no compulsory labour ; all these were freely offered, and produced an electrical effect among our population ; the public mind was violently agitated, ordinary avocations were neglected, distant visits were paid by persons anxious to canvass with each other the whole merits of the new measure, and its probable results on their future welfare.

The first vessels obtained their complement of emigrants with astonishing rapidity. The agents had in fact several hundred names enrolled of eager candidates for emigration, for whom no accommodation could be found in the vessels then about to proceed. The chagrin of the disappointed candidates was great, but they were consoled by the assurance that other and early opportunities would be afforded them.

Meantime there arose in the minds of the more shrewd and calculating, a certain measure of distrust and caution, which prompted them to wait the issue of the first experiment, before resolving on that more extended measure of expatriation, to which, by the eagerness of the emigration agents, they were invited.

For this purpose they determined to delegate certain persons to proceed with the first emigrant ship to Jamaica, Trinidad, and Demerara, under an express understanding that such delegates were to be taken away free of expense, maintained while absent, and returned to Sierra Leone also free of expense. . . .

The enthusiasm created in the public mind on the arrival of the first emigrant vessels, subsided rather rapidly after they had sailed ; a calm survey of the whole matter induced a general idea that the comforts and advantages of Sierra Leone were not outweighed by the prospects held out by emigration.

The delegates sent to Demerara returned to this colony in the Superior. They landed in a uniform of fine blue cloth, with scarlet cuff and collar, elegant forage caps, a scarlet waist-band, and fine cloth trousers. These adornments proved, in the event, to be a very great mistake ; intended, as they no doubt were, to allure

less than one third part of the whole number of adult Emigrants embarked'. This provision was not contained in the Sierra Leone Emigration Act of 13 Jan. 1843 which repealed the Act of 28 Dec. 1841, but it was incorporated in an Act of 12 Oct. 1843, amending the Act of 13 Jan. 1843.

[1] See *Report from Committee on West India Colonies 1842*, p. 593; *Papers relative to West Indies: Antigua, Trinidad, St. Lucia, Grenada*, p. 75.   [2] Ibid., p. 77.

emigrants, they had precisely an opposite effect; the scheme partook too much of artifice and delusion.[1]

The failure was attributed in part to the fact that emigration was conducted by private enterprise.

Towards the end of 1842, the emigration from Africa seemed to have come to an end. It was proposed, therefore, by the representatives of the West India body in this country, that in order to inspire confidence, the Government should employ transports of its own, which should be kept permanently sailing between Sierra Leone and the West Indies, thus securing a certain communication both ways, giving greater facilities for sending coloured delegates from the West Indies to explain the advantages of those colonies, and also for giving a free passage back, after a certain period, to any immigrants who might wish to return to their own country.[2]

. . . to a certain degree this experiment succeeded, for the emigration did revive. . . . This degree of success, however, was not sufficient to justify the continuance of the experiment, and the transports were, by the wish of the local authorities, relinquished. After this period, any suitable private ships which the owners were willing to send on the chance of procuring emigrants were licensed . . . .[3]

The causes which checked emigration were described as follows:

. . . the resident population did not emigrate, and for some time there was considerable difficulty in persuading liberated Africans to do so, partly from their natural fickleness, and partly because their countrymen, who desired their services in Sierra Leone, terrified them with the most incredible falsehoods . . . . Complaints were frequent, of the interference of the resident population, of the caprice of the Africans, and of the refusal of the Government to use any form of compulsion.[4]

The role played by emigration in the disposal of Liberated Africans was well illustrated in the Report on the Blue Books for 1849–50:

The following Return will show the number of captured Africans brought up to and in charge of the Local Government of the colony of Sierra Leone, during the years 1849 and 1850 respectively, and their disposal:—

Remaining in Liberated African Department and Hospital on Dec. 31		Number of captured Africans landed in the Colony		Total for each year	Disposal						
Year	Number	Year	Number		Emigrated	Enlisted	Located[1]	Absconded	Died	Remaining on Dec. 31	Total
1848	1,011	1849	2,203	3,214	2,240	71	466	17	278	142	3,214
1849	142	1850	1,867	2,009	1,612	120	158	15	83	21	2,009

[1] Having refused to emigrate or enlist.

Showing that, of 5,223 captured Africans brought to the colony during the last two years, 3,852 have emigrated to the West Indies.[5]

[1] Report from the Officer administering the Government of Sierra Leone to Lord Stanley, 30 Jan. 1842, *Report from Committee on West India Colonies*, p. 600. See also *Report from Committee on West Coast of Africa*, Part I, p. 562; *State of Colonial Possessions 1850*, pp. 187–9.

[2] Colonial Land and Emigration Commission, *Report 1845*, pp. 25–6. See also ibid. *1854*, p. 264: '. . . the Government, in 1843, took the management of the emigration into its own hands. A government agent was appointed to collect emigrants, who were taken to Jamaica, British Guiana, and Trinidad, in Government transports, and shortly afterwards a system which had prevailed of maintaining the liberated African for six months at the Government expense, was discontinued, the people being apprised that they would have to provide for their own support unless they chose to emigrate. Some restrictions on the emigration of the resident population which had been complained of by the West India body, were also removed on the recommendation of the Governor . . . .'   [3] Ibid. *1848*, pp. 31–2.

[4] Ibid. *1854*, pp. 264–5.   [5] *State of Colonial Possessions 1850*, p. 189.

As emigration depended on the number of captured slaves currently emancipated, it practically came to an end in 1852.[1]

The statistics concerning emigration from Sierra Leone to the West Indies are unreliable[2] and contradictory. But it seems that 12,826 went in 1841–50,[3] 1,229 in 1851–3, 839 in 1860–3, and altogether 14,894 in 1841–72.[4] This total includes 381 people who emigrated from the Kroo Coast[5] and it includes also Maroons, Nova Scotians, and Kroomen who emigrated from Sierra Leone.[6] Whether it also includes all those who died at sea it is impossible to tell. But it seems safe to say that a slight majority of the captured slaves landed in Sierra Leone after 1840 emigrated to the West Indies. Some of them returned to Sierra Leone, but their number is not known.[7]

TABLE 5. *Immigration into the British West Indies from Sierra Leone, 1841–72*[1]

Year	Brit. Guiana	Jamaica	Trinidad	Other islands	Total	Year	Brit. Guiana	Jamaica	Trinidad	Other islands	Total
1841	415	592	170	—	1,177	1849	—	228	255	1,405[2]	1,888
1842	148	292	514	—	954	1850	428	177	471	447[3]	1,523
1843	239	301	476	—	1,016	1851	453	317	—	46[4]	816
1844	378	339	246	—	963	1852	140	—	—	—	140
1845	1,425	42	420	—	1,887	1860	—	—	226	—	226
1846	278	—	—	—	278	1861	—	390	—	—	390
1847	457	—	399	—	856	1863	—	—	—	223[5]	223
1848	821	1,148	207	—	2,176	Total	5,182	3,826	3,384	2,121	14,513

[1] See Colonial Land and Emigration Commission, *Report 1850*, pp. 130–3; *1861*, pp. 80–5; *1873*, pp. 64–9.
[2] 95 to St. Kitts, 234 to St. Vincent, 711 to Grenada, 365 to St. Lucia.
[3] 261 to Grenada, 186 to St. Lucia.   [4] Tobago.   [5] St. Kitts.

Causes of Reduction. Among the first to call attention to the apparently small proportion of captured slaves surviving in the Colony was James

[1] See also Colonial Land and Emigration Commission, *Report 1853*, p. 50: 'The importation of liberated Africans, which ceased with the Brazilian slave trade, has not revived.'

[2] The 'Heads of Instructions for the Government Emigration Agent for Sierra Leone', to be sure, provided that detailed quarterly returns be sent to the British Government, but the statistics were apparently imperfect; see, for example, ibid. *1848*, p. 31.

[3] According to the Report on the Blue Books for 1849 and 1850 (*State of Colonial Possessions 1850*, p. 189), 'the Total Number of Emigrants of all Classes from the Colony of Sierra Leone to the West Indies' was 14,113 from Apr. 1841 to Nov. 1849.

[4] According to Emigration Commission, *Report 1873*, p. 68, the total number of emigrants from Sierra Leone to the West Indies was 21,118 in 1835–72, but this figure is evidently wrong and is not supported by the detailed data shown ibid., pp. 64–7.

[5] 108 in 1847 and 273 in 1853. I have omitted these emigrants in Table 5.

[6] These emigrants, however, were not numerous. See, for example, Colonial Land and Emigration Commission, *Report 1854*, p. 263: 'We are unable to state how many of the last class [Kroomen] left Africa in the earlier years of the emigration. We imagine, however, that the proportion cannot be very large, as out of about 6,500 emigrants despatched from Sierra Leone since 1848, (when the expense was first defrayed through this board by the British Government) not a hundred appear to have belonged to the resident population.' According to ibid. *1849*, pp. 35, 118, all 3,176 emigrants who sailed from Sierra Leone between 19 Jan. 1848 and 2 Mar. 1849 'except one have been liberated Africans, still under the care of Government'.

[7] According to ibid. *1852*, p. 209, about 550 'Africans and Kroomen' returned from British Guiana to their native country in the years 1842–50. See also ibid. *1851*, p. 38: 'About 302 Africans have availed themselves of the opportunity of returning from British Guiana to Sierra Leone by vessels employed in this service, and we are glad to perceive that the arrangement under which this was done is considered by the Government of British Guiana to be cheaper than any

Macqueen. In his letters on Sierra Leone to the Earl of Liverpool, dated 12 November 1824, he reproduced the figures of the 1820 and 1822 censuses as quoted by Hodgson from the *Missionary Register*, and said:

This, my Lord, is a very remarkable return. It exhibits a decrease of 107 on the number of liberated Africans, notwithstanding the addition to their numbers of 1,557 in that space, (*Par. Paper*, No. 389–1824) being above 20 per cent.! and of 113 in the number of disbanded soldiers, being nearly 10 per cent. The Nova Scotians also have dwindled down in numbers above one half in a few years! Will our Sierra Leone Sophists shew me in the annals of mankind any thing to equal this, more especially in a place where the population has the blessed benefit of 'The Marriage Tie', and where it is so religiously observed. Is death, debauchery, or cruelty the cause of this terrific decrease of the human species in this unhappy spot? . . .

. . . according to Parliamentary Papers, No. 556, Session 1823, and No. 389, Session 1824, from 1820 to March 1823, about 5,400 Negroes were carried into the place, of whom only 3,976 were to the 1st January 1823, delivered over to the authorities as liberated, the remainder standing classed as 'natives'. The total number of Negroes, according to Sir James Yeo, carried into Sierra Leone, previous to 1816, was upwards of 20,000, and from the Parliamentary Return of last year already referred to, greatly above 8,617, have been carried into the place (8,617 have been proceeded against in the Commission Court) to the end of 1822, making together 28,617—yet we find only eleven or twelve thousand, at the utmost, in the colony. What has become of all the rest ?

But let us take the population, according to the *New Times*, at 16,671, Jan. 1st, 1823. According to Mr. Macaulay (*Exposure*, p. 14,) 6,000 negroes had been brought to Sierra Leone, of whom, according to the Special Report, p. 63, 1,900 had entered the army, leaving in 1814, 4,100. To the end of 1822 (Par. Pap. 389–1824) 9,570 more were brought in and liberated, which should have made the number, at the later period, 13,670, and which, added to the other classes of the population, and the captured Negroes not liberated, would give a population of 18,673, instead of 16,671, shewing still a decrease of 2,002, instead of an increase.[1]

In a letter 'to Zachariah Macaulay, Esq.', dated 4 February 1825, he wrote furthermore:[2]

. . . '*Par fas et nefas*,' you have during the last sixteen years carried into Sierra Leone above 30,000 Negroes, yet you cannot now produce us above eleven or twelve thousand of these! Under your sway, the Nova Scotian Blacks were dwindled down in thirty years, from nearly 1,500[3] to 722. In the space of 18 months, the Disbanded African Soldiers decreased from 1,223 to 1,110, and in the same space of time, the Liberated Africans, notwithstanding the addition of nearly 1,600 to their ranks, decreased from 8,076 to 7,969, being at the rate of nearly 20 per cent. In your own words, I may ask you, 'Could this have been the case, had they given them the brief time, necessary to provide for their own subsistence ? What have been the proximate causes of all this frightful accumulation of misery and death. Without all question, these have been severity of treatment, and scantiness of food. Let us consider this unexampled waste of human life. Will the Parliament and the people of Great Britain, suffer this system to continue ? It is Quite Impossible. They will demand that the nuisance should be forthwith removed.'[4]

other that the colony could adopt. It is, we understand, expected that a considerable number will also return by one of these ships from Jamaica.'

[1] Macqueen, *Colonial Controversy*, pp. 102–3.   [2] Ibid., p. 214.

[3] The Nova Scotian Blacks landed in Sierra Leone in 1792 numbered 1,131; they were reduced by mortality during the first rainy season and later through emigration and never again attained their original numbers.

[4] This was apparently what Macaulay had written concerning the decrease of the slaves in the West Indies. For Macqueen's own opinion on the causes of mortality in Sierra Leone and the West Indies see p. 14 above.

Many of Macqueen's assumptions are absolutely wrong.

(1) The Parliamentary Paper No. 389, Session 1824, *An Account of the Number of Slaves Captured and Condemned at Sierra Leone from 5th January 1814 to 21st April 1823*, shows that from 1820 to the end of that period 4,902 slaves were seized and 3,976 delivered to Colonial Authorities. An accompanying Note says:

> The greater difference between the Number seized and the Number delivered to the Colonial Authorities, in 1821 and 1822, is accounted for principally by the accidental loss of the Yeanam Slave ship, whereby the greater number on board were drowned . . . .

I do not know where Macqueen found the figure 'about 5,400', but there is no doubt that all those who 'were carried into the place' alive were delivered to the authorities and that none were classed as natives.

(2) The total number of Liberated Africans carried into Sierra Leone previous to 1816 was not upwards of 20,000. Those landed in that period numbered 7,865.[1] The total number of captured slaves landed prior to 1823 was 16,815[2] (possibly even less)[3] and not 28,617.

(3) Macqueen assumes that the number of Liberated Africans decreased between 8 July 1820 and 1 January 1822 from 8,076 to 7,969 or by 107, 'notwithstanding the addition in their numbers of 1,557 in that space'. But it is very doubtful whether the Liberated Africans did actually decrease in that period. The number returned at the census of 31 December 1818 was 6,406. A Note accompanying the census of 1820 says that 943 Liberated Africans were 'landed here in 1819 and 1820' (between the two censuses). It is out of the question, therefore, that the number of Liberated Africans had actually increased between the two censuses by 1,670. On the other hand, the number landed between 8 July 1820 and 1 January 1822 was 1,285.[4] It seems most unlikely, therefore, that the number of Liberated Africans should have decreased in this intercensal period. As stated above,[5] I am inclined to think that the number of Liberated Africans was overstated at the census of 1820 and included many Natives.

(4) Macqueen, who assumes that at the 1822 census many Liberated Africans were returned as Natives, put the number of Liberated Africans for the end of 1822 at possibly 11,000 or 12,000.[6] But if, as I think, the number of Liberated Africans was not understated at the census of 1 January 1822, the total hardly exceeded 10,400 at the end of 1822.

---

[1] See Table, p. 116 above.   [2] See ibid.

[3] The number of captured slaves landed prior to June 1819 was apparently 12,102 (see p. 101 above). From June 1819 to 31 Dec. 1822 the number (according to Foreign Office Returns) was 3,759. Macqueen himself came near the truth when he suggested in the next paragraph of his letter that 6,000 had been brought up to (July) 1814 and 9,570 thereafter, i.e. altogether about 15,600.

[4] The figure 1,557 given by Macqueen covers the whole years 1820 and 1821.   [5] See p. 86.

[6] The *Missionary Register 1822*, p. 508, said that between 8 July 1820 and 1 Jan. 1822 'the number of Liberated Africans . . . has in fact greatly increased, independently of the addition of 1,590 since the date of the last Return. We collect from these data that the number of Liberated Africans, of all descriptions, in the Colony, on the 1st of August, was upward of Eleven Thousand.' But the assumption made in the *Missionary Register* that about 1,500 Liberated Africans were wrongly counted as Natives on 1 Jan. 1822 (see pp. 85–6 above) is, it seems to me, not justified.

The problem, then, is not how to explain a difference between 28,617 Liberated Africans landed up to 31 December 1822 and 11,000 or 12,000 surviving in the Colony on that date, but rather a difference between 16,800 imported and 10,400 surviving. The explanation is not difficult. About 2,500 Liberated Africans entered the Army and Navy. The total number settled in the Colony was about 14,200. Some left the Colony after having been settled there. Finally, assuming that 15 per cent. died in the first four months after landing, the number who thus perished would have amounted to about 2,500. It may well be, therefore, that among those surviving the first four months births were nearly equal to deaths.

The Commissioners of Inquiry into the State of Sierra Leone (1827) stated that 'the total number of negroes captured and landed in Sierra Leone from 1808 to 1825, both years inclusive was 20,571'.[1] They gave, moreover, the following account:[2]

Liberated Africans settled in the colony, up to 31 December 1825, exclusive of 2,738 who entered His Majesty's service, returned to their country, or were otherwise provided for	17,833
Received into the colony between the end of 1825 and the 23d of February 1826	783
Settled in the Isles de Los and not included in the foregoing . . .	28

As against this total of 18,644, the census taken on the initiative of the Commissioners in April 1826 showed only 10,716 Liberated Africans present. The Commissioners attributed the difference to excessive mortality and to voluntary emigration (after location in a village). But excessive mortality could hardly explain more than half of the vast difference, and voluntary emigration (after location) was probably not considerable. It seems, however, that the number of Liberated Africans ascertained at the census of 1826 was somewhat too low.[3] Even so, there must have been another factor which contributed to the reduction in the number of Liberated Africans, and this probably was re-enslavement and exportation.[4]

As shown above, Chief Justice Jeffcott, in June 1830, attributed the reduction in the number of Liberated Africans exclusively to the slave-trade.[5] The Principal Secretary of State for War and the Colonies, Sir George Murray, in a Dispatch to Lieutenant-Governor Findlay, dated 26 October 1831, refuted Jeffcott's charge.

In the first place, he has represented that the number of Africans imported into the Colony, and liberated by the Mixed Commission Courts, within the last ten years, exceeds 22,000; and that from 1808 to 1829, the number of Africans liberated by the Court of Vice Admiralty, is 13,000; this would give a total of 35,000 souls.

---

[1] *Report*, First Part, p. 52.   [2] Ibid., p. 20.

[3] But Kenneth Macaulay very much overstated the number of Liberated Africans when he said that it was 13,000 in 1823 and 'at least 16,000' in 1825 (see *Sierra Leone vindicated*, p. 9).

[4] Crooks, referring to the Commissioners' statement that 21,944 persons (negroes) had arrived in the Colony from 1787 to 23 Feb. 1826 and that only 13,020 were ascertained at the census of Apr. 1826, said: 'The difference between the numbers probably arises from the fact that numbers entered the military and naval services of the Crown; some 3,000 emigrated to Gambia, and some returned to the West Indies, with the sanction of the Government, whilst others emigrated from the Colony and joined the native tribes surrounding it. Add to this the deaths and the fact that the birth-rate was in these days low, and the whole of this apparent decrease of 8,924 is not difficult to account for' (*History of Sierra Leone*, pp. 135–6). But there was practically no emigration to the Gambia prior to 1829 or to the West Indies prior to 1841.   [5] See p. 126 above.

Now the Official Returns transmitted to this Department, are imperfectly made out; they do not include the year 1829. But assuming the numbers imported in that year to have been 2,500, which is nearly the average of the three preceding years, it would appear, from the Returns in this Office, that the total number of liberated Africans, from the year 1808 to the present time, whether condemned by the Court of Vice Admiralty, or by the Mixed Commission Courts, is not 35,000, as Mr. Jeffcott has stated, but only 28,481. The difference is 7,519. I observe also, that in the 20th page of the printed Report of the Commissioners of Inquiry, the number of imported Africans, up to December 1825, is stated at 17,833—a statement altogether incompatible with Mr. Jeffcott's supposition, that in May 1830 they amounted to 35,000.

Thus, then, I cannot but suppose, that the Judge has much exaggerated, of course unintentionally, the Total number of Africans delivered into the charge of His Majesty's Officers at Sierra Leone; it is, I think, not less evident that he has over-rated the rule of increase by births.

His statement is, that within one of the most fatal years known in the Colony, the proportions of births to deaths was as seven to one; and reasoning upon this fact, he conceives that the whole imported population ought to have increased by one-half, so as to give 52,500 souls for the population of liberated Africans and their progeny, which the Colony ought now to contain.[1]

Sir George Murray then shows why Jeffcott must have overstated the excess of births over deaths[2] and concludes:

In estimating the deduction from the stock of imported Africans, Mr. Jeffcott makes no allowance for the obvious defects in the Returns, and the impossibility under which he laboured, at the time of making his Charge, of ascertaining the existing numbers with precision. Neither does he advert to voluntary emigrations from the Colony, nor to the enlistments for the King's Military Service, as causes for diminishing the numbers of the imported Africans. He is entirely silent also respecting the destructive effect upon the lives of these people, which is known to result from their sufferings during the period of their detention in Slave ships. Had allowance been made for these circumstances, Mr. Jeffcott might perhaps have found cause to hesitate in declaring his conviction from the Bench, that, but for the Slave Trade practised in the Colony, the actual population would have been 30,000 at least greater than it is.[3]

The Royal Committee of Enquiry appointed to investigate the 'charge' by Chief Justice Jeffcott 'Humbly showeth'

That with reference to the first object to which the attention of this Committee is called, viz. 'The Statement that the Number of Africans imported into the Colony, and liberated by the Mixed Commission Courts, exceeds 22,000'. It appears to this Committee, from the official Return produced, that the number of Africans received by the Liberated African Department from the Mixed Commission Court, to the 31st May 1830, is 23,539; and that the number emancipated in that Court is 22,422, leaving a balance of 1,117, who have been received by the Liberated African Department without emancipation.

That with reference to the second object of this Committee's attention, viz. 'That from 1808 to 1829, the Number of Africans liberated by the Court of Vice-Admiralty, is 13,000'. It would appear by the Return produced by the Registrar of that Court, that the number is only 12,114; it therefore appears that an error of 886, has been made in this statement.[4] But it will further appear by the Returns of the Registrars of the Mixed Commission and Vice-Admiralty Courts, that the collective number who have been liberated in the Colony, exceeds the number stated in the Charge of Chief Justice Jeffcott to the Grand Jury, in June 1830, by 653; and by the Returns of Mr. Thomas Cole, the Assistant Superintendent of Liberated Africans, it is further

---

[1] *Charge delivered by Jeffcott*, pp. 6–7.   [2] See p. 111 above.   [3] *Charge delivered by Jeffcott*, p. 7.
[4] There is no such error. The figure 12,114 covers only the years 1808–19.

apparent that 37,456 have been received by that department, exceeding the number stated in the Charge, by 2,456.[1]

The Committee was non-committal concerning the question whether voluntary emigration was an important factor and concerning Jeffcott's statement regarding the ratio of births to deaths; it added, however, that 'even admitting the deaths to be more than the births, still the great deficiency, in the opinion of the Committee, is chiefly attributable to the system of kidnapping which has prevailed for so many years'.

Viscount Goderich, the successor of Sir George Murray, in a Dispatch to Lieutenant-Governor Findlay, dated 18 January 1832, said:

In Sir George Murray's Despatch of the 26th of October 1830, is to be found a recapitulation of the statements contained in Mr. Jeffcott's Charge to the Grand Jury. The results to which those statements came was, that the number of liberated Africans in Sierra Leone would, but for the Slave-trade carried on there, have amounted to 52,500 souls, including the progeny of that class of persons; whereas, in fact, the entire number was not above 17 or 18,000; so that the whole loss exceeded 35,000. Mr. Jeffcott did not, indeed, assert or suggest that any such number had been actually carried off by the Slave-trade. His statement was, that the number of Africans liberated by the Courts of Admiralty and Mixed Commission, amounted to 35,000. . . .

It appears then by the Returns from the Liberated African Department, that from the year 1808 to the 31st of May 1830, the number of liberated Africans settled in the Colony, was 33,595. It further appears, that the total number found in the Colony when the census of the 30th June 1830 was taken, was 23,888. The actual deficiency, therefore, was 9,707. Now supposing the number of births and of deaths to have been precisely equal, the result would be that the whole of this deficiency must be accounted for either on the supposition that 9,707 had quitted the Colony voluntarily, or by assuming that they had been removed from it by violence or fraud.[2]

He then points out that (according to Cole) of the 33,595 Liberated Africans located in the Colony from 1808 to 1830 one-fifth or 6,719 had died (5,039 within the first four months after arrival and 1,680 thereafter),[3] 'which reduces the entire number unaccounted for, to 2,988'.

Let the various circumstances to which I have thus adverted, be combined together. Allow for the rapid mortality consequent upon the diseases engendered, and the sufferings endured in the slave ships; for the disproportion of sexes; and for voluntary returns of the Africans to their native country, whether from the natural love of home or to escape from ill-usage; and much of the difficulty disappears of accounting for the deficiency of 9,707 souls upon a period of 23 years, upon a population of 33,595. Mr. Jeffcott's Charge to the Grand Jury, therefore, when thus brought to the test of sober inquiry and calculation, must, I fear, be considered as highly exaggerated . . . .[4]

Before discussing the opinions on the causes of the reduction in the number of Liberated Africans it is necessary, first of all, to deal with the various statements concerning the size of this reduction.

Sir George Murray's argument on this question was full of mistakes.

[1] *Charge delivered by Jeffcott*, p. 9. [2] Ibid., p. 33.

[3] See p. 108 above. He adds: 'This calculation, however, supposes that after allowing for the mortality occasioned by the diseases generated in the slave ships, the remaining population did not produce a number of births exceeding the number of deaths, but remained stationary.' Thus he assumes that all the 6,719 people died from diseases generated in the slave ships, which probably is a correct interpretation of Cole's statement. [4] *Charge delivered by Jeffcott*, pp. 35-6.

The average number imported in 1826–8 was not 'nearly 2,500' but about 3,259.[1] His estimate of 2,500 for 1829 was far too low; the figure was actually 4,857. His observation 'that in the 20th page of the printed Report of the Commissioners of Inquiry, the number of imported Africans, up to December 1825, is stated at 17,833' is wrong; they stated there that the number of Liberated Africans settled in the Colony, exclusive of 2,738 who entered His Majesty's service, &c., was 17,833, and they said explicitly (on page 52 of their report) that 'the total number of negroes captured and landed in Sierra Leone from 1808 to 1825' was 20,571. By adding to this figure the number of Africans landed in 1826–9 (14,635), one arrives at a total of 35,206, as compared with the total of 28,481 assumed by Sir George Murray.[2] The number of Liberated Africans landed between January and May 1830 was 2,250, and the returns of the Assistant Superintendent of Liberated Africans, Cole, showed in fact that 37,456 'have been received by that department' up to 31 May 1830. Of these, 33,595 had been settled in the Colony, as shown in the Returns from the Liberated African Department.

Chief Justice Jeffcott was certainly wrong in putting the number of Liberated Africans 'in the whole Colony' at 17,000 or 18,000. He may have been misled by the fact that the number of Liberated Africans 'under Charge of the General Superintendent' on 1 July 1829 was 17,882. This figure comprised only those settled in the villages and excluded those living in Freetown or employed up the river. The total number of Liberated Africans on 31 December was given as 21,205,[3] but even this figure was not all-inclusive. According to Viscount Goderich there were on 30 June 1830, 23,888 in the Colony.

Viscount Goderich says that the reduction in the number of Liberated Africans from 1808 to 30 June 1830 was 9,707, and suggests that 6,719 may be attributable to excess of deaths over births and the remaining 2,988 possibly to 'voluntary returns of the Africans to their native country'. He says, however, at the same time: 'That the Slave-trade has been extensively carried on at Sierra Leone, is a fact which the evidence has unhappily placed beyond the reach of controversy'. There can in fact be hardly any doubt that several thousand Liberated Africans were re-enslaved and exported. I am therefore inclined to think that, leaving out of consideration mortality in the first four months after arrival, births were at least as numerous as deaths.

In 1841–2 the same question was discussed again in the Report from the Select Committee on the West Coast of Africa. On 30 April 1841 Colonel Jones, Superintendent Assistant of Liberated Africans, was examined:[4]

What number of negroes have been emancipated, both prior to the year 1819, and since that period, by the mixed commissioners at this place?—From the year 1819 (when the Courts of Mixed Commissions were first established) to 1840, 59,531 negroes have been emancipated. Previous to the former year, commencing with

---

[1] The total number of Africans landed in these three years was 9,778.

[2] Sir George Murray was also wrong in assuming that 35,000 minus 28,481 is 7,519.

[3] See *Report from Committee on Sierra Leone and Fernando Po*, pp. 118–19.

[4] *Report*, Part II, p. 323.

1808, the date of the abolition of the slave trade by Great Britain, 11,278 negroes received their freedom from the Vice Admiralty Court of this colony.[1]

Of that number, how many are now living here ?—37,029 on the 31st December 1840.
How many males ?—20,709.
How many females ?—16,320.

Governor Doherty, as General Superintendent of Liberated Africans, submitted the following statement referring to 30 June 1840:[2]

Total number emancipated	.	.	49,933
Remaining at this date .	.	.	37,733
			12,200

Commissioner R. R. Madden, in his report dated 31 July 1841, after having pointed out that (according to Colonel Jones) 70,809 negroes had been emancipated and 'of this number 37,029 were living in the colony on the 31st December 1840', said:

Here is a frightful decrease to be accounted for of no less than 33,780 persons; and the superintendent states, in his replies respecting those who may have left the colony, he is unable to afford the required information on this subject.

None of the negroes had been at this period sent to the West Indies.[3]

With respect to the total number of negroes emancipated, as given in Colonel Doherty's returns, namely, 49,933, an apparent discrepancy with those of the acting Governor, Mr. Carr, and the assistant-superintendent, Mr. Jones, will be observed, as given in their replies to my queries on this subject. Both these gentlemen state the numbers emancipated by the Courts of Admiralty, prior to the establishment of the Mixed Courts in 1819, at 11,278, and the numbers subsequently emancipated at 59,531, namely, from 1819 to 1840.

This apparent discrepancy arises only from the different modes of computing the number liberated, in one case their being taken into account from the date of registration, and in the other from that of liberation by the sentence of the Mixed Courts, in which interval I know from my own experience in the superintendence of these negroes elsewhere, the mortality is frequently considerable.[4]

Colonel Doherty, in a report to Under-Secretary Hope, dated 27 October 1841, made the following Observations on Commissioner Madden's report:

The great decrease in the numbers of the emancipated people is then adverted to; and it astonishes Dr. Madden more than it ought to have done, because he did not persevere in searching further for causes that might account for it. It is largely accounted for by the known fact of the extraordinary number of deaths which always happen within a year after importation; and I beg leave here to annex the copy of a return which, in consequence of a particular occurrence, I was induced to preserve, showing very strikingly the rate of this mortality as it occurs at the Kissy hospital. It is partly accounted for by the numbers who have at different periods been sent by Government to the Gambia; and by enlistments, all our black regiments having for years been recruited at Sierra Leone from liberated Africans; and it is accounted for by the disproportion existing between the sexes, and by the number of males who constantly emigrate from the colony, driven from it by that cause, and allured by the fertile lands that border on the peninsula along its eastern frontier.[5]

Finally, Macgregor Laird, in a Memorandum submitted to the Committee on 11 July 1842, stated:

Up to 1819, the number of liberated Africans located in the colony was . 11,278
From that time to the 30th June 1840 51,524

---

[1] Acting Governor Carr answered the same question: 'Prior to the year 1819, 11,278 were emancipated by the mixed courts, and since that period the returns of those courts give 59,331.' See *Report*, Part II, p. 327. [2] Ibid., p. 316. [3] Ibid., p. 249. [4] Ibid., p. 314. [5] Ibid., p. 363.

The population now is supposed to be 50,000 souls. It is clear that, making all allowances for the excess of males over females among the liberated Africans, some powerful cause has been in operation to prevent a race, above all others prolific, from increasing and multiplying under the protection and patronage of the British Government, and which has made so many of its inhabitants eager to escape beyond its bounds.

That cause, it is believed, arose from three separate sources:

1st. From the poverty of the soil, which is incapable of producing exportable produce, or repaying the labour employed in its cultivation.

2d. From the non-existence of any national character in the population, Maroons, Nova Scotians, and liberated Africans, from all quarters of the Continent, being mixed together, with no common bond of unity or feeling.

3d. From the unhealthiness of the climate, preventing an efficient European superintendence being established, on the part of the Government, over these mixed and incongruous elements, and deterring the capital and skill from flowing into the colony from Great Britain, as it would naturally have done under more favourable circumstances.

Any one of these causes would have been sufficient to prevent the colony ever attaining a flourishing state; the three combined are quite sufficient to account for its present melancholy condition.

It is incapable of supplying any exportable produce, from the poverty of the soil; from the same reason it is incapable of maintaining its present population, artificially introduced. Its existence depends alone on the lavish expenditure of the British Government . . . .[1]

It is again necessary, first of all, to deal with the various statements concerning the size of the reduction in the number of Liberated Africans.

Colonel Doherty's statement that the total number of negroes emancipated up to 30 June 1840 amounted to 49,933 was wrong. The figure 49,933 actually covered only the Liberated Africans registered from June 1819 to June 1839,[2] and it was misleading to compare this number with the 37,733 Liberated Africans living on 30 June 1840 in the Colony, since many of them had arrived before June 1819 or after June 1839. The difference of 12,200 given by Colonel Doherty is absolutely meaningless.

It was, on the other hand, a mistake of the Committee to ask Colonel Jones and Acting Governor Carr (1) 'What number of negroes had been emancipated?' and (2) 'Of that number, how many are now living here?' Many thousands of those emancipated by the Courts at Sierra Leone had been landed elsewhere, and what the Committee evidently wanted to know was how many negroes had been landed in Sierra Leone and how many of these were still living there. Commissioner Madden, in comparing the number of negroes emancipated until 31 December 1840 (70,809) with the number of those living in Sierra Leone on that date (37,029), found 'a frightful decrease to be accounted for of no less than 33,780 persons', while Colonel Doherty, who likewise thought that the two figures were comparable, said that the difference 'astonishes Dr. Madden more than it ought to have done'.

Macgregor Laird came nearer the truth by pointing out that 'up to 1819, the number of liberated Africans located in the colony was 11,278'[3]

---

[1] Ibid., Part I, pp. 570–1.

[2] See *Correspondence with British Commissioners relating to Slave Trade, 30 June to 31 Dec. 1839*, p. 5.   [3] The number 'located' in the colony was actually smaller.

and 'from that time to the 30th June 1840, 51,524',[1] but he was wrong in comparing the sum of these two items (62,802) with the total population 'supposed to be 50,000 souls' since the total population was actually only about 41,000 and the number of Liberated Africans 37,733.

The number of Liberated Africans landed up to 31 December 1840 is not known exactly, but it may be put at about 67,000 of whom about 60,000 were settled in the Colony. The number living in the Colony on 31 December 1840 was about 37,000. The difference is very great indeed. While about 28,000 or 29,000 Liberated Africans had been settled at Sierra Leone in 1830–40, the number of Liberated Africans in the Colony had increased by hardly 16,000. Assuming that 15 per cent. of those settled in the Colony from 1808 to 1840 had died in the first four months after arrival, there would still remain a difference of about 14,000, which could be explained only by an excess of deaths (excluding deaths in the first four months) over births, voluntary emigration, and re-enslavement. As kidnapping in the 1830s was probably less frequent than in the preceding period, it would seem that either mortality had increased or that fertility had decreased since 1829. Colonel Doherty, who had erroneously assumed that the reduction was much greater still than it actually was, tried to explain it even without taking account of re-enslavement.[2] But his argument is by no means convincing. However, all figures are so uncertain after 1833 that it seems impossible to draw any final conclusions.

6. *Miscellaneous Immigrants*

(1) Immigration of freed slaves to Africa under American auspices was initiated by a coloured native of the United States, Paul Cuffee, who had 'heard of the encouragement offered to the Settlers at Sierra Leone by the African Institution'.[3]

Captain Paul Cuffee . . . arrived at Sierra Leone, in the brig Traveller, on the 2d of February, 1816, having on board seven families from America, amounting to thirty-four persons. . . .

On his application to the Governor, grants were made of four lots of land to the heads of families which he had brought with him . . . .[4]

---

[1] This was the number registered from 1819 to 30 June 1840; see *Correspondence with British Commissioners 1841*, p. 7.

[2] A similar attempt was made by Crooks in *History of Sierra Leone*, pp. 175–6.

[3] Claude George, p. 187; see also *Handbook of Sierra Leone*, p. 35.

[4] *Eleventh Report of African Institution 1817*, pp. 39–40; see also *Seventh Report 1813*, pp. 32–3, *Tenth Report 1816*, pp. 35, 70–1, *Twelfth Report 1818*, p. 139. Reports about the number of people whom Cuffee brought to Sierra Leone vary. According to an obituary in the *Boston Recorder*, reproduced in *The Royal Gazette and Sierra Leone Advertiser*, 27 June–25 July 1818, Cuffee arrived in Sierra Leone on 6 Dec. 1815, 'accompanied by nine families, eighteen adults and twenty children, making thirty-eight souls' (4 July, p. 128). Claude George says (p. 187) that Cuffee 'had taken with him nine families of fifty persons'. Butt-Thompson relates (p. 141) that Cuffee brought 'eight freed Negroes at their own charges and thirty at his own expense. . . . Three times in the next two years did Paul Cuffee bring here parties of settlers, totalling, with those first landed, nearly two hundred men, women and children.' I did not find any evidence of this additional immigration. Nor did I find any corroboration of the following statement by Claude George (p. 214): 'The latter half of the year 1817 witnessed several accessions to the population of our Colony. Several natives of Jamaica and Barbadoes desirous of settling down in the Colony obtained permission of the Government, through the Admiralty, and several seamen on board the transport *Friends* were added to the number of colonists.'

(2) In January 1819 eighty-five convicts who had taken part 'in the insurrection which broke out at Barbadoes on the 18th April 1816'[1] were landed at Sierra Leone. As the circumstances under which they came are somewhat complicated and have often been misrepresented I shall reproduce here extracts from some relevant documents.[2]

Earl Bathurst to Lieutenant General Sir James Leith, Governor of Barbadoes, 7 November 1816. I have had the honor of receiving your dispatch No. 12, stating the difficulty under which you labour as to the disposal of certain Negroes who had been condemned to death on account of the part borne by them in the late Insurrection in Barbadoes.

Considering on the one hand the great objections which exist to the return of these Individuals into the Mass of the Negro population of this Colony, and on the other that the number already executed are fully adequate for any purpose of punishment, or public example, I can have no difficulty in acceding to your recommendation that these now under consideration, and those who upon Trial may be found Guilty— should be transported from the Island. Some difficulty exists as to the selection of the place to which they could with best inconvenience be removed, but it appears to me that the Settlement of Honduras to which Negroes similarly situated have formerly not unfrequently been transported from Jamaica is that to which they could be conveyed with the least danger and expense. . . .

You will however delay the removal of these Negroes to Honduras for a month or Six Weeks after the receipt of this despatch in order that there may be sufficient time to apprise His Majesty's superintendent of the measures now in contemplation.

Earl Bathurst to Lieutenant Colonel George Arthur, Superintendent and Commander in Chief of Honduras, 31 March 1817. I have had the honor of receiving your dispatch of the 26th February announcing the arrival at Belize on board the Transport Frances Mary of 124 Negroes from Barbadoes, and announcing, the general alarm which had been created throughout the Settlement by the prospect of these persons being landed in the Colony.

I cannot but regret the non-arrival of the Instructions which I addressed to you on the 7th November last, as I cannot but believe that the feelings excited in the Colony by their unexpected arrival would have been altogether obviated had time been allowed for preparing the Minds of the Inhabitants for their introduction.

Altho' I cannot contemplate the probability of any danger from their Settlement in Honduras, their numbers being comparatively small, and the means of effecting mischief being cut by their separation from their more criminal associates, yet after the objections shewn to their introduction by the Inhabitants, I feel but little disposition to place these Negroes in a situation in which they may be considered objects of general apprehension and as such may be deprived of all means of amendment or reform.

If therefore they shall not already have been disposed of in the Settlement in a manner satisfactory to you, you will consider yourself authorized to send them to Sierra Leone, on board the Transport which has conveyed them to Honduras, but if they shall actually have landed in the Settlement, I can see no adequate reason for disturbing the arrangements which you have made, unless there shall have been any thing in their conduct since their landing to justify the alarm entertained by the Inhabitants on their first arrival.

Lieutenant Colonel George Arthur, 21 September 1818. I certify that on the 17th day of February 1817 the Ship Frances Mary anchored in the Port of Belize Honduras having on board 123 Convicts and other dangerous characters Stated to be concerned in the Insurrection in the Island of Barbadoes: that by my direction these people were not Suffered to Land until the British Settlers had an opportunity of Stating their Situation and Making their Appeal to the Right Hon[ble] Earl

---

[1] *The Royal Gazette and Sierra Leone Advertiser*, 12 June 1819, p. 195.

[2] See C.O, 267, vol. xlix, Nos. 185, 187, 206.

Bathurst: that from considerable Sickness making its appearance and the Necessity of heaving down the Transport, the convicts were afterwards landed on certain Keys called the Triangles, distant about three Leagues from Belize: That in consequence of the Sickness increasing and the difficulty of provisioning the Convicts at that Distance, they were removed to Moho Key, Since which time on the representation of the Medical Officer of the Necessity of their being put to some Work for the preservation of their Health they have chiefly been employed in felling Underwood there and draining the Ground in the Neighbourhood of it . . . that the orders from Earl Bathurst for removing the Convicts in the Frances Mary to Sierra Leone reached me on the 5 Aug last and that Instructions were given on the following day to the Master to prepare for Sea immediately: that twenty seven of the Convicts have died since their arrival in the Settlement, that Eight have been detained to be employed by Government[1] and that Eighty Eight remain in charge of Mr. Mathewson to be landed at Sierra Leone. . . .

William Vesey Munnings, President and Commander in Chief of the Bahamas to Governor MacCarthy, 21 November 1818. I have the honor to state to your Excellency—that the Transport Ship Frances Mary, David Mathewson Master, which Sailed from Honduras in September last (agreeably to the directions of the Earl Bathurst signified to Lieutenant Colonel Arthur Superintendant of that Settlement) bound to Sierra Leone, with 88 persons being Convicts and others concerned in the late Insurrection at Barbadoes, arrived in this Port in distress on the 26th ultimo; and upon a Survey of the Ship under the authority of the Vice Admiralty Court, she was found to be so much damaged and decayed as not to be Sea worthy nor worth the Expence of being repaired, and by a Decree of the Court, she has been Condemned and Sold by the Marshal, for the benefit of the Owners or others concerned.

Under these circumstances in order to carry Earl Bathurst's intentions into effect, I have caused the Ship Speculation, William Martin Master to be chartered for the purpose of conveying these Convicts (being now 86 in number according to the List inclosed two having died on the passage from Honduras) to Sierra Leone within the Government or Command of your Excellency. . . .

Governor MacCarthy to Earl Bathurst, 16 January 1819. I have the honor to avail myself of the opportunity of a Liverpool Vessel, sailing this day (the 'Union') for England, to inform your Lordship, that the hired ship 'Speculator' from Nassau, Bahama Islands, anchored yesterday Evening in this Harbour, having on board 85 Convicts, and other dangerous persons concerned in the Insurrection in the Island of Barbadoes—a Mr. Peebles Surgeon of the Militia of the Bay of Honduras, and entrusted by Lieut. Colonel Arthur, superintendent of that Settlement, with the charge of those people, delivered to me a letter from His Honor William Vesey Munnings—President and Commander in Chief of the Bahamas . . . .

I propose accordingly, to land them on Monday 18th Inst. and to treat and consider them as Government Apprentices; divide them in small Parties in Keeping them at Public Works in Freetown, in the Captured Negroes' Towns, and also at the Isles de Loss and the Gambia. . . .

Same to same, 23 January 1819. I have the honor to acquaint your Lordship that agreeable to the intentions expressed in my letter No. 185 a duplicate of which is enclosed, I lost no time in making out the necessary dispositions for the disposal of the Convicts and other persons brought from the Bay of Honduras they were accordingly landed and disposed of on the 18th and 19th Instant and every one of them is now I hope usefully employed either in the Country Towns or in Freetown.

Same to same, 25 June 1819. I had the honor of receiving your Letter of the 7th April last, conveying to me the very gratifying information of your approbation of the arrangements I adopted with respect to the disposal of the persons concerned in the Insurrection at Barbadoes and signifying the pleasure of His Royal Highness 'that in any or all of those cases in which the good conduct of the convicts may have

[1] See also *The Royal Gazette and Sierra Leone Advertiser*, 12 June 1819, p. 195: '. . . six valuable artificers and two boatmen . . . were retained at Honduras'.

been either satisfactorily proved to me, or has fallen under my own observations, that I should afford them such remission of their original sentence or such other indulgence as may be best calculated to mark the approbation of their good conduct.'

In returning my thanks for the expression of your approbation of my exertions in that case, it affords me very great pleasure to state, that the conduct of those men has been hitherto very proper, and that they have showed themselves deserving of the very kind manner in which they have been treated. I shall with satisfaction and perfect confidence gradually take off the only restraint under which they have been kept, that of not removing from the inland Towns to which they have been attached, without leave, and working at their different Trades for His Majesty at very Low Wages.[1]

(3) Some of the early settlers of Liberia came first to Sierra Leone.

In January 1820 some American missionaries arrived from New York with 89 free coloured people from the United States and proceeded to Sherbro to occupy a tract of land that had been purchased by the missionaries from the King of Sherbro in 1818. The climate, however, proved so unhealthy that in a short time the agents and one-fourth of the settlers had succumbed, and it was decided to abandon the location and seek a more healthy one. They proceeded to Freetown and were given temporary accommodation at Fourah Bay until they had settled their plans. They finally decided on a settlement at Cape Mesurado, now a part of Liberia, and on the 25th April 1822 the American flag was flown there.[2]

Later on there was some small emigration from Liberia to Sierra Leone.[3] The numbers of survivors of these various groups are given as follows:

	1 Jan. 1822	Apr. 1826	1837	31 Dec. 1840[4]	31 Dec. 1844[7]	1847[10]	1848[10]	1850[10]	1851[10]	1860[10]
West Indians . .	85[1]	141[2]	100[3]	33[5]	106[8]	104	123	91	95	164
Liberians . .	—	—	—	73[6]	82[9]	90[11]	90	121[12]	64[12]	50[12]

[1] 'West Indians and Americans' (48 men, 19 women, 10 boys, 8 girls); see 'Census 1 Jan. 1822'. According to Kenneth Macaulay, *Sierra Leone vindicated*, p. 16, 'Exiles from Barbadoes . . . together with a few North-American Blacks who have settled in the colony'.

[2] 'West Indians and Americans' (71 men, 35 women, 16 boys, 19 girls); see *Report of Commissioners of Inquiry*, 1827, First Part, p. 21, and Appendix A, No. 38. The Commissioners say with regard to the 85 negroes imported in 1819 from Barbados (ibid., p. 15): 'No documents have been kept from which information could be obtained respecting the influence of the climate upon them; it has been therefore found necessary on this subject to inquire of the negroes themselves, more particularly of Samuel Lane, an intelligent man, whose statement . . . accounts (though not so satisfactorily as might be wished), for 60 of the original number. Of these 60, 34 are known to be living, and 26 supposed to be dead. Whether the remaining 25 or any part of them have left the colony, or still remain in it, seems uncertain; and as they have never been distinctly specified in the census, there are no means of ascertaining the fact.' This statement was misunderstood by Commissioner R. R. Madden who said: 'Of these [85] persons not above 34 were living in 1827' (*Report from Committee on West Coast of Africa*, Part II, p. 247).

The Commissioners of Inquiry, 1827, did not mention any other immigration than that from Barbados, and it is therefore impossible to tell how they obtained the high figure of 141 'West Indians and Americans'.

[3] 'West Indians and Americans'; estimate by Henry William Macaulay, *Report from Committee on Aborigines*, 1837, Minutes, p. 92.

[4] See *Report from Committee on West Coast of Africa*, 1842, Part II, pp. 325, 328.　　　　[5] From Barbados.

[6] 30 males and 43 females.　　　　[7] See *Reports made in 1844 and 1845 by Butts*, &c., pp. 38–41.

[8] 58 males and 48 females.　　　　[9] 34 male and 48 female Americans or settlers from Liberia.

[10] See *State of Colonial Possessions 1847*, p. 198; *1848*, p. 304; *1850*, p. 185; *1851*, p. 182; *1860*, Part II, p. 24.　　　　[11] 'American black people from Liberia.'　　　　[12] 'Americans.'

Most of these figures appear to be untrustworthy.

[1] 'They were employed for two or three years on the public works, and then set at liberty: they proved a very industrious, well-ordered set of people' (*Report from Commissioners on West Coast of Africa*, 1842, Part II, p. 247). See also *Reports made in 1844 and 1845 by Butts*, &c., p. 26.

[2] *Handbook of Sierra Leone*, p. 35.

[3] Henry William Macaulay, on 14 June 1842, told the Committee on the West Coast of Africa: '. . . the distance between Sierra Leone and Liberia is so short, that many of the disappointed colonists from the latter have lately established themselves at Freetown' (*Report*, Part I, p. 321; see also ibid., Part II, p. 247).

III. Total Population

1. *Colony*

In the early days the population fluctuated considerably. The first black and white settlers from England who came on 9 May 1787 numbered 377. They had been reduced to 65 (or slightly less) when in February and March 1792 nearly 100 whites arrived from England and 1,131 negroes from Nova Scotia.[1] By the end of the year the total population had dropped to about 1,150, and it was lower still when on 30 September 1800 about 550 Maroons arrived from Nova Scotia with a detachment of 45 white soldiers. They were reinforced in February 1801 by a detachment of 50 white soldiers of the Royal African Corps.

According to the census of 29 March 1802 there were 1,641 people in the Colony, including 95 military. 'In the year 1807, the population amounted to 1,871 persons.'[2] From then on it increased by leaps and bounds through the importation of slaves captured on board ships. The census of April 1811, it is true, showed only 1,917 civilians 'within the walls of Sierra Leone' (Freetown), but the Liberated Africans were not included, and the total population of the Colony must have been about 3,500.[3] 'The population of the Colony on 9th July 1814 was estimated to amount to 5,520.'[4] In a report dated 26 August 1816, the Assistant Secretary to the Settlements and Schools of the Church Missionary Society on the Western Coast of Africa, who had left Sierra Leone on 7 June 1816, related:

The number of inhabitants in the Colony is calculated, I am told, on a moderate scale, at between 9,000 and 10,000. But there being no census, I could not obtain an accurate return of the number of adults or children. . . .

Free Town appears to be in an improving state. It may contain, including the adjoining towns, upwards of 3,000 people, or about one-third of the population of the whole Colony. . . .

Adjoining Free Town is the Kroomans Town, which contains, it is said, 700 inhabitants.[5]

[1] The Directors of the African Institution said: '. . . the whole population . . . previous to the year 1801, never exceeded 1,200 persons of all ages' (*Special Report 1815*, p. 19). But the population actually exceeded 1,200 in March 1792.

[2] Hoare, p. 310.

[3] Walker says that the population of the Colony in 1811 'amounted to nearly 4,500, of which 2,500 were liberated slaves' (*Church of England Mission*, p. xxix), but he evidently misinterpreted a statement in the *Sixth Report of the African Institution 1812* which said (p. 74): 'The report [of Commissioners on Coast of Africa] states that there are 400 houses within the walls of Freetown, Sierra Leone, containing 1,917 inhabitants. This is entirely exclusive of the slaves who have been liberated under the sentence of the Court of Admiralty, and who are supposed now to amount to upwards of 2,500.' Actually the number of slaves liberated under the sentence of the Court of Admiralty up to the day when the Directors of the African Institution submitted their report (25 Mar. 1812) was only 2,361, and the number of Liberated Africans living in the Colony on that date can hardly have exceeded 2,000.

The African Institution, on the other hand, evidently understated the population when it said in an answer to a query proposed by Viscount Castlereagh: 'The population of that colony in 1809, did not exceed 1,500 souls' (*Papers relating to Slave Trade*, 1819, p. 19).

[4] *Handbook of Sierra Leone*, p. 34. First Colonial Surgeon Charles Stormouth, in a petition to Earl Bathurst, 22 June 1819, certainly understated the population of the Colony when he said that on 1 Sept. 1815 it 'amounted to 5,000' (C.O. 267, vol. xlix, No. 201).

[5] *Missionary Register 1816*, p. 401.

The number of people living outside Freetown was certainly over-stated.

The official statements concerning the population in 1817 are somewhat confusing. In answering a Resolution of the House of Commons adopted on 14 June 1824, which asked among other things for the census returns of 1817, the Colonial Secretary wrote that no census was taken in 1817,[1] but reproduced in the same document[2] a Note which indicated that the population at the 'Census (March 1817)' was 7,313. The explanation is to be found in two tables transmitted by Earl Bathurst to the Church Missionary Society. The first showed the 'Population of Free Town, Sierra Leone (Exclusive of those Persons, liberated from Slavery, who are at present resident therein)' according to 'Census taken in March, 1817'. The second gave an 'Account of the Captured Negroes in the Colony of Sierra Leone' dated 1 April 1817.[3] The first table showed 2,183 inhabitants of Freetown; the second (which was not based on a census) showed 5,130 Captured Negroes (including 1,438 living in Freetown). The total of 7,313 thus excluded the people living outside Freetown who were not captured slaves; it excluded also 'the European Officers and Soldiers, and the Native Troops', and the Kroomen.[4] It was possibly incomplete even as regards some groups included.[5]

The census taken on 31 December 1818 showed a total civilian population of 9,565 (excluding apparently the military pensioners and their families). A Note accompanying the Return said:

The increase of Population in the grand Total, since last Census (March 1817), is 2,252; including 1,190 Negroes landed since that period, and the Kroomen.

The *Missionary Register* added the following footnote to the figure 2,252:

But there being, at the time of the former Return, 650 Kroomen then in the Colony but not reckoned in the Return, the actual increase, the Kroomen being reckoned in both cases, is 1,602.

Actually, the total of 9,565 ascertained on 31 December 1818 included 34 Europeans and Nova Scotians living outside Freetown and 746 Kroomen. The groups enumerated in 1817, therefore, had increased from 7,313 to 8,785 or by 1,472. Including the Kroomen there was an increase from about 7,963 to 9,531 or by about 1,568. (The Liberated Africans had increased from 5,130 to 6,406.)

The census of 8 July 1820 showed a total civilian population of 12,509. A Note accompanying the Return said:

The Increase of Population in the Peninsula since last Census, 31st December, 1818, is 2,956[6] Persons; which includes 943 liberated Africans, landed here in 1819 and 1820, from Slave Vessels; 85 Persons from Barbadoes, last from Honduras; and 1,030 discharged Soldiers and Families of the 2nd and 4th West India Regiments

[1] See *Accounts relating to Sierra Leone*, 1825, p. 40.   [2] See ibid., p. 14.
[3] See *Missionary Register*, Aug. 1817, pp. 355–6.
[4] 'The Census is exclusive of an average of 650 persons, Natives of the Kroo Country, constantly resident in the Colony, who are hired as porters, labourers on the King's works, &c.'
[5] Only 421 Maroons were listed as against 610 at the next census (31 Dec. 1818).
[6] Should read 2,944.

and Royal African Corps; Thus making an Increase of 888[1] by Births, and Natives coming to the Colony for Employ or Protection.

As shown above, I am inclined to think that a number of Natives was omitted at the census.

The census of 1 January 1822 showed a total civilian population of 15,081. The large increase was probably due in part to a more complete enumeration of the Natives. The census return was accompanied by the following Note dated 'Secretary's Office, Freetown, August 1st 1822':

1,590 Africans, Males and Females, have been received from Slave Vessels and established in the Villages since the 1st January last, making a total Population of 16,671 Persons at the present Date.[2]

TABLE 6. *Civilian Population by Districts, Sierra Leone, 31 December 1818, 8 July 1820, and 1 January 1822*[1]

Parish or District	Principal town	Founded	Population		
			1818	1820	1822
St. George . . .	Freetown	1787	4,430	4,785	5,643
St. Charles . . .	Regent	1812	1,177	1,218	1,551
St. Patrick . . .	Kissey	1817	860	1,033	1,069
St. Andrew . . .	Gloucester	1816	356	563	697
St. James . . .	Bathurst	1818	222	469	393
St. Peter . . .	Leopold	1817	308	469	420
St. John . . .	Charlotte	1818	205	268	420
St. Thomas . . .	Hastings	1819	—	195	171
St. Michael . . .	Waterloo	1819	—	353	519
Arthur	Wellington	1819	—	456	547
St. Paul	Wilberforce	1812	203	409	595
St. Henry . . .	York	1819	—	297	494
St. Edward . . .	Kent	1819	167	296	418
Leicester . . .	Leicester	1809	69	78	30
28 Native Villages . .	..	..	1,141[2]	1,468[2]	1,964
Islands in river . .	..	..	213	115	..[3]
St. Ann . . .	Gambia Island	1820	—	37	..
Banana Islands . .	..	1820	—	—	150
Total . . .	..	..	9,565[4]	12,509	15,081

[1] For year of foundation see *Report of Commissioners of Inquiry*, 1827, First Part, p. 33; for population, see *Missionary Register 1820*, p. 381, *Accounts relating to Sierra Leone*, 1825, pp. 13–21. Figures exclude Isles de Los, acquired in 1818.

[2] Villages in peninsula.

[3] No Return received.

[4] Including 214 'Church Missionary Society Christian Institution, Leicester Mountain'. See also *Sierra Leone Almanac 1822*, p. 60: '1820. Church Missionary Society removed their establishment, from Leicester Mountain to Regent, and the buildings have been appropriated as a General Hospital for Liberated Africans since.'

The census returns of April 1826, as revised by the Commissioners of

[1] Should read 876.

[2] The population on 1 Aug. cannot, of course, be obtained by adding to the census figure of 1 Jan. the number of Liberated Africans established in the villages in the meantime. The *New Times* quoted by Macqueen (*Colonial Controversy*, pp. 102–3) made an additional mistake by stating that the population was 16,671 on 1 Jan. 1823, while Governor MacCarthy in his Dispatch to Earl Bathurst, 14 Sept. 1823 (C.O. 267, vol. lviii, No. 340), erroneously said that 'the population had increased on the 1st January 1822 to 16,671'.

Inquiry,[1] showed a civilian population of 17,354.[2] In the following five years the influx of Liberated Africans was extraordinarily large. The census taken on 30 June 1831 in the villages showed a population of 22,783 (excluding Europeans), and the census taken in the third quarter of that year in Freetown showed a total population of 7,839.[3] The returns of the censuses taken from 1833 to 1931 are summarized in Table 7. It appears that the civilian population in 1840 (42,765) was about three times as large as in 1822, the increase being due exclusively to the importation of captured slaves. But in 1841–51 many newly liberated Africans emigrated to the West Indies, and the influx of captured slaves was small thereafter. In the 1850s apparently fewer strangers than usual came to the Colony and more people migrated from the Colony.[4] The population seems to have increased again after 1858 but—leaving out of consideration newly acquired territories—it was not much larger in 1880 than in 1840. In studying Table 7 (p. 159), it should, however, be remembered that the censuses were somewhat defective, and the fluctuations from year to year probably do not convey a true picture of the facts.[5]

[1] See *Report*, First Part, Appendix A, No. 38.

[2] The population was understated in the annual *Blue Books* (*1826*, p. 136; *1827*, p. 64):

	1826	1827
Whites.	87	87
Liberated Africans in their Villages (Dec.)	10,123	11,891
King's Troops (1826, 480 Whites, 820 Natives; 1827, 20 Officers, 714 Soldiers)	1,300	734
Resident Strangers:		
Kroomen from the Neighbourhood of Cape Palmas	1,100	900
Foulahs and others from the Coast to the North of Sierra Leone and from the Interior	400	400
Coloured Inhabitants of Freetown and its Vicinity including the Liberated Africans who have left their villages	3,500	3,500
Total	16,510	17,512

'N.B. There are a few Timmanee Villages in the Peninsula, which are not included; neither are the Isles de Los.'

According to these returns the civilians would have numbered only 15,210 and 16,778 respectively. There must have been at least 21,000 by the end of 1827. Kenneth Macaulay, on the other hand, overestimated the population when he said that on 1 Jan. 1826 it 'had increased to upwards of 20,000' (*Sierra Leone vindicated*, p. 46).

[3] See C.O. 267, vol. cxi. In *Blue Book 1831*, pp. 114–15, the total population of Freetown is given as 8,524 (including 36 Aliens and Resident Strangers) and the total population of the rest of the Colony as 23,130. These figures may refer to the end of 1831. In *Blue Book 1832*, pp. 114–15, 'the population of Freetown is filled up from the Census taken for 1831', while the population of the rest of the Colony is put at 21,076, which probably was an understatement.

[4] In his Report on the Blue Book for 1854, Acting Governor Dougan said: '. . . there has been a considerable decrease of alien residents, and since the passing of the alien children ordinance it has had the effect of driving very many persons from the colony, and transient native traders are now extremely cautious in bringing with them persons under age. There are very many absentees trading in the neighbourhood of Lagos, between which place and this port there is a very great and increasing traffic in palm oil, sprung up within the last three years . . . . There is also a very great inducement for trading in the neighbouring rivers, the produce trade, particularly in ground nuts, having considerably increased . . . .' (*State of Colonial Possessions 1854*, p. 188.)

[5] The figures for Strangers are particularly uncertain. In 1831 only 36 'Aliens and Resident Strangers' were listed in Freetown and none elsewhere. No figures whatever are entered for 1832–5, and the *Blue Book* for 1832 said: 'There is a Constant Ingress and Egress of Native Strangers principally of the Foulah and Mandingo Nations, who come to the Colony for the purposes of Trade and remain from One to six Weeks. There is another class of Natives denominated

All figures up to 1860 covered only the peninsula (including Banana Islands), so far as it belonged to the Colony.[1] The Isles de Los and Sherbro were excluded. In 1861 a portion of Quiah was acquired, and this territory was included in the Return for 1868[2] which showed a total

"Kroomen" who come to the Colony to seek for Labour and are principally employed in Merchants Stores, Timber Factories, and as Domestic Servants. They return to their Country after remaining in the Colony about three Years, and are replaced by fresh Adventurers.' It is possible, however, that prior to 1836 at least the Kroomen were included in the general population, i.e. the total population excluding Aliens and Resident Strangers. (The 1835 Blue Book showed for Freetown 7,041 males, 5,117 females, and no strangers; the 1836 Blue Book showed 5,646 males, 4,941 females, and 1,176 strangers.) From 1836 on, the headings in the Blue Books said 'Aliens and Resident Strangers, not included in preceding Columns', and in some years, for example 1844, all Strangers were entered separately. But in other years most strangers seem to have been included in the general population. Thus, for 1847, the Blue Book gives as general population 45,006 and as Aliens and Resident Strangers 655 (all in Freetown), while the Report on the Blue Book shows a general population of 41,343 (Europeans, Maroons, Nova Scotians, Americans from Liberia, West Indians, and Liberated Africans), 3,334 resident Strangers (Kroomen, Mandingo Sousoos, Foulahs, Sherbros and others), and 'about' 1,000 Aliens and transient strangers. For 1848 the Blue Book gives as general population 45,320 and as Aliens and Resident Strangers 1,191, while the Report on the Blue Book shows a general population of 41,879, as resident Strangers 3,441, and as non-resident Aliens 1,191. For 1850 the Blue Book gave as general population 44,472 and as Aliens and Resident Strangers 1,000, while the Report on the Blue Book showed as general population 41,396, as Kroomen 560, and as Native Strangers 3,516. To what extent Aliens and Resident Strangers were omitted altogether it is difficult to tell. The Commissioner of Inquiry R. R. Madden, commenting on the 927 Aliens and Resident Strangers reported for 1839, said: 'I consider the number of aliens and resident strangers set down in the preceding statement as falling far short of the real number of Kroomen, Mandingoes, Akoos, Foulahs, and refugees from Liberia, settled or living as temporary residents in the colony. I believe they amount to about 2,800 in all, 1,873 more than is set down in the above return' (*Report on West Coast of Africa*, 1842, Part II, p. 248). He, therefore, put the total population for 1839 at 42,000.

For 1851, 1855, 1858, and 1860 no Aliens and Resident Strangers are entered in the Blue Book. In 1851 they were no doubt included in the general population (44,501) since the Report on the Blue Book shows as total population 44,501 including 555 Kroomen and 1,766 Native Strangers. It is probable that the Aliens and Resident Strangers who then were few were likewise included in the general population in 1855 and 1858, and they certainly were so in 1860 (41,624) since the Report on the Blue Book shows as total population 41,624 including 363 Kroomen and 1,984 Native Strangers.

I computed the general population for 1881 and 1891 by deducting from the total population the Whites on Ships in Harbour and the (Coloured) Transient Traders and Strangers, and for 1901–1921 by deducting all persons on Ships in Harbour and the Transient Traders and Strangers, but entered for all these years as Strangers only the Transient Traders and Strangers. I computed the general population for 1931 by deducting all persons on Ships in Harbour and the few (108) 'Itinerant Strangers' whom I assumed to have been all enumerated in Freetown.

[1] The area was given for 1831 as 195 square miles (see *Blue Book 1831*, p. 114), for 1833–5 as 339 square miles (see ibid. *1833*, p. 118; *1834*, p. 118; *1835*, p. 118), for 1836–8 as 389 square miles (see ibid. *1836*, p. 118; *1837*, p. 118; *1838*, p. 118), for 1839–41 as 327 square miles (see ibid. *1839*, p. 134; *1840*, p. 134; *1841*, p. 134), for 1843 as 289 square miles (see ibid. *1843*, p. 134). Commissioner Madden said in 1841: 'The extent of territory now comprising the settlement is about 300 square miles' (*Report from Committee on West Coast of Africa*, Part II, p. 246). This figure was also given in most official documents up to 1861 (see, for example, *Statistical Tables, Colonial Possessions 1860*, p. 425), and in some even later (see *Colonial Office List 1862*, p. 60; *1863*, p. 71; *1864*, p. 77; *1865*, p. 84; *1866*, p. 88; *1867*, p. 116; *1868*, p. 123; *1869*, p. 126; *1870*, p. 129; *1871*, p. 131; *1872*, p. 127; *1873*, p. 132; *1874*, p. 130; *1875*, p. 133; *1876*, p. 147; *1877*, p. 158; *1878*, p. 171; *1879*, p. 173; *1880*, p. 178; *1881*, p. 183; *1882*, p. 186; *1883*, p. 192; *1884*, p. 187; *1885*, p. 189).

[2] The total area of the Colony was now given as 468 square miles (see, for example, *Statistical Tables, Colonial Possessions 1862*, p. 453 to *1879–81*, p. 376; *Colonial Office List 1866*, p. 9, *1867*, p. 9, *1868*, p. 9, *1869*, p. 9, *1870*, p. 11, *1871*, p. 11, *1872*, p. 12, *1873*, p. 12, *1874*, p. 12, *1875*, p. 14, *1876*, p. 18 to *1886*, p. 18; *Blue Book 1884*, p. 232). In 1883 the Sulyma District (later called

TABLE 7. *Population of Sierra Leone, 1833–1931*[1]

Year	Excluding Aliens and Resident Strangers			Aliens and Resident Strangers[2]		Total
	Freetown	Rest of Colony	Colony	Freetown	Rest of Colony	
1833	9,937	22,074	32,011	..	..	32,011
1834	11,412	22,111	33,523	..	..	33,523
1835	12,158	22,641	34,799	..	..	34,799
1836	10,587	25,091	35,678	1,176	609	37,463
1837	..	25,206	..	..	290	..
1838	13,523	25,418	38,941	1,392	289	40,622
1839	13,435	25,698	39,133	585	342	40,060
1840	13,546	28,848	42,394	195	176	42,765
1841	..	30,370	..	..	25	..
1842	11,700	28,139	39,839	1,675	2,133	43,647
1843	12,569	26,227	38,796	1,152	1,853	41,801
1844	12,580	28,653	41,233	1,950	1,752	44,935
1845	16,349	27,273	43,622	185	1,131	44,938
1846	14,195	27,540	41,735	227	1,168	43,130
1847	16,228	28,778	45,006	655	—	45,661
1848	17,020	28,300	45,320	1,170	21	46,511
1849	16,033	27,848	43,881	2,518	10	46,409
1850	16,679	27,793	44,472	1,000		45,472
1851	18,027	26,474	44,501	—	—	44,501
1855	16,022	24,361	40,383	..	..	..
1858	14,587	23,731	38,318	..	..	..
1860	18,035	23,589	41,624	—	—	41,624
1868	20,027	29,202	49,229	1,947	4,198	55,374
1871	13,937	23,152	37,089	893	954	38,936
1881	20,739	38,342	59,081	1,084	273	60,438
1891	28,582	43,920	72,502	1,091	528	74,121
1901	33,149	41,530	74,679	1,135	423	76,237
1911	33,247	40,851	74,098	455	376	74,929
1921	43,409	40,667	84,076	551	141	84,768
1931	55,250	41,064	96,314	108	—	96,422

[1] See *Blue Book 1833*, pp. 118–19, to *1838*, pp. 118–19; *1839*, pp. 134–5, to *1847*, pp. 134–5; *1848*, pp. 218–19; *1849*, pp. 134–5; *1850*, pp. 138–9; *1851*, pp. 138–9; *1855*, pp. 162–3; *1858*, pp. 159–60; *1860*, pp. 164–5; *1868*, pp. 174–5; *1871*, pp. 172–3; *Census Report 1881*, p. 6, and 'Recapitulation'; *1891*, p. 16, and 'Recapitulation'; *1901*, pp. 20, 31; *1911*, pp. 21, 39–40; *1921*, pp. 20, 40–1; *1931*, pp. 40, 72. The figures prior to 1855 exclude troops in garrison (they numbered 239 in 1851, and 306 in 1854; see *Blue Book 1851*, p. 49, *1855*, p. 62). The figures for 1881–1931 exclude the population on board ship in harbour (for 1881 only Whites).

[2] See footnote 5, pp. 157–8 above.

population of 55,374.[1] For the area covered by the census of 1840 this Return showed an increase from 42,765 to 47,655; in 1871 the population was returned (far too low) as 38,936 and in 1881 as 46,418.

The censuses of 1881–1931 did not all refer to the same areas. In

South Eastern District) was acquired by treaty, and the total area of the Colony was now estimated at 3,000 square miles (see *Blue Book 1885*, p. 232, *1886*, p. 250, *1887*, p. 246, *1888*, p. 244, *1889*, p. 242; *Colonial Office List 1886*, p. 246, *1887*, pp. 18, 262, *1888*, pp. 16, 254, *1889*, Table facing p. 18, and p. 212, *1890*, Table facing p. 18) or 4,000 square miles (see *Blue Book 1890*, p. 248, *1891*, R, pp. 1–2, to *1911*, R, pp. 1–2; *Colonial Office List 1890*, p. 215, *1891*, p. 222, *1892*, p. 194, *1893*, p. 201, *1894*, p. 205, *1895*, p. 205, *1896*, p. 209, *1897*, p. 212, *1898*, p. 210, *1899*, p. 233).

[1] Including 5,160 (3,039 residents, 2,121 strangers) in Quiah and 2,559 (1,725 residents, 834 strangers) in Bulama.

order to make the results comparable they may be summarized as follows:

	1881	1891	1901	1911	1921	1931
(a) Peninsula, including Quiah . . .	53,862	58,448	..	..	..	..
(b) Peninsula, excluding Quiah . . .	46,418	..	67,782	68,115	79,561	90,168
(c) as (b) and Bonthe, York Island, Tassoh Island . . .	..	..	74,351	74,808	85,163	96,573
(d) Total area covered by census . .	60,546	74,835	76,655	75,572	85,163	96,573

2. Protectorate

In the last years of the nineteenth century the population of the Protectorate was 'variously estimated at from 750,000 to 2,000,000'.[1] In 1901 it was estimated at 949,827, in 1911 at 1,327,560, in 1921 at 1,455,510, and in 1931 at 1,672,058.[2] The estimate for 1901 was no doubt too low, and the more recent estimates are quite uncertain. To what extent the population may have increased between 1921 and 1931 will be discussed in the section 'Population Growth'.

3. Colony and Protectorate

The total population shown in the census reports of 1921 and 1931 was as follows:[3]

	Colony		Protectorate		Total	
	1921	1931	1921	1931	1921	1931
'Resident' Africans . .	84,054	95,558	1,454,859	1,671,055	1,538,913	1,766,613
Maritime[1] Africans . .	—	84	—	—	—	84
'Resident' non-Africans .	990	864	651	1,003	1,641	1,867
Maritime[1] non-Africans .	119	67	—	—	119	67
Total . .	85,163	96,573	1,455,510	1,672,058	1,540,673	1,768,631

[1] Persons on board ship in harbour.

The area of the Colony and Protectorate was given in 1931 as 27,928 square miles. The number of inhabitants per square mile would therefore appear to have been 63. In the Colony it was 372, in the Northern Pro-

[1] Colonial Office List 1900, p. 211; 1901, p. 255.

[2] These were the estimates made in the years in which censuses were taken in the Colony. The estimates made in intercensal years were quite erratic. 'The population of the Colony and Protectorate of Sierra Leone was estimated at 1,680,000 at the end of 1905' (Statistical Tables, Colonial Possessions 1905, p. 488). 'The total population of the Colony and Protectorate of Sierra Leone was estimated at 1,208,100 at the end of 1907' (ibid. 1907, p. 430). Governor Leslie Probyn, in an address delivered before the African Society on 6 Feb. 1907, said that in Sierra Leone 'there are about 2,000,000 inhabitants' ('Sierra Leone and the Natives of West Africa', p. 253; see also ibid., p. 255). The Medical Report for 1915 spoke (p. 41) of 'the population of 1,100,000 dwelling within the 34,000 square miles comprising the Colony and Protectorate of Sierra Leone'; the Medical Report for 1916 said (p. 43): 'The entire area of the Colony and Protectorate is 24,908 square miles with a population of 1,403,132 persons.'

[3] See Census Report 1921, p. 8; 1931, pp. 20-1, 72-3, 82.

TABLE 8. *Population Density, Sierra Leone, 1931*[1]

Districts	Area sq. m.	Natives	Non-natives	Total	Population per sq. m.
COLONY					
Total	259	95,558	864	96,422	372
NORTHERN PROVINCE OF PROTECTORATE					
Port Loko	1,836	169,954	808	170,762	93
Kambia	1,154	108,342	392	108,734	94
Karene	2,656	150,047	51	150,098	57
Bombali	2,765	244,220	464	244,684	88
Koinadugi	5,514	109,778	30	109,808	20
Total	13,925	782,341	1,745	784,086	56
SOUTHERN PROVINCE OF PROTECTORATE					
Moyamba	2,665	131,815	560	132,375	50
Bonthe	1,350	97,822	204	98,026	73
Pujehun	2,129	122,779	202	122,981	58
Bo	2,150	168,264	734	168,998	79
Kenema	1,774	133,932	445	134,377	76
Kailahun	1,548	156,751	362	157,113	101
Kono	2,128	74,086	16	74,102	35
Total	13,744	885,449	2,523	887,972	65
PROTECTORATE					
Total	27,669	1,667,790	4,268	1,672,058	60
COLONY AND PROTECTORATE					
Total	27,928	1,763,348	5,132	1,768,480	63

[1] See *Census Report 1931*, pp. 20-1, 82-3, 165.

vince of the Protectorate 56 (varying between 20 in Koinadugi District and 94 in Kambia District), in the Southern Province 65 (varying between 35 in Kono District and 101 in Kailahun District).

For 31 December 1939 the population has been given as 2,000,000.[1] But this is apparently a mere guess.

IV. COMPOSITION OF AFRICAN POPULATION

Origin The origin of the African population up to 1860 is discussed in the section 'Early Colonization'. The results are summarized in Table 9. No data apparently are available for the following two decades. The results of the censuses from 1881 to 1931 are summarized in Table 10 (p. 163).

The decrease in the number of Liberated Africans from 1881 to 1891 is in part due 'to the fact that the children of some of their descendants have described themselves as Natives' (children of strange tribes born in Sierra Leone).[2] This explains also in part the enormous increase in the number of Natives. The apparently large increase in the number of 'Other

[1] See *Statistical Year-Book of the League of Nations 1942/44*, p. 12.
[2] See *Census Report 1891*, p. 6.

TABLE 9. *Civilian African Population by Origin, Sierra Leone, 1802-60.*[1]

Origin	29 Mar. 1802	Apr. 1811	31 Dec. 1818	8 July 1820	1 Jan. 1822	Apr. 1826	31 Dec. 1844	1847	1848	1850	1851	1860
Nova Scotians	904	982	691	730	722	578	597	568	560	49	112	69
Maroons	515	807	610	594	601	636[2]	470	460	462	15	73	22
Liberated Africans	—	..	6,406	8,076[3]	7,969	10,714	36,990	40,026	20,619	20,243	20,461	15,782
Descendants of Liberated Africans[4]	—	..							19,624	20,766	21,250	22,593
Military Pensioners	—	—	..	1,216	1,103	949	382	..	291	..	..	..
West Indians	—	—	..	..	85	141	106	104	123	91	95	164
Liberians	—	—	—	—		—	82	90	90	121	64	50
Kroomen	60	100	746[5]	727[5]	947[5]	947[6]	717	730	743	560	555	363
Other Natives[7]						3,276	2,970	2,604	2,698	..	..	..
Native Strangers	40		997	1,046	3,526			1,000[8]	1,191	3,516	1,766	1,984
Total	1,519	1,889	9,450	12,389	14,953	17,241	44,659[9]	44,911[10]	46,401	45,361	44,376	41,493[11]

[1] See for 1802, *Report from Committee on Petition of Sierra Leone Company*, 1804, p. 127; 1811, *Report of Commissioners on Coast of Africa*, 1811, p. 8; 1818–22, *Accounts relating to Population, &c. of Sierra Leone*, 1825, pp. 13–21; 1826, *Report of Commissioners of Inquiry*, 1827, First Part, Appendix A, No. 38; 1844, *Reports made in 1844 and 1845 by Butts*, &c., pp. 38–41; 1847–60, *State of Colonial Possessions 1847*, p. 198, *1848*, pp. 304–5, *1850*, p. 185, *1851*, p. 182, *1860*, Part II, p. 24. The data do not all refer to the same area. Those for 1811 cover only Freetown, those for 1818 cover only the Peninsula. Those for 1820, 1822, and 1826 exclude the Isles de Los.

[2] The census showed actually 681 Maroons; see *Report of the Commissioners of Inquiry*, First Part, p. 14.

[3] The survivors of the 85 convicts who arrived in 1819 from Barbados may be included in this group.

[4] Descendants of Liberated Africans born in Colony.

[5] Excluding Kroomen employed in His Majesty's ships or up the river in the timber trade; see *Report of the Commissioners of Inquiry*, First Part, p. 17.

[6] Taken from 1822 census.

[7] The figures are most defective. I suppose that in 1850, 1851, and 1860 the resident Natives who were not Kroomen were entered as Colony-born Descendants of Liberated Africans or as Native Strangers.

[8] About.

[9] The total of the various items is only 42,315.

[10] The total of the various items is only 45,582.

[11] The total of the various items is only 41,027.

TABLE 10. *African Population by Origin, Colony of Sierra Leone, 1881–1931*[1]

Origin	1881	1891	1901	1911	1921	1931
Liberated Africans and their Descendants (Creoles) . . .	35,430	33,212[2]	33,518[3]	31,078	28,222	32,848
Mulattoes and persons of mixed blood				204	358	150
Natives, i.e. children of strange tribes born in Sierra Leone. .	3,384	6,729	8,037	42,587	55,230	62,548
Other Africans	21,068	33,807	33,430			
West Indians	393	863	1,177	799	244	96
Total	60,275	74,611	76,162	74,668	84,054	95,642

[1] See *Census Report 1881*, 'Recapitulation'; *1891*, 'Recapitulation'; *1901*, p. 30; *1911*, p. 39; *1921*, p. 40; *1931*, pp. 73, 78.

[2] There was 'a small number of persons of mixed blood estimated to be about 450' (*Census Report 1891*, p. 5), most of whom were probably included in the above figure.

[3] There was 'a small number of persons of mixed blood' (ibid. *1901*, p. 6), 'most of whom would be classified as Creoles' (Descendants of Liberated Africans); see ibid. *1911*, p. 11.

Africans' was due in part to the incomplete enumeration of Sherbro in 1881.[1] The increase in the number of West Indians was 'due to more West Indian troops being now stationed here than in 1881'.[2]

The increase in the number of Natives from 1891 to 1901 was said to have been again only apparent.[3] There would have been a considerable increase instead of a slight decrease in the number of 'Other Africans' if the greater part of Sherbro had not been omitted at the 1901 census.[4]

At the 1911 census the distinction of 'Natives, i.e. children born of strange tribes in Sierra Leone' was dropped.

. . . as in 1901, 8,036 persons had been classified under this head, it is obvious that in 1911 the remaining classifications must have been augmented in numbers in order to make up for the elimination of the 'Natives' heading. In Freetown alone 1,263 persons were ranked as Natives in 1901; examination has been made of the Census returns for Freetown of that year, and judging by the names it is estimated that between 500 and 600 persons, returned in that year as Natives, should probably have been returned as Creoles. In other districts similar search has been made with similar results . . . . [5]

The increase in the number of 'Other Africans' (including Natives) would have been greater if Kikonkeh had not been omitted, by mistake, from the 1911 census, and if the Isles de Los had not been ceded to France.

The 1911 census report defined the 'Descendants of Liberated Africans or Creoles' as follows:

These people are the descendants of (1) original settlers brought to the Colony in 1787 and subsequent years, (2) the Nova Scotian and (3) Maroon Immigrants, and

[1] The number of Mendis and Sherbros enumerated in 1891 was 14,963 as compared with 5,970 in 1881. See *Census Report 1891*, p. 5.

[2] Ibid., p. 6; see also ibid., p. 4. The further increase in 1891–1901 was attributed to the same cause (see ibid. *1901*, p. 8), and the decrease in 1901–11 to a reduction in the West Indian troops (see ibid. *1911*, p. 12). The drop in 1911–21 was 'due to the withdrawal of the West Indian Regiment' (ibid. *1921*, p. 12).

[3] '. . . there is little doubt that many liberated Africans, Mendis, Timmanees, &c., have been described under this head' (ibid. *1901*, p. 7).

[4] The number of Mendis and Sherbros enumerated in 1901 was only 10,893. See ibid.

[5] Ibid. *1911*, p. 11. The census report assumed that about 10 per cent. of those counted as 'Natives' in 1901 should have been returned as 'Creoles'.

(4) the Liberated Africans who were domiciled here under the provisions of the Acts for the abolition and suppression of the slave trade.[1]

The 1921 census report used the same terminology, but the 1931 census report stated:

An innovation of some importance was introduced by the use of the term 'Sierra Leonean' in order to distinguish the Colony Non-native African from the Protectorate native tribesman and native 'foreigner'.

These Colony Africans, locally and incorrectly known as Creoles, were officially classified in previous censuses as 'Liberated Africans and their descendants'. This term, however, has lately fallen into disuse, and it is clear that it is not a suitable description, nor is it acceptable to these people. Accordingly, instructions were received that the term should not be applied in this Census and that 'Sierra Leonean' should be substituted.

The feelings and views of the Africans concerned can be easily understood. They do not wish to be known indefinitely by a name which merely connotes their former unfortunate status. The Colony Africans are a separate people and are becoming a distinct type. They have lost association and affinity with their various tribes, but as yet have not a name which gives them a sufficient ethnological or ethnographic description; the official adoption, therefore, of the name 'Sierra Leonean' from their country of settlement is an appropriate choice.[2]

But this innovation was not a success as many people described themselves as Sierra Leoneans who should have been counted as Natives or as Mulattoes.

. . . now that the term Sierra Leonean has been introduced, a large number of persons not entitled to use it apply it to themselves or, in ignorance, really think it applies to them. There is a marked and growing tendency for the educated native to style himself 'Creole' both in the Colony and the Protectorate. A large number have been to Christian schools and, becoming Christians, adopt Christian names and lose identity with their tribes. The progeny of non-natives and natives also class themselves as non-natives.

Another point to notice both in this connection and as a matter of social importance, is the very prevalent practice of fosterage. A very large number of native children in Freetown and in the Colony are acquired by Sierra Leoneans from their parents or guardians on the understanding that they are to be educated. They are useful acquisitions and perform domestic and other work. They are, no doubt, for the most part sent to school or taught a smattering of 'book', but their position is merely that of servants. A great number of these children probably do not return to the Protectorate after school age: they remain in Freetown or elsewhere in the Colony and perhaps obtain casual employment, or they remain with the family they lived with and worked for and usually take that family's name. Most of those who do return to the Protectorate become unsettled and more than likely drift back to the Colony. These persons lose all touch with their families and tribe and become self-styled 'Creoles'.

A considerable number of Colony-born natives insist on calling themselves 'Creoles', either through false pride or ignorance. There is, of course, an increasing number of these natives of all tribes, and many natives have been Colony-born for two or three generations. The greater number call themselves 'Creoles' or Sierra Leoneans. Their births are registered in Freetown or in the registration district in which they reside, but there is no registration by tribe. Many become Christians and are the children of Christianized parents. They live amongst non-natives and adopt non-native habits and customs. They sever themselves from their tribes and know no allegiance to any tribal ruler and become in fact, if not 'de jure', non-natives.

[1] *Census Report 1911*, p. 11. [2] Ibid. *1931*, p. 4.

For Census purposes there is very little more than the word of the person concerned to go by in deciding whether he or she is a Sierra Leonean. Although enumerators were instructed to explain that natives should enter themselves by the name of their tribe, whether born in the Colony or not, and care was taken to examine Schedules for errors of this kind, it is thought that many Colony-born natives were returned as Sierra Leoneans.[1]

It appears that many show a certain amount of reluctance in classifying themselves as 'mixed blood', or Mulatto, and seem to prefer the adoption of the new name 'Sierra Leonean'.[2]

The 1931 report intimates that the increase in the number of descendants of Liberated Africans was, therefore, smaller than appears from a comparison of the number of 'Sierra Leoneans' ascertained in 1931 (32,846) and the number of 'Liberated Africans and their Descendants' found in 1921 (28,222), but suggests that a considerable part of the increase was not due to a change in terminology.

The increase amongst Sierra Leoneans is partly due to persons returning from the Protectorate . . . who have no doubt, returned to the Colony owing to lack of trade. A large number may, for the same reason, have returned from adjacent Colonies.[3]

This may be so. But nearly four-fifths of the apparent increase occurred among females, and the number of females who returned from the Protectorate cannot have been very great. I am, therefore, inclined to think that the apparent increase was largely due to the inclination of native women to classify themselves as Sierra Leoneans.

		Colony			Protectorate		
		Males	Females	Total	Males	Females	Total
Descendants of Liberated	} 1911[1]	13,235	17,843	31,078	1,494	1,460	2,954
Africans . . .	} 1921[2]	13,447	14,775	28,222	1,958	1,877	3,835
Sierra Leoneans . .	1931[3]	14,440	18,408	32,848	1,632	1,414	3,046

[1] See *Census Report 1911*, pp. 10, 24.   [2] See ibid. *1921*, pp. 10, 24.
[3] See ibid. *1931*, pp. 19, 73. Figures include 2 persons on board ship in harbour.

The number of Africans in the Colony recorded as West Indians declined from 244 in 1921 to 96 in 1931 'owing to emigration. There is no likelihood of any increase and those remaining are becoming absorbed in the local population. Indeed, many are Colony-born and it is possible that some have already been returned as Sierra Leoneans.'[4]

'The mulattoes also show a very marked decrease' (from 358 to 150). But in 1921 'it may have happened that many returns were entered as "mixed blood" which referred to pure Africans whose parents were merely of different tribes, or a non-native and a native African'. In 1931, on the other hand, many Mulattoes and (other) persons of mixed blood classified themselves as Sierra Leoneans. Of those who did not do so, 109 were European-African, 28 Syrian-African, 3 Indian-African, and 9 European-Asiatic.[5]

The African population of the Protectorate consists almost entirely of Natives. Of the 3,265 non-native Africans enumerated in 1931, 3,046 were

[1] Ibid., pp. 46–7.   [2] Ibid., p. 47.   [3] Ibid., p. 46.   [4] Ibid., p. 47.
[5] See ibid. The last group certainly should not have been counted as Africans.

recorded as Sierra Leoneans, 141 as Mulattoes, 6 as West Indians, and 72 as other African non-natives.

The decrease in the number of Sierra Leoneans (1921: 3,835 descendants of Liberated Africans) was probably 'due to a large number returning to the Colony owing to the recent slump in trade and also in a few cases to Government retrenchment'.

Mulattoes are said to have increased from 37 to 141. Of these, 115 are returned as African-Asiatics (Syrian). 'These are for the greater part children.'

The number of West Indians declined from 18 to 6. 'Emigration is the probable cause of the decrease and possibly West Indians of Sierra Leone birth now class themselves as Sierra Leoneans.'

The 72 other African non-natives 'include Liberians, American negroes and persons returned as Nigerians, Gold Coasters and Gambians'.[1]

TABLE 11. *African Population by Origin, Protectorate of Sierra Leone, 1911-31*[1]

Origin	1911	1921	1931
Natives	1,323,151	1,450,903	1,667,790
Liberated Africans and their descendants	2,954	3,835	3,046
Mulattoes and persons of mixed blood	105	37	141
West Indians	26	18	6
Other African non-natives	76	66	72
Total	1,326,312	1,454,859	1,671,055

[1] See *Census Report 1911*, pp. 24, 29; *1921*, pp. 24, 31; *1931*, pp. 83, 167.

Birthplace. The birthplace was ascertained for the first time in 1911. But the returns were not satisfactory.

With regard to the Headquarters District,[2] it must be remarked that complete accuracy in discriminating between places of birth, whether in the Colony or the Protectorate, cannot always be guaranteed; owing to the similarity of many village names in the Colony with those in the Protectorate, and owing to the lack of local knowledge on the part of the Census Compilers, mistakes may have been made . . . .[3]

The 1911 figures were also defective in other respects.[4]

The 1921 Census Officer discussed very fully the changes in the numbers of Colony-born and Protectorate-born persons in the Colony and added: 'Comment on other figures shown in the . . . Table is not called for.'[5] This is an error. At the 1911 census 791 persons (including 14 Europeans) were recorded in the Colony as born in 'British Colonies' (outside West Africa and Asia), and the Compiler of Census stated:

Those born in British Colonies are, with rare exceptions, persons born in West Indian Colonies, and these again are for the most part West Indian soldiers born in either Jamaica or Barbadoes.[6]

[1] *Census Report 1931*, p. 166.
[2] This District comprised over 30 per cent. of the total population of the Colony.
[3] Ibid. *1911*, p. 18.
[4] The total number of persons in the Protectorate born in Europe is given as 125 (see ibid., p. 28), while the number of Europeans in the Protectorate born in Europe is given as 126 (see ibid., p. 25).   [5] Ibid. *1921*, p. 17.   [6] Ibid. *1911*, p. 18.

This explanation seems plausible as 800 persons (including 1 European) were returned as West Indians by origin. But in 1921, owing to the withdrawal of the West Indian Regiment, the West Indians numbered only 245 (including 1 European). Yet the census showed for the Colony 2,311 persons (including 4 Europeans) as born in 'British Colonies' (outside West Africa and Asia). This high figure certainly called for comment and I suspect that it was utterly wrong. The 1931 census report shows for the Colony only 52 persons born in the West Indies and 58 persons born in 'Other British Colonies' (i.e. British Colonies excluding West Africa, West Indies, and Asia). These figures may be correct. But the 1931 figures were inaccurate in other respects.[1]

Another defect of the 1911 and 1921 census figures is that no birthplace data are given separately for Africans. Table 12 must, therefore, be accepted with great reserve.

TABLE 12. *African Population by Birthplace, Sierra Leone, 1911–31*[1]

Birthplace	Colony			Protectorate[2]		
	1911[3]	*1921*[4]	*1931*	*1911*[5]	*1921*[6]	*1931*
Colony	43,009	42,913	47,786	2,452	2,812	2,207
Protectorate . . .	26,465[7]	31,702	40,080	556	939	890
West Africa[8] . . .	4,345	7,132	6,883	139	120	93
Other British Colonies .	777	2,307	795	11	82	64
Europe	4	—	3	—	3	1
Syria	—	—	—	—	—	5
America	68	—	11	3	—	5
Total	74,668	84,054	95,558	3,161	3,956	3,265

[1] Computed from *Census Report 1911*, pp. 8–10, 17, 24–5, 28; *1921*, pp. 9, 16, 24–5, 30; *1931*, pp. 49, 168–9.

[2] Only non-natives (mostly descendants of Liberated Africans).

[3] I deducted from the total population (by birthplace) the resident European population (by birthplace), and I assumed that of the 52 'Floating' Europeans those of European nationality were born in Europe and the 1 American in America. As regards 183 non-Europeans born in Asia, I assumed that they were all Asiatics. Since the total number of Asiatics was 202, I assumed that 19 were born in the Colony.

[4] I deducted from the total population the European population. As regards 28 non-Europeans born in Asia I assumed that they were all Asiatics. The other 170 Asiatics were assumed to be born in the Colony.

[5] I deducted from the total non-native population the European population. As regards 85 non-European non-natives born in Asia I assumed that they were all Asiatics. The other 10 Asiatics were assumed to be born in the Protectorate.

[6] I deducted from the total non-native population the European population. As regards 252 non-European non-natives born in Asia I assumed that they were all Asiatics. The other 149 Asiatics were assumed to be born in the Protectorate.

[7] Including 114 'Birth place not stated but probably Protectorate'.

[8] Including non-British territories.

It appears that of the 95,558 Africans enumerated in 1931 in the Colony 47,786 or 50·0 per cent. were born in the Colony, 40,080 or 41·9 per cent. in the Protectorate, 4,054 or 4·3 per cent. in Liberia, and 3,638 or 3·8 per cent. elsewhere. Of the 61,783 Natives only 17,647 or 28·6 per cent. were Colony-born, of the 32,846 'Sierra Leoneans' 29,977 or 91·3 per cent.

[1] See ibid. *1931*, p. 6.

TABLE 13. *African Population by Race and Birthplace, Sierra Leone, 1931*[1]

Birthplace	Freetown				Rest of Colony				Total Colony				Protectorate	
	Natives	Sierra Leoneans	Other non-natives	Total	Natives	Sierra Leoneans	Other non-natives	Total	Natives	Sierra Leoneans	Other non-natives	Total	Sierra Leoneans	Other non-natives
Colony	6,905	18,789	130	25,824	10,742	11,188	32	21,962	17,647	29,977	162	47,786	2,197	10
Protectorate	20,929	1,027	35	21,991	17,642	421	26	18,089	38,571	1,448	61	40,080	759	131
Nigeria	48	469	198	715	14	101	34	149	62	570	232	864	14	25
Gold Coast	72	108	48	228	15	26	8	49	87	134	56	277	6	6
Gambia	95	120	35	250	19	26	7	52	114	146	42	302	4	3
French Guinea	827	167	30	1,024	309	45	8	362	1,136	212	38	1,386	25	4
Liberia	3,816	75	73	3,964	40	32	18	90	3,856	107	91	4,054	1	5
Other African Colonies	225	212	142	579	83	36	4	123	308	248	146	702	38	16
Africa	32,917	20,967	691	54,575	28,864	11,875	137	40,876	61,781	32,842	828	95,451	3,044	200
West Indies	—	1	38	39	—	1	7	8	—	2	45	47	—	10
Other British Colonies	2	2	42	46	—	—	—	—	2	2	42	46	—	—
Syria	—	—	—	—	—	—	—	—	—	—	—	—	—	5
Europe	—	—	3	3	—	—	—	—	—	—	3	3	1	—
America	—	—	10	10	—	—	1	1	—	—	11	11	1	4
Outside Africa	2	3	93	98	—	1	8	9	2	4	101	107	2	19
Total	32,919	20,970	784	54,673	28,864	11,876	145	40,885	61,783	32,846	929	95,558	3,046	219

[1] See *Census Report 1931*, pp. 49, 168-9.

For the Natives in the Protectorate the birthplace has not been ascertained, but they were, of course, nearly all born in the Protectorate. Of the 3,046 'Sierra Leoneans' 2,197 or 72 per cent. were born in the Colony.

Sex. From the early 1810s till the early 1850s there had been a large preponderance of males among Africans in the Colony because there was a large excess of males over females among the slaves captured on sea and settled in Sierra Leone. But when the influx of captured slaves came to an end the preponderance of males decreased. The changes in the sex ratio of Africans from 1818 to 1881 were as follows:[1]

Year	Males	Females	Females to 100 males	Year	Males	Females	Females to 100 males
1818 (a)	5,629	3,821	68	1846 (a)	22,629	20,386	90
1820 (a)	7,722	4,680	61	(b)	21,706	19,914	92
1822 (a)	9,444	5,509	58	1847 (a)	24,952	20,614	83
1831 (b)	17,988	13,544	75	(b)	24,362	20,549	84
1833 (b)	18,442	13,485	73	1848 (a)	25,257	21,144	84
1834 (b)	19,450	13,988	72	(b)	24,263	20,947	86
1835 (b)	20,180	14,529	72	1849 (a)	24,961	21,350	86
1836 (b)	19,895	15,678	79	(b)	23,436	20,347	87
1838 (b)	20,477	18,362	90	1850 (b)	23,966	20,395	85
1839 (b)	21,754	17,280	79	1851 (a)	23,703	20,673	87
1840 (b)	23,840	18,471	77	1855 (a)	21,068	19,210	91
1842 (b)	21,989	17,734	81	1858 (a)	19,660	18,551	94
1843 (b)	19,553	19,105	98	1860 (a)	21,070	20,423	97
1844 (a)	24,425	20,335	83	1868 (b)	26,109	22,995	88
(b)	22,127	18,931	86	1871 (b)	18,455	18,527	100
1845 (a)	23,039	21,741	94	1881 (a)	30,964	29,311	95
(b)	22,214	21,250	96				

(a) Total African population. (b) Resident African population.

Some of the changes in the sex ratio—for example, the mysterious excess of females in Freetown in 1838 and the wild fluctuations of the ratio in the rural districts in 1842–7[2]—are difficult to explain. The

[1] See *Blue Book 1831*, pp. 114–15; *1833*, pp. 118–19 to *1838*, pp. 118–19; *1839*, pp. 134–5 to *1847*, pp. 134–5; *1848*, pp. 218–19; *1849*, pp. 134–5; *1850*, pp. 138–9; *1851*, pp. 138–9; *1855*, pp. 162–3; *1858*, pp. 159–60; *1860*, pp. 164–5; *1868*, pp. 174–5; *1871*, pp. 172–3; *Census Report 1891*, p. 3.

[2] The following figures may illustrate those changes:

Year	Freetown			Rest of the Colony		
	Males	Females	Females to 100 males	Males	Females	Females to 100 males
1836 (b)	5,573	4,922	88	14,322	10,756	74
1838 (b)	6,172	7,261	118	14,305	11,101	78
1839 (b)	7,079	6,270	89	14,675	11,010	75
1842 (b)	5,784	5,818	101	16,205	11,916	74
1843 (b)	6,421	6,029	94	13,132	13,076	100
1844 (b)	6,351	6,079	96	15,776	12,852	81
1845 (b)	8,473	7,742	91	13,741	13,508	98
1846 (b)	7,061	7,030	100	14,645	12,884	88
1847 (b)	8,580	7,562	88	15,782	12,987	82

(b) Resident African population.

Minutes of the Select Committee on the Slave Trade show that the fall in the preponderance of females since 1842 attracted attention at the time. The Reverend Edward Jones, on 22 June 1848, was asked to state the reasons.

> Can you tell us why it is that the females are now in Sierra Leone more equal in numbers to the males than they were some years ago ?—I can hardly say what is the real cause of it, because I have no data as to the proportions of their arrivals of late years, but I have seen cargoes.
> Have females come from other parts of the coast to marry the men that are there ? —No ; they have only been brought in as slaves ; but in some cargoes of late years the majority have been females and children ; it varies ; sometimes they are all boys ; some all men ; sometimes mostly women.[1]

Other changes may not have been genuine but due to defective returns.[2]

In 1871 the number of females was reported to be about equal to the number of males. But from 1891 on, each census again showed a large excess of males. In his report on the 1891 census the Colonial Secretary said:

> Somehow or other it has been generally believed that the number of females in the Colony exceeds that of the males, but the Census shows, that, with the exception of the Eastern Division of Freetown there are more males in every district and station than females.[3]

The belief that there was an excess of females may have arisen from the fact that among the 'Creoles' (Liberated Africans and their descendants), who in 1860 still constituted practically the sole population of the Colony, the former excess of males, owing partly to emigration, had turned into a large excess of females. But by 1891 the 'Creoles' had become a minority, and among the other Africans, who had immigrated into the Colony, only about two-fifths were females. As a consequence thereof, there were in 1891 in the whole population of the Colony only 88 females to 100 males. The censuses of 1901 and 1911 showed ratios of 84 and 86 females to 100 males, although among the 'Creoles' there were about 4 females to every 3 males.

The 1921 returns are very puzzling. The number of male 'Creoles' in the Colony (13,609) was about the same as in 1911 (13,329), but the female 'Creoles' showed a decrease from 17,953 to 14,971. The ratio of female to 100 male 'Creoles' had dropped from 135 to 110 and the ratio of females to 100 males among all Africans from 86 to 76. The 1921 census report gives no explanation for the decline in the number of female 'Creoles', and I cannot conceive of any plausible explanation for such a large decrease.[4] The figures for 1931 are not very helpful. They showed, as

[1] *Third Report*, p. 121.

[2] It is hard to believe, for example, that the numbers of male resident Africans in Freetown in 1860, 1868, and 1871 should have actually been 8,864, 10,731, and 6,540 respectively and the numbers of female resident Africans 9,054, 9,194, and 7,295 respectively.

[3] *Census Report 1891*, p. 4. In the Eastern Division of Freetown there were 2,100 males and 2,113 females; see ibid., p. 3.

[4] It is possible that the figures of males and females by races in the 1921 census report are all wrong. This report gives as total numbers of males and females in the Colony 47,564 and 37,599

stated above, an enormous increase for females (from 14,971 to 18,491) and a small increase for males (from 13,609 to 14,507). But I do not consider this to be conclusive proof that the number of female 'Creoles' had been grossly understated in 1921, since many women returned in 1921 as Natives may have classified themselves in 1931 as 'Sierra Leoneans' ('Creoles'). It should be noted, however, that the sex ratio among the 'Sierra Leoneans'—127 females to 100 males—showed in 1931 a smaller preponderance of females than that ascertained in 1901 and 1911 among the 'Creoles'. For the other Africans the ratio was 67 females to 100 males,[1] and for the total African population 84 females to 100 males.

The early estimates of the sex ratio among the Natives in the Protectorate show an enormous preponderance of females. The results for 1911 may be summarized as follows:[2]

Adults			Children		
Males	Females	Females to 100 males	Males	Females	Females to 100 males
319,924	435,940	136	90,336	123,553	137

The Compiler of Census makes the following comment:

A marked feature is the preponderance in all the districts of females over males. This is attributed to (1) former inter-tribal warfare and hostile invasions in the past from tribes living on the borders of the Protectorate; (2) emigration to the Colony and other parts of West Africa. At the same time, if reliance is to be placed upon the figures relating to the boy and girl population given in some districts, it is clear that there is a larger female than male birth-rate in the Protectorate.[3]

Actually no reliance whatever can be placed upon any of the figures. As stated above,[4] the Commissioners of the Koinadugu and Karene Districts entered for each tribe 50 per cent. more women than men. The Commissioner of the Railway District listed 50 per cent. more females

respectively (see pp. 2, 3, 6, 12, 14, 16, 40) and as excess of males 9,965 (see p. 7). But it shows at the same time (see pp. 8–10):

Races	Males	Females
Europeans .	817	94
Asiatics . .	148	50
Africans . .	47,623	36,431

which means a total of 48,588 males and 36,575 females or an excess of 12,013 males. The 1931 census report, in fact, gives as total numbers of males and females in 1921, 48,469 males (excluding 119 on board ship) and 36,575 females (see pp. 20, 21, 26). But if the totals shown in the 1921 census report (47,564 and 37,599) are correct—and this seems quite likely as the tables giving the population by districts, by occupation, by age, and by birthplace all show these totals —it may well be that the number of male 'Creoles' was overstated by 1,024 and the number of female 'Creoles' understated by 1,024. In this case the ratio of female to 100 male 'Creoles' would have been 127 in 1921 (and not 110).

[1] The 1931 census report says (p. 48): '... there has been a steady decline in native masculinity since 1901, the increase in females being probably due to immigration.' The *ratio* of females to 100 males among Natives (as distinct from Sierra Leoneans) had in fact gradually increased from 1901 to 1931 but there is no evidence that more female Natives than male Natives had immigrated.

[2] See *Census Report 1911*, pp. 29, 34–6. The sex of children is given only for 4 of the 7 Districts.

[3] Ibid. p. 29. Yet the Compiler states at another place (p. 8) that 'the male births in the Protectorate more than double the female births'!

[4] See p. 34.

both for the adults and the children among the Mendes (the main tribe of the District). The Commissioners of the Northern Sherbro District and of the Sherbro District reported for each tribe 33⅓ per cent. more females than males both among adults and children. That the sex ratio in the Protectorate with a native population of 1,323,151 cannot have been affected essentially by emigration to the Colony may be inferred from the fact that among the total population of the Colony there were only 17,732 male and 8,619 female Protectorate-born.[1]

In 1921 no attempt was made to estimate the sex ratio among native children. The number of men was put at 425,173 and the number of women at 599,199. The Census Officer stated:

> The women outnumber the men, but by a smaller margin than in 1911.[2]

This is an error. The excess of women over men had increased from 116,016 to 174,026, and the ratio of women to 100 men from 136 to 141.[3] The Census Officer says that the excess of women 'is attributable largely to the emigration of the men to the Colony and elsewhere'. Yet, there were in the Colony only 18,626 male and 13,076 female Protectorate-born.[4]

TABLE 14. *African Population by Sex, Sierra Leone, 1891–1931*[1]

| Race | Sex | Colony | | | | | Protectorate 1931 | Total 1931 |
		1891	1901	1911	1921	1931		
Creoles[2]	Males	15,002	14,473	13,329	13,609	14,507	1,632	16,139
	Females	18,210	19,045	17,953	14,971	18,491	1,414	19,905
	F. to 100 M.	121·4	131·6	134·7	110·0	127·5	86·6	123·3
Others	Males	24,682	26,939	26,872	34,014	37,512	794,010	831,522
	Females	16,717	15,705	16,514	21,460	25,132	873,999	899,131
	F. to 100 M.	67·7	58·3	61·5	63·1	67·0	110·1	108·1
Total	Males	39,684	41,412	40,201	47,623	52,019	795,642	847,661
	Females	34,927	34,750	34,467	36,431	43,623	875,413	919,036
	F. to 100 M.	88·0	83·9	85·7	76·5	83·9	110·0	108·4

[1] See *Census Report 1891*, p. 5; *1901*, p. 7; *1911*, p. 10; *1921*, p. 10; *1931*, pp. 19, 46, 73.
[2] 1891–1921 Liberated Africans and their descendants; 1931 Sierra Leoneans. Figures for Colony include persons of mixed blood.

The estimates for 1931 were more realistic. According to the census report 793,877 Natives were returned as males and 873,913 as females.[5] Since 179·8 per 1,000 are said to have been boys, 177·7 per 1,000 girls, 298·5 per 1,000 men, and 344·0 per 1,000 women,[6] there was a slight excess of males among children, while the ratio of women to 100 men was 115 (as compared with 141 in 1921). The census report says:

> In 1921 there were 709 adult males to 1,000 adult females, while the present census shows 838[7] adult males to 1,000 adult females. It is not suggested that such

---

[1] See *Census Report 1911*, p. 17.   [2] Ibid. *1921*, p. 31.
[3] In the Northern Province the number of men was put at 141,737 and the number of women at 255,128, showing a ratio of 180 women to 100 men!   [4] See ibid., p. 16.
[5] See ibid. *1931*, p. 85.   [6] See ibid., pp. 87–8.   [7] Should read 868.

a vast physical change has occurred in the population, the difference being accounted for in the closer survey of the population.[1]

In the whole of Sierra Leone there were, in 1931, 123 females to 100 males among the Sierra Leoneans and 108 females to 100 males among the other Africans. It would seem that the large preponderance of females among the Sierra Leoneans is due in part to the inclination of females to be classified in this way.

Age. As Sierra Leone is the only British Dependency in Africa for which detailed age figures are available, and this for several decades, these data deserve particular attention. The results are shown in Table 15.[2] The census reports for 1891, 1911, 1921, and 1931 contain comments on the age statistics.

1891. The returns published give the 'Age Division Tables' which have been prepared for the first time from the Census results of this Colony in compliance with the instructions of the Registrar General of England who is desirous of obtaining uniformity in the tabulation of the Census of the British Empire. The returns speak for themselves.[3]

1911. The accurate ascertainment of the ages of the population in a Colony like this is one of the most difficult tasks, and after the age of 20 is mostly a matter of guess work in the case of aboriginal natives, as none of these know their own age.[4]

1921. It is never easy to gather accurate information as to the ages of the members of the community embracing many illiterates, and in a country where registration of births and deaths have not reached the perfection which only care and time bring about, and in the present Census the difficulties have been very greatly increased by the enormous influx of illiterates. Too much reliance, therefore, should not be placed on the . . . Table, especially as regards ages over 60.[5]

Practically all the features of the 1911 corresponding Table are here reproduced; the drop from Infants under 1 year to Infants between 1 and 2 years bearing eloquent testimony to the high infant mortality; the gradual and steady rise from that point to the quinquennial period 26–30, and the great preponderance of that period; the sudden drop in the next succeeding quinquennial period and the curious recovery in the period 36–40; the steady decrease up to the 66–70 period, and then the great fall to half the number for the 71–75 period, and the steady decrease thereafter. Every quinquennial period, however, between 6–10 and 81–85 shows an increase on the 1911 corresponding figure.[6]

1931. It is very difficult, . . . in any country, to obtain correct age statistics and, in a Colony such as Sierra Leone, the population of which contains so many illiterates and semi-literates, it is not possible to obtain even a moderately correct return. This applies, chiefly, to the native section of the community, amongst which by far the greater number of illiterates are found. It applies to a degree to literates, natives and Sierra Leoneans. Even amongst the latter, though there does not seem to be any deliberate intention to mis-state ages, there seems to be, amongst the older ones, a certain amount of disinterestedness; they are hazy about their ages and do not appear to think it a matter of any importance and, in many cases, give their ages as 'about' a certain age, instead of exactly.

[1] Ibid., p. 85.

[2] It is much to be regretted that the data for 1891–1921 were not tabulated by races. If this had been done the authors of the census reports would not have had to resort to mere guesswork in discussing the coming and going of Sierra Leoneans, and it would also have been possible to appraise correctly the changes in the sex ratio of Sierra Leoneans from census to census.

[3] Ibid. *1891*, p. 17.   [4] Ibid. *1911*, p. 14.

[5] Ibid. *1921*, p. 13.   [6] Ibid., p. 15.

The ages of natives are only approximate; even the literate ones are not always able to give their exact ages and are worse offenders than the Sierra Leoneans in the use of the term 'about'. It might be said that none of the illiterate natives up to 30 know their own ages within five years; and over that, within ten years. Many have no idea what is meant when asked, and, in those cases, the enumerators were asked to enter what they considered to be the reasonable age. As it is very difficult to tell the age of an African native, especially between the ages of thirty to forty-five or fifty, and, as the 'reasonable view' differs in the case of different enumerators, the returns so entered may be taken as only within five of the correct age. As to children, infants may be more or less correctly entered, but, from walking age to five and five to ten, the age given is only 'approximate'. . . .[1]

A feature which is worthy of notice is that, though the proportion of males to females amongst the natives is rather against a high birth-rate and the distribution amongst the Sierra Leoneans in favour of a high birth-rate, the proportion of young children to adults is greater in the former than in the latter case.

. . . Another point is the difference in numbers between this [one-year] and the under-one-year group, and the inference to be drawn is obvious—a deplorably high infant mortality. [2]

Some of these comments are either injudicious or erroneous.

(1) The great difference between the numbers of children reported to be one year and under one year old is by no means a proof of high infant mortality. It is obvious that the numbers of one year old children have been understated at each census. Evidently the numbers of children under one have also been understated, but it is impossible to estimate even approximately by how much. It is clear, moreover, that in 1901 and 1911 either the number of children aged 6–10 was understated or that of children aged 11–15 overstated.

Age (years)	1891	1901	1911	1921	1931
0	1,430	1,054	1,189	1,271	1,663
1	891	872	907	828	1,195
2–5 (average)	1,559	1,206	1,233	1,454	1,785
6–10 (average)	1,532	1,199	1,287	1,365	1,688
11–15 (average)	1,493	1,476	1,407	1,411	1,478

(2) The 1921 census report speaks of 'the curious recovery in the period 36–40' in 1911 and 1921. But such a recovery occurred at each census in the periods 36–40 and 56–60, and with one exception (1921) also 46–50, evidently because an unduly large number of people were reported to be 40, 50, and 60 years old. It was wrong also, therefore, to speak of a 'steady decrease' from 36–40 to 66–70 years.

(3) The statement that every quinquennial period between 6–10 and 81–85 showed in 1921 an increase on the 1911 figure is likewise wrong. There were in 1921 fewer people aged 46–50, 56–60, and 66–70 than in 1911.

(4) The ratio of young children to adults was in 1931 not higher among the Natives than among the Sierra Leoneans. There were 12 children under 6 to 100 adults among the Natives and 18 among the Sierra Leoneans.

[1] *Census Report 1931*, p. 32.　　　　[2] Ibid., p. 33.

TABLE 15. *Population by Sex and Age, Colony of Sierra Leone, 1891–1931*[1]

Age (years)	Males							Females						
	Total population					Sierra Leoneans	Other Africans	Total population					Sierra Leoneans	Other Africans
	1891	1901	1911	1921	1931	1931	1931	1891	1901	1911	1921	1931	1931	1931
0	687	521	547	646	836	299	529	743	533	642	625	827	314	505
1	418	382	473	421	581	247	328	473	490	431	407	614	281	330
2	639	474	580	579	669	278	387	623	380	518	637	743	252	482
3	707	698	662	769	1,104	309	790	722	653	605	700	898	328	561
4	743	635	640	783	741	312	424	704	539	683	743	1,043	459	582
5	1,010	651	603	845	831	360	468	1,086	794	691	759	1,110	502	603
6–10	3,770	2,979	3,277	3,465	4,018	1,818	2,174	3,890	3,016	3,160	3,361	4,421	1,891	2,509
11–15	3,818	3,998	3,810	3,743	3,990	1,857	2,116	3,645	3,380	3,215	3,311	3,398	1,660	1,729
16–20	4,124	4,440	3,976	4,561	5,693	1,679	3,970	4,002	3,734	3,654	3,714	3,915	1,701	2,199
21–25	4,320	5,090	3,789	5,341	5,167	1,217	3,877	3,409	3,770	3,254	4,105	4,139	1,420	2,688
26–30	5,247	6,073	5,767	6,715	6,659	1,191	5,374	3,971	4,096	4,387	4,561	5,129	1,511	3,573
31–35	2,371	3,116	2,970	4,080	4,225	782	3,352	1,956	2,151	2,109	2,708	3,046	1,049	1,972
36–40	4,102	4,510	4,559	5,321	5,976	952	4,955	3,051	3,157	3,242	3,315	4,013	1,415	2,562
41–45	1,751	1,966	2,087	2,645	3,090	691	2,319	1,226	1,508	1,302	2,159	2,140	921	1,202
46–50	2,253	2,248	2,765	2,734	3,314	665	2,605	1,859	2,017	2,013	1,875	2,516	1,203	1,307
51–55	731	955	963	1,234	1,559	408	1,127	623	1,039	848	1,012	1,357	671	682
56–60	1,130	1,147	1,302	1,204	1,758	511	1,233	1,129	1,229	1,264	1,175	1,537	864	671
61–65	435	478	583	616	905	305	595	466	578	601	612	924	516	408
66–70	525	402	453	468	695	265	427	552	583	562	569	788	531	257
71–75	206	235	151	239	323	125	197	267	229	232	292	433	308	125
76–80	284	220	163	177	205	39	166	265	316	237	246	368	265	103
81–85	96	147	85	78	85	26	59	83	212	101	118	154	109	45
86–90	114	90	70	41	52	23	29	119	173	120	80	124	93	31
91–95	29	76	15	17	5	—	5	30	39	28	28	32	23	9
96–100	34	34	24	6	4	—	2	28	50	47	22	25	20	5
101–	4	6	8	—	2	2	2	8	11	15	14	7	3	4
Not stated	327	285	678	836	3	2	—	30	122	610	451	17	5	12
Error[2]	—	—	—	—	62	75	-13	—	—	—	—	152	93	59
Total	39,875	41,856	41,001	47,564	52,552	14,438	37,497	34,960	34,799	34,571	37,599	43,870	18,408	25,215

[1] See *Census Report 1891*, p. 7; *1901*, p. 9; *1911*, p. 15; *1921*, p. 14; *1931*, pp. 32, 50. I corrected two arithmetical errors in age group 41–45 of the 1911 Report.

[2] 'Error in compilation.'

As the figures for individual years of age under 6 are obviously erroneous and in view of the tendency to state ages in numbers ending with 0, it seems advisable to show the census returns for broader age groups.

Age (years)	Total population					Sierra Leoneans 1931	Other Africans 1931
	1891	1901	1911	1921	1931		
Males							
0–5	4,204	3,361	3,457	4,043	4,762	1,805	2,926
6–15	7,588	6,977	7,096	7,208	8,008	3,675	4,290
16–25	8,444	9,530	7,765	9,902	10,860	2,896	7,847
26–35	7,618	9,189	8,737	10,795	10,884	1,973	8,726
36–45	5,853	6,476	6,616	7,966	9,066	1,643	7,274
46–55	2,984	3,203	3,668	3,968	4,873	1,073	3,732
56–65	1,565	1,625	1,955	1,820	2,663	816	1,828
66–	1,292	1,210	1,029	1,026	1,371	480	887
Females							
0–5	4,351	3,389	3,570	3,871	5,235	2,136	3,063
6–15	7,535	6,396	6,375	6,672	7,819	3,551	4,238
16–25	7,411	7,504	6,908	7,819	8,054	3,121	4,887
26–35	5,927	6,247	6,496	7,269	8,175	2,560	5,545
36–45	4,277	4,665	4,544	5,474	6,153	2,336	3,764
46–55	2,482	3,056	2,861	2,887	3,873	1,874	1,989
56–65	1,595	1,807	1,865	1,787	2,461	1,380	1,079
66–	1,352	1,613	1,342	1,369	1,931	1,352	579

The figures now are quite informative. Comparing the numbers in each 10-year age group with the numbers in the next younger age group at the preceding census it appears that the males aged 16–25 in 1901, 1921, and particularly in 1931 had been largely reinforced by immigration. The same is true of the males aged 26–35 in 1921, and, to a smaller degree, of the females aged 16–25 in 1921 and 1931. Many other interesting conclusions might be drawn from the above table, and the experience of the Colony of Sierra Leone shows beyond any doubt that, though accurate age data may not be obtainable, the broad outlines of the age composition can be ascertained through censuses in a West African Colony.

The estimates of the native age composition in the Protectorate are so uncertain that it is not worth while to discuss the returns.

Conjugal Condition. The founders of the Colony were anxious to abolish polygamy. In their Rules and Instructions to the Superintendent and Council for the Settlement issued about the end of 1791 the Directors of the Sierra Leone Company said:

78. ... You will take every proper means of discouraging Polygamy ; where it has been already engaged in, the toleration of it seems unavoidable, but new engagements of this sort among those who settle in our lands, we think ought by no means to be permitted. The common arguments for it appear to us quite ill founded, and the practice subversive of domestic peace as well as good order and morals.[1]

The Maroons had been only three months in the country when, on 14 January 1801, the following Resolution was passed:

The Governor and Council think it expedient for the more effectual prevention of Polygamy, in time to come among the Maroons as well as for ascertaining the

[1] Evans, p. 72.

Nature of the connexion by drawing a marked line of distinction between concubinage and Matrimony, and importing to the latter the requisite solemnity and dignity: to

Resolve 1st That every Marriage henceforth to be contracted among the Maroons, be solemnized by The Governor of this Presidency; or in his absence by the Senior Member of Council on the spot during the vacancy occasioned by the want of a Chaplain

2nd That no Marriage henceforth contracted be valid or legitimate, or communicate to the offspring of Such Marriage the Rights of Inheritance or succession, unless solemnized as above.[1]

But in the following year the Directors of the Company stated with respect to the Maroons:

The Suppression of Polygamy among them has been hitherto deemed an Experiment too hazardous to be tried . . . .[2]

However, after the transfer of the Colony to the Crown the Governor and Council passed a new Act,[3] and in 1824 it was reported:

All the settlers are married according to the rules prescribed by the Established Church; and the institution of marriage gains ground even among the captured negroes . . . .[4]

Finally, the 1931 census report said:

Plurality of wives is permissible by ordinary native law, but it is not prevalent in the Colony, the excess of males over females making this impossible. A few of the richer natives, tribal headmen and others possess several wives, but many of the poorer ones are bachelors. . . . In the Protectorate chiefs and rich men, as a rule, have a large number of wives and others as many as they can pay for. As the preponderance of females over males is not great, many poor men have no wives and the resulting social evil is obvious.[5]

Amongst the Sierra Leoneans polygamy is not recognized except, of course, by the Mohammedan section.[6]

Statistics are very scanty. The census report for 1891 showed the conjugal condition of the total male and female population by age groups.[7] It appears that, of the males 16 years and over, 67 per cent. were returned as bachelors, 29 per cent. as husbands, and 4 per cent. as widowers, and, of the females 16 years and over, 48 per cent. as spinsters, 38 per cent. as wives, and 14 per cent. as widows. There were 108 wives to 100 husbands. It is obvious that a considerable number of husbands and wives must have been returned as never married.

The 1901 census report did not mention conjugal condition, and the reports for 1911 and 1921 said:

1911. It was decided that it was impracticable in this Colony to obtain information concerning . . . condition as to marriage . . . .[8]

1921. No attempt was made to gather statistics as to marriage; in a Colony where Christian and Mohammedan marriage co-exists with marriage under native custom, and where moreover the records of registration of both Christian and Mohammedan

[1] Sierra Leone, *Acts 1800–27*, pp. 3–4.
[2] *Report from Committee on Petition of Sierra Leone Company 1802*, p. 21.
[3] 8 Oct. 1808, see *Acts 1800–27*, pp. 50–6.   [4] *West-African Sketches*, p. 169.
[5] *Census Report 1931*, p. 12.   [6] Ibid., p. 13.
[7] See ibid. *1891*, pp. 8–9.   [8] Ibid. *1911*, p. 3.

marriages may be called in question, it was felt that such an attempt would be foredoomed to failure, or at the least would, if carried through, have produced entirely misleading and unreliable results.[1]

The 1931 census report, after having explained the difficulties of ascertaining the conjugal condition of the Natives, stated:

With regard to the African non-native ['Sierra Leoneans', etc.], over 90 per cent. of these are Christian, the greater part being literate; they have now several generations of civilization behind them and profess to observe all the customs and conventions of Christian civilization, of which monogamous marriage is one. There should therefore be no reason whatever why fairly reliable returns should not be obtainable. Accordingly, marriage statistics of non-natives are included in this Census, but those of native Africans excluded.[2]

But the returns for the African non-natives proved to be quite unreliable. Assuming that all people under 16 were single, there were, among the males 16 years and over, 60 per cent. bachelors, 35 per cent. husbands, and 5 per cent. widowers or divorced, and, among the females 16 years and over, 50 per cent. spinsters, 32 per cent. wives, and 18 per cent. widows and divorced. There were 127 wives to 100 husbands.[3] The census report made the following comment:

Table XXX (Returns for the African non-native marriages) reveals such a low ratio of married males to females, such extraordinary figures under widowhood and, in general, such a low ratio of married to single that the reliability of the table is most decidedly open to question.[4]

V. Composition of Non-African Population

1. European Population

The European population, which at one time (1792) had exceeded 100, numbered only about two dozen when, on 30 September 1800, the Maroons arrived from Nova Scotia with an escort of forty-five white soldiers under the command of two lieutenants of His Majesty's 24th Regiment. This detachment, together with the Maroons who arrived at the critical moment, quelled the insurrection of the Nova Scotians. But the Sierra Leone Company, in anticipation of this insurrection, had already applied in London for a permanent garrison.

As a farther security for the peace and permanence of the Company's establishment, the aid of a small military force was deemed necessary by the Directors, to whom representations of such necessity had come from the Governor and Council.[5]

Such a military force was available in Goree.

In August, 1800, a Corps of Infantry was raised for the defence and protection of the island of Goree.

---

[1] *Census Report 1921*, p. 1.   [2] Ibid. *1931*, p. 35.

[3] See ibid., p. 51. The 'Sierra Leoneans' included 3,228 husbands and 4,148 wives. The great preponderance of wives can be explained in only a small measure by migration of husbands into the Protectorate since among the 'Sierra Leoneans' in the Protectorate there were 550 husbands and 477 wives (see ibid., p. 170).

[4] Ibid., p. 35.   [5] *Report of Sierra Leone Company 1801*, p. 9.

The Regiment was officially styled by the name of its Colonel, 'Fraser's Corps of Infantry', in accordance with custom. It eventually became the Royal African Corps (in 1804).[1]

When the British Government received the request from the Company, the Secretary of State, on 15 November 1800, wrote to Lieutenant-Colonel Frazer:

You are to send a Detachment of fifty men from the Corps under your Command, in the charge of a proper officer to Sierra Leone, as an additional means of security to that interesting Settlement.[2]

The Records of the Royal African Corps contain the following entry:

2nd. February, 1801.—A Detachment under command of Lieutenant W. Laidlow, consisting of 3 sergeants, 1 drummer, and 46 rank and file, embarked at Goree for Sierra Leone.[3]

Dispatches from the Colony, dated 28 February 1801, said:

The detachment of troops from Gorée destined to do duty at Sierra Leone had arrived there, and enjoyed good health.[4]

But mortality among these soldiers soon became very great. Colonel Frazer wrote on 17 October 1801 to the Secretary of State:

The Garrisons at Senegal and Sierra Leone have been very sickly. At the latter place I am sorry to find we have already lost one-third of the Detachment.[5]

The Directors of the Company reported:

Out of about 50 Soldiers . . . who lately were sent thither from Goree, the Governor and Council observe, not without some Surprize as well as Concern, that no less than Ten died within Six Months after their Arrival, and that Five Women and Two Children also died. But the Governor and Council state, that the Men were, with only one Exception, much given to Liquor; and that no small Part of the Corps to which they belonged had been formed from the Invalids of other Regiments.[6]

In January 1802, after the attack by the Natives (18 November 1801) in which Lieutenant Laidlow and four men were killed, 'about Sixty-five additional British Troops had arrived from Goree'.[7] The detachment consisted on 1 February of 2 officers and 94 non-commissioned officers and men,[8] but by 1 January 1803 the number of non-commissioned officers and men was reduced to 57.[9] Mortality had again been appalling. Captain Hallowell, who had been sent by the Admiralty to Africa with orders to examine into the state of the settlement, stated before a Committee of the House:[10]

The Officers of the African Corps attribute the Sickness of their Troops in the last Rains to their Quarters not being tight and proof against the Weather. . . . Out

---

[1] Crooks, *Historical Records of the Royal African Corps*, p. 1.

[2] Ibid., p. 5. [3] Ibid., p. 15.

[4] *Report of Sierra Leone Company 1801*, p. 40. [5] Crooks, *Records*, p. 19.

[6] *Report from Committee on Petition of Sierra Leone Company 1802*, p. 15.

[7] Ibid., p. 12. See also Crooks, *Records*, pp. 19–21.

[8] See ibid., p. 21. According to the Population Return of 29 Mar. 1802, the detachment consisted of 89 officers and men and 6 women and children; see *Report from Committee on Petition of Sierra Leone Company 1804*, p. 127.

[9] See Crooks, *Records*, p. 21.

[10] *Report from Committee on Petition of Sierra Leone Company 1804*, pp. 75–6.

of Ninety-two Non-commissioned Officers and Privates who arrived there Twelve Months ago, only Forty-seven now remain alive; and many of these are so feeble and emaciated, that there is every Reason to fear they may fall a Sacrifice to the Climate during the next Rains,[1] if they have not better Accommodation than they now occupy. The annexed State of the Detachment, given to me by the Commanding Officer, will shew the Accuracy of these Particulars.

A Return of Detachment of the African Corps stationed at Sierra Leone, from 15th January 1802 to 8th January 1803:

Commissioned Officers		Ser-jeants	Drum-mers and Fifers	Rank and file				Alterations for the Year				
Cap-tain	Lieu-tenant			Present and fit for duty	Sick in hos-pital	Sick in quar-ters	Total	Men dead	Women dead	Children dead	De-serted	Dis-charged
1	1	5	2	26	6	8	40	42	4	1	1	2

The Secretary to the Company, Zachary Macaulay, made the following 'Remarks' on the 'Observations of Captain Hallowell':[2]

The Mortality in the Detachment of Troops at Sierra Leone is greatly to be deplored, and may have been owing to a Want of suitable Accommodation; but certainly in no small Degree to the Carelessness, Obstinacy, wasted Constitutions, and drunken Habits of the Soldiers and their Wives.[3] But it may be fairly asked, Has even the Mortality of Soldiers which has taken place at Sierra Leone, considerably exceeded the Proportion of Deaths of Soldiers at Goree, notwithstanding the superior Accommodations enjoyed there and in some Places in the West Indies, during the last War?

In 1803 mortality was much lower. Acting Governor Ludlam wrote on 21 September to Macaulay:

The Soldiers have suffered little compared with former Years; Three out of Thirty-five have died since the Rains began.[4]

In 1804 the garrison at Sierra Leone was again reinforced.

1st September, 1804.—The Monthly Return of the Companies at Goree under Command of Major R. Lloyd shows one officer and 50 men as embarked for Sierra Leone the 20th August, 1804.[5]

[1] The Governor and Council of Sierra Leone had written on 12 January 1803 to Captain Hallowell that of the 47 non-commissioned officers and men 'there is not One Man who in Europe would be reckoned effective, the Whole being actually sick, or so extremely debilitated by Sickness, as not to be able to perform any Service requiring greater Exertion than that of using a Musket in one or other of the Blockhouses in case of an Attack' (Report from Committee on Petition of Sierra Leone Company 1804, p. 50).   [2] Ibid., p. 76.

[3] The Directors, in describing conditions in February 1803, said in a statement submitted to the Committee: 'Many of the European Soldiers had fallen Victims chiefly to Intemperance, which in that Climate proves almost always fatal. Their Fatigue also was considerable, although Care was taken that the Night Duty should be performed by the Black Colonists' (ibid., p. 42). See also ibid., p. 6: 'The Sickliness and Mortality which for some Time existed (principally amongst the Military) has in a great Degree subsided; and there seems Reason to believe, that it arose rather from the Condition of the Troops when they entered the Colony, their Habits of Intemperance, and the imperfect Accommodation which could be afforded them, than from any Disorder necessarily connected with their Residence in that Situation.' Finally, Captain William Day, of the Royal Navy, when asked 'To what Cause do you attribute the great Mortality you have described among the African Corps?' answered: 'In a very great Measure to Intemperance'. (See ibid., p. 115.)

[4] Ibid., p. 128. See also ibid., p. 55.

[5] Crooks, Records, p. 36. See also ibid., p. 37.

Mortality among these newly arrived soldiers was excessive.

29th May, 1805.—Major Lloyd, at Goree, reports to Secretary of State that the troops at Goree as well as at Sierra Leone are tolerably healthy, although nineteen of the fifty men lately detached to the latter place have fallen victims to the unhealthiness of the climate.[1]

But in 1806 conditions were more favourable,[2] and in 1807 no death occurred among the troops.[3] On 9 August 1808 Colonel Lloyd reported from Goree to the Secretary of State that he had 'sent to the Colony of Sierra Leone a Reinforcement of 2 subalterns, 1 assistant surgeon, and 71 men',[4] and the company at Sierra Leone consisted on that date of 6 officers and 115 non-commissioned officers and men. In the meantime mortality had become excessive again. In a Dispatch to the Secretary of State, dated 9 March 1810, Major Maxwell said:

The Honourable Captain Forbes, who commands the Company of the Royal African Corps stationed at Sierra Leone, has reported to me the miserable state of the barracks allotted to the troops. Betwixt the 25th June, 1808, and 24th December, 1809, forty-three out of 109 have died, a mortality which he attributes in a great measure to the wretched lodging.

I trust your Lordship will direct comfortable quarters to be prepared for the military doing duty in that Colony; and that a measure so essential to the health of troops in all climates, and especially in that of Sierra Leone, will be carried into execution before any additional force is sent there.[5]

Mortality was much lower in 1810. On 1 November the non-commissioned officers and men at Sierra Leone numbered 69 (21 Sergeants, Drummers, and Rank and File, 22 Limited Service Men, and 26 Commuted Punishment Men).[6] Three weeks later Colonel J. W. Gordon wrote from London to Lieutenant-Colonel Torrens:

In calling the attention of the Commander-in-Chief to the composition of the Royal African Corps, which is, and ever has been, I believe, formed principally of deserters, convicts, and men whose sentences of punishment have been commuted for service in Africa, I am quite at a loss to suggest any remedy to amend it effectually, being aware that no other description of person will knowingly enlist as a private in it, but if it were possible to obtain a proportion of steady old soldiers for the purpose of being made non-commissioned officers, I should hope that a due check might be given to the turbulence of the bad men and render the circumstances in which this Corps is placed detached in three separate stations.[7]

In the meantime (May 1810) the Commander-in-Chief had 'approved of a portion of Black Men being enlisted for the Corps and formed into a Company on the present establishment of the Corps'.[8] Henceforward an increasing number of negro soldiers were stationed in Sierra Leone. But there remained still a white garrison. The available data on the strength of

[1] Ibid., p. 40.
[2] In Dispatches from the Colony dated 29 Oct. 1806 'the soldiers are said to have experienced less sickness than before' (*Report from Committee on Petition of Sierra Leone Company 1807*, p. 7).
[3] See extract of letter from Governor Ludlam, 1 Jan. 1808 (*Report of Directors 1808*, p. 15). It should be noted, however, that the number of men in 1807 was probably less than 50.
[4] Crooks, *Records*, p. 54.   [5] Ibid., p. 75.   [6] See ibid., p. 79.
[7] Ibid., pp. 80–1. The three stations were Senegal, Goree, and Sierra Leone.
[8] See p. 117 above.

the European forces and their mortality in 1810–24 may be summarized as follows:[1]

	Officers		Non-Commissioned Officers, Drummers, and Privates				Officers		Non-Commissioned Officers, Drummers, and Privates		
Year	Number	Deaths	Joined during the year	Total number	Deaths	Year	Number	Deaths	Joined during the year	Total number	Deaths
1810	—	—	—	69	3	1818	11	1	14	52[1]	16
1811	—	—	2	98	11	1819	25	—	6	—	5
1812	26	3	324	304	40	1820	25	5	—	20	—
1813	31	3	9	71	23	1821	26	—	—	—	—
1814	36	4	37	111	26	1822	25	2	—	—	—
1815	43	2	31	144	23	1823	25	7	—	—	—
1816	45	2	1	116	32	1824	19	6	—	—	2
1817	15	2	3	97	39						

[1] Including the Gambia.

In April 1817 the white garrison was depleted by the transfer of a detachment of the Royal African Corps to the Cape of Good Hope,[2] and the Monthly Return of May 1819 stated:

> Owing to the frightful loss of life among the European troops stationed in Western Africa, the Government decided to withdraw the Detachments of the Royal African Corps serving there, and to garrison the Settlements with black troops.[3]

But unfortunately, after a few years, new white troops were sent into the Colony.

> In 1823, however, a war having broke out with the Ashantees, the white soldiers formerly disbanded at the Cape of Good Hope were hastily re-embodied and sent to the defence of Cape Coast Castle; the survivors of these were subsequently transferred to the Sierra Leone Command, and, with several drafts of commuted punishment men from England,[4] formed into the Royal African Colonial Corps, which thus again consisted of Europeans of the most degraded class.[5]

[1] See 'Return shewing the Number of Troops', &c., *Papers relating to Sierra Leone 1830*, pp. 90–3. It should be noted, however, that the returns were defective and incomplete. They excluded, for example, the numerous deaths among the white non-commissioned officers of the 2nd West India Regiment listed in the Dispatch from Lieutenant-Colonel Sutherland to Governor MacCarthy, 8 Sept. 1823 (C.O. 267, vol. lviii, No. 341). See also Major Tulloch, *Statistical Reports on Sickness, Mortality, & Invaliding among the troops in Western Africa*, &c., p. 3: 'It is to be regretted that on this coast, where the baneful effects of climate on the European constitution exhibit themselves in their most concentrated form, and where it would have been of the utmost importance to trace the diseases of each station with the same minuteness as in previous Reports, the materials are neither so ample as those from other colonies, nor admit always of the same arrangement as has been hitherto adopted. The unceasing occupation of their professional duties in so unhealthy a climate left medical officers little time for making the proper distinction between the diseases of white and black troops; and their death has frequently prevented information from being obtained at those periods when the mortality was at its greatest height, and when an accurate statement of the particular circumstances under which it occurred would have been most interesting and useful.'
[2] See Crooks, *Records*, pp. 101–2.　　　　[3] Ibid., p. 109.
[4] See also Extract from the Report of Dr. Barry, Deputy Inspector of Hospitals, to the Director-General, quoted from Boyle, *Medico-Historical Account of the Western Coast of Africa*, p. 293: 'In 1824 the headquarters of the Royal African Corps were stationed at Chatham, in order to complete their establishment prior to their embarkation for the western coast of Africa. . . . The regiment sailed from Portsmouth on the 4th of January, and, after a month's voyage, arrived at Sierra Leone . . . the soldiers were subsequently distributed to the garrisons of Sierra Leone, Gambia, and Isles de Los.'　　　　[5] Major Tulloch, *Statistical Reports*, p. 6.

For 1825 the strength and the mortality of European troops from Remittent Fever was reported as follows:[1]

1st quarter		2nd quarter		3rd quarter		4th quarter	
Strength	Deaths	Strength	Deaths	Strength	Deaths	Strength	Deaths
138	—	289	13	585	161	522	37

The Surgeon to the Royal African Colonial Corps, William Ferguson, reported:

The extent of sickness and mortality has been great beyond all former experience, but not greater than was expected, considering the habits and description of the men; who, not deterred by the dangers arising out of natural causes, seemed to court destruction by perseverance in excessive intemperance and debauchery, and by fearless exposure to sun, rain, and dew, by day and night.[2]

But the Commissioners of Inquiry who visited Sierra Leone in 1826 held a different view:

In the end of February 1825, 108 soldiers of the Royal African Corps were sent to the Isles de Loss; these were young men, between 17 and 30 years of age, who had enlisted under General Turner, and accompanied him to the Coast. When those islands were visited by the Commissioners, in March 1826, 52 of them had died, and there were but few of the survivors who did not suffer from the effects of disease; yet the officer who had commanded them the greater part of the time, stated their conduct to have been exemplary; in fact the means or opportunity of committing excess were not within their reach. When it is remembered that the situation of Crawford's Island was thought so favourably of as to have been recommended as a station for convalescents, and when the conduct and circumstances of the men amongst whom this mortality occurred, are duly considered,—sufficient cause will be found (after making every allowance for the badness of the water) to justify a doubt whether any situation on the north-west coast will prove otherwise than destructive to European constitutions.[3]

The Commissioners stated furthermore 'that the ration issued to the white troops upon the Coast generally, is not of a description well calculated to enable them to resist the injurious influence of the climate, or

---

[1] See *Papers relating to Sierra Leone 1830*, p. 79.

[2] Quoted from Boyle, p. 294. Concerning the high mortality among the military in 1826 see *The Sierra Leone Gazette*, 23 Sept. 1826, quoted in *Missionary Register 1827*, pp. 8–9.

[3] *Report*, First Part, p. 108. Major Tulloch reports that the detachment arrived at the Isles de Loss on 23 Feb. 1825 and consisted of 103 men. Of these, 62 died between 21 Mar. 1825 and 20 Sept. 1826, while 21 were invalided to England during the same period. '. . . such of the Europeans as survived were withdrawn, scarcely any being fit for duty; and the fate of this detachment has afforded a useful though melancholy instance, of how little avail are supposed advantages in locality, or even the temperance and good conduct of a garrison, in contending against a climate so inimical to the constitution of Europeans' (*Statistical Reports*, p. 14). But see also letter from Colonial Surgeon Boyle to Lieutenant-Governor Findlay, 14 Dec. 1830 (C.O. 267, vol. civ): 'The Isles de Loss have been condemned as being generally unhealthy somewhat unjustly it appears on account of the fatality which occurred among the troops stationed there by the late General Turner; when it is known that in the Barrack room originally intended for thirty black soldiers only—a room whose dimensions are 80 feet by 18 without windows or any openings in the rear for the admission of air, 120 white soldiers were as it were imprisoned by means of a double row of Bedsteads. The Officers appartments, on the contrary, are extravagant in the extreme, they are tastefully arranged and extensive and altho' the Services of but two or three Officers were contemplated or required the messroom is sufficiently ample in its dimensions to dine a party of between 30 and 40 persons.'

to recover from its effects'.[1] Major Tulloch finally complained also about the poor accommodation provided for the troops.

In a climate so remarkable for its insalubrity and the extreme inclemency of the rainy season, it was obviously essential to the health and efficiency of the troops that all the buildings occupied by them should be of the most substantial description. Such, however, was the state of decay and dilapidation during the earlier years included in this Report, that, in 1821, the medical officer reported it was fortunate the troops were natives, for, had they been Europeans, he felt convinced the whole of them would be carried off in the course of twelve months; and fatally was this prediction verified, when, in 1824 and 1825, that description of force was employed without any improvement having been effected in this respect.[2] Many of the officers even could then obtain no better accommodation than rude huts, incapable of affording shelter from the inclemency of the rainy season, and in which it was not uncommon to find the husband, wife, and children lying in the last extremity of fever in the same room.

It has been necessary to advert to this important fact, because, baneful as the climate of this colony unquestionably proves to the European constitution, even under the most favourable circumstances, it would be improper to attribute the heavy loss sustained by the white troops to that cause alone, when it might, in some measure, have been induced by so powerful an accessory.

At Sierra Leone, however, these defects were remedied in 1826, by the erection of new buildings, which are stated to be good, ample, and commodious.[3]

In the meantime the British Government had decided to send no new white recruits to the Royal African Corps. On 21 January 1826 Earl Bathurst wrote to Major-General Turner:

Having taken into my consideration the casualties which have occurred during the preceding year among the troops stationed on the Western Coast of Africa, it has appeared to me that it would be most expedient that the Royal African Corps should in future be recruited with blacks, provided that you should find it practicable to enlist them in the settlements under your government, either from the natives, or from those Africans who may have been more recently introduced into the colony; and I rely upon your zeal for carrying this measure into effect.[4]

Thereupon Liberated Africans were again enlisted. Two years later it appeared feasible to consider the withdrawal of all European troops. On 26 August 1828 Sir George Murray wrote to Lieutenant-Governor Lumley:

You are aware that for some time past it has been in contemplation to reduce the present establishment of the Royal African Corps. It has been conceived, that under existing circumstances, the tranquility of the colony could be secured by the employment of a militia force, and it will accordingly be your duty to suggest for my consideration the means which you may judge best calculated for embodying a force of that description.[5]

---

[1] Report, *Second Part*, p. 19.

[2] See also statement by merchant John M'Cormack, 1 July 1830: 'When the European troops first came out, they had no barracks prepared for them, they were cribbed up during the rainy season for a length of time in the river, where they could take no exercise, and where they could not get sufficient fresh air; the barracks were built up in the rains and covered in in the rains, and the men were put in when the damp was running down the walls; and to prevent, as far as they could, the effect of this damp, an iron wheelbarrow was trundled into rooms, full of coal, wood or charcoal, lighted' (*Report from Select Committee on Sierra Leone and Fernando Po*, p. 58).

[3] *Statistical Reports*, p. 6.   [4] *Papers relating to Sierra Leone 1830*, p. 49.

[5] Ibid., p. 50.

Thereupon, there was passed on 3 August 1829 'An Act to embody and constitute a Militia in the Colony of Sierra Leone, under certain Regulations',[1] and 'in 1830 the white troops were removed'.[2]

In the first three decades of the nineteenth century the European military in most years far outnumbered the European civilians. Thus, according to the census of 29 March 1802, there were 89 officers and men with 6 women and children as compared with 22 male and 5 female civilians.[3] In April 1811 the European civilian population within the walls of Freetown consisted of 22 men, 4 women, and 2 children.[4] In March 1817 there were 49 men, 12 women, and 7 children in Freetown.[5]

The censuses of 1818, 1820, 1822 and 1826 showed the following results:[6]

Date	Freetown and Suburbs					Elsewhere					Colony				
	Boys	Men	Girls	Women	Total	Boys	Men	Girls	Women	Total	Boys	Men	Girls	Women	Total
31 Dec. 1818	1	78	2	7	88	1	20	1	5	27	2	98	3	12	115
8 July 1820	—	82	2	7	91	1	19	1	8	29	1	101	3	15	120
1 Jan. 1822		94		10	104		16		8	24		110		18	128
Apr./May 1826		93		6	99		10		4	14		103		10	113

The Commissioners of Inquiry, in submitting the total numbers of Europeans ascertained at the censuses of 1817–26, said:

Of the Europeans, not military, who have from time to time arrived at or become resident in the colony, the information which it was practicable to obtain is of so vague a nature, that it is found difficult to offer any satisfactory observations as to the increase or decrease of their numbers . . . .[7]

The data call indeed for some explanation. That the official figure for the end of 1818 was much higher than that for March 1817, in spite of a high mortality in 1818, must have been due to a large influx of newcomers.[8] That the official figure for July 1820 was hardly larger than that of December 1818, in spite of the establishment of the Courts of Mixed Commission in 1819,[9] was evidently due to the fact that the 1820 figure refers to the rainy season when many Europeans are absent from the Colony.

[1] *Sierra Leone Acts 1811–48.*

[2] *Handbook of Sierra Leone*, p. 38. See also Major Tulloch, *Statistical Reports*, p. 6.

[3] See *Report from Committee on Petition of Sierra Leone Company 1804*, p. 127.

[4] See *Report of Commissioners on Coast of Africa*, 1811, p. 8.

[5] See *Missionary Register 1817*, p. 355.

[6] See *Accounts relating to the Population*, &c. of Sierra Leone, 1825, pp. 13–21; *Report of Commissioners of Inquiry*, 1827, Appendix A, No. 38.

[7] *Report*, First Part, p. 19.

[8] The writer of a letter to *The Royal Gazette and Sierra Leone Advertiser* said that there were already in Jan. 1818, 124 European civil residents in the Colony (see *The Royal Gazette*, 20 Feb. 1819, p. 164). This must have been an overstatement.

[9] The members of the British-Spanish Commission arrived on 7 June 1819; see ibid., 19 June 1819, p. 201. See also ibid., 1 Apr. 1820, p. 359: 'Letters from that colony state, that in consequence of the arrival of the Commissary, Judges, the Commissioners, their secretaries, and the other persons attached to their suite, together with various officers, both in the civil and military departments, the white population had increased in an extraordinary degree; so that, in the early part of last June, it consisted of 118 individuals, men, women, and children . . . .' It is interesting to note in this connexion that of the Europeans enumerated on 31 Dec. 1818 only 94 were reported to have been present in the Colony on 24 Aug. 1819; see ibid. p. 357.

That the official figure for the beginning of 1822 was only slightly higher than that for July 1820 suggests that the permanent European population had decreased somewhat in the meantime. It increased, however, in the following year.

This colony has at present the advantage of a number of European residents far beyond what it has had at any former time. Most of the mercantile gentlemen who visited England at the commencement of the rains of 1822, are returned, and many new settlers are come out, either prepared to fix themselves permanently, or to make trial of the suitableness of the place to their particular objects. . . . The civil service of the colony has been strengthened by the arrival of some additional officers ; and the military department has received a valuable accession, in the arrival of Lieutenant-Colonel Sutherland, with several other officers of the 2d West-India Regiment. . . . The Church Missionary Society . . . has this season sent Missionaries and teachers adequate to an entire new establishment, if a new one were wanted ; but happily the health and efficiency of those already occupied in similar pious and beneficent labours, give to this welcome reinforcement the more acceptable character of companions and assistants in that honorable course.

But the most gratifying improvement consists in the increased number of European ladies ; Lieutenant-Colonel Sutherland, and most of the other gentlemen who have the advantage of being married, having brought their ladies with them. . . . Now that it has been seen that a rainy season can be passed, like the last, without a single death, or barely one in the general European society of the colony, we may trust that our fair countrywomen will not give way to the terrors caused by exaggerated reports, and that they will as freely face this as any other climate in company with the partners of their affections.[1]

But the heavy mortality of 1823 reduced the European population considerably,[2] and though the ranks of civilian men were, of course, soon filled up again, the census taken upon the request of the Commissioners of Inquiry in April 1826 showed only 103 males and 10 females.

About one-half of the Europeans at present in the colony, may be stated to be employed solely in situations under the Government, or the Church Missionary Society ; and the other half in some way engaged in or connected with trade.[3]

In the following five decades the European population fluctuated without showing any definite trend (Table 16).[4]

The European male residents enumerated at the censuses increased from 76 in 1871 to 129 in 1881, 177 in 1891, and 263 in 1901. The corresponding figures for females were 31, 34, 33, and 46 respectively. The

---

[1] *The Royal Gazette and Sierra Leone Advertiser*, 15 Feb. 1823, p. 25.

[2] See pp. 293–8 below.

[3] *Report of Commissioners of Inquiry*, 1827, First Part, p. 19. The *Blue Books* for 1826 and 1827 show only 'about' 80 males and 7 females (see *Blue Book 1826*, p. 136 ; *1827*, p. 64).

[4] The figures for 1843–5 may be too high. The 1844 *Blue Book* listed for Freetown 120 males and 30 females. Shreeve said (p. 51): 'The following is an extract from the Census to 31st December, 1844 of Europeans and Mulattos, taken by the author from the General Census . . .

	Men	Women	Total
Resident Europeans	59	22	81
Do Mulattos	7	8	15
Sick British Sailors	6	0	6
Foreign Seamen, the crews of condemned slave vessels, &c. .	48	0	48.'

The official figures for Europeans, therefore, included at least in 1844 Mulattoes. (The returns of the census taken in the third quarter of 1831 in Freetown showed 80 Europeans and 118 Mulattoes.)

TABLE 16. *Civilian European Population by Sex, Sierra Leone, 1831–71*[1]

Year	Males	Females	Year	Males	Females	Year	Males	Females	Year	Males	Females
1831	85	10	1839	75	24	1847	74	21	1858	82	25
1832	91	11	1840	62	21	1848	83	27	1860	100	31
1833	74	10	1842	88	28	1849	71	27	1868	99[2]	26[3]
1834	62	23	1843	98	40	1850	84	27	1871	76	31
1835	68	22	1844	136	39	1851	94	31			
1836	83	22	1845	113	45	1855	85	20			
1838	83	19	1846	80	35	1857	83	22			

[1] See *Blue Book 1831*, p. 114; *1832*, p. 114; *1833*, p. 118, to *1838*, p. 118; *1839*, p. 134, to *1847*, p. 134; *1848*, p. 218; *1849*, p. 134; *1850*, p. 138; *1851*, p. 138; *1855*, p. 162; *1857*, p. 152; *1858*, p. 159; *1860*, p. 164; *1868*, p. 174; *1871*, p. 172. The figures from 1855 on include the military.
[2] Including 1 in British Quiah and 11 in Bulama.   [3] Including 6 in Bulama.

TABLE 17. *European Population by Sex, Sierra Leone, 1881–1931*[1]

Population	Sex	Colony						Protectorate		
		1881	1891	1901	1911	1921	1931	1911	1921	1931
Resident . .	Male	129	177	263	588	698	308	140	204	173
	Female	34	33	46	62	94	112	30	46	58
	Total	163	210	309	650	792	420	170	250	231
On board ships	Male	108	14	142	52	119	67	—	—	—
Total . .	Male	237	191	405	640	817	375	140	204	173
	Female	34	33	46	62	94	112	30	46	58
	Total	271	224	451	702	911	487	170	250	231

[1] See *Census Report 1891*, pp. 3, 5; *1901*, p. 6; *1911*, pp. 8, 23; *1921*, pp. 8, 22; *1931*, pp. 21, 73, 165. The population on board ships is not given by sex for 1881; I assumed that, as in subsequent years, all were males.

increase in the number of males from 1871 to 1881 was due in part to the fact that the census of 1871 covered only the Peninsula.[1] To what extent the rise in this and the two following decades was due to a reinforcement of the military it is impossible to tell.[2] The enormous increase in the number of males to 588 in 1911 was largely due to this cause.

The total resident European population amounts to 650 persons as against 309 persons, showing a gain of 341 persons.[3] The increase is to be attributed chiefly to the larger military element, there being now stationed in Freetown a complete company of Royal Artillery.

At the same time, owing to the establishment of the railway and the expansion generally of the trade of the Colony, the number of Europeans in the service of the Colonial Government has been greatly increased, and it is fairly certain that in 1901 the number of Europeans engaged in trade was considerably less than the 130 so

[1] According to *Census Report 1881*, p. 6, the number of white residents enumerated in the sub-stations was 29 in 1881.
[2] The total number of Government Officers (including Africans) increased from 679 in 1881 to 1,176 in 1891, and to 2,545 in 1901. *Census Report 1891*, p. 12, said: 'The principal reason for the large increase is the augmentation of the Military and Police in the Colony.' *Census Report 1901*, p. 15, stated: 'The large increase of 1,369 is accounted for by the augmentation of the Military establishment in the Colony, and also by the opening of the Government Railway.'
[3] According to *Medical Report 1907*, p. 6, there was an 'increase in the actual European resident population from 300 in 1906 to 550 in 1907'.

engaged, shown by the recent Census, although no figures are available for purposes of comparison.[1]

The soldiers in 1911 were no less than 354, or 60 per cent. of the total male European population. By 1921 their number had decreased to 293, but the total male European population had risen to 698, owing mainly to an increase in the number of 'Commercial Agents and Employees' from 130 to 235.[2] The 1931 census, however, showed only 308 male Europeans. The heavy drop was due in a large measure to the withdrawal of the Imperial Garrison from Freetown in 1929, the number of soldiers being reduced to 18. But, owing to the slump, the number returned under 'Commercial' was only 101 as compared with 235 in 1921.[3]

In the meantime the number of females had increased steadily from 33 in 1891 to 112 in 1931. Their proportion among the total European resident population fluctuated somewhat but was in 1931, with 36 per cent., higher than ever before (excepting, of course, the period 1787–91).

In the Protectorate the number of resident Europeans was estimated in 1901 'at between 50 and 100'.[4] It increased to 170 in 1911 and to 250 in 1921, but declined to 231 in 1931. The rise between 1911 and 1921 was 'due to the extension of the Railway, the opening up of the country to trade'. The number returned as commercial increased from 51 to 108.[5] The decline between 1921 and 1931 was explained as follows:

> The decrease is due for the greater part to the recent trade depression, causing a consequent reduction in the numbers of persons following commercial pursuits, and to the transfer of part of the Sierra Leone Battalion of the Royal West African Frontier Force to the Colony . . . .
>
> Persons engaged in commerce have decreased from 108 to 61 or by 47 and soldiers from 26 to 9 or by 17.[6]

It is interesting to note that the proportion of females in the Protectorate was in 1931 hardly smaller than in the Colony.

According to the census reports the numbers of European Government Officials present in Sierra Leone were 97 in 1911, 141 in 1921, and 142 (including 6 females) in 1931, while the Military numbered 381, 319, and 27 respectively, and the resident non-official civilians 342, 582, and 482 respectively.[7] The annual Medical Reports show in addition the 'total number of European officials resident in the Colony and Protectorate during any portion of the year' in 1907–38, the average number of European officials in 1908–38, the total number of European Military in 1909–25, the average strength of the European Military in 1924–7, the total number of European non-officials in 1909–38, and the average number of European non-officials in 1926–38. The data are summarized in Table 18. The figures for Government Officials and Military are fairly accurate for

---

[1] *Census Report 1911*, pp. 8–9.   [2] See ibid. *1921*, p. 9.

[3] See ibid. *1931*, pp. 64, 69. The actual decrease in the number of people engaged in commerce may have been somewhat smaller. 'It is possible that banking, shipping and other kindred occupations were classed under "Commercial" in 1921.'

[4] Ibid. *1901*, p. 6.   [5] See ibid. *1911*, p. 25; *1921*, p. 25.

[6] Ibid. *1931*, p. 185.

[7] See ibid. *1911*, pp. 9, 25; *1921*, pp. 8, 25; *1931*, pp. 69, 190–1.

TABLE 18. *European Population by Occupation, Sierra Leone, 1907–38*[1]

Year	Average Government Officials	Total Government Officials	Total Military	Total Non-Officials	Total
1907	..	135	..	..	..
1908	100	160	..	..	..
1909	99	155	344	121	620
1910	77	171	361	299	831
1911	120	192	374	343	909
1912	225	230	389	184	803
1913	131	244	738	285	1,267
1914	204	328	603	303	1,234
1915	158	258	698	245	1,201
1916	172	272	597	269	1,138
1917	110	244	636	210	1,090
1918	97	227	574	277	1,078
1919	102	202	679	295	1,176
1920	133	233	495	300	1,028
1921	144	214	..	..	..
1922	109	209	285	591	1,085
1923	102	188	291	420	899
1924	164	198	300	430	928
1925	180	200	283	350	833

Year	Average Government Officials	Average Imperial Troops	Average Non-Officials	Total Government Officials	Total Non-Officials
1924	164	278	..	198	430
1925	180	283	..	200	350
1926	184	268	299	234	390
1927	250	248	299	300	369
1928	280	..	301	320	380
1929	251	..	325	302	420
1930	260	..	318	296	398
1931	177	..	343	261	494
1932	176	..	292	240	434
1933	155	..	285	218	400
1934	144	..	306	208	442
1935	145	..	399	207	511
1936	145	..	356	211	504
1937	167	..	416	227	565
1938	196	..	372	250	495

[1] See *Medical Report 1907*, p. 6; *1908*, pp. 7–8; *1909*, pp. 5–7; *1910*, pp. 6–7; *1911*, pp. 7, 10; *1912*, p. 10; *1913*, pp. 7–8; *1914*, pp. 8–9; *1915*, pp. 8–9; *1916*, p. 10; *1917*, p. 8; *1918*, pp. 6–7; *1919*, pp. 7–8; *1920*, p. 7; *1921*, p. 8; *1922*, pp. 11, 16; *1923*, pp. 10, 13; *1924*, pp. 10, 12, 14; *1925*, pp. 7, 10; *1926*, pp. 9, 12; *1927*, pp. 9–10, 13; *1928*, p. 9; *1929*, p. 9; *1930*, pp. 5–6; *1931*, pp. 5–6; *1932*, pp. 5–6; *1933*, pp. 5–6; *1934*, pp. 5–6; *1935*, pp. 4–5; *1936*, pp. 5–6; *1937*, pp. 5–6; *1938*, pp. 5–6; *Colonial Reports, Sierra Leone 1917*, p. 14; *1920*, p. 21.

most years,[1] but those for non-officials are, at least from 1919 to 1924, incomplete or merely estimated.

1919. The figures for the non-official Europeans include those of the well-known Trading Firms and Missionary Societies only. There are a small number of others of whom it is difficult or impossible to obtain accurate figures.[2]

1922. It is not practical to obtain even an approximate figure for total unofficial European residents for 1922.[3]

The non-officials, moreover, apparently comprise sometimes only men.[4]

The number of English in the Colony increased from 104 in 1881 to 195 in 1901 and to 595 in 1921, but dropped again to 195 in 1931. Taking the Colony and Protectorate together, the number of English declined between 1921 and 1931 from 711 to 298 while the number of other Europeans rose from 331 to 353. In 1921 the 94 Swiss were the most numerous group next to the English, but by 1931 their number had decreased to 30. The French numbered 91 in 1921 and 87 in 1931. The American community declined from 67 to 53. There was, on the other hand, an increase in the number of Scotch from 34 to 69 and of Irish from 31 to 53. While no Germans were present in 1921, they totalled 21 in 1931. Of the 651 Europeans enumerated in 1931, 566 were born in Europe, 44 in the United States, and 41 elsewhere.[5]

White children have always been few in Sierra Leone. Only 17 of the 651 Europeans enumerated in 1931 were under 16 years of age. Of the 472 adult male Europeans 242 were single and 223 married; of the 162 adult female Europeans 49 were single and 111 married. The proportion of bachelors is much smaller among the British than among the other Europeans. Of the male British subjects (including children) 135 were single and 185 married; of the non-British Europeans 116 were single and only 38 married. The great preponderance of bachelors among the non-British Europeans is possibly due to the fact that the great majority of European mercantile agents and clerks were non-British. Of the 324 British males 135 were Government Officials, 49 mercantile managers, agents, and clerks, and 24 ministers of religion, missionaries, and lay teachers; of the 157 non-British males 1 (American) was a Government

[1] The average number of Government Officials for 1912 seems too high. *Medical Report 1914* gives the total number of Government Officials at one place (p. 8) as 328, at another place (p. 9) as 285; *Medical Report 1918* gives similarly at one place (p. 7) 227, at another (p. 6) 185. *Medical Report 1925* gives 283 at one place (p. 7) as the total resident Imperial Military and at another place (p. 10) as the average strength of the Imperial Troops.

[2] Ibid. *1919*, p. 8.

[3] Ibid. *1922*, p. 16. See also *Colonial Reports, Sierra Leone 1920*, p. 21; *Medical Report 1923*, p. 13, *1924*, p. 14.

[4] When the total number of non-officials rose from 398 in 1930 to 494 in 1931, *Medical Report 1931*, p. 6, said: 'The large increase in the total number resident is surprising in view of the heavy retrenchment in staff of the trading firms but is largely accounted for by the mining developments in the Protectorate. Also the wives of Government Officials have been added to this list, which does not appear to have been done before.' But according to the 1931 census the persons occupied in mining in the Protectorate numbered only 15, and even the figures of non-officials for 1931 (total 494, average 343) do not seem to have been all-inclusive since on census date there were 482 non-officials in Sierra Leone.

[5] Including 5 Spanish women who were natives of the Canary Islands (see *Census Report 1931*, p. 63).

Official, 86 were mercantile managers, agents, and clerks, and 24 ministers of religion, missionaries, and lay teachers. Of the 170 European females 6 (British) were Government officials and 60 (32 British, 28 non-British) were missionaries and lay teachers. None of the Europeans followed an agricultural pursuit.[1]

Of the 651 Europeans 285 lived in Freetown, 135 in the rest of the Colony, 84 in the Northern, and 147 in the Southern Province of the Protectorate.[2]

2. *Asiatic Population*

Until 1911 the census reports distinguished merely between whites and blacks, and until 1901 the classification by nationalities suggests that all whites were of European descent. But among the whites returned in 1901 there were 41 Syrians and 1 Egyptian.

In 1901 the population was censused under the classifications 'Whites' and 'Blacks'; in the former were included a number of Asiatics, who, though white in colour, were not such in social surroundings; accordingly this anomaly has been dealt with in the recent Census by dividing the population under three headings, 'Europeans', 'Asiatics' and 'Africans.'[3]

The first Syrians came in the 1890s. The 1901 census showed 38 male and 3 female Syrians,[4] and the 1911 census 136 males and 39 females.[5] There were in addition in the Protectorate 81 males and 10 females.[6]

Syrians have increased from 41 persons in 1901 to 175 in 1911, and the statistics relating to the Protectorate will show that they are penetrating there also; their increased numbers in this Colony are probably due to the fact that many of them have been driven here from French Guinea owing to a prohibitive tax imposed upon them in that country. They come from Beyrout, Tripoli and other places in Syria, and are known as 'Coral men' among the natives of this Colony, whom they show a tendency to rival as petty traders, and they are currently reported to prosper here.[7]

The Syrians continued to increase in the years preceding the first World War,[8] but their growth in the Colony was checked by riots which occurred in 1919. They numbered, in 1921, 132 males and 45 females.[9]

Syrians have not increased at a rate at all comparable with the increase shown in the 1901–1911 inter-censal period, when they increased from 41 to 175; they have added no more than 2 to their number. But they have succeeded in establishing themselves as traders in the Colony as well as in the Protectorate and to their success in this direction is to be attributed in no small degree the engendering in the minds of a certain section of the African community of a jealousy which led to the Anti-Syrian riots in 1919. That they do not show an increase larger than 2 is due to some extent to the considerable exodus of Syrians after the Riots.[10]

But in the Protectorate the number of Syrians had increased by 1921 to 283 males and 103 females.[11]

In the 1920s the increase of Syrians was enormous. Their number rose in the Colony from 177 to 413, and in the Protectorate from 386 to 753.

---

[1] See ibid., pp. 69, 190–1.   [2] See ibid., pp. 68, 189.   [3] Ibid. *1911*, p. 8.
[4] See ibid. *1901*, p. 6.   [5] See ibid. *1911*, p. 10.   [6] See ibid., p. 24.
[7] Ibid., p. 10.
[8] *Medical Report 1913*, p. 75, says that there were in Freetown 212 Syrians as compared with 145 at the 1911 census.
[9] See *Census Report 1921*, p. 9.   [10] Ibid., p. 10.   [11] See ibid., p. 24.

All the male Syrians [in the Colony] are engaged in produce, general merchandise, cotton goods or petty trading. Some are thriving merchants and are astute business men. A considerable number have been residents in the Colony for some years and have places of business, both in the Colony and Protectorate. Many have brought their wives and females[1] out; and, even despite the recent legislation enforcing a deposit of £60 before landing, they appear to be on the increase.[2]

Marteroy, in an article 'Freetown 1899–1938', characterized the change that had occurred in those 40 years as follows:

This eastern part of the town is almost a counter part of Beyrouth or any other Syrian town. In 1899 very few Syrians were trading here, you could see them round the corners of the trade 'stream line' streets sitting on small boxes in front of a larger box, not too large,—where they were selling imitation coral beads,—they used to be called for years 'corals', but now with the help of many Sierra Leonean householders who let and later sold their freeholds to Syrians, the latter to-day run nearly the whole petty trade in Kissy, East and Little East Streets—no more little boxes with coral beads on them. With another help, the credit given to them by the Commercial Firms, the Syrians have to-day neat shops and you will meet them all along the railway line and in the Mining Districts also where they do trading and deal in gold.[3]

Apart from the Syrians there are few Asiatics in Sierra Leone. Of the 599 Asiatics enumerated in 1921, 563 were Syrians, 19 Indians, 15 Arabs, and 2 Greeks. Of the 1,216 Asiatics recorded in 1931, 1,166 were Syrians, 25 Indians, 23 Arabs,[4] and 2 Greeks. While the 651 Europeans comprised only 17 children, the 1,216 Asiatics included no less than 308.[5] The great majority of these children were born in Sierra Leone.[6] Of 714 male adult Asiatics 376 were single and 311 married; of 194 female adult Asiatics only 24 were single and 156 were married.[7]

Of the 1,216 Asiatics 400 lived in Freetown, 44 in the rest of the Colony, 279 in the Northern and 493 in the Southern Province of the Protectorate.[8]

3. Total Non-African Population

The number of resident non-Africans in the Colony increased from 852 in 1911 to 990 in 1921 but decreased to 864 in 1931. The Protectorate showed an increase from 265 in 1911 to 651 in 1921, and to 1,003 in 1931. While up to 50 years ago practically all non-Africans in Sierra Leone were Europeans, and while in 1921 the Europeans still constituted about two-thirds of the non-African population, the proportion had dropped by 1931 to about one-third.

The numbers of non-native officials (including those on leave) by sex and age on 1 January 1930 to 1 January 1938 are shown in Table 26.

[1] Should read 'children'.

[2] *Census Report 1931*, p. 59. See also ibid., p. 176.   [3] Marteroy, pp. 84–5.

[4] The Arabs are mostly of African birth and might be more correctly termed Moors. See *Census Report 1931*, pp. 31, 59, 176.

[5] These were nearly all Syrian children. (Of the 133 Asiatic children in the Colony all but one Indian child were Syrians; see ibid., p. 60.)

[6] The total number of Asiatics born in Sierra Leone was 233 (including 227 Syrians), and this figure probably includes few adults.

[7] 'All Syrian women over eighteen years of age [in the Colony] are returned as married' (ibid., p. 35).

[8] See ibid., pp. 60, 180.

TABLE 19. *Resident Non-African Population by Nationality, Sierra Leone, 1881–1931*[1]

Nationality	Colony						Protectorate			Total		
	1881	1891	1901	1911	1921	1931	1911	1921	1931	1911	1921	1931
EUROPEANS												
English	104	114	195	424	595	195	80	116	103	504	711	298
Welsh	1	4	1	11	8	6	2	1	3	13	9	9
Scotch	2	11	19	38	22	49	11	12	20	49	34	69
Irish	6	31	26	75	29	38	10	2	15	85	31	53
Brit. Colonial	2[2]	2[3]	4[4]	2[5]	3[6]	5[7]	—	—	1	2	3	6
Armenian	—	—	—	—	—	—	—	1	2	—	1	2
Austrian	—	—	1	—	—	—	1	—	—	1	—	—
Belgian	—	—	2	—	—	—	—	—	—	—	—	—
Danish	—	—	—	—	—	1	—	—	—	—	—	1
Dutch	1	—	1	3	—	2	—	—	—	3	—	2
French	15	26	34	37	55	62	9	36	25	46	91	87
German	9	1	6	20	—	14	12	—	7	32	—	21
Greek	1	2	—	—	—	2	2	—	2	2	—	4
Italian	1	7	1	4	—	3	—	1	—	4	1	3
Norwegian	—	—	—	—	—	5	—	—	—	—	—	5
Portuguese	4	—	—	—	—	—	—	—	—	—	—	—
Russian	—	—	—	—	—	3	—	—	—	—	—	3
Spanish	—	1	—	—	—	5	—	—	—	—	—	5
Swedish	1	—	—	—	—	—	—	—	—	—	—	—
Swiss	12	6	9	19	60	11	11	34	19	30	94	30
American	4	5	10	17	20	19	32	47	34	49	67	53
Total	163	210	309	650	792	420	170	250	231	820	1,042	651
ASIATICS												
Arab	—	—	—	2	15	6	2	—	17	4	15	23
Greek	—	—	—	1	2	2	—	—	—	1	2	2
Indian	—	—	—	24	4	23	2	15	2	26	19	25
Syrian	—	—	41	175	177	413	91	386	753	266	563	1,166
Total	—	—	41	202	198	444	95	401	772	297	599	1,216

[1] See *Census Report 1881*, p. 6; *1891*, p. 5; *1901*, p. 6; *1911*, pp. 8, 10, 24; *1921*, pp. 8–9, 23–4; *1931*, pp. 59, 63, 177, 186.
[2] West Indian.
[3] 1 Maltese, 1 Canadian.
[4] 1 Canadian, 2 West Indian, 1 Australian.
[5] 1 West Indian, 1 Australian.
[6] 1 West Indian, 2 Australian.
[7] 1 South African, 3 Australian, 1 New Zealand.

TABLE 20. *Resident Non-African Population by Nationality (or Race) and Sex, Sierra Leone, 1921 and 1931*[1]

Nationality (Race)	1921 Colony M.	F.	Protectorate M.	F.	Total M.	F.	Total	1931 Colony M.	F.	Protectorate M.	F.	Total M.	F.	Total
EUROPEANS														
English	543	52	106	10	649	62	711	147	48	82	21	229	69	298
Welsh	5	3	1	—	6	3	9	5	1	2	1	7	2	9
Scotch	16	6	12	—	28	6	34	34	15	17	3	51	18	69
Irish	19	10	2	—	21	10	31	22	16	12	3	34	19	53
British Colonial	3[2]	—	—	—	3	—	3	3[3]	2[4]	—	1	3	3	6
Armenian	—	—	1	—	1	—	1	—	—	1	1	1	1	2
Danish	—	—	—	—	—	—	—	1	—	—	—	1	—	1
Dutch	—	—	—	—	—	—	—	1	1	—	—	1	1	2
French	49	6	34	2	83	8	91	57	5	23	2	80	7	87
German	—	—	—	—	—	—	—	11	3	6	1	17	4	21
Greek	—	—	—	—	—	—	—	2	—	2	—	4	—	4
Italian	—	—	—	1	—	1	1	3	—	—	—	3	—	3
Norwegian	—	—	—	—	—	—	—	2	3	—	—	2	3	5
Russian	—	—	—	—	—	—	—	—	3	—	—	—	3	3
Spanish	—	—	—	—	—	—	—	—	5	—	—	—	5	5
Swiss	54	6	31	3	85	9	94	10	1	15	4	25	5	30
American	9	11	16	31	25	42	67	10	9	13	21	23	30	53
Total	698	94	203	47	901	141	1,042	308	112	173	58	481	170	651
ASIATICS														
Arab	10	5	—	—	10	5	15	5	1	14	3	19	4	23
Greek	2	—	—	—	2	—	2	2	—	—	—	2	—	2
Indian	4	—	10	5	14	5	19	20	3	2	—	22	3	25
Syrian	132	45	283	103	415	148	563	282	131	561	192	843	323	1,166
Total	148	50	293	108	441	158	599	309	135	577	195	886	330	1,216

[1] See *Census Report 1921*, p. 24; *1931*, pp. 59, 63, 177, 186.
[2] 1 West Indian, 2 Australian.
[3] 2 Australian, 1 New Zealand.
[4] 1 South African, 1 Australian.

TABLE 21. *Resident European Population by Birthplace, Sierra Leone, 1911–31*[1]

Birthplace	Colony 1911	1921	1931	Protectorate 1911	1921	1931	Total 1911	1921	1931
Sierra Leone	1	1	5	1	4	5	2	5	10
Africa (non-Brit.)	2	15	6	—	1	—	2	16	6
Europe	593	729	378	126	196	188	719	925	566
America	17	27	14	34	43	32	51	70	46
India	22	8	5	2	—	3	24	8	8
Asia (non-Brit.)	1	10	—	2	1	—	3	11	—
Brit. Colonies	14	4	12	5	5	3	19	9	15
Total	650	794[2]	420	170	250	231	820	1,044[2]	651

[1] See *Census Report 1911*, pp. 9, 25; *1921*, pp. 9–10, 25; *1931*, pp. 66, 187–8.
[2] Including 2 floating population not born in Europe.

TABLE 22. *Resident European Population by Birthplace and Sex, Sierra Leone, 1931*[1]

Birthplace	Colony		Protectorate		Total		Total
	Males	Females	Males	Females	Males	Females	
England. .	144	47	78	19	222	66	288
Wales . .	5	1	3	2	8	3	11
Scotland	28	14	18	3	46	17	63
Ireland . .	19	16	9	3	28	19	47
Malta . .	2	—	—	—	2	—	2
Denmark .	1	—	—	—	1	—	1
France . .	57	5	21	2	78	7	85
Germany .	10	3	6	1	16	4	20
Greece . .	3	—	3	1	6	1	7
Holland . .	1	1	—	—	1	1	2
Italy . .	3	—	1	—	4	—	4
Norway . .	2	3	—	—	2	3	5
Russia . .	—	3	—	—	—	3	3
Switzerland .	9	1	16	1	25	2	27
Europe .	284	94	155	33[2]	439	127[2]	566[2]
Sierra Leone .	4	1	3	2	7	3	10
South Africa .	—	1	—	1	—	2	2
Canary Islands	—	5	—	—	—	5	5
French West Africa .	1	—	—	—	1	—	1
Africa. .	5	7	3	3	8	10	18
Canada . .	—	—	1	—	1	—	1
West Indies .	3	2	—	1	3	3	6
U.S. America .	6	8	10	20	16	28	44
Mexico . .	—	—	1	—	1	—	1
South America	—	—	—	1	—	1	1
America .	9	10	12	22	21	32	53
Cyprus . .	1	—	—	—	1	—	1
India . .	5	—	3	—	8	—	8
Asia . .	6	—	3	—	9	—	9
Australia .	3	1	—	—	3	1	4
New Zealand .	1	—	—	—	1	—	1
Oceania .	4	1	—	—	4	1	5

[1] See *Census Report 1931*, pp. 66, 187–8.   [2] Including 1 not stated.

TABLE 23. *Asiatic Population by Birthplace, Sex, and Race, Sierra Leone, 1931*[1]

Birthplace	Colony Arabs M.	Arabs F.	Greeks M.	Greeks F.	Indians M.	Indians F.	Syrians M.	Syrians F.	Total M.	Total F.	Protectorate M.	Protectorate F.	Total M.	Total F.	Total
Arabia	1	—	—	—	—	—	—	—	1	—	2	—	3	—	3
India	—	—	—	—	19	—	—	—	19	—	—	—	19	—	19
Syria	—	—	—	—	—	—	235	81	235	81	474	133	709	214	923
Asiatic Turkey	—	—	1	—	—	—	—	—	1	—	—	—	1	—	1
Other Asiatic Countries	—	—	1	—	—	—	—	—	1	—	—	—	1	—	1
Asia	1	—	2	—	19	—	235	81	257	81	476	133	733	214	947
Sierra Leone Colony	1	1	—	—	—	—	37	44	38	45	21	10	59	55	114
Sierra Leone Protectorate	—	—	—	—	1	—	7	5	8	5	60	46	68	51	119
South Africa	—	—	—	—	—	3	—	—	—	3	2	—	2	3	5
French Guinea	1	—	—	—	—	—	2	1	3	1	4	4	7	5	12
Morocco	2	—	—	—	—	—	—	—	2	—	6	1	8	1	9
Other African Colonies	—	—	—	—	—	—	—	—	—	—	7	1	7	1	8
Africa	4	1	—	—	1	3	46	50	51	54	100	62	151	116	267
West Indies	—	—	—	—	—	—	1	—	1	—	1	—	2	—	2

[1] See *Census Report 1931*, pp. 60, 178–9.

TABLE 24. *Non-African Population by Sex and Age, Sierra Leone, 1931*[1]

Age (years)	Colony Europeans M.	Europeans F.	Asiatics M.	Asiatics F.	Protectorate Europeans M.	Europeans F.	Asiatics M.	Asiatics F.	Total Europeans M.	Europeans F.	Europeans Total	Asiatics M.	Asiatics F.	Asiatics Total
0–5	2	1	29	35	4	4	56	50	6	5	11	85	85	170
6–10	2	2	24	19	1	—	28	14	3	2	5	52	33	85
11–15	—	—	17	9	—	1	18	9	—	1	1	35	18	53
16–20	13	1	31	14	3	3	66	25	16	4	20	97	39	136
21–25	42	9	31	22	27	3	102	18	69	12	81	133	40	173
26–30	61	31	33	14	45	9	67	39	106	40	146	100	53	153
31–35	55	18	36	7	30	13	81	11	85	31	116	117	18	135
36–40	39	27	30	9	31	14	54	14	70	41	111	84	23	107
41–45	48	13	32	4	19	5	38	7	67	18	85	70	11	81
46–50	24	5	20	1	8	1	37	4	32	6	38	57	5	62
51–55	15	4	9	—	5	1	15	1	20	5	25	24	1	25
56–60	5	1	9	1	—	1	10	1	5	2	7	19	2	21
61–65	2	—	3	—	—	2	2	1	2	2	4	5	1	6
66–70	—	—	3	—	—	1	1	—	—	1	1	4	—	4
71–75	—	—	1	—	—	—	1	1	—	—	—	2	1	3
76–80	—	—	—	—	—	—	1	—	—	—	—	1	—	1
Not stated	—	—	1	—	—	—	—	—	—	—	—	1	—	1
Total	308	112	309	135	173	58	577	195	481	170	651	886	330	1,216

[1] See *Census Report 1931*, pp. 32, 194.

TABLE 25. *Non-African Population by Sex and Conjugal Condition, Sierra Leone, 1931*[1]

Conjugal condition	Colony British M.	British F.	Other Europeans M.	Other Europeans F.	Asiatics M.	Asiatics F.	Protectorate British M.	British F.	Other Europeans M.	Other Europeans F.	Asiatics M.	Asiatics F.
Single	77	25	74	8	175	72	58	8	42	16	373	88
Married	131	54	21	24	129	62	54	20	17	13	182	94
Widowed	2	—	1	1	4	1	—	1	1	—	20	13
Divorced	2.	—	—	—	1	—	1	—	—	—	2	—
Total	212	79	96	33	309	135	113	29	60	29	577	195

[1] See *Census Report 1931*, pp. 61, 68, 180, 189.

TABLE 26. *Non-Native Officials by Sex and Age, Sierra Leone, 1930–8.*[1]

Date 1 Jan.	20–24 years		25–29 years		30–34 years		35–39 years		40–44 years		45–49 years		50–54 years		55– years		Age unknown		Total	
	M.	F.	M.	F.	M.	F.	M.	F.	M.	F.	M.	F.	M.	F.	M.	F.	M.	F.	M.	F.
1930	6	—	46	2	62	1	55	5	64	1	34	1	12	—	1	—	3	—	283	10
1931	6	—	37	—	63	2	40	4	70	2	32	1	13	—	3	—	1	—	265	9
1932	5	—	29	—	54	1	31	4	61	—	32	2	18	—	4	—	1	—	235	7
1933	2	—	30	2	50	—	39	4	44	—	27	1	13	1	—	—	—	—	205	8
1934	3	—	25	1	47	2	40	3	39	—	27	1	10	1	1	—	—	—	192	8
1935	7	—	17	—	37	2	49	—	33	4	33	1	10	—	2	—	—	—	188	7
1936	6	—	21	1	35	1	47	2	26	4	40	—	8	—	1	—	—	—	184	8
1937	7	—	28	1	49	3	54	—	31	3	53	2	13	1	3	—	—	—	238	10
1938	4	—	28	—	39	2	46	2	34	4	40	—	16	—	1	—	—	—	208	8

[1] See *West Africa, Vital Statistics of Non-Native Officials 1930*, p. 1, to *1938*, p. 1.

VI. Birth and Death Registration

1. *1791–1913*

Registration of births and deaths was planned from the very beginning of the Colony. The 'Rules and Instructions from the Directors of the Sierra Leone Company to the Superintendent and Council for the Settlement', issued about the end of 1791, stipulated:

> You are to take care also that a Register shall be kept of all births, deaths and marriages either of settlers or others, and that a Bill of mortality be made up with as much exactness as possible, and transmitted to us once a year at least, and still oftner at the first.[1]

> You are to desire that in every case of death or material sickness, at the first the causes of disorder shall be reported to you, that they may be notified to us.[2]

The minutes of a Council Meeting held on 3 July 1792 relate:

> The Superintendent moved, that a person be appointed as a Sexton, and that the people be desired in case of any Births or Deaths that they immediately inform him of it, or they will not be intitled to any more provisions supposing they should be found to deceive this person, and that the Sexton be immediately to inform the Store Keeper whenever a death or birth takes place as he may stop the provisions.

> The Superintendent purposed a Clerk to be appointed to perform the duty of the Church, this man may also be appointed Sexton.[3]

When Governor Clarkson left for a 'short cruise to sea' he wrote, on 6 October 1792, to William Dawes:

> ... I must request that you will endeavour to comply with the following directions—

> To endeavour to collect a true statement of the births, deaths, christenings, marriages, etc., Mr. King and Mr. Strand I have employed to collect this information, agreeable to a form I have made out for them.[4]

On 15 June 1794 the Council resolved

> That Mr. Thomas Jones School Master be appointed Clerk in the Room of Henry Beverhout at the former salary of £15 a year, and that Mr. Jones be enjoined to keep

---

[1] Evans, p. 59.   [2] Ibid., p. 68.   [3] C.O. 270, vol. ii, pp. 59–60.

[4] *Diary of Clarkson*, p. 74. On 10 Sept. Clarkson had written in his Diary: 'Gave to the Rev Melville Horne all the books and papers connected with my late situation, such as the accounts of baptisms, marriages, etc.' (ibid., p. 46). But see also entry of 23 Sept.: 'After service I delivered over to Mr. Horne an additional account of the Registers of Christenings and Marriages, but could not furnish him with the deaths, as the black preachers in general buried the dead of those belonging to each sect' (ibid., p. 55).

every exact and particular Register of all Births, Marriages, and Deaths within the Colony.[1]

But the records evidently remained incomplete.

In the last year [1797], the mortality of the Nova Scotian blacks has been greater than in any former year, the first excepted. But neither their deaths nor births can be accurately stated at present; as they are unwilling to give the necessary intelligence.[2]

After the arrival of the Maroons compulsory registration of births and deaths was formally established by an Act of 7 March 1801[3] which read as follows:

Whereas both the public Good of this Colony, and the Interests of Individuals require that an authentic Register of Births and Deaths be kept within the same The Governor and Council, enact, declare, and Resolve

1st That every Settler in this Colony being the Father of an Infant born in Marriage shall within 28 days after the Birth of such Infant give notice thereof to one of the Persons hereinafter mentioned, and on failure of giving such notice either verbally or in writing, shall forfeit the sum of Four Dollars.

2nd That the Mother of the Infant be required to give this notice, subject to the above penalty on failure thereof in case the father should be dead or absent from the Colony, at the time of the birth of the said Infant, and also in cases of Bastardy, whether the reputed father be living or no.

3rd That in case of the death of any Settler in this Colony, the surviving Husband or Wife, or if there be no Survivor of this Class, the Father or Mother, or if no Surviving Father or Mother the Relation of the person deceased, be required to give notice of such death within 28 days after knowledge thereof under the penalty of four Dollars, on failure of Giving such notice.

4th That any person giving Information of the birth of an Infant, being the Offspring of any Settler in this Colony; or of the death of any Settler in default of due notice thereof by the party of whom such notice is required, and within 28 days after the Expiration of the time limited in either and every such Case be entitled to a Reward of four Dollars.

5th That notice be given in the cases aforesaid by the parties of whom such notice is required if resident in the district of Freetown, to the Secretary for the time being at Fort Thornton; and if resident in the district of Granville Town to the Justice of the Peace for that district.

6th That the aforesaid Resolutions have the force and Authority of a Byelaw in this Colony.

It seems that at first some efforts were made to enforce this Act. The data for 1807 (57 births and 36 deaths)[4] came possibly near the truth. But the Act of 1801 covered only Freetown and Granville Town, and when, with the influx of Liberated Africans from 1808 on, other villages were established, registration was not extended to these new localities,[5]

---

[1] C.O. 270, vol. ii, p. 177.

[2] *Report of Sierra Leone Company 1798*, p. 3.

[3] Sierra Leone, *Acts 1800–27*, pp. 10–11.

[4] See *The Royal Gazette and Sierra Leone Advertiser*, 3 Jan. 1818, p. 21.

[5] When in a Resolution adopted on 17 June 1824 the House of Commons asked for 'An Account of the Number of Births in the Colony of Sierra Leone; distinguishing Males from Females, in the years 1817, 1818, 1819, 1820, 1821, 1822, and 1823 respectively', the Colonial Secretary replied: 'No general Record of Births has ever been kept, nor is there any means of ascertaining, or even estimating the Total Number in the years specified' (*Accounts relating to the Population, &c. of Sierra Leone*, 1825, p. 41).

and there is no evidence that it was carried on systematically in Freetown and Granville Town.[1] The Commissioners of Inquiry (1826) who were much interested in the population trends among the various groups of people tried to obtain figures at least of marriages, baptisms, and burials, and they secured from the rector of the parish of St. George, Freetown, some carefully prepared tables comprising a long period.[2] The covering letter, dated 3 June 1826, read as follows:

In compliance with the desire expressed by you, in a communication dated 22nd Day of April last, I beg to transmit for your inspection, Returns of the Baptisms, Marriages, and Burials, which have been registered in this Parish, from the date of the earliest records to the present Time; as far as I have been able to ascertain them.

In so doing I request permission to offer a few remarks relative to the subject of Burials; which I hope may be of some use by way of explanation.

With very few exceptions, the Burials registered are those of the Established Church. There are, however, a very limited number of instances, in which the Funeral Rites have been performed by some one or other of the Dissenting Teachers; according to a privilege granted them, by the late Sir Charles MacCarthy. Some Judgment may be formed of their comparative number, from the fact, that out of 205 Burials registered in the Year 1825, 10 only were of this description.

It may be proper to state, on the other hand, that a very considerable number of the Soldiers of the Royal African Colonial Corps, were buried, during the Year 1825, at whose funeral I was not called to officiate. None of these are registered in the records of the Parish.

With respect to the Seamen (who constitute a very large proportion of the European Burials) I would just observe, that *some* of them are understood to be Natives of some part of America, or of the East Indies. But as the Register very rarely affords any assistance in discovering this, I have reluctantly been compelled to enter them all (with the very few exceptions alluded to) as Europeans. The catalogue of European Burials (of itself sufficiently large) has thus been unavoidably swelled, beyond its due limits.

There are probably other inaccuracies in classing the Individuals, whose Births, Marriages, or Burials are recorded, for it was frequently found impossible to determine with any certainty, to which class they properly belonged, owing to the scantiness of information on the subject.

[1] The annual Blue Books requested the entry of marriages, births, and deaths. The first Blue Book from Sierra Leone (*1824*, p. 147) listed the marriages of 1823, but showed neither births nor deaths. The Blue Books for 1825 and 1826 gave no figures and said: 'This cannot be ascertained in time for the furnishing of these returns and is very incorrectly kept' (ibid. *1825*, p. 142); 'There is no mode of obtaining these, at present' (ibid. *1826*, p. 136). The Blue Book for 1827 showed the total numbers of marriages, births, and deaths, but said: 'The return of Births & Deaths cannot be relied upon as the Records of the Colony only furnish Accounts of Baptisms & Christian Burials' (ibid. *1827*, p. 64). The Blue Books for 1828, 1829, and 1831 showed figures for most parishes, but the data were incomplete, while the Blue Book for 1830 merely said: 'Cannot be correctly given' (ibid. *1830*, pp. 114–15).

[2] See *Report*, Appendix A, No. 19. The tables consisted of a Return of Marriages registered in the parish from 12 Oct. 1795 to 31 Dec. 1825; a Return of Baptisms registered in the parish from 1 Apr. 1796 to 31 Dec. 1825 (1800–3 'No Baptisms registered'); a Return of Burials registered in the parish from 1 Jan. 1809 to 31 Dec. 1825 (with a Note 'Previous to the first of the above dates, no register of Burials appears to have been preserved'). The Commissioners received also from a Wesleyan preacher a table showing 'Baptisms and Burials according to the Register Book at the Mission House' which started in 1815 and ended in May 1826 (see ibid., Appendix A, No. 20), but this table as well as the scanty data published for some years in *The Royal Gazette and Sierra Leone Advertiser* (see, for example, 1 Aug. 1818 and 8 July 1820) and in the *Missionary Register* (see, for example, *1820*, p. 382; *1826*, p. 260; *1827*, p. 538) are much less instructive than the document from the rector of Freetown.

The return of baptisms registered was as follows:

Year	Euro-peans	Maroons	Nova Scotian Settlers	Liberated Africans	Natives	Ameri-cans	Total
1796	—	2	38	—	—	—	40
1797	1	—	9	—	—	—	10
1798	—	—	7	—	—	—	7
1799	—	—	4	—	—	—	4
1804	2	9	14	—	—	—	25
1805	4	2	16	—	—	—	22
1806	1	6	20	—	—	—	27
1807	9	15	22	—	1	—	47
1808	1	34	26	—	2	—	63
1809	3	41	29	—	3	—	76
1810	6	18	27	—	2	—	53
1811	2	45	26	—	6	—	79
1812	8	17	19	345	5	1	395
1813	6	4	10	108	5	—	133
1814	9	18	32	128	17	—	204
1815	7	26	17	—	18	—	68
1816	1	13	9	13	5	4	45
1817	12	12	12	3	3	—	42
1818	1	7	1	2	1	1	13
1819	7	14	13	493	2	—	529
1820	10	11	25	136	5	—	187
1821	7	13	9	16	8	—	53
1822	8	19	27	42	3	—	99
1823	15	7	14	34	3	—	73
1824	5	8	6	13	7	—	39
1825	12	9	6	25	4	1	57
Total	137	349[1]	439[1]	1,358	100	7	2,390

[1] Totals do not agree with items.

The return of burials registered showed:

Year	Euro-peans	Mulat-toes	Maroons	Nova Scotian Settlers	Liberated Africans	Natives	Ameri-cans	Total
1809	28	1	11	22	—	6	3	71
1810	20	—	17	31	—	6	2	76
1811	3	1	11	32	—	4	1	52
1812	44	1	18	28	6	3	1	101
1813	—	—	2	2	—	—	—	4
1814	12	—	14	18	1	1	—	46
1815	44	1	9	15	4	4	—	77
1816	7	1	3	8	1	—	3	23
1817	42	2	8	18	3	1	2	76
1818	37	4	15	24	2	3	—	85
1819	20	7	7	12	6	3	—	55
1820	74	6	23	16	11	6	2	138
1821	73	1	20	20	20	4	6	144
1822	65	3	13	19	14	13	3	130
1823	123	6	11	27	26	8	2	203
1824	70	1	8	26	17	14	3	139
1825	86	8	27	44	14	20	5	205[1]
Total	748	43	217	362	125	96	33	1,625

[1] Including 1 Krooman.

As pointed out by the rector, the figures concerning Europeans are defective. But the figures concerning the Liberated Africans are still less conclusive. They cover only Freetown, where few Liberated Africans lived;[1] the baptisms, moreover, in some years evidently included a large number of adults.

The Instructions issued on 16 November 1826 by the Lords Commissioners of His Majesty's Treasury[2] provided that figures of births and deaths among Liberated Africans be reported quarterly. But these reports were not prepared regularly,[3] and the Committee of Enquiry constituted to investigate the 'Charge delivered by Mr. Chief Justice Jeffcott to the Grand Jury of Sierra Leone, on the Subject of the Slave Trade' complained in their report dated 26 October 1830 that 'the Returns which have been presented to them' were 'very imperfect'.[4]

Thereupon Viscount Goderich, in a Dispatch to Lieutenant-Governor Findlay dated 18 January 1832, urged the promulgation of a law to improve these birth and death records.

To determine the actual number of births and deaths since the year 1808, by any reference to the Population Returns, is unfortunately impracticable, it being evident that no such Returns have ever been made with even a plausible approach to accuracy.[5]

It should be required that every birth and death occurring among them [Liberated Africans], should be reported to the Managers of the different Settlements, or to the Authorities of Freetown, by whom the Returns should be transmitted to the Assistant Superintendent of liberated Africans, who again should be bound to make periodical Reports on the subject to the Colonial Secretary, for your information. You will immediately adopt the necessary measures for procuring the concurrence of the Council in the promulgation of a law, to be framed in such a manner as may give full effect to this instruction.[6]

The Lieutenant-Governor decided to use this opportunity for reviving birth and death registration as a whole, and on 7 June 1832 the Council passed 'An Act to enforce the Due Registration of Births and Deaths within this Colony'.[7] The Act provided for compulsory registration of every birth and death occurring in the Colony. Registers of births and deaths were to be kept 'for the Parish of St. George, by the Colonial Chaplain, and for the Parishes, Districts, and Villages by the managers or superintendent under whose charge such Parishes, Districts, and Villages may be, such managers and superintendents in all cases keeping distinct and separate Registers for each Parish or District under their care'.

Birth registration, thereupon, improved in Freetown in 1833, but for 1834 and 1835 all data were again quite incomplete. The head of the Statistical Department, Board of Trade, George Richardson Porter, in a letter to the Chairman of the Select Committee on the Accounts of Colonial

---

[1] This may explain why no baptisms or burials were recorded prior to 1812.

[2] See p. 21 above.

[3] For the first quarter of 1827, 76 births and 73 deaths were recorded; for later years see p. 110 above.

[4] See p. 111 above.   [5] *Charge delivered by Jeffcott*, pp. 34-5.   [6] Ibid., p. 40.

[7] Sierra Leone, *Acts 1829-40*, pp. 76-80. The Preamble read: 'Whereas it would tend to the private, as well as public advantage of the Population of this Colony, if the Registering of Births and Deaths which may occur within the jurisdiction of the same, were more strictly enforced.'

Receipt and Expenditure dated 7 July 1837, wrote as regards the year 1835:

Births and Deaths evidently incorrect:

White Population	90
Black ditto	34,709
	34,799

Births 244, or 1 in 142.
Deaths 80, or 1 in 435; cannot apply to White population only.[1]

But for 1836, when 891 births and 1,387 deaths were reported,[2] registration was evidently much more complete. It deteriorated, however, soon again. In many years data were lacking from some parishes, and the returns from most parishes were evidently incomplete.[3] It seems, moreover, that as a rule baptisms and burials were still recorded instead of births and deaths.[4] When the Select Committee on the West Coast of Africa, on 30 April 1841, asked the Acting Governor 'Is there a register of births, deaths, and marriages kept here?' he answered: 'There is a register of marriages, but births and deaths are generally ascertained by the number of burials and baptisms.'[5] Several years later Governor Macdonald, in his report on the Blue Book for 1846, wrote:

It is . . . extremely difficult, in fact impossible, to arrive at a correct computation of the births and deaths. The statement given in the Population Return under these heads is only baptisms and burials, not births and deaths. Very many children are not baptized at all; and as the births are not reported or registered, no account is taken of them. On the other hand, numbers of the native population die, particularly amongst the newly-imported Africans, who are buried privately, according to their own country custom; sometimes in the bush and often in the floors of their own dwellings.

An ordinance was passed many years ago for compelling the registration of births and deaths; it has, however, never been enforced; nor would it be an easy matter to have its provisions carried out effectually, for the coloured inhabitants view with an extraordinary degree of jealousy and distrust any legal enactment of this nature. I shall, however, not lose sight of this very important subject, and shall, at an early

---

[1] Report from Select Committee, p. 197. It is interesting to note that, as a witness before the Committee, Porter stated on 12 June 1837:
'I should say, now we have a Bill for the registration of births and deaths in the Mother Country, it would be exceedingly desirable that a similar record should be kept as nearly as possible in the same form in each of the colonies, to be transmitted to this country, and laid before Parliament' (ibid., p. 100).

[2] Births were not returned from one very small locality.

[3] The lack of co-ordination may be inferred from the fact that the total number of deaths reported from outside Freetown in 1842 was 112, while the General Superintendent recorded 409 deaths among Liberated Africans in the second half of 1842 (see Correspondence relative to Emigration of Labourers from the West Coast of Africa, p. 114).

[4] The printed headings in the annual Blue Books call for births and deaths. According to the Blue Books for 1832, 1834, 1835, 1838, 1839, 1844, and 1846 the figures in the Births column refer to baptisms; according to the Blue Books for 1839, 1844, and 1846 the figures in the Deaths column refer to burials. But the figures certainly referred to baptisms and burials also in other years. (The Statistical Tables for 1837–9 list all figures as representing baptisms or burials; see Tables of Revenue, Population, &c., Supplement to Part VIII, Colonies 1839, p. 194.) How incomplete the figures for baptisms themselves were may be inferred from the fact that while the Blue Book for 1835 listed in its Population Return (pp. 118–19) 244 baptisms, it gave on the next page a return of 'baptisms by the several Dissenting Preachers' which showed 898 baptisms. (No such return is given for any other year.)

[5] Report from Select Committee, Part II, p. 327.

period, bring the matter before the notice of the Legislative Council, with the view of some amendment being made in the existing law, so as to ensure its efficient working.[1]

For 1853–6 birth and death figures are completely lacking.[2]

Thereupon a new attempt was made to enforce registration. On 9 February 1857 an Ordinance[3] was passed 'to provide the means for a complete Register of Titles to Lands, Births, Deaths, Baptisms, Burials, Marriages, and other matters of Her Majesty's subjects in the colony of Sierra Leone, whereby evidence of title to property may be more easily obtained and statistical information afforded for purposes of public interest and utility, and whereby also crime may be more readily discovered and more efficiently suppressed'.[4] According to this Ordinance the Colonial Secretary had to furnish 'to the registrar general a sufficient number of register books for making entries of all births, deaths, baptisms, burials, and marriages of Her Majesty's subjects in this colony'. The same Ordinance provided, apart from the establishment of 'an office at Freetown for the registration of . . . births, deaths, baptisms, burials, marriages', the appointment of 'one person in each district to be registrar of births and deaths'.

But registration of births and deaths remained inadequate,[5] and for many years returns are not available from one or another district. The reports on the Blue Books for the quarter of a century during which the Ordinance of 1857 was in force contain no comment on registration, but finally, in 1883, it was found necessary to amend the Ordinance. The

[1] State of Colonial Possessions 1846, pp. 138–9.
[2] See Blue Book 1853, pp. 153–4; 1854, pp. 156–7; 1855, pp. 162–3; 1856, pp. 155–6.
[3] No. 4 of 1857, reprinted in Ordinances of Sierra Leone in Force 1857, pp. 263–83.
[4] Preamble, ibid. This Ordinance was to come into operation on 1 Apr. 1857. 'An Ordinance to repeal certain Ordinances' (reprinted ibid., pp. 297–9) which was passed on that very date repealed the Act of 1832. The Registration Ordinance of 1857 was amended on 22 Feb. 1858 (No. 1 of 1858, reprinted in Ordinances of Sierra Leone 1858–60, pp. 17–21).
[5] See in this connexion Dr. James Africanus B. Horton, Staff Assistant-Surgeon of H.M. Forces in West Africa, Political Economy of British Western Africa; with the Requirements of the Several Colonies and Settlements (1865), pp. 21–2:
'IV.—The Transfer of the Registrar of Births, Marriages, and Deaths from the Legal to the Medical Profession, and the Establishment of a Health Officer.
'The beneficial result which will arise from this transfer cannot be overrated. Ever since the formation of this office, the population have been kept perfectly ignorant of the rationale of the registration—viz., the rate of mortality, the different causes of death, the proportion of births to deaths, the amount of legitimate or illegitimate births; the causes of periodic endemic diseases—in fact, there has never been a generalised summary published, half-yearly or yearly, for the benefit of the people. It is certainly impossible for the legal mind to classify diseases, to trace their causes and to point out their remedy. This truth is acknowledged in England, where none but medical men have the appointment. The books in the office as it now stands are almost a dead letter to the population, but which might hereafter be used for references, and may serve as a means for drawing up a comparative statement of the health of the colony at various periods.
'A medical officer of health should also be attached to the registrar's office; and I think no place requires this appointment more than Sierra Leone. The officer thus appointed should be made to give a half-yearly report to the Town Corporation of the state of the colony; and should recommend the best means of averting any danger. A legal mind could not cope with these facts; and now that no plea can be made against the non-existence of efficient public medical men in the colony, I think that the Executive cannot do better than give the office to Dr. Smith, a Sierra Leone bird, and a promising general practitioner.'
See also Horton, Physical and Medical Climate (1867), pp. 254–5.

new Ordinance[1] for all intents and purposes, repealed the Ordinance of
1857 (as amended in 1858) so far as the registration of births and deaths
is concerned.

'The Births Deaths and Burials Registration Ordinance, 1883' provided that registrars should be appointed for Freetown, the Mountain
District, the First Eastern District, the Second Eastern District, the Western District, the Sherbro District, and the Isles de Los. It was much more
comprehensive than the former Acts and was, moreover, accompanied by
very elaborate 'Regulations for the Discharge of the Duties of Registrars
and Deputy-Registrars of Births and Deaths in the Settlement of Sierra
Leone'. It was supplemented in 1884 by 'An Ordinance to provide for
payment of certain fees to the Registrars of Births and Deaths'[2] and was
amended twice.[3] It remained in force until 1906.

Returns were furnished from 1884 onwards from all districts covered
by the Ordinance of 1883, but registration itself remained quite incomplete.
The 1891 census report said with regard to Freetown:

> There is much reason to believe that not all births are registered, as only the
> intelligent portion of the community (and these form but a small proportion) who
> are aware of the advantages of registration, make it a point to do so. The masses
> register only to comply with the law, and as, within the past few years there has
> been a large influx of Aborigines to the capital in order to obtain either freedom or
> employment, it must be expected that through ignorance of the law or indifference
> thereto many births have not been reported.[4]

But registration was more incomplete still in some rural districts.

> 1891. Colony. The registration system here is not as perfect as it should be, owing
> partly to difficulties which are always to be found in partially civilized communities.
> The untutored native seldom complies with the law on the subject and it is not
> generally easy to compel him to do so.[5]
> 1892. Colony. . . . the registration system, so far as births are concerned, is, on
> account of local circumstances, defective.[6]
> 1894. Freetown. . . . there is no doubt . . . that a large number of deaths are still
> unregistered.[7]
> 1898. Colony. Owing to defective registration and the ignorance and prejudice
> of a large class of the population, particularly the aborigines, who crowd into the
> Colony, statistics regarding public health are very unreliable and no definite con-
> clusion can be arrived at.[8]
> 1899. Colony. The registration laws call for much more strict enforcement. Not
> only have the deaths in the past been registered in a very careless and perfunctory
> manner, but it is very doubtful whether a large number of births do not entirely
> escape registration.[9]
> 1900. Colony. I have again to call attention to the large excess of deaths over
> births registered. A partial explanation of this may be that a certain proportion of

---

[1] No. 23 of 1883 (9 Nov.), 'An Ordinance to amend the Ordinances relating to the Registration
of Births, Deaths and Burials in the Settlement of Sierra Leone', see *Sierra Leone Ordinances
1879–92.*
[2] No. 6 of 1884 (9 May), ibid.
[3] See No. 7 of 1893 (2 Mar.), ibid. *1893–8*, and No. 1 of 1895 (10 Jan.), ibid.
[4] *Census Report 1891*, pp. 3–4.   [5] *Colonial Reports, Sierra Leone 1891*, p. 17.
[6] Ibid. *1892*, pp. 16–17. See also ibid. *1893*, p. 6.
[7] Ibid. *1894*, p. 6.   [8] Ibid. *1898*, p. 21.
[9] *Selections from Colonial Medical Reports for 1898 and 1899*, p. 383. See also *Colonial Reports,
Sierra Leone 1899*, p. 40.

births escape registration, and until an effort is made to enforce penalties for non-registration of births, it will be impossible to come to a conclusion as to how far this factor accounts for this anomalous state of matters.[1]

1901. . . . I cannot but think that a considerable proportion of births escape registration, and I would urge the necessity of taking strict measures to enforce registration, which should not be a difficult matter, in Freetown at any rate.[2]

1902. Colony. A Table showing the distribution of births and deaths for the whole Colony is attached. It must, however, be pointed out that there is great reason to believe that in the outlying districts a number of deaths escape registration,[3] so that the . . . figures must be taken as only approximate so far as the whole Colony is concerned.

Freetown. Here, however, we have to deal with statistics which are much more accurate, and so far as deaths are concerned may be relied on. All burials take place in one or other of the cemeteries, and a list of burials is furnished weekly by the Cemetery clerk to the Registrar, who is then able to take steps to ensure registration. As it is not easy to get rid of a dead body, it is thus unlikely that many deaths escape registration. . . .

On the other hand it is extremely doubtful whether the number of births registered represent the actual number born, for there is considerable reason to believe that a certain proportion escape registration. Attention has been drawn to this on previous occasions, and it is essential that the Registration laws should so be altered as to ensure more complete and satisfactory registration of births. A bill to amend the laws on this subject is in course of preparation.[4]

1904. Except in Freetown . . . where the provisions of the Registration Ordinance are complied with, the returns cannot be considered complete and are therefore useless for statistical purposes.[5]

1905. Colony. . . . it is extremely probable that a number of deaths and births in the outlying districts escape registration.

Freetown. The statistics are more accurate, especially as regards deaths, and may be relied upon. A new Ordinance which will ensure more accurate registration of births has now been prepared, and will be placed before the Legislative Council at an early date.[6]

The Ordinance of 1883 was indeed repealed by the Ordinances of 27 October 1905[7] and 8 September 1906.[8] But the change in the law did not yield more accurate registration of births in Freetown. Moreover, compulsory registration which so far had been prescribed for the whole Colony became confined to Freetown. However, the Births and Deaths Registration Consolidation and Amendment Ordinance 1906 provided for 'permissive registration' wherever registration was not compulsory, and voluntary registration became available also for the Protectorate.

In the case of births or deaths occurring outside the Districts to which this Ordinance applies either in the Colony or Protectorate any person, who, if such birth or death had occurred within any such district, would have been required to inform

[1] Principal Medical Officer Dr. Prout, *Medical Reports 1900 and 1901*, p. 4.
[2] Ibid., p. 42. [3] See also *Medical Report 1902*, p. 23. [4] Ibid., p. 5.
[5] *Colonial Reports, Sierra Leone 1904*, p. 30. See also ibid. *1905*, p. 43.
[6] *Medical Report 1905*, p. 3.
[7] No. 31 of 1905, 'An Ordinance to consolidate and amend the General Laws establishing and regulating the office of Registrar-General of the Colony of Sierra Leone', *Sierra Leone Ordinances 1904–6*.
[8] No. 9 of 1906, 'An Ordinance to consolidate and amend the law relating to the Registration of Births and Deaths in the Colony of Sierra Leone', ibid. This Ordinance was amended by Ordinances No. 7 of 1907 (26 Mar.), *Sierra Leone Ordinances, &c. 1907*, p. 17, and No. 8 of 1909 (6 May), ibid. *1909*, pp. 19–22. The Ordinance as it stood after the enactment of the latter amendment is reprinted in *Revised Edition of the Ordinances of Sierra Leone 1811–1908*, vol. iii, pp. 1017–38.

TABLE 27. *Registered Births and Deaths, Colony of Sierra Leone, 1827–1918*[1]

Year	Births Freetown	Births Elsewhere	Deaths Freetown	Deaths Elsewhere	Year	Births Freetown	Births Elsewhere	Deaths Freetown	Deaths Elsewhere
1827	198		451		1876	463	151	486	233
1828	47	371	112	78	1877	482	664	463	634
1829	..	228	185	86	1878	483	641	517	611
1831	..	495	..	650	1879	484	780	605	702
1832	11	485	39	539	1880	498	746	541	739
1833	304	527	108	200	1881	490	758	574	726
1834	29	516	45	521	1882	510	764	643	783
1835	9	235	50	30	1883	544	747	700	802
1836	223	668	209	1,178	1884	556	803	680	755
1837	551	1,382	168	1,204	1885	541	833	672	811
1838	212	1,127	70	525	1886	526	851	668	792
1839	18	446	132	109	1887	497	844	661	816
1840	264	563	169	436	1888	550	808	540	708
1841	93	433	113	143	1889	505	745	695	668
1842	133	548	114	112	1890	525	724	792	739
1843	157	451	75	148	1891	629	699	660	708
1844	50	1,355	31	1,248	1892	573	637	779	605
1845	189	508	145	284	1893	591	695	679	615
1846	34	1,200	24	871	1894	647	698	800	684
1847	517	1,060	282	743	1895	615	815	847	658
1848	573	872	117	787	1896	645	896	878	754
1849	613	772	143	489	1897	587	1,057	878	897
1850	653	845	190	425	1898	668	1,169	869	814
1851	269	911	104	368	1899	548	946	927	841
1852	253	678	97	179	1900	572	863	787	839
1857	610		270		1901	410	928	957	891
1858	187	271	440	324	1902	534	906	868	955
1859	263	701	809	1,130	1903	553	941	839	903
1860	304	443	523	570	1904	602	912	962	898
1861	490	470	636	349	1905	638	761	1,071	1,085
1862	439	111	499	132	1906	557	623	850	598
1863	443	473	584	502	1907	583	348	810	382
1864	434	472	562	448	1908	635	622	848	538
1865	447	372	571	353	1909	549	603	747	606
1867	425	327	720	350	1910	582	786	939	611
1868	463	380	644	292	1911	501	615	740	574
1869	484	174	647	227	1912	587	743	751	592
1870	557	287	693	369	1913	590	600	779	558
1871	590	39	735	128	1914	666	661	997	640
1872	538	243	818	389	1915	721	738	992	699
1873	461	66	706	284	1916	706	715	1,058	918
1874	510	..	527	..	1917	774	771	1,046	841
1875	530	101	493	246	1918	695	761	2,118	1,277

[1] See Sierra Leone, *Blue Book 1827*, p. 64; *1828*, pp. 104–5; *1829*, pp. 114–15; *1831*, pp. 114–15; *1832*, pp. 114–15; *1833*, pp. 118–19, to *1838*, pp. 118–19; *1839*, pp. 134–5, to *1847*, pp. 134–5; *1848*, pp. 218–19; *1849*, pp. 134–5; *1850*, pp. 138–9; *1851*, pp. 138–9; *1852*, pp. 160–1; *1857*, pp. 152–3; *1858*, pp. 159–60; *1859*, pp. 164–5; *1860*, pp. 164–5; *1861*, pp. 165–6; *1862*, pp. 166–7; *1863*, pp. 180–1; *1864*, pp. 190–1; *1865*, pp. 206–7; *1867*, pp. 174–5; *1868*, pp. 174–5; *1869*, pp. 188–9; *1870*, pp. 180–1; *1871*, pp. 172–3; *1872*, pp. 178–9; *1873*, pp. 178–9; *1874*, pp. 183–4; *1875*, pp. 206–7; *1876*, pp. 206–7; *1877*, pp. 198–9; *1878*, pp. 183–4; *1879*, pp. 192–3; *1880*, pp. 188–9; *1881*, pp. 196–7; *1882*, pp. 198–9; *1883*, pp. 218–19; *1884*, pp. 232–3; *1885*, pp. 232–3; *1886*, pp. 250–1; *1887*, pp. 246–7; *1888*, pp. 244–5; *1889*, pp. 242–3; *1890*, pp. 248–9; *1891* R, pp. 1–2, to *1918* R, pp. 1–2. Figures given in Medical Reports and in Annual Colonial Reports differ for some years essentially from those in Blue Books.

the Registrar, may, if he so thinks fit, inform the Local Registrar . . . of such birth or death, and such Local Registrars shall register the particulars . . . .

Unless otherwise ordered by the Governor, 'Postmasters in the Colony and, in the Protectorate the District Commissioners and Postmasters, shall be the Local Registrars'. In accordance with this Ordinance the new 'Regulations for the Registration of Births and Deaths' issued in 1908 stipulated:

1. There are two systems of registration of births and deaths.
(1) Compulsory registration applicable to the City of Freetown District and such other districts as are from time to time constituted under the Ordinance.
(2) Permissive registration carried on by Local Registrars of places outside the districts to which the Ordinance applies.

Under the latter system Local Registrars are required to register births and deaths occurring in their respective districts only on application and on receipt from the Informant of an appointed fee of 6d., in stamps, for each birth or death registered.

Official reports say with regard to registration in the following years:

1906. Owing to the fact that registration outside Freetown is not compulsory, the figures . . . cannot be relied upon.

In Freetown . . . the provisions of the Registration Ordinance are enforced.[1]

1907. Registration being voluntary in the outlying districts of the Colony many cases of deaths and births are not registered.

In Freetown, however, registration is compulsory and the figures are fairly reliable.[2]

. . . in the Protectorate . . . births, deaths, and marriages are not registered.[3]

1908. Accurate vital statistics can only be obtained by compulsory registration, which is now limited to Freetown and Bonthe.[4]

The Births and Deaths Registration, Consolidation and Amendment Ordinance of 1906 provided for the establishment, when desired, of registration districts for the purposes of voluntary registration. Up to the end of 1908, 14 such districts had been established.[5]

1911. Registration in the Colony is not . . . reliable owing to the law not being compulsory.

In the City of Freetown registration is more or less compulsory and is therefore more reliable, and the figures may be taken as showing approximately the true state of things as regards birth and death rates.[6]

1913 . . . registration of deaths was compulsory in only one town, Freetown . . . .[7]

2. *1913–45*

Legislation. The Ordinance of 1906 was repealed in 1913 by 'An Ordinance to consolidate and amend the law relating to the Registration of Births and Deaths'[8] which came into force on 1 January 1914.[9] It was amended in 1924, 1929, and 1931,[10] and again in 1942 and 1945. Its main

[1] *Colonial Reports, Sierra Leone 1906*, p. 36. See also ibid. *1907*, p. 30.
[2] *Medical Report 1907*, p. 4. See also ibid. *1909*, p. 5; *1910*, p. 5.
[3] *Colonial Reports, Sierra Leone 1907*, p. 31.   [4] Ibid. *1908*, p. 43.
[5] Ibid., p. 44. See also *Blue Book 1907*, Section R, p. 2.   [6] *Medical Report 1911*, p. 5.
[7] Ibid. *1913*, p. 5. See also *Colonial Reports, Sierra Leone 1913*, p. 26.
[8] No. 13 of 1913 (25 July), reprinted in *Ordinances, &c. 1913*, pp. 23–41, and in *Revised Edition of the Ordinances of Sierra Leone 1909–13*, pp. 2250–72.
[9] See *Colonial Reports, Sierra Leone 1914*, p. 29.
[10] See Ordinances No. 12 of 1924 (13 June), 'An Ordinance to Amend Sundry Ordinances as a Preliminary to the Preparation of a Revised Edition of the Laws', *Sierra Leone Ordinances, &c. 1924*, pp. 28–34; No. 28 of 1929 (7 Dec. 1929), 'An Ordinance to Amend the Births and Deaths

provisions for ensuring birth and death registration, before the amendment of 1942, were as follows:

Registration Districts and Registrars

3. (1) The Governor-in-Council may by Order divide the Colony or the Protectorate or any part of the Colony or the Protectorate into districts for any of the purposes of this Ordinance, and may from time to time alter the districts so appointed and create new districts by dividing the same by amalgamating one district or a part of one district with another or a part of another district, or by adding to existing districts any part of the Colony or the Protectorate which is not already comprised in any existing district, or may abolish any one or more of the said districts provided that no district shall comprise a part of the Colony and a part of the Protectorate.

4. The Governor shall from time to time appoint in writing fit and proper persons to be Registrars of Births and Deaths for each district created under section 3 and Registrars of Births or of Deaths or of Births and Deaths, as the case may be, for each chiefdom or part of a chiefdom with regard to which an Order in Council has been made under section 38 A (2) and may appoint for each district or each such chiefdom or part of a chiefdom one or more Deputy Registrars to act for and under the control of the Registrar, and may by writing at any time revoke any appointment made under this section.

Birth and Death Registration in the Colony

A Registrar shall inform himself carefully of every birth and death which happens in his district.

In the case of a child born alive, (1) the father and mother, (2) the occupier of the house in which the birth occurred, each person present at the birth, and the person having charge of the child, shall within 14 days register the child. The parent who neglects to do so shall be liable to a fine not exceeding £5.

When a death occurs, (1) the nearest relatives of the deceased present at the death or in attendance during the last illness of the deceased, (2) every other relative of the deceased dwelling or being in the same district as the deceased, (3) each person present at the death and the occupier of the house in which the death took place, (4) each inmate of such house and the person causing the body to be buried shall within 3 days register the death. Persons under (1) who neglect to do so shall be liable to a fine not exceeding £5.

Special Provisions as to certain Districts

28. (1) This part of this Ordinance shall apply only to Freetown, Kissy, Congo Town, Murray Town and Wilberforce.

(2) It shall be lawful for the Governor in Council by Order to declare that this part of this Ordinance or any provisions thereof shall no longer apply to Freetown, Kissy, Congo Town, Murray Town and Wilberforce or to any one or more of the said places.

(3) It shall be lawful for the Governor in Council by Order to apply this part of this Ordinance or any of the provisions thereof to any other district.

Registration Ordinance, 1924', *Sierra Leone Royal Gazette*, 9 Dec. 1929, pp. 1394–1402, reprinted in *Supplement to the Laws of Sierra Leone, 1925–30*, pp. 15–22 (cap. 16); and No. 9 of 1931 (13 Aug.), 'An Ordinance to Amend the Births and Deaths Registration Ordinance, 1924', reprinted in *Sierra Leone Ordinances, &c. 1931*, pp. 39–42. The Ordinance as it stood on 1 January 1925 is reprinted in *Laws of Sierra Leone in Force 1925*, vol. i, pp. 89–111 (cap. 16).

29. It shall be lawful for the Governor to appoint for each district to which this part of this Ordinance applies a fit and proper person, who shall be called the Registrar's Officer, and likewise to remove such Registrar's Officer at his pleasure.

37. . . . any person, who shall knowingly bury or cause to be buried or be concerned in burying the body of any . . . deceased person or still-born child without an order of the Coroner or a certificate of the Registrar authorising the same, shall be liable to a penalty not exceeding ten pounds.

38. The provisions of this part of this Ordinance shall be auxiliary to and not in derogation of the other parts of this Ordinance and all the provisions of the other parts of this Ordinance shall have full force and effect in the districts to which this part of this Ordinance applies, save in so far as the same are actually or impliedly superseded or affected by any provision of this part of this Ordinance.

The provisions for live-born children apply also to still-born children.

Registration of Births and Deaths in the Protectorate

38 A. (1) The provisions of this Ordinance shall apply in the case of all non-natives[1] born or dying in a district of the Protectorate created under section 3 of this Ordinance in the same manner as they apply in the case of all persons born or dying in such a district in the Colony, but with the modifications specified in the next succeeding section.

(2) It shall be lawful for the Governor in Council, on the request of the Paramount Chief concerned, by Order to declare that the provisions of this Ordinance shall apply

(a) in the case of all natives[2] born, or

(b) in the case of all natives dying, or

(c) in the case of all natives born or dying in any chiefdom or part of a chiefdom, and thereupon the said provisions shall apply accordingly, and with respect to the said chiefdom or part of a chiefdom as they apply with respect to a district, but with the modifications specified in the next succeeding section.

The Governor in Council may at any time revoke an Order made under this sub-section.

Births have to be registered within 21 days and deaths within 7 days.

Optional Registration

41. Where any native is born or dies in the Protectorate within a district created under section 3 or within a chiefdom or part of a chiefdom with regard to which an Order in Council has been made under section 38 A, then notwithstanding that it may not be necessary, having regard to the provisions of this Ordinance, that information should be given to a Registrar, any person who would have been required to inform a Registrar if the giving of information to the Registrar were necessary, may, if he so thinks fit, give information of such birth or death to the Registrar of the district or chiefdom or part of a chiefdom, as the case may be, and such Registrar shall, on receipt from such informant of the appointed fee, register the particulars hereinbefore required to be registered, and, as regards the registration of such birth or death, the provisions of this Ordinance, so far as the same are applicable to registration under this section, shall apply.

Central Administration

41 A. The Chief Registrar's Office shall be in Freetown.

41 B. (1) The Chief Registrar's Office shall be the Registry for, and depository of, all registers, certificates and records and copies thereof as are directed by this Ordinance to be delivered to, and deposited with, the Chief Registrar, or to be registered at his office, and of all registers, certificates and records and copies thereof

---

[1] 'Non-native' means any person who is not subject to a Tribal Authority in the Protectorate.

[2] 'Native' means any member of the aboriginal races or tribes of Africa, ordinarily resident within the Protectorate, whether employed in the service of His Majesty or not.

relating to the registration of births and deaths which before the first day of July, 1930, were in the custody of the Registrar-General.

(2) The Chief Registrar, and every Registrar, shall use such official seal as the Governor may by Order determine.

41 C. All Registrars and other registration officers appointed under the provisions of this Ordinance shall be deemed to be officers of the department of the Chief Registrar, and shall be under his direction and control, and such Registrars and other officers shall comply with, and conform to, such orders and directions as they may from time to time receive from the Chief Registrar, in addition to the specific duties imposed upon them by this Ordinance.

41 D. The Chief Registrar shall cause indexes of all registers, certificates, records and copies thereof, deposited in the Registry, to be made and kept in the Registry.

Such indexes shall contain such particulars, and shall be prepared in such form, and by such officer or officers, as the Chief Registrar shall from time to time direct.

41 E. The Chief Registrar shall furnish, on or before the thirty-first day of January in every year, to the Governor, a general abstract of the number of births and deaths registered during the preceding year, in such form as the Governor may direct.

Headings of Registers

Schedule A (Birth): No.; When and where born; Name, if any; Sex; Name, surname and race of father; Name, maiden surname and race of mother; Rank or profession of father; Signature, description and residence of informant; When registered; Signature of Registrar; Name, if added after registration of birth.

Schedule B (Death): No.; Date of death; Place of death; Name and surname; Sex; Age; Rank or profession; Abode; Cause of death; Name of certifying medical practitioner, if any; Duration of illness; Place of burial; Signature, description and residence of informant; When registered; Signature of Registrar.[1]

The Chief Registrar, Deputy Registrar, and Registrars receive no salary, but the Registrars are entitled to the following fees:

	£	s.	d.
(a) For registering a birth or death	0	0	6
(b) For registering a birth or death at private residence.	0	1	0
(c) For entering the baptismal or other name of child upon certificate produced after registry of birth	0	0	6
(d) For taking, attesting and transmitting a declaration made by an informant respecting a birth in another district	0	0	6
(e) Upon the registration of a birth, when the child is more than three months old and not more than twelve months old	0	1	0
(f) Upon the registration of a birth, when the child is more than twelve months old	0	2	0
(g) Upon the registration of a death with the authority of the Registrar-General after the expiration of twelve months	0	2	0
(h) For registering a still-birth	0	0	6

Registration of births and deaths in due time at the Registrar's Office is free of charge. But a fee has to be paid for delayed registration of birth (when the child is more than 3 but not more than 12 months old, 5s.,

[1] The questionnaires have changed considerably in the course of time. The Birth Schedule attached to the Act of 1832 asked for Date of birth; Christian name of infant; Name of father; Name of mother; If born in wedlock; Religion. The two latter questions were dropped in the Schedule attached to the Ordinance of 1857. The Schedule attached to the Ordinance of 1883

when the child is more than 12 months old, 10*s*.), for registration of death after 12 months (10*s*.), for entering the name of a child after registration of birth (1*s*.), for searching the registry books of births or deaths (for every half hour and fraction thereof 1*s*.), for a certified extract from the registry of births or deaths (2*s*. 6*d*.).

The 'Regulations for the Discharge of the Duties of Registrars and Deputy-Registrars of Births and Deaths' of 16 April 1884 had been rescinded and replaced in accordance with the Ordinance of 8 September 1906 by 'Regulations for the Registration of Births and Deaths'[1] issued on 8 July 1908. These new regulations were amended by the 'Births and Deaths Registration (Amendment) Ordinance, 1931'.[2] The main rules as they stand to-day are as follows:

3. There are four systems of registration—

(1) Compulsory registration in the case of all persons born or dying in the Colony.

(2) Compulsory registration in the case of all non-natives born or dying in a district in the Protectorate created under section 3 of the Ordinance.

(3) Compulsory registration in the case of all natives born, or all natives dying, or all natives born or dying within a chiefdom or part of a chiefdom in the Protectorate declared under section 38 A (2) of the Ordinance.

(4) Optional registration in the case of all natives born or dying in the Protectorate to whom section 41 of the Ordinance applies.

Under the last system Registrars are required to register births and deaths occurring in their respective districts only on application and on receipt from the informant of an appointed fee of sixpence, in stamps, for each birth or death registered.

The Registrar must have a known office within the district for which he is appointed, and must fix or cause to be fixed in some conspicuous position on or near the outer door of such office a notice painted on a board in black letters on a white ground, in the following form:—

```
                    Office
                    of the
         Registrar of Births & Deaths
         For the District of.........
         .................... Registrar.
         Hours of Attendance, 8 a.m.—2 p.m.
```

11. Before beginning the entry of a birth in the register book the Registrar, in order to secure a proper registry, should satisfy himself:—

(1) That the place where the birth occurred is within his district, or, if such birth took place out of his district, that he is furnished with an attested declaration within the provisions of section thirteen of the Ordinance.

added the questions Where born, and Rank or profession of father. The Schedule attached to the Ordinance of 1906 asked in addition for the race of the father and the mother. The Death Schedule of 1832 asked for Date of decease; Name of deceased; Name of father; Name of mother. The 1857 Schedule dropped the two latter questions, but asked for Age; Rank or profession, and country; Cause of death. The 1883 Schedule dropped the question concerning 'country', but asked Where died. The 1913 Schedule asked also for Abode; Name of certifying medical practitioner, if any; Duration of illness; Place of burial.

[1] Regulation No. 6 of 1908, 'Regulations for the Registration of Births and Deaths made under Section 33 of The Births and Deaths Registration Consolidation and Amendment Ordinance 1906', *Ordinances, &c., 1908*, Regulations, pp. 6–13, reprinted in *Laws of Sierra Leone in Force 1925*, vol. iii, pp. 6–14. [2] Ordinance No. 9 of 1931 (13 Aug.).

(2) Of the exact date of birth, observing that if more than three months have elapsed since the date of birth, it can only be registered after a solemn declaration made by the informant.

If more than twelve months have elapsed from the date of birth it can only be registered with the written authority of the Chief Registrar, and the 'fact of such authority' must appear in the register.

(3) That the 'informant' is legally qualified to sign the register, and is acquainted with all the particulars required to be registered.

12. The only persons legally qualified to sign as informants, in case of births, are those appearing in the first column of the table below ; and the terms to be used, when describing their qualifications in the register, should be after the following pattern :—

Persons qualified to sign as informants in the Register of Births.	Specimens of terms in which the qualifications should be recorded in the Register.
1. Either of the parents.	1. *'Father' or 'Mother.'
2. The occupier of the house in which the birth took place.	2. 'Occupier.'
3. If birth took place in a prison hospital or other public institution.	3. 'Chief Resident Officer' or 'Medical Dresser.'
4. Person present at the birth.	4. 'Nurse present at birth.'
5. Person having charge of the child.	5. 'Guardian.'
6. Person finding a new-born child.	6. 'First having charge of child.'

* The putative father of an illegitimate child need not sign as such. He may, if so qualified, be entered as qualified under 'Occupier' or 'Present at birth,' etc., and should state his qualification in either of these terms, but not as father.

13. Still-births shall not be registered except in those districts and places to which Part IV of the Ordinance applies.[1]

14. If there is more than one child at birth, a separate entry must be made for each child in the order of priority of birth ; the exact time of each birth should be added, if it can be ascertained.

15. If the Registrar has reason to believe the child to be illegitimate, he shall (unless otherwise required pursuant to the provisions of section eleven of the Ordinance) leave the columns for 'name, surname and race of father' and 'rank or profession of father' blank. Terms denoting illegitimacy should not, except within the provisions of section eleven, be entered in the register.

16. Before beginning the entry of a death in the register book, the Registrar, in order to secure a proper registry, should satisfy himself :—

(1) That the place where the death occurred is within his district.

(2) That the death occurred within three days or seven days, as the case may be, or, if the notice is given pursuant to the provisions of section twenty of the Ordinance, then within fourteen days of the date of registry. If more than twelve months have elapsed from the date of death, it can only be registered with the written authority of the Chief Registrar, and the 'fact of such authority' must appear in the register.

(3) That the informant is legally qualified to sign the register, and has at least 'knowledge of any of the particulars required to be registered.'

17. Except when a registered medical practitioner furnishes the information, the entry must be signed by the informant in the presence of the Registrar.

18. The sex of the deceased should be ascertained from the informant and be entered 'male' or 'female,' as the case may be.

19. The age should be stated in figures, writing under the figures the word 'years,' and the ages of children who die in their first year should be stated in 'months,' 'days,' 'hours' or 'minutes.'

[1] Freetown, Kissy, Congo Town, Murray Town, and Wilberforce.

Persons qualified to sign as informants in the Register of Deaths.	Specimens of terms in which the qualifications should be recorded in the Register.
1. Nearest relative present at death.	1. 'Father present at death.'
2. Nearest relative in attendance during last illness of the deceased.	2. 'Mother in attendance during last illness.'
3. Relative dwelling in same district as deceased.	3. 'Cousin dwelling in same district.'
4. Some person present at the death.	4. 'Present at death.'
5. Occupier of house in which death took place.	5. 'Occupier.'
6. Inmate of house in which death took place.	6. 'Inmate.'
7. Person finding dead body.	7. 'Having a knowledge of the particulars.'
8. Person taking charge of dead body.	8. (Death not having occurred in a
9. Person causing the body to be buried.	9. house.)

20. In cases of deaths occurring in prisons, hospitals, or other public institutions, the former 'rank' or 'profession' of deceased should be given where possible.

21. In cases of married women and children who have not followed any occupation, the column (6) 'rank or profession' should be filled thus:—'Wife,' 'widow,' 'son,' 'daughter' (as the case may be) 'of a surgeon,' 'labourer,' etc. (as the case may be).

22. In cases of 'cancer,' the situation of the cancer should be given; in cases of 'injuries,' it should be stated how such injuries were caused; in cases of 'poisoning,' 'hanging,' 'gun-shot wounds,' 'drowning,' etc., it should be stated whether accidental, homicidal or suicidal.

23. The Registrar should furnish the printed forms of certificates of cause of death supplied to him by the Chief Registrar to all registered medical practitioners who reside within his district. This includes all army surgeons whose regiments are stationed in the district, as well as the medical attendants of lunatic asylums and public institutions situated within his district.

24. When the Registrar has been furnished with a certificate of death by a registered medical practitioner, he should copy the cause of death from it into the proper column of his register book, adding the word 'certified.' When a certificate is so furnished, it shall not be necessary for any person to sign the register as informant, but the column headed 'signature, description and residence of informant' should be filled thus:—'Information received from   registered medical practitioner' with his residence. At the same time it is open to a qualified informant in such cases to give information and to sign the register. For every death registered as 'certified' the Registrar should send to the Chief Registrar a corresponding certificate of death with his certified copies at the end of each of the quarters specified in section forty-five of the Ordinance.

25. If the deceased had no medical attendant, the Registrar should ascertain, as accurately as possible, from the qualified informant the cause of death, and enter it in the proper column, adding 'uncertified, no medical attendant.'

26. Should the Registrar ascertain that a registered medical practitioner has been in attendance, but has not furnished a certificate within the provisions of subsection (2) of section twenty-seven of the Ordinance, he should send such medical practitioner a requisition within the provisions of section twenty-one. The Registrar should not in the meantime leave this column of the entry in his register book blank, but should enter the 'cause of death' from the statement of the qualified informant, adding the word 'uncertified,' and taking care to leave room for entering the certified cause of death, with the addition of the word 'certified.' The date of entry of the certified cause of death should be given in figures, after the words 'certified,' thus:—2/4/07.

27. If the attendance of the medical practitioner has not been such as to enable him to certify to the cause of death, the Registrar should add the word '*no medical attendant*' after the word '*uncertified.*'

28. If the certified '*cause of death*' be added to any entry after the quarterly returns to which it belongs have been furnished, a certified copy of the amended entry should be transmitted, as soon as practicable after the receipt thereof, to the Chief Registrar's office.

29. The Registrar is not to sign as informant in his own register.

30. Every entry should be made in order from the beginning to the end of the books. If any space or leaf in a register is accidentally passed over, or a partial entry made in mistake, it should be cancelled, and an accurate copy of such space or partial entry, with the cancelling lines, should appear in its proper position in the certified copies. Spaces should not be left blank for expected entries, nor entries be commenced to be completed at a future time. Care should be taken to fill in the heading of each leaf of the register.

31. If an informant can write, he must sign his name, qualification and residence. If he cannot write, the Registrar will write the informant's name, qualification and residence, leaving a space between the name and surname for the mark which must be affixed by the informant in presence of the Registrar, thus:—

His

John   ×   Smith,

mark.

Father,

Gloucester Street, Freetown.

32. The Registrar must distinctly understand that in no case can the signature or mark of an informant be written into a register book by any person, subject to section twenty-four hereof, but by the informant himself and in his own presence.

33. The Registrar should carefully ascertain the mode in which the names and surnames are usually spelled by the informants themselves before making the entry in the register.

The Births and Deaths Registration Ordinance, 1913, provided for the following Districts to become Registration Districts of the Colony: Freetown, Kissy, Songo Town, York, Murray Town, Wellington, Tombo, Hamilton, Wilberforce, Hastings, Kent, Tassoh Island, Regent, Waterloo, Bananas Island, The Port of Sherbro District.[1]

As before, provision was made, in addition to compulsory registration in the above-mentioned Districts, for permissive registration 'in the case of births or deaths occurring in the Protectorate, or in parts of the Colony not comprised in any district'. Furthermore, special provisions were made for Freetown, particularly as regards the registration of still-births which were henceforward registrable.

[1] See Schedule C of Births and Deaths Registration Ordinance, 1913. On 31 Dec. 1913 (see *Revised Edition of the Ordinances of Sierra Leone 1909–13*, pp. 2273–4), Local Registrars were appointed for these Districts (2 for Freetown). Their professions were: Resident Compounder, 2; Keeper Lunatic Asylum, 1; Minister of Religion, 4; Medical Dispenser, 6; Postmistress, 1; Trader, 2; Wesleyan Catechist, 1.

The Statute Law Revision Ordinance, 1924 changed the name of the last-named district into 'the Sherbro Judicial District'. The Registration Districts (Colony) Order in Council, 1935 (No. 12 of 1935, 19 Sept., *Sierra Leone Ordinances*, &c., *1935*, p. 109) provided for the redivision of the Colony into the following Registration Districts: Freetown, Wilberforce, Regent, Kissy, Wellington, Hastings, Waterloo, Songo Town, Makomba, Russell, Kent, York, Sussex, Hamilton, Tassoh Island, Sherbro Judicial District, Banana Islands.

A Governor's Order of 24 December 1913[1] approved the appointment of the Senior Clerks to District Commissioners in six Districts of the Protectorate and the Senior Customs Clerk in a seventh District to become District Registrars. The Districts concerned were Koinadugu, Karene, Railway, Ronietta, Headquarters (Protectorate portion), Northern Sherbro, and Sulymah.[2]

The Births and Deaths Registration (Amendment) Ordinance, 1929, realized many of the recommendations embodied in a *Report of the Committee appointed by His Excellency the Governor to advise on the Amendment of the Births and Deaths Registration Ordinance, 1924 (Cap. 16), with a view to placing the Registration of Births and Deaths under the Control of the Deputy Director, Sanitary Service.* At its meetings held in September and October 1926 the Committee came to the following main conclusions:

The Committee are unanimously of opinion that the entire machinery of registration of births and deaths should be placed under the control of the Deputy Director of Sanitary Service as Principal Registrar, and that in any registration district where there is a medical officer he should be appointed Registrar.

Under the existing Ordinance registration of births and deaths is compulsory throughout the Colony, but we consider that the law relating to this should be strengthened in various respects. In view of the great importance of registration of births and deaths for efficient public health administration, we consider that all possible steps should be taken to increase the efficiency of existing registration and gradually to extend compulsory registration to the Protectorate, starting with the more important sanitary districts. The new Ordinance should empower the Governor in Council to create new registration districts in the Protectorate as well as in the Colony.

We consider that registration of non-natives might be made compulsory throughout the Protectorate, but some extension of time will be necessary to prevent undue hardship in the case of persons living at a considerable distance from the nearest registration office. With the exceptions noted, registration in the Protectorate should remain permissive. . . .

We recommend that the various special provisions applied to Freetown should also be applied to Kissy, Congo Town, Murray Town and Wilberforce, where social conditions are practically the same as in Freetown.

Registration of births should be within fourteen days instead of forty-two days as at present. A penalty for failure to register births is very necessary. Under the existing Ordinance, if there is failure to register a birth within the statutory period of forty-two days, the Registrar may require the parents or other responsible persons to attend at his office to give the necessary information and register the birth, and only in the event of failure to comply with this requirement is there any penalty (sec. 7).

Registration of deaths should be within three days instead of five days as at present. As in the case of registration of births there should be a specific penalty for the mere failure to register.[3]

[1] See *Revised Edition of the Ordinances of Sierra Leone 1909–13*, p. 2272.

[2] The number of registration districts in the Protectorate was 13 in 1923, 11 in 1926, 14 in 1927, 16 in 1928, and 15 in 1929 (see *Medical Report 1923*, p. 25; *1926*, p. 7; *1927*, p. 8; *1928*, p. 7; *1929*, p. 7).

[3] Sierra Leone, *Sessional Paper*, No. 2 of 1927, pp. 1–2. The Committee was, I think, mistaken in assuming that no such penalties were provided in the Births and Deaths Registration Ordinance. Section 39 said: 'Every person required to give information concerning any birth, still-birth or death . . . who . . . fails to comply with any requisition of the Registrar made in pursuance of this

The Ordinance of 1929, which came into force on 1 July 1930, transferred the duties connected with the registration of births and deaths from the Registrar-General to the Deputy Director of the Health Service as Chief Registrar of Births and Deaths. It extended the special provisions which in 1913 had been made in regard to birth and death registration in Freetown to Kissy, Congo Town, Murray Town, and Wilberforce, and empowered the Governor to appoint a Registrar's Officer for each of these special Districts.[1] It provided, in addition to compulsory registration of all persons born or dying in the registration districts of the Colony, for compulsory registration of 'all non-natives born or dying in a district of the Protectorate created under section 3 of this Ordinance'.[2] The Ordinance also empowered the Governor in Council by Order to introduce compulsory birth and death registration of Natives in any Health District of the Protectorate on the request of the Paramount Chief[3] concerned.

The 'Births and Deaths Registration (Amendment) Ordinance, 1931' substituted 'chiefdoms or parts of chiefdoms' for 'health districts' as the areas in the Protectorate in which compulsory registration of births and deaths of Natives may be brought into force at the request of a Paramount Chief. This extended the potential areas of compulsory registration for Natives somewhat, as the so-called Health Districts only comprised small parts of a chiefdom.[4]

Ordinance . . . shall be liable to a penalty not exceeding forty shillings for each offence; and the parent of any child who fails to give information concerning the birth of such child as required by this Ordinance shall be liable to a like penalty; and a person required by this Ordinance to give information concerning a death in the first instance, and not merely in default of some other person, shall, if such information as is required by this Ordinance is not duly given, be liable to the same penalty.'

The Committee had proposed furthermore: 'We recommend that a section should be inserted in the Public Health Ordinance (Cap. 171) requiring the notification of all births to the Sanitary Authority within thirty-six hours. This might be applied at first to Freetown only, with power to extend it by Order in Council to any other part of the Colony. This action is quite distinct from registration and is for the purpose of bringing infants within the reach of the infant welfare organization as early as possible after birth. There is ample justification for this in the extremely high mortality very soon after birth. In 1925 there were in Freetown 134 deaths of infants under fourteen days per 1,000 registered births, i.e. 45 per cent. of all deaths under twelve months. It is clearly necessary for the health visitors to get into touch with infants at the earliest possible moment after birth, and this can only be attained by early notification to the Medical Officer of Health.' (Ibid., p. 2.) But this recommendation was not accepted. See also *Medical Report 1932*, p. 45; *1933*, p. 23; *1934*, p. 70.

[1] The special provisions comprise Sections 28–38 of the Ordinance as it now stands.

[2] The Protectorate (Births and Deaths Registration Districts) Order in Council, 1930 (No. 22, reprinted in *Supplement to the Laws of Sierra Leone 1925–30*, p. 517) stipulates that 'the districts specified in the second column of Schedule B to the Protectorate (Administrative Divisions) Order in Council, 1930 [No. 21, reprinted ibid., pp. 726–8] are hereby created districts within the meaning of section 3 of the Births and Deaths Registration Ordinance, 1924'. The number of registration districts in the Protectorate increased from 15 in 1930 to 22 in 1931; see *Medical Report 1931*, p. 12.

[3] Paramount Chief means a chief who is not subordinate in his ordinary jurisdiction to any other chief.

[4] None of the Health Districts, or Health Areas as they were called after 1931 (see Ordinance No. 8 of 1931, 13 Aug., 'An Ordinance to Amend the Public Health (Protectorate) Ordinance, 1926', *Sierra Leone Ordinances, &c., 1931*, pp. 37–8), comprised a radius of more than one mile and a half, and the smallest areas comprised a radius of only half a mile (see Order in Council No. 20 of 1931, 27 July, ibid., Orders in Council, pp. 68–7).

For some years apparently no applications for the introduction of compulsory registration were made by Paramount Chiefs. But 'during 1934 requests were secured from many chiefs in the more important towns, especially in those where a medical nucleus exists'.[1] The Governor thereupon issued the 'Births and Deaths Registration (Chiefdoms) Order in Council, 1935',[2] which stipulated that 'the provisions of the Births and Deaths Registration Ordinance, 1924, shall apply with the modifications specified in section 38 B thereof in the case of all natives born or dying in the parts specified in the second column of the Schedule of the chiefdoms specified in the first column thereof'. Compulsory registration for Natives was thus introduced in nineteen Health Areas.[3]

The position as it was up to 1942 may be summarized as follows. All births and deaths occurring in the Colony, and all births and deaths among non-natives (Colony-born Africans, Europeans, and Asiatics) occurring in the Protectorate were compulsorily registrable.[4] Births and deaths of Natives in the Protectorate were compulsorily registrable only in the nineteen small Health Areas where chiefs had made suitable request to Government; all other births and deaths of Natives in the Protectorate were voluntarily registrable. The African population of the registration area comprised 6 or 7 per cent. of the total African population.[5]

An Ordinance of 26 June 1942[6] changed the legal position completely so far as the Protectorate was concerned. It repealed Part IV A of the Births and Deaths Registration Ordinance, 1924 (Sections 38 A, B, 'Registration of Births and Deaths in the Protectorate') and also Part VI A (Sections 41 A–E, 'Central Administration, etc.'); it deleted the definitions of 'Chiefdom', 'Native', and 'Non-native'; it cancelled all references to the Protectorate in Sections 3 (1) and 4,[7] and in the Schedules. The text of the new Ordinance gives no clue as to its purpose. But the 'Objects and Reasons' of the Bill[8] show the intentions of the Administration.

---

[1] *Medical Report 1934*, p. 15.

[2] Order in Council No. 20 of 1935 (16 Nov.), *Sierra Leone Ordinances, &c., 1935*, pp. 121–2.

[3] The number of registration districts in the Protectorate increased thereby to 25 (see *Medical Report 1935*, p. 15).

[4] *Colonial Reports, Sierra Leone 1937*, p. 13, stated erroneously: 'Registration is not compulsory outside Freetown'.

[5] The African population subject to compulsory registration consisted of the whole African population of the Colony (1931 · 95,558), the non-native African population of the Protectorate (1931: 3,265), and a very small proportion of the native population of the Protectorate.

[6] No. 13 of 1942, 'An Ordinance to Amend the Births and Deaths Registration Ordinance, 1924', *Sierra Leone Ordinances 1942*, pp. 43–4. On the motion of the Director of Medical Services the Bill was read a first time on 12 May, and a second and third time on 19 May. See *Legislative Council of Sierra Leone, Minutes of Meeting 12th of May, 1942*, p. 18; *19th of May, 1942*, pp. 16–17.

[7] Subsection (1) of Section 3 of the Principal Ordinance (see p. 208 above) was 'amended by the deletion of the words "or the Protectorate or any part of the Colony or Protectorate" and "or Protectorate" and by the deletion of the proviso thereto'. Section 4 (see ibid.) was 'repealed and replaced as follows':

'4. The Governor may from time to time appoint persons to be Registrars of Births and Deaths for each district created under section three of this Ordinance and may appoint for each such district one or more Deputy Registrars to act for or under the control of the Registrar of the District.'

[8] *Sierra Leone Royal Gazette*, 4 May 1942, Special Supplement, pp. 49–50.

The Principal Ordinance originally applied only to the Colony and was amended so as to provide for the Protectorate as well. It has been decided that provisions for the registration of births and deaths in the Protectorate should be made under the Tribal Authorities Ordinance, 1937,[1] and it is therefore proposed to repeal all reference to the Protectorate now existing in the Principal Ordinance.[2]

But in many respects the text of the new Ordinance cannot be reconciled with its objects.

(1) Why was Subsection (1) of Section 38 A[3] repealed ? It provided for (compulsory) registration of non-native births and deaths in the Protectorate, and Tribal Authorities could not become Registration Authorities for non-natives.

(2) If it was 'proposed to repeal all reference to the Protectorate now existing in the Principal Ordinance', why was Part VI (Section 41)[4] not repealed ? It provided for optional registration of native births and deaths in the Protectorate and hung in the air since Section 3 was no longer applicable to the Protectorate. If it was not repealed, why were the definitions of 'Chiefdom' and 'Native' deleted ?

(3) Why was Part VI A (Section 41 A–E)[5] repealed ? It dealt with the Central Administration and constituted the basis of the registration system in the Colony.

I am inclined to think that Subsection (1) of Section 38 A was repealed inadvertently and that it had been the intention to repeal Part VI instead of Part VI A.

The new Ordinance abolished compulsory registration of non-native births and deaths in the Protectorate, and since there were no provisions for optional registration, non-native births and deaths were no longer registrable. For non-natives in the Protectorate the position, therefore, was again the same as prior to the enactment of the Births and Deaths Registration Consolidation and Amendment Ordinance 1906.

The new Ordinance abolished likewise the existing compulsory registration of native births and deaths in the Protectorate, and the plan of substituting a new system of compulsory registration has not been carried out. The Medical Report for 1942 said euphemistically:

The re-organised system of registration in the Protectorate has not yet begun to function owing to delay in the printing of the required forms and registers.[6]

The Medical Report for 1943 did not mention the subject.

[1] The Tribal Authorities Ordinance of 25 June 1937 (No. 8, reprinted in *Sierra Leone Ordinances, &c., 1937*, pp. 42–50), which was to apply to the Protectorate, provided:
'Subject to the provisions of any Ordinance or other law for the time being in force, a tribal authority may (subject to the general or specific directions of the tribal authority, if any, to whom it is subordinate), issue orders, to be obeyed by natives within its area to whom the orders relate, for all or any of the following purposes:—
(i) requiring the birth or death of natives within its area to be reported to it or to such person as it may direct.'
[2] See also *Medical Report 1941*, p. 4: 'It is proposed to re-organize Birth and Death Registration in the Protectorate and substitute for the present system one whereby Native Administrations and Tribal Authorities will be the Registration Authorities and Birth and Death Registration will be made compulsory throughout the territory. It is hoped thereby in time to get reasonably complete figures for the whole country.'   [3] See p. 209 above.
[4] See ibid.   [5] See pp. 209–10 above.   [6] *Medical Report 1942*, p. 5.

But the position of registration in the Protectorate—no legal basis for any non-native registration, and provisions for native optional registration based on a section which had been repealed—was intolerable in the long run. 'An Ordinance to Amend Certain Ordinances'[1] of 15 June 1945, therefore, deleted Section 41 and substituted the original text of this section as it was in force until 1930. Since the original text provided for optional registration of both native and non-native births and deaths in the Protectorate the legal position now is: All births and deaths occurring in the Colony are compulsorily registrable; all births and deaths occurring in the Protectorate are voluntarily registrable.

Degree of Completeness. Prior to the enactment of the Ordinance of 1913 birth and death registration had been compulsory in Freetown but voluntary in the rest of the Colony and in the whole Protectorate. The new Ordinance made registration compulsory in the whole Colony, but for a long time registration was hardly enforced outside Freetown.

1914. Freetown is the only centre in which statistics of any value are obtainable.[2]

1916. Freetown. There is reason to believe that in the operation of the Act, the registration of births is defective, and it has been arranged that the Sanitary Sub-Inspectors should assist in checking the birth returns in order that importance of registration should be brought more forcibly to the notice of delinquents.

The . . . figures [for 1912–16] show a tendency to an increase in the birth rate, but this is probably more apparent than real, as year by year the native becomes more alive to the obligations required of him by law.[3]

Colony. . . . the [birth and death] figures given must . . . be accepted with caution as the present system of registration can be hardly described as effective.[4]

1920. There is a large population of Protectorate natives living in Freetown and the Colony, many of whom will not trouble to register the births of children.[5]

Sherbro District (Colony). The death rate shows great improvement if taken from the Registrar's figures; only eighty-four deaths were registered. On the other hand, ninety-three people were buried in the three cemeteries. Forty-six births, only, were registered, which is probably less than half the number which took place. If, approximately, only eighty per cent. of deaths and sixty per cent. of births are registered, it is quite time that some drastic change took place, especially as 1921 is the year of the decennial census. The remedy for this state of affairs would be for the local Registrars of Births and Deaths, who are mostly Dispensers, to be placed under the sole control of the Principal Medical Officer instead of the Registrar General.[6]

1921. Freetown. . . . the registration of deaths is probably correct, as bodies have to be buried   [7]

---

[1] No. 11 of 1945, *Sierra Leone Royal Gazette*, 21 June 1945, Supplement No. 2, pp. 120–3. The Ordinance was issued in connexion with the preparation of a Revised Edition of the Laws.

[2] *Medical Report 1914*, p. 10. See also ibid. *1915*, p. 48.

[3] Ibid. *1916*, p. 80. The apparent increase was in reality due to the fact that the Medical Officer of Health related the number of births for each year to the population of 1911, though it had increased considerably in subsequent years.

[4] *Colonial Reports, Sierra Leone 1916*, p. 20. See also ibid. *1918*, p. 14.

[5] Ibid. *1920*, p. 22. See also ibid. *1918*, p. 14; *1919*, p. 6; *1921*, p. 22.

[6] Senior Medical Officer, *Medical Report 1920*, p. 20.

[7] *Colonial Reports, Sierra Leone 1921*, p. 22. See also *Medical Report 1923*, p. 25: 'Registration of deaths is apparently quite complete, in view of the necessity to obtain a burial permit. . . .' See furthermore ibid. *1926*, p. 7: '. . . deaths can be considered as accurate, as one cannot be buried without a permit, which is only obtained by registration.' See, finally, ibid. *1930*, p. 13: 'The figures for deaths can be relied upon; every death must be registered before burial is allowed, all

But complaints about incomplete registration of births in Freetown did not cease.

> 1922. Owing to the non-registration of many births the 'available' birth rate is undoubtedly much below the actual birth rate . . . .[1]

When in 1923 the number of registered births increased, the Medical and Sanitary Department pointed out that there is 'no doubt that many births still escape registration', but added:

> The question of improving the system of registration of births and deaths is under consideration. Already, as a result of warnings to the public, there has been an appreciable increase in the number of births registered in Freetown, 853 in 1923 as compared with 744 in 1922.[2]

The further increase in birth registration in 1924 and 1925 was accompanied by similar comments.

> 1924. There was an increase in the number of births registered from 853 in 1923 to 982 in 1924, but in spite of the efforts of the Registrar's officer, assisted by the sanitary staff, registration of births must still be regarded as incomplete.[3]
> 1925. The increase in births registered noted last year has continued. There is no reason to suppose that this is a natural increase, and it is attributable to the activity of the Registrar's officer, assisted by the sanitary inspectors.[4]

In 1926 and 1927 the number of births registered declined again (from 1,102 in 1925 to 1,074 and 1,010 respectively).

> 1926. In the previous year the Registration Officer appointed for Freetown and Cline Town[5] made occasional visits to premises and defaulters were summoned before the Police Magistrate; fines were inflicted and the object in view was realised. This Officer has not been as active in the above Districts as he has been in the previous year; he is a Sanitary Inspector and it is probable that all his attention was paid to the duties of his substantive appointment and consequently he had no time to carry out the duties of Registration Officer.[6]
> . . . births . . . are only registered as the spirit moves the parents, or as they are rounded up by inspectors and infant welfare nurses. Legislation is being enacted which will strengthen our hands as regards birth registration, by lessening the period in which a child must be registered and by putting the control of registration of births and deaths completely in the hands of the Sanitary Department.[7]
> 1927.[8] Even in Freetown, owing to the floating Protectorate population, registration of births is not fully carried out . . . .[9] It is hoped that an Ordinance will shortly be enacted placing the control of registration entirely in the hands of the Sanitary Department and strengthening the law in various respects.

the cemeteries in Freetown being under control.' The only loophole apparently is that, if the burial takes place outside Freetown, registration of the death can be avoided. See 'Report of the Chief Registrar', *Medical Report 1934*, p. 13: '. . . the rigid control of cemeteries results in the detection of all deceased persons, other than those who are removed from the city just prior to death or immediately after death . . . .'

[1] Ibid. *1922*, p. 29. Literally the same, ibid. *1928*, p. 8.

[2] Ibid. *1923*, p. 25.

[3] Ibid. *1924*, p. 26. See also ibid., p. 60, the remark of the Infant Welfare Nurse: 'There are still many unregistered births.'

[4] Ibid. *1925*, p. 23.

[5] Cline Town is a suburb of Freetown.

[6] *Report of the Registrar General 1926*, p. 7.

[7] *Medical Report 1926*, pp. 7–8.

[8] Ibid. *1927*, p. 8.   [9] Literally the same, ibid. *1929*, p. 7.

The Medical Report for 1927 was not the first to call attention to the particular inadequacy of birth registration on the part of the natives coming from the Protectorate. But in that year the Infant Welfare Service apparently had classified for the first time the births and infant deaths in Freetown, excluding Cline Town, according to race. The results were published for 1927–9. They are as follows:[1]

| | Births | | | Infant deaths | | | Infant mortality rate | | |
Races	1927	1928	1929	1927	1928	1929	1927	1928	1929
Creoles	542	..	558	111	128	135	204	247	242
Aborigines	206	..	257	146	160	141	708	632	549
Croos	114	..	123	51	39	52	447	339	423
Various	19	..	30	2	2	1	..	..	..
Total	881	915	968	310	329	329	357	364	337

The high infant mortality rate ascertained in 1927 for the Natives from the Protectorate was considered a clear indication of 'a failure to register births on the part of aborigines . . . . The birth and death statistics as regards the Creole element in Freetown may be considered as fairly accurate.'[2]

In any case there cannot be the least doubt that until 1930, when the duties of birth and death registration were transferred from the Registrar-General to the Deputy Director of the Health Service as Chief Registrar, the total number of births registered lagged very much behind the actual number of births. But it is difficult to estimate the proportion of births which were not registered. The new Chief Registrar, it is true, 'surveyed the registers for the preceding years' and made 'a minute examination of the returns for two years at opposite ends of the intercensal period'.[3] He reported as follows:

A careful search of the registers for the years 1922 and 1929 revealed the fact that only 72·4 per cent. and 72·5 per cent. respectively of the deaths of children under one year of age could be traced as births in the birth registers.[4]

But this method of ascertaining the deficiency of birth registration does not necessarily lead to accurate results. The 1931 census report rightly states: 'It cannot be said, however, that this figure represents the true percentage of births registered, and it is possible that a number of children whose deaths were registered in the Colony were born in the Protectorate.'[5]

---

[1] See ibid. *1927*, p. 82; *1928*, pp. 87–8; *1929*, pp. 86, 88.
[2] Ibid. *1927*, p. 82.
[3] *Census Report 1931*, p. 25.
[4] 'Report of the Chief Registrar of Births and Deaths', *Medical Report 1932*, p. 18.
[5] *Census Report 1931*, p. 25. Of the 55,358 persons enumerated in 1931 in Freetown 22,004 were born in the Protectorate (see ibid., p. 31). The age composition of those born in the Protectorate is not given, but of the 841 children under one year enumerated in Freetown not less than 459 were of native tribes (see ibid., p. 50). The number of infants brought to Freetown by immigrants may, therefore, have been considerable. Other infants may have been brought there in different circumstances. In discussing the increase in the infant mortality rate in 1928, the *Medical Report (1928*, p. 8) says that it 'may be due, in part, to the success and popularity of the infant welfare clinics, because a great number of infants are brought to Freetown from Colony

On the other hand, certainly some children who died under one year were registered neither at birth nor at death. It is possible, of course, that these two factors offset each other and that the proportion of births registered was actually 72 per cent. in 1929.[1] But if this was so, it is impossible that the proportion should have been likewise 72 per cent. in 1922, since the number of births registered increased from 1922 to 1929 by 47 per cent. while the population increased only by 17 per cent.

Let us now consider the development of birth registration in Freetown from 1930 on.

For the first six months of 1930 the registration of births and deaths was [still] under the control of the Registrar-General and during that period there was no machinery for enforcing the registration of births.[2]

The birth figures for 1931 (1,263) and 1932 (1,276) were considered to come much nearer the truth. The Medical and Sanitary Department stated in its report for 1931:

In Freetown every precaution has been taken to secure the registration of births during the year. Ninety-five per cent. of the deaths of children under one year were traced in the birth registers, and this figure is probably a fair indication of the percentage of total births which were registered.[3]

But the Chief Registrar of Births and Deaths was more cautious. He said that the excess of deaths over births (117) 'may be accounted for— at least in part—by the difficulty still found in securing the registration of all births among aborigines from the Protectorate'.

The birth-rate for Freetown was 22·73 per 1,000 as compared with 22·04 per 1,000 in 1930. Although every effort has been made to secure the registration of all births these figures cannot be considered more than approximately accurate.[4]

His successor, however, in his report for 1932, stated:

In 1931, which was the first complete year during which registration was under the control of this department, 95 per cent. of the deaths of children under one year of age at Freetown were traced as births in the births registers, and the number of births registered increased by 161 or 14·6 per cent. It is probable that the percentage registered of births which took place lies between 87 and 95 per cent.[5]

The registration figures of births and deaths at Freetown represent fairly accurately the number of births and deaths which actually took place. Every precaution has been taken to secure registration of births; it is probable that at least 90 per cent. of those which take place are registered.[6]

villages to these clinics in a moribund condition'. Finally 'of the large number of native women in Freetown and the Colony, who are not settlers, many, when they become expectant mothers, go to their homes in the Protectorate to be delivered. It is the regular custom for native women to return to their own families for this purpose. They return to their husbands later and bring the children with them but the births are not registered. . . . Some of these die in the Colony as infants . . . and their deaths are registered.' (*Census Report 1931*, p. 25.)

[1] In 1931 about 40 per cent. of the African population in Freetown were Creoles (see ibid., p. 50). The number of Creole births registered in 1929 in Freetown (excluding the suburb Cline Town) was 558 and the total number of African births registered 938. Assuming that the Creole births were all registered and that they constituted 40 per cent. of all births, the total number of births would have been 1,395. The proportion of births registered would then have been 67 per cent. Since certainly also some Creole births escaped registration, I see no reason to assume that more than 72 per cent. of all births were registered.

[2] *Medical Report 1930*, p. 13.   [3] Ibid. *1931*, p. 12.
[4] Ibid., p. 76.   [5] Ibid. *1932*, p. 18.   [6] Ibid., p. 16.

The figures contained in this statement are quite contradictory, and only one thing is certain. It is out of the question that as many as 95 per cent. of the infants deceased in Freetown in 1931 were traced in the birth registers. A number of infants deceased in 1931 were born in 1930 when birth registration in Freetown was still quite defective, and even if registration had been complete at Freetown in 1930 and 1931, the children born elsewhere and dying in the capital would probably have been too numerous to permit the tracing of 95 per cent. of the deceased children in the birth registers. If something like 90 per cent. of the births occurring in 1931 in Freetown were registered, the proportion of infants deceased whose birth could be traced in the registers must have been less than 90 per cent.

The Blue Books for 1933–8 stated, year-in, year-out, that 'it is probable that 95 per cent. of the births which take place at Freetown are registered'.[1] But I suspect that this statement was based on the opinion expressed by the Medical and Sanitary Department in its report for 1931. The official birth-rate averaged 22·6 in 1933–8 as in 1931–2, against 20·8 in 1924–30. I am inclined, therefore, to assume that the proportion of births registered in 1933–8 was between 80 and 90 per cent.[2] In recent years registration seems to have been still more defective. The Medical Report for 1940 said:

It is . . . more than probable that the recent influx of population is of a type that will not effect registration and the numbers of births and deaths registered are probably short of the actual total of these occurrences particularly in the case of births.[3]

In the Colony outside Freetown the number of births registered oscillated in 1920–31 between 769 and 950, leapt to 1,163 in 1932, was again only 948 and 934 in 1933 and 1934 respectively, and oscillated in 1935–43 between 981 and 1,153. The number of deaths registered oscillated in 1920–35 between 789 and 1,068, in 1936–8 between 1,109 and 1,205, and in 1939–43 between 1,221 and 1,622. The official comments on the completeness of birth and death registration are unfavourable.

1927. Registration.—In the colony it is nominally compulsory, but difficult to enforce outside Freetown.[4]

1931. In the case of births, there is less supervision over natives from the Protectorate than is exercised in Freetown and probably a greater proportion are left unregistered. Unfortunately, all the Colony cemeteries are not yet controlled, and it is possible that a number of deaths have not been registered. Legislation on this matter is considered.[5]

When in 1932 the numbers of registered births and deaths showed increases of 39 and 9 per cent. respectively over 1931 the Chief Registrar stated:

Registration figures of births and deaths for the rest of the Colony cannot yet be regarded as representing even the numbers of births and deaths which actually

---

[1] See, for example, *Blue Book 1938*, Section O, p. 2. In ibid. *1939* O, p. 2, the figure was raised to 97.

[2] Assuming that in 1924–30, 72 per cent. of all births were registered, the birth-rate would have been 28·9. Assuming that in 1933–8 between 80 and 90 per cent. of all births were registered, the birth-rate would have been between 25·1 and 28·2.

[3] *Medical Report 1940*, p. 10.   [4] Ibid. *1927*, p. 8; literally the same, ibid. *1929*, p. 7.

[5] 'Report of the Chief Registrar', ibid. *1931*, p. 77.

take place. The conditions are rural, the population scattered and the villages far apart; so it is probable that a number of burials take place outside the cemeteries which are not yet under control. But propaganda can be conducted through the schools and village headmen to indicate the benefits of registering. Extension of the number of special districts and the appointment of Registrars' Officers, when circumstances permit, to ascertain and enforce registration of births and deaths should also do much to improve the numerical value of the returns. The registrars, who are all paid fees by Government according to the numbers registered, will be encouraged to take more interest, and the cemeteries brought under control as early as possible so that burials may not take place without a certificate from the local registrar. In certain districts the presence of police officers may also be of assistance although so far their co-operation has of necessity been limited owing to shortage of staff.[1]

This increase . . . in the number of births registered over the previous year is to be attributed to greater zeal on the part of the registrars at Waterloo, Wellington and Songo Town, which showed increases of . . . 344 per cent., 51 per cent. and 25 per cent., respectively, on the previous year's figures. These very high percentage increases are indicative of what can be done on the part of a keen registrar to improve registration in his district.

Births exceeded deaths registered by 159, the latter figure possibly approximating the number of deaths which escaped registration.[2]

Omissions of births and deaths as a whole were still considered to be numerous owing to the fact that outside the 'special districts' (Kissy, Congo Town, Murray Town, and Wilberforce) the Registrars were either Government Dispensers or 'private individuals carrying on other occupations and without the machinery necessary for enforcing registration'.[3]

Two reforms were introduced in 1934 and 1935.

. . . the Births and Deaths Registration (Fees) Rules, 1934, is an important minor measure which, it is hoped, will have far-reaching consequences. By these rules, fees formerly payable by informants in respect of the registration of births or deaths have been waived; copies of register entries, if requested at the time of registration, are now also free . . . . It is hoped that these concessions will induce people to come forward for registration, as it was considered that the people were reluctant to pay even the small sum of 6d. from their very meagre earnings.[4]

The Order in Council of 19 September 1935 rescinded the division of the Colony into registration districts as provided in the Ordinance of 1913 and redivided the Colony into seventeen districts, one Registrar being appointed for each. The Registrars were 'chosen from the Medical Officers or from educated citizens in non-medical stations'.[5]

But the effects of these reforms upon registration were practically nil.

1935. . . . the present organisation now covers the whole of the Colony, though it must still be pointed out that the figures obtained cannot be taken as a true indication of the morbidity[6] of the people. Only in Freetown do the figures in any way approximately disclose true conditions owing to rigid control of cemeteries

---

[1] *Medical Report 1932*, p. 17. See also ibid. *1933*, p. 12; *1934*, p. 13.

[2] Ibid. *1932*, p. 17. If 159 deaths escaped registration, about 14 per cent. of all deaths would not have been registered.

[3] Ibid., p. 14. See also ibid. *1933*, p. 25: '. . . the registrars are Government dispensers, school teachers or traders and difficulty is often experienced in finding a literate person capable of making the entries in the registers.'

[4] Ibid. *1934*, p. 13.   [5] Ibid. *1935*, p. 12.

[6] Should evidently read 'mortality'.

and the detection of live births by the Sanitary Inspectors and Health Visitors in the course of their daily duties.[1]

. . . no reliance can be placed on the figures obtained from the registration districts in the Colony outside Freetown. At the best, they represent but a proportion of the births or deaths taking place, and cannot be used for the compilation of any accurate figures. The machinery exists but only time and custom will induce the African to register, and this desirable object is better achieved by persuasion than by coercion.[2]

1937. Although the Colony is well served with registries the figures so far obtained are far from complete and it is only in Freetown that the figures can be regarded as reasonably accurate.[3]

The figures obtained from registrations in the Colony outside of Freetown are much too incomplete for the compilation of even very approximate rates.[4]

The Chief Registrar most probably had conclusive evidence that registration outside Freetown was quite incomplete. But, as will be shown later, the official birth- and death-rates were very much higher than in Freetown, and it seems somewhat doubtful whether birth registration is actually far more adequate in Freetown than in the rest of the Colony.

In the Protectorate registration prior to 1930 was not compulsory, and little use was made of permissive registration. The number of births registered in 1919–30 oscillated between 17 and 212, and the number of deaths registered between 1 and 216.

1923. Vital statistics for the Protectorate are not available. Registration of births and deaths is permissive and there are thirteen registration districts, but very few births or deaths are registered.[5]

1927. In the Protectorate registration is permissive and practically non-existent.[6]

In July 1930 compulsory registration was provided for all non-natives (including Colony-born Africans), but not before 1931 was any machinery established to enforce it. For Natives registration remained optional.

1930. Owing to the apathy of the native in matters appertaining to public health, it is unlikely that he will exercise this option to any great extent and this elementary form of registration is to be regarded as a preliminary to the introduction later of compulsory registration for natives in well established medical districts. In the meantime much useful work can be accomplished by means of propaganda to pave the way to this desirable end : the Ordinance provides for the application of a clause embodying such compulsory registration on the request of a native chief.[7]

---

[1] *Medical Report 1935*, p. 12. Almost literally the same ibid. *1936*, p. 13.

[2] Ibid. *1935*, p. 14. Almost literally the same ibid. *1936*, p. 14.   [3] Ibid. *1937*, p. 12.

[4] Ibid. *1937*, p 14. See also ibid. *1938*, pp. 12–13; *1940*, p. 10. Unfortunately the publication of the figures was sometimes also done very carelessly. Thus, the Medical Reports (*1941*, p. 4; *1942*, p. 5; *1943*, p. 5) showed the deaths for 1941 as follows:

	M.	F.	Total
Freetown	1,271	862	2,133
Rest of Colony	949	493	1,622
Total	2,220	1,355	3,755

Since *Blue Book 1941* O, p. 2, gives as total death figures 2,133, 1,622, and 3,755 respectively the registered female deaths in the Colony excluding Freetown numbered probably 673 and in the whole Colony 1,535. I entered these figures in Table 29 below. (I was, however, not able to correct similar mistakes in the Protectorate figures for 1941.)

[5] *Medical Report, 1923*, p. 25.   [6] Ibid. *1927*, p. 8. See also ibid. *1929*, p. 7.

[7] Ibid. *1930*, p. 12.

The number of registered births leapt from 55 in 1930 to 557 in 1931 and the number of registered deaths from 17 to 452. The Chief Registrar attributed the increase in the number of birth registrations to 'a change in some registrars and the fact that a number of births of over three months up to and over one year have been registered'. He said that the increase in the number of deaths was 'due almost entirely to the appointment of new deputy registrars and the watchful eye of the Protectorate Medical Officers who act as Registrars for their districts'.[1] But these explanations are evidently inadequate. The increases were due in part to the introduction of compulsory registration for non-natives. Since, however, the total non-native population, according to the 1931 census, numbered only 4,268, and since registration of non-native births and deaths was incomplete,[2] the majority of the births and deaths registered in 1931 must have occurred among Natives and must have been registered voluntarily.

In 1932 the numbers of registered births and deaths dropped by more than one-half. The official comments are contradictory. The report on 'Public Health', neglecting the facts, said:

. . . the increase of recorded deaths in the Protectorate can easily be taken as demonstrating greater assiduity on the part of Registrars of Births and Deaths, who are now controlled by the Health Department.[3]

But the Acting Chief Registrar stated:

The marked decrease in the number of births and deaths recorded is to be attributed to lack of funds on the part of natives desiring to register optionally.[4]

For the native population, which numbered 1,667,790 persons in 1931, registration is optional or permissive, and at present practically non-existent: the fact that a fee of sixpence is charged for registering the birth or death of a native is a strong deterrent rather than an inducement for them to come forward and register, especially as they are unable owing to lack of education to realize the possible benefits of registering.[5]

In 1933–5 registrations of births and deaths were more numerous than in 1932 but still fewer than in 1931.

The Chief Registrar reported:

1933. In the Protectorate, comprising ninety-five per cent. of the total population of this territory, registration of births and deaths is compulsory only for non-natives, i.e. Europeans, Asiatics and Colony-born Africans. This non-native population numbered 4,268 persons at the Census of 1931. Registration is optional for the aboriginal natives, who numbered 1,667,790 persons; and is at present practically non-existent owing to the fees charged for registering. As the result of recent consultations with the Provincial Commissioners, it is expected that several applications will be received at an early date from the Paramount Chiefs for compulsory and free

[1] *Medical Report 1931*, p. 77.
[2] See Report of Acting Chief Registrar, ibid. *1933*, p. 16: 'The number of non-natives living near enough to towns with registration offices to make registration possible is not known.'
[3] Ibid. *1932*, p. 10. See also ibid. *1933*, p. 9; *1934*, p. 9. [4] Ibid. *1932*, p. 18.
[5] Ibid., p. 17. Another, certainly not less important, reason for the little use made of optional registration was that the opportunity for such registration was lacking almost everywhere. See ibid., p. 18: '. . . the present elementary system of compulsory and optional registration . . . only applies to comparatively small and isolated districts where trading activities attract the presence of non-natives . . . .'

registration for the aboriginal natives, as provided for in the Ordinance. This will be confined in the first instance to health areas where machinery for enforcement is already available.[1]

1934. During 1934, although registration was compulsory for the non-native residing in the Protectorate (i.e. Syrians, Colony-born Africans, Europeans, etc.), only ·4 per 1,000 of the total Protectorate population of approximately 1,672,058 people were subject to compulsory registration. As previously pointed out compulsory registration can be applied to the native of the Protectorate only on request of the Paramount Chiefs. During 1934 requests were secured from many chiefs in the more important towns, especially in those where a medical nucleus exists. These requests will increase the number of people covered, from ·4 to ·7 per 1,000.[2]

The figures obtained from such a small proportion of the populace can in no way express the conditions in the Protectorate, while the gross figures registered merely record a greater or lesser willingness to inform registrars of births and deaths which have occurred.[3]

These comments are not very helpful. The Chief Registrar said in his report for 1933 that optional registration is 'practically non-existent owing to the fees charged for registering'. But these fees were abolished in 1934 and optional registration did not increase. The Chief Registrar said repeatedly[4] that as long as compulsory registration was confined to non-natives it covered only 0·4 per 1,000 of the population and that when, upon requests from many chiefs in the more important towns, it was expanded, it covered 0·7 per 1,000 of the population. But the non-native population actually comprised 2·5 per 1,000 of the population of the Protectorate, and by the end of 1935 native registration had become compulsory in 19 Protectorate towns.

The comments in the reports for the following years are likewise not very informative.

1936. During the year it was not found possible to extend the scope of the organisation to embrace more Protectorate towns, but it will be seen . . . that something has been achieved by the stations opened in December, 1935.[5]

In the Pujehun District of the Protectorate good results have been obtained, but where Permissive Registration only is in force, only time and education can change the present lack of interest.[6]

1937. No extension of registration was effected in the Protectorate during 1937. There was a general decrease in the registrations effected in the Protectorate during the year.[7]

Where permissive registration only is in force in the Protectorate little interest is displayed in it by the inhabitants and even where it has been made compulsory at the request of a Paramount Chief the figures obtained are far from complete.[8]

1938. . . . the number of births and deaths . . . are not representative of the births and deaths which occurred.[9]

The Chief Registrar apparently believed that the increase in the numbers of registrations was due to the extension of compulsory registration. But I very much doubt whether, for example, the 'good results' obtained in the Pujehun District actually occurred in the areas where registration was compulsory. The numbers of births and deaths registered in four

---

[1] Ibid. *1933*, p. 12.   [2] Ibid. *1934*, p. 15.   [3] Ibid., p. 13.
[4] See ibid. *1934*, pp. 13, 15; *1935*, p. 12.   [5] Ibid. *1936*, p. 14.
[6] Ibid., p. 13.   [7] Ibid. *1937*, p. 14.
[8] Ibid., p. 12.   [9] Ibid. *1938*, p. 13.

selected and in the other twenty-one Districts of the Protectorate were as follows:[1]

Districts	Births				Deaths			
	1935	1936	1937	1938	1935	1936	1937	1938
Bandajuma[1] . .	5	—[2]	7	481	7	—[2]	2	292
Pujehun . .	191	1,572	800	822	43	60	14	15
Potoru[1] . .	15	240	354	612	10	120	40	108
Sulima. . .	16	244	229	167	—	9	5	6
All others . .	250	397	453	663	366	544	504	699
Total . .	477	2,453	1,843	2,745	426	733	565	1,120

[1] Opened in Dec. 1935.   [2] Registrar not available.

It appears that while registration of births increased enormously in the Pujehun District, registration of deaths remained negligible. Such a development may take place in an area where registration is voluntary. But it seems inconceivable that under a compulsory system death registration should be evaded almost completely, whereas regulations as to registration of births should be obeyed. Since also in the other Districts where great progress was made it affected mainly births, it seems likely that the increase in registration occurred mostly in areas where native registration remained voluntary.[2] Absolute clarity would, of course, have been easily obtained if the returns had distinguished between areas where registration was compulsory and areas where it was not. It is significant, however, that the abolition of compulsory registration in 1942 did not affect the amount of registration. The number of registered births, after having dropped from 2,963 in 1939 to 2,017 in 1941, was 1,951 in 1942 and 2,042 in 1943. The number of registered deaths was even much higher in 1942 (1,662) and in 1943 (1,610) than in any previous year.

Surveys. Apart from current birth and death registration very little has been done to obtain data on fertility and mortality in Sierra Leone.

In 1923 Dr. Easmon, African Medical Officer at Bo, made an investigation into the infant mortality at various places in the Central and Southern Provinces. The method he used has not been reported, but he apparently succeeded in ascertaining how many of 793 children had died within 12 months.[3]

Two attempts to secure information on fertility and mortality were made at the time of the 1931 census.

. . . a questionnaire was circulated amongst the Medical officers of the Colony and Protectorate containing a number of questions dealing with social customs and habits, diet and conditions of living in general and asking their opinions on the effects these factors have on such subjects as birth-rate, infantile, and child mortality, adult life in general and the general trend of the population.[4]

[1] See *Medical Report 1935*, p. 15; *1936*, p. 15; *1937*, p. 15; *1938*, p. 14.

[2] It was unfortunate that the towns in which registration for natives was made compulsory were nearly all places where registration offices for non-natives had been established because trading activities attracted the presence of non-natives. This certainly was very convenient for the Administration, but there is no reason to assume that these were necessarily the towns where compulsory registration appealed most to the natives.

[3] See ibid. *1923*, p. 25.   [4] *Census Report 1931*, p. 11.

In addition to requests for information on the foregoing, Medical officers were asked to endeavour to collect some figures dealing with fertility rates of women. In making this request, it was suggested that the method used in obtaining figures should be the same as that used in Nyasaland for the last Census (1926), which the Chief Census Officer of the Gold Coast proposed using for this Census.

The Nyasaland method was as follows:—

One hundred married women were selected in each district who, by reason of age, were not likely to have any further children. Each was asked to state (1) the number of children born to her, (2) the number of still-born, (3) the number who died as infants, (4) the number who died before puberty. . . .

Attention is drawn to the term 'married women'. The term 'married couple' was used in the case of Nyasaland, but is possibly indefinite, as applied to Sierra Leone. It should be emphasized that statistics would not be so valuable based on information concerning each 'marriage' or each married couple and it was pointed out that the details given should be those relating to married women, who may have had several 'husbands'. They refer to the fertility of the woman and not the male parent. District Commissioners were also asked to assist and the response was good.[1]

In the Protectorate 833 women in nine of the twelve Districts were questioned; in the case of two Districts the figures were collected by the District Commissioners.

No figures were returned for the rural districts of the Colony. In the case of Freetown and Kissy Districts, the figures for 200 non-native and 100 native and non-native women were taken. . . . The figures were collected by the Medical officers of the district and the Resident Medical officer of the Princess Christian Hospital.[2]

I shall discuss the results of these investigations in the following section.

VII. African Fertility, Mortality, and Population Growth

1. *Fertility*

Introduction. It has been shown that in earlier times the opinion rightly or wrongly prevailed that fertility among the Liberated Africans was low. The Colonial Secretary, in his report on the 1881 census, expressed the view that fertility among the African population as a whole was low.

The number of Infants is disproportionate to the population, but I take it the chief cause of so small an infantile record, and consequently so gentle an increase of the population amongst a people whose prolific tendencies are indisputable, arises from the fact that mothers nurse their children for periods of from one to three years, whilst amongst the Mohammedan population polygamy may operate to a small extent.[3]

His successor, in the report on the 1891 census, wrote:

Infants have increased by 875 but this cannot be considered as proportionate to the population. A reason for this was given in the report of 1881 namely the long period in which native mothers nurse their infants, to which also may be added the fact that the mortality among infants in this Colony is very great.[4]

But quite apart from the fact that the number of 'Infants' had increased between 1881 and 1891 in exactly the same proportion as the total population, the term 'Infants' is far too vague to permit the drawing

[1] Ibid., pp. 15–16.
[3] Ibid. *1881*, p. 10.
[2] Ibid., p. 16.
[4] Ibid. *1891*, p. 12.

of any conclusions concerning fertility. It may suffice to mention that in the Peninsula 45 per cent. of the children under 6 were counted in 1891 as infants and in the rest of the Colony 84 per cent.[1]

The census reports for 1901, 1911, and 1921 do not discuss fertility, but the 1931 report deals very fully with this topic. The answers to the questionnaires circulated amongst the Medical Officers of the Colony and the Protectorate, in so far as they bear on fertility, are summarized as follows:

Birth-rate. The most important question is the prolificacy of the race, the birth-rate and factors affecting it. To the question 'Are the women in your district naturally prolific?' the reply from all the Medical officers was in the affirmative. The next step in an enquiry of this kind should be to find out whether there is any check or restriction in the birth-rate, whether there exist many cases of infertility, and to what cause they are attributed.

Infertility. It has been suggested that excessive sexual intercourse may be a cause of infertility. The Medical officers stationed in Freetown and the Colony state that they frequently receive complaints from women of infertility but, on the other hand, some of the Medical officers in the Protectorate state that such complaints are never made, and others that they seldom receive them. The Medical officers in Freetown deal with both the native and the non-native class and it is presumed that requests for advice on this matter are received from both. An important point to note is that amongst the natives in the Colony, and especially in Freetown, there is a large preponderance of males. This is distinctly a low birth-rate factor, excessive intercourse, as far as women are concerned, probably causing barrenness.

In the Protectorate the women are not so ready to come to the European doctors with complaints of this nature, although infertility exists.

Causes of Infertility. The most common causes of infertility are stated to be gonorrhœa and its complications, syphilis and malaria, which give rise to relative sterility; the last and over-indulgence in sexual intercourse causing impotency in males.

Preventive Checks. As far as can be ascertained, there are very few preventive checks practised, but the procuring of abortion is not unknown. It probably takes place occasionally in the case of young girls and young unmarried non-native women. Women who have been unfaithful to their husbands and native women who have become pregnant by intercourse within the prohibited degree of relationship (a wide one) probably also have recourse to it.

Among the few abortifacients known, one is said to be a 'medicine' made from benniseed; another a decoction of thymol leaves (tea bush), fignut leaves and spice. Other methods are the manipulation of the womb through the abdomen, and, as one Medical officer states, the proximation of the anterior abdominal wall to the steam emanating from the boiling of husk rice.

Ordinarily the native woman will not employ means to this end. She is not averse from bearing children in, or even out of, wedlock. She considers the gift of a child a blessing, and barrenness a curse.

Involuntary abortion is said by the Medical officers of Freetown to be uncommon, but conflicting opinions are given by the Medical officers in the Protectorate. Some say that it is common and others that it is not. All admit, however, that there are many causes predisposing to it—hook-worm, malaria, gonorrhœa, syphilis and anæmia all causing lowered fertility and vitality.

Polygamy. Medical officers, for the most part, are inclined to condemn polygamy on the ground that it tends to produce impotency in the male through excess. In this country the moral code is not rigid and, where there are a large number of wives to one man, the probability is that the neglected wives will not remain faithful.

[1] See *Census Report 1891*, p. 11.

They run the risk of the contraction of venereal disease and, in turn, infect their husbands. A husband with venereal disease will infect many wives, who may again consort with other men and so continue to spread the disease. Sterility and lowered vitality are the result.

To quote one Medical officer on the effect of polygamy: 'It is responsible' he states, 'for impotency in the males and relative infertility in the females. Unfaithfulness with consequent venereal infection—the husband is infected and the vicious circle is created which is almost impossible to break—infection from wife to husband and husband to other wives. One-birth sterility is common amongst these women.'

It would appear, therefore, that polygamy has a very important bearing on the subject of the birth-rate.[1]

Period of Suckling. Another factor bearing on the question of the birth-rate is the long period of suckling. This, it seems, continues up to the third year after birth and, ordinarily, intercourse is not supposed to take place while the child is on the breast. This practice will, of course, act as a check and limit the potential rate.

It seems from the foregoing that, although there are a number of checks, conditions, on the whole, are not unfavourable to a moderately high birth-rate.[2]

Lord Hailey made the following comment on this investigation:

Information bearing on the 'social and moral well-being of the population' was sought by the circulation of a questionnaire to medical officers . . . . None of these questions, however, can be answered without ample objective data; opinions, particularly on such matters as the effects of unfamiliar sexual customs, are of little value unless supported by facts, and doubly doubtful if they are offered in explanation of phenomena whose existence is itself merely assumed. A detailed study of questions of this type, extending over a comparatively small area, would certainly have had more scientific value than impressions recorded in reply to general questions of the nature of those indicated.[3]

The surveys made by Medical Officers and District Commissioners, questioning altogether 833 women past child-bearing age in the Protectorate, showed that they had borne 4·9 children on an average. Excluding still-born the average was 4·5, varying between 3·1 in the Kono District and 6·3 in the Bombali District. The number of women returned as barren was only 19, but as in five Districts, with 493 women questioned, not a single woman was returned as barren, the data concerning barrenness were evidently defective. The figures, on the whole, suggest a low fertility. But the surveys by Medical Officers in the Colony covering 300 women— mostly non-natives, i.e. descendants of Liberated Africans—revealed a still lower fertility. The average number of live-born was here only 4·0. Not more than three women were returned as barren. The census report makes the following comment:

It should be noted that the information sought was details of marriages in which the whole period of child-bearing had elapsed. The conditions will, therefore, relate to the past rather than the present generation. There is no reason, however, to believe that conditions have changed very materially, if at all, within recent years so far as the Protectorate is concerned.[4]

[1] Ibid. *1931*, pp. 11–12. See also *Papers relating to the Health of Native Populations* (1931), p. 138: 'The percentage of sterility amongst native women would possibly reveal a very serious state of affairs. It is to a very large extent the outcome of this corralling of wives by the big men and forms one of the most serious obstacles to the free growth of the tribe and is a much more serious factor than any damage done by initiatory rites at puberty.'

[2] *Census Report 1931*, p. 13.   [3] Hailey, *African Survey*, pp. 119–20.

[4] *Census Report 1931*, p. 16.

But the number of women questioned was far too small to permit the drawing of any conclusions with regard to fertility either in the past or in recent times.

TABLE 28. *Fertility and Child Mortality, Sierra Leone Surveys, 1931*[1]

Areas	Women ques-tioned	Barren women	Children born			Children deceased		Children born per woman			Infant mortality rate
			Live-born	Still-born	Total	In infancy	Later, but before puberty	Live-born	Still-born	Total	
Prot. Southern Province	460	14	1,790	142	1,932	545	233	3·9	0·3	4·2	304
Prot. Northern Province	373	5	1,923	238	2,161	379	181	5·2	0·6	5·8	197
Protectorate Total	833	19	3,713	380	4,093	924	414	4·5	0·5	4·9	249
Colony	300	3	1,198	50	1,248	307	112	4·0	0·2	4·2	256

[1] See *Census Report 1931*, pp. 16–17.

Venereal Diseases. Dr. Thomas Winterbottom, Physician to the Colony of Sierra Leone in 1792–6, wrote:

The venereal disease is frequently met with among the natives, though there is great reason to believe that in every instance it had been first communicated by Europeans.[1]

Gonorrhœa is the most usual form of the venereal disease which occurs upon this coast, and it appears to be rather more frequent among the Soosoos and Mandingos, than among the Bulloms and Timmanees.[2]

About a hundred years later, in 1901, Acting District Surgeon Dr. Maxwell said:

A large number of cases in continuous attendance are syphilitic, late secondary or tertiary. These cases generally yield to appropriate treatment. Chancres are not often seen—probably are not severe in a circumcised population—and one has no opportunities of observing them in women. So many cases of tertiary syphilis are seen in women where the history points to the disease having commenced in early puberty before sexual connection can have been a cause, that it seems probable that the ceremony of clitoridectomy may be the cause of its spread ; this is supported by the fact that one can in certain districts map out fairly accurately the syphilitic and non-syphilitic towns. Evidently an infected operator or infected knife might spread the disease very widely, and I cannot otherwise account for the existence of tertiary symptoms in women who are still virgins. It is peculiar that congenital syphilis is rarely seen.[3]

Gonorrhœa is prevalent, but only cases with the usual severe sequelæ are seen.[4]

Diseases of the Generative System are common in women, and frequently cause sterility. Exact diagnosis can rarely be made, as they object to examination, but these cases may not unfairly be associated with the prevalence of gonorrhœa and syphilis.[5]

The more recent medical reports throw little light on the prevalence of venereal diseases. They show, as a rule, merely the number of cases

---

[1] Winterbottom, vol. ii, p. 32.   [2] Ibid., p. 34.

[3] The rarity of the congenital form of this disease is also mentioned in several later reports. See, for example, *Medical Report 1910*, p. 27 ; *1913*, pp. 7, 33.

[4] 'Diseases prevalent among the Native Population', *Medical Reports 1900 and 1901*, pp. 12–13. See also *Selections from Colonial Medical Reports 1898 and 1899*, pp. 386, 390.

[5] *Medical Reports 1900 and 1901*, p. 14.

treated. Instructive comments are rare; a few examples may serve as an illustration.

1905. Syphilis and Gonorrhœa have as usual been very prevalent and play an important part in the causation of ill-health.[1]

1910. Syphilis. This disease is met with throughout the country, but from the comparatively small number of cases that come up for treatment I am not in a position to say that it is prevalent to any alarming extent.[2]

1912. Syphilis. In 1912, 513 cases were treated as against 286 during the previous year. It may be confidently stated that the disease is much more prevalent than these returns would appear to show, and it may be added that its study is of considerable interest, since it is now more appreciated that the course of certain other tropical affections, such as leprosy and skin diseases, is considerably modified by the co-existence of a syphilitic contamination.[3]

1913. Koinadugu District. Venereal Disease. This is rapidly on the increase, probably owing to the opening up of the district by the railway and by traders.[4]

1917. It is scarcely necessary to say how vitally lowering these diseases are, and probably they account, partly, at any rate, for the low birth rate and high infantile mortality.[5]

1923. Gonorrhœa and syphilis show a steady increase in the numbers treated.[6]

The figures in these diseases are only the cases treated by Government medical officers and one fears they are not all representative of the true numbers.[7]

Whether the disease be gonorrhœa or syphilis, the native through indifference or persistent negligence fails to come for treatment until almost incapacitated; in the meantime he may be spreading the disease far and wide.[8]

1926. These figures [cases treated] are of little assistance in estimating the prevalence of venereal diseases, as the native rarely reports unless complications arise. Gonorrhœa is regarded by him with slightly less concern than is a cold in the head by the European.[9]

In the last years before the war the numbers of cases treated, particularly for gonorrhœa, increased again,[10] and the report for 1938 said:

Venereal disease is stated to be gradually gaining a foothold in [mining] camps and is a difficult problem in view of the itinerant nature of camp women, it is however engaging serious attention. The sudden recruiting of labour at camps far apart precludes examination before engagement. It is further deplorable to note, to quote the Medical Officer, Maroc, that these dangerous conditions are now being spread about the neighbouring villages which formerly were practically free from such pollution.[11]

Birth-rates. The early official birth-rates are not worth while quoting because birth registration was very defective and because the rates were computed by relating the number of registered births to the population ascertained at the preceding census without taking account of the population changes in intercensal periods. But the Medical Report for 1932

---

[1] *Medical Report 1905*, p. 11.   [2] Principal Medical Officer, ibid. *1910*, p. 10.

[3] Ibid. *1912*, p. 8.   [4] Ibid. *1913*, p. 34. See also ibid. *1914*, p. 32.

[5] Ibid. *1917*, p. 24.

[6] The numbers of cases of gonorrhœa treated in 1920–6 were 1,143, 1,087, 969, 1,126, 1,248, 1,523, and 1,701 respectively, and of syphilis 472, 687, 647, 723, 919, 1,005, and 874 respectively.

[7] See also *Handbook of Sierra Leone*, 1925, p. 71: '. . . both in the Colony and in the Protectorate the ravages of venereal disease compel the closest attention of the Medical Authorities.'

[8] *Medical Report 1923*, p. 8. See also ibid. *1924*, p. 9; *1925*, p. 6.

[9] Ibid. *1926*, p. 7. See also, for example, ibid. *1929*, p. 7; *1932*, p. 13.

[10] 1934–8: 2,234, 2,526, 2,756, 3,174, and 3,708 gonorrhœa, 476, 566, 769, 566, and 1,469 syphilis; see ibid. *1938*, p. 12.

[11] Ibid., p. 66.

TABLE 29. *Registered Births and Deaths, Sierra Leone, 1919–43*[1]

Year	Live-born			Still-born	Total deaths			Deaths under one year		
	Male	Female	Total		Male	Female	Total	Male	Female	Total
					FREETOWN					
1919	..	..	729	..	..	..	879	..	..	225
1920	..	..	716	50	..	..	1,035	..	..	..
1921	395	325	720	66	528	398	926	..	..	..
1922	..	..	744	97	..	..	1,161	..	..	311
1923	465	388	853	62	753	579	1,332	..	..	373
1924	492	492	982	61	643	500	1,143	..	..	316
1925	..	..	1,102	61	..	..	1,124	..	..	321
1926	552	522	1,074	59	720	511	1,231	162	156	318
1927	515	495	1,010	71	724	566	1,290	202	153	355
1928	530	506	1,036	78	772	617	1,389	198	179	377
1929	588	505	1,093	..	865	585	1,450	202	147	349
1930	552	550	1,102	75	741	617	1,358	195	176	371
1931	629	634	1,263	52	772	608	1,380	202	163	365
1932	635	641	1,276	77	708	692	1,400	179	169	348
1933	691	687	1,378	87	686	543	1,229	168	149	317
1934	690	649	1,339	136	774	587	1,361	176	136	312
1935	707	651	1,358	..	740	635	1,375	163	145	308
1936	766	671	1,437	..	728	569	1,297	177	126	303
1937	686	658	1,344	..	807	652	1,459	182	145	327
1938	726	737	1,463	..	765	613	1,378	137	145	282
1939	731	705	1,436	..	751	645	1,396	..	..	273
1940	691	719	1,410	..	853	687	1,540	..	..	..
1941	743	762	1,505	..	1,271	862	2,133	..	..	312
1942	809	810	1,619	..	1,330	871	2,201	..	..	314
1943	905	976	1,881	..	1,175	741	1,916	..	..	314
				COLONY EXCLUDING FREETOWN						
1919	..	..	698	..	..	..	796	..	..	..
1920	..	..	785	..	..	..	1,023	..	..	..
1921	439	403	842	..	553	515	1,068	..	..	..
1922	..	..	830	..	..	..	869	..	..	..
1923	366	403	769	..	487	397	887	..	..	198
1924	425	400	825	..	441	346	789	..	..	163
1925	..	..	888	..	..	..	831	..	..	167
1926	449	416	865	..	458	341	799	115	87	202
1927	445	482	927	..	493	372	865	116	85	201
1928	498	452	950	..	550	490	1,040	130	121	251
1929	484	445	929	..	599	408	1,007	153	94	247
1930	406	384	790	..	437	402	839	98	99	197
1931	433	405	838	6	540	385	925	100	91	191
1932	563	600	1,163	15	544	460	1,004	112	107	219
1933	495	453	948	..	532	444	976	126	97	223
1934	480	454	934	..	578	445	1,023	124	94	218
1935	569	462	1,031	..	584	465	1,049	141	103	244
1936	580	520	1,100	..	669	524	1,193	152	129	281
1937	516	546	1,062	..	613	496	1,109	132	134	266
1938	547	526	1,073	..	638	567	1,205	144	126	270
1939	575	532	1,107	..	716	522	1,238	..	..	..
1940	570	583	1,153	..	761	618	1,376	..	..	..
1941	544	528	1,072	..	949	673	1,622	..	..	..
1942	502	479	981	..	940	641	1,581	..	..	..
1943	572	557	1,129	..	686	535	1,221	..	..	..

[1] See *Blue Book 1919* R, p. 2, *1939* O, p. 2, *1940* O, p. 2, *1941* O, p. 2; *Colonial Reports, Sierra Leone 1919*, p. 6, *1920*, p. 22; *Medical Report 1921*, p. 27, *1923*, pp. 24–5, *1924*, p. 26, *1925*, p. 23, *1926*, p. 8, *1927*, p. 9, *1928*, p. 8, *1929*, p. 8, *1930*, p. 13, *1931*, pp. 12–13, 77–8, *1932*, pp. 17, **19,**

TABLE 29. *Registered Births and Deaths, Sierra Leone, 1919–43* (cont.)

Year	Live-born			Still-born	Total deaths			Deaths under one year		
	Male	Female	Total		Male	Female	Total	Male	Female	Total
					TOTAL COLONY					
1919	..	..	1,427	..	..	..	1,675	..	..	..
1920	..	..	1,501	..	..	..	2,058	..	..	..
1921	834	728	1,562	..	1,081	913	1,994	..	..	..
1922	..	..	1,574	..	..	..	2,030	..	..	..
1923	..	..	1,632	..	..	..	2,219	..	..	571
1924	917	892	1,807	..	1,084	846	1,932	..	..	479
1925	..	..	1,990	..	..	..	1,955	261	227	488
1926	1,001	938	1,939	..	1,178	852	2,030	277	243	520
1927	960	977	1,937	..	1,217	938	2,155	318	238	556
1928	1,028	958	1,986	..	1,322	1,107	2,429	328	300	628
1929	1,072	950	2,022	..	1,464	993	2,457	355	241	596
1930	958	934	1,892	..	1,178	1,019	2,197	293	275	568
1931	1,062	1,039	2,101	58	1,312	993	2,305	302	254	556
1932	1,198	1,241	2,439	92	1,252	1,152	2,404	291	276	567
1933	1,186	1,140	2,326	..	1,218	987	2,205	294	246	540
1934	1,170	1,103	2,273	..	1,353	1,031	2,384	300	230	530
1935	1,276	1,113	2,389	..	1,324	1,100	2,424	304	248	552
1936	1,346	1,191	2,537	..	1,397	1,093	2,490	329	255	584
1937	1,202	1,204	2,406	..	1,420	1,148	2,568	314	279	593
1938	1,273	1,263	2,536	..	1,403	1,180	2,583	281	271	552
1939	1,306	1,237	2,543	..	1,467	1,167	2,634	..	..	..
1940	1,261	1,302	2,563	..	1,614	1,305	2,916	..	..	..
1941	1,287	1,290	2,577	..	2,220	1,535	3,755	..	..	..
1942	1,311	1,289	2,600	..	2,270	1,512	3,782	..	..	..
1943	1,477	1,533	3,010	..	1,861	1,276	3,137	..	..	..
					PROTECTORATE					
1919	..	..	29	..	..	..	3	..	..	..
1920	..	..	17	..	..	..	1	..	..	..
1921	..	..	28	..	..	..	32	..	..	..
1922	..	..	44	..	..	..	14	..	..	..
1923	29	21	50	..	6	2	8	..	..	..
1924	21	21	42	..	8	2	10	..	..	..
1925	..	..	212	..	..	..	216	..	..	..
1926	46	63	109	..	62	66	128	2	4	6
1927	..	..	67	..	..	..	69	3	4	7
1928	44	39	83	..	25	17	42	2	1	3
1929	..	..	117	..	..	..	98	..	..	..
1930	..	..	55	..	..	..	17	..	..	..
1931	276	281	557	..	219	233	452	38	31	69
1932	135	109	244	..	112	73	185	14	4	18
1933	198	160	358	..	182	127	309	26	24	50
1934	173	160	333	..	186	134	320	27	16	43
1935	223	254	477	..	202	224	426	35	46	81
1936	1,182	1,271	2,453	..	415	318	733	82	64	146
1937	935	908	1,843	..	318	247	565	43	37	80
1938	1,390	1,355	2,745	..	560	560	1,120	103	104	207
1939	..	..	2,963	..	..	..	1,287	..	..	..
1940	..	..	2,700	..	..	..	1,460	..	..	..
1941	1,190	1,150	2,017	..	752	559	1,170	..	..	..
1942	986	965	1,951	..	907	755	1,662	..	..	..
1943	984	1,058	2,042	..	889	721	1,610	..	..	..

1933, pp. 15, 19, 1934, pp. 15–16, 1935, p. 15, 1936, pp. 14–15, 1937, p. 15, 1938, p. 14, 1939, p. 6, 1940, p. 10, 1941, pp. 3–4, 1942, p. 5, 1943, p. 5; *Report of Registrar General 1923*, pp. 3, 5, 1924, p. 5, 1926, pp. 3–4, 6, 10, 1928, pp. 3–6, 11; *Census Report 1931*, p. 24.

TABLE 30. Birth- and Death-rates, Colony of Sierra Leone, 1919–41[1]

Year	Freetown				Colony excluding Freetown				Total Colony			
	Mid-year population	Birth-rate	Death-rate	Infant mortality rate	Mid-year population	Birth-rate	Death-rate	Infant mortality rate	Mid-year population	Birth-rate	Death-rate	Infant mortality rate
1919	(42,079)	17·3	20·9	309	(41,021)	17·0	19·4	..	(83,100)	17·2	20·2	..
1920	(43,129)	16·6	24·0	349	(41,021)	19·1	24·9	..	(84,150)	17·8	24·5	..
1921	(44,189)	16·3	21·0	333	41,021	20·5	26·0	261	85,210	18·3	23·4	..
1922	(45,259)	16·4	25·7	418	41,021	20·2	21·2	217	86,280	18·2	23·5	..
1923	(46,359)	18·4	28·7	437	41,021	18·7	21·6	257	87,380	18·6	25·3	350
1924	(47,469)	20·7	24·1	321	41,021	20·1	19·2	198	88,490	20·4	21·8	265
1925	(48,589)	22·7	23·1	291	41,021	21·6	20·3	188	89,610	22·2	21·8	245
1926	(49,719)	21·6	24·8	296	41,021	21·1	19·5	234	90,740	21·3	22·3	268
1927	(50,859)	19·9	25·4	351	41,021	22·6	21·1	217	91,880	21·1	23·4	287
1928	51,878	19·9	26·8	364	41,064	23·1	25·3	264	92,942	21·3	26·1	316
1929	53,080	20·6	27·5	319	41,064	22·6	24·5	266	94,144	21·4	26·0	295
1930	54,311	20·3	25·0	336	41,064	19·2	20·4	249	95,375	19·8	23·0	300
1931	55,569	22·7	24·8	289	41,064	20·4	22·5	228	96,633	21·7	23·9	265
1932	56,857	22·4	24·6	272	41,064	28·3	24·4	188	97,921	24·9	24·5	233
1933	58,175	23·6	21·1	230	41,064	23·0	23·7	235	99,239	23·4	22·2	232
1934	59,523	22·4	22·8	233	41,064	22·7	24·9	233	100,587	22·5	23·7	233
1935	60,903	22·3	22·5	227	41,064	25·0	25·5	236	101,967	23·4	23·7	231
1936	62,314	23·0	20·8	210	41,064	26·7	29·0	255	103,378	24·5	24·0	230
1937	63,758	21·0	22·8	243	41,064	25·8	27·0	250	104,822	22·9	24·5	246
1938	63,572	23·0	21·5	192	41,093	26·1	29·3	251	104,665	24·2	24·6	217
1939	64,329	22·3	21·7	190	41,096	26·9	30·1	256	105,425	24·1	25·0	..
1940	65,447	21·5	23·5	180	..	28·0	33·2	232	..	..	..	..
1941	80,000	18·8	26·7	207	..	25·5	38·6	220	..	..	..	..

[1] See Blue Book 1920, p. 168, 1939 O, p. 2, 1940 O, p. 2, 1941 O, p. 2; Medical Report 1921, p. 27, 1922, p. 29, 1923, p. 24, 1924, p. 26, 1925, p. 23, 1926, p. 8, 1927, p. 8, 1932, p. 20, 1937, p. 16, 1938, p. 15, 1939, pp. 5–6, 1940, p. 10; Census Report 1931, p. 25. The figures in parentheses and the birth- and death-rates were computed by the author.

revised the official birth-rates for Freetown, by relating the number of
births registered in 1928 and subsequent years to the town's estimated
mid-year population which was computed by assuming that in the intercensal period 1921–31 the population had increased in geometrical proportion, and the official birth-rates until 1938 were calculated on the
assumption that the population had increased since 1931 at the same rate
as in 1921–31. If this method is applied to the years 1919–27, it appears
that the birth-rate averaged in 1919–23 17·0, in 1924–30 20·8, and in
1931–7 22·5. From 1938 on the position becomes somewhat obscure. If
it had been assumed that the population had continued to increase at the
same rate as in 1921–31, the population figures for mid-year 1938–41 should
have read 65,236, 66,747, 68,294, and 69,877, and the birth-rates would
have been 22·4, 21·5, 20·6, and 21·5 respectively. But the Medical Reports
for 1938–40 reckoned with a population of 63,572, 64,329, and 65,447
respectively, and the Blue Book for 1941 assumed a population of 80,000.[1]
The official birth-rates for 1938–41, therefore, were 23·0, 22·3, 21·5, and
18·8 respectively.[2] The average official birth-rates for 1938–41 are 21·4,
while the computation, assuming a geometrical population increase, shows
an average of 21·5. In each case the average rate is lower than in 1931–7.

Thus it would seem that if omissions in registration have been as few
as stated by the Administration the actual average birth-rate in 1931–41
would have been 23 or 24. The official reports, for many years, have
given as an explanation of this extraordinarily low birth-rate the large
excess of males over females caused by the influx of young labourers
without wives coming to Freetown from the Protectorate.[3] But since,
according to the 1931 census, the females aged 16–45 years constituted not
less than 24 per cent. of the total population, it cannot possibly be said
that the sex and age composition in the town tended to reduce the birth-
rate. It seems therefore that either fertility was extremely low in Freetown
or that birth registration was more defective than the authorities estimate
it to be. I am inclined to accept the second alternative. But even so,[4]
fertility in Freetown would appear to be low.

In the rest of the Colony the population changed so little between 1911
and 1931 that this factor caused no difficulties in computing the birth-
rate. The official rate averaged here 19·1 in 1919–23, 22·2 in 1924–34,
and 26·3 in 1935–41. In recent years it has been much higher than in
Freetown although the sex and age composition was less favourable than
in the capital[5] and although, according to the Chief Registrar, even in
recent years the birth figures 'obtained from registrations in the Colony
outside of Freetown are much too incomplete for the compilation of even

[1] The Medical Report for 1940 had already stated (p. 10) that the population 'including immigration figures is more probably not far short of 80,000'.
[2] No birth-rates have been published in more recent years either for Freetown or for the rest
of the Colony.
[3] See, for example, *Medical Report 1927*, p. 8; *1929*, p. 8; *1931*, p. 12.
[4] Assuming that omissions were not 5 but 20 per cent., the actual average birth-rate in Freetown
would have been 27 or 28 in 1931–41.
[5] According to the 1931 census the females aged 16–45 years constituted 22 per cent. of the
total population.

very approximate rates'. It may well be, therefore, that fertility outside Freetown is not low. But it is impossible to reach any definite conclusion. No attempt has ever been made to estimate the proportion of omissions in registration outside Freetown. Moreover, the birth-rates have been computed on the assumption that the population has remained the same since 1931, and it would be rash to rule out the possibility that the population has increased in the 1930s.[1] If this were the case the official birth-rates for the last decade would be unduly high.

Nothing whatever is known about fertility in the Protectorate.[2]

Still-births. The 1931 census report, as shown above, stated: 'Still-birth is considered, by most Medical officers, to be uncommon.' The surveys made at the same time, mainly by Medical Officers, did not confirm this view. The 1,133 women questioned stated that 430 or 8 per cent. of their children were still-born. The percentage varied in the Districts of the Protectorate between 5 and 22; in the Colony (Freetown and Kissy) it was only 4. The author of the census report, who probably did not expect so high proportions of still-births in the Protectorate, said:

... with regard to still-births, it is probable that a considerable number of these are really live-births which survive only a very short time and are given as still-births by the mothers.[3]

But this explanation does not seem plausible.

Although registration of still-births became compulsory in Freetown in 1914 the available statistics are scanty. The proportion of still-births was 6·8 per cent. in 1920–8 and 6·3 per cent. in 1930–4, but the data were considered to be incomplete. When, in 1930, 75 still-births had been registered the Medical Report stated:

Native women are very loath to disclose the fact of not having carried a baby to full term; so this figure is probably much below the number of still-births which took place.[4]

The Chief Registrar was anxious to get a more complete record of still-births, and in 1934 the proportion of registered still-births rose in fact to 9·2 per cent. of all births.

During the year 136 still-births were registered. This is a large increase over 1933 when only 87 were detected. This increase in figures is due to the greater vigilance of the sanitary inspectors who have been instructed to obtain particulars of all births occurring in their districts.[5]

But he thought it 'still probable that a good many still-births are not disclosed'.[6]

It is to be regretted that none of the more recent reports contains any data concerning still-births in Freetown.

[1] It certainly has increased since the outbreak of the war.
[2] I venture this statement in spite of the fact that the Acting Commissioner of the Northern Province wrote on 6 May 1930 to the Colonial Secretary: '... one cannot walk through Protectorate villages without being struck with the number of children one sees in proportion to the size of the village and I am confident that the birth-rate is high' (*Papers relating to the Health of Native Populations*, pp. 132–3).   [3] *Census Report 1931*, p. 18.
[4] *Medical Report 1930*, p. 13. Similar statements are to be found in the 'Report of the Chief Registrar', ibid. *1931*, p. 76; *1932*, p. 17; *1933*, p. 15.
[5] Ibid. *1934*, p. 15.   [6] Ibid., p. 13.

Compulsory registration of still-births was introduced on 1 July 1930 in four other towns of the Colony. There 6 still-births were registered in 1931[1] and 15 in 1932. No data are available for other years.

No still-births have ever been registered in the Protectorate.

2. *Mortality*

General Mortality. A hundred years ago Dr. Robert Clarke, Senior Assistant Surgeon to the Colony of Sierra Leone, wrote:

As an example of the diversity of opinion which exists, I may here introduce the following replies given to queries addressed to two medical gentlemen long resident in the Colony. I quote from Dr. Madden's Report, which contains much valuable information respecting the western coast of Africa.[2]

Query. Do you conceive the health of the settlement has improved, or the contrary has happened of late years ?

Dr. F. I think it has improved.

Dr. A. I do not conceive it has improved of late years, particularly since 1837.

Query. Are the natives subject to many, or few diseases ?

Dr. F. Comparatively few.

Dr. A. Yes, to many.

Query. Are diseases of the lungs common ?

Dr. F. Not common.

Dr. A. Very common.[3]

The position in the Protectorate is apparently about the same to-day as it was in the Colony a century ago, the only difference being perhaps that the better informed doctors to-day realize our complete ignorance of the state of health.

Speaking broadly, there are as yet no figures of disease incidence available for the Protectorate of Sierra Leone. The reasons for this state of affairs are chiefly the large area involved and the necessary allotment of the available medical staff to the larger district headquarters. It is true that figures are obtainable from certain hospitals such as that at Daru, and to a lesser extent from the dispensaries, and that there have been periodical examinations for special diseases, e.g. ancylostomiasis at some of the Protectorate schools. Again special surveys for the purpose of research have been made of individual diseases in limited areas, e.g. schistosomiasis in the Konno District, goitre in part of Konno and Koinadugu districts, trypanosomiasis in a part of the Ribbi River country and so on.

Such instances apart, there is little known as regards the country, so that it is impossible to say, as things now are, in which areas particular diseases are present and what is the comparative incidence of the several diseases either regionally in the country or numerically among the population.[4]

Other documents indicate that their authors are not aware of the lack of adequate information.

. . . the increase in population has been followed step by step by an increase in physical well-being. The general level of physique is considerably above the

---

[1] 'The remarkably low figure is consequent upon the fact that native women are intensely unwilling to record such a thing' ('Report of the Chief Registrar', ibid. *1931*, p. 77).

[2] See *Report on West Coast of Africa*, Part II, pp. 352, 354, 357–9.

[3] Clarke, *Sierra Leone*, p. 15.

[4] Statement by Dr. B. Blacklock, *Correspondence relating to A General Survey of Disease* (Sessional Paper No. 4 of 1927), p. 3.

standard of thirty years ago. The people are better fed, better housed, better dressed than they used to be, and in consequence they are stronger, happier, and a trifle more industrious.[1]

Children are exposed to a number of risks and the mortality amongst them appears to be fairly high. As in infant mortality, bronchial troubles are responsible for many deaths. So also are malaria, incorrect feeding and malnutrition due, no doubt, to ignorance and superstition.

Children also suffer from many minor and serious complaints, the chief being helminthiasis and intestinal parasites, ankylostome infection, diarrhœa, dysentery from drinking polluted water and schistosomiasis, all of which cause lowered vitality and predisposition to death.

Adult mortality is not abnormally high in the Protectorate, but is relatively so for a people living the 'simple life' and free from such positive checks to population as war, famine and pestilence. There are a number of conditions to notice which might be considered to contribute to the rate. General primitive conditions, customs, habits and conditions of living, insanitary conditions, pollution of water and over-crowding in houses are conducive to many illnesses. Lack of care as regards exposure to disease, superstition, ignorance and failure to seek medical aid at the commence-ment of a disease may be responsible for many cases of death.

Malaria, venereal disease, ankylostomiasis, rheumatism, yaws, and, in some districts, schistosomiasis, improper food, and especially neglect during childhood are the chief factors contributing to lowered vitality and an increased adult mortality. As to fatal diseases themselves, a Medical officer in the Protectorate states that 'there are no specially fatal diseases in this area. The native would appear to possess a high immunity from endemic disease when he has reached the adult stage. Pulmonary tuberculosis, though not very common, is very fatal.'

In the view of the Medical officers, the principal fatal diseases are tuberculosis (chiefly pulmonary), acute pulmonary diseases, dysentery and many cases of leprosy reported by District Commissioners but not mentioned by Medical officers. They may be cases of tertiary syphilis or other diseases mistaken for leprosy, such as leucodermia.[2]

With regard to general health, this varies in different districts but it would appear that the general health of the natives is not good, though they must be possessed of a fairly high natural vitality in order to withstand the conditions under which they live and are reared, and the risks to which they are exposed. There are, however, too many minor and endemic diseases and too many persons infected with one or other of them. Those already mentioned have the greatest incidence and effect on the general health. To recapitulate, customs and habits, conditions of living and insanitary conditions of villages (other than in the 'Sanitary Districts'), polluted water, and overcrowding in houses have their evil effects on the general health and are conducive to many illnesses, and the importance of their bearing, at least on infant and child mortality, cannot be too greatly stressed.

Pulmonary complaints, malaria and intestinal parasitic complaints (chiefly ankylostomiasis or hook worm) are very prevalent and take their toll chiefly of the younger life. The latter two are almost universal and, though not often fatal in adults, tend to cause chronic anæmia, producing debility and a lowering of resistance to other diseases.[3]

Mortality records in the Protectorate have been throughout much less adequate than they were in the Colony a hundred years ago.

For the Colony, on the other hand, our knowledge of morbidity and mortality has been enlarged in the course of time. I shall deal here first with conditions in Freetown.

[1] The Commissioner, Central Province, to the Colonial Secretary, 25 Apr. 1930, *Papers relating to the Health of Native Populations*, p. 135.
[2] *Census Report 1931*, pp. 13–14.   [3] Ibid., p. 15.

Since death registration, no doubt, was incomplete until the end of the nineteenth century it is impossible to tell how high mortality actually was, but it seems to have been excessive. Complaints about unsanitary conditions and the ignorance of the African 'doctors' were numerous.

1881. Unfortunately . . . the [house] owners are not always in possession of the means to effect the timely repairs which property in the tropics constantly requires, more especially in a Colony where the average rainfall is 160 inches and the dilapidation into which they have fallen is painfully visible as one walks the streets and contrasts strongly here and there with the newly painted dwelling of some more fortunate individual.[1]

1887. The large number of deaths among the natives in Freetown during 1887 is surprising . . . being 591[2] . . . . This great mortality being due to the baneful effects of so-called 'country medicine' and the persistent practice of the majority of the people in seeking the advice of ignorant 'country doctors' and of other unqualified persons who trifle with the use of drugs.[3]

1892. The excess (203) of registered deaths over births is principally in Freetown.[4] The Colonial Surgeon is unable to account for this excess beyond stating that it may be due to quackery and country medicine . . . .

The insanitary domestic arrangements of Freetown no doubt contribute to the death-rate, and the registration system, so far as births are concerned, is, on account of local circumstances, defective. In the earlier years of Sierra Leone the colonists underwent great privations, which, according to medical reports, would be sufficient to cause disease even in the present day. It is said that the native, after adopting European habits and clothing, becomes more liable to disease and early death than while he remained in his original state.[5]

1897. Taking the population of Freetown proper at 30,033, we arrive at a death rate of 29 per thousand. This must be regarded as a very heavy death rate . . . . There must then be factors existent in our midst to account for this high mortality, and I think there can be no question that the principal of these are the insanitary conditions under which we live . . . . There is no doubt in my mind that were it not that the general climatic conditions allow of a life which is largely open air, and that many dwellings are so constructed and many so ricketty as to allow of very free ventilation, we should have even a higher death rate than at present.[6]

1898. Taking . . . the population at 30,033 as determined at last census, this mortality [866 deaths] gives us a death rate of 28·83 per 1,000, as against 29 in 1897.

This must be regarded as showing no improvement . . . . I must confess that no other result could be anticipated, for . . . the sanitary condition of the Town remains the same, and until we are able to point to some progress in sanitation, it is not only useless to expect any improvement in the death rate, but we need not be surprised if at times it exceeds the very high figure at which it at present stands. It ought also to be pointed out that there is a fallacy in the death rate to which I omitted to draw attention last year, and that is that as all small pox cases are removed to the Small Pox Hospital, the deaths which took place there are registered at Kissy. The majority of these deaths are, however, to be entered against the City, which would make the death rate considerably higher than it appears.[7]

[1] *Census Report 1881*, p. 5.
[2] Mortality would not have been high if deaths had not actually numbered more than 591. (The non-European population of the town was 21,737 in 1881 and 29,834 in 1891.)
[3] *Report on the Medical Department for 1887*, p. 6. See also *Selections from Colonial Medical Reports for 1898 and 1899*, p. 386.
[4] In Freetown 573 births and 779 deaths had been registered.
[5] *Colonial Reports, Sierra Leone 1892*, pp. 16–17.
[6] Dr. Prout, *Sanitary Reports on Freetown 1897 and 1898*, p. 4.
[7] Ibid., pp. 30–1. The 'number of patients removed to the Small Pox Hospital, Kissy' was 47 in 1897 and 85 in 1898; see ibid., pp. 18, 37.

For 1899–1901 the Principal Medical Officer, assuming again a population of 30,033, computed death-rates of 30·7, 29·8, and 31·9 respectively.[1] In his report for 1902 he revised the population figures on the basis of the 1901 census returns and gave as death-rates for 1896–1902: 27·2, 26·7, 26·2, 27·6, 26·4, 28·9, and 24·9 respectively. He revised at the same time his opinion on mortality.

The average death-rate for the past seven years is thus 26·8, by no means an high death-rate for a tropical city . . . .[2]

Since about the beginning of this century death registration in Freetown has been fairly complete, and as the population in 1911 (34,090) was about the same as in 1901 (34,463) there are no difficulties in computing the death-rate.[3] The number of deaths registered in these 11 years oscillated between 740 and 1,071 and averaged 876. This would suggest an average death-rate of 26. In 1912–17 the number of deaths registered oscillated between 751 and 1,058 and averaged 915. The population increased during this period, and the average death-rate may have been about the same as in 1901–11. For the rest of the Colony death registration was too incomplete to permit the computation of informative death-rates. Comments on morbidity and mortality in Freetown or in the whole Colony were as follows:

1900. The number of natives availing themselves of the Dispensary steadily increases, though the opportunities of continuous observation of disease are not as complete as one would wish, especially in medical cases, as frequently the patients, feeling no immediate benefit, resort to their own native medicines and charms.[4]

1905. Apart from the deaths under the age of five years, the principal causes of death are debility, respiratory diseases, and diseases of the alimentary system. Deaths from debility and respiratory diseases predominate in the earlier part of the year, and this is due to the prevalence of very strong Harmattan winds, which have a great effect on the incidences of respiratory diseases.[5]

The pernicious system of cesspits still exists unchecked in our midst, and I have no doubt whatever that it accounts for a considerable proportion of the sickness and mortality among the inhabitants of Freetown. On a still night the fœtid smell emanating from the cesspits and the sewage-soaked soil is appalling, and as most of the homes are uncemented on the ground floor, the sleeping inhabitants get the full benefit of it.[6]

1912. It is a fact which impresses the mind of the medical observer in West Africa that the persistent negligence of the native to treat himself in time accounts for the existence of a considerable amount of disease of a general nature, as well as illnesses

[1] In 1899 '157 cases were removed to the Small-pox Hospital, Kissy. Of these 34 died.' In 1900 and 1901 the cases were only 8 and 9 respectively. See *Selections from Colonial Medical Reports for 1898 and 1899*, p. 383; *Medical Reports 1900 and 1901*, pp. 4, 6, 41, 44.

[2] *Medical Report 1902*, p. 6. As death registration, at least for the earlier years, was defective, the average death rate was actually higher.

[3] The official death-rates in this period are in part far too low because the Administration assumed that the population had increased very much. See, for example, ibid. *1909*, p. 44: 'The estimated population of Freetown on the 31st December, 1909, was 39,531, and there were 760 deaths . . . during the year, giving a death rate of 19 per thousand . . . .'

[4] Dr. Maxwell, 'Diseases prevalent among the Native Population', *Medical Reports 1900 and 1901*, p. 12.

[5] *Colonial Reports, Sierra Leone 1905*, p. 44.

[6] Principal Medical Officer, *Medical Report 1905*, p. 7. See also ibid., p. 15; *1906*, p. 6; *1907*, p. 9; *1908*, p. 13.

due to local or climatic causes. This is true of the Colony and Protectorate of Sierra Leone, in spite of the fact that here the people of Freetown have continued so long under European influence. To this want of promptness may be added an obstinate and continued disregard of the simple, obvious rules of health, and an inveterate hankering after the futile methods of 'native treatment.'[1]

1916. Any medical man who has used his microscope conscientiously is in a position to confirm this statement, that it is the exception to find a person in Sierra Leone free from some pathogenic parasite, whether it be of skin, tissues, blood or intestines.[2]

. . . it is practically impossible to find a really healthy person in Sierra Leone.[3]

The history of sanitation in Freetown for the last eighteen or twenty years practically resolves itself into a series of reports on the insanitary condition of the City, and recommendations for its improvement. In the year 1898 Dr. Prout, Medical Officer of Health, submitted to the Municipality a report on 'the Sanitary Department and the health of the City for the year 1897.' This report contained a number of excellent recommendations for improving the sanitary conditions, *few of which have however been carried into effect.*[4] Sir Ronald Ross in his book 'The prevention of malaria,' commenting on the disappointments experienced about the year 1900 that so little was being done in British possessions to combat malaria, makes the following statement:—'Even in Sierra Leone where the way had been pointed out exactly, and where the disease was the principal enemy of the colony *little had been done.*' In 1902, in spite of the work done, the object lessons given, and the assistance rendered by men sent out from England, the work was stopped for financial reasons,[5] and it was reported 'that the local authorities did not appear very anxious to continue.' The Medical Reports for Sierra Leone since that time have contained suggestions and recommendations, but in spite of these and other reports (including Professor Simpson's), *sanitation in Freetown does not seem to make very rapid progress.* The chief reason has of course been lack of funds, and with the present unsettled state of affairs in Europe, it cannot be said that the sanitary outlook of Sierra Leone will be particularly bright for some time to come. A vast amount of good can be, and has been done by rigid sanitary inspection, the execution of minor sanitary works, the introduction and subsequent increase of a pipe-borne water supply, etc.; but, without the expenditure of large sums of money on drainage (surface and subsoil), the universal adoption of the pan latrine system, or the introduction of a water carriage system, the closure of all wells so that the pipe-borne supply becomes the only water available, etc., conditions must remain unsatisfactory.[6]

In 1918 the number of deaths in Freetown was more than twice as high as in any prior year (except 1905). In the rest of the Colony the number of registered deaths increased much less but this may have been due to defective registration.

---

[1] Ibid. *1912*, p. 6.   [2] Ibid. *1916*, p. 8.

[3] Ibid., p. 9.

[4] Dr. Prout had expected a different course of events. 'I trust that within a few years it will no longer be possible to call this City by a term which I saw used in a medical journal recently, a designation perhaps severe, but not wholly unmerited, "the filthy Capital of the West Coast of Africa"' (*Sanitary Report on Freetown 1897*, p. 15).

[5] See in this connexion also Dr. Prout's comment: 'It has been repeatedly claimed by Major Ross, that Freetown could be made healthy at a comparatively slight outlay. . . . It seems to me that statements as to the feasibility of carrying out sanitary improvements at slight expense are calculated to do a great deal of harm, and are opposed to all experience; and the sooner it is realised that progress in sanitation cannot be effected without the expenditure of considerable sums of money, the more rapid will be the progress made. Chambers of Commerce meet and pass classic resolutions, but very rarely do they make practical suggestions as to the means of raising money for this purpose, and still more rarely do they suggest taxing themselves' (*Medical Report 1902*, p. 17).   [6] Ibid. *1916*, p. 64. See also ibid., pp. 70, 75–6; *1917*, p. 57.

During the year under review the Colony and Protectorate were visited by a severe epidemic of influenza. It is estimated that two-thirds of the population contracted the disease, and that during the month of September, 3 per cent. of the native population died from this cause.[1]

In no locality was it possible to obtain complete reports of cases, and therefore a true prevalence rate cannot be computed. An attempt was made in Freetown to ascertain to what extent certain groups of individuals were affected, but the data obtained was most unreliable and scanty. There is reason to believe that at least 70 per cent. of the population was affected in Freetown. In the Protectorate it would seem as if the proportion was at least as high as in Freetown. Every chiefdom was affected.

Case Mortality. This can hardly be determined with any approach to accuracy as the number of cases and the number of deaths are both conjectural figures. From data available it has been calculated that the case mortality all over was about 4 per cent.[2]

In 1919–25 the average death-rate of Freetown was 23·9 and in 1926–32 25·6. The corresponding rates for the rest of the Colony were 21·8 and 22·5. The increase outside Freetown may not have been genuine; registration here was incomplete and probably improved in the course of time. In Freetown the authorities considered the number of deaths which escaped registration to be negligible, and, when the number of registered deaths rose from 1,124 in 1925 to 1,450 in 1929, the Medical Department attributed this increase to immigration.

1929. There have been no epidemics of any kind in recent years, and the increase in the number of deaths during the last few years may be due to an actual increase in the population by immigration from the Protectorate.[3]

But it seems impossible that population increase alone could have caused the rise in the number of deaths by 29 per cent. within four years— excluding infant deaths the number increased by as much as 37 per cent. —and when the death-rate continued to be high the Medical Department stated:

The high crude death-rate is coincident with the excess of male over female deaths recorded. There is abundant evidence that many of the immigrants meet with adverse circumstances and are compelled to adopt an extremely low standard of living.[4]

But this argument is by no means convincing. The ratio of males to 100 females was 118 in 1931, as compared with 129 in 1921,[5] and the ratio of male to 100 female deaths in 1928–32 was 124. Yet, whatever may have been the causes of the apparent increase in the death-rate from 1919–25 to 1926–32, the authorities considered it to be genuine. They continued to complain about the insanitary conditions in the capital and in addition repeatedly emphasiz d the pernicious effects of overcrowding.

1922. An investigation was made during the year into the question of housing and overcrowding in Freetown. The inquiry showed more strongly than ever the

[1] Colonial Reports, Sierra Leone 1918, p. 14. See also ibid.: '. . . an epidemic of influenza which visited the Colony in the latter part of the year, and to which 1,072 deaths are attributed.'
[2] Medical Report 1918, p. 55. See also ibid., pp. 21–2, 33.
[3] Ibid. 1929, p. 8. See also ibid. 1927, p. 8; 1928, p. 8.
[4] Ibid. 1931, p. 12.　　　　[5] See Census Report 1921, p. 6; 1931, p. 22.

FERTILITY, MORTALITY, AND POPULATION GROWTH 245

urgent need for new building regulations in Freetown as well as the necessity for legal powers to deal with unhealthy houses and unhealthy areas.[1]

1923. Tuberculosis.—This for the last four years shows a steady and somewhat alarming increase; the increase is more evident amongst the Creole population, which is not surprising in Freetown, when one realizes the overcrowding of houses, want of air space and ventilation, and the apparent overcrowding in the houses themselves.[2]

1926. There is general overcrowding in Freetown. Most houses are improperly ventilated. In fact it is difficult to understand how the people are able to live throughout the night in rooms without ventilation of any sort and often with the addition of an open kerosene flame in the room.[3]

1930. The housing conditions in the poorer districts of Freetown are very bad. The majority of the houses are small, packed close together, inadequately ventilated and roofed with thatch. In many, the main structure is dilapidated beyond repair and incapable of supporting a corrugated iron roof. Owing to the poverty prevailing in recent years it has not been possible to enforce the provisions of the Freetown Improvement Ordinance of 1926.[4]

1931. There is considerable congestion in the native quarters in Freetown and five persons to a room is common in 'strangers' lodging houses'.[5]

Complaints about overcrowding have not been less intense in recent years.

1936. A survey on overcrowding in one section in Freetown has been completed. A report has been forwarded depicting an undesirable conglomeration of slum houses with all its evil sequelæ.[6]

1938. The overcrowded slum quarters of Freetown are a matter of considerable concern and Government has appointed a committee to consider the steps to be taken to ameliorate this unsatisfactory position.[7]

[1] Medical Report 1922, p. 27; see also ibid. 1923, pp. 22–3. Conditions had apparently deteriorated. See ibid. 1916, p. 79: 'Investigations made during the year under review, although failing to expose any very flagrant case of overcrowding, certainly pointed to the fact that with an appreciable increase of the population overcrowding was certain to occur.' See furthermore ibid. 1917, p. 57, and ibid. 1933, p. 43: 'Writing in 1922, the Director of Medical and Sanitary Service observed that Freetown was "an excellent example of an originally well laid out town allowed to sink into its present insanitary, overcrowded, irregular condition through lack of power to regulate building . . . . Originally, its streets and building plots were admirable but through encroachments, sub-letting, sub-dividing, and other causes, streets and plots shrank, resulting in the most striking insanitary feature of the city. . . ."'
[2] Ibid. 1923, p. 8. See also ibid., p. 21.
[3] Ibid. 1926, p. 56. See also ibid., p. 22; 1927, p. 20; 1929, p. 19.
[4] Ibid. 1930, p. 28. The deterioration of housing conditions may be illustrated also by the following figures:

| Year | Inhabited houses | | | | Population | |
	Stone	Frame	Wattle	Total	Total	Per house
1911	305	5,964	423	6,692	33,702	5·0
1921	506	5,503	503	6,512	43,960	6·8
1931	499	5,714	371	6,584	55,358	8·4

See Census Report 1911, p. 22; 1921, p. 20; 1931, p. 28. 'Frame houses are timber-framed on concrete or stone and mortar dwarf walls and roofed with corrugated iron sheets or palm tile thatch, the floors being either of concrete or native timber boarding, and window openings fitted with glazed casements or boarded hinged shutters according to the means of the occupant. "Wattle and daub" houses are of brittle construction and rapidly become dilapidated unless constantly repaired, which should not be allowed' (Medical Report 1933, p. 44).
[5] Census Report 1931, p. 29.
[6] Medical Report 1936, p. 36. See also ibid. 1933, p. 44.
[7] Ibid. 1938, p. 5.

1939. The Committee found that in the sections surveyed—

(a) there was undoubtedly overcrowding,

(b) many houses at present inhabited are barely fit for habitation, even if a very low standard is taken,

(c) some which are inhabited are totally unfit for habitation, and

(d) that a scheme for slum clearance is necessary.[1]

. . . an increase in the influx of labourers from the Protectorate causing the congestion of the slum areas to become even more acute than before.[2]

1940. The influx of labourers to Freetown and the Colony has resulted in overcrowding both in Freetown and some of the Colony villages.[3]

1941. . . . in Freetown an increase in the number of cases of cerebro-spinal fever is disquieting in view of the serious state of overcrowding existing in the town.[4]

A still further influx of labour has taken place from the Protectorate into Freetown and the Colony and housing conditions are extremely unsatisfactory. It is estimated that the increase in numbers since the outbreak of war is in the vicinity of 35,000 and of this number only a very small fraction has been housed by employers. The remainder are overcrowding the already crowded slum areas of Freetown and in some cases the Colony villages. An obvious solution would appear to be to enlist all the permanent labour employed in the Army, Navy and Air Force and house them as Labour Battalions in specially constructed camps.[5]

1942. The formation of Labour Battalions has not yet had any appreciable effect on the overcrowded conditions under which labourers live in Freetown and Colony villages adjacent to works . . . .

No work was done with regard to slum clearance as there is no means in Freetown of replacing houses demolished.[6]

Freetown continues to be greatly overcrowded. A serious degree of overcrowding also exists in those colony villages which are in proximity to military establishments and works; this increase of population in the Rural Areas has resulted in the erection of large numbers of temporary buildings the sanitary control of which has been extremely difficult. These conditions have fortunately not, so far, led to any outbreak of disease.[7]

1943. Overcrowding in Freetown is as great as ever.[8]

Other complaints referred to water pollution[9] and to insanitary conditions in schools.[10]

Notwithstanding the fact that the official reports do not suggest any cause for a reduction in mortality, the official death-rate for Freetown was in every year from 1933 to 1939 lower than in every year from 1922 to 1932. It averaged only 21·9 as compared with 25·6 in 1926–32 (and 23·9 in 1919–25). In the rest of the Colony, on the other hand, the average official death-rate was 27·1 as compared with 22·5 in 1926–32 (and 21·8 in 1919–25). Whether the increase was genuine it is impossible to tell because it is not known to what extent registration improved. But it is

---

[1] *Report of the Slum Clearance Committee 1939*, p. 2.

[2] *Medical Report 1939*, p. 10.   [3] Ibid. *1940*, p. 11.

[4] *Appendix to Address delivered by Governor Sir H. C. Stevenson, Legislative Council, 4 Nov. 1941*, p. 10.

[5] *Medical Report 1941*, p. 6. See also ibid., p. 7.   [6] Ibid. *1942*, p. 6.

[7] *Appendix to Address, 3 Nov. 1942*, p. 11.   [8] Ibid., 23 Nov. 1943, p. 11.

[9] See *Medical Report 1937*, p. 39: 'The water supply of Freetown gives cause for considerable anxiety and has for some time shown definite signs of pollution.' See also *Preliminary Report on the Freetown Water Supply* (1945), pp. 4–7. See furthermore *Outline of the Ten-Year Plan for the Development of Sierra Leone* (1946), p. 8: 'The improvement of water supplies, both in the Colony and the Protectorate, is a vital need.'

[10] See *Medical Report 1934*, p. 38; *1936*, p. 36; *1938*, pp. vi. 27; *1941*, p. 6; *1942*, p. 5; *1943*, p. 5.

noteworthy that the death-rate outside Freetown was higher than in the capital for every year from 1933 on. In his report for 1933 the Chief Registrar said with regard to Freetown:

The crude death rate was 21·1 per 1,000. This is lower than last year (24·6) but still high and is coincident with excess of males over females in the population . . . and the attraction of sick persons to the two largest institutions affording medical treatment.[1]

But outside Freetown, the official death-rates in 1936–9 were 29·0, 27·0, 29·3, and 30·1 respectively. Since the Chief Registrar held the opinion that 'the figures obtained from the registration districts outside Freetown at the best . . . represent but a proportion of the births and deaths taking place', he must have assumed that the death-rate actually exceeded 30. The situation is quite puzzling. The Chief Registrar thinks that the Free-town death-rate of 21 represented actual conditions; he considers it high and thinks that it would be lower if it were not for the large immigration of labourers from the country who meet in Freetown with adverse circum-stances, and the influx of sick persons to institutions affording medical treatment. At the same time he thinks that in the mostly rural districts outside Freetown the death-rate is very much higher.

It is most difficult to give a satisfactory explanation. The great decline in the Freetown death-rate from 1926–32 to 1933–9 may have been due to an actual decline of mortality and (or) to an overstatement of the population in the latter period. But the official reports do not suggest that the factors affecting mortality have improved and I see no reason to assume that population increase has been overestimated.[2] As regards the rural districts there cannot be any doubt, I think, that mortality was very high. It may well be that the population has been underestimated but registration has been so emphatically denounced as being incomplete that it is difficult to believe that the official death-rates should have been higher than the actual death-rates.

In 1940 and 1941 the death-rates both in Freetown (23·5 and 26·7) and in the rest of the Colony (33·2 and 38·6) were much higher than in the preceding years.[3] The year 1941 was apparently very unfavourable. Owing to the large immigration from the Protectorate due to war condi-tions and the needs of the military there was a serious shortage of food. 'An unusually severe rainy season has not been without its effects on health and pneumonia has been prevalent.'[4] It may be, however, that the

[1] Ibid. *1933*, p. 13.   [2] It was probably underestimated in 1938 and 1939.

[3] The number of deaths over one year increased in Freetown from 1,123 in 1939 to about 1,286 in 1940 and to 1,821 in 1941. The corresponding figures for the rest of the Colony were about 955, 1,108, and 1,386 respectively.

[4] *Appendix to Address delivered by Governor H. C. Stevenson, Legislative Council, 4 Nov. 1941*, p. 10. See also *Parliamentary Debates House of Commons*, 3 Nov. 1943, vol. 393, No. 116, cols. 653–4:

'Major Lyons asked the Secretary of State for the Colonies whether he has had an opportunity of personally inquiring into the responsibility for the deplorable conditions of health, lack of fresh water, bad drainage and housing at Freetown; and whether he can give the House an assurance that he is satisfied that improvement has been effected and will be sustained until these serious short-comings have been completely rectified?

'Colonel Stanley: The present very unsatisfactory conditions at Freetown are primarily due to

official death-rates for 1940 and 1941 (at least outside Freetown) are too
high because the population to which the deaths were related was possibly
understated.

No death-rates have been published for later years.[1] The number of
registered deaths was very high both in Freetown and in the rest of the
Colony in 1942 but dropped in 1943. It is interesting to note that the ratio
of male to female deaths was extraordinarily high in 1941–3, owing, of
course, to the large influx of male labourers.

Medical and Sanitary Staff. Complaints about the inadequacy of the
medical services are very old. The Commissioners of African Inquiry
reported in 1811 as regards the 'Medical Department':

> The extreme importance of this branch of an establishment in a tropical climate,
> is so obvious that it is unnecessary to dwell upon it.
>
> The vote of Parliament very liberally appoints a first and second Surgeon, an
> Apothecary and his Assistant. And were these offices always filled in a suitable
> manner, they might be sufficient to effect their purpose.
>
> But unfortunately such is the disproportion of the salaries to the abilities required
> for the due discharge of the first two offices, that no competent persons can be found
> to accept them.[2]

Ex-Governor Campbell stated on 22 June 1840 at the Anti-Slavery
Convention:

> During the greater part of my administration, there was but one Colonial Surgeon,
> Dr. Aitkin, for a population of 40,000, with an Hospital at Kissey, containing from
> 700 to 900 poor creatures, taken from slave-vessels. An assistant was sent out, who
> on his arrival was, from his habits of intemperance, incapable of performing an
> operation, and soon afterwards died of delirium tremens. It is not possible for one
> man, or even five, properly to discharge the duty in such a climate, and hundreds
> consequently die for want of medical aid and vaccine lymphe, in procuring which I
> had the greatest difficulty.[3]

The situation was apparently still the same in 1868.

> That it is the duty of a paternal Government to look after the health of the poor
> inhabitants of the country is undoubted; but we find that whilst there are two
> colonial surgeons in the capital, the districts are left unsupplied. The poor

the enormous strain suddenly thrown upon the Administration of Sierra Leone by the exigencies
of war and the consequent great increase in its population. I am satisfied that the Administration
is doing its best to improve conditions as quickly as possible, but its efforts are very seriously
hampered by acute shortage of skilled personnel and of essential materials, adequate supplies of
which cannot be expected to be available for a long time to come.

'... I am just as interested as my hon. and gallant Friend in getting this matter right. I would
like to point out, also, that the demands of the Services in Freetown are very large and that it is
important that they should have priority.'

[1] The Blue Book showed birth- and death-rates still for 1941, but the Medical Report for that
year said (p. 3): 'Due to the large and unknown immigration into Freetown to meet labour requirements it is impossible to give a population estimate of any value and consequently no birth or
death rates are given this year.'

[2] 'Report of the Commissioners sent out by His Majesty's Government, to investigate the state
of the Settlements and Forts on the Coast of Africa', *Papers relating to African Forts*, 1816, p. 129.
The Commissioners proposed a rise of the salaries of the two surgeons from £350 to £600, and from
£300 to £400 respectively (see ibid., p. 130).

[3] *Proceedings*, p. 504. An increase in the medical staff had already been urged, for example, by
Governor MacCarthy in his Dispatch of 26 June 1823 to Earl Bathurst (C.O. 267, vol. lviii, No. 322)
and by Dr. Barry in his statements to the Commissioners of Inquiry in 1826 (see *Papers relating
to Sierra Leone 1830*, p. 66).

inhabitants get sick and die without the chance for life being given them . . . . The consequence is that the death rate is still constantly high, and the authorities take no means for effectually diminishing it.[1]

But the ratio of Medical Officers to population did not change. They numbered four in 1895. After the Proclamation of the Protectorate (1896) the medical staff was, of course, reinforced, though by no means in proportion to the extension of the area or the population.

1900. The Medical staff consisted during the year of four Assistant Colonial Surgeons, for service in the Colony proper, five District Surgeons in the Protectorate, and myself. In addition there were two medical men who were District Commissioners and who acted as District Surgeons during the greater part of their time, making a total of twelve.[2]

1905. In concluding what will in all probability be my last Annual Report on this Colony, I would venture to express the opinion that very considerable progress has been made in all directions in connection with the work of the Medical Department.

When I arrived, in 1895, there were three medical officers in the service besides myself; there are now fifteen. Additional dispensaries have been opened, and regular visits are now paid to outlying and hitherto unvisited districts.

The Colonial Hospital has been improved and extended, a maternity ward has been added, new quarters for the staff have been built, a resident European matron has been appointed, and the emoluments and conditions of service of the nursing staff have been much improved.

A Nursing Home for Europeans, with trained European nurses, was started in 1899, and has been of the greatest value to the community.

The greater part of the Lunatic Asylum has been rebuilt, medical officers have been stationed in different parts of the Protectorate, and the natives show, by the increasing numbers which attend, a great and growing appreciation of the benefits of European treatment.[3]

Progress, no doubt, had been conspicuous in the Colony, but in the Protectorate, which comprised about 94 per cent. of the total population, only a tiny proportion of the inhabitants had access to medical facilities.

Karene District. Dr. Arbuckle draws attention to the fact that the District Hospital is in the most sparsely populated part of the District, and consequently that the people do not derive the benefit that they might were it situated in a more thickly populated area. This is unfortunately true, and while it is to be regretted, yet the considerations of a centrally situated Head-quarters and the obligation on the part of the Government to provide medical attendance for government officials are more than a set-off against what is nevertheless a philanthropic suggestion.[4]

Unfortunately, in several districts patrolling for any purpose is not always possible, owing to local medical duties. Medical Officers in the Protectorate are now called upon to carry out the following varied duties as well as their ordinary purely medical work, viz.:—

(a) To patrol their districts and instruct the natives in sanitation.

(b) To patrol for purposes of vaccination.

(c) To assist in the study of entomology.

(d) To study the prevalence, etc., of such diseases as Syphilis, Leprosy, Sleeping Sickness, etc.

(e) To select and inspect sites for quarters and report on water supplies.

(f) To make special study of blood-sucking flies as to their prevalence and localities.

[1] Horton, *West African Countries*, p. 228.
[2] Principal Medical Officer Dr. Prout, *Medical Reports 1900 and 1901*, p. 3.
[3] Dr. Prout, *Medical Report 1905*, p. 18.   [4] Ibid. *1906*, p. 12.

(*g*) To specially report on each of these.

(*h*) To act as Deputy District Commissioners.

Taking into consideration the various duties Medical Officers are now called upon to perform in connection with the practice of their profession in the Protectorate, I think it is high time that they should be completely exempted from taking any part in purely administrative duties. As to Deputy District Commissioners' duties, it now frequently happens that a Medical Officer has to give up most of the time that he could have given, with much more benefit to the country, to some of the other and more congenial subjects with which he is expected to deal.[1]

In 1910 two Sanitary Officers were appointed, and there were in addition eighteen Medical Officers.[2] By 1914 the number of Medical Officers had risen to twenty-six.[3] During the First World War many Officers were seconded for Service with the Cameroons Expeditionary Forces or for other war services outside the Colony.[4] Sanitary activities were confined more or less to the capital and even there were scanty. Hospital facilities were unsatisfactory.

1916. Freetown and Bonthe, the former the chief port in the Colony of Sierra Leone, the latter a port in the island of Sherbro, also included in the Colony, have all along practically formed the Alpha and Omega of sanitary development, and it is not to be wondered at, as, apart from being the most important ports in either Colony or Protectorate, the funds available for sanitary requirements have not been able to extend much beyond them.[5]

Houses and compounds in Freetown are inspected about once in five weeks, which is not frequently enough . . . .[6]

When patients suffering from infectious disease report at the Colonial Hospital, they are isolated in a small hut near, until the diagnosis has been determined. This hut is used for all cases of infectious disease and is totally inadequate. There is only one compartment, and only cases of a similar nature can be isolated at the same time. . . .

The cases are removed to the Infectious Diseases Hospital at Kissy on stretchers which may or may not be fly- and mosquito-proof.[7]

The only Infectious Diseases Hospital of importance is that established at Kissy, a very long journey from Freetown, and it is in such an unsatisfactory state, the buildings being old, dilapidated and quite unsuited for infectious cases, that it is hardly worthy of the name it bears. Other features of the place are its association with the Hospital for Incurables and its burial ground in the bush in the heart of the compound.[8]

In 1921 the medical staff was still much depleted. It consisted of 11 European and 7 African Medical Officers as compared with 22 European and 3 African Medical Officers in 1914.[9]

The Medical Report for 1921 said:

There is provision for sixteen Public Vaccinators for the Colony and Protectorate . . . . As a class, they are unsatisfactory in that they are for the most part semi-illiterate, unreliable and their methods are crude in spite of attempts at careful training.[10]

[1] Principal Medical Officer, *Medical Report 1909*, pp. 10–11.

[2] See ibid. *1910*, p. 3.   [3] See ibid. *1914*, p. 3.

[4] See ibid. *1915*, p. 3; *1916*, p. 4; *1917*, p. 3; *1918*, p. 3; *1919*, p. 3.

[5] Ibid. *1916*, p. 43.   [6] Ibid., p. 45; see also ibid., p. 65.

[7] Ibid., p. 69.   [8] Ibid., pp. 56–7. See also ibid. *1921*, p. 27.

[9] See ibid. *1921*, p. 5. There was in addition, as in 1914, a sanitary staff with one Medical Officer of Health and 2 Sanitary Officers.

[10] Ibid., p. 14.

In the greater part of Sierra Leone sanitary work is necessarily unorganized, without continuity and with little regular plan. Things are often done by one man, undone by the next; some are keen on sanitation, others not, but usually, with the best of wills and energy, sanitation shows signs of amateurism. At present it cannot be helped, one must look to a better future, resulting from a larger sanitary staff and better sanitary legislation.[1]

The financial condition of the Colony is so bad that it is useless recommending anything that will cost money unless it is absolutely necessary.[2]

In 1925 the medical staff was again enlarged,[3] though not to pre-war level. A Lady Medical Officer (Dr. M. G. Blacklock) was appointed and medical inspection of schoolchildren was introduced.[4] This most necessary work proved to be quite successful.[5]

1929. It is satisfactory to note that since school medical inspection was instituted in 1925 there has been a gradual improvement in the health and sanitary environment of the children.[6]

A School Clinic was opened in Freetown on 19 February 1930,[7] and the Medical Report for this year contained for the first time a long, very interesting chapter on the 'School Medical Service'.[8] It appears that 1,621 children were examined in Freetown, 1,050 in the rest of the Colony, and 368 in the Protectorate, and that 1,519 children were treated in the School Clinic. But sixteen months after the opening of the clinic the school medical service came practically to an end.

1931. The financial stringency caused by the world-wide economic depression rendered necessary the abolition of the appointment of the Lady Medical Officer on the 17th June, 1931.[9]

1938. No organised school medical service now exists in Sierra Leone. The School Medical Officer has not been replaced since her retrenchment in 1932,[10] as it is considered that under present conditions the services of any new medical officer are more urgently required in other spheres.[11]

The medical and sanitary staff had in fact been reduced in the meantime also in other respects. The number of Medical and Sanitary Officers had declined from 30 in 1930 to 27 in 1931, 26 in 1932, 23 in 1933–5, and 21 in 1936. It rose to 23 in 1937, and to 24 in 1938. It was in 1938 lower than 25 years earlier, although the population had increased in the meantime, and although the inhabitants of the Protectorate, through the impact of European civilization, had become more exposed to certain diseases.[12] Two quotations may illustrate the effects of the curtailment of staff and funds.

1932. In the absence of adequate funds, directly due to the financial depression through which the whole world is passing, it is impossible to envisage the carrying out of any important sanitary works.[13]

[1] Ibid., p. 15.   [2] Ibid., p. 27.
[3] See ibid. *1925*, p. 1.   [4] See ibid., pp. 2, 22.
[5] See ibid., pp. 58–66; *1926*, pp. 20–2; *1927*, pp. 19, 90–2; *1928*, pp. 19–20, 93–6; *1929*, pp. 90–2.
[6] Ibid. *1929*, p. 18.   [7] See ibid. *1930*, p. 28.   [8] See ibid., pp. 91–103.
[9] Ibid. *1931*, p. 21.   [10] Should read 1931.   [11] Ibid. *1938*, p. 27.
[12] It should be realized, furthermore, that the tasks of the Medical and Sanitary Officers had grown enormously in the meantime, through various circumstances such as, for example, the development of mining.
[13] Ibid. *1932*, p. 44. See also, for example, ibid. *1931*, p. 21; *1934* p. 37.

1938. The normal revenue of Government however is such that no large and comprehensive campaigns against the major endemic diseases is possible without outside financial assistance and such must ultimately be provided.[1]

For some years now routine inspection of schools has been in abeyance on account of lack of staff. It was possible however during the year to make an inspection of the sanitary circumstances of all the Freetown schools. . . . It can be said that with few exceptions the sanitary condition of the schools was extremely poor. The buildings are for the most part in bad repair, poorly lighted and badly planned. Overcrowding is common and sanitary conveniences poor in type, insufficient and badly maintained. There is little prospect of teaching the elements of hygiene to children so long as they have to be educated in such deplorable surroundings. Here again almost intolerable conditions have to be accepted because better cannot be afforded from local resources.[2]

A matter of concern in connection with Protectorate hospitals is the degree to which these institutions are overcrowded. Most of these hospitals, which are all more or less of a standard type, were designed for twelve beds but it is rare to find any of them with less than eighteen patients and some have accommodated as many as twenty-six.[3]

However, the outlook in 1938 was more promising.

The re-creation of the post of Senior Health Officer, a post abolished some years ago as a measure of economy, is an important step towards laying the foundations of a more satisfactory health service in the Protectorate. . . . An important part of his duties will be the closer control and supervision of health conditions of native labourers in mining areas. Hitherto this important aspect of the Health Services in the Protectorate has not received the attention it should have and inspections have been too infrequent. While some companies have shown every disposition to give the housing of their labour the consideration it deserves, others have not shown the same disposition to co-operate.[4]

Freetown and the Colony continue to absorb an unduly high proportion of the total expenditure on Medical and Health Services but the needs of the Protectorate are now receiving greater consideration. Two new dispensaries were opened this year and two more are planned for next year. The reconstruction of the Bonthe Hospital is also to be undertaken next year[5] and new wards will be built at the hospitals at Bo and Pujehun. That at Bo will be of a temporary nature pending a more extensive reconstruction later. Despite these however the inadequacy of the hospital facilities in the Protectorate are only too obvious and a definite programme of expansion and improvement has been drawn up and agreed to.[6]

---

[1] *Medical Report 1938*, p. v.   [2] Ibid., p. vi.   [3] Ibid., p. 32.

[4] Ibid., p. v. See also, for example, ibid. *1934*, p. 38; *1937*, p. 41; *1938*, pp. 64–6. The development of mines in the Protectorate is of comparatively recent date. The Medical Report for 1930 said (p. 28): 'Hitherto, with the exception of the labourers from the Protectorate employed by the Government and commercial firms, the shipping companies have been the chief source of employment of labour. This year, over 1,000 labourers were engaged in operations commenced by the Sierra Leone Development Company in connection with the iron ore deposits at Marampa.' *Colonial Reports, Sierra Leone 1938*, p. 35, stated: 'An average number of 13,534 Africans was employed in mining and prospecting throughout the year and additional numbers were engaged in such accessory services as police work, building and construction, etc.' It is obvious that an important part of the duties of the new Senior Health Officer 'will be the closer control and supervision of health conditions of native labourers in mining areas'. But it is hard to consider at the same time his appointment as 'an important step towards laying the foundations of a more satisfactory health service in the Protectorate' (with a territory about the size of Ireland and with about $1\frac{3}{4}$ million inhabitants).

[5] Bonthe is actually in the Colony, but the hospital there is 'in effect a Protectorate hospital both as regards type and the bulk of the population served by it' (*Medical Report 1938*, p. 32).

[6] Ibid., p. v. See also ibid., p. 32.

The Medical Report for 1939 said more cautiously that the programme 'has been submitted to Government and provisionally approved',[1] and the Governor, on 3 November 1942, said in the Legislative Council:

In the course of my tours in the Protectorate it became obvious to me how much requires to be done as regards medical and health services and education. My predecessor, Sir Douglas Jardine, had realized this, but unfortunately the progress of the five-year plan for the improvement and extension of medical and health services, which was drawn up by his direction, has been seriously hindered by the impossibility of getting building materials or skilled labour. Nevertheless the question has by no means been forgotten and a programme for providing better services will be actively pursued when times are more propitious.[2]

A year later, on 29 November 1943, the Director of Medical Services stated in the Legislative Council:

Priority is now being given to the provision of medical facilities in the Protectorate, where they are much more urgently required than in the Colony.[3]

In the meantime the medical staff had been reduced considerably.

1940. During the year three European Medical Officers were released for military service with West African Troops operating in East Africa, one European Medical Officer retired on pension and one resigned from the service. A retired Senior Medical Officer was re-employed to fill one vacancy, and a local Medical Practitioner has been engaged on contract to fill temporarily another of the vacancies. The Department is, however, three short of establishment which is a considerable proportion in a small Department.[4]

Malnutrition. The Medical Reports for a very long time dealt mainly with food shortages[5] and with outbreaks of beri-beri.[6] But once medical school inspection was introduced the reports began to deal with malnutrition in general.

1925. As judged from inspection there appears to be a considerable amount of mal-nutrition among these children [under 12].[7]
1926. The staple food in Sierra Leone is rice. . . . The native diet here undoubtedly contains too great a proportion of carbohydrates and too little protein.[8]
That the people are living on a diet deficient of Vitamin A. is certain, that their diet is deficient in calcium is probable . . . .[9]
1927. That the diet of the general population of this country, as in other African countries, is deficient in certain substances has been pointed out by many authorities.

---

[1] Ibid. *1939*, p. 15.
[2] *Address delivered by Governor Sir H. Stevenson in Legislative Council, 3 Nov. 1942*, p. 2.
[3] *Legislative Council Debates, No. I of Session 1943–4*, p. 34. It should be noted, however, that the total cost in 10 years of the Medical and Health Services schemes approved for assistance under the Colonial Development and Welfare Acts will be about £3 per head in the Colony and about 7s. in the Protectorate.
[4] *Medical Report 1940*, pp. 1–2. See also ibid. *1941*, pp. 1, 6; *1942*, p. 1; *1943*, p. 1.
[5] See, for example, ibid. *1906*, p. 13; *1909*, p. 39; *1910*, pp. 30, 38; *1917*, p. 36; *1919*, pp. 25–6.
[6] See, for example, ibid. *1901*, p. 48; *1902*, p. 24; *1910*, pp. 10, 20, 31–2; *1911*, p. 9; *1912*, pp. 8, 21; *1913*, pp. 6, 20; *1919*, pp. 13, 22–3, 32; *1921*, p. 10; *1922*, pp. 10, 59–66; *1923*, pp. 9, 52–61, 63–4, 87–8; *1929*, pp. 19, 23, 25; *1931*, pp. 12, 81–118; *1939*, p. 1; *1940*, pp. 2–3.
[7] Ibid. *1925*, p. 61. See also ibid. *1927*, p. 90; *1929*, p. 91; *1930*, p. 92. At an examination of schoolchildren in 1930 it was ascertained that in Freetown 13·4 per cent. showed evidence of avitaminosis, in the rest of the Colony only 1·2 per cent., and in the Protectorate 3·1 per cent. (see ibid. *1930*, p. 99, and *Review of Present Knowledge of Human Nutrition in Sierra Leone*, p. 29).
[8] *Medical Report 1926*, p. 23.   [9] Ibid., p. 57. See also ibid. *1927*, pp. 29–32.

The effort to make up the deficiency by prescribing medicines containing such substances as vitamins seems an expensive and inadequate method of dealing with the problem. The real solution would seem to be widespread education in vegetable culture, in poultry keeping and in sheep and goat farming.[1]

1929. Owing to the sparse population scattered throughout the Protectorate, schools there consist largely of boarders and as a result of this a rather serious situation has arisen.

In some mission schools a vague arrangement has been made by the mission authorities with the local chiefs that the chief should supply food for the children and in return the mission authorities will open and staff a school in the town. At some such schools the children were found to be almost starving and at others the managers had been forced to send the children home as no food could be obtained for them.[2]

1931. The normal native diet is probably suitable and sufficient for non-working persons, but for the labourer working a normal six hours a day it is hardly sufficient.[3]

. . . these very early infantile deaths are due to congenital debility, the result of maternal deficiency diet. . . . The extraordinary prevalence of A.–avitaminosis among pregnant women . . . is sufficient evidence of the dietetic deficiency and maternal depletion that goes on during pregnancy. The liberal use of Oleum Morrhœae and vitamin A concentrated with Marmite is very helpful but cannot make up for the ill-feeding from which these women suffer through ignorance and poverty.[4]

The Medical Reports called attention repeatedly to the increase in the number of patients attending for avitaminosis the various hospitals and dispensaries.[5]

1932	1933	1934	1935	1936	1937	1938
221	327	455	1,311	969	2,186	2,624

The report for 1938 said:

The general impression of the nutrition of the people of this country is that in rural areas of the Protectorate it varies from time to time and from place to place but it may be said that in the undisturbed tribal communities the diet is fairly satisfactory and evidence of malnutrition is comparatively rare. On the other hand, in the Colony proper, i.e. Freetown and the adjacent villages there is some evidence of malnutrition, the result of qualitative defects in the diet, which are caused by a combination of ignorance, poverty and an insufficient supply of essential foods. The main qualitative defects in the Colony diet are an insufficiency of protein especially good class protein such as meat and fish coupled with a deficiency of the vitamin B complex, vitamin A and sulphur.[6]

It is noteworthy that in the undisturbed tribal communities of the Protectorate—though 'ignorance' there is certainly not less prevalent than in Freetown and the adjacent villages which have been under European influence for a century and a half—the diet is fairly satisfactory. There is ample evidence that conditions are not so good in some areas of the Protectorate which are in closer contact with European civilization. It seems, moreover, that the diet was much more satisfactory also in the

---

[1] *Medical Report 1927*, p. 92.   [2] Ibid. *1929*, p. 92.   [3] *Census Report 1931*, p. 14.
[4] *Medical Report 1931*, p. 64. See also ibid. *1934*, p. 68.
[5] See ibid. *1933*, p. 10; *1934*, pp. 5, 10–11; *1935*, pp. 4, 9, 11; *1936*, p. 10; *1937*, pp. 5, 10, 12; *1938*, p. 10.
[6] Ibid. *1938*, p. 5.

Colony before the advent of the Europeans. The Senior Medical Officer, Dr. E. J. Wright, said in 1937 in the summary of his very valuable *Review of Present Knowledge of Human Nutrition in Sierra Leone*:

In the 17th Century the people were of fine physique and lived on a mixed diet and apparently had sufficient animal food although in no great quantity. In the early and middle 18th Century it would seem that they still had a satisfactory diet, but towards the end of this period—1792, the diet appeared to be wanting in animal food.

In the early and middle 19th Century the diet was satisfactory, but towards the close of this period it was deteriorating through lack of husbandry in the Colony.

The present Century shewed that beri-beri was chiefly an institutional disease and was eradicated by attention to the balance and method of preparation of the diet. Goitre was found to be endemic in the Kono and Koinadugu districts of Sierra Leone but could not be definitely attributed to Iodine deficiency. School children were found to be suffering in considerable numbers from malnutrition. . . . The present dietary of the people is . . . ill balanced with an undue proportion of carbohydrate resulting in malnutrition and disease.[1]

The Second World War which removed tens of thousands of people from their native homes in the Protectorate increased considerably the incidence of malnutrition.

1941. The large increase of population and the demands for local produce on the part of His Majesty's Forces in Freetown has caused not only a rise in prices but also a shortage of protective foodstuffs for civilian needs with the result that there is definite evidence of an increase in nutritional defects. This has particularly affected mothers and small children among whom there has been more ill health than usual.[2]

1942. While there has been no notable increase in avitaminosis during the past twelve months, the incidence of the condition still remains considerably higher than it was before the outbreak of war.[3]

Referring to the large number of neo-natal deaths in Freetown, recent medical reports said:

. . . a considerable number of them, and also still births, may be ascribed to malnutrition of the mothers.[4]

Smallpox. Dr. Winterbottom said that 'the Small Pox, from the concurrent testimony of authors', is a disease 'supposed to have originated in Africa'.

However just these speculations may be, it is certain, that at the present day, the small-pox is so far from being endemical on the western coast of Africa, on the windward part of it at least, that it is always imported thither by Europeans. . . . It is about twelve years since its last appearance in the river Sierra Leone, or on the Bullom shore. It was very fatal in the higher branches of the river Sierra Leone, in the year 1773, and about seventeen years ago it appeared in the river Sherbro, where it proved very fatal, especially to old people.[5]

---

[1] *Review*, pp. 43–4. As regards the deterioration of the diet among the Creoles, see *Medical Report 1909*, pp. 50–1.

[2] *Appendix to Address delivered by Governor Sir H. C. Stevenson, Legislative Council, 4 Nov. 1941*, p. 10.   [3] Ibid. *3 Nov. 1942*, p. 11.   [4] *Medical Report 1942*, p. 5; *1943*, p. 5.

[5] Winterbottom, vol. ii, p. 132. Referring to 'the general health of the Colony during the last three years' the *Report of the Directors of the Sierra Leone Company*, submitted 26 Mar. 1801, said (p. 27): 'The small-pox has twice appeared in the Colony, though without its usual degree of malignity. A great part of the Colonists caught the infection, but only three died.' See also Macaulay's Journal, 14 Sept. 1798, Knutsford, pp. 209–10. Regarding a severe epidemic in 1817 see *Missionary Register 1817*, pp. 252, 486, and *Twelfth Report of African Institution 1818*, p. 52.

When Staff Surgeon Dr. Fergusson and Colonial Surgeon Dr. Aitkin, both stationed in Freetown, were asked in 1841 by the Select Committee 'Has the small-pox made much ravages among the natives of the adjoining country of late years?' they answered:

Dr. Fergusson. There have been three epidemic visitations of it in the last 10 years; the ravages on each occasion were great.[1]
Dr. Aitkin. Yes, in 1837 and 1839.[2]

The report on the Blue Books for 1881 and 1882 said:

An outbreak of small-pox occurred in the dry and early portion of 1882, during which period there were some 118 admissions to the small-pox hospital, and the mortality for the whole year (1882), was 22½ per cent. of the admissions.

But for the energy of the Sanitary Department in finding and reporting cases, and their subsequent skilful treatment, there is no doubt a larger percentage would have been recorded.

The Colonial Surgeon, Dr. W. Hume Hart, in his annual report says:—
'Small-pox has made frightful ravages in this Colony, persons attacked with the confluent form rarely recover, and those who have not been properly treated for a milder form bear life-long scars on their faces. These scars I have observed in every village in the Timmanee country, and they represent many deaths among the less favoured victims of this scourge.'

Further on he adds:—
'From the way it is constantly recurring it would seem to be a disease endemic, and subject to frequent exacerbation, rather than an epidemic visitor to this Colony.'[3]

Devastating epidemics occurred apparently in the Koinadugu District in the early years of this century. The Medical Officer of the District said in his report for 1909:

There were 443 vaccinations performed .... This number is only about one-tenth of the number that should be vaccinated yearly, except that the district is, owing to the appalling epidemics of from 4 to 6 years ago, more protected than other districts in the Protectorate. Coming from the Mendi or Timne country one notices what a much greater proportion of Kurankos, Limbas, and Yalunkas are pock-marked. The longer dry-season, accompanied by stronger winds, is probably a cause of greater frequency of Small-pox in this district than in the country near the sea.[4]

The last severe outbreak of smallpox in Freetown took place in 1905,[5] but many more or less serious epidemics have been reported from elsewhere, particularly in 1915–17[6] and 1932–5. Little is known about the incidence of the disease at the earlier outbreaks, but detailed figures of notified cases and deaths have been published for the last one.[7]

Cases					Deaths				
1932	1933	1934	1935	1936	1932	1933	1934	1935	1936
998	2,378	2,333	1,599	391	20	288	313	259	51

[1] *Report from Committee on West Coast of Africa*, Part II, p. 353.
[2] Ibid., p. 358. See also footnote 4 to p. 110 above.
[3] *Colonial Possessions Reports 1881–3*, pp. 175–6.
[4] *Medical Report 1909*, p. 37. See also ibid. *1907*, p. 24.
[5] See ibid. *1905*, pp. 6, 14–15.
[6] See ibid. *1915*, pp. 5, 7, 46; *1916*, pp. 6, 25–6, 29–30, 48–9, 68; *1917*, pp. 5, 31, 34–7, 54–5.
[7] See ibid. *1932*, p. 80; *1933*, p. 37; *1934*, p. 33; *1935*, p. 37; *1936*, p. 39. It should be realized, of course, that not all cases and deaths were notified; see ibid. *1932*, p. 35.

There is no evidence that smallpox in any period has claimed an excessive number of victims in Sierra Leone, and at least since 1905 there was apparently no severe outbreak over a very wide area. It is doubtful, on the other hand, whether the incidence of the disease has decreased in the course of the last generation. The reason for this lack of progress in recent times is probably the failure of extending systematic vaccination outside Freetown. In 1909–13 the number of vaccinations performed (including Freetown) averaged 8,512 or about 6 per 1,000 of the population. But the Medical Reports of that period do not suggest that the numbers of vaccinations were considered to be too low.[1] In 1914 and 1915 the vaccinations, owing to the depletion of the medical staff, numbered only 6,032 and 6,880 respectively. In October 1915 there occurred an epidemic 'of somewhat serious dimensions', but the Acting Principal Medical Officer thought that through a temporary increase in vaccinations started several months after the outbreak the situation could be saved.

Vigorous measures were taken to vaccinate the population, and isolation and disinfection carried out systematically. Unfortunately, the infection has spread, but the disease is in a very mild form, and this feature, added to the extensive vaccination, which is being carried on up to date of writing this report,[2] will ensure comparative freedom for some years.[3]

But the hopes of a comparative freedom for some years were not fulfilled. In 1916 'the disease was prevalent in most parts of the Protectorate', and the medical authorities at last realized that systematic and constant vaccination on a vast scale was needed.

. . . the outbreak was sufficiently serious to enforce compulsory vaccination in some areas, and the figures for vaccination results in the year under report are gratifying to a degree. The effort to vaccinate the entire population is being pushed to the utmost by provision of extra Vaccinators, both for the Colony and Protectorate.

A system of training Protectorate natives to vaccinate among the people of their own tribes has been started, and greater success is anticipated than in sending strangers among them.[4]

.The number of vaccinations rose in fact to 87,705 in 1916 and to 105,988 in 1917.[5] The number of native vaccinators was increased from 1 in 1915 to 8 in 1917, and to 16 in 1919,[6] and 'the scheme suggested by the Governor, for the selection and training of young men from the more important native tribes in the Protectorate to work among their

[1] Vaccination 'was kept up fairly regularly during the year in the Colony and Protectorate' (ibid. 1909, p. 8). Vaccination 'was carried on fairly regularly during the year throughout the Colony and Protectorate' (ibid. 1910, p. 8).
[2] The report was dated 22 May 1916.   [3] Ibid. 1915, p. 7.   [4] Ibid. 1916, p. 6.
[5] It should be noted, however, that 33,685 of the vaccinations of 1916 were performed in Freetown. 'Although these figures appear to be high, there are still a large number of unvaccinated persons to be seen in the town' (ibid., p. 68). Compulsory vaccination, therefore, was apparently not very effective in Freetown though the vast majority of the people were vaccinated. In the remainder of the Colony and in the Protectorate where nearly all cases occurred (in Freetown there were only 69 cases with 12 deaths) the number of vaccinations was 54,020 or less than 4 per cent. of the population. The number of vaccinations in Freetown has apparently not been published separately for 1917.
[6] See ibid. 1917, p. 54; 1919, p. 53.

own people' seemed also to achieve good results. There were at first only six.

> . . . this number was gradually increased until thirteen in all had been trained and returned to their various countries, the salaries of these youths, together with the cost of increased lymph supply and the provision of uniforms, entailing a considerable augmentation of the estimate for the year, but the good work done by them— they are mostly sons of chiefs—has justified their selection and appointment . . . .'[1]

But from 1918 on the number of vaccinations dropped every year until in 1920 it amounted to only 26,672 (including Freetown). Even in 1921 'when Smallpox became epidemic in the City'[2] (Freetown) the total number of vaccinations rose to not more than 35,989 (including 14,708 in Freetown); it dropped to 21,517 in 1923, and averaged 11,729 in 1924–31. The main cause for the breakdown of the vaccination service was the destruction of the organization built up in 1916–19. The Medical Reports said:

> 1921. There is provision for sixteen Public Vaccinators for the Colony and Protectorate: three are usually stationed in Freetown, the remainder at Bonthe and in the Protectorate. As a class, they are unsatisfactory in that they are for the most part semi-illiterate, unreliable, and their methods are crude in spite of attempts at careful training. The attempt was made to train Protectorate natives and station them in the districts from which they came, but the candidates do not possess the standard of education required for carrying out vaccination and supervision of outbreaks of Smallpox. It is hoped that better provision will soon be made for carrying out these important public health functions.[3]
>
> 1922. Reference was made in the last annual report to the failure of the scheme for training Protectorate youths to be public vaccinators. Approval was given during the year to abolish as soon as possible the rank of vaccinator, except in Freetown, and transfer this work to the sanitary inspectors. For this reason provision was made to increase the establishment of sanitary inspectors from twenty-four to thirty in 1923. The staff of vaccinators was reduced from sixteen to eight at the end of the year.[4]
>
> 1923. The staff of vaccinators . . . was abolished at the end of the year, with the exception of one post in Freetown. In future vaccination will be carried out by sanitary inspectors, and it is hoped that this change besides effecting a considerable saving, will lead to increased efficiency.[5]
>
> 1924. Owing to the abolition of specially appointed vaccinators in the Protectorate, the number of vaccinations during the last two years shows an apparent falling off. Vaccination is now being carried out more efficiently and under close supervision by sanitary inspectors and dispensers, and every effort is being made to increase the amount done.[6]

The meaning of the last comment is not clear. The falling off in the number of vaccinations was not 'apparent' but real, and the proportion of unsuccessful and of not inspected vaccinations remained high.

		1922	1923	1924
Vaccinated .	.	26,448	21,517	9,636
Successful .	.	9,795	10,294	4,925
Unsuccessful	.	6,302	4,266	2,052
Not inspected	.	10,351	6,957	2,659

---

[1] *Medical Report 1917*, p. 54.   [2] Ibid. *1921*, p. 17.   [3] Ibid., p. 14.
[4] Ibid. *1922*, p. 21.   [5] Ibid. *1923*, p. 17.   [6] Ibid. *1924*, p. 21.

The new system may have effected a considerable saving, but the number of vaccinations for many years was so low that it is doubtful whether the money spent on vaccinations outside Freetown was not wasted altogether. By 1931 the total number of vaccinations (including Freetown) had dropped to 8,391. In 1932, when after a lapse of ten years a severe outbreak occurred, the number of vaccinations jumped to 266,147. About 11 per cent. of the population of the Protectorate were vaccinated in that year. However, the Assistant Director, Health Service, realized that this was not enough.

> . . . although the epidemic has now passed away, security can be achieved only by the continuance of a vigorous campaign of vaccination, while immunity from mass infection can be expected only when 1,000,000 people have been so vaccinated, and thereafter an annual figure of 50,000 has been maintained to cope adequately with the natural increment of life.[1]

But no such vigorous campaign was initiated, and although the epidemic spread considerably in 1933 and 1934 the number of vaccinations dropped to 57,141 and 53,827, and the Medical Report for 1934 said:

> In the absence of a definite extensive and expensive anti-smallpox campaign which would have cost at least £30,000 over a period of five years, and which in these times of financial depression could not be justified, the activities of the Health Department were concentrated on those centres of infection which occurred among the main routes of traffic and which therefore were calculated seriously to affect or to impede the normal course of trade. It is to be expected that the disease will now soon burn itself out, and that the normal annual vaccinations performed will serve to prevent all but the sporadic cases which will continue to occur in the more remote districts, or in those areas where the people flee from vaccination.[2]

TABLE 31. *Vaccinations against Smallpox, Sierra Leone, 1909–39*[1]

Year	Total	Year	Free-town	Else-where	Year	Free-town	Else where
1909	7,443	1916	33,685	54,020	1928	3,441	10,512
1910	6,536	1917	105,988		1929	2,449	8,460
1911	8,432	1918	63,700		1930	6,336[2]	7,179
1912	10,778	1919	47,702		1931	2,039	6,352
1913	9,371	1920	26,672		1932	82,618[3]	183,529
1914	6,032	1921	14,708	21,281	1933	2,118	55,023
1915	6,880	1922	26,488		1934	5,385	48,442
		1923	21,517		1935	13,498	30,811
		1924	9,636		1936	8,448	21,634
		1925	10,367		1937	21,622	16,330
		1926	5,560	8,109	1938	30,173	19,308
		1927	4,240	9,149	1939	28,898	33,312

[1] See *Medical Report 1909*, p. 8; *1910*, p. 8; *1911*, p. 8; *1916*, pp. 6, 68; *1918*, p. 54; *1920*, p. 16; *1921*, p. 22; *1924*, p. 21; *1925*, p. 19; *1926*, p. 17; *1927*, p. 16; *1928*, p. 16; *1929*, p. 15; *1930*, pp. 21, 93; *1931*, p. 22; *1932*, p. 81; *1933*, p. 37; *1934*, p. 33; *1935*, p. 37; *1936*, p. 39; *1937*, p. 37; *1938*, p. 26; *1939*, p. 3.

[2] This figure may include a number of vaccinations of children in rural schools of the Colony.

[3] The figures given in *Medical Report 1932* (pp. 34, 38, 81) are quite confused and contradictory. The figure of 82,618 evidently comprises a number of vaccinations performed outside Freetown, and the same is probably also true of the figures for the following years.

[1] Ibid. *1932*, p. 38.   [2] Ibid. *1934*, p. 33.

Actually the annual vaccinations in 1935–8 averaged only 40,456, of which 18,435 were performed in Freetown. In 1939, when there were some outbreaks in mining areas, the total number of vaccinations rose to 62,210, including 28,898 in Freetown.[1]

Thus very little has been done to render the people outside Freetown immune from smallpox. The Principal Medical Officer, in his report for 1907, had stated with regard to the York District:

There was no outbreak of Small-pox during the year, and there was no vaccination performed.[2]

The policy of the Medical Department has not changed essentially since.

Malaria. Thirty years ago the Principal Medical Officer expressed the opinion that this disease was waning, particularly in Freetown,[3] but these expectations were not fulfilled.

1920. Nearly a quarter of a century after the cause of Malaria was discovered, Freetown is still very malarious, and yet, there can be no doubt that the complete abolition of malaria in the town is perfectly feasible. Against the cost of such an undertaking has to be considered the capitalised cost of labour and material now being expended on temporary measures.[4]

Freetown is very malarious still to-day, and recent medical reports suggest that conditions in the country as a whole are far from improving.

1932. Malaria is undoubtedly the greatest predisposing factor in the mortality and morbidity rates amongst children throughout the whole Colony and Protectorate; and in the adult it plays a prominent part on its own account but chiefly as an influence in lowering resistance to other diseases.[5]

1935. Amongst the general populace malaria shows a marked increase . . . .[6]

1936. The incidence of malaria is about the same [as in 1935] . . . .[7]

1937. Malaria still holds pride of place and there has been an increase of over 2,000 cases.[8]

1938. There has been a considerable increase in the number of cases of malaria . . . .[9]

Among all the problems that the Public Health Service is faced with in these parts malaria easily continues to take first place.[10]

Inadequate funds and inadequate knowledge of local conditions are apparently the main reasons why the fight against malaria has failed so far.

. . . in the light of modern knowledge of malaria control any extensive anti-larval measures are at present economically impossible. . . . Further research into the local malaria problem is essential before any large expenditure could be contemplated.[11]

[1] The total numbers of vaccinations have not been published since 1939, but the Governor stated in November 1944: 'Smallpox has been prevalent since March. It was first notified in the Pujehun District; it appears to have spread to Kailahun, Karene and Kono districts, with sporadic outbreaks in other areas. Additional staff was despatched to the Protectorate and approximately 173,902 vaccinations were performed.' (*Address delivered by Sir Hubert Stevenson in the Legislative Council, 7 Nov. 1944*, p. 19.)

[2] *Medical Report 1907*, p. 25.   [3] See ibid. *1911*, pp. 5–6, 9; *1912*, p. 7.

[4] Ibid. *1920*, p. 19.   [5] Ibid. *1932*, p. 31.   [6] Ibid. *1935*, p. 4.

[7] Ibid. *1936*, p. 5.   [8] Ibid. *1937*, p. 5.   [9] Ibid. *1938*, p. 10.

[10] Ibid., p. v. See also ibid. *1939*, p. 2, and *Appendix to Address delivered by Governor Sir H. C. Stevenson in the Legislative Council, 3 Nov. 1942*, p. 11.

[11] *Medical Report 1939*, p. 2.

Leprosy. Cases of this disease have been noticed and described by many medical officers in the course of the last 150 years, but the number of patients treated has been small throughout and little is known still to-day about the actual incidence. I shall first give some quotations from medical reports published in the course of the last decades.

1907. Kaballa District. Leprosy was . . . found to be fairly common in the district . . . .

I strictly advised Chiefs not to keep a case of leprosy in the towns.[1]

1908. Protectorate. Leprosy seems to be on the increase, and it may be necessary to found Leper Colonies to treat and control these patients.[2]

Moyamba District. Looking back over a period of some ten and a half years I find evidence of this disease having made extensive inroads amongst the aboriginal population. . . . I . . . have advised them [Chiefs] to establish Leper Reservation Colonies. Some such scheme is, I am persuaded, urgently required for as matters are at present the afflicted mate with the healthy, and it is not unusual to see children of quite tender years with early signs of this disease.[3]

1910. From the observations of the Medical Officers, this [leprosy] seems to be most prevalent in the Karene and Kaballa districts,[4] in both of which several cases were met with during patrols. In every instance advice was given as to the necessity for segregation, which the Chiefs promised to follow.[5]

1911. From the observations of Medical Officers, this disease does not seem to be on the increase in Sierra Leone.[6]

1912. It is possible that a serious attempt at the segregation of lepers on a larger scale than is at present attempted would disclose a much wider distribution of the disease than is apparently suspected in Sierra Leone.[7]

1913. Within the Colony the segregation of Lepers is compulsory; but . . . such compulsory segregation is purely nominal, as the majority of them escape after a few days, whilst in the Protectorate segregation is not enforced either by the Government or the Native Administration.

The whole subject is at present under consideration.[8]

1914. . . . I am in favour of compulsory segregation, and I think it might be carried out, partly by means of local settlements in the more infected areas and partly by means of a central settlement near Freetown . . . .[9]

1916. Apart from the authority which the Governor has under the Prisons Ordinance to remove a case of leprosy from a prison to a hospital for incurables or other suitable place, there is no legislation whatever on the subject, and lepers cannot be brought under any kind of restraint, unless they are agreeable to it, which few, except very advanced cases, are; but something should be done for the protection of the general public . . . .[10]

Freetown. Leprosy in all stages is frequently met with. On account of the difficulty of guarding these cases at the leper hospital, isolation of all cases has not been possible.[11]

1917. Leprosy, while not uncommon in this country, is a disease which could be brought under reasonable control by getting the chiefs and people interested in what seems to me to be the simplest means of preventing its transmission to other members of the community, namely by making the chiefs and headmen responsible to report to the District Commissioners the appearance of all cases of the disease in their towns (they can all recognise it) and by compelling them to provide, a short

[1] Medical Officer, Kaballa, *Medical Report 1907*, p. 24. See also ibid. *1908*, p. 36.
[2] Ibid. *1908*, p. 11.   [3] Medical Officer, Moyamba, ibid., p. 31.
[4] For Karene District, see also *Selections from Colonial Medical Reports for 1898 and 1899*, p. 391.
[5] *Medical Report 1910*, p. 10. See also ibid., pp. 34, 36.
[6] Ibid. *1911*, p. 9.   [7] Ibid. *1912*, p. 8.   [8] Ibid. *1913*, p. 6.
[9] Principal Medical Officer, ibid. *1914*, p. 7.
[10] Ibid. *1916*, p. 48.   [11] Ibid., p. 68

distance outside the town, proper accommodation for the patients, and the requisite amount of food and clothing. . . .[1]

But neither this 'simplest' plan nor compulsory segregation through medical authorities was carried out.

1921. The same two cases are still in the Kissy leper ward.[2] Other cases under treatment were two prisoners in Freetown, four noted by the Medical Officer, Moyamba, five by the Senior Medical Officer, Bonthe, with one death and two others elsewhere by Dispensers. The last named officer remarks 'Leprosy is prevalent'.[3]

The Medical Report for 1930, in an historical survey on leprosy in Sierra Leone, says that 'the treatment of leprosy on modern lines was started in 1922 by Dr. Cummings at Kissy'.[4] The reports for 1922 and 1923 relate:

The lepers, two in number, had a change in their usual experience. Active treatment was started in the last quarter of the year on both these patients. . . .[5]

It is hoped that when the natives begin to realize that the new methods of treatment hold out promise of cure they will bring their cases more readily to the various dispensaries, as has already happened in India, and that in time real progress will be made in the eradication of this disease.[6]

But progress at first was very slow.

1924. Twenty-five new cases were reported during the year. Of these only five could be persuaded to submit to any treatment and all these five absconded after only one injection of Moogrol or Gorli seed oil. One nodular case remaining from 1923 continued to do well on Moogrol.[7]

In 1925–8 the numbers of cases reported from all stations were 58, 43, 80, and 129 respectively.[8] In the latter year the Medical Department began to realize that the situation was more serious than had been thought.

1928. During the year Professor Blacklock completed a survey of diseases in the Northern Province of the Protectorate. He reported that 183 cases of leprosy were seen . . . .

Up to the present information as to the prevalence of leprosy in Sierra Leone has been limited, but, in view of Professor Blacklock's report, it must now be considered to be a disease of great importance involving a problem which will have to be dealt with.

As Professor Blacklock says in his report—'although it would be premature to endeavour to assess the total amount of leprosy existing, it is clear that the number of lepers must be very large.'[9]

Recommendation. Provision for leper settlements for the Colony and Protectorate. These are necessary to cope with the increased number of lepers coming forward for treatment.[10]

1929. Owing to the setting up of clinics for this disease, and the propaganda work carried out by Professor Blacklock during his survey of disease in the Protectorate many more cases are presenting themselves for treatment. It is difficult, however,

---

[1] Senior Sanitary Officer, *Medical Report 1917*, p. 54.

[2] The numbers of lepers segregated in the Kissy ward at the end of the years 1912–20 were 3, 2, 1, 2, 2, 4, 3, 3, and 2 respectively (see *Medical Report 1913*, p. 25; *1915*, p. 20; *1916*, p. 25; *1917*, p. 28; *1918*, pp. 38–9; *1919*, p. 16; *1921*, p. 23). The numbers who escaped were nearly equal to the numbers of new admissions, but in 1921 and 1922 none were admitted and none escaped.

[3] Ibid. *1921*, p. 23.   [4] Ibid. *1930*, p. 39.

[5] Ibid. *1922*, p. 19.   [6] Ibid., *1923*, p. 21.

[7] Ibid. *1924*, p. 9.   [8] See ibid. *1925*, p. 6; *1926*, p. 7; *1927*, p. 17; *1928*, p. 7.

[9] Ibid., pp. 16–17.   [10] Ibid., p. 22.

to induce them to stay long enough to derive much benefit from treatment, and a hint as to the formation of a settlement has been sufficient to cause the whole attendance at a clinic to vanish.[1]

A scheme for the establishment of a leper settlement in the Colony and one in each Province of the Protectorate has had to be postponed for financial reasons.[2]

1930. Leprosy cases are presenting themselves for treatment in increasing numbers . . . .[3]

In Sierra Leone, Colony and Protectorate, there exists a larger amount of leprosy than is realized or returned in the Annual Medical Report.[4]

Leprosy under section 43 paragraph 7 of the Public Health Ordinance, is a notifiable disease and under section 53 the Sanitary Authority has power to remove to and detain a case in a suitable place. From the earliest times leprous cases have been received into the Kissy Hospitals and since 1910 males only in a ward set apart in the Male Infirmary. There is however no means available to force them to stay in, and the few cases sent in by the Sanitary Authority go away whenever it pleases them.[5]

Funds do not at present permit of the establishment of farm-colonies for lepers where adequate treatment and supervision could be given.[6]

From 1931 on the number of cases treated decreased again:[7]

	1928	1929	1930	1931	1932	1933	1934	1935	1936	1937	1938
In-patients .	21	26	24	21	19	17	16	23	14	13	21
Out-patients .	108	418	497	272	223	189	196	222	181	113	118

1931. Leprosy shows a marked reduction in new cases reporting for treatment . . . . This is no indication of any reduction in the incidence of the disease. There has been less travelling by Medical Officers, and the disappointing results of the treatment has undoubtedly affected the attendance of many sufferers.[8]

1932. Cases reported in 1932 again show a decrease . . . . Here again the figures do not indicate the prevalence of this disease, and in Sierra Leone chiefs have so far not set up those leper villages which are to be found in any other Colony in West Africa. It is thus somewhat impossible to estimate the extent of leprosy in the Protectorate, but it would be safe to estimate that its percentage would not fall much below that of Northern Nigeria, both countries being inhabited by people who in the far distant past spring from the parent tree, whose climates are similar, and whose habits are in the main the same.[9]

1934. A leprosy survey has been commenced and reliable figures should be available early in 1935. Until those figures are available it would be unwise to make any further statements as to the incidence of the disease, but it is known to be spreading in the Colony and the Protectorate.[10]

1935. The leprosy survey which was commenced in 1935, and which was continued throughout the year, has now been completed. The figures which have been submitted from the various districts show that there are, approximately, 3,600 known cases of leprosy in the Colony and Protectorate. The question of leper settlements is now under consideration, and it is hoped that definite progress will be reported in the next annual report.[11]

---

[1] Ibid. 1929, p. 7. See also ibid., p. 33: 'After one or two visits the majority are never seen again, disappointed perhaps in not having been speedily cured. No lasting good will be done with such patients until proper colonies or treatment centres are started in the respective districts and close to tribal groups.'

[2] Ibid., p. 16.   [3] Ibid. 1930, p. 22.   [4] Ibid., p. 40.
[5] Ibid.   [6] Ibid., p. 22.
[7] See ibid. 1928, p. 55; 1929, p. 59; 1930, p. 72; 1931, p. 49; 1932, p. 58; 1933, p. 61; 1934, p. 53; 1935, p. 58; 1936, p. 61; 1937, p. 61; 1938, p. 44.   [8] Ibid. 1931, p. 11.
[9] Ibid. 1932, p. 13.   [10] Ibid. 1934, p. 11.   [11] Ibid. 1935, p. 10.

1936. During the year Dr. E. Muir, Medical Secretary to the British Empire Leprosy Relief Association, visited the Colony and undertook a tour of inspection. Dr. Muir put forward several suggestions which are being embodied in the Leper Settlements which are now under consideration. Several Paramount Chiefs have expressed their willingness to assist in the erection of these settlements and two are being proceeded with at once.[1]

1937. Two leper settlements have been commenced in the Southern Province. It is proposed to run these settlements on a tribal basis so as to isolate the infectious cases in the various districts. If these settlements are a success it is hoped to considerably extend the tribal settlements in the near future.[2]

The reports for 1938–43 do not indicate that these settlements have ever been put into operation.[3] The leprosy survey of 1935–6 revealed approximately 3,600 known cases. If the percentage of lepers does 'not fall much below that of Northern Nigeria' the actual number of lepers in Sierra Leone would be at least 10,000. It is probably much higher.

The Medical Report for 1928 had stated that leprosy 'must now be considered to be a disease of great importance involving a problem which will have to be dealt with'. It has not as yet been dealt with.

Infant Mortality. The special mortality of infants was apparently not discussed in official documents prior to the last decade of the nineteenth century. The census report for 1891 stated that 'the mortality among infants in this Colony is very great'.[4] But this was probably, at least so far as the territory outside Freetown is concerned, a mere guess. The data from Freetown for 1897–1941[5] are summarized in Tables 29, 30, 32, and 33. The Medical Department, for a long time, apparently did not realize that the rates computed by relating registered infant deaths to registered births grossly overstated infant mortality, since birth registration was much more incomplete than death registration.

1897. . . . by far the larger number [of the 296 deaths under 5 years] take place at the age of 12 months or under, namely 235 . . . . The births in Freetown amounted to 587, which thus give us an infantile mortality of 400·8 to every thousand births during the year. If we remember that in addition to this there were 37 still-births, which are not registered at all,[6] we gain an idea of the enormous mortality which is taking place annually among the children of this Town.[7]

---

[1] *Medical Report 1936*, p. 11. See also Rogers and Muir, *Leprosy* (3rd ed., 1946, p. 30): 'In Sierra Leone 3,656 cases were known in 1936 and Muir estimated the true number at 18,000, 10 per mille.'   [2] *Medical Report 1937*, p. 11.

[3] See also in this connexion *Outline of the Ten-Year Plan for the Development of Sierra Leone* (1946), p. 8: 'The exact incidence of this disease has not been accurately assessed, but sufficient is known to justify the establishment of at least one leper settlement as soon as possible. It is felt that this problem can be best dealt with in co-operation with a Mission.'

[4] *Census Report 1891*, p. 12.

[5] It seems that figures were lacking even in Freetown for every year prior to 1897, except 1895. See Dr. Prout, *Sanitary Report on Freetown 1897*, p. 5: '. . . I find that the infantile mortality for that year (1895) was 375·6 per 1,000 births, and looking at the death rate since 1891, it is probable that this is a constant condition, though I have not been able to go into the figures.'

[6] In 1898 'there were 40 still-births, and as these are not registered, and are only ascertained from the cemetery books, it is extremely probable that this figure does not represent the total number' (ibid. *1898*, p. 32). The numbers of still-births thus ascertained in 1899–1902 were 26, 27, 24, and 46 respectively; see *Medical Report 1902*, p. 8. Registration of still-births was introduced in 1914.

[7] *Sanitary Reports on Freetown 1897 and 1898*, p. 5.

1898. ... 251 [deaths] took place at 12 months or under .... The total number of births registered in Freetown during 1898 was 668, which gives us an infantile mortality of 357·7 to every 1,000 births.

While then the total number of infantile deaths is greater, the increased number of births gives us a slightly diminished infantile mortality. There is, however, no cause for congratulation in this; the infantile mortality is appalling, and calls for serious reflection on the part of those responsible for the health of the Town ....[1]

1899. I have in every annual report since 1895 drawn attention to the enormous infantile mortality which takes place in Freetown, amounting this year to 428·3. I have pointed out that this enormous loss of life takes place principally within the first few hours after birth, and is evidently connected with the process of parturition. Apart from this, there is an enormous amount of maternal disease and sterility, due to the mismanagement of labour and the puerperium. I have also drawn attention to the fact that very few cases are attended by duly qualified medical men, and that the majority are left to the tender mercies of midwives, whose principal qualifications for the post are an appalling ignorance, and very often a capacity for getting intoxicated at the most critical stage of labour.[2]

1901. The infantile mortality is exceptionally high. In Freetown alone it is as high as 578·8 per thousand births. A large number of these deaths occur in connection with labour, and the Government are now erecting a Maternity Ward in the Colonial Hospital, and steps are being taken to establish a Maternity Home with the idea of training and registering midwives. In fact every endeavour will be undertaken by the Government to put a stop to the present heavy loss of life at birth.[3]

1902. I have in a special report on this subject attributed the mortality to the mismanagement and prolongation of labour, which is principally due to the type of midwives who practise in the Colony, who are quite untrained and are unfitted for their work. An additional cause is the habit of inducing abortion which undoubtedly exists to some extent, and to the prevalence of syphilitic disease. The ignorance of the midwives and of the mothers as to the early care and proper feeding of infants is also a factor to be borne in mind.[4]

1903. There was a heavy infantile mortality, which, it is hoped, the establishment of the maternity ward at the Freetown Hospital will greatly obviate.[5]

1906. Freetown. Of the total number of deaths [852] ... no fewer than 242 were infants below the age of 12 months, an appalling figure, which speaks volumes on the question of the proper—or rather improper care and feeding of infants. It is hard to impress on the natives the fact that their foolhardy substitutes for normal infant food—and a mother incapable of suckling her own child seems a rarity here—is slowly but surely driving them to race suicide. Another factor having a certain amount of influence in keeping up this high figure is the lack of properly-trained midwives.[6]

To ensure some relief from this condition one can only hope that in the future the natives themselves will realise its importance and provide a suitable maternity home and children's hospital. It is their only salvation.[7]

Protectorate, Karene District. Dr. Arbuckle gives some startling figures relating to infantile mortality, which, considering the outdoor life the children lead, is terrible. He estimates the death-rate of children at 362 per 1,000.[8]

[1] Ibid., p. 32.

[2] Extracts from Report of the Medical Department for 1899, *Selections from Colonial Medical Reports for 1898 and 1899*, pp. 384–5. In earlier reports Dr. Prout had also drawn attention to the large number of infant deaths from malaria; see *Sanitary Reports on Freetown 1897 and 1898*, pp. 6, 32. As regards malaria among infants outside Freetown, see Dr. Maxwell, 'Diseases prevalent among the native population', *Medical Report 1900*, p. 13.

[3] *Colonial Reports, Sierra Leone 1901*, p. 27. The *Medical Report* for this year calls attention to the fact that the official infant mortality rate may be swelled by defective birth registration.

[4] Dr. Prout, *Medical Report 1902*, pp. 8–9.   [5] *Colonial Reports, Sierra Leone 1903*, p. 21.
[6] See also *Medical Report 1905*, p. 4.   [7] Ibid. *1906*, p. 4.   [8] Ibid., p. 11.

Table 32. *Infant Mortality in Freetown, 1897–1918*[1]

Year	Births	Deaths					Infant mortality rate
		Within 24 hours	1 day to 1 week	1 week to 1 month	1 month to 1 year	Total under 1 year	
1897	587	56	48	27	104	235	400
1898	668	69	49	34	99	251	376
1899	565	58	36	148		242	428
1900	462	45	37	143		225	487
1901	417	48	43	144		235	564
1902	544	49	54	33	118	254	467
1903	553	..	..	..	..	254	459
1904	602	..	..	..	..	240	399
1905	642	55	61	39	141	296	461
1906	557	44	47	35	116	242	434
1907	588	60	28	21	101	210	357
1908	632	58	38	25	101	222	351
1909	549	55	35	22	76	188	342
1910	581	58	39	23	94	214	368
1911	501	43	30	14	69	156	311
1912	587	39	43	23	90	195	332
1913	590	45	33	29	114	221	375
1914	666	55	53	33	93	234	351
1915	721	..	..	..	..	219	304
1916	706	101		34	102	237	336
1917	774	..	..	..	..	300	388
1918	695	..	..	..	..	404	581

[1] See, for 1897–1904, *Sanitary Reports on Freetown 1897 and 1898*, pp. 20, 39, *Medical Report 1902*, pp. 8, 37, *1916*, p. 81, *Colonial Reports, Sierra Leone 1903*, p. 21, *1904*, p. 30, *1913*, p. 25; for 1905–13, *Medical Report 1905*, pp. 4, 34, *1906*, pp. 4, 30, *1907*, pp. 4, 52, *1908*, pp. 5, 57, *1909*, pp. 5, 71, *1910*, pp. 5, 61, *1911*, pp. 5, 62, *1912*, pp. 12, 55, *1913*, pp. 10, 56; for 1914–18, *Colonial Reports 1914*, p. 28, *1915*, p. 25, *1917*, p. 15, *1918*, p. 13, *Medical Report 1914*, p. 68, *1916*, pp. 81, 88. I computed the infant mortality rates from the official basic figures.

1907. Freetown. This high infant death rate is, in my opinion, due chiefly to three potent causes—viz., 1, Malaria, 2, Carelessness in the management of child-birth, 3, Insanitary surroundings, and I may add 4, Ignorance as to feeding, clothing, and cleanliness of infants . . . .[1]

In the absence of data, it is assumed that the last is the most prolific cause of death. It should also be the most easily remedied. In the meantime, this high death-rate is a matter of serious import to the natives of Sierra Leone, as, owing to the fact that the deaths are in excess of the births, the descendants of the original people who first settled in the Colony are gradually dying out. The more intelligent natives realize this, and also that unscientific midwifery plays a prominent part in the high death-rate of children. The Government some years ago opened a special midwifery ward at the Colonial Hospital to remedy this evil, but the effect it has had on the mass of the people has been inappreciable owing to the ignorant conservatism of the people, which has, so far, prevented them from enjoying to the full the benefits of the institution.[2]

1908. Freetown. The infantile death-rate . . . although decreasing, is undoubtedly high, and is due to several causes, malaria being one. Another is ignorance as to the proper feeding, care, and cleanliness of the children in the first few months of their existence . . . .

The maternity ward of the Colonial Hospital has still to overcome the prejudices of the people, who are reluctant to discontinue the employment of native midwives,

[1] Principal Medical Officer, *Medical Report 1907*, p. 5.
[2] *Colonial Reports, Sierra Leone 1907*, p. 32.

whose methods of treatment are often a compound of ignorance and superstition. It is, however, doing much by training native women and girls to be nurses and midwives, and will thus in time inspire more confidence and increase its sphere of usefulness.[1]

1909. Freetown. Native children are not weaned until they are about 18 months old, but the natural food of the child is supplemented at an early age—a few months after birth in the case of the poorer natives—by a gruel made of maize—not a very digestible food at the best of times. This is given to very young children by the mother 'drenching' the child with it.

Some years ago the Government opened a special midwifery ward at the Colonial Hospital and, at first, it was very little used. Now, however, the natives of all classes, even the highest, make use of it, and it is hoped that its good effects will be as far reaching as they are beneficial.[2]

1912. Freetown. It would appear from these figures [infant mortality rates 1903–1912] that there has been a steady decrease of infant mortality in Freetown.[3] This may be due, in some degree, to the improvements in the sanitary condition of this city in the last few years, but until women can be properly trained as midwives, and encouraged to practise among the masses, and until the people of Sierra Leone are educated sufficiently to appreciate the simple, proper methods of feeding and rearing of infants and young children, I fear the Infant Mortality will continue to remain abnormally high.[4]

1915. The Infantile Mortality—that is the proportion which the deaths of infants under 12 months of age bears to 1,000 births—for Freetown is as follows:—

Males	364
Females	385
Both Sexes	374

If these figures are correct[5]—and they must be taken with some degree of reserve— they show an appalling infantile mortality, but the conditions under which the native lives are in many respects appalling.[6]

1916. On account of the doubtful nature of the data available, due to faulty registration, the infantile mortality rate for 1916 (335·6 per 1,000 births) may be taken with a certain amount of reserve, but the figure nevertheless is exceptionally high, and merits some attention.

. . . the excessive mortality of the first three months of life is almost entirely due to premature birth and enfeebled vitality (marasmus, atelectasis, convulsions). Although a large number of deaths in the early days of infancy is due to the immature condition of the child at birth, a number of deaths undoubtedly occur through the carelessness and inefficiency of the local midwives in attendance. The number of deaths from *Trismus Neonatorum* certainly points to absence of aseptic measures at birth. In 1912 a committee of medical men and ladies interested in the subject, formed for the purpose of enquiring into the causes of the high infantile mortality in this colony, made the following statement in their report:—'Whilst the treatment of normal cases by native midwives seems to be satisfactory on the whole, in abnormal cases there is much improvement to be desired.' Under the Medical, Midwives, Dentists and Druggists (Amendment) Ordinance, 1914, legislation has been extended to midwives, and it is hoped that in this way more adequate control and supervision will be exercised over the training and work of the midwives, thereby

---

[1] Ibid. *1908*, pp. 44–5.   [2] Ibid. *1909*, pp. 44–5.

[3] This impression was caused by an arithmetical error. The infant mortality rate in 1912 was not 268, as assumed by the Principal Medical Officer, but 332. It was higher than in 1911 (311).

[4] Principal Medical Officer, *Medical Report 1912*, p. 13.

[5] They were apparently incorrect. According to *Colonial Reports, Sierra Leone 1915*, p. 25, the births numbered 721 and the infant deaths 219. This indicates an infant mortality rate of 304. According to *Medical Report 1916*, p. 81, the infant deaths in 1915 numbered only 210, indicating an infant mortality rate of 291.   [6] Ibid. *1915*, p. 48.

leading to a decrease in the infantile mortality in the colony. . . . It appears there
is a tendency for the natives, especially the creoles, to commence artificial feeding
far too early, and doubtless the presence of convulsions and diarrhœa can to a large
extent be attributed to this.[1]

The statements in the Medical Reports for 1915 and 1916 suggest that
the Medical Department was no longer ready to accept the excessive ratio
of registered infant deaths to registered births as a proof of excessive
infant mortality. But how much the official infant mortality rates which
for two decades created the impression of an excessive infant mortality
differed from reality it is impossible to tell. The average number of
registered infant deaths was 247 in 1897–1906, 198 in 1907–11, and 221 in
1912–16. The average infant mortality rates were 448, 346, and 340
respectively. From 1897 till 1911 the population had hardly changed,
but it increased thereafter. The number of registered infant deaths decreased from 1897–1906 to 1907–11 by 20 per cent., and the infant mortality rate by 23 per cent. In the following quinquennial period (when
population increased) the average number of registered infant deaths
increased by 12 per cent. while the average infant mortality rate decreased
by 2 per cent. These figures seem to indicate that infant mortality decreased considerably from 1897–1906 to 1907–11, but little, if at all,
thereafter. The figures do not suggest a change in the proportion of births
that were not registered. The ratio of registered births to population
averaged about 18. If we assume that one-third of the births were not
registered and that all infant deaths were registered the infant mortality
rate would have been about 300 in 1897–1906 and about 230 in 1907–16.
But both assumptions are, of course, arbitrary.

The Medical and the Colonial Reports for 1917–21 do not discuss infant
mortality in Freetown.[2] When in 1922 the infant mortality rate was 418,
the Medical Report said:

Owing to the non-registration of many births . . . the infantile mortality rate . . .
appears a good deal higher than it really is.[3]

In 1923 the rate was higher still (437) in spite of an improvement in
birth registration. Of the deceased infants 45 per cent. were under 14
days old.

It is natural to suppose that bad methods of midwifery and ignorance and carelessness in the treatment of the newly-born infant have a great deal to do with such
deaths, but there are no doubt various other causes, including perhaps syphilis,
and research is needed.

The fact that the rest of the Colony, which is entirely rural, has a much lower
infant mortality suggests that urban life, especially such conditions as congestion
of buildings and overcrowding, together with the insanitary conditions that are
inevitably associated, have much to do with the high rate prevailing in Freetown.[4]

Research was indeed needed, and as such research was not made, it is
impossible to tell the real reasons for the excessive infant mortality in

[1] *Medical Report 1916*, p. 81.
[2] The infant mortality rates in these years were 388, 581, 309, 349, and 333 respectively, the
high rate for 1918 being due to the influenza epidemic.
[3] Ibid. *1922*, p. 29.   [4] Ibid. *1923*, p. 25.

1923. But it seems safe to say that neither bad methods of midwifery nor carelessness in the treatment of the newly born infants, nor syphilis, nor congestion of buildings and overcrowding can have brought about such an increase in infant mortality in one single year. Mortality of people over one year was likewise excessive in 1923 and there were probably some factors impairing the health of the total population including infants.[1]

From 1924 onwards infant mortality was apparently much lower. The number of infant deaths, which had been 373 in 1923, averaged 347 in 1924–32 and 313 in 1933–7. The infant mortality rate dropped from 437 in 1923 to 315 in 1924–32, and to 229 in 1933–7. Since the population is said to have increased between 1924 and 1937 by about one-third, the decrease in infant mortality was probably greater than the decrease in registered infant deaths. But since birth registration improved considerably, the decrease in infant mortality was much less than the decrease in infant mortality rates.[2] The actual infant mortality rate was probably lower in 1924–32 than in 1917–23 but possibly about as high as in 1912–16 when, according to the above very rough estimate, it was about 230.[3] In 1933–7 it may have been about 200. It is doubtful, however, whether infant mortality actually was much lower in 1933–7 than in 1912–16 or in 1924–32. The Chief Registrar in his report for 1933 said:

The infant mortality rate or proportion of deaths under one year of age per 1,000 live births was high—230, but again shows a decrease compared with 272 in 1932 and 289 in 1931. This decline may be due in some part to the more accurate registration of age, which is checked now by comparison with birth certificates which must be produced, if available, before the deaths of infants and very young children are registered. On the other hand, it may represent a real improvement due to the activities of the health visitors and infant welfare clinics.[4]

It is difficult, in fact, rightly to appraise the effects of infant welfare work upon infant mortality in Freetown. Table 32 indicates that in 1897–1916 mortality was particularly great in the first week of life. No such data are available for 1917–22, but it appears that in 1923, when infant mortality was extraordinarily high, 183 children died under one month and 190 between one month and one year.[5] The Infant Welfare Centre with clinic was opened on 22 February 1924.[6] The District Nurse, every week, 'was given a list of the births registered, every one of which she made it a duty to visit first'.[7] But since birth registration was frequently delayed, she had probably seldom an opportunity of helping infants in

[1] See also ibid., p. 8: 'The general health of both European and African officials was not so satisfactory as in 1922.'

[2] See, for example, ibid. *1925*, p. 24: 'The diminution in the infant mortality rate in Freetown as compared with 1924 is due solely to the increase in the number of registered births ....' (The same situation arose in 1931, but the *Medical Report* then said: 'The rate was high but showed a welcome decrease when compared with former years'; ibid. *1931*, p. 13.)

[3] The 300 women questioned in Freetown and Kissy in 1931 said that they had 1,198 live-born children of whom 307 or 256 per 1,000 had died in infancy (see Table 28 above). Since all these women were past child-bearing age, most of their children had probably been subject to infant mortality during the first quarter of this century.

[4] Ibid. *1933*, p. 15.   [5] Computed from ibid. *1923*, p. 24.
[6] See ibid. *1924*, p. 59.   [7] Ibid., p. 60.

the first month of their lives.[1] Deaths under one month remained high
in 1924 (189) and 1925 (173). Infant deaths over one month were only
127 and 148 respectively.[2] But the number of deaths over one month rose
again and oscillated in 1927–32 between 160 and 191. The figures of
deaths between one month and one year (assuming that death registration
was complete) may have overstated somewhat mortality at that age because until 1933 some deaths of children over one year were returned as
infant deaths,[3] but there is no reason to assume that the errors were
greater in 1927–32 than in earlier years. When infant welfare work had
been in operation for one year, the Deputy Director of Sanitary Service
wrote:

> We have not yet got the confidence of the expectant mothers to any extent nor
> have the bad methods of midwifery, ignorance and carelessness in treatment of the
> newly born been eliminated. In the near future, with two more welfare centres,
> a lady medical officer, and more trained midwives, vastly improved figures are to
> be expected.[4]

But these expectations were not fulfilled. Infant mortality, to be sure,
was lower in 1924–37 than in 1917–23, but there is no evidence that it
was notably lower than in 1912–16, which means that it was very high.
The causes have been discussed in various official reports. A few quotations
may serve an as illustration.

> 1926. I am of opinion that malaria is not responsible for the very high infant
> mortality which exists among children here of under 14 days, and that syphilis is
> not an important factor at this age . . . . I have come to the conclusion that, as the
> children are often born in a weakly state, the cause of this mortality must be a general
> condition and not a specific disease.[5]

> 1929. I doubt very much whether there will ever be a marked further reduction
> in these figures [infant mortality rates] until the people are better fed. All the
> information so far gathered goes to show that underfeeding and badly balanced
> diets are the fundamental causes of the high infant death-rate—more than half of
> which has been traced to deaths during the first month of life and which are un-
> doubtedly mostly due to congenital debility.[6]

> 1937. Infant mortality rate is still alarmingly high . . . the main causes being
> due to inadequate living or malnutrition of expectant mothers, improper feeding
> of young infants, ignorance and superstition.[7]

Infant mortality in Freetown fluctuated very much, and the comments
of the Chief Registrar throw little light on the causes.

> 1936. The figure 210 per 1,000 . . . is the lowest ever recorded in this Colony[8] and
> low when compared with rates for former years when ante-natal and child welfare

---

[1] Conditions in this respect improved somewhat in the course of time. But *Medical Report 1934*
still said (p. 70): 'It is unfortunate that births are so often registered late because, as a result, a
large number of children under two weeks, children amongst whom the mortality is greatest, are
not seen in time to be assisted, as their whereabouts are unknown.'

[2] Computed from ibid. *1925*, p. 23.

[3] The average number of deaths registered as occurring between 6 and 12 months dropped from
74 in 1927–32 to 56 in 1933–8.

[4] Ibid. *1924*, p. 27.

[5] Dr. E. J. Wright, ibid. *1926*, p. 54. See also ibid. *1931*, p. 64.

[6] Dr. M. G. Blacklock, ibid. *1929*, p. 87.

[7] Ibid. *1937*, p. 36. See also ibid. *1936*, pp. 36, 43; *1938*, p. 63.

[8] Should read 'Freetown'. The rate in the Colony was 230.

work did not exist. The utilisation of these now well organised services leads one to expect a gradual reduction through the succeeding years.[1]

It is doubtful, however, whether antenatal work had anything to do with the low record in 1936. The deaths of children under two weeks in 1931–6 numbered 175, 163, 153, 152, 155, and 183 respectively.

TABLE 33. *Deaths in Early Childhood, Freetown, 1927–38*[1]

Year	Under 24 hrs.	1–7 days	1–2 wks.	2–4 wks.	1–3 mths.	3–6 mths.	6–9 mths.	9–12 mths.	Total under 1 yr.	1–2 yrs.	2–3 yrs.	3–4 yrs.	4–5 yrs.
1927	113		56		44	56	86		355	..	..	..	..
1928	186				62	42	87		377	..	..	..	..
1929	189				51	50	59		349	..	..	..	..
1930	124		76		53	53	65		371	..	..	..	..
1931	57	118		30	58	45	57		365	..	..	..	..
1932	52	111		23	38	37	87		348	..	..	..	..
1933	44	75	34	38	34	40	30	22	317	50	26	26	9
1934	60	69	23	22	38	37	33	30	312	83	40	26	14
1935	42	81	32	21	33	39	33	27	308	80	42	35	21
1936	49	93	41	18	25	34	22	21	303	65	39	19	13
1937	34	84	38	20	29	59	36	27	327	92	53	30	15
1938	30	85	40	18	33	24	29	23	282	66	32	17	18

[1] See *Medical Report 1927*, pp. 9, 23; *1928*, p. 8; *1930*, p. 15; *1931*, p. 17; *1932*, p. 23; *1933*, p. 23; *1934*, p. 18; *1935*, p. 17; *1936*, p. 17; *1937*, p. 17; *1938*, p. 16.

1937. The hope that the decline in the infant mortality rate in Freetown which has taken place in the past few years would continue has not been realized and the figure has risen to 243 per 1,000 which is the highest recorded for five years. Of the 327 infant deaths registered 25·6 per cent. died within a week of birth,[2] 47·7 per cent. within two weeks, 53·8 per cent. within a month and 62·9 per cent. within three months. . . . These figures, though no doubt exaggerated due to defective birth registration,[3] can only be described as appalling and indicate the crying need for greatly increased Ante-Natal, Maternity and Infant Welfare Services.[4]

As a matter of fact both the number of deaths under three months (205) and the proportion of deaths under three months (63 per cent.) were lower in 1937 than in every year from 1928 to 1936, and the high infant mortality rate of 1937 was due only to the enormous rise in the number of deaths over three months (122 in 1937 as against 77 in 1936). This increase probably had the same reason as the simultaneous increase in the mortality of older children and of adults. The Senior Medical Officer therefore was probably right in saying·

The increase in the Infant Mortality Rate this year is considered due to the scarcity of rice during the year and exceptionally poor quality of staple food as evidenced by the great prevalence of food deficiency disease throughout the year.[5]

[1] Ibid. *1936*, p. 14.
[2] Should read '10·4 per cent. died on the first day, 36·0 per cent. within a week of birth', &c.
[3] These percentages are not affected at all by defective birth registration. As regards the infant mortality rate the position is as follows. If—as I am inclined to think—only 80 or 90 per cent. of the births were registered, the official infant mortality rate (243) may have overstated infant mortality considerably. But if—as stated by the Administration—95 per cent. of the births were registered, the exaggeration due to defective birth registration was small and might perhaps be disregarded altogether, as probably some infant deaths also escaped registration.
[4] Ibid. *1937*, p. 13.   [5] Ibid., p. 79.

In 1938–40 infant mortality in Freetown was apparently lower than in any former period. The official rate averaged 187. The progress, however, was checked again in 1941 when, owing probably to malnutrition, it rose to 207. It declined to 194 in 1942 and to 167 in 1943.

For the rural districts of the Colony figures concerning infant mortality are available from 1921 on. The official rate varied in 1921–41 between 188 and 261 without showing a definite trend.[1] It averaged 235. In 1921–32 the ratio of infant deaths registered to births registered was much lower in the rest of the Colony than in Freetown. The Medical Department attributed the difference to better housing and sanitary conditions in the rural districts.[2]

1932. As would be expected, the infant mortality rate in the rural areas is considerably below that in Freetown, namely, 188 as compared with 272 per 1,000 live births; hence the prior claim and necessity for child welfare activities in the densely populated area of Freetown.[3]

But when in 1933 the infant mortality rate in the rest of the Colony leapt to 235 (while that of Freetown dropped to 230) the Chief Registrar abandoned comparisons between the rural and the urban areas since 'infant mortality rates for the Colony outside Freetown are not reliable, the registration figures probably not representing even approximately the true position'.[4] There is in fact no evidence that infant mortality in 1921–32 was lower than in Freetown. The fact, on the other hand, that in recent years the official infant mortality rate in the rural districts has been very much higher than in the capital is no proof that infant mortality was actually higher. Birth and death registration has been all the time so defective outside Freetown that it is impossible to draw any final conclusion from the official figures.

In the Protectorate registration of infant deaths is practically non-existent. A survey of infant mortality was made on a very small scale in 1923.

Dr. Easmon, African Medical Officer at Bo, has recently made an investigation into the infant mortality at various places in the Central and Southern Provinces. He found that out of 793 births 254 infants died within twelve months, an infant mortality rate of 320.[5]

The 833 women questioned in 1931 had 3,713 live-born children, of whom 924 or 249 per 1,000 died in infancy. But the census report states that the figures 'refer to deaths during suckling, which covers a period of two years or even more'.[6]

The report summarizes furthermore the answers to the questionnaires circulated in 1931 amongst the Medical Officers:

It does not appear that the number of weak babies born is great, but, nevertheless, the infantile mortality is said to be heavy. It is chiefly due to lack of intelligent post-

[1] According to *Blue Book 1942* O, p. 3, it rose to 298 in 1942.
[2] See *Medical Report 1923*, p. 25, quoted p. 268 above.
[3] Ibid. *1932*, p. 17. See also ibid. *1938*, p. v: 'Infant welfare work has been carried on in Freetown for a number of years but so far little serious attempt has been made to extend it to rural areas in the Colony or to the Protectorate'.
[4] Ibid. *1933*, p. 16. [5] Ibid. *1923*, p. 25. [6] *Census Report 1931*, p. 18.

TABLE 34. Deaths by Age and Sex, Freetown, 1897–1914[1]

Year	Under 1 year Male	Female	1 to 5 years Male	Female	5 to 15 years Male	Female	15 to 25 years Male	Female	25 to 45 years Male	Female	45 to 65 years Male	Female	65 years and over Male	Female	Total
1897	119	116	30	31	28	20	36	38	144	64	67	62	58	52	865
1898	126	125	30	29	15	12	40	33	123	69	72	63	62	67	866
1902	126	128	24	24	21	24	49	39	127	84	71	54	38	56	865
1905	147	149	55	40	20	18	63	30	166	93	103	82	44	59	1,069
1906	124	118	29	33	16	9	49	42	147	74	84	55	30	40	850
1907	118	92	36	25	20	19	56	37	126	74	64	67	32	50	816
1908	118	104	37	42	13	22	40	29	127	88	67	60	32	61	840
1909	105	83	42	30	11	16	20	34	146	77	76	48	26	46	760
1910	119	95	34	48	18	14	47	42	164	69	95	69	55	67	936
1911	92	64	31	26	12	15	36	17	148	62	78	64	44	58	747
1912	102	93	32	39	14	13	27	14	125	77	71	54	41	49	751
1913	119	102	41	31	16	16	29	24	117	78	71	55	33	46	778
1914	132	102	35	32	17	17	56	22	120	80	94	59	37	56	859

[1] See Sanitary Reports on Freetown 1897 and 1898, pp. 20–1, 39–40; Medical Report 1902, pp. 37–8; 1905, pp. 35–6; 1906, pp. 30–1; 1907, pp. 52–3; 1908, pp. 57–8; 1909, pp. 71–2; 1910, pp. 61–2; 1911, pp. 62–3; 1912, pp. 55–6; 1913, pp. 56–7; 1914, pp. 68–9.

TABLE 35. Deaths by Age and Sex, Freetown, 1933–8[1]

Year	Under 24 hours Male	Female	1 day to 1 year Male	Female	1 to 5 years Male	Female	5 to 15 years Male	Female	15 to 25 years Male	Female	25 to 45 years Male	Female	45 to 65 years Male	Female	65 years and over Male	Female	Total
1933	31	13	138	135	62	49	26	20	40	31	205	120	130	68	63	98	1,229
1934	37	23	139	113	90	73	25	29	38	39	216	111	165	101	64	98	1,361
1935	22	20	142	124	78	100	27	26	43	33	197	120	135	106	92	110	1,375
1936	25	24	152	102	70	66	30	38	40	22	187	95	150	104	77	115	1,297
1937	22	12	159	134	89	101	40	31	31	27	187	126	185	101	96	118	1,459
1938	14	16	125	127	67	66	32	41	35	39	211	109	176	94	104	122	1,378

[1] See Medical Report 1933, p. 14; 1934, p. 24; 1935, p. 20; 1936, p. 20; 1937, p. 20; 1938, p. 17.

natal care. Babies are given food of an unsuitable kind too soon after birth and often during the first month. Foo-foo (made from cassava) and corn-pap is usually given and, a little later, rice. Cow's or goat's milk is never used. Digestive troubles follow a starchy diet of this nature and, at times, prove fatal.

This improper food results in a retardation of growth, produces a weak child and impairs its chances in life. Some of the Medical officers are rather divided in their opinions here. One Medical officer states that 'it is difficult to imagine how any feeding such as is described can be good for any baby' but that 'it requires proof that it causes harm.' The adult population has good physique and it may be presumed that they went through this régime.

Improper care also is responsible for a number of infectious complaints, such as malaria, helminthiasis and other abdominal parasitic complaints. Without doubt some of the habits and customs of natives are responsible for part of the infantile mortality, amongst them being the early use of native medicines, the superstitious aversion from modern medical aids (gradually being overcome), ignorance of ordinary hygiene and the fatalistic belief, at times, that sickness is due to a 'swear' or ju-ju.[1] Conditions of living, such as overcrowding in houses and lack of fresh air, also play a part. Such conditions, however, are improving in the Protectorate.

The chief causes of infant mortality are quoted as being malaria, broncho-pneumonia, diarrhœa, convulsions, helminthiasis, intestinal troubles, improper nourishment and exposure.[2]

Adult Mortality. Detailed statistics concerning deaths by age in Freetown were published for 1897, 1898, 1902, and for every year from 1905 to 1914. The great excess of male deaths at age 25 to 45 was attributable in a large measure to an excess of males in the population. No such statistics are available for 1915–32. The data for 1933–8 show an excessive mortality of men aged 45 to 65 years. Although, according to the 1931 census, males of that age exceeded females by only 5 per cent. male deaths exceeded female deaths by 64 per cent.

For the rural districts of the Colony and for the Protectorate death statistics by age are not available.

3. Population Growth

Colony. The African population increased very much in the second, third, and fourth decades of the nineteenth century owing to the importation of captured slaves, although mortality among them, especially in the first months after arrival, was excessive. In the following three decades the population apparently remained about stationary, but this may have been due to emigration. The census of 1871 covered only the Peninsula excluding Quiah, and for this area the census of 1881 showed an increase of 7,482 or nearly 20 per cent. The Colonial Secretary made the following comment:

I am inclined to think that the real increase of souls on the peninsula in the past decade should not be estimated at more than 5,000. On the other hand it must be remembered that large numbers of Sierra Leone people have since migrated to

---

[1] Referring to the welfare work done among the infants of immigrants from the Protectorate to Freetown, the Medical Report for 1932 said (p. 45): 'Indeed it is with this section that the Health Visitors find most difficulty in recording progress. The Senior Health Visitor reports that "the mortality is highest amongst the country people who rely very much on the treatment of their native doctors," chiefly owing to their illiteracy and lack of education.'

[2] *Census Report 1931*, p. 13.

various parts of the West African Coast, some as labourers, a large number as traders. The adjoining northern rivers contain many Sierra Leone traders, and a great number have carried their trading operations into portions of Quiah and the surrounding country, including Sherbro, who are not enumerated in this Census. As a set off against this however we have an increased number of transient traders and strangers, from the neighbouring tribes, amongst us.[1]

The Colonial Secretary, I think, underestimated the omissions at the 1871 census,[2] and the population increase was probably much less than 5,000. On the other hand, the number of transient traders and strangers had not increased; it amounted in 1881 to only 1,300 as compared with 1,847 in 1871.[3] That 'large numbers' should have emigrated from the Peninsula does not seem likely.[4]

Between 1881 and 1891 the population of the Peninsula, including Quiah, increased from 53,862 to 58,448 or by 4,586. But while the population of Freetown increased by 8,102, the population of the other districts decreased by 3,516.

The construction of the fortifications for the defence of Freetown harbour and the building of additional Barracks at Tower Hill during the past five years gave employment to large numbers of the labouring classes. The Sierra Leone Coaling Company also employ a great many labourers.

It may be stated that the strength of the Troops in garrison in 1891 is 30 officers and 664 non-commissioned officers and men as compared with 9 officers and 135 men in 1881.

The decrease . . . in the other Districts proves, that there were grounds for the opinion which has been current for some time that the villages are being deserted. This may be attributed to the low price given for ginger which is the principal article of export cultivated by the villagers, and also to the more remunerative employment obtainable elsewhere.[5]

In the out-stations 16,387 persons were counted as compared with 6,684 in 1881. But this apparent increase was due almost entirely, if not entirely, to incompleteness of the 1881 census in the Sherbro District.[6]

In 1901, 67,782 people were enumerated in the Peninsula as compared with 58,448 in 1891. But Quiah had in the meantime been included in the

[1] Ibid. *1881*, pp. 4–5.   [2] See p. 26 above.
[3] See *Blue Book 1871*, pp. 172–3; *Census Report 1881*, 'Recapitulation'. In the whole Colony there were according to the 1881 census 1,357. Their number, of course, changed considerably from year to year. See *Colonial Possessions Reports 1881–3*, p. 181:
    'In 1881 1,809 strangers, comprising caravans of various sizes, arrived in Sierra Leone from the towns and countries of Sego, Bouré, Futha, Falaba, &c. in the interior.
    'In 1882 the number increased to 2,609. These strangers, who bring amongst other articles gold, ivory, and oxen, are quite distinct, coming as they do from a great distance, from the ordinary trader of the country immediately adjoining this Settlement.'
[4] There had been, on the other hand, some immigration into the Colony. The Report on the Blue Book for 1871 said: 'The population of Sierra Leone, which for ten years past had been diminishing year by year, is now being recruited by families that had gone to the Bullom Shore and the neighbouring districts to avoid the penalties of the Road Tax and the House Tax' (*Colonial Possessions Reports 1873*, Part II, 2nd Division, pp. 11–12).
[5] *Census Report 1891*, p. 4.
[6] The total population enumerated in the Colony outside Freetown was 44,802 as compared with 38,615 in 1881. The Census Officer in charge of the 1921 census, who was not aware of the fact that if allowance is made for the imperfection of the 1881 census in Sherbro the population outside Freetown showed a marked decrease, took great pains to describe the economic causes of the apparent increase (see ibid. *1921*, p. 4).

Protectorate. The population increase in the Peninsula excluding Quiah may, therefore, have amounted to something like 15,000.

At the same time it must be admitted that if it were not for the immigration into the Colony from the Protectorate, the population of the Peninsula would be stationary if not actually diminishing.[1]

In the out-stations only 8,873 persons were counted as compared with 16,387 in 1891. But if one accepts the estimate of the Registrar-General for those portions of the Bonthe District which were not included in the 1901 census (18,263),[2] there was in the out-stations a population increase of 10,749. Nevertheless the Registrar-General stated for the Colony as a whole:

Infant mortality is very great in this Colony, and the registration returns show that the deaths considerably exceed the births; and the inevitable conclusion is that the population of the Colony is kept up only by a constant stream of immigration on the part of male persons coming from the Protectorate in search of work in the Colony.[3]

If the population of the Colony (including the whole of Sherbro) increased in 1891–1901 by about 25,000, while deaths considerably exceeded births, immigration from the Protectorate must have been enormous during this period. But the registration returns were quite incomplete and it may well be that births actually exceeded deaths. The Colonial Report for 1898, after having pointed out that the population enumerated in 1891 was 74,835, said:

Owing to the immigration of natives from the Protectorate and natural increase, the population of the Colony may be estimated at about 100,000, and that of Freetown at about 40,000; but the population of Freetown fluctuates considerably, owing to the influx during the dry season of natives from the Protectorate, who come to seek employment as labourers.[4]

Immigration. There is a great influx into the Colony from the Protectorate annually of natives seeking labour after their crops have been harvested, and until it is time for them to return home to prepare their farms for the ensuing crop. This period extends from about the end of October till March. A portion of these natives remain and take up their abode in the Colony.

Emigration. A considerable number of natives still emigrate annually down the coast seeking labour at the Congo and elsewhere; but the majority of these usually return after an absence of from two to three years.[5]

The population enumerated in the Colony in 1911 was 75,572 as compared with 76,655 in 1901. If account is taken only of those areas which were covered by both censuses there was an increase from 74,351 to 74,808.[6] The Compiler of Census made the following comment:

The last ten years have been years of great trade development, the imports being double and the exports treble in 1910 of what they were in 1900, so that the stagna-

[1] *Census Report 1901*, pp. 3–4.   [2] See ibid. *1901*, p. 5; *1911*, p. 5.   [3] Ibid. *1901*, p. 4.
[4] *Colonial Reports, Sierra Leone 1898*, p. 21. According to the 1901 census the population of Freetown was only 34,463 (as compared with 30,033 in 1891). If one accepts the estimate of the Registrar-General for those portions of the Sherbro District which were not included in the 1901 census the population of the Colony in the area covered by the 1891 census would have been at least 100,000 in 1901. But it is difficult to believe that the population of those portions should actually have increased from 9,036 to 18,263, and I, therefore, think that the total population was less than 100,000 and the population increase less than 25,000.   [5] Ibid., p. 27.
[6] This small increase was due to the increase in the number of Europeans and Asiatics.

tion in the population, especially in that of Freetown, which is the chief port and the terminus of the railway, is all the more remarkable.

In only one district is any considerable increase of population shown and that is in the Mandokia sub-district of the Headquarters District; this is to be attributed to immigration on the part of natives of the Protectorate who come into this district for farming purposes.

The two districts of Kissy and Kissy (Regent) show heavy decreases in population amounting to over 11 per cent. and 17 per cent. respectively. These two districts consist entirely of villages that were founded in the early days of the Colony for the settlement of liberated Africans, and although they have been invaded by aboriginal natives of Protectorate origin, yet they are still chiefly inhabited by Creoles, and there can be no doubt that the depopulation of these villages is to be attributed to the decrease in the Creole population . . . . [1]

After having given other examples of population decreases in Creole villages,[2] the Compiler of Census points out that the total Creole population in 1911 was shown to be 31,282 (including 204 Mulattoes) as compared with 33,402 in 1901, 'a decrease of 2,120 persons amounting to about 6·3 per cent'. But he thought that a number of Creoles had been returned in 1901 as Natives[3] 'and the conclusion to be arrived at is that the real decrease in the Creole population is probably something like 3,000 persons, or a decrease nearer 10 per cent. than 6 per cent.'[4]

It is interesting to enquire how this decrease is to be accounted for, whether it is due to emigration or decreased birth-rate, or how. From the results of the Protectorate Census it will be observed that 2,944 persons have been returned as Creoles, and that 2,446 persons have been returned as having been born in the Colony, and it may be taken for granted that these 2,446 persons were for the most part Creoles. Consequently even if it be assumed that all these 2,446 Creoles were included in the Colony population 10 years ago, it will not account for the whole of the decrease. As a matter of fact, although the establishment of the railway and the development of the Protectorate have undoubtedly induced an increased number of Creoles to settle there during the last 10 years, still it is well known that in 1901 there were many hundreds of Creoles living in the Protectorate as traders, artisans, etc. It is clear, therefore, that the decrease in the Creole population cannot be attributed to any great degree to emigration to the Protectorate.

Judging from the notices in the local papers from time to time advertising for native clerks from other West African Colonies, there is no doubt that there is a certain amount of emigration beyond the limits of the Colony and Protectorate, but it is impossible to say in what numbers Creoles emigrate elsewhere.

The registration returns show that the deaths exceed the births, but the system of registration of births and deaths is imperfect, and there is nothing to show that there is heavier mortality among the Creoles than among the rest of the population.

Assuming that the race is not dying out, but that its reduced numbers are due to emigration elsewhere, one thing is certain, viz., that although the Colony has progressed commercially in the last 10 years, economic circumstances appear to be against the Creoles, and many are compelled to go elsewhere to earn a livelihood, and, as the general population has not declined, it is clear that their places are being filled by others.[5]

The males outnumber the females by 6,430 . . . Seeing that the Census of 1901 showed also a preponderance of males over females (6,767), it may be taken that the dominating factor determining this male preponderance is immigration from the Protectorate.[6]

---

[1] *Census Report 1911*, p. 7.   [2] See ibid.   [3] See p. 163 above.
[4] Ibid. p. 11. A decline of 3,000 to 31,282 would indicate a decrease of 8·8 per cent.
[5] Ibid., pp. 11–12.   [6] Ibid., p. 8.

278SIERRA LEONE

This argument, for various reasons, is not convincing.

(1) Whether there was a natural decrease among the Creoles it is impossible to tell. The Medical Report for 1909, it is true, said:

. . . there has been occurring for several years among the descendants of the liberated Africans and original settlers an increasing death rate, a falling birth rate, a diminution in the number of families among the married people, and an increase in sterility.[1]

The Colonial Report for the same year said that 'owing to the fact that the deaths are considerably in excess of the births, the race is gradually dying out'.[2] But the only known fact was that among the *total* population *registered* deaths were considerably in excess of *registered* births. The Compiler of Census rightly considered the registration returns to be not conclusive and seemed inclined to think that Creole births exceeded Creole deaths. But his argument that 'there is nothing to show that there is heavier mortality among the Creoles than among the rest of the population' is not to the point. Even if mortality was not heavier among the Creoles than among the rest of the population, deaths among the Creoles might have exceeded births either if fertility among the Creoles was lower, or if deaths exceeded births also among the rest of the population. It should be noted, moreover, that the Medical Department was apparently of the opinion that important factors tended to raise the mortality among the Creoles above that of the rest of the population.

Puerperal Fever is one of the principal causes of death among the creole population of the Colony, but it is infrequent among the aborigines.[3]

I have been rather struck within recent years with the increasing number of cases of Cancer of various organs, especially of the breast, that have, in the course of my practice, come under my observation, and this, particularly so, among the descendants of the liberated Africans . . . .

From the fact that this disease is rarely seen or met with among the hundreds of female aborigines who are treated regularly every year in the Colonial Hospital, and that the medical officers of the Protectorate districts, especially those who are stationed in large towns where there are established dispensaries, at which the natives have been encouraged to attend for treatment, have in their official returns not shown the presence of new growths among their patients, we can safely assume that Cancer as a disease is very rare among the aborigines.[4]

As a rule the Creole part of the population seem to be much more careless as regards clean surroundings than the natives, and are not so ready to clean up when their attention is drawn to insanitary conditions, paying much less attention to arguments in favour of sanitation.[5]

(2) Contrary to the opinion of the Compiler of Census a decrease of the Creoles by 3,000 can be attributed in a large measure to emigration to the Protectorate. According to the Protectorate census 2,944 persons were

[1] *Medical Report 1909*, p. 24. The descendants of the original settlers were, of course, numerically negligible. According to the census of 1860 they numbered 91 (including 22 Maroons), and while their number probably was understated in 1860 it seems doubtful whether at the beginning of this century more than half a dozen families were known to be descended from the original settlers.

[2] *Colonial Reports, Sierra Leone 1909*, p. 45.　　[3] *Medical Report 1909*, p. 23.

[4] Dr. W. Renner, 'The Spread of Cancer among the Descendants of the Liberated Africans or Creoles', ibid., pp. 48-9.

[5] Ibid. *1910*, pp. 28-9. See also ibid., p. 31.

returned as Creoles, and 2,446 as persons born in the Colony. The former figure was greater than the latter because it included children of Creoles born in the Protectorate.[1] But both figures exclude, of course, those Creoles who had been in the Protectorate in 1901 and had died in the meantime, and also all those Creoles who had emigrated to the Protectorate since 1901 and had died before 1911.

(3) Assuming that births equalled deaths among the Creoles there would have been a total emigration of about 3,000, of whom the majority went to the Protectorate.[2] It is doubtful whether there is justification for drawing therefrom the conclusions that economic circumstances were against the Creoles, that many were compelled to go elsewhere to earn a livelihood and that their places were clearly being filled by others. The Creoles were nearly all descendants of immigrants, and migration to the Protectorate or elsewhere was not necessarily the result of adverse economic circumstances in the Colony.[3] The reduction in their numbers was not greater among males than among females. Emigration from the Protectorate into the Colony was very slight during this period,[4] and it is doubtful whether there was any increase at all in the number of able-bodied non-Creole African men.[5]

From 1911 to 1921 the population of the Colony rose considerably, but the increase was confined to Freetown with 44,142 people in 1921 as compared with 34,090 in 1911. The Census Officer made the following comment:

While some part of the increase in the population of the Colony may safely be attributed to the growing wealth of the country and the consequent gravitation of the inhabitants to the Capital where work and wages were more easily obtainable . . . one must seek for some cause or causes other than this to explain the whole increase. . . . In addition to the constant immigration of natives from the Protectorate during the Great War, thousands of men were recruited in the Protectorate for service in the Carrier Corps and the Inland Water Transport in East Africa, Cameroons, Mesopotamia and elsewhere. On the conclusion of their service they were repatriated to Sierra Leone and have in many instances remained in Freetown. Having through force of circumstances seen something of the world and something of the doubtful attractions of civilisation, they are at present unwilling to return to their uneventful and peaceful lives in their own villages in the Protectorate, but prefer to eke out a precarious existence in the crowded capital of the Colony.[6]

[1] Of the total 3,426 non-Natives enumerated in 1911 in the Protectorate 881 were under 16 years of age; see *Census Report 1911*, p. 27.

[2] '. . . in recent years a considerable number of Sierra Leoneans have migrated into the Protectorate, or have sought employment down the coast' (*Colonial Reports, Sierra Leone 1911*, p. 34).

[3] It should be noted also that many Creoles may have been employees of commercial firms which extended their business to the Protectorate.

[4] See in this connexion ibid. *1901*, pp. 35–6: 'Emigration is discouraged by the Government. The Protectorate needs population greatly, and every endeavour must be made to prevent those who should work the soil and help to develop their own country from leaving it to seek work in the gold mines where, perhaps, the temporary high wages are the temptation.'

[5] The Compiler of Census said with regard to the population of the Colony: '. . . the number of persons from 11 to 50 is less by 2,376 in 1911 than it was in 1901. The inference to be drawn seems to be that immigration from the Protectorate, though marked, has not been quite so prevalent during the last decade as it was in the previous one' (*Census Report 1911*, p. 16). He evidently did not realize the fundamental change that had occurred, inasmuch as the extraordinarily large immigration from the Protectorate which had taken place in the 1890s had practically ceased.

[6] Ibid. *1921*, pp. 4–5.

But the statistics of the population by birthplace tell another story. Since the number of Colony-born in Freetown was in 1921 about the same as in 1911, there cannot have been a marked gravitation of the inhabitants of the Colony to the capital. Since the number of Protectorate-born males in Freetown increased by only 2,376 while the number of Protectorate-born females increased by 3,383, the men recruited in the Protectorate for war service who after their repatriation remained permanently in Freetown cannot have been very numerous.[1] There was, on the other hand, a remarkable influx from other countries. The number of people in Freetown returned as born in West Africa (outside Sierra Leone) and in British Colonies (outside West Africa) increased from 4,199 (2,545 males and 1,654 females) to 8,466 (4,837 males and 3,629 females).

The Creole population in the Colony declined again between 1911 and 1921. The decrease this time amounted to 2,702 or 8·6 per cent. The Census Officer made the following comment:

That the native of the Colony, or Creole, is slowly but steadily decreasing in numbers cannot be gainsaid. . . .

The result of the Protectorate Census shows that 3,835 persons have been returned as natives of the Colony, or Creoles. This figure shows an increase of 891 over the corresponding figure for 1911, and is brought about by the extension of the Railway, the opening of new administrative Districts, and branches of commercial houses, but it cannot make up for the great decrease within the Colony.

A certain amount of emigration to other Colonies and Countries does undoubtedly take place, but while one cannot gather accurate particulars of the numbers of Creoles who so emigrate, it is safe to say that this emigration cannot be held responsible for the whole decrease.[2]

But the position concerning the Creoles is quite puzzling. According to the census returns the number of male Creoles (including Mulattoes) in Sierra Leone (Colony and Protectorate) increased from 14,899 in 1911 to 15,588, while the number of female Creoles decreased from 19,442 to 16,864. These figures apparently suggest that there was no male emigration to other colonies and countries[3] but a very considerable female emigration. It may be, however, that the number of female Creoles was understated in 1921.[4]

The development in 1921–31 was in some respects similar to that in 1911–21. The population of Freetown increased from 44,142 to 55,509

---

[1] See also in this connexion *Medical Report 1916*, p. 80: 'During the years 1915 and 1916 there have been at times temporary increases in the population owing to the return of large numbers of carriers from the Cameroons, many of whom were for a time allowed to take up residence in Freetown before going back to the Protectorate. Subsequently, action was taken to have these men sent up country as soon as possible after their arrival.' That the Census Officer misjudged the position of the repatriated recruits from the Protectorate may be inferred from the following fact. He says that 'the Mendi rise from 10,832 to 11,304 . . . may be mainly attributed to the return of Carrier Corps men and Inland Water Transport men from the seats of war' (*Census Report 1921*, p. 12). Actually the number of male Mendi in the Colony decreased from 7,568 in 1911 to 7,392 in 1921, while the number of female Mendi increased from 3,264 to 3,912. The Census Officer says furthermore (ibid., p. 33) that the Mendi 'emigrate to the Colony in considerable numbers'. Since the number of Mendi in the Protectorate was estimated in 1921 at 557,674, the numbers who had emigrated to the Colony in 1911–21 were negligible.   [2] Ibid., p. 11.

[3] The increase in the number of male Creoles was 689. In view of the ravages of the influenza epidemic it is quite unlikely that the natural increase should have exceeded this number.

[4] See pp. 170–1 above.

while the population of the rest of the Colony again remained stationary. The census report made the following comment:

> The general increase is due to immigration from the Protectorate, a large number of Sierra Leoneans having returned to the Colony from the Protectorate, the figures for the latter showing a large decrease. A number of emancipated slaves are said to have come to the Colony following the passing of the Ordinance for the abolition of slavery in 1926.
>
> Many other natives have been attracted to the Colony as settlers, but chiefly to Freetown in search of work. Much of the population is a floating or shifting one, coming or going on business or visits, and much of the increase in 1921 probably remained and attracted others and a small natural increase may also have taken place, though this would not appear to be the case if the registration figures for births and deaths are reliable.[1]

The most marked differences between the periods 1911–21 and 1921–31 were the following:

(1) While the Colony-born population both in Freetown and in the rest of the Colony had been in 1921 about the same as in 1911 but had increased somewhat in the Protectorate, the Colony-born population increased between 1921 and 1931 in Freetown by 7,109 and decreased in the rest of the Colony by 2,319, and in the Protectorate by 575. These figures suggest that in 1921–31 there was a considerable migration from the rural districts of the Colony into Freetown and that, as stated in the census report, a large number of Colony-born had returned from the Protectorate to Freetown. To what extent the increase in the total number of Colony-born in Sierra Leone (4,215) was due to natural increase and to what extent to the return of former emigrants to other colonies and countries it is impossible to say.

(2) While the Protectorate-born population in the rural districts of the Colony had slightly decreased in 1911–21 it increased by 2,532 in 1921–31. It seems therefore that Protectorate natives went not only as in 1911–21 to Freetown but settled also in the rural districts of the Colony.

(3) While the number of people in Freetown born outside Sierra Leone had increased enormously in 1911–21 it decreased considerably in 1921–31. It seems therefore that a number of strangers who had come to Freetown before 1921 had left Sierra Leone in the meantime.

(4) While the Creole population in Sierra Leone had decreased considerably in 1911–21 (as in the preceding decades) it increased in 1921–31 by 3,629. This increase may have been due in a small measure to the fact that some natives in 1931 were returned erroneously as 'Sierra Leoneans' (Creoles). But the bulk of the increase was probably caused by either natural increase or return from abroad.[2]

Nothing is known about the population growth in the Colony between the census of 1931 and the outbreak of the Second World War. The Administration assumed that the population of Freetown continued to increase at the same rate as in 1921–31 and that the population of the

---

[1] *Census Report 1931*, p. 23.

[2] See Luke, 'Some Notes on the Creoles and their Land', p. 65: 'Part of the recent increase may be due to Creoles and their families returning from the Coast on pension or as result of retrenchment during the financial crisis of the depression of 1929–1933.'

TABLE 36. *Population Increase, Colony of Sierra Leone, 1911–31*[1]

Area	Sex	Born in Colony			Born in Protectorate			Born elsewhere			Total		
		1911	*1921*	*1931*	*1911*	*1921*	*1931*	*1911*	*1921*	*1931*	*1911*	*1921*	*1931*
Freetown	Male	8,226	9,848	..	7,110	9,486	..	3,196	5,496	..	18,532	24,830	30,011
	Female	10,517	8,953	..	3,276	6,659	..	1,765	3,700	..	15,558	19,312	25,347
	Total	18,743	18,801	25,910	10,386	16,145	22,004	4,961	9,196	7,444	34,090	44,142	55,358
Rest of Colony	Male	11,044	12,837	..	10,622	9,140	..	803	757	..	22,469	22,734	22,541
	Female	13,242	11,446	..	5,343	6,417	..	428	424	..	19,013	18,287	18,523
	Total	24,286	24,283	21,964	15,965	15,557	18,089	1,231	1,181	1,011	41,482	41,021	41,064
Total	Male	19,270	22,685	..	17,732	18,626	..	3,999	6,253	..	41,001	47,564	52,552
	Female	23,759	20,399	..	8,619	13,076	..	2,193	4,124	..	34,571	37,599	43,870
	Total	43,029	43,084	47,874	26,351	31,702	40,093	6,192	10,377	8,455	75,572	85,163	96,422

[1] See *Census Report 1911*, p. 17; *1921*, p. 16; *1931*, pp. 22, 31. Figures for 1911 and 1921 include the Maritime Population. The data for 1911 include Bendu and Mocolo (with 764 inhabitants), which were not covered by later censuses.

rural districts remained stationary. Since the outbreak of the war the population of the Colony has increased enormously.

1940. . . . recent years have seen a large influx of labourers and their dependants into the town. This immigration is unrecorded and estimates of the numbers vary between 10,000 and 15,000.[1]

1941. The construction of numerous Naval, Military and Air Force works through-out the Colony has altered the whole fabric of Society. There has been an influx of labour from the Protectorate, which, with dependents and 'others' may be estimated at 30,000, or some 20 per cent. of the former population.[2]

1942. The abnormal conditions caused by the influx of labour from the Protec-torate persist. It is estimated that the population of the Rural Areas has increased by at least 50 per cent.[3]

In the Colony the 'Monthly Totals of African Employees working for Employers employing not less than Ten Africans' were as follows (in thousands):[4]

Year	Jan.	Feb.	Mar.	Apr.	May	June	July	Aug.	Sept.	Oct.	Nov.	Dec.
1940	10·9	10·1	10·4	10·8	10·8	10·1	13	15·5	19	23·4	23·4	25·7
1941	27·3	27·8	28	30	28	25	30	26	29·6	29·3	32	33·1
1942	41·1	44·7	42·7	42·8	41·4	41·9	45	48	49	48·1	50·5	45·3
1943	43·4	39·9	37·8	35·4	31·1	34·5	36·3	38	34·5	33·8	33	29

The number increased from 10,000 or 11,000 in the first half of 1940 to over 50,000 in November 1942. It decreased thereafter and amounted on 31 August 1944 to 27,607.[5]

In his Address of 23 November 1943 the Governor, after having shown the decrease from November 1942 to May 1943, said: 'The main reason advanced for this fall is the normal seasonal return of labour to the farms accelerated by difficulties in getting food.'[6] But this was evidently not the main reason. The Labour Report for 1943 stated:

During the period covered by this report there was a considerable easing off in the demand for labour, the principal causes being the completion of certain works, the closing down of a number of service works due to the change in the strategic position of Freetown during the course of the year, as well as the policy of service works in limiting the numbers of African workmen under each European supervisor.[7]

The Admiralty and War Department continued to employ the bulk of the labour in the Colony, although there was a sharp decrease in the numbers employed by the War Department at the end of the year. In December, 1943, the former employed 8,212 African artisans and labourers and the latter 4,826, compared with 14,577 and 26,974 respectively for the corresponding period of 1942.[8]

[1] Medical Report 1940, p. 10.

[2] Appendix to Address delivered by Governor Sir H. C. Stevenson in Legislative Council, 4 Nov. 1941, p. 1. As shown, p. 246 above, the Medical Report for 1941, referring probably to the end of the year, said: 'It is estimated that the increase in numbers since the outbreak of war is in the vicinity of 35,000.' This would have implied an increase of at least 30 per cent.

[3] Appendix to Address delivered by Governor Sir H. C. Stevenson in Legislative Council, 3 Nov. 1942, p. 1.

[4] See Report on the Labour Department 1941 and 1942, p. 2; 1943, p. 2.

[5] See Address delivered by Governor Sir Hubert Stevenson in Legislative Council, 7 Nov. 1944, p. 18.

[6] Appendix to Address, 23 Nov. 1943, p. 9.

[7] Report on the Labour Department 1943, p. 1.

[8] Ibid., p. 4. This statement suggests that of the 45,300 African employees working in December 1942 for employers employing not less than ten Africans 41,551 worked for the Admiralty and War Department, and of the 29,000 employed in December 1943 only 13,038.

As shown above, the population of Freetown had been estimated in 1940–1 at 80,000. It must have been much larger in the second half of 1942. In 1944 it was estimated at 87,000.[1]

Protectorate. Nothing definite can be said about the population growth in the Protectorate. At the time when the 1901 census was taken in the Colony the Native population of the Protectorate was put at 949,827. Ten years later it was estimated at 1,323,151. An increase in population had been expected.

> The causes, which in years gone by militated against the growth of the population have, under the settled form of government which now obtains, been removed, and there are signs that the population is gradually increasing.[2]

But the increase, of course, cannot have been as great as suggested by the above figures.

> It is not easy to make comparisons with estimates of population made in 1901 owing to change of districts, but generally speaking it may be assumed that, no doubt owing to more accurate information, the increase of population shown by the recent Census is accounted for by a larger number of persons having been allowed to each house than in 1901. For instance, in the Karene District, where an exact comparison can be made with the year 1901, the population was arrived at by allowing 9 persons to each house on a house computation of 40,583 houses, rendering a population of 366,081, while in 1901 a population of 200,000 was returned on a basis of 5 persons to a house living in 40,000 houses. Consequently the great increase of population must not necessarily be attributed to actual increase in numbers, but more probably is due to inaccurate estimates made in 1901.[3]

The estimated number of Natives in the Protectorate was 1,450,903 in 1921 or 127,752 more than in 1911. Considering that the influenza epidemic claimed many victims and that there was emigration to the Colony and elsewhere[4] it seems doubtful whether the increase was actually as large. The Census Officer does not discuss this problem, and the great changes in boundaries make it impossible to reach any final conclusion.

In 1931 the Native population of the Protectorate was estimated at not less than 1,667,790. The census report said:

> The native population appears to have increased by 216,887 since 1921, but, as both census figures were arrived at by estimate, it can only be called an apparent increase. What part of it is real it is impossible to say.[5] The Northern Province accounts for 215,391 of this increase and the Southern Province 1,496.[6]

[1] See *Preliminary Report on the Freetown Water Supply*, p. 9. 'The 1944 figure is stated to include some 20,000 persons who have come to Freetown during the war, and it is anticipated that many of these will leave the City as work declines. The estimated post-war population figure is 75,000 . . . .'

[2] *Colonial Reports, Sierra Leone 1905*, p. 58. See also ibid. *1904*, p. 38.

[3] *Census Report 1911*, p. 29. See also ibid. p. 32, concerning the Koinadugu District: 'At the time of the Census of 1901 it was estimated that there were 56,386 inhabitants in this district, but the estimate made was of a rudimentary description, and the population of 125,529 estimated by the recent Census is no indication that the population has doubled itself during the last decade, or even increased appreciably.'   [4] See ibid. *1921*, p. 31.

[5] This cautious point of view seems to have been abandoned later by the authorities. See, for example, *Colonial Reports, Sierra Leone 1932*, p. 13: 'The difference must be taken as an actual increase due to natural increment and not to migratory or other causes.'

[6] *Census Report 1931*, p. 83. Since Toli Chiefdom, with a native population of 1,186 in 1931, was transferred in 1927 from the Northern to the Southern Province (see ibid., p. 128), even the small increase in the Southern Province would be fictitious.

It is obvious that the population of the Northern Province cannot have actually increased by 38 per cent. Some comments in the census report throw light on the position.

The native population of the Port Loko and Karene Districts was estimated in 1921 at 307,900. The figure for the same area in 1931 was 387,719,[1] or 26 per cent. larger. The 1931 census report states for Port Loko that 'there appears to be an increase in the population',[2] but intimates that part of the increase was due to a more accurate estimate of the number of persons per house. For Karene the District Commissioner remarks: 'My impression is that, if there has been an increase, it is a very small one.'[3]

In the 1921 area of the Bombali District the reported population increased from 173,350 to 284,844 or by 64 per cent. 'It cannot be said that this increase is a natural one.'[4]

In the 1921 area of the Koinadugu District the reported population increased from 85,700 to 110,964, or by 29 per cent. 'As to the general increase in population, this is attributed to (a) immigration of Fula and Temne, (b) a slight natural increase and (c) larger basis on which to form a closer estimate. With reference to the last, the Limba are given as 9 persons per house as against 8 in 1921 and the Korankos as 5 against 4·5 in 1921 . . . .'[5]

It seems, therefore, that the population of the Northern Province increased actually in 1921–31, but much less than indicated by the 'census' figures.

In the Southern Province, where according to the 'census' figures the population was the same in 1931 as in 1921, it increased probably also slightly. The census report states that in the Moyamba and Bo Districts the population in 1931 was underestimated.[6] As to the Kono District, where the population was reported to have decreased from 167,450 to 102,741[7] or by 39 per cent., the District Commissioner is of opinion that 'the population was grossly overestimated in 1921',[8] and that the Kissi population was underestimated in 1931.[9]

In view of the apparently much larger population increase in the Northern than in the Southern Province it is interesting to note that the survey made in 1931 showed a similar result. The 373 women questioned in the Northern Province had 1,923 live-born children, of whom 560 died before puberty. The 460 women questioned in the Southern Province had only 1,790 live-born children, of whom not fewer than 778 died before puberty. The average number of children reaching adult life was 3·7 in the Northern Province and only 2·2 in the Southern Province. The figures for the Southern Province would suggest that the population there is dying out. But the surveys comprised too few cases to permit the drawing

[1] Computed from ibid., pp. 83, 123.   [2] Ibid., p. 107.   [3] Ibid., p. 119.
[4] Ibid., p. 123. See also p. 38 above.   [5] Ibid., p. 128.   [6] See ibid., pp. 133, 148.
[7] Taking account of the changes in area.   [8] Ibid., p. 164.
[9] The Kissi population was given as 10,160 in 1921 and as 3,801 in 1931, although the Kissi Chiefdom Toli (with 1,186 inhabitants in 1931) had been transferred in the meantime from the Koinadugu District.

of any conclusions. The official opinion seems to be that the population of the Protectorate was increasing notably.

Whatever may be the case in certain other less-well-developed portions of the Empire the native population of Sierra Leone is certainly neither decreasing nor stationary. For a number of years now it has been, and still is, increasing. This fact is brought out by the steadily increasing returns of revenue derived from house tax and by the land hunger that is already evident in many of the more populous chiefdoms. Villages that had their origin as outlying farm hamlets of a larger native town now contain more huts than the parent settlement and are themselves throwing out clusters of houses on the extreme confines of their farm lands. . . . If additional testimony of this fact were required, the rapid and almost total denudation of the Protectorate of forest is at once an eloquent if also an unfortunate witness of the fact. Another and rather more welcome sign of congestion is the attention that is being more and more paid to grassland which has hitherto been considered too poor to cultivate. . . .

The increase of population has its main source in the cessation of native inter-tribal wars. It is now thirty years since there was a native raid, with its consequent denudation of an area, restricted though it might be, of effective men, women, and children. In place of this form of activity the Pax Britannica has brought trade and the opportunity for the native to sell his produce. Wealth that is wealth in which all could share has not so much been increased as created for the first time.[1]

It will appear that, though people are naturally prolific, conditions exist which restrict the growth of the population. However, the evidence generally goes to prove that the population tends to keep above the 'static'. In favour of its growth, it may be said that subsistence is sufficient if not very efficient, marriage is almost universal (amongst natives at least); it does not take place too young and pre-puberty intercourse is not common; the eliminating checks of war, famine and pestilence are not present; and preventive checks, such as abortifacients and the using of contraceptives, are rare. On the other hand, the main factors operating to restrict the population are the diseases already mentioned. The chief toll is taken in infant and child life due to lack of intelligent ante-natal and post-natal care and the many risks to which infants and children are exposed.[2]

Actually the official population estimates up to 1940 did not differ essentially from the 1931 census result (1,672,058), the figures being 1,702,726 for 1939 and 1,714,112 for 1940. But the estimate was raised to 1,791,404 in 1941 and to 1,801,917 in 1942.[3] In view of the large influx of labour from the Protectorate to the Colony in 1940–2 it is most unlikely that the population of the Protectorate was larger in 1942 than at the outbreak of the war.

VIII. Non-African Mortality[4]

1. *Mortality of Europeans*

Mortality of Europeans in the eighteenth century has been discussed in the section 'Early Colonization' and mortality of European military during the first quarter of the nineteenth century in the section 'Composition of non-African Population'. As regards mortality of European

---

[1] The Commissioner, Central Province, to the Colonial Secretary, 25 Apr. 1930, *Papers relating to Health of Native Populations*, pp. 134–5.   [2] *Census Report 1931*, p. 15.

[3] See *Blue Book 1939* O, p. 4; *1940* O, p. 4; *1941* O, p. 4; *1943* O, p. 4.

[4] Data concerning non-African births are apparently not available. European births are rare; only 10 European residents in 1931 were born in Sierra Leone. But there were 233 Asiatics born in the country.

civilians in the first quarter of the nineteenth century, the Commissioners of Inquiry reported in 1827:

The information given in the Medical Report of the Church Missionary Society, published in 1825, may be cited as indicating the effect of climate upon the Missionaries and others sent out by that body to the Coast of Africa, and almost exclusively to Sierra Leone.

It appears that between the month of March 1804 and August 1825, 89 individuals, mostly in the prime of life, arrived upon the Coast, of whom 51 were males and 38 females. Of this number 54 had died, seven returned to England in good health, 14 in ill health, and 14 remained at the time upon the Coast; of those who died 32 were males and 22 females; two were lost at sea. It was endeavoured to ascertain in what proportion the resident Europeans generally, had suffered from the effects of climate, but on this subject no authentic information was attainable. The principal medical officer says respecting them, 'It is now impossible to frame such a statement, as nearly the whole of the colonists have been occasionally treated by the medical officers, there being no private practitioner in these colonies.' In Sierra Leone, however, it is the general opinion that neither the officers of the civil establishment, the merchants, nor other Europeans suffer in the same proportion as the military officers, or the individuals sent out by the Church Missionary Society.[1]

These figures, of course, are not quite conclusive as no data are given concerning the duration of the sojourn of the missionaries in Sierra Leone. Death statistics are altogether very scanty and uncertain up to 1885, and even when census data became available there was still the difficulty of appraising correctly the average number of Europeans present.

It is a very difficult matter, in view of the uncertainty of the actual number of European residents in Freetown, or the Colony, and the frequency with which they change, to arrive at an accurate idea as to the actual death-rate, and it has hitherto not seemed to me advisable to do so on figures which are more or less imaginary.[2]

Another difficulty arose from the fact that it was not always clear whether the death figures covered only residents or also strangers.

This explains in part why, particularly in the period from 1818 to 1823, opinions on mortality of Europeans differed widely, though this was due probably as much to wilful misrepresentation. I must confine myself to quoting a few examples.

1818. *Star* (London), 5 November. Our late accounts from Sierra Leone, have been melancholy in the extreme. The white inhabitants, exclusive of military, do not exceed 30 persons, and of these one-third fell victims to the fever during the rainy season . . . .[3]

Hampshire Gazette (Southampton). A letter from Sierra Leone, states the following particulars of the number of Europeans, and the sickness in the Colony, somewhat at variance with the accounts which have appeared in the London Journals:—
. . . The number of Europeans here may be estimated at from fifty to sixty—between thirty and forty arrive yearly—those merely make up for the number who perish—a month after the death of an European he is forgotten—not one out of one hundred survive to return to Europe.[4]

'Africanus' to the Editor of the *Royal Gazette*, 7 January 1819. . . . I, as well as most of your Readers, know whence all these lies proceed. This Colony has from its very infancy called forth the animosity of all dealers in human blood . . . they have

[1] *Report*, First Part, p. 109.
[2] Principal Medical Officer, *Medical Reports 1900 and 1901*, p. 4.
[3] Quoted from *The Royal Gazette and Sierra Leone Advertiser*, 20 Feb. 1819, p. 164.
[4] Quoted from ibid.

had recourse to quotations from private letters either written by themselves or by vile wretches paid by the Havannah Slave Dealers . . . .

The last rainy season was peculiarly unhealthy . . . but Mr. Editor great as that loss undoubtedly was, it did not bear even the usual proportion of the casualties experienced in tropical climates . . . .

In order to trump up a frightful appearance the inventors of lies decreased the Europeans to thirty, whereas the actual number in this Colony in January, 1818, was one hundred and twenty-four, exclusive of the Officers of the Royal African Corps and European Soldiers,—it is now 115. . . .

The total number of Europeans who died in the Peninsula, in 1818, was eight men, three women, and two children . . . .[1]

The English papers no doubt had overstated mortality,[2] but 13 deaths among a European population which (in view of absences during the rainy season) probably averaged less than 100 was certainly an excessive number.[3]

1819. *Avocat sans Causes* to the Editor of the *Royal Gazette*, 30 September. I trust the following calculation will stand the test of enquiry:—

On the 31st of December, 1818, we had in the Colony a grand total of Europeans, exclusive of the military forces, of *one hundred and fifteen*—from that number we lost six men by *death*, two women and two children.

Twenty men and two ladies have left the Colony, and either returned to Europe, gone to the Gambia on their private affairs, or for the benefit of their health.

Among the number of those who died, *three only* had resided in the Colony *above one year* . . . the others had not experienced a rainy season.[4]

Ci-devant Avocat sans Causes to the Editor of the *Royal Gazette*, 15 October. I have lived on the peninsula of Sierra Leone for sixteen years!—Some years we have (that is the inhabitants, whether white or black) been healthy, and in other years rather sickly. In 1805 we had a severe and long rainy season: it was a very sickly season to the inhabitants: 1807 was little better, and 1812 and 16 were rather worse; but this last year, I must confess, was worse than any.[5] The rains began early—were

---

[1] *The Royal Gazette and Sierra Leone Advertiser*, 20 Feb. 1819, p. 164. See also ibid., 6 Mar., pp. 171-2; 12 June, p. 197; 19 June, p. 199; 26 June, p. 203; 4 Sept., p. 247.
'Investigator' in his letter to the Editor of *The Times* (London), dated 3 Jan. 1820, said: 'These comfortable assurances appear to have been kindly intended to keep up the spirits of the commissioners for repressing the illegal traffic in slaves; for they are inserted in the *Royal Gazette* of the 12th, 19th, and the 26th of June, and the commissioners, with their suites, arrived there on the 7th of that month' (*The Royal Gazette*, 1 Apr. 1820, p. 358).

[2] In a Dispatch to Under-Secretary of State Henry Goulburn, dated 8 June 1819, Governor MacCarthy wrote that the Surveyor who was returning on leave to England 'will I hope dispel the false alarms created by the exaggerated reports on the insalubrity of the colony' (C.O. 267, vol. XLIX). In a further Dispatch to Earl Bathurst, dated 24 Aug. 1819, he pointed out 'the dread actually existing among the greatest part of the Europeans, and principally those who have not resided here above a few Months, of the extreme danger of the climate, an alarm which owes its origin to the nefarious publications so widely circulated at home' (ibid.).

[3] It may well be that the European population averaged much less than 100, because, as stated above (see p. 185), the European population in January 1818 was certainly smaller than indicated by 'Africanus'. It should be realized, on the other hand, that mortality was probably swelled by an unusually large proportion of newcomers who experienced their first rainy season in 1818. See in this connexion Boyle (1831), p. 150: 'The success or accuracy of the result of any attempt to generalise the average annual mortality among the European residents at Sierra Leone, is rendered exceedingly doubtful, from the very great difference of risk between the newly-arrived European who has not had fever, and the one who has had it, however short or long a period either may have been in the colony; and, also, from the nature of the engagements of the different individuals, whether leading to great exposure soon after their arrival or otherwise.'

[4] *The Royal Gazette*, 2 Oct. 1819, p. 262.

[5] See also Yellow Fever Commission (West Africa), *Second Report*, p. 34: 'The earlier years of the existence of this Colony have been marked by seasons of extreme unhealthiness especially so in 1807, 1809, 1812, 1815 and 1819'.

severe[1]—and continued with violence for a longer period than usual. The sickness and mortality in every year have been chiefly confined to those recently arrived; and I understand, every drunken sailor, and all unfortunate poor and wretched creatures, let loose from ships and captured 'slavers,' have been crammed in the bills of mortality to present a more formidable aspect, and a more *glorious* service to those who have crawled through the torrents of rain and yet live! . . .[2]

Médecin malgré lui to the Editor of the *Royal Gazette*. . . . A correct list of those who died in the Colony of Sierra Leone in the months of June, July, and August—total No. 53. . . .[3]

Ci-devant Avocat sans Causes to the Editor of the *Royal Gazette*. . . . Suppose 53, or even more died, pray what inference can be drawn either for or against this climate ? It is a fact that more than one-half of the number were sea-faring persons, and, consequently, did not belong to the Colony; and if any estimate is to be made of the healthiness or unhealthiness of this place, the whole of the sailors who arrive here in ships of war and merchant vessels ought to be added to the number of the Colonists, otherwise no correct idea can be formed of the number who might be expected to perish amongst a certain number of Europeans residing in the Colony. . . .[4]

Médecin malgré lui to the Editor of the *Royal Gazette*. . . . I will demand—of the whole European population, civil and military, in number about 130, how many escaped disease of climate in the last rainy season ? I answer 20 at the utmost. . . . If this be called a healthy climate, with what place is the comparison made ? and what place is unhealthy ?[5]

Editorial *Royal Gazette*. The following extract from the Liverpool Mercury, of the 22nd October, will delight him [*Médecin malgré lui*]. We lost *five* Europeans, who were included in the Census of December 1818; yet Médecin and his friends swell the list in August to *thirty-five*.—How many departed this troublesome world by the *kind assistance* of Médecin ?

Africa—A letter from Sierra Leone, (Aug. 24) states, that not only Europeans but natives have fallen victims to the epidemic fever occasioned by the severe rainy season. The doctors reckon that thirty-five Europeans died in July and August, and many were ill when the last accounts came away.[6]

'Investigator' to the Editor of *The Times*, 3 January 1820. Letters from that colony state, that . . . the white population . . . in the early part of last June . . . consisted of 118 individuals, men, women, and children, of whom 94 had been attacked by the fever, and no less than 54 had perished between that period and the 24th of August, when the accounts were dated. The rainy or sickly season is not over till the month of October, and the fever still raged with great violence. . . .[7]

'Africanus' to the Editor of the *Royal Gazette*. . . . the Fatal List of Dead and dying transmitted from Freetown to London, in August last . . . a list published in the

---

[1] See also *The Royal Gazette*, 7 Aug. 1819, p. 230. See furthermore *Missionary Register*, Oct. 1819, p. 454: 'The Rains of the present year, on the Western Coast of Africa, have been unusually severe and uninterrupted, beyond those of any season in the memory of man; and sickness and mortality have prevailed, therefore, more than ordinarily, among Natives as well as Europeans.'

[2] *The Royal Gazette*, 30 Oct. 1819, p. 271. In the course of his letter he says furthermore that *Avocat sans Causes* made a mistake and that only two residents who had been longer than a year in the Colony had died.

[3] Ibid., 6 Nov. 1819, p. 274.   [4] Ibid., 13 Nov. 1819, p. 279.

[5] Ibid., 27 Nov. 1819, p. 287. This is from a letter comprising over 3,000 words. The major space of the *Royal Gazette* in those weeks was taken up by the discussion of mortality among Europeans, and I cannot do justice to all contributors. But I want to quote at least the concluding paragraph of another lengthy letter on the subject 'to the Printer of the Royal Gazette'. It reads: 'I know you are dying with curiosity to know who I am. I am too modest to tell you my name, after saying so much in my own praise; but I will help you to guess, by giving you my occupation in French, after the fashion of your other tiresome Correspondents, who I hope have, like me, made up their minds never to write to you more. *Sage Femme*.' (4 Dec. 1819, p. 291.)

[6] Ibid., 27 Nov. 1819, pp. 287–8.

[7] Reprinted ibid., 1 Apr. 1820, p. 359. The figure 118 is apparently meant to include the military.

London newspapers of November last . . . amounts to *Fifty-three*: from a careful journal kept, I find that, taking in children soldiers,[1] sailors, and strangers, of all descriptions, whose names were *not* of course included in the Census of 31st December, 1818, the correct number was *thirty* . . . .[2]

Same to same, 22 March 1820. The following will, I believe, be found an exact copy of the *fatal* list transmitted to Europe in August last.[3] It was ushered into the world with an eloquent preamble, stating, that the whole of the white population, in the early part of June, did not exceed *one hundred and eighteen* souls, men, women, and children—of that number *ninety-four* had been attacked with fever—*fourteen* had died in July—*sixteen* between the 1st and 12th of August, making thirty in six weeks, besides two gentlemen in May, Captain Neale and Mr. Barrett, also a great number of individuals in June, whose names could not be procured, but that they amounted to more than *twenty-three*, mostly in the hospital, consisting of non-commissioned officers, mechanics, and poor persons.

I will state *plain facts.*—The census taken on the 30th December, 1818, did not include the military officers, non-commissioned officers or private men, nor their families, excepting such officers as held civil employments. The undermentioned persons were not in the census, and most of them not in the colony for months after, viz. Capt. Neale, Mr. Barrett . . . .[4]

. . . I will, however, to prevent further cavilling transmit to you the list of Europeans included in the census of December, 1818, and their disposal on the 1st September last.[5]

He then reproduces a table 'Census of Europeans in the Colony of Sierra Leone, taken 31st of December 1818: exclusive of the Military',[6] in which he showed what had become of each person by 24 August 1819. He revised this list later[7] and found finally that 94 were present in the Colony on that date, that 21 had sailed, and that only 6 had died in the Colony.[8] This was the beginning of the fight between 'Investigator' and 'Africanus'.[9] It is unnecessary here to enter into the details of this elaborate discussion, but it may be useful to reproduce two statements made after the termination of the controversy, the one by the editor of the *Royal Gazette* and the other by the Deputy Inspector of Hospitals, Dr. Nicoll:

(1) It was stated, that our population consisted only of *one hundred and eighteen* Europeans, of all descriptions;—that in June, out of *that number*, we lost 23 persons —in July 14—in August 16, grand total from 1st June 53!—All in the short period of eleven weeks . . . .

[1] This means apparently military and their children.

[2] *The Royal Gazette*, 19 Feb. 1820, p. 336.

[3] 'Investigator' says that the copy used by 'Africanus' was not exact (see ibid., 15 Apr. 1820, p. 373).

[4] Here follows a long list of other names. His 'Observations on that List' indicate that of the 30 persons who according to his 'careful journal' died in the Colony between 1 June and 22 August 1819, 10 were civilian residents, 5 children of military (including 4 children of officers), and about 15 soldiers or sailors.   [5] Ibid., 25 Mar. 1820, pp. 354–5.

[6] See ibid., 1 Apr. 1820, p. 356.   [7] See ibid., 3 Apr. 1820, p. 364.

[8] His statements as regards five more persons are not clear.

[9] See Editorial Note, ibid., 25 Mar. 1820: 'The grand controversy between *Investigator* and *Africanus* being interesting to most of our readers, we propose printing the Letters, in toto, in extra sheets each week. To these we will subjoin some explanatory notes for the benefit of our correspondents at home:—truth, and nothing but the truth, is *all* we ask.' The discussion is to be found in the issues of 25 Mar., 1, 3, 15, 22, and 29 Apr., 20 and 27 May, and 3 and 17 June ibid., pp. 354–5, 357–64, 370–4, 376–84, 393–6, 399, 401–4, 413–14, 416. Most of these Letters were first published in Jan. and Feb. 1820 in *The Times* (London).

Now let us *once* more repeat what we said before, over and over again, and is known to every one in the colony. On the 31st December, 1818, the population consisted of *one hundred and twenty eight,* and did not include any of the military officers or soldiers, or their families, nor persons who came here in January, February, March, April, May, and June following. In June *three* persons died . . . they were not in the colony when the census was made; *eleven* died in July, and only *two* of that number were in the list . . . *nineteen* died in August, *four* of whom only were included in the *list* . . . . Total number of Europeans died in that period *thirty-three,—* out of which number *six* belonged to the census, and *one* only a colonial officer.

The correspondents of *Investigator* refer to the Census, and from *one hundred and eighteen* persons kill *fifty-four,* whereas *six* died, making then a difference of *forty-eight* !¹

(2) On the 31st of December, 1818, there were one hundred and twenty-eight, of which eighteen sailed before the rainy season for England, two of which died, and of the remaining number, one hundred and ten, eight perished, giving a proportion of dead, as 7½ per cent., or very nearly one in 13.²

The principal questions which require an answer are the following:

(1) How many Europeans died altogether in the Colony in June? 'Africanus' and the editor of the *Royal Gazette* state that only three non-commissioned officers who had come in April and May with the 4th West India Regiment and were drunkards, died. 'Investigator' claims that twenty-three died. It seems likely that the actual figure was higher than three and lower than twenty-three.³

(2) How many Europeans died altogether in the Colony from 1 July to 24 August? There is a consensus of opinion that the total number was about thirty.

(3) How many died of the European civil residents enumerated at the census of 31 December 1818?⁴ 'Africanus' and the editor of the *Royal Gazette* say that six died in the Colony up to 24 August 1819. Dr. Nicoll says that in 1819 eight died in the Colony and two more who had sailed before the rainy season for England. *Avocat sans Causes* said on 2 October 1819 that ten had died. All these statements may be true.⁵

(4) How many died of the European civil residents who had come since 31 December 1818? 'Africanus' and the editor of the *Royal Gazette* say that four died in the Colony up to 24 August 1819. This statement may be true.

(5) How many of the European civil residents died altogether in the Colony? This question cannot be answered since it is not known how many of the newcomers died before 1 June or after 24 August.

As regards European mortality in 1820, the *Royal Gazette* reported.

We have, with little variation, the same favorable condition of health to acknowledge with increased thankfulness to providence. A couple of gentlemen have had

¹ Editorial, *Royal Gazette,* 24 June 1820, pp. 419–20.

² 'Extracts from the Half-yearly Report, Dated 1821, of the late Dr. Nicoll', Boyle (1831), pp. 149–50.

³ I suspect that 'Africanus' kept his journal only from July on.

⁴ The census returns reproduced in the *Royal Gazette* of 8 July 1819 and in many other documents showed only 115 European civil residents. The same number was given by *Avocat sans Causes* (ibid., 2 Oct. 1819). I know of no explanation for the figure 128 used by so many contemporary writers.

⁵ It would be surprising, however, if actually not a single death had occurred before 17 July. ('Africanus' gives as dates of death 17 and 23 July, and 1, 3, 4, and 10 Aug.)

slight attacks of fever in consequence of the late accessions of rain, but without any material inconvenience. We trust, therefore, that the season usually considered so unhealthy is now at a close, without any casualty to produce an alteration in the general feeling of gratitude and satisfaction for the present and confidence for the future.[1]

The truth may be inferred from the following statement by Dr. Nicoll:

About one in twelve, or nearly nine per cent. of the better class of society died . . . .

As is usually the case in other countries, the mortality fell heavy on the poorer class of Europeans, unprovided with good accommodations, without the means of procuring articles of comfort suitable to the climate, and who were not guarded in their general conduct, nor restricted as to regular habits of temperance.[2]

The high mortality of 'the poorer class of Europeans' appears also in the following 'Return of the Number of Europeans (exclusive of Military) received into Military Hospital, Sierra Leone, and the Number of Deaths in each Year; between 20th June 1819 and 20th December 1825':[3]

Years	Seamen and Marines of Royal Navy		Seamen of Merchant Vessels		Distressed Europeans		Total treated	Total died
	Treated	Died	Treated	Died	Treated	Died		
1819	8	—	—	—	—	—	8	—
1820	17	2	—	—	190	40	207	42
1821	16	—	—	—	106	26	122	26
1822	36	—	68	26	81	12	185	38
1823	36	2	91	32	47	15	174	48[1]
1824	6	2	49	11	23	8	78	21
1825	24	7	—	—	3	1	27	8

[1] Total does not tally with sum of items.

The large numbers of 'Distressed Europeans' sent to the Military Hospital in 1820 and 1821 suggest that the figures may include some seamen of merchant vessels.[4] But the vast majority of seamen dying in those years perished outside the Hospital.

Hy. Williams to the Editor of the *Morning Post* (London), April 1821. In the *Morning Post* of the 24th instant, I observe in an article respecting Sierra-Leone, an assertion that, in two months, out of 85 seamen, 65 were buried from the merchant ships. At the season mentioned, December and January, I had four vessels loading there, whose crews amounted to 68; three of those vessels have arrived home—one with the loss of two men—the others one each. The fourth vessel with a crew of 26, were all well on the 11th February, nearly loaded.

That the climate of that colony is unhealthy, is beyond a doubt; but there are those who seem determined to lose no opportunity of making the most of that unhappy circumstance, without being scrupulous as to the correctness of their statements.[5]

'Observations on the Timber Trade of Sierra Leone' (From a Correspondent). . . . Malicious reports had been designedly circulated in London and Liverpool, that

[1] Editorial, *Royal Gazette*, 7 Oct. 1820, p. 457.

[2] Boyle, pp. 149–50. According to Rankin, vol. ii, p. 324, the total number of deaths in 1820 was 19. This figure includes 5 officers (see p. 182 above). Mortality of civilians evidently was very high in 1820.   [3] See *Papers relating to Sierra Leone 1830*, p. 69.

[4] See in this connexion letter from Dr. A. Nicoll to Governor MacCarthy, 16 Dec. 1822; Dispatch from Governor MacCarthy to Earl Bathurst, 1 Feb. 1823; and letter from Dr. Barry to Governor MacCarthy, 22 Sept. 1823 (C.O. 267, vol. lviii, Nos. 305, 341).

[5] *The Royal Gazette*, 11 Aug. 1821, p. 636.

this beneficial trade in timber was attended with the most imminent danger to the crews of vessels; and that, in short, the river Sierra-Leone was but the grave of seamen. . . . The number of deaths has been much exaggerated . . . and it has even been absurdly asserted in this colony, as well as in England, that 65 perished out of 85. Now the fact is, that upwards of two hundred and fifty seamen were employed, last season, in the timber trade of Sierra-Leone; twenty three died here after being sent down the river, and about the same number (poor fellows!) fell victims to the ravages of the fever, without having benefited from medical aid, or obtained comfort of any kind in their respective vessels up the river. The sickness and mortality were confined to certain ships, and generally to those in certain situations; and from an attentive consideration of all the circumstances of their peculiar hardship and misery, it will appear only surprising that so few died, and so many lived to circulate tidings the most false, and injurious to the prosperity of a trade very likely to be productive of the greatest good to this hard struggling and rising colony.[1]

The excessive mortality of seamen on timber vessels caused the Board of the Governor and Council to pass, on 20 October 1823, 'An Act for the preservation of White Seamen, while in the River Sierra Leone'.[2] The Preamble read as follows:

Whereas most ruinous consequences have been occasioned by the deaths and sickness of White Seamen belonging to Merchant vessels, resorting to the port of Freetown, Bance Island, and other parts of the River Sierra Leone, and particularly of those White Seamen employed in the Timber Trade; and there being much reason to apprehend the same has been often caused by the parsimony of the Owners and Masters of such vessels, in not employing native labourers to assist in the very heavy and laborious duties necessarily attending the loading of such vessels, and in not supplying such White Seamen with proper and sufficient food. And Whereas, from the increased general trade of this Colony, as well as that of the Timber trade thereto, it is highly requisite for the protecting the interest thereof, as well as for the cause of justice and humanity towards such White Seamen, that a remedy should be provided for the evils herein set forth:[3]

The action of the Government was probably prompted by the yellow fever epidemic which ravaged the Colony from late in 1822 to the middle of 1823.[4] I shall submit some of the available evidence in chronological order.

[1] Ibid., 1 Sept. 1821, pp. 647–8.

[2] Printed ibid., 15 Nov. 1823, pp. 181–2. See also Dispatch from Governor MacCarthy to Earl Bathurst, 25 Oct. 1823 (C.O. 267, vol. lviii, No. 345).

[3] The Act, which was to come into force on 1 May 1824, apparently had not much effect. On 24 Apr. 1826 the Medical Officer Ferguson stated before the Commissioners of Inquiry: 'The fifth class (merchant seamen and private soldiers) afford numerous and melancholy examples of the effects of climatorial influence, from the rapid increase of the African timber trade; during the last two years the number of merchant seamen visiting the colony has increased nearly tenfold, and during the last year there have been on an average nearly four hundred European troops in the colony. I have attended but a small proportion of the sick merchant seamen; but my limited opportunities of observation with regard to them, lead me to say generally, that they are exposed to the same morbid causes, and are liable to the same diseases in as severe types as the European soldiers, who have been the more immediate objects of my medical charge; the most prominent of those diseases is the bilious remittent fever; other complaints, forming a very minute proportion, either in frequency of occurrence or in mortality . . .' (Papers relating to Sierra Leone 1830, p. 78). See also, for example, the editorial in The Royal Gazette, 11 Sept. 1824, quoted pp. 298–9 below, and Missionary Register, Sept. 1824, p. 400.

[4] See statement by Dr. Barry before the Commissioners of Inquiry in 1826: 'During the dry season of 1823 the colony was visited by the yellow fever, attended by those peculiar symptoms which always mark the disease within the tropics. Symptoms of the same description appear to

Editorial, *Royal Gazette*, 3 May 1823. The tornado season has at length set in, and most sincerely do we trust, that its anticipated good effects may be realized, in the mitigation of the sickness and mortality which has afflicted this town during the greater part of the last month. In former years, April was found to be one of the most healthy; this year, however, it has unhappily been otherwise. Natives and Europeans seem to have suffered with undistinguishing severity. It is therefore to be hoped, that the tornadoes may have a salutary influence in lessening the violence of the prevailing Endemic; and, in the mean time, too much caution cannot be observed in guarding against all unnecessary exposure.[1]

Letter from Sierra Leone, 15 May 1823. The Colony is very sickly at present, and the Medical Gentlemen have declared that the yellow fever has been brought here by the ship Caroline, from the Mediterranean, or the United States' ship Cyane, from St. Thomas's.[2] What a scene of woe does this colony present just now! Widows lamenting the deaths of their husbands, families mourning for the loss of parents. Every thing seems to conspire against this unfortunate colony, which is now visited with one of the most baneful fevers that was ever seen in this or any other place. Trade is depressed beyond all former precedent, and nothing but misery and despair seems to be depicted in the countenance of the few Europeans who yet remain. Nearly eighty gentlemen have died within six weeks.

The colony contains about one hundred, or one hundred and ten Europeans.[3]

Mr. Philip Vaughan to the Secretary of the Church Missionary Society, 18 June 1823. . . . I shall, therefore, proceed to inform you how awfully Death has been executing the Decree of Heaven—in a manner, indeed, before unknown even to the oldest inhabitant.

The following is the number of Europeans, who have died since my arrival in the Colony[4]:—

In the month of December, 7—January, 2—February, 9—March, 11—April, 12—May, 24—and (to the date of this Letter) June, 12: Total 77. . . .

Very few of the Europeans who have recently died, have fallen victims to the fever of the climate. The Medical Men have not ascertained the character of the disease. Almost all die of the black vomit; and very few that have died have had more than three or four days of illness.[5]

Senior Missionary Nyländer to the Church Missionary Society, 6 July 1823. The Governor, who has been absent since November, is daily expected. He will be astonished to see the Colony almost empty of Public Officers—no Lawyer—no

have occurred in the year 1815, and it is very probable that this colony, similar to those of the West Indies will be occasionally liable to its visitation, its origin in all instances has been involved in obscurity. The disease, during the year 1823, did not appear to be contagious, nor were the black population subjected to its influence' (*Papers relating to Sierra Leone 1830*, p. 66).

[1] *The Royal Gazette*, 3 May 1823, p. 70. In no issue of the preceding six months had ill-health or mortality been mentioned, and only two deaths (a naval man on a schooner, 24 Feb., and a Missionary, 16 Apr.) had been recorded. When the yellow fever had raged for some months in the Colony, an editorial of 15 Feb. 1823 (p. 25) gave the glowing description of the condition of the European population quoted p. 186 above.

[2] See also Dispatch from Governor MacCarthy to Earl Bathurst, 26 June 1823 (C.O. 267, vol. lviii, No. 322): 'The dry season from December to June being comparatively healthy, and no equal number of Europeans having died at Sierra Leone, at any former period, it has been conjectured, that the Bilious malignant remittent Fever—of the same nature as that of the West Indies, and which has raged with such violence at Sierra Leone since the end of March was imported in the Month of February by the United States Frigate 'Cyane': by others the infection is attributed to a Merchant Vessel, which came direct from Malta for Timber—having no correct information on that point, I shall await my return to that Colony, and the report of a Board of Enquiry, until I offer an opinion.'

[3] Reprinted in *Royal Gazette*, 18 Oct. 1823, p. 166. This letter had apparently been published in a London paper.

[4] 3 Dec. 1822 (see Walker, *Church of England Mission*, p. 184).

[5] *Missionary Register*, Sept. 1823, p. 379. See for details ibid. July 1823, pp. 292–4, 298–307, Aug., pp. 367–8, Sept., pp. 369–71, 379–83.

Judge—no Secretary—only one Writer, and three Members of Council—no Chaplain—one Schoolmaster—only three Medical Men—and a few Missionaries![1]

Editorial, *Royal Gazette*, 12 July 1823. We have to offer an apology to our friends for having allowed so very long a period to elapse between our last and our present Number. To our fellow-colonists, the circumstances which caused the interruption of our labours are but too well known, and therefore do not require an explanation.[2]

It is with great satisfaction that we now congratulate ourselves on our anticipation, that the setting-in of the Rains would dissipate all vestiges of the malignant fever which raged for so long a period. We can now safely say, that we have no sick among the European or native Inhabitants . . . .[3]

Dr. William Barry, Surgeon to the Forces and Acting Deputy Inspector of Hospitals, to Governor MacCarthy, 10 August 1823. At the termination of last year when Your Excellency embarked for the Gold Coast; the Colony of Sierra Leone enjoyed good health, the Rainy season had passed over with such favorable circumstances, as scarcely to warrant the appellation of a sickly one.

The fevers which had occurred presented no peculiar type and the deaths were confined with a very few exceptions to the lower orders of society.

The very superior accommodations which the towns of Sierra Leone now afford, and that confidence which all ranks enjoy under your paternal sway, will doubtless prove of vital importance to the Colony—the general salubrity of which has considerably improved; strange as this assertion may appear after the late melancholy events, I do conscientiously believe, that it proceeds from no erroneous impression for I consider the late awful visitation, only as one of those pestilential blasts whose destructive influence has occasionally been experienced in all our intertropical possessions.

In referring to the records of this office as far back as the year 1816, no detailed case of fever presents itself which appeared to have any resemblance to the one which has so lately committed such horrible ravages, and threatened destruction to the whole of the white population of this interesting establishment. Had any desease similar to the one now under consideration occurred, some trace of it would have been transmitted to us by oral tradition at least, even had it been possible that it should have escaped the observation of those most upright and scientific officers, Doctor Erly, and the late Doctor Nicoll, who were, during that period in charge of the department, and so ably answered the Director General's injunctions in preserving an accurate and consecutive series of the Medical occurrences of this Colony. In the year 1815 a fever appears to have prevailed of a most destructive character and by the histories of the cases noted by Staff Surgeon Cook at that period we find the desease running a rapid and fatal course, attended with great irritability of stomach; in one, the similarity of the one in question is very evident from the following concluding passage in the Statement of a fatal case.

'Some hours before death the skin was deeply tinged with yellow, the eyes were much suffused, the tongue covered with a thick brown fur, and a considerable quantity of *black fluid* was thrown from the stomach.' With the most careful scrutiny I have examined the Medical Registers since that period, but have not been able to detect one instance where this last symptom prevailed, until the present year, when it formed a striking feature of the desease, and uniformly preceded a fatal termination. From the foregoing statement it would appear that Fever has assumed two very different characters on this Coast, the one, that of remittent of uncertain duration and termination, and the other a fever similar to that described by authors

[1] Ibid., Sept. 1823, p. 408. Actually Governor MacCarthy had been informed, of course, of the great mortality. He wrote on 26 June from the Gambia to Earl Bathurst (C.O. 267, vol. lviii, No. 322): 'I must also postpone until I reach Sierra Leone to mention the manner in which I shall fill up, *pro tempore*, all the vacancies in the Civil Department.'

[2] The explanation was probably the prevailing epidemic. No number of this weekly paper had been published since 24 May.

[3] *The Royal Gazette*, 12 July 1823, p. 110.

as the 'Bulam' in which the Black vomit is the predominant feature, and which runs its fatal course in a few days. The latter the occasional visitant of the dry season, the former the continual companion of the wet. Whether they are modifications one of the other rendered more malignant from Atmospherical variations, or terrestial exhalation has not been satisfactorily ascertained. It certainly appeared during the late invasion that the slightest excitement, even external injury was cause sufficient to induce the desease, and that the air, either from the abstraction of some salubrious principle, or from the addition of some deleterious one had partaken of the nature of the atmosphere in some crowded Hospital where the slightest scratch becomes Gangrenous and phagedenic.

With regard to the nature of the fever, it is a standard opinion of Medical writers, that it has its rise in general from the decomposition of animal and vegetable substances, or that its origin may be traced to a marshmiasmal origin.

. . . The desease generally terminated fatally on the fourth or fifth day, at which period the surface of the body, assumed a dingy yellow appearance. In some instances there was low muttering dilerium, in others an oblivious cloud appeared thrown over the recollection; and it became some times not a difficult task to raise a smile on the countenance, when it bore but too evidently the marks of approaching dissolution.

It becomes an interesting question whether we have any evidence of the importation of the Malady which if ascertained would demonstrate the necessity of future strict quarantine; which would subject the mercantile world to much inconvenience and perhaps cases be destructive to the Crews.

The American sloop of War the 'Cyanne', and Merchant Vessel the Caroline, have both become objects of suspicion. I trust however that it will appear, that we have no authority either the one or the other as being the cause of our late dreadful Malady.

The Cyanne arrived here on the twenty fourth of February, but we have indisputable proof of the desease having existed prior to the arrival of that vessel. . . .

The Caroline arrived from the Mediterranean on the 4th November. The Crew were inspected by the Colonial Surgeon Mr Shower who reported in the most positive terms the good health and excellent appearance of the Sailors . . . .

It is worthy to remark that the European females and children were perfectly exempt from this desease, and no cases of malignant fever occurred among the natives, the Maroons or any of the black settlers.

The heretofore much dreaded rains were anxiously looked out for, and as we had anticipated, the desease disappeared; about the commencement of July we had a return of a few days of fine but not particularly hot weather, when a Gentleman who was then convalescent from the Sierra Leone remittent was seized with the malignant desease, which terminated fatally on the fourth day, his death being preceded by symptoms similar to those, I have before enumerated—this solitary case was the last that presented itself.

Your Excellency will perceive that I have not been able to throw much light on the origin of the late fever, which in all countries have been involved in obscurity. For 'shadows clouds and darkness rest upon it' and I cannot conclude in words more appropriate than those used by the celebrated Doctor Bancroft when speaking of the epidemic of the West Indies 'It is still involved in so much obscurity, and placed so little within our power, that neither human ingenuity, nor patriotic zeal, with their most persevering efforts, has as yet been able to hinder its appearance or perhaps materially to check its ravages.'[1]

The Governor to the Church Missionary Society, 13 September 1823. . . . according to the official Report of the principal Medical Officer, not one man of colour, not a woman, or a child, died of that disease . . . . Another no less important mistake is that of comparing the number of those who died with the Census taken on the 1st of January 1822; whereas, at the period of the fatal disease, there were upward

[1] C.O. 267, vol. lviii, No. 327.

of 300 Europeans here. In making such returns, remarks ought to be inserted. I have been too much engaged to look at the List; yet, I am inclined to believe, that, from the Census referred to, not above 20, if so many, died. I will transmit it by a future opportunity.[1]

Editorial, *Royal Gazette*, 13 September 1823. We scarcely need to call the attention of our readers to an extract of a Letter from Sierra Leone. The heavy losses we suffered by the malignant fever which raged at the time it was written, should have inspired a little more caution into the writer. He ought not to have allowed his *fears* or *malice* to get so far the better of his judgment, as to write a downright falsehood—and that for no earthly purpose than to cause the most painful feelings in the minds of our relatives, or of those friends of Africa who conceive, truly or not, that the promotion of the civilization of Africa is, in a great measure, linked to our fate. The 'scene of *woe*' was then sufficiently distressing to satisfy our most bitter enemy. Why then magnify it to a degree unparalleled even in our annals? Why state that out of the population of Sierra Leone, which in the Census of 1822 was 110 males and 18 females (Europeans) exclusive of the Military, 80 had died; when it was known to every individual, that the greater portion of those who died were not at Sierra Leone at the time the Census was taken? However averse we feel to recall, to absent or present friends, the loss of relatives; yet it is a duty we owe to *truth*, to prove our assertions by facts, which we shall do in our next, by giving from official documents the list of those who were present on the 1st January 1822, and those alone could be included in the census. . . .[2]

Editorial, *Royal Gazette*, 20 September 1823. Our duty to our fellow-colonists induced us, in our last number, to express in strong terms, the indignation we justly felt at the cruel and exaggerated reports which had been circulated in England, and which we then pledged ourselves to disprove from official documents. We will now endeavour to redeem that pledge.

By the census taken on the 1st January, 1822, it appears there were 94 Europeans then resident in Freetown, and in the country towns and villages 16; making a total, which agrees with the writer of the letter, of 110. Now, of the 94 then residing in Freetown, 24 have died: but we may remark, that Dr. Nicholl died at Accra on the Gold Coast, Mr. R. Munro drowned himself in a fit of insanity, and the Rev. S. Flood died on his passage to Europe,[3] and are included in the 24; of the number 16, mentioned as living in the mountains, the Rev. William Johnson is the only death, and he also died on his passage to England, having left the Colony in good health.[4] Thus the grand total of deaths among those who were present on the 1st January 1822, to this day, is 25, and not 80 out of 110 persons as our friend states. . . . From this plain statement of facts, we trust our friends in Europe will, in future, be a little more cautious in receiving and circulating the dreadful accounts which some persons, from motives it would be difficult to develope, occasionally think it worth their while to publish about the ravages of Death in this Colony.[5]

Editorial, *Royal Gazette*, 27 September 1823. In our last, we exposed the fallacy of the statement of the Navigator to the Isles de Loss, as to the male European population . . . . We have to account for the European females who were noticed in the census, and who, from motives easily seen through, are unnoticed by the Navigator. On the 1st of January, 1822, we had 18 European Ladies in the Peninsula; 10 residing in Freetown, and 8 in the Mountains. We lost one out of the 10 (Mrs. Lisk who died on her passage to Europe); the remaining 9 are either in the Colony, or have returned to their friends; from the 8 in the Mountains, 3 have gone

---

[1] *Missionary Register*, Jan. 1824, p. 5. The Governor apparently did not send any further information.   [2] *The Royal Gazette*, 13 Sept. 1823, pp. 146–7.

[3] He was sick when he boarded the ship and died three days later; see *Missionary Register*, July 1823, pp. 293, 304.

[4] '. . . there can be no doubt but that he carried with him on board the seeds of the fatal disease' (ibid., p. 302), and he died after seven days (see ibid., p. 293).

[5] *The Royal Gazette*, 20 Sept. 1823, p. 151.

to England, and 5 to this day are residing there. Thus after nearly two years, and the most fatal dry season ever experienced by the oldest inhabitants, out of a population of 128, we have lost, including all casualties, 26 individuals—a severe loss undoubtedly, and which will long be deplored by those who wish well to Africa.[1]

Editorial, *Royal Gazette*, 18 October 1823. We have again inserted an extract of two letters from Sierra Leone.[2] The same regard is paid to *truth* as in the former report. The medical officers did *not state* that the fever which was raging at the time, was *imported* by the Caroline or the American frigate; they have given it as their opinion, that the fever was not *imported*—that it was not contagious. It is also hinted that, out of a population of 100 or 110, we lost 80 Europeans. Since that period, on a reference to the shipping returns, it will appear that about 30 have either returned to Europe, or gone to Cape Coast, or Cape de Verd Islands, and only two or three have arrived; yet *strange,—wonderful strange,*—we have now upwards of 100 Europeans in the Colony, exclusive of the Military and sailors.[3]

The questions that arise are as follows:

(1) How many Europeans died in 1823 in the Colony? According to the Missionary Philip Vaughan 7 died from 3 to 31 December 1822 and 70 from 1 January to 18 June 1823. How many died in the following months has not been reported. According to *Handbook of Sierra Leone* the epidemic of yellow fever 'proved fatal to 89 Europeans'.[4] It seems, therefore, likely that the total number of deaths in the Colony in 1823 was approximately 100. The statement that 'nearly eighty gentlemen have died within six weeks' was undoubtedly wrong.

(2) How many of the 128 European civil residents enumerated at the census of 1 January 1822 died up to September 1823? The Governor was 'inclined to believe that . . . not above 20, if so many, died'. The editor of *The Royal Gazette* stated that 22 had died in the Colony, 1 on the Gold Coast, and 3 on their passage to Europe. But the survivors, of course, had not been exposed to death in the Colony during the whole period. Some of those who had left the Colony before the rainy season of 1822 had not returned, and, according to the editor of *The Royal Gazette*, about 30 had sailed before the rainy season of 1823 and were not in the Colony in September.

(3) How many died of the European civil residents who had come since 1 January 1822? It is impossible to answer this question. The editor of *The Royal Gazette* said that 'the greater portion of those who died were not at Sierra Leone at the time the Census was taken'.[5] But this greater portion included also people who were not civil residents.[6]

As regards mortality during the rainy season of 1824, the editor of *The Royal Gazette* stated on 11 September:

During the last week there have been experienced, in various parts of the Peninsula, heavy thunder storms, attended with vivid lightning—sure presages of the termination of the wet weather. In congratulating our fellow colonists on this prospect of

---

[1] *The Royal Gazette*, 27 Sept. 1823, p. 155.

[2] For the letter of 15 May concerning mortality see p. 294, above.

[3] Ibid., 18 Oct. 1823, p. 167.   [4] *Handbook* (1925), p. 36.

[5] Among the new-comers who died between March and June 1823 were 3 wives and 2 children of missionaries; see *Missionary Register 1823*, pp. 299, 367, 380.

[6] In 1823, 7 officers died, and there occurred in addition in the Military Hospital 2 deaths of Seamen and Marines of the Royal Navy, 32 deaths of Seamen of Merchant Vessels, and 15 deaths of Distressed Europeans (some of the latter probably not being civil residents).

the approach of the dry season, we should, however, be truly grateful to Divine Providence for the general healthy period since the commencement of the rainy months, and which has in a great degree divested them of their terrors, even to *new* comers and *alarmists*. The number of Europeans in the colony during such time has been equal to those of any preceding year, while the deaths among the higher classes have not exceeded four or five, and the casualties of the lower order, including seamen, have been, compared with any former period, equally small, and this not-withstanding our having had (in addition to several merchantmen in the general trade) two ships loading Timber up the river during the heaviest rains of the season— a circumstance which, in adverting to, we must condemn as an unnecessary exposure of the lives of the mariners engaged in navigating such vessels . . . .[1]

How many of 'the lower order, including seamen,' died it is impossible to tell. In the Military Hospital there occurred in 1824, 8 deaths of Distressed Europeans and 11 deaths of merchant seamen. But merchant seamen were excluded from this hospital in the course of the year.[2]

The effect of mortality on the number of civilian residents in those years is difficult to appraise. They numbered 128 on 1 January 1822. Few apparently died before the outbreak of yellow fever; most of those who had gone to England before the rainy season returned; and there were many new-comers. It is possible, therefore, that, although the epidemic had claimed some victims by 15 February 1823, the Colony had then 'the advantage of a number of European residents far beyond what it has had at any former time'. On 18 October, when both the epidemic of yellow fever and the rainy season were over, the editor of *The Royal Gazette* said that although since April about 30 Europeans had sailed and only 2 or 3 had arrived there were 'upwards of 100' civil residents in the Colony. This statement can have been correct only if the civil residents on 15 February had been something like 160.[3] But if their number had been as high as that, the editor's statement that the number of Europeans during the rainy season of 1824 'has been equal to those of any preceding year' can hardly have been correct.

In 1825 *The Royal Gazette* did not mention mortality at all, although, owing to the ravages of 'intermittent fever' among the military, more Europeans died in Sierra Leone than in any earlier or later year, and as I did not have access to *The Royal Gazette* for the following decades, I shall confine myself to quoting from other sources.

1825–1830. From 1825 to 1830, the deaths of the governors averaged more than one a year.[4]

[1] *The Royal Gazette*, 11 Sept. 1824, p. 351. [2] See ibid., 22 Jan. 1825, p. 427.
[3] The Governor said that 'at the period of the fatal disease, there were upward of 300 Europeans here', but this figure included all Europeans who were not resident civilians, and it may have been an overstatement.
[4] *Report from Committee on West Coast of Africa*, 1842, Part II, p. 252. See also *Handbook of Sierra Leone* (1925), p. 69: 'West Africa has throughout its known history borne the reputation of being unhealthy for Europeans, and of the four West African Colonies probably none (in this respect) stinks in the nostrils of uninformed opinion as vilely as Sierra Leone. That this Colony at one time did deserve to be called "The White Man's Grave" cannot be doubted; a glance at the Table of Governors . . . will show that from the foundation of the Colony up to the year 1885 no less than ten Governors (in addition to eight Acting Governors) died while on the coast, or on their way to England; no account is taken of the many more who must have died shortly after landing in England; and if Governors were thus penalised it is unlikely that lesser men escaped more lightly.'

1827. If Sierra Leone be free from the stagnant waters which are supposed to influence the climate of St. Mary's, and less subject to the periodical fogs which are considered to be so injurious on the Gold Coast; these comparative advantages seem to be counterbalanced by the greater quantity and longer duration of the rains, and the consequent exhalations which take place at the commencement of the dry season. Freetown is supposed to suffer particularly from this cause, for being situated near the foot of the mountains, it becomes in some measure a receptacle for the decayed vegetable matter which the continued rains wash from their sides.

Freetown, as well as the rest of the peninsula, enjoys an advantage which none of the other settlements possess, in a constant and plentiful supply of excellent water.[1]

1829. But in addition to the annual sickly season, which generally carried off several Europeans, particularly new comers, the coast was again visited in 1829 with an epidemic, similar to that of 1823, which greatly reduced the number of the Europeans at Sierra-Leone, not sparing even the oldest settlers.[2]

1831. Respecting the habits of the male Europeans it must be confessed, that they would be injurious to health, on many grounds, in any climate, but they are especially inimical to it in Sierra Leone. They are too frequently loose, careless, and dissipated; and, although some improvement has occurred in the last few years, there is still an abundance of room for amendment.[3]

1840. Either 16 or 17 Europeans died . . . .[4]

1841. Those who are not absolutely ill, are always ailing; in fact, all the white people seem to belong to a population of invalids. The sallowness of their complexion, the listlessness of their looks, the attenuation of their limbs, the instability of gait, and the feebleness of the whole frame, that are so observable in this climate, are but too evident signs, even where organic disease has not yet set in, that the disordered state of the functions which goes under the name of impaired health exists, and in none is it more painfully evident than in the general appearance of the European women and children in this colony. Indeed to the latter, the climate is allowed to be almost universally fatal.[5]

Freetown, in fact, is placed in a focus of pestilential vapours, concentrated there by the circumstances of its position; and at particular seasons these vapours are to be seen a few feet above the level of the soil, before the sun has been sufficiently powerful to dispel them.

At other places in the peninsula where fresh water mingles with the sea, as in the neighbourhood of King Tom's Point, the exhalation that arises from the stagnant waters in the shallows there at sunset, and I am told before sunrise, are most offensive, and cannot fail to be most prejudicial to health.[6]

1847. The comparative healthiness which the colony had enjoyed for some years previously to 1847 had begun to excite hopes that some permanent improvement had taken place in its climate.

The fearful epidemic however, in the forms of yellow fever and of malignant remittent fever which visited the colony during that year, has shown that such hopes were delusive, and that the settlement still merits the fatal celebrity which it has acquired.

In the rainy season of that year 11 European residents were carried off by yellow fever, 6 by remittent fever, and 6 by other diseases, no doubt partly aggravated if not induced by climatorial influence.[7]

[1] *Report of Commissioners of Inquiry*, 1827, First Part, p. 105.

[2] Fox, p. 191. For details concerning this yellow fever epidemic see Augustin, *History of Yellow Fever*, pp. 314–16.   [3] Boyle, p. 30.

[4] Statement of Colonial Secretary before Committee on West Coast of Africa, 26 Apr. 1841, *Report*, Part II, p. 354. The number of Europeans in the Colony on 31 Dec. 1840 was only 83 as compared with 99 in 1839.

[5] Report of Commissioner of Inquiry R. R. Madden, ibid., p. 244.   [6] Ibid., p. 245.

[7] *State of Colonial Possessions 1847*, p. 196. The European population apparently decreased in the course of the year from 115 to 95.

1848. During the year 1848 the colony has been comparatively healthy, only nine deaths have occurred among the resident white population, and of those only two can be attributed to fever or direct climatorial influence.[1]

1859. ... the [yellow] fever broke out in April, 1859, and became epidemic in May. There had been an influx of Europeans during the past year, and 106 fell victims to the disease between April, 1859, and January, 1860.[2]

1865. In the *Statistical Report of the Health of the Navy for 1865*, (published in 1868), pp. 196–208, it is stated that 'during Michaelmas' of that year, a very malignant type of yellow fever was prevailing on shore at Sierra Leone, causing a mortality of seventy-five per cent. amongst the European population.[3]

1866. The epidemic of 1866, was one of the severest experienced in the colony in many years. Between the months of April and October, one hundred Europeans died at Freetown.[4]

1872. During my brief experience of Sierra Leone (that is since February of this year), 24 Europeans have died out of a population of 98.[5] The medical officers assert that this is the highest death-rate in any part of Her Majesty's dominions. I find, however, that the extraordinary sickness and mortality is confined to Freetown. The mountain district, according to the Registrar-General's Returns, appears to be as healthy as any part of England, or indeed as Madeira, the climate of which it closely resembles.

I therefore venture to suggest, for your Lordship's consideration, whether the seat of Government might not properly be removed to the mountain villages of Leicester or Regent, which are only three or four miles from Freetown; or at least whether a vote might not be sanctioned for building a few substantial bungalows for Government officials in the healthy districts lying above the vapours that rise from the Freetown river, and above the range of the more active malarial influences.

Though no expense will be spared to keep the town clean, I fear the Government must not be too sanguine as to the result. With the exception of the Mahomedans, the habits of the people, and of some of the European residents—as the medical officers point out in the Reports I had the honour of transmitting to your Lordship in Despatch No. 136, of the 20th November, 1872—are very bad. One of the main duties I have urged upon the Sanitary Inspector and his staff is that of teaching the inhabitants the dry-earth system; but it will take considerable time before it can be expected to be generally adopted.

There is another reason why we must not expect too much from Government action in this matter. Your Lordship and other Secretaries of State have frequently written on this subject, and my predecessors have tried many experiments to improve the health of Freetown. As a result of many years' observations, it is alleged that sickness sometimes breaks out in the cleanest parts of the town, whilst apparently dirty localities escape.

For my own part, having narrowly watched the phenomena affecting public health here, I venture to express the opinion that owing to its situation Freetown is radically unhealthy. It is near the mouth of a broad river laden with vegetable decomposition, which is partially driven back to the town twice every day by the tide; and at its rear it is hemmed in by a range of hills, which tend to keep the products of evaporation suspended over the streets. During my morning walks up Leicester Hill I frequently observe the river vapours lying motionless over the houses of Freetown.

[1] Ibid. *1848*, p. 304.

[2] Augustin, p. 322. See also Yellow Fever Commission (West Africa), *Second Report*, p. 35: 'Yellow Fever was epidemic in Freetown and carried off 106 Europeans during this year.'

[3] Augustin, p. 324.

[4] Ibid. See also Lamprey, p. 595, Yellow Fever Commission (West Africa), *Second Report*, p. 35, and *Handbook of Sierra Leone* (1925), p. 40. I suspect that mortality in 1859, 1865, and 1866 has been overstated.

[5] 'This excessive mortality does not include all the victims of the pestilence, as many died on shipboard in trying to escape from the colony' (Augustin, p. 326).

The general conclusion at which I have arrived respecting the state of the public health in these Settlements is that they are unsuited for European residents.

I venture to repeat what I said in my Despatch of the 11th of October, 1872:—
'Wherever it can possibly be done, I would strongly recommend dispensing with the service of Europeans on this coast.'

Fortunately this can be done, and to a much greater extent than is generally imagined. It is no disparagement to the other members of my Legislative Council to mention the fact that the two ablest members of that body are both pure negroes. The best scholar on the Coast—a man who knows Hebrew, Greek, Latin, French, German, Italian, and Arabic, and is well read in the literature of these languages—is Mr. Blyden, a pure negro. The most intelligent clergy of the Church of England in the various Settlements are the native pastors. Among the most trustworthy clerks in the public service are the native officials.[1]

From 1886 on, European death figures are available for each year, but they were for some time not all-inclusive. The Medical Report for 1902 contains a table which 'shows the number of European deaths since 1886, the first column comprising those landed on account of illness or for burial, and the second the deaths which took place among the actual residents of the City [Freetown], differentiating between those which took place from climatic or other causes'.[2] But the first column is headed 'Landed for Burial', and 'those landed on account of illness' seem to have been included in some years among the deceased residents.[3] From 1901 on, the military deaths which formerly had been included among the deaths of residents were given separately. Thus the Medical Report for 1909 showed the European deaths, distinguishing (1) 'Landed from Vessels',[4] (2) 'Resident in Freetown', and (3) 'Garrison'. The Medical Report for 1910 showed the European deaths in 1901–10, distinguishing (1) 'Landed from Vessels', (2) 'Protectorate', (3) 'Colony', and (4) 'Military (Freetown)', but gave for the Protectorate figures only for 1910, noting 'Not previously recorded', and entered under Colony the same figures as had been given in prior reports under Freetown. It seems safe, therefore, to assume that up to 1909 all statistics excluded the deaths of civilians resident outside Freetown. Tables 37 and 38 summarize the statistics for 1886–1909.

If these figures can be trusted,[5] mortality in 1886–91, with the exception of 1889, was low. It was unfavourable in most years from 1892 to 1900.

---

[1] Governor Pope Hennessy to the Earl of Kimberley, 31 Dec. 1872, *Colonial Possessions Reports 1873*, Part II, 2nd Division, pp. 19–20. A similar plea for the employment of many more negroes in Government service had been made as far back as 22 Apr. 1830 by Acting Governor Fraser in a Dispatch to Under-Secretary of State Hay (see C.O. 267, vol. cii), in reply to a Dispatch from the latter, 13 Dec. 1829 (see C.O. 268, vol. xxviii, pp. 313–14).   [2] *Medical Report 1902*, p. 9.

[3] The table shows for 1894, 15 deaths of residents in Freetown, but the Assistant Colonial Surgeon reported (*Colonial Reports, Sierra Leone 1894*, p. 10): 'The number of deaths among Europeans was 16 (including one case on board a steamer in port, and three cases that died within 36 hours after landing in Freetown from the rivers).' The table shows for 1900 likewise 15 deaths of residents in Freetown but of these 'two were landed very ill and died here' (*Medical Report 1900*, p. 5).

[4] This term continued to be used in a loose manner. *Medical Report 1905*, p. 5, gave for 1896–1902 as 'Landed from Vessels' the same figures as had been given in earlier reports for 'Landed for burial', although the figure, at least for 1900, included only those landed for burial and excluded those who 'were landed very ill and died' in Freetown. Later figures, on the other hand, apparently excluded those landed for burial. See, for example, *Colonial Reports, Sierra Leone 1923*, p. 25: 'Two Europeans died on board ships in Freetown Harbour in addition to the above.'

[5] It is hard to believe that not one resident European died in 1886.

TABLE 37. *European Deaths, Sierra Leone, 1886–1900*[1]

Year	Landed from vessels	Resident in Freetown		Total	Year	Landed from vessels	Resident in Freetown		Total
		'Climatic'	Otherwise				'Climatic'	Otherwise	
1886	3	—	—	3	1894	1	13	2	16
1887	4	—	2	6	1895	—	4	2	6
1888	1	1	3	5	1896	3	5	2	10
1889	—	3	6	9	1897	2	13	—	15
1890	2	3	1	6	1898	2	8	4	14
1891	5	3	2	10	1899	—	3	6	9
1892	4	6	2	12	1900	4	8	7	19
1893	5	4	4	13					

[1] See *Medical Report 1902*, p. 9.

TABLE 38. *European Deaths, Sierra Leone, 1901–9*[1]

Year	Landed from vessels	Resident in Freetown		Garrison		Total
		'Climatic'	Otherwise	'Climatic'	Otherwise	
1901	—	5	2	3	—	10
1902	3	3	—	1	1	8
1903	2	2	2	2	3	11
1904	3	2	3	2	2	12
1905	3	2	2	1	—	8
1906	3	2	1	1	1	8
1907	2	3	3	2	3	13
1908	1	1	6	3	2	13
1909	3	3	—	—	—	6

[1] See *Medical Report 1909*, p. 6.

In these nine years deaths among the residents of Freetown, who probably averaged less than 200,[1] numbered 93 or about 10 per year. Some quotations may illustrate the view of the administration.

1893. On the whole the health of the European population was good, there being only eight deaths registered among the residents.[2]

1894. The public health during the year was most unsatisfactory; a good deal of sickness was prevalent among the natives and European residents.[3]

1895. The public health generally was fairly good in 1895 as compared with the previous year.

The number of deaths among Europeans was only six as against 16 in 1894; but there were a considerable number of serious cases invalided.[4]

1896. The Public Health throughout the Colony was fairly good. . . .

The number of deaths among Europeans was, however, 11, as against 6 in the previous year, and 6 European Officials died, while 6 were invalided.[5]

1897. The number of deaths among Europeans was 19, as against 11 in the previous year, and six in 1895.[6]

[1] According to the censuses of 1891 and 1901 the European residents in Freetown numbered 185 and 228 respectively (see *Census Report 1891*, pp. 3, 5; *1901*, pp. 4, 6; *Colonial Reports, Sierra Leone 1902*, p. 20). Many Europeans who at the time of the census (April) were in Freetown went on leave during the rainy season.

[2] Report of Colonial Surgeon, quoted ibid. *1893*, p. 13.

[3] Report of Assistant Colonial Surgeon, quoted ibid. *1894*, p. 10.   [4] Ibid. *1895*, p. 13.

[5] Ibid. *1896*, p. 18. The 11 deaths probably refer to the whole Colony.

[6] Ibid. *1897*, p. 22. The 19 deaths probably refer to the whole Colony.

From the beginning of this century, mortality, as in the Gold Coast, was considerably lower.[1] The Annual Colonial Report for 1905 said:

There were eight deaths among Europeans during the year.

Of these, five occurred among the European population resident in Freetown, and three were landed from steamers. Taking the European population of Freetown at 270,[2] the number as ascertained at the last census, these five deaths give a death rate of 18·5 per 1,000, the lowest recorded for many years. If the two deaths from rheumatic fever and chloroform poisoning be excluded, we obtain a death rate of 11·1 per 1,000 from climatic causes. In connection with the death rate, attention may be called to the trite but most misleading description, 'Sierra Leone, or the White Man's Grave.' With the exception of the Gambia, Sierra Leone (especially the Protectorate) is probably much more healthy than any other British Colony on the West Coast, not excluding Northern Nigeria. The expression 'White Man's Grave' became well-known in olden days, when all the places on the coast were under the Sierra Leone Government.[3]

It has been occasionally claimed that the improvement in European mortality followed the establishment of bungalows on Hill Station, an elevated place which certainly had great advantages as compared with Freetown. It is important, therefore, to note that the reduction in mortality occurred several years before the opening of Hill Station.

1905. . . . a mountain railway has been constructed, and a cantonment built on the hills, thus permitting of the Europeans residing in the hills and of their segregation from infected natives.[4]

The bungalows are now complete, and the health of those who are fortunate enough to reside there has been very satisfactory.[5] One or two cases of malarial fever have occurred there, but these have been invariably in officers who have been recently in the Protectorate, and I am not aware of any case being acquired in the cantonment.

It is much to be regretted that no European firm has yet seen its way to build a residence for their employés at Hill Station, though a large and desirable site has been reserved for them. It is to be hoped that this reluctance will soon be overcome.[6]

[1] Some statements in the official reports at the beginning of this century are not quite clear. *Colonial Reports 1902*, p. 19, say: 'The European death rate can only be given for Freetown, and does not include members of the garrison. Eight deaths were registered in Freetown during the year.' But the 8 deceased include 2 belonging to the garrison. *Colonial Reports 1903*, p. 21, says: 'Eleven Europeans, including three persons belonging to the garrison and two persons who died on board ship, were buried at Freetown during the year.' The persons belonging to the garrison actually numbered 5. *Medical Report 1902*, p. 10, gives as death-rates of Europeans resident in Freetown for 1891 and 1899–1902, 26, 33, 56, 37, and 19 respectively.

[2] This figure includes 41 Syrians and 1 Egyptian, while the 5 deaths probably refer to Europeans only.

[3] *Colonial Reports, Sierra Leone 1905*, pp. 44–5. See also ibid. *1906*, p. 37.

[4] Principal Medical Officer, Dr. Prout, *Medical Report 1905*, p. 18.

[5] Three years earlier the Principal Medical Officer said: 'So far as those who will have the good fortune to live on the hills is concerned, there can be no doubt that this is the most important step in the direction of health preservation which has yet been taken. At the same time I must confess that I am not one of those who think that the European is the only factor to be considered in this matter. While it is essential that those upon whom the administration of the Colony devolves, and those upon whom its material prosperity depends, the merchants, should be placed in as favourable conditions as possible, and while we cannot fail to recognise that under the conditions in town, surrounded by native dwellings, swarming with infected children, this is at present impossible, yet it should not be lost sight of that the improvement of the health of the natives is of equal importance, and the measures which have been indicated should be carried on *pari passu* with the present scheme' (ibid. *1902*, pp. 18–19).

[6] Ibid. *1905*, p. 8.

1907. . . . the number of deaths from climatic causes among the Europeans resident in the Colony was more than in the previous two years; this increase is very probably due to the increase in the actual European resident population from 300 in 1906 to 550 in 1907, the number of deaths from these causes being five gives a death rate of nine for 1,000 from climatic diseases, which compares most favourably with former years.[1]

The improvement in the health of Europeans is to a large extent due, in my opinion, to residence at Hill Station, where for the past three years a large number of the European officials on duty at headquarters reside.[2]

Hill Station with its railway, undoubtedly the finest and the most successful anti-malarial measure ever carried out by any West African Colony, continues its good repute for its almost complete freedom from fever, mosquitos and other insect pests.[3]

With all the advantages to health and comfort, so far as Europeans are concerned, that accrue from this great sanitary scheme, it seems to me inexplicable that up to the present the Cable Company is the only European firm in Freetown that has taken advantage of the opening of Hill Station as a residential site by erecting a bungalow there for the use of its European staff. We are accustomed to hear so much talk about what certain people at home have done for West Africa, and the interest they seem to have taken in measures having for their object the improvement of the health conditions prevailing there, that one cannot help being struck with the apathy and indifference shown in this particular instance. But, when a large firm does not supply even quinine for the use of its European staff, it would be too much to expect them to go to the expense of building residential bungalows at Hill Station.[4]

From 1910 to 1927 the statistics are more complete than for any earlier or later period. One set of figures showed the deaths, distinguishing (1) 'Landed from Vessels'; (2) Colony and Protectorate, Non-Military;[5] (3) Colony and Protectorate, Military.[6] Apart from that, figures were published showing the deaths of Government Officials, of Military, and of non-officials.[7] The data in the second series for some years differ from those given in the first set.

---

[1] This statement is quite misleading. The death figures refer to Freetown and not to the Colony. The number of deaths from 'climatic causes' was higher than in the previous five years. The European resident population of Freetown did of course not increase from 300 in 1906 to 550 in 1907. The Annual Colonial Report for 1906 (p. 37) put it at 450, and the Report for 1907, in discussing mortality, said (p. 32): 'The number of Europeans in Freetown in 1907 was estimated to be 550, but this is a very rough estimate, and any inferences based on those figures must necessarily be speculative.' The 1911 census showed only 506 European residents in Freetown (see *Census Report 1911*, p. 9). [2] Principal Medical Officer, *Medical Report 1907*, p. 6. [3] Ibid., p. 10.

[4] Ibid., p. 11. All efforts to interest private firms in Hill Station failed. See, for example, ibid, *1913*, p. 7: 'The total number of residents at Hill Station was 65, made up as follows:—Government Officials 57, Military 5, Missionaries 2, The African Cable Company 1.' While nearly one-quarter of all Government Officials resided in Hill Station, only 1 per cent. of the non-officials lived there. Nor were the hopes fulfilled that mosquitoes would be prevented from breeding on the hill. In 1914, when 48 Government Officials resided there, the Medical Report said (p. 9): 'Although the general health of the residents was satisfactory, no less than ten officials suffered from malarial fever, the diagnosis in each case being confirmed microscopically.'

[5] For 1910 separate figures were given for Colony and for Protectorate.

[6] For 1910–12 the heading was 'Military (Freetown)'. According to the 1911 census there were 299 European soldiers in Freetown and 55 in Wilberforce; see *Census Report 1911*, p. 9.

[7] Some such figures had also been published for earlier years. For 1900 five deaths were reported. 'This, however, must be regarded as absolutely abnormal, as for many years there were no deaths among European officials' (*Medical Reports 1900 and 1901*, p. 5). In 1901 no European Official died. Of the 10 deaths 'three took place among the military, three among the mercantile community, two were ministers of religion, one was a mechanic, and one a child of $3\frac{1}{2}$ months'

From 1928 on, the Medical Reports show only the deaths of resident civilians, distinguishing between Government Officials and non-officials.

TABLE 39. *Deaths of Europeans, Sierra Leone, 1910–27*

	A¹							B²			
	Landed from Vessels		Colony and Protectorate								
			Civilian		Military						
Year	'Climatic'	Other	'Climatic'	Other	'Climatic'	Other	Total	Officials	Military	Non-officials	Total
1910	—	—	9	2	2	2	15	2	..	..	..
1911	2	5	2	1	—	1	11	1	..	..	..
1912	—	5	3	3	3	2	16	4	5	2	11
1913	—	—	4	1	3	2	10	3	5	2	10
1914	—	—	4	1	3	—	8	—	3	5	8
1915	1	1	7	3	2	—	14	2	2	10	14
1916	3	3	2	1	3	4	16	1	9	6	16
1917	—	12	4	2	1	3	22	2	..	..	..
1918	—	46	—	6	3	7	62	6	56³	..	..
1919	3	3	4	6	2	—	18	1	2	9	12
1920	—	2	5	3	—	—	10	4	—	5	9
1921	—	1	5	3	—	—	9	2	—	6	8
1922	1	1	5	4	1	1	13	2	2	7	11
1923	—	—	4	1	2	—	7	—	2	..	..
1924	1	—	3	2	2	—	8	1	1	7	9
1925	1	1	3	2	—	1	8	2	1	3	6
1926	2	2	1	6	1	—	12	1	—	8	9
1927	3	1	4	2	—	1	11	3	1	5	9

[1] See *Medical Report 1911*, p. 11; *Sierra Leone, Colonial Reports 1920*, p. 22, *1927*, p. 26.
[2] See *Medical Report 1910*, p. 7; *1911*, p. 9; *1912*, p. 11; *1913*, p. 8; *1914*, p. 9; *1915*, p. 8; *1916*, p. 10; *1917*, p. 7; *1918*, pp. 6–7; *1919*, pp. 7–8; *1920*, pp. 8, 10; *1921*, pp. 8, 11; *1922*, p. 16; *1923*, p. 13; *1924*, p. 14; *1925*, p. 7; *1926*, pp. 9, 12; *1927*, pp. 9–10, 13.
[3] Garrison 10, Ex-Transport 46.

TABLE 40. *Deaths of European Civilians, Sierra Leone, 1928–38*[1]

Civilians	1928	1929	1930	1931	1932	1933	1934	1935	1936	1937	1938
Officials	1	1	—	1	—	1	—	3	—	1	—
Non-officials	4	5	5	3	6	3	—	3	4	1	3
Total	5	6	5	4	6	4	—	6	4	2	3

[1] See *Medical Report 1930*, pp. 5–6; *1933*, pp. 5–6; *1936*, pp. 5–6; *1938*, pp. 5–6.

The figures in Tables 37–40 comprise only deaths occurring in Sierra Leone. The yearly *Vital Statistics of Non-Native Officials*, on the other hand, include deaths on leave. The data are summarized in Table 41. It appears that the average death-rate in 1921–38 was 9 for 1,000.

There was no marked change in mortality among European officials in the course of the last two decades, and it is interesting to note that there was apparently likewise no definite trend in the incidence of malaria. The numbers of days lost through malaria in 1921–38 per 100 resident European officials were 651, 541, 312, 271, 223, 264, 198, 233, 173, 202, 145, 210, 243, 413, 391, 459, 231, and 251 respectively.[1] The numbers averaged, in

(*Medical Reports 1900 and 1901*, p. 42). The deaths of European Officials in 1902–9 were 1, 0, 0, 1, 1, 2, 2, and 2 respectively (see ibid. *1902*, p. 10; *Colonial Reports 1903*, p. 21, *1904*, p. 30; *Medical Report 1905*, p. 6, *1906*, p. 5, *1907*, p. 7, *1908*, p. 7, *1909*, p. 7). Of the 12 European residents in Freetown deceased in 1908, 2 were Officials, 5 Military, and 5 'Commercial, &c.' (see ibid. *1908*, p. 14). Of 5 European residents in the Colony (and Protectorate ?) deceased in 1909, 2 were Officials and 3 'Commercial, &c.' (see ibid. *1909*, pp. 6, 7, 12).

[1] See ibid. *1925*, p. 5; *1930*, p. 11; *1935*, p. 9; *1938*, p. 10.

the three 6-year periods 1921–6, 1927–32, and 1933–8, 377, 194, and 331 respectively.

TABLE 41. *Deaths of Male Non-Native Officials, Sierra Leone, 1921–38*[1]

Year	Average number	Deaths	Death-rate per 1,000	Year	Average number	Deaths	Death-rate per 1,000	Year	Average number	Deaths	Death-rate per 1,000
1921	229	3	13	1927	250	3	12	1933	198	2	10
1922	206	2	10	1928	269	1	4	1934	190	—	—
1923	193	1	5	1929	283	4	14	1935	186	4	22
1924	199	4	20	1930	275	—	—	1936	186	2	11
1925	217	3	14	1931	249	5	20	1937	237	2	8
1926	246	1	4	1932	221	1	5	1938	214	—	—

[1] See *West Africa, Vital Statistics of Non-Native Officials, Returns for 1921*, p. 2, to *1938*, p. 2. Figures prior to 1930 apparently include females.

2. Mortality of Asiatics

Figures concerning mortality have hardly ever been published. In 1910 there were reported 6 deaths of Syrians, of whom 3 succumbed to yellow fever.[1] In 1933 the number of recorded deaths among Syrians was 13.[2] Both statements no doubt understated mortality.

[1] See ibid. *1910*, pp. 5, 47.   [2] See ibid. *1933*, p. 30.

CHAPTER III

GAMBIA[1]

I. CENSUS-TAKING

1. Up to 1931

CENSUSES were taken in 1851, 1871, and thereafter every ten years up to 1931. From 1901 on they included the Protectorate. Each census has been authorized by an enabling Ordinance *ad hoc.*[2] The census of 1931 was taken in accordance with the following Ordinance:[3]

1. This Ordinance may be cited for all purposes as The Census Ordinance, 1930.

2. (*a*) A Census of the Colony and Protectorate of the Gambia shall be taken in the year one thousand nine hundred and thirty-one.

(*b*) In the Island of St. Mary the Census shall be taken on the 24th day of April and in the manner provided in sections six, seven and eight hereof.

(*c*) In the Protectorate the Census shall be taken between the 24th day of March and the 24th day of May (both inclusive), and in such manner as the Census Commissioner, to be appointed under the provisions of this Ordinance, may direct; and such particulars shall be given and such returns made as the said Census Commissioner may direct.

3. The duty of taking such Census shall be performed by a Census Commissioner appointed by the Governor, and such other persons as may be appointed by the Governor or by this Ordinance as Enumerators.

4. There shall be a Clerk to the Census Commissioner who shall be nominated by the Governor.

5. In the Protectorate the Travelling Commissioners shall be the Enumerators for their respective Provinces and it shall be lawful for the Governor to appoint such assistant Enumerators at such remuneration as he may think fit.

6. (1) Schedules to be approved by the Governor shall be prepared by the Census Commissioner for the purpose of being filled up by or on behalf of the several occupiers of dwelling houses in the Island of St. Mary, with the following particulars, and no other, namely, particulars showing the name, sex, age, race, religion, profes-

---

[1] The Gambia consists of (1) the Island of St. Mary administered as a Colony; (2) the rest of the Colony (British Kombo, the Ceded Mile including Albreda, the territories of Brefet and Bajana, and MacCarthy Island) which around 1900 was placed under the Protectorate system of administration; and (3) the Protectorate (a long narrow strip of territory on each bank of the river Gambia). In the official statistics the Gambia has been subdivided for several decades into two areas only, viz. (1) the Island of St. Mary, and (2) the Protectorate, comprising both the areas of the Colony administered as part of the Protectorate and the Protectorate proper. All recent data referring to 'the Colony' cover, therefore, only the Island of St. Mary. This island to-day 'contains few inhabitants outside the Town of Bathurst and therefore practically speaking the figures given for the Island are in effect those for the Town of Bathurst' (*Census Report 1931*, p. 3).

[2] See Ordinance No. 1 of 1851 (28 Mar.), listed in *Blue Book 1851*, p. 56; No. 4 of 1871 (23 Mar.), reprinted in *Ordinances of the Gambia 1818–79*, pp. 390–2; No. 2 of 1881 (14 Mar.), reprinted ibid. *1879–82*, pp. 24–5; No. 3 of 1891 (14 Mar.), *Gambia Ordinances 1889–1904*; No. 2 of 1901 (6 Mar.), ibid.; No. 1 of 1911 (6 Feb.), *Government Gazette, Colony of the Gambia*, 11 Feb. 1911, pp. 60–3. The census of 1921 was authorized by Ordinance No. 16 of 1920 (31 Dec.), ibid. 31 Dec. 1920, pp. 358–60, reprinted in Colony of the Gambia, *Ordinances, &c., 1920*, pp. 43–6.

[3] Ordinance No. 6 of 1930 (11 Aug.), 'An Ordinance for taking the Census of the Colony and Protectorate of the Gambia', *Government Gazette*, 15 Aug. 1930, pp. 351–3, reprinted in *Ordinances, &c., 1930*, pp. 13–17. The wording of this Ordinance was the same as that of the Census Ordinance, 1921.

sion or occupation, degree of elementary education, condition as to marriage, relationship to head of family, and birth place of every living person who abode in every house on the night of the Census Day, and showing also whether any such person was blind or deaf and dumb, or imbecile, or lunatic; and also, where the occupier is not in occupation of a whole house, the number of rooms occupied by him.

(2) Every enumerator for the Island of St. Mary shall in the course of the week previous to the Census Day leave or cause to be left at every dwelling house within his district one or more of the said schedules, for the occupier or occupiers thereof or of any part thereof; and in every such schedule shall be plainly expressed that it is to be filled up by the occupier with or for whom it is left, and that the Enumerator will collect all such schedules within his district on the day next following the Census Day.

(3) Every occupier with or for whom any such schedule has been so left, shall fill up the schedule to the best of his or her knowledge and belief, so far as relates to all persons dwelling in the house, storey, or apartment occupied by him or her and shall sign his or her name thereto, and shall deliver the schedule so filled up, or cause the same to be delivered, to the Enumerator when required so to do.

(4) If any such occupier wilfully refuses or without lawful excuse neglects to fill up the schedule to the best of his or her knowledge and belief, or to sign and deliver the same as by this Ordinance required, or wilfully makes, signs, or delivers, or causes to be made, signed, or delivered, any false return of all or any of the matters specified in the schedule, he or she shall be liable on summary conviction to a fine not exceeding five pounds and in default of payment to imprisonment for a period not exceeding thirty days.

(5) In this section the expression 'dwelling house' shall include every building and tenement of which the whole or any part is used for the purpose of human habitation, and where a dwelling house is let or sub-let in different stories or apartments and occupied distinctly by different persons or families, a separate schedule shall be left with or for, and filled up by, the occupier of each such distinct storey or apartment.

7. The Enumerators for the Island of St. Mary shall visit every house in their respective districts, and shall collect all the schedules so left within their districts, from house to house, and so far as may be possible on the day next following the Census Day and shall complete such of the schedules as on delivery thereof to them appear to be defective, and correct such as they find to be erroneous, and shall add thereto an account, according to the best information which they are able to obtain of all the persons present within their district on the night of the Census Day, but not included in the schedule collected by them.

8. The Census Commissioner shall obtain, by such ways and means as appear to him best adapted for that purpose, returns of the particulars required by section six hereof with respect to all persons who during the night of the Census Day were travelling or on shipboard, or for any other reason were not abiding in any house in the Island of St. Mary of which account is to be taken by the Enumerators and other persons as aforesaid, and such returns shall be included in the abstract directed by section eleven hereof to be made.

9. Every enumerator shall take an account of the inhabited houses, and of the houses then building and therefore uninhabited and of all other uninhabited houses within his province or district.

10. Every Enumerator shall make a summary in accordance with instructions issued under this Ordinance of the contents of the schedules collected by him, and shall deliver such summary to the Census Commissioner and shall sign a declaration, in a form prescribed by the Governor, to the effect that the summary has been truly and faithfully made up by him, and that to the best of his knowledge the same is correct.

11. The Census Commissioner shall examine all the summaries so delivered to him, and shall satisfy himself how far the Enumerators have duly performed the

duties required of them by this Ordinance and shall cause any inaccuracies which he may discover in the summaries to be corrected so far as may be possible, and shall, on or before the expiration of one month after the taking of the Census, or such other time as may be fixed by the Governor, return all the summaries to the Governor, together with an abstract of the said returns which shall be printed and laid before the Legislative Council within six months next after the taking of the Census.

12. The Master or keeper of every gaol, hospital or other public institution shall be the Enumerator of the inmates thereof, and shall conform to such instructions as may be sent to him for obtaining the returns required by this Ordinance so far as may be practicable, with respect to such inmates.

13. Any Enumerator or person bound under this Ordinance to act as Enumerator, making wilful default in any matter required of him by this Ordinance, or making any wilful false declaration, shall on summary conviction be liable for each offence to a fine not exceeding five pounds, or in default of payment to imprisonment for any period not exceeding thirty days.

14. The Enumerators and other persons employed in the execution of this Ordinance shall be authorised to ask all such questions as are necessary for obtaining the returns required by this Ordinance; and if any person refuses to answer or wilfully gives a false answer to such questions, or any of them, he shall on summary conviction be liable for each offence to a fine not exceeding five pounds, or in default of payment to imprisonment with or without hard labour for any period not exceeding thirty days.

15. It shall be lawful for the Governor to make Order for the payment out of the revenue of the Colony of such sum or sums as may be necessarily incurred in taking the Census and generally in carrying out the purposes of this Ordinance.

16. It shall be lawful for the Governor-in-Council to make, alter, or revoke rules or regulations for the better carrying out of the purposes and provisions of this Ordinance and to attach suitable penalties for the breach thereof.

A 'Census Schedule and General Instructions for use in the forthcoming Census' were 'published for general information' on 15 April 1931.[1]

The persons to be included in this schedule are all those who are alive on the night of Friday the 24th April, 1931, and who, whether as members of the family or as visitors, boarders, or servants:—

(1) pass the night in the dwelling of this household or establishment, or
(2) arrive and are received into the household or establishment on Saturday the 25th of April, 1931, before the collection of the schedule, not having been already enumerated elsewhere. No one else may be included.

The headings of the schedule read as follows:

Name.
Relationship to Head of Household, e.g., Head, Wife, Son, Daughter, Stepson, Niece, Visitor, Boarder, Servant, etc.
Religion (if Christian enter Denomination).
Sex: Male, Female.
State whether Married, Unmarried, Widowed (if marriage dissolved, 'Divorced').
Age last Birthday.
Race.
Birthplace, If born outside the Colony, state the name of the Island, Country, State, Province, etc.
Nationality. State whether British born, Naturalized British Subject, American, French, Danish, etc., etc., etc.
Occupation or Means of Subsistence.
Whether able to Read.

[1] Colony of the Gambia, *Government Gazette*, 15 Apr. 1931, pp. 124–5.

Whether able to Write.

Whether able to speak English.

If suffering from serious infirmity, state nature (e.g., Blind, Deaf-Mute, Insane, Loss of Limb).

At the bottom of the schedule was to be entered 'the number of rooms occupied by the above persons'.

Official comments on completeness and accuracy are available for the last five censuses. The census of 1891, which covered only the Colony,[1] was considered incomplete.

> The Census returns are not a correct index of the population which apparently only amounts to 14,266, and, it is needless to add, that except in Bathurst, and perhaps British Combo, the difficulties of obtaining any correct statistics are stupendous.[2]
>
> The numbers must of course be taken as approximately only.[3]

The Superintendent of the 1901 census reported:

> It was thought desirable to enumerate the Colony of the Gambia[4] apart from the Protectorate; for whereas in the former where every house could be visited and the people were more enlightened, fairly accurate returns could be made of the several particulars required, it would have been practically impossible to obtain such details in the latter, owing to the insufficient staff of workers that could have been placed at the disposal of the Travelling Commissioners who were directly responsible for the returns of places within their respective districts.
>
> His Excellency the Governor therefore sent a Circular Despatch to the Travelling Commissioners with instructions that they were only required to give particulars as to the number of males over 15 years of age and females over 15 years of age, and of boys under 15 years of age and girls under 15 years of age. This so far simplified matters that the Commissioners were able to make their returns without seriously interfering with their usual duties.[5]

The Annual Colonial Report for 1904 suggested that the population had been very much understated.[6]

> It would ... at any time be a difficult matter to obtain correct figures, and if such an attempt were made trouble might arise, as the natives are suspicious and would at once jump to the conclusion that fresh taxation of some sort was about to be introduced by the Government. Moreover, a large portion of the population in the Protectorate is continually on the move, owing to the numbers of strange farmers who come into British territory for the planting season only, and to the Fulahs who cross the boundary with their cattle for pasturage; and these people it is impossible to enumerate.[7]

The Commissioners of the 1911 census said:

> In the Island of St. Mary ... the Census was taken on the night of April 2nd. ...[8]
>
> In the Protectorate a period of two months extending from March 1st to April 30th was allowed for the taking of the Census by the Travelling Commissioners of the

[1] i.e. St. Mary's Island, British Kombo, Ceded Mile, MacCarthy Island, Tenderbah, Bai, Kansala, Brefet, and Bajana.

[2] *Colonial Reports, Gambia 1891*, p. 5. It is hard, however, to see why the difficulties of enumerating the population, for example in MacCarthy Island, which has an area of 7 square miles and had been under British administration for nearly seventy years should have been stupendous. There is, moreover, no evidence that the population of the Colony actually exceeded 14,266.

[3] Archer, Treasurer of the Colony, *The Gambia Colony and Protectorate*, p. 85.

[4] i.e. St. Mary's Island, British Kombo, Ceded Mile, MacCarthy Island.

[5] *Census Report 1901*, p 3.   [6] See p. 331 below.

[7] *Colonial Reports, Gambia 1904*, p. 30. See also Archer, p. 137.   [8] *Census Report 1911*, p. 1.

respective Provinces, and in the case of two of the Provinces, it was found necessary to extend the time in accordance with the provisions of Section II (c) of the Census Ordinance, 1911.

Those portions of the Colony known as McCarthy's Island, the Ceded Mile and British Kombo, which at the Census of 1901 were included as parts of the Colony as distinct from the Protectorate, have since that time been made subject to the Protectorate system by Section 4 of the Protectorate Ordinance, 1902, and have for the purpose of the present Census been treated as part of the Protectorate. . . .[1]

It was not attempted to obtain in the Protectorate information in such detail as was done in Bathurst, our object in the main being to secure an accurate enumeration of persons and houses with distinction of sexes, races and religion, and such other particulars, as we were advised could be sought without rousing opposition or animosity among the people. . . . The almost universal ignorance of the people as to their ages made it impossible to obtain exact information on this head, and it was thought sufficient to divide the people roughly into those under and over 15 years, in order to obtain a general idea of the adult and infant population.

. . . On the whole, the work seems to have proceeded smoothly and satisfactorily, and the results may be taken as very reasonably accurate. In only one instance was it found necessary to inflict fines on the people of a town for deliberately refusing to give the required information under Section 6 of the Census Ordinance. . . .

The difficulties of enumeration in this Province [Upper River], which is large and scattered and contains a great number of small towns and villages, were considerable, and there is little doubt that the true population is much larger than the returns show.[2]

The difficulties in the way of obtaining particulars from semi-civilized un-educated people with any approach to accuracy and without causing offence are obvious. The methods adopted by the Travelling Commissioners varied slightly in each Province, but the results in each case have been successful and have far exceeded the expectation of those best fitted to judge.[3]

The Commissioner of the 1921 census reported as regards the Protectorate:

I think the work entailed in the various Provinces must have been a good deal more thoroughly done on this occasion than on the last if one is to account satisfactorily for the very big increase in the population. . . . Difficulty of a kind similar to that met with in 1911 was again found but I do not think to the same degree and herein may partly lie the explanation. It is at any rate obvious that many of the older and wiser who remembered the taking of the 1911 Census would be able to assure their fellow tribesmen that a count of heads would not necessarily be followed by conscription or, say, the levying of a poll-tax.

. . . As showing the difficulty of obtaining the kind of information fairly easily had in Bathurst, [Commissioner] Dr. Hopkinson speaks of the people (especially the women) of Upper and Lower Baddibu being 'surprised and confused by what was asked of them' so that he has felt justified in adding 6 per cent. to the figures actually obtained in the case of the women there.

. . . with the best intentions in the world quite reliable results cannot be expected from the Protectorate in all the existing circumstances. The most indeed that even Dr. Hopkinson can say is 'on the whole I think that the count is fairly accurate—at any rate it is the best obtainable. *It is almost certainly an under estimate.*'

[Commissioner] Colonel Wannell . . . shows that the Census having been taken when it was, quite a number have not been accounted for.—He writes 'I took the Census of the Wharf Towns in May, just before the 24th,[4] when the time expired. During May quite a few native traders, agents and dealers and also one or two

---

[1] This implied that from 1911 on the census returns for these districts are much less detailed than the earlier censuses.   [2] *Census Report 1911*, pp. 2–3.   [3] Ibid., p. 4.

[4] The census was to be taken in the Island of St. Mary on 24 Apr. and in the Protectorate between 24 Mar. and 24 May.

white agents shut down and went to Bathurst.—These would not only escape
coming into my Returns but they would also not be in the Bathurst figures, as they
would arrive in Bathurst after April 24th.'[1]

The Commissioner of the 1931 census stated concerning the Protectorate:

Every endeavour was made to get as accurate figures as possible and Capt. Doke
the Travelling Commissioner for the MacCarthy Island Province states 'no difficulty
was experienced in the collection of these figures from the natives and no fear was
expressed that they were being taken for any ulterior purpose.' And one can I think
state that the figures are reliable.[2]

'Expenditure in connection with Census, 1931', was £103. 2s. 2d.[3] This
would indicate a cost per 1,000 enumerated persons of only 10s. 4d.

2. 1944

A census for very peculiar reasons was taken in Bathurst in 1944. The
Governor, in an address to the Legislative Council, on 25 January 1944,
said:

At the meeting held on the 18th of January the Commissioner of the Island of
St. Mary informed you that Government did not propose to proceed with the
Vagrancy Ordinance at this sitting. I have delayed further consideration of the bill
for this reason. It is now becoming obvious that a more drastic measure is required
of dealing with the crowds of people who come pouring into Bathurst from the
Protectorate, or from French country, and make themselves a nuisance to the
permanent inhabitants, a menace to public health, and greatly add to the problems
of administration. Under the appropriate Defence Regulations, which contain provisions not very dissimilar from those in the bill for the Vagrancy Ordinance, nearly
2,000 undesirables were removed from Bathurst during 1943, but I doubt very much
whether the population has in fact been reduced by that number. It, therefore,
seems to me that we must tackle our problem from another angle, and first decide
who has a reasonable claim to live in Bathurst, either permanently or for a limited
period, and give them suitable identity cards, so that we can, if necessary, make it
illegal for anyone who has not such credentials to live in Bathurst at all. Broadly,
what I have in mind is to take a census of Bathurst in the course of which information
would be obtained regarding the claims of each individual to be allowed to live in
the capital. There are those who have very strong claims because of their traditional
family connections with the place, or because of their occupation. There are others
with less strong claims which require further investigation, or whose only claim is
temporary employment in Bathurst: and there are others again who are possibly
only transitory, but quite legitimate, visitors. For these three groups of persons we
might issue three classes of card—let us call them for convenience Red Cards, White
Cards, and Blue Cards. Persons in possession of red cards would, subject to what
I have to say later, be regarded as having very strong claims to live in Bathurst as
long as they like: those in possession of white cards would be allowed to live in
Bathurst for a period of perhaps twelve months, when their cases would come up
for re-consideration: and those in possession of blue cards would be permitted to
live in Bathurst only for a short time, at the end of which they would have to have
their cards renewed for a further short period if they had a reasonable claim to
remain. Persons not in possession of one of these cards would be reckoned as having
no claim at all to live in Bathurst; if they did not leave voluntarily steps could be
taken if necessary to remove them; and, after a certain date, it would be an offence
to live in Bathurst without one of the cards referred to. So far as I can see, it is only
by adopting some such scheme as this can we remove permanently from the capital
the loafers and work-shy who have neither the right nor the excuse to cumber our

[1] Ibid. *1921*, p. 2.   [2] Ibid. *1931*, p. 4.   [3] See *Blue Book 1931*, p. 37.

streets, and can we distinguish between them and the traditional inhabitants of Bathurst, whose claim to remain, if they choose, in the surroundings to which they and their forbears have for several generations been accustomed, must be given the most careful and sympathetic consideration.[1]

The population of Bathurst has got to be reduced to an absolute maximum of 8,000 souls. I cannot think that this number will not very much more than cover what may for convenience be described as the 'red card' people, and possibly also many of the 'white card' people.[2]

The census was taken in accordance with the following Ordinance :[3]

1. This Ordinance may be cited as the Bathurst Census Ordinance, 1944.
2. In this Ordinance, unless the context otherwise requires—
    'Bathurst' means and includes the whole of the Island of Saint Mary in the Colony of the Gambia;
    'Commissioner' means the Census Commissioner appointed under this Ordinance;
    'Dwelling house' means and includes
     (a) every building or tenement of which the whole or any part thereof is used for the purpose of human habitation, and
     (b) where such building or tenement is let or sub-let in different storeys or apartments and occupied distinctly by different persons or families, every such distinct storey or apartment.

3.—(1) A Census of Bathurst shall be taken in the year One thousand nine hundred and forty-four.

(2) The Census shall be taken in the manner provided by this Ordinance and upon such day as the Governor shall by Proclamation appoint.

4. For the purpose of taking the Census the Governor shall appoint—
(a) a Census Commissioner;
(b) a Clerk to the Commissioner; and
(c) such Enumerators as may be necessary at such remuneration as he shall think fit.

5.—(1) The Commissioner shall prepare schedules, which shall be submitted to the Governor for approval, to be filled up by or on behalf of the several occupiers of dwelling houses.

(2) Every such schedule shall contain the following particulars relating to every living person who abode in the dwelling house on the night of the Census Day—
(a) name;
(b) sex;
(c) age;
(d) race;
(e) religion;
(f) profession or occupation;
(g) married or single;
(h) relationship to occupier;
(i) birth place;
(j) how long such person has resided in Bathurst;
(k) where ascertainable, how long such person's forbears have resided in Bathurst; and
(l) degree of education,
and shall also show whether any such person is blind or deaf or dumb, or imbecile or lunatic, and, where the occupier is not in occupation of a whole house, the number of rooms occupied by him.

[1] Legislative Council, *Meeting held 25th January, 1944*, p. 6.   [2] Ibid., p. 7.
[3] Ordinance No. 12 of 1944 (6 Oct.), 'An Ordinance to Provide for taking the Census of Bathurst'. *Gambia Government Gazette*, Supplement, 16 Oct. 1944.

6.—(1) Every Enumerator shall, three days before the Census Day, leave or cause to be left at every dwelling house within the area allocated to him one or more schedules for the occupier or occupiers thereof or of any part thereof.

(2) In every schedule it shall be plainly stated that such schedule is to be filled up by or on behalf of the occupier with whom or for whom it is left, and that the Enumerator will, on the day next following the Census Day, collect or cause to be collected all such schedules within the area allocated to him.

7.—(1) Every occupier with or for whom any schedule has been left shall fill up such schedule to the best of his knowledge, information and belief, so far as relates to all persons dwelling in the house, storey or apartment in his occupation and shall sign his name or make his mark thereto, and shall deliver the completed schedule or cause the same to be delivered to the Enumerator when required so to do.

(2) Any occupier who wilfully refuses or without lawful excuse neglects to fill up any schedule to the best of his knowledge, information and belief, or to sign and deliver the same in accordance with the requirements of this Ordinance, or who wilfully makes, signs or delivers, or causes to be made, signed or delivered, any false return of all or any of the particulars contained in any such schedule, shall be guilty of an offence against this Ordinance, and shall be liable on summary conviction to a fine not exceeding five pounds or, in default of payment, to imprisonment for a period not exceeding one month.

8.—(1) The Enumerators shall visit every house in their respective areas, and shall collect therefrom all schedules left thereat, from house to house, and so far as may be possible on the day next following Census Day.

(2) The Enumerators shall to the best of their ability complete such of the schedules as on delivery thereof to them appear to be defective or incomplete, and shall correct such as they find to be erroneous, and shall add thereto an account, according to the best information that they are able to obtain, of all the persons present within their respective areas on the night of the Census Day but who are not included in the schedules collected by them.

9. The Commissioner shall obtain, by such ways and means as appear to him best adapted for that purpose, returns of the particulars required by Section 5 of this Ordinance in respect of all persons who during the night of the Census Day were travelling or on shipboard or who were not for any reason abiding in any house in Bathurst but who are normally resident in Bathurst, and such returns shall be included in the abstract for which provision is made by section 12 of this Ordinance.

10. Every Enumerator shall take an account of the inhabited houses and of the houses in course of construction and therefore uninhabited and of all other uninhabited houses in the area allocated to him.

11. Every Enumerator shall make a summary, in accordance with such instructions as may be issued by the Commissioner, of the contents of the schedules collected by him, and shall deliver such summary to the Commissioner and shall sign a declaration, in a form prescribed by the Governor, to the effect that the summary has been truly and faithfully made by him, and that the same is correct to the best of his knowledge, information and belief.

12. The Commissioner shall examine all summaries delivered to him and shall satisfy himself how far the Enumerators have duly performed their duties under this Ordinance and shall cause any inaccuracies which he may discover in the summaries to be corrected so far as may be possible, and shall, on or before the expiry of one month after the Census Day, or such other time as may be fixed by the Governor, return all the summaries to the Governor together with a report and an abstract of the said returns which shall be printed and laid before the Legislative Council within six months next after the Census Day.

13. The master, keeper or person in charge of every gaol, hospital or other public institution shall be the Enumerator of the inmates thereof, and shall comply with such instructions as may be given by the Commissioner for obtaining

the return of such particulars required by this Ordinance as are applicable to such inmates.

14. Any Enumerator who makes wilful default in any matter required of him by this Ordinance or who wilfully makes any false declaration or return shall be guilty of an offence against this Ordinance and shall be liable on summary conviction to a fine not exceeding five pounds or, in default of payment, to imprisonment for a period not exceeding one month.

15.—(1) The Enumerators and other persons engaged in carrying out the provisions of this Ordinance are authorised to ask all such questions as are necessary for obtaining the particulars and returns required hereby.

(2) Any person who refuses to answer or who wilfully gives a false answer to any question or questions put to him by an Enumerator or other person engaged in carrying out the provisions of this Ordinance or who obstructs any Enumerator or other such person shall be guilty of an offence against this Ordinance and shall be liable on summary conviction to a fine not exceeding five pounds or, in default of payment, to imprisonment for a period not exceeding one month.

16. The Governor is hereby authorised to pay out of the revenue of the Colony such sum or sums of money as may be necessary to defray the expenses incurred in taking the Census and generally in carrying out the provisions of this Ordinance.

17. The Governor-in-Council may make Regulations for the better carrying out of the provisions of this Ordinance.

The Governor, under Section 3 of the Ordinance, proclaimed that 'the Census of Bathurst shall be taken upon Tuesday the 14th day of November, 1944'.[1]

The Instructions printed on the schedule said that it was to be completed by the Occupier 'in respect of all persons living or sleeping on his premises on the night of the Census Day. Any persons who are normally resident in the household, but are temporarily out of Bathurst, should ALSO BE INCLUDED in the schedule.'

The headings of the schedule read as follows:

1. Name.
2. Sex.
3. Age.
4. Race or Nationality.
5. Religion (stating denomination if Christian).
6. Profession or Occupation.
7. Married or Single.
8. Relationship to Head of Household (Occupier) e.g. wife, son, servant, lodger, etc.
9. Birth-place (Country Province etc.).
10. Number of years in Bathurst.
11. Number of years family lived in Bathurst.
12. Whether able to:—(a) Read (b) Write (state Arabic or English).
13. Whether able to speak English.
14. Educational standard attained (standard, class, Cambridge Exam: Matric, or Degree).
15. Whether defective (blind, deaf, dumb, imbecile or lunatic).

The Report of the Census Commissioner does not comment on the accuracy of the returns but, as was to be expected in view of the objects of the census, apparently many people born outside the Colony stated that they were born in Bathurst, and it seems also that numerous persons

---

[1] Proclamation No. 4 of 1944 (8 Nov.), *Gambia Government Gazette*, 9 Nov. 1944, pp. 233–4.

who were born elsewhere overstated the length of their residence in the town.[1] Far too many people were recorded as married, but this may have been due to wrong tabulation.

II. Total Population

1. *St. Mary's Island*

The present British Dependency, the Gambia, dates from April 1816, when St. Mary's Island, an island a few miles above the entrance of the Gambia in the Ocean, was acquired. In its origin the new settlement was purely a military post, but it grew rapidly in the first few years. In March 1818 the civil population already outnumbered the military, the resident population, including the garrison, amounting to nearly 600.[2] On 3 January 1819 the civil population was 704.[3] By 1820 it had increased to upwards of 1,000,[4] and in 1823 it numbered 1,845.[5] A census made in June 1826 by the commandant at the request of Major Rowan, Commissioner of Inquiry into the State of the Colony of Sierra Leone,[6] showed a civil population of 1,867. They were all living in Bathurst with the exception of 30 natives residing in a neighbouring hamlet.[7] The population rose to 2,825 in 1833[8] and to 3,586 in 1838, the increase being due in part to the removal of liberated Africans from Sierra Leone to the Gambia.[9] The population did not increase essentially in the following three decades. At

[1] As persons temporarily out of Bathurst were to be included in the schedule without being described as such it is quite possible that many householders, in view of the objects of the census, included people who had been away for a long time.

[2] See Gray, *History of the Gambia*, pp. 306, 322; see also Governor MacCarthy to Earl Bathurst, 29 Mar. 1818 (C.O. 267, vol. xlvii, No. 141).

[3] See *Fourteenth Report of the African Institution, 1820*, p. 81. There were 393 men, 213 women, and 98 children.

[4] See Gray, p. 310.

[5] See Martin, *History of Colonies*, p. 553. Major William Gray, who had been in Bathurst in 1818 and again in November 1821, wrote after his second visit:
'That this infant colony has answered, nay, exceeded the most sanguine expectations of all concerned, is strongly proved by the very great and rapid increase of its population, not only by the considerable augmentation of the number of British merchants, but by an immense influx of the inhabitants of Goree, who, not finding employment under the French Government there, and being excluded from the trade of the Gambia, except through the medium of Saint Mary's, or a small factory belonging to the French at Albreda (than which they are not allowed to go higher up the river) are daily emigrating to Bathurst.
The troops, inhabitants, and merchants are abundantly supplied with beef, mutton, poultry, fish, fruit, milk, butter, palm-wine, and all the African vegetables by the natives of the surrounding towns, who, feeling the advantage of such intimacy with the settlement, flock to it in great numbers, and consume a large proportion of the European articles imported into the colony' (Gray and Dochard, *Travels in Western Africa*, pp. 367–8).

[6] The Gambia at that time was a Dependency of Sierra Leone.

[7] See *Report of the Commissioners*, Second Part, p. 7. The figure of 1,845 in 1823 included 309 strangers. 'As was inevitable in an infant colony . . . a certain number of undesirable characters congregated in Bathurst. In 1824 a purge by the commandant removed some of the least estimable members of the community' (Gray, p. 320). The census of 1826 showed only 7 'Strangers, Native traders'. This explains the small population increase between 1823 and 1826.

[8] Including discharged soldiers located at Fort Bullen.

[9] In 1826 'the number of liberated Africans at St. Mary's was not precisely known, but supposed to be under 100' (*Report of the Commissioners of Inquiry*, 1827, Second Part, p. 8). In 1834 they apparently numbered about 1,800 (see Alexander, *Narrative of a Voyage*, vol. i, p. 69), and in 1841 approximately 800 (see *Report on the West Coast of Africa*, 1842, Part II, p. 187).

TABLE 1. *Population of St. Mary's Island, 1823–1944*[1]

Sex	1823	June 1826	1828	1829	1830	1831	1832	1833	1838	1839
Males	1,101[2]	1,021[3]	850	913	1,181	1,053	1,276[4]	1,541[5]	1,645	1,614
Females	744[6]	846	842	808	1,035	1,017	1,134	1,284[7]	1,820	1,719
Total	1,845	1,867	1,854[8]	1,920[9]	2,227[10]	2,080[11]	2,410[4]	2,825[12]	3,586[13]	3,514[14]
Europeans[21]	45	30	43	31	24	28	31	36	50	42

Sex	1845	31 Mar. 1851	1 Apr. 1871	4 Apr. 1881	5 Apr. 1891	1 Apr. 1901	2 Apr. 1911	24 Apr. 1921	24 Apr. 1931	14 Nov. 1944
Males	1,903	2,359	2,139	2,790	2,841	4,911	4,087	5,253	7,966	11,574
Females	1,786	1,903	2,452	3,348	3,398	3,896	3,613	3,974	6,404	9,578
Total	3,880[15]	4,262	4,591[16]	6,138	6,239	8,807[17]	7,700[18]	9,227[19]	14,370[20]	21,152
Europeans[21]	50	180	55	100	62	193	230	260	274[22]	101

[1] See Martin, *History of the Colonies*, p. 553; *Report of the Commissioners of Inquiry*, 1827, Second Part, p. 7; *Blue Book 1828*, pp. 111–12, *1829*, pp. 114–15, *1830*, pp. 114–15, *1831*, pp. 114–15, *1832*, pp. 118–19, *1833*, pp. 118–19, *1838*, pp. 118–19, *1839*, pp. 118–19, *1845*, pp. 114–15, *1851*, pp. 134–5, *1871*, pp. 226–7; *Census Report 1881*, Table, *1891*, Table, *1901*, pp. 7, 9–10, *1911*, pp. 1, 5, *1921*, pp. 1, 4, *1931*, pp. 1, 6–7, *1944*, pp. 4–5.
[2] Including 152 Sailors and 295 Strangers.   [3] Including 131 Sailors and 7 'Strangers, Native traders'.
[4] Including 37 Aliens and Resident Strangers.   [5] Including 60 Aliens and Strangers.
[6] Including 14 Strangers.   [7] Including 25 Aliens and Strangers.
[8] Including 162 Aliens and Resident Strangers.   [9] Including 199 Aliens and Resident Strangers.
[10] Including 11 Aliens and Resident Strangers.   [11] Including 10 Aliens and Resident Strangers.
[12] Including 85 Aliens and Resident Strangers.   [13] Including 121 Aliens and Resident Strangers.
[14] Including 181 Aliens and Resident Strangers.   [15] Including 191 Aliens and Resident Strangers.
[16] Including 279 Aliens and Resident Strangers.
[17] Including an exceptionally large number of persons temporarily present. The number of persons on ships in harbour was 599.
[18] Including 404 'persons on board ships in the harbour and river', of whom 40 were Europeans.
[19] Excluding 'some 70 or 80' prisoners in gaol.   [20] Including 76 in the harbour.
[21] Included in totals.   [22] Non-Africans.

the outbreak of the cholera in May 1869 it numbered about 4,250, of whom more than one-quarter died within a month, while many others left for the mainland. But the gaps were filled immediately,[1] and the census of 1871 showed a population of 4,591. According to the censuses of 1881 and 1891 it amounted to 6,138 and 6,239 respectively. The census of 1901 showed a population of 8,807, but the large increase over 1891 was due in part to the temporary presence of military and naval forces.

The Census was taken of what may be aptly described as the 'population de fait' as distinguished from the 'population de droit'. That is to say, it was a Census of the persons who slept or abode in the several towns or harbours on the night of Monday, April 1st, 1901.

If the Census had been taken of the latter the results for Bathurst . . . would have been a somewhat diminished one. For, owing to the Gambia Expedition which had then just come to a successful termination, there were on that night officers and men of the 2nd Central African Regiment with the wives of the men, and a few officers and men of the 3rd West India Regiment in the town, and H.M.S. 'Dwarf' and H.M. Troopship 'Dwarka' in the harbour.[2] There were, however, some persons comprised in the latter class who were at that time absent from Bathurst in the Protectorate for the purpose of trade or barter. These would, however, make a very

[1] On 23 June 1870 the Administrator reported: 'Population. Suffered considerably by the epidemic, but it being of a migratory character, no very great change is perceptible' (*State of Colonial Possessions 1869*, Part II, p. 15).
[2] Among the people enumerated at this census were 14 Military Officers, 26 Naval Officers, 365 Soldiers, 269 Sailors, and 279 'Carriers, Gambia Expedition'; see *Census Report 1901*, pp. 12–13. The carriers were all strangers. 'In order to secure as much secrecy as possible, the carriers were recruited in Sierra Leone' (Gray, p. 470).

small total as compared with the large increase caused by the expedition as stated above.[1]

It will be noticed that there is a large number of whites in the Colony when the Census was taken. But in this number are included 72 officers and men of H.M.S. 'Dwarf', 11 officers of H.M. Troopship 'Dwarka', and 24 military officers serving with the troops, making a total of 107. All of them have now left the Colony.[2]

It should be realized, moreover, that, quite apart from such extraordinary events, the population fluctuated considerably in the course of each year.

1859. The population of the island of Saint Mary's during the greater part of the year has of late risen to 9,000. It consists for the greater part of nomade tribes of men who come down the river for work without their families.[3]

1868. A large number of natives emigrate to Bathurst from the Upper River for work during the dry season [November to May].... They are the usual day labourers. They leave towards the rains for the purpose of putting in their ground-nut crops.[4]

1892. The population is a shifting one. Between November and June Bathurst is denuded of a large number of persons who go up the river to trade, and the figures given by a census taken in the month of April, when Bathurst is abnormally empty, do not represent what should fairly be considered as the real number of inhabitants of the town.[5]

1908. It must ... be remembered that the population of the town is a floating one, and that between planting seasons, i.e., January to May—a large number of labourers and traders come into Bathurst, and this way the population for the time being is considerably increased.[6]

1919. A large portion of the Bathurst population spends from early in December to the end of May up the river trading.[7]

Although the population at the 1901 census had been swelled by a large number of persons temporarily present, the Administration expected that the 1911 census would show a much higher figure.

1908. The last census was taken in 1901 and the population was then returned as 8,807 for Bathurst. At this date it can be assumed that, with the additional settlers who have come to St. Mary's Island during the past seven years, that number is below the mark.[8]

1910. According to the census of 1901 the population of Bathurst was returned as 8,807. This number has undoubtedly considerably increased since then.[9]

But the census of 1911 did not fulfil those expectations.

1911. Contrary to the opinion expressed in the 1910 Report, the population of the Island of Saint Mary was found to be smaller than at the time of the 1901 census, being 7,700 compared with 8,807 in 1901.[10]

[1] Census Report 1901, p. 4.   [2] Ibid., p. 5.
[3] State of Colonial Possessions 1859, Part II, p. 11.   [4] Ibid. 1868, Part II, p. 17.
[5] Colonial Reports, Gambia 1892, p. 5. Captain Hewett related in 1862: 'At a certain time in the year the merchants quit Bathurst and ascend the river to bespeak the crops of ground-nuts, and then a general migration of the whole white, brown, and black population occurs, and also at another period when they travel to collect the promised cargoes. These expeditions, though difficult and arduous, are of necessity taken, as the negro has not the slightest idea of the flight of time, and if his house was well found in edible stores, would, unless urged, and even bullied, neglect his crops altogether, and the merchant would consequently be obliged to send vessels home only half loaded. On these occasions whenever you inquire for a Gambiote, the reply will be "Gone to buy grun-nuts"' (Hewett, European Settlements on the West Coast of Africa, p. 270). See also Horton, West African Countries (1868), p. 75.
[6] Colonial Reports, Gambia 1908, p. 22.   [7] Medical Report 1919, p. 10.
[8] Colonial Reports, Gambia 1908, p. 22. See also ibid. 1909, p. 18.
[9] Ibid. 1910, p. 20.   [10] Ibid. 1911, p. 16.

The Census Report for 1911 stated:

The total population was returned as 7,700, showing a decrease of just over 1,000 since the last Census in 1901. This decrease is accounted for mainly, if not entirely, by the presence in Bathurst in 1901 of soldiers, sailors and other people taking part in the Gambia Expedition of that year. It is also to be noted that at the date of the Census, which took place in the height of the trading season, a very considerable number of people engaged in trade were away from Bathurst at the various stations in the Protectorate. On the whole, we are of opinion that there has been no decrease, but rather a slight increase in the resident population of the town.[1]

This explanation cannot be considered adequate. The Administration knew that most of the people connected with the Gambia Expedition had left the island shortly after the 1901 census day; moreover, in 1908–10, it had stated explicitly that the population exceeded 8,807 considerably. Furthermore, the number of sailors present in 1911 (287) was larger than the number present in 1901 (269). As regards the argument that 'at the date of the Census [2 April], which took place in the height of the trading season, a very considerable number of people engaged in trade were away from Bathurst at the various stations in the Protectorate', it may be remembered that only three years earlier the Administration had stated that between January and May 'a large number of labourers and traders come into Bathurst, and this way the population for the time being is considerably increased'.[2]

During the following decade the Administration believed that the population increased very little.[3] The Medical Report for 1920 estimated it at 8,309.[4] But the 1921 census showed it to be 9,227. The Commissioner of Census did not explain this unexpected result, but said:[5]

A considerable increase is shown in the population of Bathurst, the figures on the last taking of the Census being 7,700 as compared with the 9,227 on this occasion.[6] A remark in this connection made in the three Commissioners' Report for 1911, applies with equal force now, viz., that the trading season which continued till an unusually late date this year would naturally account for a number of persons being absent from Bathurst at various stations in the Protectorate.

But since the excess of males ascertained at this census was exceptionally large—it amounted to nearly one-third—it is hard to believe that those temporarily absent exceeded those temporarily present.

During the following ten years the Administration reckoned again with a moderate increase, and the Medical Report for 1930 estimated the

[1] *Census Report 1911*, p. 1.

[2] The official descriptions of these population movements are altogether quite puzzling. It was stated in 1868 and 1908 that the population is swelled at the time when the census is taken by labourers (and traders) coming temporarily to Bathurst, while it was stated in 1892, 1911, and 1919 that the population is reduced by the absence of traders from Bathurst at that time. What actually happened it is difficult to tell. Most of the censuses show a marked excess of males over females, while some show a considerable excess of females over males. The fact that the numbers of women and of children had decreased between 1901 and 1911 suggests that the Commissioners' 'opinion that there has been no decrease, but rather a slight increase in the resident population of the town' was erroneous.

[3] See, for example, *Colonial Reports, Gambia 1917*, p. 11; *1918*, p. 10.

[4] See *Medical Report 1920*, p. 7.   [5] *Census Report 1921*, p. 1.

[6] '... owing to a regrettable oversight the number of prisoners in gaol was not returned so that to this total should be added some 70 or 80.'

population at 11,054.[1] But the 1931 census showed it to be 14,370. The Census Commissioner made the following comment:

It will be noticed how the population of Bathurst has increased. It has very nearly doubled since 1911 and has increased more than half as much again since the 1921 Census. It is not possible to say to what this great increase is due. No doubt it is to a large extent due to a natural rise in the birth rate but at the same time the tendency which seems to be becoming more pronounced for Protectorate natives to come to Bathurst to seek employment may also be a contributing factor. And I think one should also bear in mind that between 1911 and 1921 the War and the influenza epidemic must have caused a big wastage and therefore the figures of the 1921 Census are probably lower than they would otherwise have been if those two events had not intervened and the proportionate increase in the 1931 Census over the 1921 Census would not have been so pronounced.[2]

It is obvious that the 'natural rise in the birth rate' can have affected only the number of children, and that if the increase of the total population in 1921–31 was actually 56 per cent., as indicated by the census figures, immigration was not a contributory but the main cause. The total population in 1921 was 9,227. Assuming that only 20 per cent. of them had died by 1931 and that there had been no emigration and no immigration, there would have been by 1931, 7,382 persons over 10 years of age. But there actually were 11,586. Protectorate natives went to Bathurst in 1921–31; however, the main influx came from Senegal, the number of people born in this French Colony and enumerated in St. Mary's Island having risen from 1,322 in 1921 to 2,989 in 1931 (while the number of people from the Protectorate rose only from 1,517 to 2,100).

For 1932–41 the population of St. Mary's Island was given in the Medical Reports as follows:[3]

	1932	1933	1934	1935	1936	1937	1938	1939	1940	1941
'Europeans and Whites'	191	198	200	183	193	232	233	261	..	..
'Africans'	14,169	14,132	14,045	14,215	14,141	14,069	14,163	14,245	11,868	12,816
Total.	14,360	14,330	14,245	14,398	14,334	14,301	14,396	14,506	..	..

The report for 1940 contained the following comment:

The reduced figure as compared with previous years for the population is based on the Housing Survey completed late in 1939, and reflects the reduction of population following the financial depression in Bathurst during the preceding years.

For 1942 the Medical Department put the African population at 14,900, and for 1943 it estimated the total population at 14,900.[4] The Report on Development and Welfare (June 1943) expressed likewise the opinion that the population was in 1942 slightly larger than in the 1930s.

[1] See *Medical Report 1930*, p. 22.   [2] *Census Report 1931*, p. 3.
[3] See *Medical Report 1932*, p. 14; *1933*, p. 6; *1934*, p. 7; *1935*, p. 11; *1936*, p. 10; *1937*, p. 10; *1938*, p. 30; *1939*, pp. 3–4; *1940*, p. 3; *1941*, p. 3. In *An Economic Survey of the Colonial Empire* (*1937*), p. 109, the population at the end of 1937 was estimated at 12,153.
[4] See *Medical Report 1942*, p. 3; *1944*, p. 8.

Since that date [census 1931] the population has varied between 12,000 and 14,000 rising to not less than 15,000 during 1942 when accurate figures could not be obtained.[1]

The Commissioner of the 1944 census reported:

The grand total for Bathurst is 21,152, probably a great deal more than was expected.[2]

It is difficult to understand why the Administration was not aware of the enormous increase in the population of Bathurst. The number of houses had risen since 1931 by 13 per cent.,[3] and it was known that over-crowding was appalling and that numerous people slept in the streets. The reports of the Labour Department, moreover, contained many details concerning migration into the capital. They suggest also that at the time when the population was estimated at some 15,000 it was larger even than at the census of 1944. A few quotations may serve as illustration:

1942. The War Department had to undertake extensive works and to finish them as soon as possible. The Gambia was naturally anxious to supply the man-power. It had a total of about 50,000 adult males, of which the great majority were employed in agricultural pursuits. At the busiest season in the years before the war, there were scarcely 7,000 workers industrially employed in Bathurst and its neighbour-hood. Of these 7,000 workers, perhaps more than 80% were unskilled, and a large proportion, perhaps 50% were seasonal immigrants from French and Portuguese territories. Yet during 1942, when foreign immigration had practically ceased, the War Department and allied concerns were employing close on 20,000 workers, of whom a high proportion, 30 or 40% were classed as artisans.[4]

Strenuous effort had to be made towards the middle of the year to induce Protec-torate workers to return to their farms;[5] it was considered that 7,000 workers would suffice to carry on the necessary military works, whilst the others did their share by cultivating food-crops. Undoubtedly a good many workers did return to their farms, but no certain figures are available. Towards Xmas their presence on the farm was again necessary and there was even a temporary shortage of labour in Bathurst. Food was hard to get and rents were high, and therefore earnings did not go very far.[6]

On 17.11.42, there was a police round-up of persons found sleeping in the street. Such of them as could not produce satisfactory proof of employment were enlisted in the Army. In all, 117 labourers were enrolled, though approximately 800 males were rounded up. It was alleged by some employers that this action led to a flight of labourers from Bathurst, and it was certainly noticeable that less persons were to be seen sleeping out of doors after the round-up. However, it appears that in fact labourers were returning to their homes for the Xmas season, and since then they have begun to come back to Bathurst in fairly large numbers. Sleeping-out is due to the overflowing of available accommodation.[7]

1943. With the end of hostilities in the North African campaign, several works undertaken by the services were either closed or curtailed. The labour situation

---

[1] *Development and Welfare in the Gambia*, chapter xvi, p. 8. See also ibid.: 'The present posi-tion is that some 15,000 people are living in a town . . . .' See, furthermore, ibid., p. 10: '. . . the pre-war population of between 12,000 and 14,000.'

[2] *Census Report 1944*, p. 2. See also *Medical Report 1944*, p. 8: 'The resident population figure has varied beyond all expectation, the census at the end of 1944 . . . showing over 21,000 population in Bathurst whilst the estimated population was only 14,900 in 1943.'

[3] See *Census Report 1944*, p. 3.   [4] *Report of Labour Department 1942*, p. 1.

[5] The production of ground-nuts in the Protectorate had decreased from 48,000 tons in 1938 to 18,000 tons in 1942. '. . . the principal cause of it must be attributed to the absence from their farms of the many thousands of workers who were engaged in War Department undertakings' (ibid., p. 2).

[6] Ibid., p. 3.   [7] Ibid., p. 4.

therefore fluctuated and many of the unskilled and semi-skilled were without work and had to return home to the Protectorate to farm.[1]

The Labour Officer has on several occasions co-operated with the Police Department in round-ups of vagrants in Bathurst. These men were sent to the Army for enlistment. Aliens found in these round-ups were deported.[2]

The police have taken steps to comb out unauthorised persons staying in Bathurst, and have had no difficulty in finding them in fairly large quantities. On the other hand, since the first rains at the beginning of June, a great deal of unskilled labour has returned to the Protectorate. A large concern employing over 5,000 labourers earlier in the year, reported in June, that their roll has fallen to 1,639 in spite of all their efforts to retain them.[3]

The 1943 report shows furthermore the number of unskilled and skilled workers employed in Bathurst and Yundum during the year.[4]

	Jan.	Feb.	Mar.	Apr.	May	June	July	Aug.	Sept.	Oct.	Nov.	Dec.
Unskilled	6,128	6,703	7,992	8,771	4,908	4,724	4,644	5,038	3,985	3,085	3,298	3,243
Skilled	3,436	3,982	4,117	3,760	3,311	5,932	3,633	3,854	3,075	2,720	3,270	3,206
Total	9,564	10,685	12,109	12,531	8,219	10,656	8,277	8,892	7,060	5,805	6,568	6,449

The returns of 1944 are not strictly comparable with those of 1931 since the recent census was taken in the late autumn and since it covered also persons temporarily absent.

It was taken at the end of the rains at a time when farms were still being reaped in the Protectorate and before the trade season had opened, so that the figures should not include the considerable number of annual immigrant casual labour which finds its way into Bathurst in the dry season. The Census therefore hoped to embody all those who actually dwell and make a livelihood in Bathurst, for on these figures any controlled movement of population would have to be based; and for this reason any normal inhabitants of Bathurst who happened to be away at the time of the Census were also included in the returns. The figures appertain to civilians only, no account being taken of any Services, i.e. enlisted personnel, for whom allowance should be made if necessary, but these are too few to influence the total to any appreciable degree.[5]

After having shown that the population had risen from 14,370 to 21,152, the Census Commissioner said:

This large increase of 50% in thirteen years is partly attributable to the wartime influx of foreigners and Protectorate persons mostly male workers attracted to Bathurst by the considerable demand for labour, and by the large amount of money in circulation engendered by Services Works and Salaries. It will be noticed that there is a predominance of males over females, namely a surplus of two thousand, which is in accordance with the supposition of a regular (as opposed to seasonal) migration of male labour to Bathurst.[6]

In order rightly to appraise the position it must be realized that the very large increase between 1931 and 1944 may have been due to (1) natural increase, (2) net immigration before the war, and (3) net immigration during the war. The vital statistics show an excess of deaths over births. Since birth records are probably more incomplete than death records, there may have been an actual natural increase but it cannot

[1] See also *Report of Department of Agriculture 1943-4*, p. 3: '. . . we are able to report a return to the land of much of the civilian labour previously employed on construction work . . . .'
[2] *Report on Labour Department 1943*, p. 1.
[3] Ibid., p. 6.   [4] See ibid., p. 7.   [5] *Census Report 1944*, p. 2.   [6] Ibid.

have been large. As regards net immigration before the war the available
material does not permit the drawing of final conclusions. According to
the census of 1944, 10,942 people were born in Bathurst, and 5,041 who
were born elsewhere had resided over five years in the town.[1] If these
figures were correct, it would seem that the population at the outbreak
of the war was considerably larger than in 1931 (14,370) and that there
had been a considerable net immigration in 1931–9. On the other hand,
if in fact only 5,169 of the people enumerated in 1944 had been less than
five years in Bathurst, net immigration in 1940–4 would not have been
extraordinarily large. But it may well be that, in view of the purposes
of the census, numerous people wrongly claimed to have been born in
Bathurst or to have resided there for over five years. There is, moreover,
the disturbing factor of the inclusion of the temporarily absent in 1944.

Net immigration in 1931–44 came mostly from the Protectorate. The
number of people born there and counted in Bathurst increased from
2,100 to 4,479, while the number of people born outside the Gambia
increased only from 4,864 to 5,698.[2] The sex distribution does not support
the Census Commissioner's view that the immigrants were mostly male
workers. The number of males increased between 1931 and 1944 from
7,966 to 11,574, while the number of females increased from 6,404 to
9,578. The excess of males was 1,562 in 1931 and 1,996 in 1944. This
rise was no doubt due in part to the inclusion of persons temporarily
absent in 1944.

2. *The Rest of the Colony*[3]

MacCarthy Island. This river island, 158 miles distant from St. Mary's
Island, was acquired in April 1823. 'A Black sergeant, with thirteen
Black soldiers, were left to occupy and protect it.'[4] When the missionary
William Moister visited it in May 1831 he found there two towns, the
original native town Morcunda inhabited by Mandingoes and the English
settlement Fort George 'garrisoned by a few black soldiers' and 'inhabited
chiefly by discharged soldiers and liberated Africans'. The only European
resident was the British Commandant of the island.[5] The Blue Book for
1831 listed 350 blacks (198 males, 96 females, and 56 children) and noted:
'There is also a Village inhabitated by Natives supposed to Contain from
200 to 300.'[6] When Moister made his second visit, in March 1832, the
Commandant had left.[7]

I visited [17 March] every house in the settlement . . . and, at the same time,
I took a census of the population, according to the request made by the Governor.
The inhabitants of Fort George amounted to about two hundred: but the Mandingo
town, at a short distance, to which I could not gain access for this purpose, is much
more populous.[8]

[1] See *Census Report 1944*, p. 7.   [2] See ibid., p. 4.
[3] This is the part of the Colony which by Ordinance No. 7 of 1902 was definitely placed under
the Protectorate system of administration. No separate census data are available for this area
since 1911.   [4] Fox, *History of the Wesleyan Missions*, p. 279.
[5] See Moister, *Memorials*, pp. 80–3.   [6] *Blue Book 1831*, pp. 114–15.
[7] He evidently had left already before the date to which the figures given in the 1831 Blue Book
refer.   [8] Moister, *Memorials*, p. 109.

But the Blue Book for 1832 showed a total coloured population of 514 (Fort George 224 males and 99 females, Fort Campbell 63 males and 38 females, Mandingo Town 40 males and 50 females).[1] It said concerning Mandingo Town: 'This Village has decreased in Population for a Considerable time past as the Mandingoes have been leaving to settle on the Main land.'[2] It seems, however, unlikely that the population of Mandingo Town was actually as small as shown in the Blue Book for 1832 (and 1833).

The population of the island increased very much in the next four years through the transfer of more liberated negroes from Sierra Leone and probably also by immigration from the mainland. The Blue Book for 1833 gave the following details:[3]

	Whites		*Blacks*		*Mulattoes*		*Total*	
	M.	F.	M.	F.	M.	F.	M.	F.
Fort George	2	1	376	110	2	1	380	112
Falots or Fort Campbell . .	—	—	77	28	3	5	80	33
Mandingo Town . . .	—	—	55	73	—	—	55	73
Total	2	1	508	211	5	6	623[1]	218

[1] Including 108 Aliens and Resident Strangers (73 in Fort George, 12 in Fort Campbell, and 23 in Mandingo Town).

According to a 'census' taken in 1836 the population, excluding Mandingo Town, amounted to 1,162 (7 white males, 777 coloured males, and 378 coloured females). The column 'Aliens and Resident Strangers, not included in preceding Columns' contained the following remark:

One Mandingo Town population about 350 established before the Island was in possession of the British also a number of laborers who come from Tillibunco varying from 60 to 100.[4]

The total population of the island, therefore, appears to have been about 1,600 in 1836, and it is doubtful whether at any prior or later time it was larger than that. The Report from the Select Committee on the West Coast of Africa stated in 1841: 'The population on M'Carthy's Island amounts to about 1,200 souls, 800 of which are males and 400 females.'[5] The census of 1851 showed a population of 1,171 (8 white males, 637 coloured males, and 526 coloured females).[6] The 1860s seem to have proved particularly fateful to the island.

[1] See *Blue Book 1832*, pp. 118–19.

[2] The Missionary Macbrair wrote on 24 Jan. 1836 that the town 'was once a considerable native settlement; but it has been greatly reduced since the British settled here, on account of their mutual jealousies' (*Sketches of a Missionary's Travels*, p. 247).

[3] See *Blue Book 1833*, pp. 118–19.

[4] Ibid. *1836*, pp. 118–19. All subsequent Blue Books up to 1850 show the 1836 figures for the island, excluding Mandingo Town, and list in addition 410 Aliens and Resident Strangers (as the population of Mandingo Town).

[5] *Report*, Part II, p. 179. The great preponderance of males was probably due in part to the presence of about 400 Liberated Africans; see ibid., p. 187. But there were also on the island (apart from 173 soldiers, probably not included in the population) pensioners of the 2nd West India Regiment and discharged men from the Royal African Corps; see Archer, p. 43.

[6] See *Blue Book 1851*, pp. 134–5.

TABLE 2. *Population of the Colony of the Gambia now under Protectorate Administration 1871–1911*[1]

Sex	1871	1881	1891	1901	1911	1871	1881	1891	1901	1911
	MacCarthy Island					Ceded Mile				
Males . . .	647	504	499	465	..	2,201	2,289	1,806	1,184	..
Females . .	616	404	407	332	..	1,716	1,758	2,401	1,027	..
Total. . .	1,263[2]	908	906	797	852	3,917[3]	4,047	4,207	2,211	2,642
Europeans .	1	2	2	5	..	1	3	—	—	..
	British Kombo					Total				
Males . . .	2,319	1,632	846	823	..	5,167	4,425	3,735[5]	2,472	..
Females . .	2,100	1,425	859	818	..	4,432	3,587	4,292[6]	2,177	..
Total. . .	4,419[4]	3,057	1,705	1,641	1,963	9,599[7]	8,012	8,027[8]	4,649	5,457
Europeans . .	—	—	—	—	..	2	5	2	5	..

[1] See *Blue Book 1871*, pp. 226–7; *Census Report 1881*, Table, *1891*, Table, *1901*, pp. 9–10, *1911*, p. 2.
[2] Including 860 Aliens and Resident Strangers.   [3] Including 953 Aliens and Resident Strangers.
[4] Including 544 Aliens and Resident Strangers.
[5] Including 270 in Tenderbah, 222 in Bai, and 92 in Kansala, Brefet, and Bajana.
[6] Including 306 in Tenderbah, 232 in Bai, and 87 in Kansala, Brefet, and Bajana.
[7] Including 2,357 Aliens and Resident Strangers.
[8] The 1891 Total for the area included at the other censuses was 6,818.

1860. . . . at Macarthy's Island the population is fast dying out . . . .[1]

1861. The population is dying out, especially the male sex. By a census made by the present active and intelligent Civil Commandant there were seven females to one male.[2]

1866. . . . orders were given for the withdrawal of the officer and thirty men who formed the garrison of MacCarthy Island. These troops left the island on 18 May 1866. The only official, who was left upon the island, was . . . a native [doctor] of Sierra Leone. . . . The members of the mercantile community . . . were all . . . Africans. . . . In June a [European] Manager arrived . . . .[3]

1869. On 9th April, the first case of cholera occurred at M'Carthy's Island . . . having a population of from 300 to 400 inhabitants. The disease extended rapidly, and great numbers of the people fell victims to it. The natives were so terrified by such a fatal disease amongst them, that many fled the island; some went over into the main land, others went lower down the river, carrying disease and death with them wherever they went.

The disease disappeared on 28th April, at which time there were 98 deaths registered, and it is to be supposed that a great many were buried without any registration, thus making the high ratio of mortality at from one-third to one-fourth of the whole population.[4]

But, strange to say, the population was returned at the census of 1 April 1871 as 1,263, with an excess of males over females. However, depopulation soon started again.

1873. At McCarthys Island there was an exodus of 100 Foulahs—who were previously settled on the Island[5]—to a place called Dorna at which their

[1] Governor D'Arcy to the Duke of Newcastle, 24 July 1861, *State of Colonial Possessions 1860*, Part II, p. 31. See also Horton, *West African Countries*, p. 83: '. . . the unhealthiness of the place has led to unparalleled yearly depopulation . . . .'
[2] Governor D'Arcy to the Duke of Newcastle, 25 Aug. 1862, *State of Colonial Possessions 1861*, Part II, p. 24.   [3] Gray, *History of the Gambia*, pp. 434–5.
[4] Report by Robert Waters, M.D., 4 June 1869, *Papers Relating to the Outbreak of Cholera in the Gambia*, p. 15; see also ibid., p. 23.
[5] See also Hewett, *European Settlements on the West Coast* (1862), p. 275: 'The Foulahs, or the Fellahs, a wandering pastoral tribe, occasionally visit the island, and erect temporary huts in the grove.'

Chief Moleo established them & founded a new home for this scattered race of people.[1]

1876. Writing in 1876 of MacCarthy Island the Superintendent [of the Wesleyan Mission] reported that 'the troops have been withdrawn and the younger and more intelligent portion of the inhabitants have either removed to Bathurst or are endeavouring to earn a rather precarious living at one or other of the many trading ports in the river'.[2]

By 1881 the population had declined to 908. In 1901 it numbered only 797, and in 1911 852. For 1922, 1927, and 1930 the population of George-town alone was given as 1,297, 709, and 1,163 respectively,[3] but according to the tax assessments of 1934–9 the number of native inhabitants of the whole island was only 744, 632, 679, 600, 678, and 787 respectively.[4]

Mainland Territories. Two years before the acquisition of MacCarthy Island, a plot of ground had been purchased at the river's mouth close to Cape St. Mary. A house was erected there as a station for convalescents.[5] The population, according to the 1851 census, was 54.[6]

The next acquisition was Barra Point (Ceded Mile) in 1826.

Barra Point was first occupied in June 1826, when a tract of land upon the northern bank of the river was ceded to His Majesty by the 'King of Barra'. This tract of land is one mile in breadth, and about thirty-six miles in length. . . . But the King of Barra reserved a small portion of it (about 400 yards by 300) at Albrida, where the French factory is established. . . . At Barra Point, a small battery has been formed, and it is occupied by a few black troops.[7]

For a long time only a very small part of this tract was occupied by the British. There was a small garrison at Fort Bullen and a number of discharged soldiers.[8] The total population, according to the 1851 census, was 206.[9] In 1857 Albreda was ceded by France to Britain, and the British Administration was gradually extended a little.

There was a small garrison at Fort Bullen up to 1870,[10] a settlement of liberated Africans and discharged soldiers and a Wesleyan mission close to that fort at Berwick Town, and a small settlement of European and other traders at Albreda and the adjacent village of Juffure. . . . But outside of these small areas no attempt at all was made by the Colonial Government to administer the Ceded Mile. . . .[11]

At the 1871 census the population was returned as 3,917, and in 1891 as 4,207, but it dropped to 2,211 in 1901[12] and was 2,642 in 1911.

In 1840 the King of Kombo 'ceded to Great Britain the district which thereafter came to be known as British Kombo or Kombo St. Mary. The

---

[1] *Blue Book 1873*, p. 138. The population was given there as 1,185 or 78 less than in 1871.

[2] Gray, pp. 483–4.

[3] See *Medical Report 1922*, p. 22; *Government Gazette*, 31 Aug. 1927, p. 326, 14 June 1930, p. 246.

[4] See *Report on MacCarthy Island Province 1935*, p. 23; *1937*, p. 18; *1939*, p. 18.

[5] See *Report of the Commissioners of Inquiry*, 1827, Second Part, p. 6.

[6] 36 male and 16 female coloured, 1 male and 1 female white; see *Blue Book 1851*, pp. 134–5, *State of Colonial Possessions 1852*, p. 206.

[7] *Report of the Commissioners of Inquiry*, 1827, Second Part, pp. 4–5.

[8] At the enumeration of 1833 (which excluded the military) the discharged soldiers located in Fort Bullen were included in the figures for St. Mary's Island; see *Blue Book 1833*, p. 118.

[9] 131 male and 74 female coloured, 1 male white. See ibid. *1851*, pp. 134–5; *State of Colonial Possessions 1852*, p. 206.

[10] 'In 1870 all imperial troops were removed from the Gambia . . .' (Archer, p. 77).

[11] Gray, p. 480.   [12] See also ibid., p. 484.

area thus ceded, which was slightly enlarged by another treaty in 1853, comprised about twenty-five miles of the mainland adjoining St. Mary's Island and included the plot of ground at Cape St. Mary which had been acquired in 1821'.[1] The primary object of the acquisition of this district in 1840 had been the location of Liberated Africans. 'In 1853 Colonel O'Connor had settled a number of pensioners from the West India Regiments in the district. . . . But side by side with these settlers there lived a number of Mandingos and other indigenous people, who were already in the district at the time of its annexation.' Afterwards 'a number of Soninki refugees came over the border and built villages. In addition to them a number of members of different African tribes settled *en bloc* in various parts of British Kombo.'[2] Thus the population of British Kombo rose from 1,246 in 1859[3] to 4,419 in 1871. But by 1871 it may already have declined. Dr. Horton related in 1867:

British Combo comprises, besides Combo, all Sabbajee, the territory conquered from the Marabouts. In it are scattered irregularly the following towns which are occupied by British subjects—viz., Newcastle, Albert Town, Hamilton Town, Jassewang, and Coto, besides a few other Mandingo villages. These British towns are not really now worth the name of towns; they are merely scattered villages, containing from a hundred to two hundred inhabitants, the majority of them old and decrepit, and entirely unfit to hold their ground against a Marabout force of even one-fourth their number. The property and wealth of the country is at Bathurst; the young and robust, as soon as they are capable of distinguishing between *meum* and *tuum*, go off to Bathurst for occupation.[4]

The census of 1881 showed a population of only 3,057.

. . . in 1880 the Superintendent of the Wesleyan Mission reported that in nearly all the villages, which had been founded by Colonels O'Connor and D'Arcy [successor of O'Connor], there were left scarcely a dozen, and very often less than a dozen, English-speaking Africans.[5]

Depopulation continued. The number of inhabitants dropped to 1,705 in 1891 and to 1,641 in 1901. For 1911 it is given as 1,963.

The total population of the Colony, excluding St. Mary's Island, at the censuses of 1871–1911, was 9,599, 8,012, 8,027, 4,649, and 5,457 respectively.

3. *The Colony*

The total population of the Colony at the censuses of 1871–1911 was 14,190, 14,150, 14,266, 13,456, and 13,157 respectively. The Acting Registrar explained the slight increase in 1881–1891 as follows:

The increase of population during the intervening decennial was only 116. If the figures representing the populations of Tenderbah, Bai, and other newly-acquired districts[6] were eliminated the result would show an appreciable decrease in the population.

While the populations of Bathurst and the Ceded Mile district have remained almost stationary, that of British Combo has decreased at the rate of 50 per cent.

---

[1] Gray, p. 367.   [2] Ibid., pp. 481–2.

[3] See *Blue Book 1859*, pp. 226–7. There were 812 male and 434 female coloured.

[4] Horton, *West African Countries*, p. 79.   [5] Gray, p. 484.

[6] Apparently Tenderbah, Bai, Kansala, Brefet, and Bajana with altogether 1,209 inhabitants in 1891.

Emigration no doubt is the chief producing cause, as it is a well-known fact that within the last few years there has been a gradual exodus of the aboriginal people of British Combo, who have either gone to settle in Foreign Combo, or have found homes on French territories.

It is difficult to comprehend why the Colony which, it is conceded, possesses advantages favorable to the growth of its population, such as a congenial climate and an immunity from serious epidemics, and in which the sexes are fairly balanced, should not have increased its population at the natural rate within the last decade. But in a Country like the Gambia where the bulk of the population consist of people engaged in trade, agriculture, and other occupations of an unsettled character, perhaps this result is not much to be wondered at.[1]

The Superintendent of the 1901 Census said with regard to the population decrease in 1891–1901:

The total population of the Colony according to the Census returns is as follows:—

Males 7,383, females 6,073, total 13,456 as against males 6,576, females 7,690, total 14,266 returned for the census taken in 1891, showing a decrease of 810. This may be accounted for partly by the fact that since 1891 the Protectorate has been taken under the Government of the Colony and therefore a large number of persons have settled there either permanently or temporarily during the trade season for the purpose of trade, and partly by the fact that a good many of the natives, fearing that the Census was being taken for the purpose of impressing them as carriers in the Expedition or for the purpose of a poll-tax, left the Colony and took refuge in the Protectorate.[2]

This explanation seems quite inadequate. Taking the figures given by the Superintendent it appears that the male population rose in 1891–1901 by 807, while the female population dropped by 1,617. The increase in the number of males was apparently attributable to the influx of men connected with the Gambia Expedition. What needed an explanation was the enormous decline in the number of females by more than one-fifth, which certainly could not be explained by the fact that a large number of persons went to the Protectorate for trading purposes and that a good many of the natives fearing that the census was being taken for the purpose of impressing them as carriers or for the purpose of a poll-tax left the Colony. But the figures given by the Superintendent are not at all comparable, because for 1891 they include the population in the districts acquired in the 1880s while for 1901 they exclude them. If no account is taken of the population of these districts (584 male and 625 female inhabitants), the male population shows for 1891–1901 an increase of 1,391 and the female a decrease of 992. The explanation of the Superintendent then appears still less to the point.

Between 1901 and 1911 the population of the Colony decreased by 299; but, as stated above, the figure of 1901 had been swelled by a large number of soldiers and carriers connected with the Gambia Expedition.

4. *The Protectorate*

Apart from the small tracts of territory ceded by native chiefs and included in the Colony, other areas along the banks of the Gambia came under British protection. But the limits of these protected areas remained

---

[1] *Census Report 1891*, Letter of Transmittal.   [2] Ibid. *1901*, p. 5.

vague until the conclusion of an Arrangement between the British and French Governments in 1889.

> Prior to the demarcation of the Anglo-French frontier, the total area of the Gambia Settlements, including St. Mary's island, British Combo, the Ceded mile, McCarthy's island, and other islets in the river, was taken to be not more than 69 square miles . . . . Outside the settlements, the sphere of British influence was wholly undefined.[1]

The census of 1891 was still confined to the Colony. The Colonial Report for 1892 said:

> Population and Vital Statistics. These statistics are not satisfactory. They only pretend to deal with the town of Bathurst, British Combo, The Ceded Mile and M'Carthy Island, and no information is available about the population in the territory stretching on both banks of the river for 250 miles.[2]

'In January 1893 two travelling commissioners were appointed, one for each bank of the river, to travel through the country and ascertain what there was, either in the shape of towns, or people or anything else, within the boundary, for there was absolutely no data of any sort to work upon, with the object of establishing some form of civilized Government and to put a stop if possible to slave-dealing within the Protectorate.'[3] On the basis of such explorations the first estimate of the Protectorate's population was made in 1895.

> It is difficult to estimate the population in the Protectorate, but a rough estimate based on the number of huts in those parts of the Protectorate visited by commissioners, which is about two-thirds of the whole of the Gambia Protectorate, would give a population of about 75,000, and I think the population of the whole is, at the lowest estimate, 100,000.[4]

But while the population of the Protectorate in 1895 was considered to be at the lowest 100,000, it was estimated in 1898 and 1899 at 200,000.[5]

The first count in the Protectorate was made in 1901. It yielded a population of 76,948.

> This return can only be regarded as approximate, as many of the natives, being under the impression that the numbering of the people meant the imposing of a poll tax, ran across the boundary to French territory. Allowing for these absentees, I think that the population of the Protectorate may fairly be estimated at 90,000.[6]

In 1903 it became 'possible to arrive at a more accurate estimate of the population'. The population of the Island of St. Mary was put at 8,807.[7] 'The districts of British Kombo, the Ceded Mile, and McCarthy Island having been placed under the Protectorate system for administrative purposes,[8]

---

[1] Lucas, *Historical Geography of the British Colonies*, vol. iii, p. 260.

[2] *Colonial Reports, Gambia 1892*, p. 5.

[3] Ibid. *1894*, p. 8. The first Protectorate Ordinance was passed in 1894.   [4] Ibid. *1895*, p. 6.

[5] See *Statistical Tables, Colonial Possessions 1897–8*, p. 502; *1899*, p. 410; *1900*, p. 428.

[6] *Colonial Reports, Gambia 1901*, p. 17. See also ibid. *1902*, p. 11; *1903*, p. 30.

[7] This was the figure ascertained at the 1901 Census.

[8] The two small districts of Brefet and Bajana acquired in the 1880s were placed under the Protectorate system in 1895, the Ceded Mile in 1896, and MacCarthy Island in 1897. 'After 1897 the only parts of the Gambia, outside of St. Mary's Island, which had not been brought legally under the protectorate system, were the Kombo, Fuladu and the districts above MacCarthy Island' (Gray, p. 484). By Section 4 of the second Protectorate Ordinance (No. 7 of 1902) the whole of the Gambia, with the exception of St. Mary's Island, was placed under the Protectorate system.

their returns have been included in those of the Protectorate.'[1] The population of the Protectorate was estimated at 154,911.

Another estimate, yielding at least 144,000, was made in 1904.

The population in April, 1901, when the last Census was taken, gave a return for the Colony and Protectorate of 90,404, but, at that time no portion of Fulladu was under British protection; the population of this territory was, in 1904, estimated at 24,484,[2] which increases the total to nearly 115,000. These figures, however, can at best be only approximate, and it may fairly be assumed that the population exceeds the number stated by at least 25 per cent.[3]

The Colonial Reports for 1905 and 1906 gave again the estimate made in 1903.[4] The report for 1907 showed as population of the Protectorate only 137,516,[5] and the reports for 1908–10, 152,000.[6] The count made in 1911 suggested that the estimates of 1908–10 had been too high.

Previous to the census, the population of the Protectorate (including those parts of the Colony administered under the Protectorate system) was estimated at 152,000; the census in 1911 proved this estimate to be excessive, for the population was found to be 138,401. These figures give a total of 146,101 inhabitants of the Colony and Protectorate of the Gambia.[7]

But this conclusion was not justified. The 1911 count was certainly incomplete, though more complete than that of 1901.

In 1919 the population of the Protectorate was estimated at about 232,000,[8] but this was a gross overestimate. The count in 1921 showed a population of 201,303, and there is no evidence that this count was incomplete.

[1] *Colonial Reports, Gambia 1903*, p. 30.

[2] The Commissioners of the 1911 census, however, reported: 'Since the date of the last Census . . . the Districts of Fulladu, East and West have been added to the Upper River Province. The population of these combined districts amounts to 14,240' (*Census Report 1911*, p. 2).

[3] *Colonial Reports, Gambia 1904*, p. 30.

[4] See ibid. *1905*, p. 27; *1906*, p. 20. 'The population of the Colony may be taken to be 8,807. It is difficult to say definitely what the population of the Protectorate is. It has, undoubtedly, increased since the census of 1901, but not to any great extent, and I believe 155,000 may be taken as a fairly reliable estimate' (ibid.). The position is altogether quite confused. When the estimate of 163,718 was first made, it was assumed that the total area of the Colony and the Protectorate was 3,061 square miles and the Colonial Report for 1903 said (p. 31): 'This gives an estimated population of 53·4 to the square mile.' The figures probably excluded Fulladu. The report for 1904, which included Fulladu, stated (pp. 30–1): 'The area of the Colony [and Protectorate] is said to be 3,700 square miles; if 25 per cent. be added to the population as at present estimated [115,000] for temporary settlers, such as strange farmers and herdsmen, a return of nearly 39 persons to the square mile will be obtained, and this I consider may be regarded as fairly accurate.' The report for 1905 which reckoned with a total population of 163,718 (as the report for 1903) but with an area of 3,700 square miles (as the report for 1904) said (p. 27): 'This gives a population of a little over 44 to the square mile.'—A 'Return of Districts and their Boundaries together with the names of all Towns in each District' (*Government Gazette*, 25 Aug. 1906, pp. 297–318) gave as population of the Protectorate 144,765.

[5] See *Colonial Reports, Gambia 1907*, p. 21. The Protectorate Medical Officer, in his report for 1907, even said: 'Population. I do not know exactly but believe about 100,000' (*Medical Report 1907*, p. 25).

[6] See *Colonial Reports, Gambia 1908*, p. 22; *1909*, p. 18; *1910*, p. 20. In *Blue Book 1908*, p. 67, the population of the Protectorate was given as 152,695, and ibid. *1910*, p. 71, as 157,713. A 'Return of Provinces and their Boundaries together with the names of all Towns in each Province for the year 1909' (*Government Gazette*, 13 Nov .1909, pp. 469–89) showed a population of 150,029.

[7] *Colonial Reports, Gambia 1911*, p. 16.

[8] See ibid. *1919*, p. 2.

According to the 1931 count the population of the Protectorate numbered only 185,150, a decrease of 8 per cent. since 1921. The comment of the Census Commissioner is not very illuminating:

Owing to administrative changes whereby the boundaries of the Provinces have been changed and the number of Provinces reduced from five to four, it is not possible to make a comparison with the 1921 census figures as a whole, but in regard to MacCarthy Island Province, I may quote the remarks of Capt. Doke in his covering report 'taking the districts of the MacCarthy Island Province as it was formerly the total of the Census this year is only 17,979 as compared with 26,171 of the last census. A decrease of 8,172. It is hard to give definite reasons for such a decrease but it must be remembered that the last figures were taken at a time of great prosperity when many were attracted into the country.'

And Capt. Leese, O.B.E., Senior Travelling Commissioner, states 'Kombo and Foni Province in 1921 was made up of five Kombo, six Foni, and one Kiang (Kiang West) districts, in these twelve districts the census taken that year showed a population of 35,425; this year the Census returns for the same districts show one for 43,827—an increase of 8,402. In only one district namely Foni Karanai is there a decrease; this occurred in the years 1923–4–5 when a number of deaths from sickness took place and the people in the villages most affected becoming frightened moved away from the District, the population dropping from 1,725 (1921 census) to 1,475. Since 1925 there has been a gradual increase but the figure is still about 200 below that of 1921. The population in all the remaining districts has been steadily increasing.'[1]

This comment, it seems to me, is quite inadequate. The boundaries had been changed but the Colonial Report for 1930 shows for each of the four Provinces which constituted the Protectorate in 1931 the returns of 1921.[2] A comparison of the data for the two years yields the following result:

Year	North Bank	South Bank	Upper River	MacCarthy Island	Protectorate
1921	63,237	48,660	34,011	55,393	201,301
1931	47,636	48,888	35,372	53,254	185,150

It appears that in three of the four Provinces the population in 1931 was about the same as in 1921, while the North Bank Province shows a decrease of 25 per cent. It seems unlikely that the population should actually have dropped so considerably, and I suspect that the population had been overstated in 1921. The Commissioner of the 1921 census, it is true, said that the Commissioner of the North Bank Province 'evidently has a positive genius for this kind of work in spite of its laboriousness',[3] and the Commissioner of the Province stated that the count was 'almost certainly an under estimate'. Moreover, the population was given for 1930 as 64,183,[4] i.e. even a little higher than for 1921. On the other hand, the detailed figures of the 1931 count inspire much more confidence than those of 1921.

It is quite improbable that in 1921 the number of houses and huts should have been nearly equal to the number of people over 15 years,

[1] *Census Report 1931*, pp. 4–5.   [2] See *Colonial Reports, Gambia 1930*, pp. 4–5.
[3] *Census Report 1921*, p. 2.   [4] See *Government Gazette*, 14 June 1930, p. 269.

1921						1931					
	Males		Females				Males		Females		
Houses and huts	Under 15 years	Over 15 years	Under 15 years	Over 15 years	Total	Houses and huts	Under 15 years	Over 15 years	Under 15 years	Over 15 years	Total
27,588	19,059	13,440	13,084	17,654	63,237	20,509	9,520	15,295	8,631	14,190	47,636

and the number of boys so much greater than the number of girls and also of men. Moreover, the tax assessment figures published for 1935–9 showed a still very much lower population in the North Bank Province than even the count of 1931.[1]

In order rightly to appraise the results of the counts in the Protectorate, it must be realized that they show the situation in April and that the population in the second half of each year is swelled by the presence of a more or less considerable number of 'strange farmers' who take part in the cultivation of ground-nuts. As far back as 1852 Governor MacDonnell, in a Dispatch to Sir John S. Pakington, stated:[2]

It is a fact, that at least one third of the produce exported is raised by natives, who travel from distances of 500 and even 700 miles in the interior to visit the Gambia,[3] along the banks of which they hire, from the various chiefs in whose countries they settle, small tracts of ground, which they cultivate. Most of these visitors from the interior remain from two to three years near the Gambia, till, by their labour and the produce of their farms, they have earned sufficient to enable them to purchase those goods, the desire for which had induced them to leave their homes. They then form themselves into parties, from 20 to 100 strong, and return whence they had come, to spread amongst their countrymen welcome tidings of a safe market for the produce of labour, and to exhibit the goods which they had themselves secured by their own energy and industry.

When travelling became safer the 'strange farmers' usually did not stay away from their homes for so long a period. But otherwise the system has not changed. The Colonial Report for 1903 stated:

Practically the whole of the male population is engaged in this industry for about eight months of the year. At the commencement of the planting season [June] a number of what are termed 'strange farmers' come into the Protectorate, often from a great distance. When a 'strange farmer' arrives at a village he reports himself to the chief or headman, stating the amount of land he wishes to cultivate, which is generally about double the quantity taken up by the local planter; a farm is given

[1] The decrease by 15,600 in the population figure of the North Bank Province was undoubtedly the most important and the most unexpected result of the 1931 count. While the report on the census did not mention this decrease at all, it dwelled at length on the decrease by 250 in the population figure of Foni Karanai. It stated that this decrease was due to mortality and emigration in 1923–5, and that 'since 1925 there has been a gradual increase'. But I doubt whether this explanation is correct, since according to *Government Gazette*, 31 Aug. 1927, p. 346, the population in 1927 (1,773) was slightly higher than in 1921 and very much higher than in 1931. This would suggest that the decrease occurred between 1927 and 1931, or rather between 1927 and 1930 since the population was given ibid., 14 June 1930, p. 269, as 1,475—strange to say, exactly the figure 'ascertained' at the 1931 count.
[2] *State of Colonial Possessions 1851*, p. 198.
[3] Earl Grey was mistaken when he wrote: 'The Governor states that ground-nuts . . . are raised chiefly by the natives of countries far in the interior . . .' (*Colonial Policy*, vol. ii, pp. 288–9), but the substitution of 'chiefly' for 'at least one third' is to be found, of course, wherever Earl Grey's book has been used as source for MacDonnell's statement.

to him and he immediately sets to work. For the four or five months the crop is growing the headman or landlord into whose care he has been given has to house and feed him until it is reaped, when half the nuts are taken by the landlord in payment for board and lodging for the five months and the other half are the property of the 'strange farmer',[1] who, as soon as he has sold them, disappears, and is often not heard of again for years. The number of 'strange farmers' visiting the Protectorate during the planting season of 1903 was nearly 6,000.[2]

The number of 'strange farmers' fluctuated enormously.[3]

1912	1913	1914	1915	1916	1917	1918
6,525	9,940	14,908	32.220[1]	9,315	20,727	20,509
1919	1920	1921	1922	1923	1924	1925
22,440	24.150	22,048	20,566	17,383	14,188	14,652
1926	1927	1928	1929	1930	1931	1932
13,553	17,237	20,640	18,874	16,592	9,736	..
1933	1934	1935	1936	1937	1938	1939
14,500	8,361	13,306	9,754	13,477	9,195	4,615

[1] See also *Development and Welfare in the Gambia*, Chapter vii, p. 3: '. . . in 1915 the record number of 32.220 "strange farmers" arrived in the Gambia. As the total able-bodied male population of the Gambia is only in the neighbourhood of 50,000, it will be appreciated that the arrival of over 32,000 "strange farmers" had a great effect on production, and the year 1915 saw the record export crop of groundnuts—96,151 tons.'

The main factor determining the influx was apparently the price of ground-nuts in the preceding year. When this price was high, the influx increased but it was influenced, of course, also by prices in the adjoining territories.[4]

[1] These terms seem to vary. *Colonial Report 1919*, says (p. 8): 'They are fed and housed. In return they either work two days a week for their landlords and give him one-tenth of the produce of the land or work three days and retain the whole.' The *Report on the Social and Economic Progress of the People of the Gambia, 1939*, says (p. 12): 'Each year a fluctuating number of natives from the neighbouring French territories enters the Colony to engage, on a share-cropping basis, in the production of groundnuts and some of these immigrants obtain alternative work in the wharf towns transporting nuts between stores for the buyers and loading ships.'

[2] *Colonial Reports, Gambia 1903*, p. 15.

[3] For 1912–31 see *Report of the Department of Agriculture 1930–1*, p. 49, *1931–2*, p. 5; for 1933–9 see Table 4. (For supplementary figures see p. 776 below.)

[4] Thus, the enormous drop in the numbers of strange farmers in 1939 was due to the fact that in the preceding years nut prices had been much higher in the Senegal than in the Gambia. See *Report on the North Bank Province 1939*, p. 15; *Report on the South Bank Province 1939*, p. 11; *Report on the MacCarthy Island Province 1939*, p. 5; *Report of the Upper River Province 1939*, p. 19.

When the number of strange farmers fell in 1931 to 9,736, the Director of Agriculture said:

'It is with much regret that I have to record a serious drop in the number of Strange Farmers coming into the Colony to grow ground-nuts. . . .

'In my report for 1924 I wrote as follows:—"Their importance can hardly be over-estimated, as there is not the slightest doubt that upon the labours of these farmers depend in no uncertain measure the material prosperity of the Gambia. Their presence makes all the difference between a good or bad year, both in respect to the crop of groundnuts grown, and to the general trade in cotton piece goods. Before returning home these farmers convert about half of their earnings into cotton piece goods which they trade with over the border. This heavy drop in their numbers is a serious economic loss both directly and indirectly to the revenue of the Colony" ' (*Report of the Department of Agriculture 1931–2*, p. 6).

The Director of Agriculture says furthermore (ibid., p. 11) that 'the whole prosperity of the entire community depends entirely upon the quantity of groundnuts raised and exported each year', but this statement, it seems to me, is not exact. In some years, when exports were enormous, the misery was great because prices were too low.

It would, however, be a mistake to assume that the numbers of 'strange farmers' convey a true picture of the amount of temporary migration into the Protectorate.

(1) Some 'strange farmers' are accompanied by their wives.[1]

(2) Some 'strange farmers' do not leave the country after having sold the nuts. Thus, the Colonial Report for 1912 stated:

While some of these immigrants only visit the Protectorate to sow and harvest a crop of ground-nuts, very many of them become permanent residents.[2]

(3) Some 'strange farmers' do not come from abroad but are native Gambians who cultivate ground-nuts far from their homes. The Colonial Report for 1919 said:

In thickly populated districts it is on occasion necessary for some of the inhabitants to migrate for farming purposes to other parts of the Province or Protectorate, where they are treated in the same manner as the 'strange farmers'. . . . They return to their districts after having sold their crop of ground-nuts.[3]

The number of Gambian and of other 'strange farmers' has been given for three of the four Provinces of the Protectorate as follows:[4]

| | North Bank | | South Bank | | MacCarthy | |
Year	Gambians	Others	Gambians	Others	Gambians	Others
1934	813	1,056	. .	. .	. .	. .
1935	1,004	1,205	1,695	1,644	788	2,390
1936	787	869	1,487	1,332	683	1,749
1937	984	1,530	1,578	2,033	846	2,844
1938	599	1,210	1,524	1,680	724	1,348
1939	468	491	708	946	253	960

The 'strange farmers' coming from other districts of the Gambia are, of course, included in the census figures of their home districts where they stay in April.

[1] See Census Report 1921, p. 2: 'During the rains about 8,000 "Strange Farmers" come into the [Upper River] Province to plant ground-nuts—about half of these bring a wife and in some cases two. This means that from July to December, the population of the Province is raised by 12,000 to 13,000 people.' (The population, according to the census taken in the spring of 1921 was 34,011; see ibid., p. 10.)

[2] Colonial Reports, Gambia 1912, p. 20. In the Report on the South Bank Province for 1939 part of the decrease in the resident population was attributed to 'the return home of foreigners who had settled for some time in the Gambia and who found a prolonged period of low prices and bad trade offered little inducement for them to stay' (p. 11). See also Report on the Upper River Province 1934, p. 8.

[3] Colonial Reports, Gambia 1919, p. 10. See also ibid. 1925, p. 6, and 1926, p. 9:
1925. 'The Strange Farmers who contributed materially to the harvest numbered 14,192, as against 14,188 in 1924. The majority of them were not from the Sudan [should read "the Senegal"] as in former years, but from other parts of the Gambia.'
1926. 'Amongst the so-called strange farmers only about one half are Senegalese; the others come from different parts of the Gambia.'

[4] See Report on North Bank Province 1938, p. 8, 1939, p. 15; Report on South Bank Province 1938, p. 16, 1939, Appendix 2; Report on MacCarthy Island Province 1938, p. 22, 1939, p. 19. No figures seem to be available for Upper River Province. (For 1945 see p. 776 below.)

Many passages in the administrative reports suggest that in former times the official figures for 'strange farmers' included only foreigners. Thus, the Report of the Department of Agriculture for 1930–31, p. 49, contained a Table 'Number of Immigrant or "Strange Farmers" entering the Gambia annually to plant Groundnuts' (see also, for example, Colonial Reports, Gambia 1919,

(4) 'Strange farmers' are not the only ones to migrate into the Gambia. The *Report on the Upper River Province* for 1934 said:

> A considerable number of Natives come in from French Senegal and French and Portuguese Guinea during the Trade Season looking for work.[1]

It should be noted moreover that, especially in recent times, the influx of 'strange farmers' from abroad has been offset by the efflux of Gambians who went as 'strange farmers' to adjoining French territories. Two quotations from the annual reports on the South Bank Province may serve as an illustration:

> 1935. The figures [of residents] show that the decreases occurred chiefly in the Foni, Kiang and Jarra districts, from whence there is known to have been increased emigration to French Senegal. The majority of emigrants were young farmers lured away by reports of high prices for groundnuts.[2]
>
> 1939. . . . 1,753 young men from the Province went to French Territory to grow groundnuts during the farming season, having been attracted by the high prices offered in French Territory in the previous two years. . . . This efflux amounted to 1,753 as against a total influx of 1,654 of which only 946 were foreigners, so that on balance more came in than went out.[3] This must be the first time this has happened for a very long time.[4]

The Report on Development and Welfare in the Gambia said:

> In immediately pre-war years the numbers have shown signs of decreasing, partly due no doubt to the fact that the countries of origin of the 'strange farmers' are being developed and now offer opportunities of earning money equivalent to those which are available in the Gambia. During the first three years of the war, the entry of 'strange farmers' into the Gambia was discouraged, and in 1941 the poll tax which they are called upon to pay was increased from 8/- to 16/-. In 1943, however, the adherence of the Senegal to the cause of the United Nations and the need for increasing the local production of groundnuts without undue interference with the food cultivation campaign made it necessary once again to encourage the admission of 'strange farmers' and the tax on them was again reduced to 8/-.[5]

Recent Reports of the Department of Agriculture state:

> 1939–40. There was a slight fall in the acreage under groundnuts due variously to a decrease in the number of strange farmers from neighbouring territories, to a movement of some of the young Gambian farmers in the reverse direction and to increased cultivation of food crops.[6]
>
> 1941–2. Groundnuts.—Purchases for export during the 1941–42 season only just reached 18,000 tons of undecorticated nuts being the lowest crop on record since groundnuts have been the staple export of the Gambia. Apart from the poor growing season, the drop was variously due to a marked decline in the number of strange farmers, the success of the campaign to grow more food crops, the loss of man-power ... and the development of oil extraction as a local industry. In addition, rigid frontier control prevented any nuts coming in from neighbouring territories.[7]

p. 8; *1920*, p. 6; *1922*, p. 5; *1927*, p. 13). But it is practically certain that the figures actually included always also the native Gambians who came from other districts of the Protectorate.

[1] *Report*, p. 8.   [2] *Report on South Bank Province 1935*, p. 5.
[3] Should read 'more went out than came in'.
[4] Ibid. *1939*, pp. 11–12. When the population of MacCarthy Island Province dropped from 45,342 in 1938 to 42,356 in 1939, it was stated that 'the reduction in 1939 was due to people leaving to farm in French territory where better prices were obtainable for their produce' (*Report on MacCarthy Island Province 1939*, p. 5). The number of 'strange farmers' in the Province in 1939 was only 1,181, of whom 960 were foreigners.
[5] Chapter vii, p. 3.   [6] *Report 1939–40*, p. 2.   [7] Ibid. *1941–2*, p. 2.

1943–4. The number of strange farmers coming into the Gambia did not reach expectations. In the previous seasons of the present war, alien strange farmers had been discouraged but in the season under review the strangers tax was reduced to the pre-war level. However only 3,205 alien strange farmers came in against an estimated figure of 5,000.[1]

1944–5. Owing to the high price [of groundnuts] a great number of strange farmers came into the country.[2]

In the following season the number was greater still. On 6 November 1945 the Governor said in the Legislative Council:

The number of strange farmers increased from nearly 11,000 last year to over 19,000 this year.[3]

The area of the Gambia is 4,003 square miles.[4] According to the 1931 census the number of inhabitants per square mile was 49·8. In St. Mary's Island it was 3,265,[5] in the Protectorate 46·3.

TABLE 3. *Population Density, the Gambia 1931*[1]

Administrative Divisions	Area, sq. m.	Population total	Population per sq. m.
Island of St. Mary (Colony) . . .	4·42	14,370	3,265
North Bank Province	814	47,636	58·5
South Bank Province	1,088	48,888	44·9
MacCarthy Island Province . . .	1,186	53,254	44·9
Upper River Province	911	35,372	38·8
Protectorate	3,999	185,150	46·3
The Gambia	4,003	199,520	49·8

[1] See *Census Report 1931*, p. 13; *Blue Book 1938*, p. 116.

More recent population figures for the Protectorate have been ascertained in connexion with the annual tax assessments made in the various Provinces in July/August. They show (1) the 'resident population', (2) the 'strange farmers', and (3) the 'total population'. The 'total population' which is the sum of the two groups does, however, not represent the population present at the time of the tax assessment, as the 'resident population' apparently excludes not only the 'strange farmers' but also other persons temporarily present.[6] It probably excludes too persons

[1] Ibid., *1943–4*, p. 2.   [2] Ibid. *1944–5*, p. 3.

[3] Legislative Council, *Meeting held 6th November, 1945*, p. 12. (See also p. 776 below.)

[4] See *The Dominions Office and Colonial Office List 1940*, p. 314: 'The Island of St. Mary has an area of about 2,500 acres [4 sq. m.] . . . . The area of the Protectorate, including that of the parts of the Colony administered as Protectorate, is 3,999 sq. miles . . . .' However, in the Table facing ibid., p. civ, the total area is given as 4,068 sq. m. This error is apparently due to the fact that 'the total area of the Colony is about 69 square miles' (see ibid., p. 314) and that the compiler of the Table added 'the total area of the Colony' to 'the area of the Protectorate, including that of the parts of the Colony administered as Protectorate' and thus counted the latter twice. *An Economic Survey of the Colonial Empire (1937)*, p. 546, and *Statistical Abstract of the British Empire 1928–37*, p. 3, give similarly as area of the Gambia 4,069 sq. m., while the more correct figure of 4,002 sq. m. appeared still ibid. *1924–33*, p. 3.

[5] In 1944 it was 4,786.

[6] See, for example, *Report of the Upper River Province 1936*, p. 6: 'The [resident] population figures do not include lodgers and strange farmers, who spend only the farming season in the

temporarily absent even if they work as 'strange farmers' in another part of the Province.

The figures of the South Bank Province are said to have been reliable since 1933.[1] For the other Provinces they must be considered inaccurate.

TABLE 4. *African Population of the Protectorate of the Gambia, 1933–9*[1]

Province	1933	1934	1935	1936	1937	1938	1939
	Resident Population						
North Bank	..	..	30,687	34,319	37,703	31,905	34,036
South Bank	65,462	64,592	59,993	58,243	60,242	58,297	57,775
MacCarthy Island	38,492	37,542	38,156	37,527	38,937	45,342	42,356
Upper River	42,134	42,523	41,419	40,871	41,596	46,898	42,736
Total	..	..	170,255	170,960	178,478	182,442	176,903
	Strange Farmers						
North Bank	2,564	1,869	2,209	1,656	2,514	1,809	959
South Bank	4,177	2,825	3,339	2,819	3,611	3,204	1,654
MacCarthy Island	4,101	1,787	3,178	2,432	3,689	2,072	1,181
Upper River	3,658	1,880	4,580	2,847	3,663	2,110	821
Total	14,500	8,361	13,306	9,754	13,477	9,195	4,615

[1] See *Report on North Bank Province 1936*, p. 5, *1938*, pp. 7–8, *1939*, pp. 14–15; *Report on South Bank Province 1939*, Appendix 11; *Report on MacCarthy Island Province 1934*, p. 5, *1935*, pp. 6, 23–4, *1938*, pp. 8, 21–2, *1939*, pp. 18–19; *Report of Upper River Province 1937*, pp. 4, 15, *1938*, p. 5, *1939*, p. 19, Appendix A. The number of strange farmers in Upper River Province 1938 has been computed by deducting the resident population given ibid. *1938*, p. 5, from the total population given in *Colonial Reports, Gambia 1938*, p. 17. (Otherwise no use has been made here of the figures in the annual Colonial Reports. For some years they evidently include strange farmers, for others not. The figures for North Bank and Upper River Provinces read in *Report 1936*, p. 7, 37,970 and 45,718 respectively, but ibid., p. 15, 35,970 and 43,718 respectively; the figure for South Bank Province 1937 reads ibid. *1937*, both on pages 9 and 19, 73,853 instead of 63,853.) (For supplementary figures see p. 776 below.)

North Bank Province 1935. At the time of the assessment of taxes the Chiefs were asked to make a count of the people in their districts and gave as a total for the Province the figure 30,687. In 1931 the Census revealed the population of the Province to be 47,636. It is probable that the decrease is due to errors in the Chiefs' workings, although it must be admitted that no grave errors were discovered in any village where checks were made.[2]

MacCarthy Island Province. 1934. The figures for yards and huts can be taken as correct but those for the population are untrustworthy and are probably below the correct numbers. The local people have a rooted objection to counting heads or allowing others to do it, as it is supposed to bring ill luck.[3]

Gambia, or the influx of merchants, buyers and labourers etc. who come to the Wharf Towns from outside the Province during the Trade Season.'

In comparing the post-censal and the 'census' figures for the various Provinces it should be realized furthermore that in 1932 the Jarre Districts were transferred from MacCarthy Island Province to South Bank Province, and Fuladu West from Upper River Province to MacCarthy Island Province (see *Report on MacCarthy Island Province 1938*, p. 2). The area of South Bank Province increased thereby from 1,088 to 1,294 sq. m., while that of MacCarthy Island Province decreased from 1,186 to 1,101 and that of Upper River Province from 911 to 790 sq. m. (see *Colonial Reports, Gambia 1933*, p. 5).

[1] See *Report on South Bank Province 1938*, pp. 16–17.
[2] *Report on North Bank Province 1935*, p. 9.
[3] *Report on MacCarthy Island Province 1934*, p. 5.

1936. As has been noted in previous reports, the figures for population which depend entirely on the statements of the yard-owners are probably somewhat underestimated; but on the other hand, the stability of the totals obtained during the last three assessments 1934, 37,542; 1935, 38,156; and 1936, 37,527, would seem to point to the fact that the figures are not as unreliable as has previously been assumed.[1]

1938. As has been noted in previous reports, the figures for population which depend entirely on the statements of the yard-owners are probably somewhat underestimated. During assessment the numbers of men and women, boys and girls were called for separately. This more accurate form of assessment accounts for the increase in population, which in the last three years has been recorded as follows:—1936, 37,527; 1937, 38,937; and 1938, 45,342.[2]

Upper River Bank Province 1938. The assessment for the 1939 taxation was carried out with greater despatch and efficiency than usual owing to the Seyfolu and Alkalolu arranging to have their statistics written up either by the Court Clerk or a literate member of the village, then checking the accuracy of the figures whilst they were read to the Commissioner.

The 1938 assessment shows a population of 46,898, an increase of 5,302 over the previous year. It is estimated that the increase is due merely to a more efficient method of assessment and that actually a decrease of about 3,000 took place. In previous years children have not been counted separately from adults with the result that many very young children were not accounted for. The figure for boys in Wuli District is considered quite inaccurate owing to a misunderstanding over the instructions given to the Seyfu, there is, however, no reason to doubt the accuracy of the total figure for males.[3]

The total population of the Gambia on 31 December has been estimated as follows:

Year	Population	Source
1933	208,094[1]	*Statistical Abstract British Empire 1924–33*, p. 3.
1935	197,811[2]	*Statistical Abstract British Empire 1926–35*, p. 3.
1936	190,739[3]	*Economic Survey of the Colonial Empire (1936)*, p. 104.
1937	192,818[4]	*Statistical Abstract British Empire 1928–37*, p. 3.
1937	200,601[5]	*Economic Survey of the Colonial Empire (1937)*, p. 109.
1938	205,000	*Statistical Year-Book of the League of Nations 1942/44*, p. 12.

[1] This figure evidently represents the sum of the 1931 census figures for the Colony and North Bank Province and the 1933 assessment figures for the resident population of the other Provinces.

[2] This figure evidently represents the sum of the Africans in the Colony and in the Protectorate (the latter comprising both the resident population and the strange farmers). The decrease from 1933 to 1935 (in spite of the inclusion of the strange farmers in the 1935 figures) is due to a drop in the figures for North and South Bank Provinces. For the decrease in the North Bank Province see p. 338 above. In the South Bank Province the decrease was attributed to 'increased emigration to French Senegal' and to a greater 'incidence of sickness and disease' (see *Report on South Bank Province 1935*, p. 5).

[3] 'The estimated population at the end of 1936 was 14,141 in the Colony and 176,598 in the Protectorate, making a total of 190,739.' The figure for the Colony excludes the non-Africans; as to the figure for the Protectorate I do not know its origin.

[4] This figure, unlike the one for 1935, excludes the 'strange farmers'. This explains the apparent decrease from 1935 to 1937.

[5] 'The estimated population at the end of 1937 was 12,153 in the Colony and 188,448 in the Protectorate, making a total of 200,601.' I do not know the reasons for the low estimate in the Colony and the high estimate in the Protectorate as compared with 1936.

[1] Ibid. *1936*, p. 5. The same *mutatis mutandis* ibid. *1937*, p. 7.
[2] Ibid. *1938*, p. 8.
[3] *Report of the Upper River Province 1938*, pp. 5–6.

III. Composition of the Population

1. *Introduction*

The returns of the early counts subdivide the resident civil population into Europeans, Mulattoes, and Blacks, but from 1836 on no separate figures seem to have been published for Mulattoes except in 1901.[1] The number of people returned as Europeans at the enumerations in St. Mary's Island in the nineteenth century varied between 30 and 62, except in 1851 (180) and in 1881 (100). The high figures for 1851 and 1881 were apparently due to the temporary presence of numerous visitors,[2] and between the various counts there were times (after epidemics) when the number of European residents was smaller than 30. At the census of 1901 the number of Europeans, owing to the Gambia Expedition, rose to 193.[3] It dropped thereafter, but reached 230 in 1911[4] and 260 in 1921.[5] The report on the 1931 census subdivided the population of St. Mary's Island into Africans and non-Africans. The non-African population numbered 274, but it included 57 persons born in Syria (while the 47 persons from Syria ascertained at the 1921 census had not been counted as Europeans).[6] The resident European population had apparently declined between 1921 and 1931. The 1944 census showed again a non-African population of 274. It included 173 Syrians.[7] How many of these were born in Syria has not been reported, but there is no doubt that the number of such persons has increased very much since 1931. Only 101 Europeans were enumerated in 1944. This figure seems extraordinarily low even considering that only civilians were counted.[8]

The bulk of the non-Africans in the Gambia have always lived in St. Mary's Island. The census reports for 1921 and 1931 do not list any non-

---

[1] The numbers of people returned as Mulattoes in St. Mary's Island in 1823, 1826, and 1829–33 were 135, 122, 167, 186, 161, 143, and 126 respectively and in MacCarthy Island, in 1833 and 1835, 11 and 15. The adults were all immigrants—domestic servants in the families of European merchants whom they had accompanied from Goree and other parts of Senegal or mechanics from the same places (see *Report of the Commissioners of Inquiry*, 1827, Second Part, p. 7). The number of Mulattoes in 1901 was 116 in St. Mary's Island and 5 in MacCarthy Island (see *Census Report 1901*, p. 10).

[2] Of the 180 Europeans ascertained in 1851, 167 were males and only 13 females. In his report for 1868 the Governor said: 'Population is much the same as the previous year, but I fail to find 167 white males, as appears in the Blue Book for 1867' (*State of Colonial Possessions 1868*, Part II, p. 17). Up to 1867 the Blue Books had in fact shown the figures of the 1851 census, but in the Blue Book for 1868 (p. 226) the number of Europeans was given as 47 (39 males and 8 females). Of the 100 Europeans enumerated in 1881, 41 were French or Italian seamen on board ships at the Port of Bathurst; see *Census Report 1881*, Table.

[3] The total number of Europeans resident in the Colony in 1898–1901 was 63, 80, 71, and 88 respectively; see *Colonial Reports, Gambia 1902*, p. 12.

[4] Including 40 'on board ships that happened to be in the harbour' (*Census Report 1911*, p. 1).

[5] The number of persons on board ships is not given but it must have been considerable. The number of Danes enumerated at this census was 52 as compared with 0 in 1911 and 2 in 1931.

[6] That in earlier times Syrians were counted as Africans appears also from the fact that the *Colonial Report* for 1906 said (p. 15) that 'of the 547 natives admitted' into the General Hospital '14 were Syrian traders'.   [7] See *Census Report 1944*, p. 5.

[8] See in this connexion *Report on Labour Department 1943*, p. 3: 'Registration by Europeans under the Compulsory Service Ordinance (No. 11 of 1942) was ordered in January, 1943. Registration was carried out without difficulty and some 360 persons of both sexes have been registered. Of this number sixty-five have since left the Colony and are not expected to return.'

Africans outside Bathurst, and the tables in the Blue Books state explicitly that there are no whites in the Protectorate.[1] But this is a mistake. To judge from the Medical Reports quite a few Europeans have been living in Georgetown and some places on the mainland, and Syrians are also to be found in various Protectorate towns.[2]

As apart from some data concerning nationality the recent census reports give no separate figures for Africans and non-Africans in St. Mary's Island and no such separate figures whatsoever for the Protectorate,[3] most of the data in the following paragraphs will necessarily cover the total population.

2. African Population

Birthplace. Of the 14,370 persons enumerated in 1931 in St. Mary's Island 7,406 were recorded as born on the island, 2,100 in the Gambia Protectorate, 1,138 in other British possessions in Africa (mainly Sierra Leone), 3,027 in French possessions in Africa (mainly Senegal), 234 elsewhere in Africa (mainly Portuguese Guinea), and 250 in other continents, while the place of birth was not stated for 215 persons. The 13,905 persons recorded as born in Africa were probably all Africans. Of the 250 persons recorded as born in other continents apparently only 6 were Africans (born in America). Of the 215 persons for whom the place of birth was not stated apparently 185 were Africans, and these were doubtless all or nearly all born in Africa.

Of the 21,152 persons enumerated in 1944 in St. Mary's Island 10,975 were returned as born in Bathurst, 4,479 in the Gambia Protectorate, and 5,698 elsewhere.[4] The Census Commissioner says that 'one half only of the population of Bathurst is in fact Bathurst born. The 1931 figure was 8,260 (then shown as "British born subjects") compared to 10,975 to-day, quite an appreciable increase.'[5] Actually the increase in the number of persons returned as born in Bathurst was much greater than the Census Commissioner supposed it to be. He was not aware of the fact that the number born in Bathurst had been ascertained in 1931 and that it amounted to 7,406. According to the census returns the number of people born in Bathurst had increased in 1931–44 by 48 per cent. and the number of people born elsewhere by 46 per cent. But, as stated above, I am inclined to think that many people born elsewhere pretended to be born in the capital.

Data concerning the birthplace of the population of the Protectorate are not available.

[1] See, for example, *Blue Book 1938*, p. 116.
[2] *Census Report 1911*, p. 6, lists 16 British, 15 French, 15 Portuguese, 3 Spaniards, 12 Swiss, 1 American, 31 Syrians, and 6 Jews. References to Europeans living in the Protectorate are also to be found, for example, in *Medical Report 1910*, p. 16; *1911*, p. 7; *1912*, pp. 13, 32; *1913*, pp. 14, 31; *1915*, p. 21; *1916*, p. 20; *1917*, p. 20; *1918*, p. 12; *1920*, pp. 23–4; *1923*, pp. 16, 20; *1924*, pp. 13, 16; *1925*, pp. 22, 26; *1926*, pp. 41, 43; *1927*, p. 41; *1928*, pp. 43–4; *1935*, p. 47. According to ibid. *1922*, p. 22, the European population of Georgetown then numbered 14 (all males). As regards Syrians in Protectorate towns see ibid. *1920*, p. 24; *1927*, p. 41; *1928*, p. 44.
[3] Including the parts of the Colony placed under the Protectorate system of administration.
[4] See *Census Report 1944*, p. 4. The figure of Bathurst born given there does not agree with that shown ibid., p. 7 (10,942).   [5] Ibid., p. 3.

TABLE 5. *British and Foreign Population by Birthplace, St. Mary's Island, 1921 and 1931*[1]

Birthplace	1921			1931		
	British	Foreign	Total	British	Foreign	Total
Island of St. Mary	4,389	2	4,391	7,406	—	7,406
Gambia Protectorate	1,255	262	1,517	2,100[2]	—	2,100
Gold Coast	35	4	39	42	—	42
Nigeria, Northern	3	—	3	37[2]	—	37
Nigeria, Southern	31	—	31	—	—	—
Sierra Leone	825	—	825	1,059[3]	—	1,059
Conakry (French Guinea)	1[4]	13	14	—	14	14
Liberia	—	30	30	—	7	7
Morocco	14[5]	23	37	—	24	24
Portuguese Guinea	87	66	153	—	214	214
Senegal	209[6]	1,113	1,322	—	2,989	2,989
Teneriffe	—	3	3	—	13	13
Africa Total	6,849	1,516	8,365	10,644	3,261	13,905
United Kingdom	123	—	123	81	—	81
Denmark	1[4]	52	53	—	2	2
France	8[5]	43	51	1[4]	89	90
Germany	—	1	1	—	1	1
Spain	—	—	—	—	6	6
Switzerland	5[5]	22	27	—	3	3
Europe Total	137	118	255	82	101	183
Syria	6	41	47	25[7]	32	57
'America'	—	5	5	3	2	5
West Indies	8	2	10	5	—	5
America Total	8	7	15	8	2	10
Others and not stated	107	438	545	4	211[8]	215
Total	7,107[9]	2,120	9,227	10,763[10]	3,607	14,370

[1] See *Census Report 1921*, p. 6; *1931*, p. 8.   [2] British Protected Persons.
[3] Including 253 British Protected Persons.   [4] Naturalized British Subject.
[5] Including 1 Naturalized British Subject.   [6] Including 5 Naturalized British Subjects.
[7] Including 2 Naturalized British Subjects.   [8] Including 12 Norwegians.
[9] Including 10 Naturalized British Subjects.
[10] Including 3 Naturalized British Subjects and 2,390 British Protected Persons.

TABLE 6. *African and Non-African Population by Birthplace and Nationality, St. Mary's Island, 1931*[1]

Birthplace	British subjects		British protected	French		Portuguese	Others and not stated		Total	
	African	Non-African	African	African	Non-African	African	African	Non-African	African	Non-African
Africa	8,254	—	2,390	3,027	—	214	20[2]	—	13,905	—
West Indies	3	2	—	—	—	—	—	—	3	2
Elsewhere America	1	2	—	—	—	—	2	—	3	2
Others and not stated	2	109	—	—	121	—	183	40	185	270
Total	8,260	113	2,390	3,027	121	214	205	40	14,096	274

[1] Computed from *Census Report 1931*, pp. 7–8. For further details concerning non-Africans see Table 9.
[2] 13 Spaniards (from Teneriffe), 7 Liberians.

Nationality. Of the 14,096 Africans enumerated in 1931 in St. Mary's Island 8,260 were recorded as British subjects, 2,390 as British protected persons (mainly from the Gambia Protectorate), 3,027 as 'French protected persons', and 214 as 'Portuguese protected persons'. The remaining 205 Africans were mostly persons whose nationality had not been ascertained.

The 1944 census report does not show the Africans by nationality.

Sex. In St. Mary's Island the ratio of females to males has changed considerably at the various censuses, but from 1901 on there has always been an excess of males. In 1931 the ratio of females to 100 males was 80·4; in 1944 it was 82·8. As regards the Protectorate the Commissioners of the 1911 census stated: 'The balance between Males and Females is strikingly even in the Protectorate as a whole, there being just over 1,000 more males than females.'[1] The Commissioner of the 1921 census said: 'The same may, I think, be said now as in 1911, in regard to males and females "even in the Protectorate" being evenly balanced.'[2] But this was an error. There was in 1921 an excess of 10,000 males, and there were only 90·2 females to 100 males. In 1931 the ratio was 91·0 to 100. In the Gambia as a whole there were in 1931 90·2 females to 100 males.

Age and Conjugal Condition. The proportion of children (under 15) in St. Mary's Island, 1931, was 28·4 per cent., the proportion of men between 15 and 50, 36·6 per cent., the proportion of women between 15 and 50 24·7 per cent., and the proportion of old people (over 50) 10·3 per cent. The percentage of children was much higher in the Protectorate; it amounted in 1931 to 36·8. The ratio of children to 100 women was 94 in St. Mary's Island, 124 in the Protectorate, and 122 in the Gambia as a whole.

The number of girls was about equal to the number of boys. But there were in St. Mary's Island only 72·6 women to 100 men, in the Protectorate 88·3, and in the whole of the Gambia 86·9. Among the people between 25 and 50 years there were in St. Mary's Island only about 5 females for each 9 males.

The census reports distinguish only between single and married people,[3] but the large number of old single women suggests that widowed persons have been counted as single. Of the adult males in St. Mary's Island, 1931, only 34·6 per cent. were returned as married and of the adult females 51·5 per cent. Of the men between 20 and 30 only 15 per cent. were married.[4] The total number of wives exceeded the total number of husbands by 8 per cent.

For the Protectorate data concerning conjugal condition are not available.

---

[1] *Census Report 1911*, p. 3.　　　　[2] Ibid. *1921*, p. 2.

[3] Yet, the 1931 Instructions for filling in the schedule were quite explicit in this respect: 'Each person, whether infant, child, or adult should be entered as unmarried, married, widowed, or divorced. Divorced persons, who have married again, should be entered as "married" and not as divorced. As to whether a man or woman are married or not, the statements made by them should be accepted. The entry "divorced" should only be made when a legal divorce, by English or Mohammedan law, has been obtained.' (The 1944 Instructions said nothing concerning conjugal condition.)

[4] It should be borne in mind, however, that many Mohammedans wedded in conformity with the rites of their faith may have been returned as single because they were not civilly married.

TABLE 7. *Total Population by Sex and Age, the Gambia, 1921 and 1931*[1]

	Males						Females					
	Under 15 years		Over 15 years		Total		Under 15 years		Over 15 years		Total	
	1921	1931	1921	1931	1921	1931	1921	1931	1921	1931	1921	1931
Island of St. Mary .	1,251	2,004	4,002	5,962	5,253	7,966	1,256	2,078	2,799	4,326	4,055	6,404
Protectorate .	42,256	34,786	63,511	62,142	105,767	96,928	35,391	33,335	60,145	54,887	95,536	88,222
Total . .	43,507	36,790	67,513	68,104	111,020	104,894	36,647	35,413	62,944	59,213	99,591	94,626

Continued — Total column:

	Total	
	1921	1931
Island of St. Mary	9,308	14,370
Protectorate	201,303	185,150
Total	210,611	199,520

[1] See *Census Report 1921*, pp. 8–9; *1931*, pp. 10–11.

TABLE 8. *Total Population by Conjugal Condition, St. Mary's Island, 1921 and 1931*[1]

	Males				Females			
	Single		Married		Single		Married	
Age (years)	1921	1931	1921	1931	1921	1931	1921	1931
Under 5	374	630	—	—	392	707	—	—
5–10	471	732	—	—	481	715	—	—
10–15	406	642	—	—	383	655	—	—
15–20	513	771	3	7	360	618	43	114
20–25	552	780	57	82	251	391	151	366
25–30	637	886	141	217	197	298	210	378
30–35	339	506	169	328	105	156	145	296
35–40	286	408	241	373	125	139	159	265
40–45	150	205	156	284	106	79	103	192
45–50	138	155	139	254	120	80	84	176
50–55	60	63	94	169	69	71	56	125
55–60	44	60	70	129	92	73	52	106
60 and over	64	63	149	222	256	191	115	212
Total	4,034	5,901	1,219	2,065	2,937	4,173	1,118	2,231

[1] See *Census Report 1921*, p. 8; *1931*, p. 10.

The 1944 census report gives merely the following data concerning age and conjugal condition:[1]

	Under 5	5–10	10–15	15–20	20–30	30–40	40–50	50–60	Over 60	Total
Total .	2,028	1,845	1,890	2,139	5,044	3,279	2,585	1,305	1,037	21,152
Married .	—	—	—	1,299	3,475	2,361	1,181	573	341	9,230

It appears that the proportion of children (under 15) in St. Mary's Island had decreased since 1931 from 28·4 to 27·2 per cent., while the proportion of adults between 15 and 50 had increased from 61·3 to 61·7 per cent., and the proportion of old people (over 50) from 10·3 to 11·1 per cent. Thus the changes were very slight. Moreover, the apparent decrease in the proportion of children may have been due to inclusion, in 1944, of the people temporarily absent who no doubt were mostly adults.

While in 1931 only 41·8 per cent. of all adults were reported as married, the proportion in 1944 was 60·0 per cent.! But the figures for 1944 are obviously wrong. Of 2,139 persons between 15 and 20, 1,299 or over three-fifths were shown as married. Even if the females at that age were as numerous as the males (which is most unlikely), and even if one-quarter of the males and three-quarters of the females were married (two quite fantastic assumptions), the married people would constitute only one-half of the total population at that age.

3. Non-African Population

For the Protectorate no figures concerning the non-African population are available. In St. Mary's Island there were in 1921, 260 Europeans

TABLE 9. Non-African Population by Birthplace and Nationality, St. Mary's Island, 1931[1]

Birthplace	British	French	Norwegians	Spaniards	Swiss	Danes	Germans	West Indians	Americans	Not stated	Total
United Kingdom .	81	—	—	—	—	—	—	—	—	—	81
France .	1[2]	89	—	—	—	—	—	—	—	—	90
Spain .	—	—	—	6	—	—	—	—	—	—	6
Switzerland .	—	—	—	—	3	—	—	—	—	—	3
Denmark .	—	—	—	—	—	2	—	—	—	—	2
Germany .	—	—	—	—	—	—	1	—	—	—	1
West Indies .	2	—	—	—	—	—	—	2	—	—	4
Elsewhere in America .	2	—	—	—	—	—	—	—	2	—	4
Syria .	25[3]	32	—	—	—	—	—	—	—	—	57
Not stated .	2	—	12	—	—	—	—	—	—	12	26
Total .	113	121	12	6	3	2	1	2	2	12	274

[1] Computed from Census Report 1931, pp. 7–8. [2] Naturalized British Subject.
[3] Including 2 Naturalized British Subjects.

[1] See Census Report 1944, p. 6.

TABLE 10. *European Population, St. Mary's Island, 1910–39*[1]

Year	Average Government Officials	Total Government Officials	Total General Population	Europeans and Whites
1910	25	50	96	146
1911	30	57	186	243
1912	24	51	142	193
1913	32	53	120	173
1914	34	56	93	149
1915	28	44	84	128
1916	27	52	95	147
1917	28	41	101	142
1918	29	47	90	137
1919	27	49	138	187
1920	33	55	172	227
1921	38	75	163	238
1922	48	63	155	205
1923	45	65	145	210
1924	42	66	150	218
1925	53	64	150	214
1926	50	72	123	172
1927	53	72	116	188
1928	48	72	119	180
1929	54	82	116	198
1930	50	71	124	195
1931	48	65	120	185
1932	45	60	131	191
1933	51	63	135	198
1934	50	65	135	200
1935	57	69	114	183
1936	59	69	126	193
1937	62	69	163	232
1938	61	71	162	233
1939	64	72	189	261

[1] See *Medical Report 1919*, pp. 7, 9; *1920*, pp. 2–3, 6; *1921*, pp. 4–6, 11; *1922*, pp. 6–7; *1923*, pp. 6–7; *1924*, p. 7; *1925*, p. 7; *1926*, pp. 8–9; *1927*, pp. 7–8, 21; *1928*, pp. 9–10, 21; *1929*, pp. 9–10, 21; *1930*, pp. 10–11, 22; *1931*, pp. 8–9, 15; *1932*, pp. 8, 14; *1933*, pp. 6–7; *1934*, pp. 6–7; *1935*, pp. 11–12; *1936*, pp. 10–11; *1937*, pp. 10–11; *1938*, pp. 9–10; *1939*, pp. 3–4. The total (Europeans and Whites) does not always agree with the sum of the Government Officials and the general population.

TABLE 11. *Non-Native Officials by Sex and Age, Gambia, 1930–38*[1]

Date 1 Jan.	20–24 years M.	20–24 years F.	25–29 years M.	25–29 years F.	30–34 years M.	30–34 years F.	35–39 years M.	35–39 years F.	40–44 years M.	40–44 years F.	45–49 years M.	45–49 years F.	50–54 years M.	50–54 years F.	55– years M.	55– years F.	Age unknown M.	Age unknown F.	Total M.	Total F.
1930	1	—	9	—	13	—	12	1	9	1	12	1	4	—	2	—	1	—	63	3
1931	—	—	12	—	10	—	14	2	10	1	12	—	2	—	2	—	—	—	62	3
1932	1	—	9	1	12	—	14	2	12	—	7	—	7	—	1	—	—	—	63	3
1933	—	—	6	—	12	—	13	2	11	—	7	—	7	—	2	—	—	—	58	2
1934	—	—	7	1	7	—	10	1	11	1	8	—	8	—	—	—	—	—	51	3
1935	1	—	8	2	8	—	7	—	13	1	11	—	7	—	—	—	—	—	55	3
1936	1	—	9	1	9	1	9	—	13	—	9	1	5	—	—	—	—	—	55	3
1937	—	—	9	—	11	2	8	—	11	—	15	1	4	—	—	—	—	—	58	3
1938	—	—	7	1	15	1	7	—	12	—	13	1	6	—	—	—	—	—	60	3

[1] See *West Africa, Vital Statistics of Non-Native Officials 1930*, p. 1, to *1938*, p. 1.

and 47 Syrians. The figure for Europeans was probably obtained by adding the number of persons recorded as born in the United Kingdom (123), Denmark (53), France (51), Switzerland (27), Germany (1), and America excluding the West Indies (5).[1] According to the 1931 census report the number of non-Africans was 274, including 57 persons born in Syria. According to the 1944 census report there were in St. Mary's Island 101 European civilians (49 British, 30 French, and 22 of other nationalities) and 173 Syrians. Table 9 shows the distribution of the non-Africans in 1931 by birthplace and nationality.

The Medical Reports show the number of 'Europeans and Whites', and separately the number of 'European Officials' and the (Estimated) 'General European Population (excluding Government Officials)' from 1910 onwards. The results are given in Table 10. Finally, the Colonial Office published each year, from 1930 to 1938, the number of non-native officials by sex and age. The results are summarized in Table 11.

IV. BIRTH AND DEATH REGISTRATION

Legislation. Compulsory registration of births and deaths was provided by an Ordinance of 12 May 1845.[2] This Ordinance was amended six times.[3] The main provisions ensuring the registration of births and deaths as they stand to-day are as follows:

Registration of Births and Deaths

In the case of a birth (1) the father, (2) the mother, (3) the occupier of the house in which the birth occurred, shall verbally or in writing

---

[1] The Medical Reports show the European population by sex and occupation in 1921-5 (see *Medical Report 1921*, p. 5; *1922*, p. 7; *1923*, p. 7; *1924*, p. 7; *1925*, p. 7).

Year	Government Officials		Residents		Employees of mercantile firms		Missionaries		Total	
	Males	Females	Males	Females	Males	Females	Males	Females	Males	Females
1921	71	4	11	17	123	—	6	6	211	27
1922	47	3	6	22	115	—	5	7	173	32
1923	62	3	1	21	110	—	5	8	178	32
1924	54	14	2	21	118	—	4	5	178	40
1925	60	4	1	30	107	—	3	9	171	43

According to ibid. *1926*, p. 8, there were 166 white males and 29 females. According to the *Blue Books* (*1927*, p. 85, *1928*, p. 87, *1929*, p. 91, *1930*, p. 94), the white males in 1927–30 numbered 166, 175, 173, and 149 respectively and the white females 32, 40, 43, and 44 respectively.

[2] No. 8 of 1845, 'Ordinance for establishing a Registry of Births, Deaths, and Marriages, in the British Settlements on the Gambia', reprinted in *Laws and Ordinances of the British Settlements in the Gambia* (1852), pp. 99–103.

[3] See Ordinances No. 5 of 1883 (12 Sept.), reprinted in *Ordinances of the Settlement on the River Gambia*, 1883–5, pp. 5–7; No. 11 of 1886 (20 Dec.), *Gambia Ordinances 1867–88*; No. 7 of 1916 (15 Mar.), No. 9 of 1916 (15 Mar.), and No. 5 of 1919 (22 Apr.), *Government Gazette*, 22 Mar. 1916, pp. 103–7, 109–10, 30 Apr. 1919, pp. 97–8; No. 41 of 1940 (5 Dec.), *Ordinances, &c.*, *1940*, pp. 189–191. The Ordinance as it stood after the enactment of the Ordinance of 1886 is reprinted in *Ordinances of the Colony of the Gambia 1900*, vol. i, pp. 136–42. The Ordinance as it stood before the enactment of the Ordinance of 1940 is reprinted in *Revised Edition of the Ordinances of the Colony of the Gambia* (1942), vol. i, pp. 47–55 (cap. 13).

give notice to the Registrar within 14 days (the mother or the occupier, within one calendar month after the birth) or shall be liable to a fine not exceeding £5.

In the case of a death (1) the occupier of the house in which the death occurred, (2) the nearest neighbour of the deceased, shall verbally or in writing give notice to the Registrar within 14 days or shall be liable to a fine not exceeding £5.

Headings of Registration Forms

Schedule B (Birth): No.; When Born; Name, if any; Sex; Name and Surname of Father; Name and Maiden Name of Mother; Rank or Station in Life of Father; Signature, Description and Residence of Informant; When Registered; White, Black, or Mulatto; Signature of Registrar; Baptismal Name if added afterwards.

Schedule C (Death): No.; When Died; Name and Surname; Sex; White, Black, or Mulatto; Rank or Station in Life; Cause of death; How long ill; Age; Signature, Description, and Residence of Informant; When Registered; Signature of Registrar.

The Colonial Registrar[1] receives no remuneration for his services in this capacity. Registration of births and deaths in due time is free of charge, but a fee of 1s. has to be paid for delayed registration. The payment of a fee is moreover demanded for searching the registry (for each name within ten years, 1s.; every year beyond, 6d.) and for a certified extract from the registry (2s. 6d.). All fees received by the Registrars are to be paid into the Treasury for public use.

Registration Area. The 1845 'Ordinance for establishing a Registry of Births, Deaths, and Marriages, in the British Settlements on the Gambia' provided (section 2) that after the appointment of a Colonial Registrar it shall be lawful for the 'Governor or officer administering the government from time to time, to establish by proclamation the provisions of this Ordinance in any British settlements on the Gambia, or any dependency of the same, or so much of the said provisions as may be applicable to or can be enforced in the same, and to appoint at MacCarthy's Island, or any other settlement or dependency as aforesaid, a Deputy Registrar of births, deaths, and marriages....' Registration thereupon was established forthwith in St. Mary's Island,[2] and apparently in 1852 in MacCarthy

---

[1] The Legal Adviser is also Colonial Registrar and Curator of Intestate Estates; see *Blue Book 1938*, p. 92.

[2] On 1 June 1845 'a correct Register was first commenced' (ibid. *1845*, p. 115). In a Dispatch to Earl Grey, dated 29 July 1850, Governor MacDonnell stated: 'The establishment of a Registry of Births, Deaths, and Marriages, in Bathurst, at my suggestion, some years ago, has furnished more certain data from whence to draw inferences than previously existed ...' (*State of Colonial Possessions 1849*, p. 219). This statement suggests that some kind of registers were kept before 1845, though the Ordinance of that year was enacted 'Whereas, no means have hitherto been provided for the registering of births, deaths, and marriages within these settlements, and it is highly expedient that means should now be provided for establishing the same'. Birth and death figures had in fact been published for earlier years. The numbers of births (or baptisms) recorded for Bathurst in 1828–36, 1838, and 1839 were 30, 53, 18, 59, 73, 71, 59, 72, 92, 121, and 139 respectively and the numbers of deaths 34, 59, 38, 71, 105, 102, 98, 116, 160, 280, and

Island[1] and in 1862 in Barra Point, Cape St. Mary's, and Kombo District, but it is doubtful whether it was maintained for any length of time in the three latter areas.

An amendment enacted on 12 September 1883 repealed the above-quoted section of the 1845 Ordinance and stipulated merely that 'it shall be lawful for the Officer Administering the Government of the Settlement from time to time to establish by Proclamation the provisions of the . . . Ordinance of the 12th May 1845 at Macarthy's Island, or so much of the said provisions as may be applicable to the same, and to appoint from time to time a Deputy Registrar of Births, Deaths, and Marriages at Macarthy's Island . . .'. The Governor thereupon, on 10 June 1884, issued a Proclamation[2] ordering 'that the provisions of the . . . Ordinance of the 12th May 1845 are hereby extended to the Settlement of Macarthy's Island so far as they remain unrepealed by the amending Ordinance of the 12th of September 1883'.

The 'Ordinance to make further and better provision for the registration of Births, Deaths, and Marriages in the British Settlement on the River Gambia' of 20 December 1886 provided in addition:

> The Manager of British Combo shall be virtute officii Deputy-Registrar for the district of British Combo and from the Proclamation of this Ordinance the provisions of the Ordinance of the 12th May 1845 . . . and of the Ordinance of 12th September 1883 amending the same shall, so far as applicable, be extended to the district of British Combo.

But registration had already been re-established in British Kombo in September 1884 and was also reintroduced in MacCarthy Island and the Ceded Mile. In his report for the year 1884 the Administrator states that 'registration now extends to the whole Settlement',[3] and it was maintained until 1915, though probably with some interruptions outside St. Mary's Island. The returns of births and deaths in 1845–1914 are summarized in Table 12.[4]

More detailed statistics, available for 1859–66, are summarized in Tables 13 and 14.[5]

Until 1906 registration had been confined at best to the area of the Colony as constituted in 1853.

Other dependencies of the Colony, such as Bai and Kansala, furnished no returns.[6]

271. From MacCarthy Island 63 deaths were reported in 1836, but the number of births was not known. (See *Blue Book 1828*, pp. 111–12; *1829*, pp. 114–15; *1830*, pp. 114–15; *1831*, pp. 114–15; *1832*, pp. 118–19; *1833*, pp. 118–19; *1834*, pp. 118–19; *1835*, pp. 118–19; *1836*, pp. 118–19; *1838*, pp. 118–19; *1839*, pp. 136–7.)

[1] In a report quoted by Governor MacDonnell (29 July 1850) Staff-Surgeon Dr. Kehoe said: 'It is to be regretted that an accurate register of the deaths among European civilians has not been kept at MacCarthy's Island' (*State of Colonial Possessions 1849*, p. 220). For 1852 figures are available.

[2] Reprinted in *Ordinances 1883–5*, p. 98.   [3] *Report on the Gambia Blue Book 1884*, p. 14.

[4] Most of the gaps in the table are caused by gaps in the official publications, but some are due to the fact that the set of the *Government Gazette* which I used was incomplete for 1884–91 and 1897–9.

[5] They are given in Horton, *Physical and Medical Climate* (1868), pp. 260–7. He says (p. 260): 'The following tables of the mortality of the River Gambia from 1859 to 1866 were kindly furnished me by Mr. Thomas Johnson, the registrar of births, marriages, and deaths, expressly for this work.' The death figures are shown also by months.   [6] *Colonial Reports, Gambia 1893*, p. 5.

Table 12. *Registered Births and Deaths in the Colony of the Gambia, 1845-1914*[1]

Year	*Births*	*Deaths*
St. Mary's Island		
1845	98	101
1846	137	118
1847	100	106
1848	85	192
1849	89	179
1850	102	137
1851	114	185
1852	141	165
1853	118	227
1854	109	160
1855	99	189
1856	74	177
1857	114	204
1858	138	304
1859	111	199
1860	127	180
1861	88	201
1862	131	194
1864	69	252
1865	93	195
1866	102	224
1867	87	253
1868	111	328
1869	615	26
1870	55	285
1871	67	283
1872	..	530
1873	101	245
1875	71	416
1878	101	368
1879	78	344
1880	103	408
1881	..	460
1882	86	339
1883	77	389
1884	126	358
1887	193	466
1888	225	325
1889	232	240
1891	285	345
1892	242	334
1893	216	286
1894	217	335
1895	259	282
1896	304	270
1900	316	350
1901	304	340
1902	332	266
1903	297	371
1904	314	303
1905	271	299
1906	271	281
1907	257	296
1908	297	306
1909	285	264
1910	294	302
1911	262	258
St. Mary's Island (*cont.*)		
1912	261	262
1913	254	282
1914	274	297
MacCarthy Island		
1852	27	54
1853	31	61
1854	25	55
1855	80	179
1856	24	35
1857	16	49
1858	21	54
1859	16	55
1860	26	60
1861	18	43
1862	33	43
1864	21	70
1865	29	61
1866	28	49
1867	31	58
1868	33	90
1870	11	54
1871	26	41
1873	18	54
1879	13	43
1887	32	52
1888	41	41
1889	23	50
1891	41	38
1892	33	40
1893	23	54
1894	35	23
1895	27	21
1896	28	26
1902	10	15
1903	22	31
1904	36	33
1905	28	33
1906	35	23
1907	29	25
1908	20	17
1909	24	15
1910	33	38
1911	20	31
1912	23	33
1913	20	25
1914	19	14
Ceded Mile		
1862	4	5
1864	5	6
1865	4	5
1866	5	2
1867	—	—
1870	1	4
Ceded Mile (*cont.*)		
1887	44	200
1888	77	131
1889	69	110
1891	69	197
1892	54	134
1893	58	166
1894	66	150
1895	58	131
1896	28	44
1900	7	38
1901	12	18
1902	18	44
1903	26	26
1904	3	5
1905	7	9
1906	5	19
1907	17	13
1908	11	8
1909	8	10
1910	4	10
1911	7	1
1912	7	12
1913	7	17
1914	4	13
British Kombo		
1862	15	19
1864	13	19
1865	13	30
1866	14	21
1868	30	103
1870	10	16
1873	28	86
1884	2	33
1887	24	153
1888	37	87
1889	45	132
1891	28	77
1892	62	151
1893	35	121
1894	28	69
1895	32	65
1896	20	55
1900	29	39
1901	32	22
1902	43	85
1903	63	67
1904	18	40
1905	25	35
1906	27	36
1907	26	52
1908	22	56
1909	18	39
1910	32	35
1911	17	28
1912	12	29
British Kombo (*cont.*)		
1913	11	11
1914	9	8
Colony[2]		
1852	168	219
1853	149	288
1854	134	215
1855	179	368
1856	98	212
1857	130	253
1858	159	358
1859	127	254
1860	153	240
1861	106	244
1862	183	261
1863	115	414
1864	108	347
1865	139	291
1866	149	296
1867	118	311
1868	174	521
1869	615	26
1870	77	359
1871	93	324
1873	147	385
1879	91	387
1884	128	391
1885	232	512
1886	220	566
1887	293	871
1888	380	584
1889	369	532
1890	348	719
1891	423	657
1892	391	638
1893	332	611
1894	341	575
1895	381	503
1896	381	392
1897	325	365
1898	340	439
1899	360	429
1900	353	431
1901	348	380
1902	403	410
1903	408	495
1904	371	381
1905	331	376
1906	338	359
1907	326	386
1908	351	387
1909	339	330
1910	363	385
1911	306	318
1912	303	336
1913	292	335
1914	306	332

[*For notes to table see opposite*

TABLE 13. *Registered Births by Sex, St. Mary's Island, 1859–66*

	1859	1860	1861	1862	1863	1864	1865	1866[1]
Male	58	65	47	64	46	53	51	48
Female . . .	53	63	41	67	45	25	42	44
Total . . .	111	128	88	131	91	78	93	92

[1] 1 Jan. to 30 Sept.

TABLE 14. *Registered Deaths of Black and Coloured Population by Sex and Age, St. Mary's Island, 1859–66*

	Male					Female					
Year	1 to 7	7 to 20	20 to 40	40 and up-wards	Total	1 to 7	7 to 20	20 to 40	40 and up-wards	Total	Total
1859	47	13	37	19	116	31	11	24	13	79	195
1860	34	15	36	22	107	29	16	11	19	75	182
1861	34	16	40	21	111	37	9	17	11	74	185
1862	39	11	55	14	119	27	17	15	9	68	187
1863	68	25	44	34	171	65	14	31	35	145	316
1864	51	16	56	26	149	40	11	31	17	99	248
1865	44	8	34	13	99	30	11	24	14	79	178
1866[1]	41	9	33	22	105	33	7	12	17	69	174

[1] 1 Jan. to 12 Oct.

Notes to table opposite]

[1] See for 1845–62 *Blue Book 1845*, pp. 114–15, *1846*, pp. 218–19, *1847*, pp. 114–15, *1848*, pp. 114–15, *1849*, pp. 134–5, *1850*, pp. 134–5, *1851*, pp. 134–5, *1852*, pp. 134–5, *1853*, pp. 218–19, *1854*, pp. 226–7, *1855*, pp. 226–7, *1856*, pp. 226–7, *1857*, pp. 226–7, *1858*, pp. 226–7, *1859*, pp. 226–7, *1860*, pp. 226–7, *1861*, pp. 226–7, *1862*, pp. 228–9; for 1863 *State of Colonial Possessions 1865*, Part II, p. 16; for 1864–80 *Blue Book 1864*, pp. 226–7, *1865*, pp. 226–7, *1866*, pp. 226–7, *1867*, pp. 210–11, *1868*, pp. 226–7, *1869*, pp. 226–7, *1870*, pp. 226–7, *1871*, pp. 226–7, *1873*, pp. 138–9, *1875*, pp. 134–5, *1878*, pp. 128–9, *1879*, pp. 120–1, *1880*, pp. 134–5; for 1881–2 *Colonial Possessions Reports 1880–2*, p. 134, *1883–4*, p. 185; for 1883–4 *Report on Blue Book 1884*, pp. 12–14; for 1885 *Colonial Reports, Gambia 1890*, p. 5; for 1886 *Blue Book 1886*, pp. 138–9; for 1887–9 *Report on Blue Book 1887*, pp. 8–9, *1888*, p. 12, *1889*, pp. 16–17; for 1890–3 *Colonial Reports, Gambia 1890*, p. 5, *1891*, p. 6, *1892*, p. 5, *1893*, p. 5, *Government Gazette* 1892, 1893, Monthly Returns; for 1894–1906 *Blue Book 1894*, pp. 164–5, *1895*, pp. 160–1, *1896*, pp. 164–5, *1897*, pp. 170–1, *1898*, p. 48, *1899*, p. 48, *1900*, p. 48, *1901*, p. 54, *1902*, p. 57, *1903*, p. 61, *1904*, p. 61, *1905*, p. 61, *1906*, p. 67, *Government Gazette* 1894–6, 1900, Monthly Returns; for 1907–11 *Blue Book 1907*, p. 67, *1908*, p. 67, *1909*, p. 67, *1910*, p. 71, *1911*, p. 75, *Government Gazette* 1907–12, Monthly Returns, *Medical Report 1909*, p. 8, *1919*, p. 6; for 1912–14 *Colonial Reports, Gambia 1912*, pp. 15–16, *1913*, pp. 14–15, *1914*, p. 15. The figures computed from the Monthly Returns of Births and Deaths, published in the *Government Gazette*, do not always tally with the (probably revised) totals given in the *Blue Books* and other documents.

Deaths apparently include still-births at least from 1887 on. To what extent births include still-births is not clear. The still-births in the Colony in 1887–96 numbered 54, 30, 19, 35, 33, 35, 26, 27, 30, and 32 respectively; and in 1900–14, 31, 24, 36, 45, 39, 24, 31, 13, 32, 24, 27, 28, 26, 29, and 27 respectively. See *Report on Blue Book 1887*, p. 9, *1888*, p. 13, *1889*, p. 17; *Colonial Reports, Gambia 1890*, p. 6, *1891*, p. 7, *1892*, p. 5, *1893*, p. 6; *Government Gazette* 1894–6, 1900–2, Monthly Returns; *Medical Report 1909*, p. 9, *1919*, p. 6.

[2] The figures for the Colony comprise in 1852–61, 1871, and 1879 St. Mary's Island and MacCarthy Island; in 1867 St. Mary's Island, MacCarthy Island, and Ceded Mile; in 1884 St. Mary's Island and British Kombo; in 1868 and 1873 St. Mary's Island, MacCarthy Island, and British Kombo; in 1900–1 St. Mary's Island, Ceded Mile, and British Kombo; in 1862, 1864–66, 1870, 1887–9, 1891–7, and 1902–14 St. Mary's Island, MacCarthy Island, Ceded Mile, and British Kombo. For other years the territory covered is uncertain.

After the placing of MacCarthy Island, the Ceded Mile, and British Kombo under the Protectorate system of government, registration became practically non-existent also in these areas. The Colonial Report for 1905 said:

> At present no reliable returns are obtainable in regard to the births and deaths which take place in the Protectorate, as the chiefs and people view anything in the form of registration with great suspicion, looking upon it as regards themselves as the thin edge of the wedge for the introduction of a poll tax, and as regards their cattle as an intention on the part of the Government to levy a tax on them. It is hoped, however, that by constant and careful explanation the chiefs and headmen may be induced to keep such a record as will at least enable an approximate estimate to be formed as to the births and deaths in their districts.[1]

But the Report for 1906 stated:

> An endeavour is being made to introduce a very simple system, under which a record of births and deaths will be kept by the Headmen and Alimamis of towns, but it has not been in force long enough yet to be able to tell if it will answer.[2]

The Report for 1907 told the following story:

> At the beginning of the year the Chiefs and Headmen in the Protectorate were given red and blue books with pencils to match, and had it carefully explained to them that they were to enter all deaths in the red book and all births in the blue book. This they promised to do. A return was made at the end of the year, and the estimated population of each province with the return of births and deaths taken from these books is given hereunder:—

Province	Population	Births	Deaths
Upper River. . .	49,685	1,892	1,388
McCarthy Island . .	19,459	964	615
North Bank . . .	49,325	1,417	956
South Bank . . .	12,004	621	476
Kommbo and Fogni .	7,043	443	334

The natives view with suspicion the counting of the people and their cattle, and did not take to the idea of entering in a book every birth or death, but the object was carefully explained to them, and with the assurance that the imposition of a poll-tax was not intended, all the Headmen have made entries in their books. It is too much to say that the present returns can be regarded as accurate, but it is very probable that in a few years these books will give a good idea of the number of births and deaths every year in each district.[3]

The total births and deaths recorded in the Colony and Protectorate in 1907–10 were as follows:[4]

1907		1908[1]		1909[1]		1910[2]	
Births	Deaths	Births	Deaths	Births	Deaths	Births	Deaths
5,594	4,068	4,126	2,902	3,218	2,280	2,509	1,610

[1] 'Exclusive of births and deaths in the Protectorate Districts of South Bank and Upper River Province.'
[2] 'Exclusive of births and deaths in the Protectorate Districts of South Bank, McCarthy Island and Upper River Province.'

---

[1] *Colonial Reports, Gambia* 1905, p. 28.   [2] Ibid. *1906*, p. 20.   [3] Ibid. *1907*, p. 21.
[4] See *Statistical Tables relating to Colonies 1909*, p. 463; *1910*, p. 463.

Recording obviously deteriorated steadily. The Colonial Reports for 1908 and 1909 did not mention the subject at all, and the report for 1910 merely said: 'The number of births and deaths in the Protectorate proper is not obtainable.'[1]

The 'Registration of Births, Deaths and Marriages (Amendment) Ordinance 1916' (No. 7) repealed all prior provisions relating to the registration area and substituted the following:

The Ordinance shall apply to the Island of St. Mary and MacCarthy Island, but it shall be lawful for the Governor-in-Council by Order to apply this Ordinance or any part thereof, with such modifications as may be deemed necessary, to any other place or district in the Protectorate.

The Legal Adviser shall *virtute officii* be Colonial Registrar, but it shall be lawful for the Governor to appoint Deputy Registrars for and in respect of MacCarthy Island and any other place or district to which this Ordinance may be applied as aforesaid.

The Colonial Report for 1916 made the following comment:

In the few areas outside the Island of St. Mary, to which a system of registration has been applied, it has not been found to be productive of any useful result, and in 1916 an Ordinance was passed, No. 9 of that year, with the object of confining the compulsory system to places sufficiently advanced to follow it.[2]

Even so, it might have been expected that all births and deaths occurring in the Island of St. Mary and MacCarthy Island would be compulsorily registrable, but registration was apparently not carried out in the latter island. For some years, it is true, registration was enforced in the chief town.

The registration of births and deaths is carried out in Georgetown only. It is compulsory and reliable, being done through the headman to the dispenser, who acts as registrar.[3]

But birth data have been published only for 1921–7, and death data only for 1921–6.[4] Moreover, the Medical Report for 1935 stated explicitly:

Registration of Births and Deaths is only compulsory in Bathurst itself.[5]

[1] *Report*, p. 20. No further attempt seems to have been made to establish registration on a large scale in the Protectorate. The *Colonial Report* for 1922, it is true, says (p. 9) that 'a careful return from the North Bank Province for 1922 gives 1,628 births and 905 deaths'. But these figures were probably not obtained through registration.

[2] *Colonial Reports, Gambia 1916*, p. 13. At the same time interest in vital statistics seems to have vanished. While the *Government Gazette* for several decades up to 1914 had published detailed monthly returns, the *Gazette* for 1915 contains only data for the two quarters ending March and June, and the *Gazette* for 1916 only a half-year return for January to June. Subsequent issues gave no vital statistics.

[3] 'Annual Medical Report for the Protectorate and Georgetown, 1923' (*Medical Report 1923*, p. 21; literally the same in the report for 1924, ibid. *1924*, p. 17). See also ibid. *1920*, p. 23: 'The Dispenser [in Georgetown] acts as registrar of births and deaths, Meteorological registrar, and also as Inspector of Nuisances.'

[4] The births and deaths registered in Georgetown were (see ibid. *1923*, p. 21; *1924*, p. 17; *1926*, p. 44; *1927*, p. 45):

	1921	1922	1923	1924	1925	1926	1927
Births .	39	33	28	32	27	19	35
Deaths.	38	53	53	49	65	73	..

[5] Ibid. *1935*, p. 11.

In recent years, however, two attempts were made to extend the registration area.

(1) The 'Native Authority Ordinance, 1933'[1] provided:

9. Subject to the provisions of any law for the time being in force, a Native Authority may, subject to the general or special directions of the Native Authority, if any, to whom he is subordinate, issue orders to be obeyed by natives within the area:

(j) requiring the birth or death of any native within his jurisdiction to be reported to him or such other person as he may direct.

But there is no evidence that such an order has ever been issued.

(2) An Order made by the Governor-in-Council on 1 May 1937[2] provided that those sections of the Births, Deaths, and Marriages Registration Ordinance which refer to births and deaths shall be in force in two towns of North Bank Province (Kerewan and Jawarra), four towns of Mac-Carthy Island Province (Kau-ur, Kuntaur, Georgetown, and Bansang), one town of Upper River Province (Basse), and one town of South Bank Province (Bakau).[3] A Notice of 31 May 1937[4] said:

In exercise of the powers vested in him by section 3 of the Births, Deaths and Marriages Registration Ordinance, 1886 (Cap. 52), the Governor has appointed the persons holding the office of Sanitary Inspector in the Towns of Jawarra, Kuntaur, Basse and Bakau, and the office of Dispenser in the Towns of Kerewan, Georgetown, Kau-ur and Bansang to be Deputy Registrars of births and deaths for the purposes of the said Ordinance.[5]

The results obtained in the two towns of the North Bank Province were as follows:[6]

Towns	1937 (1 July to 31 Dec.)		1938			1939		
	Births	Deaths	Popu-lation	Births	Deaths	Popu-lation	Births	Deaths
Kerewan .	30	24	675	42	25	730	30	42
Jawarra .	10	9	576	30	20	588	20	22

No data have been published for any of the other towns and the Administration seems to be sceptical even as regards the returns from Kerewan and Jawarra.

1938. Vital statistics are recorded in the Island of St. Mary only as, owing to the illiteracy of the people, the collection of reliable data in the Protectorate is impossible.[7]

[1] No. 3 of 1933 (22 Feb.), 'An Ordinance to provide for the Recognition and Establishment of Native Authorities in the Protectorate and to prescribe their Powers and Duties', Government Gazette, 28 Feb. 1933, pp. 121–6, reprinted in Ordinances, &c., of the Colony of the Gambia 1933, pp. 9–17.

[2] See Order No. 6 of 1937, Supplement to Government Gazette, 15 May 1937, Ordinances, &c., of the Colony of the Gambia 1937, p. 163. See also Notice No. 268 of 31 May 1937, Government Gazette, 31 May 1937, p. 178.

[3] By Order No. 9 of 1937 (21 July; Supplement to Government Gazette, 31 July 1937) the same provision was made for another town of South Bank Province (Waslunga).

[4] See Notice No. 267, Government Gazette, 31 May 1937, p. 178, and 'Corrigendum', Notice No. 310, ibid. 15 June 1937, p. 197.

[5] By Notice No. 373 (ibid., 31 July 1937, p. 258), the Sanitary Inspector at Bakau was appointed to be Deputy Registrar in the Town of Waslunga.

[6] See Report on the North Bank Province 1938, pp. 11–12; 1939, p. 15.

[7] Colonial Reports, Gambia 1938, p. 14.

1939. Registration is compulsory in Bathurst. It has been introduced into the Protectorate but it is too unreliable at the moment to be of any statistical value.[1]

Even assuming that the Order of 1937 was fully enforced, the registration area would comprise hardly more than 10 per cent. of the total population of the Gambia.

The Medical Report for 1944 summarized the present unsatisfactory position as follows:

The births and deaths of non-natives are compulsorily registrable in the whole of the Gambia, but compulsory registration of the total population is applied to the Island of St. Mary and MacCarthy Island only. Endeavour is also made to introduce non-compulsory registration at certain larger centres in the Protectorate.[2]

Degree of Completeness. Official opinion on the completeness of birth and death registration has varied considerably in the course of time.

1849. . . . there is some question as to the accuracy of the registrar's entries of seamen's deaths [in Bathurst] . . . .[3]

The birth and death returns for 1858–61 were considered 'imperfect'.[4]

1868. The registered births appear to be only a third of the deaths, but this is accounted for by the fact that an order is requisite before a body can be buried, whereas, although it is compulsory to register the birth of a child, yet the natives frequently neglect, and do not take the trouble to do so.[5]

1873. This great difference between the Births & Deaths [in Bathurst] may in a measure be set down to the neglect of the half Civilized inhabitants & others to Register the Births of their Children.[6]

1875. It is difficult to ascertain whether there has been since [1871] any increase or decrease in the population, in consequence of the roving nature of many of the natives as well as their neglect to register births and deaths.[7]

1879. This number by no means represents the total births, in the settlement [Bathurst]. More than half, I believe, of the parties concerned do not come to have the births of their Infants registered.[8]

In his report for 1883 the Administrator said that he had 'no reason to question the fullness of the Registrar's figures as to deaths in the island of St. Mary, to which alone it may be fairly stated that the Ordinance of 12th May 1845 has applied', but that 'a comparison between the return of the Registrar and that compiled from information received from the heads of the different Christian bodies, represented by a total in the Settlement in 1881 of 3,825 against the Mohammedan and "Pagan"

---

[1] *Medical Report 1939*, p. 3.   [2] Ibid. *1944*, p. 7.

[3] *State of Colonial Possessions 1849*, p. 222.

[4] See *Statistical Tables Colonial Possessions 1858*, p. 420; *1859*, p. 417; *1860*, p. 431; *1861*, p. 438; *1862*, p. 459.

[5] *State of Colonial Possessions 1868*, Part II, p. 17.

[6] *Blue Book 1873*, p. 138. See also ibid. *1874*, p. 138.

[7] Ibid. *1875*, p. 134. Literally the same ibid. *1876*, p. 134; *1877*, p. 110; *1878*, p. 128; *1879*, p. 120; *1880*, p. 134. For incompleteness of birth and death returns in 1869–81 see also *Statistical Tables Colonial Possessions 1868–70*, p. 384; *1871–5*, p. 352; *1876–8*, p. 334; *1879–81*, p. 386. No figures whatsoever have been published for 1874, 1876, and 1877, and some of the published figures are quite erratic. For 1869 the number of registered births is given as 615 and the number of registered deaths as 26. It is out of the question that as many as 615 births should have been registered. On the other hand, the number of registered deaths due to cholera alone was 1,174 in St. Mary's Island and 98 in MacCarthy Island.

[8] Statement of Colonial Registrar in *Blue Book 1879*, p. 121.

elements who totalled 10,825, will readily show how little operative the above Act has been for the years given'.[1]

The amendment of 20 December 1886 made the Registration Ordinance a common informer's Ordinance, and the number of births registered in the Colony rose from 220 in 1886 to 293 in 1887 and 380 in 1888. The Registrar, in his report for 1888, made the following comment:

The total number of births registered in the Colony during the year under review was 380, being 87 in excess of the births registered in the preceding year; of these, 225 were registered at Bathurst, 37 at British Combo, 77 on the Ceded Mile districts, including Albreda, and 41 at McCarthy's Island. . . .

It is obvious that the statistics of births cannot be said to be quite accurate or reliable, although the figures showed an improvement on the returns of previous years. Taking Bathurst, for example, where it was only natural to expect that the returns would be full and complete, the register showed that only 225 births were registered, or 3·6 per cent. of the entire population, computing on the basis of the figures of the last decennial census.

In 1885 the registry returns [of the Colony] showed an excess of deaths over births of 280; in 1886 of 346; in 1887 of 578; and in 1888 of 204. Assuming the relative proportion of deaths to births to be correct, the obvious inference would be that the population is actually dying off at a rate by which it will be extinct in a short time; but it is manifest that the contrary is the fact, and I am therefore bound to assume that the returns of births were not as full and reliable as might be desired, and that a great many births occurring in the Colony, more especially among the Aboriginal population, were not registered. Section 8 of the Registration Ordinance of 1886 provides that a moiety of all penalties and forfeitures recovered under the Registration Ordinances after a summary conviction shall be paid to the person prosecuting to conviction; but as far as I know there has not been a single instance in which information has been given to the police or the responsible authorities against any parties contravening the provisions of the Ordinances. It is a well-known fact that the Joloff and other cognate tribes, which form the great bulk of the population, are averse to litigation, and no pecuniary inducement would make them assume the rôle of a common informer.[2]

There is, however, no evidence that birth registration was very defective either in St. Mary's Island (birth-rate 36) or in MacCarthy Island (birth-rate 45). The large excess of registered deaths over registered births in the Colony was due, it seems to me, to the constantly high mortality in St. Mary's Island and to the quite incomplete registration of births in the Ceded Mile and in British Kombo.[3]

Death registration was again considered complete for the whole Colony.

It being indispensably necessary previous to the interment of a corpse to give notice thereof, and obtain a burial permit, there is no room for evading the provisions of the law as regards the registration of deaths, and the returns under this head may therefore be implicitly relied on.[4]

---

[1] *Colonial Possessions Reports 1883–84*, pp. 185–6. The comparison between the returns of the Registrar and the information from the heads of the Christian bodies is not so simple. The former comprised only the Island of St. Mary (6,138 inhabitants) and showed for 1882 and 1883, 86 and 77 births respectively. The figures from the Christian bodies were 196 and 159 and apparently included also some baptisms of adults. But there is, of course, no doubt that the Registrar's records were quite incomplete.   [2] *Report on Blue Book 1888*, p. 12.

[3] How incomplete birth registration had been in the Colony as a whole in 1887 may be inferred from the fact that the number of registered live-births was only 239 while in the same year 274 infants 'succumbed to convulsions consequent upon teething, diarrhœa, and other infantile ailments' (ibid. *1887*, p. 9).   [4] Ibid. *1888*, p. 13. See also ibid. *1889*, p. 17.

In the following year the Registrar repeated his complaints about the incompleteness of birth registration.

As the present writer has more than once pointed out in previous reports, it is impossible to place absolute reliance upon these figures notwithstanding the pains which have been taken to attain perfect accuracy. According to the records of births, the population of the Colony has been steadily on the decrease during the *decennium*, while the contrary is an uncontrovertible fact, discovered by observation and experience.

Going further back to the registered returns for the five years preceding 1889, the figures show that the population has been progressively on the decrease.

In view of the fact that the Colony has been visited by no formidable epidemic since 1869, the climate congenial, and the sexes fairly balanced, I am loth to believe that a population so circumstanced must have decreased as the returns would indicate.

Assuming the correctness of the birth returns, the proportion of births to population is 2·7 per cent., while the proportion of deaths . . . is 3·7 per cent.

It must be borne in mind, however, that only births occurring in Bathurst and in the sub-districts are recorded, those which might have occurred in places beyond the area of registration, in which the parents might have been temporarily living either for the purposes of trade, or, which is more often the case, to avoid the expensive native customs consequent on the birth of a child, are, of course, not recorded.[1]

The Administrator made the following comment:

It will be observed from the tenour of the Registrar's report that the statistics given cannot be relied upon as giving an accurate idea of the state of the Gambia population.

The Registrar is of opinion, in spite of returns to the contrary, that the population is increasing, but although the disparity between the birth and death-rate is, doubtless, in reality not so great as would appear from the figures given (369 births, 532 deaths), yet I am inclined to the belief that the Registrar is too sanguine in his view of the excess of the birth-rate.[2]

The 1891 census showed in fact that the Registrar had been mistaken when he considered a steady increase of the Colony's population during the decennium 'an uncontrovertible fact, discovered by observation and experience'. Actually the population had decreased since the 1881 census from 14,150 to 13,057.

Similar comments on incomplete birth registration and adequate death registration were made in the early 1890s,[3] but when in 1896 the number of deaths dropped considerably it was said that 'it is difficult for the registrar to get perfect information relating to births and deaths'.[4] The Medical Report for 1907 said likewise that 'it is more than probable . . . that a number of births and deaths escape registration especially in the more out of the way parts'.[5] This was particularly the case in the Ceded Mile. But the low figure of births registered in that year in St. Mary's Island (257, including still-births) suggests that birth registration was also quite defective there. Moreover, birth registration seems even to have deteriorated in St. Mary's Island. It may suffice to mention that in 1918 only 218 live-births were registered as against 157 deaths of infants and 89 deaths of children between 1 and 5 years.

[1] Ibid , p. 16.   [2] Ibid., p. 18.
[3] See *Blue Book 1890*, p. 143; *Colonial Reports, Gambia 1890*, p. 6; *1892*, p. 5; *1893*, p. 5.
[4] Ibid. *1896*, p. 4. See also ibid. *1903*, p. 31; *1905*, p. 28.
[5] *Medical Report 1907*, p. 5. See also ibid. *1910*, p. 8.

The Medical Reports for 1926, 1927, and 1928 stated: 'Registration is compulsory and reliable for Bathurst.'[1] But although the numbers of births and deaths registered in 1929 were much higher, the Medical Reports then began to take a more sceptical view.

1929. Registration is compulsory and not reliable for Bathurst.[2]
1930. Registration is compulsory, but the figures may not be absolutely accurate.[3]
1931. Registration is compulsory in Bathurst, but the figures may not be accurate.[4]

Subsequent Medical Reports took again a more favourable view:

1935. Registration ... in Bathurst ... is for the most part reliable.[5]
1938. Registration ... in Bathurst ... is reliable.[6]

The Annual Colonial Report for 1931 said:

The statistics indicate ... that more births are being registered from year to year and this is undoubtedly due to the fact that parents, including the illiterates, are beginning to realize the value of certificates of birth to their children in adult years.[7]

The Annual Colonial Reports for 1934–7 stated that 'whereas all deaths taking place in Bathurst are registered (certificates of deaths and burial permits being required in all cases),[8] in some instances births of infants, in particular to illiterate parents, are not reported'.[9] The 1937 report added that 'with the new scheme for registration of Unqualified Midwives our [birth] returns should be much more useful in 1938 than in previous years', and the 1938 report stated: 'Registration of births is more accurate than previously as all midwives are now registered.'[10]

But it seems that birth registration in Bathurst is in fact still quite defective. The Medical Report for 1944 stated:[11]

The Colonial Registrar has expressed the opinion that the registration of deaths is about 100% accurate.[12] The accuracy of birth registration is probably about

---

[1] *Medical Report 1926*, p. 7; *1927*, p. 6; *1928*, p. 8. See also ibid. *1921*, p. 7; *1925*, p. 6.

[2] Ibid. *1929*, p. 8. On 13 Mar. 1930 the Colonial Registrar issued a Notice, in which he said: 'Several cases have occurred recently in which there has been a failure to register a birth. Persons whose duty it is to register the birth, render themselves liable to penalties if they fail to do so' (Notice No. 94 of 1930, *Government Gazette*, 15 Mar. 1930, p. 87). He issued a similar Notice on 27 Jan. 1936 (see Notice No. 88 of 1936, ibid. 15 Feb. 1936, p. 66).

[3] *Medical Report 1930*, p. 10.   [4] Ibid. *1931*, p. 8.

[5] Ibid. *1935*, p. 11.   [6] Ibid. *1938*, p. 9.   [7] *Colonial Reports, Gambia 1931*, p. 7.

[8] See 'The Public Health Ordinance, 1912' (16 May, reprinted in *Revised Edition of the Ordinances of the Colony of the Gambia*, 1926, vol. i, pp. 327–64, cap. 56):

'88.—(i) No corpse shall be buried without first obtaining from the Victoria Hospital a permit, signed by the Senior Medical Officer or other person authorised by him to sign, and every applicant for a permit shall answer, to the best of his knowledge and belief, all questions which may be put to him by the Senior Medical Officer or such other authorised person.

'(ii) Any person offending against the provisions of this section shall be liable to a penalty not exceeding twenty pounds.

'89.—(i) A Medical Register of Deaths shall be kept at the Victoria Hospital, in which shall be recorded the names of all persons dying in the Island of Saint Mary, together with such particulars as may be prescribed.

'(ii) Such particulars shall be entered by the proper officer in every case, prior to the issue of a burial permit to an applicant, and such applicant may be required to sign the Medical Register as informant of the death so recorded.'

[9] See *Colonial Reports, Gambia 1934*, p. 12; *1935*, p. 12; *1936*, p. 12; *1937*, pp. 15–16. See also ibid. *1932*, p. 10; *1933*, p. 10.   [10] Ibid. *1938*, p. 14.   [11] *Medical Report 1944*, p. 8.

[12] The Medical Department apparently does not share this opinion as it says (ibid.): '... the number of deaths may be taken as accurate enough for most purposes ....'

80% only, though this figure is probably increasing as education increases. Minor discrepancies occur since some births are still registered as much as sixteen years later in order to obtain the birth certificate required before entry to school.

V. Native Fertility, Mortality, and Population Growth

1. *Introduction*

The vital statistics of the Gambia have been affected all through by the incompleteness of registration, and for a number of years no records at all seem to have been available. But apart from these defects attributable to ill functioning of registration, the vital statistics have suffered from defects which can only be explained by incompetence or lack of interest on the part of officials responsible for presenting the returns.

(1) Very often it is not stated whether a figure refers to Bathurst only or to the whole Colony, and very often the same figure is given in some documents as referring to Bathurst and in others as referring to the Colony.[1]

(2) Very often the same figure is given in some documents for live-births and in others for total births, including still-births; the same is true of deaths. As the number of still-births is large, the error is serious. Very often the excess of deaths over births has been computed by deducting the number of live-births from the number of deaths including still-births.

(3) Very often the same figure is given in some documents for 'Total deaths under 5 years' and in others for 'Deaths over 1 and under 5 years'. The same is true of 'Total deaths under 1 year' and 'Deaths over 1 week and under 1 year'. The infant mortality statistics, therefore, are quite chaotic.[2]

[1] Some very startling changes in the official birth- and death-rates are due to the fact that the computer was not aware of the area to which his basic figures referred. Thus the rise in the birth-rate from 18·92 in 1915 to 37·92 in 1916 and the corresponding rise of the death-rate from 22·49 to 36·88 (still shown, for example, ibid. *1928*, p. 17) were due to the fact that though the birth and death figures all referred to Bathurst alone they were related for 1915 to the population of the Colony and for 1916 to the population of Bathurst.

[2] Thus, the infant mortality rates for 1902–7 are given ibid. *1907*, p. 8, as 139, 158, 146, 132, 102, and 126, but ibid. *1928*, p. 17, as 263, 245, 307, 274, 204, and 266. At the latter place the data for 1908–14 are given as follows:

Year	Live-births	Deaths under 5 years	Deaths under 1 year	Deaths under 1 week	Deaths under 24 hours	Still-births	Infant mortality rate
1908	351	155	77	23	—	32	284
1909	339	101	50	11	17	24	230
1910	363	40	68	34	11	27	311
1911	306	29	43	15	1	28	127
1912	303	42	66	6	—	26	354
1913	292	20	50	22	3	29	295
1914	306	27	59	16	5	27	263

Deaths under 5 include deaths under 1 for 1908 and 1909, but exclude them for 1910–14. The infant mortality rates for 1908–10 and 1914 were apparently computed by relating the sum of 'Deaths under 1 year', 'Deaths under 1 week', and 'Deaths under 24 hours' to the number of live-births; the infant mortality rate for 1911 was apparently computed by relating 'Deaths

(4) Very often the same figure is given in some documents for deaths of Africans, in others for deaths of non-Europeans, and in still others for deaths of the total population.[1]

How chaotic the position is still to-day appears from the following data for Bathurst given in the Blue Book for 1941 and the Medical Reports for 1941–4:[2]

Source	Year	Popula-tion	Births	Still-births	Deaths	Deaths under one	Birth-rate	Death-rate	Infant mortality rate
B.B.	1941	(14,370)	378	..	421	74	26	29	194·9
M.R.	1941	12,816	378	45	372	92	29·3	29·1	243·3
M.R.	1942	14,900	490	66	591	77	37·31	39·66	157·14
M.R.	1943	14,900	539	70	533	112	40·87	35·77	176·25
M.R.	1944	21,152	592	73	423	77	27·98	19·99	130·06

The birth figures for 1941 are the same in the Blue Book and in the Medical Report, but as the population figures to which the births are related differ considerably, the birth-rates differ considerably. The death figure for 1941 is much lower in the Medical Report than in the Blue Book, but the figure for infant deaths is much higher.

The birth-rate in the Medical Report for 1941 was computed by relating 'births' to population, while in the Report for 1942 the sum of 'births' and 'still-births' was related to the population. For 1943 the birth-rate was computed by relating the sum of 'births (live)' and still-births to the population, and for 1944 by relating 'births (live)' to population.

All birth-rates and death-rates for 1941–3 are far too high because the population was grossly understated.

2. Fertility

For the Gambia as a whole birth figures are available only for the year 1907, when 5,594 births were recorded for a population which then was estimated at about 146,000. This would mean a birth-rate of about 38, but the population was certainly underestimated, and the recorded births possibly did not represent a higher birth-rate than 32. However, the birth records themselves may have been incomplete. The figures for 1908–10 covered only two or three of the five Provinces and inspire less confidence still. In fact, the only birth data which deserve attention are those for St. Mary's Island, and as the figures prior to 1901 are scanty and in many years obviously defective, only those for this century will be discussed here.

under 1 year' to the sum of the live- and still-births; that for 1912 was apparently computed by relating the sum of 'Deaths under 5 years' and 'Deaths under 1 year' to the number of live-births; that for 1913 by relating the sum of 'Deaths under 5 years', 'Deaths under 1 year', 'Deaths under 1 week', and 'Deaths under 24 hours' to the sum of live- and still-births!

[1] Since the early vital statistics show, as a rule, only the total number of births and deaths, and since births and deaths of Asiatics (Syrians, &c.) have almost never been given separately, I shall use throughout in this section figures referring to the total population. The error thus introduced is small, as births to non-Africans have been rare and as the number of deaths among the small non-African population is, of course, low.

[2] See *Blue Book 1941*, p. 99; *Medical Report, 1941*, p. 3; *1942*, p. 3; *1944*, p. 8.

The number of births (including still-births) registered in St. Mary's Island oscillated in 1901–14 between 254 and 332 and averaged 284. As the population was about 8,000, this would suggest a birth-rate (including still-births) of about 35. The number of live-births oscillated in 1915–28 between 205 and 307, and in 1929–41 between 315 and 429; it rose in 1942 to 490, in 1943 to 539, and in 1944 to 592. The birth-rate hardly ever exceeded 30 in the last 30 years.

Official comments on fertility are very scanty, but the emphasis laid on incompleteness of birth registration suggests that the Administration thinks that fertility has been much higher than indicated by the birth figures. The Report on the Blue Book for 1889 gave still another reason for the small number of births registered in the Colony, viz. temporary absence of the parents.[1]

TABLE 15. *Registered Births and Deaths, St. Mary's Island, 1915–42*[1]

Year	Live-born	Still-born	Total deaths	Deaths under one year	Year	Live-born	Still-born	Total deaths	Deaths under one year
1915	249	30	266	77	1929	315	44	458	105
1916	292	22	284	73	1930	350	45	383	89
1917	307	30	332	72	1931	422	..	370	97
1918	218	45	617	157	1932	339	..	356	86
1919	216	42	257	86	1933	331	..	369	96
1920	205	44	369	112	1934	351	..	442	98
1921	222	62	337	111	1935	386	44	452	120
1922	295	50	437	148	1936	357	50	431	132
1923	255	52	412	127	1937	370	42	420	94
1924	291	57	513	137	1938	429	52	377	79
1925	262	48	329	112	1939	407	47	325	64
1926	281	42	335	100	1940	379	49	313	50
1927	278	45	357	88	1941	378	45	372	92
1928	263	56	407	104	1942	490	66	591	77

[1] All data for 1915–30 are taken from *Medical Report 1929*, pp. 8, 17; *1930*, pp. 10, 19. For live-born and total deaths 1931–9, 1941–2, and still-born and deaths under 1 year 1935–42, see ibid. *1931*, p. 15; *1932*, p. 14; *1933*, p. 6; *1934*, p. 7; *1935*, pp. 10–11; *1936*, pp. 9–10; *1937*, pp. 9–10; *1938*, pp. 9, 30; *1939*, p. 3; *1940*, p. 3; *1941*, p. 3; *1942*, p. 3. For deaths under 1 year 1931–4, see *Blue Book 1931*, p. 98; *1932*, p. 99; *1933*, p. 99; *1934*, p. 103. For live-born and total deaths 1940, see ibid. *1940*, p. 112. Figures for 1943–4 are shown p. 360 above.

As regards the Protectorate, the Acting Governor, in a report dated 26 July 1930, stated:

Maternity is still the normal function it should be, and so normal is it usually that the birth of a child merely causes a few hours' interruption in a woman's occupation. The bearing of children is relatively easy and it is very rarely indeed that a death of a woman in child-birth occurs.[2]

It must be borne in mind that the *raison d'être* of marriage among these people is the propagation of children, and it is extremely unlikely that a form of [circumcision] operation would be carried out which might interfere with the bearing of children.[3]

[1] See p. 357 above. *Medical Report 1944*, p. 8, mentions 'the custom of some tribes whereby the wife returns to her own home for the birth'.
[2] *Papers relating to the Health of Native Populations*, p. 142.
[3] Ibid., p. 143. But see also the statement of the Acting Colonial Surgeon (1890): 'I regret to have to say that I have certain knowledge that abortion is frequently carried on by herbalists in a manner known to the profession . . .' (*Report on Blue Book 1889*, p. 14).

The proportion of still-births among all births amounted in the Colony in 1887–96 to 8·8 per cent. and in 1900–14 to 8·5 per cent.[1] In St. Mary's Island the proportion amounted in 1915–30 to 14·2 per cent. and in 1935–44 to 11·1 per cent. Even if the number of live-births should have been understated considerably, still-births would appear to be very frequent.

In view of the lack of adequate birth data, particularly for the Protectorate, opinions on the frequency of venereal disease deserve special interest.

When the Colonial Surgeon D. Robertson was asked in May 1841 by the Committee on the West Coast of Africa 'Do syphilitic diseases prevail in the interior of the country ?' he answered: 'I think not. I have never seen a case from the interior of the country.'[2]

In his elaborate report for 1907 the Protectorate Medical Officer stated:

Tertiary Syphilis. This fortunately is rare in the Protectorate . . . .
Other Venereal Disease. Gonorrhoea is comparatively common, more so among the Foulahs than the other peoples, and of course commoner still among the inhabitants and neighbours of the numerous trading stations along the river. Primary and secondary syphilis are still distinctly rare.[3]

In the following year he said:

. . . there has been, I am sorry to say, during the last few years some increase in the number of cases of venereal diseases, which I see, especially gonorrhoea and soft sores, but also to a less extent syphilis . . . .[4]

The Medical Report for 1919 stated likewise that venereal diseases 'are rife' and 'are on the increase',[5] and subsequent reports contained similar complaints.[6] A few quotations may illustrate the apparently deteriorating situation.

1924. Venereal Diseases are well known to be extremely common in Bathurst but few of the natives avail themselves of Hospital treatment.[7]
1925. Protectorate. Venereal Disease.—This is so widespread as to be almost universal. The supposed infrequency of syphilis is a myth . . . .[8]
1926. Protectorate. Venereal Disease.—Still remains—attacking enormous numbers of the population, and is a great cause of disability.[9]
1927. Protectorate. Venereal diseases, especially gonorrhoea, are extremely prevalent, and, owing to neglect of the natives in seeking early treatment, severe complications are frequently met with.[10]

The reports for 1928–37 do not discuss the subject, but the reports for 1938 and 1939 said:

1938. Gonorrhoea past or present is almost universal in the population of Bathurst though it is not quite so common in the Protectorate.[11]
1939. Venereal diseases cause much concern.[12]

---

[1] These proportions should, however, be accepted with great reserve. Registration of still-births outside St. Mary's Island was apparently more incomplete even than registration of live-births. Moreover, in computing the percentages, I have assumed that registered births included still-births. But this was evidently not always the case. (The number of births registered in British Kombo in December 1907 and in MacCarthy Island in April 1909 was nil while the number of still-births registered was 1; see *Government Gazette*, 18 Jan. 1908, p. 22, 22 May 1909, p. 240.)

[2] *Report*, Part II, p. 223.   [3] *Medical Report 1907*, p. 35.   [4] Ibid. *1908*, p. 11.
[5] See ibid. *1919*, p. 4.   [6] See ibid. *1920*, pp. 2, 23; *1923*, p. 21.
[7] Ibid. *1924*, p. 6. See also ibid. *1925*, p. 6.   [8] Ibid., p. 23.
[9] Ibid. *1926*, p. 42.   [10] Ibid. *1927*, p. 42.   [11] Ibid. *1938*, p. 9.   [12] Ibid. *1939*, p. 3.

3. *Mortality*

General Mortality. In the Gambia as a whole the number of deaths recorded in 1907 was 4,068 or 28 per 1,000 of the estimated population and possibly something like 23 per 1,000 of the actual population. But it is doubtful whether the death records were complete. No all-inclusive figures are available for other years. In St. Mary's Island and the other parts of the Colony mortality has been frequently excessive. The greatest single disaster was probably the heavy cholera epidemic in 1869. In MacCarthy Island 98 deaths from cholera were recorded from 9 to 28 April. In Doomasangsang, a place midway between MacCarthy Island and Bathurst, there were 80 deaths from cholera. 'It has broken out with the same virulence at Albreda.' In Bathurst, between 5 May and 21 June, '1,174 deaths [were] registered, and it is to be supposed that some were interred without any registration'. The deaths from cholera in MacCarthy Island, Doomasangsang, and Bathurst were about 300 per 1,000 of the population.[1]

Since the influenza epidemic of 1918 mortality in St. Mary's Island has apparently never been excessive but has been all the time high. In 1920–41 the number of registered deaths oscillated between 325 and 513 without showing any marked tendency; in 1942 it rose to 591, but dropped to 533 in 1943 and to 423 in 1944. If the 1921 and 1931 census figures may be trusted, the death-rate on the whole has been lower since 1924 than in former years. Yet it would never have been lower than about 23 prior to 1939, and it would have been about 30 as recently as 1934–7 and possibly again in 1942. The Administration, it is true, has stated repeatedly that the death-rate does not convey a true picture of the mortality of the residents of Bathurst because many of the deceased are strangers.

> . . . it should be noted that the death rate in Bathurst is raised very considerably by the fact that the chief hospital of the Colony is situated there, that people come from all over the Colony for treatment, and that many of them are in a moribund condition when they reach Bathurst.[2]

This is certainly true. But it should also be noted that more than three-fifths of the total population of Bathurst are between 15 and 50 years, that the death records are possibly incomplete, and that there is a consensus of opinion that Bathurst is still to-day a very unhealthy town. The Island of St. Mary, a considerable part of which is liable to annual flooding, was uninhabited when the Europeans arrived and probably would have remained uninhabited or practically so if they had not come. That many thousands of Africans went to live there was either because

---

[1] See *Papers relating to the Outbreak of Cholera in the Gambia*, pp. 15, 25. See also Gray (pp. 445–6): 'It is impossible to estimate the number of deaths, which occurred between MacCarthy Island and Bathurst as the disease travelled down the river. Some villages may have escaped altogether, but when once the plague found its way into one of the many over-crowded stockaded villages, which the wars had brought into existence, it must have worked terrible havoc. It is known, for instance, that at the trading post at Dumasansan in Jarra the cholera carried off eighty persons out of a population of 300. Therefore it may well be that in the course of about three months one-quarter of the people living on the river banks fell victims to cholera.'

[2] *Colonial Reports, Gambia 1938*, p. 14.

they were compelled to do so (the Liberated Africans) or in order to secure British protection and to gain a livelihood. As far back as 1821, five years after the arrival of the British, Major William Gray emphasized the necessity and at the same time the difficulty of ameliorating the situation.

It is possible that much benefit might result from so shutting up the mouths of Newt and Crooked Creeks, and the one adjoining the latter, as to prevent the high flood-tides in the rainy season from entering them, as it would, if effectually done, reclaim from inundation and its consequent bad effects, a large space in the almost immediate vicinity of the town. But it remains to decide whether the ground about them is lower than high-water mark, in which case it would be impossible to remedy the present evil in any other way than raising the level of the surface, a work that would be attended with considerable expense and difficulty.[1]

After another five years the Commissioners of Inquiry into the State of the Colony of Sierra Leone stated:

Attempts have been made, by drainage, to overcome this evil in the immediate vicinity of the town, but the means hitherto employed have proved totally inadequate; and it is greatly to be feared that any effectual corrective must be attended with much labour and great expense.[2]

The amount of capital already invested in buildings, both by the government and by individuals, will perhaps be deemed sufficient to justify an attempt to remove these causes [which render the island so unhealthy]; but such an undertaking would be attended with considerable expense. For nothing can be done towards its accomplishment but by extensive and judicious drainage . . . . It is therefore a subject of regret that Barra Point had not in the first instance been selected for the settlement, instead of St. Mary's. The advantage which the latter place possesses as a roadstead is by no means sufficient to compensate for its disadvantages in other respects, or for the poverty of the soil and badness of the water.[3]

The present situation may be illustrated by a few quotations from recent medical reports.

1930. The more our circumstances are studied the clearer it becomes that a decided and sustained policy is required in Sanitation and Hygiene in several directions. I.—One is the complete suppression of anopheline breeding spots within town precincts. Our street drains are still largely grassy earth pits from some of which water has to be swept out and which land crabs honeycomb with mosquito nurseries. In such things we have slipped over a quarter of a century without progress! One result is that we stagger along with a heavy death rate, while a promising birth rate is annually pitted against conditions that defeat both arrival and survival of infants. . . .[4]

1935. The year 1934 ended in gloom following the visitation of a grave outbreak of Yellow Fever. This focussed attention on the insanitary condition of Bathurst and showed clearly that a perfect nidus existed for the growth of any epidemic.[5]

For the most part housing conditions can only be described as wretched and primitive in the extreme.[6]

---

[1] Gray and Dochard, p. 367.   [2] Report, First Part, p. 104.

[3] Ibid., Second Part, p. 5. See also, for example, Alexander, Narrative of a Voyage (1837), p. 70: 'But why a settlement has been founded amidst swamps, when higher up, and with plenty of water for ships of large size, there are dry and healthy spots, I cannot comprehend. However, Bathurst in this respect resembles our settlements elsewhere: we fix ourselves on the first spot that presents itself eligible for commerce, seemingly regardless if we perish in the pursuit of wealth.'

[4] Medical Report 1930, p. 16.   [5] Ibid. 1935, p. 6.

[6] Ibid., p. 16; see also ibid., p. 17. A vivid description of these housing conditions is to be found ibid. 1922, p. 12: 'Poor housing on damp sites in neglected parts of the town contributes to all our high mortality figures. It is still unfortunately true that families in the rainy

Until Bathurst is raised to allow of adequate free drainage health conditions can never be good. It is useless to complete cures and return patients to an environment which means almost certainly a recurrence of their disease. This problem stands easily first and the health of Bathurst is dependent on its solution.[1]

1936. The greatest problem in Bathurst remains as always that of adequate drainage. The Reclamation scheme has most unfortunately been held over at least for some years. Bathurst without adequate drainage will present the picture of flooding and ill-health so often described in previous Reports.[2] It is impossible to over-stress the importance of this.[3]

The unfortunate postponement of the Reclamation Scheme leaves us with our greatest problem still unsolved—and therefore in a dangerous position. Linked up with the actual problem of reclamation and level raising is the equally important problem of housing. Nearer and nearer to us year by year creeps Plague.[4] We are in no position to withstand it—and shall not be until the miserable hovels so prevalent here are razed to the ground and proper rat-proof buildings erected in their stead.[5]

1937. Mosquito borne disease will however remain the greatest problem in Bathurst until such time as the Reclamation Scheme, and its concomitant, re-housing of the population, are completed. No sanitary regime, no matter how well supervised can hope to eliminate mosquito borne diseases till such time as proper drainage of the town can be provided and this cannot be done till the centre of the township is raised to a higher level than its periphery. Pumps ameliorate the condition but they do not cure it. The only absolute cure is complete reclamation; and until this scheme is carried out Bathurst cannot be rendered free from the dangers of Malaria and Yellow Fever, nor can such advancements as septic tank latrines for general use be contemplated.[6]

Everything depends on the Reclamation Scheme. Nothing of real value can be initiated till this matter is decided, one way or another. Reclamation, as was remarked before, offering the only possible real cure for most of the ills to which Bathurst is liable.[7]

Lord Hailey described the situation in 1938 as follows:

The health conditions of the capital are far from satisfactory. A reclamation scheme to improve the level of a part of the town which is submerged in the rainy season has been postponed, and the existing conditions of bad drainage are aggravated by bad housing. . . . Malarial infection is prevalent; there are also important problems of sewage disposal in Bathurst and the riverine towns.[8]

A Report on Development and Welfare in the Gambia, prepared by the Commissioner for Post-War Development, Mr. K. W. Blackburne, with the assistance of a local Development Committee, describes in detail recent developments.

season are sometimes beaten to find a large enough dry area to make a fire on either outside their houses or inside for days on end. Sometimes the bed is almost the only article above water. There are areas in Bathurst on which no people ought to have been given sites till the level was sufficiently raised.'

[1] Ibid. *1935*, p. 21.

[2] To quote only one example. In the *Sanitary Report on Bathurst* for the two weeks from 22 Nov. to 5 Dec. 1910 the Senior Sanitary Officer said (p. 6): 'Reclamation, filling up of swamps and low-lying land in the town, was in 1902 and in 1905, and is now, and will remain till it is done, the most important sanitary large work required in Bathurst. . . . I presume the work would be quite simple, and the only difficulty be how and where to find the money.'

[3] *Medical Report 1936*, p. 7.

[4] There have so far only occurred a few small outbreaks of plague in the Protectorate. See ibid. *1922*, p. 9; *1930*, p. 13.

[5] Ibid. *1936*, p. 21.

[6] Ibid. *1937*, p. 7.

[7] Ibid., p. 20.

[8] Hailey, pp. 1170-1.

Between 1936 and 1939 there was considerable correspondence between the
Colonial Office and the Gambia in regard to the administrative feasibility and the
financing of the scheme and in 1938 it was suggested that an application should be
made to the Colonial Development Fund for a free grant of £350,000 towards the
total cost [£553,300]. In the same year the Secretary of State enquired whether it
would be possible to move the town of Bathurst to another site. The then Governor
replied that no other suitable site existed and that the removal of the town, in which
much capital had been sunk, would arouse formidable opposition. At that time the
possibility of moving *a part* of the population of the town to another site was
apparently not considered.

No decision in regard to the reclamation and drainage scheme had been reached
by the summer of 1939 and, on the outbreak of war, the execution of the scheme was
deferred owing to the necessity for avoiding any diversion of machinery from the
United Kingdom.

. . . Early in 1941, Dr. G. W. M. Findlay of the Wellcome Institute of Scientific
Research visited the Gambia in connection with his investigation into yellow fever
in Africa. In his report he referred to Bathurst as follows:—

'Clearance of over-crowded areas is being carried out in Lagos but in Bathurst
the population, massed on the Island of St. Mary, still lives in one of the worst
tropical slums in Africa. Until Bathurst is removed from the water-logged Island
and rebuilt on the Atlantic coast it will continue to be a disgrace to the Colonial
Empire.'

The passing of the Colonial Development and Welfare Act in 1941 and the
invitation of the Secretary of State to prepare a comprehensive plan of development
offers at last an opportunity to remove this disgrace. The situation in Bathurst has,
however, changed so vastly from that obtaining before the outbreak of war that the
reclamation and drainage scheme of 1935 no longer appears to be the best solution.

The greatest changes which have occurred in the years since the beginning of
the war are the increase in the population of the town and the reduction of the area,
already totally inadequate, available for their houses. . . .

The increase in population is bad enough by itself, but there is another new and
important factor to be considered. In 1941, and again in 1942, it became necessary
for a part of the town to be evacuated to make room for a flying boat base and for
oil tanks. Approximately 32 acres of the town was cleared in this way and the
inhabitants of the cleared area, unable to find alternative building land in the town,
merely added to the overcrowding problem. This land is being leased to the Air
Ministry and the Admiralty for a long period and for all practical purposes the
inhabitable area of Bathurst has now been reduced permanently by nearly 8%.
Moreover it appears likely that still further land will be required in order to create
an anti-amaryl area around the flying boat base. This may involve the clearance
of a further considerable area of densely inhabited land. . . . A count in 1942 disclosed
that about 10% of the population were sleeping in the streets, while an unascertained number of others were sleeping in private yards and out-houses without the
knowledge of the owners. Before the war there were two open spaces in the town,
the King George V Memorial Playing Ground and MacCarthy Square. The former
is included in the area now occupied as a flying boat base, leaving MacCarthy Square,
6 acres in extent, as the sole recreational ground and open space. . . .[1]

With the object of finding a permanent solution of the problem of overcrowding in Bathurst 'the Governor appointed a Committee in 1942 to
draw up plans for the development of the Kombo area.[2] At the same
time he invited the Commissioner of the Island of St. Mary and the acting

---

[1] *Development and Welfare in the Gambia, June 1943*, chapter xvi, pp. 7–8.

[2] The 'Report of the Committee Appointed to draw up Plans for the Future of a Portion of
Kombo St. Mary' is reprinted ibid., chapter xvii, pp. 5–15.

Senior Medical Officer to investigate possible improvements in the layout of Bathurst.'[1] The main conclusions reached by these two officers were:

The total area available in the Island without large scale reclamation only allows, on well laid out lines, for a maximum of 1,600 houses accommodating 7,500 to 8,000 people. If the Town of Bathurst is to become a modern township this number should not be exceeded. If on the other hand it is considered feasible to carry out extensive reclamation it must be considered whether this should not rather be directed to providing a modern land aerodrome as was done at Singapore. This would bring aerodrome, flying boat base and sea port together, would make operation quicker and more economical and would enable complete sanitary control to be maintained over the whole traffic area.

It is not suggested therefore that reclamation, if undertaken, should be directed to providing more residential accommodation on the Island. The land which can be satisfactorily used for this purpose should be so used and should house those people whose business requires that they should remain in Bathurst, up to the numerical limit indicated above. The proposals indicated on the attached plan therefore are for housing this limited population in a dignified town providing adequate facilities for human development and healthy recreation. The remainder of the inhabitants should be accommodated on the mainland together with all such Government and commercial activities as do not need to remain in close contact with the Port. It does not appear economic in these days of rapid transport to spend large sums reclaiming unsuitable land for housing when suitable land exists only six or eight miles away and there is no counter-balancing advantage in favour of the former area.[2]

The plan thereupon proposed by the Government was summarized by the Governor as follows:

Broadly, the proposal is to abandon the old reclamation and drainage scheme; to produce a smaller and better Bathurst; to provide alternative accommodation in the Kombo for surplus population; to develop healthy residential areas in Kombo St. Mary for European and African alike, and to remove to the mainland virtually all Government offices, Government officers' quarters, and Government House.[3]

In the meantime the always serious problem of malaria in Bathurst has been aggravated through the war. The Medical Report for 1942 said:

The influx of a large number of a susceptible population into an overcrowded and hyper-endemic malaria area has had the natural result of increasing the malarial problem. Malaria has been and remains our greatest and most difficult hygienic problem.[4]

The report listed the following 'Factors leading to the increase in Malaria'.

1. The introduction of new strains of malaria parasite into Bathurst, against which natives of Bathurst have no immunity. These new strains were brought in by labourers from the protectorate, and by the large numbers of troops coming from other parts of West Africa.

2. The virulence of all strains of malaria parasite, whether imported or indigenous, must have been greatly increased by repeated passage through a population of non-immunes—i.e. the labourers and troops mentioned above, also the large number of Europeans entering Bathurst.

[1] Ibid., chapter xvi, p. 10.   [2] Ibid., p. 11.
[3] Legislative Council, *Meeting held 16th November, 1943*, p. 18. Recently it has become doubtful how much of this plan will in fact be carried out.
[4] *Medical Report 1942*, p. 4.

3. The presence of a large reservoir of infection in a non-immune population, leading to high incidence of infection amongst mosquitoes.

4. Insufficient mosquito control measures.

5. Lowered general resistance to disease of the populace, due to overcrowding, poor sanitation and subnutrition.[1]

As regards the Gambia as a whole, I shall first submit some data concerning smallpox, sleeping-sickness, and tuberculosis.

Smallpox. This disease was apparently introduced by Liberated Africans.

Towards the close of 1835, a vessel left Sierra Leone, bringing three hundred of these unfortunate creatures to the Gambia. . . . On the above occasion, many of them had been attacked with small-pox before they were sent on board; but no medical aid was present, and the fatal disorder spread fearfully amongst them. Twenty-seven died at sea, and a great part of the remainder subsequently perished at St. Mary's. The small-pox was thus introduced into the island, and numbers of the resident Negroes were hurried into eternity.[2]

Another epidemic of smallpox occurred in Bathurst in 1880–1,[3] and in 1887 'there was a general outbreak of small-pox all over the British Settlement'.[4] At the same time the Administrator stated: 'Small-pox is more or less prevalent every year.'[5]

In 1906 conditions were bad in the Protectorate.

No case of small-pox was known of in Bathurst during the period under report, but in the Protectorate it broke out in several places and carried off a large number of persons, especially children.[6]

In the Protectorate, especially in Combo, Fogni, and the South Bank Provinces there was a good deal of small-pox.[7]

---

[1] *Medical Report 1942*, p. 14. See also *Development and Welfare in the Gambia*, chapter x, pp. 16–18.

[2] Macbrair, *Sketches of a Missionary's Travels* (1839), p. 301 (see also the declaration of the master of the vessel, 18 Dec. 1835, *Report from the Committee on the West Coast of Africa*, 1842, Part II, p. 201). Macbrair adds: 'A similar specimen of wholesale manslaughter took place during the preceding year, when a full vessel of these hapless victims were sent in a diseased state to M'Carthy's Island; where no proper shelter or attendance was provided for them, and many accordingly died from neglect. If the amount of the present population were compared with the large number of liberated Africans that have been sent to this colony, the mortality would appear frightful indeed!' The removal of Liberated Africans from Sierra Leone to the Gambia began in 1818. 'By the year 1836 the liberated Africans in the Gambia under charge of the Government were no less than 2,386' (Archer, p. 39); they constituted then nearly one-half of the total population of the Colony. 'When Lieutenant-Governor Mackie assumed office in 1838, he utterly condemned this system of indiscriminate immigration and refused to receive any more liberated Africans from Sierra Leone' (Gray, p. 364). On 23 May 1841 Lieutenant-Governor Huntley stated before the Committee on the West Coast of Africa that the total number of negroes emancipated by the Mixed Commissioners at Sierra Leone and who had been transferred to the Gambia and established in this settlement was 2,914, and that of these about 1,400 were living there (see *Report*, Part II, p. 212). The Commissioner, R. R. Madden, drew the following conclusion: '. . . by the above returns and making allowance for those who were fortunate enough to escape from the settlement, it appears that nearly one-half of the whole number brought here must have perished' (ibid., p. 187).

[3] See *Colonial Possessions Reports 1879–80*, p. 216; *1880–2*, p. 134. The number of deaths from smallpox is not given, but the death-rate of Bathurst in each of these two years was approximately 70.

[4] *Report on Blue Book 1887*, p. 14. See also ibid., p. 9. The total number of registered deaths from smallpox in the Colony was 146 out of a total of 817 deaths excluding still-births (death-rate approximately 60), but for 224 deaths the cause was 'unclassified and undefined'.

[5] Ibid., p. 8.   [6] *Colonial Reports, Gambia 1906*, p. 15.   [7] Ibid., p. 20.

In the following years there were apparently only small outbreaks in the Protectorate,[1] and it was stated that 'small-pox is not nearly so rife as it used to be'.[2] But in 1914–15 smallpox was again more prevalent in the Protectorate,[3] and in 1921–3 the situation was unsatisfactory also in the Colony.

1921. An epidemic of small-pox occurred in Bathurst in March, and the disease lingered on amongst a well vaccinated population until the end of the year. There were many cases of a mild type, and it is suspected that some of these did not come under observation at all. Thirty-five people were attacked by the disease, of whom six died.[4]

Small Pox has been a troublesome disease all over the Colony throughout the year.[5]

1923. Smallpox broke out in town [Bathurst] in mid-March and was not over till the end of July. In that interval 36 patients were isolated and treated with a case mortality of 11·1 per cent.[6]

There was one case only of Smallpox in Georgetown, but many cases in the Protectorate in the beginning of the year.[7]

For some years thereafter recorded cases were few, but a serious epidemic occurred again in 1928.

Smallpox must be reckoned as endemic in the Protectorate but infection is also frequently carried over the border from Senegal. This latter happened during March in Central Badibu, where 75 deaths, all children, occurred. During the second and third quarters of the year many cases were reported on both sides of the River. During October 279 further cases were reported from North Bank Province.[8]

Then came a series of most favourable years, but 1936 and 1937 were again bad.

1936. Protectorate. A serious outbreak of Small Pox occurred during June and July. . . . Many cases were concealed and the actual number of deaths is uncertain.[9]

1937. An outbreak, involving practically the whole of the Protectorate, occurred during March to June. Totals of cases and deaths are not available owing to the wide spread nature of the epidemic.[10]

In 1941 '355 cases were reported with 46 deaths'.[11]

In 1944 'there was a minor outbreak of smallpox in Bathurst and the Protectorate which lasted from March to May'; reported cases numbered 171.[12]

Sleeping-sickness. No case of this disease seems to have been discovered by Europeans before 1902. Captain Todd, in a report on animal diseases of the Gambia, dated 18 December 1906, stated:

This disease [tsetse fly disease] has existed in the Gambia for a number of years. Some of the old and more intelligent natives remember in their youth that cattle died

[1] See ibid. *1907*, pp. 18, 21; *1908*, p. 20; *1911*, p. 17; *1917*, p. 12; *Medical Report 1907*, p. 10; *1908*, p. 3; *1909*, pp. 10, 25; *1910*, pp. 6, 10.

[2] *Colonial Reports, Gambia 1908*, p. 23.

[3] See *Medical Report 1914*, pp. 6, 15, 25, 27; *1915*, pp. 7, 15.   [4] Ibid. *1921*, p. 4.

[5] Ibid., p. 7. 'All over the Colony' probably means 'all over the Gambia'. In 1922 there were 24 reported cases with 2 deaths; see ibid. *1922*, p. 6.   [6] Ibid. *1923*, p. 11.

[7] Ibid., p. 21. See also *Report on Upper River Province 1923*, p. 5: 'Smallpox has been bad in the Province all through the season and there is still a good deal of it about.'

[8] *Medical Report 1928*, p. 12. See also ibid., p. 44.

[9] Ibid. *1936*, p. 46. The reported cases were 140 with 24 deaths; see ibid., p. 9.

[10] Ibid. *1937*, p. 8; see also ibid., p. 13.   [11] Ibid. *1941*, p. 4.

[12] See ibid. *1944*, p. 10.

of this sickness. It was not until 1902 that it was proved to be caused by a trypano-some in the blood. In this year Doctors Dutton and Todd made an expedition to the Gambia to study sleeping sickness, and found trypanosomes in the blood of horses and many other animals, as well as in man. . . .

The disease is transmitted to animals by the testse fly (*Glossina palpalis*), which is found from one end of Gambia to the other.[1]

But the natives had evidently been aware of the spread of sleeping-sickness long before 1902. In his comprehensive Report on the Protectorate for 1907 the Protectorate Medical Officer said:

A practice which seems to be peculiar to the natives of this part of Africa, is that they are in the habit of removing in youth certain glands of the neck, as a preventive of Sleeping Sickness. This operation all the inhabitants of the Gambia firmly believe saves those who undergo it from this dreaded disease . . . .[2]

Sleeping sickness is endemic but fortunately rare, and native report says that in earlier times it was much more prevalent than it is at the present day.[3]

Three years later he discussed the situation more fully.[4] I can give here only a very brief extract.

Since I have been in the Protectorate (since 1902) I see, perhaps, half-a-dozen cases a year, all of which have eventually terminated fatally . . . .

. . . I remember patients from the following places:—Faraba in the Upper River, Lamin Koto, McCarthy Island and Sami in the McCarthy Island Province, Salikenni (2) in Baddiboo, Albreda in Niumi, Kaiaff and Kwinella in the South Bank, Man-dowa and Willimissa in Kiang, and two cases in Bathurst, either from Bathurst itself or some adjacent town in Kombo.

One may say therefore that no part of the Gambia is safe from the disease, and its presence must always be a constant menace. . . .

Native tradition asserts that in earlier times the disease was much more prevalent in the Gambia than it is now, and whole districts, now desirable dwelling-places, are said to have been uninhabitable. In the Protectorate, this particularly applies to Nianija, which, in former days bore such evil name that its inhabitants were few or non-existent, but it is now a rich and fairly thickly populated country inhabited mainly by Turankos, a branch of the Foulah race and a prosperous people, who are the owners of large quantities of cattle. Accounts too of the slave-trade and the frequent awful mortality among the slave-gangs and slave-ship cargoes from this disease, all provide additional evidence to show in those days sleeping sickness was a much commoner disease in the Gambia, one of the chief centres of the export trade in slaves, than it is now.

The general conditions favourable to the incidence of the disease must, one would think, be much the same round the Uganda Lakes or in the Congo as in the Gambia: the actual morbid agent, the Trypanosome, is the same, the same carrier, the Tsetse fly (more particularly G. palpalis) is present. Yet in one place the disease is decimat-ing (or worse) the people, in the other, though fatal to those it attacks, it is un-common. Our people no doubt have the advantage over the inhabitants of Uganda in the matter of stamina, as the Gambia natives are a fine strong people of good physique and constitution; many are quite wealthy, all are comfortably off and there are certainly nowadays no very poor or absolutely destitute, for everyone can get enough to eat, and nearly all live really well. . . .

[1] *Second Report on the Animal Diseases of the Gambia*, pp. 1–2.

[2] *Medical Report 1907*, pp. 30–1.

[3] Ibid., p. 43. See also the statement of the Senior Medical Officer ibid., p. 21: 'There is no doubt that the Gambia is an endemic area for sleeping sickness although the disease is by no means at the present time common; efforts should be made to encourage the people to bring all such cases to Hospital for the Atoxyl treatment is most encouraging.'

[4] See Dr. Emilius Hopkinson, 'Report on Sleeping Sickness in the Gambia', ibid. *1910*, pp. 17–21.

The situation of the towns too, probably compares favourably with what is the case in Uganda. . . .

Although all these are favourable factors on the side of general resistance to disease, one can hardly believe that to them alone is due our present comparative freedom—long may it continue—from the scourge of Sleeping Sickness. So that taking everything into consideration—the established presence on the Gambia of the Trypanosome, of myriads of its carriers, the Tsetse flies, and of its results, cases of disease—I am driven more to the belief (and hope) in a degree of acquired immunity among our people.

Doctors Todd and Wolbach in their 'First Report of the Expedition to the Gambia, 1911', said:

The expedition reached Bathurst . . . on the 4th of February, 1911. . . . it travelled about 550 miles, and it palpated the necks of 12,298 natives drawn from ninety-five towns and villages. Trypanosomes were found in seventy-nine persons. If to these be added twenty-one persons with much enlarged glands, whom it was impossible to puncture and who were almost certainly infected, a total of one hundred is obtained; consequently, at least, 0·8 per cent. of the whole population of the Gambia are probably infected with trypanosomes.

. . . so far as it was possible, examples of every type of country, included in the 5,000 square miles of the Colony and of the Protectorate of the Gambia, were visited.[1]

The natives of all the tribes know the disease well . . . .

Every headman was questioned; but none gave any hint of a tradition that sleeping sickness had ever been more prevalent than it is at present, and none knew when the disease first came to the Gambia, though they all agreed that it had been in the country for two or three generations.[2]

Many tribes along the West Coast of Africa practice gland excision as a preventive of sleeping sickness . . . .[3]

The fact that trypanosomiasis has been present in the Gambia and elsewhere on the West Coast of Africa for many years, in places where *Glossina palpalis* exists, without assuming the epidemic form which it has taken in the Congo Free State and in Uganda, of itself, suggests that the West Coast natives may have acquired some immunity of it.[4]

In the following 15 years only few cases of sleeping-sickness were ascertained.

1914. . . . there was no evidence of any marked increase in the cases of the disease.[5]

1915. No case of trypanosomiasis was found among the sick examined and treated by the Senior Medical Officer during these tours of inspection [in the Upper River Province, MacCarthy Island Province and the South Bank Province]. Records are still being kept, as far as possible, of the progress of the cases of Sleeping Sickness investigated by Dr. Todd in 1911, but there is still no obvious spread of the infection,[6]

1916. Five patients were treated in Bathurst for trypanosomiasis of whom two died. No deaths from this cause were reported from the Protectorate, and of the few chronic cases known to exist there, some appear to have recovered.[7]

1919. The tsetse fly abounds in many parts of the Protectorate. The natives appear to have become immune to a great extent. Four cases of sleeping sickness and two deaths were reported in Bathurst in 1919.[8]

1920. Trypanosomiasis is not prevalent in Bathurst, and exists only in very mild form in the Protectorate.[9]

[1] 'First Report', pp. 248–9.   [2] Ibid., p. 252.
[3] Ibid., p. 254.   [4] Ibid., p. 282.
[5] *Medical Report 1914*, p. 14.   [6] Ibid. *1915*, p. 20.
[7] *Colonial Reports, Gambia 1916*, p. 14. See also *Medical Report 1916*, pp. 12–13.
[8] *Colonial Reports, Gambia 1919*, p. 5.   [9] *Medical Report 1920*, p. 5.

1923. Protectorate. Cases of Trypanosomiasis . . . are occasionally seen.[1]

1924. Protectorate. Despite innumerable blood examinations, in no human case has the trypanosome been demonstrated.[2]

Between 1927 and 1934 the number of recorded cases increased from 45 to 900.[3] This, however, was generally attributed to an increasing readiness of the patients to present themselves for treatment.

1927. The number of cases treated in Georgetown Hospital in 1927 was nineteen, as compared with twelve in 1926. As only hospital figures are available, it cannot be assumed that this means that the disease is actually on the increase; in fact, it seems more probable that cases are now coming to Hospital which were formerly hidden away in the villages. At the same time it is highly probable that this disease will eventually be found to be far more prevalent than is at present apparent, as it is certain that the cases reported represent only a very small minority of those which actually exist.[4]

1929. 122 cases recorded and all acquired infection in the Protectorate . . . . The recorded cases are double those of 1928—but this probably means that those affected having the advantages of modern treatment present themselves more readily.[5]

26 cases with 10 deaths treated as In-Patients at the [Georgetown] Hospital, and 18 as Out-Patients. The latter figure is exactly double that of last year, so that there is reason to believe that this disease is on the increase in Georgetown and the surrounding district.[6]

1930. 121 cases were treated in Bathurst with tryparsamide as against 61 in 1929. It does not follow that the complaint is more common; it is more likely that patients present themselves for treatment more readily.[7]

1933. 610 cases were treated in Bathurst and Georgetown as against 580 cases in 1932, and 366 cases in 1931. It is confidently believed that this increase in attendance is due to increased faith in modern treatment, and that there is no real increase in the incidence of the disease.[8]

From 1935 on the opinion gained ground that sleeping-sickness was on the increase and that preventive measures would be advisable.

1935. 1,106 cases with 32 deaths. . . . A rapid survey of the Upper River Province was made during the rains. The incidence there is low . . . . Further down river in the swampy country round the creeks the number of cases rises rapidly. Although undoubtedly many more cases are presenting themselves for treatment than formerly I am of opinion that there has been considerable spread of the disease.[9]

1936. 1,972 cases with 34 deaths. Of these cases a thousand were treated at Bwiam[10] and Kaiaf. There are several endemic areas in the Gambia. Trypanosomiasis is still on the increase. On the river itself travellers report a marked increase in the number of tse-tse flies in some areas.[11]

1937. Trypanosomiasis is still the great danger to this Colony. A survey of the North Bank Province was made early in the year and much of value discovered. At

[1] *Medical Report 1923*, p. 21. Only 3 cases were recorded in 1923; see ibid. *1936*, p. 7.

[2] Ibid. *1924*, p. 16.

[3] See ibid. *1927*, p. 5; *1934*, p. 5.

[4] Medical Report for the Protectorate, ibid. *1927*, p. 42.

[5] Report of Senior Medical Officer, ibid. *1929*, p. 7.

[6] Report of Medical Officer Protectorate, ibid., p. 43.

[7] Report of Senior Medical Officer, ibid. *1930*, p. 8.

[8] Report of Acting Senior Medical Officer, ibid. *1933*, p. 5.

[9] Report of Senior Medical Officer, ibid. *1935*, p. 9; see also ibid., p. 14.

[10] See also ibid. *1936*, p. 5: 'It was decided after due consideration to erect the hospital at Bwiam on the Bintang Creek—seventy miles from Bathurst. This position was decided on largely because Sleeping Sickness was so prevalent in that area.'

[11] Report of Senior Medical Officer, ibid., p. 8.

present, however, it is impossible to undertake an Anti-Trypanosomiasis Campaign, but this is not being lost sight of and it is hoped that plans for such a Campaign will be formulated during 1938 and put into operation in 1939. The chief difficulty will be the matter of finance.[1]

2,025 cases, with 37 cases dealt with in Government Dispensaries by African Dispensers not included. . . . Trypanosomiasis is still on the increase.[2]

Preventive measures must be envisaged. A survey of the population of the North Bank Province of the river as to incidence of the disease[3] showed a percentage of three (to be confirmed) varying from under one per cent to nearly twelve per cent in one village. It appears, however, that the disease is especially prevalent between the Bintang and Jawarra creeks and the sea, *i.e.* Niumi and Kombo and Foni districts.

There are areas of high incidence, however, around MacCarthy Island, e.g. Kuntau-ur, Kudang and Jessadi.

The disease is found almost everywhere and only requires suitable situation of villages near fresh water swamp and thick bush to cause a higher incidence.[4]

1938. Trypanosomiasis loomed large in last year's report. It is still as important as ever. Dr. Lochhead in his survey of the North Bank Province . . . made several recommendations. It has not been felt desirable, however, to advise the carrying out of these except the clearing around villages, until much fuller information is obtained as to whether the disease is on the increase or decrease, the types of glossina spreading the infection and their habitat. . . . Large numbers of the inhabitants of the area affected are now receiving treatment, but financial difficulties preclude free treatment on a massive scale.[5]

Trypanosomiasis is common in large areas of the country.[6]

1939. A very thorough survey of the North Bank was made by Dr. Bowesman in May and June. He made complete examinations of over 12,000 people in less than two months, every single suspect being examined microscopically. He found that the average infection rate was 3·21 per cent. of those examined. This is probably somewhat higher than the actual rate as practically all sick people of the district were brought to him whilst by no means all of the population was examined.

Further investigations were made in the South Bank Province, but it was only possible to select a few villages at random. The infection rate appears to be roughly the same as in the North Bank Province.[7]

1940. Number of cases treated during the year were 2,032. It is estimated that of these 107 were French subjects from the Senegal and Cassamance who took advantage of our treatment centres.[8]

1941. Number of cases treated during the year were 1,025. It is hoped that during 1942 another survey and a treatment campaign will be carried out in co-operation with the Royal Army Medical Corps.[9]

1942. 1,272 cases were treated at hospitals. A further 615 cases were treated at the nine dispensaries. A further 183 cases were treated by a combined Army and Civil team working on Trypanosomiasis survey in North and South Bank Provinces.[10]

---

[1] Report of Acting Senior Medical Officer, ibid. *1937*, p. 6.

[2] Ibid., p. 8.

[3] For details see Report by Dr. J. L. Lochhead, ibid., pp. 84–7. The total number of persons examined was 7,151.

[4] Ibid., pp. 12–13.　　　　　　　　　　[5] Ibid. *1938*, p. 7.

[6] Ibid., p. 8.　　　　　　　　　　　　　[7] Ibid. *1939*, p. 2.

[8] Ibid. *1940*, p. 2.　　　　　　　　　　[9] Ibid. *1941*, p. 2.

[10] Ibid. *1942*, pp. 2–3. See also *Development and Welfare in the Gambia*, chapter x, p. 18: 'In 1942 it became necessary to station a considerable number of troops, including Europeans, in the North Bank Province. Alarmed by the prevalence of disease in the area, the military authorities arranged for a team under the direction of Captain D. MacGowan, R.A.M.C., to carry out a survey and treatment campaign in the Province. The Gambia Government provided the African staff, but the whole cost of the campaign was met from Army funds.'

Captain MacGowan's survey yielded the following results:[1]

Area	Total examined	Glands punctured	Trypano-somiasis found	Infection rate per cent.
North Bank (Civilians) . .	3,160	424	43	1·4
Bintang-Buiam Area . . .	2,648	360	57	2·2
Kanfinda-Sintet Area . . .	1,489	237	83	5·5

Captain MacGowan reached the following conclusion:

It is obvious from the surveys of Lochhead and Bowesman and the present survey that a regular trypanosomiasis campaign covering the whole of the Gambia is urgently required. Other West African colonies, Gold Coast and Nigeria, and also French West Africa, have had an organised service working for some years and the results justify the labour expended. The present survey has only touched the fringe of the problem, but it has shown the deplorable conditions present in many areas of the Colony.[2]

The Medical Report for 1944 said:

A total of 1,567 cases were treated with twelve deaths, the latter recorded in late cases admitted to Hospital or Asylum.[3]

After malaria this remains our chief disease problem since the time effective yellow fever protection became available. With the exception of the Island of St. Mary it is prevalent in all parts of the country, and in the barrierless surrounding French and Portuguese territories. It is now recognised that long-continued endemicity has resulted in a stage of quiescence in most infected subjects. . . . While the term 'immunity' is scarcely applicable, it is apparent that a very high degree of tolerance has been achieved, probably broken down by the addition of intercurrent disease or other lowering circumstance.[4]

Tuberculosis. 'Tuberculosis has been introduced by the European in a community highly susceptible to the disease.'[5] The Senior Sanitary Officer, in his report for 1913, wrote:

While looking through the old Colonial Hospital records of 40 years ago one is struck by the frequency with which entries suggesting tuberculosis occur; the diagnosis phthisis, consumption, hæmophthysis appear frequently both for Europeans and natives. . . .

It may be that cases of tuberculosis . . . were then but little less rare or common than at present.[6]

But the Medical Reports following the First World War stated repeatedly that the incidence was increasing,[7] and the report for 1925 said:

Far above everything else in seriousness is the problem of Tuberculosis.[8]

The Medical Report for 1927 said again that the records showed 'an undoubted increase'.

Unfortunately, it is exactly what must be expected in so susceptible a people unless and until housing conditions and social hygiene improve.[9]

The reports for 1931 and 1932, however, stated that this complaint 'is not very rife'.[10] But from 1935 on opinion again became more unfavourable.

[1] See *Medical Report 1942*, pp. 9–11.   [2] Ibid., p. 11.   [3] Ibid. *1944*, p. 10.
[4] Ibid., pp. 6–7.   [5] Ibid. *1919*, p. 4.   [6] Ibid. *1913*, p. 24.
[7] See ibid. *1919*, p. 4; see also ibid. *1924*, p. 10.   [8] Ibid. *1925*, p. 23.
[9] Ibid. *1927*, p. 10.   [10] See ibid. *1931*, p. 10; *1932*, p. 10.

1935. Pulmonary Tuberculosis (Bathurst). The bad housing conditions, the state of Bathurst during the rains, the prevalence of Malaria, and Helminthic diseases, all contribute to lowering the resistance of the African to this disease.[1]

Tuberculosis (Protectorate). The housing conditions of the wharf towns leave much to be desired and serve as a potential source in the spread of this disease. Housing conditions generally in the Protectorate are poor and no town planning exists.[2]

1944. It is probable that the incidence compares with the increasing numbers reported from other Colonies.[3]

Hospitals. The history of hospital accommodation in the Gambia can perhaps best be characterized by quotations from two reports. In a Dispatch dated 3 July 1855 Governor O'Connor wrote to Lord John Russell:

The Colonial Hospital was opened for the reception of patients in July 1854. The internal economy and the whole arrangements of this valuable building afford universal satisfaction.

British and Foreign seamen, European and native inhabitants, instead of being crowded in miserable huts or lodgings, surrounded by filth, and subjected to a noisome atmosphere, with little or no ventilation, are now amply accommodated in spacious airy wards, and furnished with every comfort the sick can require.

Two colonial surgeons, one English, the other French, are in daily attendance on the patients.[4]

I have enjoyed extensive and numerous opportunities of visiting many Colonial and Military Hospitals, and I am satisfied none are better calculated to answer every useful and sanatory purpose required than the one now in full operation at the Gambia.[5]

The Medical Report for 1938 stated:

The Victoria Hospital, Bathurst, is . . . the main hospital of the Colony. It was erected in 1854. There have been several additions to it since then,[6] but it is a most unsatisfactory building and should be replaced as soon as funds permit by a much more extensive building planned on modern lines.[7]

The main recommendations for Bathurst are new African and European Hospitals. Preventive medicine is more important than curative but there is no real approach to good sanitation and hygiene except through propaganda and the main element of this is successful individual treatment when necessary. Belief in our sanitation follows faith in our system of medicine, and this cannot be really efficient in inadequate insanitary buildings.[8]

'The Medical Department and most of the staff are concentrated at the Victoria Hospital at Bathurst. . . . The Protectorate area, containing the greater part of the population, has long been starved of medical care.'[9]

It was not until 1935 that any noticeable effort was made to provide medical and health services in the Protectorate. Prior to that date there had been a small

[1] Ibid. *1935*, p. 15. See also ibid. *1936*, p. 14. [2] Ibid. *1935*, p. 46.
[3] Ibid. *1944*, p. 11. [4] *State of Colonial Possessions 1854*, p. 191.
[5] Ibid., p. 192. See also ibid. *1858*, Part II, p. 15; *1861*, Part II, p. 25; *1873*, Part II, 2nd Division, p. 37; *Report of Colonel Ord* (1865), p. 7. As regards the terrible conditions in the early military hospitals in St. Mary's Island and MacCarthy Island, see Poole (1850), vol. ii, p. 137; Burton (1863), vol. i, pp. 155–6.
[6] See, for example, *Colonial Reports, Gambia 1891*, p. 11; *1900*, p. 13; *1902*, p. 9; *1904*, p. 23; *1907*, p. 16; *Medical Report 1912*, p. 10.
[7] *Medical Report 1938*, p. 7. See also *Development and Welfare in the Gambia, June 1943*, chapter x, p. 1: 'The present hospital in Bathurst . . . stands to-day almost unchanged from the time when it was built in 1854 although it has been quite unsuited to meet modern requirements for many years.'
[8] *Medical Report 1938*, pp. 27–8. [9] Hailey, pp. 1170–1.

hospital at Georgetown, MacCarthy Island Province, and a dispensary at Basse. Between 1935 and 1938 hospitals were opened at Bansang, near Georgetown,[1] and at Bwiam in the South Bank Province, the latter being established mainly to deal with yaws and trypanosomiasis. At the same time a number of dispensaries were established in various parts of the Protectorate, and African Sanitary Inspectors were stationed at the principal river ports.[2]

Health. Opinions on the health of the African population have varied considerably in the course of time. The Colonial Surgeon Robertson, when questioned in May 1841 by the Committee on the West Coast of Africa, took a favourable view:

> Are the natives a long-lived people ?—I have seen many apparently old men.
> Are they subject to many or few diseases ?—They are subject but to few diseases.[3]

Sir Richard Burton, on the other hand, said in 1862 with particular reference to the garrison:

> It has been a favourite theory that the Jamaican negro and others withstand the heat and miasmata of Africa better than the white man; the contrary is probably the case. The semi-civilised African dies of phthisis much more readily than the Englishman; and if exposed to hardship, he becomes, to use a homely but forcible expression, rotten after the first year. In enduring the fatigues of actual warfare he is, I believe, inferior to the acclimatised European. Although negroes have a singular immunity from yellow fever—none were attacked at Sierra Leone during the five epidemics from 1837 to 1859—the small-pox is a scourge to them, and they die like sheep of dysentery and bilious remittent.[4]

A few extracts from the official reports in later years may serve as illustrations.

> 1865. . . . in the rains, the Europeans die,—and in the cold weather, the Africans; badly clad, badly housed, and ill-fed, they yield to the cold north-east wind, which blows night and day without intermission.[5]
> 1868. The stamina of the people is at a very low ebb from the depressing influence of the climate, as well as from the nature of their trade, and none of the energy, spirit, or determination of the Saxons is to be found in the native African. The constant petty wars and cruelty of the natives in the country surrounding these settlements afford no prospect of even keeping up the standard of the population.[6]
> 1875. There was much privation felt among the natives of the upper river, many of whom died from starvation. The scarcity of food was owing to two causes, the native wars prevented in some cases the culture of provisions, and predatory bands of so-called warriors scoured the country, pillaging as they went.[7]
> 1882. The census taken in 1881 showed the population of the Settlement to be 14,150. The numbers, I think, do not increase, principally owing to the rate of mortality amongst children, which is a high one, and the natural unhealthiness of a fœtid region known as 'Halt Die', where there is a large native settlement.[8] Small-

---

[1] See also *Medical Report 1938*, p. 6: 'The Protectorate Hospital at Bansang was completed during the year . . . The hospital at Georgetown has now reverted to its original use as a prison.'

[2] *Development and Welfare in the Gambia*, chapter x, p. 2.

[3] *Report*, Part II, p. 223.   [4] Burton, vol. i, p. 158.

[5] *State of Colonial Possessions 1865*, Part II, p. 16.

[6] Ibid. *1868*, Part II, p. 17.   [7] Ibid. *1876*, Part I, p. 140.

[8] See also *Colonial Possessions Reports 1883-4*, p. 186: '. . . the people live on the swampy malarial delta of a tropical African river, which for a certain number of months is almost covered, more frequently than not, with water.' As far back as 1835 the missionary Macbrair had said with regard to St. Mary's Island (p. 208): 'There are also two small villages, Jollar Town and Moka Town; the latter consisting of a few huts, situated in a marsh,—a disgrace to the authorities that could be so cruel as to locate any human beings in such an unhealthy place.'

pox is unhappily not an uncommon disease amongst the natives, occasionally assuming an epidemic form and becoming a formidable evil.[1]

1883. To a large consumption of fruit in July and August can be attributed, I am told, much of the mortality among children. Poor food, indifferent clothing and housing, combined with a very damp climate during certain portions of the year, for many, indeed, of the dwellings in this island are miserable places of abode, must, if they do not originate, at least nurse disease in those of tender years, and contribute later in no small degree to the death-rate.[2]

1887. It is feared that the [population] ratio is not an increasing one, owing to the unfavourable conditions of life in the Settlement, but more especially in Bathurst, which is not susceptible of any satisfactory system of drainage. Small-pox is more or less prevalent every year, and the mortality amongst infants at all times is great.[3]

Among the native community malarial fever and diarrhœa prevailed, arising from various causes, such as dampness (particularly at Half Die, where the embankment gave way during the high tide, and that part was inundated by the sea), want of sufficient food and proper clothing, and badly ventilated habitations.[4]

1889. The diseases most commonly fatal amongst the natives I have found to be acute lung and kidney diseases. Intermittent fever amongst them is very common, but not fatal. Alcoholism and venereal diseases of the most virulent types are extremely prevalent.[5]

1898. The natives suffer also [as the Europeans] from fever in the rainy season, and in addition, contract consumption and chest affections during the months of December and January when the winds are sometimes very cold.[6]

1903. Although Bathurst was free from any epidemic disease, the death-rate of the town was higher than in the previous year. This, however, may be attributed to the increased number of cases of pneumonia and dysentery[7] due to the exposure and discomfort the poorer classes of the community suffered in the month of August, when, owing to the exceptional heavy rainfall, the lower portions of the town were under water for several days, and the people were unable to light fires for the purpose of cooking their food or drying their clothes.[8]

1904. The diseases most commonly fatal among West Africans are acute liver and kidney diseases, pneumonia, and phthisis.[9]

1918. The influenza epidemic was very serious. It began in September and lasted about four weeks, with the result that 6 Europeans and 317 natives died in Bathurst. It is estimated that there were 7,800 deaths in the Protectorate from influenza.[10]

1919. Tuberculosis, Venereal Disease and Amoebic Dysentery are on the increase. The increase is due to trade.[11]

Malaria has decreased enormously.[12]

Sufficient stress has not been laid in the past on the fact that the population of Bathurst is largely migratory. A large portion of the Bathurst population spends from early in December to the end of May up the river trading. This migration brings a double element of danger, both from the fact that disease acquired up

[1] *Colonial Possessions Reports 1881–3*, p. 158. [2] Ibid. *1883–4*, p. 186.
[3] *Report on Blue Book 1887*, p. 8. [4] Ibid., p. 14.
[5] Statement of Acting Colonial Surgeon, *Report on Blue Book 1889*, p. 14.
[6] *Colonial Reports, Gambia 1898*, p. 12.
[7] See in this connexion the statement of the Colonial Surgeon Dr. Sherwood, *State of Colonial Possessions 1861*, Part II, p. 26: 'I regret to say that dysentery, a disease almost unknown in this Colony a few years ago, has within the two last been very prevalent amongst the natives. The great mortality in these cases I attribute to the natives having so many remedies of their own for this class of diseases, that they never think of consulting the colonial surgeon until their own remedies are exhausted; hence much valuable time is lost, and the majority of cases are carried to the hospital but to die.'
[8] *Colonial Reports, Gambia 1903*, p. 31. [9] Ibid. *1904*, p. 32.
[10] Ibid. *1918*, p. 11. For further details see *Medical Report 1918*, pp. 8–9, 28–32.
[11] Ibid. *1919*, p. 4; see also ibid., pp. 5, 12. [12] Ibid., p. 5.

the river is brought back into the Town, and that during the rainy season there is serious overcrowding in Bathurst. This occurs just at the time when it is most undesirable.[1]

In 1920, when the official death-rate had reached the excessive height of 49·8, the Medical Department stated: 'The Health of the general population was very good.'[2] In the following year the official death-rate was still 44·5. 'Except for the epidemic of Small Pox . . . this community enjoyed remarkably good health.'[3] But in 1922 a new Senior Medical Officer took charge of the Department. The first report issued by him spoke of 'the atrociously high figure' of infant mortality and deplored the 'perfect holocaust of infant life'.[4]

In 1924–7 epidemics of relapsing fever caused great concern.

1924. A serious outbreak of epidemic, diagnosed as relapsing fever, broke out in three villages in the North Bank Province, causing the deaths of 685 people out of a total of 2,790.[5]

1925. The occurrence of several outbreaks of Relapsing fever in South Bank Province is of serious import. This fever is much more serious than the usual form, causing a very high mortality.[6]

1926. Endemic in the South Bank Province with a very high mortality. Exact number of cases and deaths difficult to estimate.[7]

1927. . . . an attack of relapsing fever in the South Bank Province . . . caused over 200 deaths . . . .[8]

In his Dispatch to the Secretary of State for the Colonies, dated 26 July 1930, the Acting Governor stated with regard to the population of the Gambia as a whole:

The standard of health cannot be called low and it has not deteriorated during the last thirty years. Their physique is good on the whole, although their diet is lacking in the essential qualities that produce stamina.

A recently retired Commissioner of nearly thirty years' experience in the Gambia, who was also a fully qualified medical practitioner, states that during the last fifteen years he has noticed one change which is not for the better, and that is in the children in the larger towns where the people are more in touch with a slightly more civilized mode of existence. The children in those towns are generally of a poorer type physically than the normal active children of the country, and lack the average child's interest in life. This deterioration is attributed to the replacement of the normal rice or millet meal or pap by the universal use of bread and biscuit and other more easily prepared foods of modern days.[9]

The Committee on Nutrition in the Colonial Empire said:

In a country having conditions of imperfect sanitation, a vast amount of malaria and a high incidence of parasitic infection,[10] trypanosomiasis and tuberculosis, it is

[1] *Medical Report 1919*, p. 10.   [2] Ibid. *1920*, p. 3.
[3] Ibid. *1921*, p. 5. See also *Colonial Reports, Gambia 1921*, p. 2: 'Much has been done to improve its [Bathurst's] condition . . . and its death-rate is now only 44·5 per 1,000.'
[4] *Medical Report 1922*, p. 11.
[5] *Colonial Reports, Gambia 1924*, p. 10. See also *Medical Report 1924*, p. 9.
[6] Ibid. *1925*, p. 22.
[7] Ibid. *1926*, p. 6. See also ibid., p. 41, and *Colonial Reports, Gambia 1926*, p. 11.
[8] Ibid. *1927*, p. 11.
[9] *Papers relating to the Health of Native Populations*, pp. 141–2.
[10] See *Medical Report 1938*, p. 9: 'Almost every inhabitant of the Gambia harbours intestinal parasites of some sort. In Bathurst ankylostomiasis is the commonest. . . . Askaris is the rural worm of the lower river, whilst tape worms become increasingly common as one proceeds up river.'

difficult to estimate the precise influence which the customary diet of the people has on their health. Nevertheless, the high infant mortality, the marked prevalence of dental caries and the frequent manifestations of vitamin A and D deficiency are clear evidence of dietary inadequacy. Beriberi is comparatively rare, but mild cases of neuritis are not uncommon. A characteristic is the physical and mental lethargy of the native farmer which is undoubtedly due, in part at least, to lack of proper food.[1]

Conditions deteriorated during the war. The Medical Report for 1942 said:

The general health of the population particularly in Bathurst deteriorated throughout the year. This is attributable to the vicious circle set up by war conditions—overcrowding, malnutrition, malaria.[2]

The influx of population placed a strain on the food resources of the Gambia that it was unable to bear. The Gambia was never self supporting but before the war there was no marked evidence of mal-nutrition. In fact, conditions were rapidly improving owing to the great increase in market gardening and utilization of dry season vegetable crops. . . . The supplies of meat, fish, fruit and vegetables, however, were insufficient to meet the new demands and the effect both of lack of quantity and quality made itself very obvious in tne wet season—August to October, 1942. There was definite evidence of both protein and vitamin deficiency in both European and African.[3] . . . There has been also shortage of staple food reserves. The African depends largely on imported rice which has not been forthcoming and he has not taken kindly to a change over to cassava and maize.[4]

Infant Mortality. In St. Mary's Island the ratio of registered deaths under one year to 1,000 registered live-births was 295 in 1915–44. As birth registration is said to have been more defective than death registration, infant mortality may have been lower than a comparison of the number of infant deaths with the number of births suggests, but infant mortality in the Gambia has been considered excessive until recently. Official documents of the 1880s listed infant mortality as the main cause preventing population increase,[5] and in the following decades infant mortality was discussed frequently in administration and medical reports.

1889. The rate of infant mortality is very high in the Gambia, and owing to apathy on the part of adult relatives, and want of proper treatment, numbers often succumb to diseases, which, under favourable circumstances, ought not to result fatally.[6]

1891. It is to be regretted that infant mortality formed so large an item in the death roll. Many of the ailments, under which a large number of children succumbed, were, if not preventible, readily amenable to medical treatment. I am of opinion

[1] *First Report*, Part II, p. 33. See also ibid.: 'In general, the diet is excessive in carbohydrate, and deficient in the protective food substances, animal fat and protein, mineral salts and vitamins.'

[2] *Medical Report 1942*, p. 2.

[3] See also *Development and Welfare in the Gambia*, chapter vii, p. 2; chapter x, pp. 22–3.

[4] *Medical Report 1942*, pp. 5–6. As regards the change over to maize see also *Report of Labour Department 1942*, pp. 5–6: 'Maize, though not found unsavoury by local Africans, is difficult to prepare and needs a good deal of hard pounding before it is ready to eat. For that reason it is unpopular with the average worker not accompanied by his wife. . . . The difficulty in preparing maize for consumption was realised, and the necessary tools, time and labour were in different cases provided. The Army has been able to issue some of its labour with rice, and perhaps other labourers felt that invidious distinctions were being drawn.'

[5] See Report of Administrator Dr. Gouldsbury, dated 22 June 1881, *Correspondence relating to the Expedition to the Upper Gambia*, p. 34; *Report on Blue Book 1888*, p. 11.

[6] *Report on Blue Book 1889*, p. 15. See also *Colonial Reports, Gambia 1890*, p. 6.

that this abnormal rate of mortality, may be attributed to the criminal negligence of ignorant and superstitious parents, who would resort to quacks or to charms, and such like agencies, to propitiate malevolent influences rather than obtain proper medical relief for their sick children.

Parents of this class would apply for medical assistance only when the innocent patients are in a moribund condition.[1]

1909. The death rate of babies still remains high. Midwifery is a branch of Medical Work that is neglected in the Gambia, and so far it has not been possible to train Midwives; the lives of many babies and not a few mothers are undoubtedly lost on this account.[2]

1912. . . . the infant mortality still keeps high. I attribute this not so much to accidents or mis-management at child-birth, but to the ignorance and carelessness displayed later in feeding.

Few women are able or willing to suckle their infants, and more or less indigestible food stuffs are substituted.

An attempt is now being made to form classes for instructing women in Midwifery and the feeding of children, but so far there is little interest displayed.[3]

1914. . . . infantile mortality remains very high; a fact which is largely attributable to the conservative ignorance of the native nurses.[4]

1916. Infantile mortality did not drop appreciably below the high figure at which it normally stands. Out of a total number of 314 births there were 22 still births and 74 deaths of infants of less than one year in age.[5]

1917. It is satisfactory to note that there was a distinct drop in infantile mortality, as compared with previous years.[6]

1918. Infantile mortality was at even a higher figure than usual. Out of a total number of 263 births there were 50 still-births, and 138 deaths of infants of less than one year in age.[7]

1920. The infant mortality is high, being influenced by the large number of still births, deaths of infants soon after birth, and the prevalence of *tetanus neonatorum*.[8]

1922. Taking now the infant mortality rate, which 'is looked upon by Sanitarians as affording the most important index as to the general sanitary conditions,' we find it stands at the atrociously high figure of 502.

In plain words infants (up to one year) in 1922 were dying at the rate of 502 for every 1,000 born—a perfect holocaust of infant life! The average figure since 1916 is 452. . . . As far back as 1909 the Medical Report for this Colony called special attention to the high rate of loss of mothers and babies, when the infant mortality works out at 241. What added emphasis 502 calls for![9]

The Medical Officer of Health gave as causes of this high mortality, tetanus,[10] 'exhaustion from diarrhœa', fatal 'convulsions', poor housing on damp sites, and illegitimacy. He laid particular stress on the latter factor.

There is also the question of illegitimacy. Its influence *per se* almost halves an infant's chances of life. Though the amount of it in Bathurst is not known, it can

---

[1] *Colonial Reports, Gambia 1891*, pp. 6–7. See also ibid. *1893*, p. 6; *1895*, p. 6; *1896*, p. 4; *1898*, p. 12.   [2] *Medical Report 1909*, p. 8.

[3] Senior Medical Officer ibid. *1912*, p. 7. See also ibid. *1913*, p. 6.

[4] Ibid. *1914*, p. 8.

[5] *Colonial Reports, Gambia 1916*, p. 13. The data for this and all subsequent years comprise only Bathurst.

[6] Ibid. *1917*, p. 11. In this year there were registered 337 births (including 30 still-births) and 72 infant deaths. The infant mortality rate was never again so low until 1931.

[7] Ibid. *1918*, p. 11. But birth registration was evidently incomplete.

[8] *Medical Report 1920*, p. 2.   [9] Ibid. *1922*, p. 11.

[10] 'In the quinquennium 1917–1921, 26 per cent. of infant deaths were due to tetanus' and in 1922, 32 per cent.

by no means be considered a negligible factor. No doubt its effect is in direct ratio to its extent.[1]

There are proofs that the illegitimate birth rate in Bathurst is amazingly high,[2] and as is well known, the fact of illegitimacy bears seriously in infant welfare. It is not possible however to give exact figures or rates in this matter. Beyond doubt the baneful influence works lethally both before as well as after birth. Indeed there is a strong nexus between the illegitimacy rate and the still-birth rate, and I dare suggest even some with the tetanus rate.

All three rates are very high. They illustrate poignantly the dire effect of public morals on public health. They further indicate that the massive problem behind child welfare is that of the illegitimate parent,—even grandparent![3]

But when it became possible to give exact figures the situation appeared quite different.

Study of infant mortality has unearthed one remarkable and unexpected fact, which is that the well known ill effect of illegitimacy on infant welfare seems in Bathurst to be entirely reversed. The illegitimate infant mortality rate for 1923 was 325 as contrasted with a legitimate infant mortality rate of 590!

The explanation is manifold, but lies wholly in the peculiarities of the life and customs of the people, which, though capable of effecting an *apparent* mitigation of calamity, are yet in reality sordid to a degree socially unjustifiable, and immoral to boot.[4]

In the following year the Senior Medical Officer reported:

The infant mortality rate is 317 against 471 of last year, and against a mean rate of 454 for 1921–1925. It is a remarkable decline for one year . . . .

This decline is attributable very largely to the almost phenomenal success of the [Mother and Child Welfare] Clinic.[5]

Actually the decline in the official infant mortality rate was attributable very largely to an arithmetical error,[6] and if the ratio of registered infant deaths to registered births was a true indication of infant mortality the success of the Mother and Child Welfare Clinic was not 'almost phenomenal', but nil, since this ratio was much higher than a decade earlier. But the excessive official infant mortality rates in 1918–25 may have been due in part to particularly defective birth registration in those years. Whether infant mortality was essentially lower in 1926–36 than in 1918–25 it is impossible to tell, but there was apparently a reduction in recent years.

4. *Population Growth*

Some reference to official opinion on population growth in the Colony has been made above in dealing with Total Population, Birth and Death

[1] Ibid. *1922*, p. 12.

[2] The proportion of illegitimate births had always been 'amazingly high'. Thus, in 1888, 364 of 380 registered births had been 'illegitimate', and in 1889, 354 of 369 (see *Report on Blue Book 1888*, p. 12; *1889*, p. 16). The Administrator made the following sensible comment on the 1888 figure: 'I may be permitted to observe that a large majority of the children thus irregularly born were the offspring of Mahomedan parents, who are wedded together in conformity with the rites and tenets of that faith' (ibid. *1888*, p. 12; see also *Colonial Reports, Gambia 1891*, p. 6, *1893*, p. 5).

[3] *Medical Report 1923*, p. 14.   [4] Ibid. *1924*, p. 11.

[5] Ibid. *1925*, p. 12. See also ibid. *1942*, p. 12: 'The beneficial effects of the clinic are shown by the lowering of infantile mortality from 571 [sic] per 1,000 in 1924 to 220 in 1931.'

[6] The number of infant deaths was not 83 (as stated ibid. *1925*, p. 24) but 112 (as stated ibid., p. 6), and the infant mortality rate was not 317 but 427. (This correct rate was given in *Medical Report 1928*, p. 17, and in subsequent reports.)

Registration, and Mortality, but a brief summary will not be out of place.

In his Report on the Blue Book for 1865 the Administrator, Colonel D'Arcy, said that the large excess of registered deaths over registered births speaks 'very unfavourably for the salubrity of the Settlement'.[1]

If it was not for the constant mainland supply of immigrants to St. Mary's, who, after long residence, become civilized British subjects, the inhabitants of the Settlement would soon die out; in this particular we have profited by the adversity experienced by the Yúloff countries to the northern sea-board: the town is now full of labourers, and British Combo is richly cultivated by poor people, who have been tried in the furnace of misfortune; naked and friendless, flying before the Mahommedan sword, they have found a refuge in our territory.[2]

In his Report for 1888 the Administrator stated:

Owing to the high rate of infant mortality and the carelessness of the negro in regard to sanitary precautions generally, there is no doubt that the population is not increasing to any great extent . . . .[3]

A year later, after having expressed 'the belief that the Registrar is too sanguine in his view of the excess of the birth-rate',[4] he said:

The census taken in 1871 returned the population of the Settlements at 14,190, and in 1881 at 14,150, and I believe these figures to show a fairly accurate representation of the actual state of things; in other words, that the birth and death rate are nearly equal. In spite of the existence of polygamy it is a rare occurrence to find a large family. The present King of Barra, who has had no lack of wives, and is now about 55 years of age, has but two children living; most of the others died in infancy, and this is a history which is but too common in the Gambia.[5]

When the census of 1891 showed a decrease in population this was attributed to emigration.[6]

In 1909 the registered births exceeded for the first time the registered deaths in the Colony, and this was duly noted in the Colonial Report for that year.[7] But this was to remain quite an exception. The Medical Report for 1923 stated:

Figures were given last year to show that only thrice in the last twenty-two years have births been more numerous than deaths, viz., 1909 by 10, 1916 by 10 and 1917

[1] Horton, after having shown that from January 1859 to September 1866, 812 births and 1,665 deaths (977 male and 688 female) had been registered, said: 'The total deaths here exceed the total births by 837; or the total mortality of the male inhabitants alone, from 1859 to September 30, 1866, exceeded the total male and female births during the same period by 156. The inhabitants occupying the unhealthy town of Bathurst are fast dying out; there is little or no immigration into it. The population is barely 6,000, and at this rate of mortality, with so small a register of births, within fifty years from the present there will scarcely be found living in that area a single individual now among its inhabitants, nor even their offspring yet unborn. *They will all die out.* Do the local authorities require any more forcible argument for the necessity of rigid sanitary reforms? Within eight years the deaths exceeded the births by 837. The inhabitants might truly say "*We do not live; we die*" ' (*Physical and Medical Climate*, pp. 267–8).
[2] *State of Colonial Possessions 1865*, pp. 16–17. See also the statement ibid. *1868*, Part II, p. 17 (quoted p. 376 above), and *Colonial Possessions Reports 1880–2*, p. 133.
[3] *Report on Blue Book 1888*, p. 11.   [4] See p. 357 above.
[5] Ibid. *1889*, p. 19.
[6] See pp. 328–9 above; see also Archer, pp. 85–6.
[7] See *Colonial Reports, Gambia 1909*, p. 18.

by 73.[1] It may not be pleasing, but it is plausible, to liken the life of Bathurst to that of a cancer which, unable to maintain the vitality of its own cells, involves neighbouring ones in the common disaster. Bathurst cannot maintain its own life and it only continues its career by imported lives.[2]

If the ratio of deaths to births were an adequate gauge of the vitality of the inhabitants of Bathurst, the situation would have been alarming all through, since it could still be said at the outbreak of the Second World War that only thrice in the last 22 years (in 1931, 1938, and 1939) have births been more numerous than deaths. But it should be remembered that birth records are probably more incomplete than death records.

As regards the Protectorate, the Administrator Dr. Gouldsbury, in his report dated 22 June 1881, suggested that the population was 'if not stationary, actually decreasing in numbers' owing to infant mortality, polygamy, and wars.[3]

A year later, pointing to the fact that the population in the Colony had not increased since 1871, he said:

This circumstance is anything but encouraging to those who look upon a rapidly increasing population as one of the most potent agents in the civilization and moral and social advancement of the native, and I fear the story told by the census of 1881 as regards the Settlement would, in its broad outlines, be applicable to the greater portion of the surrounding territories.[4]

In the Colonial Report for 1895 the Governor said:

The Mahommedan system of a plurality of wives, the custom of purchasing as wives girls from their parents, and the practice of prolonged suckling by mothers of infants, together with want of care, all tend to retard a very large annual increase in the population.[5]

In 1902 an increase was attributed to immigration.

The population remained stationary, excepting, perhaps, in certain parts of the Protectorate where there has been a considerable influx of natives, who, having been attracted by the conditions of British rule, have crossed the frontier.[6]

In a report sent to the Secretary of State for the Colonies on 26 July 1930 the Acting Governor expressed a more favourable opinion.

The bulk of the races forming the population of the Gambia are sufficiently virile and their numbers are definitely on the increase.[7]

But the results of the 1931 census did not support this view, and there is no conclusive evidence that the population of the Gambia has increased in the course of the last 25 years.

[1] The large excess of births over deaths computed for 1917 was due to an arithmetical error. It had been assumed for many years that deaths in 1917 numbered only 232 while they actually numbered 332. The correct figure appears for the first time in *Medical Report 1928*, p. 17.
[2] Ibid. *1923*, p. 13.
[3] *Correspondence relating to the Expedition to the Upper Gambia*, p. 34.
[4] *Colonial Possessions Reports 1880–2*, p. 133.
[5] *Colonial Reports, Gambia 1895*, p. 6.
[6] Ibid. *1902*, p. 11.
[7] *Papers relating to the Health of Native Populations*, p. 141.

VI. Mortality of Europeans[1]

In the nineteenth century there were many years in which mortality, owing to some epidemic, was excessive.[2]

1816. Of the fifty European soldiers who occupied St. Mary's Island in April, eight 'died during the first rains'.[3]

1825. Of a contingent of 199 European soldiers who arrived in Bathurst in May just at the beginning of the rainy season, 160 had died by 21 December.[4]

1826. A new draft of 200 soldiers arrived, again at the beginning of the rainy season. Deaths numbered 116 between 21 June and 21 December. Of the 123 survivors (out of a total of 399) 33 were permanently unfit for any further service.[5]

1834. 'Out of about 50 Europeans [in Bathurst] no less than ten or twelve have been carried to the house appointed for all living.'[6]

1837. Apparently more than one-half of the Europeans died of yellow fever.[7]

---

[1] Fertility of European women, while in the Gambia, is practically nil. According to the official reports not a single birth occurred in 1912–38. For earlier times births have been reported occasionally (3 in 1868, 1 in 1901, 1 in 1905, 1 in 1906, 1 in 1908, 2 in 1909, 1 in 1911; see *State of Colonial Possessions 1868*, Part II, p. 20; *Government Gazette* 1901, 1906, 1908, 1909, 1911, 1912, Monthly Returns; *Colonial Reports, Gambia 1905*, p. 28).

[2] The following summary shall serve merely as an illustration. It is not based on a thorough perusal of the medical literature.

[3] Fox, p. 261.   [4] See Gray, p. 308.

[5] See Gray, p. 309. In July 1827 it was decided that white troops could not be stationed in the Gambia and the survivors were withdrawn and replaced by African troops; see ibid. The high mortality of the white soldiers in 1825–6 has, of course, attracted a great deal of attention, and has often been explained by some such statement as that they were 'the greatest rascals under the sun, the offscourings of the army, and were drunk day and night, sleeping in the dews and drinking new rum, old palm wine, or anything they could lay their hands upon' and that the officers were 'equally reckless and insubordinate' (see, for example, Burton, vol. i, p. 158). But these were certainly only contributory factors, and Governor MacDonnell probably came nearer the truth when he said in a report written in 1852: 'I have . . . not been surprised to learn from the Second Report on Quarantine, that more than twenty-six years back, when 420 white soldiers were stationed here for a space of only nineteen months, 279 died, of whom 234 fell victims to the fever of the climate. An entire regiment stationed in quarters more indifferent than those which are now represented as inadequate, a regiment composed as the condemned corps in question was, of the worst and most dissipated characters, and stationed literally in a swamp, which Bathurst then was, might all have perished in that space of time without there being any more real grounds for surprise at such mortality than there would be at death ensuing from a draught of poison or a bullet' (*State of Colonial Possessions 1851*, pp. 206–207).

[6] Letter from Fox dated 10 Nov. 1834; Fox, *History of the Wesleyan Missions*, p. 366.

[7] The reports are somewhat contradictory. Fox (Aug./Sept. 1837) relates (p. 434) that yellow fever raged in Bathurst. 'Not less than *one-half* of the Europeans then residing at St. Mary's, were in a few short weeks numbered with the dead; exclusive of the naval officers and crews of Her Majesty's ships, and of other Europeans and Americans, of merchant-vessels, besides a number of Mulattoes, and a great number of the natives. . . . It was indeed a season never to be forgotten by those who witnessed it, or lived to survive its effects.' Two medical officers, in a report dated July 1840, say that in St. Mary's Island 'the embankments frequently give way, thereby inundating the settlement, as was the case in 1837, when nearly all the Europeans and a great number of the native inhabitants died of [remittent] fever. It also occurred in 1838 and 1839, both of which years proved extremely unhealthy' (*Report from the Committee on the West Coast of Africa*, Part II, p. 197; see also ibid., pp. 180, 222). Burton (1862) says (vol. i, p. 169) that 'in 1837 and 1839 bilious remittent deepened to yellow fever at Bathurst and Macarthy's Island', but suggests (p. 158) that not a single native was attacked by yellow fever.

1848. 'Of seven [civilian] Europeans who remained on the [MacCarthy] island during the rainy season of 1848 six died, including the two medical officers.'[1]

1859. After the yellow fever epidemic lasting from August to October only six or ten Europeans were left in Bathurst.[2] Deaths were heavy also in MacCarthy Island.[3]

1866. 'In August, 1866, a further epidemic of yellow fever visited the colony, and fourteen of the thirty Europeans resident at the time in Bathurst died.'[4]

1872. An epidemic of yellow fever reduced the number of whites to twenty-six.[5]

1878. 'Out of a small European community, averaging between 50 and 60 persons for the year, including the floating population of ships, 13 persons died, of which number 10 died during the last quarter of the year.

'Of the resident European community, averaging 33 persons for the year, 7 died . . . .'[6]

1900. Epidemic of yellow fever during June, July, and August. 'The deaths amongst the European section of the community were 9, or at the rate of 140 per thousand. Of these six were due to yellow fever . . . .'[7]

1911. Several outbreaks of yellow fever. 'Nine Europeans succumbed to this disease, of whom three were officials; and five other Europeans, all non-officials, died from other causes, making a total of 14 deaths, compared with two in 1910.'[8]

Very much has been written about the insalubrity of St. Mary's Island and MacCarthy Island for Europeans, and there cannot be the least doubt that the selection of these two places as practically the only places in the

---

[1] *State of Colonial Possessions 1849*, p. 220.

[2] 'The new Governor [D'Arcy] landed to find himself in the midst of an outbreak of yellow fever, the first after an interval of twenty-two years. It lasted from August to October, by which time only ten Europeans were left in the Colony' (Gray, p. 416). Governor D'Arcy himself, in a Dispatch to the Duke of Newcastle, dated 24 May 1860, said: 'Here let me pause a moment, and bring to your Grace's mind the position of the colony last September, with but six Europeans alive; some of those convalescent; one military officer fit for duty . . .' (*State of Colonial Possessions 1859*, Part II, p. 11). Two years later (25 Aug. 1862) he reported: 'I account for the British mercantile houses not increasing solely to the fact that the capitalists at home have not yet recovered from the shock the reputation of the place received in August 1859, when the Gambia was visited by so serious an epidemic. Before the merchants had embarked on their usual summer vacation, saving by the trip the expense of home agency, and at the same time renovating their health by the change, the epidemic overtook the travellers, and many were cut off in their prime, when a few days would have removed them from the coast' (ibid. *1861*, Part II, p. 28). See also Burton, p. 149, and Archer, p. 60.

[3] Governor D'Arcy in a Dispatch to the Duke of Newcastle, dated 24 July 1861, said: 'Previous to my visit to Macarthy's Island I was inclined to recommend the abandonment of this station, owing to the sad mortality last year of three assistant surgeons in as many months, and in consequence of the alarming decrease in population . . .' (*State of Colonial Possessions 1860*, Part II, p. 31). See also Burton (1862), p. 169: 'In 1860, the medicoes died off in rapidest succession, and the non-professionals, out of decency, followed suit.'

[4] Archer, p. 77.   [5] See *Colonial Possessions Reports 1874*, Part I, p. 134.

[6] Ibid. *1877–9*, p. 218.

[7] *Colonial Reports, Gambia 1900*, p. 15. But according to the Monthly Returns in the *Government Gazette* the European deaths in 1900 totalled 19.

[8] *Colonial Reports, Gambia 1911*, p. 17. For further details see *Medical Report 1911*, pp. 33–6; *West Africa, Report on Certain Outbreaks of Yellow Fever in 1910 and 1911*, pp. 18–22.

Gambia where Europeans reside was unfortunate from the viewpoint of health. But some improvement has been made in the course of time.

The earliest report on mortality in 'normal' years was apparently made by the Medical Officer, Dr. Kehoe, in 1850. Concerning the civilian population in Bathurst he says:

The total number of European deaths at Bathurst (not including the military) during the five years ending December 1849 was 23. Of these, 12 occurred amongst sailors casually trading to the coast, leaving 11 as the total number of deaths amongst the resident European population. The European residents amount on an average to 50 persons. The ratio of deaths, therefore, during this period has been 4·40 per cent. But on analyzing these deaths it appears, that one was death from extreme old age; one was upwards of 60 years of age, and had been 40 years in the colony; one was accidental death, found drowned; one accidental death, taking an overdose of colchicum; one small-pox, and one an infant; leaving but five deaths which can be at all attributed to climatorial influence. Of these, three were cases of fever, all occurring in the first year of residence in persons who had not previously been in any tropical country. . . .

The ratio of mortality, though large, gives, I consider, a very inadequate idea of the injurious influence of the climate on Europeans. Few can reside for any length of time at the Gambia without their constitution being impaired for life; a considerable number return to Europe when they find their health to be seriously affected. Even the great number of persons invalided home scarcely gives a full idea of the impairment of health.[1]

In his report for 1851 Governor MacDonnell stated:

The improved drainage of Bathurst, the gradual filling up of swampy and low sites by the accumulation of the materials that always follow increase of population and buildings, show that much may be done to improve the general sanitary condition of the town; and I am happy to think that exertions made by myself to direct public attention to this subject are bearing their fruits, and will no doubt in a few years render this place as much healthier than it is even now, as it has already become healthier than it was twenty years ago.[2]

No parallel . . . exists between the Bathurst of that day [1825–26] and of the present period.[3]

Captain Hewett (1862) said that MacCarthy Island was 'the most insalubrious spot in the most pestilential climate in the world',[4] and that 'the climate of Bathurst is undoubtedly more deadly and injurious to the European constitution than that of almost any other place in the world'.

. . . still, unhealthy as the climate is now, it has much improved since the swamp nearest the town has been reclaimed, previous to which, and when medical men did not so well understand the nature of the fevers, the average duration of human life was three months; but, if the year in which I was there may be taken as a criterion, it is now five years,—ten out of fifty white people having died in one month.[5]

In 1889 Administrator Carter expressed the following opinion 'based upon nearly 14 years experience gained in Sierra Leone, the Gold Coast, and the Gambia':

Taken as a whole, the climate of the Gambia is decidedly superior to that of any other British Settlement in West Africa, though at certain seasons intermittent and

---

[1] *State of Colonial Possessions 1849*, p. 220.   [2] Ibid. *1851*, Part I, p. 206.
[3] Ibid., p. 207.   [4] Hewett, p. 274.
[5] Ibid., pp. 284–5. He probably meant to say 'ten out of fifty white people having died in one year'. He reached the conclusion that Bathurst 'must ever remain what it now is—the white man's grave' (ibid., p. 286).

remittent fevers are very prevalent, few Europeans escaping an attack of one or other of these forms between the months of July and October.[1]

A year later, however, referring to native mortality from August to October, he said:

If the death-rate is so high amongst the native population, the effect of such a climate on the European constitution may readily be imagined. It is fortunate that a radical change takes place in December, otherwise few would rally from the extreme depression of the vital forces which occurs to the strongest, after an experience of these months.[2]

In 1897 Administrator Llewelyn stated:

The unhealthiness of Bathurst, owing to its low-lying position, during the rainy season, July to October, is well known. During those four months the climate is, perhaps, the most trying on the west coast of Africa, and in the dry season the great diurnal variations in temperature are equally trying to some constitutions.[3]

In the following year he reported:

I may here also remark that the year 1897 was, I believe, the first on record in which no death occurred amongst the European population . . . .[4]

In the next year he said:

I believe the climate in Bathurst between July and October is as bad as the worst season on any part of the West Coast, but, fortunately, few Europeans are then here. During the remainder of the year it is fairly healthy, but it is necessary always to be careful and remember you are on the West Coast of Africa.[5]

The Colonial Reports for 1902 and 1903 said:

The climate of the Gambia is admittedly the best on the British West African Coast, and for some eight months in the year—November to May, known as the dry season—is really pleasant. In other months, during the rains, it is, however, probably as unhealthy as other places on the coast. During this period the atmosphere is hot, damp, and depressing.[6]

There is no doubt that the climate of the Gambia, for at any rate six months of the year, is less unpleasant than that of other parts of the West African coast. Much cannot be said in favour of the remaining portion of the year.[7]

Housing conditions are unsatisfactory.

In many instances European quarters are most unsatisfactory especially as regards situation. Many of these are rat and bat infested, due to the old type of building and unoccupied ground floor rooms.[8]

Mortality figures for Europeans are summarized in Table 16. In order rightly to appraise mortality it must be borne in mind that many Europeans are absent from the Colony in the sickly season. Reports about the proportion of the Europeans who leave the country vary.

1868. . . . it is no wonder that the merchants, on the approach of the rainy season, escape for their lives to Europe, leaving their clerks to feed on the deadly miasma.[9]

1891. . . . about half of these [permanent European residents] are absent in Europe every year during the rainy season . . . .[10]

[1] Report on Blue Book 1888, p. 19.   [2] Ibid. 1889, p. 19.   [3] Colonial Reports, Gambia 1896, p. 5.
[4] Ibid. 1897, p. 4. But see 'Report on Blue Book 1872' (Colonial Possessions Reports 1875, Part I, p. 92): 'No mortality occurred among the white residents.'
[5] Colonial Reports, Gambia 1898, pp. 12–13.   [6] Ibid. 1902, p. 13.
[7] Ibid. 1903, p. 32. See also, for example, ibid. 1904, p. 33; 1905, p. 29; 1906, pp. 21, 24.
[8] Medical Report 1935, p. 16.   [9] Dr. Horton, West African Countries, pp. 240–1.
[10] Colonial Reports, Gambia 1891, p. 5.

TABLE 16. *European Deaths in the Gambia 1878–1939*[1]

Year	Deaths	Year	Deaths	Year	Deaths	Year	Deaths	Year	Deaths
1859	14	1887	6	1901	4	1915	—	1929	1
1860	5	1888	5	1902	2	1916	—	1930	2
1861	6	1889	2	1903	2	1917	—	1931	1
1862	4	1890	4	1904	—	1918	6	1932	1
1863	8	1891	4	1905	2	1919	2	1933	1
1864	2	1892	2	1906	3	1920	1	1934	4
1865	5	1893	3	1907	2	1921	2	1935	—
1866[2]	20	1894	5	1908	4[4]	1922	1	1936	—
1878	13[3]	1895	2	1909	2[4]	1923	4	1937	6
1879	1	1896	4	1910	2[5]	1924	3	1938	14[6]
1880	2	1897	—	1911	14	1925	5	1939	3
1882	3	1898	4	1912	3	1926	3		
1883	9	1899	1	1913	2	1927	5		
1884	5	1900	19	1914	1	1928	5		

[1] See Horton, *Physical and Medical Climate*, pp. 260–4; *Colonial Possessions Reports 1877–9*, p. 218, *1879*, p. 205, *1879–80*, p. 216, *1883–4*, p. 186; *Report on Blue Book 1884*, pp. 14–15, *1887*, p. 9, *1888*, p. 13, *1889*, p. 17; *Colonial Reports, Gambia 1890*, p. 6, *1891*, p. 5, *1893*, p. 6, *1896*, p. 5, *1897*, p. 4, *1898*, p. 12, *1901*, p. 17, *1902*, p. 12, *1903*, pp. 25–6, *1904*, p. 24, *1905*, pp. 23–4, *1907*, p. 17; *Government Gazette* 1892, 1894–5, 1900, 1906–7, Monthly Returns; *Medical Report 1919*, pp. 7, 9, *1920*, pp. 2–3, *1921*, pp. 4, 6, *1922*, p. 17, *1923*, pp. 6–7, *1924*, pp. 7–8, *1925*, p. 7, *1926*, pp. 9, 21, *1927*, p. 21, *1928*, p. 21, *1929*, pp. 10, 21, *1930*, p. 22, *1931*, p. 15, *1932*, pp. 8, 14, *1933*, p. 6, *1934*, p. 7, *1935*, pp. 11–12, *1936*, p. 10, *1937*, p. 10, *1938*, pp. 9–10, *1939*, pp. 3–4. No European Government official died in 1897, 1903–5, 1908, 1910, 1912, 1914–19, 1921, 1922, 1926–9, 1932–3, 1935–9; one died in 1907, 1909, 1913, 1920, 1923, 1924, 1925, 1930, and 1931; two died in 1901 and 1934; three died in 1911.   [2] From 1 Jan. to 12 Oct.
   [3] Including 6 deaths from ships.   [4] Including 1 from ships.   [5] From ships.
   [6] Including 12 deaths of non-residents as the result of an aeroplane accident.

1898. The rainy and unhealthy season for Europeans lasts for four months, July to October, but as business is then at a standstill, nearly all the Europeans leave the Colony for Europe, and this sensible arrangement reduces the mortality rate considerably.[1]

1903. July to October is regarded as the unhealthy season. All business is then more or less at a stand-still and as many Europeans as possible, both official and mercantile, leave the Colony for a change, to Europe.[2]

1905. . . . during the rainy season—July to October—this number [European population] is reduced by quite half owing to officials, merchants and others proceeding to Europe.[3]

1906. Some 100 Europeans are employed as clerks both in Bathurst and up the river for about seven months, and, as a rule, their health is fair, but quite three-fourths of them go home for the rainy season, and all of those that remain out are withdrawn to Bathurst by the second week in June.[4]

1907. More than half of the European community consisting of officials, merchants, and their assistants, leave the Colony during the rainy season—July to November.[5]

1908. During the rainy season, July–November, the leading mercantile agents and almost all their clerks leave the Colony . . . .[6]

Since in the nineteenth century the number of Europeans, including those temporarily absent, seldom exceeded 50, mortality in most years was very high. But it has been much lower since 1911.

[1] *Colonial Reports, Gambia 1898*, p. 12.   [2] Ibid. *1903*, p. 32.   [3] Ibid. *1905*, p. 24.
   [4] Ibid. *1906*, p. 24.   [5] Ibid. *1907*, p. 25. See also ibid., p. 17.
   [6] Ibid. *1908*, p. 31. See also *Medical Report 1913*, p. 7.

CHAPTER IV

GOLD COAST AND TOGOLAND[1]

I. Census-taking

Censuses (or at least counts) were taken in 1891 and thereafter every ten years up to 1931. 'At the Censuses of 1891 and 1901 legislation had not been considered politic',[2] but on the occasion of the 1911 census 'it was thought that the time had arrived when legal powers should be given to officers concerned with the Census and a legal duty to supply information should be imposed on the public'.[3] Thus, enabling Ordinances *ad hoc* were enacted for the censuses of 1911[4] and 1921.[5] But in 1930 'it was considered that from now on a definite ordinance should be placed among the Statutes of the Colony and with this end in view Ordinance No. 21 of 1930[6] was passed'.[7] The text of this Ordinance was very similar to the Ordinances of 1911 and 1921. It read as follows:

1. This Ordinance may be cited as the Census Ordinance, 1930.

2. The Governor in Council may from time to time as he may think fit by Order direct a census to be taken of the inhabitants and livestock of the Colony or any part thereof specified in such Order.

3. (1) It shall be lawful for the Governor to appoint a census officer, who, subject to the control of the Governor, shall have the general supervision and management of the census, and shall appoint a sufficient number of persons duly qualified to act as enumerators for taking the census and also any other officers necessary for the purpose of carrying this Ordinance into effect.

(2) Notice of the appointment of such enumerators and any other officers shall be published in the *Gazette*.

---

[1] In *An Economic Survey of the Colonial Empire*, as in most other British official publications, 'the Gold Coast' comprises the Gold Coast Colony, its dependencies Ashanti and the Northern Territories, and Togoland under British Mandate. In this volume the term Gold Coast covers the Gold Coast Colony (called for brevity sake the Colony), Ashanti, and the Northern Territories, but not Togoland.

[2] In 1891 it was 'decided that it was unnecessary and inexpedient to pass an Ordinance for the purposes of the Census as had been done at Sierra Leone' (*Census Report 1891*, p. 7). 'The reasons may be summarised thus:—that it was anticipated that in the peculiar mode of computation which would be adopted in the interior towns and villages, it would be difficult to enforce such an Ordinance generally and (2dly) that it was inexpedient to press an Ordinance with a penal operation which would most probably excite fear and opposition amongst the majority of the natives who laboured under the misapprehension that the ulterior object arrived at by the Government was the imposition of a Poll Tax' (ibid., p. 40).

[3] *Census Report 1911*, p. 1.

[4] No. 1 of 1911 (28 Jan.), reproduced ibid., p. 11.

[5] The census of 4 Apr. 1921 was authorized in the Colony by Ordinance No. 23 of 1920 (1 Sept.) which was almost identical with Ordinance No. 1 of 1911. It was applied to Ashanti by Ordinance No. 13 of 1920 and to the Northern Territories by Ordinance No. 9 of 1920 (19 Sept.). (These three Ordinances are reprinted in *Census Report 1921*, pp. 18–20.) The necessary powers to extend the census to Togoland were taken under Proclamation No. 24 of 1921 (15 Sept., Gold Coast, *Government Gazette*, 24 Sept. 1921, pp. 1247–8).

[6] 'An Ordinance to make provision for taking a Census of the inhabitants and livestock of the Colony as and when required' (19 Dec. 1930), *Gold Coast Gazette*, 27 Dec. 1930, pp. 2214–15; reprinted in *The Gold Coast, 1931*, vol. i, pp. 127–8. However, this Ordinance, possibly by mistake, was not included in *The Laws of the Gold Coast in Force 1936*.

[7] *The Gold Coast, 1931*, vol i, p. 127.

4. The census officer shall cause to be prepared and printed, for the use of the persons to be employed in taking a census, such forms and instructions as he may deem necessary, and in particular schedules to be filled up with such details as the Governor may consider necessary in order to insure, as far as possible, the completeness and accuracy of the census returns.

5. The enumerators and other persons employed under this Ordinance shall have authority to ask all persons all such questions as may be necessary for obtaining any of the particulars required by this Ordinance, and every person refusing to answer, or knowingly giving a false answer to any such question shall for every such refusal or false answer be liable to a fine not exceeding five pounds.

6. Every person who—

(a) without lawful excuse refuses or neglects to fill in any schedule of details as and when he may be required by the census officer or any officer acting on his behalf so to do ; or

(b) fills in any such schedule with details which he knows to be false ;

shall be liable to a fine not exceeding five pounds.

7. Upon the completion of any census the census officer shall cause an abstract of the returns to be furnished to the Governor.

Similar Ordinances, Ashanti No. 9 of 1930,[1] Northern Territories No. 5 of 1930,[2] and British Sphere of Togoland No. 4 of 1930,[3] were enacted to apply *mutatis mutandis* to these Dependencies.[4]

In accordance with sections 2 and 3 of these Ordinances a Government Notice to the effect that a census would be taken was issued on 23 February 1931,[5] couched in the following terms:

A census of the Colony, Ashanti, Northern Territories and Togoland under British Mandate, will be taken on Sunday the 26th April, 1931. Each occupier, or head of a house, will be required to furnish a return of all people who slept in his or her house or premises on that night.

2. Similar arrangements will be made by the Census Officers as in 1921 and the forms on which the Census will be taken are as follows:—

Form 'A' for villages and small towns (Africans only)
Form 'B' for certain selected large towns (Africans only)
Form 'C' for all non-Africans
Form 'D' for collecting data as to Religions
Form 'E' for inhabited houses.

3. *Foodstuffs.*—District Census Officers will take a census as to the prices of the principal native foodstuffs on Census day, viz., 26th April.

4. Captain A. W. Norris has been appointed Census Officer, with office at Accra (P.O. Box 560), and further information may be obtained from him, or from any District Census Officer.[6]

Form 'A' asked for the following data for 'every person, whether a stranger or a native of the town or village, who slept in the town or village on the night of census taking':

I. Tribe or State.
II. Place of Origin: African of Gold Coast or Alien African.
III. Sex and Age (whether under 15, 15–45, or 46 and over).

---

[1] *Gold Coast Gazette*, 27 Dec. 1930, pp. 2224–5.
[2] Ibid., pp. 2227–8.
[3] Ibid., pp. 2231–2.
[4] These three Ordinances were likewise enacted on 19 Dec. 1930.
[5] *Gold Coast Gazette*, 7 Mar. 1931, p. 383; reprinted in *The Gold Coast, 1931*, vol. i, p. 128.
[6] The forms are reproduced ibid., pp. 125–6, 129–38.

IV. Education in or over Standard IV.

V. Infirmities: Lepers, Blind, Deaf and Dumb, Mentally deranged.

Form 'B'[1] asked for the same data as Form 'A' and in addition for the name; the specific age of children (up to 1 year old, age to be stated in months; between 1 and 5 years; 6–15 years); the occupation; and the industry.

Form 'C' (for non-Africans) asked for the name; relationship to head of household; religion; sex; marital condition; age; race; birthplace; nationality; occupation; industry; whether able to read, write; whether able to speak English; if suffering from serious infirmity, nature of infirmity.

Form 'D' was intended for the use of the various missions only, which had been asked, in order to obtain greater accuracy, to fill in the details called for. These were for each town or village: Children baptized; Adult full members; Adults under Instruction; Total.

Form 'E' asked for each inhabited house or compound: Name of Occupier; Type of Building.

The Chief Census Officer, 1931, says: 'In each census report a greater degree of accuracy has been claimed for the accompanying statistics than for previous figures. The present is no exception.'[2] I shall try to show briefly the actual position at the various censuses.

1891. No census was taken; only a count was made. The returns were compiled in a large measure by the Native Kings who received from the Governor the following letter dated 22 December 1890:[3]

King,

The Queen has expressed a wish to know how many subjects she has in the Gold Coast Protectorate, and has instructed you to obtain this information for her and send it to the District Commissioner.

2. I ask you, therefore, to number the people of all the towns and villages in your country, and when you have done this to let the District Commissioner of   know how many males and how many females you have in your country.

3. I understand the way you count your people is to divide each town or village into companies, which are again sub-divided into families. The heads of families are then directed to drop into a calabash, or similar article provided for the purpose, a grain of corn or a cowrie, according to the number of their people—and that these calabashes are then collected and the contents counted. You will, therefore, I know, have no difficulty in doing what I ask you.

4. I wish you to clearly understand that I am not asking you to do this in order to tax your people, or for any purpose but your good. The Government in requiring this information has no intention to tax you or interfere with your country, and I only want the information to give to the Queen. As a loyal King you will, I am sure, help me. You will see that it is for your advantage that I should know how many people belong to your country in the same way that a shepherd counts his sheep to know how many look to him for protection and care.

5. In those of your towns where you have Hausas living, you must not forget to include them in the numbers.

[1] This form was used for the urban population comprising 377,075 of the 2,866,715 African counted in the Gold Coast, and 6,396 of the 293,671 Africans counted in Togoland.

[2] *The Gold Coast, 1931*, vol. i, p. 123.

[3] *Census Report 1891*, pp. 37–8.

6. In order that you may be able to say how many males and how many females
you have, I wish you to give instructions that when the numbering takes place
different articles are to be used for each sex—that is to say, Indian Corn for males,
and Cowries or Kernels for females.

I am, King,

Your good Friend,

W. BRANDFORD GRIFFITH,

Governor.

It seems that almost only in the sixteen principal towns with a total
population of about 70,000 was a count made by enumerators in the
employ of the Administration. In these towns the population was to be
subdivided into male adults, female adults, male children, and female
children, into Whites, Mulattoes, and Blacks, into Christians, Mahommedans, and Pagans, and into occupations (8 groups)[1] while for the rest
of the country merely the total number of males and of females was
ascertained.[2]

The Secretary of the Census Committee (Assistant Colonial Surgeon)
reported:

It soon became evident to the Committee that the accuracy of the Census Returns
would be problematical, if not impossible, for, in addition to the absence of any
Census records or reliable data for their guidance, the following difficulties presented
themselves:—

(i) The great dread of the native population of all Census enumerations, founded
on the belief—the outcome of experience when not under British rule—that
all such enumerations were but the harbingers of taxation in some form or
other.

(ii) The poverty of the materials at the disposal of the Committee for the collection of such data as could be obtained, and the physical difficulties to be met
in collecting the necessary information, arising from the absence of convenient
means of travelling and the scattered situations of the towns, villages and
hamlets in the several Districts.

(iii) The large numbers of mechanics and labourers which were being drafted
from the Colony during the time of the Census operations—a drainage which
had been going on for some time before also to supply the labour markets of
the Oil Rivers, the Niger Protectorate, the Cameroons, Fernando Po, and,
greatest of all, the Congo Free State.

In order to adapt itself to the peculiar circumstances of the Colony—and it cannot
for a moment be denied that the circumstances of this Colony, so far as Census
purposes are concerned, are peculiar—the Committee found it necessary to extend
the period for taking the Census from one day, April 5th, to six days, April 13th to
18th. As a matter of fact, in one case, Axim, the Census was taken before the period
stated, and in some other cases, a very long time after, e.g., Cape Coast, Elmina,
Saltpond.[3]

The total estimated population according to the Returns received, is 768,882
for the whole Colony, exclusive of Quahoo and Krepi, viz.: 357,584 males and
409,511 females, 1,787 unclassified. But it must be apparent to any one with a
knowledge of the Country that these figures do not accurately represent the population, and the inaccuracy is especially great as regards the interior parts of the Colony.
Most, if not all, of the people of the interior are engaged in farming and other agricultural pursuits, and spend most of their time during the day on their farms, where
a rude hut shelters them from the heat of the mid-day sun, and they return to their

---

[1] See Form B, reprinted in *Census Report 1891*, p. 133.

[2] See Form A, reprinted ibid., p. 38.   [3] Ibid., p. 8.

homes at night. This applies especially to the female portion of the community and the children, *e.g.*, Axim, Aowin, Wassaw, Yankumasi and Denkera. Consequently it was very difficult for the paid enumerators to get at these people, and the Returns supplied by the Native Chiefs are all more or less influenced by that dread of taxation already referred to.

This inaccuracy is not equal in all the Census Districts, however, and in the case of most of the principal towns along the littoral, in the Aquapim, Krobo, Osudoku, and Aquamu sections of the Volta Census District; in the Accra section of the Accra Census District; and in the Winneba and Saltpond Census Districts, the Returns may be regarded, for all practical purposes, as fairly accurate. As regards Kwitta, the Returns must be regarded as inaccurate, due to the Political complications in the District at the time.

I would propose to make the following additions to the populations of the Census Districts to get a more approximately accurate account, viz.:— . . . 205,000, making a total of 973,882, to which I would add 500,000 for the unestimated Districts of British Krepi and Kwahu, making a grand total of 1,473,882 inhabitants for the Colony and Protectorate, or approximately 1½ millions.[1]

The total of 1,473,882 was obtained as follows:[2]

	Accra	Ada	Axim	Cape Coast	Kwitta	Pram- pram	Salt Pond
Returns .	91,612	46,869	39,870	87,873	36,230	10,908	138,828
Additions .	30,000	10,000	15,000	40,000	10,000	5,000	10,000
Total .	121,612	56,869	54,870	127,873	46,230	15,908	148,828

	Se- kundi	Was- saw	Volta	Winne- bah	Ata- bubu	Krepi, Kwahu	Total
Returns .	29,863	73,683	128,608	80,164	4,374	—	768,882
Additions .	5,000	50,000	20,000	10,000	—	500,000	705,000
Total .	34,863	123,683	148,608	90,164	4,374	500,000	1,473,882

The Secretary of the Census Committee was, no doubt, right in distrusting the accuracy of the returns from most districts, but since many figures were evidently obtained by guessing[3], overstatements were probably on the whole about as frequent as understatements, and his scheme of making huge additions to the figures even of those Districts where he regarded the returns, for all practical purposes, as fairly accurate was certainly wrong. As regards Kwahu (Quahoo) and Krepi, he raised the total of 480,000 given in the preceding Blue Books[4] to 500,000, but both guesses were wide of the mark.

It would seem from the [1901] figures, that the addition of 500,000 proposed by the Census Committee of 1891 for the unestimated districts of Kwahu and British Krepi, was excessive, being almost 400,000 more than the numbers returned for 1901.[5]

[1] Ibid., p. 9.   [2] See ibid., pp. 9, 41.

[3] The population, for example, of the town of Sefwhi Whyawsu was returned as 11,000 males and 22,000 females; see ibid., p. 90.

[4] See Gold Coast Colony, *Blue Book 1887* R, p. 1; *1888* R, p. 1; *1889* R, p. 1.

[5] *Census Report 1901*, p. 5. The 1911 census returns showed the population of these two Districts to be 58,525; see ibid. *1911*, p. 7. The *Blue Books* 1887–9 had given for Kwahu 30,000 and for Krepi 450,000.

The cost of the count was £231. 13s. 9d.[1] or 6s. per each 1,000 inhabitants. This money was probably spent exclusively for the remuneration of the enumerators in the employ of the Administration.

1901. The methods of counting the population were in 1901 practically the same as in 1891. The Kings were again asked as in 1891 to return the number of inhabitants by sex.[2] The forms used by the enumerators in the employ of the Administration were more primitive than at the earlier count and asked merely for a distinction between males and females; Whites, Mulattoes, and Blacks; and occupations (7 groups).[3] But it is doubtful whether even these scanty details were obtained. In any case, unlike the report for 1891, the report for 1901 shows hardly more than the number of males and of females.[4]

While the enumeration area in 1891 comprised only the Colony, excluding the Districts of British Krepi and Kwahu, it covered in 1901 (on principle) the whole Colony, Ashanti (annexed in 1901), and the Northern Territories (as constituted in 1901).

The Census Committee reported:

It was found to be impossible to take the Census on the day suggested by the Right Honourable the Secretary of State, and, in order that the enumeration of the people in the various districts might be simultaneous throughout the Colony, it was deemed advisable to postpone the day for the Census-taking until June the first.[5]

The total population of the Colony, including Ashanti and the Northern Territories, is, according to the returns received, 1,338,433; but the Committee were of opinion that these returns in many instances, were unreliable. Particular towns, well known to members of the Committee, were found to be either over-, or under-estimated, in most cases the latter. That there should be inaccuracies will not appear remarkable, when the difficulties of collecting the necessary information are recognised. There is the native repugnance to any census enumeration, due partly to superstition and partly to a fear of taxation. Again there is the absence of experienced enumerators; Commissioners in charge of a wide district with a small staff at their disposal and few facilities for rapid travelling have been compelled to accept the returns of the Local Chief, or of illiterate Policemen for the scattered villages under their control. Another difficulty is the fact that there is often great divergence between the Political and Tribal divisions of the Colony. Many villages refused to send Census returns to the District Commissioner, on the ground that their King resided in another District. On the other hand some kings sent in returns of the number of their subjects, gathered not merely from their own but also from adjoining districts. Moreover in places where farming is general, it sometimes occurred that a considerable portion of the population—women and children specially—were at work on their plantations many miles away from their villages and out of reach of the enumerators.

In view of these considerations, the Committee, following the precedent set by the Census Committee of 1891, decided that a more correct estimate of the population in certain of the census districts would be obtained by making the following additions, viz:— . . .[6]

---

[1] See *Census Report 1891*, p. 41.

[2] See Form A, reprinted in *Census Report 1901*, p. 64.

[3] See Form B, reprinted ibid., p. 65.

[4] The only additional information is the total number of Europeans in each District of the Colony (but not in Ashanti or the Northern Territories) and data on occupation for ten towns. See ibid., pp. 7–8.

[5] Ibid., p. 3.   [6] Ibid., pp. 4–5.

These additions worked out as follows:[1]

	Accra	Adda	Axim	Cape Coast	Dix-cove	Kwitta	Pram-pram
Returns .	143,141	46,487	18,130	100,282	11,725	174,224	13,404
Addition .	10,000	10,000	15,000	30,000	5,000	—	5,000
Total .	153,141	56,487	33,130	130,282	16,725	174,224	18,404

	Salt-pond	Sekon-di	Volta River	Was-saw	Win-neba	Total
Returns .	57,820	22,600	163,997	80,603	62,937	895,350
Addition .	30,000	3,000	10,000	20,000	10,000	148,000
Total .	87,820	25,600	173,997	100,603	72,937	1,043,350

The Census Committee stated furthermore:

The great development of the Mining industry and the construction of the Sekondi–Tarkwa Railway since the last Census has naturally largely increased the number of White men in the Colony.

The Committee have endeavoured to get as accurate a return as possible of the number of White men, and to classify their nationalities and professions.

From some districts the returns appear to be very accurate, but from others they are not so satisfactory.

As no record has been kept at the different ports of entry, of the number of White men landing in the Colony, it has been found impossible to check these returns.

In the case of the Railway and of the leading Gold Mines, accurate returns have been supplied. But there must be many men not belonging to any known company, who have escaped the notice of the Enumerator.[2]

The Cape Coast District has a population numbering 100,282 and an increase of 12,409 on the last Census. The District Commissioner, however, thinks that the population is really far greater. Owing to illness in one case and heavy rains in another the enumerators were unable to complete the Denkera portion of the district; but they made rough estimates of the villages they were unable to visit.

The District Commissioner is of the opinion that, in the Denkera district alone, if 20,000 were added to the numbers given by the enumerator the result would still be under the correct figure. In a district like Cape Coast where so many carriers are employed it is particularly difficult to arrive at a correct estimate of the population.

It is almost impossible to believe that the returns from Saltpond and Axim can be correct. The former shows a decrease of 80,998 and the latter a decrease of 21,740. The mines may have drawn many workmen from these districts into others, but that would hardly account for so remarkable a decrease. I am inclined to think that though doubtless the returns of 1901 are considerably under the true figure, yet the population of Saltpond and Axim was not nearly as large as stated in 1891.[3]

The Census Committee refers only quite incidentally to the enumeration in Ashanti and the Northern Territories, and it seems that a count was actually made only in small sections of these Dependencies. For most Districts of Ashanti the population is given in thousands[4] and 'it was reported that the only returns that are of any use as a census return are

---

[1] See ibid., pp. 5, 19.   [2] Ibid., p. 5.

[3] Ibid., pp. 5–6. The population ascertained in 1891 in Saltpond District was 138,828 and in Axim District 39,870. The Secretary of the 1891 Census Committee had proposed to add 10,000 in Saltpond and 15,000 in Axim 'to get a more approximately accurate account'!

[4] This was also true, as in 1891, for some areas of the Colony.

those of British Gaman and Wenchi'.[1] The inhabitants of these two Districts numbered only 13,890 and 8,488[2] and comprised only about 7 per cent. of the population of Ashanti. As regards the Northern Territories, the Census Report gave as total population 107,432 (55,098 males, 52,334 females).[3] But the Chief Commissioner reported in 1902:

A census was taken of this hinterland last year with fairly satisfactory results, especially when one considers the very short time these territories have been under our rule; the total counted adult population amounted to 107,964, there being 2,000 more males than females.

In order to get a more approximately accurate account 104,000 was added to the above numbers as a considerable portion of the country was not counted. Only the adult population has been included in these figures; it was suggested, therefore, that 50 per cent should be added for children, viz., 106,000, so that the estimated total population of the Northern Territories amounts to 317,964.[4]

It is with great satisfaction I am able to report that in the districts of Mamprusi, Dagomba, Gonja, Kintampo, Bole, Wa, and Grunshi, the chiefs gave every assistance, and readily accepted my assurance that the counting had nothing to do with the bringing in of a tax or making additional calls upon them for free labour.

In Dagarti the enumerators were received in many places with considerable suspicion; whenever this took place the counting was not proceeded with. The Fra-Fra district I did not attempt, as it would not have been safe to send anyone to count them without an escort, which would have defeated its own object.[5]

The Census Committee evidently thought that the figure of 107,432 given in their report included children and covered the total area of the Northern Territories, but it evidently comprised only adults; and the 1911 census report says: 'It was found, on examination, that the estimated population of certain Districts had been omitted from that report.'[6]

The cost of the count (remuneration of enumerators) was £254. 6s. 0d.[7] or 3s. 10d. per 1,000 inhabitants. Even considering that only £21. 17s. 0d. of this money was spent in the Northern Territories and nothing in Ashanti, it appears that the expenditure in the Colony was lower than in 1891, but the returns furnished by the enumerators were also much poorer.

1911. A census was taken of all Whites and Indians, and of the Africans in thirty-two towns and villages of the Colony. All other Africans in the Colony and those in Ashanti and the Northern Territories were merely counted, but more details were ascertained than on former occasions. The total population of each town or village was to be shown by sex and age (5 years and under, 6 to 15, 16 to 45, 46 and over), by tribe or race, and by religion.[8] In the towns and villages where a census was taken additional

---

[1] *Census Report 1911*, p. 25. *Colonial Reports, Gold Coast 1902*, p. 46, said that the returns from Ashanti were 'very incomplete'.

[2] See *Census Report 1901*, p. 56. *Census Report 1911*, p. 25, says: 'The totals for these Districts were 6,945 and 4,244 respectively as against 14,369 and 5,168 at the recent census' (I am sure I do not know why the 1901 figures were halved).

[3] See *Census Report 1901*, p. 56.

[4] *Colonial Reports, Gold Coast 1906*, p. 34, said: 'A discrepancy in the figures placed before the Committee was discovered in 1906, from which it is apparent that the population of the Northern Territories has been understated by 210,532.' This understatement, as shown above, was pointed out by the Chief Commissioner already in 1902.

[5] *Colonial Reports, Northern Territories of the Gold Coast 1901*, p. 11.

[6] *Census Report 1911*, p. 49.   [7] See *Census Report 1901*, p. 52.

[8] See Form A, reprinted in *Census Report 1911*, p. 15.

information was obtained concerning occupation, education, and infirmities.[1] In most of these places the census was apparently taken by paid enumerators in the employ of the Administration, but 'in certain large towns and notably at Accra the enumeration of the population was carried out successfully and without friction by the Chiefs and Elders of the Quarters and Companies'.[2] The Chiefs and Headmen were in charge of the enumeration also in the rest of the Colony and were expected to have 'the voluntary assistance of educated natives, of the representatives of Missions and of Trading Firms, residing or working in the village'.[3]

In Ashanti and the Northern Territories considerations of expenditure and different social conditions to a great extent rendered inapplicable the procedure followed in the Colony. The Chiefs are with very few exceptions illiterate, Missions and Trading Firms are not widely established, and there are few educated natives whose assistance is available. The Census therefore in the Dependencies had to be taken under the personal supervision and often by the personal efforts of the Commissioners and their Staff, and this entailed upon them a heavy burden of work and responsibility in addition to their other duties.[4]

The census report gives the following additional details about the taking of the census:

The Census night for the Colony and its Dependencies was the night of Sunday, April 2nd. In the towns and in most of the large villages this date was strictly observed, but in the outlying portions of the Colony and in many parts of Ashanti and the Northern Territories, the enumeration, owing to the small staff available, could not be completed on the appointed date.

The number of enumerators appointed under the Ordinance was 323 . . . . The rates of pay varied from 5/- to 10/- according to local conditions, but in several cases, and notably in the Central Province, services were given gratuitously. . . .

In the Western Province, it was necessary to appoint travelling Supervisors and Enumerators to explain the census forms and assist Chiefs and Headmen in the work of enumeration and in making out the returns. The rate of pay was £6 with an allowance of £2 for a carrier, the work occupying about a month. Eight enumerators of this class were appointed. Axim, Tarquah, and Seccondee Districts received one each, Ancobra District two, and Western Frontier three.

In the Central and Eastern Provinces where many of the Chiefs are literate and where there are a far greater number of educated natives than in the Western Province, the enumeration was undertaken by the Chiefs themselves or under their direction. It is worthy of note that the most reliable returns were received from these Provinces.

In Ashanti eighty two clerks were appointed as enumerators. In the Northern Territories the only assistance it was found possible to provide was an extra clerk for each Province. These clerks had to be obtained from the Coast and though the rate of pay was six pounds a month inclusive and an allowance for four hammockmen and one carrier was granted, there was considerable difficulty in obtaining suitable persons.[5]

The section of the report which deals with the accuracy of the returns is particularly valuable.

[1] See Form B, reprinted ibid., pp. 18-19. See also ibid., pp. 2-3, and p. 400 below. Special Forms, C and D, reprinted ibid., pp. 20-1, were used for the first time for Indians and for Whites respectively.
[2] Ibid., p. 2. [3] Ibid., p. 13.
[4] Ibid., p. 3. [5] Ibid., pp. 1-2.

The following extracts concerning the accuracy of the Census are taken from the Reports of the Chief Commissioners and, in the Colony, of Provincial Commissioners:—

THE COLONY

The Western Province.—'In my opinion the Returns fall short of the actual population of this Province by twenty per cent. I am confident the travelling enumerators have not carried out their duties with any degree of accuracy and the inherent belief held by all classes of the native community that there were ulterior motives with regard to the taking of the Census tended to keep the returns of the Census as low as possible.'

The Central Province.—'The District Commissioners are of opinion that numerically the returns sent in are generally accurate.'

The Eastern Province.—With the exception of the Addah and Quittah and, perhaps, the Birrim Districts a high degree of accuracy has been obtained, special reference being made to the good work done in the Volta River and Akwapim Districts. The return for the Birrim District is considered disappointing but there is little in the Commissioner's report to suggest that the actual population is greatly in excess of the number recorded. In the case of the Addah District it is reported that the Northern portion across the Volta with an estimated population from two to four thousand was not visited by the Enumerators. The return for the Quittah District is inaccurate. In 1891 the population was recorded as 36,230, but it was reported that there was great difficulty in taking a census owing to political complications. In 1901 the population was returned as 174,224, figures which have never been accepted with complete confidence. At the recent census the total recorded is 36,960. Adequate arrangements appear to have been made for enumeration but the District Commissioner was transferred before the census was taken. On his return he found that no steps had been taken to enumerate the people in the Central Division, and he was compelled to improvise machinery for the work. He reports that the Enumerators experienced considerable trouble, that there was a universal fear of a hut tax and that in some cases on the approach of an Enumerator villages were deserted. He adds that 'in the opinion of competent observers a large addition should be made to the figures obtained, many new villages have been built and old ones have grown to the dignity of towns'.[1]

ASHANTI

'The total falls short of expectations (as is usually the case), but I can safely say that throughout Ashanti numbers have been underestimated, for some cause or another—the main underlying feeling being one of nervousness of the Census being taken as a basis for possible future taxation.'

THE NORTHERN TERRITORIES

'It is reported that the returns for the Southern and North Western Provinces are considered to be fairly accurate, but that in the North Eastern Province it is estimated that only two-thirds of the inhabitants have been enumerated.'[2]

[1] *Report on the Eastern Province 1912*, p. 7, says: 'The population of the Province at the last Census was 442,232, though in some instances the returns were considered disappointing the actual population at the time of the year the census was taken is probably not much larger than the recorded total.' But there cannot be any doubt that the omissions, particularly in Quittah, were enormous.

[2] It is very doubtful whether the returns for the Southern and North-Western Provinces can really be considered even fairly accurate. See the following comment on the figures obtained for the Northern Territories (*Colonial Reports, Northern Territories 1911*, p. 12):

'These figures must not be taken as giving an accurate idea of the population of the Protectorate. This will be readily understood when it is borne in mind that only three special enumerators were appointed . . . .

'The fear of taxation amongst the natives throughout the Protectorate deterred numbers from

It is also stated that no Census was taken in 26 towns of the Zouaragu District [North Eastern Province]. The Commissioner estimates the population of these towns at 56,000.

The accuracy of a census depends of course upon the honesty and intelligence of the enumerators. In many of the towns and important villages of the Colony considerable interest was taken in the work by the community generally, and a good class of enumerator was often available. . . .

Away from the towns, however, and in Ashanti and the Northern Territories reliance in the long run had to be placed upon Chiefs and Headmen. In small villages the Headman and his Elders have no doubt personal knowledge of the names and numbers of every family, but in the towns and larger villages it is hardly possible that this should be the case. The enumeration undertaken by Chiefs and Headmen is not likely on the whole to be as accurate as the return obtained by special enumerators on Form B.

The Census, therefore, cannot lay claim to any result comparable in accuracy and detail with a census in more civilised communities. Indeed the attempt to reach such a standard was impossible. There is not a sufficient number of educated natives out of employment, who possess the qualities necessary to obtain reliable returns. There is also the question of expense, not on account of the numbers to be enumerated but on account of the extent of country to be covered. The expenditure on transport alone for a staff adequate to take accurate statistics of the Colony and its Dependencies in the short time available would itself have placed any attempt at an elaborate and ambitious census outside the range of practical politics. The money could doubtless have been spent but adequate value would not have been obtained for it.

The general opinion is, as the extracts from the reports show, that the actual population is in excess of the numbers recorded on the returns, and without doubt this is the case. It is probable however that, assuming an honest attempt has been made to get at the numbers of the people, the difference between the actual and recorded population is not a very great one. The Colony and its Dependencies are now better known and more extensively travelled than in former years, and it is not probable that villages of any importance have been overlooked. It is possible of course that hunting or farming villages buried deep in the forest were not reached by enumerators or have not been included in the returns from the Chiefs, but it is easy to exaggerate their numbers and to overestimate the allowance to be made for them. The imagination of the Native peoples the Forest with Spirits and the imagination of the Official peoples it with men, but experience tends to dispel the fears or hopes of either.

In 1891 and 1901, estimates of the population unrecorded or under-enumerated were added to the total on the returns. . . . If the returns of the recent census are any guide, these estimates of previous years are not only valueless but mischievous. It has therefore been decided on the present occasion to accept the recorded population as comparatively accurate and to make no estimated additions. Such additions to be of any value should be estimated on a more trustworthy basis than mere

putting in an appearance to be counted, which is not to be wondered at, as in the adjacent territories of France and Germany all natives are taxed.

'It was only possible to get a rough enumeration of the people in some parts of the North-Western Province and in the northern portion of the North-Eastern Province, as the towns in those parts of the country consist of large numbers of compounds, scattered over extensive areas, and it is estimated that only about two-thirds of the people in the latter Province have been counted.'

See also *Census Report 1911*, p. 31: 'With regard to the excess of males over females in the North Western and Southern Provinces, the Commissioners attribute it, to a great extent, to the young girls and women being hidden from the enumerators, so much so that the commissioner of the Southern Province recommends that 2,000 [nearly 35 per cent.] be added to the number given for females between the ages of 6 and 15, in addition to the 15 per cent recommended to be added to the other totals of that sex.'

personal impression, and, if they are to be made at all, should be assessed by those, who having been engaged in the task of enumeration, have acquired the local experience on which only a reliable estimate can be founded.[1]

The cost of the enumeration was £523. 2s. 0d.,[2] of which £27. 8s. 9d. was spent at headquarters. The expenditure per 1,000 inhabitants was 7s.

1921. The procedure was, in principle, the same as in 1911.

On the advice of the Honourable the Secretary for Native Affairs, Mr. Furley, c.m.g., o.b.e., it was decided 'not to attempt any elaboration or extension of the scope of the Census beyond the lines on which it was conducted in 1911 . . . as the results of the 1921 Census would be more easily comparable with those of 1911 and will be of more value and interest if they are obtained by the same procedure'.

The procedure followed in 1911 was, roughly, a house to house Census on a Form, called B, of the largest and most important towns in the Colony, shewing particulars of tribe, sex, age (in four age groups) religion, whether literate or illiterate, blind, deaf and dumb or mentally deranged. An attempt was also made to classify the occupations of the inhabitants of these selected towns. The enumeration of the remainder of the African population was taken on a Form, called A, which required no particulars of the occupations, education or infirmities of the population. The Census of Indians was taken on a Form, called C, which required particulars as to name, sex, age, birthplace, religion, occupation and civil conditions as to marriage.

All the other non-African races were enumerated on a Form called D, which required, in addition to the particulars collected from Indians, a statement as to Nationality.

A Form, called E, . . . was used to collect particulars as to inhabited houses in towns and villages. It appears that in some cases an enumeration of houses was undertaken before and indeed as a check to the subsequent Census of the population.

Where the voluntary assistance of Europeans and educated Natives was easily obtainable, some reliance could be placed on the statistics obtained, but in most of the Colony, and in the whole of Ashanti and the Northern Territories, considerable difficulty was experienced in obtaining reliable returns, especially from the outlying villages where the population was, and still remains, illiterate. In the Census Report for 1911, Mr. Harper the Chief Census Officer, suggested that at the next Census, Form B, should be simplified, but, on the understanding that absolute accuracy could not be effected in every case, it was agreed to make no change in 1921.

Again following Mr. Furley's recommendation, the schedule of Occupations was revised, and reduced, and the classification of tribes as published in the Civil List was adopted.

A column was added to Form A headed 'Education' but no change was considered necessary in the other Forms.[3]

However, Special Forms, B, C, and D, were used in the five towns of Accra, Cape Coast, Secondee, Axim, and Coomassie which differed from the ordinary Forms B, C, and D inasmuch as they contained extra age columns for children up to one year old in which the age was to be stated in months.

The Census Day was to be 24 April, but 'The Census Ordinance, 1920' (like 'The Census Ordinance, 1911') provided that 'it shall be lawful for the Governor in Council by order or proclamation to postpone until any later time the doing of any matter or thing required by this Ordinance to

---

[1] *Census Report 1911*, pp. 4–7. See also ibid., p. 26: 'The Census Reports for those years suggest that in the former case [1891] the estimate is the impression of the Assistant Colonial Surgeon who drafted the Report, and that in the latter case [1901] it is the opinion of certain residents of Accra who were formed into a local Committee.'

[2] See ibid., p. 24.

[3] *Census Report 1921*, p. 21.

be done at or by any particular time'. An Order of 14 March 1921[1] informed the public that 'Census Officers in remote districts have been granted discretionary powers to take the Census between March 24th and May 24th'.

Unlike the 1911 census report, the report for 1921 is somewhat vague regarding the personnel connected with the taking of the census. Concerning the attitude of the people towards the enumeration the report says:

Northern Territories. On this occasion . . . the attitude of the people was at least more favourable than on previous occasions. The Chief Commissioner of the *Northern Territories* reports that in Eastern Gonja (Salaga and Yeji), 'The people did not like it (the Census) and frequently ran away, but the chiefs usually succeeded in bringing them back and counting would then proceed'. In Western Gonja (Bole) 'they often tried to make out that all had been counted, when in reality only a half had'. In the Dagarti area of Wa the people are said to have been 'shy and elusive'. In Tumu there was some trouble owing, it is said, to the lack of influence of the Chiefs of the Issala Grunshis, a tribe of a 'generally suspicious and sensitive character'. But in Lorha, the District Commissioner reported the attitude of the people to be 'admirable'.

Ashanti. The Chief Commissioner of *Ashanti* reports that on this occasion there was less suspicion amongst the people as to the objects of the Census.

The Colony. In the *Colony*, the Commissioner of the *Western Province* states that some of the Chiefs and people thought the Census a preliminary to the imposition of a Poll Tax and that some fishermen at Chama took to sea to avoid enumeration, but that in two cases only were prosecutions taken under the Census Ordinance.

In the Winnebah District of the *Central Province*, some of the Chiefs also connected the enumeration with taxation, but otherwise the enumerators met with no trouble in this Province.

In the *Eastern Province*, there was, it is said, a certain amount of suspicion at first which, allayed by the explanations of the District Commissioners, changed to one of 'contemptuous indifference'.[2]

Togoland. It was inevitable that the people should construe the Census as a preliminary to the imposition of a head, or hut, tax which has been collected by the Germans before the war and has since been reimposed by the French in the area under their administration. The District Officers did their best to assure them that there was no such intention on the part of the British Government, but nevertheless, it is certain that the number of able-bodied men is considerably more than the Returns show.[3]

The Chief Census Officer says in conclusion:

The attitude of the people towards the Census on this occasion may therefore be considered to have been comparatively favourable, but even so, the conditions existing in the Gold Coast to-day absolutely prohibit the collection of accurate and entirely reliable statistics of population.

The Census was in fact an addition to the ordinary duties of the Political and other officers, and in 1921 as in 1911, some officers must be presumed to have been so fully occupied by their ordinary duties that the Census received from them less attention than it deserved.

It would be idle to deny the unpopularity of the Census amongst all officers who had to carry it through. Yet I imagine no Political Officer would be found to deny the value of such information though it can be truthfully described in no higher terms than 'fairly accurate' or even probably 'fairly accurate'.[4]

---

[1] Reprinted ibid., p. 22.   [2] Ibid., pp. 15–16.
[3] Ibid., p. 138.   [4] Ibid., p. 16.

As regards the accuracy of the enumeration in various areas he stated:

Northern Territories. The Chief Commissioner of the *Northern Territories* wisely does not definitely commit himself.[1] Many villages were counted in 1921 which could not be dealt with in 1911 owing to the wildness of the inhabitants. In that year, the population of these villages could only be roughly guessed and the estimate would appear to have been, from present data, very unreliable. One finds that in parts of the Tumu Area, even in 1921, the only practical method of enumeration was extremely primitive. The Chiefs' messengers brought to the District Census Officer calabashes filled with beans, ground nuts and stones representing the numbers of males, females and children in the more remote villages. Such methods, admittedly unavoidable in the circumstances, are not favourable to accuracy.

Ashanti. The Chief Commissioner of *Ashanti* says it is not possible to speak 'with any great confidence' of the accuracy of the actual figures, and considers that until the survey is completed an 'accurate Census is not likely to be attained'. The particulars relative to education and religion should be received he thinks, 'with a good deal of caution, and in fact they are not wholly reliable'.

The Colony. As regards the *Colony* the estimates are, as one would expect, more optimistic. The Central Province, the smallest, and in a sense the oldest Province is, man for man, probably the most enlightened Province of the three. The Commissioner states that the accuracy obtained in 1921 was far greater than in 1911, and in 1911 the result was considered to be generally accurate, in fact the most satisfactory of all.

In many cases a trial Census was taken, and the results approximated very closely to the later and final figures. The result of the highly commendable care and trouble taken by the Census Officers and all who assisted them in this Province is that the Commissioner can state that 'a very satisfactory degree of accuracy has been obtained'.

In the *Eastern Province* which is much larger than the Central Province, the same favourable conditions exist, but in a smaller degree. The Commissioner, after stating that some villages were no doubt included in the purview of the Census for the first time, considers that the result is 'very fairly accurate'. In Accra Municipal Area probably the most favourable conditions exist and in my opinion a satisfactory degree of accuracy should have and has been obtained.

The *Western Province* is the largest, probably the wealthiest, and without doubt unfortunately the most backward of the three Provinces. Conditions here are more like those which confronted the Census Officers in Ashanti, and it is absolutely impossible to obtain, under present conditions, the same degree of accuracy as in the other two Provinces. In 1911, the Census was described as 'Unfortunate' and the error was estimated to be 20 per cent.

I am inclined to consider that that estimate was too optimistic. On this occasion in spite of the inexperience of the staff, all of whom are reported to have taken great personal interest in the difficult task, the Commissioner considers the result to be accurate to 'within 10 per cent of the actual numbers'.[2]

Togoland. It was not found possible to collect age statistics in Southern and Northern Mamprussi, where even the bare enumeration was rendered extremely difficult owing to the wildness of the people, especially of the Konkombas.[3]

Not even the number of huts or houses was ascertained in these two Districts. Particulars about the distribution by tribes were made available only for the Ho District, the Eastern Dagomba District, the Northern Mamprussi District, and the town of Kete-Kratchi; particulars about education were lacking entirely. Data about occupation were apparently collected only in the towns of Ho and Kete-Kratchi.

[1] See also *Census Report 1921*, p. 129: 'The Chief Commissioner does not give any estimate of the accuracy of the results of this Census.'
[2] Ibid., pp. 16–17.   [3] Ibid., p. 141.

For the Gold Coast as a whole the Chief Census Officer, 1931, reckoned with 'an error of 5 per cent under-estimation in the 1921 figures'.[1]

The cost of the enumeration was £4,118. 0s. 6d.[2] or £1. 15s. 10d. for each 1,000 enumerated people. The expenditure per head was small compared with that devoted to census purposes in the Union of South Africa or Basutoland, but it was larger than at any other census that has been taken so far in a British West African Dependency.

1931. The procedure followed in 1931 differed somewhat from that at earlier censuses.

(1) The 'method of counting by cowries or stones or similar convenient articles was still in force in 1921 in certain areas but the census recently taken seems to have dispensed with these substitutes and educated persons were employed in their stead'.[3]

(2) 'In previous censuses the return for the religions of the people had been collected from the individuals concerned, but the results were considered so unsatisfactory that it was decided that the figures for the present census should be obtained from the various mission bodies functioning in the country.'[4]

(3) The same form as for Europeans was used for Asiatics.

(4) Some of the forms contained additional questions. Form A, used for Africans in villages and small towns, asked for place of origin and for infirmities (but no longer distinguished between children under and over 6 years). Form B, used for Africans in certain selected large towns, was similar to Special Form B of 1921, but contained additional questions concerning industry, place of origin, and lepers.[5] Form C, now used for all non-Africans, was completely changed and adapted to the pattern of European censuses.

As to the completeness and the accuracy of the 1931 returns, the census report states:

A majority of the census officers were of the opinion that the figures collected by them are lower than they should have been by from 2 per cent to 10 per cent. No particular reasons were given for reaching this conclusion but it is probable that the knowledge that reluctance to count any valuable property is common throughout

---

[1] *The Gold Coast, 1931*, vol. i, p. 147.   [2] See *Census Report 1921*, p. 44.

[3] *The Gold Coast, 1931*, vol. i, p. 125.

[4] Ibid., p. 177. This procedure, which had been recommended by the Chief Census Officer, 1921 (see *Census Report 1921*, p. 46), was, theoretically, a retrogression and proved a failure in practice. As regards the figures for Christians, the census report says (vol. i, p. 178): 'Although the . . . statistics were rendered by the various missions themselves to the Census Officer, the return is not necessarily correct, as a certain confusion seems to have occurred, headquarters being looked upon as the returning authority by some of the smaller out-lying parishes. The result is that the totals fall short to a small extent of their true amount. At the same time the geographical boundaries of the missions are not necessarily the political ones. This is particularly the case with the returns for the trans-Volta area, which includes not only the whole of the British mandated area of Togoland but also that portion of the Eastern Province of the Colony which lies to the east of the Volta River.' Figures for Mohammedans are lacking for many districts and are incomplete in others. The figures of 'Presumed Animists' are useless as they were obtained by deducting from the total population the numbers of Christians and Mohammedans. (Where no figures were available for Mohammedans all non-Christians were counted as Animists.)

[5] But see ibid., p. 136: 'In the event this form proved too elaborate nor was its meaning as indicated in the instructions generally understood.'

the Gold Coast and that the necessity of taking the count over a period of time automatically causes an error in the final computation prompted the expression of this fear. At the same time it must not be forgotten that there was a certain inducement for chiefs especially in the Colony to exaggerate. Not only do population figures form the basis of representation in the Provincial Councils, but they also usually provide the numbers on which the issue of gun permits, etc., are based and at the same time to certain chiefs, especially the northern ones, an exaggeration of the number of one's subjects adds glory and power to the monarch.

It may be safely assumed that the accuracy of the 1931 census in so far as the actual numbers are concerned is greater than that of any previous census. This cannot however be said of the details. The analyses made later in this report will show how inaccurate these latter unfortunately remain.[1]

The actual cost of the enumeration amounted to £3,274. 0s. 5d.[2] or £1. 0s. 8d. per 1,000 enumerated persons. The expenditure varied considerably district by district. In Mampong District it was only 1s. 11d. per 1,000, in Aowin District £3. 18s. 4d.

An explanation of these variations lies not so much in the better organisation of the census taking by individual officers as in the nature of the area covered and in the political conditions obtaining in the different census districts. The very low expenditure in the Mampong District is noteworthy, but is probably explained by the fact that the native organisation is excellent and that the distribution of the villages is most even.[3]

While in 1891 and 1901 only counts were made, partial censuses were taken in 1911, 1921, and 1931. But the proportion of the population covered by those censuses has been small. In 1931 it comprised 14 per cent.

II. TOTAL POPULATION

1. *The Colony*

In his report on the Blue Book for the year 1846, Lieutenant-Governor Winniett stated:

There has not been any census of the native population of this colony ever been attempted to be taken; from certain data, however it may be safely assumed that the aggregate number of the population of those districts which acknowledge and are amenable to the jurisdiction of this Government is not less than 275,000, scattered over a territory of about 6,000 square miles.[4]

The Blue Book for 1849 said:

A Census of the Population of this Settlement was attempted to be taken this year but from the Suspicious and jealous eye with which the Natives view giving any information to Government Officials especially respecting numbers caused this important measure to fail.

The Population is however rapidly increasing and the peaceful and continued prosperity of the Settlement, which in the absence of Statistical information, renders

---

[1] *The Gold Coast, 1931*, vol. i, pp. 123–4. See in particular ibid., p. 169: 'Probably more inaccurate information was returned on the subject of occupations than for any other subject on which data and statistics were required at the census-taking of 1931.' For inaccuracy of age data see ibid., p. 166.

[2] See ibid., p. 144. 'The above expenditure does not include any estimate of departmental assistance or of the voluntary help given by the people, the chiefs, the Chambers of Commerce, the mine managers and the missions' (ibid., p. 145). [3] Ibid., p. 144.

[4] *State of Colonial Possessions 1846*, p. 146. See also ibid. *1847*, p. 203; Gold Coast Colony, *Blue Book 1846*, pp. 80–1, *1847*, pp. 82–3.

it impossible to form an accurate estimate of, may be Stated at fully 5 per Cent above that Assumed to have been the Population in 1846 Viz 275,000 (as Stated in the Blue Book of that Year) . . . .[1]

In his report on this Blue Book Acting Lieutenant-Governor Fitzpatrick wrote:

. . . I find the population is estimated at 288,500.[2] I have no means of corroborating or correcting this estimate, but I apprehend it can scarce be an exaggeration, as, with the exception of a few sea-side towns, the vast district extending from Assinee to Pram Pram and back to Ashantee, is all under the jurisdiction of the British authorities.[3]

But in the following year Lieutenant-Governor Bannerman wrote to Earl Grey:

Upon the subject of population, where no census has been taken, and especially throughout such an extensive country, it would be impossible to state anything with certainty regarding actual numbers. My own opinion is that there has been exaggeration upon this point, as the country is far from being thickly populated; although, taking into account the immense space over which our jurisdiction extends, even without exaggeration the number must be great. . . . Since the last Report to your Lordship, the territory formerly under the Danish flag has been added to our rule. This has nearly doubled the amount of population claiming English protection. . . .[4]

In his report on the Blue Book for 1851 Governor Hill took account of the increased area and population.

. . . taking into consideration the opinions of men who have resided many years in this country, and travelled much, I am led to conclude that the total number may be put down as at least amounting to 400,000 under British protection, occupying about 8,000 square miles of country.[5]

This report, dated 26 April 1852, was the first to put the population of the Gold Coast at 400,000, a figure which, as we shall see presently, became the standard estimate of the Administration for a whole generation. But a week earlier, another event had occurred that brought forward a quite different figure which played as important a role in British official publications as the figure of 400,000 did in the Gold Coast.

At a general meeting of the chiefs and head men of the towns and districts upon the Gold Coast under British protection, held at Cape Coast Castle on the 19th day of April 1852, in the presence of his Excellency Major Hill, Governor and Commander-in-Chief, and the civil and military officers of his Government, it was unanimously resolved and agreed upon,

I. That this meeting, composed of his Excellency the Governor, his Council, and the chiefs and head men of the countries upon the Gold Coast under British protection, constitutes itself into a Legislative Assembly . . . .

V. That . . . the chiefs and head men do, for themselves and their people, voluntarily agree to pay annually to the Government the sum of 1s. sterling per head for every man, woman, and child residing in the districts under British protection.

VI. That the collection of this tax be confined to officers appointed by his Excellency the Governor, assisted by the chiefs, who, in consideration of annual stipends to be paid to them by the Government, agree to give in their several

[1] *Blue Book 1849*, pp. 78-9.   [2] That is 275,000 plus 5 per cent.
[3] *State of Colonial Possessions 1849*, p. 93.
[4] Ibid. *1850*, pp. 197-8. The Danish forts and possessions were ceded on 17 Aug. 1850.
[5] Ibid. *1851*, Part I, p. 185.

districts their cordial assistance and the full weight of their authority in support of this measure, and to aid the tax-gatherers in taking a census of the population, and in collecting the tax.[1]

The Blue Book for 1852 reported:

No Census of the Population of this Colony has ever yet been effected although several fruitless attempts have been made.—The causes of these failures have arisen from the suspicions with which those Persons possessing Domestic Slaves have viewed the taking of their numbers which they imagine to be for the purpose of manumitting them[2]. . . . By a Poll Tax which is now being collected their numbers will be ascertained without arousing the suspicions above alluded to, but as it will not be completed in time for this present Blue Book it can only be left to conjecture as hitherto, although it would appear by the collection as far as it has already that the Population has been over computed and that it will not exceed 300,000, thinly scattered over a Territory of about 8,000 Square Miles.[3]

Governor Hill, in his report on this Blue Book, therefore reduced his former estimate of at least 400,000, though he was sceptical concerning the completeness of the tax census.

When the collection of the tax is completed we shall be enabled to arrive at a more correct estimate of the numbers enjoying the protection of Great Britain; but, so far as I can judge at the present time, I am inclined to believe that the supposed total of inhabitants has been exaggerated, and does not exceed 300,000 persons, although it would not be advisable to take the numbers down on the books of the collectors as altogether correct, nor until I can secure the services of a competent person, well acquainted with the country and people, to superintend those receivers, who, although the best agents I could possibly secure for their respective districts, are yet generally not the energetic men I should have selected had it been possible to procure better.[4]

In 1853, the first year for which the tax was collected, the revenue was stated to have been £7,567. 6s.[5] or 151,346 shillings. The Blue Book reported:

From the amount collected in the form of a Poll Tax from the Natives of the Gold Coast all of whom pay it (with the exception of the Assin Tribes who were exempted in consequence of the Ashantee Forces over-running their Country during its collection), the Population may be rated at 151,346 thinly scattered over a Territory of about 8,000 Square Miles.[6]

However, in his report on this Blue Book, Governor Hill maintained his estimate of 300,000.

It is impossible to arrive at any correct conclusion as to the number of persons enjoying the protection of the British Government; but as 151,347 have paid the poll tax, which I am satisfied has been very imperfectly collected, and many tribes in the Leeward district have not paid it at all, I am inclined to believe that the total population may be fairly estimated at 300,000 persons . . . .[7]

The Blue Books, for several years more, in the section on population referred to the poll tax.

---

[1] 'Poll Tax Ordinance, 19th April 1852', reprinted in *Ordinances, &c. relating to Her Majesty's Forts and Settlements on the Gold Coast* (1860), pp. 34–7, and in *Ordinances of the Settlement of the Gold Coast* (1874), pp. 1–4.
[2] See also *Blue Book 1850*, pp. 76–7, *1851*, pp. 82–3; *State of Colonial Possessions 1851*, Part I, p. 185.				[3] *Blue Book 1852*, pp. 84–5.
[4] *State of Colonial Possessions 1852*, p. 197.				[5] See *Blue Book 1853*, p. 28.
[6] Ibid., pp. 79–80.				[7] *State of Colonial Possessions 1853*, p. 182.

1854. The only Census attempted is that by the Poll Tax Collectors and from that Collection as stated in the Blue Book for 1853, the number of Persons returned for the Tax would appear to be 151,346 omitting the Assin Country said by some to contain upwards of 30,000 (but returned for the Poll Tax of 1855 as only between three and four thousand) . . . . The Poll Tax Collection of 1854 was too partial to be referred to.[1]

1856. There are no means of telling the amount of Population. The Poll Tax could not be relied on even if every part of the Protected Territory paid it.[2] This Tax was paid more generally in 1852–1853 than in any other year and the number of persons returned that year for the Tax would appear to be 151,346 omitting the Assin Country which however would not add more than 5,000.[3]

1860. During the year 1860 only £1,601 Poll Tax was paid[4] on a population of 32,020 which the best informed believe to be but a fifteenth of the whole population of the British Protectorate.[5]

In his report on the Blue Book for 1860 Governor Andrews made a similar estimate.

There can be no doubt that the population for the extent of territory is sparse— for hours together you may travel in the interior and not meet with a human being. The population I am persuaded has been much exaggerated when I have seen it noted down as high as 900,000; probably the proximate number would be 450,000

[1] *Blue Book 1854*, p. 110; literally the same ibid. *1855*, p. 117. The amount of tax collected in 1854 was £3,624. 15s. 9½d. (see ibid. *1854*, p. 24). '. . . the collection of the Poll Tax which had always been difficult was much resented by the people. It was the cause of a rising at Christiansborg and in the east in 1854 which resulted in the bombardment and partial ruin of Teshie, Labadi, and Christiansborg' (*Census Report 1921*, p. 10). See also *State of Colonial Possessions 1854*, p. 198.

[2] 'A considerable proportion of the payments was in cowries' and the accounts were rather confused; see ibid., pp. 197–9.

[3] *Blue Book 1856*, p. 120; literally the same ibid. *1857*, p. 122, *1858*, p. 118, *1859*, p. 108. 'At a meeting held at Cape Coast 25th February 1856 attended by the Chiefs and people of the Windward Districts presided over by Major Ord R.E. the Commissioner of Enquiry some exemptions were made in respect of children of a certain age and of some widows and infirm persons' (ibid. *1857*, p. 4). These exemptions were embodied in an 'Ordinance to explain and amend an Ordinance commonly called the Poll Tax Ordinance' of 10 May 1858 (reprinted in *Ordinances, &c. relating to Her Majesty's Forts and Settlements on the Gold Coast*, pp. 63–6, and in *Ordinances of the Settlement of the Gold Coast*, pp. 40–3), which stipulated among other things:
'V. The following persons shall be exempt from payment of the said tax:—
1. Infants under two years of age.
2. Poor women having no husband or head of family to pay the tax for them.
3. Aged persons unable to work, and having no relative or head of family to pay for them.'
On the same day (10 May 1858) there was enacted an 'Ordinance to provide for the Establishment of Municipalities in the Coast Towns of Her Majesty's Settlements on the Gold Coast' (reprinted in *Ordinances, &c. relating to Her Majesty's Forts and Settlements on the Gold Coast*, pp. 68–72), which stipulated among other things:
'XXVIII. The inhabitants of every town to which this ordinance shall be applied, and which shall pay out of the town rate to the Government its fair proportion towards the maintenance of magisterial, medical, and educational establishments within the district, shall be exempt from the payment of the poll tax.'
This Ordinance was repealed by Ordinance No. 1 of 1861 (7 Jan., reprinted in *Ordinances of the Settlement of the Gold Coast*, pp. 90–1). One reason for the repeal of the Ordinance which had been applied to 'the towns of Cape Coast and James Town, Accra' was that 'Her Majesty's revenue has been seriously diminished by the nonpayment of the proportion of the rates provided by such Ordinance to be paid in lieu of poll tax'. This would suggest that while the Ordinance was in force no poll tax was paid in those towns.

[4] Including £133 from Assin; see *Blue Book 1860*, p. 26.

[5] Ibid., p. 136. '. . . the receipts fell off to 1,552 *l.* in 1861, since when, partly from the antipathy which is entertained to it, and partly from the disturbances which have occurred, and the consequent distress to which they have given rise, no attempt has been made to levy the tax' (*Report of Colonel Ord*, 1865, p. 21). The Poll Tax was formally repealed by the 'Statute Law Revision Ordinance, 1886' (No. 1 of 1886, 11 Feb., *Gold Coast Ordinances 1879–1892*).

distributed by 200,000 living on the Seabord, and within a day's journey from the coast; the remainder scattered in various interior parts of the Protectorate.[1]

Some Blue Books of the 1850s, therefore, had accepted the figure of 151,346 taxpayers in 1853 as representing the total population, but no report on the Blue Books and apparently no other official document from the Gold Coast made the same mistake. In the meantime, however, this population figure had crept into British official publications and stood there for two decades.[2]

The Blue Book for 1861 merely said that 'there are no means of telling the Population',[3] and no Blue Book was prepared for any of the years 1862–6. But the difficulties of estimating the population at that time were anyway enormous. The *Colonial Office List*, in its first issue of 1862, said:

The British territory, strictly speaking, is limited to the forts and to the distance of a cannon-shot around them;[4] beyond these the British Government has no dominion; but British influence extends over an area variously estimated at from 6,000 to 8,000 square miles, inhabited by a population estimated at from 250,000 to 400,000 people. Justice is administered to this large population by their own consent, and under the sanction of an Act of Parliament, by British magistrates.[5]

The territory under British protectorate was reduced by a Convention with the Dutch Government which came into effect on 1 January 1868. The *Colonial Office List* reported:

A diminution in the population under British protection and its area followed. Probably 200,000 souls were within the protected territory, and an average area of 4,500 square miles.[6]

---

[1] *State of Colonial Possessions 1860*, Part II, p. 35.

[2] Thus the *Statistical Tables relating to the Colonial Possessions of the United Kingdom* gave, year-in, year-out, from the first issue (1854) to the thirteenth issue (1867) 151,346 as the total population of the Gold Coast exclusive of Assin Country; the *Statistical Abstract for the Colonial Possessions of the United Kingdom* from the First Number (published in 1865) to the Eleventh Number (published in 1875) gave as population of the Gold Coast in 1858 151,346; the *Colonial Office List for 1866* as well as all the *Lists* from 1867 to 1875 showed in the Table 'Colonial Possessions' (though not in the Text) 151,346 as the population of the Gold Coast. See also the following passage in a Memorandum by Assistant Colonial Secretary Evans (Gold Coast, *Census 1883*, Enclosure No. 2, pp. 3–5):

'In volume III of the "General Report on the Census of England and Wales", for the year 1861, (page 194) I find that the population of the Gold Coast was given in a return for the year 1858 at 151,346 (including 70 whites) excluding Assin, "which is not supposed to contain more than 5,000 persons".

'It is also stated in this volume (page 194) "that the same return (151,346) is given in "Parliamentary paper No. 147 Session 1863".

'I am unable to find the Return or Parliamentary paper referred to or any record showing how or by whom this return was compiled.'

A glance at the annual Blue Books for any of the years 1853–60 would have shown the Assistant Colonial Secretary how and by whom this return was compiled.

[3] *Blue Book 1861*, p. 110.

[4] See also *Colonial Office List 1865*, p. 40: 'The British territory is limited by an Order in Council, passed in 1864, to Fort William, Fort Victoria, the whole of Cape Coast Castle, and the land adjacent thereto being within 500 yards of the principal gate or entrance to the Castle.' See furthermore *Report of Colonel Ord* (1865), p. 16: 'The territory on the Gold Coast which is recognised as British consists of a large number of forts and posts, many of them abandoned or in ruins, which have come into our possession either by settlement, capture, or purchase, during the last 200 years, together with the line of the sea-coast adjacent to them.'

[5] *Colonial Office List 1862*, p. 61.

[6] Ibid. *1873*, p. 136. Payne, *Lagos Almanack and Diary for 1878* says (p. 133) that 'the amount of population was estimated in 1868 at about 252,000'.

But in 1872 the British Protectorate was extended even beyond the limits recognized before 1868.

The interchange of territory in 1868 was not effected without some bloodshed; and, owing to this, it did not work well. The Dutch Government at length agreed to transfer to the British Crown the whole of their possessions on the coast of Guinea. By the Royal Convention signed at the Hague in February, 1872, Her Majesty's Gold Coast Colony has been doubled in extent and population.[1]

These and other changes in boundaries affected, however, very little the current opinion on the size of the population, and the estimate which was repeated most frequently in the official publications of the Gold Coast was the one of 400,000 made in 1852.[2] Its origin, and the fact that it was made before the Poll Tax became effective was apparently forgotten when Administrator Moloney wrote on 3 October 1882:

The number of the population of the Gold Coast is wholly unascertained. Since the time of the imposition of the poll tax in 1852, an estimate of 400,000 as a population has been handed down as a legacy.

He added:

In 1881 when the census of Her Majesty's Empire was being taken generally, it was hoped that something more approximate in the shape of an estimate of the supposed population would have been secured. No action in the matter was taken. The assistance and co-operation of commissioners, heads of the different religious bodies, and of other influential persons have now been invited, and it is to be hoped that their labours will bring forth something.[3]

The first effort to collect population statistics on the Gold Coast was then made, quite reluctantly, on the insistence of the Secretary of State. In a 'Memorandum on the Census of the Gold Coast Settlement and Protectorate, 1883' Assistant Colonial Secretary Evans reports (19 December 1883):

. . . in 1880 a Circular despatch dated 27th April 1880 was received from the Secretary of State directing that a Census of the Gold Coast should be taken in April 1881.

To this despatch Governor Ussher replied (in a despatch No. 194 dated 16th August 1880) 'that the endeavours to take a Census of the Gold Coast would result in certain failure'[4]—He added that he believed the population 'to be not less than 400,000'—

In despatch General dated 11th October 1880, the Right Honorable the Secretary

---

[1] *Colonial Office List 1873*, p. 136. See also Payne (1878), p. 133: 'This increases the Gold Coast Colony from about 6,000 square miles to 14,000 square miles.'

[2] See, for example, 'Medical Report for the year 1858', *State of Colonial Possessions 1858*, Part II, p. 26, ibid. *1867*, Part II, p. 20, *1868*, Part II, p. 23, *1869*, Part II, p. 17; *Blue Book 1867*, p. 96, *1868*, p. 96, *1869*, p. 96, *1870*, p. 106, *1871*, p. 112, *1872*, p. 124, *1880*, pp. 212–13, *1881*, p. 198, *1882*, p. 198. The population was estimated to be 'between 400,000 and 500,000' in *Colonial Possessions Reports 1876–8*, p. 149, and 'about 500,000' ibid. *1879*, p. 208.

[3] Ibid. *1880–2*, p. 113.

[4] The opinion that it was impossible to take a census of the Gold Coast was also expressed five years later by the Colonial Secretary in his report upon the Blue Book for 1884: '. . . no means exist whereby a census could be taken of the Gold Coast Settlement, the natives of which are suspicious of their numbers being counted, having, perhaps, a lively recollection of the old days when the poll tax was in force, besides which there are many other practical difficulties in the way of taking a census of the Gold Coast, even supposing that the native was not adverse to it' (ibid. *1884–6*, p. 8).

of State acknowledged receipt of Governor Ussher's reply and asked for 'as close an estimate as possible of the supposed population on the Gold Coast'.

On 30th January 1882 a Circular was issued by Governor Sir Samuel Rowe's direction to all District Commissioners with a view of obtaining some basis for arriving at an estimate of the population of the Colony—

On 28th August 1882, in a Circular letter addressed to all District Commissioners and to the heads of the Missionary Societies on the Gold Coast, Captain Moloney asked for information as to the population. There were many promises of assistance in reply to this Circular but practically no results.

On 20th September 1882 Captain Moloney issued another Circular letter in which he asked for the supply of information on a variety of points and amongst others for the number of inhabitants.[1]

As shown above, Administrator Moloney, in his report dated two weeks after the issue of the third Circular Letter, was not very optimistic regarding the results of his efforts. But the Secretary of State did not relax.

In a despatch General dated 6th April 1883 received at Lagos on the 10th May 1883, the Right Honorable the Secretary of State referred to the previous despatches on the subject of the 1881 Census and stated that the Registrar General had requested to be furnished with the census Returns of the Gold Coast.

Sir Samuel Rowe replied to the above in a despatch No. 166 dated 15th May 1883 —and on the 21st May 1883 a further Circular was issued at his request by the Lieutenant Governor to all the District Commissioners, and this Circular produced the Returns from which the numbers (135,761) shewn in the statement furnished to your Excellency by Mr. Simpson were derived.[2]

The statement furnished by Acting Colonial Secretary Simpson was dated 10 December 1883.[3] It consisted of a Table called 'Estimates of the Population of the Undermentioned placès furnished by the Commiss^{rs} of Districts with a view to taking a Census of the Settlement on the Gold Coast and its Dependencies 1883'. For several Districts no returns whatever had been received, the available returns were not all-inclusive, and no claim was made that the 'Total (from Returns Received)' of 135,761 had any statistical value. Thus, the Circular of 21 May 1883 was hardly more effective than its predecessors, and when the Secretary of State in a Dispatch dated 12 October 1883 once more asked for census figures, Governor Rowe sent the following 'Memorandum on the Census of the Gold Coast Settlement and Protectorate, 1883',[4] dated 21 December, which apparently was not affected by the recent returns from the District Commissioners:

In a despatch dated 23 April 1873 Sir Robert (then Colonel) Harley, then Administrator in Chief of the Government of the West Africa Settlements forwarded to the Secretary of State a return which I furnished of the number of fighting men who had assembled belonging to the Fanti tribes at Dunquah on 14th April 1873.

This estimate had a fair claim to accuracy. A good deal of it was the result of the actual counting by myself of the people there present.

[1] Gold Coast, *Census 1883*, Enclosure No. 2, pp. 7–10.

[2] Ibid., pp. 10–12.

[3] Two months earlier, on 12 Oct. 1883, Acting Colonial Secretary Evans said in his report on the Blue Book for 1882:

'Population. No reliable information exists on this head. It has been estimated that the population of the Colony and Protectorate is about 400,000. Endeavours are being made to obtain more accurate statistics' (*Colonial Possessions Reports 1881–3*, p. 145).

[4] Gold Coast, *Census 1883*, Enclosure No. 1.

This number did not include any of the people of Aowin or Appolonia who were too far off to join in this assembly or any of the people of Wassaw or any of the people of Axim or of Secondee who with the rest of the Ahanta tribes and the Elminas embraced the cause of the Ashantis and held aloof.

In a despatch dated 14th December 1873 Sir John (then Captain) Glover stated to Lord Wolseley that he estimated that the force with which he should cross the Prah river would be at the lowest estimate 16,000 effectives.

The numbers given by Sir John Glover had reference to the fighting men of the Accras and to those tribes inland of Accra which had not taken part in the engagement at Dunquah. They did not include any of the people on the eastward side of the Volta as the tribes with Sir John Glover were at that time fighting with the Awoonahs.

The totals of the numbers above given as 56,000 fighting men from the Western part of the Settlement and 16,000 from the Eastern part give a total of 72,000. To multiply these numbers by six, as allowing for every fighting man the existence of one woman and 4 old people and young children, does not appear to me unreasonable, this would give a population of $72,000 \times 6 = 432,000$.

The Ahanta tribes who did not join the Fantu camp at Dunquah number in all fully 50,000 people.

The population of Elmina town was calculated, from taxation returns by the Dutch, to be 12,000 at the time of their occupation.

It is said that many of the people have left Elmina. If the Dutch calculation was correct, and we admit the possibility of one half having left, that would still leave 6,000.

The population of the Sea Coast towns of Appolonia as computed by Mr. Evans (from the returns furnished by Mr. Schnerr in 1869) numbers over 33,000.

If this be so an allowance of 15,000 for the inland villages of the District is not excessive, they are numerous and populous—that would give 48,000 as the total population of Appolonia.

Of the population of the country of Aowin on the Western limits of the colony but little is known to us, but I estimate it to be fully 20,000 people.

In 1873 the fighting men of Wassaw were estimated to number 10,000; if we allow 50,000 as the entire population of the country I do not think the Estimate is in excess of the numbers.

The numbers of the population of the Beach villages between the Volta and the Eastern Limits of the protectorate, consisting of Awoonahs, Somes, and Afflohoos, are not less than 10 or 15,000.

The Supreme Court of the Gold Coast Colony has jurisdiction over all the districts of Awoonah, those which are inland of the Quittah Lagoon and Creek, as well as over those on the sea side of it, though it is not thought desirable at present that the Commissioner of the Quittah district should interfere in the internal administration of that part of the Awoonah country.

The population of this district I should suppose to be not less than 30,000.

The estimate of the entire population of these districts as shown in the accompanying table amounts to over 651,000. I much regret my inability to offer more complete information, but the Estimate thus given is the result of careful calculation and enquiry.

It is not put forward as being absolutely accurate—it is only offered as the best result I have been able to attain, and as subject to daily correction from farther work and extended observation.

He said in his accompanying dispatch, likewise dated 21 December 1883:

I incline to the idea that the estimate which I have given in the attached memorandum and which puts the total number of the population of the Gold Coast Settlement at 651,000 will not be found to be exaggerated.

It will be noticed that the total of 651,000 was arrived at as follows:

Central Districts, 72,000 fighting men × 6	432,000
Wassaw, 10,000 fighting men × 5	50,000
Other tribes and districts:	
50,000 + 6,000 + 48,000 + 20,000 + 15,000 + 30,000 . . .	169,000
	651,000

The total of 651,000 was given also in the annual Blue Books for 1883–5, 339,188 being allocated to the Western and 311,812 to the Central Province.[1] The area was estimated in the Blue Book for 1883 at 18,784 square miles and in the Blue Books for 1884–6 at 20,000 square miles.[2]

A completely new estimate was given in the Blue Book for 1887. It showed a population of 1,406,450—402,400 for the Western and 1,004,050 for the Central Province. The Blue Book contained the following comment:

The area of the Gold Coast and the Protected Territories is estimated at 29,401 Square Miles.[3]

No regular Census has ever been taken on the Gold Coast, and there are almost insuperable difficulties in the way of doing so. The year's Returns have been compiled from information supplied by the several District Commissioners of the Colony, and the various Missionary bodies as well as by reference to official records.[4]

The Blue Books for 1888 and 1889 gave identically the same figures and text.[5] The Blue Book for 1890 said merely that 'the population is estimated at 1,600,000'.[6]

This was the situation with which the Census Committee was confronted when the count, made in 1891, showed a population of 765,000—excluding Kwahu and Krepi with a population estimated in 1887 at 480,000. The Secretary of the Committee, as shown above, put the population of Kwahu and Krepi at 500,000, estimated the omissions in the remainder of the country at 205,000 and thus arrived at a total of 1,470,000.

The second count, made in 1901, showed a population of 895,000, and

---

[1] See *Blue Book 1883* R, p. 1, *1884* R, p. 1, *1885* R, p. 1; see also *Colonial Possessions Reports 1884–6*, pp. 124–5. In *Blue Book 1886* R, p. 1, the population is given, apparently owing to an arithmetical error, as 661,000. The Blue Books contain also figures by Districts.

However, while the Blue Book for 1884 showed the population to be 651,000, the Colonial Secretary in his report upon this Blue Book said: 'The population of the Colony is, of course, considerable, and I think may be guessed to be not less than 475,000' (*Colonial Possessions Reports 1884–6*, p. 8).

[2] In the *Blue Books 1846–9* the area was given as 6,000 square miles. After the cession of the Danish possessions (1850) this estimate was raised to 8,000 square miles. But *Statistical Tables Colonial Possessions 1860*, p. 420, gave again 6,000 square miles, and this estimate was repeated every year until and including *Tables 1876–8* (p. 317); it appeared likewise in *Statistical Abstract for the Colonial Possessions* from the First to the Twentieth Number (published in 1884), and in *Colonial Office List 1866 to 1875* (in the Tables 'Colonial Possessions')—irrespective of all changes in boundaries. *Colonial Office List 1876* (p. 18) to *1885* (p. 18) gave 15,000 square miles.

[3] During the last decade of the nineteenth and the first decade of this century the area was frequently given as 39,060 square miles; see, for example, *Statistical Tables Colonial Possessions 1888–90* (p. 366) to *1900* (p. 403), *Statistical Abstract for the Colonial Possessions 1877–91* (p. 5) to *1887–1901* (p. 6). See also in this connexion *Colonial Reports, Gold Coast 1892*, p. 28: 'The area of the Colony has been variously estimated from 29,401 square miles . . . to 39,060 square miles . . . . It is probable that a mean between the two—say 35,000 square miles—will more nearly approximate to accuracy.' But even 29,401 square miles were apparently an overestimate.

[4] *Blue Book 1887* R, p. 1.

[5] See ibid. *1888* R, p. 1; *1889* R, p. 1.

[6] Ibid. *1890* R, pp. 1–2.

the Census Committee estimated it at 1,043,000. A comparison of the
returns and estimates of 1891 and 1901 yields the following results:[1]

Districts	Returns		Estimates	
	1891	1901	1891	1901
Accra	91,612	103,651	121,612	} 153,141
Kwahu	..	39,490	} 500,000	
Krepi	..	} 163,997		} 173,997
Volta River	128,608		148,608	
Ada	46,869	46,487	56,869	56,487
Axim	39,870	18,130	54,870	33,130
Cape Coast	87,873	100,282	127,873	130,282
Kwitta	36,230	174,224	46,230	174,224
Prampram	10,908	13,404	15,908	18,404
Saltpond	138,828	57,820	148,828	87,820
Sekundi	29,863	34,325	34,863	42,325
Wassaw	73,683	80,603	123,683	100,603
Winneba	80,164	62,937	90,164	72,937
Total	764,508[1]	895,350	1,469,508[1]	1,043,350

[1] Excluding 4,374 in Atabubu.

The 'returns' were certainly too low in 1891 for Kwitta and seem to have
been too high for Axim and Saltpond. Whether the total came near the
truth it is impossible to tell. But it probably came nearer the truth than
the excessive estimate of the Census Committee. At the 1901 count the
population of Kwitta was probably overstated, but it was probably understated, for example, in Saltpond. The total population was very likely
greater than the returns indicate, and the Census Committee's estimate
was probably not too high.

The total returned at the enumeration of 1911 was only 853,766. The
population this time was very much understated in Kwitta,[2] but the
figures seem to have been far too low also in some other Districts. A
comparison, District by District, of the results of 1911 and 1901 is not
feasible owing to changes in boundaries, but it is possible to compare the
results by Provinces for each enumeration from 1891 to 1931 and by
Districts for 1911 to 1931 (see Tables 1 and 2).

If the estimate of the Commissioner of the Western Province for 1911
is correct that 'the Returns fall short of the actual population of this
Province by twenty per cent', and if the same assumption is made for
the Eastern Province, the total population would have been about
1,000,000. But it is safe to say that the population was larger than that.
It probably exceeded 1,150,000.

The total population enumerated in 1921 was 1,174,971. It was reported
to have been understated again in the Western Province. It seems unlikely
that the population was less than 1,300,000.

[1] See *Census Report 1891*, pp. 9, 41; *1901*, pp. 5, 19, 22.
[2] The native population of Kwitta had been given in 1887, 1891, 1901, and 1911 as 106,900,
36,230, 174,224, and 36,945 respectively. (*Census Report 1901*, p. 6, says concerning population
density: 'Of individual districts, Kwitta is easily first, with a population of 181 to the square
mile.' It was indeed easy for Kwitta to be first with a population put at 174,000.) The native
population of Kwitta and Addah was given in 1911 as 77,394, and in 1921 as 177,625.

TABLE 1. *Resident African Population of Gold Coast Colony by Provinces, 1891–1931*[1]

Provinces	1891	1901	1911	1921	1931
Western . .	143,406	133,038	163,540	205,080	284,902
Central . .	306,755	221,039	247,306	302,626	431,384
Eastern . .	314,024[2]	541,253	441,820	664,207	855,076
Total . .	764,185[2]	895,330	852,666	1,171,913	1,571,362

[1] See *The Gold Coast, 1931*, vol. ii, p. 1. Some figures differ slightly from those given in earlier census reports (see footnotes to Table 3). [2] Excluding Kwahu and Krepi.

TABLE 2. *Resident African Population of Gold Coast Colony by Districts, 1911–31*[1]

District	1911	1921	1931	District	1911	1921	1931
WESTERN PROVINCE				CENTRAL PROVINCE			
Sekondi .	44,757	54,164	73,821	Cape Coast .	86,891	93,427	136,044
Tarkwa .	36,367	44,525	60,983	Saltpond .		71,468	103,265
Ankobra .	38,071	33,053	46,173	Western Akim	93,034	32,164	63,381
Sefwi .		26,008	42,060	Winneba . .	67,111	105,567	128,694
Aowin .	15,620	6,571	9,941				
Axim .	28,725	40,759	51,924	Total . .	247,036	302,626	431,384
Total .	163,540	205,080	284,902				

District	1911	1921	1931
EASTERN PROVINCE			
Accra . .	73,047	99,603	136,696
Akwapim . .	88,047	79,917	86,380
Akim-Abuakwa .	46,768	90,306	140,677
Kwahu . .	41,783	41,693	59,026
Volta River			162,100
New Juaben	114,781	175,063	26,526
Kete-Ada . .	77,394	177,625	243,671
Total . .	441,820	664,207	855,076

[1] See *The Gold Coast, 1931*, vol. ii, pp. 31, 58, 78.

The total population enumerated in 1931 was 1,573,770. There is no evidence that it was understated.

Table 3 shows the population at the enumerations from 1891 to 1931, as given in the more recent census reports.[1]

From the census date 1931 on, the Principal Registrar has computed the population by assuming that the 'resident' African population increased each year by one-tenth of the difference between the 1931 and 1921 returns, i.e. by 39,938, and that the numbers of the 'resident' non-African population and the maritime population had not changed since 1931. The result for mid-year 1940 was 1,943,265.[2]

[1] Some of these figures should be revised; see footnotes to Table 3.
[2] From 1941 onwards the mid-year population of the Gold Coast and Togoland has been estimated to be equal to that computed for mid-year 1940. See *Blue Book 1941*, p. 107; *1942*, p. 107; *1943*, p. 105; *1944*, p. 111.

TABLE 3. *Population of the Gold Coast Colony, 1891–1931*[1]

	1891	1901	1911	1921	1931
'Resident' Africans. . . .	764,185[3]	895,330[5]	852,666[7]	1,171,913	1,571,294[10]
Maritime[2] Africans . . .	—	—	—	1,157	68
'Resident' non-Africans . . .	428[4]	716[6]	1,389[8]	1,530[9]	2,304
Maritime[2] non-Africans . . .	—	—	—	371	104
Total	764,613	896,046	854,055	1,174,971	1,573,770

[1] See *Census Report 1921*, Appendices, pp. 5, 11, 19; *The Gold Coast, 1931*, vol. i, p. 256, vol. ii, pp. 1–2; *Report of the Principal Registrar 1933*, p. 13.

[2] Persons enumerated on ship-board. Such persons were apparently not enumerated before 1921.

[3] The population shown in *Census Report 1891* was 768,882, including 4,374 in Atabubu. But from *Census Report 1901* on, the population for 1891 is given as 768,559 including Atabubu or 764,185 excluding Atabubu.

[4] There was only a partial count of whites in 1891, and *Census Report 1921*, Appendices, p. 19, still said regarding non-Africans: 'No figures available for 1891.' See also p. 439 below.

[5] The population shown in *Census Report 1901* was 895,350. But from *Census Report 1911* on, the population for 1901 is given as 895,330.

[6] *Census Report 1901*, p. 7, gives 646 as the number of Europeans on the Gold Coast, excluding 'officials and others who were travelling in the Colony at the time of the Census' and excluding those in Ashanti and the Northern Territories. 'An addition of 53 to 70 might fairly be made to represent this deficiency.' *Census Report 1921*, Appendices, p. 19, gives as Resident non-Africans in the Colony 716 'made up as follows:—646 for the Colony with an addition of 70 to represent those in Ashanti and the Northern Territories and others not enumerated'.

[7] *Census Report 1911* gives (p. 49) as 'Population' 853,766, and (p. 55) as 'Native Population' 852,396. The figure of 852,666 given from *Census Report 1921* on, as representing the 'Resident African Population' is 270 higher than the figure given in *Census Report 1911* for the Native Population because the Central Province is, I think erroneously, entered with 247,306 instead of 247,036.

[8] This figure represents the number of whites (including Syrians).

[9] This figure is given erroneously in *The Gold Coast, 1931*, vol. i, p. 254, and vol. ii, p. 2, as representing the total non-African population.

[10] *The Gold Coast, 1931*, vol. ii, p. 1, gives as Resident African Population 1,571,362, but this figure, erroneously, includes the Maritime Population.

2. Ashanti

No official estimate of the population seems to have been made before the annexation of Ashanti to the Crown in 1901. In that year the native population was estimated at 335,651.[1] This does not include Kintampo with about 10,000 inhabitants which then formed part of the Northern Territories. The Census Committee pointed out that the population figure implied a density of only 11 per square mile, 'which is obviously much below the true ratio'.[2] But it probably overestimated the area.[3] However, the Administration remained convinced that the population had been understated in 1901.

Until a reliable census of Ashanti has been taken the native population can only be roughly guessed at. It has generally been reckoned at 500,000, and this figure must be supplemented by several thousand immigrants from the north, such as Moshis, Dagombas, Dagatis, Grunshis, Hausas, &c. Ashanti, moreover, numbers a large floating population of these people, who come for purposes of trade.[4]

[1] See *Census Report 1901*, p. 56.   [2] Ibid., p. 6.

[3] The area at that time was usually put at 32,200 square miles (see, for example, *Statistical Tables Colonial Possessions 1900*, p. 403).   [4] *Colonial Reports, Ashanti 1909*, p. 14.

But the count of 1911 showed a total population of only 287,814, including Kintampo. The Chief Commissioner said that the population was underestimated, and he was certainly right. The figures for 1921 and 1931 were 406,640 and 578,702 respectively, the total for 1921 being no doubt too low. 'Owing to the changes in titles and areas since 1911 comparisons with the figures obtained at the Census taken in that year are not possible.'[1] But for 1921 and 1931 the figures for Provinces and Districts are fairly comparable (see Table 4). Table 5 shows the population at the enumerations from 1901 to 1931, as given in the more recent census reports.

From the census date 1931 on, the Principal Registrar computed the population by assuming that the African population increased each year by one-tenth of the difference between the 1931 and 1921 returns, i.e. by 17,189, and that the figure for the non-African population did not change. The result for mid-year 1940 was 737,696.

3. Northern Territories

No official estimate of the population seems to have been made before 1901, when these districts were constituted a distinct Administration under a Chief Commissioner. For 1901 the number of adults, on the basis of a count made in part of the Northern Territories, was estimated at 211,964, and 50 per cent. or 106,000 were added for children. The Colonial Report for 1901 said:

The total figure of 317,964 given by Lieutenant-Colonel Morris would indicate a population of rather over 8·3 per square mile, the area of the Territories being about 38,000 square miles.[2] This is a sparse population. I am doubtful, however, whether, adults only having been counted, an addition of 50 per cent. is sufficient for children.[3]

The Colonial Report for 1909 gave still another reason why the total arrived at was too low.

The native population of the Northern Territories was roughly estimated at 318,000 in 1900, but little reliance can be placed on these figures, as a considerable portion of the most densely-populated parts of the Protectorate was underestimated.[4]

But the Report for 1910 was more cautious.

It is of little use speculating as to what our population is at present. As accurate a census as is practicable will be taken in April, 1911. It is probable that we shall find our previous estimates excessive. There is no district that can be described as 'densely populated' in the usually accepted sense, but there is a vast variation in the population of the various districts.[5]

Actually, the count of 1911 showed a population of 361,819, excluding Kintampo (which on 1 January 1907 had been transferred to Ashanti), as

---

[1] *The Gold Coast, 1931*, vol. i, p. 149.

[2] This was apparently an overestimate. Yet *Statistical Tables Colonial Possessions 1900*, p. 403, gave an area of 48,000 square miles.

[3] *Colonial Reports, Northern Territories 1901*, p. 5. *Colonial Reports, Gold Coast 1906*, p. 34, said that the inhabitants of the Northern Territories 'probably number at least 1,000,000'! (See also ibid. *1909*, p. 30: 'Roughly estimated there are probably nearly 3,000,000 inhabitants of the Gold Coast, including Ashanti and the Northern Territories.')

Colonial Reports, Northern Territories 1909, p. 12.   [5] Ibid. *1910*, p. 11.

against 317,964 in 1901, including Kintampo, and the 1911 count itself was quite incomplete. If the estimate that only two-thirds of the people in the North-Eastern Province had been enumerated was correct, an addition of about 80,000 should be made on this account alone.[1] The enumeration of 1921 showed a population of 530,391 and that of 1931 a population of 717,382, the figure for 1921 being no doubt too low. The native population figures by Districts for 1911, 1921, and 1931 are shown in Table 6. The population at the enumerations of 1901 to 1931, as given in the more recent census reports, is shown in Table 7.

From the census date 1931 on, the Principal Registrar computed the population in the same manner as for Ashanti, reckoning with a yearly increase of 18,692 Africans. The result for mid-year 1940 was 890,283.

4. *Gold Coast*

The count of 1901 showed a native population of 1,338,433. But it was probably somewhat understated in the Colony, and the returns for the Northern Territories included apparently not more than one-third of the population. If the Chief Commissioner's estimate for the Northern Territories based on the partial count is substituted for the original returns, the figure for the native population would be raised to 1,548,965. It is safe to say that it exceeded 1,750,000.

The returns for 1911 showed a native population of 1,501,793. The figures were apparently incomplete in every section of the country. Assuming that the omissions amounted to one-fifth in the Western and Eastern Provinces of the Colony and in Ashanti, and to one-third in the North-Eastern Province of the Northern Territories, the native population would have been about 1,800,000. It was no doubt much larger than that.

The returns for 1921 showed a total population of 2,112,002. The omissions were much smaller than in 1911 but it seems unlikely that they amounted to less than 200,000.

The returns for 1931 showed a total population of 2,869,854. There is no evidence that it was understated.

From the census date 1931 on, the Principal Registrar computed the population by assuming that the 'resident' African population increased each year by one-tenth of the difference between the 1931 and 1921 returns, i.c. by 75,810, and that the 'resident' non-African population and the maritime population did not change. The result for mid-year 1940 was 3,571,244. But quite apart from the fact that the difference between the returns of 1931 and 1921 was swelled by an understatement of the population in 1921, it is uncertain whether the actual increase in the 1930s was similar to that in the 1920s. The official figures for recent years may, therefore, be wide of the mark.

5. *Togoland*

According to the 1921 count the population was 187,959, but the returns were very incomplete. The 1931 enumeration showed a population

---

[1] The native population enumerated in this Province was 163,472. See *Census Report 1911*, p. 58.

TABLE 4. *African Population of Ashanti by Districts, 1921 and 1931*[1]

	Western Province					Eastern Province						Total
Year	Ahafo	Kintampo	Sunyani	Wenchi	Total	Ashanti-Akim	Kumasi	Mampong	Obuasi	Bekwai	Total	
1921	9,256	28,782	36,672	39,039	113,749	29,757	149,114	47,491	66,082		292,444	406,193
1931	15,776	43,410	66,976	58,106	184,268	55,235	172,196	50,295	39,718	76,366	393,810	578,078

[1] See *The Gold Coast, 1931*, vol. i, p. 150.

TABLE 6. *African Population of Northern Territories by Districts, 1921 and 1931*[1]

	Northern Province							Southern Province				Total
Year	Kusasi	Navrongo	Zuarungu	Lawra-Tumu	Mamprusi	Wa	Total	Western Dagomba	Eastern Gonja	Western Gonja	Total	
1911		149,618		51,559	13,854	64,884	279,915	63,976	10,328	7,587	81,891	361,806
1921		257,949		84,264	21,944	43,168	407,325	93,944	18,152	10,934	123,030	530,355
1931	110,614	120,870	133,981	93,125	46,523	72,323	577,436	100,433	23,683	15,723	139,839	717,275

[1] See *The Gold Coast, 1931*, vol. ii, pp. 186, 204.

TABLE 8. *Population of the Gold Coast, 1901–31*[1]

	Colony		Ashanti		Northern Territories		Gold Coast		
Year	Africans	Non-Africans	Africans	Non-Africans	Africans	Non-Africans	Africans	Non-Africans	Total
1901	895,350	646	345,891	..	307,724	..	1,548,965	716	1,549,681
1911	852,396	1,389	287,591	223	361,806	13	1,501,793	1,625	1,503,418
1921	1,171,913[2]	1,530[3]	406,193	447	530,355	36	2,108,461[2]	2,013[3]	2,110,474
1931	1,571,294[4]	2,304[5]	578,078	624	717,275	107	2,866,647[4]	3,035[5]	2,869,682

[1] I have revised here some figures given in Tables 3, 5, and 7. See footnotes to these Tables.
[2] Excluding 1,157 on board ships. [3] Excluding 371 on board ships.
[4] Excluding 68 on board ships. [5] Excluding 104 on board ships.

TABLE 5. *Population of Ashanti, 1901–31*[1]

	1901	1911	1921	1931
Africans . . .	345,891[2]	287,814[4]	406,193	578,078
Non-Africans . .	—[3]	223	447	624
Total . . .	345,891	288,037	406,640	578,702

[1] See *The Gold Coast, 1931*, vol. ii, pp. 1–2.

[2] 'Includes a rough estimate of 10,240 for Kintampo which in 1901 was included in the administrative area of the Northern Territories.'

[3] No count was made of the small number of non-Africans; see footnote 6 to Table 3.

[4] The figure of 287,814 is given, from *Census Report 1921* on, as representing the African Population. But this, I think, is a mistake. According to *Census Report 1911*, pp. 57, 75, the native population was 287,591 and the white population 223.

TABLE 7. *Population of Northern Territories, 1901–31*[1]

	1901	1911	1921	1931
Africans . . .	307,724[2]	361,806	530,355	717,275
Non-Africans . .	—[3]	13	36	107
Total . .	307,724	361,819	530,391	717,382

[1] See *The Gold Coast, 1931*, vol. ii, pp. 1–2.

[2] The Chief Commissioner's estimate was 317,964. The figure 307,724 excludes 10,240 for Kintampo which became part of Ashanti.

[3] No count was made of the few non-Africans; see footnote 6 to Table 3.

TABLE 9. *African Population of Togoland, 1921 and 1931*[1]

Year	Northern Section					Southern Section	Total
	Eastern Dagomba	Kete-Krachi	Kusasi	Mam-prusi	Total	Ho	
1921	58,929	25,244	12,093	4,518	100,784	87,155	187,939
1931	91,523	20,521	41,101	14,997	168,142	125,529	293,671

[1] See *The Gold Coast, 1931*, vol. ii, pp. 220, 238.

of 293,714. Table 9 gives a comparison of the returns for Africans in the two years by districts. The number of non-Africans was 20 in 1921 and 43 in 1931.

From 1931 on the population has been computed in the same manner as for the Gold Coast, the yearly increase in the African population being put at 10,573. The result for mid-year 1940 was 391,516. But in view of the gross understatement of the population in 1921, the figures for recent years may be far too high.

6. Gold Coast and Togoland

According to the 1921 enumeration the population was 2,299,961. In view of omissions in the Gold Coast and particularly in Togoland it seems unlikely that the actual population was less than 2,550,000. The

TABLE 10. *Population Density, Gold Coast and Togoland, 1931*[1]

Districts	Area, sq. m.	Africans	Non-Africans[2]	Total	Population per sq. m.
COLONY, WESTERN PROVINCE					
Ankobra	2,149	46,173	46	46,219	21·5
Aowin	1,272	9,941	2	9,943	7·8
Axim	1,518	51,924	28	51,952	34·2
Sefwi	2,610	42,060	18	42,078	16·1
Sekondi-Dixcove	367	73,821	435	74,256	202·3
Tarkwa	1,683	60,983	155	61,138	36·3
Total	9,599	284,902	684	285,586	29·8
COLONY, CENTRAL PROVINCE					
Cape Coast	2,125	136,044	120	136,164	64·1
Saltpond	690	103,265	48	103,313	149·7
Western Akim	951	63,381	37	63,418	66·7
Winneba	917	128,694	93	128,787	140·4
Total	4,683	431,384	298	431,682	92·2
COLONY, EASTERN PROVINCE					
Accra	618	136,696	1,009	137,705	222·8
Akwapim	834	86,380	44	86,424	103·6
Birim (Akim-Abuakwa)	} 4,747	140,677	72	140,749	} 42·1
Birim (Kwahu)		59,026	17	59,043	
Kete-Ada	2,146	243,671	47	243,718	113·6
New Juaben	52	26,526	105	26,631	512·1
Volta River	1,258	162,100	28	162,128	128·9
Total	9,655	855,076	1,322	856,398	88·7
ASHANTI, WESTERN PROVINCE					
Ahafo	1,434	15,776	—	15,776	11·0
Kintampo	5,141	43,410	8	43,418	8·4
Sunyani	2,416	66,976	21	66,997	27·7
Wenchi	2,077	58,106	5	58,111	28·0
Total	11,068	184,268	34	184,302	16·7
ASHANTI, EASTERN PROVINCE					
Ashanti-Akim	4,580	55,235	20	55,255	12·1
Kumasi	3,169	172,196	457	172,653	54·5
Mampong	3,349	50,295	10	50,305	15·0
Obuasi	} 2,213	39,718	87	39,805	} 52·5
Obuasi (Bekwai)		76,366	16	76,382	
Total	13,311	393,810	590	394,400	29·6
NORTHERN TERRITORIES, NORTHERN PROVINCE					
Kusasi	807	110,614	3	110,617	137·1
Lawra-Tumu	3,840	93,125	8	93,133	24·3
Mamprusi	2,014	46,523	3	46,526	23·1
Navrongo	1,551	120,870	20	120,890	77·9
Wa	3,462	72,323	6	72,329	20·9
Zuarunga	781	133,981	9	133,990	171·6
Total	12,455	577,436	49	577,485	46·4

TABLE 10. *Population Density, Gold Coast and Togoland, 1931[1]—contd.*

Districts	Area, sq. m.	Africans	Non-Africans[2]	Total	Population per sq. m.
NORTHERN TERRITORIES, SOUTHERN PROVINCE					
Western Dagomba . . .	6,754	100,433	50	100,483	14·9
Eastern Gonja . . .	5,053	23,683	7	23,690	4·7
Western Gonja. . .	6,224	15,723	1	15,724	2·5
Total	18,031	139,839	58	139,897	7·8
TOTAL GOLD COAST					
Colony	23,937	1,571,362	2,304	1,573,666	65·7
Ashanti	24,379	578,078	624	578,702	23·7
Northern Territories. .	30,486	717,275	107	717,382	23·5
Total	78,802	2,866,715	3,035	2,869,750	36·4
TOGOLAND					
Eastern Dagomba . .	5,503	91,523	4	91,527	16·6
Kete-Kratchi . . .	3,949	20,521	2	20,523	5·2
Kusasi	420	41,101	—	41,101	97·9
Mamprusi . . .	705	14,997	—	14,997	21·3
Northern Section . .	10,577	168,142	6	168,148	15·9
Southern Section . .	2,464	125,529	37	125,566	51·0
Total	13,041	293,671	43	293,714	22·5
GOLD COAST AND TOGOLAND					
	91,843	3,160,386	3,078	3,163,464	34·4

[1] See *The Gold Coast, 1931*, vol. ii, pp. 2–3, 23.
[2] Excluding 104 Maritime Population in the Colony.

1931 enumeration showed a population of 3,163,568. The population for mid-year 1940 has been computed at 3,962,760 (86,392 yearly increase of African resident population since 1931). This may be an overstatement.

The area of the Gold Coast is 78,802 square miles and that of Togoland 13,041 square miles. According to the 1931 enumeration the number of inhabitants per square mile was 36 4 in the Gold Coast. In the Colony it was 65·7 (Western Province 29·8, Central Province 92·2, Eastern Province 88·7), in Ashanti 23·7 (Western Province 16·7, Eastern Province 29·6), in the Northern Territories 23·5 (Northern Province 46·4, Southern Province 7·8). While it exceeded 100 in 8 of the 17 Districts of the Colony and in 2 of the 6 Districts of the Northern Province of the Northern Territories, it was less than 5 in 2 of the 3 Districts of the Southern Province of the Northern Territories (Western Gonja 2·5, Eastern Gonja 4·7). In Togoland the number of inhabitants per square mile was 22·5. In the Northern Section it was only 15·9 (in Kete Kratchi not more than 5·2), in the Southern Section 51·0. In the Gold Coast including Togoland the average density was 34·4.

The Chief Census Officer made the following comment:

A closer scrutiny of the district areas and their density return reveals an interesting fact concerning the incidence of population. The districts within the forest belt where the population is least are those adjacent to the western frontier; this zone of scarcity of inhabitants sweeps across the country to the eastern frontier outside and to the north of the forest zone and widens with an ever increasing diminution of population to the north until it reaches the Northern Province where the population becomes denser than in most parts of the country.

The reason for this is somewhat difficult to establish especially with regard to the forest zone. The writer would suggest tentatively that the western frontier districts not having been developed in time for the cacao boom retained the conditions which prevailed elsewhere in the forest zone prior to that boom, conditions which as one receded further westward into the forest made habitation by man increasingly difficult. Outside and to the north of this forest belt is a country which in the rainy season is mostly under water and the high ground of which, where villages alone can be constructed, is in the dry season in some places almost entirely destitute of water. Such districts as Kintampo, Northern Mampong, most of Krachi, Eastern and Western Gonjas are to all intents and purposes uninhabitable and they form by creating a belt of territory without people, a very serious obstacle to the complete opening up and progress of the thickly populated north. The same situation is encountered in most of the Mamprusi district and after leaving the high plateaux of the Dagomba country one descends into a swampy or barren zone which forms that district. Conditions north of the White Volta and westward along the parallel of that river's eastward sweep are completely different. The country is a well-watered one even in the dry season. . . . That country supports a dense population . . . .

The rapidity with which the country has been developed since the beginning of the century has created a number of large towns in the area exploited. Their growth has been considerable, but it is rather in the number of townships than in the size of individual towns that this growth has been most marked.[1]

The largest towns in 1931 were Accra with 60,726 inhabitants, Kumasi with 35,829, Cape Coast with 17,685, and Sekondi with 16,953.[2]

III. Composition of African Population

Area of Origin. At the enumerations of 1911 and 1921 an attempt was made to group the population by tribes, but the returns were scanty and uncertain[3] and they provide hardly any adequate information on the area of origin. The forms used in 1931 contained for the first time a special column 'Place of Origin, African of Gold Coast or Alien African'. In this column was to be written 'where possible the name of the country or Province inhabited by the tribe'. If, for example, the person was a Krobo, the entry was to be 'Eastern Province Colony'; if he was a Mendi, 'Sierra Leone'. The Chief Census Officer considered the people who did not belong to an indigenous tribe as 'immigrants' and divided these immigrants into 'Subjects of other British West African Colonies', 'Subjects of French West African Colonies', &c.[4] I doubt whether this interpretation was correct. I do not think that the fact that a child belonged to an alien tribe necessarily meant that it was born outside the Colony and that it was

---

[1] *The Gold Coast, 1931*, vol. i, p. 157.   [2] See ibid., vol. ii, p. 18.
[3] See *Census Report 1911*, pp. 38–9, 69–72; *1921*, pp. 60–1, 72–3, 86–94, 118, 140, 159, Appendices, pp. 15–16.   [4] See *The Gold Coast, 1931*, vol. i, p. 154.

TABLE 11. *African Population by Area of Origin, Gold Coast and Togoland, 1931*[1]

Area of origin	Residence: Gold Coast						Residence: Togoland		
	Gold Coast Colony			Ashanti	Northern Territories	Total	Northern Section	Southern Section	Total
	Western Province	Central Province	Eastern Province						
Gold Coast Colony (a)	222,508	389,608	748,286			1,360,402			
Gold Coast Colony (b)	25,804	6,933	6,809	20,293	1,131	60,970	136	4,774	4,910
Ashanti	3,217	2,703	9,522	465,106	1,746	482,294	208	108	316
Northern Territories	7,454	4,624	7,664	22,659	653,104	695,505	1,119	493	1,612
Gold Coast	258,983	403,868	772,281	508,058	655,981	2,599,171	1,463	5,375	6,838
Togoland (British)	—	974	10,210	1,221	—	12,405	141,406	111,348	252,754
Gambia	13	5	7	—	—	25	—	—	—
Sierra Leone	1,630	59	807	299	—	2,795	} 1,867	} 2,101	13
Nigeria	6,846	10,518	24,970	15,036	6,378	63,748			3,955
West Indies (British)	—	1	—	—	—	1	—	—	—
Other Brit. Dependencies	8,489	11,557	35,994	16,556	6,378	78,974	143,273	113,449	256,722
French West Africa	14,277	15,227	37,806	52,734	46,136	166,180	23,406	6,696	30,102
Liberia	3,078	732	2,792	201	—	6,803	—	9	9
Unclassified Aliens	75	—	6,203	529	8,780	15,587	—	—	—
Total Aliens	17,430	15,959	46,801	53,464	54,916	188,570	23,406	6,705	30,111
Grand Total	284,902	431,384	855,076	578,078	717,275	2,866,715	168,142	125,529	293,671

[1] Computed from *The Gold Coast, 1931*, vol. ii, pp. 1, 21–2, and *Report on the Administration of Togoland 1931*, p. 68.
(a) Residing inside the Province of their origin.
(b) Residing outside the Province of their origin.

a subject of another country. All that can be said, it seems to me, is that such a child was of alien origin.

Of the 2,866,715 Africans enumerated in 1931 in the Gold Coast, 78,974 originated from other British Dependencies (mainly Nigeria and Togoland) and 188,570 from other countries (mainly French West African Dependencies). Of the inhabitants of the Western Province of the Colony not more than 78·1 per cent. originated from that Province; the corresponding percentages for the Central and Eastern Provinces were 90·3 and 87·5 respectively. Of the inhabitants of Ashanti 80·5 per cent. originated from Ashanti. Of the inhabitants of the Northern Territories 91·1 per cent. originated from these Territories. The differences are due in part to internal migration. There were in the Colony 15,442 people originating from Ashanti and 19,742 from the Northern Territories. There were in Ashanti 20,293 from the Colony and 22,659 from the Northern Territories. But there were in the Northern Territories only 1,131 from the Colony and only 1,746 from Ashanti. While 42,401 inhabitants of the Colony and Ashanti originated from the Northern Territories, only 2,877 inhabitants of the Northern Territories originated from the Colony or Ashanti. The proportion of inhabitants of the Northern Territories originating from other West African British Dependencies was also very small. But in view of the fact that the Northern Territories are generally considered to be a country with a large excess of emigration, it is noteworthy that the number of Africans living in the Northern Territories and originating from foreign colonies was very large. They constituted 7·7 per cent. of the total population as compared with 5·1 per cent. in the Gold Coast Colony; in Ashanti, however, the percentage was 9·2.

Of the 293,671 Africans enumerated in 1931 in Togoland, 10,806 originated from other British Dependencies (mainly Gold Coast and Nigeria) and 30,111 from other countries (mainly French West African Dependencies). The number of Togolanders residing in other British Dependencies was obviously greater than the inflow of Africans from the Empire into Togoland, since 12,405 Togolanders were recorded in the Gold Coast alone.[1] But there was certainly a favourable balance of migration in the intercourse with French Dependencies.

Little is known about the occupation of the people originating from other British Dependencies and other countries. The census reports convey the impression that employment at the mines played a very important part. But in the period covered by these reports only a small proportion of the immigrants went to the mines. Table 12 shows the average number of Africans (including local labourers) employed in the mines from 1905 to 1938–9. It appears that the number was 12,465 in 1905, oscillated in 1906 to 1918 between 13,580 and 18,466, and in 1919 to 1932–3 between 10,439 and 13,227, and that it rose thereafter to 39,122 in 1938–9.[2] The

[1] This figure, moreover, is very likely incomplete since not a single Togolander was recorded in the Northern Territories.
[2] The average number employed (including Europeans) was 38,887 in 1938, 40,452 in 1939, 39,770 in 1940, 30,900 in 1943, and 29,545 in 1944; see *Blue Book 1938*, p. 137; *1939*, p. 137; *1940*, p. 137; *1943*, p. 131; *1944*, p. 136.

sources from which the labour was drawn have been published for 1904, 1911 to 1928–9, and 1931–2 to 1933–4. The figures given for those employed at any time during the first six months of 1904 were as follows:[1]

Natives belonging to the Gold Coast				Natives from other British Colonies			Foreign Natives		
Ashanti	Fanti	Krepe	Appolonians	Mendi	Lagos	Hausas	Kroo Boys	Bassas	Total
2,766	6,545	1,934	242	743	1,187	399	2,382	846	17,044

It appears that 67 per cent. belonged to the Gold Coast while 14 per cent. came from other British Dependencies and 19 per cent. from foreign countries.

TABLE 12. *Average Number of African Mine Labourers employed on Gold Coast, 1905–38*[1]

Year	Number	Year	Number	Year	Number	Year	Number
1905	12,465	1914	15,204	1922–3	10,929	1931–2	11,839
1906	13,580	1915	14,824	1923–4	11,995	1932–3	12,319
1907	14,739	1916	14,846	1924–5	13,096	1933–4	16,453
1908	15,206	1917	16,004	1925–6	13,227	1934–5	26,535
1909	15,395	1918	13,582	1926–7	10,734	1935–6	33,403
1910	18,466	1919	11,732	1927–8	10,719	1936–7	35,350
1911	18,383	1920	10,439	1928–9	11,353	1937–8	37,783
1912	16,921	1921	11,243	1929–30	12,140	1938–9	39,122
1913	15,094	1922[2]	12,605	1930–1	12,380		

[1] See *Report on the Mines Department 1905*, p. 14; *1906*, p. 15; *1907*, p. 14; *1908*, p. 13; *1909*, p. 13; *1910*, p. 13; *1911*, p. 14; *1912*, p. 13; *1913*, p. 12; *1914*, p. 12; *1915*, p. 10; *1916*, p. 10; *1931–2*, p. 7; *1938–9*, p. 16. Some figures do not represent the average number but the number employed on a given day.   [2] First quarter.

The figures for later years are summarized in Table 13. They show that though the proportion of natives from French West Africa has been increasing, the majority of the native mine labourers belonged all the time to the Gold Coast.

It should be realized, however, that conditions may have changed in recent years[2] and also that apart from those employed in the mines there were immigrants working as wood-cutters for the mineral industry.[3] Even so, the number of immigrants employed in the cocoa industry has been certainly much larger, all the time, than the number employed directly or indirectly by the mineral industry.

[1] See Gold Coast, *Report on Mines Department 1903–4*, p. 30.

[2] Apparently the only pertinent statement in recent years is to be found in *Report on the Labour Department 1939–40*, p. 3: 'An enquiry was . . . made into the territorial sources of labour in the mining industry. The figures for the whole of the Gold Coast were as follows: Colony and Ashanti, 32·5 per cent; Northern Territories and contiguous French territories, 55 per cent; other West African territories, 12·5 per cent. The high proportion of Colony and Ashanti labour was unexpected.' The proportion of Colony and Ashanti labour was about the same as in 1933–4, although the total number of natives employed in the mining industry had doubled in the meantime. Whether the proportion coming from French territories has changed it is impossible to tell.

[3] It is not clear to what extent such workers have been included in the figures of labourers employed in the mines.

TABLE 13. *African Mine Labourers Employed on Gold Coast by Country of Origin, 1911–33*[1]

Date or Period[2]	Natives from Gold Coast				Natives from other British Dependencies				Natives from foreign countries				Total
	Ashanti	Northern Territories[3]	Other	Total	Nigeria	Sierra Leone	Other[4]	Total	French Colonies	Liberia	Togoland[5]	Total	Total
31 Dec. 1911	2,543	2,421	7,628	12,592	1,276	663	222	2,161	539	1,470	365	2,374	17,127
31 Dec. 1912	2,480	2,359	7,426	12,265	1,503	677	149	2,329	665	1,367	256	2,288	16,882
Year 1913	2,133	2,900	6,285	11,318	1,711	489	66	2,266	1,092	1,050	373	2,515	16,099
Year 1914	1,965	4,215	5,555	11,735	1,992	385	98	2,475	1,508	1,233	418	3,159	17,369
Year 1915	1,871	4,070	4,607	10,548	2,209	449	58	2,716	2,722	946	415	4,083	17,347
Year 1916	1,832	3,605	4,330	9,767	2,109	440	62	2,611	3,359	1,061	359	4,779	17,157
Year 1917	1,891	3,591	5,269	10,751	2,579	471	38	3,088	3,863	1,260	348	5,471	19,310
Year 1918	1,820	3,152	4,653	9,625	2,597	380	30	3,007	3,445	1,083	228	4,756	17,388
Year 1919	1,633	2,530	3,626	7,789	1,836	303	20	2,159	3,079	909	196	4,184	14,132
Year 1920	1,397	2,122	2,782	6,301	1,280	405	73	1,758	2,004	900	287	3,191	11,250
31 Dec. 1921	2,256	2,136	3,456	7,848	1,717	289	96	2,102	1,981	1,281	186	3,448	13,398
Year 1922-3	1,690	2,493	3,128	7,311	1,277	220	21	1,518	2,058	1,043	263	3,364	12,193
Year 1923-4	1,557	2,441	3,702	7,700	1,443	238	25	1,706	2,225	961	403	3,589	12,995
Year 1924-5	1,729	2,868	4,385	8,982	1,971	225	23	2,219	2,702	928	470	4,100	15,301
Year 1925-6	1,547	2,020	4,914	8,481	2,067	227	175	2,469	2,532	750	112	3,394	14,344
1926-7	842	2,492	3,071	6,405	1,022	179	22	1,223	2,040	643	423	3,106	10,734
1927-8	1,027	2,707	3,253	6,987	1,036	134	37	1,207	1,807	416	302	2,525	10,719
1928-9	1,427	2,883	3,412	7,722	1,005	142	6	1,153	1,818	474	186	2,478	11,353
1931-2	947	2,580	3,538	7,065	942	145	—	1,087	3,858	492	113	4,463	12,615
1932-3	1,417	3,152	3,527	8,096	947	101	240	1,288	4,940	613	89	5,642	15,026
1933-4	1,487	5,070	5,226	11,783	1,053	149	58	1,260	6,132	599	108	6,839	19,882

[1] See *Report on the Mines Department 1911*, p. 15; *1912*, p. 14; *1913*, p. 13; *1914*, p. 13; *1915*, p. 11; *1916*, p. 11; *1917*, p. 12; *1918*, p. 12; *1919*, p. 12; *1920*, p. 23; *1921*, p. 17; *1922-3*, p. 28; *1923-4*, p. 26; *1924-5*, p. 32; *1925-6*, p. 38; *1926-7*, p. 31; *1927-8*, p. 24; *1928-9*, p. 25; *1931-2*, pp. 13-14; *1932-3*, pp. 13-15; *1933-4*, pp. 10-12.

[2] The data for 1911, 1912, and 1921 refer to 31 Dec. Those for 1913-20, 1922-3, and apparently also 1923-4 to 1925-6 are meant to cover all labourers employed during the year. Those for 1931-2 to 1933-4, and apparently also those for 1926-7 to 1928-9, 'are in respect of Africans employed at the actual time of enquiring into their nationality, and are not to be taken as being an average for the year'; the inquiries were apparently made at different dates in different mines.

[3] From 1924-5 on (possibly from 1921 on) including Togoland under British Mandate.

[4] 1911-19 Gambia; 1932-3 'Cardo 201, Fulani 37, Br. Guiana 1, West Indies 1'.

[5] 1921 to 1933-4 Togoland under French Mandate.

Sex. No attempt seems to have been made before 1891 to estimate the number of males and females, but when the first count was made in that year it was apparently expected that it would show a large excess of females. The Secretary of the Census Committee reported:

... it will be seen that of the total classified population, viz.: ... 767,095, there is only a predominance of (409,511 females, 357,584 males) 51,927 females in the entire Colony, the proportion being one male to every 1·145 females.[1]

He suspected that a greater proportion of women than men had evaded enumeration. Therefore, the estimated figures which were to supplement the returns of the count assumed a greater predominance of females:[2]

	Males	Females	Females to 100 males
Returns	357,584	409,511	114·5
Addition for omissions . . .	92,000	113,000	122·8
'Children and Old' in Atabubu[1] . .	787	1,000	127·1
Krepi and Kwahu	225,000	275,000	122·2
Total	675,371	798,511	118·4

[1] Not classified according to sex in the census returns.

It seems, however, that already in the original returns the predominance of females had been overstated, as it was particularly great in those areas for which the population is given in round figures, i.e. where the population had been estimated or guessed.[3]

The returns of 1901 again did not fulfil the expectations of a great predominance of females. The Census Committee made the following comment:

It will be seen . . . that the sexes are fairly evenly divided, there being a slight preponderance of females. The ratio for the Colony, including Ashanti and the Northern Territories, is 1 male to 1·18 females. The returns for the Northern Territories show a preponderance of males (viz.: 55,098 males, 52,334 females or 1 female to 1·05 males) as do also those for Sekundi (11,998 males, 10,602 females, or 1 female to 1·13 males), Axim (9,303 males, 8,827 females, or 1 female to 1·05 males) and Dixcove (5,878 males, 5,847 females). The figures for the Northern Territories are unreliable, while in the other districts the unusual number of males is probably to be accounted for by the influx of labourers and servants consequent on the development of the mining industry and the construction of the Railway. The excess of females to males is most noticeable in the Kwitta district, where the ratio is 1 male to 1·26 females; Accra and Volta River districts come next with 1 male to 1·17 females.[4]

The last sentence contains, of course, an error. It is obvious that if the excess of females for the whole country was 18 per cent., Kwitta cannot have been the only district where the excess was larger than that. As a matter of fact, the ratio of females to 1 male was 1·42 in Saltpond (23,915 males, 33,905 females)[5] and 1·32 in Ashanti (144,436 males, 191,215 females).[6] But it should be remembered that Ashanti, Saltpond, and

[1] *Census Report 1891*, p. 10.   [2] See *Blue Book 1891* S, p. 1.
[3] See *Census Report 1891*, pp. 42–105. I have quoted above the example of Sefwhi Whyawsu where the population was returned as 11,000 males and 22,000 females.
[4] Ibid. *1901*, p. 6.   [5] See ibid., p. 19.   [6] See ibid., p. 56.

Kwitta were areas where the count was particularly defective. Yet, as the Census Committee again thought that the proportion of omissions was larger among women than among men, the sum of 148,000 which was added in consideration of omissions was subdivided into 48,000 males and 100,000 females, and the population figures were raised to 660,263 males and 826,170 females,[1] giving a ratio of 125 females to 100 males.

The sex ratio returned at the 1911 enumeration differed essentially from the earlier results. They showed for the whole country a small excess of males.[2]

Sex	Colony	Ashanti	Northern Territories	Total
Males	427,277	141,012	187,157	755,446
Females . . .	425,119	146,579	174,649	746,347
Females to 100 males .	99·5	103·9	93·3	98·8

The Census Officer thought that for the Colony immigration 'would appear to be the main factor in the change which has arisen in the proportion between the sexes since the censuses of 1901 and 1891'.[3] But this explanation is inadequate. The number of males had apparently increased since 1901 from 412,729 to 427,277 or by only 3·5 per cent., while the number of females had apparently decreased from 482,621 to 425,119 or by 11·9 per cent. If immigration had been the main factor in the change of the sex ratio, then in the absence of immigration the number of males would presumably have decreased enormously, but I have nowhere found any suggestion that there was such a decrease. The fact alone that according to the returns the male population of Kwitta decreased between 1901 and 1911 from 76,992 to 18,025, and the number of females from 97,232 to 18,920, shows the futility of seeking for any specific cause of the apparent change in the sex ratio. But there still remains the question whether the sex ratio found for the Colony at the 1911 enumeration can have been approximately correct. I am inclined to answer this question in the affirmative. The excess of males was negligible and there had been for a decade or more a notable immigration of males.

. . . as the excess occurs in the agricultural and mining districts it can be satisfactorily explained by the number of imported labourers. . . . Both in the mining and agricultural districts it appears that the imported labourers are unaccompanied by their women.[4]

The sex ratio in Ashanti calls for no comment. The apparently large excess of males in the Northern Territories was, I suppose, due to omission of females at the count.

The Commissioner of the North Western Province considers the excess may be also, to a certain extent, attributed to the severe epidemics of the cerebro-spinal meningitis that visited his Province three times during the past decade, when more women than men succumbed to its ravages; and also to the raids of Samory and Babatu when hundreds of women were captured. The latter explanation would not, however, account for there being fewer girls than boys in the groups 1 to 5 and 6 to

---

[1] See *Statistical Tables Colonial Possessions 1901*, p. 437.
[2] See *Census Report 1911*, pp. 55–8.   [3] Ibid., p. 30.   [4] Ibid., p. 30.

15, as Samory's last raid took place early in 1897, and Babatu had not raided the country for some years previous to that date.[1]

The sex ratio at the 1921 enumeration did not differ essentially from the results of 1911. The returns showed for the whole country a slightly larger excess of males (see Table 14). In the Colony there was, as in 1911, a small excess of females over males in the Eastern and Central Provinces and a considerable excess of males over females in the Western Province (110,406 males and 94,674 females, i.e. only 85·8 females to 100 males). This preponderance of males was particularly large in the Tarquah District with 27,288 males and 17,237 females, and within this District in the mining villages with 7,589 males and 3,515 females.[2]

The excess of males in Ashanti is greater than appears from the figures in Table 14 since the 5,632 people whose sex was not specified were mostly males. It is safe to say that there were not more than 96 females to 100 males. The 1911 returns had shown an excess of females. The Chief Commissioner attributes this change to an increased number of immigrants from the North, and the Census Officer of the 1911 census writes: 'At the last Census the number of foreign natives in Ashanti was 31,204, the number is now 43,839 or if the Railway labourers are included 47,532, that is to say an addition of 16,278 in the last ten years.'[3]

For the Southern Province of the Northern Territories both the statistics and their presentation are quite inadequate. No figures by sex are available for Western Gonja. For Western Dagomba and Eastern Gonja the figures read as follows:[4]

District	Boys	Men	Girls	Women	Total males	Total females	Total
Western Dagomba.	21,913	25,275	20,467	26,289	42,380	51,564	93,944
Eastern Gonja .	3,846	5,553	3,293	5,460	9,399	8,753	18,152

The census report says 'it is obvious that the males in every recorded group outnumber the females'.[5] This is not correct. In Western Dagomba the women outnumber the men. Moreover, the 'Total males' are the sum of the boys and girls and the 'Total females' the sum of men and women.[6] The census report adds:

The Deputy Chief Commissioner has no comments to make, but it is recorded that in 1911 the same condition existed and it was thought then that many girls and young women had been hidden from the enumerators. Probably the same thing occurred in 1921.[7]

[1] Statement by Acting Chief Commissioner Northern Territories, quoted ibid., p. 31. It should be noted, moreover, that the (very imperfect) count of 1901 which was taken before the epidemics of cerebrospinal meningitis showed also an excess of males over females in the Northern Territories.   [2] See ibid. *1921*, pp. 106–7.
[3] Ibid., p. 118.   [4] See ibid., Appendices, p. 10.   [5] Ibid., p. 131.
[6] The same mistake appears ibid., p. 130. In compiling Table 14 I have assumed that the totals are wrong and have entered for Western Dagomba 47,188 males and 46,756 females. I have thus obtained a total excess of 16,275 for the Northern Territories. But it should be noted that in the 'Final Review', ibid., p. 158, the total excess of males in the Northern Territories is given as only 6,659. The Chief Census Officer, therefore, accepted the figures for Total males and Total females as correct and reckoned with an enormous excess of females over males in the Southern Province!   [7] Ibid., p. 131.

TABLE 14. *African Population by Sex, Gold Coast and Togoland, 1921 and 1931*[1]

District	Males		Females		F. to 100 M.	
	1921	1931	1921	1931	1921	1931
COLONY, WESTERN PROVINCE						
Ankobra	18,142	24,146	14,911	22,027	82	91
Aowin	3,346	5,262	3,225	4,679	96	89
Axim	20,353	25,794	20,406	26,130	100	101
Sefwi	12,141	22,248	13,867	19,812	114	89
Sekondi	29,136	39,857	25,028	33,964	86	85
Tarkwa	27,288	32,615	17,237	28,368	63	87
Total	110,406	149,922	94,674	134,980	86	90
COLONY, CENTRAL PROVINCE						
Cape Coast	45,854	68,522	47,573	67,522	104	99
Saltpond[2]	34,528	53,980	36,183	49,285	105	91
Western Akim	15,180	34,070	16,984	29,311	112	86
Winneba	53,261	64,947	52,306	63,747	98	98
Total	148,823	221,519	153,046	209,865	103	95
COLONY, EASTERN PROVINCE						
Accra	53,389	73,493	46,214	63,203	87	86
Akwapim	39,727	44,067	40,190	42,313	101	96
Akim-Abuakwa	44,893	75,651	45,413	65,026	101	86
Kwahu	20,780	30,656	20,913	28,370	101	93
Kete-Ada	88,660	116,289	88,965	127,382	100	110
Volta River	83,715	94,937	91,348	93,679	109	99
Total	331,164	435,093	333,043	419,983	101	97
ASHANTI						
Western Province	56,096	94,182	57,653	90,086	103	96
Eastern Province[3]	146,132	204,159	140,680	189,651	96	93
NORTHERN TERRITORIES, NORTHERN PROVINCE						
Navrongo	134,107	181,112	123,842	184,353	92	102
Lawra-Tumu	43,136	46,227	41,128	46,898	95	101
Mamprusi	11,193	23,184	10,751	23,339	96	101
Wa	22,825	36,307	20,343	36,016	89	99
Total	211,261	286,830	196,064	290,606	93	101
NORTHERN TERRITORIES, SOUTHERN PROVINCE						
Western Dagomba	47,188	52,580	46,756	47,853	99	91
Eastern Gonja	9,399	12,887	8,753	10,796	93	84
Western Gonja[4]	..	7,963	..	7,760	..	97
Total	56,587	73,430	55,509	66,409	98	90

[1] See *Census Report 1921*, Appendices, pp. 9–10; *The Gold Coast, 1931*, vol. ii, pp. 31, 58, 78, 147, 159, 186, 204, 220, 238.

[2] Excluding, in 1921, the population (757) of 9 villages omitted in Census.

[3] Excluding, in 1921, 5,632 persons (Regiment 1,592, Police 181, Prisons 166, Railway Labourers 3,693) whose sex was not specified.

[4] Sex of population (10,931) not specified in 1921.

TABLE 14—*contd.*

District	Males		Females		F. to 100 M.	
	1921	1931	1921	1931	1921	1931
TOGOLAND, NORTHERN SECTION						
Eastern Dagomba .	30,893	48,613	28,036	42,910	91	88
Kete-Krachi . .	12,302	10,470	12,942	10,051	105	96
Kusasi . . .	6,332	21,533	5,761	19,568	91	91
Mamprusi . .	2,447	7,545	2,071	7,452	85	99
Total . . .	51,974	88,161	48,810	79,981	94	91
TOGOLAND, SOUTHERN SECTION						
Ho . . .	42,435	62,303	44,720	63,226	105	101
GOLD COAST AND TOGOLAND						
Colony . . .	590,393	806,534	580,763	764,828	98	95
Ashanti . . .	202,228	298,341	198,333	279,737	98	94
N. Territories .	267,848	360,260	251,573	357,015	94	99
Gold Coast . .	1,060,469	1,465,135	1,030,669	1,401,580	97	96
Togoland . .	94,409	150,464	93,530	143,207	99	95
Grand Total .	1,154,878	1,615,599	1,124,199	1,544,787	97	96

In the Northern Province of the Northern Territories there was an excess of males in each of the four Districts, the total being 211,261 males and 196,064 females, or only 92·8 females to 100 males. The census report says:

In every case there are more males than females. For this, no doubt the reason given in the report on the Southern Province may be partly responsible. It has been suggested that the mortality from Cerebro Spinal Meningitis is higher amongst females than males. Mention was also made of the raids of Samory and Babatu—the last took place in 1897, in which many women were captured.

The numerical superiority of males is, however, a remarkable fact because it is well known that many male natives of the Protectorate are employed in Ashanti and the Colony and they are not as a rule accompanied by their women.[1]

For the Gold Coast as a whole my computation yields an excess of 29,800 males and a ratio of 97·2 females to 100 males. This ratio would have been reduced to about 96·7 if the 5,632 people in Ashanti whose sex was not specified had been included. The Chief Census Officer, who reckons with an excess of only 20,184 males,[2] i.e. with a ratio of 98·1 females to 100 males, says:

I am unable to explain this excess, but it will be noted that the excess occurs in the less civilised portions of the area and it [may] very well be true that in those parts the numbers of women were deliberately withheld. In the Western Province the large male excess is no doubt explained by the numbers of males employed on the Mines, Railway construction and other works who are not as a rule accompanied by a corresponding number of women. There were 11,104 males employed on the Mines alone.[3] The same may be said of Ashanti. In the Northern Territories however

---

[1] *Census Report 1921*, pp. 132–3.   [2] See footnote 6 to p. 429 above.

[3] This is a mistake. There were 11,104 people in the mining villages in the Tarquah District (6,328 men, 2,523 women, and 2,253 children). The average daily number of natives employed during the first quarter of 1921 in the mines in the Western Province was 7,087. (See *Census Report 1921*, pp. 107–8.)

the case is somewhat different for a very large additional number of males (the total of these males and females is approximately estimated at 50,000) are resident in the Colony and Ashanti, employed on the construction works already referred to.— No explanation is advanced by the Chief Commissioner, though I specially remarked on the fact and I regret that I am unable to evolve any satisfactory explanation owing to my ignorance of local conditions. It has been remarked that the mortality amongst women, caused by Cerebro Spinal Meningitis of which there have been several epidemics in this area, is much higher than amongst men.[1]

In Togoland there was in 1921 a negligible excess of males.

In 1931 the preponderance of males was even larger than in 1921, and it is very much to be regretted that the comments in the census report are vague and less instructive than on former occasions. I shall first make a few remarks on the changes which occurred in the sex ratio between 1921 and 1931.

Colony, Western Province. The preponderance of males decreased; the ratio of females to 100 males rose from 85·8 to 90·0. The change was most conspicuous in the Tarkwa District, where the ratio rose from 63 to 87. This change can be explained in part by the decrease in the amount of labour employed in the gold-mines,[2] but I suspect that the enormous increase appearing in the number of females—from 17,237 to 28,368—was partly due to incomplete counting of women in 1921. The reductions in the ratios of females from 114 to 89 in Sefwi District and from 96 to 89 in Aowin District may be due to an influx of male strangers attracted by the development of the cacao planting industry in those areas.

Colony, Central and Eastern Provinces. The preponderance of females changed into a preponderance of males; the ratio of females to 100 males decreased in the Central Province from 102·8 to 94·7 and in the Eastern Province from 100·6 to 96·5. The most conspicuous changes occurred in the Western Akim and the Akim–Abuakwa Districts where the ratios dropped from 112 to 86 and from 101 to 86 respectively. The changes may be due in part to the development of the cacao planting industry, and —to a small extent—to the opening of the diamond fields.[3]

Ashanti. The preponderance of males increased slightly; the ratio of females to 100 males declined from about 96 to 93·8.

Northern Territories. In the Northern Province the considerable preponderance of males changed into a slight preponderance of females; the ratio of females to 100 males rose from 92·8 to 101·3. It is hard to believe that the basic figures are correct. The apparently increasing preponderance of males in the Southern Province is probably due to defects in the 1921 count.

Togoland. The Northern Section shows an increasing preponderance of males and the Southern Section a decreasing preponderance of females. The returns in 1921 were so incomplete that it is not worth while commenting on these changes.

---

[1] *Census Report 1921*, pp. 158–9.

[2] The number of Africans employed in the gold mines of the Gold Coast decreased from 10,313 in 1921 to 7,121 in 1930–1; see *Report on the Mines Department 1937–8*, p. 16.

[3] The number of Africans employed on diamond fields of the Gold Coast increased from 125 in 1921 to 3,392 in 1930–1. See ibid.

The enumeration of 1931 reveals for the Gold Coast and Togoland an excess of 70,000 males over females, the ratio of females to 100 males being 95·6. Such a great preponderance of males can only be the result of two factors: an enormous excess of male net immigration over female net immigration or an unusually high mortality of females. There was no doubt a considerable excess of male net immigration over female net immigration, but it was, I think, not large enough to explain the large excess of males. I shall first reproduce the scanty available data concerning the sex ratio of people originating from another area than the area of residence:[1]

Area of residence	Area of origin	Males	Females	Males per cent.
Colony, Eastern Province, excluding Accra District	Northern Territories	5,873	3,130	65·2
	Nigeria	9,468	6,272	60·2
	French Colonies	16,160	7,846	67·3
Togoland, Ho District	Outside Togoland	8,424	5,757	59·4

According to the 1931 enumeration the number of Africans in the Gold Coast and Togoland originating from other countries was 289,218. Assuming that 65 per cent. were male and 35 per cent. female, there would have been about 188,000 males and 101,200 females originating from outside the Gold Coast and Togoland. Excluding these people there would have been a slight excess of females. The position in the various sections of the country would have been as follows:[2]

Section	(1) Males	(1) Females	(2) Males	(2) Females	(3) Males	(3) Females	(4) Males	(4) Females
Colony .	806,534	764,828	111,419	59,995	17,112	9,222	712,227	714,055
Ashanti	298,341	279,737	73,432	39,540	11,378	6,126	236,287	246,323
N. Terr.	360,260	357,015	41,711	22,460	28,608	15,405	347,157	349,960
Togoland	150,464	143,207	25,804	15,113	8,063	4,342	132,723	132,436

It is interesting to note that by deducting the people originating from other areas and by adding the people residing in other areas of the Gold Coast and Togoland the ratio of females to 100 males rises in the Colony from 01·8 to 100·3, in Ashanti from 93·8 to 104·2, in the Northern Territories from 99·1 to 100·6, and in Togoland from 95·2 to 99·8. But this computation ought to be supplemented, of course, by adding the people (originating from the Gold Coast or Togoland) residing in other British Dependencies or in foreign countries. No data concerning emigration are available, but it is safe to assume that among these emigrants males exceeded females. The actual excess of male net immigration over female net immigration was, therefore, probably not larger than the excess of

---

[1] See *The Gold Coast, 1931*, vol. i, p. 156; *Report on the Administration of Togoland 1931*, p. 68.

[2] (1) Residents; (2) Originating from elsewhere; (3) Residing elsewhere (in Gold Coast or Togoland); (4) Resident in Gold Coast or Togoland and originating from the area shown in the first column, i.e. (1) — (2) + (3). I have assumed that of the people entered in (2) and (3) 65 per cent. were males and 35 per cent. females, except for the Ho District where I have used for (2) the actual figures.

males over females in the resident population, and it would seem that
without immigration and emigration the number of females would have
been just about equal to the number of males. This unusual position can
only be explained by an unusually high mortality of females. It has been
suggested that more females than males died in the epidemics of cerebro-
spinal meningitis, and it is possible that other factors, too, augmented
female mortality. But it is also possible, of course, that omissions of
females were more numerous than omissions of males.

More recent figures for males and females have been published in the
Statistical Abstract for the British Empire. They read as follows:[1]

Country	Census 1931		31 Dec. 1933	
	Males	*Females*	*Males*	*Females*
Gold Coast 'exclusive of the man-dated areas'	1,467,554	1,402,196	1,639,947	1,405,254
Togoland	150,497	143,217	164,034	156,122

Country	31 Dec. 1935		31 Dec. 1937	
	Males	*Females*	*Males*	*Females*
Gold Coast 'exclusive of the man-dated areas'	1,690,298	1,540,252	1,948,379	1,798,333
Togoland	175,691	165,563	. .	. .

The figures for the Gold Coast proper are all wrong. The males for 1933
are evidently inclusive of Togoland, while the females are exclusive of the
mandated area (and even so are too low). The males and females for 1935
are both exclusive of the mandated area, but the excess of males over
females is grossly overstated; it is out of the question that the males could
have increased between 1931 and 1935 by 223,000 and the females by
138,000. The males and females for 1937 are both inclusive of the mandated area; they were obtained by adding 258,081 to both the males and
the females given for 1935!

Age. 'The grouping of the population by ages is difficult since the
estimates of Age are almost impossible to ascertain with any degree of
accuracy.'[2] It appears in fact that in many Districts the distinction
between children (under 15) and adults (15 and over) was inadequate.
The Central Province of the Colony, the Northern Territories, and Togoland show a suspicious preponderance of male children. The most striking
example is provided by the Northern Province of the Northern Territories,
where the ratio of females to 100 males was 85·7 among children and 113·6
among adults.[3] The Chief Census Officer makes the following comment:

No satisfactory explanation is readily available for the preponderance of adult
females in the Northern Territories, beyond the possible fact that the youth of the
country is at work in the Southern areas.[4]

[1] See *Statistical Abstract 1924 to 1933*, pp. 3, 285; *1926 to 1935*, pp. 3, 303; *1928 to 1937*, pp. 3, 309.
[2] *The Gold Coast, 1931*, vol. i, p. 166.
[3] In the Lawra–Tumu District the ratios were 80 and 122 respectively. See ibid., vol. ii, p. 4.
[4] Ibid., vol. i, p. 162.

A more satisfactory explanation, it seems to me, is that the distinction between children and adults was not carried through in the same manner for both sexes since, as in many other African countries, females who should have been counted as children were considered to be adults.

Although apparently a number of children were counted as adults, the proportion of children among the total population was high. It amounted in the Gold Coast and Togoland to 40 per cent., varying between 35 per cent. in the Western Province of the Colony and 43 per cent. in the Northern Section of Togoland.

The distinction between young adults (15–45) and old adults (46 years and over) seems to have suffered in some Districts from an understatement of old adults. It seems incredible, for example, that in the Northern Section of Togoland the latter should have constituted only 9 per cent. of the total population.[1] The proportion for the whole of the Gold Coast and Togoland was 12·1 per cent.

In the urban areas a distinction was also made between children under one, from 1 to 5, and from 6 to 15. The results may be summarized as follows:[2]

Males					Females				
Up to 1 year	1–5 years	6–15 years	16 years and over	Total	Up to 1 year	1–5 years	6–15 years	16 years and over	Total
5,616	23,600	43,596	133,304	206,116	5,158	24,023	40,372	107,802	177,355

The Chief Census Officer makes the following comment:[3]

The age group 0–1 year should be the annual grouping with the greatest number of individuals and there should normally appear if shown in graph form a gradually descending curve. The present returns, however, if one takes the age group 1–5 years and divides by four to establish a comparison with the preceding age group 0–1 year, show an inclination upwards for this group level, the curve then descending as usual.

The following table shows this tendency:—

	0–1 year	1–5 years	Annual average of 2nd group
Gold Coast	9,160	40,715	10,178
Ashanti	995	4,385	1,096
Northern Territories . .	436	1,637	409
Togoland	183	886	221
Total	10,774	47,623	11,905

But the Chief Census Officer obviously made a wrong assumption. The age group 1–5 years comprised 5 and not 4 years, and the annual average of the second group was not 11,905 but 9,525. The ratio of children under

[1] Within this Section the proportion varied between 6 per cent. in Mamprusi and 20 per cent. in Kete-Krachi. In Tunda Division (Mamprusi), with a population of 375, only 3 women 46 years and over were recorded; in 8 villages of this Division all 74 females over 15 were recorded as under 46. (See ibid., vol. ii, p. 236.)

[2] See ibid., p. 7.   [3] Ibid., vol. i, p. 166.

TABLE 15. *African Population by Sex and Age, Gold Coast and Togoland, 1931*[1]

Provinces	Males			Females			Males Total	Females Total	Total	Females to 100 Males				Children to 100 Women
	Under 15 years	15 to 45 years	46 years and over	Under 15 years	15 to 45 years	46 years and over				Under 15 years	15 to 45 years	46 years and over	Total	
GOLD COAST COLONY														
Western Province	49,024	80,478	20,420	49,734	68,754	16,492	149,922	134,980	284,902	101·4	85·4	80·8	90·0	115·9
Central Province	90,124	101,889	29,506	86,242	97,935	25,688	221,519	209,865	431,384	95·7	96·1	87·1	94·7	142·7
Eastern Province	166,291	206,418	62,384	166,740	197,271	55,972	435,093	419,983	855,076	100·3	95·6	89·7	96·5	131·5
Total	305,439	388,785	112,310	302,716	363,960	98,152	806,534	764,828	1,571,362	99·1	93·6	87·4	94·8	131·6
ASHANTI														
Western Province	36,194	46,622	11,366	36,512	42,252	11,322	94,182	90,086	184,268	100·9	90·6	99·6	95·7	135·7
Eastern Province	79,246	101,200	23,713	79,740	88,757	21,154	204,159	189,651	393,810	100·6	87·7	89·2	92·9	144·6
Total	115,440	147,822	35,079	116,252	131,009	32,476	298,341	279,737	578,078	100·7	88·6	92·6	93·8	141·7
NORTHERN TERRITORIES														
Northern Province	126,240	136,302	24,288	108,216	149,730	32,660	286,830	290,606	577,436	85·7	109·9	134·5	101·3	128·5
Southern Province	29,612	34,925	8,893	26,258	31,836	8,315	73,430	66,409	139,839	88·7	91·2	93·5	90·4	139·1
Total	155,852	171,227	33,181	134,474	181,566	40,975	360,260	357,015	717,275	86·3	106·0	123·5	99·1	130·5
TOTAL GOLD COAST														
Total	576,731	707,834	180,570	553,442	676,535	171,603	1,465,135	1,401,580	2,866,715	96·0	95·6	95·0	95·7	133·3
TOGOLAND														
Northern Section	38,244	41,876	8,041	34,007	38,942	7,032	88,161	79,981	168,142	88·9	93·0	87·5	90·7	157·2
Southern Section	26,167	29,003	7,133	25,612	30,375	7,239	62,303	63,226	125,529	97·9	104·7	101·5	101·5	137·7
Total	64,411	70,879	15,174	59,619	69,317	14,271	150,464	143,207	293,671	92·6	97·8	94·0	95·2	148·4

[1] See *The Gold Coast, 1931*, vol. ii, pp. 4-7, 14-17. The form used in urban areas treated as children those under 16, while that used in the rest of the country drew the limit at 15 years. The headings of this table are, therefore, slightly inaccurate.

1 to children 1–5, therefore, does not suggest that the number of children under 1 was understated.

This, however, does not imply that the figures for children in the urban areas were fairly accurate. The ratio of girls to 100 boys was 91·8 in the first year of age, 101·8 in the group 1–5, and 92·6 in the group 6–15. The ratios in the first and third group certainly arouse suspicion. The preponderance of males in the third group is probably due to the fact that a number of girls aged 14 or 15 were counted as adults.

There were in the Gold Coast 133, and in Togoland 148, children per 100 women. In the Western Province of the Colony the ratio was only 116: 100, in the Northern Section of Togoland 157: 100. Leaving out of consideration the women 46 and over whose offspring were probably mostly adults, it appears that there were in the Gold Coast 167 and in Togoland 179 children per 100 women. In the Western Province of the Colony the ratio was only 144, in the Northern Section of Togoland 186.[1]

Conjugal condition. 'Statistics concerning the marital condition of the inhabitants of the Gold Coast are not obtainable.'[2] Opinions on the frequency of marriage and the age at marriage are to be found in the census reports for 1911, 1921, and 1931.

1911. As a general rule women marry at the ages of sixteen to eighteen, and men at the ages of eighteen to twenty. Among the educated classes and in the Coast towns the age is later, women at eighteen and men rarely before twenty-five.[3]

1921. Colony, Eastern Province. The Commissioner reports that the average marriage age for males is 22 and for females 18. The more literate and the small professional classes marry later in life.[4]

Central Province. . . . the Commissioner is of opinion that 'it is still safe to say that almost every man over 19 and every woman over 16 is living in a state of marriage or concubinage'. This is universally true in the Gold Coast . . . .[5]

Western Province. The Commissioner reports that he is inclined to place the marriage age at from seventeen to nineteen years in the case of males and fifteen to eighteen in the case of females. This is a little lower than in the other two

[1] Concerning the Central Province (in which the ratio in 1931 was 180:100) the 1921 census report said: '. . . we find there were 65,670 women of this age and 131,613 children or 2 children to every woman, a low proportion which is not borne out by observation and shews the futility of similar calculations' (*Census Report 1921*, p. 71). Actually a proportion of 2 children to every woman 15 to 45 is extraordinarily high.

The Chief Census Officer 1931 shows the ratio of children to every woman 15 to 45 for each of the 40 districts of the Gold Coast and Togoland and says (*The Gold Coast*, 1931, vol. i, p. 223): 'The figures shown cannot be taken as absolutely accurate but their similarity is most striking. One very noticeable feature is the Navrongo rate, which is apparently inexplicable.' But the differences between the various districts are in fact considerable.

	More than 2·10	2·01 to 2·10	1·91 to 2·00	1·81 to 1·90	1·71 to 1·80	1·61 to 1·70	1·51 to 1·60	1·41 to 1·50	Less than 1·40
Number of districts . .	1	4	4	6	5	8	6	3	3

The districts with the lowest ratios were Navrongo (0·98), Zuarungu (1·05), and Sekondi-Dixcove (1·15).

[2] *The Gold Coast, 1931*, vol. i, p. 168.   [3] *Census Report 1911*, p. 33.
[4] Ibid. *1921*, p. 56.   [5] Ibid., p. 72.

Provinces and the reason is that the people are much more primitive and the standard of living is not so high.[1]

Northern Territories, Southern Province. Females usually marry at puberty, but the marriage age of males is most often later.[2]

Northern Province. Generally speaking males marry at about eighteen, females at puberty.[3]

Togoland. The marriage ages in the Ho District are said to be 18 years among males and 16 for females. In the other parts of the area, males marry when they can afford to, which is probably earlier than 18 amongst the more primitive tribes and females at puberty.[4] One can safely say that every woman is either married or living in concubinage.[5]

1931. The Gold Coast, as is the case in other countries of a similar cultural state, does not regard the bachelor or the spinster with favour; and the religion of animism which is so involved with ancestor-worship practically enforces not only marriage but child-production. It can therefore be safely stated that almost the total adult population of the country is married, in the case of males over the age of 25, and in the case of females about the age of 16 or 17.

No figures are possible to prove this statement, however; it can only be deduced from reasoning and observation.[6]

But, unfortunately, it is impossible to estimate the usual age at marriage and the frequency of marriage by 'reasoning and observation'.[7] There is, moreover, some evidence that numerous adult females are neither married nor living in concubinage.[8]

Opinions concerning the prevalence of polygamy seem also ill founded. The Report on Togoland for 1920–1 stated: 'Polygamy is universal, the average being about two wives to every man.'[9] The 1921 census report said that 'monogamy is not the fashion in West Africa'[10] and spoke of 'the general repugnance with which the African regards monogamy'.[11] The 1931 census report said that the practice of polygamy 'prevails throughout the country and in the conditions of the home-life of these people is almost an essential institution'.[12] But it is obvious that in a country where adult males are as numerous as adult females polygamy cannot be very common if actually almost all men marry young.

[1] *Census Report 1921*, p. 100.

[2] Ibid., p. 131.   [3] Ibid., p. 133.

[4] See also *Report on Togoland 1929*, p. 30: '. . . the women of the tribesi n the Northern Section . . . marry shortly after reaching the age of puberty as also do the men. In fact it is regarded as a disgrace for an adult of either sex to remain unmarried.'

[5] *Census Report 1921*, p. 143. See also *Report on Togoland 1920–1*, pp. 7, 11.

[6] *The Gold Coast, 1931*, vol. i, p. 169.

[7] A member of the House of Commons who apparently used this method said on 9 Dec. 1942: 'Boys of 18 are very different to-day from what they were in my young days. At that time 18 was a common age at which to be married.' (*Parliamentary Debates*, vol. ccclxxxv, col. 1608.) Actually at that time only 2 or 3 per 1,000 males aged 18 in Great Britain were married.

[8] See *Report on Togoland 1929*, p. 29; *1930*, p. 31; *1936*, p. 43; *1937*, p. 34. It may be mentioned incidentally that Administration officers are apt to cause confusion by clinging to the terminology of missionaries who prefer to call concubinage what in reality is polygamy. Actual concubinage is apparently rare in the Gold Coast.

[9] Ibid. *1920–1*, p. 11. See also, for example, ibid. *1924*, p. 10; *1926*, p. 13; *1928*, p. 22; *1930*, p. 29.

[10] *Census Report 1921*, p. 56.   [11] Ibid., p. 72.

[12] *The Gold Coast, 1931*, vol. i, p. 169.

IV. Composition of Non-African Population

1. *Total Non-African Population*

The chapter 'Non-African Population' in the 1931 census report begins as follows:

The total number of non-Africans in the Gold Coast at the time of the census-taking was 3,182. This can be compared with previous censuses as follows:—

	1891	*1901*	*1911*	*1921*	*1931*
Gold Coast Colony . .	428	716	1,389	1,530	2,408
Ashanti	—	—	223	447	624
Northern Territories . .	—	—	13	36	107
Togoland	—	—	—	20	43
	428	716	1,625	2,033	3,182

The increase in the decade is therefore 1,149 or 56·5 per cent and can be accounted for to a large extent by the influx of females and Syrians. The number of the former has risen from 208 to 626, whilst that of the latter from 116 to 570, of whom 180 are females, these two accounting therefore for 692 or 60·2 per cent of the total accretion.[1]

This introduction is not quite accurate.

(1) The figure of 428 for 1891 was not ascertained at the count. The count merely revealed that there were 206 whites (and 1,200 Mulattoes) in the sixteen principal towns.[2] According to the Medical Report for 1891, the 'total number of Europeans resident during the year' consisted of 65 Official and 428 Commercial.[3] The Chief Census Officer, 1931, erroneously assumed that the figure of 428, given for Commercial Europeans, represented the total number of non-Africans. How large the actual number of non-Africans was on the date of the count it is impossible to tell.

(2) The number of Europeans returned in the Colony at the 1901 count was 646. The census report contained the following comment:

No returns . . . are given for Ashanti and the Northern Territories, nor is any reckoning made of officials and others who were travelling in the Colony at the time of the Census. An addition of 53 to 70 might fairly be made to represent this deficiency.[4]

The figure of 716 (646+70), therefore, does not represent the number of non-Africans in the Colony but the number of Europeans in the whole of the Gold Coast. There were at that time also some Syrians in the Colony,[5] who probably were not enumerated.

(3) In 1911 and 1921 the West Indians were reckoned as Africans, in 1931 as non-Africans. The number counted in 1911 is not known.[6] In 1921 there were apparently 38 West Indians,[7] in 1931, 20.[8]

[1] Ibid. p. 254.
[2] See *Census Report 1891*, pp. 16, 134.
[3] See ibid., p. 169.
[4] Ibid. *1901*, p. 7.
[5] In Cape Coast 2 deaths of Syrians (1 male, 1 female) were recorded in 1898 and 1 (female) in 1900; see Gold Coast, *Medical Report 1911*, p. 187.
[6] There were in the Eastern Province of the Colony apparently 7 males and 3 females; see *Census Report 1911*, p. 70.
[7] See ibid. *1921*, pp. 61, 73, 87–93.
[8] In order not to complicate matters I have neglected in the two following paragraphs this difference in the allocation of West Indians.

(4) The numbers of non-Africans enumerated at the censuses of 1921 and 1931 in the Colony were 1,901 and 2,408 respectively. The former figure included 371 persons on board ship, the latter 104. It is misleading to compare the 1921 figure of 1,530 which excludes persons on board ship with the 1931 figure of 2,408 which includes persons on board ship. For the Gold Coast and Togoland the 'increase in the decade' was not 1,149 or 56·5 per cent.; it was 1,045 or 51·4 per cent. excluding shipping population and 778 or 32·4 per cent. including shipping population.

(5) The Census Officer overlooked that there were 44 female Syrians in the country in 1921. The total number of female non-Africans rose from 208 in 1921 to 626 in 1931 and the number of male Syrians from 72 to 390. The increase of females and Syrians, therefore, accounted for 736 (not 692) or 70·4 per cent. of the total accretion.

From the 1911 census on it is possible to group the non-Africans according to sex and nationality. The development in the Colony may be summarized as follows:[1]

Nationality	1911			1921			1931		
	Males	Females	Total	Males	Females	Total	Males	Females	Total
European	1,242	97	1,339	1,311	143	1,454	1,491	348	1,839
Syrian	31	15	46	42	22	64	282	114	396
Other	4	—	4	12	—	12	49	—	49
Total .	1,277	112	1,389	1,365	165	1,530	1,822	462	2,284

It appears that in the Colony the number of non-Africans increased from 1,389 in 1911 to 1,530 in 1921, and to 2,284 in 1931. The figures for Syrians were 46, 64, and 396 respectively. The few other non-Europeans were in 1911 all Turks, in 1921 all Indians, and in 1931 nearly all Indians.

In Ashanti the number of non-Africans rose from 223 in 1911 to 447 in 1921 and to 624 in 1931. In 1911 all non-Africans were of European nationality.[2] But in 1921 there were 52 Syrians (30 male, 22 female),[3] and 2 (male) Indians. By 1931 the number of non-European non-Africans had increased to 176 (mostly Syrians).

In the Northern Territories the number of non-Africans rose from 13 in 1911 to 36 in 1921 and to 107 in 1931. In 1911 and 1921 all non-Africans were of European nationality; in 1931 they included 8 Syrians and 1 Indian.

In the Gold Coast the number of non-Africans rose from 1,625 in 1911 to 2,013 in 1921, and to 3,015 in 1931. The figures for Syrians were 46, 116, and 570 respectively. The few other non-Europeans were in 1911 all Turks, in 1921 all Indians, and in 1931 nearly all Indians.

In Togoland the number of non-Africans rose from 20 in 1921 to 43 in 1931. They were all of European nationality.

A more detailed comparison of the returns of the last three censuses is hampered by the fact that the report for 1911 does not show the non-

[1] See Census Report 1911, p. 73; ibid. 1921, pp. 55, 68, 99; The Gold Coast, 1931, vol. ii, p. 23. Figures exclude West Indians and persons on board ship.
[2] See Census Report 1911, p. 75.   [3] See ibid. 1921, p. 119.

African population of Ashanti by sex, and that neither this report nor the report for 1921 give any data concerning the number of non-African children. I must, therefore, confine myself to a very few supplementary remarks.[1]

There were in 1921 in the Gold Coast and Togoland 1,480 British males, 345 other non-African males, and 208 non-African females. The corresponding figures for 1931 were 1,472, 963, and 623. While the number of British males remained stationary, the numbers of other males and of females trebled. The increase in the number of non-British males by 618 was half due to the increase in the number of Syrians from 72 to 390. The increase in the number of females by 415 was largely due to the increase in the number of British females from 149 to 371; the Syrian females increased from 44 to 180, the other females from 15 to 72.

TABLE 16. *Non-African Population by Nationality and Sex, Gold Coast and Togoland, 1921 and 1931*[1]

Nationality	1921		1931		1931						1931	
	Gold Coast		Gold Coast		Colony		Ashanti		Northern Territories		Togoland[2]	
	M.	F.	M.	F.	M.	F.	M.	F.	M.	F.	M.	F.
British.	1,461	148	1,455	370	1,118	298	270	54	67	18	17	1
Austrians	—	—	1	1	1	1	—	—	—	—	—	—
Belgians	4	1	1	—	1	—	—	—	—	—	—	1
Bulgarians	—	—	1	—	1	—	—	—	—	—	—	—
Danes .	3	—	2	—	1	—	1	—	—	—	—	—
Dutch .	7	2	29	5	24	5	3	—	2	—	9	—
French	73	6	137	16	107	14	29	2	1	—	1	3
Germans	1	1	63	13	47	10	16	3	—	—	5	5
Greeks.	7	—	24	2	`22	2	2	—	—	—	—	—
Italians	59	—	98	5	64	4	26	1	8	—	—	—
Lithuanians .	1	—	—	—	—	—	—	—	—	—	—	—
Norwegians .	1	—	—	—	—	—	—	—	—	—	—	—
Rumanians .	—	—	1	—	—	—	1	—	—	—	—	—
Russians	—	—	1	—	1	—	—	—	—	—	—	—
Spaniards	—	—	1	—	—	—	—	—	1	—	—	—
Swedes	—	—	1	—	1	—	—	—	—	—	—	—
Swiss .	78	2	125	16	91	10	33	6	1	—	—	—
Americans .	25	3	13	4	12	4	1	—	—	—	1	—
Total Europeans .	1,720	163	1,953	432	1,491	348	382	66	80	18	33	10
Arabs .	—	—	1	—	1	—	—	—	—	—	—	—
Chinese	—	—	1	—	1	—	—	—	—	—	—	—
Indians	14	—	56	—	46	—	9	—	1	—	—	—
Syrians	72	44	390	180	282	114	100	66	8	—	—	—
Turks	—	—	1	1	1	—	—	1	—	—	—	—
West Indians	..	..	17	3	17	3	—	—	—	—	—	—
Total Non-Europeans.	86	44	466	184	348	117	109	67	9	—	—	—
Total .	1,806[3]	207[3]	2,419	616	1,839	465	491	133	89	18	33	10

[1] See *Census Report 1921*, p. 137, Appendices, p. 20; *The Gold Coast, 1931*, vol. i, pp. 255–6, vol. ii, p. 23 This table does not include the maritime population, which comprised in 1921, 371 non-Africans and in 1931, 104 (male) non-Africans (68 British, 1 Dane, 1 German, 2 Portuguese, and 32 Americans).
[2] In 1921 all non-Africans (19 males, 1 female) were British.　　　　　[3] Excluding West Indians.

Of the 138 children enumerated in 1931, as many as 128 were Syrians.[2] Of the 531 persons between 15 and 25 years, 164 were British, 164 Syrians, and 203 of other nationalities. Of the 2,389 persons over 25 as many as 1,672 were British, only 278 were Syrians, and 439 were of other nationalities.

[1] All figures exclude West Indians.　　　[2] The 50 children from 5 to 15 were all Syrians.

Of the 2,380 non-African males over 15 years, 1,181 were unmarried, 1,157 married, 33 widowed, and 9 divorced. The percentage of married was 49. Of the 560 non-African females over 15 years 118 were unmarried, 425 married, and 17 widowed. The percentage of married was 76.[1]

Most non-Africans live in the Colony where in 1931 they constituted 0·15 per cent. of the total population. In Ashanti the proportion was 0·11 per cent., in the Northern Territories and in Togoland only 0·015 per cent.

No data are available concerning the country of birth.

TABLE 17. *Non-African Population by Nationality and Age, Gold Coast and Togoland, 1931*[1]

Nationality	Up to 15 years	15 to 25 years	25 to 35 years	35 to 45 years	45 to 55 years	Over 55 years	Total
British	7	164	766	620	258	28	1,843
Austrians	—	—	1	1	—	—	2
Belgians	—	—	1	1	—	—	2
Bulgarians. . . .	—	—	—	1	—	—	1
Danes	—	—	1	1	—	—	2
Dutch	—	3	32	6	2	—	43
French	1	70	59	16	10	1	157
Germans	—	25	23	12	17	9	86
Greeks	—	2	15	7	1	1	26
Italians	—	8	55	32	7	1	103
Rumanians	—	—	—	—	1	—	1
Russians	—	—	—	1	—	—	1
Spaniards	—	—	1	—	—	—	1
Swedes	—	—	—	1	—	—	1
Swiss	2	59	59	16	3	2	141
Americans. . . .	—	2	6	8	2	—	18
Total Europeans . .	10	333	1,019	723	301	42	2,428
Arabs	—	—	—	—	—	1	1
Chinese	—	—	—	1	—	—	1
Indians	—	32	11	8	3	2	56
Syrians	128	164	145	89	30	14	570
Turks	—	2	—	—	—	—	2
West Indians . . .	—	3	4	3	8	2	20
Total non-Europeans . .	128	201	160	101	41	19	650
Total	138	534	1,179	824	342	61	3,078
Gold Coast . . .	138	528	1,158	814	338	59	3,035
Togoland	—	6	21	10	4	2	43

[1] See *The Gold Coast, 1931*, vol. ii, pp. 25, 30. This table does not include the maritime population.

2. *European Population*

Available data on the numbers of Europeans in the period from 1846 till the end of the century may be summarized as shown opposite.[2]

[1] See *The Gold Coast, 1931*, vol. ii, p. 29. These figures include West Indians.
[2] See *State of Colonial Possessions 1846*, p. 146, *1847*, p. 203, *1858*, Part II, p. 21; Gold Coast Colony, *Blue Book 1849*, pp. 78–9, *1850*, pp. 76–7, *1851*, pp. 82–3, *1852*, pp. 84–5, *1853*, pp. 79–80, *1854*, p. 110, *1855*, p. 117, *1860*, p. 136, *1861*, pp. 110, 133, *1867*, p. 96, *1868*, p. 96, *1869*, p. 96, *1870*, p. 106, *1871*, p. 112, *1872*, p. 124; *Statistical Tables Colonial Possessions 1860*, p. 420; Gold Coast Colony, 'Medical Report 1891', quoted in *Census Report 1891*, p. 169; *Medical Report 1895*, pp. 15, 24, *1896*, pp. 12, 21, '*1897*', pp. 171, 191, 204, *1899*, pp. 2–3; *Colonial Reports, Gold Coast Colony 1898*, p. 26, *1900*, p. 23.

Year	Males	Females	Year	Males	Females	Year	Officials	Non-officials
1846	34	3	31 Dec. 1854	28	3	1891	65	428[8]
1847	33	7	31 Dec. 1855	26	2	1895[9]	224	545
1849	30	2	1858	57[1]	13[2]	1896[9]	183	615
1850	27	4	1860	57[3]	13[4]	1897[9]	160	362[10]
1851	30	3	1861	61[5]	14	1898[11]	122	230
1852	40	1	1867–9	100[6]		1899	166	400[12]
1853	40	2	1870–2	70[7]		1900	468	1,512

[1] Including 18 missionaries.   [2] Including 12 females belonging to missions.

[3] '3 are carrying business on their own account and 6 are Agents for European Houses. . . . The other Europeans are Missionaries and the officers Civil and Military of the Government.'

[4] Including 11 wives of missionaries.

[5] 22 officers civil and military; 13 merchants, agents of mercantile houses, and clerks; 6 tradesmen; 3 farmers; 17 missionaries.

[6] 'The European population may be estimated at about 100; of these about 20 are in the Civil and Military Service of the Government, about 10 or 15 Merchants or Agents of European Houses and their Clerks, and the remainder Missionaries.' (I suspect that the number of missionaries was overestimated.)

[7] '22 are in the Civil and Military service of the Government; 16 are Merchants or Agents of European Houses & their Clerks; and the remainder, Missionaries.'

[8] Commercial.   [9] 'Total Strength.'   [10] 'Estimated.'

[11] 'In a constantly changing population it is out of the question to keep accurate statistics. The above figures do not include European officials employed in the Northern Territories, who number at least 25, neither does it include prospectors who are constantly moving about the Colony and adjoining territories.'

[12] 'Estimated . . . the actual number of Non-Official Europeans in the Colony is unknown.'

The enormous increase in the number of Europeans in 1900 was due to the development of gold-mining,[1] but the figures for this year are apparently still more uncertain than for prior years.[2] From 1902 on the figures become more detailed and somewhat more accurate.

This is the first year in which an accurate return of the Europeans resident in the Colony, Ashanti, and the Northern Territories, has been obtained.[3]

But the data for non-officials remained apparently incomplete.

1903. The return of the population, deaths and invaliding, though fairly accurate, is not quite complete, as some companies failed to send in their returns although frequently written to for them; and many of the mines have been shut down during the year.[4]

1909. The European population recorded was somewhat under the previous year although an increase in officials occurred. The returns under Mining Companies showed a decrease on the previous year of 174 but the records under this head are always unreliable and some difficulty is experienced in obtaining information.

The number under Mining Companies including other Concessions is probably very much higher than represented.[5]

[1] See Report on Mines Department 1903–4, p. 3:
'In 1900, as the result of the South African output of gold being temporarily stopped and also owing to the reports of the extraordinary richness of the reefs in the Colony, a tremendous rush for Concessions started and continued until the end of 1901.

'During these two years Concession-hunters wandered over the country taking up every bit of land in districts where old workings had been discovered.'

[2] The figure for officials seems extraordinarily high. For 1901 the 'total strength' is given as 188 (see Medical Report 1901, p. 11; Colonial Reports, Gold Coast 1901, p. 31). No figures of non-officials seem to have been published for 1901. (The census figures for 1901 were incomplete.)

[3] Medical Report 1902, p. 13.   [4] Ibid. 1903, p. 16.   [5] Ibid. 1909, p. 6.

1910. The strength of the first group [Government Officials] is steadily increasing year by year; that of the others, however, varies considerably and much difficulty is experienced in obtaining as accurate figures regarding it as are available in the case of Government Officers. The system in vogue is unsatisfactory. It depends for its success on the courtesy of individuals; but, although their courtesy is not called in question, such a method of obtaining statistics is bound to prove faulty. A suggestion was recently put forward that arrivals and departures other than those over the seaboard of the Colony might be regarded as a negligible quantity, and that what is required is an accurate record of embarkations and disembarkations. This could be provided by the agents of the different Shipping Companies or the Pursers of ships landing and embarking passengers; in existing conditions, the required information is only obtainable through the courtesy of these officials. It has been suggested that the question of some form of legal enactment should be considered.[1]

The data for 1902–44 are summarized in Table 18. The official reports show the average number of resident Government Officials present and also the total number of resident Government Officials including those on leave. Until 1941 the military were apparently counted as Government Officials. The figures for non-officials refer to the total number including those on leave, but data are available also for the average number of mining employees. Such persons as contractors, medical practitioners, and lawyers, and in fact all breadwinners who were not either employed by the Government or by a mining company or by a mission were probably counted as 'employees of trading firms'. Wives of non-officials were probably grouped with their husbands. But the wives of officials were apparently included among the females of the group 'employees of trading firms',[2] so that the females of this group probably comprise the female employees of trading firms, and the wives (and daughters) of all persons not employed by a mining company or a mission.

The total number of resident Europeans (including those on leave) fluctuated in 1902–10 between 1,692 and 1,953 and rose to 2,645 in 1914. It was lower again during the First World War, but jumped to 3,182 in 1919. In 1920–34 it fluctuated between 2,818 and 3,693 and rose thereafter to 4,975 in 1938, but declined to 4,788 in 1939, 4,287 in 1940, 3,729 in 1941,[3] 3,467 in 1942, 3,377 in 1943, and 3,147 in 1944. The number of Government Officials increased until 1914 and, after a setback during the First World War, continued to rise until 1930; it declined thereafter and never again reached the level of 1926–30. The number of commercial employees fluctuated very much; it was particularly large immediately after the First World War, in the late 1920s, and before the outbreak of the Second World War. The number of mining employees was very large early in this century and again before the outbreak of the First World War; it was low from 1915 to 1933 but rose enormously in the following years. The number

[1] *Medical Report 1910*, p. 10.
[2] Ibid. *1931–2* (p. 13) and *1932–3* (p. 12), it is explicitly stated: 'Wives of officials appear under Merchants, Females.'
[3] *Medical Report 1941* says (p. 2): 'In 1941, the total resident was 3,729 as compared with 4,287 in 1940, i.e., a decrease of 558. This decrease is due to the non-inclusion of military figures and the opening-up of leave.' But this explanation is not convincing. The number of Government Officials decreased only by 82, and persons on leave were supposed to be included in the figures of residents.

TABLE 18. *European Population by Occupation, Gold Coast (and Togoland), 1902–44*[1]

Period[2]	Average Government officials	Average mining employees	Total Government officials M.	F.	Total Employees of trading firms M.	F.	Total Employees of mining companies M.	F.	Total Missionaries M.	F.	Total
1902	..	..	286		373		778		96		1,830[3]
1903	..	..	326		335		1,043		92		1,796
1904	..	611	351		305		1,222		75		1,953
1905	..	504	388		272		1,157		94		1,911
1906	..	576	399		255		992		119		1,765
1907	..	538	370		538		883		86		1,877
1908	..	590	413		434		759		162		1,768
1909	..	500	438		574		585		118		1,715
1910	..	672	475		422		660		135		1,692
1911	..	770	566		605		922		152		2,245
1912	510	712	586		668		953		160		2,367
1913	573	564	740		796		928		126		2,590
1914	646	537	768		733		1,020		124		2,645
1915	631	475	700		677		481		148		2,006
1916	468	450	589		671		642		109		2,011
1917	489	415	597		718		718		139		2,172
1918	413	336	515		681		578		49		1,823
1919	522	292	653		1,902		561		66		3,182
1920	620	273	775		1,506		465		72		2,818
1921	612	266	768		1,556		541		74		2,939
Jan. to Mar. 1922	692	279	741		1,565		518		77		2,901
1922–3	719	279	979		1,410		521		88		2,998
1923–4	689	281	994		1,425		527		97		3,043
1924–5	680	286	846		1,482		434		104		2,866
1925–6	761	266	994		1,529		469		112		3,104
1926–7	783	269	1,046		1,861		440		134		3,481
1927–8	835	268	1,202		1,737		486		152		3,577
1928–9	881	284	1,227	53	1,339	373	454	3	103	56	3,608
1929–30	972	286	1,256	67	1,313	410	451	16	112	68	3,693
1930–1	936	267	1,242	71	1,139	380	438	15	135	88	3,508
1931–2	819	232	1,076		935	430	357	14	142	93	3,047
1932–3	639	261	941		903	407	428	22	155	103	2,959
1933–4	617	365	857		885	474	658	24	146	101	3,145
1934	599	623	847		909	502	928	24	174	107	3,491
1935	594	839	832		957	543	1,306	57	175	99	3,969
1936	607	908	865		1,073	549	1,446	95	180	120	4,328
1937	632	977	901		1,205	660	1,564	119	199	143	4,791
1938	690	1,023	931		1,288	712	1,586	140	193	125	4,975
1939	..	..	926		..	..	..	..	..	..	4,788
1940	..	..	964		..	..	..	..	..	..	4,287
1941	..	..	882[4]		..	..	1,280		..	..	3,729[4]
1942	..	..	850[4]		..	..	..		..	..	3,467[4]
1943	..	..	817[4]		..	..	..	..	..	..	3,377[4]
1944	..	..	826[4]		..	..	..	..	..	..	3,147[4]

[1] See *Medical Report 1909*, pp. 6–8, *1910*, pp. 9, 11, *1911*, pp. 7, 10, *1912*, pp. 10, 13, *1913*, pp. 11, 13, *1914*, pp. 13–14, *1915*, p. 11, *1916*, pp. 9–10, *1917*, pp. 8, 10, *1918*, pp. 20–1, *1919*, pp. 8–9, *1920*, pp. 7–8, *1921*, pp. 7, 9, *1922–3*, pp. 6, 8, 37–8, *1923–4*, pp. 7–8, *1924–5*, pp. 10–11, *1925–6*, pp. 9–10, *1926–7*, p. 14, *1927–8*, p. 18, *1928–9*, pp. 15, 17, *1929–30*, pp. 17–19, *1930–1*, pp. 17, 19, *1931–2*, pp. 11, 13, *1932–3*, pp. 11, 13, *1933–4*, pp. 12, 14, *1934*, pp. 7, 9, *1935*, pp. 9–10, *1936*, pp. 11–12, *1937*, pp. 9–10, *1938*, pp. 9–10, *1939*, p. 4, *1940*, p. 5, *1941*, pp. 2, 5, *1942*, p. 4, *1943*, p. 5, *1944*, p. 5; *Report on the Mining Department 1904*, p. 5, *1905*, p. 14, *1906*, p. 15, *1907*, p. 14, *1908*, p. 13, *1909*, p. 13, *1910*, p. 13, *1911*, p. 14, *1912*, p. 13, *1913*, p. 12, *1914*, p. 12, *1915*, p. 10, *1916*, p. 10, *1931–2*, p. 7, *1938–9*, p. 16.

[2] The data for 1902–21 and 1939–44 refer to calendar years; those for 1922–3 to 1933–4 refer to the years ending 31 Mar.; those for 1934–8 refer to calendar years, except the figures of average mining employees which refer to the years ending 31 Mar. 1935–31 Mar. 1939.

[3] Including 297 Gold Coast Railway.   [4] Excluding military.

of missionaries (including their families) fluctuated very much until 1918 when it was extremely low; it increased steadily in the following years and has been larger since 1928 than in any prior year.

The censuses throw some light on the nationality of the European population. The results may be summarized as follows:[1]

Year	British	French	German	Italian	Swiss	American	Other	Total
1911	1,290	18	154	61	17	16	19	1,575
1921	1,629	79	2	59	80	28	26	1,903
1931	1,843	157	86	103	141	18	80	2,428

The proportion of British rose from 82 per cent. in 1911 to 86 per cent. in 1921, but dropped to 76 per cent. in 1931. The rise in 1921 was due to the disappearance of the Germans, the drop in 1931 to a considerable influx of foreigners of various nationalities, particularly Germans and French. The percentage of British among male Europeans was 85 in 1921 and 74 in 1931; the percentage of British among female Europeans was 91 in 1921 and 84 in 1931. Of the Europeans between 15 and 25 years enumerated in 1931 only 49 per cent. were British, of those over 25 years 80 per cent.

The Colonial Office has published for each year from 1930 to 1938 the number of non-native officials by sex and age. The results are summarized in Table 19.

TABLE 19. *Non-Native Officials by Sex and Age, Gold Coast and Togoland, 1930–8*[1]

Date	20–24 years		25–29 years		30–34 years		35–39 years		40–44 years		45–49 years		50–54 years		55– years		Age unknown		Total	
1 Jan.	M.	F.	M.	F.	M.	F.	M.	F.	M.	F.	M.	F.	M.	F.	M.	F.	M.	F.	M.	F.
1930	53	3	194	16	243	25	246	12	210	6	130	2	55	1	12	1	4	2	1,147	68
1931	46	1	170	13	212	23	262	18	197	8	141	1	47	2	15	1	1	1	1,091	68
1932	26	1	157	11	175	21	239	16	200	11	124	3	51	2	14	—	—	—	986	65
1933	16	1	135	4	163	18	194	10	159	12	111	5	39	1	6	—	—	—	823	51
1934	9	—	116	4	170	20	160	13	159	10	104	5	41	2	7	—	—	—	766	54
1935	8	—	100	4	162	14	161	18	157	11	122	6	44	—	7	1	—	—	761	54
1936	8	—	89	5	154	10	155	19	177	12	120	8	52	—	4	1	—	—	759	55
1937	20	—	69	5	160	7	157	19	192	14	136	7	59	2	6	1	—	—	799	55
1938	25	—	87	7	142	8	175	16	181	9	126	6	64	1	9	—	—	—	809	47

[1] See *West Africa, Vital Statistics of Non-Native Officials 1930*, p. 1, to *1938*, p. 1.

V. BIRTH AND DEATH REGISTRATION

1. *The Colony*

For a very long time the introduction of birth or death registration was considered to be impossible everywhere in the Colony owing to 'the superstition of the natives',[2] and the only available birth and death data were the scanty figures furnished, quite irregularly, by the various religious bodies.

1881. No Act exists for the compulsory registration of births, marriages, and deaths. The Government have to look, with what results the foregoing statistics

[1] See *Census Report 1911*, pp. 39, 73, 75; ibid. *1921*, Appendices, p. 20; *The Gold Coast, 1931*, vol. ii, p. 23. Figures for 1921 and 1931 include Togoland.

[2] See, for example, *State of Colonial Possessions 1867*, Part II, p. 20.

will show, to the superintendents of the different religious bodies for information, so far as each for his own flock will supply.[1]

The possibility of establishing native birth and death registration was apparently suggested for the first time in 1886 by Dr. Rowland, Axim, and by Dr. Waldron, Quittah. Dr. Rowland said:

As there is not any system of registration of births and deaths it is impossible to estimate the increase of population or the mortality. I think that the Inspector of Nuisance might act as registrar.[2]

Dr. Waldron's report has not been published. But we have the following comment by the Chief Medical Officer of the Colony:

In Dr. Waldron's Sanitary Report for Quittah he complains of the absence of what we shall never be able to obtain on this coast, viz., reliable factors for the preparation of statistics showing the mortality amongst the natives. The Registrar of Births and Deaths at Lagos pretends to supply such data, but I analysed his figures for two years, and found them utterly incorrect, and therefore, of course, dangerously misleading. Dr. Waldron advocates enforced registration. It would not succeed, and for this reason, that there is nothing in the world natives abhor, deprecate, and actually resist so much as official inquiry into the *arcana sacra* of their domestic life.[3]

The number of cases treated at the surgery during the year was 1,529; of these the pauper or out-door patients numbered 546. Out of this large number only six deaths are recorded, and 10 per 1,000 of the whole population. This surely must be merely approximative, as it is literally impossible to ascertain the true death rate of a people who practise secret domiciliary sepulture, as all the tribes on the coast do. In the other villages of the district Dr. Waldron was informed that the mortality ranged from 30–35 per 1,000. That is more like the figure he would have found at Quittah had he the means of ascertaining correct data.[4]

Governor Griffith was likewise of the opinion that registration was not practicable. In a Dispatch dated 9 August 1886 he wrote:

Dr. Waldron advocates enforced registration of births and deaths, but I do not consider it is practicable at present. The information which would be afforded by a system of reliable registration would be valuable, no doubt, but the matter must lie over until the Colony is more advanced in intelligence upon this and other questions of equal, if not greater, importance and value.[5]

A few months later, the Chief Medical Officer said:

As I have often before remarked, it is utterly impossible to obtain any reliable information respecting the death rate and still more so of the amount and nature of sickness which prevails amongst the people on this coast. Hence, with the exception of those treated in hospital . . . , I leave them completely out of consideration, and simply because incorrect statistics, like those of the Registrar of Births and Deaths of Lagos, are worse than useless—they are misleading.[6]

In the following year (22 July 1887) he wrote:

As I have often stated in other reports, both here and at Lagos, it is utterly impossible to obtain anything approaching reliable data respecting either the sick or death rate of the native population of the towns on this coast.

The people have the strongest possible repugnance against the 'white man's' interference in their domestic affairs, and especially against his knowing anything concerning the sickness and deaths occurring in their families. They even endeavour

---

[1] *Colonial Possessions Reports 1880–2*, p. 114.   [2] Ibid. *1884–6*, p. 120.

[3] Ibid., p. 111. See also ibid., p. 109.   [4] Ibid., p. 112.

[5] Ibid., p. 106.   [6] Ibid., p. 249.

to conceal cases of small-pox, preferring to treat the patients at home to sending them to the contagious diseases hospital. Even the inspector of nuisance or other native official who may be instructed to make inquiries on this subject will not obtain anything more than partial information. To compile statistics from such data would be to follow the example of the registrar of births and deaths of Lagos, whose figures, when I analysed them in 1883–4, made Lagos appear to be as healthy as Southsea or Brighton; his death rate was about 17 per 1,000.[1]

But before another year had passed, death registration, on a very limited scale to be sure, was established. The 'Cemeteries Ordinance, 1888'[2] provided that the Governor 'may by proclamation in the *Gazette* declare any Government Cemetery to be a Public Cemetery for any town or place' and 'may appoint a Registrar of Deaths for any town or place where a Public Cemetery has been declared', who 'shall keep a register of all burials in such Public Cemetery'. Any person 'desirous of interring a corpse in a Public Cemetery' was to furnish the Registrar of Deaths with the particulars required to be registered. Public Cemeteries were thereupon proclaimed in Christiansborg (20 April 1888), Accra (1 September 1888), Ada (3 January 1890), and Big Ada (22 May 1890).[3]

The Ordinance of 1888 was repealed by the 'Cemeteries Ordinance, 1891'[4] which was amended twice.[5] The Ordinance of 1891 extended the provisions of the 1888 Ordinance to private cemeteries inasmuch as (1) the registrar of deaths appointed for any town or place where a public cemetery has been declared shall 'keep a register of all burials in any public or private cemetery in or adjacent to such town or place' and that 'any person desirous of interring a corpse in a public or private cemetery in or adjacent to any town or place for which a registrar of deaths has been appointed, shall furnish such registrar' with the particulars required to be registered. Public cemeteries were proclaimed in Cape Coast (31 December 1894 and 1 July 1899), Axim (23 March 1899 and 1 April 1905), Saltpond (8 September 1899), Tarquah (30 June 1903), Elmina (20 July 1903), Kpong (1 September 1906), Secondee (21 December 1907), Winnebah (5 February 1909), Bato and Dodowah (16 February 1909),[6] Quittah (5 July 1910), Labadi (13 August 1911), Akuse (24 August 1911), Brewe, Axim (4 December 1911), Aburi (21 March 1912), Dunkwa (16 April 1912).[7] In the first decade following the issue of the 1888 Ordinance Registrars of Deaths were appointed, therefore, in only 5 towns, in the second decade in 6 towns, but in 1909–12 in 8 towns.

[1] Gold Coast, *Sanitary and Medical Reports for 1886 and 1887*, pp. 32–3.

[2] No. 7 of 1888 (9 Mar.), 'An Ordinance to provide for interments in cemeteries and to prohibit intramural sepulture', Gold Coast, *Government Gazette*, 31 Mar. 1888, pp. 75–7.

[3] See *Ordinances of the Gold Coast Colony in Force 1898*, vol. ii, p. 1144.

[4] No. 9 of 1891 (6 Aug.), Gold Coast, *Government Gazette*, 31 Aug. 1891, pp. 302–8.

[5] See Ordinances No. 16 of 1892 (14 Nov.), ibid., 30 Nov. 1892, pp. 413–16, and No. 4 of 1909 (15 Feb.), ibid., 13 Mar. 1909, pp. 135–7. The Ordinance as it stood after the enactment of the Ordinance of 1909 is reprinted in *Ordinances of the Gold Coast Colony in Force 1909*, vol. i, pp. 646–55. In accordance with this Ordinance the Governor, on 19 Mar. 1892, made Rules as to Burials in Cemeteries, Gold Coast, *Government Gazette*, 31 May 1892, p. 144, reprinted in *Ordinances of the Gold Coast Colony in Force 1898*, vol. ii, p. 1144. See also 'Rules for the Regulation of Cemeteries', 31 May 1892, Gold Coast, *Government Gazette*, 31 May 1892, p. 148.

[6] See *Ordinances of the Gold Coast Colony in Force 1909*, vol. i, p. 656.

[7] See *Laws of the Gold Coast Colony in Force 1919*, vol. iii, pp. 154–5.

Figures of burials furnished by the Registrars of Deaths were given in
the annual Blue Books, from 1890 on, and also, sometimes, in the Medical
Reports, but for about a decade after the enactment of the Ordinance of
1888 no comment on the adequacy of registration seems to have been
published. However, in his report for 1899 the Acting Chief Medical
Officer said:

No death rate can be calculated for Native Officials or Natives, owing to lack of
information; but an attempt at an estimate can be given for Accra, assuming that
there are 20,000 inhabitants, the burial rate was 731, gives 36.5 per thousand as the
death rate, which is probably far below the real.

Attempts are being made so that in future more correct estimate of the natives'
death rate may be given.[1]

The Registrar of Deaths for Accra apparently did not share the opinion
that the records were incomplete since he thought that the figures
indicated 'better sanitary conditions and surroundings'.[2] But though in
1900 the number of burials rose to 901 he now said that the figure did not
'necessarily represent the real number of deaths'.[3]

The question was discussed anew in the Medical Report for 1907.

There is no registration of births or deaths, therefore native vital statistics are
scientifically valueless. At some of the larger coast towns records are kept of the
number of permits issued for burials in public cemeteries, but these records do not
give reliable information as to the number of deaths which occur, and they provide
no information whatever as to their cause; the latter is obtained from the hospital
records which only show a fraction of the actual death rate. . . .

A complete registration scheme can hardly be made applicable except to the more
important towns; but in the absence of the all-important information which would
be derived therefrom, it will not be possible to estimate the extent of any general
or special mortality, an accurate knowledge of which would direct endeavour to
combat and suppress disease. Such a result can only be arrived at by compulsory
registration of the cause of death; and in the present state of civilization of the
natives generally, this would not, as a rule, be possible except in the situations I have
indicated above. Elsewhere, for the present, at least, the most that can be hoped
for is a simple record of numbers. Registration of births is also important and should
not present many difficulties. The whole question is occupying the attention of the
Colonial Government, and it is probable that in the near future, measures, as fully
comprehensive as are possible in the existing circumstances, will be adopted. The
work involved should form part of the duties of the various Medical Officers of
Health.[4]

The Medical Report for 1908 showed that the 'Burial Permit Records
for Accra, Ada, Cape Coast, Elmina, Sekondi and Saltpond' gave as totals
in the seven years 1902–8 1,781, 1,718, 1,405, 1,712, 1,361, 1,517, and 1,159
respectively, and it made the following comment on the low figure for
1908:

It will be seen that . . . the number of deaths . . . obtained from the Registrar of
Burial permits for . . . six towns in the Colony is considerably less than in any
preceding year since 1902 even with the addition of 157, the number of bodies
buried under special plague precautions by the Medical Authorities.[5]

[1] 'Medical Report 1899', p. 255.   [2] Ibid., p. 293.
[3] *Medical Report 1900*, Appendix 'Public Cemeteries', p. 3.   [4] Ibid. *1907*, p. 6.
[5] Ibid. *1908*, p. 10. This comment is particularly interesting as it shows that the burial permit
records did not even include all burials sanctioned by the authorities.

The burial statistics were compiled apparently with special care in Cape Coast. Registration started here in 1895. The data for 1895–1911 may be summarized as follows:[1]

Year	Natives	Europeans	Syrians	Year	Natives	Europeans	Syrians	Year	Natives	Europeans	Syrians
1895	223	14	—	1901	501	23	—	1907	241	1	—
1896	348	11	—	1902	444	12	—	1908	258	1	—
1897	263	10	—	1903	397	7	—	1909	267	—	—
1898	324	5	2	1904	285	2	—	1910	327	—	—
1899	317	7	—	1905	267	—	1	1911	266	2	—
1900	461	14	1	1906	255	—	—				

The figures show great fluctuations, but this does not necessarily mean that they are misleading. Quite apart from the fact that mortality may have varied considerably, the population itself fluctuated very much. According to the enumeration returns the number of natives increased from 11,575 in 1891 to 28,948 in 1901 and decreased to 11,269 in 1911.[2]

Cape Coast was in its zenith towards the close of the nineteenth century, and there is no doubt that the population has much diminished. The number of ruins in the town . . . alone bears this out. One meets with a great many cases where members of families have left Cape Coast to earn their livelihood. Merchants complain of loss of trade.[3]

Of the 268 people buried in 1911, 28 were under 1 year and 42 between 1 and 5 years; females between 15 and 35 numbered 37 (males of this age only 20).

The Medical Officer of Health, Cape Coast, in his report for 1911, made the following comment:

There is no compulsory death notification, but in every case of burial in any cemetery, in or adjacent to the town, authority for such burial must first be obtained.[4]

Placing the control of death registration—as far as it exists—under the Medical Officer of Health is likely to greatly assist the early detection of epidemics and

---

[1] See *Medical Report 1911*, p. 187.

[2] See *Census Report 1891*, p. 134; *1911*, p. 50.   [3] *Medical Report 1911*, p. 185.

[4] Professor W. J. Simpson, in 1909, had described the position as follows: 'In the Gold Coast towns there is no compulsory registration of deaths. It is only since the outbreak of plague that every death in Accra has to be reported and the deceased examined by a medical man before a permit for burial is given. Previous to this there was registration when burial was to take place in particular cemeteries, but there was no compulsion to bury in these cemeteries. In other towns this system still exists. Burials often take place outside the towns in the bush.' (*Report on Sanitary Matters in various West African Colonies and the Outbreak of Plague in the Gold Coast*, p. 13.) Professor Simpson, however, it seems to me, overstated the differences between the legal position in Accra and other towns. Under 'The Infectious Diseases Ordinance, 1908' (No. 2 of 1908, 13 Apr., Gold Coast, *Government Gazette*, 11 May 1908, pp. 424–32; reprinted in *Ordinances of the Gold Coast Colony in Force 1909*, vol. iii, pp. 1717–24) the Governor, on 5 June 1908, had issued the following 'Rules for the Removal of Sick Persons and Corpses at Accra' (Gold Coast, *Government Gazette*, 5 June 1908, p. 514; reprinted in *Ordinances of the Gold Coast Colony in Force 1909*, vol. iii, p. 1732):

'1. No sick person shall be removed from within the municipal area of Accra without permission in writing from a Government Medical Officer.

'2. No corpse shall be removed from within the said municipal area without similar permission.

'3. No authority for burial shall be given by the Registrar of Deaths for Accra unless the application be accompanied by a certificate from a Government Medical Officer as to the cause of death.'

It can hardly be said that these Rules established compulsory notification of deaths in Accra. Nor can it be said that there was registration in other towns only when burial was to take place in particular cemeteries. Registration was prescribed when burial was to take place in any cemetery in or adjacent to the town.

fatal infectious diseases. In order that any unusual mortality or, as far as possible, any death of a suspicious nature may be known at the earliest possible moment, the Assistant Registrar of Deaths sends daily a report of registered deaths to the Medical Officer of Health.[1]

The majority of natives do not know their exact ages, but in a town such as Cape Coast it is possible to arrive at a fairly correct solution, in most cases from historical associations, by comparison with the known age of some relative or otherwise. The Assistant Registrar has instructions to obtain all ages as approximately as possible.

One notices the very small number of recorded deaths of infants. There is no birth registration, hence the number of births is not known, but common observation in the streets of Cape Coast makes it evident that a large number of women are pregnant. The cause is evidently not due to a low birth rate. On the other hand it is almost impossible to accept the theory that the infant mortality is low. The only remaining explanation is that deaths of infants are not registered. It is difficult to get definite evidence of deaths of infants when not registered; for, although registration is not compulsory and it is no offence to bury a body in the bush, provided the place is not 'in any town or adjacent to it,' yet it seems to be, according to native views, to some extent a reproach to lose an infant, whilst a quiet burial removes the necessity for funeral customs—always an expense—and of burial fees. There is also the idea, I understand, that the death of an infant is not of the same importance as that of an adult or even of an older child. Formerly it was the custom to bury within the house or its precincts. This is now a statutory offence, and although it seems unlikely that such a practice is at the present time carried out with regard to adults, I have reason to believe that it is still done in the case of infants.

In the case of children over five years of age and of adults, the table . . . is probably nearly a correct record of the deaths in Cape Coast during 1911.[2] I believe that very few such bodies are removed without registration. As one would expect, there is a considerable number of deaths of women at the child-bearing ages.

It is impossible to get a reliable death-rate. The population is not definitely known (there are numerous fallacies in the census figures), nor is the number of deaths of those under five years of age.[3]

'The Cemeteries Ordinance, 1891' was repealed in 1912 by 'An Ordinance to make provision for the Registration of Births, Deaths and Burials and to amend the Law relating to the Regulation of Cemeteries'.[4] This Ordinance introduced compulsory registration of births and deaths but again only in towns or places where a public cemetery had been declared and for which a registrar had been appointed. In accordance with this Ordinance, the Governor, on 18 April 1912, made Rules concerning Forms, fees, and appointment of officers.[5] As regards appointments the Rules stipulated:

The Senior Sanitary Officer or his Deputy to be Registrar for the Colony of the Gold Coast.

In any place or town to which this Ordinance may apply, excepting towns under the Town Councils Ordinance, the Medical Officer in charge of the station to be the Deputy Registrar.

In towns under the Town Councils Ordinance the Medical Officer of Health to be the Deputy Registrar.

[1] *Medical Report 1911*, p. 186.

[2] Professor Simpson (p. 13) had expressed the opinion that the death records of Cape Coast were utterly incomplete, but he came to this conclusion mainly because he thought that the population of Cape Coast then still numbered '25,000 or 30,000'.

[3] *Medical Report 1911*, pp. 187–8.

[4] No. 3 of 1912 (27 Mar.), Gold Coast, *Government Gazette*, 11 May 1912, pp. 462–71: reprinted in *Laws of the Gold Coast Colony in Force 1919*, vol. i, pp. 599–609 (chapter 55).

[5] See Gold Coast, *Government Gazette*, 27 Apr. 1912, pp. 406–11.

While these Rules envisaged only the appointment of Medical Officers and Medical Officers of Health, administration officers were in fact also appointed as Deputy Registrars. Thus, on 3 September 1912 the Acting Governor made the following appointments:

The Medical Officer of Health at Accra to be Deputy Registrar for the town of Labadi.
The District Commissioner at Elmina to be Deputy Registrar for the town of Elmina.
The District Commissioner at Aburi to be Deputy Registrar for the town of Aburi.[1]

Seventeen public cemeteries were proclaimed between 1 July 1912 and 1 April 1926, but they were mostly situated in towns in which there had been already a public cemetery. For the first time such cemetery was proclaimed only in Kwanyako (29 April 1916),[2] Somanya (30 June 1922), Nsawam (22 November 1923), and Koforidua (12 June 1925).[3] The number of registration areas increased only from 16 in 1912 to 19 in 1925.[4]

The Medical Reports for 1912 and 1913 said:

1912. Vital statistics in this Colony at present are in their infancy, and the figures will be included in the Report of the Senior Sanitary Officer, who is the Chief Registrar under the Ordinance.
The Ordinance only began its operations in earnest in the last quarter of the year, and has met with many difficulties, as it takes a long time to get the Native accustomed to a new law.[5]
1913. For the first time in the history of this Colony a Report on Vital Statistics for certain areas of it, where Ordinance No. 3 of 1912 is enforced as far as it is possible, has been submitted by the Registrar of Births and Deaths—Senior Sanitary Officer.[6]

So far as deaths are concerned the statistics were somewhat improved through the new Ordinance. The numbers registered in 1911–14 were as follows:[7]

Town	Population Census 1911	Deaths			
		1911	1912	1913	1914
Accra . . .	19,844	782	913	777	780
Cape Coast . .	11,306	268	236	261	247
Secondee. . .	9,122	118	136	160	211
Winnebah . .	5,870	208	164	179	230
Elmina . . .	5,098	88	58	67	89
Kpong . . .	4,213	61	52	34	94
Saltpond. . .	3,553	80	118	114	108
Quittah . . .	3,416	26	34	55	52
Axim . . .	3,307	44	89	100	97
Akuse . . .	3,107	69	59	66	55
Tarquah . . .	2,423	107	122	239	339
Dunkwa . . .	2,364	33	52	64	49
Dodowa . . .	2,307	8	13	16	37
Labadi . . .	2,130	—	—	79	95
Aburi . . .	1,609	—	51	90	83
Addah . . .	1,582	40	42	34	31
Total . . .	81,251	1,932	2,139	2,335	2,597

[1] Gold Coast, *Government Gazette*, 21 Sept. 1912, p. 1209.
[2] See *Laws of the Gold Coast Colony in Force 1919*, vol. iii, p. 155.
[3] See *Gold Coast Gazette*, Supplement, 29 July 1922, pp. 447–8; 8 Dec. 1923, p. 1436; 4 July 1925, p. 1050.   [4] No Deputy Registrar was apparently appointed for Kwanyako.
[5] *Medical Report 1912*, p. 7.   [6] Ibid. *1913*, p. 8.
[7] See ibid. *1911*, p. 92; *1912*, p. 112; *1913*, p. 87; *1914*, p. 105.

In the fourteen towns for which comparable data are available the number of registrations rose from 1,932 in 1911 to 2,088 in 1912, 2,166 in 1913, and 2,419 in 1914. But there were still in 1914 some towns such as Quittah, Dodowa, Elmina, and Akuse where death registration was obviously quite incomplete. Birth registration was much less adequate still. The total numbers of births and deaths registered in the sixteen registration areas from 1913 to 1925/6 were as follows:[1]

	1913	1914	1915	1916	1917	1918	1919
Births . . .	1,331	1,984	2,199	2,103	2,031	2,045	1,927
Deaths . . .	2,335	2,597	2,692	3,050	3,164	5,083	2,524
Still-births. . .	76	..	..	..	102	103	102

	1920	1921	1922–3	1923–4	1924–5	1925–6
Births . . .	2,075	2,963	2,880	2,867	2,841	2,771
Deaths . . .	3,223	2,916	3,092	3,106	3,028	3,289
Still-births. . .	95	153	144	110	119	124

The Registration Reports for 1919 to 1922–3 said:

1919. The registration of births is somewhat disappointing. The Ordinance has been in force for several years yet section 10 which enjoins on the parents, or other responsible persons in default of them, the duty to register a birth within 14 days, is much neglected. In Secondee, a town with about 12,000 inhabitants and a fair proportion of women, only 71 births were registered giving a birth-rate of 5·9 per 1,000 living.

This omission may be the result of ignorance, though native Chiefs have more than once been requested to instruct the people in the matter, or it may be due to an unfounded fear of being charged a fee as for burial permits. The necessity for the latter ensures registration of a death, unless the body is disposed of in secrecy or beyond the town boundary, but neglect to register a birth entails no disadvantage unless proceedings are instituted by the Deputy Registrar.

Hitherto there has been, and still is, reluctance to prosecute rather than to secure the desired object by personal persuasion and education. The Medical Officer of Health in Accra, during the last quarter of the year effected an improvement through the Sanitary Inspectors, who made inquiries and gave reasonable warning to register or to obtain post-registration certificates.

A few prosecutions resulted in a very considerable increase of births registered as compared with previous months.[2]

The death rate of young children like any other criterion of sanitation fails as an index unless the figures are tolerably complete . . . .'[3]

[1] See *Report on Registration 1921*, p. 3; *1922–3*, p. 32; *1923–4*, p. 14; *1924–5*, p. 15; *1925–6*, p. 14. Figures are available, from the first quarter of 1922 on, for Koforidua, from June 1924 on, for Somanya, and from July 1924 on, for Nsawam. The total numbers of births and deaths registered in the 17 (19) registration areas were:

	Jan. 1922 to Mar. 1922	Apr. 1922 to Mar. 1923	Apr. 1923 to Mar. 1924	Apr. 1924 to Mar. 1925	Apr. 1925 to Mar. 1926
Births . . .	759	2,990	2,941	3,011	2,914
Deaths . .	700	3,283	3,285	3,591	3,814
Still-births . .	42	151	117	124	142

[2] Ibid. *1919*, p. 4. The numbers of births registered in Accra in the 12 months of 1919 were 43, 41, 33, 48, 35, 26, 36, 43, 72, 151, 95, and 86 respectively; see ibid., p. 11.   [3] Ibid., p. 6.

1920. The registered deaths exceed the figure for births by 1,215, a condition which cannot be accepted as fact. In only 5 registration areas, *viz.* Accra, Addah, Quittah, Dodowah, and Axim, did the registered births exceed the deaths.

. . . . The Small-pox epidemic doubtless acted in a manner calculated to prevent registration . . . a general dislocation occurred of routine measures so that births which in normal times would have been discovered by Sanitary Inspectors probably escaped notice, and vigilance in enforcing registration no doubt suffered. At the same time the number of post-registrations was 67 and these are commonly the result of warning or advice by the Sanitary Inspectors.

. . . It is impossible to believe that only 3 births occurred in Tarquah and only 66 in Seccondee.

Chiefs are all aware of the regulation but apparently failed to impress their people.[1]

In Accra the total number of births registered during the year was 714 . . . and the number of deaths 1,314 . . . . On its face value this represents a natural decrease of population to the extent of 600, which is most unlikely to be an index of the true condition.

. . . the Medical Officer of Health in a memorandum on Vital Statistics for Accra Municipality during the period January to June, 1920, remarks:—

'It must be remembered, however, that although all deaths have to be registered before a burial permit can be obtained from the Deputy Registrar of Deaths, many births remain unregistered either through ignorance of the law, or, less frequently, from studied evasion of same . . . .'[2]

The absence of any registered deaths within 24 hours of birth again indicates defective registration in 3 of the large towns.[3]

1921. The number of Births is the highest so far recorded. . . . It also exceeds the figure for 1920, *viz.*, 2,075 by 888, an encouraging fact which probably results from the issue of a circular to various Deputy Registrars drawing attention to the common neglect of registration and recommending prosecution in cases where persuasion and efforts at enlightenment fail. Advice and warning by the Sanitary Inspectors in the course of their routine duties has the effect of stimulating registration and post-registration.

In five of the 16 registration areas the number of births registered is less than in 1920, but in four of these there is no Medical Officer actually resident. In some towns the increase is considerable *e.g.*, Cape Coast shows 470 births as compared with only 112 last year; Winnebah has 294, and Saltpond 226, as compared with 183 and 103 respectively last year.[4]

In Quittah with a population of 9,839, exceeding that of Seccondee, only 62 deaths were registered. A Medical Officer has now been stationed there and registration will probably be progressively more complete.

. . . it is highly probable that [in Accra] many of the births are still unregistered . . . .[5]

In order to know how far such factors as the total and neo-natal infant mortality (under one month) vary in the different towns it is of essential importance to have accurate and complete birth registration. Such knowledge would reveal the areas where concentrated effort was most required and would be most productive . . . . [6]

1922 (1st quarter). The high number of births recorded, goes to prove that the time spent by the Sanitation Staff in showing the uneducated African the advantages of registration, has not been wasted.[7]

[1] *Report on Registration 1920*, p. 3.   [2] Ibid., p. 4.

[3] Ibid., p. 5. In Accra 91 deaths under 24 hours were registered, in the three other large towns (Seccondee, Cape Coast, and Tarquah) none; see ibid., p. 9. Similar conditions prevailed in subsequent years; see ibid. *1921*, pp. 5–10; *1922–3*, pp. 7, 28, 31; *1923–4*, pp. 5, 13; *1924–5*, pp. 6, 14.

[4] Ibid. *1921*, p. 3. It should be noted, however, that in Tarquah with 6,300 inhabitants only 27 births were registered, and in Addah with 5,900 inhabitants only 54; see ibid., p. 11.

[5] Ibid., p. 4.   [6] Ibid., p. 7.

[7] Ibid. *1922–3*, p. 3. The births registered in 16 towns in the first quarters of 1919–22 were 511, 482, 519, and 727 respectively, and the deaths registered 631, 506, 729, and 670 respectively; see ibid., pp. 3, 8.

1922-23. The . . . figures do not represent the actual number of Births, as birth registration continues to be very unpopular amongst the uneducated classes, who make every possible attempt at concealing them.

The [death] figures are far more accurate than that for births, owing to the difficulty in concealing a death. Besides, no burials are allowed at any public cemetery without previous registration.

Some corpses are, however, removed to the 'bush' for burial, and no record of these deaths is available.[1]

Tarquah, with a population of 6,301 records only 2 births, while Elmina and Axim with populations of 5,252 and 3,781 record 214 and 156 births respectively. Tarquah, during the greater part of the year under review did not have the advantage of a Government Medical Officer, the duties of Deputy Registrar of Births and Deaths being carried out by a Medical Officer employed by the Gold Mines.[2]

The remarks made elsewhere in this report regarding the accuracy of birth registration do not apply to Accra, the staff there being large enough to see that very few births escape registration.

151 Still-births were recorded in the 17 registration towns; to this figure Accra contributed 68. This figure is considerably in excess of that recorded last year—104.[3] The increase being probably due to compulsory notification previous to burial.[4]

'The Births, Deaths and Burials Ordinance, 1912' was repealed by 'The Births, Deaths and Burials Ordinance, 1925'.[5]

2. Ashanti

On 9 February 1909, three years before birth and death registration was introduced in the Gold Coast Colony, the Chief Commissioner of Ashanti made the following 'Rules with respect to Registration of Births and Deaths in Ashanti':[6]

Whereas by section 27 of the 'Ashanti Administration Ordinance, 1902',[7] as amended by section 11 of the 'Ashanti Administration (Amendment) Ordinance, 1907,'[8] it is enacted that it shall be lawful for the Chief Commissioner, subject to the approval of the Governor, to make rules with respect to the registration of births and deaths in Ashanti, and that to the breach of any such rules may be attached a penalty not exceeding Twenty-five pounds, or in default three months imprisonment with or without hard labour;

Now, therefore, I Francis Charles Fuller . . . Chief Commissioner of Ashanti, by virtue of the hereinbefore recited authority do hereby make the following rules:—

1. Every birth or death occurring within the town of Coomassie shall be reported by the responsible person to the Police Officer on duty at the Central Police Office.

2. All reports must be made within twenty-four hours of the occurrence between the hours of 8 a.m. and 5 p.m.

3. The Police Officer shall keep Registers for the purpose of entering therein all such reports—to be called 'The Register of Births' and 'The Register of Deaths'. Entries shall be made in accordance with Schedules A. and B. hereto.

[1] Ibid., p. 25.   [2] Ibid., p. 26.

[3] The Registrar assumed erroneously that the figure of 104 still-births in 1921 referred to all the registration towns; it actually referred to Accra alone. The total number of still-births registered in 1921 (16 towns) was 153 and in 1922-3 (17 towns) 151. It dropped in 1923-4 to 117.

[4] *Report on Births and Deaths 1922-3*, p. 28.   [5] See pp. 457-8 below.

[6] Gold Coast, *Government Gazette*, 13 Mar. 1909, pp. 137-8; reprinted in *Ordinances of Ashanti with Rules and Orders made thereunder in Force 31 Dec. 1909*, pp. 58-9.

[7] No. 1 of 1902, Ashanti (1 Jan.), Gold Coast, *Government Gazette*, 1 Jan. 1902, pp. 4-11.

[8] No. 3 of 1907, Ashanti (25 Oct.), ibid., 2 Nov. 1907, pp. 809-11. This Ordinance added '(21) The registration of births and deaths' to the matters with respect to which 'it shall be lawful for the Chief Commissioner to make, amend, and revoke rules'.

4. No fees shall be charged for the registration of births or deaths.

5. The person held responsible under these rules shall be the Head of the house or compound within which the birth or death takes place.

6. Any responsible person failing to report either a birth or a death within twenty-four hours shall render himself liable to a fine not exceeding forty shillings or in default to imprisonment not exceeding one month with or without hard labour.

7. The Police Officer shall allow search to be made at any reasonable time in any Register of Births or Register of Deaths in his custody upon payment of a fee of 1/- and shall upon request give a certified copy of any entry in such book upon a further payment of 1/-.

8. These Rules shall come into force on 1st of July, 1909.

These Rules were revoked on 26 June 1912 by new Rules[1] which, however, differed from the earlier ones only in as much as they substituted for the 'Police Officer' the 'Provincial Medical Officer or person appointed by him'.[2] The new Rules were extended to the towns of Obuasi, Kintampo, and Sunyani by Rules made on 30 September 1912[3] which, like the Rules of 26 June 1912, came into force on 1 January 1913.

The following figures have been published concerning births and deaths registered in Coomassie from 1913 to 1925–6:[4]

	1913	1914	1915	1916	1917	1918	1919
Births	..	72	126	96	69	37	32
Deaths	81	262	400	440	469	803	374
Still-births	..	..	..	..	..	..	..

	1920	1921	1922–3	1923–4	1924–5	1925–6
Births	63	25	48	26	439	581
Deaths	331	423	400	398	498	428
Still-births	2	..	8	11	17	14

According to the enumerations of 1911 and 1921 Coomassie had a population of 18,853 and 20,268 respectively,[5] and it is obvious that registration, particularly of births, was incomplete for many years. The Registration Report for 1924–5 said:

The Senior Sanitary Officer, Kumasi, states that the method of registration in Kumasi is unsatisfactory and obsolete, and that in consequence the vital statistics are of little value.

In order to improve registration it is intended that when the proposed new Births, Deaths and Burials Ordinance for the Colony is passed, a similar ordinance will be brought into force in Ashanti.[6]

The deaths of infants under one year registered numbered 34 giving an infantile mortality of 77. This rate is low and is most probably due to all births not having

[1] See Gold Coast, *Government Gazette*, 28 Sept. 1912, p. 1283.

[2] An 'Amendment of Rules with respect to the Registration of Births and Deaths in Coomassie' (Rule No. 2 of 1920, Ashanti, 19 Feb., ibid., 28 Feb. 1920, p. 212) substituted for the 'Provincial Medical Officer or person appointed by him' the 'Medical Officer of Health'.

[3] See ibid., 23 Nov. 1912, pp. 1615–16. The Rules of 26 June and 30 Sept. 1912 (combined), as they stood prior to the Amendment of 1920, are reprinted in *Laws of Ashanti in Force 1919*, pp. 84–5.

[4] See Gold Coast, *Medical Report 1913*, p. 87; *Report on Registration 1920*, p. 11, *1921*, p. 8; *Report on the Kumasi Public Health Board 1926–7*, p. 42.

[5] See *Census Report 1921*, Appendices, p. 13.   [6] *Report on Births and Deaths 1924–5*, p. 6.

been registered as it is most unlikely that the infant mortality in Kumasi can be less than that in Accra where it is 203.[1]

No data on births or deaths seem to have been published for either Obuasi, Kintampo, or Sunyani prior to 1926.

3. *Northern Territories*

No provision for registration of native births or deaths was made until 1929.

4. *Togoland*

No provision for registration of native births or deaths was made until 1926.[2] 'The British Sphere of Togoland Administration Ordinance, 1924',[3] it is true, stipulated that the laws for the time being in force in the Northern Territories of the Gold Coast were to be applied to the Northern Section of Togoland and the laws for the time being in force in the Gold Coast Colony to the Southern Section of Togoland, but there was no law concerning birth and death registration in the Northern Territories and no registrar was appointed in the Southern Section in the first years during which The British Sphere of Togoland Administration Ordinance was in operation.

5. *Gold Coast and Togoland*

Legislation. 'The Births, Deaths and Burials Ordinance, 1912' which regulated birth and death registration in the Colony was repealed by 'An Ordinance to make further and better provision for the Registration of Births, Deaths and Burials, as also with respect to cemeteries, and for purposes connected therewith'.[4]

The principal changes effected by this Ordinance are the following:—

(1) All births and deaths of non-natives to be compulsorily registered;
(2) All births and deaths of Africans in certain areas (to be defined) to be compulsorily registered;
(3) The free issue of a Birth Certificate on registration of a birth;
(4) The registration of death and the issue of the Burial Certificate, at the place of death only;
(5) Provision is made to enable non-compulsorily registered births and deaths of Africans to be registered, if so desired;
(6) The duty to bury a corpse is imposed on certain specified persons; and
(7) Express provision is made with respect to cremations.[5]

This Ordinance was introduced to bring up to date the provisions contained in Ordinance No. 3 of 1912 relating to the subject of birth and death registration

---

[1] Ibid., p. 7. The infant mortality rate would, of course, have been lower and not higher if all births had been registered. Registration of infant deaths was evidently more incomplete still than registration of births. See also ibid. *1925–6*, p. 6.

[2] The Order of 20 October 1909 which introduced notification of all deaths in the German Protectorate of Togoland applied only to some towns situated in the territory which came under French Mandate. See Kuczynski, *Cameroons and Togoland*, p. 383.

[3] No. 1 of 1924, Togoland (1 Apr.), *The Gold Coast Gazette*, 23 Apr. 1924, pp. 529–52; reprinted in *Laws of Ashanti, The British Sphere of Togoland and the Northern Territories of the Gold Coast in Force 1928*, vol. i, pp. 217–42.

[4] No. 26 of 1925 (30 Dec.), *The Gold Coast Gazette*, 31 Dec. 1925, pp. 1964–88. The Ordinance resembled in many respects the 1917 Ordinance of Nigeria.

[5] *Colonial Reports, Gold Coast 1925–6*, p. 44.

(as recommended by Sir William Simpson during his visit to the Colony in 1924) and, as far as possible, to secure uniformity in registration throughout the Gold Coast.[1]

The Ordinance issued originally, on 30 December 1925, for the Colony alone was applied, therefore, to Ashanti by Ordinance of 23 January 1926[2] and came into force in both territories on 1 June 1926. It was extended to the Northern Territories by the 'Births, Deaths and Burials Ordinance, 1929'.[3] Finally, the 'Ordinances Extension Ordinance, 1935'[4] declared the Births, Deaths and Burials Ordinance of 1925 (as amended in the meantime) to extend to the whole of the Gold Coast and Togoland.

The 'Births, Deaths and Burials Ordinance, 1925' itself was amended in 1926,[5] 1929,[6] 1936,[7] and 1939.[8]

Section 58 of the Births, Deaths, and Burials Ordinance provided that the Governor in Council may make Regulations,[9] and the first Regulations

[1] *Medical Report 1926–7*, p. 7.

[2] No. 1 of 1926, Ashanti, 'The Ashanti Administration Amendment Ordinance, 1926', *The Gold Coast Gazette*, 30 Jan. 1926, pp. 117–18. This Ordinance, which repealed the Ashanti 'Rules with respect to Registration of Births and Deaths' of 1912, applied to Ashanti 'The Births, Deaths and Burials Ordinance, 1925, and all regulations made or to be made thereunder', and stipulated in particular: 'The Principal Registrar of Births, Deaths and Burials for the Gold Coast Colony shall be the Principal Registrar of Births, Deaths and Burials for Ashanti; and his office at Accra shall serve for Ashanti business as it serves for the Gold Coast Colony business.'

[3] No. 10 of 1929, Northern Territories (16 June 1929), ibid., 22 June 1929, pp. 1189–1217; reprinted in *Ordinances of the Gold Coast, &c., 1929*, pp. 211–39. This Ordinance was almost identical with the 'Births, Deaths and Burials Ordinance, 1925' in force in the Colony and Ashanti.

[4] No. 30 of 1935 (27 Apr.), 'An Ordinance to amend certain Ordinances of the Gold Coast Colony and to extend such Ordinances as amended and certain other Ordinances of the Gold Coast Colony to the Gold Coast Colony, Ashanti, and the Northern Territories as though they were a single territory', *Gold Coast Gazette*, Supplement, 10 May 1935, pp. 2007–56; reprinted in *Ordinances of the Gold Coast, &c., 1935*, pp. 545–94. This Ordinance repealed 'The Births, Deaths and Burials Ordinance, 1929' passed in the Northern Territories.

[5] See No. 30 of 1926 (14 Dec.), *The Gold Coast Gazette*, 29 Jan. 1927, pp. 138–9; reprinted in *Ordinances of the Gold Coast, &c., 1926*, pp. 143–5. The Ordinance, as it stood after the enactment of this Amendment Ordinance, is reprinted in *Laws of the Gold Coast Colony in Force 1928*, vol. i, pp. 92–120 (chapter 11).

[6] See No. 36 of 1929 (25 Dec.), *The Gold Coast Gazette*, 31 Dec. 1929, pp. 2455–6; reprinted in *Ordinances of the Gold Coast, &c., 1929*, pp. 109–10.

[7] See No. 19 of 1936 (20 Mar.), 'Statute Law Revision Ordinance, 1936', *Gold Coast Gazette*, Supplement, 18 Apr. 1936, pp. 436–41; reprinted in *Ordinances of the Gold Coast, &c., 1936*, pp. 52–6. The Ordinance, as it stood after the enactment of this Ordinance, is reprinted in *Laws of the Gold Coast Enacted on or before 1 Sept. 1936*, vol. i, pp. 957–86 (chapter 58).

[8] See No. 32 of 1939 (27 Dec.), reprinted in *Annual Volume of the Laws of the Gold Coast 1939*, p. 153.

[9] '58. (1) It shall be lawful for the Governor in Council to make regulations for the further, better, or more convenient, effectuation of any of the provisions or purposes of this Ordinance, and in particular (but without derogating from the generality of the provision last aforesaid) with respect to any or all of the following matters:—

(*d*) The revocation or amendment or variation of, or the addition to, any of the forms, fees, or provisions set forth in the Schedules, and the substitution therefor of other forms, fees, and provisions;

(*f*) The government and guidance of the Registrars;

(*g*) The prescription of the manner in which entries shall be made in registers;

(2) All regulations made under subsection (1) shall be published in the *Gazette*, and shall thereupon have the like force and effect as if enacted herein, either immediately or on and from such other date as may therein or in that regard be provided.'

I have omitted in subsection (1) Regulations referring to cemeteries.

were made on 3 February 1926.[1] They came into force on 1 June 1926, and have been amended four times.[2] The main provisions referring to registration as they stand to-day are as follows:

3. Every Registrar shall at the beginning of each month forward to the Principal Registrar true copies, certified under the hand of the Registrar, of all entries made in the Register of Births and in the Register of Deaths and Burials during the preceding month. These copies shall be in the form of Form A in the case of births and of Form B in the case of deaths.

5. Entries in all Registers shall be made in order, and shall be numbered consecutively from the beginning to the end of each calendar year; the entries for each year beginning with Number 1. Each entry shall be made in the proper space in the Register; and the Registrar shall enter his signature in the proper column after each entry.

6. In cases in which no certificate of death signed by a qualified medical practitioner is produced, Registrars shall ascertain as accurately as possible from the person registering the death the cause of such death.

Almost identical Regulations were issued on 24 August 1929 for the Northern Territories.[3]

The main provisions of the Births, Deaths, and Burials Ordinance ensuring the registration of births and deaths are as follows:

Principal Registrar, Registrars, and Registry Offices

4. The Governor may by order—

(1) appoint Registry Offices and direct for what areas and for what parts of the territorial waters of the Gold Coast and in relation to what class of persons each such office shall be the proper office for the registration of births and deaths under this Ordinance;

(2) appoint a Principal Registrar of Births, Deaths, and Burials; and

(3) appoint such Registrars and Assistant Registrars of Births, Deaths, and Burials as he may think proper.

Birth and Death Registration

3. (1) Births and deaths are registrable under this Ordinance in the following cases:—

(a) All births and deaths occurring amongst non-natives[4] in the Gold Coast or in the territorial waters of the Gold Coast;

(b) All births and deaths occurring amongst Africans[5] in any area or in any part of the territorial waters of the Gold Coast defined in an order made under subsection (2).

(2) The Governor in Council may by order direct that all births and deaths

[1] No. 3 of 1926, *The Gold Coast Gazette*, 13 Feb. 1926, pp. 168–70; reprinted in *Laws of the Gold Coast Colony in Force 1928*, vol. iii, pp. 33–5.

[2] See Regulations No. 1 of 1930 (7 Feb.), *The Gold Coast Gazette*, 15 Feb. 1930, pp. 230–1, reprinted in Gold Coast Colony, &c., *Proclamations, &c., 1930*, pp. 93–4; No. B 2 of 1935 (25 June), *Gold Coast Gazette*, Supplement, 1 July 1935, p. 2206, reprinted in *Proclamations, &c., 1935*, Part II, p. 55; No. B 27 of 1935 (29 July), *Gold Coast Gazette*, Supplement, 10 Aug. 1935, p. 2312, reprinted in *Proclamations, &c., 1935*, Part II, p. 89; No. 33 of 1944 (4 Sept.), *Gold Coast Gazette*, Supplement, 16 Sept. 1944, p. 426, reprinted in *Annual Volume of the Laws of the Gold Coast 1944*, p. 232. The Regulations as they stood after the enactment of No. B 27 of 1935 are reprinted in *Laws of the Gold Coast in Force 1936*, vol. iii, pp. 166–9.

[3] Regulations No. 6 of 1929, Northern Territories, *The Gold Coast Gazette*, 7 Sept. 1929, pp. 1630–3; reprinted in Gold Coast Colony, &c., *Proclamations, &c., 1929*, pp. 511–14.

[4] 'Non-native' means any person who is not an African.

[5] 'African' means a person belonging to any of the coloured races of Africa.

occurring amongst Africans in any area or in any part of the territorial waters of the Gold Coast defined in such order shall be registered.

(3) The birth of a still-born child is not registrable under the Ordinance.

A Registrar shall keep himself informed of all births and deaths occurring and registrable in his office.

When a registrable birth occurs, (1) the parent, (2) the person having charge of the child, (3) the occupant of the house in which the birth took place, shall within 21 days register the birth or shall be liable to a fine not exceeding £20.

When a registrable death occurs, the relatives of the deceased present at the death or in attendance during the last illness of the deceased, every person present at the death, and the occupier of the house in which the death took place, and in default of such occupier the person causing the body to be buried shall within 24 hours register the death or shall be liable to a fine not exceeding £20.

When a birth or death occurs which is not (compulsorily) registrable, any person desiring that it shall be registered may register it.

Burials

Unless the Coroner, District Commissioner, or Medical Officer of Health orders otherwise, no body of any deceased African or of any still-born African child shall be buried or otherwise disposed of within any area in which African deaths are registrable and no body of any deceased non-native or of any still-born non-native child shall be buried or otherwise disposed of anywhere within the limits of the Gold Coast without a certificate for burial signed by the Registrar. Penalty: a fine not exceeding £20.

Headings of Registers

Birth (Form A): No.; Name in full; sex; father's name, occupation, nationality, and religion; mother's maiden name and nationality; when born; where born; signature in full, or name in full and mark duly witnessed, of informant, and relationship, if any, to the child; date of registration; signature of Registrar.

Death (Form B): No.; name in full; age (years, months, days); sex; nationality and tribe; address in full; occupation; religion; residence at death; period of continuous residence in registration area; last place of residence before arrival in registration area, giving address in full, if obtainable; date of death; cause of death; duration of illness; date of registration; signature in full, or name in full and mark duly witnessed, of informant; full name and qualifications of qualified medical practitioner certifying cause of death; place of burial; signature of Registrar.

The Principal Registrar and the Registrars receive no salary for their services in this capacity.[1] Registration of births and deaths in due time

---

[1] By an Order of 5 July 1926 (No. 26 of 1926, Colony, *The Gold Coast Gazette*, 17 July 1926, pp. 938–9; reprinted in *Laws of the Gold Coast Colony in Force 1928*, vol. iii, pp. 16–17) the Acting Governor of the Gold Coast Colony appointed the Deputy Director of Sanitary Services, Accra, to be the Principal Registrar, and 2 District Commissioners, 10 Medical Officers of Health, and 11 Medical Officers to be Registrars in the Colony. He appointed on the same day (Order No. 6 of

is free of charge. But a fee has to be paid for a delayed registration of birth (when the child is more than 2 but not more than 12 months old, 2s. 6d., when the child is more than 12 months old, 5s.), for registering a death after the expiration of 3 days (2s. 6d.), for entering the name of a child after registration of birth (1s.), for correcting an error of fact in a register (2s.), for each inspection of any entry in any register, or for each search of registers and indexes in any Registry Office (4s.), for every search in the indexes and registers in the custody of the Principal Registrar (general search £1, particular search 10s.), for each certified copy of an entry in a register (2s.).

Registration Area. All births and deaths occurring in the Gold Coast or Togoland among non-Africans are compulsorily registrable. Births and deaths of Africans are compulsorily registrable only in so far as they occur in districts for which a special order has been made by the Governor in Council under section 3 (2). Two such Orders, one for the Colony and one for Ashanti, were made on 5 July 1926. The Order for the Colony[1] read as follows:

All births and deaths occurring amongst Africans in the areas specified in the schedule to this order, shall be registered.

Schedule

EASTERN PROVINCE

The towns of Accra, Ada and Keta, together with the territorial waters adjacent to the said towns.
The towns of Aburi, Akuse, Dodowa, Koforidua, Kpong, Labadi, Nsawam and Somanya.

CENTRAL PROVINCE

The towns of Cape Coast, Elmina, Saltpond and Winneba, together with the territorial waters adjacent to the said towns.

WESTERN PROVINCE

The towns of Axim and Sekondi, together with the territorial waters adjacent to the said towns.

1926, Ashanti, *The Gold Coast Gazette*, 17 July 1926, p. 945; reprinted in *Laws of Ashanti*, &c., *in Force 1928*, vol. ii, p. 68) 1 Medical Officer of Health and 4 Medical Officers to be Registrars in Ashanti. Other appointments were made in the Colony by Orders 31 of 1929, 17 and 21 of 1932, 32 of 1933, and 48 and 60 of 1942; in Ashanti by Orders 4 of 1931 and 23 of 1935; in the Northern Territories by Orders 3, 4, 7, and 8 of 1920, 2 of 1921, 9 of 1932, and B 17 of 1935; in Togoland by Order 2 of 1929. From July 1935 to July 1942 the distribution of Registrars was as follows (see *Laws of the Gold Coast in Force 1936*, vol. iii, pp. 134–6):
    Colony: 1 District Commissioner, 7 Medical Officers of Health, 9 Medical Officers;
    Ashanti: 1 Senior Health Officer, 1 Medical Officer of Health, 3 Medical Officers, 2 Sanitary Inspectors;
    Northern Territories: 1 Medical Officer of Health, 3 Medical Officers;
    Togoland: 1 Medical Officer of Health.
    In July 1942 two additional Medical Officers of Health were appointed as Registrars in the Colony; see *Annual Volume of the Laws of the Gold Coast 1942*, pp. 185, 193–4.
    In March 1945 the Medical Officer of Health, Accra, who is the Registrar for Accra, became Registrar of the two areas in the Colony (Aburi and Dodowa) for which the District Commissioner, Mampong, had been Registrar; see Order No. 10 of 1945, *Gold Coast Gazette*, Supplement, 3 Mar. 1945.
    [1] No. 13 of 1926, *The Gold Coast Gazette*, 17 July 1926, p. 941; reprinted in *Laws of the Gold Coast Colony in Force 1928*, vol. iii, p. 16.

The towns of Aboso, Abontiakoon, Adja Bepo, Dunkwa, Prestea and Tarkwa.

In so far as the boundaries of the towns mentioned in this schedule have been defined under the Towns Ordinance, the said boundaries as so defined shall be the boundaries of the said towns for the purpose of this schedule.

The Order for Ashanti[1] covered the towns of Bekwai, Kintampo, Kumasi, Obuasi, and Sunyani.

The Medical Report for 1926–7 says that 'registration was extended to a large number of small centres on the coming into force of the amended Births, Deaths and Burials Ordinance No. 26 of 1925, on the 1st of June, 1926',[2] and the Report on Births and Deaths for 1926 states:

During the year seven new registration areas were opened viz., Abosso and Prestea in the Colony, and Obuasi, Bekwai, Kumasi, Kintampo and Sunyani in Ashanti. Registration in these Ashanti towns commenced on 1st June, 1926, under the same Ordinance as had hitherto been applicable only in the Colony (sensu restricto). Registration began at Abosso and Prestea on the same date.

Thus registration of Births and Deaths is now being carried out in 26 towns.[3]

The population of the 26 towns wherein registration of births and deaths is now compulsory is approximately 208,775 being 58.246 more than last year.[4]

But both reports, it seems to me, overstate the extension of the registration area. Registration had been introduced in Kumasi in 1909, and in Obuasi, Kintampo, and Sunyani in 1913, and for Kumasi with 25,000 inhabitants birth and death data had been regularly published in the same manner as for the nineteen registration towns of the Colony. In 1928–35 Orders extended registration to the following towns:

Colony, Eastern Province: Dzelu Kope (7 October 1932), Big Ada (1 November 1933);[5]

Colony, Central Province: Oda (6 November 1929);[6]

Colony, Western Province: Takoradi (22 September 1932);[7]

Ashanti: Mampong (29 April 1935), Wenchi (29 April 1935);[8]

Northern Territories: Salaga (6 August 1929), Tamale (6 August 1929), Bawku (25 July 1935), Wa (25 July 1935);[9]

Togoland: Ho (21 August 1929).[10]

Thus the number of registration areas increased from 28 in 1926 to 39 in 1935.[11] No new registration area was constituted in 1936–41, though the urgency of extending registration was stressed repeatedly.

[1] No. 5 of 1926, Ashanti, *The Gold Coast Gazette*, 17 July 1926, p. 944; reprinted in *Laws of Ashanti*, &c., *in Force 1928*, vol. ii, p. 67.

[2] *Medical Report 1926–7*, p. 12.

[3] Registration was apparently not carried out in Abontiakoon and Adja Bepo.

[4] *Report on Births and Deaths 1926*, pp. 3–4.

[5] See Orders No. 12 of 1932, Colony, and No. 19 of 1933, Colony, *Gold Coast Gazette*, 22 Oct. 1932, p. 1591, 11 Nov. 1933, p. 567.

[6] See Order No. 13 of 1929, Colony, ibid., 16 Nov. 1929, p. 1986.

[7] See Order No. 9 of 1932, Colony, ibid., 1 Oct. 1932, p. 1467.

[8] See Order No. 24 of 1935, Ashanti, ibid., Supplement, 11 May 1935, pp. 2112–15.

[9] See Orders Nos. 5 and 6 of 1929, Northern Territories, and B 8 and B 9 of 1935, Gold Coast, ibid., 17 Aug. 1929, pp. 1516–17, Supplement, 17 Aug. 1935, pp. 2331–2.

[10] See Order No. 1 of 1929, Togoland, ibid., 31 Aug. 1929, p. 1601.

[11] A list of the thirty-nine registration areas is given in *Laws of the Gold Coast in Force 1936*, vol. iii, pp. 134–5. The registration areas of Accra and Kumasi were changed by Order in Council No. 10 of 1944 (3 Apr.), *Gold Coast Gazette*, Supplement, 15 Apr. 1944, p. 257.

1936. The areas with the chief claims for early inclusion are Yendi in the Northern Territories, and Bibiani and Bogosu in the Western Province of the Colony. The latter two areas are closely associated with important mining concerns.[1]

1937. No new registration areas were added during the year. Several areas, however, somewhat urgently call for inclusion, namely—Swedru in the Central Province of the Colony; Bibiani and Bogosu in the Western Province of the Colony, both of which towns are closely associated with important mining concerns; and Yendi in the Mandated Area of Togoland.[2]

1938. No new registration areas were added during 1938; but Yendi in the Mandated Area of Togoland, Bogosu and Bibiani in the Western Province and Swedru in the Central Province of the Colony are somewhat overdue for inclusion.

It is hoped to bring Swedru and Bibiani within the scope of the provisions of the Births, Deaths and Burials Ordinance in the near future.[3]

Finally, in July 1942, Bibiani and Bogosu were included in the registration area.[4]

Degree of Completeness. The reports of the Principal Registrar covered 26 registration areas in 1926–8, 28 in 1929, 30 in 1930–2, 31 in 1933–4, and 35 from 1935 on.[5] The population of these towns was estimated in mid-year 1940 at 355,780, or 9 per cent. of the total population of the Gold Coast and Togoland.

The Registration Ordinance of 1925 which came into force on 1 June 1926 had a marked effect on the number of registrations of births. In the nineteen towns included in the vital statistics of 1925–6 the number of births registered increased from 2,914 in the twelve months ending 31 March 1926 to 3,900 in the calendar year 1926 and to 4,729 in 1927. In Accra alone the figure rose from 1,082 in 1925–6 to 1,700 in 1926, and to 2,246 in 1927.[6] But in at least a dozen of the twenty-six towns included in the 1927 statistics birth registration was utterly incomplete, and the same was true of death registration in at least half a dozen towns. The official rates for all towns were 22·8 for births and 19·9 for deaths. The Principal Registrar stated:

. . . in the case of birth rates in particular, little reliance can be placed on statistics received from several areas where the legal provisions relating to birth registration are very inadequately enforced.

The registration of births was satisfactory in several of the larger townships, more especially where a Medical Officer of Health was stationed.[7]

But the figures do not support this view. Of the six large towns in which a Medical Officer of Health was Registrar, at least three (Cape Coast, Tarkwa, and Kumasi) had very incomplete birth registration. Registration of both births and deaths improved in the course of time, but the comments of the Principal Registrar leave no doubt that birth registration in particular was never satisfactory (until 1939) and that the degree of completeness has fluctuated.

[1] *Report of Principal Registrar 1936*, p. 1.   [2] Ibid. *1937*, p. 1.   [3] Ibid. *1938*, p. 1.

[4] See Order No. 8 of 1942 (16 May) and Order No. 11 of 1942 (25 July), *Annual Volume of the Laws of the Gold Coast 1942*, pp. 227–8.

[5] They did not cover the towns of Abontiakoon, Adja Bepo, and Dzelukope. The town of Big Ada was included in the Ada registration area; see *Report of Principal Registrar 1933*, p. 1.

[6] See *Report on Births and Deaths 1925–6*, p. 14; *1926*, p. 18; *1927*, p. 11.

[7] Ibid., p. 4.

1928. There is some justification for assuming that the majority of deaths that take place in registration areas are duly recorded while the reverse is the case as regards births. Where, however, the importance is not adequately appreciated by the local authority, registration even of deaths is notably deficient; as, for example, at Ada in the Colony from which centre reports were received of only 74 deaths during the year 1928 giving an estimated death rate of 4·5 which figure is, of course, entirely erroneous.[1]

It is, however, necessary to bear in mind that while death registration, at any rate as regards numbers, is more or less complete, this is far from being the case in birth registration . . . .[2]

1929. Birth registration has improved, but in areas where no Medical Officer of Health is stationed the figures are still deficient.

Registration at Ada and Keta is very lax. The birth rate for these two places being only 5·4 and 6·5 respectively.

The collective rate for . . . 15 areas with an estimated population at mid-year, 1929, of 210,107, was 30·9 per thousand as compared with 24·2 in the previous yearly period.

In most registration areas it can be assumed that the majority of deaths are recorded.

In some areas, notably Ada and Keta, where 42 and 56 deaths were recorded giving death-rates of 4·2 and 2·6, death registration is very lax. In these areas the local authority would apparently not appreciate the importance of the measure, for, after all, it is on these data alone that a sound national system of preventive medicine can be evolved.[3]

1930. Birth registration is improving, but in areas where no Medical Officer of Health is stationed the figures are still deficient. Parents of children apparently have no aversion to registering their births, but as it requires a little effort on their part it is necessary to keep the advantages of birth registration continually before them in order to ensure that a proper record is kept and progress in birth registration maintained.[4]

1931. Whereas birth registration may be somewhat incomplete in some areas, it is probable that death registration is much more nearly complete owing to the fact that it is necessary for the members of the general public to obtain permits from Registrars or Deputy Registrars of Births and Deaths before the body of the deceased can be disposed of.[5]

1932. . . . it is impossible as yet to carry out registration in the more rural areas owing to the lack of trained staff.

During 1932 some 9,376 births were registered as compared with 8,239 for 1931.

This total shows the very satisfactory increase of 1,137 over the total for last year. There is no doubt but that the general public are appreciating, more and more, the advantages to be gained by the registration of the births of their children.

The combined crude birth-rate of the thirty registration areas is estimated at 34·7 for 1932 as compared with 31·3 for the previous twelve-monthly period.[6]

It is considered that the general public is taking more interest in, and appreciating more fully, the benefits resulting from the compulsory registration of births and deaths.

These advantages are continually kept before the public in all the larger centres.[7]

1933. Every endeavour is made to encourage the registration of all births occurring in registration districts but there is little doubt but that this is deficient still in certain areas as, for example, Sekondi.[8]

---

[1] For Keta the official death-rate was only 4·0.

[2] *Report on Births and Deaths 1928*, pp. 4–5.

[3] *Report of the Principal Registrar 1929*, pp. 3–4.   [4] Ibid. *1930*, p. 2.

[5] Ibid. *1931*, p. 2. But see also ibid. *1932*, p. 2: 'It is of course easier to dispose of the body of a young infant in some of the more rural centres without registration than that of an adult . . . .'

[6] Ibid., p. 1.   [7] Ibid., p. 4.   [8] Ibid. *1933*, p. 2.

There can be little question . . . that a proportion of the still-births especially of premature children, does not come to the notice of the local Registrar, the Health Authority.[1]

There are good grounds for believing that the general population is now well aware of the value of birth registration and the health personnel has to devote far less time during house-to-house visits in persuading parents to fulfil their legal duty in this respect.

The rate (34 per 1,000 persons living) was well maintained showing a very small fall from that of the previous year.[2]

1934. Although there is a growing appreciation of the value of birth registration amongst the better educated sections of the population, a fair proportion of births even in towns of the size of Accra would not be registered were it not for the persuasive efforts of the sanitary inspectors, health visitors and district midwives in the course of their domiciliary visiting. In times, therefore, of epidemic or when the health staff are engaged in special anti-malarial surveys, etc., and less opportunity occurs for routine domiciliary inspections, a larger proportion of births remain unregistered . . . .[3]

1935. It is considered that among the better educated classes the value of birth registration is becoming yearly more apparent. In all centres, however, were it not for the constant vigilance of officers of the Health Branch of the Medical Department many births would not be registered. It is essential continually to keep the importance of birth registration before a large section of the community. When the Health Branch staff is busily engaged on epidemic disease prevention it is not uncommon to find a corresponding fall in the number of births registered in the affected centres.[4]

1936. Among the better educated classes birth registration is valued, and evasion is rare. Among the less well educated, however, the necessity for the registration of all births has continually to be kept before the people, or evasion is the rule rather than the exception. All Health Branch staff during routine visits of inspection stress the importance of birth registration to parents and guardians. Naturally, in those years—such as that under review—when routine work is not upset by outbreaks of serious infectious disease there is more time available for such propaganda, resulting in a corresponding upward tendency in the total number of births registered.[5]

1937. If the highest recorded crude [birth] rate, namely 94·3 at Somanya is compared with the lowest 9·7 at Obuasi it is considered that some further explanation is required.

Somanya is a very busy road centre, in a thickly populated area, into which many children are brought for voluntary registration of birth.

Obuasi, on the other hand, is an important mining town where males exceed females in a proportion of some 166–100.[6] Obuasi, as a general rule, returns the lowest birth-rate in the Gold Coast.

As the years pass, birth registration is increasingly less frequently evaded by the better educated classes of the community. Such is not the case, however, with the less-educated and non-educated sections of the public. As in the past, unceasing vigilance and propaganda by all members of the Health Branch staff is required to keep the necessity for the registration of all births before the general public.

In those years when the absence of outbreaks of serious infectious diseases causes no break in the routine work of the Health Branch, the attention of the public can continually be kept to the essential nature of birth registration. Unfortunately, the year under review was exceptional, and sporadic outbreaks of yellow fever demanded much of the attention of the staff. When these considerations are reviewed, it must be considered that the total number of births registered was

[1] Ibid., p. 3. [2] Ibid., p. 9.
[3] Ibid. *1934*, p. 2. [4] Ibid. *1935*, p. 2. [5] Ibid. *1936*, p. 2.
[6] This certainly is no sufficient explanation for a birth-rate of only 9·7. In 1938 the birth-rate of Obuasi was 13·1.

satisfactory, and indicates an increasing recognition of the necessity for this measure.[1]

1938. All that is claimed for the rates contained in this summary and report is that they increase in reliability annually and their value steadily grows.

Birth and death registration are still in their infancy in the Gold Coast, but it is considered that a commencement has been made on sound lines and promises well for the future.[2]

The large majority of the inhabitants of the registration areas are illiterate, and to such the necessity for the registration of all births conveys but little. The Health Branch inspectorate staff has, therefore, always to be on the alert and by means of unceasing propaganda to keep the importance of this necessary measure well before the general public. When routine work is not upset by reason of outbreaks of serious infectious disease, education of the public proceeds without break, but in years such as that under review, when sporadic outbreaks of smallpox and yellow fever scattered over wide areas necessitated the extensive travelling of staff in certain localities this measure was, perhaps, not so prominent as could be desired.

It can be considered, therefore, that the results achieved indicate an increasing recognition of the necessity for the registration of all births in the mind of the general public, the better educated of which rarely, if ever, evade their responsibility. From time to time, recourse is made in certain areas to propaganda through the local chiefs. In this measure, the Administrative Officers have been most helpful.

As a rule, death registration is more complete in the more backward areas than is the registration of births.[3]

In view of the uncertainty of the population figures and the peculiar, urban, character of the registration areas it is very difficult rightly to appraise the returns. It should be noted, however, that while the official birth-rate fluctuated in 1931–8 between 31·5 and 34·7 it rose to 36·2 in 1939 and to 38·1 in 1940. This seems to indicate that registration improved considerably in those two years. But in 1941–3 the numbers of births registered were again considerably lower than in 1940. As there is no reason to assume that birth registration was complete in 1940, many births must have remained unregistered prior to 1939 and in 1941–3. As regards death registration it is impossible to tell how numerous omissions are. But the large increase in the numbers of deaths registered in 1942 and 1943 suggests that registration was more defective prior to the Second World War than the administration assumed it to be.

Surveys. Apart from birth and death registration in a number of towns little has been done to obtain data on fertility and mortality in the Gold Coast. I know only of three such sample surveys.

(1) The Medical Report for 1924–5 contains 'A Report on the Birth-rate and Infant Mortality in the Koforidua District'[4] by the Senior Medical Officer Dr. O'Brien. It begins as follows:

The register of births has been so little patronised locally, that in order to obtain information with regard to the Birth-rate and Death-rate of infants, I resorted to the tedious method of questioning individuals with whom I came in contact.

The figures from which the following averages, and percentages are derived, were obtained from the women who came to the dispensary. These were of two classes:—

(1) Those who came to consult me with regard to some illness of their own, these included a number of completely or partially barren women out of proportion to the general population.

---

[1] *Report of the Principal Registrar 1937*, p. 2.   [2] Ibid. *1938*, p. 1.
[3] Ibid, p. 3.   [4] *Medical Report 1924–5*, pp. 70–3.

(2) Those in normal health who brought sick children for treatment.

Though I kept no count of their relative numbers, I can say that the latter were much in excess of the former.

Only females of sufficient age and over to have co-habited with a man for a year were questioned. This age I judge at the lowest to be about 16, for from my observations I gather that the first menstruation appears late here, between the 14th and 15th year, and that marriage rarely takes place before six menstrual periods have passed. . . .

The total number of women questioned is 1,000.

. . . In some cases the number of children stated to have been born was so great, that a low estimate of age had to be reconsidered. Several women noting my surprise at the fecundity they claimed, volunteered the information that since marriage they had had a child every eighteen months.

The following information was obtained from each woman.

1. Total number of children born.
2. Total number alive.
3. Number of those amongst the deceased children who had been able to walk about.
4. Number of miscarriages.

I shall discuss the results in the following sections.

(2) The Report on the Administration of Togoland under British Mandate for 1928 said:

. . . a recent endeavour was made with the active co-operation of the Na of Yendi to estimate the local infantile birth and death rates by questioning parents in their compounds, but either no information or only misleading information was obtainable.[1]

(3) Shortly before the 1931 census the Director of Medical and Sanitary Services initiated a large number of sample surveys, in the course of which 5,854 women were questioned.

Before the actual taking of the Census a questionnaire was circulated to all Medical and Health officers, who were requested to obtain the following information from each of a hundred 'old women' (i.e. those who had passed the menopause):—

(a) The number of children they had born.
(b) The number still born.
(c) The number born alive.
(d) The number who died before walking.
(e) The number who died before puberty.

The figures obtained related to a more extended period of the past than the last decade.

The general conditions of life, however, have not altered to any perceptible extent from the point of view of the statistician except in the larger centres. The results may, therefore, be considered as being fairly representative. The 'old women' were taken haphazard, and barren women were not excluded.[2]

I shall discuss the results in the following sections.

VI. Native Fertility, Mortality, and Population Growth

1. Fertility

Natality. Lieutenant-Governor Bannerman, in his report on the Blue Book for 1850, and the Colonial Surgeon Dr. Clarke, in his report for the year 1858, pointed out that polygamy reduces very much the number of

---

[1] *Report 1928*, pp. 42-3. [2] *The Gold Coast, 1931*, vol. i, p. 212.

births,[1] and the latter said furthermore that 'abortion is sometimes practised'. He said specifically:

Abortion is sometimes resorted to when a woman who is suckling becomes pregnant, on the grounds of the injury done to the baby at the breast, and because generally they are too poor to rear the child upon spoon meat.[2]

In the following decades fertility was apparently not discussed in official documents. But the Report on Togoland for 1920–1 states that 'as is usual with Africans' the natives in Togoland 'are prolific'.[3] 'The women generally have about six children.'[4] The 1923 report says that the 'birth-rate is reported to be approximately 80 to 100 per 1,000'.[5] More valuable figures were obtained at the investigation made in the Koforidua District in 1924–5, which covered 1,000 women (of all ages) who came to the dispensary. According to their statements they had had 4,088 pregnancies, of which 422 resulted in miscarriages.[6] Women over 40, numbering 72, had had 572 pregnancies, of which 79 ended in miscarriages. These figures indicate a very high fertility. But they were not confirmed by the survey made in 1931 which showed that 141 women in Koforidua Town and District who had passed the menopause had given birth to 633 children, the ratio of births to 1 woman being 4·5 as compared with 6·8 according to the earlier inquiry. It should be noted, moreover, that at only 11 of the 54 surveys made in 1931 was the ratio of births to women as high as, or higher than, in the early investigation for Koforidua District.[7] For the country as a whole the ratio was 5·8. All these figures include still-births. The number of live-births to 1 woman was 5·3, oscillating between 2·7 in the Volta River District and 7·9 in the Lawra District.[8] The proportion of barren women was only 4·6 per cent. In the Western Province of the Colony 'the percentage of barren women works out at 2·2, but the Medical Officers and others who collected the information for this province stated that they had the greatest difficulty in obtaining replies on this point'.[9] However, the data concerning barrenness were apparently defective also in other areas. In Ashanti 25 of the 100 women questioned in Kintampo District were reported to be barren, while not a single one of the 560 women questioned in six other Districts was so reported. On the other hand the 75 women in the Kintampo District who were not barren stated that they had amongst them 716 children (including 43 still-born), a figure which appears incredibly high. The Chief Census Officer reaches the conclusion

[1] See p. 528 below.   [2] State of Colonial Possessions 1858, Part II, p. 27.
[3] Report on Togoland 1920–1, p. 7. See also ibid. 1923, p. 38.
[4] Ibid. 1920–1, p. 11. See also ibid. 1924, p. 10.   [5] Ibid. 1923, p. 31.
[6] Of the 1,000 women 48 'said that they had borne no living children', but this figure does not mean much, as the great majority of the women came to the dispensary with sick children for treatment, while all others came because they were ill and 'these included a number of completely or partially barren women out of proportion to the general population'.
[7] See The Gold Coast, 1931, vol. i, pp. 214–17.
[8] A group of 100 women questioned in the Tamale District reported 859 live-births, but another group of 100 women in the same District reported only 538. In the Bawku District one group of 100 women reported 635 live-births, while another group of 100 women reported only 303. Such results make it seem doubtful whether the women were really 'taken haphazard', as stated in the census report.
[9] Ibid., pp. 215–16.

'that the average number of children per woman is, apparently, lower in the more advanced Provinces, i.e. the Eastern and Central Provinces of the Colony, than in the less advanced areas'.[1] But the number of children per woman was high only in the Western Province and Ashanti, where evidently many barren women wrongly reported children, and the difference between the Northern Territories and the Eastern and Central Provinces of the Colony is slight.[2] The Chief Census Officer says furthermore:

There are numerous factors which affect the birth-rate, differing considerably from those at work in more civilised countries. The conditions in the Gold Coast generally can be considered favourable to a high birth rate.[3]

The meaning of this statement is not clear. The results of the sample surveys suggest that fertility in the first three decades of this century was lower the Gold Coast than in eastern Europe, India, or China, and similar to that prevailing in England a generation earlier. 'Civilization', therefore, does not seem to be a decisive factor. It might be argued, of course, that conditions in the Gold Coast generally can be considered to be as favourable to a high birth-rate as in India or China, but it would be probably just as correct to say that conditions in Sweden generally can be considered favourable to a high birth-rate.

TABLE 20. *Fertility and Child Mortality, Gold Coast and Togoland Surveys, 1931*[1]

District	Women questioned	Barren women	Children born			Children deceased		Children born per woman			Infant mortality rate
			Live-born	Still-born	Total	Before walking	Later, but before puberty	Live-born	Still-born	Total	
Colony, Eastern Province.	1,411	87	7,512	494	8,006	1,074	1,264	5·3	0·4	5·7	143
Colony, Central Province .	531	26	2,643	325	2,968	453	747	5·0	0·6	5·6	171
Colony, Western Province.	684	15	3,942	316	4,258	584	1,225	5·8	0·5	6·2	148
Ashanti . . .	1,010	38	6,049	563	6,612	875	1,450	6·0	0·6	6·5	145
Northern Territories .	1,318	35	7,339	459	7,798	1,641	1,816	5·6	0·3	5·9	224
Togoland . . .	900	70	3,666	607	4,273	688	628	4·1	0·7	4·7	188
Total . . .	5,854	271	31,151	2,764	33,915	5,315	7,130	5·3	0·5	5·8	171

[1] See *The Gold Coast, 1931*, vol. i, pp. 214–17.

As regards the birth-rate in the registration towns the Medical Department, in an 'Historical Survey, 1013–33', says·

In 1913 the average birth-rate for the registration districts in the Colony was 10·6 per thousand living persons. This figure was more than doubled in 1923–24 when the rate had increased to 21·9. In 1933 it amounted to 34. Better registration accounts for much of this increase, but the reduction in the loss of fœtal life from malaria and other infections owing to improved hygienic conditions no doubt constitutes a not unimportant factor.[4]

Since 1933 the birth-rate in the registration districts has risen, being 36 in 1939, and 38 in 1940. These rates are high considering (1) that

[1] Ibid., pp. 217–18.
[2] In Togoland, however, fertility appeared to be very low. (Concerning miscarriages and abortions see *Report on Togoland 1924*, p. 55; *1925*, pp. 60, 75.)
[3] *The Gold Coast, 1931*, vol. i, p. 223.   [4] *Medical Report 1933–4*, p. 4.

TABLE 21. *Registered Births and Deaths, Gold Coast and Togoland,*
1919–44[1]

Years	Live-born			Still-born	Total deaths			Deaths under one year		
	Male	Female	Total		Male	Female	Total	Male	Female	Total
1919	983	944	1,927	102	1,487	1,037	2,524	..	..	..
1920	1,058	1,017	2,075	95	1,909	1,314	3,223	..	..	..
1921	1,450	1,513	2,963	153	1,708	1,208	2,916	..	..	..
Jan. to Mar. 1922	399	360	759	42	422	278	700	..	..	..
1922–3	1,516	1,472	2,988	149	1,987	1,296	3,283	..	..	..
1923–4	1,459	1,482	2,941	117	1,991	1,294	3,285	..	..	..
1924–5	1,488	1,523	3,011	124	2,164	1,427	3,591	..	..	..
1925–6	1,423	1,491	2,914	142	2,240	1,574	3,814	..	..	..
Apr. to Dec. 1926	1,835	1,837	3,672	140	2,260	1,376	3,636	..	..	..
1927	2,800	2,774	5,574	216	3,093	1,791	4,884	356	323	679
1928	2,783	2,756	5,539	218	3,139	2,043	5,182	425	339	764
1929	3,693	3,783	7,476	280	3,454	1,997	5,451	471	380	851
1930	4,090	3,964	8,054	320	3,752	2,220	5,972	493	443	936
1931	4,080	4,159	8,239	343	3,765	2,207	5,972	511	425	936
1932	4,726	4,650	9,376	392	3,687	2,218	5,905	516	438	954
1933	4,794	4,820	9,614	..	3,981	2,283	6,264	530	427	957
1934	4,794	4,843	9,637	..	4,025	2,525	6,550	562	455	1,017
1935	4,966	5,140	10,106	432	4,827	3,004	7,831	673	612	1,285
1936	5,591	5,631	11,222	501	4,972	3,030	8,002	632	571	1,203
1937	5,655	5,579	11,234	590	5,257	3,174	8,431	728	582	1,310
1938	5,601	5,664	11,265	559	4,789	2,741	7,530	623	523	1,146
1939	..	..	12,621	568	..	..	8,079	..	..	1,382
1940	..	..	13,548	645	..	..	7,894	..	..	1,491
1941	..	..	12,627	685	..	..	8,467	..	..	1,388
1942	..	..	12,560	709	..	..	9,441	..	..	1,482
1943	..	..	12,983	881	..	..	10,449	...	..	1,670
1944	..	..	13,526	904	..	..	10,093	..	..	1,694

[1] See *Report on Births and Deaths 1919*, p. 3; *1920*, p. 3; *1921*, p. 3; *1922–3*, pp. 3, 25; *1923–4*, p. 3; *1924–5*, p. 3; *1925–6*, p. 3; *1926*, pp. 3, 7–12; *1927*, pp. 3–6, 20–1; *1928*, pp. 3–5, 19–20; *1929*, pp. 3–5, 19–20; *1930*, pp. 3, 18–19; *1931*, pp. 2, 9, 16; *1932*, pp. 2, 9, 16; *1933*, p. 16; *1934*, p. 20; *1935*, p. 18; *1936*, pp. 3, 18; *1937*, pp. 3, 11–12, 17; *1938*, pp. 2–4, 20; *Medical Report 1939*, p. 4; *1940*, p. 5; *1941*, p. 4; *1942*, p. 4; *1943*, p. 5; *1944*, p. 5.

registration even in recent years was probably incomplete, (2) that, owing to the preponderance of men, the proportion of women at child-bearing age amongst the urban population is low, and (3) that 'pregnant women tend to return to their native villages for childbirth in order to obtain the assistance of their mother, family, native doctor, ancestors and the tribal deity'.[1] There are, however, two factors which may swell the official birth-rate artificially.

(1) The population of the twenty registration towns which showed an increase between 1921 and 1931 is computed by assuming that the yearly increase since 1931 has been equal to one-tenth the difference between the 1931 and 1921 census returns. But the population of the five towns which showed a decrease between 1921 and 1931 and the population of the ten towns which were not enumerated separately in 1921 are assumed to have remained the same as they were in 1931. As a consequence thereof the total population of the registration towns appears to have been 24·6 per cent. higher in 1940 than in 1931, while the official estimate for the whole country shows an increase of 25·3 per cent. It is quite

[1] *The Gold Coast, 1931*, vol. i, p. 213. See also, for example, *Report on Registration 1919*, p. 4; *Report on the Kumasi Public Health Board 1926–7*, p. 40.

TABLE 22. *Births and Deaths Registration Area, Gold Coast and Togoland, 1931–44*[1]

Year	Dis-tricts	Mid-year population	Live-born	Deaths	Birth-rate	Death-rate
		29 REGISTRATION DISTRICTS[2]				
1931	29	258,912[3]	8,188	5,933	31·6	22·9
1932	29	267,989	9,329	5,882	34·8	21·9
1933	29	275,369	9,419	6,180	34·2	22·4
1934	29	282,738	9,338	6,364	33·0	22·5
1935	29	289,902	9,511	7,337	32·8	25·3
1936	29	297,207	10,308	7,275	34·7	24·5
1937	29	304,639	10,118	7,513	33·2	24·7
1938	29	311,787	10,140	6,791	32·5	21·8
		TOTAL REGISTRATION AREA[4]				
1931	30	261,198[3]	8,239	5,972	31·5	22·9
1932	30	270,357	9,376	5,905	34·7	21·8
1933	30	280,847	9,549	6,223	34·0	22·2
1934	31	292,666	9,637	6,550	32·9	22·4
1935	31	299,830	9,905	7,559	33·0	25·2
1936	35	325,433	11,222	8,002	34·5	24·6
1937	35	333,159	11,234	8,431	33·7	25·3
1938	35	340,600	11,265	7,530	33·1	22·1
1939	35	348,190	12,621	8,079	36·2	23·2
1940	35	355,780	13,548	7,894	38·1	22·2
1941	35	355,780	12,627	8,467	35·5	23·8
1942	35	355,780	12,560	9,441	35·3	26·5
1943	35	355,780	12,983	10,449	36·5	29·4
1944	35	355,780	13,526	10,093	38·0	28·4

[1] Computed from *Report Principal Registrar 1931*, p. 15; *1932*, p. 15; *1933*, p. 15; *1934*, p. 14; *1935*, p. 12; *1936*, p. 12; *1937*, p. 12; *1938*, p. 14; *Medical Report 1939*, p. 4; *1940*, p. 5; *1941*, p. 4; *1942*, p. 4; *1943*, p. 5; *1944*, p. 5. The population figures exclude non-Africans.

[2] Abosso, Aburi, Accra and Labadi, Akuse, Axim, Bekwai, Cape Coast, Dodowa, Dunkwa, Elmina, Ho, Keta, Kintampo, Koforidua, Kpong, Kumasi, Nsawam, Obuasi, Oda, Prestea, Salaga, Saltpond, Sekondi, Somanya, Sunyani, Tamale, Tarkwa, and Winneba.

[3] Census 26 April 1931.

[4] 1931 and 1932, including the registration district of Ada; 1933, excluding the registration district of Ada, which on 1 Nov. 1933 was enlarged to include the adjoining town of Big Ada, but including the new registration district of Takoradi; 1934 and 1935, including the enlarged Ada registration district and the Takoradi District; 1936–44 as 1935, but including also the new registration districts of Bawku, Mampong, Wa, and Wenchi from which figures for the complete year were not available in 1935.

unlikely that the population of the registration towns should have increased less than the rest of the country.

(2) The figures of registered births include a number of births that occurred outside the registration areas. The Principal Registrar reported for 1938:

The high rates recorded for Mampong (98·3) and Somanya (103·4) call for comment. Both these places are situated on busy trade routes, and a large percentage of the total numbers of births registered in each were births voluntarily registered from the surrounding rural areas.[1]

[1] *Report of Principal Registrar 1938*, p. 3. The birth figures include also the few non-African births, while the population to which the birth figures are related comprise only Africans.

The conclusions to be drawn from the available data may be summarized as follows: Fertility in urban areas is apparently high; as regards rural areas there is no evidence that fertility is low, but whether it is moderate or high it is impossible to tell.

Sex ratio. Among the live-births registered in 1919–38 there were only 99·7 males to 100 females. The Chief Census Officer, 1931, says that 'there are no obvious grounds for thinking that African parents refrain from registration in the case of male children, and have no objection with regard to female'.[1] Yet, the sex ratio at birth is very puzzling.

Still-births. The proportion of registered still-births[2] among all births was 4·0 per cent. in 1919–32, 4·5 per cent. in 1935–40,[3] and 5·8 per cent. in 1941–4, but registration of still-births was evidently incomplete,[4] particularly in earlier years. According to the sample surveys made in 1931 the proportion of still-births was 8·1 per cent. The Chief Census Officer says that the still-birth rates 'are highest in the more advanced Provinces',[5] and the proportion was actually only 5·8 per cent. in the Northern Territories as compared with 14·2 per cent. in Togoland. But in more backward regions many women may not have reported still-births. It is hard to believe, for example, that the 100 women questioned in the Lawra District had actually 793 live-born children and only 1 still-born.

Venereal Diseases. These diseases are apparently somewhat less common in the Gold Coast than in other British West African Dependencies, and this may be a reason for higher fertility. As regards syphilis it has been reported for some time that it is comparatively rare. For gonorrhœa the evidence is much more unfavourable.

1897. One of the gravest features in connection with the health of the General native population is the prevalence of untreated syphilis. So far as my own observation goes there is no effective native remedy for this disease and natives have not the patience to persist in a prolonged course of European treatment. Many indeed do not present themselves to the District Medical Officer until the disease has made terrible ravages in their system and the large number of men and women whose lives are crippled in this way must affect considerably the economic condition of the native community and of the Colony as a whole.[6]

1906. Although this disease [syphilis] is very common in certain towns, it is possible to travel for days and pass through villages that do not present a single case, and the disease is rare in the Northern Territories.[7]

1912. Gonorrhœa. There was an increase in the number of cases of this disease.

The natives have many methods of treating this disease, and patent medicines also are freely used by the educated ones.

Syphilis. There was a large increase in the number of cases treated and the disease seems to be on the increase.[8]

---

[1] *The Gold Coast, 1931*, vol. i, pp. 221–2.

[2] 'The accepted definition of a still-birth is a child born after the twenty-eighth week of pregnancy which, after complete expulsion from the mother, did not breathe or show any signs of life' (*Report on Births and Deaths 1927*, p. 6).

[3] The numbers of still-births have not been published for 1933 and 1934.

[4] See *Report of Principal Registrar 1933*, p. 3.   [5] *The Gold Coast, 1931*, vol. i, p. 219.

[6] Acting Chief Medical Officer in Gold Coast, 'Medical Report 1897', p. 175. See also ibid., p. 174; *Medical Report 1895*, p. 29; *1899*, p. 4; *1901*, p. 25.

[7] Ibid. *1906*, p. 9.   [8] Ibid. *1912*, p. 9.

1913. Syphilis. There is a marked decline in the number of cases, but what its significance may be it is difficult to say.

I am not inclined to think it is on the decrease.[1]

Both syphilis and gonorrhœa are prevalent, but, as is commonly found in other countries, the patients do not realize the seriousness of the condition and the necessity for continuance of treatment, in order to prevent the resulting serious consequences to themselves, as well as to the community at large.[2]

1914. Gonorrhœa. . . . this disease is on the increase. The fact that so few females apply for treatment does not indicate that it is not common amongst them.[3]

Syphilis. There would appear to be a gradual decline in the number of cases treated.

It would be idle to think that the disease is on the decrease.[4]

In the Colony and Ashanti venereal disease is undoubtedly prevalent, and to an extent which is quite inadequately represented by hospital statistics. The increasing facilities for travelling, and the cosmopolitan character of the large towns and industrial centres, probably tend to disseminate all forms of venereal disease.

In commenting upon the health of Coomassie, Dr. A. J. R. O'Brien, the Medical Officer of Health, dilates at some length upon the question of venereal disease among adults. Dr. O'Brien quotes Dr. C. V. Le Fanu as writing:—'I am not over-stating facts when I say that almost every male adult over 20 suffers from gonorrhœa. I might say the same of female adults, although I should say it is less common among them.' In the villages outside Coomassie the disease also appears to be prevalent, so much so that a native chief appealed for legislation as a means of dealing with the spread of gonorrhœa. According to Dr. O'Brien, syphilis 'is common and becoming more so every day': salvarsan was tried in 8 cases with marked success.

The large proportion of resident Hausas, the fact that Coomassie is a large garrison town, and also, I am afraid, the rapid 'civilisation' that is overtaking this cosmopolitan place, are factors which may account for the serious condition of things to which Drs. Le Fanu and O'Brien draw attention.[5]

1915. Gonorrhœa. This disease still increases steadily, and no doubt the increase is even greater than the figures suggest, for many cases seek no medical advice and others undergo native treatment.[6]

Syphilis. The foregoing remarks on gonorrhœa apply equally well to this disease; in fact the two diseases are frequently found co-existent in the same patient.[7]

1916. Both forms of venereal disease are undoubtedly very prevalent. Efforts are made to explain the serious nature of the disease, and the need for early and continuous treatment.[8]

1919. Venereal Diseases. The extent of these amongst the general population is not truly indicated by the hospital and dispensary returns. Female cases in particular are no doubt much underestimated.[9]

1920. . . . . a very considerable proportion of apparently healthy African males in the Gold Coast is affected with gonorrhœa. No data are at present available with regard to the women.[10]

1921. . . . [in] the Volta River District . . . according to the Acting District Commissioner '. . . venereal diseases are reported to be almost universal . . . .'[11]

As regards Venereal Disease which is reported to be prevalent through the Colony and certain parts of Ashanti, one can only say that the problem for a population of a little over two million does not appear to be so hopelessly insoluble as in the

[1] Principal Medical Officer, ibid. *1913*, p. 10.   [2] Senior Sanitary Officer, ibid., p. 26.
[3] Principal Medical Officer, ibid. *1914*, p. 11.   [4] Statement by same, ibid., p. 12.
[5] Senior Sanitary Officer, ibid., p. 39. See also, for example, *Colonial Reports, Ashanti 1916*, p. 19; *1919*, p. 17.   [6] *Medical Report 1915*, p. 8. See also ibid. *1913*, p. 10.
[7] Ibid. *1915*, p. 9.   [8] Ibid. *1916*, p. 13.   [9] Ibid. *1919*, p. 16.   [10] Ibid. *1920*, p. 54.
[11] *Census Report 1921*, p. 64. It is interesting to note that according to the surveys made in 1931 the Volta River District showed the lowest fertility.

thickly populated countries in Europe, America and the East. To the laymen there appears to be no reason to discriminate between venereal and other infectious diseases, except that from the population point of view, venereal diseases are probably more dangerous. 'The native attitude appears to be one of indifference, unless sterility results, then of course it is too late'; but the venereal clinics at Accra and other towns will be at least of some benefit to the community.[1]

1922. Syphilis was unknown among the natives of this district [Accra] until recently.[2]

There was a fairly increased number of attendances in gonorrhœa patients. The increase is more noticeable in the female patients. . . . The male attendance in gonorrhœa should have been higher, as I am certain that about 50 per cent of all the men in the district are in one way or the other suffering from gonorrhœa.[3]

1923. The most important disease in the Southern Section [of Togoland] is venereal.[4]

Venereal disease is practically negligible in the Northern Section.[5]

1925. Syphilis. Steady progress has been made in stamping out venereal disease in the Colony.[6]

1928. Gonorrhœa appears to be increasing in the Northern Territories, especially in places like Navrongo and Zuarungu, where it is known as the 'Kumasi disease.' This is due to the opening up of the country by roads.

Syphilis is, however, not at all prevalent there according to the reports of medical officers.[7]

1929. The control of syphilis is dependent on a whole population with at least a twentieth century appreciation of the disease, its dangers and consequences to the race: this is scarcely likely to be acquired, except by a negligible proportion of the general population of British West Africa, for many decades if not centuries, for it means not only the acquisition of a high standard of general medical knowledge, but a complete alteration in their standard of life and living. Syphilis, under these conditions of lack of control, probably means the slow disappearance of a race owing to still birth and other ante-natal effects, and it is to be hoped that there is at least some cross immunity from yaws, and that the difference between the two diseases is the survival in the tropics of a dermatropic strain by natural selection as against a strain altered by constant attack of drugs though still giving a type of immunity common to the two diseases.[8]

1930. There is a marked decrease in the number of cases of venereal diseases treated at the Accra Venereal Clinic. It is to be feared that this does not mean a decrease in incidence but is due to the fact that the African Medical Officer on the permanent staff, who took over from an African private practitioner in temporary part-time employment, found that a very large number of yaws and other cases not strictly venereal in origin had been included in the previous returns.[9]

1931. Medical Officers are generally of the opinion that although gonorrhœal infection is common, the incidence of syphilis is low. It is thought to exist to a greater proportionate extent in the Colony and Ashanti than in the Northern Territories, where both gonorrhœa and syphilis are known as 'Kumasi Sickness,' an expression which would seem to indicate definitely that the people of the last-named area consider the diseases to be directly due to the return of emigrants.[10]

From these figures [of cases treated] it would appear as if the incidence of gonorrhœa was declining. This is not the view taken by most Medical officers, one of whom gives his opinion for his own area that 'one would probably be right in assuming that most of the adult males have gonorrhœa.' Another Medical Officer after stating

---

[1] *Census Report 1921*, p. 163. See also ibid., pp. 81, 106.

[2] 'Report on the Venereal Clinic in the Accra Native Hospital 1922–3', *Medical Report 1922–3*, p. 78.   [3] Ibid., p. 80.   [4] *Report on Togoland 1923*, p. 29. See also ibid. *1924*, p. 53.

[5] Ibid. *1923*, p. 30.   [6] *Medical Report 1925–6*, p. 8.   [7] Ibid. *1928–9*, p. 13.

[8] Director of Laboratory Services, ibid. *1929–30*, p. 105.

[9] Ibid. *1930–1*, p. iii.   [10] *The Gold Coast, 1931*, vol. i, p. 220.

his view on the prevalence of the disease remarks naïvely:—'gonorrhœa is all that is left to remind them of their former days of prosperity. This they prefer to take to the Oman Council in the hope of obtaining pecuniary solace rather than to the Medical Officer for cure,' meaning thereby that they prefer to sue the infecting party for damages before the native tribunal.

There would appear to be general agreement amongst Medical officers that there is a real decrease in syphilis.[1]

1938. Hospital figures in the Gold Coast give no true index to the incidence of gonorrhœa. Comparatively few report the condition and it is rare to get the full co-operation of a patient in the treatment of its less acute manifestations.

Because of this the sequelæ of the disease such as arthritis, stricture, etc., appear in very much larger numbers than in Europe.

A considerable amount of working time is lost and disability ranging from general ill-health to actual crippling often results.

Gonorrhœa is responsible for a great deal of chronic ill-health among female Africans.

Syphilis is not a common disease. In parts of the Northern Territories it is only seen among the indigenous population in those who have returned from the mines or from the larger urban communities.[2]

1939. Syphilis is not a common disease. . . .

Gonorrhœa, its complications and sequelæ, on the other hand, is extremely common.[3]

1944. Venereal diseases are very common in the Colony particularly in the coastal towns and measures to deal with this problem are under consideration. Fortunately syphilis is, as yet, not a common disease, but there is likely to be an increased incidence after the war and this possibility is not being overlooked.[4]

2. General Mortality

Introduction. There are no data whatsoever concerning general mortality outside the registration towns, as the few sample surveys covered only births and child deaths and did not inquire into mortality of adults. Since there is a consensus of opinion that the urban registration figures do not permit the drawing of any conclusions concerning mortality in other areas, all statements about mortality in the Gold Coast and Togoland, as a whole, are mere guesses.

In his report on the Blue Book for 1851 Governor Hill said that the population increase must be great 'as there are no causes to diminish the numbers, excepting a decay of nature from old age'.[5] But such a favourable view of native mortality on the Gold Coast has never been taken again. In his report for 1858 the Colonial Surgeon Dr. Clarke suggested that mortality was very high, and that this was not due to 'war, pestilence, or famine', but to an enormous infant mortality and to 'the easy access to spirits, and its enormous consumption in these settlements'.[6] Alcoholism

---

[1] *Medical Report 1931-2*, pp. 8-9.   [2] Ibid. *1938*, p. 8.

[3] Ibid. *1939*, pp. 3-4. See also ibid. *1940*, p. 4; *1941*, p. 3.

[4] *General Plan for Development in the Gold Coast*, p. 6. See also Saunders (1945), p. 157: 'Even before the war, gonorrhœa was spreading to areas previously unaffected, but the spread appears to have been accelerated by war conditions. Syphilis, formerly rare, appears to have become more common.'

[5] *State of Colonial Possessions 1851*, Part I, p. 185.

[6] Ibid. *1858*, Part II, p. 26. See also ibid., p. 24: 'I regret to say that drunkenness is a widespread vice among the natives, a circumstance chiefly dependent upon the cheapness of the spirits imported from the United States and the Brazils.'

and the frequency of deaths from violence were occasionally complained of in the following decades.

1867. Wife murder appears common in the eastern districts. Human sacrifice, I regret to state, still exists in parts, but it is severely punished when practicable.

The standard of morality is low, and the vile 'customs' of the natives, still existing, appear to have no object but drunkenness, riot, and dissipation. These 'customs' take place on certain occasions, such as burial of the dead, &c. The most objectionable is the 'yam custom' or 'Black Christmas', which takes place in August, and at such seasons, unless restrained, the natives generally fight, and resorting to arms many deaths are the result. They are gradually being abolished in the towns of Cape Coast and Accra, and I trust will soon disappear from them for ever.[1]

1901. Kwitta. Within the last quarter, it would appear that wounding has assumed the form of an epidemic. An average of two severe cases of wounding per week have been admitted into hospital during the last two months of the year. Excessive drinking is mainly responsible for these cases. Invariably, they are the outcome of some drunken affray, following upon that institution known as the 'funeral custom,' whose *raison d'être* is the opportunity it affords for unlimited drinking of cheap spirits. . . .

Alcoholism, judging from out-patient experience, claims a great number of victims and is greatly on the increase.[2]

But according to the Chief Census Officer, 1931, alcoholism is apparently no longer a notable cause of death. After having estimated 'the per capita consumption of alcoholic drinks per annum' at 'a trifle under 10 gallons' he said:

In spite of this apparently large consumption of alcohol the average African of the Gold Coast is certainly not a 'toper'; although acute bouts of drunkenness on occasions of festivity and funerals are sometimes indulged in. From no district in the Gold Coast is excess in alcoholic drink reported, and no record of any influence on adult, infantile or child mortality.[3]

A more important factor affecting mortality in earlier times was probably the burying of corpses within dwelling-houses. I shall confine myself to quoting from reports of the years immediately preceding the enactment of 'An Ordinance to provide for interments in cemeteries and to prohibit intramural sepulture'.[4]

The old and pernicious practice of burying the dead in the midst of towns is now condemned all the world over as insanitary, for it has been proved by chemical analysis that morbific exhalations are constantly given off from the surface of grave-yards. Hence it is that in all large towns in Europe, and especially in England, well-kept cemeteries are established in suitable positions in or outside their suburbs.

In Accra, however, where the native hovels are allowed to be built in such close proximity that a wheelbarrow could hardly pass through some of the narrow, foul-smelling alleys intersecting them, the disgusting custom of domiciliary sepulture

[1] Administrator Ussher, *State of Colonial Possessions 1867*, Part II, p. 21.
[2] 'Report on the Hospital at Quitta 1901', Gold Coast, *Medical Report 1901*, pp. 25–6.
[3] *The Gold Coast, 1931*, vol. i, p. 238.
[4] See p. 448 above. The establishment of cemeteries had been urged as far back as 1859 by Colonial Surgeon Dr. Clarke. He described conditions as follows (*State of Colonial Possessions 1858*, Part II, p. 25): 'The mass of the inhabitants bury their dead in the basement floor of their houses; a practice not confined to the pagan part of the population, but also practised by many respectable and wealthy families. This hurtful custom cannot be too soon discontinued. It is not done by the natives of the interior, but by all accounts it has been an ancient custom on the coast towns. . . . I may here mention that several persons have been buried in the floor of the medical store of the Colonial Hospital, in the surgery, and in the kitchen used by the female prisoners.'

is still carried on, and as no grass nor other herb can be grown over such graves it is easy to comprehend how tainted the atmosphere must be in the neighbourhood of such centres of putrid fermentation. It is, I am convinced, the cause of much of the sickness which prevails amongst Europeans who have to reside permanently in the town. In the absence of data on the vital statistics of the native population, for they are utterly impossible to obtain, we are unable to gauge the effects of this pernicious custom on their health. But it can easily be understood. Just fancy for one moment sitting down to one's meals every day as these people do over a spot where a corpse, perhaps more, lies rotting six feet below, and then multiply such instances by the hundred and you will very easily comprehend the evil effects which the deadly emanations arising from such a mass of decomposing animal matter must exert in places where fresh air has little or no access, where vegetation is absent, and where no effectual precautions are taken to prevent the ascent of poisonous gases from the graves below. . . .

There is a remedy for this, and that is to provide the people with a walled in cemetery for their own special use, then an Ordinance against domiciliary sepulture could be put into force; but until the people are given a decent burial ground of their own it would be useless making any effort to carry the provisions of such an Ordinance into effect; as useless, indeed, as it would be to try and stop them latrining around and about the town while they are unprovided with a sufficient number of public latrines.[1]

Ada District. If anything will wean the people from the dangerous and disgusting practice of domiciliary sepulture the establishment of public cemeteries will do so more effectually than any other remedy can do.[2]

Ada Station. The necessity for a Government public cemetery has been urged in former reports. Intramural sepulture still continues in this district. There is a small private cemetery belonging to the Basel Mission Society and in which none but Christians are interred. It is well known the number of Christians is very small and therefore the majority of the natives are buried anywhere, in the bushes and houses. There being no public cemetery, the provisions of 'Ordinance No. 7 of 1888' 'to provide for interments in cemeteries and to prohibit intramural sepulture' cannot be enforced.[3]

Unfortunately public cemeteries were established in only five towns during the first decade after the enactment of the 1888 Ordinance and in only six more towns during the second decade,[4] a fact which was the more regrettable as the natives apparently were quite ready to bury their dead in such cemeteries.

It is satisfactory to note that the action taken by the Government in 1891, in requiring the establishment of cemeteries in the principal towns and villages, is being appreciated by the natives. Formerly it was the practice of the native to bury his relations within his dwelling house, but this practice is fast becoming a thing of the past, and the cemeteries established by the orders of the Government are now being freely used, many of the graves being marked with rude memorials to distinguish them. Cemeteries are kept up at the expense of the Government in Accra, Christiansborg, Cape Coast, Elmina, and Adda.[5]

---

[1] 'Sanitary Report on the Station of Accra 1885', *Colonial Possessions Reports 1884–6*, pp. 109–10. Referring to this report the Right Hon. Edward Stanhope, M.P., wrote to Governor Griffith (ibid., pp. 321–2):

'Even at the capital, Accra, . . . such urgent wants as a cemetery . . . have still to be postponed.

'. . . I cannot refrain from observing that it is not worthy of a civilised Government to leave such evils unredressed while receiving a large annual surplus revenue. . . .

'The Colony has a considerable sum of money available for such services . . . .'

[2] 'Sanitary Report on Addah District' (1887), Gold Coast, *Sanitary and Medical Reports for 1887 and 1888*, p. 11.   [3] 'Sanitary Report on Ada Station 1888', ibid., p. 46.

[4] See p. 448 above.   [5] *Colonial Reports, Gold Coast 1895*, p. 8.

The 1885 Sanitary Report on Accra, quoted above, complained about overcrowding, and such complaints and complaints about inadequate housing conditions have been quite frequent.

1869. It [the Settlement] would be pre-eminently healthy among West African Colonies, but for the many barbarous and unhealthy customs of the natives, and their indifference to sanitary arrangements, as well as their unwillingness to consent to such improvements as tend to do away with their dilapidated tenements. These are invariably treated as sacred, or 'family houses,' and give the towns a ruinous appearance, besides being a prolific source of disease from the dirt and animal matter accumulated in and around them. I should much dread any outbreak of cholera in the towns of the Gold Coast.[1]

1891. In Accra, for example, the houses are built in very close proximity to each other, and are most defectively constructed from a hygienic point of view, and also overcrowded, so that it is difficult to understand why the vitality of the people has not been more seriously affected by the continuous inhalation of impure air, especially during the night hours.[2] This question of physical and physiological overcrowding, especially in the larger towns of the Colony, is one of serious importance. The older towns or parts of the towns of Accra and Cape Coast may be excused for the condition of things in this respect now existing in them, but such comparatively modern towns as Kwitta and Saltpond have no excuse whatever . . . .[3]

1919. Shortage of housing accommodation is a sinister feature of most coast towns at present. Evacuation of dilapidated buildings, and prosecutions for overcrowding, are unjustifiable in the absence of reasonable accommodation elsewhere. Labourers in the large centres often have to spend a very considerable proportion of their monthly wages on a small room shared with others, or a few square feet of verandah.[4]

Governor Guggisberg, on 3 March 1927, in an address to the Legislative Council, described the sanitary conditions during the first decade of this century as follows:

Throughout the country no sanitation worthy of the name existed. In Accra, the capital, and in all the coast towns the conditions were very bad. The conservancy system was primitive in the extreme, and methods obtained for the disposal of refuse which to-day would be absolutely taboo. The water supply—which is of the first importance in the Tropics—was rain water collected from the roof in storage tanks. The tanks were frequently dry, and foul water from polluted wells was often sold at as much as 6d. a gallon. Housing was extremely bad. No attempt had been made at town-planning. The native quarters consisted of dark, ill-ventilated mud hovels crowded together; ideal *foci* for epidemic diseases. The merchants lived over their stores surrounded by insanitary native compounds. Government officials lived in bungalows made in England, brought out and re-erected outside the towns.

It is no wonder that under the above conditions mortality was high. Water being scarce, it was carefully stored by the natives, and hidden away in unprotected vessels which generally swarmed with mosquito larvæ. Malaria was extremely common, diarrhœa and dysentery rife. Though no reliable records are obtainable,

---

[1] Administrator Ussher, *State of Colonial Possessions 1869*, Part II, p. 18. See also ibid. *1858*, Part II, pp. 24–5.

[2] Actually mortality was excessive. In Accra and Christiansborg, with a combined population of 19,082 according to the 1891 count, 664 natives were buried in public cemeteries in 1891, 768 in 1892, and 812 in 1893. In addition many were buried in the Wesleyan Cemetery, Accra, in the Basel Mission Cemetery, Christiansborg, and in the Mohammedan Cemetery, Accra. See Gold Coast, *Blue Book 1891* T, p. 1; *1892* T, p. 1; *1893* T, pp. 1–3. Finally there may have been quite a few burials in other private cemeteries and in the 'bush'. As shown above (p. 449), the Acting Chief Medical Officer, in his report for 1899, said that the official Accra burial rate of 36·5 per 1,000 was probably far below the real death-rate.

[3] *Census Report 1891*, p. 12.   [4] *Medical Report 1919*, p. 18.

the death-rate, and especially infantile mortality, must have been appalling. The paths in the vicinity of the towns, and the streets in the towns themselves, were extremely bad, generally congested with livestock, and thick with dust laden with the germs of dust-borne diseases.[1]

As regards medical services he said:

During the first decade of the century the Medical Department was in a primitive state. Activities were chiefly confined to the principal towns lying along the coast line where hospitals of a sort had been established and where efforts were being made to introduce modern medicine and surgery. The hinterland at this time was very imperfectly opened up; there were no motor roads, and means of transport were scarce and unreliable. A few Medical Officers were sent off to the bush and to three or four of the towns lying in the Northern Territories.[2]

To make matters still worse the quality of the Medical Officers left much to be desired. In a report dated 30 April 1901 the Principal Medical Officer Dr. Henderson wrote:

I regret to say that the majority of the Medical Officers sent out during the last twelve months were what I can only describe as the dregs of the profession; men who cannot get anything to do in England, and take whatever offers; this is borne out by the fact that, for various and discreditable causes, so many have had to be sent home after at most a few weeks in the Colony. Sending out such men puts the Colony to great expense, and brings discredit on the Department.[3]

But when shortly afterwards the medical staffs of all the West African Colonies and Protectorates were amalgamated into one service and the salaries raised, more and better doctors went to the Gold Coast, and after the outbreak of plague in 1908 and the epidemic of yellow fever in 1910 the medical staff was further increased.[4]

This, however, was the last permanent rise in the number of Medical Officers. In its 'Historical Survey, 1913–33', the Medical Department reports:

. . . the number of qualified medical officers of all grades and in both hospitals and health branches has varied very little; the relevant figures being 66, 57 and 69 for the years 1913, 1923–24[5] and 1933–34 respectively.[6]

At the outbreak of the recent war the ratio of Medical Officers to the population was smaller than 25 years earlier. Their activities outside the towns lying along the coast have been feeble all through,[7] and little is

[1] *The Gold Coast, A Review of the Events of 1920–6*, p. 181.   [2] Ibid.
[3] Gold Coast, *Medical Report 1900*, p. 19. This possibly explains why, according to *Colonial Reports, Gold Coast 1899*, p. 22, even in the towns the large majority of the natives still resorted to the 'Native Medicine Man'.   [4] See *A Review of the Events of 1920–6*, p. 182.
[5] By 1923–4 pre-war conditions had not been restored. In his address of 3 Mar. 1927 Governor Guggisberg said: 'After the war we experienced the utmost difficulty in obtaining Medical Officers and it was not until 1926 that our establishment was brought up to strength' (ibid., p. 184).
[6] Gold Coast, *Medical Report 1933–4*, p. 4. As a matter of fact the relevant figures varied enormously. See, for example, ibid. *1935*, p. 3: 'Staff of medical officers—other than administrative officers—numbered 66 on 1st January, 1935 . . . as compared with a staff of 90 on 1st April, 1929 . . . .' The number increased again from 1936 on, but was reduced considerably after the outbreak of the war.
[7] See also in this connexion Hailey, p. 1169: 'While many hospital buildings have been erected in the important towns, at considerable expense, dispensaries in rural areas are as yet few, and it appears that the initiative is left largely to the local native authorities, who, in the absence of a regular "native treasury" system, have no means of making the necessary provision for them.'

known therefore concerning the incidence of such diseases as leprosy or sleeping-sickness. Even serious epidemics occurring not far from the places where the Officers are stationed may escape their notice.

That epidemics within fifty miles of Accra involving serious loss of life do still remain undetected for considerable periods owing to the dearth of Health Officers is clearly established by the history of the outbreak of yellow fever at Asamangkese in 1926. Briefly, Asamangkese is an important cocoa centre situated about forty miles as the crow flies north-west of Accra.

The population consists of about 4,800 African inhabitants living in about 800 compounds.

From the information subsequently received, it would appear that the disease was introduced into Asamangkese in May and that it was causing many deaths before the end of that month.

In spite of this, however, the epidemic was not discovered until towards the end of July . . . .[1]

Recent General Mortality. Since the late 1920s official reports on health and mortality in general have been more or less unfavourable. A few quotations may serve as an illustration.

1929–30. The health of the general African community throughout the year was, generally speaking, and as compared with previous years, fair.[2] The term fair is used purely in a comparative sense, for the Gold Coast is no exception to the well-known fact that the health of Africans in Africa is really much poorer than that of Europeans in Europe. High infantile mortality, diet deficiencies, with low resistance to infection and high mortality, parasitic diseases of various kinds which sap vitality, prevail everywhere. Some parts are worse off than others.

The lack of good water supplies in the Northern Territories and in certain areas of the Eastern Province of the Gold Coast is a serious handicap in many respects to the health of the people in those parts. The improvement of public health is not merely a problem of treating diseases but is bound up with the whole problem of raising the standard of living all round.[3]

1933–34. Up to the present there are little statistical data to show that the trade depression has had an adverse effect on the health of the population as a whole. On the other hand, the setback to housing and sanitation which was referred to in the last year's report was still more noticeable in the year under review. Unless a measure of prosperity returns and makes it possible to regain at least the standards achieved before the slump—including adequate staff of medical and health officers—

---

[1] *Medical Report 1926–7*, p. 20.

[2] The medical staff was apparently larger in 1929–30 than ever before and ever thereafter. See, in this connexion, ibid. *1931–2*, p. 5: 'It is . . . in the outlying areas that the effect of a reduced staff has been most severely felt. Not only were Medical Officers withdrawn from Bekwai, Bawku, Wioso, Mpraeso and Kete Krachi, but Salaga, Kibi, Sunyani and even Saltpond were deprived of the services of a Medical Officer for varying periods. This curtailment of ordinary medical services involved a corresponding reduction in the health services in these areas. The brunt of the economy measures fell therefore with a very serious double effect on the more remote stations where the Medical Officer must perform the dual function of Medical Officer and Health Officer.' For further retrenchments of staff see, for example, ibid. *1933–4*, pp. 8, 44.

[3] Ibid. *1929–30*, p. 10. In striking contrast to this statement the Census Officer, 1931, said: 'The general health of the population of the Gold Coast and its dependencies can at least be considered fair, if not good. . . . From general observations by officers long resident in the country and from the data collected in the towns it would appear that the people under normal conditions of family life enjoy a state of health favourably comparable with other similar countries, but they are subject to epidemics of outstanding virulence' (*The Gold Coast, 1931*, vol. i, pp. 224–5). I am inclined to think that the statement would have been more correct if it had ended: '. . . as they are less subject to epidemics of outstanding virulence.' I doubt whether the Gold Coast compares favourably with other similar countries as regards non-epidemic diseases (malaria, leprosy, tuberculosis).

there is little doubt but that the death-rate will tend to increase. A note of warning is sounded by the actual increase in the death-rate of 1933 and by the fact that the number of patients whose condition was attributed to hunger has risen from thirty-six in 1932–33 to sixty-eight in 1933–34.[1]

1935. It is with regret that a serious set-back has to be recorded in the health of the people of the Gold Coast in the year under review. Some indication of this was manifest early in 1935 when the returns of deaths in the registration areas scattered throughout the Colony were compiled. The Principal Registrar of Births, Deaths and Burials pointed to the fact that a slight but definite rise had taken place in the death-rate in 1934. During 1935 this increase amounted to the alarming figure of three per thousand of the population living in 31 registration districts. Furthermore, all but four of such areas showed an increased death-rate; while in one populous centre, the rate rose by over 50 per centum above the corresponding rate for the previous year.

It is difficult to hazard an explanation for this, but it might be desirable to mention certain factors.[2]

The factors listed in the report are (a) Immigration of Undernourished and Diseased Elements; (b) Low Standard of Hygiene, especially in Rural and Mining Areas; (c) Increased Facilities for the Dissemination of Disease; (d) Malnutrition; (e) Specific Diseases. I shall deal below with specific diseases and shall briefly discuss here the other factors.

(a) The large preponderance of male deaths in the registration areas had attracted the attention of the Principal Registrar for many years, but he had attributed it to a preponderance of males in the urban population due to male immigration.

1927. The large preponderance of male deaths over deaths in the opposite sex is accounted for by the fact that considerable immigration of male workers takes place from other colonies.

For example, conservancy work is largely carried out by Kroos who come to the Gold Coast in large gangs in search of work and as a rule bring one woman to every fifty men and boys.

Labourers and carriers frequently come from the Haute Volta and Senegal in search of work in the mines and on cocoa farms; it is the exception rather than the rule for such gangs to be accompanied by their womenfolk.[3]

Two years later he thought that deaths from accidents were a contributing factor.

1929. Of the total [registered deaths] 3,454 were males and 1,997 were females.

These figures give a proportion of 172·9 male deaths, to every 100 female deaths.

The chief reason for this disproportion between the two sexes, as in former years, is the immigration of male labourers from the Kru Coast and French Territory. By far the larger proportion of accidental deaths are naturally male and this also tends to increase the disproportion.[4]

In his next report, in discussing 'the age distribution of deaths at six large stations', he pointed to the conditions under which the immigrants lived in towns as a further factor.

1930. The preponderance of deaths in the 25–45 group as usual is very high. The reasons for this are as follows:—

(a) Labour immigration swells this age group.

(b) The 'heat and burden of the day' is, to a very great extent, borne by this

[1] *Medical Report 1933–4*, p. 11.   [2] Ibid. *1935*, p. 4.   [3] *Report on Births and Deaths 1927*, p. 5.
[4] *Report of Principal Registrar 1929*, p. 4. See also ibid. *1930*, p. 3.

category; exposure, strain, under-nourishment, effects of excesses, etc., all play a part.

(c) By far the greatest proportion of accidental deaths affects this age group.[1]

But for several years more there is little evidence that the Administration was aware of the fact that the condition in which the immigrants arrived was apparently the decisive factor.[2]

1933. As might be expected, the health conditions in the more important towns compare favourably with those in the more primitive rural areas.

Not only is groundwork sanitation of higher standard in the former including pure water supplies, satisfactory disposal of waste and good housing and town planning—to mention but a few points—but far more constant supervision is exercised by health officers and their staffs than is possible in the 'bush' inhabited mostly by an illiterate and ignorant peasantry.

Hence, one would anticipate that the expectation of life would be greater in urban than in rural areas and vital statistics would appear in a more favourable light than would be the case if means existed for securing a random sample of the populace as a whole.

This factor is corrected to some extent artificially owing to the existence of hospitals in the larger areas where registration is in vogue; since sick persons may be attracted from the countryside and may die in the medical institutions (including the mental hospital) in towns.

Furthermore, the congregation of numbers of persons in townships where congested districts are to be found may raise the general death-rate owing to the higher mortality from respiratory disease, for example, pulmonary tuberculosis, the incidence of which is definitely influenced by overcrowding and bad housing.[3]

... the excess of male over female deaths is particularly marked in the age group 25–45 when the hazard suffered by men, especially those employed in mining, influences the rate more markedly.[4]

Finally, in his report for 1934, the Principal Registrar said:

Unfortunately, a not inconsiderable proportion of these immigrants enter the Colony in an emaciated condition, frequently suffering from helminthiasis, malaria, trypanosomiasis and a host of other maladies. Crowded together in gangs in ill-ventilated huts, they provide fertile soil for Kock's bacillus and the recovery rate in such cases is practically nil.[5]

Subsequent reports stated:

1935. ... these centres [registration areas] often draw to themselves large numbers of immigrant males, in the 'vulnerable' 25–45-year group, seeking employment. These men are often in a very poor condition, frequently diseased, and their influx tends considerably to raise the local death rate.[6]

It is unfortunate that a large proportion of the immigrants are in such a poor physical condition on arrival. Many are diseased. They crowd together into insanitary dwellings, and their death rate from respiratory diseases is high. They are particularly prone to develop pulmonary tuberculosis; and the immigrant infected with trypanosomiasis is, and will be, a factor of the greatest importance.[7]

It is considered that the increased death rate for 1935 was to no small extent due to an exaggerated movement of immigrant labour—attracted by signs of

[1] *Report of Principal Registrar 1930*, p. 4.

[2] This is the more surprising, as the terrible condition in which the immigrants arrived had attracted the full attention of the local authorities of Kumasi; see *Reports on the Eastern and Western Provinces of Ashanti 1930–1*, p. 17.

[3] *Report of Principal Registrar 1933*, p. 1.

[4] Ibid., p. 4. In 1931–8 the ratio of male deaths to 100 female deaths was 168 at age 15 to 25; 314 at age 25 to 45; and 216 at age 45 to 65.

[5] Ibid. *1934*, p. 2.   [6] Ibid. *1935*, p. 1.   [7] Ibid., p. 2. See also ibid., p. 4.

increasing prosperity—in greater numbers than could properly be absorbed into steady employment.

If Koforidua be taken as an example, i.e. the town among the more important centres which registered the largest proportional increase in the number of deaths, it is found that those occurring in total 'strangers' to the Gold Coast increased by some 44 per centum over the number of deaths in the same category reported for 1934.[1]

1936. It is to be deplored that so many of these immigrants arrive in such a poor physical condition. A large percentage are undernourished, and many are diseased. They overcrowd into insanitary dwellings on the trade routes and on arrival in the larger centres, and often fall an easy prey to respiratory diseases in general and to pulmonary tuberculosis in particular.

Some two per centum of immigrants from the North were found, after blood-examination at Kumasi, to be suffering from trypanosomiasis.[2]

1937. Large numbers of immigrant labourers flock into the centres in search of employment. Many of these labourers, arriving in a very poor physical condition, do much to swell the local morbidity and mortality rates.[3]

It is unfortunate that so many of these immigrant labourers arrive in such a poor physical condition. A considerable proportion are actually diseased; many are in such an enfeebled state that they are unable to take up employment on arrival—a high proportion are undernourished.

The inferior type of labourer, in past years, has largely depended on finding work on the cocoa farms, and in the handling and movement of the cocoa crop. The hold-up of the cocoa crop, experienced towards the end of 1937, to a very great extent deprived this class of labourer of his chances of employment.[4]

Members of this class of the community are very subject to the effects of want, undernourishment, strain, exposure, insanitary overcrowding, the total lack of health knowledge bearing on self-preservation and the evil results of the universal spitting habit.

They have practically no resistance to pulmonary infections; helminthic infestations are very common, and malaria is almost universal. There can be little wonder, therefore, that they frequently fall victims to pneumonia or pulmonary tuberculosis.[5]

1938. . . . many of these registration areas have industrial attractions which ensure a steady annual influx of immigrant labourers. These men, the majority of whom are referable to the 25–45 years age group, are often undernourished and sick on arrival and . . . profoundly influence the mortality returns.[6]

In most of the important areas, local deaths arrange themselves fairly readily under one or two arbitrary heads, e.g. those occurring in the local stable population which are comparatively constant, and the larger number occurring in the 'floating' stranger population which is subject to wide fluctuations depending on many factors, both health and economic.[7]

Yearly the conditions under which the stable section of the population lives steadily improve. The floating section of the population, which influences the mortality-rate so profoundly, requires specially devised means of succour.[8]

Steady improvement has been taking place, especially in the larger centres, in the conditions under which the stable sections of the population live, but to cause a further drop in the death-rate, which is deeply influenced by the presence of immigrant labourers, more attention to the care of this class, the individuals of which arrive in an under-nourished and often diseased condition, is greatly needed.[9]

[1] Ibid., p. 7.   [2] Ibid. *1936*, p. 2.   [3] Ibid. *1937*, p. 1.
[4] Ibid., p. 2. See also ibid., p. 3.   [5] Ibid., p. 5.
[6] Ibid. *1938*, p. 1. See also ibid., p. 5, and *Medical Report 1937*, p. 29; *1938*, pp. 4–5.
[7] *Report of Principal Registrar 1938*, p. 3.   [8] Ibid., p. 9.
[9] *Medical Report 1938*, p. 5.

The reasons for the deplorable condition in which so many migrant labourers arrive in the towns are not far to seek. Major Orde Browne, in his report on Labour Conditions in West Africa (1941), states:

Labour for the various employment centres is largely migrant, the bulk of it coming from the Northern Territories, Nigeria, or the French colonies. The reasons governing this movement are the general shortage of money and the seasonal scarcity of food in the north. . . . Since there is no recruiting and no contract, the men have to make their own way and pay their own expenses on the journey; no medical inspection is carried out and no facilities for repatriation exist. The travellers support themselves on the journey by providing themselves with a little food with which to start out, and by carrying fowls and other local products to trade on the road; beyond this they have to depend upon casual employment and the conspicuous hospitality of the country-people.[1] A journey of four or five hundred miles in such conditions is naturally a severe ordeal and a large proportion therefore arrive at their destination worn out and emaciated . . . .

Generally, the picture now presented is that of a labour force amounting to many thousands moving without supervision or help pathetically lacking in the essentials for their long and exacting journey.[2]

TABLE 23. *African Deaths by Age and Sex, Gold Coast and Togoland, 1931–8[1]*

Year	First 24 hours		1 day to 1 year		1 to 5 years		5 to 15 years		15 to 25 years		25 to 45 years		45 to 65 years		65 years and over		Total
	M.	F.	M.	F.	M.	F.	M.	F.	M.	F.	M.	F.	M.	F.	M.	F.	
1931	55	25	456	400	358	349	188	167	375	205	1,514	470	524	266	295	325	5,972
1932	40	34	476	404	379	327	182	148	351	205	1,366	460	530	239	363	401	5,905
1933	51	35	479	392	380	380	190	159	402	238	1,509	431	602	268	368	380	6,264
1934	60	43	502	412	411	407	181	150	331	250	1,583	535	591	279	366	449	6,550
1935	50	50	623	562	505	448	231	233	412	240	1,905	593	624	335	477	543	7,831
1936	48	43	584	528	516	481	286	224	483	289	1,820	615	751	344	484	506	8,002
1937	49	24	679	558	501	478	281	240	461	298	1,987	630	780	342	519	604	8,431
1938	49	34	574	489	415	400	234	173	498	247	1,809	566	720	302	490	530	7,530

[1] See *Report Principal Registrar 1931*, p. 16; *1932*, p. 16; *1933*, p. 16; *1934*, p. 20; *1935*, p. 18; *1936*, p. 18; *1937*, p. 17; *1938*, p. 20.

It is very difficult to estimate the actual mortality of the immigrants into the towns, but the scanty available data indicate that it is excessive. According to the 1931 census there were in the then thirty registration areas 77,633 males and 59,077 females at ages 15–45.[3] The numbers of registered deaths of persons 15–45 in 1931 were 1,889 males and 675 females. The death-rate was, therefore, 24·3 for males and 11·4 for females. If we assume that the death-rate of the non-immigrant male population aged 15–45 was 15 and that the immigrants constituted one-third of the male population aged 15–45, the death-rate of the immigrants aged 15–45 would have been 43.[4]

[1] See also, for example, *Medical Report 1934*, p. 21: 'It is usual for these labourers to find little or no work *en route* and their dietary is largely restricted to a handful of kola nuts and water from pools and streams.'

[2] Orde Browne, pp. 91–2. See also *Report on the Labour Department 1938–9*, pp. 3–4.

[3] Computed from *The Gold Coast, 1931*, vol. ii, pp. 32–246.

[4] This rate, of course, does not cover the deaths of migrant labourers who leave the town after having contracted a fatal disease. See in this connexion *Report on the Labour Department 1938–9*, p. 4: 'The worst case of all is where a boy contracts some serious illness in the south and he has the homing instinct. He feels that he must go back to his country to die. It is cases such as these which are so pathetic for often he never arrives home but dies on the way.'

(b) The Principal Registrar has pointed out many times that health conditions are much better in the towns than in the rural areas.[1] The Medical Report for 1935 in discussing the rise in mortality stated:

Contributory factors probably include insanitary conditions in the rural—as against town—areas particularly where, in mining regions, collections of hovels have grown up with no pretence of plan and without any of the necessary sanitary requirements. . . .

Meanwhile the standard of hygiene in the countryside of the Colony and Ashanti is steadily becoming worse.[2]

This report said furthermore:

The Senior Health Officer, Western Province, reports that:—

'Village sanitation in practically every rural area in the Province is in the most appalling condition, and has to be seen to be believed. It is heart-breaking work against an impassable barrier of indifference and open hostility.'

The Senior Health Officer, Ashanti, reports a serious fall in the standard of rural sanitation in Ashanti since 1928. For this he holds the financial depression of the last few years mainly responsible. There are no legal sanctions to insist on the elevation of the standard of rural sanitation to a reasonable and safe minimum. Education and moral suasion will take years to achieve tangible results. So many of the inhabitants of rural centres of any importance are 'strangers,' owing no allegiance to the local Chiefs, that co-operation is difficult to obtain.[3]

The following reports said:

1936. As pointed out in last year's report the sanitary conditions in the rural areas and in the areas surrounding the mines are deteriorating and this will continue until the successful establishment of local sanitary authorities with sufficient powers.[4]

1937. As in previous years, it must be stressed that the 'pin-point' sanitation of a few centres only, is a most unsatisfactory system. These centres become infected, again and again, from the uncontrolled surrounding rural areas; free movement is checked, and trade is impeded.[5]

But conditions in many towns are likewise unsatisfactory.

. . . most of the larger centres in the Gold Coast are of considerable antiquity and occupy classical West African sites extensively complicated by lagoons, or sites consisting of alternating well-drained and low-lying areas, the latter usually accommodating sluggish streams, swamps and pools the drainage of which very often presents considerable difficulties.[6]

(c) As regards increased facilities for the dissemination of disease the Medical Reports said:

1935. Yet another possible cause of the increased morbidity and death-rate in the Colony as a whole is attributed to the opening up of the country resulting in a much more fluid population. In former times a village in the Northern Territories, for example, might be invaded by such a severe outbreak of, say, sleeping sickness that the population became decimated before the disease burnt itself out. Towns and villages in the same district might, at the same time, remain unaffected owing to the complete isolation of the stricken village. Nowadays, through the construction of roads and the considerable increase in transport facilities, few towns or villages are so remote as not to have contact with the outside world. In addition, the stories

[1] See, for example, the passage in *Report of Principal Registrar 1933* (p. 1) quoted p. 482 above. See also ibid. *1935*, p. 1; *1936*, p. 1; *1937*, p. 1; *1938*, p. 1.
[2] *Medical Report 1935*, p. 4.   [3] Ibid., p. 27.
[4] Ibid. *1936*, p. 4.   [5] Ibid. *1937*, p. 30.   [6] Ibid. *1938*, p. 15.

of financial reward and adventure of persons who have returned from working in the Government service, in the mines or cocoa plantations, all act as incentives to the inhabitants of distant parts to migrate and offer their labour.[1]

1936. The opening up of trade routes and increased motor transport facilities continue to play their rôle in the dissemination of disease. This is the inevitable result of development and can only be met by more vigorous efforts at prevention whether by facilities for treatment or other methods.[2]

(d) Malnutrition has been discussed a great deal in official reports, and though it would seem that conditions are better than in many other British dependencies in Africa, the problem has caused some concern in recent years. A few quotations may serve as illustration:

1920. The neglect of cultivation of the ordinary foods of the country is bringing about consequences which may be far-reaching. Already the occurrence in hospital of some cases of grave illness or death attributable to deficiency of important factors in the normal diet—'Deficiency Disease'—have helped to bring this subject into a salutary prominence. The tendency of certain classes to live on an unvaried diet of one or two articles which are often lacking in the minute but essential elements for full nutrition, and the increasing temptation to others to live on the cheaper forms of imported canned provisions, are matters for immediate reform not by statute but by the influence of administrative officers and by instruction and encouragement towards greater production of ordinary farm crops and improved methods of preserving grain and other produce. The cultivation of such an important food as the pulses seems to be particularly neglected.[3]

1927. Tinned foods of various descriptions are being used more and more in lieu of local foodstuffs.

In spite of this, however, deficiency diseases are negligible both in numbers and in degree of severity.

Among 1,233 deaths recorded in Accra, for example, during the year, there was only one from beri-beri and a doubtful fatal case of rickets.

Instances are reported from time to time of death from starvation, but these are rare and there is usually some other factor involved for example, chronic ulceration, ankylostomiasis, trypanosomiasis, etc. There is little difficulty in obtaining a well-balanced diet with all the necessary food elements.[4]

1929. It is well known that in many centres in the Gold Coast large sections of the community have made very radical changes in their dietary, of late years tinned meat and fish being partaken of in increasingly large quantities.

The present is referred to by one influential chief as 'the day of the tin and the bottle.'

So far, little deterioration can be noted as a result of this change and it must be left to the future to be made clear.[5]

1930. It may be stated generally that foodstuffs procurable throughout the Gold Coast are sufficiently varied and plentiful to admit of a well balanced diet. . . .

There is however, a tendency to overload the diet with carbohydrates and to reduce proteins and fats.

Tinned foodstuffs, especially the cheaper brands, are much in favour in the large towns, but there is as yet no proof that the consumption of these foodstuffs has done a great deal of harm, the diet, apparently being supplemented by a sufficient quantity of articles containing the necessary accessory food factors.[6]

1931. In so far as the bulk of the population of the Gold Coast and its Dependencies is concerned, there would appear to be little reason to suspect that dietaries are deficient in calorific value; although under exceptional circumstances, as for

[1] Medical Report 1935, p. 5.   [2] Ibid. 1936, p. 4.
[3] Ibid. 1920, p. 22. See also Census Report 1921, p. 164.
[4] Medical Report 1927-8, p. 31.   [5] Ibid. 1929-30, p. 45.   [6] Ibid. 1930-1, p. 40.

example during prolonged droughts or after visitations from locusts, the population may have to subsist on a semi-starvation diet for a period. This occasional privation is probably confined to local areas in the Northern Territories.

Judging from the fact that diseases of the respiratory system, apart from pulmonary tuberculosis, occupy first place amongst the list of the chief causes of registered deaths and to the fact that these diseases are particularly common in many tribes in the Northern Territories, there would appear to be grounds for belief that there is a distinct lack of vitamin A in the average diet of the indigenous African and more particularly amongst Northern Territory tribesmen.[1]

1934. Although mortality and morbidity from deficiency diseases do not figure to any great extent in the returns, and the majority of the inhabitants appear sufficiently nourished, yet reports from medical officers in many areas point to deficiency and monotony in diet as a factor lowering health and resistance to disease, children being the chief sufferers.[2]

1935. Nutrition is probably another important factor affecting public health, although it is very difficult to assess its true importance. . . .

There is little doubt but that an appreciable proportion of the population, especially in the arid areas in the Northern Territories, suffers from some degree of under or faulty nutrition. A visit to an 'ulcer' ward and to the welfare centres provides graphic evidence of this.[3]

1936. In some districts of the Northern Territories the people are undoubtedly under-nourished. In certain areas the result of the impoverishment of the soil and in others the debilitating effects of disease and lack of satisfactory water supplies result in an inability to farm extensively. As a consequence there is a scarcity of food to carry on during the long dry season. This follows season after season until the inhabitants are in a miserably under-nourished condition.[4]

The dietary of the general bulk of the population is considered to lack protein and animal fat and to be deficient in fresh fruit and vegetables. The dietary of a people generally deprived of all dairy produce must leave gaps which are difficult to fill, particularly with respect to the diet of the infant at weaning and thereafter.[5]

The Committee on Nutrition in the Colonial Empire reported:

Broadly speaking, the diet is deficient in those animal and vegetable foodstuffs which provide fat, good protein, vitamins and mineral matter. It is believed, but not proved, that the calcium content of the diet is poor. The protein content is generally very low. This is especially noticeable in the miners' diet. There is also a definite deficiency of vitamin C in the diet of many of the poorer classes.[6]

As regards the effects of the war on nutrition the Medical Report for 1944 says:

Since the outbreak of the war . . . there has been little general indication that the incidence of malnutrition has increased to any appreciable extent. It can safely be said, it is thought, that malnutrition is at present not so generally noticeable as it was during the slump period of twelve years ago, i.e. before food farming had become more general. Difficulties of transport and rising costs, however, do make it a matter of considerable difficulty for the average African to feed himself adequately in the larger centres. Again, the African, who has accustomed himself largely to European habits of diet, finds it increasingly difficult to maintain these under present conditions.[7]

---

[1] Ibid. *1931–2*, p. 33. See also ibid. *1932–3*, p. 34; *1933–4*, p. 38; and, for the details of the diet, *The Gold Coast, 1931*, vol. i, pp. 229–32.

[2] *Medical Report 1934*, p. 7. See also ibid. *1935*, p. 28.   [3] Ibid. *1935*, p. 5.

[4] Ibid. *1936*, p. 4.   [5] Ibid., p. 31. See also *Report of Principal Registrar 1938*, p. 8.

[6] *First Report*, Part II, pp. 35–6.

[7] *Medical Report 1944*, p. 6. See also ibid., pp. 4–5.

The discussion of the causes of rising mortality was provoked mainly by the increase in the death-rate of the registration towns from 21·8 in 1932 to 25·2 in 1935. The rate remained high in 1936 and 1937, being 24·6 and 25·3 respectively.[1] It dropped in 1938 to 22·1 and amounted in 1939–41 to 23·2, 22·2, and 23·8 respectively. The Medical Department attributed the decline in 1938 mainly to 'the almost complete absence of the harmattan during the year' and 'the drop in the number of immigrant labourers, who generally arrive in an undernourished or diseased condition'.[2] It attributed the increase in 1941 mainly to the fact that 'there has been a considerable influx of population into the registration areas for industrial and other reasons'.[3]

The death-rates in many registration areas are affected indeed decisively by the high mortality of immigrant labourers. They are swelled, moreover, by the influx of other people in poor health.

Many registration areas contain hospital facilities, and five of the largest, namely —Accra, Cape Coast, Sekondi, Koforidua and Kumasi very busy infant welfare centres. There is a very appreciable influx of the seriously sick into such registration areas from the surrounding countryside, which reacts powerfully upon the local mortality rates.[4]

The death figures include, moreover, a number of deaths which occur outside the registration areas and are registered voluntarily.

Finally, the official death-rates are unduly (though only slightly) raised by including the deaths of non-Africans in the numbers of deaths which are related to population figures excluding non-Africans.

The death-rates are, on the other hand, reduced by the fact that 'a person hopelessly ill is frequently removed from a town by his relatives and friends, to die and be buried in the village of his ancestors'.[5]

The uncertainty regarding completeness of death registration and regarding the accuracy of population figures are still other factors which render it difficult to say anything definite with respect to mortality of the population residing in the registration towns, but it may be permissible tentatively to draw the conclusion that mortality is not very high. Whether it has improved or not in the course of time it is impossible to tell.

I shall now discuss the prevalence of some of the more important diseases.

Smallpox. Very little is known about the prevalence of smallpox in early times. Residents questioned by the Select Committee in 1841 apparently

[1] *The Gold Coast Handbook 1937* conveyed a wrong picture of the actual events when it said (p. 138): 'The health of both European and African population continues on its upward trend, although a slight set-back was noted in 1933, when the general death-rate showed a very small increase over that for the previous year.' It is true that in 1933 the general death-rate showed a very small increase over that for the previous year and that in 1934 the general death-rate showed likewise only a very small increase over that of the previous year, but in 1935 it showed a very large increase over that of the previous year.

[2] *Medical Report 1938*, p. 4.

[3] Ibid. *1941*, p. 1. The enormous rise of the death-rate to 26·5 in 1942 and to 29·4 in 1943 may be due in part to a further influx of population, in part to an understatement of the population (which was assumed to be equal to that of 1940), and in part to improved registration.

[4] *Report of Principal Registrar 1937*, p. 1.   [5] *The Gold Coast, 1931*, vol. i, p. 213.

had not noticed very many cases among natives.[1] The Colonial Surgeon, Dr. Clarke, in his report for 1858, said:

Rumours were current at different times during the year of the appearance of smallpox at various stations, but these statements were greatly exaggerated, and in most instances unfounded. At least I saw no case of smallpox during the year, and I feel satisfied that I should have detected such cases, notwithstanding that the natives do everything in their power to conceal its presence by the immediate removal of the afflicted persons into the bush. I may here mention the remarkable fact, that few persons among the population whom I have had ample opportunities of observing in different parts of the protected territory are marked with smallpox.[2]

Governor Andrews, on the other hand, in his report on the Blue Book for 1860, stated:

I am informed that in many parts of the interior this disease at times, makes sad ravages, causing the people to die by hundreds, and is probably one of the principal causes in rendering the population as sparse as it is.[3]

The Report on the Blue Book for 1888 states that 'outbreaks of smallpox occurred in the eastern and north-eastern districts amongst the native population'.[4]

The Medical Report for 1896 was apparently the first to declare that smallpox was endemic.

Small pox is endemic on the Gold Coast, as a rule the coast towns are comparatively free from it, but during the year under review there were outbreaks in the Axim District, at Cape Coast, Saltpond, Winneba and in the Volta River District.[5]

The report for the following year said:

Small-pox is endemic in this Colony. During the year there were 261 cases recorded with 48 deaths . . . . These numbers however are very far from indicating the prevalence of the disease—as many cases occur in the bush villages and towns which do not come under Official observation.[6]

Since 1897 many more or less serious outbreaks have been reported[7] but it is impossible to tell whether the number of deaths in the country as a whole was considerable in any year. The Medical Reports for 1910 and 1912, for example, said:

1910. 162 cases are reported as having been treated in Hospital . . . as compared with 217 cases . . . in 1909. This represents but a small proportion of cases that actually occurred, as a large number are concealed in the bush and never heard of.[8]

In Ashanti there were frequent small and scattered outbreaks, but it is impossible to obtain reliable information, and statistics are out of the question,[9]

1912. Twenty-three thousand, two hundred and thirty-two successful vaccinations were performed, but it cannot be said that as yet any efficient and organized attempt has been made to rid the Colony of Small-Pox. The disease is endemic and breaks out from time to time; when it has assumed noticeable proportions or it is accidentally or otherwise brought to the notice of the Authorities, a Medical Officer is sent

[1] See Report from Select Committee on the West Coast of Africa, Part II, pp. 98, 101, 103, 106, 108, 110.   [2] State of Colonial Possessions 1858, Part II, p. 22.
[3] Ibid. 1860, Part II, p. 37.   [4] Report on Blue Book 1888, p. 10.
[5] Gold Coast, Medical Report 1896, p. 5.   [6] 'Medical Report 1897', p. 175.
[7] See in particular 'Medical Report 1898', p. 318; Medical Report 1900, p. 18; 1901, p. 12; 1908, p. 10; 1909, pp. 35–6, 39; 1910, p. 34; 1917, p. 18; 1920, pp. 13–14; 1924–5, p. 8; 1925–6, p. 14; 1929–30, pp. 13, 28; 1930–1, pp. 9, 11; 1939, p. 1; 1941, p. 1; Colonial Reports, Ashanti 1908, pp. 17–18; 1909, p. 15; 1910, p. 13.
[8] Medical Report 1910, p. 50.   [9] Ibid., p. 51.

to the district to vaccinate and take other preventive measures; and in the meantime, except in Ashanti, where a native Public Vaccinator is employed, and the Northern Territories, where these duties are performed by a Senior Sanitary Inspector, prophylaxis is confined to the vaccination of Government employees and prisoners.[1]

It was apparently an epidemic in the capital in 1920 which induced the authorities to make the long delayed efficient and organized attempt to rid the Colony of smallpox. The Medical Report for 1920 stated:

The year will be memorable on account of the severe epidemic of Small-pox which occurred in Accra and district, causing much dislocation of routine work of the Department and the usual interference with peaceful pursuits in many other directions as the result of quarantine and local restrictive measures.[2]

A Vaccination Ordinance which had come into force on 1 January 1920 was applied to certain towns and districts,[3] and the number of vaccinations performed which had been only 14,700 in 1918 and 21,467 in 1919 rose to 221,386 in 1920. It was much smaller again in the following years, but when in 1925-6 considerable outbreaks of the disease caused new concern the number rose to 311,927,[4] and it has remained on a fairly high level thereafter. *The Gold Coast Handbook 1937* said:

The incidence of smallpox has shown a diminution in recent years, but it is too early to say whether this is due to the intensive vaccination campaign which has been carried out during the past fourteen years or to improved sanitary conditions and residual immunity from earlier epidemics.[5]

It should be realized, moreover, that since the publication of the *Handbook* the incidence of smallpox has apparently increased. In 1939 there were outbreaks in the Western and Central Provinces of the Colony and in the Northern Territories. 'Seventy deaths occurred among the 389 smallpox cases.'[6]

In 1941 the number of known cases was very much larger.

The outstanding event of the year was an extensive outbreak of smallpox. The area involved was considerable, but cases occurred sporadically, and there was no tendency for the outbreak to assume epidemic proportions in any locality. The areas involved were the Central Province of the Colony and the Northern Territories. Three hundred and forty-three cases occurred in the Central Province, of which 106 died. In the Northern Territories 1,127 cases were reported with 66 deaths.[7]

In 1942 known cases were still more numerous, but mortality apparently was lower.

There was a recrudescence on a large scale of the outbreak of Smallpox in the Northern Territories which had shown signs of dying out towards the end of the previous year. New areas where the vaccination rate was low became involved and the whole of the Northern Territories was declared an infected area. The areas chiefly affected were Eastern and Western Dagomba, Navrongo-Mamprusi, Wa, Lawra, Tumu and Kusasi. The outbreak died out towards the end of the year, the last case being reported in early December. Some 1,649 cases with 82 deaths were recorded.[8]

---

[1] *Medical Report 1912*, p. 93.   [2] Ibid. *1920*, p. 13.
[3] See Orders in Council No. 8 of 1920 (14 Apr.) and No. 21 of 1920 (24 July), Gold Coast, *Government Gazette*, 21 Apr. 1920, pp. 459-60; 7 Aug. 1920, pp. 984-5.
[4] See *Medical Report 1923-4*, p. 12; *1925-6*, p. 15.   [5] *Handbook*, p. 138.
[6] *Medical Report 1939*, p. 1.   [7] Ibid. *1941*, p. 1.   [8] Ibid. *1942*, p. 1.

The situation may perhaps be summarized as follows: There is no conclusive evidence that smallpox at any time claimed an excessive number of victims on the Gold Coast; epidemics have become more rare, but minor outbreaks and sporadic cases are still quite frequent.

Cerebrospinal Meningitis. This is another disease which in former times was a more important cause of death than it is now. The Acting Principal Medical Officer, in his report for 1906, said:

> The most remarkable occurrence in connection with the native health was the outbreak of Cerebro-Spinal Meningitis in the Northern Territories, and it would appear that this disease took on a virulent epidemic type in places, in one case decimating a village.
>
> Sporadic cases of this disease have been observed from time to time. The existence of this disease was denied at Cape Coast in 1900, although diagnosed by a Medical Officer. In the year 1905 I diagnosed a case of this disease at Cape Coast and satisfied myself by a post-mortem examination that it was correctly diagnosed. The recurrence of this disease will be closely watched and investigated.[1]

The Acting Senior Medical Officer Dr. Le Fanu, in his report on the Northern Territories for 1906, said:

> Reports from the various stations in the Northern Territories have for the most part been quite satisfactory. In February and March, however, an epidemic disorder was the cause of large numbers of deaths. In Gambaga there were nine deaths amongst the Soldiers alone during these months. In Wa and Kintampo, especially in the former, the same disease was observed, and there also resulted in many deaths. One death from the same cause was reported from Yeji. Dr. Collier, in his report on Tizza, a town in Lobe Dagarti, stated that on his arrival there he found it practically deserted, and on making enquiries he elicited the fact that over 400 natives had fallen victims to an epidemic disorder, which in its clinical signs bore a strong resemblance to cerebro-spinal meningitis.
>
> On my march from Gambaga to Yeji, during the month of February, I noted some undoubted cases of this disease in the towns I passed through.[2]

Contemporaneous reports do not estimate the incidence, but the Medical Report for 1920 says that the number of deaths from cerebrospinal fever in 1906 was 20,000.[3] If actually 5 or 6 per cent. of the population of the Northern Territories perished through this disease in 1906, it is noteworthy that 'reports from the various stations in the Northern Territories have for the most part been quite satisfactory' and that so experienced a doctor as Dr. Le Fanu apparently did not realize that the epidemic disorder in February and March had been a disaster of the first magnitude in the Protectorate of which he was the responsible Medical Officer. But it must be remembered that the Northern Territories at that time had been only a few years under British administration and that the Lobi Dagarti country in particular was only just coming under control.

The disease apparently claimed also a very large number of victims in the two following years. The Colonial Report for 1907 stated:

> An epidemic of cerebro-spinal meningitis swept over the North Western part of the country, and over 10,000 deaths must have occurred in the Grunshi, Dagarti, and Lobi country, whole families dying in a single day.[4]

[1] Ibid. *1906*, p. 8.   [2] Ibid., p. 29.   [3] See ibid. *1920*, p. 18.
[4] *Colonial Reports, Northern Territories of the Gold Coast 1907*, p. 18. 'Medical Report on the Northern Territories 1907' ibid., p. 21, says: 'The number of cases of cerebro-spinal meningitis

What happened in 1908 is not clear at all.

Cerebro Spinal Meningitis was not prevalent in the Northern Territories as in previous years.[1]

There was a brief epidemic of this disease reported from the Northern Territories: 27 cases, of which 9 were fatal.[2]

There was a slight increase in the number of cases of Cerebro Spinal Meningitis in these Territories; the Tumu district suffering most severely from the outbreak which only lasted a short time.[3]

Yet, according to the Medical Report for 1920 the number of deaths in 1908 was estimated at 6,000.[4]

Other epidemics of cerebrospinal meningitis occurred in 1919 and 1920.

1919. An outbreak of a virulent type occurred in the North-West Province of the Northern Territories from February to May. The first cases reported were at Lorha, early in February, and, by the middle of March, the disease had spread 20 miles, 18 miles, and 10 miles respectively along the main trade routes. The direction of the prevailing breeze, *viz.*, the dry and dusty Harmattan from the North-East, in a period of exceptional drought, was doubtless a factor in accelerating its spread. One of the first reported cases was at a caravan ferry on the Volta River, suggesting a direct connection with French Haut Sénégal where the disease was already epidemic.

With the advent of the rains in April the outbreak suddenly declined and all restrictions were raised in the first week in May.

Cerebro-spinal Fever was epidemic in the North-West Province of Northern Territories in the successive years 1906, 1907 and 1908, and the disease is to be regarded as really endemic, in that region at least, atypical or undetected cases (and unverified cases reported by administrative officers of sudden deaths amongst apparently healthy children) occurring at any time, with outbreaks in the dry season.

The Chiefs were called in and instructed to report daily, cases and deaths.

The total number of known cases was 1,041 with 986 deaths, a case mortality of 94·8 per cent.

After the first fortnight the majority of cases were infants and young persons, and the recoveries recorded were, as is usual, chiefly in the concluding weeks.[5]

1920. The Northern Territories again experienced a serious epidemic of Cerebro-spinal Fever, the previous epidemic years in that Dependency having been 1906, 1907, 1908 and 1919. In these successive outbreaks the range has tended to increase and in 1920 for the first time Ashanti has been the scene of this disease in epidemic form.[6] Its endemic existence in the Northern Territories is accepted, but the reasons for epidemic outbreaks in certain years and not in others is unknown, and perhaps the most important new feature is the extension of its range.

The earliest known cases dated from about the middle of January in the more distant parts of the North-Western Province. Further investigation however renders it probable that in the North-Eastern Province as well as in Ashanti the beginnings of the epidemic wave were coincident in all three areas.

The number of ascertained deaths was approximately 3,000.[7]

The 1921 census report said in the section on the Northern Territories:

. . . Cerebro-Spinal Fever is endemic and occurs epidemically from year to year during the Harmattan season. The mortality from that disease is high, aided in

which occurred was much less than in the previous years . . . .' According to *Medical Report 1920*, p. 18, the number of deaths in 1907 was estimated at 8,000.

[1] Statement by Principal Medical Officer, ibid. *1908*, p. 11.
[2] Statement by same, ibid., p. 18.
[3] Statement by Senior Medical Officer, Northern Territories, ibid., p. 41.
[4] See ibid. *1920*, p. 18.   [5] Ibid. *1919*, pp. 15–16.
[6] See also *Colonial Reports, Ashanti 1920*, p. 15.   [7] *Medical Report 1920*, p. 18.

great measure 'by the nature of the peoples' dwellings which foster the disease and render epidemics sooner or later inevitable'.[1]

In his Final Review the Chief Census Officer stated:

Cerebro Spinal Meningitis which appears to have been diagnosed for the first time in the Gold Coast in 1900 amongst East African Carriers in the Ashanti War,[2] is now endemic and epidemic in the Northern Territories and Ashanti. In the Colony it is mainly sporadic.[3]

From 1922 to 1938 only sporadic cases were reported. But the Medical Department was aware of the fact that an epidemic may easily recur.

For several years past the case incidence has been represented by a few scattered cases, nothing like an epidemic outbreak having taken place.

Usually cases occur in the colder part of the year during the 'harmattan' season when a great deal of over-crowding results for the purpose of maintaining warmth.

It is a disease, however, which demands respect for the conditions over wide areas are conducive to an epidemic outburst at any time.[4]

A recrudescence was in fact noted in 1939.

1939. Outbreaks of epidemic cerebro-spinal meningitis occurred in the Northern Territories . . . . Three hundred and fifty-eight cases of cerebro-spinal meningitis were reported during the period January to April with only 86 deaths. There was a slight recrudescence of the disease in November and December.[5]

In 1940–4 the numbers of reported cases were 77, 25, 255, 367, and 923 respectively and the numbers of deaths 25, 11, 140, 144, and 191.[6]

Malaria. Unlike smallpox and cerebrospinal meningitis, malaria, though perhaps not very frequently a direct cause of death, apparently impairs the health of the natives to-day as much as in former times.

Malaria still continues to be the most important, general factor adversely affecting the public health. Infection can be considered to be almost universal. Every pathological condition throughout life is complicated by it; and it calls for early exclusion before any diagnosis can be made. It is also the most important factor when labour inefficiency and lost time is considered. The general standard of physical well-being is very low in the Gold Coast, and towards this end malaria plays an important part.[7]

I shall now discuss some diseases which may have gained in importance in recent times.

Yellow Fever. This disease, of course, had for a long time been a prominent cause of death among non-natives, but until 1926 Africans were considered to be practically immune against it. The total number of non-native cases reported in 1910–25 was 92 with 71 deaths, while among Africans who were at least a thousand times as numerous only 59 cases had been recorded with 26 deaths. But in 1926 alone not less than 57 cases of Africans (with 13 deaths) were ascertained.[8] Of these 50 (with 8 deaths)

---

[1] *Census Report 1921*, p. 131.
[2] *Medical Report 1900*, which says that smallpox was 'brought down by native carriers and others returning from Kumasi and other parts of Ashanti' (p. 13), does not mention cerebrospinal meningitis.
[3] *Census Report 1921*, p. 163.   [4] *Medical Report 1933–4*, p. 24.   [5] Ibid. *1939*, p. 1.
[6] See ibid. *1940*, p. 1; *1941*, p. 1; *1942*, p. 1; *1943*, p. 1; *1944*, pp. 1–2.
[7] Ibid. *1937*, p. 14; see also ibid. *1938*, p. 15; *1939*, p. 2; *1940*, p. 3; *1941*, p. 3. 'It would seem, from all sources of information available, that there was an actual increase in the incidence of malaria in 1943' (ibid. *1943*, p. 4).
[8] See *Report on Yellow Fever in Accra 1927*, p. 3.

were seen in Asamangkese where, as shown above,[1] the disease was introduced in May but was not discovered until towards the end of July.

> . . . the epidemic was not discovered until towards the end of July, when twenty-
> eight cases were seen. In the following month a further twenty cases occurred and
> the outbreak virtually came to an end in September, during which month only two
> cases were reported. . . .
> The members of the Rockefeller Commission who carried out very careful and
> comprehensive investigations with regard to this outbreak were of the opinion that
> over a thousand cases or twenty-five per centum of the total population of the town
> suffered from the disease between May and September.[2] This was based upon
> a mortality of sixteen per centum in the fifty cases studied and from reliable infor-
> mation including a statement that eight out of a total of fourteen persons living in
> one compound had died of the disease.
> The case mortality of fifty per centum in persons over thirty years of age suggested
> very strongly that many mild and probably unrecognised cases of yellow fever occur
> in children—a hypothesis of many years standing.[3]

Governor Guggisberg, in his address of 3 March 1927 to the Legislative
Council, said:

> There is naturally great difficulty in discovering exactly how many deaths occurred
> among the townspeople, but the Medical Officer of Health, who conducted careful
> enquiries towards the end of the epidemic after the confidence of the people had been
> gained, and examined the various cemeteries, could discover only 87 deaths, some
> of these deaths being probably due to other causes than yellow fever. However,
> eight deaths out of fifty cases amongst natives were diagnosed.[4]

Eight years later the Acting Director of Medical Services, Dr. Selwyn-
Clarke, in a paper presented to the Pan-African Health Conference in
Johannesburg, said:

> For many years white residents were regarded as non-immunes and the local
> Africans as immunes.
> That the West African is almost as liable to the disease as a European, was
> demonstrated in no uncertain manner in 1926 in the Gold Coast.
> It is estimated that, in that year, in one comparatively small town situated about
> sixty miles inland from the port of Accra, 1,500 of the 6,000 inhabitants sickened
> with yellow fever and 150 died.[5]

In 1927, 88 cases among Africans were reported with 25 deaths and the
Medical Report stated:

> The health of the general African community compared favourably on the whole
> with the record of previous years, the continuance of the yellow fever outbreak
> from the previous year being the chief cause for anxiety. It should, however, be
> noted that the incidence of the disease as compared with the total population of the
> country was not serious.[6]

Recorded cases were few in subsequent years but recent Medical Reports
emphasize that many cases may not be noticed by the authorities.

> 1935. On the whole 1935, from the viewpoint of the incidence of yellow fever,
> is to be considered satisfactory.

---

[1] See p. 480.
[2] See also *Report on Yellow Fever in Accra 1927*, p. 4: '. . . over a thousand cases and over a
hundred deaths are believed by the Rockefeller Yellow Fever Commission to have occurred prior
to the discovery of the outbreak.'
[3] *Medical Report 1926–7*, pp. 20–1.   [4] *A Review of the Events of 1920–6*, p. 194.
[5] *Medical Report 1935*, p. 89.   [6] Ibid. *1927–8*, p. 12.

The term 'incidence' in this connexion is intended to mean the 'known' incidence, or merely those cases which come to light. The whole of the Gold Coast is an endemic area.

Mosquito control is confined to the ports, the larger centres and some of the larger villages and towns on certain of the important trade routes.

The rest of the country is more or less a 'closed book'; an outbreak may, or may not, come to knowledge.

The complete picture is rather like that within the crater of a volcano. The whole contents may be actively molten, but it is only where the gas bells burst on the surface (i.e. the isolated outbreaks which come to knowledge) that any indication of the real state of affairs can be appreciated. Only in three centres in the Northern Territories can efficient mosquito control be said to exist.[1]

1936. As in previous years, stress must again be laid on the fact that the cases which came to light must represent but a small percentage of those which actually occur up and down the country. The whole of the Gold Coast is an endemic area, and we have little knowledge of the general incidence of the disease.[2]

1937. During the year the worst outbreak of yellow fever occurred since 1927. There were 75 reported cases and 69 deaths. The brunt of the outbreak fell on the African community in the Eastern Province. Four fatal Syrian and two fatal European cases occurred. The prolonged dry season and consequent storage of water in the villages made the epidemic difficult to control.

Owing to this outbreak the full extent of which it is difficult to estimate and to climatic, economic and other causes, the general improvement recorded in 1936 suffered a setback. An increase took place in the general and infantile mortality rates.[3]

With regard to yellow fever many more fatal cases must have occurred than came to official notice. The rise in the death rate of African officials from ·38 per cent of the average number resident in 1936 to ·7 in 1937 was largely due to yellow fever and is a clear indication of what must have been happening amongst the general population especially in the affected areas.[4]

The areas principally involved lie to the north and north-east of Accra in the Shai and Krobo districts. In January, 1937, an outbreak occurred in Accra, and subsequent investigations revealed the fact that extensive outbreaks had occurred in the hinterland to the north and north-east in isolated villages impossible of control with a strictly limited staff. . . .

In addition to the area principally involved sporadic cases occurred in the Central Province, the Western Province and in the Northern Territories. Ashanti, to the best of our knowledge, completely escaped.

As stressed in previous years, the cases coming to light can only have been a small percentage of those which actually occurred.

Investigations following the appearance of the disease in one, or other, of the larger centres have, as in the past, revealed extensive implication of rural areas the satisfactory control of which is not possible. Information concerning such outbreaks is rarely, if ever, supplied by the Chiefs responsible. Mosquito control requires to be extended; but with the staff available it is considered that the limit of control is being reached.

Mosquito control is confined to the ports, the larger centres, the more important towns and large villages on the major trade routes. Vast rural areas, however, are completely closed books, and an extensive outbreak may occur in such without any indication of any trouble, unless, of course, a case is imported into one of the larger centres and recognised, thus setting investigations in train.

The total elimination of yellow fever from the Gold Coast cannot be envisaged save after years of steady development of the country and through the education

[1] Ibid. *1935*, p. 14.   [2] Ibid. *1936*, p. 17.   [3] Ibid. *1937*, p. 3.
[4] Ibid., p. 4. Six out of an average of 3,750 resident African officials died of yellow fever in 1937; see ibid., p. 11.

and the co-operation of the people. The long period which must elapse before these desiderata are attained is fraught with a steadily increasing anxiety. Communications improve yearly; and it is a matter of economic difficulty for the machinery of prevention to keep pace with rapid development.[1]

1938. As in former reports, it must be stressed that the number of cases which come to light must be a small percentage only of the total number which occur annually. So much of the country is uncontrolled, or only superficially controlled from a sanitary standpoint, that this is inevitable.

There is some indication that a generation of Africans is arising in these well-controlled centres which must be considered as being hardly less susceptible to yellow fever than the average European.[2]

The Medical Department no doubt is right in suspecting that the reported cases represent only a small fraction of the cases which actually occur. But in order rightly to appraise the position, three facts, I think, should be borne in mind.

(1) The number of reported cases has been all the time so small that even if only 1 per cent. of all cases had been reported, yellow fever would not have been an important cause of death among Africans.

(2) The epidemic of yellow fever in Asamangkese was a terrible shock to the Medical Officers because no such epidemic had ever been recorded in a purely African community and because this outbreak remained unnoticed for several months. They may therefore have drawn too far-reaching conclusions from this single event. The investigation by the members of the Rockefeller Commission was no doubt 'very careful and comprehensive', but their estimate that over 1,000 cases and over 100 deaths occurred prior to the discovery of the outbreak was based 'upon a mortality of sixteen per centum in the fifty cases studied and from reliable information including a statement that eight out of a total of fourteen persons living in one compound had died of the disease'.[3] Dr. Selwyn-Clarke reports that '1,500 of the 6,000 inhabitants sickened with yellow fever and 150 died'. But he also stated that only 28 cases were seen towards the end of July, that only a further 20 cases occurred in August, and that 2 cases were reported in September. This would imply that all but 22 of 1,500 cases occurred before the epidemic was discovered and that 90 per cent. of the diseased had recovered before any Medical Officer was on the spot. This may, of course, have been the case, but we cannot be at all sure that it was so.[4]

(3) The Medical Department, in 1927, made the following comment on the increase in the number of cases reported in 1926:

It will be observed that the disease which hitherto in this country had appeared to have a greater incidence on so-called non-immunes or individuals of the white race affected Africans in a much greater degree during the year.

The explanation is hard to find but it is suggested that, either as the result of

---

[1] *Medical Report 1937*, pp. 16–17.　　　　[2] Ibid. *1938*, p. 19.

[3] The total number of compounds in Asamangkese was about 800.

[4] According to Governor Guggisberg, the Medical Officer of Health who examined the various cemeteries could discover only eighty-seven deaths, some of which were probably due to other causes than yellow fever. If we assume that mortality was not lower before the Medical Officers arrived than thereafter (when it was 16 per cent.), the total number of cases may not have exceeded 500.

TABLE 24. *Cases and Deaths of Yellow Fever, Gold Coast, 1910–44*[1]

Year	Cases			Deaths		
	European	Syrian	African	European	Syrian	African
1910	12	—	3	11	—	3
1911	6	—	3	5	—	—
1912	3	—	7	3	—	—
1913	10	—	10	5	—	2
1914	9	—	10	4	—	5
1915	1	—	1	1	—	1
1916	5	—	1	4	—	1
1917	3	—	2	3	—	2
1918	2	—	2	1	—	—
1919	6	—	5	5	—	2
1920	1	—	1	1	—	—
1921	3	—	1	3	—	1
1922	4	—	6	4	—	4
1923	15	—	4	14	—	2
1924	7	1	—	5	1	—
1925	3	1	3	—	1	3
1926	8	—	57	5	—	13
1927	14	5	88	10	5	25
1927–8	14	3	67	10	3	19
1928–9	2[2]	—	—	2[2]	—	—
1929–30	—	—	—	—	—	—
1930–1	1	—	1	—	—	1
1931–2	8	2	10	6	2	4
1932–3	—	—	3	—	—	2
1933	3	—	4	3	—	1
1934	—	—	2	—	—	2
1935	—	—	7	—	—	4
1936	—	—	3	—	—	3
1937	2	4	69	2	4	63
1938	5	1	9	5	1	9
1939	—	—	2	—	—	2
1940	1	—	1	1	—	1
1941	—	—	4	—	—	4
1942	—	—	1	—	—	1
1943	—	—	2	—	—	2
1944	—	—	1	—	—	1

[1] See *Report on Yellow Fever in Accra 1927*, p. 3; Gold Coast, *Medical Report 1927–8*, p. 23; *1928–9*, p. 21; *1929–30*, p. 25; *1930–1*, p. 22; *1931–2*, p. 18; *1932–3*, p. 17; *1933–4*, p. 21; *1934*, p. 14; *1935*, p. 15; *1936*, p. 17; *1937*, p. 17; *1938*, p. 18; *1939*, p. 2; *1940*, p. 3; *1941*, p. 3; *1942*, p. 1; *1943*, p. 2; *1944*, p. 4.   [2] Including apparently 1 Japanese.

comparative immunity from epidemics for a considerable period a relatively non-immune race of Africans has come into being, or that epidemics, which in the past went unrecognised either through faulty death registration or from the remoteness of towns and villages from medical aid, now are discovered owing to improved death registration, to the very considerable improvement in lines of communication and means of transport which allow of rapid transit to areas hitherto untraversed, and to the increased medical and sanitary personnel stationed in various parts of the Colony.[1]

But not a single epidemic of any magnitude has been reported since 1926.

[1] *Medical Report 1926–7*, pp. 19–20.

Sleeping-sickness. This disease was detected as far back as 1895 in that portion of Togoland which later came under British mandate.[1] The German Government Medical Officer, Dr. Hintze, reported in 1904:

From the middle of the 1890's, in the Boëm and Tapá regions at the Western frontier of the Protectorate sporadic cases of sleeping-sickness appeared, which increased in numbers in the course of the last few years.

The disease was apparently confined to two foci separated from each other by a several days' journey and consisting of a few villages. After a slow increase (from 1896) the epidemic reached its peak in the years 1902–3 and thereafter declined rapidly. As far as could be ascertained the number of fatal cases did not amount to more than about 110 or 120; thus here the disease has evidently not reached the extent which has been reported from the east of the continent, particularly from Uganda.

Of the 10 cases still surviving in September 1903, one-half succumbed to their sufferings before the end of the year; 5 were isolated in January 1904 on a mountain fit for this purpose. In all of them *Trypanosoma Ugand.* was ascertained. On 1 April only one patient was still alive.[2]

The last patient died shortly thereafter and only few new cases were reported in the following years. But in the second half of 1908 it was ascertained that the disease had spread considerably in the Misahöhe District. Other cases were discovered in the Kete-Kratchi District, and by the end of March 1909 the total number of cases ascertained in both districts was 164. In 1909–10, 98 more cases were ascertained. The total number of patients brought into the sleeping-sickness camp prior to 1 April 1913 was 568. On 31 March 1913 the patients in the camp numbered 86. In addition 341 persons who formerly suffered from sleeping-sickness were under observation.[3]

On the Gold Coast (excluding Togoland) 'there is no record of the occurrence of the disease prior to 1903',[4] and the cases recorded in 1903–6 numbered only 1, 6, 7, and 3. But the Acting Principal Medical Officer, in his report for 1906, said: 'The cases of Sleeping Sickness coming under notice are an infinitesimal proportion to the actual cases which must occur.'[5] In 1907, 34 cases were 'seen', mostly in Kumasi,[6] but they were 'not all confirmed microscopically',[7] and in 1908, 16. In 1909 the number rose to 45,[8] and the Governor of Ashanti reported to the Secretary of State that 'the prevalence of sleeping sickness, a disease which is probably endemic, was the cause of much anxiety and expense'.[9]

Early in the year two cases of sleeping sickness (*Trypanosomiasis Gambiensis*) were reported by the Medical Officer, Kintampo. On investigation, it was proved that the disease was all too prevalent in the neighbourhood of Kintampo and had been the cause of several deaths some two years previously; besides these, cases cropped up in various places, notably at Sunyani, the headquarters of the Western

---

[1] As regards the question whether or not sleeping-sickness was prevalent on the Gold Coast in earlier times see, for example, Gold Coast, *Medical Report 1912*, p. 8; *1923–4*, p. 23; *1925–6*, pp. 61–2; *1933–4*, pp. 100, 102; *Report of the Accra Laboratory 1915*, pp. 41–3.

[2] *Medizinal-Berichte über die deutschen Schutzgebiete 1903/4*, pp. 171–2.

[3] See Kuczynski, *The Cameroons and Togoland*, pp. 392–3.

[4] Gold Coast, *Medical Report 1908*, p. 18.   [5] Ibid. *1906*, p. 9.

[6] See ibid. *1907*, p. 13. See also *Colonial Reports, Ashanti 1907*, pp. 4, 15.

[7] *Medical Report 1908*, p. 18.   [8] See ibid. *1909*, p. 16.

[9] *Colonial Reports, Ashanti 1909*, p. 3.

Province, where the European Medical Officer became infected after a three months' residence and had to be invalided to England.

The fact that the attention of the Government was drawn to the prevalence of sleeping-sickness in Ashanti proved by far the most important event of the year as regards public health. An expert, Dr. Kinghorn, has been at work investigating the disease, with the result that trypanosomes have been discovered in about one per cent. of natives examined.[1] Serious as this may seem, it would appear from native evidence that the disease is by no means of recent importation and that it has not yet been experienced in an epidemic form. The *Glossina palpalis* being prevalent throughout Ashanti, it is to be hoped that some degree of immunity will be found to have been acquired by the people of the country. Clearing operations on a large scale were put into force and a fly-proof hospital erected.[2]

Though in 1910 most cases were again seen in Ashanti,[3] the menace to the Gold Coast as a whole was recognized.

During 1910, about 50 cases of Sleeping Sickness were treated in the different Hospitals, and 11 deaths recorded. Towards the end of the year 107 cases were reported under observation or treatment by the Medical Officers in various districts ....

Glossina Palpalis is universal and widespread in almost every part of the Colony, from Anum on the eastern border to Berekum and Sunyani on the west, extending into the Gonja district, and even probably as far north as Gambaga. Dr. Kinghorn reports it pretty universal throughout the northern and western provinces of Ashanti and the Banda District. He states that the extent of the disease in the Western province bears a strict relation to the comparative frequency of Glossina Palpalis. In Wenki 5 per cent. of the inhabitants were found to be infected.

On the Togoland border Dr. Claridge states that the whole district is adapted to the tsetse fly and that Glossina Palpalis is present everywhere.

Dr. Beringer points out the widespread prevalence of this fly throughout the Gonja District .... Whole villages in this District are reported to have been deserted by the Natives on account of Sleeping Sickness prevalent there.

Dr. Rice has called attention to the prevalence of the fly all along the Coomassie Kintampo road, and it has long been known to be exceedingly plentiful in the Kintampo District. It would appear therefore that Glossina Palpalis is far more widely spread throughout the Colony and Protectorates than any other variety of tsetse. It is found almost universally throughout the whole of the forest and semi-forest country.

Taking into consideration the widespread distribution of Glossina Palpalis it seems extraordinary that Trypanosomiasis has not made greater headway or taken on an epidemic form. Whether human Trypanosomiasis is endemic and the Natives to some extent become immune, or whether we are dealing in this Colony with a strain of infection of low virulence, are hypotheses to neither of which I care to commit myself.

The seriousness and the possibilities of Sleeping Sickness, as far as the Gold Coast is concerned, are now well recognized, and every effort is being made to cope with a situation that at first sight strikes one as being well-nigh superhuman.[4]

In his report for 1911 the Senior Sanitary Officer stated under 'Recommendations for future work':

It is to be hoped that before long this menace to the future prosperity of the Colony will be dealt with in the same systematic and scientific precision with which it is already being fought in Togoland.

[1] Dr. Kinghorn examined 9,171 natives amongst whom he found 92 cases; see *Medical Report 1911*, p. 49.
[2] *Colonial Reports, Ashanti 1909*, pp. 14–15.
[3] See *Medical Report 1910*, p. 34; *Colonial Reports, Ashanti 1910*, p. 13.
[4] Acting Senior Sanitary Officer, *Medical Report 1910*, pp. 46–7.

It is high time that we established a Special Sleeping Sickness Service, passed laws as to compulsory segregation and notification, and established a segregation camp.[1]

The reports of the following years show that these suggestions were not accepted.

1912. I am still of the opinion, which I have expressed several times before, that it is the duty of the Government to establish a Segregation Camp in a fly-free belt in Ashanti, and there make arrangements for the isolation and treatment of persons infected with this disease. To leave them in their native villages, a source of infection to others, to face a lingering and certain death, is both inhuman and impolitic.

I have no information as to the recent progress of this disease, but the reports of Doctors Kinghorn and Wade, quoted last year,[2] pointed to one per cent. of the population of Ashanti being infected.[3]

1913. Sixty-one cases were under treatment and of these fifteen died. There were, however, in addition to these cases, 120 known cases scattered through the Western and Northern Province of Ashanti.[4]

I have had an opportunity of seeing Dr. Wade's Report on his tour in the Western Province of Ashanti. As a result of his investigations he draws attention to the fact that the disease follows trade routes, and that the more remote the village from the main road, the freer from infection. This is of importance from a preventive point of view, and should receive attention.[5] The percentage of cases found infected out of the large number examined (110 in 39,742) would not appear to be by any means large, but is sufficient to serve as a warning of its presence, in order that effective measures might be taken to prevent its spread.[6]

1914. There is very little to add to what was said in last year's report on this subject. The lack of funds and the withdrawal of troops has resulted in less clearing being done in bush stations than formerly.

The segregation of officials, the initiation of extra-urban rest houses in country districts and the general improvement in housing conditions have all tended to minimise the risk of Europeans becoming infected.

In the case of natives, however, it cannot be said that much has been done to meet the added risks of dissemination due to the increased facilities with which traders and others can now travel about the country.[7]

In the years following the First World War the situation was not considered to be serious.

1918. Trypanosomiasis does not call for any special mention. There is no evidence that it is on the increase and no special measures beyond the clearing of bush and undergrowth around towns and at fords and watering places, have been taken.[8]

1924–5. There are no definite figures relative to the incidence of trypanosomiasis in the Gold Coast. Dr. Young, Director of the Medical Research Institute, in his report on tsetse fly and trypanosomiasis in Ashanti states that 'sleeping sickness is by no means a rare disease in Ashanti, but it is undoubtedly chronic and probably many spontaneous recoveries take place.'

The Medical Officer at Wa in the Northern Territories in a report on the incidence of sleeping sickness in the Lorha District concludes that sleeping sickness though not uncommon is not on the increase.[9]

1926–7. Unlike in East Africa this disease is not commonly met with in man on the Gold Coast.[10]

[1] *Medical Report 1910*, p. 66.   [2] See ibid. *1911*, p. 49.
[3] Senior Sanitary Officer, ibid. *1912*, p. 64.   [4] Ibid. *1913*, p. 9.
[5] See also *Report of the Accra Laboratory 1915*, p. 41.
[6] Senior Sanitary Officer, *Medical Report 1913*, p. 22.   [7] Ibid. *1914*, pp. 33–4.
[8] Ibid. *1918*, p. 25. See also ibid. *1919*, p. 13; *1920*, p. 13; *1921*, p. 12.
[9] Ibid. *1924–5*, p. 15. See also ibid. *1925–6*, p. 61.   [10] Ibid. *1926–7*, p. 21.

1927–8. A small number of cases of this disease was reported principally from Ashanti. The Medical Officer, Kintampo, reported that several small foci existed in the Western Province of Ashanti, wherein five per centum of the population were infected.

Taking the Colony as a whole it is impossible to give even an approximate figure for the percentage of population infected with this disease.[1]

1928–9. The disease on the Gold Coast is fortunately not the scourge it is in other parts of equatorial Africa and does not call for very special methods to deal with it.[2]

Unlike in some sister colonies e.g., Nigeria, human sleeping sickness is not a problem of any magnitude in the Gold Coast.

Only twenty-six deaths among the 5,182 recorded were certified as having been due to this malady during 1928—a ratio of 0·5 per centum.[3]

From 1928–9 to 1937 the number of cases treated showed a steady increase.[4]

	1927–8	1928–9	1929–30	1930–1	1931–2	1932–3	1933–4	1934	1935
Cases	59	94	121	224	250	685	1,179	1,973	3,885
Deaths	4	18	23	16	28	45	77	112	106

	1936	1937	1938	1939	1940	1941	1942	1943	1944
Cases	4,820	5,162	5,085	5,095	5,676	4,322	3,948	3,610	4,092
Deaths	132	156	151	156	142	172	127	125	112

But for some years more sleeping-sickness, while attracting increased attention, did not cause much concern.

1929–30. Human trypanosomiasis has attracted more attention than in previous years, and a greater number of cases are recorded, but it would be entirely premature to conclude that it is on the increase. In all probability the correct explanation is that greater facilities have occurred for observing the disease which for generations has been endemic in certain areas on the Gold Coast.[5]

It is not possible from these figures to say if there is a true increase in the incidence of the disease. A slight increase certainly appears in the figures for the past three years. This may be a true increase; on the other hand it may be that more sufferers are coming forward for treatment or that more cases are being diagnosed.

In previous reports it was pointed out that the disease on the Gold Coast was of a very chronic type from which a very large number of people recover by natural resistance and was fortunately not the urgent problem it was elsewhere. It was also pointed out that it not infrequently happens that the disease is accidentally discovered in a patient who is being examined for some other ailment,[6] which would indicate that a closer search would probably reveal many more cases, and that it is more prevalent than the above figures would show.[7] In any case the position does not at present seem one to cause alarm.[8]

This disease does not occupy a very prominent position in the Gold Coast, but we cannot afford to lose sight of its importance. The highest figures were returned from Kumasi which shew 58 cases with 17 deaths. Tamale reports eleven cases with two deaths.

The Medical Officer of Health, Kumasi, stresses the point that all these cases occurred in immigrants from the north and that no indigenous cases arose in Kumasi during 1929–30.

[1] Ibid. 1927–8, p. 24.   [2] Ibid. 1928–9, p. 11.   [3] Ibid., p. 22.
[4] See ibid. 1929–30, p. 12; 1938, p. 6; 1939, p. 3; 1940, p. 3; 1941, p. 3; 1942, p. 3; 1943, p. 4; 1944, p. 4.   [5] Ibid. 1929–30, p. v.
[6] See ibid. 1928–9, p. 11.   [7] See also ibid., p. 67.   [8] Ibid. 1929–30, p. 12.

In no part of the Gold Coast does trypanosomiasis constitute a menace, but it is considered that a survey of both the north and south banks of the river Volta in the Kete Krachi, Mampon and Eastern Gonja districts would be useful and interesting and would probably reveal an infection rate of from 2 to 3 per centum of the population.

Prevention resolves itself into keeping a sufficient clearing of the bush round villages, towns and fords on main traffic routes.[1]

1930–1. Judging from the incidence and death-rates during the past few years, trypanosomiasis would not appear to give cause for any anxiety in the Gold Coast.[2]

Up to the present it has not been proved that trypanosomiasis can be considered a great menace in any part of the Gold Coast.

However, every year brings to light more cases and the disease certainly cannot be ignored and should be the subject of continued research.

In the light of our present knowledge, therefore, it is extremely difficult to indicate the distribution and case incidence.

The highest incidence of the disease appears to be in the fishing villages along the middle two-thirds of the course of the Volta River, in the Kete Krachi, Mampong, Eastern Gonja and Kintampo districts.[3]

1931–2. It is a remarkable fact that the areas in the Northern Territories and Ashanti to the north and south of the Black Volta are very thinly populated. Many officers consider that this is due to the continued drain of ill-health[4] and death caused by the disease. In a recent article in the *West African Medical Journal* (January, 1932) Saunders and Morris concluded that the original depopulation of these areas was brought about by Ashanti raids although the disease may have contributed in maintaining the resulting scarcity of people.[5]

Less than 0·7 per centum of all registered deaths in the Colony and its Dependencies during 1931–32 were recorded as being due to trypanosome infection, the majority being males.

There is no evidence that the incidence of the disease or the severity of the type justify the diversion of funds utilised at the moment for the control of malaria, yellow fever, diseases of the alimentary tract, and so on.

Clearing of bush from the neighbourhood of much used fords, for 50 yards around towns and villages and in and around residential areas constitutes the major methods of prevention.[6]

The year 1933 apparently marked the turning-point in the attitude of the medical officers towards sleeping-sickness. Although there was still a marked reluctance to take the spread of the disease very seriously, nevertheless it aroused anxiety.

1932–3. Fortunately there were no epidemics, although a rapid increase which has taken place in the number of cases of Sleeping Sickness seen in the Northern Territories and Ashanti, is causing anxiety.[7]

During the past year there has been a rapid increase in the number of trypanosomiasis cases reported and treated, the incidence per 10,000 of all cases treated having risen from 6·56 in 1929–30 to 33·11. Last year the figure was 12·61.

It might be considered that this is not an alarming rate, but it may be a definite warning that the disease has spread. On the other hand, the increase may be due to better diagnosis with consequential better treatment leading in its turn to increased attendances.

It would appear to be concentrated chiefly in a few areas, the most important

[1] *Medical Report 1929–30*, p. 26.   [2] Ibid. *1930–1*, p. 11.   [3] Ibid., p. 24.
[4] See also ibid. *1928–9*, p. 67: 'Epidemics of sleeping sickness may bring the danger into prominent notice, but the insidious effect of the milder form of the disease may be no less serious amongst the comparatively small population of the Gold Coast . . . .'
[5] Ibid. *1931–2*, pp. 6–7.   [6] Ibid., p. 19.   [7] Ibid. *1932–3*, p. iii.

being the Nakpanduri–Bende area of Northern Togoland[1] close to the French frontier and east of Gambaga in the Northern Territories. Another area in which cases appear to be increasing is the Sunyani district in Ashanti.[2]

During 1932–33 a total of 48 deaths from trypanosomiasis were registered or 0·84 per centum of the total number of deaths registered. From the above figures neither the incidence nor the severity of the type of the disease would appear to render it a problem of urgent importance. But registration is not universal, and more cases are being seen annually by medical officers.

Certain districts in Ashanti and the Northern Territories to the north and the south of the Black Volta show a comparatively high rate of incidence, say, 3 per centum. And in certain limited areas a case incidence as high as 10 per centum has been recorded.

With the evidence at our disposal trypanosomiasis is a problem which at present does not demand a very large diversion of sorely needed and often inadequate funds, from more pressing items affecting the public health elsewhere. It is, however, one which cannot be disregarded. The Medical branch section of this report strikes a warning note.[3]

1933–4. Trypanosomiasis was described in the Report for 1932–33 as 'causing anxiety'. This anxiety was in no way dispelled as the result of thorough surveys carried out during the year. The surveys revealed a high infection rate in certain areas in the Protectorate of the Northern Territories and the British Sphere of Northern Togoland. In the past ten years the incidence per thousand of all cases treated has increased by over seventeen times. It must be remembered, however, that part at least of this increase is due to the special attention directed towards the disease.[4]

During the year 117 deaths from trypanosomiasis were registered; of these 109 or 93·2 per centum were in males. Of the above total number of deaths 69, or some 59 per centum, were registered in Kumasi.

Death registration, however, is not general throughout the Gold Coast and the above figures cannot be considered as representing the real incidence of the disease.[5]

Realizing the dangers of infection and the risk to which the people were exposed unless segregation measures of infected cases were undertaken, the chief and people of Nakpanduri, a village 23 miles east of Gambaga, constructed on their own initiative a special sleeping sickness camp and hospital on a site near the summit of a scarp, some 400 metres above sea-level. . . .[6]

In a special report on 'Trypanosomiasis in the Gold Coast', the Acting Director Medical and Sanitary Service, Dr. Selwyn-Clarke, said:

It must be remembered that a considerable amount of attention has been paid to the problem of human trypanosomiasis in the Gold Coast in the past few years and that officers have been specially detailed to make surveys of the incidence of the disease. The very marked increase in the number of cases reported cannot therefore be attributed entirely to the occurrence of localised epidemics.[7]

It is particularly desirable to emphasise that there is no desire to minimise the danger to the Colony of trypanosomiasis.

At the same time it is necessary, especially in times of reduction in staff and funds, to obviate the temptation to divert large sums of money and much time and energy to a disease which is of far less vital economic importance to the inhabitants and far less easy or certain to prevent and cure than, say, malaria.

It is interesting to compare the number of cases dealt with within the main zones

[1] For details concerning the spread of sleeping-sickness in Togoland see Kuczynski, pp. 539–47.
[2] *Medical Report 1932–3*. p. 6.   [3] Ibid., p. 18.   [4] Ibid. *1933–4*, p. 9.
[5] Ibid., p. 22. It is noteworthy that the number of deaths of patients treated in the whole country was only 77 although not fewer than 117 deaths were registered in the registration towns alone.
[6] *Report on Togoland 1933*, pp. 51–2.   [7] *Medical Report 1933–4*, p. 101.

in the Colony and its dependencies. Infection is rare in the coastal zone and the incidence of cases of sleeping sickness in 1933–34 was in the ratio of 7·1 per ten thousand patients treated.

In the forest belt the ratio showed an increase to 84·6 per ten thousand patients treated, whilst the incidence in the savannah belt was in the ratio of 87·3 per ten thousand. It would be as well to recall the fact that there is some evidence to suggest that in both coastal and forest cases a certain proportion of the sufferers are immigrants from endemic or epidemic areas in the Northern Territories of the Gold Coast or from neighbouring French territory.

There is little doubt that the Northern Territories and neighbouring regions are responsible for the bulk of the cases met with; for even in the Sunyani-Kintampo district of Ashanti where infection not uncommonly occurs, many of the patients seen are from the Protectorate or beyond and may have been infected there.[1]

Summary. (a) Writing in 1928, Dr. Saunders and Mr. Morris stated: 'We are not of the opinion that trypanosomiasis in the Gold Coast constitutes a serious or immediate danger to the stability or economic condition of the people. . . .

'We are however, of the opinion that trypanosomiasis constitutes a continual drain of death and ill-health; and also that there is a potential danger of extension, if the development of the country were to progress in such a way as to expose large numbers of people to the fly.'

This statement still holds good and care should be taken to maintain a proper balance when considering the apparent forty-five-fold rise in the case incidence of trypanosomiasis in the past 10 years. At the same time the presence of considerable numbers of persons in the Colony carrying the trypanosome in their blood-stream must give rise to no little concern and calls for a determined effort to limit infection as far as possible.

(b) It is not possible to indicate to what extent the apparent increase has resulted from (i) focussing attention in recent years on the disease, (ii) detailing officers whose principal duty has been to search for cases and, lastly, (iii) the unabated immigration from French territory—part of which is known to be heavily infected—of labourers many of whom have contributed to the numerous cases of death from the disease recorded during the year. The majority of cases seen are adult males of whom a large proportion are immigrants.

(c) Investigations suggest that the northern portion of Togoland under British mandate (Mamprusi under mandate) is a hyper-endemic area with an infection rate in the neighbourhood of 11 per cent.

(d) The Sunyani District of the Western Province of the Colony of Ashanti is another region where the infection is known to have existed for many years. Cases have also been reported where infection was believed to have occurred on the outskirts of Kumasi in the centre of forest belt of Ashanti.

(e) Cases occurring in the coastal belt of the Colony proper are believed to be to a very large extent imported. . . .

Recommendations. (a) A careful watch should be kept on the incidence of the disease, and investigations directed towards the discovery and, if possible, eradication of hyper-endemic foci should continue to be pursued. . . .

(d) Whilst the advisability of definite, planned anti-trypanosomiasis operations is undoubtedly a matter that allows of no argument, care must be exercised to ensure that large sums of money and numbers of personnel are not diverted from being used to deal with other vital medical and health problems of equal or much greater importance.[2]

1934. Trypanosomiasis continues to cause anxiety and there is some reason to think that it may be increasing although to what extent is very difficult to say. The figures for incidence per 10,000 of all cases treated by the Medical Department have steadily gone up during the past ten years, but whether there is a true increase of incidence is doubtful owing to the fact that the confidence of the people in European

---

[1] *Medical Report 1933–4*, pp. 101–2. [2] Ibid., pp. 106–7.

medicine is steadily increasing and medical officers are probably more alive to the disease and more accurate in diagnosis.

An outbreak, with an estimated infection rate at present of about seven per cent of the population, is going on in the Southern Mamprussi and Kusasi areas of Northern Togoland (population about 15,000) . . . .[1]

A small outbreak was reported towards the end of 1934 from the village of Kwale in the Tumu section of the Lawra area . . . . The whole available population of 126 was examined and 59 cases (47 per cent) were found infected.

The danger of the spread of trypanosomiasis in and from the Northern Territories is recognised but it is believed that extension of our present methods will control spread.[2]

1935. At Lawra and in the Lawra-Tumu district the medical officer devoted much of his time to the work and gained the complete confidence of the people so that the number of cases treated rose from 150 in 1934 to 1,161 in 1935.

A certain amount of evidence was forthcoming during the year that sleeping sickness was making headway in districts other than those where it was known to be hyperendemic. When the wholesale clearance of forest for cocoa and food farms is realised, it will be readily appreciated that conditions are becoming rapidly more favourable for the breeding of the fly vector.

Approval has been given for the appointment in 1936 of an experienced medical officer, of a medical entomologist with considerable local knowledge and of the necessary staff of nurses, dispensers and laboratory technicians. A complete survey will be made of the Protectorate followed later by a similar survey of Ashanti and the Colony proper. When the results of the survey have been collated, it should be possible to attack the problem in a more effective manner.[3]

This disease continues rightly to cause considerable anxiety. . . .

Two points . . . may well be stressed. The first is to what extent are we opening out fresh tracts of tsetse country by forest clearing resulting in the growth of secondary bush and the formation of savannah ? The second is a plea that the trypanosomiasis question should not distract attention from diseases such as tuberculosis, which in the towns and increasingly so in rural areas, has taken its toll for years and will continue to do so in the future, requiring the most strenuous efforts in the improvement of housing conditions and the elevation of the general standard of environmental sanitation for its control.

Trypanosomiasis is no new disease to the Gold Coast ; cases if carefully looked for could often be found in the Colony as well as in Ashanti and the Northern Territories.

Tsetse has always abounded in many areas. It will be found, it is thought, that the percentage of infected flies has risen in many localities, and that the main factor is the human element, i.e., the infected immigrant. Trypanosomiasis has now been added to the schedule of 'infectious diseases.'[4]

A Committee appointed by the Governor 'to discuss the problem created by the apparent increase in the prevalence of the disease known as human trypanosomiasis' reported:

General Situation. The Committee does not consider that the present situation throughout the Colony need give rise to undue concern. The disease is undoubtedly a drain upon the people and can, in certain circumstances, become dangerous, but there is, on the whole, no cause for panic.

Apparent Increase in Prevalence. Hospital figures show a relatively considerable increase in the number of cases of trypanosomiasis treated by the medical officers of the Colony during recent years. This increase, however, does not necessarily mean that there has been a serious increase in the incidence of the disease among the people of the Gold Coast. The figures available should be interpreted with much

---

[1] *Colonial Reports, Gold Coast 1934–5*, pp. 14–15. See also *Medical Report 1934*, p. 5.
[2] Ibid., p. 6.   [3] Ibid. *1935*, p. 6.   [4] Ibid., p. 16.

caution. There have certainly been isolated outbreaks in a few areas (such as Mamprusi) but it would be a mistake to suppose that a corresponding increase throughout the Colony is thereby indicated.

Explanation of Apparent Increase. There are various factors which tend to explain the rise in the number of cases observed or reported. Since 1924 the medical officers have become more aware of and interested in the disease. Diagnosis is now more accurate and more efficient means of treatment are available. This has in turn engendered a feeling of confidence among the natives. The more cases a medical officer cures, the more cases he is given an opportunity of treating. The Africans, impressed by the good results already obtained, are coming forward in greater numbers to the various hospitals. The success of the treatment camp at Nakpanduri, for instance, may be attributed in large measure to the enormous increase of confidence in European medicine.

Estimate of Actual Rate of Increase. In spite of the foregoing remarks, it is probable that there has, in recent years, been a slight increase in the prevalence of the disease. The opening up of communications, which has led to more speedy movements of the population and the introduction thereby of infected people into other areas, is naturally a factor making strongly for such an increase. A wide survey repeated from time to time would give data to answer this question.

Incidence of Disease. The incidence of trypanosomiasis in the most seriously infected focus, which lies in the Northern Territories, varies between 4 and 10 per cent. 7 per cent may be taken as an average for the area. This is, of course, a figure which gives rise to anxiety.

. . . The rate of infection is not so high in Ashanti as in the Northern Territories, and it has been established that the majority of cases treated in Ashanti hospitals are immigrants from the north. However, the Ashanti themselves are by no means immune to the disease and numbers of them have been infected. The percentage of infection in northern Ashanti is about ·6.[1]

In an Appendix to the Report of the Committee Dr. G. Saunders and Mr. K. S. Morris said:

We are not of the opinion that trypanosomiasis in the Gold Coast constitutes a serious or immediate danger to the stability or economic condition of the people. Even if we carry out the illegitimate procedure of adding together the two Makongo surveys we get a percentage infection of only about 11 per cent. The infected areas in the Kamerun vary from 38 per cent to 78 per cent (Jamot, 1925), reaching 80 per cent in some riverside villages.[2]

1936. Sleeping sickness continues to be a cause of anxiety. . . .

The returns indicate an increase in Western Mamprussi, South-Eastern Gonja and in the vicinity of Dunkwa, especially in the villages along the road between Dunkwa and Bibiani where it is spread by Northern Territories boys looking for work in the mines. This last fact is significant.[3]

It is regretted that owing to the difficulty of obtaining an Entomologist, the recommendation of the Committee on Human Trypanosomiasis which met in July, 1935 . . . to conduct a careful survey in the Northern Territories and Ashanti, could not at once be given effect to, but this difficulty has now been overcome and it is hoped to commence an extensive survey in 1937.[4]

[1] *Medical Report 1935*, p. 79.

[2] Ibid., p. 85. But S. Deutschman, Member of the Health Section of the League of Nations Secretariat, rightly said (*Epidemiological Report*, Oct.–Dec. 1936, p. 201):

'. . . generally speaking, the number of cases of the disease recorded is the largest where the efforts for their discovery are greatest and most widespread.

'It would be unfair not to take this into account in a superficial comparison of the apparent situation in the eastern part of Equatorial Africa (Belgian Congo, Cameroons, French Equatorial Africa, etc.), where the campaign has been carried out extensively for a long time, and in West Africa, where unknown foci of the disease are only now being discovered.'

[3] *Medical Report 1936*, p. 6.   [4] Ibid., p. 7.

Full data are not yet available and prolonged discussion, until such are forth-coming, must be fruitless and possibly misleading.[1]

Fly is plentiful throughout the Gold Coast wherever conditions are suitable. More cases of trypanosomiasis are being seen yearly. This increase is considered to be both actual and due to an increased faith on the part of the people in the efficacy of modern treatment. There is little sign, yet, of any increase in the virulence of the infecting strain. Immigration and movement of population, it is considered, is increasing yearly. Towards the end of the year a survey was carried out at Kumasi at the disinfesting station on the Great North Road, and the blood of all immigrants was examined for trypanosomes. Some two per centum were found to be infected. This ratio, although apparently small, represents a large number when the total number of immigrants passing south is considered. This figure cannot be guessed at. At the disinfesting station, where the survey was carried out, some 38,106 immigrants were dealt with during the year, but this total only represents the stream approaching Kumasi by one of many routes.[2]

The survey began work in the latter half of 1937. The Medical Reports for 1937 and 1938 said:

1937. It is too soon to forecast results but the investigators are optimistic about the possibility of effective control in the Lawra area.[3]

1938. The situation is now more satisfactory; spread has been checked and we can look forward to obtaining effective control within a reasonable period of time.[4]

But the scanty information published about the activities of the survey team[5] suggests that its investigations of the prevalence of the disease are still in a preliminary stage, and until a thorough survey has been carried through it will be impossible to say anything definite concerning the incidence of sleeping-sickness on the Gold Coast. Governor Burns, in a *General Plan for Development in the Gold Coast*, dated 26 July 1944, summarized the position and the intentions of the Government.

The prevalence of trypanosomiasis, especially in the Northern Territories, makes this disease a serious menace to the health of the people. Areas available for farming are restricted and the prevalence of the tsetse fly endangers the cattle industry. Both these factors, again, have their reactions on health by limiting the diet of the people.

It is intended to elaborate existing schemes and to bring areas already cleared, and mass treated, on to a maintenance basis at the earliest possible moment to permit the extension of similar operations to other areas. This will permit the processes of survey, treatment and clearing to be extended more rapidly to other districts, until a full knowledge of the incidence of the disease over the whole area of the Gold Coast has been obtained. Again, *Glossina submorsitans* appears to be extending its range widely, and entomological research into this factor will be necessary. The details of a five-year anti-trypanosomiasis campaign are now being worked out and I hope shortly to address you on the subject.[6]

[1] Ibid., p. 19.
[2] Ibid., p. 20. The numbers of immigrants crossing the ferries across the River Volta from the Northern Territories into Ashanti in the years 1935–6 to 1939–40 were 101,071, 90,127, 101,891, 108,071, and 61,163 respectively; see *Report on the Labour Department 1938–9*, p. 42; *1939–40*, p. 6. In 1942–3, 1943–4, and 1944–5 they numbered 63,809, 124,129, and 98,453 respectively; see ibid. *1942–3*, p. 4; *1943–4*, p. 4; *1944–5*, p. 4.
[3] *Medical Report 1937*, p. 6.   [4] Ibid. *1938*, p. 6.
[5] See ibid., pp. 104–7; *1939*, p. 3; *1940*, p. 3; *1941*, p. 3; *1942*, p. 1; *1943*, p. 2; *1944*, p. 2.
[6] *General Plan*, p. 6.

Leprosy. The Medical Report for 1922–3 was apparently the first to discuss this disease.[1] It has since attracted increasing attention, but very little is known as yet about its incidence.

1922–3. The incidence of leprosy in the Gold Coast is an unknown quantity, and until a suitable staff is available nothing can be done to cope with the disease.

No one doubts that there is a considerable number of lepers going about the country, carrying out their usual daily avocations—the Medical Officer of Health of Accra in his annual report for 1922 produces the photograph of a leper selling vegetables. Leprosy is not a notifiable or a legally infectious disease, and this Department has not the legal power to enforce any measures to prevent its spread.[2]

1923–4. The number of lepers in the Gold Coast is not known. . . . A British Empire Leprosy Relief Association has been founded in London to assist in dealing with leprosy in the Empire. This should do a great deal to stimulate anti-leprosy work in the Colonies.[3]

1924–5. It is notoriously difficult to get correct figures for Leprosy but there is little doubt that the disease is widespread.[4]

1925–6. 446 cases were seen and treated during the year as compared with 96 for the previous year. This increase does not indicate wider prevalence of the disease in the Colony, but results rather from the increased interest taken by Medical and Political Officers in the distribution of the disease.

Inquiries in reply to a questionnaire issued by the British Empire Leprosy Relief Association, revealed:—

(a) that no definite and reliable information is as yet available regarding the extent or distribution of the disease throughout the Colony and its dependencies;

(b) that it is less widely distributed, and the number of cases is comparatively fewer than in the other British West African possessions;

(c) that there is no evidence of its increase in recent years.[5]

1926–7. During the year under review 668 cases were treated with one death. . . . The increase in numbers is due to the efforts being made to collect patients for treatment, furthermore there is no doubt that the hope of relief which has been raised by observing the excellent effects of injections in yaws and other diseases has induced patients to come for treatment. The actual incidence of the disease is not accurately known and is difficult to estimate but so far proof has not been obtained that it is increasing.[6]

1927–8. During the year 830 cases were treated with one death, an increase of 162 cases on the previous year's record. This is due not to any increased incidence but to the fact that sufferers are coming forward in greater numbers voluntarily for treatment.

Early in 1926, the Secretary of the British Empire Leprosy Relief Association visited the Gold Coast Colony. As a result it was decided to form a Central Branch of the association at Accra with subsidiary branches for Ashanti and the Northern Territories at Kumasi and Tamale, and it was further decided that a whole time specially trained Medical Secretary to the Local Branch should be appointed and paid by Government . . . .[7]

1928–9. In the report for 1927–28, it was pointed out that a whole time specially

[1] I am here leaving out of consideration the somewhat vague remarks by the Colonial Surgeon Dr. Clarke in *State of Colonial Possessions 1858*, Part II, p. 23.

[2] *Medical Report 1922–3*, p. 47. The Acting Deputy Director of Sanitary Services recommended ibid., p. 49, 'one additional Medical Officer of Health to investigate the incidence of Leprosy'. But see ibid. *1923–4*, p. 16: 'Provision for one additional Medical Officer of Health was made in the 1923–24 Estimates. No appointment has, however, yet been made. In addition two vacancies in the Medical Officer of Health grade . . . still remain unfilled. Medical Officers were not keen on entering the Sanitary Branch of the Medical Department, and the Secretary of State has not found suitable candidates in Britain.'

[3] Ibid. *1923–4*, p. 14.   [4] Ibid. *1924–5*, p. 9.   [5] Ibid. *1925–6*, p. 8.
[6] Ibid. *1926–7*, pp. 11–12.   [7] Ibid. *1927–8*, p. 17.

trained Medical Secretary to the local branch of the British Empire Leprosy Relief Association was to be appointed for the purpose of making a leprosy survey of the Colony. Dr. M. B. Duncan Dixey was selected and arrived in the Colony early in the year and has spent his whole time travelling through various districts. Togoland, the Colony proper, Ashanti and the Northern territories have been visited and a valuable body of facts has already been collected. When these are digested a more accurate idea of the prevalence of the disease will have been obtained and plans can then be formulated for extending relief to sufferers.[1]

In his report for the year 1928–9 Dr. Dixey states that in the Ho district the leprosy incidence appears to be about 7 per 1,000,[2] and that 'it appears that leprosy is very prevalent in the Northern Territories'.[3] 'Starvation may play a part in predisposing to the disease in the Northern Territories though not in the Colony, farther south.'[4] In his report for 1929–30 Dr. Dixey said:

The results of the surveys have been interesting, and demonstrate to date that there is definitely a higher leprosy incidence in some areas, than in others . . . .

An impression is also gained that there is a greater relative prevalence of leprosy than was formerly believed.[5]

The Medical Report for 1929–30 said:

1929–30. It is prevalent in the Northern Territories and, generally speaking, amongst poorer tribes who live in regions where water is scarce, the quality of the food poor, and sanitation primitive. From this fact the conclusion is obvious that the problem of leprosy is largely secondary to the much wider problem of raising the whole standard of living of the tribes residing in such areas.[6]

The Medical Report for 1930–1 stated:

1930–1. During the year there was a great increase in most stations in the number of cases of leprosy attending for treatment.

This is an example of a disease apparently on the increase whilst in reality due to increased interest in the problem on the part of Medical Officers, increased confidence on the part of the lepers themselves and also without doubt due to the great improvement to patients after treatment in the early stages of the disease.

The incidence of the disease varies widely in the various districts of the Colony, Ashanti and the Northern Territories, but to give any actual figures of the total number of lepers would be quite impossible at this juncture.[7]

Dr. Dixey in his report for 1930–1 said:

In April, a circular was sent by the Honourable the Director of Medical and Sanitary Service to all Medical Officers and Medical Officers of Health asking for information in regard to leprosy and leprosy work in their respective districts. From the replies received to this circular and from the results of previous surveys in various parts of the Colony it is possible to give some idea of the prevalence of leprosy in the various parts of the Colony, Ashanti and the Northern Territories, and the means which are being undertaken to combat this problem. This general survey, while admittedly incomplete, gives a clue as to where the leprosy incidence is highest, and where leper settlements are most needed at the present time. Altogether over 4,300 lepers have been seen of whom 2,160 have received treatment.

The largest number of cases have been noted in Ashanti and the Northern Territories; fewer cases have been seen in the Eastern Province and in Togoland, and fewer still in the Central and Western Provinces.[8]

[1] Ibid. *1928–9*, p. 13.   [2] See ibid., p. 128.   [3] Ibid., p. 129.   [4] Ibid., p. 131.
[5] Ibid. *1929–30*, p. 196.   [6] Ibid., p. 15. See also ibid., p. 29.
[7] Ibid. *1930–1*, p. 27.   [8] Ibid., p. 150.

Leprosy is prevalent throughout the Gold Coast and British Togoland.
Among the chief difficulties to contend with are:—

(a) The apathy of the people in many parts of the country.

(b) The slow and non-spectacular results of treatment.

(c) The anæsthetic type of leprosy predominates, and may partly account for this apathy.

(d) The paucity of Medical Officers and the distances to treatment centres for many of the patients.[1]

Dr. Dixey had terminated his survey shortly before the taking of the 1931 census (or count) which also asked for the number of lepers. The Census Officer, 1931, made the following comparison of the results of the two inquiries:[2]

	Census Returns	Dr. Dixey's Returns
Colony, Western Province	235	104
„ Central Province.	270	80
„ Eastern Province.	451	369
Ashanti, Western Province	325 ⎫ 1,011	1,056
„ Eastern Province	686 ⎭	
Northern Territories, Northern Province .	1,774 ⎫ 2,524	1,702
„ „ Southern Province .	750 ⎭	
Togoland	547	859
Total	5,038	4,170

The discrepancies are not irreconcilable. Dr. Dixey made no claim that his figures represented the true incidence of the disease, and the extreme difficulty in accurate diagnosis together with a certain reluctance on the part of the people to reveal the presence of this disease effectively prevented accuracy at the Census.

According to the above figures the ratio per mille of the population who are recognised as lepers is as follows:—

	Lepers	Population	Ratio per mille
Gold Coast Colony . .	956	1,571,362	0·6
Ashanti	1,011	578,078	1·7
Northern Territories .	2,524	717,275	3·5
Togoland	547	293,671	1·8
Total. . . .	5,038	3,160,386	1·6

The Census Officer was certainly right in suggesting that no conclusions concerning the prevalence of leprosy should be drawn from Dr. Dixey's returns. First of all, they did not cover the whole country. In Western Dagomba (Northern Territories), for example, where the incidence is high, he listed only 520 cases. The explanation is to be found in the following passage from his report:

At Tamale [Western Dagomba] through the energy of Dr. Gillespie, 520 lepers have been seen . . . .[3]

It is obvious that the lepers seen in Tamale comprised only part of all lepers in the District. But this is not the only reason why he found not more than 1,702 cases in the Northern Territories.

[1] *Medical Report 1930 1*, p. 158.   [2] *The Gold Coast, 1931*, vol. i, p. 228.
[3] *Medical Report 1930–1*, p. 152.

In the Northern Territories and particularly in the Northern Province where the population is dense, the water supply is a difficulty in the dry season, shortages of food occur and sanitation is absent, leprosy is very prevalent. The number of lepers seen is large and many more would appear were there a larger Medical staff to see and treat the cases.[1]

In Togoland he found altogether 859 cases, of which 776 in the Ho District. But the figure of 776 represented in fact the total number of persons who, since the formation of the Leper Settlement at Ho (1926), had been there under treatment, and of whom 58 had been rendered symptom-free and 12 had died. On the other hand, his figures for the rest of Togoland represented only a very small fraction of all cases.

As regards the census returns, the position is somewhat obscure. The Census Officer, in the table reproduced above, entered for Togoland 547 cases. But according to the detailed census tables the number of cases actually enumerated was 1,114 (including 450 in the Ho Leper Settlement).[2] For the Southern Province of the Northern Territories he entered altogether only 750 cases, while the detailed report shows for the Western Dagomba District alone 816 cases[3] (excluding Tamale, for which the number is not given). Even according to the certainly quite incomplete census the incidence, therefore, was higher than shown by the Census Officer. The 'ratio per mille' for Togoland, for example, should read 3·8 instead of 1·8.

Subsequent Medical Reports said:

1931–2. The observation made in a previous report that the problem of Leprosy is intimately bound up with the problem of raising the whole standard of living of the tribes chiefly affected may again be stressed. Unless the standard can be raised special measures are bound to be seriously handicapped.[4]

Some 5,038 lepers were enumerated during the Census in April, 1931, giving a leprosy rate of 1·6 per mille of the whole population, varying from 0·6 in the Colony to 3·5 in the Northern Territories.[5]

1932–3. The old difficulty of maintaining regular treatment in stations outside the Ho and Accra Leper Settlements still exists. Medical officers from various centres throughout the Colony report that they are unable to persuade lepers to continue treatment for any length of time.

Numbers of cases were reported from various places such as Bawku, Lawra, and Sunyani.

The Medical Officer, Lawra, reported that the disease was prevalent throughout his district and caused much disfigurement but few cases came forward for treatment.

As pointed out in previous reports the problem of leprosy is bound up with the general problem of raising the whole standard of living of the tribes chiefly affected. Expenditure on it is limited by its relative importance to other more pressing problems and the Colony's financial resources.[6]

It is difficult to be sure of the true incidence of leprosy in the Gold Coast. Some 5,000 lepers were enumerated during the Census in April 1931, but this figure cannot be considered as conclusive for many reasons.

The above figures, such as they are, point to an incidence of about 1·5 per mille of the general population. . . .

In the Northern Territories the case incidence per mille is probably about six times as high as that of the Colony. Settlements are maintained at Accra, Kumasi, Yendi,

[1] Ibid., p. 151. [2] See The Gold Coast, 1931, vol. ii, pp. 221–46.
[3] See ibid., pp. 205–14. [4] Medical Report 1931-2, p. 9.
[5] Ibid., p. 22. [6] Ibid. 1932-3, p. 9.

Ho (the principal one) and Navrongo, the settlement at Navrongo being organised and run by the White Fathers.

Efforts are made to persuade lepers in the infective stage to enter these settlements and to submit to voluntary segregation. In the advanced stages not much persuasion is required as a rule.[1]

1933–4. Owing to shortage of staff nothing has been added to our previous information with regard to the incidence of this disease.

. . . It is generally accepted that the incidence of this disease is in the region of 1·5–2 *per mille*, and that the percentage increases the further north one proceeds.[2]

After having pointed out that the increase in the 'incidence' of sleeping-sickness in the Gold Coast was due in part to more thorough surveys, Dr. Selwyn-Clarke said:

In this connexion, it might be desirable to refer to the apparent increase of over 100 per cent in the number of cases of leprosy recorded in the Annual Medical and Sanitary Report for 1928–29 over that of the previous year. The period covered by the report in question happened to coincide with the appointment of a leprosy medical officer by the British Empire Leprosy Relief Association.

Since the abolition of that special post leprosy has diminished, on paper, to a very considerable extent. Before the appointment (1927–28) the number of cases of leprosy treated was 668, this rose to 1,427 in 1928–29 and to 3,224 in 1930–31. The leprosy medical officer resigned at the end of 1931 and the figure for 1933–34 has fallen to 1,494.[3]

1935. Owing principally to staff shortage nothing useful has been added in recent years to our knowledge with respect to the incidence of this disease.[4]

The report for 1936 still contained the statement that 'no staff has been available to increase our knowledge with respect to the incidence of this disease',[5] but it contained at the same time another statement which indicates that the Department had realized in the meantime that to wait for an improvement in 'the whole standard of living of the tribes chiefly affected' was a policy which could not possibly be recommended any longer.

A revision of our policy with regard to leprosy appears to be necessary.[6]

This change in the attitude of the Medical Department was caused by 'A short Report on Anti-Leprosy Work in the Gold Coast with suggestions for its further development', by Dr. E. Muir, Medical Secretary, British Empire Leprosy Relief Association. Dr. Muir said:

Leprosy may be considered from four points of view, viz., the æsthetic, charitable, medical and public health. According to the first, deformed and disabled lepers are an eye-sore in the town, and a place of refuge is therefore created for them to which they can be removed. From the charitable point of view these victims are looked upon as unfortunates and charitably disposed people supply comforts in the form of food, treats, left-off clothing, etc. The medical standpoint is shown when lepers attend hospital and dispensary for treatment, either of the leprosy itself or of its complications and accompanying diseases. Attendance however tends to be irregular, and while a few receive benefit, the majority are but little improved. The public health point of view is that which endeavours to probe down into the causes of leprosy, to study it as it exists in the villages and to devise means which, however

---

[1] *Medical Report 1932–3*, p. 21.

[2] Ibid. *1933–4*, p. 25. See also ibid. *1935*, p. 18; *1936*, p. 22.

[3] Ibid. *1933–4*, p. 101. Actually 668 cases were treated in 1926–7 and 830 in 1927–8.

[4] Ibid. *1935*, p. 18.   [5] Ibid. *1936*, p. 22.   [6] Ibid., p. 8.

long they may take to bear fruit, will in the end deal effectively with the disease and bring about its control.

From the æsthetic and charitable points of view I consider that something is being accomplished in the Gold Coast. From the medical side very little is being done except by a few keen doctors who are distressed at the frequency of the disease and are seeking to do what little they can in addition to their many other pressing duties. From the public health standpoint something is being accomplished by the isolation of some 400 lepers, about one-third of which may be considered as highly infectious cases. But, in the absence of any clear indication of the actual incidence and distribution of leprosy in the country it is difficult to say to what extent the spread of the disease is likely to be limited by the partial removal of these cases from contact with the public.[1]

He pointed out the need of a survey:

So far no satisfactory estimate of the incidence of leprosy is available. The 1931 census report shows as much as 4 per cent in some villages; but these figures are acknowledged by public health workers to be unreliable. Short surveys of very limited extent have been carried out by two medical officers in recent years; but these were not extensive enough to give the necessary data for forming an effective and comprehensive programme.[2]

He submitted a plan for carrying out 'a series of sample surveys in selected areas',[3] and the Medical Department thought that his views on policy and his suggestions 'merit our closest consideration and must be the basis of our future efforts'.[4] But apparently nothing was done.

1938. Owing to staff shortage, our knowledge as to the incidence of leprosy in the various localities, and generally, has not been materially increased during recent years. The incidence progressively increases as one proceeds north. Calculations based on the generally held supposition that there are about two lepers per mille of population shew the total number of lepers in the Gold Coast to be between 7,000 and 8,000. This estimate, it is considered, is on the low side.[5]

The Medical Reports for 1939–44 do not mention any survey work, and Governor Burns, in a *General Plan for Development in the Gold Coast*, said:

As regards leprosy we have no certain information of the present incidence of the disease. In an incomplete survey, abandoned in 1931, it was estimated that the incidence of leprosy was roughly one per mille of the population. The position, however, remains somewhat obscure. It is feared that the problem is greater than was at first thought, and I consider that a fresh survey should be undertaken as soon as staff conditions permit. Only then will we be able to appreciate the magnitude of the problem that lies ahead.[6]

Tuberculosis. The early medical reports do not suggest that tuberculosis was frequently discovered.[7] But in the last years before the First World War the number of registered deaths attributed to this disease attracted attention.

Cape Coast. Causes of deaths as entered in the Register are of little scientific value. But it may be noted that 'Consumption' is frequently given as a cause of death.

---

[1] Ibid., p. 85. [2] Ibid. [3] See ibid. [4] Ibid., p. 9.

[5] Ibid. *1938*, p. 25; see also ibid. *1937*, p. 21. Rogers and Muir said that the number 'may be provisionally placed at 20,000 or 5·55 per mille' (*Leprosy*, 2nd ed., p. 30; 3rd ed., p. 29).

[6] *General Plan* (1944), p. 5.

[7] A notable exception is the 'Report upon the Colonial Hospital and Dispensary, Elmina, for the Year, 1895' which said: 'In regard to the Medical cases it appears from analysis of the out-patient record that Tuberculosis in all its forms is common in this locality' (Gold Coast, *Medical Report 1895*, p. 29).

That this is so, is borne out by the Medical Officer's statement for the third quarter of the year that 'The number of cases of tuberculosis is quite remarkable'.[1]

The Medical Report for 1913 said:

The official returns show 141 cases of tuberculous disease as having been treated during the year, with 15 deaths. Judging from the figures obtained from the Death Registers, tuberculous disease would appear to be much more common than the above figures indicate. The total number of deaths in the Registration Districts of the Colony attributed to this disease is 244 (174 male, 70 female). In Cape Coast alone the registered deaths from this disease number 30 males and 23 females, giving a percentage of 37·2 per cent. males and 37 per cent. females to total deaths registered.[2]

When in 1914 the number of cases treated rose to 272, the Medical Report said:

I regret to say there is a marked increase in the number of cases treated, and fear that the disease is on the increase. The increase may, however, be due only to the fact that many more people suffering from it applied for treatment.[3]

In the mining districts where the case incidence of phthisis is comparatively high —especially among natives from the Northern Territories—there is need, I think, of special care in the housing and care of those employees who are working underground.[4]

Subsequent reports expressed the opinion that the disease was on the increase.

1916. Reports shew that tubercular disease is on the increase, especially in the larger towns. No special preventive measures are yet taken against this disease, beyond the general improvement in sanitary conditions, and the attention that is paid to better ventilation, light and air space in buildings. Other means for prevention are at present under discussion.[5]

1917. Death returns shew that tuberculosis is on the increase and certainly the average native house and mode of life are ideal for the spread of the disease. During the year it was made an infectious disease under the Infectious Diseases Ordinance and notification by all Government Medical Officers made compulsory.[6]

1918. There is a decrease all round in the number of deaths from this disease registered during the year, but this can only be an apparent fall, as influenza most certainly accounted for the deaths of a number of tubercular subjects who would have died from tuberculosis had not influenza supervened. The general concensus of opinion is that the disease is on the increase, and the medical officer of one of the mining companies has been so impressed with this that he has opened an isolation building for the treatment of his cases. It is an unfortunate fact however that cases of tuberculosis of the lungs are seldom seen until the disease is well advanced. The onset of the disease is so often insidious and lacking in any acute symptoms that it is not until some alarming sign obtrudes itself that relief is sought.[7]

The increase of tuberculosis . . . requires special attention and the formation of cliniques and sanitoria should be considered.[8]

1919. Although there is only a small increase in the number of these cases recorded the idea appears prevalent that this disease is distinctly on the increase.[9]

---

[1] *Medical Report 1911*, p. 189.   [2] Ibid. *1913*, p. 25.

[3] Principal Medical Officer, ibid. *1914*, p. 12.

[4] Senior Sanitary Officer, ibid., p. 38. The numbers of deaths due to tuberculosis registered in Tarkwa in 1913–18 were 46, 78, 113, 112, 137, and 139 respectively; see *Report on Births and Deaths 1921*, p. 9.

[5] *Medical Report 1916*, p. 13.   [6] Ibid. *1917*, p. 18. See also ibid., p. 7.

[7] Ibid. *1918*, p. 27.   [8] Ibid., p. 30.   [9] Ibid. *1919*, p. 7.

There is much reason to regard as well-founded the belief that Pulmonary Tuber-culosis is steadily on the increase, whether actual figures can be quoted to prove it or not. A large number of the cases which come for treatment are already in a hopeless condition.[1]

1920. Three hundred and fifty-five cases were treated as compared with two hundred and sixty-nine in the previous year. From these figures and those of previous years it appears that this disease is distinctly on the increase.[2]

Statistical evidence is at present insufficient to prove a real increase, but the number of untreated cases is probably much in excess of the advanced ones which seek relief. As the Vital Statistics also of each of the larger towns show *Tuberculosis* to be a relatively frequent cause of death there is strong presumptive evidence that this disease is one of increasing importance.[3]

As all these reports deal practically only with the larger towns, two passages from the 1921 census report may be quoted here:

Colony, Central Province. The most prevalent diseases in his [the Commissioner's] opinion are Tuberculosis, Venereal Diseases, Dysentery, Malaria and Guinea worm ....[4]

Colony, Western Province. Tuberculosis, venereal diseases, tropical ulcers and fevers of different sorts ... are found all over the Province ....[5]

Subsequent Medical Reports said:

1923-4. In the Gold Coast increasing numbers of the people are drifting from their former simple isolated village life into the larger trading and mining centres where they live together with other races in denser communities, and come in contact with diseases which are new to the pathological environment to which they have been accustomed.

One would imagine that once introduced into a susceptible race tuberculosis would rapidly spread under the conditions of housing favoured by the African.

It has been my experience, however, that, though the disease runs a sub-acute or acute course in Africans actually infected, it does not spread so rapidly as one would expect. I attribute this mainly to the tropical sun, and the fact that the climate and simple life of the African have habituated him to a practically wholly outdoor life. The risk of spread is, however, becoming greater since the people, in increasing numbers, are obtaining employment in more sedentary indoor occupa-tions and in the dust-laden atmosphere associated with underground mining.[6]

1925-6. 571 cases of this disease, with 76 deaths, were treated in the various hospitals during the year as compared with 414 cases, with 51 deaths, for the previous year. Though this increase may be partly accounted for by the increase in the number of Africans seeking medical treatment there is a consensus of opinion among Medical Officers that the disease is steadily becoming more prevalent in the Colony with each succeeding year. The high mortality is due to the fact that the disease, being of comparatively recent introduction, assumes the characters of an acute infection as the Natives have not yet had time to become 'tuberculized'.[7]

---

[1] Ibid., p. 16.   [2] Ibid. *1920*, p. 7.   [3] Ibid., p. 19.
[4] *Census Report 1921*, p. 81.   [5] Ibid., p. 106.
[6] Deputy Director of Sanitary Services, *Medical Report 1923-4*, p. 14. In the same year out of an average of 726 indentured labourers from the Northern Territories 34 died from tuberculosis and altogether 104 from causes other than accidents (see *Report on the Mining Department 1923-4*, pp. 9, 25). The Secretary for Mines made the following comment: 'The tuberculosis cases were in all human probability suffering from this disease before they left their homes—this is inferred with some justice from the comparatively short time which elapsed, in nearly every case, between the arrival on the mine and the death of the sufferer' (ibid., p. 9). See also ibid., p. 6: 'All recruits for the mines from the Northern Territories are now medically examined before they are allowed to travel. This will eradicate the unfit, and the deplorably high mortality rate ....' See, further-more, *Medical Report 1924-5*, pp. 20-1.
[7] Ibid. *1925-6*, p. 8.

The Medical Officer of Health Tarkwa, in his Annual Report, states as follows:—

'This disease, in Tarkwa Town and in the Mining Areas, is, by far, the most serious question that has to be faced.

'The total number of deaths at all ages registered in Tarkwa during 1925–26 was 126 of which 58 were certified as due to Pulmonary Tuberculosis. The "killing disease" both in Tarkwa Town and in the neighbouring Mine Areas is Tuberculosis. In the two Mine Areas where I have acted as Medical Officer for the past 6 months the most typical cases are to be seen in the young adolescent and in the elderly mine employee who has usually worked with the Companies for years'.[1]

1926–7. The number of deaths from tuberculosis continues to increase in spite of the improvement in housing conditions in many of the larger areas.

The Medical Officer, Tarkwa, in his report for 1926–27 states that pulmonary tuberculosis is the chief fatal disease in that town. This statement is substantiated by the fact that seventy-five or 39·4 per centum of those who died suffered from pulmonary tuberculosis. Of the deaths from this disease forty-nine or 65·3 per centum occurred in employees of the mines.

This is a serious state of affairs and would seem to point to the necessity of early action being taken to improve housing conditions and other factors affecting the health of the mine labourers and of the local population.[2]

Phthisis. This continues to be a serious menace to public health owing to the almost complete absence of immunity among the African population resulting in a heavy case mortality rate amounting, according to the writer's observations to nearly one hundred per centum.

The menace of this white plague is not fully realised and unless adequate steps are taken to control it the results will one day be disastrous to the prosperity of the Colony.[3]

1927–8. Tuberculosis. Again shows an increase. The advance although somewhat disquieting is not yet of sufficient proportion to cause serious alarm, for it should be noted that the number of cases of tuberculosis relative to the total number of all cases shows a very small increase only. It is difficult to estimate accurately the extent to which tuberculosis is really increasing.[4]

1928–9. The number of cases of tuberculosis relative to the total number of all cases treated shows a slight drop on the previous year and although the table would indicate a steady general increase it does not justify dogmatic conclusions or that expensive experiments should be made which might later prove failures.

It is believed that the resistance of the African to the pulmonary form of the disease, once the disease is established, is generally speaking low, although some officers aver that the African has a greater degree of natural immunity than he is usually credited with, cases of the chronic type seen in Europe with arrestment of the disease being occasionally seen. Certainly labourers from Northern parts coming to Coast towns and mining centres and living under altered conditions of diet and housing do suffer severely.[5]

Members of the West African Medical Staff are generally agreed that the indigenous African has little or no immunity to this disease and a number are definitely of the opinion that cases are more frequently met with in practice at the present day than hitherto.

In his Annual Report for 1928–29, the Medical Officer of Health, Winneba, writes as follows:—

'Pulmonary tuberculosis is becoming a serious menace against which little can be done unless the native can be taught that his salvation lies in personal hygiene and sanitary dwelling places.'

---

[1] *Medical Report 1925–6*, p. 15.   [2] Ibid. *1926–7*, p. 24.
[3] Acting Medical Officer of Health Dr. Selwyn Clarke, *Report on the Kumasi Public Health Board 1926–7*, p. 30.
[4] *Medical Report 1927–8*, p. 16.   [5] Ibid. *1928–9*, pp. 12–13.

The Medical Officer of Health, Kumasi, in his Annual Report for the same period writes:—

'During the year there was a very definite increase in these cases of pulmonary tuberculosis. The majority were in labourers recently from the Northern Territories.

'The mortality rate of the disease was very high. Dust and starvation are probably potent predisposing causes and occurring on the way down to Kumasi and overcrowding undoubtedly helps to spread it here.

'The whole problem is beginning to assume serious proportions in this relatively non-immune population.'[1]

1929–30. The above table[2] does not support the view that tuberculosis is a very urgent problem, or that expensive experiments should be undertaken. With close attention to general sanitation and especially to housing conditions it is believed that the disease can be kept under control.[3]

For many years, Tarkwa, as the centre of the mining industry, has returned by far the highest percentage of cases of pulmonary tuberculosis of any station in the Gold Coast. A Medical officer specially trained in tuberculosis is now in residence there. He writes as follows:—

'This disease continues to be a very serious problem, the measure of which is not indicated by the number of cases diagnosed amongst out-patients.

The victim rarely reports until his symptoms are severe, and then probably is most unwilling to enter hospital although he may be febrile, wasted and with extensive involvement of at least one lung.

The housing conditions in the district are largely such as to assist the spread of the disease, especially in the villages formerly belonging to the mines which have since ceased work.'[4]

The increased number of cases of pulmonary tuberculosis returned from several of the larger centres should probably be put down to the increasing number of cases of pulmonary tuberculosis coming in to these centres for treatment and would appear to be increasing *pari passu* with the increased number of general patients applying for treatment.

If this is the case the outlook is hopeful, for the general sanitation of the country is improving year by year.[5]

1930–1. Tuberculosis does not appear to be increasing to any degree. The percentage of cases of Tuberculosis to all cases seen has shown no increase during recent years.[6]

In the past eight years there has been practically no variation in the percentage column, and the figures do not suggest that the tuberculosis problem is a very pressing one. Year by year sanitation and preventive medicine are having more attention and this fact should gradually lead to a lowering of the case incidence.[7]

In the large, more advanced and populous centres there is some indication that a slight degree of immunity is being acquired. This, however, is not marked and generally it may be stated that the average African has little or no resistance to the disease.

If one is right in the conclusion that the disease is making no marked headway and that the case incidence is practically stationary and this conclusion would appear to be correct from figures returned, then the future must be considered hopeful.

[1] Ibid., pp. 25–6.
[2] The table showed that while the number of cases of tuberculosis treated had increased the percentage of cases of tuberculosis among all cases treated in 1923–4 to 1929–30 was 0·53, 0·50, 0·58, 0·66, 0·68, 0·65, and 0·64 respectively.
[3] Ibid. *1929–30*, p. 14.　　　　　　　　[4] Ibid., pp. 30–1.
[5] Ibid., p. 33. It was realized a few years later that the general sanitation of the country was deteriorating; see p. 485 above.
[6] Ibid. *1930–1*, p. iii.　　　　　　　　[7] Ibid., p. 13.

Year by year conditions improve and enlightenment of the general population advances.[1]

1931–2. The incidence of Tuberculosis in the Colony appears to vary little from year to year although it is always high in the mining areas. The close association everywhere between the gold mining industry and a high rate for Tuberculosis is exemplified in the mining areas of the Gold Coast . . . .[2]

The chief focus is situated in the mining area and the Senior Health Officer noted that 25 per cent of all registered deaths in Tarkwa in males were due to Pulmonary Tuberculosis. If death registration were general throughout the country there might be cause for alarm at a death rate of 12 per cent which was the figure for all male deaths registered in the Colony. But at present registration is confined to only about 30 of the towns in the Colony (and even in these the figures are unreliable), and these towns are centres where overcrowding and unsuitable dieting exist and are most likely to favour spread. They contain less than one-twelfth of the population of the whole country and one would expect to find in them a higher incidence of Pulmonary Tuberculosis than in the rural areas in which the bulk of the population resides.

There is no evidence of an increased incidence of the disease in the whole Colony, but cases are being noted more widely than heretofore. Increased transport facilities are doubtless a contributing factor.[3]

Pulmonary tuberculosis followed closely upon non-tuberculous diseases of the respiratory system in being one of the most important causes of death in 1931–32. Furthermore, the ratio of deaths from this affection to deaths from all causes rose from 11·5 in 1930–31 to 12·5 in 1931–32.

Deaths from pulmonary tuberculosis are more than twice as common amongst males as amongst females and the labourer employed on mines or who has been so employed contributes an altogether disproportionate number of deaths to the total bill of mortality.[4]

1932–3. The problem remains one of the most important to be faced. The causes for the high incidence of this disease are not far to seek. Insanitary housing, over-crowding, exposure, a vitamin-deficient dietary, lack of immunity, predisposing debilitating diseases, uncleanly habits and a total ignorance of the rudimentary laws of hygiene are all important factors.

The opinions of medical and health officers are almost equally divided as to whether the disease is really on the increase or not. In the larger centres it would seem that the disease is just being 'held', the race between pulmonary tuberculosis and improved sanitation being very close. It is possible that a degree of immunity is in process of being purchased 'at a price'.

In the less advanced rural areas a slow increase may be taking place, the source of infection often being returned ex-mine labourers.[5]

1933–4. The actual number of cases of the various forms of tuberculosis seen— and the large proportion of these were pulmonary in type—was slightly smaller than in the previous year but it would be very unwise to infer from this that the disease was on the decline; there is little doubt, moreover, that the reverse is the case in view of the increased proportion of deaths reported to have taken place from the disease to deaths due from all causes in the registration areas in the Gold Coast Colony.

After non-tuberculous diseases of the respiratory system, pulmonary tuberculosis was once more the chief killing disease and its toll was especially severe in Tarkwa and the mining areas.[6]

1934. Although case mortality is high (and in all probability definitely higher than shown owing to the fact that many victims of the pulmonary form find their

[1] *Medical Report 1930–1*, p. 29.   [2] Ibid. *1931–2*, p. iii. See also ibid. *1932–3*, p. iii.
[3] Ibid. *1931–2*, p. 8.   [4] Ibid., p. 22.
[5] Ibid. *1932–3*, p. 22. The Medical Report for 1943 quoted these three paragraphs and said (p. 3): 'In our present state of knowledge little more can be added.'
[6] Ibid. *1933–4*, pp. 9–10.

way back to their villages to die), yet it is to be noted that the case incidence does not seem to vary much from year to year.

The increase in gold-mining activities with its known close association with phthisis is bound to bring this special problem into greater prominence on the Gold Coast as time goes on.[1]

1935. Of all the diseases met with in the Colony, tuberculosis is believed to constitute one of the greatest menaces to the indigenous population.

It should be pointed out that the figures of cases treated in no way represent the total for the Colony, since many patients suffering from the pulmonary form are removed by their relatives from hospitals where little can be done to cure the condition once it has acquired a firm foothold, and many labourers who became infected in the mining areas return to die in their home villages. Furthermore, if all cases of the pulmonary type of the disease—forming by far the greatest proportion of all varieties—could be traced, it would probably be found that considerably over ninety per centum had succumbed within two years, usually a much shorter period. Lack of immunity, mass infection, faulty nutrition and the existence of other debilitating diseases, e.g., worms, malaria, yaws, etc., all act as factors in this tragedy.[2]

As a 'killing' disease entity, tuberculosis takes pride of place, and is only exceeded by the combined disease category of 'pneumonia, broncho-pneumonia and bronchitis'. It is unnecessary, therefore, to stress its importance.

Whether tuberculosis is generally on the increase is hard to say. Tuberculisation of the community in the populous centres is believed to be considerable and it is possible that a degree of resistance may be in the process of being acquired. Generally, resistance to the infection is practically non-existent. In the more rural areas it is thought that tuberculosis is on the increase: in such areas, however, death registration does not apply. Most of the labour is drawn from these areas and the returning, tuberculous ex-worker must do much to spread the disease in his community.

Undoubtedly the deep mining industry influences the problem. To what degree, it is difficult to sum up, for the mine labourer is not compounded and, usually, on the first signs of the establishment of the disease he leaves the mine. Frequently, after a stay of varying period in some overcrowded and insanitary local village, he proceeds back to his country to die before he arrives home.[3]

The future of tuberculosis in the Gold Coast resolves itself into a race between sanitation in its widest application and the disease. Tuberculosis is not a showy 'tropical' disease and for this reason may fail to receive the public attention it merits. It is capable of killing throughout the length and breadth of the Gold Coast, and from a health standpoint is the most important problem for the future.[4]

1936. The disparity between the figures for males and females can readily be explained. The male age group which provides some 42·2 per centum of all cases is the 25–45-year group.[5] Most of the immigrant and labouring classes are contained in this category. On these men fall in the greatest degree the effects of undernourishment, exposure, strain, overcrowding in insanitary hovels, ignorance of the

[1] Ibid. *1934*, p. 5.   [2] Ibid. *1935*, p. 7.   [3] Ibid., p. 19. See also ibid. *1933–4*, p. 26.
[4] Ibid. *1935*, p. 20. See also ibid. *1941*, p. 3; *1943*, p. 3.
[5] The total numbers of deaths from tuberculosis in the registration towns in 1933–8 were as follows:

	Deaths from Tuberculosis						Per cent. of all deaths					
	1933	*1934*	*1935*	*1936*	*1937*	*1938*	*1933*	*1934*	*1935*	*1936*	*1937*	*1938*
Male . . .	536	519	647	632	639	658	13	13	13	13	12	14
Female . . .	169	176	220	221	207	167	7	7	7	7	7	6

(See *Report of Principal Registrar, 1933*, p. 6; *1934*, p. 31; *1935*, p. 31; *1936*, p. 31; *1937*, p. 31; *1938*, p. 33.)

rudimentary laws of health and the universal spitting habit. Many suffer from concurrent debilitating diseases, and their power of resistance to the infection is almost non-existent. A more fertile soil for the implantation of infection would be difficult to find.[1]

Many sufferers, when the cause of their complaint is obvious, make an attempt to return to their homes. Some succeed in doing this, others die *en route.*

Whatever happens, the chances of their propagating the infection are legion. Year after year the process continues, and it is little to be wondered at that the consensus of opinion indicates a steady increase of the infection in the rural areas in which the majority, if not all, of the labouring classes have their homes.[2]

When the whole field of prevention is reviewed it is considered that tuberculosis is the most direct threat to the future of the peoples of the Gold Coast. Diseases such as trypanosomiasis will rise and fall in incidence and virulence in certain localities as in the past, but tuberculosis will continue taking its toll anywhere in the Gold Coast, necessitating elevation in every phase of sanitation and in the economic status of the people before its progress can be checked.

Tuberculosis is apt not to receive the publicity it undoubtedly warrants, and tends to be relegated to the background in the public opinion in the face of such threats as are presented by well-advertised diseases as yellow fever and the aforementioned trypanosomiasis.[3]

1938. Tuberculosis. The seriousness of this problem needs no stressing. It has now resumed its place at the head of the list of killing diseases.

Out of a total of 453 cases of pulmonary tuberculosis 226 deaths occurred, i.e. a mortality of 50 per cent.[4]

There is little statistical evidence to prove that the incidence of the disease is increasing, generally, in the larger centres; but in the more rural areas it is considered that an increase is probably taking place. . . . The question of pulmonary tuberculosis may well present the most difficult and important health problem for the future.

The improvement of every factor constituting general environmental sanitation will play its part in the struggle, with particular emphasis on housing and the abolition of congested areas. Elevation of the general economic status of the people and the improvement of their dietary will be powerful adjuncts towards the desired end.[5]

1940. Investigation of the problems associated with pulmonary tuberculosis is being made as the disease appears to be on the increase. Its prevention and treatment in a country like the Gold Coast presents a variety of difficult problems. Malnutrition among some of the labouring classes, poor housing accommodation with overcrowding, and a desire by the infected persons to return to their homes all militate against limiting the depredations of the disease. In addition, the humid climate is considered to be a factor adversely affecting the prospects of recovery. Notwithstanding these difficulties, however, it is hoped that preventive measures with increased facilities for treatment will in time be introduced which will assist in limiting the spread and diminishing the incidence of this disease.[6]

1942. The preliminary report on the prevalence of silicosis and tuberculosis among the mine-workers has been published, and shows the existence of both of these

[1] See also *Medical Report 1944*, pp. 3–4: 'Tuberculosis of the Respiratory System.—Two thousand and eighty-six cases were treated with 309 deaths. . . . Of the total deaths recorded 276, or 89 per cent, were male deaths; in 1943 the percentage was 91. The marked disparity between the sexes is capable of ready explanation. The class of person chiefly affected is the itinerant labourer (for whom there is no female counterpart). On such class falls, to a very large extent, the brunt of the effects of overcrowding, lack of resistance, a faulty dietary, exposure, overstrain, ignorance of the rudimentary laws of health, the deadly results of the universal spitting habit, predisposing diseases, etc.'

[2] Ibid. *1936*, p. 23. See also ibid. *1937*, pp. 21–2; *1938*, pp. 25–6.

[3] Ibid. *1936*, p. 24.   [4] Ibid. *1938*, p. 7. See also ibid., p. 25.

[5] *Report of Principal Registrar 1938*, p. 6.   [6] *Medical Report 1940*, p. 3.

diseases in this section of the community. It also suggests that tuberculosis is prevalent to such an extent among the general population as to justify an investigation of this aspect of the problem. Preliminary estimates have been completed for the establishment of a mobile unit and, if the unit can be obtained, it is hoped that survey work among the general population will not be long delayed.[1]

1943. It has not been possible to acquire the equipment for a mobile unit to assist in the survey of tuberculosis and its associate silicosis and this will have to await the end of the war.[2]

Conclusion. The results of the preceding survey on general mortality and diseases are extremely meagre. The reasons are obvious. The Medical Sanitary Report of the Gold Coast for 1891 had stated:

The health of the natives of the littoral is reported as having been good, but reports on this subject are as a rule based on hearsay, and, therefore, not of much value. Little as we know of the actual death-rate of the native communities of the littoral, and it is very little, we are in perfect ignorance of the sickness and mortality which prevailed amongst the tribes of the interior. All that can be said is that, so far as it was known, no epidemic of infectious or other grave disease occurred amongst the natives during the past year, from which we conclude that the health was normal throughout the protectorate.[3]

The only decisive change that has occurred in the five decades since this report was written is that our knowledge of health and mortality in the larger towns has increased considerably. Most Medical Officers seem aware of the fact that still very little is known to-day about the health and mortality of the bulk of the people of the Gold Coast. It is less certain, however, whether the Administration realizes the position. The *Gold Coast Handbook 1937* said:

Immense strides have been made in the health and well-being of the people of the Gold Coast as in other parts of the tropics—since the epoch-making discovery of the mode of transmission of malaria by Ross in 1898, and the almost equally important work of the American Commission two years later which enabled effective measures to be taken against that dread disease, yellow fever. The old days when the scanty European population in the Gold Coast was decimated by tropical disease, when the mortality rate of the indigenous population was very high and when more than half the number of infants born died before attaining one year of age, have happily disappeared into the limbo of the past, never, it is hoped, to return.[4]

There is not the slightest doubt that the death-rate of Europeans (who constitute about 1 per mille of the population) has decreased enormously, but as regards the natives it is impossible to say anything definite. It is very doubtful, in particular, whether the incidence of malaria and yellow fever among Africans has decreased since the epoch-making discovery of the mode of transmission of malaria by Ross in 1898, and the almost equally important work of the American Commission two years later which enabled effective measures to be taken against yellow fever. That there is no justification whatsoever for the statement that in former times more than half the number of infants born died before attaining one year of age will be shown presently.

---

[1] *Address delivered by Governor Sir Alan Burns*, 23 Feb. 1943 (Appendix), p. 22.

[2] *Address by Sir Alan Burns*, 13 Mar. 1944 (Appendix), p. 24. See also *Medical Report 1943*, p. 2, and *General Plan for Development in the Gold Coast* (1944), p. 6.

[3] Quoted in *Census Report 1891*, p. 169.   [4] *Gold Coast Handbook 1937*, p. 133.

3. *Infant Mortality*

Some early official reports express the opinion that infant mortality was very high,[1] but prior to the First World War no attempt was made to produce figures or to estimate the rate. The Medical Officer of Health, Cape Coast, in his report for 1911, stated that only twenty-eight deaths of infants had been recorded, but thought that many deaths of infants were not registered since 'it is almost impossible to accept the theory that the infant mortality is low'.[2] The Medical Report for 1914 said:

Coomassie. The Medical Officer in his report . . . draws attention to the prevalence of dental caries in young children, and the high infantile mortality said to arise therefrom. It is suggested that the teeth decay because weaning does not take place until the child is three years old, and the 'food necessary for the development and maintenance of milk teeth is withheld.'[3]

The 1915 Report for the Northern Territories spoke of 'the heavy infant mortality'.[4] Two years later a Committee was 'appointed to investigate causes of high infant mortality in Accra'.[5] The Medical Report for 1917 said:

The Registrar of Deaths reports that the Returns for Accra shew that the infantile mortality figure for 1917 was 383·77 per 1,000, but as all births are not registered this figure is too high. Inflated figures such as the above are apparently not uncommon in countries in which registration is only partial. . . .

During the year the subject of infant mortality in Accra was enquired into by a special Committee, and the Senior Sanitary Officer, in a memorandum submitted to the Committee, estimated the infantile mortality in Accra during the year 1915 to have been 292 per 1,000.

The main conclusions of the Committee were that the excessive infant mortality is due to the improper management of labour by untrained midwives and ignorance concerning the after-treatment of both mother and child. Their chief recommendation was the establishment of a Maternity Hospital and Training Institution for midwives.[6]

The Registrar, as will be noted, was aware that the official infant mortality rate was meaningless owing to defective birth registration. Two years later he said:

The death rate of young children like any other criterion of sanitation fails as an index unless the figures are tolerably complete; in particular the 'Infantile Mortality' calculated in the authorised way as a proportion of the year's births is exaggerated if the number of births is much under-stated.[7]

When in 1922–3 the number of births registered in Accra rose to 1,134 as compared with 854 in 1921 and 714 in 1920, the Registrar declared that birth registration in Accra was almost complete, 'the staff there being large enough to see that very few births escape registration'. The infant mortality rate of 232 'can therefore be accepted as being almost accurate. It compares favourably with the infant mortality in the larger towns in

[1] See *State of Colonial Possessions 1850*, p. 198; *1858*, Part II, p. 26.
[2] *Medical Report 1911*, p. 188 (quoted p. 451 above).   [3] Ibid. *1914*, p. 30.
[4] *Colonial Reports, Northern Territories 1915*, p. 13.
[5] Gold Coast, *Medical Report 1933–4*, p. 5.   [6] Ibid. *1917*, p. 8.
[7] *Report on Births and Deaths 1919*, p. 6. See also ibid. *1920*, p. 6; *1921*, p. 6.

India.'[1] But a few years later he realized that he had misjudged the efficiency of birth registration. Owing to a change in the registration law the number of registered births rose from 1,082 in 1925–6 to 1,700 in 1926. As the number of registered infant deaths was practically the same in both periods (280 in 1925–6 and 288 in 1926), the official infant mortality rate dropped from 259 to 169. The Registrar rightly said:

> The cause of this sudden apparent decrease in the infant mortality rate is attributable, not, except in an almost negligible degree, to the Infant Welfare work presently carried out in the town, but to a more rigid enforcement of the registration of births. The number of births under one year registered during the last three months of 1926 has increased very considerably without any appreciable change either in the character or amount of the population. The number of deaths under one year and its percentage to the total deaths at all ages remain practically unchanged.[2]

But in 1927 the number of registered births, of course, increased still further. It amounted to 2,246. As at the same time the number of registered infant deaths decreased somewhat (to 250), the official infant mortality rate dropped to 111. The Registrar made the following comment:

> The table ... would afford a rough idea of the reduction of infant mortality due to improved sanitary conditions were it not for the fact that birth registration has been enforced to a much greater extent in recent years.
> Lest such satisfactory figures give rise to premature gratification and a slackening in effort, it must be acknowledged that the percentage of deaths in infants under one year to the total deaths at all ages was 21·60 or only 0·78 per centum below the average for the previous seven yearly periods.
> The explanation is not hard to seek, namely, that, whereas there has been a considerable improvement in sanitary conditions in the past ten years or more, the weak spot in the armour—the ante- and neo-natal condition of the mother and infant—still remains to be strengthened and this should include the health of the expectant mother, the conduct of the delivery and puerperium and the neo-natal care of the infant.
> While it cannot be denied that valuable infant welfare work has been done, this has had a scarcely appreciable effect on mortality figures up to the present.[3]

Since 1927 the official infant mortality rate of Accra has fluctuated without showing any definite trend. It was lower than in 1927 only in 1931 when it dropped to 95.[4] It averaged 122 in 1928–38.

From 1927 on, the numbers of registered infant deaths have been compiled for all registration areas. The picture for the whole of these towns is similar to that shown for Accra. The infant mortality rates in 1927–44 were 122, 138, 114, 116, 114, 102, 100, 106, 127, 107, 117, 102, 110, 110, 110, 118, 129, and 125 respectively. They averaged 121 in 1927–31, 108 in 1932–6, 110 in 1937–41, and 124 in 1942–4.[5]

It is very gratifying to note the intellectual honesty with which the Registrars analysed the infant mortality figures of Accra up to 1927. It

[1] Ibid. *1922–3*, p. 28.
[2] Ibid. *1926*, p. 6. Of the 1,700 births registered in 1926, 759 were registered in the last quarter; see ibid., p. 7.   [3] Ibid. *1927*, p. 6.
[4] The rate for 1931 may have been reduced by incomplete registration in Labadi which was included in Accra from 1931 on. (In 1930 the registered births in Labadi numbered 279 and the registered infant deaths only 17; see ibid. *1930*, pp. 10, 18.)
[5] The decrease from 1927–31 to 1932–6 may have been due to improved birth registration, and the increase from 1937–41 to 1942–4 (at least in part) to more defective birth registration.

TABLE 25. *Infant Mortality, Accra, 1911–38*[1]

Year	Live-born	Deaths under 1	Infant mortality rate	Year	Live-born	Deaths under 1	Infant mortality rate
1916	736	271	368	1928	1,919	288	150
1917	651	246	378	1929	2,576	349	135
1918	648	313	483	1930	2,599	293	113
1919	709	255	360	1931	2,901	275	95
1920	714	289	405	1932	2,916	321	110
1921	854	211	247	1933	2,799	329	118
1922–3	1,134	263	232	1934	2,827	321	114
1923–4	1,011	257	254	1935	2,772	389	140
1924–5	1,000	203	203	1936	2,969	352	119
1925–6	1,082	280	259	1937	2,985	387	130
1926	1,700	288	169	1938	2,837	324	114
1927	2,246	250	111				

[1] See *Report on Births and Deaths 1921*, p. 6; *1926*, p. 5; *1927*, pp. 10–11; *Report of Principal Registrar 1928*, pp. 9–10; *1929*, pp. 9–10; *1930*, pp. 8–9; *1935*, p. 13; *1938*, p. 15. Figures from 1931 on include Labadi.

certainly was a mistake to assume in 1923 that birth registration was almost complete in Accra and to conclude that the infant mortality rate of 232 was nearly accurate. But it is very difficult to judge correctly the degree of completeness of birth registration, and when the Registrar recognized his mistake he frankly stated that the drop of the official infant mortality rate to 169 in 1926 and to 111 in 1927 was due to a stricter enforcement of the registration law. The Principal Registrar's Report for 1930 still said:

> The infantile mortality rate of an area is far more readily lowered by an increased number of birth registrations, following a campaign to this effect by the local authorities, than by actual diminution in the number of infant deaths.[1]

But from then on the official reports became much less judicious.

1931. In view of the fact that infant mortality provides a useful index of local health conditions, it is pleasing to note the very considerable reduction that has taken place in the loss of infant life in the registration areas during the past ten years—the rate in Accra having fallen from 247 in 1921 to 95 in 1931.[2]

1932. The continued definite fall in the infantile mortality rate is most gratifying. It is not claimed that the figure is an exact one. It is of course easier to dispose of the body of a young infant in some of the more rural centres without registration than that of an adult; and the effect of local propaganda, from time to time, temporarily may increase the total of registered births very considerably. The results are, however, of comparative value as the factors of error are more or less constant. It cannot be disputed but that the environmental hygienic surroundings, which so materially affect infantile mortality, have greatly improved of recent years. The part played in the larger centres by continuous and active health propaganda on the part of the voluntary workers of the Gold Coast League for Maternity and Child Welfare Section of the Gold Coast Branch of the British Red Cross Society has been a large one.

The work done at the welfare centres and the Accra Maternity Hospital has been of the greatest value. It is confidently anticipated that conditions will still further

[1] *Report of Principal Registrar 1930*, p. 4. See also ibid. *1928*, p. 5; *1929*, p. 5.
[2] Ibid. *1931*, p. 2.

improve as the voluntary effort, inaugurated in most of the large towns, extends into areas at present hardly touched.[1]

1933. A brighter feature of this report is provided by the continued fall in the infant mortality rate from 232 in Accra in 1922–23 to 126 in 1933 or 116, 114, 102 and 100 in all registration districts for the years 1930, 1931, 1932 and 1933, respectively.[2]

Immense strides have been made in the Gold Coast in little more than a decade since welfare work has been carried out . . . .[3]

1934. There has . . . been a definite saving of life in infants in the past two decades as the figures for Accra . . . will prove. Briefly, the infant mortality rate in 1916 was 368, falling to 247 in 1921 and to 113 in 1934.

The figures indicate that for every thousand births registered in Accra in 1934 there were 255 fewer deaths of infants under one year of age than in 1916.[4] In other words approximately 720 lives were saved in 1934 amongst those born.[5]

On the other hand, it must be remembered that with the spread of education birth registration is far better appreciated by the general community, in consequence of which the proportion of births failing to be registered must be less than in 1916.[6]

1935. Deaths in infants under one year, registered during 1935, totalled 1,285 as compared to 1,016 in 1934, an increase of 269. The crude infantile mortality rate for 1935 was 127.

This represents a very considerable increase over the rate of 105 returned for 1934. It must be borne in mind, however, that since 1934 infant deaths from four, large, comparatively backward stations have now to be included.[7]

In viewing the increased rates returned from certain large centres one must keep in mind the lack of correction. To take the case of Accra—during 1935 a total of 365 infant deaths were registered. Of these deaths over one third occurred in the various hospitals, a large proportion of which—estimated with respect to the Princess Marie Louise Child Welfare Centre and the Maternity Hospital as being 60 and 30 per centum respectively—were 'imported' cases.[8]

The fact remains that the set-back in the health of the community which was indicated in 1934 has continued, emphatically, into 1935; to what extent the economic stress of the previous few years is responsible it is impossible to judge.

There can be little doubt, also, but that the measure of increased prosperity in the rural localities has enabled the mothers in these areas to bring their ailing children in increasing numbers into the centres for treatment.[9]

Finally, the 1938 report says:

Owing to the factor of the very sick child brought into the registration areas for treatment, the rate must be considered in excess of the true rate for the more advanced centres, but very considerably lower than the rate for the surrounding, usually backward rural areas.[10]

---

[1] Ibid. *1932*, p. 2.   [2] Ibid. *1933*, p. 9.   [3] Ibid., p. 3.

[4] The Registrar might just as well have said that the figures for Kumasi indicate that for every thousand births registered in 1924–5 there were 1,653 fewer deaths of infants under one year of age than in 1923–4 (the official infant mortality rate of Kumasi dropped from 1,730 in 1923–4 to 77 in 1924–5, the number of registered births rising from 26 to 439; see *Report on the Kumasi Public Health Board 1926–7*, p. 42).

[5] See also *Medical Report 1933–4*, p. 4.   [6] *Report of Principal Registrar 1934*, p. 3.

[7] The inclusion of these 4 towns which in 1935 reported altogether 201 births and 272 deaths cannot have had any marked influence upon the infantile mortality rate of the whole registration area.

[8] This argument is not convincing. From 1934 to 1935 deaths under 1 week increased in Accra from 138 to 176, deaths from 1 week to 1 month from 42 to 62, and deaths from 1 to 12 months from 120 to 127 (see ibid., p. 15; *1935*, p. 13). It is unlikely, therefore, that the 'imported' cases should have been responsible in a large measure for the increase in the number of infant deaths from 300 to 365. (The number of deliveries in the Maternity Hospital increased from 659 in 1934 to 750 in 1935, and the number of infant deaths from 74 to 87; see ibid. *1935*, pp. 16, 18.)

[9] Ibid. *1935*, p. 3. See also ibid. *1936*, pp. 1, 3; *1937*, pp. 1, 3; *1938*, p. 1.   [10] Ibid. *1938*, p. 4.

It is understandable that after a long period of welfare work and with a low infant mortality rate in the advanced centres the opinion now prevails that infant mortality is higher in the rural districts, but it is difficult to understand why before the initiation of welfare work and at a time when (owing to defective birth registration) the official infant mortality rate in the towns was very high it was likewise believed that the rate must be higher still in the country. In his address of 22 February 1926 to the Legislative Council Governor Guggisberg said:

In Accra, which is at present practically the only place where we can get reliable information, infant mortality has decreased by between forty and fifty deaths per thousand births since 1921.[1] To a certain extent this is satisfactory, but on the other hand the rate to-day—203—is still painfully high when compared with the 75 of England and Scotland. Also it must be remembered that Accra has advantage of a good water supply, and better drainage and other conditions than exist in the provinces, where the infant mortality must be far higher than it is here. Medical Officers generally place the infant mortality in the country districts at between 300 and 400 per thousand births.[2]

These estimates by Medical Officers have apparently not been published, but general complaints about a very high infant mortality in the country are to be found in many official reports of the 1920s.[3] However, the only available statistics including other areas than the registration towns give little support to this view. They were provided by the surveys made in 1931 at which the 5,854 women questioned were asked the numbers of their children who died before walking.[4]

The consensus of opinion is that the average African baby in the Gold Coast crawls and walks at an earlier age than the average European baby which may be taken to be at about 12 months. Although this is so the mortality rate of children dying before they can walk may possibly be compared with the infantile mortality rate elsewhere which is based on the first 12 months of life. This basis of comparison is not strictly accurate, but should provide some standard of reference for the future.[5]

The infant mortality rate, as a whole, turned out to be 171. It was lowest in the Eastern Province of the Colony where it amounted to 143 and it was highest in the Northern Territories where it amounted to 224. Some rates were extraordinarily low. Thus, the 200 women questioned in Accra stated that only 77 of their 1,032 live-born children had died before walking. The Census Officer said:

Accra . . . shows low rates, a return which possibly is not to be wondered at, when the sanitary improvements, effected in this important centre, are taken into account.[6]

---

[1] Infant deaths numbered 211 in 1921 and 203 in 1924–5. But, owing mainly to the improvement in birth registration, the official infant mortality rate dropped from 247 to 203.

[2] *Legislative Council Debates 1926–7*, p. 152.

[3] See, for example, *Census Report 1921*, pp. 106, 162–3; *Colonial Reports, Gold Coast 1926–7*, p. 34; *Medical Report 1929–30*, p. 10. For Togoland see Kuczynski, pp. 524–6.

[4] A similar question was put in 1924 to 1,000 women who came to the dispensary at Koforidua. It appeared that of 3,666 children borne by these women 924 had died before being able to walk about, and the Medical Officer concluded that the infant mortality rate was 252 per 1,000. But it seems that both the numbers of births and of infant deaths included stillborn. Moreover, the great majority of women questioned were mothers who brought sick children for treatment.

[5] *The Gold Coast, 1931*, vol. i, p. 212.   [6] Ibid., p. 214.

But as all the women questioned had passed the menopause the vast majority of the children were born at a time when sanitary conditions in Accra were quite unsatisfactory. It is, therefore, more likely that many of the 200 women questioned in Accra omitted to state deceased infants. On the whole, however, the returns look plausible.

The conclusions to be drawn from all published data may be summarized perhaps as follows:

(1) The official infant mortality rates of Accra and other registration towns computed for the period before the present registration law came into force (1 June 1926) grossly overstate mortality because birth registration was very incomplete.

(2) From 1927 on, the rates of Accra and of the registration towns as a whole indicate an infant mortality lower than that which prevailed in England 40 years ago. There is no reason to suppose that these fairly low rates understate mortality, since it is unlikely that births have been registered more completely than infant deaths. These rates suggest furthermore that mortality has not improved in the course of the last 15 years. To what extent it has improved as compared with earlier times it is impossible to tell.

(3) The surveys made in 1931 suggest that infant mortality in the first two decades of this century was not excessive in the country as a whole, but that it was higher than it has been in the registration towns during the last 15 years.

4. *Population Growth*

Lieutenant-Governor Winniett, in his report on the Blue Book for 1846, expressed the belief that the population was increasing rapidly.

During the space of the last 15 years a most extraordinary change has taken place in the aspect of the population of the various districts which have enjoyed the advantages of being within the range of British jurisdiction. Its numerical increase has been very great, as may be daily proved by the numerous new villages which are rising on every hand. It may not be saying too much to state, that during the time above mentioned the villages in the Fanti country, and among the Assins, have increased, on an average, about 15 per cent.[1]

The Blue Book for 1849 assumed a population increase of 5 per cent. since 1846. Acting Lieutenant-Governor Fitzpatrick, as shown above,[2] said that he had no means of corroborating or correcting the resulting population estimate of 288,500.

However, though there may possibly be a mistake, and a considerable one, as to the actual amount of the population, there can be no difference of opinion as to its steady and continuous increase.

Within this large territory there has been for some years past neither war, nor famine, nor pestilence, nor emigration, nor the exportation of slaves, to cause any unusual diminution of the people. Their habits are greatly improved; though heathens, and uneducated still, they are more civilized than they were; they have abandoned the practice of offering human sacrifices; they feel that they owe some

[1] *State of Colonial Possessions 1846*, p. 146. See also ibid. *1847*, p. 203, *1848*, p. 308; *Blue Book 1846*, pp. 80-1, *1847*, pp. 82-3, *1848*, pp. 74-5.
[2] See p. 405.

duty towards their slaves . . . . Add to all these protecting circumstances, a continual absorption of the Ashantee population into Fantee, and we must conclude that a very great increase of the population is going on.[1]

But Lieutenant-Governor Bannerman did not share this opinion. According to him the country was not thickly populated.

Neither, in my opinion, has the population increased to the extent within the last quarter of a century which one had a right to expect. There has been neither war, nor pestilence, nor famine. A sufficient abundance has been open to all. The people are powerful, muscular, and full of all the energies of health and strength; and, notwithstanding all these favourable circumstances, the fact is undoubted, that the increase in the population is not at all in proportion to what it would be in Europe. I believe polygamy to be one principal cause of this, and the want of medical skill another; the former, with the habits which must always attend such a state of society, make fewer births an invariable consequence; but when it is known how many children die in infancy, the conviction is evident that unskilfulness in the treatment of the young is the chief cause.[2]

Governor Hill again took another view:

The numerical increase must be great, as there are no causes to diminish the numbers, excepting a decay of nature from old age.[3]

The Medical Report for 1858 was again more sceptical.

The population has not been diminished by war, pestilence, or famine, for the Croboe revolt last year may be said to have been put down without bloodshed; nevertheless the increase of population has not been in any degree commensurate with what might reasonably be expected under such favourable circumstances. To what then is the cause ascribable? In my humble opinion the chief cause arises from the enormous mortality which continually occurs in infancy from mismanagement by the natives of their young, and by their unskilful medical treatment. Polygamy is another cause which powerfully contributes to this effect, because the habits which it engenders materially diminishes the number of births, and, undoubtedly, the easy access to spirits, and its enormous consumption in these settlements, may justly be considered extremely prejudicial to life.[4]

In the following decades the official documents contain hardly any comment on population growth, and if one may judge from the population estimates the population was assumed to have remained stationary.

Whether the returns of the counts made in 1891 and 1901 indicate a population increase or decrease in the Colony between those years it is difficult to tell. The 1901 census report, it is true, says:

In comparing the Census Returns of 1901 with those for 1891, it will be seen that in most of the Districts there has been an increase in population.[5]

But the returns actually showed a decrease in four of the twelve Districts, and there would have been a decline also in the Volta River District if Krepi had not been included in this District in the meantime. Excluding Kwitta, where the count was utterly incomplete in 1891, and excluding Kwahu and Krepi, which were not covered by the 1891 count, the total population of the Colony showed a marked decrease from 1891 to 1901, but this may have been due to an overstatement in 1891 of the

---

[1] *State of Colonial Possessions 1849*, Part I, p. 93.   [2] Ibid. *1850*, pp. 197–8.
[3] Ibid. *1851*, Part I, p. 185. See also ibid. *1853*, p. 182.
[4] Ibid. *1858*, Part II, p. 26.   [5] *Census Report 1901*, p. 5.

population of Saltpond or to an understatement of the population of this District in 1901.

The position is not less obscure for the first decade of this century. The African population enumerated in the Colony declined from 895,350 in 1901 to 852,396 in 1911. But the decrease can be easily explained by the complete failure of the 1911 count in Kwitta. For many other Districts a comparison is impossible owing to changes in boundaries, and whether for the Colony as a whole the omissions in 1911 were much more numerous than in 1901 it is hard to tell. The Census Officer expressed the following opinion:

Taking the recorded totals only and making allowance for the Quittah returns it would appear that the population of the Colony has increased. How far this increase is the result of more accurate enumeration and how far it is due to natural increase it would be futile with the data available to attempt to determine. The conditions however during the past decade, have been favourable to the growth of population. There has been an absence of tribal war, and of serious epidemics, and at the same time there has been a great advance in material prosperity. If therefore the native races are prolific, it would not be unreasonable to look for a high rate of natural increase.[1]

The enumeration of 1921 showed an African population of 1,171,913 or 319,517 more than the enumeration of 1911. There was to be sure an excess of immigration over emigration, but this was probably offset by the deaths caused by the influenza epidemic. It is safe to say, therefore, that the major part of the apparent increase was due to more complete enumeration. By far the largest increase was shown for the Eastern Province which in 1911 had returned only 441,820 Africans (as compared with 541,253 in 1901) and which now returned 664,207.[2] The report on the enumeration in this Province states:

There has been no severe epidemic since 1911 except influenza which, in the whole Colony, was considered by the Medical authorities to have been the cause of the loss of at least 4% of the population.[3] Conditions of life on the other hand have altered for the better during the decade, but I am inclined to think that the large addition

---

[1] Ibid. *1911*, p. 26. It should be noted, however, that the belief of the Census Officer in a high rate of natural increase was due, at least in part, to a misinterpretation of some census figures. He stated (ibid., pp. 31–2):

'In the case of the Colony there are 84,882 more adults than children, the proportion being roughly five children to six adults. . . .

'Ten years hence those persons in the second age group (*i.e.* those who are now from six to fifteen years of age) will have joined the adult classes (*i.e.* those over sixteen years), while those who are now 46 years and over will, it may be assumed, have passed beyond the ken of the Census Officer. Assuming, therefore, that existing conditions remain the same, the number of adults in ten years time will be the total of those who are now between the ages of six and forty-six, viz.:—545,962. Assuming again that the present ratio of six adults to five children continues, then the number of children ten years hence will be 454,965 and the total population of the Colony 1,000,927, which signifies a probable annual increase of 15,000 or 1·7 per cent.'

The Census Officer evidently assumed that none of the 545,962 people aged 6–45 in 1911 would die before 1921! If he had reckoned with a yearly death-rate of 15 per 1,000 in these age groups, he would have come to the conclusion that the population would be smaller in 1921 than in 1911. But it is impossible, of course, to derive the population in 1921 from the age composition in 1911.

[2] Excluding Addah-Quittah the figures for the Province in 1901, 1911, and 1921 were 320,542, 364,426, and 486,582 respectively; see ibid. *1921*, p. 49.

[3] See also *Medical Report 1918*, pp. 13–14; *Colonial Reports, Gold Coast 1918*, p. 45.

to the population is due more to greater care in enumeration than to natural increase.[1]

The Central Province showed an increase from 247,036 to 302,626. The Commissioner of the Province 'states that the accuracy obtained in 1921 was far greater than in 1911'. But apart from the Winnebah District, where the population was reported to have risen from 67,111 to 105,567, the increase was not great. The census report says that 'Winnebah shows the largest increase',[2] but does not offer an explanation.

The Western Province showed an increase from 163,540 to 205,080. The count was reported to have been here much less defective than in 1911. The actual increase, therefore, may have been small.

The population figures for Ashanti and the Northern Territories are less conclusive still. The return for the African population of Ashanti in 1911 was 287,591 as compared with 335,651 (excluding Kintampo) in 1901. But the 1911 count was no doubt quite defective. The enumeration of 1921 showed a population of 406,193 and the Chief Commissioner stated that the increase was 'not necessarily a natural increase'.

It is probably due to a more extensive acquaintance with the country, to the opening up by roads of districts formerly remote and to less suspicion on the part of the inhabitants as to the object of a Census.[3]

The African population of the Northern Territories had been estimated in 1901, on the basis of a partial count, at 318,000 (including Kintampo), and the quite defective count of 1911 made it appear to be 361,806 (excluding Kintampo). The total ascertained in 1921 was 530,355. Owing to the ravages of cerebrospinal meningitis and influenza the natural increase between 1901 and 1921 was probably very small.[4]

For the Gold Coast as a whole (excluding Togoland) the African population, according to the enumerations, increased from 1,501,793 in 1911 to 2,108,461 in 1921 or by 40 per cent. The large number of deaths during the influenza epidemic makes it most unlikely that the natural increase exceeded 10 per cent., and it is improbable that the excess of immigration over emigration should have accounted for more than 5 per cent. Thus there cannot be any doubt that the major part of the apparent increase was due to more accurate counting.

According to the enumeration of 1931 the African population (including Togoland) had increased since 1921 from 2,296,400 to 3,160,386 or by 38 per cent. The increase was 34 per cent. in the Colony (Western Province 39 per cent., Central Province 43 per cent., Eastern Province 29 per cent.),

[1] *Census Report 1921*, p. 49. See also *Report on the Eastern Province 1921*, p. 10: 'The increase must be considered abnormal and leads one to believe that the Census taken in 1911, could not have been accurate as naturally the methods of obtaining the correct figures in that year were more difficult of application than that in 1921, due to the difficulty of Communication and through the suspicion of the inhabitants that the information sought for by the Government was required in connection with the levying of a Poll Tax.'

[2] *Census Report 1921*, p. 67.

[3] Ibid., p. 114. See also *Colonial Reports, Ashanti 1921*, p. 29.

[4] The deaths from cerebrospinal meningitis in 1906–8 have been estimated at 34,000 (see *Medical Report 1920*, p. 18), those from influenza in 1918–19 at 29,000 or more (see *Colonial Reports, Northern Territories 1918*, p. 13; *1919*, p. 14).

42 per cent. in Ashanti, 35 per cent. in the Northern Territories, and 56 per cent. in Togoland. The Chief Census Officer explained this amazing increase as follows:

It is generally agreed that in a country where conditions are such as those which obtain in the Gold Coast the decennial increase could be estimated at 15 per cent. ....

If one reckons an error of 5 per cent under-estimation in the 1921 figures, the total of the population which could reasonably have been expected would have amounted to 2,872,903 leaving a balance of 287,483 to be accounted for by immigration.[1]

According to the enumeration returns the number of Africans originating from other British Dependencies or other countries was 289,217.

This figure is surprisingly close to the estimate given above of the immigrant population after allowing for an increase on the previous census figure based on an error of 5 per cent in the original total and a 15 per cent increase on the corrected figure in the intercensal period.[2]

But this explanation is by no means convincing.

(1) If one reckons an error of 5 per cent. under-estimation in the 1921 figures and a 15 per cent. natural increase, the total population which could have been expected would have amounted to $2,296,400 \times 1 \cdot 05 \times 1 \cdot 15 = 2,772,903$ (not 2,872,903), leaving a balance of 387,483 (not 287,483) to be accounted for by immigration.

(2) A certain proportion of the 289,217 persons originating from elsewhere had come before 1921 and was included in the 1921 Returns. There was also some emigration from the Gold Coast and Togoland. It, therefore, seems unjustified to allocate more than 200,000 of the increase in 1921–31 to net immigration.

The argument of the Chief Census Officer would have been more plausible if he had said: If one reckons an error of 12 per cent. under-estimation in the 1921 figures, the total of the population which could reasonably have been expected would have amounted to 2,957,763, leaving a balance of 202,623 to be accounted for by immigration. This would have implied that the population had increased between 1921 and 1931 from 2,572,000 to 3,160,000 or by 23 per cent.

The apparent increase of 38 per cent. was no doubt due in a large measure to understatement of the population in 1921. There was no doubt an actual increase both by excess of births over deaths and by excess of immigration over emigration. But it is by no means certain that it aggregated 23 per cent. The Chief Census Officer says that it is generally agreed that in a country where conditions are such as those which obtain in the Gold Coast the decennial increase could be estimated at 15 per cent. I do not know of any such agreement. All the basic data for estimating the natural increase in the Gold Coast are lacking, and a guess of 15 per cent. is probably too high. The scanty data available suggest that fertility is not very high and I see no reason for assuming that it should be so. There is no evidence, on the other hand, that mortality is low.

Since the census of 1931 the African population is said to have increased from 3,160,000 to 3,960,000 at mid-year 1940 or by 800,000. Immigration

---

[1] *The Gold Coast, 1931*, vol. i, pp. 146–7.   [2] Ibid., p. 154.

until the outbreak of the war was considerable,[1] but even if it should have accounted for an increase of 250,000 the balance would appear far too great to be explainable by an excess of births over deaths.

VI. NON-NATIVE MORTALITY[2]

The Commissioners of Inquiry into the State of the Colony of Sierra Leone reported in 1827:

Some information was obtained on the Gold Coast with respect to the casualties amongst the Europeans, civil as well as military, which it is believed may be relied upon. This was contained in memoranda kept by Mr. Athy, apothecary and collector of duties, and the oldest resident upon that coast, where he had long held a medical appointment under the African Company.

It appears from a list of the individuals, that between the 1st of January 1812 and April 1823, 95 officers in the Company's service arrived upon the Coast. That of these 44 died, four had been killed in action, four then remained upon the coast and 28 had returned to England, nine of whom had left the coast prior to 1816. Between April 1822 and 1825, 111 individuals arrived upon the coast, of whom 77 were military officers, 21 merchants and other civilians, eight women and five children; of these 55 had died, four were killed in action, one shot himself, 26 left the coast and 15 remained. Of those that died, 33 were military, 17 civilians, three women and two children.[3]

Mortality among Europeans remained very high until the beginning of this century and was, at certain times, much discussed in official reports.

1849. There have been about 19 cases of fever amongst the Europeans newly arrived on the Coast, and of these, in which there was no medical attendance, 6 have been fatal, and amongst the 13 who had the benefit of medical advice there has not been a single death.[4]

1852. As has been the case for four consecutive years, no person who had the advantage of medical aid has died of fever; but I regret to add, the fatal disease of this coast, 'dysentery', has carried off two of my officers, together with four young men, merchants and clerks, at Cape Coast; and I was obliged to send home on medical certificate one staff assistant surgeon with one surgeon, and the latter, I am sorry to state, died at Madeira, where he was landed in a sinking condition.[5]

1853. . . . both fever and dysentery have proved fatal to many during the year, particularly the white resident merchants.[6]

1854. . . . the year 1854 was considered for the place a healthy one; but still the proportion from among the small number of civil and military officers or other Europeans who die or are invalided, even in healthy years, is large. It is however very probable that much of this is attributable in part to indiscretions; but the nature of this climate is, that though happily sweeping epidemics are scarcely known to it, yet, generally speaking, it is ever sapping the health, and is always ready to seize fatally on anything peccant either in habits or constitution.[7]

1855. With respect to the health of these settlements, the year 1855 was considered fully an average unhealthy one, if not more than that. During part of that year one of the medical officers, having also a magisterial situation, used to visit Annamaboo in both these capacities, and the clerk of the Court writing up to him

---

[1] See, for example, *Report on the Labour Department 1938-9*, p. 42.

[2] Data concerning non-African births are apparently not available. European births must be rare since only 10 children under 5 were counted in 1931. But there were then 78 such children among Syrians.   [3] *Report*, First Part, p. 109.

[4] *State of Colonial Possessions 1849*, Part I, p. 96. The Europeans numbered 32.

[5] Ibid. *1852*, p. 198. The Europeans numbered 41.

[6] Ibid. *1853*, p. 182.   [7] Acting Governor Connor, ibid. *1854*, pp. 199-200.

on business, added in a P.S. to his letter 'The people are dying here somewhat like fowls.' In a letter shortly subsequent, he expressed himself on this latter subject to this effect, 'I have the same report to give of the health of the people as in my last letter.' I should hope that in point of indulgence in intoxicating liquors, Europeans here are as little exposed to the charge of excess as they have been at any time; but still, at times, instances of it appear. The observation of a native woman who acts often as nurse, with reference to the death of a European who formed an instance of this kind, and whose intemperance attained its end in one of the few first days of this year, was, as reported to me, to this effect, 'God did not kill him, he killed himself; God did not want him.' The effect of this climate on the health appears to me, if I may so express myself, like a snake preparing a victim for being swallowed, it quietly slavers him with poisonous saliva, and finally gulps him, unless the unhappy one has previously contrived to get leave of absence, and had the good fortune to get 'home'.[1]

1856. There was much sickness during the year, and many of the military officers were invalided home; two died here and one on his passage to England; the wife of another of the officers died here.[2]

The reports on the following Blue Books do not discuss health or mortality, but the report for 1868 again emphasized the unsuitable habits of many Europeans.

. . . it cannot be too strongly impressed on persons taking up their residence in a tropical country, and especially the Gold Coast, that an undue indulgence in stimulants, and an undue omission of constant muscular and mental exercise, is the main, and well-nigh the sole (indirect) cause of the agues, fevers and dysenteries, which are so unjustly attributed entirely to atmospheric influences.[3]

But the habits of Europeans improved. The Sanitary Report on the Station of Cape Coast for 1885 says:

Ten years ago intemperance was general throughout the whole coast . . . . Since then times, manners, and men have changed, and for the better, hence the true cause of our more temperate habits now.[4]

However mortality remained high.

1886. Accra. In April, May, and June a good deal of sickness prevailed amongst the Europeans here, resulting in seven deaths, three of blackwater fever, two of remittent fever of another type, one of phthisis and one of insolation.

Seventy Europeans have resided at Accra since January, so that the death rate up to date [21 Oct.] is 100 per 1,000. Many of these Europeans, however, resided here for short periods, some for a fortnight only, others for a month or thereabouts, so that to include them in this number obviously makes the death rate appear much lower than it would be if the permanent residents alone were considered. Six were invalided, four temporarily, two to Europe.[5]

1887. The total strength of Europeans and West Indian officials resident on the Gold Coast in 1887 was 72, out of which 4 died[6] and 15 were invalided.

Death rate, 5·4 per cent., or 54 per 1,000.

Per-centage invalided, 20·8, or 208 per 1,000.[7]

Elmina. During the second quarter an epidemic of remittent fever of great severity prevailed and caused the deaths of two Europeans in the Castle and two in the town.[8]

---

[1] Same, ibid. *1855*, pp. 254–5.   [2] Ibid. *1856*, p. 191.   [3] Ibid. *1868*, Part II, pp. 24–5.
[4] *Colonial Possessions Reports 1884–6*, p. 114.   [5] Ibid., pp. 249–50.
[6] For 1877–9, when the number was much smaller, it was reported that in each year 3 European officials died (including those who died on the passage to England); see ibid. *1876–8*, p. 149, *1879*, p. 208.
[7] Gold Coast, *Sanitary and Medical Reports for 1887 and 1888*, p. 10.   [8] Ibid., p. 15.

Quittah. In common with those on other parts of the coast, the European residents of Quittah have suffered severely during the past year; the actual mortality has been 40 per cent., and there has been, besides, much sickness of a grave but not fatal character. The deaths which have occurred have mostly been due to the adynamic form of malarial fever complicated with hæmoglobinuria which has of late been so common on the coast; deaths were also recorded from dysentery, ardent remittent fever, and in one case from sporadic yellow fever. The death (rate) of the official population was better than that of the non-official; out of five officers stationed at Quittah one died from the pernicious malarial fever spoken of above, one was invalided home with the same disease and the remaining three were from time to time visited by attacks of remittent fever of varying severity, but otherwise enjoyed fair health.[1]

1888. The total number of Europeans and officials resident on the coast was 72. Of this number the death rate was 5·5 per cent., and the invaliding rate 5·55 per cent.[2]

In 1891 conditions were better. The Medical Sanitary Report said:

Commercial Europeans. Although the death-rate during the year among the Commercial Europeans at Elmina and Kwitta was, owing to local climatic and other influences, abnormally high, respectively 12·50 and 15 per cent. . . . the death-rate of the total number resident in the protectorate was low. Out of a total of 428 resident during the year 14 died and 75 were invalided, thus giving a death-rate of only 3·27 per cent. . . . The number invalided was 74, which gives a percentage of 17·52. 47 or more than half of this invaliding occurred in the gold mining district of Tarquah, where out of 148 resident during the year 4 died, making the very low death-rate in that District 2·72 per cent. The high invaliding rate, however, of 32·4 per cent. must be taken as a set-off against the low death-rate, for had the patients who were invalided been allowed to remain in the country they would most assuredly have died. No European is ever invalided from this Coast, unless he is either found physically or mentally unfit for Service, or whose life is in imminent danger from grave sickness.

Official Europeans. Low as the death-rate was among the Commercial Europeans that of the official Europeans was still lower. Out of a total of 65 residents during the year 2 died and 10 were invalided; of the latter 2 died at sea, and, therefore, I do not include them in our death-rate, which was 3·07 per cent. . . . The invaliding rate was 15·38 per cent. The remark above made on invaliding of course applies here also.[3]

The Census Report for that year added the following comment:

Fevers of an intermittent type prevailed largely; the mortality was low but invaliding high. Affections of the liver and spleen rank next in importance, but there were only a few cases under treatment among European Officials. The climatic and other conditions engendering disease, and the hygienic precautions necessary for the preservation of health in this country are far better understood now, and the general health of Europeans in the Colony has greatly improved of late.[4]

But the years 1893–7 were apparently again very bad.

1893 (1st half). At Cape Coast during the first quarter two Europeans died and one was invalided, although the percentage of sickness was not great. In the second quarter, however, the European sick rate was very high and almost all the resident European population suffered from severe forms of Remittent Fever; two deaths occurred from Malarial remittent fever and two were invalided.

Elmina. The general health could not have been more unsatisfactory; one official began to suffer from malarial debility until removed to Aburi, four of the five traders exhibited grave and complicated forms of fever, and the missionaries generally

---

[1] Gold Coast, *Sanitary and Medical Reports for 1887 and 1888*, p. 19.
[2] Ibid., p. 25. See also ibid., pp. 31, 62–3.
[3] Quoted in *Census Report 1891*, p. 169.   [4] Ibid., p. 25.

suffered from anæmia and intermittent and remittent fevers. The prevalent diseases
were Remittent Fever of a serious type, Intermittent Fever, Diarrhœa, Dysentery,
Congestion of the Liver and Malarial Anæmia. Two deaths occurred and two were
invalided.[1]

1894. The months of November and December were most unhealthy for Europeans in the western districts of the Colony, and many deaths occurred from malignant malarial fever.[2]

1895. The general health of the Colony was extremely bad during the period, the
endemic fever assuming a pseudo-epidemic form of a malignant type closely
approaching in its clinical manifestations the Vomito Negro or Yellow Fever of the
West Indies. The death rate was enormous among Europeans and the excitement
induced thereby amounted almost to a panic and served to intensify the fatal
tendencies of the prevailing fever in the latter part of the year.[3]

1896. The general health of the Colony during the year under review shows little
or no improvement on that of the previous year. This year there were, amongst the
European population, 11 deaths of Officials, and 30 Non-Officials, as against 15
and 23 respectively during 1895. The number invalided being 23 Officials and
35 Non-Officials, against 26 and 32 in 1895. This high rate is to be attributed to the
fact that the epidemic of the malignant type of fever which prevailed during the last
half of 1895 continued during the first four months of this year, the period in which
the greater number of the deaths occurred.[4]

1897. In a total estimated European population of 522 there were 40 deaths and
78 cases of invaliding, equal to a death rate of 76·62 per 1,000 and an invaliding rate
of 155·1 per 1,000.[5]

The general health of the Colony shows a slight improvement on the two previous
years, though the death-rate still remains exceptionally high.[6] It must be remembered that the Europeans in the Colony are for the most part men in the prime of
life, as there are no European children in the Colony and a man of 50 years of age
is an exception.[7]

The death-rates for officials in 1893–7 were given as 31, 34, 67, 60, and
38 respectively.[8] Those for 1895 and 1896 may appear excessive, but a very
interesting investigation covering the years 1881–97[9] indicates that for this
period as a whole the death-rate of officials was 76 per 1,000.

The compilation of vital statistics relating to the Europeans who are or have been
in the employment of the Governments of the Gold Coast and Lagos since the
beginning of 1881 has been completed up to the end of 1897 . . . .

The column headed 'Number of years' service' contains the totals of the periods
from the date on which each European arrived in West Africa to take up his employment under one of two above-mentioned Governments to the date on which he

---

[1] Quoted in Gold Coast Colony, *Medical Report 1912*, pp. 87–8, *Medical Report 1917*, p. 12,
gives the following death rates per 1,000 for 1893:

Government Officials	31
Europeans at Kwitta, including Officials	75
Basel Missionaries	77
Catholics	115
Residents at Elmina and Cape Coast (including Govt. Officials and Catholics)	114
Mining Districts	121

[2] *Colonial Reports, Gold Coast 1894*, p. 21.

[3] Gold Coast Colony, *Medical Report 1895*, p. 3.

[4] Ibid. *1896*, p. 3.   [5] Ibid. '1897', p. 171.

[6] It was in fact much higher than in the two previous years, and the same is true of the invaliding rate.   [7] *Colonial Reports, Gold Coast Colony 1897*, p. 16.

[8] See Gold Coast Colony, 'Medical Report 1897', p. 172.

[9] *Vital Statistics respecting Europeans employed by the Governments of the Gold Coast and Lagos,
1881–1897*.

ceased to be in that Government's employ. In the case of persons whose employment falls partly outside of the years 1881 to 1897, the part before 1881 or after 1897 is not taken into account. Leave of absence to England has been regarded as incidental to the employment, and is included. Since 1883, and except in cases of invaliding, such leave of absence would ordinarily be for six months after every twelve months' service, voyages to and from England being included in the six months.[1]

The statistics have been compiled by Mr. T. E. Young, a former President of the Institute of Actuaries, from data collected from the records of the Colonial Office by Mr. C. D. Turton, a former Treasurer of the Gold Coast . . . .

Colony	Number of persons	Number of years' service	Average length of service in years	Number of deaths during service	Death rate per thousand per annum
Gold Coast	554	1,307	2·4	99	75·8
Lagos	258	522	2·0	28	53·6

As regards non-officials the death rates for 1895–7 were shown to be 42, 49, and 94.[2] But the comparatively low rates for 1895 and 1896 may have been computed from incomplete records.[3] In 1897 the death-rate was much higher than for officials. The Colonial Report for this year made the following comment:

It will be noticed . . . that the death-rate among the official class is less than that among the mercantile community. This may perhaps be attributed to the leave arrangements of the Government service whereby all European officials are permitted to proceed to Europe on leave after twelve months residential service on the Coast, and to the houses occupied by Government officials being away from the thickly populated part of the town. This is no trivial matter, for climatic conditions are such that what is at most an inconvenience in more temperate climates is a veritable calamity to the European resident in West Africa. Much of the comfort of life depends on attention to its minutiæ, and this is pre-eminently so in a country such as the Gold Coast.[4]

The numbers of deaths of officials in 1897–1901 were 6, 8, 9, 10, and 15 respectively, and those reported for non-officials 34, 17, 18, 34, and 38 respectively. The death-rates for officials were 38, 66, 54, 21, and 80 respectively, and those for non-officials (1897–1900) 94, 74, 45, and 22 respectively.[5] But the population figures, particularly those for 1900 and 1901, are so uncertain[6] that no conclusions concerning actual mortality should be drawn from the death-rates. The comments in the Medical Reports deserve attention merely because they show that at that time death-rates which appear very high were then considered to be satisfactory.

---

[1] Mortality in West Africa, therefore, was possibly higher than indicated in these statistics, as a considerable proportion of 'Number of years' service' was spent on sea and in England, and not under the more unfavourable conditions prevailing in West Africa.

[2] See Gold Coast Colony, *Medical Report 1895*, p. 24; *1896*, p. 21; '1897', p. 171.

[3] See ibid. *1895*, p. 3: 'It is impossible to obtain reliable statistics as to the sickness and deaths amongst the non-official population.'

[4] *Colonial Reports, Gold Coast Colony 1897*, p. 17.

[5] See ibid. *1897*, p. 16; *1898*, p. 26; *1899*, p. 22; *1900*, p. 23; *1901*, p. 31.

[6] It is hard to believe, for example, that the officials in 1899–1902 should have numbered 166, 468, 188, and 286 respectively. The low death-rate of non-officials in 1900 may be quite erroneous. Their number was estimated at 1,512 as against 400 in 1899.

1898. The general health of the Colony, during the year under review, showed a slight improvement on that of the three previous years . . . . The improvement is probably due to two causes:—the better circumstances under which Europeans, Official and Non-Official, live, and the Meteorological conditions. Formerly the greater number of the white residents lived in, or very near to, the native parts of the various towns, but during the last three or four years Government has, in most districts, built residences for the Officials in healthy and open situations, and the example thus set is gradually being followed by the European merchants. The meteorological conditions were also more than usually favourable to health; the rainfall was above the average, and the temperature throughout the year was below the normal.[1]

1899. The general health of the Colony during the past year was good; out of 166 European officials there were only 9 deaths and 23 cases of invaliding, and out of an estimated number of 400 Non-Official Europeans there were 18 deaths and 52 cases of invaliding.

The death rate [54·2] is slightly higher than the average death rate for Officials for the Colony, which is about 47·8 per thousand.[2]

1900. The general health of the Colony during the year 1900 showed a very marked improvement on that of the previous year; in fact, from a health point of view, it may be looked on as a record year. Amongst the European population, 1 Official and 18 Non-officials died,[3] as against 9 Officials and 18 Non-officials during 1899. 10 Officials and 45 Non-officials were invalided,[4] as against 23 Officials and 52 Non-officials during 1899. . . . The improvement in the health is, in some measure, due to the more careful and regular methods of life, which, I am glad to say, are yearly receiving more attention; and also to the meteorological conditions . . . .[5]

1901. The general health for the year was very bad . . . . Fifteen officials died during the year in a total strength of 188.[6]

Whether 1900 was a good year and 1901 a bad year it is impossible to tell. But 1902, if compared with earlier years, showed a favourable mortality. The data were more detailed and more accurate. The death-rate for the whole European community was 31 per 1,000—35 for Officials, 56 for Merchants, 23 for employees of Mining Companies, 20 for employees of the Gold Coast Railway, and 21 for Missionaries. The Principal Medical Officer made the following interesting comment:

This return is remarkable as showing such marked differences in the mortality and invaliding in the various sections of the community; and the question very naturally arises: to what is this due ? It is most undoubtedly in a very great measure attributable to the following:—

Period of service on the Coast.
Liability to sun exposure.
Nature of occupation.
Facilities for exercise.
Location of residences.

The highest rate of mortality is amongst the mercantile community; and these have the longest period of service—two to three years; many of them are also much exposed to the sun, having to work on the beach or the yards of the factories from about 6.0 a.m. till 11.0 a.m. and from 1.0 p.m. to 4.30 p.m. or 5.0 p.m. Their work is pretty hard, and the long hours and the tired feeling most men must have at the

[1] Gold Coast Colony, 'Medical Report 1898', pp. 315–16.
[2] Ibid. *1899*, pp. 2–3. The ave age death-rate in 1893–7 was given ibid. '1897', p. 172, as 47·86; it should, however, read 45·86.
[3] Actually 10 Officials and 34 non-Officials died.
[4] Actually 29 Officials and 99 non-Officials were invalided; see *Colonial Reports, Gold Coast 1900*, p. 23.   [5] *Medical Report 1900*, p. 12.   [6] Ibid. *1901*, p. 11.

end of their day's labour leaves them unfit for much exercise, in any form, and a period of rest is more generally indulged in. The residences of the merchants are almost invariably situated in the town, in the midst of the houses and huts of the natives, and I think it is now accepted as a fact that living day and night in close proximity to native dwellings is a very strong factor in the causation of malarial fevers.

The next highest rate is amongst the officials, and with them the conditions of life are somewhat different. The period of service on the Coast is only one year, with the exception of a few departments, notably the Public Works; the sun exposure is comparatively small; the hours of work are shorter and the facilities for exercise much greater, and as a rule more taken advantage of; and in most stations their residences are situated at a considerable distance from those of the natives.

Next come the mining companies and the Gold Coast Railway, and in the case of both the conditions of life are very similar. The period of service on the Coast is usually eight months, followed by at least four months' leave to Europe; the work is certainly hard, but it is active healthy exercise; and in many cases there is a considerable amount of exposure to the sun. Their residences are almost invariably in the bush and at some distance from native towns and villages. In addition to the short tour of service, the Chief Resident Engineer of the Gold Coast Railway, and the managers of the different mining companies, have the power of at once dismissing and sending home any man addicted to alcohol, or for any other serious offence. This power is freely used, and I have no doubt it has had a very marked effect in reducing the invaliding and death rate.

In the case of the missionaries they, as a rule, live under very favourable conditions, and lead quiet, peaceful lives, so that a low rate of mortality is what one would expect.

After considering all the above circumstances as to conditions of life, &c., the only conclusion one can come to is that one of the most powerful factors in reducing the mortality amongst Europeans in West Africa is a short tour of service; this is clearly shown in the case of the railway and mining companies, the employés of which, although in many ways not living under such favourable conditions as the Government officials, show a much lower rate of mortality. In view of this it is most desirable that mercantile firms should reduce the period of service for their employés at least to eighteen months.

Although the death rate was very high in one section of the community, it should be noted that the rate for the European population as a whole was only 31·14 per 1,000, and I think this may be looked on as very satisfactory.

It has taken much time and difficulty to get this return completed, principally owing to the carelessness, or unwillingness, of the mining managers; many of whom had to be asked several times before the necessary statistics could be obtained; and in others the papers were so carelessly filled in as to be useless, and had to be returned for correction. A beginning has, however, been made, and as the statistics are of such great interest, and, in view of the largely increasing European population of the Colony, of such inestimable value for life insurance and other purposes, every effort will be made to keep it up in future years.[1]

The mortality of 1902 was favourable if compared with earlier years, but it was still very high considering that nearly all Europeans belonged to age groups in which death everywhere claims the smallest number of victims. However, in 1903 the rate dropped considerably—to 22. The Principal Medical Officer who had considered the 1902 rate of 31 to be very satisfactory was diffident. The return 'may be looked upon as very satisfactory, but I fear it is too much to hope that such a very low death rate will be maintained in all future years'.[2] It was not too much to hope. The rate dropped to 13 in 1904, and never again reached the 'satisfactory'

---

[1] *Medical Report 1902*, pp. 13–14.   [2] Ibid. *1903*, p. 16.

level of 1902. All sections of the community took part in this improvement. The development of the death-rates in the first ten years for which the new statistics had been prepared was as follows:[1]

	1902	1903	1904	1905	1906	1907	1908	1909	1910	1911
Officials . . .	35·0	15·3	22·8	23·2	15·0	8·1	14·5	11·4	16·8	7·1
Merchants . .	56·3	35·8	9·8	11·0	15·7	16·7	20·7	12·2	37·9	23·1
Mining companies .	23·1	19·2	10·6	10·4	18·1	13·6	14·5	12·0	27·2	17·3
Missionaries . .	20·8	21·7	13·3	21·3	25·2	11·6	24·7	25·4	29·6	19·7
Total . . .	31·1[1]	21·7	12·8	13·6	17·6	13·3	17·0	12·8	27·2	16·5

[1] Including Gold Coast Railway.

The progress achieved was enormous, but sometimes tropical diseases took anew a heavy toll. Of the 46 deaths occurring in 1910, 15 were due to malaria, 10 to blackwater fever, and 10 to yellow fever. Living conditions on the whole had become infinitely better, but they still left much to be desired. In his report for 1911 the Senior Sanitary Officer said:

We cannot, of course, compel Europeans who are already established in native towns to move outside, but surely instructions might be issued to all local building authorities to refuse to sanction the erection of quarters for the occupancy of Europeans in native towns, and in all new townships, such as those springing up along the railways, no Europeans should be allowed to reside outside the segregation areas. Offices and factories, of course, must be built within the business area.

My experience in West Africa has taught me that, apart from a certain type of Government official, more happily becoming extinct, the bitterest opponent of sanitation is the local mercantile agent. He may live in a native town, but his quarters are usually palatial, whilst those occupied by his assistants are often such as, could the shareholders at home realise their condition, they would blush to pocket their dividends.[2]

But from 1912 on, the death-rate of the Europeans exceeded 13 only in the influenza year 1918 when it jumped to nearly 31, and it has been below 10 in every year since 1922–3.

In order rightly to appraise these rates two facts must be taken into consideration:

(1) The rates have been computed by relating the number of deaths occurring in the Gold Coast to the number of resident Europeans (including those on leave). Mortality, therefore, is somewhat higher than the death-rates indicate.

(2) That the death-rate of the Europeans is so much lower than that of the Africans is due to factors which have been characterized by the Principal Registrar in the following terms:

The majority of whites coming to the Gold Coast undergo medical examination prior to embarkation and it is rarely that anyone physically unfit is allowed to embark. Secondly, only a small percentage of whites living in the Gold Coast belong to the two extremes of life when mortality rates are normally much higher than during the wage-earning period. Thirdly, the majority of Europeans who come to these shores are in a better economic position than the bulk of the indigenous inhabitants. They are well-housed and adequately fed.[3]

[1] See ibid. *1909*, pp. 6–8; *1910*, pp. 9, 11; *1911*, pp. 8, 10.
[2] Ibid., p. 65.   [3] *Report Principal Registrar 1934*, pp. 5–6.

TABLE 26. *Deaths of Europeans by Occupation, Gold Coast and Togoland, 1902–44* [1]

Period[2]	Government officials		Employees of trading firms		Employees of mining companies		Missionaries		Total
	M.	F.	M.	F.	M.	F.	M.	F.	
1902	10		21		18		2		57[3]
1903	5		12		20		2		39
1904	8		3		13		1		25
1905	9		3		12		2		26
1906	6		4		18		3		31
1907	3		9		12		1		25
1908	6		9		11		4		30
1909	5		7		7		3		22
1910	8		16		18		4		46
1911	4		14		16		3		37
1912	8		7		11		2		28
1913	6		7		5		4		22
1914	11		9		13		—		33
1915	7		10		2		1		20
1916	4		6		3		1		14
1917	9		11		6		1		27
1918	6		19		29		2		56
1919	6		15		7		—		28
1920	7		20		4		1		32
1921	14		15		2		1		32
Jan. to Mar. 1922	2		5		1		—		8
1922–3	6		19		5		1		31
1923–4	10		11		2		1		24
1924–5	7		11		1		—		19
1925–6	8		10		3		1		22
1926–7	3		13		5		5		26
1927–8	6		16		—		5		27
1928–9	4	—	14	2	6	—	—	—	26
1929–30	5	—	12	3	3	—	—	1	24
1930–1	2	1	9	1	5	—	—	—	18
1931–2	7		12	2	3	—	1	—	25
1932–3	1		3	—	3	—	1	2	10
1933–4	3		6	—	8	—	1	—	18
1934	2		2	—	12	—	1	—	17
1935	1		2	3	10	—	—	—	16
1936	8		10	1	6	1	2	—	28
1937	7		7	2	14	—	1	1	32
1938	3		12	3	9	—	—	1	28
1939	1		..	..	..	..	..	..	14
1940	2		..	..	..	..	..	..	22
1941	5[4]		..	..	10	..	..	..	21[4]
1942	4[4]		..	..	..	..	..	..	30[4]
1943	1[4]		..	..	..	..	..	..	7[4]
1944	4[4]		..	..	..	..	..	..	19[4]

[1] See *Medical Report 1909*, pp. 6–8; *1910*, pp. 9, 11; *1911*, pp. 7, 10; *1912*, pp. 10, 13; *1913*, pp. 13–14; *1916*, pp. 9–10; *1918*, pp. 20–1; *1919*, p. 10; *1920*, pp. 7, 9; *1921*, pp. 7, 9; *1922–3*, pp. 6, 8, 37, 39; *1923–4*, pp. 7, 9; *1924–5*, pp. 10–11; *1925–6*, pp. 9, 11; *1926–7*, pp. 14, 16; *1927–8*, pp. 18, 20; *1928–9*, pp. 15, 17; *1929–30*, pp. 18–19; *1930–1*, pp. 17, 19; *1931–2*, pp. 11, 13; *1932–3*, pp. 10, 12; *1933–4*, pp. 12, 14; *1934*, pp. 7, 9; *1935*, pp. 9–10; *1936*, pp. 11–12; *1937*, pp. 9–10; *1938*, pp. 9–10; *1939*, p. 4; *1940*, p. 5; *1941*, pp. 1–2; *1942*, p. 2; *1943*, p. 5; *1944*, p. 5.
[2] The data for 1902–21 and 1934–44 refer to calendar years, those for 1922–3 to 1933–4 to the years ending 31 Mar.　　[3] Including 6 Gold Coast Railway.　　[4] Excluding military.

All the factors which tend to reduce the death-rate of Europeans as compared with that of the natives tend also to reduce their death-rate as compared with that of the Syrians. It should be noted, however, that, though the Syrians have a more unfavourable age composition and live under more unfavourable conditions, they apparently enjoy likewise a low death-rate.

TABLE 27. *Deaths of Non-Africans by Nationality and by Sex, Gold Coast and Togoland, 1931–8* [1]

Nationality	1931	1932	1933	1934	1935	1936	1937	1938
British . . .	21	5	12	12	11	17	21	19
Dutch . . .	—	—	1	1	1	1	—	—
French . . .	3	—	1	1	—	—	1	2
Germans . . .	1	—	2	1	—	—	—	1
Greeks . . .	—	—	—	—	—	1	—	—
Italians . . .	2	1	3	2	—	2	3	6
Norwegians. . .	—	—	—	—	—	1	—	—
Russians . . .	—	1	—	—	—	1	—	—
Swedes . . .	1	—	—	—	—	—	—	—
Swiss	—	—	1	1	1	2	2	—
Americans . . .	—	—	1	—	—	—	—	—
Canadians . . .	—	—	—	—	1	1	1	—
Total Europeans .	28	7	21	18	14	26	28	28
Arabs. . . .	..	—	—	3	1	—	—	—
Indians . . .	..	—	—	1	1	1	1	1
Lebanese . . .	..	—	—	—	—	—	—	2
Syrians . . .	..	4	6	11	7	5	5	6
West Indians . .	..	—	—	2	1	—	—	1
Total non-Europeans	9	4	6	17	10	6	6	10
Total	37	11	27	35	24	32	34	38
Males	31	9	24	31	20	29	31	32
Females . . .	6	2	3	4	4	3	3	6

[1] See *Report Principal Registrar 1931*, p. 16; *1932*, pp. 2, 16; *1933*, p. 30; *1934*, pp 8, 21; *1935*, pp. 6, 18; *1936*, pp. 6, 18; *1937*, pp. 7, 18; *1938*, p. 8.

CHAPTER V

NIGERIA AND CAMEROONS[1]

I. Census-taking

Censuses were taken in 1866, 1868, 1871, and thereafter every ten years up to 1931. Before 1911 the census area comprised only part of Lagos Island and some small mainland districts. In 1911, 1921, and 1931 attempts were made to enumerate the people in a wider area and to obtain population figures—based mainly on estimates or guesses—for the whole of Nigeria (including in 1921 and 1931 the Cameroons).

1. Lagos[2]

Provision for census-taking was made as far back as 1863, one year after the foundation of the Colony of Lagos. The Ordinance,[3] which introduced at the same time registration of births and deaths, was enacted 'Whereas it is expedient to provide the means for a complete register of births, deaths, and marriages, and also for taking the census of the said Settlement, whereby evidence may be more easily obtained and statistical information afforded for purposes of public interest and utility, and whereby crime may be more readily discovered and more efficiently suppressed'. It stipulated:

X. That the Registrar shall take the census of the said Settlement, and furnish a copy of the same to the Colonial Secretary on or before the twenty-eighth day of

---

[1] In *An Economic Survey of the Colonial Empire*, as in most other British official publications, 'Nigeria' comprises the Colony of Nigeria (which includes the islands and mainland constituting the Lagos Municipal Area), the Protectorate of Nigeria, and the Cameroons under British Mandate. For statistical purposes 'Nigeria' was subdivided until 1939 into (1) the Northern Provinces of the Protectorate including Northern Cameroons, and (2) the Southern Provinces of the Protectorate including the Colony and also Cameroons Province. On 1 Apr. 1939 (2) was replaced by (2) the Eastern Provinces including Cameroons Province, and (3) the Western Provinces including the Colony. In this volume the term 'Nigeria' covers the Colony and the Protectorate, but not the Cameroons.

[2] In 1862 the port and island of Lagos were erected into a Colony. In 1863 Lekki, Palma, and Badagry were added to the Colony, and Protectorate rights were established over Ado and Oke-Odan. Between 1883 and 1899 the areas of both the Colony and Protectorate were extended considerably and finally comprised about 28,000 square miles. In 1906 the Colony and Protectorate of Lagos were amalgamated with the Protectorate of Southern Nigeria and became the Western Province of the Colony and Protectorate of Southern Nigeria.

The terminology concerning Lagos used in census and vital statistics is most confusing.

(1) 'Colony of Lagos', as a rule, meant only the Colony but sometimes comprised also the protected territories.

(2) 'Settlement of Lagos' and 'Colony of Lagos' seem to have been used, as a rule, indiscriminately, but sometimes 'Settlement' comprised only 'Lagos Island' and its immediate vicinity, and sometimes included not only the protected territories but even the 'sphere of influence'.

(3) 'Lagos Island' practically never means the whole island. It comprises, as a rule, either all the western part of the island which is included in Lagos Township, i.e. the Town and Harbour of Lagos, Ikeyi, and Victoria Beach (9 square miles), or the Town and Harbour of Lagos and the immediately adjoining area ($3\frac{3}{4}$ square miles), or only the Town and Harbour of Lagos, i.e. the part of the island west of the MacGregor Canal (1·7 square miles).

(4) Ebute Metta sometimes means the town of Ebute Metta (1·2 square miles) and sometimes the whole mainland portion of Lagos Township including Iddo Island (15 square miles).

[3] No. 21 of 1863 (28 Oct.), reprinted in *Ordinances of the Settlement of Lagos* (1874), pp. 38–42.

February in every year, as the Governor for the time being shall direct, as per Schedule hereunto annexed marked (M.),[1] in order that the statistical information may be compiled in the blue book for the previous year.

'Annual' censuses under this Ordinance were taken in 1866 and 1868 but never thereafter, and Section X was repealed in 1891 by 'An Ordinance to provide for a census being taken during the current year'.[2] The 'decennial' censuses of 1871 and 1881 were apparently taken, as in many other colonies, without special legal enactment.

There is no evidence how the censuses in the 1860s were carried out. In 1871 a house-to-house enumeration was made in the town of Lagos and some places on the mainland, but the data given for other neighbouring areas were probably based on estimates.[3] The returns, particularly for the town (28,518), were lower than had been expected, since the authorities in the years preceding the census had made quite fantastic claims as to the increase of the population,[4] and the Administrator's report for 1873 gave a much higher figure.

Population. A variety of circumstances contributes to prevent any return under this head being reliable. It is believed that the population of the Island of Lagos alone is not now under 50,000.[5]

But the reports for the following years were more cautious.

[1] Schedule M provided for the following entries: Name, Sex, Age, Occupation, Religion, Infirmities.

[2] No. 6 of 1891 (16 Apr.), *Lagos Ordinances 1886-1901*. In the meantime there had been enacted 'The General Registry Ordinance, 1888', which provided: '11. The Registrar-General shall from time to time take a census of the Colony, when and as the Governor shall direct.' But the Governor never directed the Registrar-General to take a census, and 'The Registration Ordinance 1901', which repealed 'The General Registry Ordinance, 1888', contained no provision concerning the taking of censuses.

[3] In his report for the year 1871 the Governor stated:
'A census was taken during the year 1871. The population of the Island of

	Males	Females	Total
Lagos was . . .	13,520	14,998	28,518
Badagry . . .	1,148	1,343	2,491
Palma . . .	431	383	814
Leckie . . .	99	66	165
Total for Lagos Settlement .	15,198	16,790	31,988

'A census also appears to have been taken of the districts, towns, and villages surrounding Lagos, showing a population of—males, 12,665; females, 15,568; total, 28,233; which, combined with the Lagos Settlement, 31,988, makes a total of 60,221, of whom 94 are Europeans' (*Colonial Possessions Reports 1873*, Part II, 2nd Division, p. 41).

It seems strange that the Governor was not sure whether or not a census had been taken 'of the districts, towns, and villages surrounding Lagos'. A year later the Administrator reported: 'The population of Lagos, according to the census of 1871, amounted to 36,005 souls. . . . The population of the entire settlement is estimated at 60,221. . . .' (Ibid. *1874*, Part I, p. 138.) This statement suggests that the enumeration covered, apart from the town of Lagos, not only Badagry, Palma, and Leckie but the whole 'Vicinity of Lagos' with a population of 7,487 (see ibid. *1879*, pp. 215-16, and *Census Report 1881*, Enclosure No. 3, p. 2) and that the figures given for other areas were estimates.

[4] See report of Administrator Glover, dated 14 Sept. 1868 (*State of Colonial Possessions 1867*, Part II, p. 22), and report of the Acting Chief Clerk and Treasurer to the Administrator of Lagos, dated 20 May 1870 (ibid. *1869*, Part II, p. 19). The claims were based, apart from general impressions, on 'the number of persons who have crossed the Lagoon to and from the mainland'. (During the last six months of 1869, 157,765 were reported to have landed in Lagos while only 101,939 left the island!)

[5] Administrator Strahan, 12 May 1874, *Colonial Possessions Reports 1874*, Part II, p. 118.

1874. The population of Lagos is estimated at over 60,000, but the return under this head cannot be considered reliable.[1]

1875. The population at the taking of the census in 1871 was returned as . . . 60,221 but owing to the great difficulty experienced in obtaining reliable information on the subject, these numbers cannot be accepted as accurate.[2]

1876. The population of the town of Lagos has been roughly estimated at 32,358, but if the number of inhabitants in the inland and outlying districts be taken into account, the number will probably be increased to about 60,000.[3]

However, in a report dated 11 October 1880, Lieutenant-Governor Griffith suggested that omissions at the 1871 census had been serious.

The census taken in 1871 is not accepted as accurate, as it is generally asserted that the arrangements made for the purpose were carried out perfunctorily. The natives too, not having been instructed upon the question, were suspicious of it, and did all they could to obstruct the work. The census to be taken in 1881 will, I trust, be carried out satisfactorily, and so afford a reliable foundation upon which not only to base calculations as to the gain or loss of population in the future but also for other useful purposes.[4]

Therefore, when the 1881 census yielded a much higher figure (75,270) the Lieutenant Governor suggested that the increase was not genuine:

. . . it must not be forgotten that circumstances interfered to prevent the Census of 1871 being taken so as to leave an impression on the public mind that it was a fair representation of actual numbers. The Natives did not understand it. Some thought it was intended as a preliminary step towards the introduction of a poll tax. Others considered it wrong from a religious point of view . . . . The enumeration of 1871 was spread over several days, if not weeks, and nobody in Lagos believed in its accuracy, whilst not a doubt has been insinuated against the Census of this year.[5]

Such doubt was only insinuated when the 1891 census yielded a lower population for Lagos Town than the 1881 census, and the insinuation was that the 1881 returns had been faked owing to 'the fact that the enumerators in 1881 were paid by the head, according to the number of people each of them recorded'.[6] In his report of 7 November 1891 the Colonial Secretary said:

The town of Lagos was not found to be nearly so large as was anticipated, as only 32,508 inhabitants were enumerated against 37,452 in 1881. . . . At the same time it is right that I should point out that it is not thought that the population of the town has decreased, the falling off being considered to be due to a more effectual enumeration brought about by a better system of payment to the enumerators.[7]

[1] Administrator Lees, 14 June 1875, *Colonial Possessions Reports 1875*, Part II, p. 128.

[2] Acting Administrator John D'A. Dumaresq, 17 May 1876, ibid. *1876*, Part I, p. 145.

[3] Assistant Colonial Secretary, 25 May 1877, ibid. *Reports for 1876*, p. 118. See similar statement of Acting Assistant Colonial Secretary, 10 July 1878, ibid. *1876–7*, p. 135.

[4] Ibid. *1879*, pp. 216–17. See also ibid. *1876*, Part I, p. 145.

[5] *Census Report Lagos 1881*, pp. 12–13; see also *Colonial Possessions Reports 1879–81*, p. 301. The census report for 1881 says (p. 1) that the 'Census of the Settlement of Lagos and its Dependencies for 1881 . . . was successfully accomplished on the night of the 3rd and morning of the 4th April', but 'the committee appointed to prepare a method to be followed in taking the Census of 1891' said: 'In 1881 the Census extended over a very considerable period, the extent of which the committee have not been able accurately to ascertain, but ranging from 17 to 30 days' (*Colonial Reports, Lagos 1891*, p. 38).

[6] *Census of Nigeria, 1931*, vol. iv, p. 1. The rate of pay was ½d. per enumerated person; see Payne, *Lagos and West African Almanack and Diary for 1894*, p. 50.

[7] *Colonial Reports, Lagos 1890*, p. 7. 'It was originally intended that the enumerators should, as was the case in previous years, be selected from the general public.' When the number of

The Superintendent of the 1891 census does not mention the decline in the population figure but makes some comments on the completeness and accuracy of the Returns:

The Census of the Colony and Protectorate of Lagos, except so much thereof as lies to the east of the meridian of Ode, was duly taken in the month of April, 1891.[1]

In the work of enumeration a certain amount of difficulty was experienced, but not more than I think might reasonably have been expected. . . . Much of the difficulty in obtaining information was due to persons being away at their farms when the enumerator called on them.

The Commissioner for the Western District reported to me as follows:—

'I consider that in Pokra 5 per cent. at least are omitted. In the Badagry district about 3½ per cent. It is almost impossible with the very scant knowledge at our disposal to enumerate every farm and village, and until the district is properly surveyed this will always be the case.[2] . . . I think Appa is at least 10 per cent. short.'

In the Eastern District the villages of Ehinosa, Mawusa and Ofin, which are situate opposite Epe, could not be enumerated owing to the resistance opposed to the enumerator by the Epe people, who farm there, and who claimed the land as part of the Ijebu country. As there were probably only a few score of persons thus unenumerated, the Government did not consider it worth while for the enumerator to be sent back there on that account.

Some allowance should doubtless be made both in the Central and Eastern Districts for persons unenumerated, but I am not prepared to say how much.

In the town of Lagos the enumeration should be more exact, as the enumerators could visit every house, and there were several officers to supervise them. At the

applicants proved to be too small it was decided to take the census in the town through clerks in the Government service and in the 'Districts' through private applicants. But, as the Superintendent reports (see *Lagos Census Report 1891*, p. 5), the applicants were not ready to accept the terms of the Administration.

'With one or two exceptions, those whom I saw at once declined service on hearing that the pay was to be 10/- a day, and that the Government would not consent to payment by the head as was the case in former years. When I had seen about a dozen of the applicants, I found that the rest had gone away and saved me the trouble of a personal interview.

'It was then evident that Civil servants must enumerate the whole of the Central and Eastern Districts.'

'The division of the Western District into sections, and the appointment of enumerators to them, was left entirely to the discretion of the Commissioner of the district with the happiest results. Only two Civil servants were employed as enumerators in this district.' (Ibid., p. 6. The other eight enumerators were apparently taken from the general public; see ibid., p. 39.)

[1] I doubt whether this statement is correct. Ordinance No. 6 of 1891 (16 Apr.) provided: 'Subject to the provisions of this Ordinance, a census of the Colony, and of so much of the Protectorate as the Governor in Council may determine, shall be taken during the month of April, one thousand, eight hundred and ninety-one, as regards the town of Lagos, on the four days from the twentieth to the twenty-third of that month, and, as regards the remainder of the area over which the Census may extend, on the ten days from the twentieth to the twenty-ninth of that month.' An 'Order in Council limiting the extent of the Protectorate of which a Census is to be taken under the Ordinance', issued on 18 Apr. (*Lagos Ordinances 1886–1901*), ordered 'that a census of the whole Protectorate, except so much thereof as lies east of the Ode Line, shall be taken under the said Ordinance'. But according to Lagos *Blue Book 1891*, p. 26, two more Orders in Council were issued: one, on 18 Apr. 'postponing the Census as regards the Eastern District West of the Ode line and as regards the Central District except the Town of Lagos', and one on 23 Apr. 'extending the time for taking the Census in Town of Lagos'.

[2] It may have been almost impossible with the very scant knowledge at their disposal to enumerate every farm and village, but if this was so it must have been absolutely impossible to have such an exact knowledge of the omissions as to be able to estimate them in one district at 'about 3½ per cent.' But the reader will soon see that Nigeria census officials have seldom realized the extraordinary difficulty of estimating the proportion of omissions.

same time, the Census can only be regarded as affording approximate information; actual accuracy is not obtainable in the present condition of things.[1]

The Census Officer for Lagos, 1931, thinks that the population 'was possibly returned at a little too high a figure in 1881, and at too low a figure in 1891'.[2] The Medical Officer of Health who took the Medical Census of the Southern Provinces in 1930–2, on the basis of an analysis of the health conditions in Lagos since 1861, held the 'view that much more weight attaches to the 1891 and 1901 Censuses than to that of 1881'.[3] But the Government Statistician, in his report on the 1931 census, expressed still another opinion.

If one asserts that there has been unbroken inter-censal increase in the population,[4] one is forced to conclude that the 1881 figures are too high or the 1891 figures too low.

I incline to the latter view, firstly, because in 1881 the enumerators were paid at so much a head, and while they would naturally try to include every possible person in the count, the controlling authorities can have hardly been so simple as not to check any entries of fictitious names; and, secondly, because there was some sort of strike of enumerators at the beginning of the 1891 Census, so that, apparently, the work was done without enthusiasm. The Superintendent of the 1891 Census refers to errors of 5, 3½ and 10 per cent in the Districts of Pokra, Badagri and Appa, and he said that in the town of Lagos the enumeration should be more exact; but the much greater errors which have been common in counts of rural areas, even at later dates, suggest that the errors in the Districts named were under-estimated, and a like suspicion, therefore, attaches to the Lagos data.[5]

Far from considering the 1881 returns too high he thinks it probable that the actual population was 10 per cent. higher, and he assumes that the population in 1891 was about 15 per cent. higher than in 1881. This would imply that 40 or 50 per cent. would have to be added to the 1891 figure in order to obtain the actual population!

That the population of Lagos was understated in 1881 is, it seems to me, out of the question. In an African town with a constant flow of people from and to the mainland the controlling authorities were certainly not able to check to any extent fictitious entries, particularly of visitors or children. That in 1891 the would-be enumerators were quite aware of this position appears from the fact that they refused to participate in the count when they learned that they would not be paid so much a head. The assumption that the Returns for 1881 were too high seems, therefore, plausible. Although in 1891 the enumerators were paid by the day, the cost of taking the census was much higher than in 1881,[6] and I found no evidence that 'the work was done without enthusiasm'. It may well be that omissions were more numerous than the Superintendent's estimates suggest, but I see no good reason to assume that they were excessive. What seems to have been overlooked by all Nigeria officials who have

[1] *Lagos Census Report 1891*, pp. 5–6.   [2] *Census of Nigeria, 1931*, vol. iv, p. 1.

[3] See ibid., vol. i, p. 64.

[4] I shall discuss this assertion of the Government Statistician in the section 'Population Growth'.   [5] Ibid., vol. iv, pp. 63–4.

[6] In 1881 the cost of taking the census was £224. 1s. 8d. (excluding remuneration to the Registrar). In 1891 it was £331. 12s. 9d. (excluding the remuneration to the Superintendent). See Lagos, *Census Report 1881*, p. 16; *1891*, p. 40.

compared the results of the 1881 and 1891 censuses is the important fact that while in 1881 all persons found on the census day in Lagos were included, in 1891 those 'ordinarily resident in the house' were counted.[1] The numerical importance of the Visitors enumerated in 1881 appears from the following statement by the Lieutenant Governor:

Among the population there are inserted Visitors 5,017 which consist of persons who are constantly on the move from other places within or without the Settlement, engaged in business, pleasure, or in visiting their friends. It is a population which is seen every day and is constantly passing to and from the Island of Eko, or Lagos.[2]

There cannot be the least doubt that in a town such as Lagos the *de jure* population, as a rule, is smaller than the *de facto* population, and this may explain in part the difference between the census returns of 1891 and those of 1881 (and 1901).

The returns for 1881 and 1891 seem to have been based mostly on actual house-to-house enumeration. The area covered in 1881 was apparently the same as in 1871; in 1891 it was larger. But in 1901 it was restricted to the towns of Lagos and Ebute Metta.[3] The Superintendent of the 1901 census reported:[4]

The Census of the Island and Harbour of Lagos and Ebute-Metta[5] was taken on April 1st, 2nd, and 3rd.

No attempt was made to take a census of the Districts. An immense amount of preparation, and a large expenditure of money would have been required for this purpose.[6] Even then the results would hardly have been more accurate than estimates. Until the country has made very great strides in civilisation an approximately accurate enumeration is impossible.

Every effort was made to insure the census of the Island of Lagos and Ebute-Metta being as accurate as possible, but I cannot pretend that the results are strictly so.

For some sections of the town of Lagos the returns differed enormously from those of the 1891 census. The most striking example was the drop in Section 37 from 1,307 to 408. The Superintendent made the following comment:

Section 37 is obviously wrong, I discovered this too late to order a retaking.[7]

[1] See *Colonial Reports, Lagos 1891*, p. 39.   [2] Lagos, *Census Report 1881*, pp. 6–7.
[3] The report on the 1931 census of Lagos states (p. 2): 'Before 1901 the area covered by house-to-house enumeration was simply Lagos Island, exclusive of the part to the east of MacGregor Canal which is now called Ikoyi. In 1901 Ebute Metta was included in the Lagos Census for the first time.' But the area covered by house-to-house enumeration no doubt included some mainland villages in 1871. I found no evidence that any area was excluded from house-to-house enumeration in 1881; and there is conclusive evidence that no area was excluded in 1891. The Schedule as outlined in the Census Ordinance could obviously only be used for a house-to-house enumeration, and the Ordinance provided: 'Each Enumerator shall fill up such schedules, or cause such schedules to be filled up, with regard to all dwelling-houses situate within his Section . . . .' In fact, of course, house-to-house enumeration was not carried out everywhere.
[4] *Census Report Lagos 1901*, p. 1.
[5] 'The Census Ordinance, 1901' provided that 'a census of the Colony and Protectorate, or of such parts thereof as the Governor in Council may determine, shall be taken during the month of April, one thousand nine hundred and one' (Ordinance No. 6 of 1901, 30 Mar., *Government Gazette, Colony of Lagos*, 13 Apr. 1901, pp. 235–7; reprinted in *Ordinances and Orders, &c., in Force on April 30th, 1901*, vol. ii, pp. 935–6).
[6] The actual cost of the census was only £79. 18s. 4d (£71. 18s. 4d. for enumerators and £8 for stationery). See *Census Report Lagos 1901*, p. 2.   [7] Ibid., p. 5.

The Government Statistician responsible for the 1931 census who, as will be remembered, considered the 1891 census most defective said:

The 1901 Census was possibly not as good as that of 1891. At any rate, the data are not presented with the same clearness and detail.[1]

In 1906 the Colony of Lagos and its protected territory were amalgamated with the Protectorate of Southern Nigeria into the Colony and Protectorate of Southern Nigeria, but the Report on the Southern Nigeria Census, 1911[2] devotes a special chapter to the 'Census of the Lagos Municipal Area' which was larger than the area covered by the 1901 census of Lagos though smaller than the area of the earlier censuses.

The Lagos Municipal Area comprises the island of Lagos, Iddo Island, Ebute Metta and Apapa on the mainland, and Victoria (the Beach). Including the outskirts within the municipal boundary, the total area may be stated as approximately 18 square miles. Omitting the outskirts, the extent of the towns proper is about two square miles.

The total population registered for the whole area (including 1,067 shipping and 451 military population) was 73,766 . . . .

The numbers shown above were, of course, those actually registered on the schedules, which in the majority of cases were filled in by the Enumerators on behalf of illiterate people, many of whom were unduly suspicious. It is not improbable that an appreciable number of such persons were omitted from the declarations made by the heads of the families, who, notwithstanding the official assurances given to the contrary, could not disassociate the idea of subsequent taxation from the census.[3]

In 1914 the Colony and Protectorate of Southern Nigeria and the Protectorate of Northern Nigeria were formed into the Colony and Protectorate of Nigeria, and the Lagos censuses of 1921 and 1931 were taken in accordance with the Census Ordinance of 25 October 1917[4] covering the whole of Nigeria. The report on the 1921 census in the Southern Provinces, including Lagos, was published by the Census Officer Dr. P. Amaury Talbot as volume iv of his work *The Peoples of Southern Nigeria*. He does not comment on the census of Lagos specifically, but says with regard to the township census which covered thirteen townships with an aggregate population of 152,027 (of whom 99,690 were in Lagos Township):[5]

The township census was held on one day, viz. 24th April, and since the areas were small and distinct it was possible to attempt an accurate enumeration and to request much fuller information than could be supplied in the rest of the country. Each township was divided into Districts and Sub-districts, and every house was visited by an enumerator, who filled in the forms if the occupants were too illiterate

---

[1] *Census of Nigeria, 1931*, vol. i, p. 64. It may be mentioned as an example that the 1901 Report said (p. 1) that the European population of 'Lagos Island and Harbour' was 233 while this figure actually included 33 Europeans in Ebute Metta (see ibid., p. 3). The table showing the population in 1891 (ibid., p. 8) is also quite confusing.

[2] The census was authorized by 'An Ordinance for taking the Census of the Colony of Southern Nigeria from time to time' (No. 4 of 1911, 31 Jan., reprinted in Southern Nigeria, *Ordinances 1911*, pp. 17–20). (The term 'Colony' was not correct; the Ordinance applied to the Colony and Protectorate.)

[3] *Report on Southern Nigeria Census, 1911*, p. 15. The Government Statistician (1931), however, said: 'The 1911 Census clearly marked a great advance and, as regards accuracy, is probably on much the same footing as the two subsequent Censuses' (*Census of Nigeria, 1931*, vol. i, p. 64).

[4] See pp. 570–1 below.   [5] See Talbot, vol. iv, p. 10.

to do so themselves. The population, as given for the townships, may therefore be considered to be nearly correct, and probably under 5% of the inhabitants escaped the count; no allowance has been made in any statistics for those who evaded enumeration.[1]

Before the taking of the 1931 census the following Public Notice[2] was issued on 18 March 1931:

A Census of Lagos Township will be held on Thursday, April 23rd of this year.

On that day, every house in the Township will be visited by an Enumerator who will enter in a book the name, tribe, age, birthplace and religion of every person who slept in that house on the previous night. If some people happen to have gone out when the Enumerator arrives, this information will be given by their relatives. Census Enumerators will be distinguished by a Badge, and all information given to them will be regarded as strictly confidential.

Educated Householders will be provided with a separate form on a day prior to the Census date, which they will fill in for themselves and their households and deliver to the Census Official calling at their house on the 23rd April.

Educated Householders who have not received a form before the 23rd April should obtain one from the Enumerator and fill it in and return it to him without delay.

Any person refusing to give the desired information or wilfully giving false information is liable to a penalty of £5.

In the report on the 1931 census of Nigeria a special volume has been devoted to Lagos Township. The difficulties with which the authorities were confronted were great.

The preliminary arrangements made for the 1931 Census had to be altered several times owing to unforeseen circumstances, and in consequence the final preparations were unavoidably hurried. In November 1930, it was decided that the census should be a Town Council census, carried out under the supervision of Mr. Martin, Assistant Secretary of the Town Council, using the Council's staff of sanitary inspectors, reinforced if necessary by Tax Assessment clerks as enumerators. The Secretary of the Town Council, however, pointed out that Mr. Martin would not return from leave in time to assume control at the beginning of January, so this plan was abandoned.

There was some difficulty in finding a successor for Mr. Martin; and finally the present writer, although he was completely inexperienced, and knew nothing of Lagos conditions, was appointed to act under the direct control of the Government Statistician.

At the beginning of February, when the report of the Select Committee on the 1931–32 Supply Ordinance was discussed in the Legislative Council, it was suggested that the financial situation did not justify the expenditure of any money on the census. The Unofficial Members of the Legislative Council were unanimous in their opposition to a motion that the estimated expenditure on the census should be re-included in the Supply Ordinance. The matter was referred to the Secretary of State, who decided that the census should be proceeded with, but every economy should be made in carrying it out.

Accordingly the census schedule for Lagos was revised, and the more troublesome questions it included—those relating to occupation, civil condition, and physical infirmities—were struck out. A regrettable break thus occurs in the sequence of the statistics which had been obtained since 1891 for occupation and civil condition.[3]

---

[1] Ibid., p. 1.   [2] The Nigeria Gazette, 19 Mar. 1931, p. 158.

[3] Census of Nigeria, 1931, vol. iv, p. 3. The questions finally asked were confined to sex, age, tribe or nationality, birthplace, and religion. 3,361 persons found on waterside canoes, roads, and trains were not required to fill in a census schedule; the enumerators counted them, distinguishing men, women, boys, and girls; see ibid., pp. 1, 9–10.

The census day was April 23rd. The last three censuses of Lagos have all been planned to commence and finish on a single day, but as Lagos continues to increase in numbers it becomes increasingly difficult to organise a one-day census. It is likely that a system of the gradual collection of information, such as was recommended by the Government Statistician this year, will have to be adopted in the future, as there is no longer a sufficient number of Government employees available to cope with the work in a single day. This year the outskirts of the town were enumerated at several different times: the villages in the neighbourhood of Lighthouse Creek on April 1st, the Surulere area on April 28th, and the villages around Kuramo Water on May 5th.[1]

The report says with respect to the accuracy of the censuses taken so far in Lagos:

There is no doubt that all the Lagos censuses have been more or less inaccurate, and the reasons for this are not far to seek. Census taking depends for its success above all on the willing co-operation of the people counted, and that co-operation is extremely difficult to obtain in Lagos. Among illiterate people in Lagos there has always been present a fear that the census will be used as a basis for a new assessment, and will result in increased taxation. No assurance given by the Government has been quite sufficient to eradicate this fear. The people of Lagos also, in common with most Nigerian tribes, are reluctant to reveal the name and numbers of their families, and especially of their children, as they believe it is unlucky to do so. These difficulties are presumably less grave than they used to be, but they will remain formidable until a much larger number of the people are able to write, and fill up written forms correctly.[2]

An interesting attempt was made to check the completeness of the 1931 census.

Immediately after the census, the work done in a number of enumeration units was checked, in order that an estimate might be formed of the probable error in the whole municipal area. This checking continued for more than a fortnight. The check was not carried out very systematically, because only a few of the enumerators could be spared by their departments to go over their own work again.

In D division, the sub-divisions were chosen which showed little or no increase of population since 1921, or showed a very large percentage increase. Elsewhere the sub-divisions were chosen more or less at random. A systematic check, taking, say, 10 houses from each enumeration unit, was contemplated, but the staff to carry it out was not available.

Under the supervision of the Government Statistician or the census officer a checking party visited every house in each enumeration unit selected, and the householders in it were asked to confirm or vary the information they had already given. In a great many houses it was discovered that names had been omitted on the census day, because the people had not been in the house when the enumerator called and frequently houses which were locked on the census day, while their occupants were at work or at the market, were found open during the check.

Altogether the work of 46 enumerators was checked, the thoroughness of the checks varying according to the amount of the supervision it was possible to exercise over them. The highest number of omissions discovered in any single enumeration unit was 29%, and the lowest 3%, and the average number 10%.[3]

The Government Statistician concluded therefrom that the population of Lagos Township was 10 to 11 per cent. larger than ascertained by the enumerators.[4] But it seems doubtful whether this conclusion was justified.

[1] *Census of Nigeria, 1931*, vol. iv, p. 2.   [2] Ibid., pp. 1–2.
[3] Ibid., p. 6.   [4] See ibid., vol. i, p. 7.

(1) The checks were made on a very small scale.

(2) The checks were distributed most unevenly over the census area.[1]

	Lagos A	Lagos B	Lagos C	Lagos D	Ebute Metta	Rest	Total
Population, total[1]	22,365	26,357	22,672	18,799	18,398	17,517	126,108
Population of checked areas[1]	1,060	5,251	—	3,162	729	—	10,202
Omissions found in checks	99	493	—	354	119	—	1,065
Percentage addition	9·3	9·4	—	11·2	16·3	—	10·4

[1] Excluding omissions found in checks.

(3) It is most unlikely that all omissions were discovered through the checks.[2]

(4) A special check made for schoolchildren yielded a very much larger proportion of omissions than the field-checks.

The managers of schools had given a complete return of all their day-scholars as well as their boarders. In the Census Office a number of the schedules from the schools were gone through, and a comparison was made between the names of the day-scholars as recorded by their teachers and their names as they appeared in the schedules collected from their homes. Searching for the names at their home addresses was slow work, so only 547 names were checked out of a total of approximately 11,000 day-scholars. Of these only 286 were found at their home addresses. Making allowance for the fact that the school teachers may have made mistakes in the names and addresses of their pupils, a remarkably high number of school-children —between 40% and 45%—appear to have escaped enumeration.[3]

(5) A comparison of the total number of Lagos-born children recorded at the census, with the number of births registered in the years preceding the census,[4] suggests that many thousands of children were omitted at the census.

The census area was somewhat larger in 1931 than in 1921.

I estimate that between 1,000 and 1,500 persons were included in the census for the first time this year as a result of the extension of the township boundary and the addition of the thinly populated Urban Area. No administrative distinction appears to be made between the Township and the Urban Area.[5]

'The total cost of the census, exclusive of the cost of printing the census report, was £519 8s. 5d.'[6] or £4. 2s. 5d. for each 1,000 enumerated persons.

2. Southern Nigeria[7]

In 1911 an enumeration similar to that of Lagos Municipal Area was taken in some other places of Southern Nigeria, and an attempt was made

[1] See ibid., vol. iv, pp. 7, 48.

[2] See ibid., vol. i, p. 62: 'As our check itself was subject to errors of omission, it is reasonable to suppose that 10 per cent is a minimum addition to the recorded figures to get the true population of Lagos and Ebute Metta . . . .'

[3] Ibid., vol. iv, p. 6.   [4] See ibid., pp. 13–14.   [5] Ibid., p. 2.

[6] Ibid., p. 9. The cost of printing the report was £70; see ibid., vol. i, p. 91.

[7] In 1885 the British claim to a protectorate over Nigeria was recognized by the Berlin Conference, and that part of the country which was not included within the Colony and Protectorate of Lagos or the sphere of the Royal Niger Company was placed under British administration as the 'Oil Rivers Protectorate', later (1893) named the 'Niger Coast Protectorate'. When in 1900 the charter of the Royal Niger Company was revoked, the northern part of its territories became the Northern Nigeria Protectorate whilst the southern was combined with the Niger Coast Protectorate under the name of the Protectorate of Southern Nigeria.

to estimate the total population of the country. The Census Officer reported:

The total population returned for the whole Colony and Protectorate was, after adjustment, slightly over seven and three quarter millions, viz. 7,858,689 . . . .

With regard to adjustments, it should be at once explained that whilst a house to house enumeration was made in the ports and at a number of places up-country, this plan was not feasible in most of the outside districts, and in such cases estimates based upon the best available data had to be prepared by the District Commissioners. These estimates were compared at headquarters with former calculations made two or three years ago, and, where doubtful, the figures were questioned and revised, allowance being made for the much closer knowledge of some parts of the country now as compared with the time when the previous estimates were made, and for alterations in district boundaries. In only one instance (Lagos district outside the municipal area) was a 1911 original estimate increased at the chief census office, but reductions were made in the cases of Ibadan and Oshogbo in the Western Province; Onitsha in the Central; and Abakaliki, Bende, and Owerri in the Eastern Province.

It is not, of course, claimed that even the total now published is completely reliable, but judging by the very considerable amount of trouble taken by the various officers up-country, as indicated by their detailed returns, I am of opinion that the total figure may be accepted as a reasonably approximate estimate.[1]

Dr. Talbot was more sceptical regarding the 1911 figures.

In 1911 the population of the ports was enumerated, but only a rough estimate was given for the rest of the country, the inaccuracy of which can be seen by contrasting the population of towns with that obtained in 1921.[2] It must be remembered, however, that in 1911 a large part of the Southern Provinces was just coming under the control of Government, and the machinery at the disposal of the political officers was very inadequate.[3]

Finally, the compiler of the 1931 population statistics of Southern Nigeria made the following comment:

The first Census of the Southern Provinces as a whole was taken in 1911, when the figures were based mainly on estimates, except in the principal ports, where a house-to-house enumeration was made. The figures thus obtained were of a purely preliminary nature, and are of little value for comparative purposes. The Census Officer regarded the total population then returned as 'a reasonably approximate estimate.' In the light of the last two censuses this phrase should probably be read in its widest sense. For in 1911 a considerable part of the Southern Provinces was only just coming under the control of the Government, and even in 1921 and 1931, when this control had developed, the figures returned must be viewed with considerable caution.[4]

[1] *Report on Southern Nigeria Census, 1911*, p. 1. See also 'Report on the Eastern Province 1911' pp. 124-5:

'A census was held throughout the Province in April. At the port towns of Calabar, Bonny, Opobo, Brass and Degema a complete house to house census of individuals duly classified, took place while in the outlying Districts a general reckoning was made. . . .

'At certain of the port towns some amount of suspicion was latent as regards the census, which was however, allayed by letters written personally by His Excellency the Governor to the Chiefs. In other Districts the Chiefs here and there made it impossible to arrive at a correct estimate of the proportion of young women. No serious hindrances, however, were offered to the general carrying out of enumeration.'

[2] Dr. Talbot apparently took it for granted that discrepancies between the census results for towns must be due to inaccuracies in the 1911 census, and that if the 1911 results for the towns were inaccurate the 1911 figures for the rest of the country must be so *a fortiori*.

[3] Talbot, vol. iv, p. 5. [4] *Census of Nigeria, 1931*, vol. iii, p. 1.

As regards house-to-house enumeration, there is in fact no evidence that it was extended beyond the eleven principal ports[1] with an aggregate population of 109,161, including Lagos with 73,766.[2] In any case it is safe to assume that the people covered by such enumeration outside Lagos constituted less than 1 per cent. of the total population of Southern Nigeria.

In 1921 an attempt was made to extend the scope of actual enumeration.

The census of the Southern Provinces was taken in two divisions, called the Township and the Provincial census respectively. The former dealt only with the townships and non-natives, wherever they might be; the latter covered the rest of the population.[3]

As shown above, Dr. Talbot considered the results of the Township census to be nearly correct.

A very different state of affairs prevailed throughout the remainder of the country, where, although two months were allowed for the carrying out of the enumeration, statistics can only be regarded as approximate. In every case the counting was done under the superintendence of the political officers and the control of the Resident of each Province. Most unfortunately the census took place at the worst possible moment, since the political staff was at the lowest stage of efficiency it has ever reached. Not only was it seriously depleted in numbers—for many officers had just retired, including those who would have left the service earlier had it not been for the war—but a very considerable proportion was composed of new men entirely without experience of the Coast. The census in a country like Nigeria needed specially careful handling, while, in order to obtain any accuracy, a thorough knowledge of the people and of the particular locality was necessary.

Most of the Nigerian peoples share in the widespread feeling against giving the number of their family, especially of the children, in the same way as many will not give their true name; for it is thought that a person in possession of this gains power over them and can do them harm, if so inclined. Many also believe that, if the number of a family is told aloud, any evil spirit in the neighbourhood who may hear it will perhaps become jealous and cause the death of some member, most likely a child. Among the Yoruba it is a breach of etiquette to enquire after a man's family, but probably this feeling is based on the same idea as that just mentioned.

Another grave objection to the enumeration in the minds of the people was the belief that it was merely a prelude to taxation. At the present moment direct taxes are only imposed on the Yoruba Provinces, viz. Ijebu, Abeokuta, Ondo and Oyo— and part of Benin—which are all ruled by Native Administrations. The rest of the country is immediately under the political officers and is not directly taxed. Even in the Yoruba Provinces the census was thought by many to be connected with some further development of taxation.

In certain regions which are not yet under full control—for instance, the northern parts of the Cameroons Province and of Abakaliki Division—the population perforce had to be estimated. On the whole, however, the census does not appear to have suffered much from the fact that Government jurisdiction had been extended such a short time ago to a large portion of the country; in some very wild Districts such as Ogoja the enumeration was carried out with little trouble. That of the Yoruba would not appear to have been so successful as amongst the other tribes. On the whole the

[1] That it was not extended to all ports may be inferred from the following statement in the *Report on Southern Nigeria Census, 1911*, p. 4: 'Census of the Ports:—In each of the principal ports, viz: Lagos, Calabar, Warri, Bonny, Opobo, Degema, Brass, Forcados, Burutu, Sapele and Koko Town, a house to house enumeration was made, the names of each inhabitant being entered on the census schedules.' (The statement, ibid., p. 25, that the form used in Lagos was also used 'for all the ports in Southern Nigeria' is probably erroneous.)

[2] See ibid., p. 14.   [3] Talbot, vol. iv, p. 1.

least opposition to the taking of the census was experienced amongst the Ibo and those coastal regions which have been longest in touch with Europeans.

The final great disadvantage under which the census laboured was the scarcity of educated and trustworthy clerks. For the most part only new, entirely untrained and comparatively illiterate men could be obtained to go round the Districts.

It was requested that a house-to-house enumeration should be carried out, but for various reasons this was sometimes impossible and in certain parts a proportion of the population was estimated.

In every case the accepted figures have been those as finally determined by the officer on the spot and confirmed by the Resident of the Province. The percentages added to cover those not actually counted and absentees seem to be reasonable, and to err, if at all, on the conservative side; on the whole, in my opinion, the population is considerably larger than that given in this report, and it would appear safe to say that, if 10% were added to the native tribes, the result would be more accurate.[1]

The last sentence is not quite clear. The claim that the percentages added to cover those not actually counted and absentees err, *if at all*, on the conservative side can only mean, it seems to me, that the official total was not an overstatement and that it is doubtful whether it was an understatement, but this claim cannot be reconciled with the author's opinion that on the whole the population was considerably larger than the total given in the report. Finally, the statement that it would appear safe to say that, if 10 per cent. were added to the native tribes, the result would be more accurate, means, if interpreted literally, that it is safe to say that the native population was at least 5 per cent. larger than the official total, but it is possible that the author meant to suggest that 10 per cent. be added to the total for native tribes.

It is, however, doubtful whether the population as a whole had been understated. When the 1931 returns showed for the Provinces of Calabar, Onitsha, and Owerri a total population of 3,607,157 as compared with 4,448,918 in 1921,[2] the Census Officer for Southern Nigeria stated:

It is suggested by some of the Administrative Officers that the figures were over-estimated in 1921, although the Residents of these three Provinces in 1921 were all of the opinion that the Census figures were too low. As far as Onitsha and Owerri Provinces are concerned, arguments in favour of the present figures are based mainly on the density of the population as shewn by the 1921 figures; it is claimed that, in many cases, the density was absurdly high. Moreover, there is evidence to shew that, in 1921, the figures returned by District Officers in Owerri Province were subjected to considerable manipulation before publication.[3]

In 1931 the area in which an enumeration was carried out was even smaller than in 1921. It comprised merely Lagos Municipal Area and the some 2,000 non-natives living outside Lagos.[4]

---

[1] Talbot, vol. iv, pp. 1–3.   [2] See *Census of Nigeria, 1931*, vol. iii, p. 21.   [3] Ibid., pp. 4–5.

[4] In April 1930 the Governor had ruled that an enumeration (Intensive Census) should also be made of the Egba Division (Abeokuta Province). 'The Alake of Abeokuta welcomed the idea of an Intensive Census, which was to have been carried out by Native Administration Staff over a period of three months; general preparations were made and enumerators appointed. A meeting was held in Abeokuta, at which the aims of the Census were described by the Alake and the Census Officer. However, in February, 1931, this programme, too, was abandoned' (ibid., p. 2).

As regards the Intensive Census of non-natives the Census Officer says: 'There is no reason to believe that the returns are other than accurate, although there may have been a few omissions, due, for instance, to the absence of persons on trek' (ibid., p. 14).

The Southern Provinces' Section has been the Cinderella of the Census of Nigeria in 1931. The preliminary arrangements in 1929 and 1930 were interrupted by the riots in the Eastern Provinces, one of the main causes of which was said to be the attempts which were being made to enumerate the native tribes.[1] This interruption was discouraging to any who anticipated a really thorough Census of the population in the Eastern Provinces, and it is no matter for surprise that a general feeling of nervousness arose in connection with enumeration. The consequence was that a scheme for a General Census in the Southern Provinces failed to mature, and although certain proposals were discussed and approved, most of them were eventually found to be impracticable, so that the Census of the Southern Provinces finally became a mere compilation of existing data, and the results have, often, only a provisional character.[2]

As in Lagos, the officer in charge of the census was a Cadet. He reports:

The Census of the Southern Provinces suffered many early disadvantages and, indeed, throughout its course it has been beset with difficulties. It is evident to those who have experience of Census work that the officer in charge should be one who has wide experience and knowledge of the territory and people concerned. The compilation and report in this case were the work of a junior officer with only slight experience of one part of the Southern Provinces.[3]

The drawbacks that, unlike in 1921, no house-to-house enumeration of natives was carried out in any Province and that the Census Officer had not as thorough a knowledge of the country as Dr. Talbot, were probably offset by the fact that the 'existing data' on which the population estimates were based were less defective in 1931 than in 1921, but they were still quite inadequate.

Figures of the number of Adult Males have been obtained in most instances from the Tax Registers,[4] and far greater reliance may be placed on these figures than on those of the rest of the population, but even so they cannot be accepted as accurate. For, in many cases, no allowance has been made for the aged and infirm, and in some cases purely arbitrary additions have been made in respect of these classes; it would indeed be difficult to obtain a genuine estimate. Of necessity the number of Adult Males has been adopted as the basic figure in calculations from the returns, and the fact that this number itself is inexact must be borne in mind.

Women are subject to taxation only in one or two small areas of the Southern Provinces, consequently reliable records of their number are few.

The number of Non-Adults is the most highly speculative feature of the Census.[5]

The present Census consists largely of transcripts from the Tax Returns, with the addition of Adult Females and Non-Adults, and it is this addition, in the main, which has proved the stumbling block: for few calculations appear to have been based on reliable knowledge or definite data.[6]

As there was no Census proper in the Southern Provinces, apart from that in

---

[1] For details concerning these riots in which many native women were killed see *Report of the Commission of Inquiry appointed to Inquire into the Disturbances in the Calabar and Owerri Provinces, December, 1929*, and *Notes of Evidence, December, 1929*. See also Margery Perham, *Native Administration in Nigeria*, pp. 206–20.

[2] *Census of Nigeria, 1931*, vol. iii, pp. 1–2.   [3] Ibid., p. 4.

[4] See in this connexion ibid., p. 9: 'The Medical Census Officer wrote from one of the areas which he visited:—"The Census figures were compiled from the most recent Assessment Reports, and these in some cases are 6 or 7 years old".' See also ibid., vol. i, p. 3. (As regards the assessment reports in Cameroons Province see Kuczynski, *The Cameroons and Togoland*, pp. 210–12.)

[5] *Census of Nigeria, 1931*, vol. iii, p. 5. The report does not show how the other information called for (tribe, language, religion, infirmities, occupations) was obtained.   [6] Ibid., p. 4.

Lagos and a few small areas,[1] most of the data supplied as to Females and Non-Adults are based on guesses and estimates . . . .[2]

The Census Officer for the Southern Provinces discusses very fully the 'chaos of inconsistencies' appearing in these guesses and estimates. 'Without valid evidence little credence can be attached to the anomalous values of the ratios reported from the various Provinces.'

As shown above, the returns for Southern Nigeria showed a decrease in the population of the three Eastern Provinces from 4,448,918 in 1921 to 3,607,157 in 1931. The nine Western Provinces,[3] on the other hand, showed an increase from 3,922,541 to 4,886,090. These increases 'appear too great and are to be accounted for rather by over-estimation of Females and Non-Adults than by any influx of population or more accurate enumeration'.[4] As regards the three Eastern Provinces the Census Officer is inclined to think that the 1921 figures had been overestimates, but adds: 'At the same time it is admitted that the 1931 figures returned from some areas were considerably under-estimated.'[5] But nowhere does he suggest that the total returned for the whole of Southern Nigeria was an underestimate.

The Government Statistician, however, in his general report on the census of Nigeria, estimated the total population of Southern Nigeria at 20 per cent. more than the official returns. His argument ran as follows:

(1) 'There is a systematic bias towards omission.'[6]

(2) 'The estimate for the Southern Provinces population must be recast in two stages. Firstly, we must bring the reported figures for Calabar, Onitsha and Owerri Provinces, where special causes were at work in producing under-estimates of population, to the general standard of the Southern Provinces counts; and, secondly, apply a correction to the total so obtained to allow for the omissions which occur in all counts in the Southern Provinces, even in such areas as Abeokuta and the Colony, where the administration is relatively advanced.'[7]

(3) 'The reported drop in Calabar, Onitsha, and Owerri [since 1921] is between 9 and 20 per cent.'

While the 1921 figures were doubtless inaccurate, it is striking that they were considered by Dr. Talbot, the then Census Officer, as erring in defect rather than excess, as now asserted by the Residents of these Provinces. Some interesting replies have been received by Mr. Cox in answer to a memorandum containing an analysis of these and other anomalies. The most convincing supporter of the 1931 Census figures is Mr. K. A. B. Cochrane, Acting-Resident, Owerri, who holds that 'in the

---

[1] The Census Officer evidently refers here to the 'counts' of which he says (*Census of Nigeria, 1931*, vol. iii, p. 9): 'In some areas figures are said to have been obtained by Count; in the majority of cases it is claimed that Adult Males have been counted, and this probably means that transcripts have been made from the Tax Registers. Most of the "Counts" are reported probably from areas which have been covered by Assessment Reports, and the dates vary from 1921 to 1931; no information is given as to the methods by which these counts were brought up-to-date.'

[2] Ibid., p. 6.

[3] I shall follow here the procedure of the 1931 census report which distinguishes between (1) the three 'Eastern Provinces' and (2) the nine 'Western Provinces' including the Colony.

[4] Ibid., p. 4. The adult males showed an increase of 13·4 per cent., the adult females an increase of 21·1 per cent., and the non-adults an increase of 35·5 per cent.

[5] Ibid., p. 5.   [6] Ibid., vol. i, p. 7.   [7] Ibid., p. 22.

1921 Census there seemed to be a tendency, perhaps unconscious, not to record the
result of the enumeration accurately, but to make the population figures fit an ideal.
It was a case of fitting facts to theories. Two millions, and even two and a half
millions were the figures hopefully anticipated. In my opinion the final figure in 1921
for Owerri Division of 615,557 is far too high. The average density is most definitely
not 600 per square mile.' Again he says: 'I cannot believe that in 1921 the average
density of Bende District was anything approaching 350 to the square mile; I am
confident that the figure of 219,938 gives a much closer approximation to the truth,
though it is an under-estimate.' Again, in referring to the 'New Ahoada' area,
Mr. Cochrane says that, 'While I believe the 1921 figure was an over-estimate, I
believe that the present figure *may be a considerable under-estimate.*'

On the other hand, Mr. E. M. Falk, a Senior Resident of great experience, especially in the Eastern Provinces, makes some weighty comments on the divergences
of the 1921 and 1931 figures. He says (1), 'There has probably been an increase in
the population of Calabar since 1921,' and (2), 'The 1921 figures were better than
those of 1931, and probably 1929 data are the most accurate of the three.'

We need have no hesitation in considering that, whatever the value of the 1921
Census figures for the Eastern Provinces, those now given for Owerri, Onitsha, and
Calabar are far below the mark.

. . . the reported figures may be as much as 15 to 20 per cent in error.[1]

'Adopting for the number of adult males in Calabar, Onitsha and
Owerri the figures of 1921,[2] and for the per mille proportion of adult
females and non-adults, 1,100 and 1,300[3] respectively', the total rises to
4,318,000. 'As the reported (1931) figure . . . is 3,607,000, we must add
711,000 to the reported population of the Southern Provinces to bring the
figure to the standard of the Western Provinces counts. This brings the
population of the Southern Provinces on a Western Provinces' standard
to 9,204,000.'[4]

(4) In the Western Provinces 'the figures of taxable males given by
Residents are possibly correct to within 5 per cent',[5] but the figures for
women and children are much more defective. The errors in the totals are
'probably 10 per cent, sometimes less and sometimes more'.[6]

(5) Therefore, the population of the Southern Provinces is estimated
as follows:

'Southern Provinces population, on Western Provinces
standard 9,204,000
Add 10 per cent for omissions . . . . . 920,000'[7]
(10,124,000)

This argument for various reasons is by no means convincing.

(a) The Government Statistician takes no account of the essential
changes in the boundaries of the Provinces that occurred between 1921
and 1931.[8]

(b) The Government Statistician takes it for granted that there was

[1] Ibid., p. 6.
[2] 281,841, 427,415, and 573,329 respectively (see Talbot, vol. iv, table facing p. 154) as against
258,700, 351,080, and 459,848 in 1931 (see *Census of Nigeria, 1931,* vol. iii, pp. 19–20).
[3] The original returns were 1,049 and 1,323 respectively.
[4] Ibid., vol. i, p. 23. The recorded total for the Southern Provinces was 8,493,247 (including
3,607,157 for Calabar, Onitsha, and Owerri).
[5] Ibid., p. 5.   [6] Ibid., p. 6.   [7] Ibid., p. 23.
[8] I shall assume in the following discussion that these changes did not change essentially the
total population of the various Provinces.

a systematic bias towards underestimation of the population and that women and children were far more underestimated than men. There is, however, it seems to me, no reason to assume that the figures for women and children as a whole should have lagged behind reality more than those for men. The individual officers concerned chose as a rule some formula for deriving from the number of men the number of women and children, and the ratio which seemed to them the most plausible may have been just as often too high as too low. If in the Western Provinces 'the figures of taxable males given by Residents are possibly correct to within 5 per cent', it may be justifiable to argue that the estimates of women and children are correct to within 12 per cent. But I see no justification for assuming that in order to arrive at a correct estimate 5 per cent. should be *added* to the returned number of men, 12 per cent. to the returned number of women and children, and 10 per cent. to the returned total. It would be wrong in particular to overlook that in the totals, as returned, underestimates are more or less offset by overestimates.[1] The Census Officer said that the increase in the Western Provinces (from 3,922,541 in 1921 to 4,866,090 in 1931) appears too great and is to be accounted for rather by overestimation of Females and Non-Adults than by any influx of population or more accurate enumeration. But it must be remembered that in 1921, according to Dr. Talbot, the counting 'of the Yoruba would not appear to have been so successful as amongst the other tribes', and the Yoruba inhabited just those Provinces where the apparent increase in 1921–31 was particularly large.[2] It may well be, therefore, that the popu-

---

[1] The Government Statistician says that omissions occur 'even in such areas as Abeokuta and the Colony, where the administration is relatively advanced'. This may be true, but it is not less true that, on the other hand, gross overstatements occurred even in the Colony. See *Report, Colony 1937*, p. 1: 'In Ikeja the population figures, which were returned in the 1931 decennial census as 79,067, giving a density of over 400 to a square mile, had for some time been suspect and were last year reduced to 71,000. In the light of a more recent count made by the District Officer, and considered by him to be fairly accurate, the 1931 census appears to have been a gross overestimate, since there has been no epidemic or movement of population to account for the drop of about 30,000 revealed by the present estimate of 41,134.' It is amusing to note in this connexion the following passage from the Report of the Committee appointed by the Governor to examine the methods of Direct Taxation in force in Lagos and the Colony (*Report*, dated 8 Oct. 1936, pp. 8–9):
'The following figures for 1935–36 were supplied to the Committee:—

	Ikeja	Epe	Badagri
1. Population .	75,463	94,083	33,327
2. No. of persons paying tax	9,447	14,922	9,081
3. Percentage of tax-payers to population .	12%	16·9%	27·25%

'The reason given to the Committee for the small percentage of tax-payers to population in Ikeja and Epe as compared with Badagri were (a) that the inhabitants are more sophisticated and more skilled in evasion, (b) that the headmen have less influence, and (c) that the population is more shifting. . . . There is . . . no compulsion on people to pay tax prior to the collector's arrival or to remain in the village while the collector is there. Indeed in the Ikeja District it frequently happens that, on the approach of a collector, a whole village or hamlet effaces itself and remains in retirement until he is reported to have moved elsewhere.'
As a matter of fact the percentage of tax-payers in Ikeja was by no means small and only appeared so because the population had been overstated.
[2] Abeokuta, Ijebu, and Oyo Provinces were inhabited exclusively by Yoruba and they constituted the vast majority in Ondo Province and the Colony (see *Census of Nigeria, 1931*, vol. iii, p. 27). The population increased here apparently from 2,187,513 to 2,864,932 or by 31 per cent.,

lation increase, in so far as it was excessive, is to be accounted for rather by understatements in 1921 than by overstatements in 1931. On the other hand, I see no cogent reason to assume that in 1931 the population in the Western Provinces as a whole was understated rather than over-stated.

(c) The various population figures for the Eastern Provinces are as follows:

Provinces	'Census' returns 1921	Estimate 1929[1]	'Census' returns 1931	Revised 1931[2]	Estimate 1931[3]
Calabar	979,189	921,000	899,503	952,000	(1,047,000)
Onitsha	1,493,945	1,421,000	1,107,745	1,428,000	(1,571,000)
Owerri	1,975,784	1,953,000	1,599,909	1,938,000	(2,132,000)
Total	4,448,918	4,295,000	3,607,157	4,318,000	4,750,000

[1] These are the figures given by the Government Statistician; they are taken from the annual *Blue Book*. But the Report on the Southern Provinces gave for Onitsha 1,187,000; see Table 1 below.

[2] 'Adopting for the number of adult males the figures of 1921, and for the per mille proportion of adult females and non-adults, 1,100 and 1,300 respectively.'

[3] Adding 10 per cent. 'to allow for the omissions which occur in all counts in the Southern Provinces'.

The Government Statistician believed that in these Provinces 'special causes were at work in producing under-estimates of population' and that 'the reported figures may be as much as 15 or 20 per cent in error'. But it appears from the above table that he actually added 19·7 per cent. to the reported figures and that he raised the thus obtained total by another 10 per cent., so that his estimate exceeded the reported figures by nearly one-third. He was possibly right in assuming that the population of these Provinces had been understated in the 1931 returns, but he failed to present any evidence which would suggest that the understatements were excessive. The Senior Resident whom he quotes expressed the opinion that the 1921 figures for Calabar (979,000) were better than those of 1931 (900,000), and that probably the 1929 data (921,000) are the most accurate of the three. This statement does not speak against the accuracy of the Government Statistician's revised figure for 1931 (952,000), but it does not justify the addition of another 10 per cent. (which would raise the revised figure to 1,047,000). As regards Owerri Province, the Government Statistician quotes the Acting-Resident as stating that the 1921 figures were too high but that for some Districts of the Province the 1931 figures were too low. It is hard to believe that this 'most convincing supporter of the 1931 Census figures' should have agreed with an estimate which put the population of this Province one-third higher than the 1931 'census figure'.

Finally, it should be noted that none of the more recent official estimates showed for the Southern Provinces as a whole a marked increase over the

while it increased in the other four Western Provinces from 1,735,028 to 2,021,158 or by only 16 per cent.

1931 returns.[1] For the three Eastern Provinces the native population in 1942 was given as 3,621,368 as compared with 3,606,102 at the census. For the Western Provinces there was an increase in the native population from 4,883,528 to 5,206,443, but this increase was practically confined to Abeokuta and Cameroons Provinces. It may well be, of course, that all recent estimates as well as the 1931 returns were quite defective, but it is most unlikely, for example, that if in Onitsha and Owerri the populations in 1931 had been actually two-fifths and one-third higher than returned, these enormous errors should not have been corrected, at least in part, at one of the more recent estimates.

The totals for Southern Nigeria in 1911, 1921, and 1931 were 7,858,689, 8,371,459, and 8,493,297 respectively. The Census Officer in 1911 regarded the total population then returned as a reasonably approximate estimate. Dr. Talbot, who published the 1921 results, thought that the population in 1921 was probably about the same as in 1911[2] and that it had been considerably understated in 1921 and still more so in 1911. The Government Statistician, ten years later, evidently believed likewise that the population had been considerably understated in 1921[3] and estimated that the actual population in 1931 was about 20 per cent. higher than the reported figures. The Census Officer for the Southern Provinces, on the other hand, apparently did not think that the population had been understated in 1921 and evidently considered the 1931 returns so chaotic that he refrained from guessing whether the totals were too high or too low.

Until a proper count has been made in Southern Nigeria it seems impossible to appraise the margin of error in the various returns of the past. However, it is perhaps safe to say that the population was not considerably overstated in 1921, that it was not much lower in 1911 than in 1921, and that it was not lower in 1931 than in 1921. This would make it probable that the population exceeded 7,000,000 in 1911 and 7,500,000 in both 1921 and 1931. As regards the upper limit the situation is more uncertain. It is possible that, as the Government Statistician thinks, the population exceeded 10,000,000 in 1931 and that it exceeded, say, 9,500,000 both in 1911 and 1921, but I think it improbable.

The cost of the 1931 'census' of Southern Nigeria was practically nil.

The expenditure on the Southern Provinces' Administrative Census was £713, a great part of this sum being incurred in connection with the Intensive Census of the Egba Division of Abeokuta, which was subsequently abandoned.[4]

Considering that the sum of £713 includes an expenditure of £102 for the printing of the report, the actual cost of taking the 'General Census' and tabulating the results was probably less than 1s. per 1,000 returned persons.

[1] See Table 1 below. [2] See Talbot, vol. iv, p. 7.
[3] He did not explicitly say so, but since his estimate of the population of the Southern Provinces (10,124,000) exceeds the 1921 returns by 21 per cent. and since he thought that the total population of Nigeria had increased in 1921–31 only by something like 7 per cent., he evidently assumed that the 1921 population returns for the Southern Provinces had been far too low.
[4] Census of Nigeria, 1931, vol. i, p. 92.

3. Northern Nigeria[1]

The 'census returns' of Northern Nigeria 'as on the 2nd April, 1911' showed a total native population of 8,110,631. The Acting Governor, in a letter to the Secretary of State for the Colonies, said that 'the information . . . I fear is but very moderately approximate'. He expressed the opinion that the native population had been underestimated and that a more correct return would be 9,269,000.[2]

It was not stated at the time how the 'census returns' were obtained, but Mr. C. K. Meek, Census Commissioner, Northern Provinces, 1921, who incorporated the report on the 1921 census in volume ii of his work *The Northern Tribes of Nigeria*, said that 'the 1911 census was . . . merely a rough estimate of population by sex'.[3] Regarding the 1921 census he makes the following general comment:

The census of 1921 represents a very considerable advance. While it is not pretended that the count made of the natives in the provinces is anything more than approximately accurate, the statistics nevertheless furnish a great amount of valuable information.[4]

The census was taken in two parts: (a) by Provinces, (b) by Townships.

(a) In the Provinces, in view of the vast area involved, and the paucity of the staff engaged in its administration, a simultaneous enumeration was not possible. A period of two months (March 24th to May 24th) was allowed for the collection of statistics from each district, and a standard procedure was laid down by a Government circular. The Native Administrations gave a ready assistance, the existing staff of enumerators, ordinarily employed for the assessment of taxation, being augmented where this was necessary. The enumerators were instructed to obtain full information as to the occupations, language, religion, and degree of education of all natives, by tribes, within their area. No attempt was made to obtain accurately the ages of the people, as Negroes have hazy ideas on this subject; any closer approximation than that actually attempted, viz. a division into adult and non-adult, would have been wholly unreliable. Directions were given, however, by which children up to fifteen years of age could be uniformly classified, according to sex, with some degree of accuracy. No information was obtained as to civil condition, as the collection of these statistics would have thrown a great deal of additional work on a staff already overburdened. Residents were also asked for a return of all towns over 1,000 inhabitants, of missions, mining companies, and trading firms, lepers, live-stock, and an estimate of the number of acres under cultivation. (b) In the municipal areas known as townships it was possible to carry out on April 24th a simultaneous enumeration of all the inhabitants. It was also possible in these areas to obtain fairly accurate information as to age and civil condition. Each householder was required to fill up a form for his household, stating the name, nationality or tribe, sub-tribe, age and sex, civil condition, degree of education, occupation, and religion of each member of his household. Similar forms were issued to all non-natives who were residing outside the townships.[5]

[1] On 1 Jan. 1900 the territories administered by the Royal Niger Company, under Charter dated 10 July 1886, were transferred to Her Majesty's Government. A portion of these territories (from the Coast to Idda) were incorporated in the Protectorate of Southern Nigeria, the remainder being named the Protectorate of Northern Nigeria.

[2] See Northern Nigeria, *Census 1911*. For details by Provinces see Table 2, Population 1911 (a) and (b).   [3] Meek, vol. ii, p. 169.   [4] Ibid.

[5] Ibid., pp. 170–1. The report on the 1931 census of the Northern Provinces conveys a slightly different picture of the position of the 1921 census of non-natives outside townships. 'The 1921 Census was taken in two parts called A—the Township Census, and B—the Provincial Census. The former was taken and completed in all Townships on 24th April . . . . The Provincial Census,

As intercensal counts of the population have of recent years been regularly made in the Provinces by the European Political Staff and the Native Administrations, with a view to the assessment of taxation, Residents were in a position to check to some extent the decennial census returns of population. It will be readily understood, however, that with an administrative staff of only a hundred Europeans, already overburdened with multifarious duties, close supervision of all the details of enumeration was not to be expected. The distances to be travelled are so great, and the means of rapid transport so deficient, that a district officer might spend an entire year enumerating all the individuals resident in his district. The major part of the work of enumeration had therefore to be left to a small body of Muslim *malamai*, possessed of only a moderate degree of literacy, who carried out the count with the assistance of the local authorities. Many natives were no doubt omitted from the count, either unintentionally, or deliberately with a view to the concealment (as they thought) of their taxable capacity. In some Provinces it is apparent that the number of non-adult males was overstated with the same intention, for whereas the female adults are in excess of the male to a disproportionate degree, the female non-adults are correspondingly fewer than the male. Moreover, in some pagan areas the tribes are only partially under control, and in such cases the census taken was little better than an approximation based on counts made in a number of villages.

Numerous clerical errors, sometimes extending to hundreds of thousands, were made by the enumerators and overlooked by the census officers, but it is believed that these have now been all eliminated.[1]

None of the above difficulties were experienced in the enumeration of the township populations. The numbers who reside in townships being small—totalling only twenty thousand—they could be accurately reckoned; but as the conditions of township life are wholly artificial, the statistics are only of value as illustrating these artificial conditions.

No systematic enumeration was made of the mandated territory, the returns shown being based on estimates recently made by political officers during the ordinary course of their work.

The cost of taking the census was about £1,000.[2]

Mr. Meek thinks that many natives were omitted in 1921. Since the total number of natives returned was 9,994,515 he probably shares the opinion expressed by the Acting Governor in 1911 that the returns of that year (8,110,631) were quite incomplete.

The 1931 census consisted of (a) a General Census, and (b) an Intensive Census.

(a) The General Census was carried out on lines similar to those of the Provincial Census of 1921. It covered the whole of the Northern Provinces (including Northern Cameroons) with the exception of the five Townships (29,000 inhabitants), and of the households of Non-Natives and Educated Native Foreigners living outside Townships (7,600 people). Data were collected by the Administrative Staff from records available and returned by totals. The census units, of which there were some 9,000, averaging about 1,200 inhabitants, were a village area, or in the case of towns a ward, and the information called for was figures for sex and age (under 15, over 15), tribes, subdivisions or sub-tribes, language, religion, infirmities,

in which a simultaneous enumeration was not possible, had two main divisions: (a) a Census of all Non-Natives residing outside Townships was made, on a date as near to the 24th April as possible, on the same schedule as that used in Townships; (b) a Census was made of all the remaining inhabitants . . .' (*Census of Nigeria, 1931*, vol. ii, p. 3).

[1] Meek, vol. ii, pp. 171–2.   [2] Ibid., pp. 172–3.

and occupation. If there were no records established during the twelve months next preceding the census date (23 April 1931), 'a fresh count was to be made in divisions in which it was found possible to undertake it'.[1]

The report contains the following comments on the accuracy of the returns:

The Census could scarcely have been taken under more unfavourable conditions. The period was one of great financial depression and at a time when every economy had to be practised, the funds provided for Census-taking were bound to be reduced to a minimum. Added to this there was a locust invasion, which affected the whole of the Northern Provinces, and most of the time of the limited administrative staff was absorbed in supervising anti-locust measures.

In the circumstances the returns of the General Census, which called for the information to be supplied for each of the 9,000 individual census units, were much better than might have been expected.

As the details of the methods employed in each case of supplying the figures returned were not always given in the memorandum forwarding the returns, it is difficult to arrive at an entirely complete estimate of their accuracy.

In the Niger and Ilorin Provinces complete new counts were carried out for all columns of the General Census Forms. The figures of population by sex and adolescence for all Provinces are the results of a count made at some recent date; the adult males are everywhere counted annually for taxation purposes,[2] and allowing for the fact that they include all males of sixteen years and over instead of fifteen years and over, which is the age of adolescence in Census returns, the figures must be regarded as reasonably accurate. It is generally thought by officers responsible for their collection that the degree of error is certainly not more than 5%, and in most cases considerably less.[3]

Errors in enumeration must mainly be ascribed to the low degree of literacy among the enumerators, who, in addition, are unaware of the value of statistics, except for taxation purposes, while population statistics must also be affected by the superstition prevalent among Pagan tribes that enumeration would bring harm to their women and children. The latter has been reflected in the returns for Pagan areas.[4] In the Northern Emirates the degree of accuracy increases annually, and that for adult males is thought to be a high one.[5]

The following gives some of the views expressed and information supplied:—[6]

In Muri[7] the figures which were obtained through the Native Administration cannot be regarded as wholly accurate. . . . In Biu[8] adults are thought to be 2 to 3%, non-adults in all but two districts 10 to 15% below the true total; there is a local superstitious prejudice against the counting of children. . . . In Ilorin a complete new count was made; it was started on the 11th of November and completed on the 11th of March, 1931, and is thought to be reliable, as checks under European supervision revealed very little concealment. In Koton Karifi[9] it is considered that a number of persons under sixteen were enumerated as adults.[10]

---

[1] See *Census of Nigeria, 1931*, vol. ii, pp. 3, 5.

[2] But see also ibid., p. 12: 'As regards the General Census, there are now very few areas in which actual poll counts have not yet been made; the returns only showed the Hill Pagans in Dikwa Emirate, but there are possibly also certain small areas in the Mandated Territory of Adamawa Emirate. The population of the hills in Gwoza and Ashigashiya in Dikwa Emirate was estimated; the figures are based on the number of compounds which were counted for taxation purposes.' (For details as to the assessment returns in Northern Cameroons see Kuczynski, pp. 212–16.)

[3] *Census of Nigeria, 1931*, vol. ii, pp. 10–11.

[4] Pagans constituted one-third of the total population.   [5] Ibid., p. 12.

[6] I shall omit here passages referring to the figures for tribes, language, religion, infirmities, and occupation.

[7] A Division of Adamawa Province.   [8] A Division of Bornu Province.

[9] A Division of Kabba Province.   [10] See also p. 608 below.

. . . the figures for Kano Emirate[1] were compiled without a recount of the population being made except actually in Kano City. It was not considered advisable to incur the additional burden of a general census in the district during the closing period of tax collection owing to the economic conditions prevailing. 1930 taxation figures for adult males were available, and 1929 figures for adult females and non-adults. The proportion of increase or decrease of the adult male figures for 1930 over the figures for 1929 were applied to the 1929 figures for adult females and non-adults. The Resident had no reason to think that the result was other than a fairly close approximation of the true total, as the Native Administration Annual Censuses in the districts have reached a fair standard of efficiency. . . . The figures for nomad pastorals are, however, an exception; it is difficult for a Village Headman to know the whereabouts of nomad pastorals, as those present during the Census are not necessarily those by whom he is paid tax in the dry season or jangali in the rains.

. . . In Jemaa[2] it is believed that the degree of inaccuracy is less than 1 per cent, as a sleeping sickness survey was being made in the division.[3]

(b) The Intensive Census was carried out on lines similar to those of the Township Census and the census of non-natives in 1921. It covered (1) the five Townships and the households of Non-Natives and Educated Native Foreigners residing outside Townships; (2) six complete districts in Katsina Division, comprising 144 villages,[4] specially selected villages one in each of the other 16 Katsina districts, and 41 specially selected villages spread over the remainder of the Provinces.[5] The population enumerated in the Intensive Census comprised 4 per cent. of the total population of the Northern Provinces.

Katsina Division	308,062
Selected villages in all Provinces	99,328
Townships	28,948
Households of Non-Natives and Educated Native Foreigners	7,582
Train	14
Total	443,934

The questionnaire of the schedules prepared for these intensive censuses included the following:—

Street or court, Tenement Number (for Townships only, and replaced elsewhere by a single column headed 'Compound'), Number of Rooms in Tenement, Name and Surname, Tribe or Nationality, Sub-division or Sub-tribe, Sex, Age, Birthplace, Education, Occupation, Civil Condition, Number of Children Alive, Religion, and Infirmities.

Forms 6 (in English) and 6A (in Hausa and Arabic) were issued for the enumeration of the majority of the intensive census population, in which the details were entered by paid enumerators. A special Form 7, calling for the same information, was issued

---

[1] A Division of Kano Province.   [2] A Division of Plateau Province.

[3] *Census of Nigeria, 1931*, vol. ii, p. 11. For the sleeping-sickness survey in Jemaa Division see Nigeria, *Medical Report 1930*, p. 108; *1931*, pp. 95–6.

[4] 'Originally the whole of Zaria Province was included for intensive enumeration, but as the financial situation demanded sacrifices the intensive area was reduced, at first to cover the Katsina Emirate, and subsequently to the Northern portion of that Emirate alone' (*Census of Nigeria, 1931*, vol. i, p. 3).

[5] 'Forty-seven special censuses in selected village areas in all Provinces were originally undertaken. The Government Statistician had requested that there should be a minimum of one special census per division, as the figures obtained therefrom were to be used to test the accuracy of the figures supplied in the General Census for neighbouring areas. It was not, however, found possible to complete more than forty-one of these censuses.' (Ibid., vol. ii, p. 8.) Eight of the 38 Divisions were not represented.

to Educated Householders (Non-Native and Native Foreigner), for them to fill up the form in respect of their own households . . . .

A train passenger census was arranged with the Railway Authorities at Lagos, but the return for the Northern Provinces only showed fourteen persons. A Special Schedule (Form 8), with a reduced questionnaire, was used for this purpose.[1]

The census report gives additional details concerning the taking of the Intensive Census.

In Divisions the District Officer in charge, and in Townships the Station Magistrate, were in general charge of the Census, and in some cases special officers were detailed under them for census work.[2]

Towards the middle of March the preliminary enumeration of the Intensive Census areas in Katsina Emirate was started; the schedules were revised by the enumerators on the census date (23rd April). Between the 23rd March and the 23rd May the Special Intensive Censuses proceeded in selected areas in the Provinces. The enumeration of Townships was made between the middle of April and the Census date, and revised on the latter day.[3]

It was found in test censuses that an enumerator could enter fifty persons on an average per diem, and was, after experience, able to work up to an average of eighty or more. The standard of literacy of the enumerators was, it should be remembered, low; it differed considerably in the various areas. In one section of Katsina, two enumerators were employed who had never previously seen a European (a fact scarcely credible but subsequently confirmed). Further, large distances had often to be covered between households in scattered village areas. The scheme provided for one supervisor for every five enumerators. Particular care had to be taken to define clearly the limits of each enumerator's area. The number of the enumerators and supervisors employed was 278.

For the Census in Townships and Special Areas in all Provinces a course of instruction for supervisors and enumerators was held at Kakuri; where advantage was taken of this a great improvement was reflected in the returns.

In Townships the filling in of the schedules started four or five days before the Census date, and on the latter each enumerator revisited the households enumerated by him and made any necessary amendments to bring the schedules up to date by erasing entries or adding new-comers.

Remuneration of one pound for an enumerator, and two pounds for a supervisor was found to be adequate. As the classification of results and tabulation was done in the Census Office, clerical work was reduced to a minimum.[4]

[The censuses in 41 special villages] were taken between 23rd March and 23rd May, a limit of one month on each side of the census date being regarded as permissible.

These special censuses were all to have been taken under the close supervision of such European staff as the Resident was able to detail for the purpose, but the locust invasion and shortage of staff interfered with this arrangement, and the returns suffered in consequence. In some Provinces the Provincial Superintendent of Education, however, undertook that one or more special censuses should be held with the assistance of his department.

In the Katsina Division the preparations were carefully supervised by Mr. Humphreys, the second Administrative Officer attached to the Census Staff, and as a result of his attention to detail the actual census went forward without a hitch. Instructions were issued in Hausa, and a limited number of test censuses was held; these were kept at a minimum as the native enumerator is easily wearied. Serial numbers were used for compounds, starting from the household of the village or hamlet Headman, and the supervisors were responsible for seeing that every individual had been enumerated with a separate entry for each man, woman, or child. District Headmen exercised general control, and District Scribes and Central Assessment Mallams were employed as district supervisors.[5]

[1] Ibid., pp. 4-5. [2] Ibid., p. 4. [3] Ibid., p. 5. [4] Ibid., p. 7. [5] Ibid., p. 8.

In summing up 'the value of the data given in the 1931 Census Tables', the Government Statistician distinguishes two classes of accuracy for the Northern Provinces:

Class 1. The Intensive Census data of the Northern Provinces, with an accuracy approximating, and in some cases attaining to, that of the Census of India, that is, with errors in the neighbourhood of 1 or 2 per cent.

Class 2. The General Census data of the Northern Provinces, with an error of 5 per cent or less.[1]

He explains the estimate for Class 2 as follows:

For the part of the Northern Provinces included in the General Census the figures are probably mostly within 5 per cent of the truth, as is shown by the correspondence between the Intensive Census figures and the Native Administration counts in the forty-one special villages throughout the different Provinces, the latter taken, for the most part, six months before the Census. The increase shown by the Intensive Census count is, in fact, only 3·4 per cent. As there is an increase of about 0·5 per cent of population every six months, the error of the General Census count, if the Intensive Census figures are accepted as very close to the truth, may even be less than 3 per cent in error. This is possibly too favourable a view, and taking a 5 per cent additive correction as an upper limit of error, we may say that the Northern Provinces' population probably lies between 11,435,000[2] and 12,000,000 persons.[3]

He then shows the discrepancies between 'the Native Administration Counts (Autumn, 1930) and Census Counts (April, 1931)'.

Area	N. A. Count 1930	Census 1930	Difference	Percentage on N. A. Count
6 Katsina Districts	240,077	248,434	+8,357	+3·5
16 Katsina Villages	55,832	59,628	+3,796	+6·8
41 Special Villages	95,090	99,328	+4,238	+4·5
Townships.	25,334	28,948	+3,614	+14·3

The discrepancy in the Townships is large, due to the special difficulties of counting a population where everyone is not known to his neighbours, and to the ebb and flow of a fluid population, difficulties which were very marked even in the fairly systematic Census of Lagos, where 10 per cent of omission was discovered by check counts.[4]

Finally he makes the following estimate:

'Northern Provinces Census count 11,435,000
Add 3 per cent for omissions . . . . . 343,000 '[1]
                                         (11,778,000)

[1] *Census of Nigeria, 1931*, vol. i, p. 23.

The Government Statistician certainly underestimated very much the margin of error in the returns of both the Intensive and the General Censuses.

(a) The standard of literacy of the enumerators who took the Intensive Censuses was low and differed considerably in the various areas. They were employed, as a rule, for six or eight weeks, under little supervision,[5]

[1] *Census of Nigeria, 1931*, vol. i, p. 6.   [2] Persons enumerated 11,434,924.
[3] Ibid., pp. 4–5.   [4] Ibid., p. 5.
[5] While supervision by Europeans seems very desirable, enumeration by Government staff is not necessarily more effective than enumeration by Native Authorities. See in this connexion the Reassessment Report on Dan Zomo District by the Assistant District Officer (1932),

and received as total remuneration one pound without any incentive to work conscientiously. Large distances had often to be covered between households in scattered village areas. In the Katsina Emirate which comprised 70 per cent. of the population included in the Intensive Censuses the enumerators started their work towards the middle of March and completed it apparently on 23 April. The report says that 'the schedules were revised by the enumerators on the census date (23rd April)'. They may have been instructed to do so, but it is obvious that this was physically impossible. No such revision was attempted in the special village areas where the census was spread over two months and where the returns suffered particularly owing to the lack of adequate supervision. As regards Townships the special difficulties prevailing there were pointed out by the Government Statistician. The uncertainty of the returns may be inferred from the following summary:

Source	Jos	Kaduna	Kano	Lokoja	Zaria	Total
Township Census 1921[1] .	720	5,438	4,670	2,099	3,791	16,718
Latest Assessment before 1931 Census[2] . .	1,399	9,893	6,681	1,397	5,964	25,334
Intensive Census 1931[2] .	2,467	10,628	7,643	2,122	6,088	28,948

[1] See Meek, vol. ii, p. 178.   [2] See *Census of Nigeria, 1931*, vol. ii, p. 199.

It is, therefore, out of the question, it seems to me, to put the error in the Intensive Census figures at less than ±5 per cent.

(b) As regards the General Census the Government Statistician based his estimate of the margin of error on 'the correspondence between the Intensive Census figures and the Native Administration counts in the forty-one special villages throughout the different Provinces'. The former were 4·5 per cent. higher than the latter.[1] But as the Intensive Census was particularly defective in these villages, the error in the General Census figures (Native Administration count) of these villages may have been very large. In the Katsina Emirate, where the Intensive Census was apparently more accurate, the returns exceeded those of the General Census by 4·1 per cent., but the excess would have been greater if there had not been a temporary emigration.

In the figures for the Intensive Census in Katsina (308,000), there is an increase of more than 12,000 over the 1930 Native Administration count. This increase is a substantial one when the fact is taken into account that the Masu-chin rani (temporary emigrants during the dry season) had not all returned to their homes before the census date, and were not enumerated in the Intensive Census, but had been included in the Native Administration count.[2]

p. 5: 'The census and work of assessment were carried out between April 15th and May 30th during which time the Emir of Gumel visited the district and inspected the work of the District Headman. I was in the district for twenty-five days between those two dates. I tested the work of the District Headman in several hamlets by recounting with Government staff but very soon abandoned this as any discrepancies between the messengers' and the District Headman's count were invariably explained in favour of the Native Administration owing to their greater knowledge of the people dealt with.'

[1] The Government Statistician assumes erroneously that the difference is only 3·4 per cent.
[2] *Census of Nigeria, 1931*, vol. ii, p. 20.

The figures of the General Census were derived mainly from existing tax records.[1] Complete new counts were made in the Niger and Ilorin Provinces which comprise 9 per cent. of the total native population. Partial new counts were apparently made in some other Provinces, but no new count was made, for example, in the Kano Emirate (except Kano City) and Bornu Division with 24 per cent. of the total native population.[2] The new counts were, of course, not enumerations of individuals like the Intensive Censuses, but the figures so obtained were more up to date than the tax records.[3] A comparison of the totals ascertained at Native Administration counts and the Intensive Censuses in the 41 special villages yields the following results:[4]

Census	Adamawa	Bauchi	Benue	Bornu	Ilorin	Kabba	Kano Emirate
General .	5,933	6,900	14,535	2,002	2,369	6,123	9,558
Intensive .	5,296	7,132	15,462	1,732	2,295	5,273	11,524
Difference .	−637	+232	+927	−270	−74	−850	+1,966
Per cent. .	−10·7	+3·4	+6·4	−13·5	−3·1	−13·9	+20·6

Census	Kano Northern	Niger	Plateau	Sokoto	Zaria	Total
General . .	7,691	12,202	15,307	8,859	3,611	95,090
Intensive .	8,174	12,454	18,459	8,037	3,490	99,328
Difference .	+483	+252	+3,152	−822	−121	+4,238
Per cent. .	+6·3	+2·1	+20·6	−9·3	−3·4	+4·5

[1] The Government Statistician says (*Census of Nigeria, 1931*, vol. i, p. 5): 'A comparison of the recent Assessment counts also gives confidence in the General Census figures for the Northern Provinces. The recorded population . . . is as follows:—

Year	(000's omitted)	*Increase*	Year	(000's omitted)	*Increase*
1926 . .	10,233	217	1929 . .	11,047	235
1927 . .	10,450	333	1930 . .	11,282	153
1928 . .	10,783	264	1931 . .	11,435	—

'All the increases shown in the third column are annual except the last, which covers the six months period from October, 1930, to April, 1931, and is, thus, fairly consistent with the previous annual changes.'

I shall discuss the results of the Assessment counts in the section 'Total Population'. At this place it is necessary only to point out that the harmony between the General Census figures and the Assessment data is due to the fact that they are both derived from the tax records.

[2] The similarity, in many Provinces, of the 1931 census returns and the 1930 assessment counts (see Table 5 below) suggests that the part played by new counts was, on the whole, only small.

[3] The new count in Niger Province showed an increase from 456,683 (assessment count 1930) to 472,959, the new count in Ilorin Province an increase from 511,890 to 537,487. It should be noted, however, that in the following years the official population figures for these two Provinces again declined; see Table 3.

In Kano City the new count was apparently made independently of the tax records. The Census Officer, Northern Provinces, reports (ibid., vol. ii, p. 23): 'For Kano City a decennial census was taken during February and March, and completed in April, 1931. It was closely supervised by Europeans, and infinite care was taken to ensure accuracy.' The results of this new count and of the Native Administration Count 1929–30 were as follows:

	Adults		Non-Adults		
	Male	Female	Male	Female	Total
Census 1931 . .	28,082	33,260	14,751	13,069	89,162
Count 1929–30 . .	16,840	20,534	7,871	5,720	50,965

[4] See ibid., pp. 197–8.

It appears that in the Ilorin and Niger Provinces, where complete new counts had been made, the differences between the Intensive and the General Censuses (−3·1 and +2·1 per cent.) were smaller than in any other Province while in Bornu (−13·5) and Kano Emirate (+20·6) where no new counts were made the differences were particularly great. The Resident of Kano 'had no reason to think that the result [derived for the Emirate from available records of men, women, and children] was other than a fairly close approximation of the true total', but the scanty data from selected villages certainly do not support this view. In these Kano villages the records of females seem to have been particularly defective since the General Census showed 5,091 males, 3,260 women, and 1,207 girls, while the Intensive Census yielded 5,423 males, 4,016 women, and 2,084 girls. But in this respect these villages did not constitute exceptions, and there cannot be any doubt that in general the figures for females, so far as they were taken from available records, lagged considerably behind the truth.

As direct taxation in Nigeria is largely and in most units based on the number of adult males, with the occasional inclusion of adult females, the Administration devotes much greater care to obtain a correct tally of the number of adult males than of any other section of the community.[1]

It would be wrong, however, to conclude therefrom that the General census figures concerning women and children were, on the whole, more defective than those for men. I shall confine myself to confronting here the results of the General and the Intensive Censuses in the six Katsina Districts where the Intensive Census was in the personal charge of the Assistant Census Officer and therefore probably more accurate than elsewhere.

Census	Men	Women	Children	Total
General, Actual figures . .	51,181	70,599	118,297	240,077
General, Revised figures[1] .	53,197	70,599	116,281	240,077
Intensive	64,590	73,680	110,019	248,434[2]

[1] Allowing for the difference in the age of adolescence of 16 years at the General Census instead of 15 years at the Intensive Census (see *Census of Nigeria, 1931*, vol. ii, p. 34).
[2] Including Unspecified as to age.

It appears that the Intensive Census showed 21 per cent. more men, 4 per cent. more women, and 5 per cent. fewer children than the General Census. It would be unwise to generalize for the whole the results found for these six Districts, but I may be permitted perhaps to draw, quite tentatively, the following conclusions regarding the probable error in the General Census returns:

(1) The existing records of adult males are more or less unreliable and as most General Census figures of adult males are taken from such records these figures are likewise unreliable. They are, on the whole, probably too low.

[1] Ibid., vol. i, p. 20.

(2) The existing records of adult females and of children are still more unreliable than those of men, and in so far as the General Census figures of women and children are taken from such records they are, on the whole, probably much too low. But (fortunately) there are not many such records, and in the majority of cases the figures of women and children have been obtained by estimate or guessing.

(3) The Government Statistician thinks that 'the Northern Provinces' population probably lies between 11,435,000 and 12,000,000 persons'. I do not think that one can say more than that it probably exceeded 10,500,000 and probably did not exceed 12,500,000.

As regards the cost of the 1931 census of Northern Nigeria the Census Officer reports:

> The cost of the Census in the Northern Provinces, exclusive of the printing of the report, has been about £3,000.[1] Of this amount £1,800 was expended exclusively on the Intensive Census. The cost of the General Census, administration and tabulation was, therefore, about the same as in 1921 (viz., £1,000), as allowances of staff employed on Census work were charged against the Census vote.[2]

The actual cost of taking the General Census and tabulating the results was between 2s. and 3s. for each 1,000 enumerated persons. The corresponding cost for the Intensive Census was about £4.

4. Nigeria and Cameroons

I have so far discussed separately census-taking in Lagos, in the Southern Provinces, and in the Northern Provinces. I shall now summarize the position at the 1931 census adding some details referring to Nigeria as a whole (including the Cameroons).

The census was taken in accordance with the following Ordinance:[3]

1. This Ordinance may be cited as the Census Ordinance.
2. The Governor may by Order in Council direct a census to be taken of the inhabitants of Nigeria or of any part thereof specified in such Order at such time or times as he may think fit.
3. The Governor may appoint a superintendent of any census directed to be taken, who, subject to the control of the Governor, shall have the general supervision and management of the census and, subject to the approval of the Governor, shall appoint such enumerators and officers as may be necessary for the purpose of the census and the carrying into effect of this Ordinance.
4. The superintendent shall cause to be prepared and printed, for the use of the persons to be employed in taking the census, such forms and instructions as he may deem necessary, and in particular schedules to be filled up with such particulars as the Governor may consider necessary in order to insure as far as possible the completeness and accuracy of the census returns.
5. The occupier or person in charge of any premises shall fill up or cause to be filled up any schedule, left at such premises, to the best of his knowledge and belief in relation to all persons dwelling or being on the premises at the time when such

---

[1] According to the Government Statistician (see *Census of Nigeria, 1931,* vol. i, p. 91) the cost was £3,591, including £308 for the printing of the report.

[2] Ibid., vol. ii, p. 13.

[3] No. 54 of 1917 (25 Oct.), 'An Ordinance to make provision for taking the Census of Nigeria as and when may be required', *The Nigeria Gazette,* 25 Oct. 1917, Supplement; reprinted in *Laws of Nigeria in Force 1923,* vol. ii, pp. 1604–5.

Census is taken, and shall sign his name thereto and shall deliver the schedule so filled up to the enumerator when required to do so: Provided always that when any person required to fill up such schedule is illiterate, such schedule may be filled up and signed by the enumerator.

The term 'premises' in this section includes also any vessel or train, and any plantation, mining area or other place where persons are employed.

6. The enumerators and other persons employed in the execution of this Ordinance shall have authority to ask of all persons presumably able to afford the information desired all such questions as may be necessary for obtaining any of the particulars required by this Ordinance, and every person refusing to answer, or knowingly giving a false answer to, any such question shall for every such refusal or false answer be liable to a fine of five pounds.

7. Every person who—

(a) Wilfully refuses or without lawful excuse neglects to fill up and sign any schedule of particulars as and when he may be required by the superintendent of the census or any officer acting on his behalf so to do ;

or

(b) Wilfully fills up or signs any such schedule with particulars which he knows to be false, or does not believe to be true,

shall be liable to a fine of five pounds.

8. Upon the completion of any census the superintendent shall cause an abstract of the returns to be made, and furnished to the Governor.

9. The Governor may make regulations for the carrying out of this Ordinance.

The original scheme for the 1931 census, sanctioned on 1 February 1930, provided for an all-inclusive census, but this scheme 'was modified on the 12th April, 1930, under the Governor's orders, so as to exclude the Southern Provinces as a whole from Census-taking'.[1] The Order in Council authorizing the 1931 census[2] had then a very limited scope:

Direction for Census to be taken under section 2 of the Census Ordinance.

The Governor-in-Council is pleased to direct a census to be taken of the inhabitants of the Township of Lagos and of the Northern Provinces (including those parts of the Cameroons under British Mandate which are administered therewith) between the 10th day of March, 1931, and the 10th day of May, 1931.

In fact, however, an enumeration of natives was carried out only in five Townships and 201 villages of the Northern Provinces (and in Lagos).[3] For 96 per cent. of the native population of the Northern Provinces, as for 98·6 per cent. of the native population of the Southern Provinces, figures were obtained mainly from existing records, though greater efforts were made in the Northern Provinces to bring these data up to date.

The census returns showed 8,493,247 people in the Southern Provinces (including the Colony) and 11,434,924 people in the Northern Provinces, or 19,928,171 in the whole of Nigeria (including the Mandated Territory). The Government Statistician thought that the census returns understated the population considerably in the Southern Provinces and slightly in the Northern Provinces. After having added 711,000 to the 3,607,000 persons

[1] *Census of Nigeria, 1931*, vol. i, p. 2.

[2] Order No. 5 of 1931 (5 Mar.), reprinted in *1933 Supplement to the Laws of Nigeria*, p. 1322.

[3] The Intensive Censuses covered in addition the households of Non-Natives and Educated Native Foreigners in the Northern Provinces and the Non-Natives in the Southern Provinces (altogether about 10,000 people).

returned in the Eastern of the Southern Provinces, where he believed that omissions had been particularly great, he said:

I, therefore, estimate provisionally the population of Nigeria in 1931 as 22,000,000, made up as follows:—

Southern Provinces population, on Western Provinces standard	9,204,000
Add 10 per cent for omissions	920,000
Northern Provinces Census count	11,435,000
Add 3 per cent for omissions	343,000
Estimated population of Nigeria	21,902,000

This estimate is more likely to err in defect than in excess.[1]

The Government Statistician was certainly right in assuming that in many cases the population had been underestimated, but he did, it seems to me, not take sufficiently into account that in numerous other cases it must have been overstated. It is, of course, extremely difficult to estimate the errors in returns which in a large measure are based on guesses. All one can safely say, I think, is that the population of Nigeria in 1931 was probably not under 18,500,000 and not over 22,000,000.

The Administrative (General and Intensive) Censuses of 1931 were supplemented by Medical Censuses. These sample surveys were made in the Northern Provinces between 1 May 1930 and 30 January 1931 and in the Southern Provinces between 2 July 1930 and 22 January 1932. The numbers of examined persons were 9,491 and 11,023 respectively.[2]

The cost of the 1931 Administrative Censuses was nearly £5,600 (as against £9,457 in 1921), and that of the Medical Censuses nearly £2,000. These totals include the cost of printing the census reports (£730 and £334 respectively), but exclude payments on account of salaries and passages of the Government Statistician and the Census Officers.[3] Excluding the expenditure for printing the reports the cost of the Administrative Censuses was about 2s. per 1,000 returned persons and the cost of the Intensive Censuses about £4. Assuming that the cost of an actual enumeration (Intensive Census) of the total population of Nigeria would have been proportionately the same, such enumeration would have involved an expenditure of about £80,000.[4]

II. Total Population

1. Lagos

The Blue Book for 1863, the first year after the creation of the Colony, said as regards 'Population':

No Census having been taken the information required by this return cannot be furnished.[5]

---

[1] Census of Nigeria, 1931, vol. i, p. 23. [2] See ibid., vols. v and vi.

[3] See ibid., vol. i, pp. 91-2. The Census Officer for the Northern Provinces went to England with the General Census forms and the Intensive Census data which had been prepared for mechanical tabulation by the Hollerith system; see ibid., vol. i, p. 3, vol. ii, pp. 6-7, 9-10.

[4] This was the amount spent in the Union of South Africa at the 1936 census for a population half as large as that of Nigeria.

[5] Lagos, Blue Book 1863, p. 226. For estimates of the population of Lagos Town prior to the British occupation see the quotations from Burns and Talbot in Census of Nigeria, 1931, vol. i, pp. 62-3.

Governor Freeman, in a report dated 4 July 1864, made the following comment:

No calculation has been made in the Blue Book of the population of the territory, as there are no official data to go upon. I think, however, the following is not very far out:—

Lagos	40,000
Badagry	5,000
Villages between Lagos and Badagry . .	3,000
Palma District	2,000
Villages between Lagos and Palma . .	2,000

This calculation is rather under than above the mark, and does not include the inhabitants of Okeodan and Addo.[1]

This estimate covered the whole Colony but excluded the Protected areas.

The census of 1866 showed a population of 25,083.[2] The figure suggests that it refers to the Town of Lagos only. The census taken in 'Lagos and its Vicinity' in 1868 and the estimates made for the adjoining Districts in 1867–70 yielded the following results:[3]

Area	1867[1]	1868	1869	1870
Lagos	35,000	} 41,236	41,236	41,236
Villages in the Vicinity of Lagos . .	10,000			
Eastern District	25,000	25,000	25,000	25,000
Western District	25,000	25,000	25,000	25,000
Villages bordering on the Northern Frontier of the Settlement . .	15,000	25,000[2]	15,000	50,000
Total Settlement	110,000	116,236	106,236	141,236

[1] See also *State of Colonial Possessions 1867*, Part II, p. 22: 'The inhabitants of the town and island of Lagos amount to 35,000, and the roughly estimated number of the rural population being about 75,000.'   [2] Northern District.

The figures probably included not only the 'Protected' territories, but also what may be called the 'sphere of influence'.[4]

[1] *State of Colonial Possessions 1863*, Part II, pp. 41–2.
[2] See Lagos, *Blue Book 1866*, p. 228.
[3] See ibid. *1867*, p. 174; *1868*, p. 160; *1869*, p. 206; *1870*, p. 230.
[4] It is extremely difficult to define the area under British control in the nineteenth century. On 13 Mar. 1862, when British sovereignty in that part of Africa extended only over a few square miles, a Commission was passed under the Great Seal of the United Kingdom declaring that the Port and Island of Lagos, together with all the territories which do now or may hereafter belong to the Crown of Great Britain on the coast of Africa, between the 1st and 10th parallels of east longitude, and the south of the 10th parallel of north latitude, shall constitute a separate government, under the title of the Settlements of Lagos. The area thus described covered about 200,000 square miles and comprised what became later Southern Nigeria and portions of Northern Nigeria, German Cameroons, and French West Africa. In the Letters Patent of 24 July 1874, by which Lagos became an integral part of the Gold Coast Colony, the Settlement of Lagos was defined to comprise (only) all places, settlements, and territories which may at any time belong to Her Majesty in Western Africa between the 2nd and 5th degrees of east longitude. But the actual situation was then described as follows: 'The British settlements are—Badagry on the west, Lagos Island in the centre, and Palma and Leckie on the east. Sovereignty is virtually exercised over the intervening sea board; and the adjacent country, as far as we are related with the tribes by treaty, is vaguely said to be a Protectorate, but there is no regular authority exercised inland, as at the Gold Coast' (*Colonial Office List 1875*, p. 58). The area of 'Lagos' was given in *Colonial Office List* 1876–84 (see p. 18 of each issue) as 25 square miles. But in *Statistical*

The census returns for 1871–91 may be summarized as follows:

Area	1871[1]	1881[2]	1891[3]
Lagos Town . . .	28,518	37,452	32,508[4]
Vicinity of Lagos . .	7,487	15,944	21,808[5]
Northern District . .	12,401	9,563	
Eastern District . .	4,014	4,519	9,346
Western District . .	7,801	7,792	21,945
Total	60,221	75,270	85,607

[1] See Lagos, *Blue Book 1872*, p. 100; Lagos, *Census Report 1881*, Enclosure No. 3, p. 2. In *Blue Book 1871*, p. 228, the population of the Eastern District had been given as 5,814 and the total population as 62,021. The latter figure was also given in *Statistical Tables, Colonial Possessions 1868–70*, p. 364, as the 'Total Population according to the Census Return of 1871'. Owing probably to the fact that the revised figure 60,221 (which was already shown in the Governor's report for 1871; see *Colonial Possessions, Reports 1873*, Part II, 2nd Division, p. 41) appeared in the *Blue Book* for 1872, it was erroneously given in *Statistical Tables, Colonial Possessions 1876–8*, p. 309 (and also in later years), as 'Total Population according to the Census of 1872'. Talbot, vol. iv, p. 176, gives erroneously 4,014 for the Western District and 7,801 for the Eastern District. *Colonial Office List* never gave the revised figure of 60,221, but reproduced in the Text (*1874*, p. 136; *1875*, p. 58; *1876*, p. 63; *1877*, p. 69; *1878*, p. 71; *1879*, p. 75; *1880*, p. 77; *1881*, p. 80) the figure of 62,021 and gave in the 'General Statistics' either 52,051 (ibid., *1876*, p. 18; *1877*, p. 18) or 54,051 (*1878*, p. 18; *1879*, p. 18; *1880*, p. 18; *1881*, p. 18), figures for which I have no explanation.

[2] See Lagos, *Census Report 1881*, p. 2.   [3] See ibid., *1891*, p. 13.
[4] Including 276 on Ships.   [5] Central District (exclusive of Lagos Town).

Tables, Colonial Possessions 1876–78 (p. 309) and *1879–81* (p. 359) it was given as 73 square miles, and this figure appears also in *Colonial Office List 1885* (p. 18). It is possible that the figure of 25 square miles referred to the Colony only, and it is probable that the area of 73 square miles comprised portions of the Protectorate, but it evidently excluded the territories for which protectorate treaties had been concluded since 1878 (1879 Ketonu; 1884 Appa, Jakri, and Ogbo; 1885 Mahin). In Lagos *Blue Book* 1885–90 (see *1885*, p. 40; *1886*, p. 36; *1887*, p. 38; *1888*, p. 40; *1889*, p. 42; *1890*, p. 48) and in *Colonial Office List* 1886–92 (see *1886*, pp. 18, 116; *1887*, pp. 18, 141; *1888*, pp. 16, 143; *1889*, Table p. 18, and p. 144; *1890*, Table p. 18, and p. 145; *1891*, Table p. 18, and p. 150; *1892*, Table p. 18, and p. 132) the area of 'Lagos and its Protectorate' is given as 1,071 or 1,071½ square miles. This apparently was the area of the Colony and Protectorate after the conclusion of the treaties concerning Mahin (24 Oct. 1885) until the conclusion of the treaty concerning Igbessa (15 May 1888). According to the *Blue Books* it was composed as follows:

Central District

1 Lagos Island	3¾	
2 Iddo or Bruce Island	1	
3 Curamo Island from Beach Light Station to Magbon, near Leckie. . .	279	
4 Awore Protection on the Ebute Metta Mainland from Badagry Point to Woro and interior thereof	230	
		513¾

Eastern District

5 Palma and Leckie from Magbon to Shirinwon, near Leckie	63	
6 Ode Beach from Shirinwon to Ode Beach	86¾	
7 Mahin Beach from Ode Creek to Benin River	150	
		299¾

Western District

8 Badagry	108	
9 Ketonu	88	
10 Appah	62	
		258
		1,071½

The Colony consisted of small portions of each of the three Districts.

Ketonu (88 square miles) was exchanged for the Kingdom of Pokra by the Arrangement concerning the Delimitation of the English and French Possessions on the West Coast of Africa of

The censuses of 1871 and 1881 covered evidently a smaller area than the estimates for 1867–70, although the area of British sovereignty had hardly changed in the meantime.[1] I am inclined to think that the census area in 1881 was practically the same as in 1871 and that it comprised the Colony and (small) portions of the Protectorate.[2] In 1891 the census area was larger. It covered 'the Colony and Protectorate of Lagos, except so much thereof as lies to the east of the meridian of Ode'. The table in *Statistical Tables, British Colonies 1888–90*, which shows the census returns and gives as area 985 square miles, is accompanied by the following Note:

The area is exclusive of the Jebu territory of about 255 square miles, and of the territories of Pokra, Addo, Ilaro, and Igbessa, of which the area is unknown. The

10 Aug. 1889, and this cession of Ketonu caused a good deal of confusion in the statements regarding the area of Lagos and its Protectorate. It was still given as 1,071 square miles in *Colonial Office Lists* 1893-6 in the 'General Statistics' (following p. 18), but was given as 983 square miles (i.e. excluding Ketonu) in the Text of the 1893 issue (p. 136) while the *Blue Books* for 1891-3 gave as area on one and the same page (*1891*, p. 48; *1892*, p. 52; *1893*, p. 54) both 1,071½ and 984½ square miles. This area, moreover, excluded the kingdom of Pokra, the kingdoms of Addo, Ilaro, and Igbessa, acquired in 1888–91, and the Jebu territory, portions of which, aggregating 255 square miles, were incorporated in 1892 and 1894 in the Colony. Evidently by adding these 255 square miles to the area of 1885-8 minus Ketonu the area of Lagos and its Protectorate was given as 1,239 square miles in *Colonial Office List 1894*, Text (p. 138), in *Colonial Office List* 1897–1902, 'General Statistics', and in *Blue Book 1894*, p. 54, *1895*, p. 58, *1896*, p. 62, *1897*, p. 58, *1898*, p. 62, *1899*, p. 69, *1900* p.67 (though the figure of 983½ also appears 1894-7, ibid.). In *Colonial Office List* 1895–1901, Text (*1895*, p. 139; *1896*, p. 142; *1897*, p. 143; *1898*, p. 144; *1899*, p. 161; *1900*, p. 133; *1901*, p. 193) some further account was taken of the extension of the Protectorate by stating: 'the whole Colony and Protectorate probably includes about 1,500 square miles', but this figure understated considerably the actual area, even in 1895, and very much more so after Yoruba (with over 20,000 square miles) had been included in the Protectorate (1899). *Colonial Office Lists* 1902–4, Text (*1902*, p. 202; *1903*, p. 214; *1904*, p. 218) reported: 'Lagos Island has an area of 3¾ square miles, and the whole Colony about 3,420 square miles, and the Colony and Protectorate about 26,700 square miles.' The *Blue Books* for 1904 (p. 78) and 1905 (p. 82) said: 'The area of the Island of Lagos is 3¾ square miles. The area of the districts and Protectorate is unknown, but is estimated at 28,910 square miles.' *Colonial Office List 1905* (Text, p. 222) and *1906* (Text, p. 229) gave 3,420 for the Colony and 24,500 for the Colony and Protectorate, but they evidently meant to say that the area of the Protectorate alone was 24,500 square miles. In *Report on Southern Nigeria Census, 1911*, p. 2, the area of the Western Province which coincided with the former Colony and Protectorate of Lagos was given as 28,600 square miles.

[1] The only change that seems to have occurred in the area of the Colony and Protectorate between 1867 and 1881 was the extension of the Protectorate over Ketonu in 1879. But Ketonu, which according to a Dispatch of Sir Samuel Rowe, Governor of the Gold Coast, to the Earl of Derby, dated 31 May 1883, had a population of 11,895, was not included in the Lagos census of 1881; see Gold Coast, *Census 1883*, pp. 5–6. As Ketonu was transferred in 1890 to France, it was likewise excluded from the Lagos census of 1891.

[2] Talbot (vol. iv, p. 176) suggests that the totals of 60,221 (1871) and 75,270 (1881) referred to the Colony only. The Acting Assistant Colonial Secretary said in 1878 that 'if the neighbouring population under British protection be taken into account, the total population is supposed to be about 60,000' (*Colonial Possessions Reports 1876–7*, p. 135). The 'Report upon the Blue Book of the Gold Coast Colony (including Lagos) for the year 1885' states that the population of 'Lagos and its protectorate' had been estimated at 75,270 (see ibid. *1884–6*, pp. 124–5). The last statement is certainly not correct, but it seems probable that the census included, apart from the Colony, the *neighbouring* population under British protection.—The data given in *Colonial Office Lists* are somewhat confusing. The 'Population of Settlement' in 1871 is given *1873*, p. 137, as 31,988 (i.e. the total for the towns of Lagos, Badagry, Palma, and Leckie), and *1874*, p. 136, as 62,021 (i.e. the total for the whole census area). List *1885*, p. 89, gives for 'Lagos Island, 1881', 53,396 (the total for Lagos Island and mainland Vicinity), and for 'Protectorate, 1881', 21,874; *1886*, p. 116, shows correctly 'Lagos Island, 1881', 37,452, 'Vicinity and Protectorate, 1881', 37,818, while *1887*, p. 141, gives as 'population of Lagos Island' in 1881, 37,452 and as 'population of the Protectorate, as then defined,' 37,818.

population given in the Table is exclusive of the inhabitants of the above-mentioned territories.[1]

The total area of the Colony and Protectorate, excluding those territories, may in fact have covered about 985 square miles and the census returns no doubt excluded Adda, Ilaro, Igbessa, and Jebu,[2] but they excluded also all the territories east of the meridian of Ode (Jakri, Ogbo, and Mahin). Pokra, on the other hand, which was acquired in 1890, was actually included in the census.[3] In any case the census area was much smaller than 985 square miles since it excluded the major part of the Eastern District. By how much it exceeded the census area of 1881 it is impossible to tell.[4]

In 1901 the census was confined to the Town and Harbour of Lagos (39,387)[5] and Ebute Metta (2,460). But the Superintendent gave the following estimate of the population in the whole Colony and Protectorate:

Western District	60,000
Eastern District	132,000
Central District . . .	30,000
Ikorodu & Shagamu District .	65,000
Province of Ibadan & Oyo . .	610,000
Province of Ode-Ondo . .	150,000
Province of Ilesha . .	300,000
	1,347,000
Town and Harbour of Lagos and Ebute-Metta	41,847
Total	1,388,847

Allowing for over-estimating which I think is more probable than under-estimating; the population of the Colony and the Protectorate as defined by Order-in-Council, July 24, 1901, may be put down at 1¼ millions.

No comparison is possible between the Eastern and Western Districts in 1891 and 1901 as the boundaries have been much extended.[6]

But the population of the Colony and Protectorate had evidently been underestimated in 1901. For 1906 it was put at 3,000,000.[7] In the census report for Southern Nigeria 1911, it was returned as 2,152,848.[8]

---

[1] *Statistical Tables, British Colonies 1888-90*, p. 356.

[2] Adda, Ilaro, and Igbessa were definitely included in the Protectorate only in Aug. 1891 (four months after the Census) and Jebu was acquired in 1892-4. See also *Colonial Office List 1892*, p. 132: 'The population of the recently acquired territories of Addo and Llaso is estimated at 25,000.'

[3] In discussing the completeness of the census, the Commissioner for the Western District estimated 'that in Pokra 5 per cent. at least are omitted'. See also *Colonial Reports, Lagos 1891*, p. 47: 'The area of these territories [the kingdoms of Pokra, Addo, Ilaro, and Igbessa] is as yet imperfectly known, and the population has been computed for the kingdom of Pokra alone.'

[4] The largest extension probably occurred in the Western District owing to the inclusion of Appa and Pokra in the 1891 census. In 1871 and 1881 the population of this District had been returned as 7,801 and 7,792 respectively. For 1886 it was given as 23,678 (Badagry 12,068, Kotonu 8,355, Appa 3,255); see *Reports on the Resources of the Western District*, p. 18. The 1891 census returns which excluded Kotonu but included Pokra showed a population of 21,945 (including Appa with 2,153 inhabitants; see Lagos, *Census Report 1891*, p. 12).

It should be noted moreover that there are still other factors which hamper the comparability of the 1891 returns with those of former censuses. In 1871, and probably also in 1881, the towns of Leckie, Palma, and Badagry were included in the 'Vicinity of Lagos'. In 1891 Leckie and Palma were included in the Eastern District, and Badagry in the Western District.

[5] Including 420 on ships in harbour.   [6] *Census of Lagos 1901*, p. 1.

[7] See *Colonial Reports, Southern Nigeria 1906*, p. 56.

[8] See *Report on Southern Nigeria Census, 1911*, p. 2.

For the Municipal Area of Lagos the results of the censuses of 1911, 1921, and 1931 may be summarized as follows:[1]

Area	Square miles 1931	Population 1911	1921	1931
Lagos Town	1·70	56,653	77,561	90,193
Ebute Metta with outskirts and Yaba .	10·13	10,758	13,938	23,648
Ikoyi	3·53	1,749	1,276	3,953
Victoria Beach	4·00	793	955	1,082
Iddo Island	0·39	456	827	640[1]
Apapa	3·40	931	1,058	2,251
Lighthouse Creek	1·09	—	—	206
Steamers	—	1,067	1,334	774
Waterside Canoes	—	1,359	1,387	1,986
Trains	—	—	—	393
Roads	—	—	1,354	982
Total	24·24	73,766	99,690	126,108

[1] 'The decrease in the population of Iddo Island is due to the removal of Ijora Village from Iddo to Apapa' (Census of Nigeria, 1931, vol. iv, p. 13).

Prior to 1905 no systematic attempt had been made to estimate the population of Lagos for intercensal years. But the need of up-to-date population figures for computing birth- and death-rates finally induced the Governor to seek a remedy, and he directed in a Memorandum of 30 June 1905 that the yearly increase of the Town of Lagos since the census of 1901 should be assumed to be equal to the average yearly increase between 1891 and 1901, i.e. 687.[2] In accordance with these instructions the population was put for 1906 at 42,822, while the population of Ebute Metta was assumed to have remained at 2,460. In the meantime, however, a Vaccination Census had been taken in 1905[3] which showed a population of 48,467 for Lagos and 5,356 for Ebute Metta.[4] The appearance of these greatly diverging figures created much confusion. In his report for 1907 the Registrar of Vital Statistics said:[5]

By the Census of 1901, the Population of the Town (and Harbour of Lagos) was 39,387; plus average increase of 687 per annum for 6 years (4,122) as obtained during the decade 1891–1901, (calculated on that basis as directed by His Excellency the Governor in his Memo of 30.6.1905), the population for 1907—43,509.

By Vaccination Census of 1905 . . . it was found that the population was actually 50,551;[6] plus estimated increase, calculated on an average increase of 21½ per cent per annum,[7] the population for 1907 was 50,551 or with Ebute Metta Suburb—57,058.[8]

In the following year the Registrar of Vital Statistics computed the population of Lagos, according to the instructions of the Governor, at 44,196 and added:[9]

By Vaccination Census of 1905 . . . it was found that the population was actually 50,551; plus estimated increase, 687 p.a. calculated on an average increase of 21·16

[1] See Census of Nigeria, 1931, vol. iv, Census Map and p. 7.
[2] See Lagos, Blue Book 1905, p. 82.   [3] See Lagos, Medical Report 1904, p. 9.
[4] See Southern Nigeria, 'Medical Report 1906', pp. 288, 290.
[5] Southern Nigeria, Medical Report 1907, p. 17.
[6] Should read 48,467.   [7] Should read 'per decade'.
[8] Instead of adding 2 × 21½ per 1,000 as in the case of Lagos, the Registrar added, probably by mistake, 21½ per 100 for Ebute Metta.   [9] Ibid. 1908, p. 15.

per cent. per decade, the population for 1908 was 52,612, or with Ebute Metta (6,722) = 59,334.[1]

In a Memorandum of 29 October 1909, the Governor, after having explained the motives for his earlier Memorandum,[2] said:

That was in 1905. In 1906 a 'vaccination census' was held, I do not remember this being brought to my notice. The result was to show that the increase assumed by me was less than the actual and had I been referred to again I should have directed the adoption of figures of the 'vaccination census' of 1906 with an annual addition based on that census until further more reliable data are available. I am of opinion that the population of Lagos cannot now be less than 65,000 and Ebute Metta 10,000.

Thus, the instructions of 1905 were cancelled, and the population for 1909 and 1910 was computed by adding each year both for Lagos and for Ebute Metta 687 to the 1908 population derived from the Vaccination Census.[3] But the 1911 census returns showed that the population had been still underestimated considerably, and for the following years the estimates were based, of course, on the results of the census. The estimates before and after the census (used for the computation of the official birth- and death-rates) may be summarized as follows:[4]

District	1909	1910	1911	1912	1913	1914
Lagos	53,299	53,986	61,000	61,000	64,096	64,096
Ebute Metta . .	7,417	8,104	12,000	12,000	12,609	12,609
Total . . .	60,716	62,090	73,000	73,000	76,705	76,705

District	1915	1916	1917	1918	1919	1920
Lagos	65,163	66,248	67,351	68,472	..	..
Ebute Metta . .	12,819	13,032	13,249	13,469	..	..
Total . . .	77,982	79,280	80,600	81,941	83,306	84,694

But the population had again been underestimated considerably, and on the basis of the 1921 census returns it was put for the computation of the 1921 birth- and death-rates at 98,625. The estimates for 1922–30 were 102,260, 104,530, 105,763, 109,076, 111,000, 114,500, 118,500, 122,000, and 122,000 respectively,[5] no separate figures being published for Lagos Town and Ebute Metta. These estimates were quite reconcilable with the 1931 census returns which showed a total population of 126,108. Since the census of 1931, however, the estimates have become quite chaotic.

As shown above, the Government Statistician thought that the population had been understated in 1931 and also at all earlier censuses. He

[1] Thus the Registrar added for Lagos to the population of 1907 (!) 3 × 687. The figure of 6,722 for Ebute Metta was apparently obtained by a not quite successful attempt to add 2 × 687 to the population figure ascertained at the Vaccination Census (5,356).
[2] See p. 658 below.   [3] See Southern Nigeria, *Medical Report 1909*, p. 41; *1910*, p. 13.
[4] See ibid. *1914*, p. 61; *Report on the Lagos Municipal Board of Health 1915*, p. 17, *1916*, p. 14; Lagos Town Council, *Report of Medical Officer of Health 1917*, p. 9, *1918*, p. 11; Nigeria, *Medical Report 1919–21*, p. 23. From 1915 on it was assumed that the yearly increase since the 1911 census had been 1/60.
[5] See ibid. *1924*, p. 11, *1925*, p. 12, *1926*, p. 17, *1927*, p. 20; Lagos Town Council, *Report of Medical Officer of Health 1928*, p. 15, *1929*, p. 14, *1930*, p. 25.

thereupon revised the figures published for 1927–30 and estimated the population for 1931–5 as follows:[1]

District	1927	1928	1929	1930	1931	1932	1933	1934	1935
Lagos . . .	95,000	96,000	97,000	98,000	99,000	100,000	110,000	113,000	120,000
Ebute Metta .	31,000	33,000	35,000	37,000	39,000	40,000	46,000	47,000	50,000
Lagos Township .	126,000	129,000	132,000	135,000	138,000	140,000	156,000	160,000	170,000

Dr. Cauchi, Medical Officer of Health, Lagos, in a special report, explained the enormous rise in the estimate for 1933 as follows:

In order to get some idea of the increase of population going on in Lagos, a simple census (or enumeration) was held in three small areas of the township in the early part of 1934, the Government Statistician kindly checking and reporting on the result of the count. It was found that by mid-year 1933 the population of Lagos Township had increased by 12·7 per cent over the figure obtained by the 1931 census, which was held in April and which then gave a population of 139,000.[2] Assuming that what occurred in the three areas chosen for enumeration in early 1934 represents what was happening in all parts of the township as far as population growth is concerned, we get the total of 157,000 as the population figure for mid-1933 for the whole township of Lagos.[3]

But the population of the three small areas enumerated in 1934 was only about 3,000.[4] In the following year, however, Dr. Cauchi made an enumeration on a somewhat larger scale.

[1] See ibid. *1931*, p. 19; *1935*, p. 21.

[2] It actually gave a population of only 126,108. The figure of 139,000 was obtained by the Government Statistician through the following argument: 'The present 1931 count needs an addition of probably 11% to allow for omissions, this figure having been arrived at by a series of checks made in the fortnight subsequent to the Census date' (quoted ibid. *1936*, p. 23). [3] Quoted ibid.

[4] See Letter of 27 Feb. 1934 from the Government Statistician to the Medical Officer of Health (*Report of the Lagos Town Council 1933*, pp. 44–5):

'There was good reason for supposing that there has been a considerable increase in the population of Lagos and Ebute Metta since 1931 and in the last eighteen months particularly, and this impression has been confirmed by the "Health" Census which was, with your consent, carried out by Sanitary Inspectors in January and February last. The checks I carried out showed that the work was, on the whole, well done, very few people escaping the count in Ebute Metta (Sub-division E.H.) and Sub-divisions A.I. and D.H. of Lagos Island. I found it impossible to check the count in Sub-division B.S. owing to pressure of other work.

'My checks showed that the omission in the health count was about two per cent, apart from Ebute Metta (E.H.), where I failed to discover a single omission, though test counts were made in several tenements.

'The comparison of the 1931 and 1934 populations is as follows:—

Area	Census 1931 (with 10% added for omissions)	Health Census, 1934 (with 2% added except in E.H.)	Increase
A.I. Blocks iv and v. . .	341	369	28
B.S.	1,037	1,273	236
D.H., Blocks ix, x, xii and xiii .	652	676	24
E.H.	970	1,168	198
Total	3,000	3,486	486

'Thus the population would have increased on this showing by 16·2%, that is since the Census of April, 1931.

'The increase to mid-1933, the year whose health we are considering is thus $\left(\dfrac{26}{33} \times 16\cdot 2\right) =$

For a similar count to be made . . . I have chosen seventeen areas so distributed over the township as, in my opinion, to constitute a fair sample of the whole.[1]

He commented on the results as follows:

There is every evidence that the population of the township is rapidly increasing owing to immigration from the interior. As a sample census, the population of seventeen selected small representative areas in the township was carefully counted by sanitary inspectors last April. The figure thus obtained for April 1935—an aggregate of 8,743 persons—compares with a figure of 6,887 recorded for the same set of blocks in the last census held in April, 1931. The difference represents an increase of 26·9 per cent in the population of the township over a period of forty-eight months, assuming that the areas chosen for the sample census are representative of the whole township.[2]

The Government Statistician seems to have had some misgiving about applying the increase of 26·9 per cent. in 48 months found in the seventeen selected areas to the whole of the Township and put the population for mid-year 1935 at 170,000, thus assuming an increase of 22·3 per cent. for the 50 months from April 1931 to mid-year 1935. But Dr. Cauchi thought that the population had increased by even more than 26·9 per cent. in the 50 months and that it exceeded 170,000 considerably.

Assuming our sampling to be representative of the whole community, the increase to mid-1935 is thus $\frac{50}{48} \times 26\cdot9 = 28\cdot0\%$ of the 1931 census figure. The Lagos population, therefore, which was 139,000 in April 1931, has apparently increased to 177,920 (or 178,000 in round figures) in mid-1935.

The figure 178,000 as representing the Lagos Township population in mid-1935 is a crude figure as no additions have been made for omissions.[3] There is every reason to believe that real population figure is higher, and there is no doubt that immigration is responsible for a considerable proportion of this very rapid increase.[4]

Dr. Cauchi was transferred in February 1936 to Kaduna as Senior Health Officer,[5] and shortly thereafter a new Deputy Director of Health Service was appointed for Nigeria. Commenting on the above findings of Dr. Cauchi and the Government Statistician he instructed the new Medical Officer of Health, Dr. Oluwole:

Whilst I am perfectly prepared to admit with Dr. Cauchi . . . that the tide of immigration—the strength of which cannot be gauged accurately until the 1941

12·7%, so that from 139,000 in 1931, the population apparently increased to 157,000 in mid-1933.

'The increase in population is, however, due more to female than to male increase, and I find approximately that males have increased by ten per cent and females by fifteen per cent between the date of the 1931 Census and mid-1933, so that my finally adopted figures for 1933 are:—

Males	.	.	.	84,975
Females	.	.	.	70,689
Total	.	.	.	155,664

'Of this, approximately 110,000 live on Lagos Island, Iddo and Victoria Beach, while 46,000 live in Ebute Metta, Surulere, Apapa, and other villages on the mainland.'

[1] Quoted in Lagos Town Council, *Report of Medical Officer of Health 1936*, p. 23.
[2] Ibid. *1935*, pp. 11–12.
[3] Dr. Cauchi apparently was not aware that the basic figure of 139,000 had been obtained by taking account of omissions.
[4] Quoted ibid. *1936*, pp. 23–4.   [5] See ibid., p. 2.

census—may have far-reaching effects on the population figure, I feel that our data are insufficient at present to warrant any variation in the conventional method of crude calculation.

For this reason, I should be grateful if you would adopt the population at mid-year 1936 for your 1936 report, and at mid-year 1937 for your monthly reports for 1937—adding a note as to the method used.[1]

The new Medical Officer of Health, following these instructions, assumed that the population had increased each year since 1931 by a tenth of the difference between the 1931 and 1921 census figures and put the total population for 1935 at 137,335 and for 1936 as 139,977.[2] But before another year had passed the Director of Medical Services gave new instructions. The Medical Officer of Health in his report for 1937 says:

In my annual report for 1936 I explained at length why, on the suggestion of the Deputy Director of Health Service, I substituted the arithmetical progression method for that previously in use for estimating the population of Lagos since 1931. The following fresh suggestion has been received from the Director of Medical Services at the time of writing this report:—

'There has been considerable doubt as to the correct population in Lagos and various estimates have been made from time to time. It is essential that there should be uniformity as otherwise birth and death rates calculated in different offices lead to confusion. I suggest that the following figures calculated from formulae supplied by Mr. S. M. Jacob should be used:—

POPULATION

1931	.	. 139,800	1942	.	. 167,600
1932	.	. 142,500	1943	.	. 169,800
1933	.	. 145,300	1944	.	. 172,000
1934	.	. 148,200	1945	.	. 174,200
1935	.	. 150,700	1946	.	. 176,500
1936	.	. 153,300	1947	.	. 178,700
1937	.	. 155,900	1948	.	. 180,800
1938	.	. 158,500	1949	.	. 182,400
1939	.	. 160,700	1950	.	. 184,000
1940	.	. 163,000	1951	.	. 186,000
1941	.	. 165,500			

The census figure for 1941 will supply a check on the accuracy of the figures.'

The actual census figure for 1931 was 126,108; the addition of 13,692 to this to make the population 139,800 is based on the formulae referred to above. These new figures are different from those obtained and used since 1931, and which were based on another formula supplied to my predecessor by the same gentleman, the Government Statistician. For the purpose of comparison, and in the hope that the above figures will be retained until the next census, the vital statistics have been recalculated from 1931 to 1937 . . . .[3]

He then gives rates based on the above population figures. In his next report he uses the Government Statistician's forecast for 1937 and 1938 but says that the estimated population 'is for Africans only'.[4]

The Lagos Medical Department was not the only office to publish estimates of the population of Lagos Township since 1931. To save space

[1] Quoted ibid., p. 24. [2] See ibid.
[3] Ibid. *1937*, p. 25.
[4] See ibid. *1938*, pp. 23–4. This, I think, is an error. The revised census figure of 139,000 (139,800 mid-year 1931) comprised both Africans and non-Africans.

and to facilitate comparison I shall summarize here the various estimates available for mid-year 1931–7:

Source		1931	1932	1933	1934	1935	1936	1937
Lagos M.O.H.,								
Rep.	1935	138,000	140,000	156,000	160,000	170,000	—	—
,,	1936	(126,767)	(129,409)	(132,051)	(134,693)	137,335	139,977	—
,,	1937–8	139,800	142,500	145,300	148,200	150,700	153,300	155,900
Nigeria,								
Med. Rep. 1931–5[1]		141,209	140,000	155,664	161,069	170,000	—	—
,, 1936–8[2]		—	—	—	—	157,630	160,717	155,900
Colony,								
Reports 1931–7[3]		—	128,000[4]	155,664	156,000	170,000[5]	142,620[6]	155,900[7]

[1] See *Report 1931*, p. 19; *1932*, p. 10; *1933*, p. 10; *1934*, p. 13; *1935*, p. 7.
[2] See ibid. *1936*, p. 9 ; *1937*, p. 9 ; *1938*, p. 9. The deviations in 1935–6 from the figures given in the Report of the Medical Officer of Health, Lagos, are evidently due to a misunderstanding. The Nigeria Medical Report gave for Lagos Town 137,336 and 139,977, and for Ebute Metta 20,294 and 20,740, not realizing that the former figures included Ebute Metta.
[3] See *Report 1932*, p. 1; *1933*, p. 1; *1934*, p. 1; *1935*, p. 1; *1936*, p. 1; *1937*, p. 1.
[4] 1 Jan. 1933.
[5] Dec. 1935.
[6] 'As compared with the figure given for the Township last year it will be observed that there is a decrease in population of 27,380. This is due to the adoption of a new formula for estimating the population and is therefore more apparent than real.'
[7] 'The estimated population of Lagos Township shows an increase of 13,280, but since it is based solely on the application of a formula adopted by the Health Authorities, the figure should be accepted with reserve.'

For 1937 to 1944 the forecasts of the Government Statistician have been accepted all through, but they have become more and more out of date. The Medical Reports for 1943 and 1944 said:

The estimated population figures given . . . for Lagos [1942 and 1943] are based on a forecast table prepared by the Government Statistician as a result of the last census, in 1931. There is no doubt that the Lagos population, mainly owing to immigration from the province, is considerably larger . . . but the actual figures can only be guessed rather than estimated in the absence of an adequate staff to conduct a careful enumeration.[1]

War-time movement of population into urban areas, and the trend for people to drift into large towns, has caused a considerable increase in the Lagos population, but actual figures are impossible to obtain. A new census of Lagos is now long overdue.[2]

2. Southern Nigeria

The early official reports state that it is impossible to estimate the native population of Southern Nigeria.[3] On 11 January 1904 instructions were issued for the 'Collection of Intelligence respecting Districts' which dealt also with population estimates:

VI.—In estimating the population of towns an Officer should estimate the average number of persons in a house and the average number of houses in a compound; the number of compounds is easily ascertainable and consequently an approximate estimate can be made of the population. When the population of one or more towns has been thus ascertained it is easy for an Officer to make a 'preliminary estimate' of the population in a place through which he travels for the first time; the entries in the Intelligence Book should always show whether the population is based upon a 'preliminary estimate' or the reverse.[4]

[1] Nigeria, *Medical Report 1943*, p. 9.   [2] Ibid. *1944*, p. 8.
[3] See *Colonial Reports, Southern Nigeria 1899–1900*, p. 17, *1902*, p. 33, *1903*, p. 31, *1904*, p. 37, *1905*, p. 35; Southern Nigeria, 'General Abstract of Registration 1903', p. 288.
[4] *Government Gazette, Protectorate of Southern Nigeria*, 30 Jan. 1904, p. 10.

Probably, on the basis of such estimates for some districts, the total population was put for 1904 at 2,000,000.[1] But on 17 February 1905 the Acting Secretary published a detailed estimate which yielded a population of over 3 millions.[2]

The following rough estimate of the Population of Southern Nigeria, is published for general information.

The statistics have been compiled by District Officers and are estimates of the towns and villages known to them. Many parts of the Protectorate have not yet been visited, and the returns are necessarily only very approximate.

District	Men	Women	Children	Total
CALABAR DIVISION				
Calabar	54,845	70,091	32,499	157,435
Eket	92,121	112,545	36,081	240,747
Ikot-Ekpene	55,893	111,786	224,141	391,820
Total	202,859	294,422	292,721	790,002
CROSS RIVER DIVISION				
Bende	73,850	100,926	118,110	292,886
Aro-Chuku	11,843	15,481	12,602	39,926
Afikpo	36,727	44,461	31,645	112,833
Obubra	23,008	40,511	65,941	129,460
Okuni	5,590	5,575	3,620	14,785
Total	151,018	206,954	231,918	589,890
EASTERN DIVISION				
Bonny	2,632	4,916	3,671	11,219
Degema	24,105	29,205	34,080	87,390
Opobo	38,310	72,200	70,428	180,938
Brass and Akassa	9,165	11,660	3,542	24,367
Akwete	43,673	45,681	36,060	125,414
Owerri	82,030	122,420	204,400	408,850
Total	199,915	286,082	352,181	838,178
WESTERN DIVISION				
Warri	17,672	33,621	38,486	89,779
Forcados	3,255	3,200	1,078	7,533
Sapele	34,640	37,442	40,089	112,171
Benin	68,464	84,922	52,366	205,752
Ifon	20,745	28,136	20,565	69,446
Total	144,776	187,321	152,584	484,681
CENTRAL DIVISION				
Asaba	44,546	48,253	29,893	122,692
Idah	21,478	24,400	14,715	60,593
Abo	63,467	63,674	42,369	169,510
Total	129,491	136,327	86,977	352,795
TOTAL	828,059	1,111,106	1,116,381	3,055,546

[1] 'Conjectural', *Colonial Office List 1905*, Table facing p. 1.
[2] See *Government Gazette, Protectorate of Southern Nigeria*, 17 Feb. 1905, pp. 80–1.

TABLE 1. *Area and Native Population of Southern Provinces, Nigeria and Cameroons, 1918–42*[1]

Year	Colony	Abeo-kuta	Ijebu	Ondo	Oyo	Benin	Warri	Onitsha	Owerri	Calabar	Ogoja	S. Nigeria	Cameroons Province	Total
						AREA (square miles)								
1914	1,400	4,300	8,500	—	14,200	10,900	7,400	7,600	9,300	6,900	9,500	80,000	—	—
1915	1,400	7,332		3,246	16,742	8,429	8,488	7,959	8,721	6,373	11,310	80,000	—	—
1918	1,335	6,694		6,051	14,872	8,799	9,342	7,519	7,613	6,248	8,211	76,684	18,700	95,384
1919	4,006	6,316		7,861	14,381	9,200	10,260	5,311	7,543	6,234	8,014	79,126	—	—
1920	2,414	6,316		7,312	14,381	7,489	10,260	5,141	7,545	3,727	7,961	72,599	24,103	96,702
1921 (a)	1,469	4,338	2,432	7,852	15,150	8,345	9,049	4,883	7,367	6,306	8,014	75,152	16,742	91,894
1921 (b), 1922-3	1,469	4,338	2,432	7,312	14,381	7,489	10,260	5,141	7,545	3,727	7,531	72,108	24,103	96,211
1924	1,469	4,008	2,200	7,312	14,876	7,740	9,670	5,141	7,405	6,423	7,129	73,775	19,242	93,017
1925	1,469	4,338	2,432	7,852	15,150	8,345	9,049	4,883	7,367	6,306	7,517	74,338	16,742	91,062
1926	1,469	4,008	2,432	7,852	15,150	8,345	9,049	4,883	7,367	6,306	7,517	74,378	16,258	90,636
1927 (a)	1,469	4,338	2,432	7,852	14,381	8,627	9,640	4,883	7,405	6,331	7,517	74,875	16,258	91,133
1927 (b)	1,469	4,338	2,432	7,852	14,381	8,627	9,640	4,903	7,405	6,331	7,529	74,895	16,258	91,153
1928 (a) (b)	1,419	4,266	2,456	8,211	14,216	8,627	9,040	4,937	7,476	6,331	7,529	74,558	16,581	91,139
1929 (a)	1,469	4,266	2,432	8,211	14,216	8,627	6,915	4,937	9,601	6,331	7,529	74,508	16,581	91,089
1929 (b)	1,469	4,338	2,432	7,852	14,301	8,627	6,915	4,937	10,799	6,280	7,837	75,787	16,258	92,045
1930-1	1,381	4,266	2,456	8,211	14,216	8,627	5,987	4,937	10,374	6,331	7,529	74,315	16,581	90,896
1932-5	1,381	4,266	2,456	8,211	14,216	8,627	5,987	4,937	10,279	6,331	7,624	74,315	16,581	90,896
1936-7	1,381	4,266	2,456	8,211	14,216	8,589	6,334	4,937	9,970	6,331	7,624	74,315	16,581	90,896
1938-40	1,381	4,266	2,456	8,286	14,216	8,589	6,334	4,937	9,970	6,331	7,624	74,390	16,581	90,971
1941-2	1,381	4,266	2,456	8,286	14,216	8,483	6,440	4,937	9,970	6,331	7,624	74,390	16,581	90,971
						POPULATION								
1914	166,292	271,682	443,884	—	1,269,625	649,273	403,956	1,342,959	1,753,651	771,027	788,400	7,855,749	—	—
1915	166,000	551,490		164,558	1,269,435	563,611	489,618	1,342,959	1,372,707	874,291	1,061,080	7,855,749	—	—
1918	154,000	552,000		384,000	1,027,000	567,000	515,000	1,342,000	1,272,000	871,000	1,066,000	7,750,000	570,000	8,320,000
1919	182,400	348,885		427,317	1,517,900	489,022	597,971	1,928,000	1,469,000	1,034,840	923,360	8,918,695	—	—
1920	238,000	418,977	133,042	341,439	1,096,000	419,302	604,871	1,642,842	1,877,000	1,032,840	923,360	8,727,673	527,266	9,254,939
1921 (a)	223,806	319,298	182,508	375,003	1,085,297	403,102	396,231	1,493,716	1,975,438	978,788	636,219	8,069,406	299,106	8,368,512
1921 (b), 1922	225,098	319,349	182,532	388,925	1,085,485	403,148	396,444	1,493,945	1,975,784	974,434	636,251	8,081,395	294,161	8,375,556
1923	225,099	319,349	182,532	375,035	1,085,498	403,148	396,464	1,493,945	1,975,784	979,189	636,251	8,072,294	299,165	8,371,459

1924	225,099	372,169	216,630	377,236	1,081,745	463,496	400,362	1,456,959	1,854,394	917,624	615,661	7,981,375	358,018	8,339,393
1925	235,121	543,681	227,460	378,689	1,040,909	469,598	404,124	1,500,000	1,873,320	923,338	615,661	8,211,901	390,881	8,602,782
1926	225,099	543,681	215,716	375,035	1,085,498	403,148	396,464	1,493,945	1,975,784	979,189	615,661	8,309,220	354,272	8,663,492
1927 (a)	224,033	415,634	215,000	478,893	1,121,068	443,392	451,197	1,123,992	1,873,320	942,619	615,661	8,004,809	356,040	8,360,849
1927 (b)	235,121	385,314	223,000	478,846	1,121,302	368,547	323,639	1,364,099	1,873,320	942,930	615,661	7,936,779	355,787	8,292,566
1928 (a)	224,033	420,379	243,000	491,070	1,134,215	450,212	505,340	1,155,472	1,873,320	910,939	646,162	8,054,142	375,595	8,429,737
1928 (b)	224,033	390,000	243,000	491,070	1,134,215	456,096	503,340	1,170,899	1,475,750	913,942	646,162	7,650,507	366,515	8,017,022
1929 (a)	224,033	428,866	261,673	491,964	1,134,750	475,874	444,549	1,187,482	1,475,750	920,624	687,579	8,210,639	375,120	8,585,759
1929 (b)	224,033	397,650	264,673	491,070	1,134,750	475,874	445,714	1,421,109	1,953,245	920,624	687,579	8,413,321	366,372	8,779,693
1930	325,426	440,905	261,657	491,964	1,136,532	477,307	422,012	1,097,482	1,958,245	917,909	642,818	8,172,257	379,050	8,551,307
1931	323,544	434,410	305,868	462,508	1,336,609	493,126	444,368	1,107,525	1,599,497	899,080	708,499	8,115,034	374,596	8,489,630
1932–3	326,912	434,290	305,703	506,520	1,339,504	454,118	414,505	1,121,947	1,610,890	899,021	708,322	8,122,732	374,872	8,497,604
1934	334,486	434,526	305,898	462,560	1,342,259	493,215	444,533	1,107,745	1,617,281	899,503	726,233	8,168,239	384,796	8,553,035
1935	332,910	434,526	305,408	462,560	1,342,259	459,906	414,505	1,096,323	1,616,072	900,285	726,233	8,090,987	382,501	8,473,488
1936	368,495	480,114	305,408	476,968	1,342,259	461,114	414,505	1,096,323	1,616,072	900,285	725,018	8,186,561	406,388	8,592,949
1937	324,444	536,060	303,837	476,968	1,342,259	482,278	416,524	1,096,323	1,613,973	908,702	678,488	8,182,856	407,689	8,590,545
1938	327,044	536,060	306,837	476,968	1,342,259	483,277	423,524	1,096,323	1,613,973	908,858	687,657	8,202,780	445,753	8,648,533
1939	335,544	546,318	306,837	476,968	1,382,574	489,665	423,524	1,096,323	1,613,973	910,802	687,657	8,270,185	464,097	8,734,282
1940	331,544	546,318	312,937	476,968	1,382,574	492,023	434,948	1,096,323	1,613,973	910,802	681,123	8,279,533	477,258	8,756,791
1941	331,544	566,858	312,937	476,968	1,395,966	501,915	437,204	1,096,323	1,613,973	911,072	680,198	8,324,958	477,258	8,802,216
1942	331,544	566,253	312,937	476,968	1,392,073	520,187	437,204	1,096,323	1,613,973	911,072	692,019	8,350,553	477,258	8,827,811

[1] See for 1914–15 Nigeria, *Blue Book 1914* 3, p. 4, *1915* R, p. 4; 1918 *Report by Lugard on the Amalgamation of Northern and Southern Nigeria*, p. 11; 1919–20 Nigeria, *Blue Book 1919* R, p. 4, *1920*, Section 15, p. 4; 1921 (a) Talbot, vol. iv, pp. 9–10, 22; 1921 (b)–1925 Nigeria, *Blue Book 1921*, Section 15, p. 4, *1922*, p. 248, *1923*, p. 252, *1924*, p. 270, *1925*, p. 282; 1926 *Report on the Southern Provinces of Nigeria 1926*, p. 3; 1927 (a), 1928 (a), 1929 (a) *Report on the Colony 1927*, p. 1, *1928*, p. 19, *1929*, p. 18, *Report on the Southern Provinces 1927*, pp. 3, 7, 13, 19, 26, 36, 41, 48, 54, 61, 67, 75, *1928*, p. 81, *1929*, p. 55; 1927 (b), 1928 (b), 1929 (b), 1930 Nigeria, *Blue Book 1927*, p. 320, *1928*, p. 346, *1929*, p. 340, *1930*, p. 342, *Report on the Colony 1929*, p. 4; 1931 *Census of Nigeria, 1931*, vol. iii, pp. 21, 27; 1932–42 Nigeria, *Blue Book 1932*, Section 15, p. 2, to *1942*, Section 15, p. 2. In a few cases—such as 1921 (b), 1922, and 1923—the figures apparently include non-natives.

The 'estimates' by some District Officers were very rough indeed. Thus, the officer for Ikot-Ekpene put the number of women (111,786) exactly at twice the number of men (55,893), and the number of children (224,141) at almost exactly twice the number of women. Some other officers likewise overstated the number of children while others evidently understated it.

Prior to 1906 the totals for Southern Nigeria, of course, excluded the Colony and Protectorate of Lagos. Including these territories, the population 'was estimated to be about 6 millions at the end of 1906'.[1]

There are no means of ascertaining or even of estimating approximately the native population. Officers acquainted with the various parts of the hinterland have formed estimates of the population, which, added together, give the following figures:—

Western Province	3,000,000
Eastern „	1,500,000
Central „	1,585,000[2]

But in this estimate, as in the earlier estimates, the population of the Eastern and Central Provinces had been understated while that of the Western Province (formerly Colony and Protectorate of Lagos) was overstated. The estimates of the native population for subsequent years and the 1911 'census' returns showed the following results:

Province	1907[1]	1908–10[2]	1911[3]
Western . . .	2,200,000	2,200,000	2,151,483
Eastern . . .	2,200,000	2,500,000	3,296,602
Central . . .	1,600,000	2,000,000	2,407,664
Total . . .	6,000,000	6,700,000	7,855,749

[1] See *Colonial Reports, Southern Nigeria 1907*, p. 22. See also *Statistical Tables, Colonial Possessions 1907*, p. 403: 'The total population for the whole Territory of Southern Nigeria was estimated to be about 6 millions at the end of 1907.' The 'Report on the Eastern Province for the Year 1907' says (p. 19): 'The population of the known portions of the Eastern Province according to an estimate prepared in 1905 was calculated at 2,218,070. In Southern Nigeria, *Medical Report 1907*, p. 10, the native population of the Central Province was estimated at 1,900,000.

[2] See *Colonial Reports, Southern Nigeria 1908*, p. 29; *1909*, p. 22; *1910*, p. 26. *Statistical Tables, Colonial Possessions 1908*, p. 414, and *1909*, p. 423, gave 'about 6,500,000' for the end of 1908 and 'about 6,700,000' for the end of 1909.   [3] *Report on Southern Nigeria Census, 1911*, p. 2.

The estimates in the following years did not assume a population increase,[3] and Sir Frederick Lugard, in his *Report on the Amalgamation of Northern and Southern Nigeria*, dated 9 April 1919, said that Southern Nigeria had 'a population estimated at $7\frac{3}{4}$ millions (probably an overestimate)'.[4] But in the *Blue Books* for 1919 and 1920 the coloured native population was given as 8,918,695 and 8,727,673 respectively. However, the 'census' returns of 1921 yielded only 8,069,406 and those for 1931 8,115,034. The official figure for 1942 is 8,350,553.

[1] *Statistical Tables, Colonial Possessions 1906*, p. 397.
[2] *Colonial Reports, Southern Nigeria 1906*, p. 56.
[3] Southern Nigeria, *Blue Book 1913* R, p. 4, it is true, showed an increase from 7,855,749 to 7,891,000 owing to 'alteration in the boundaries of the Protectorate' and 'the opening of new territory', but the Nigeria *Blue Books* for 1914–18 gave again as coloured native population 7,855,749. *Colonial Reports, Nigeria 1915*, p. 19, gave 7,806,000 (possibly a misprint), and the following Reports (*1916*, p. 24; *1917*, p. 16; *1918*, p. 16) showed 7,856,000.
[4] *Report*, p. 5. See also ibid., p. 9.

All these data exclude the population of Southern Cameroons (Cameroons Province). Sir F. Lugard estimated it at 570,000,[1] and in the *Blue Book* for 1920 it was put at 527,266. But the 'census' returns of 1921 showed only 299,106. However, the official figures increased enormously in the course of time until in 1940 they reached 477,258.[2] Including Southern Cameroons the native population of the Southern Provinces is reported to have increased from 8,368,512 in 1921 to 8,489,630 in 1931, and to 8,827,811 in 1942.

I have dealt so far only with the native population, for which yearly estimates are available. For non-natives, except Europeans, data are scanty. According to the censuses of 1911, 1921, and 1931 the non-natives numbered 2,940,[3] 2,947, and 3,617 respectively.

3. *Northern Nigeria*

In the first years after the constitution of the Protectorate (1 January 1900) the population estimates varied a great deal. *Colonial Office List 1900* said:

The Protectorate includes the Foulah Empire . . . . The Hausa States of the Foulah Empire are Mohammedan, and are said to have the densest population of any country in the whole African Continent—estimated at 30 millions.[4]

For 1901 and 1902 *Colonial Office List* gave as population of Northern Nigeria 10,000,000,[5] for 1903 20,000,000,[6] for 1904 and 1905 10,000,000[7] or 20,000,000,[8] and for 1906 10,000,000.[9] *Statistical Tables, British Colonies* gave as estimated population at the end of 1902 10,000,000, and at the end of 1903 '8 to 10 millions'.[10] The Blue Book for 1903 said:

Native Population.—Not ascertainable.—No census has yet been taken; the population has been variously estimated at between ten and thirty millions.[11]

In the meantime, however, Sir F. Lugard, who had taken over the administration from the Royal Niger Company, had inaugurated a scheme of assessment which provided a somewhat more solid basis for population estimates. In his report for 1902 he stated:

Some progress has been made with this scheme of assessment.
Simultaneously with it a census, and a geographical survey, together with the collection of a mass of statistical information regarding products, area under cultivation,

[1] See ibid., p. 72.
[2] For details of this enormous increase which conveys a distorted picture of actual population movements, see Kuczynski, pp. 219–37. The official figures for 1941 and 1942 are the same as for 1940.
[3] Excluding Cameroons.
[4] *Colonial Office List 1900*, p. 195; literally the same *1901*, p. 245. The population of the 'Niger Territories', i.e. Northern Nigeria and Southern Nigeria, excluding the Colony and Protectorate of Lagos, had been estimated ibid. *1892*, p. 266, *1893*, p. 274, *1894*, p. 278, at 20,000,000 to 25,000,000, and ibid. *1895*, p. 280, *1896*, p. 285, *1897*, p. 294, *1898*, p. 287, *1899*, p. 315, at 20,000,000 to 35,000,000.
[5] See ibid. *1902*, Table General Statistics, and p. 255; *1903*, Table General Statistics.
[6] See ibid. *1903*, p. 272; *1904*, Table General Statistics.
[7] See ibid. *1905*, Table General Statistics; *1906*, Table General Statistics.
[8] See ibid. *1904*, p. 277; *1905*, p. 283.   [9] See ibid. *1906*, p. 291.
[10] See *Statistical Tables, British Colonies 1902*, p. 865; *1903*, p. 859.
[11] Northern Nigeria, *Blue Book 1903* R, p. 1.

&c., are being effected in a rough and ready way; but the work of fully grappling with and completing so large a task still belongs to the future. Its most effective realisation so far has been achieved in the Illorin province, since it was one of the three first taken under administrative control.[1]

Two years later he published an estimate of the population for each Province by sex. The total for the Protectorate was 9,161,700.

The assessment of towns for tribute, and the closer touch now established between the administration and the people, has enabled me to submit some rough idea of the population. The returns are, however, largely guesswork at present, but will form a basis for future revision. Except in the cases of Bornu, Bassa, Nassarawa, and Kano, I am inclined to think that the numbers are somewhat under-estimated.[2]

Probably the most accurate figures are those of Nupe, which has been most fully assessed,[3] and next to Nupe, Illorin, and Sokoto. If these were taken by themselves as a basis of calculation for the whole Protectorate,[4] the total would be 5,000,000 only, as against the total of 9,000,000 shown above. I am, however, inclined to think that the population is about what the return shows it at, viz., 9,000,000. The estimates have in almost every case been made by the Resident in Charge, who is the best judge. Barth in 1854 estimated the population at from 30 to 50 millions.[5]

Sir Frederick Lugard made, furthermore, the following comments:

Muri. The estimate of the population is, of course, largely guesswork at present.[6]

Kontagora. . . , its population is estimated by the Assistant Resident at 79,000 (females 44,650, males 34,350). An alternative estimate by Major Sharpe, C.M.G., the Resident in charge, puts the population at only 40,625.[7]

Bassa. . . . It is at present in charge of Mr. Ley-Greaves . . . who estimates its dense population at 1½ millions, but I have assumed it at a million at most.[8]

In the report for 1905–6 he stated:

Much useful work has been done in completing the statistics of provinces in the record book, which has been instituted in all provinces, and contains lists of every town, village, and district, its history, assessment, chiefs, sub-chiefs, industries, products, population and economic information, together with notes on tribes, tsetse areas, trade routes, courts, rolls of ex-soldiers, freed slaves, native craftsmen, arms, traders, &c., &c. These record books will form most valuable data for the compilation of a gazetteer for Northern Nigeria as well as for administrative and economic purposes.[9]

The census of the population is still very vague in some provinces, but the completion of the assessment during the current and next year should result in a tolerable approximation to the correct figures. The table given below is a summary of the fuller details given in Appendix 2. It will be observed that the return for the Kabba province is more than four times the estimate given last year by Captain Larymore. I am inclined to think this is an over-estimate. It includes the Egbira and Kukuruku tribes on the south frontier, who have lately been visited by the Acting Resident, but no details are given by him. The estimate for Bassa is little more than half that formerly returned, and I should think it is now approximately correct. Captain Ruxton and Mr. Gowers agree in reducing the estimate of Muri by a third from that furnished by Mr. Lobb. Nassarawa remains at its former figure, which I think is

[1] Colonial Reports, Northern Nigeria 1902, p. 53.   [2] Ibid. 1904, pp. 83–4.
[3] See also ibid. 1905–6, p. 48: 'The first rough and ready assessment of the province has been carefully revised for a considerable portion of it, and this revision will be continued during the present year. It was found that the number of hamlets was greatly in excess of that shown on the records, which resulted in an increase in the estimate of the population of this district of the province by 100 per cent. . . .' But the estimate was reduced in 1906.
[4] i.e. the population density of these three Provinces.   [5] Ibid. 1904, p. 84.
[6] Ibid., p. 57.   [7] Ibid., p. 72.   [8] Ibid., p. 77.   [9] Ibid. 1905–6, p. 5.

much too high. I should imagine the population of the Protectorate to be about 8½ millions.[1]

In a *Memorandum on the Taxation of Natives in Northern Nigeria*, dated 22 November 1906, Sir F. Lugard throws more light on how the population figures were obtained.

The task of assessment has involved a simultaneous approximate census of the population, but the figures are still very crude, nor has the proportion of the sexes, and the average number of children in relation to adults, been determined with any accuracy. Some of the figures given for the general tax are not precise, but the total at which I have arrived is probably a very nearly correct statement of the taxation as it stands to-day. The taxed population is estimated at 3,000,536 adults. If three children be allowed for every two adults (the minimum it would seem possible to assume), this would represent a taxed population of 7½ millions out of the total 9½ at which the population of the Protectorate is estimated. The two millions untaxed represent pagan tribes not under administrative control, such as the Okpotos and Munshis in Bassa and Muri (over half a million), the pagan tribes in Yola, Nassarawa, Bauchi and Zaria, &c.[2]

In his comments on the various Provinces he frequently emphasizes his belief that the number of children should be about one and a half times as large as the number of adults.

Kano. The adult population is not given, nor the number of males. The gross population is 2,330,000; if three-fifths were children, the adults would be 920,000 . . . .[3]

Nupe. The population is estimated at 61,121 adults [total population 151,890].[4]

Yola. Adults are reckoned at one-third of the population, but probably the proportion is as two to three.[5]

Kabba. The returns of population are not very reliable, the children being shown as less than half the adult population. Assuming 80,000 adults (out of a total of 233,191) . . . .[6]

Sir F. Lugard was mistaken, of course, when he thought that three children for every two adults was 'the minimum it would seem possible to assume'. I do not know of any country where the number of children has ever been as large as the number of adults, and four children for every five adults is about the maximum found anywhere. But the effect on his population estimates of Sir F. Lugard's wrong assumption was not very great, since in many cases he evidently derived the number of adults from the total estimated population and not the total population from the number of adults.[7] There was, however, a tendency to overestimate the population. This was also the impression of his successor Governor William Wallace, who said in his report for 1906–7:

In 1903 I had to bring to the notice of the Secretary of State how incorrect the estimated population was, and instead of putting it down at 20,000,000, that 10,000,000 would be much nearer the mark. Since then Sir Frederick Lugard had

---

[1] Ibid., p. 61.   [2] *Memorandum*, p. 14.   [3] Ibid., p. 32.
[4] Ibid., p. 44.   [5] Ibid., p. 54.   [6] Ibid., p. 59.
[7] Some of his figures for adults are evidently wrong. He lists, for example, for Sokoto 578,500 'Assessed Adults' (see ibid., p. 62), although 578,500 was the estimated total population of the Province (see ibid., p. 30). If he had entered a lower figure for Assessed Adults in Sokoto he would have obtained a lower total than 3,000,536. His estimate of the total population which turned out to be 9½ millions would then have been nearer to his original estimate of 8,782,183 (see *Colonial Reports, Northern Nigeria 1905–6*, p. 62).

TABLE 2. *Area and Native Population of Northern Provinces, Nigeria and Cameroons, 1904-25*[1]

AREA (square miles)

Year	Bauchi (Central)	Bornu	Ilorin	Kabba	Kano	Borgu	Konta-gora	Bassa (Munshi)	Muri	Nas-sarawa	Nupe (Niger)	Zaria	Sokoto	Yola	N. Nigeria
1904	23,200	33,000	6,300	7,800	31,000	12,000	14,500	7,000	25,800	18,000	6,400	22,000	35,000	16,000	258,000
1906	23,200	32,800	6,300	7,800	28,600	27,000		7,000	25,600	17,900	6,400	21,900	35,400	15,800	255,700
1907	23,200	32,800	6,300	7,800	28,600	27,000		7,000	25,600	17,900	12,500	15,800	35,400	15,800	255,700
1909	24,700	32,800	6,300	7,800	28,600	27,000		7,000	25,600	17,900	18,453	9,847	35,400	14,300	255,700
1910	25,200	32,800	6,300	7,800	28,600	27,000		14,000	28,000	17,900	18,453	9,847	33,000	14,300	263,200
1911 (a)	25,200	32,800	6,300	7,800	28,600	27,000		7,000	25,600	17,900	18,453	9,847	35,400	14,300	256,200
1911 (b)	23,061	35,952	6,906	6,867	30,078	16,587		7,286	25,789	17,365	6,733	22,146	32,821	13,085	244,676
1912	25,200	32,800	6,300	7,800	28,600	27,000		7,000	25,600	17,900	18,453	9,847	35,400	14,300	256,200
1913–17	23,700	33,600	6,500	8,200	29,500	27,800		6,700	28,700	16,710	16,770	13,320	35,400	11,600	255,700
1918 (a)–1920	23,700	33,600	13,588		28,600	27,000		16,936	21,231	16,770	16,770	13,320	32,600	11,600	257,355
1918 (b)	24,700	32,800	14,100		29,500	27,800		17,000	15,600	17,900	18,450	9,850	35,400	14,300	255,700
1921 (a)	23,700	33,600	11,770		29,500	27,800		16,936	19,698	16,710	17,003	13,320	32,600	11,600	254,237
1921 (b), 1922	23,700	38,100	7,050	5,390	29,500	27,800		16,936	19,698	16,710	16,333	13,320	32,600	11,700	258,837
1923	23,885	39,290	6,619	4,814	29,290	27,616		18,949	19,524	16,710	16,145	13,320	34,661	23,567	275,030
1924	23,885	39,290	6,619	4,814	29,930	27,616		19,370	19,524	14,644	16,145	13,320	34,661	22,767	272,585
1925	25,299	44,614	17,249	5,446	30,111	—		16,954	19,771	13,991	23,616	15,589	40,071	18,411	271,122

POPULATION

Year	Bauchi (Central)	Bornu	Ilorin	Kabba	Kano	Borgu	Konta-gora	Bassa (Munshi)	Muri	Nas-sarawa	Nupe (Niger)	Zaria	Sokoto	Yola	N. Nigeria
1904	920,000	1,105,000	255,000	68,000	2,192,000	25,300	79,000	1,000,000	825,000	1,500,000	150,000	230,000	521,000	290,500	9,161,700
1905	920,000	1,105,000	250,000	281,650	2,330,000	25,327	89,678	525,138	543,000	1,500,000	151,890	232,000	578,500	250,000	8,782,183
1906	920,000	403,322	179,978	118,576	2,714,000	21,873	80,182	525,150	500,801	601,005	123,566	230,000	561,298	185,000	7,164,751
1907	709,100	460,000	163,600	184,900	2,400,000	22,000	75,500	175,000	548,000	161,100	226,800	179,000	600,000	30,000	5,935,000
1909	641,651	454,000	199,959	112,369	2,571,170	21,848	76,777	256,300	427,462	287,487	232,520	144,673	1,102,658	168,983	6,714,038[2]
1910	682,651	674,230	199,959	119,939	2,855,539	121,565		205,101	494,143	351,681	253,361	402,055	1,245,000	189,904	7,811,309[2]
1911 (a)	682,314	674,230	191,427	130,940	3,172,746	121,565		205,393	494,353	354,292	257,861	402,055	1,245,705	177,750	8,110,631
1911 (b)	700,000	700,000	200,000	140,000	3,500,000	122,000		205,000	700,000	600,000	400,000	402,000	1,300,000	300,000	9,269,000
1912	908,351	700,000	319,075	140,000	3,500,000	137,195		205,320	700,000	600,000	400,000	402,000	1,300,000	300,000	9,611,941
1913, 1914	1,033,407	657,647	352,263	145,680	3,500,000	150,478		198,711	397,541	264,675	257,947	402,999	1,357,968	248,520	8,967,836
1917	761,492	700,541	488,323		2,721,236	131,928		163,739	472,625	257,462	335,267	323,375	1,473,480	251,325	8,080,793
1918 (a)	791,402	700,541	488,323		2,871,236	131,928		413,893	349,627	257,462	335,267	352,885	1,593,480	251,325	8,537,369
1918 (b)	679,700	679,700	330,100		3,398,300	118,400		471,000	407,800	582,000	388,500	390,300	1,262,300	291,300	9,000,000
1919	933,652	731,149	527,932		2,826,897	169,485		569,944	222,258	266,248	326,548	318,643	1,516,326	259,056	8,668,138
1920	916,259	767,938	486,625		2,788,186	167,633		762,645	258,656	274,417	331,865	375,819	1,622,483	337,000	9,089,526
1921 (a)	954,407	759,912	576,551		3,447,069	187,465		776,366	261,473	322,053	364,639	379,489	1,695,120	270,971	9,994,515
1921 (b), 1922	954,904	953,341	576,914		3,493,569	187,493		776,471	261,735	322,123	364,622	380,311	1,722,182	338,700	10,332,365
1923	914,941	942,538	442,655	192,782	3,526,794	182,283		759,699	269,805	322,035	336,958	379,728	1,526,812	419,948	10,216,978
1924	925,234	1,001,296	474,498	200,621	3,490,392	182,260		767,104	268,544	333,882	333,651	396,307	1,562,751	384,784	10,321,324
1925	967,849	1,038,967	521,041	203,443	3,355,503	—		772,182	270,060	345,936	361,656	403,339	1,657,763	399,770	10,297,509

[*For notes to table see opposite*

further to reduce this estimate, and from figures received from Residents he last year estimated the population at 8,782,183. This year I have had to reduce this figure still further to 7,164,751, which I should say is fairly approximate; it will, however, take some years to get correct figures, as where the country is still unassessed, mostly in pagan zones, the population is merely guessed at.[1]

The large decrease is the more noteworthy as the estimate for the most populous Province, Kano, which had been raised from 2,192,000 in 1904 to 2,330,000 in 1905 jumped to 2,714,000 in 1906.[2] Reductions to less than one-half of the previous year's estimate were made in Bornu (from 1,105,000 to 403,319), in Kabba (from 281,650 to 118,576),[3] and in Nassarawa (from 1,500,000 to 601,005).[4]

The estimates for 1907 seem quite erratic. Some Provinces (Kabba, Nupe) show enormous increases, but others (Bassa,[5] Nassarawa,[6] Yola[7]) quite fantastic decreases. The total population estimate dropped from 7,164,751 to 5,935,000.[8] For 1908 no estimates were given by Provinces and the total native population was put, as in 1906, at 7,164,751, i.e. much higher than in 1907.

The total was arrived at from assessment returns and a rough estimate made of the unadministered parts of the Protectorate. On a proper census being taken the figures may probably show a large increase.[9]

[1] *Colonial Reports, Northern Nigeria 1906–7*, p. 38.

[2] The figure for 1905 was given as the 'amended estimate of the population' by Mr. Cargill (see ibid. *1905–6*, p. 26). The *Report 1906–7* said (p. 9) merely: 'The census, which is based on the old census of 1905 by Dr. Cargill, figures out at 2,714,000.'

[3] As regards the high figure for 1905, see p. 588 above.

[4] As regards details for Nassarawa see *Report 1905–6*, p. 129; *1906–7*, pp. 18, 98. See also *Memorandum on Taxation*, p. 52: 'A great deal remains to be done in this province in applying the instructions regarding taxation. The discrepancies in the returns have rendered it very difficult for me to arrive at correct results. In some returns, for instance, the population is shown as three times as great as in others.'

[5] The population was estimated in 1904 at 1,000,000 or 1,500,000, in 1905 and 1906 at 525,000, and in 1907 at 175,000. As regards the reduction to 525,000 see p. 588 above. This estimate had been quite uncertain. 'The estimate of population allows four per sleeping hut, and one-third as children' (ibid., p. 61). See also *Colonial Reports, Northern Nigeria 1906–7*, p. 25: 'The population is estimated at 525,150, of which the Igara and Okpoto are put at 400,000, but this is considered to be overestimated. The figures will be revised as opportunity offers.'

[6] The population now was estimated at 161,100 as compared with 1,500,000 in 1905.

[7] The Report says: '. . . the Fulani population [in Yola Province] appears to be on the decrease . . .' (ibid. *1907–8*, p. 60).

[8] The Medical Report, however, says: 'The Native population is approximately given as 7,000,000' ('Report on the Public Health of Northern Nigeria 1907', p. 91).

[9] *Colonial Reports, Northern Nigeria 1908–9*, p. 13.

Notes to table opposite]

[1] See for 1904–6 *Colonial Reports, Northern Nigeria 1904*, pp. 25, 31, 42, 44, 46, 51, 55, 58, 62, 65, 69, 72, 74, 77, 84, *1905–6*, p. 62, *1906–7*, p. 99, Northern Nigeria, *Blue Book 1906* R, p. 1; 1907 *Colonial Reports Northern Nigeria 1907–8*, pp. 33, 35, 40, 43, 46, 48, 50–1, 53–4, 56–8, *Statistical Tables, Colonial Possessions 1907*, p. 399; 1909–10 Northern Nigeria, *Blue Book 1909* R, p. 1, *1910* R, p. 1; 1911 Area (a) ibid. *1911* R, p. 1, (b) *Census of Nigeria, 1931*, vol. ii, p. 19, Population Northern Nigeria, *Census 1911*; 1912–13 Northern Nigeria, *Blue Book 1912* R, p. 1, *1913* R, p. 2; 1914–18 (a) Nigeria, *Blue Book 1914* R, p. 2, *1915* R, p. 2, *1916* R, p. 2, *1917* R, p. 2, *1918* R, p. 2; 1918 (b) *Report by Lugard on the Amalgamation of Northern and Southern Nigeria*, p. 11; 1919–20 Nigeria, *Blue Book 1919* R, p. 2, *1920*, Section 15, p. 4; 1921 (a) Meek, vol. ii, pp. 177, 180; 1921 (b)–1925 Nigeria, *Blue Book 1921*, Section 15, p. 4, *1922*, p. 248, *1923*, p. 252, *1924*, p. 270, *1925*, p. 282. Boundaries changed during the period under consideration; figures for Bassa, Munshi, and Muri, and figures for Nupe (Niger) and Zaria should be read in conjunction. The Province of Kontagora was in 1924 partitioned between the provinces of Sokoto, Nupe, and Ilorin. Data up to 1921 (a) exclude Cameroons. In a few cases—such as 1921 (b), 1922—the figures apparently include non-natives; the figures for 1911 (a) comprise only natives of Northern Nigeria.

[2] Including 16,181 in the Cantonments of Zungeru (Niger Province) and Lokoja (Kabba Province), not included in the Provincial figures.

The estimates by Provinces for 1909 yielded a total of only 6,714,038, but the Chief Secretary said:

> The native population is estimated at over 8,000,000, but as it has not as yet been possible to take an accurate census, it is impossible to state the population with any great degree of accuracy. The estimate is probably under rather than over the mark.[1]

The estimate for 1910 was 7,811,309, but the Colonial Report for 1910–11 said:

> The native population is roughly estimated at 10,000,000, but until a careful assessment of land revenue and population has been completed throughout the Protectorate this figure can only be considered as approximate. It will probably prove to be under the actual number.[2]

The 'census' returns for 1911 showed a native population of 8,110,631.[3] This figure, as explained above, was considered too low and replaced by an official estimate of 9,269,000.[4] The Colonial Report for 1911 stated:

> The native population is estimated at 9,269,000, being 4,033,743 males and 5,235,257 females. These are the same figures as those given in the previous year's Report and are approximately correct; but it must be understood that they are the result of an estimate and not of a census.[5]

The report for 1912 contained the same statement and added, 'but the assessments for taxation show that the estimate is a conservative one'.[6] In the *Blue Book* for that year the revised figures of the 1911 'census' were entered for most Provinces but they were raised for some, and the total shown was 9,611,941.

The report for 1913 said: 'The native population is estimated at 9½ millions.'[7] But in the *Blue Book* the estimates were reduced considerably for some Provinces,[8] though they were raised for others, the total estimate being only 8,967,836.

The first Colonial Reports published after the amalgamation of Northern and Southern Nigeria put the native population of Northern Nigeria at 9½ millions.[9] For 1916–18 it was estimated in the Colonial Reports at 9,270,000, 8,080,793, and 8,537,369 respectively,[10] and Sir F. Lugard, in his report of 9 April 1919, put it at 9,000,000.[11] The Blue Books for 1919 and 1920 showed 8,668,138 and 9,089,526 respectively, and the 'census' returns for 1921 9,994,515.[12]

All these data exclude Northern Cameroons, which according to the 1921 returns had a native population of 261,663. Including Northern Cameroons these returns showed a native population of 10,258,815. The

---

[1] *Colonial Reports, Northern Nigeria 1909*, p. 16.   [2] Ibid. *1910–11*, p. 21.

[3] The rise was due to an increase in the estimate for Kano Province (from 2,855,539 to 3,172,746).

[4] See Northern Nigeria, *Census 1911*, and *Colonial Reports, Northern Nigeria 1910–11*, pp. 42–3.

[5] Ibid. *1911*, p. 17.   [6] Ibid. *1912*, p. 19.   [7] Ibid. *1913*, p. 13.

[8] For some Provinces the figures were equal or even inferior to the original 1911 census figures.

[9] See *Colonial Reports, Nigeria 1914*, p. 22; *1915*, p. 19.

[10] See ibid. *1916*, p. 24; *1917*, p. 16; *1918*, p. 16.

[11] See *Report on the Amalgamation of Northern and Southern Nigeria*, p. 11. Most of the changes in the totals for these years were due to changes in the estimates for Kano Province (*Blue Books 1913* to *1916* showed 3,500,000, *Blue Books 1917* and *1918* 2,721,236 and 2,871,236 respectively, Sir F. Lugard 3,398,300).

[12] The increase was again due mainly to a rise in the estimate for Kano Province (from 2,788,186 in 1920 to 3,447,069 at the census).

official estimates revealed hardly any change in the following five years, the native population in 1926 being reported as 10,232,834.[1] The 1931 census report contained the following comment:[2]

In the first five years of the decade there was a drop of 60,000 in the total for the whole of the Northern Provinces, allowing for the transfer of the Egedde district, with a population of approximately 30,000 from the Southern to the Northern Provinces.[3] The figures for some of the divisions certainly appear to have been over-estimated in 1921, and it was in the next few years that more accurate counts were taken than had been possible in the past. This is observed from a scrutiny of some of the district figures for Kano Division, where there is a decrease of over 47,000 since 1921. The total for this division in 1921 was 2,047,762; in 1928 it was 1,990,176; and in the 1931 Census it was returned as 2,000,441. It must, however, be remembered that there was a heavy mortality in the relapsing fever epidemic in 1924, but we have no record of the number of deaths.

From 1926 to 1931 the official population figures increased very much, the total numbers for natives being 10,232,834; 10,449,800; 10,783,303; 11,047,275; 11,282,155; and 11,433,099 ('census') respectively. The total increase in the $4\frac{1}{2}$ years[4] was 1,200,265 or 11·7 per cent. In Zaria Province the percentage increase was 31·6, in Benue Province 24·0, in Adamawa Province 18·8. It was, on the other hand, only 3·4 per cent. in Ilorin. The 1931 census report made the following comment:[5]

In Adamawa and Benue, where the increases are over 20%, and in Zaria, where the increase is over 30%, a more accurate enumeration is responsible for the bulk of the increase. This would appear to be the case in Katsina Division, where at the 1921 Census the total population for Katsina Emirate was returned at 625,486; it is now returned at 925,848. When the Intensive Census of the whole of this area was first proposed, the population figure stood at only 730,000.[6]

Various passages in annual reports confirm that the apparent large increases in Zaria, Benue, and Adamawa Provinces were due to closer counting, and that also the smaller increases in some other Provinces were due to this cause.

Zaria Province. 1928. Statistics show large increases in the figures of population and livestock in the Katsina Emirate and smaller increases in the Zaria Emirate.[7]

1929. The Census of Zaria Emirate, made in September and October, showed an increase of 10,000 head of population compared with last year. An increase of 1,000

---

[1] 'In 1926 approval was given for a re-grouping of the Provinces, Divisions, and Districts of the Northern Provinces, which altered the boundaries of the old Provinces of Bauchi, Bornu, Kabba, Kano, Munshi, Niger, Yola, and Zaria; abolished the Provinces of Muri and Nassarawa, the divisions of which were absorbed in the newly re-arranged Provinces, and created a new Plateau Province. Munshi and Yola Provinces were renamed Benue and Adamawa.' (*Census of Nigeria, 1931*, vol. ii, p. 17.) The only Provinces which remained unaltered were Ilorin and Sokoto.

[2] Ibid., p. 20.

[3] See also ibid., p. 17: 'In 1922 the delimitation of the natural ethnographical boundaries between the Munshi Province and the Ogoja Province (Southern Provinces) involved the inclusion of the Egedde District with a population of 38,000 in the Idoma Division of the then Munshi Province.'

[4] From Oct. 1926 to Apr. 1931; see ibid., vol. i, p. 5.

[5] Ibid., vol. ii, p. 20.

[6] The claim that the 1931 census returns from the Katsina Emirate were trustworthy seems, however, dubious. See ibid., p. 8: 'In the Katsina Census the reduction of the area of the Intensive Census, for financial reasons, was a serious handicap, as no preparation had been made for a General Census, and this had to be hurriedly undertaken at the eleventh hour.'

[7] *Report on the Northern Provinces 1928*, p. 31.

TABLE 3. Area and Native Population of Northern Provinces, Nigeria and Cameroons, 1926-42[1]

AREA (square miles)

Year	Adamawa	Bauchi	Benue	Bornu	Ilorin	Kabba	Kano	Niger	Plateau	Sokoto	Zaria	Katsina	N. Nigeria
1926 (a)	33,424	24,579	27,640	45,349	17,779	10,382	17,644	25,018	11,052	38,860	23,695	—	275,422
1926 (b)	35,136	24,576	26,354	45,349	17,779	10,382	17,644	25,018	10,539	38,860	23,695	—	275,332
1927 (a)	33,424	24,579	27,640	45,349	17,879	10,382	17,795	25,018	11,026	38,760	23,900	—	275,752
1927 (b)	33,424	24,579	27,641	45,349	17,879	10,382	17,644	25,018	11,052	38,760	23,900	—	275,628
1928 (a) (b)	33,424	24,651	27,641	45,349	17,879	10,281	17,795	25,018	11,026	38,760	23,900	—	275,724
1929 (a)	33,424	24,651	27,641	45,349	17,879	10,281	17,795	24,901	11,026	38,877	23,900	—	275,724
1929 (b)	33,424	24,651	27,641	45,349	17,879	10,281	17,795	24,948	11,026	38,830	23,900	—	275,724
1930 (a)	33,424	24,651	27,641	45,349	17,879	10,281	17,795	25,516	11,026	38,940	23,900	—	275,724
1930 (b)	35,001	25,977	28,082	45,900	18,095	10,577	17,602	25,349	10,977	39,940	24,278	—	281,945
1931 (a) (b), 1932	35,001	25,977	28,082	45,900	18,095	10,577	17,602	25,176	10,977	39,940	24,278	9,712	281,778
1933	33,765	25,977	29,318	45,900	17,719	10,953	17,602	25,176	10,423	39,965	16,490	9,466	281,778
1934	33,765	25,977	29,318	45,900	17,719	10,953	16,380	25,178	10,423	39,965	16,488	9,466	281,778
1935	33,765	25,977	29,318	45,900	17,644	10,953	16,626	25,178	10,443	39,965	16,488	9,466	281,778
1936	33,765	26,120	29,298	45,757	17,644	10,953	16,626	25,178	10,443	39,965	16,488	9,466	281,703
1937-8	33,620	26,120	29,443	45,757	17,644	10,953	16,626	25,178	10,443	39,965	16,488		281,703
1939-42	33,620	26,120	29,443	45,757	17,644	10,953	16,626	28,666	10,443	36,477	16,488		281,703

POPULATION

Year	Adamawa	Bauchi	Benue	Bornu	Ilorin	Kabba	Kano	Niger	Plateau	Sokoto	Zaria	Katsina	N. Nigeria
1926 (a)	549,137	952,877	795,899	1,053,839	519,627	411,082	2,299,682	439,275	513,048	1,666,821	1,031,547	—	10,232,834
1926 (b)	549,136	952,951	795,899	1,053,839	519,627	411,082	2,300,034	439,275	510,631	1,666,821	1,020,231	—	10,219,526
1927 (a)	569,734	951,517	816,416	1,097,914	517,516	445,964	2,335,789	445,070	518,817	1,700,557	1,050,506	—	10,449,800
1927 (b)	569,734	944,086	816,416	1,097,914	517,516	445,964	2,297,472	445,070	517,687	1,700,903	1,036,319	—	10,389,081
1928 (a) (b)	597,436	1,000,464	846,083	1,079,484	504,022	449,443	2,404,456	453,998	542,316	1,768,369	1,137,232	—	10,783,303
1929 (a)	622,085	1,006,650	888,572	1,091,224	507,495	450,204	2,435,212	458,508	544,474	1,776,761	1,266,090	—	11,047,275
1929 (b)	622,085	1,006,650	888,572	1,091,224	507,495	450,204	2,435,212	457,907	544,474	1,776,761	1,250,230	—	11,030,814
1930 (a) (b)	652,693	1,010,786	926,526	1,112,236	511,890	464,976	2,451,936	456,683	540,361	1,824,349	1,329,719	—	11,282,155
1931 (a)	652,277	1,025,236	987,208	1,118,313	537,487	462,668	2,436,505	472,969	568,315	1,815,110	1,357,037	—	11,433,099
1931 (b)	657,099	1,037,218	985,515	1,118,138	536,085	462,321	2,431,875	471,314	552,819	1,825,899	1,310,818	—	11,389,081
1932	660,538	1,029,508	990,568	1,114,368	514,313	459,652	2,425,778	457,152	588,064	1,791,762	1,304,393	—	11,336,096
1933	670,709	1,029,213	976,322	1,102,124	475,124	450,509	2,432,451	453,744	563,035	1,856,784	1,306,923	—	11,316,938
1934	657,976	984,757	986,525	1,053,573	453,347	463,531	2,374,253	461,208	540,836	1,869,160	428,142	1,039,109	11,312,417
1935	654,698	1,019,145	980,481	1,057,441	452,201	467,074	2,388,400	465,332	523,311	1,935,732	453,650	1,047,563	11,445,028
1936	669,181	1,034,160	983,273	1,063,430	464,015	484,972	2,471,530	464,494	526,032	1,937,554	449,948	1,049,230	11,597,822
1937	683,026	1,034,685	1,009,921	1,081,579	468,097	505,690	2,615,395	466,946	536,461	1,977,130	446,478	1,060,842	11,886,250
1938	682,066	1,029,771	1,021,380	1,054,462	473,345	512,213	2,638,139	471,732	553,970	1,979,274	447,939	1,076,016	11,940,307
1939	690,832	1,015,231	1,022,008	998,271	478,643	513,594	2,629,337	553,055	562,406	1,894,848	466,966	1,081,991	11,907,532
1940	690,843	1,019,238	1,047,139	1,012,255	505,856	460,595	2,675,842	556,778	556,615	1,921,839	492,607	1,124,078	12,063,985
1941	717,828	1,024,660	1,048,606	1,055,441	519,476	458,345	2,702,589	564,702	575,352	1,942,835	492,295	1,136,221	12,238,350
1942	743,651	1,036,501	1,041,134	1,060,103	530,702	462,710	2,811,131	563,350	584,909	1,938,628	509,192	1,150,939	12,432,950

[1] See for 1926 (a) to 1930 (a) Report on Northern Provinces of Nigeria 1926, p. 55, 1927, p. 57, 1928, p. 55, 1929, p. 53, 1930, p. 54; 1926 (b) to 1930 (b) Nigeria, Blue Book 1926, p. 298, 1927, p. 320, 1928, p. 346, 1929, p. 340, 1930, p. 342; 1931 (a); 1931 (b) Census of Nigeria, 1931, vol. ii, pp. 52-3, 63-6, 99-104; 1931 (b) Report on Northern Provinces of Nigeria 1931 p. 55; 1932-42 Nigeria, Blue Book 1932, Section 15, p. 2, to 1942, Section 15, p. 2.

was found in Birnin Gwari. In Katsina every effort was made to ensure a more accurate count, resulting in an increase of 117,000 in the population statistics.[1]

1930. The Census in Zaria Emirate showed a small decline in population. This suggests that the regular increases of previous years were due to a gradual improvement in the counting of a more or less stationary population. The increase of 68,278 in Katsina Emirate over the 1929 figures is due mainly to a closer counting subsequent upon the change over from the system of assessment based on farm measurements to one based on an estimate of the total income from all sources of the taxation unit.[2]

Benue Province. 1929. In the Tiv Districts marked improvement in District Administration has followed the appointment of Tiv District Scribes, which made it possible for the District Heads themselves to carry out the annual assessment census with excellent results.[3]

1930. Throughout the Province the increased efficiency of the Native Administrations was reflected in more accurate census figures being obtained, resulting in an increase of some 40,000 of all ages.[4]

Kabba Province. 1926. The Igbirra Division is progressing and a much more accurate census, showing a large increase in population, was made during the year.

In Kabba Division a fresh census resulted in an increase in the return of population furnished last year.

A new system of tax collection was inaugurated in Igbirra District, which was found to be very successful. Slips of different colours for adult males, females and exempted persons of either sex were issued and the native authority gave out that all persons were required to be in possession of such a token or were liable to a fine in the Native Courts. This brought to light an extraordinary large number of people who had formerly avoided the tax or not been counted . . . .[5]

1927. The new system of tax collection inaugurated in Igbirra Division in 1926 was extended to the other Divisions in 1927 and has been an unqualified success. . . . This method has resulted in a large increase of figures of population, by the registration of persons who had hitherto escaped taxation.[6]

Bornu Province. 1929. The increase in the number of children recorded in Dikwa Division is due to closer and more accurate methods of counting.[7]

1930. The disproportionate increase in the number of children in Dikwa Division is due to more accurate registration and to the fact that the suspicions entertained by many concerning the counting of children are gradually being overcome.[8]

From the 'census' of 1931 to the assessment of 1934 the official population figures showed a slight but steady decrease. The drop in 1931 in Zaria Province (from 1,357,023 to 1,310,818) was apparently not genuine.

The Native Administration annual census for 1931 revealed a serious decline of population in Zaria Emirate amounting to some 23,000. Apart from locust damage and failure of crops this is attributed to the high incidence of taxation in Zaria as compared with other emirates, and to meet this situation it will be necessary to write down the 1931–32 assessment.[9]

The heavy drop in 1933 in Ilorin Province (from 514,313[10] to 475,124) was likewise due to technical causes.

[1] *Report on the Northern Provinces 1929*, p. 31.   [2] Ibid. *1930*, p. 34.   [3] Ibid. *1929*, p. 11.
[4] Ibid. *1930*, p. 14. For details as to Adamawa Province see Kuczynski, pp. 214–15, 245.
[5] *Report on the Northern Provinces 1926*, p. 25.   [6] Ibid. *1927*, pp. 24–5.
[7] *Report on the Cameroons under British Mandate 1929*, p. 100.
[8] Ibid. *1930*, p. 103. The official figure for children increased from 55,845 in 1928 to 65,556 in 1929, and to 70,012 in 1930.
[9] *Report on the Northern Provinces 1931*, p. 33.
[10] The 'new count' in 1931 had shown a population of 537,487.

In May the tax registers [in the Pategi-Lafiagi Division] were carefully checked, and the names of a number of non-taxable persons, aged, infirm, absentees were removed.[1]

A similar situation was revealed in 1934 in Kano Province (decrease from 2,432,451 to 2,374,253).

Intensive counts of representative village units have been made in order to obtain a check on the general census and a better idea of the proportion of adult taxable males to the females and children. It is impossible to attempt a general census of women and children, which only leads to most misleading figures. A very much closer count has been made of adult males. The result of this has been to find that in many areas the assessment has been unduly inflated by the inclusion of youths below the taxable age amongst adult males.[2]

The official figures increased again considerably from 1934 to 1942, but the reports do not offer any explanation.

According to the returns of 1911, 1921, and 1931 there were, apart from the Natives, 5,350, 1,168, and 1,825[3] non-Natives.[4]

4. Nigeria and Cameroons

The figures of Natives and non-Natives are summarized in Tables 4, 5, and 6. In view of the comments already made it does not seem necessary further to discuss these data; it may suffice to mention that according to the most recent estimate (1942) the total population of Nigeria and the Cameroons was about 21,260,000, i.e. less than the estimate of the Government Statistician for 1931 (22,000,000). But this may be the place to point out the defects in the presentation of the population data in the various official documents.

(1) The figures given for the total population often comprise only the native population.[5]

(2) Sometimes the same figures are given for the non-Native and for the European population.[6]

(3) The yearly population estimates given for Cameroons Province in the Reports to the League of Nations differed in part considerably from those shown in the Reports on the Southern Provinces and the Blue Books.[7]

(4) The figures in the 1931 census report regarding the Cameroons are contradictory. The Census Officer, Northern Provinces, gives the population of Northern Cameroons as 394,961,[8] but according to the Government Statistician it was 422,440.[9] The former total was obtained by adding the

---

[1] *Report on the Northern Provinces 1933*, p. 25.

[2] Ibid. *1934*, pp. 32–3.   [3] Including Northern Cameroons.

[4] The 1911 census report treated all persons who were not natives of Northern Nigeria as non-Natives, while in 1921 and 1931 all Africans (and descendants of Africans) were counted as Natives. The 1931 census report showed for 1911 only 678 non-Natives (see *Census of Nigeria, 1931*, vol. ii, p. 1), but reckoned as such only the Europeans.

[5] See, for example, *Colonial Reports, Nigeria 1936*, p. 10, *1937*, p. 11; *Statistical Abstract British Empire 1926/35*, p. 3, *1928/37*, p. 3.

[6] Thus, Nigeria, *Medical Report 1935*, p. 8, shows for 1934 and 1935 a European population of 5,021 and 5,246 respectively while the same figures are given ibid. *1936*, p. 14, for the non-Native population of those two years.   [7] See Tables 1 and 5.

[8] See *Census of Nigeria, 1931*, vol. ii, p. 21.   [9] See ibid., vol. i, pp. 8, 99.

TABLE 4. *Native Population of Nigeria, 1906–20*

Territory	1906	1907	1909	1910	1911
N. Nigeria.	7,164,751	5,935,000	6,714,038	7,811,309	8,110,631
S. Nigeria.	6,085,000	6,000,000	6,700,000	6,700,000	7,855,749
Total	13,249,751	11,935,000	13,414,038	14,511,309	15,966,380

Territory	1913	1914	1918	1919	1920
N. Nigeria.	8,967,836	9,500,000	9,000,000	8,668,138	9,089,526
S. Nigeria.	7,891,000	7,856,000	7,750,000	8,918,695	8,727,673
Total	16,858,836	17,356,000	16,750,000	17,586,833	17,817,199

TABLE 5. *Native Population of Nigeria and Cameroons, 1921–42*[1]

Year	Northern Provinces	Northern Cameroons	Southern Provinces	Cameroons Province	Nigeria	Cameroons	Total
1921[2]	9,994,515	261,663	8,069,406	299,106	18,063,921	560,769	18,624,690
1921	10,046,865	285,500	8,081,395	358,914	18,128,260	644,414	18,772,674
1923	9,927,349	289,629	8,072,294	347,722	17,999,643	637,351	18,636,994
1924	10,019,328	301,996	7,981,375	358,028	18,000,703	660,024	18,660,727
1925	10,000,998	296,511	8,211,901	390,864	18,212,899	687,375	18,900,274
1926	9,920,094	312,740	8,309,220	354,101	18,229,314	666,841	18,896,155
1927	10,105,792	344,008	8,004,809	356,042	18,110,601	700,050	18,810,651
1928	10,430,954	352,349	8,054,142	366,515	18,485,096	718,864	19,203,960
1929	10,675,860	371,415	8,210,639	366,763	18,886,499	738,178	19,624,677
1930	10,907,365	394,790	8,172,257	379,050	19,079,622	773,840	19,853,462
1931[2]	11,010,668	422,431	8,115,034	374,596	19,125,702	797,027	19,922,729
1932	10,929,357	406,739	8,122,732	374,872	19,052,089	781,611	19,833,700
1933	10,914,952	401,986	8,122,732	378,825	19,037,684	780,811	19,818,495
1934	10,916,566	395,851	8,168,239	382,501	19,084,805	778,352	19,863,157
1935	11,033,800	411,228	8,090,987	406,388	19,124,787	817,616	19,942,403
1936	11,183,070	414,752	8,186,561	410,482	19,369,631	825,234	20,194,865
1937	11,463,244	423,006	8,182,856	407,689	19,646,100	830,695	20,476,795
1938	11,528,833	411,474	8,202,780	445,753	19,731,613	857,227	20,588,840
1939	11,907,532		8,270,185	464,097	..	..	20,641,814
1940	12,063,985		8,279,533	477,258	..	..	20,820,776
1941	12,238,350		8,324,958	477,258	..	..	21,040,566
1942	12,432,950		8,350,553	477,258	..	..	21,260,761

[1] For Cameroons 1921–38 see *Report on the Cameroons under British Mandate 1921* to *1937* (quoted in Kuczynski, *The Cameroons and Togoland*, pp. 222–3, 238–9); *1938*, p. 106. For all other data see Sources to Tables 1, 2, and 3. [2] 'Census'.

TABLE 6. *Non-Native Population of Nigeria and Cameroons, 1921, 1931, and 1938*[1]

Year	Northern Provinces	Northern Cameroons	Southern Provinces	Cameroons Province	Nigeria	Cameroons	Total
1921	1,168	6	2,888	59	4,056	65	4,121
1931	1,816	9	3,341	276	5,157	285	5,442
1938	..	12	..	436	7,775	448	8,223

[1] For 1921 see Meek, vol. ii, p. 180; *Report on the Cameroons under British Mandate 1921*, p. 47; Talbot, vol. iv, p. 22. For 1931 see *Census of Nigeria, 1931*, vol. i, pp. 8, 10, vol. iii, p. 27; *Report on the Cameroons 1932*, p. 100. For 1938 see *Colonial Reports, Nigeria 1938*, p. 16; *Report on the Cameroons 1938*, p. 107.

figures for the various districts. If it is correct, the population of British Cameroons would have been 769,833, and not 797,312 (as shown by the Government Statistician).

(5) An utterly misleading estimate of the population is given in the Nigeria Medical Report for 1936:

The estimate is computed on an arithmetical basis from the figures for the 1921 and 1931 census.

	1921 Census	1931 Census	1935 (mid-year)	1936 (mid-year)
Southern Provinces . .	7,856,297	7,793,355	7,793,355	7,793,355
Northern Provinces . .	10,332,365	11,434,924	11,903,512	12,013,767
Cameroons under British Mandate	294,161	374,872	409,174	417,245
Totals	18,482,823	19,603,151	20,106,041	20,224,367

Owing to the doubt existing as to whether the population had actually diminished in the Southern Provinces during the intercensal period 1921–1931, the census population is given and not one based on the later census.[1]

The first line should not read 'Southern Provinces', but 'Southern Provinces excluding Colony'; the second line should not read 'Northern Provinces', but 'Northern Provinces including Northern Cameroons'; the third line should not read 'Cameroons under British Mandate', but 'Cameroons Province'; the total should read 'Nigeria, excluding Colony, and including Cameroons under British Mandate'.

The area of Nigeria is 338,593 square miles and that of the Cameroons 34,081 square miles. According to the 1931 'census' the number of inhabitants per square mile was 56·5 in Nigeria. In the Northern Provinces it was 41·7 (varying between 19 in Niger Province and 138 in Kano Province); in the Southern Provinces it was 109·2 (varying between 56 in Ondo Province and 235 in the Colony). In the Cameroons it was only 23·4.[2] According to the estimate for 1942 the number of native inhabitants per square mile was 57·0 in Nigeria and the Cameroons. In the Northern Provinces (including Northern Cameroons) it was 44·1 (varying between 20 in Niger Province and 169 in Kano Province); in the Eastern Provinces (including Cameroons Province) it was 105·4 (varying between 29 in Cameroons Province and 222 in Onitsha Province); in the Western Provinces it was 88·7 (varying between 58 in Ondo Province and 240 in the Colony).

According to the 1931 'census' there were two towns with over 100,000 inhabitants (Ibadan, 387,133; Lagos, 126,108).[3]

[1] Nigeria, *Medical Report 1936*, p. 8.
[2] The *Annual Colonial Reports, Nigeria*, from 1932 onwards (see, for example, *1937*, p. 11) all state: 'The density for Nigeria, excluding mandated territory, is 56·5, while for mandated territory only it falls to 16·4 persons per square mile.' But the figure of 16·4 for the Mandated Territory was the one ascertained at the most deficient 'census' of 1921. (According to *Census of Nigeria, 1931*, vol. i, p. 21, the population of the Northern Cameroons, excluding the Dikwa Division, was 67,669 in 1921 and 200,588 in 1931!)
[3] See ibid., p. 12.

TABLE 7. *Population Density, Nigeria and Cameroons, 1931 and 1942*[1]

1931

Provinces	Area sq. m.	Natives	Non-Natives	Total	Population per sq. m.
NORTHERN PROVINCES					
Adamawa[2]	35,001	652,277	84	652,361	19
Bauchi	25,977	1,025,236	74	1,025,310	39
Benue	28,082	987,208	150	987,358	35
Bornu[3]	45,900	1,118,313	47	1,118,360	24
Ilorin	18,095	537,487	72	537,559	30
Kabba	10,577	462,668	58	462,726	44
Kano	17,602	2,436,505	339	2,436,844	138
Niger	25,349	472,969	98	473,067	19
Plateau	10,977	568,315	423	568,738	52
Sokoto	39,910	1,815,110	68	1,815,178	45
Zaria	24,278	1,357,037	386	1,357,423	56
Total	281,778	11,433,099[4]	1,825[4]	11,434,924	41
Excl. N. Cameroons	264,278	11,010,668	1,816	11,012,484	42
Northern Cameroons	17,500	422,431	9	422,440	24
SOUTHERN PROVINCES					
Calabar	6,331	899,080	423	899,503	142
Cameroons	16,581	374,596	276	374,872	23
Ogoja	7,529	708,499	39	708,538	94
Onitsha	4,937	1,107,525	220	1,107,745	224
Owerri	10,374	1,599,497	412	1,599,909	154
Colony	1,381	323,544	1,476	325,020	235
Abeokuta	4,266	434,410	116	434,526	102
Benin	8,627	493,126	89	493,215	57
Ijebu	2,456	305,868	30	305,898	125
Ondo	8,211	462,508	52	462,560	56
Oyo	14,216	1,336,609	319	1,336,928	94
Warri	5,987	444,368	165	444,533	74
Total	90,896	8,489,630	3,617	8,493,247	93
Excl. Cameroons Province	74,315	8,115,034	3,341	8,118,375	109
NIGERIA AND CAMEROONS					
Total	372,674	19,922,729	5,442	19,928,171	53
CAMEROONS					
Total	34,081	797,027	285	797,312	23

1942

Provinces	Area sq. m.	Natives	Native Population per sq. m.
NORTHERN PROVINCES			
Adamawa	33,620	743,651	22
Bauchi	26,120	1,036,501	40
Benue	29,443	1,041,134	35
Bornu	45,757	1,060,103	23
Ilorin	17,644	530,702	30
Kabba	10,953	462,710	42
Kano	16,626	2,811,131	169
Katsina	9,466	1,150,939	122
Niger	28,666	563,350	20
Plateau	10,443	584,909	56
Sokoto	36,477	1,938,628	53
Zaria	16,488	509,192	31
Total	281,703	12,432,950	44
EASTERN PROVINCES			
Calabar	6,331	911,072	144
Cameroons	16,581	477,258	29
Ogoja	7,624	692,019	91
Onitsha	4,937	1,096,323	222
Owerri	9,970	1,613,973	162
Total	45,443	4,790,645	105
WESTERN PROVINCES			
Colony	1,381	331,544	240
Abeokuta	4,266	566,253	133
Benin	8,483	520,187	61
Ijebu	2,456	312,937	127
Ondo	8,286	476,968	58
Oyo	14,216	1,392,073	98
Warri	6,440	437,204	68
Total	45,528	4,037,166	89
NIGERIA AND CAMEROONS			
Total	372,674	21,260,761	57

[1] Computed from *Census of Nigeria, 1931*, vol. i, pp. 8, 10, 99; vol. ii, pp. 21, 63–6, 99–104; vol. iii, p. 27; Nigeria, *Blue Book 1939*, Section 15, p. 2; *1942*, Section 15, p. 2.
[2] Including 12,530 sq. m. of Northern Cameroons.
[3] Including 4,970 sq. m. of Northern Cameroons.
[4] The sum of the figures for the Provinces differs slightly from the total.

III. Composition of Native Population

Area of Origin. Of the total native population of Nigeria and the Cameroons in 1931, 19,895,522 were recorded as 'Natives of Nigeria', i.e. persons descended from a tribe indigenous to Nigeria,[1] and 27,207 as 'Native Foreigners', i.e. persons descended from other African tribes.[2] The distribution among the Northern and Southern Provinces was as follows:[3]

Northern Provinces and Northern Cameroons		Southern Provinces incl. Cameroons Province		Nigeria and Cameroons	
Natives of Nigeria	Native Foreigners	Natives of Nigeria	Native Foreigners	Natives of Nigeria	Native Foreigners
11,422,510	10,589	8,473,012	16,618	19,895,522	27,207

A question as to birthplace of the Natives was included only in the Intensive Census in the Northern Provinces and in the Census of Lagos. It appears that the proportion of persons born outside Nigeria among the Natives of Nigeria was 2·7 per cent. in the selected areas of the Northern Provinces (2·1 in the six complete districts of Katsina Division, 7·2 in the selected villages of the other Katsina Districts, 1·1 in the selected villages of the other Divisions, 4·5 in the Townships) and 0·8 per cent. in Lagos, while the proportion of persons born outside Nigeria among the Native Foreigners was 83·4 per cent. in the selected areas of the Northern Provinces and 78·6 per cent. in Lagos.

On the basis of these samples the Government Statistician makes an interesting attempt to estimate the proportion of persons born outside Nigeria for the whole of Nigeria and the Cameroons:

The relatively high proportion of immigrants from outside Nigeria shown by all the Intensive Census villages together is due to the considerable areas of the Katsina Emirate adjacent to French territory which were included in that Census. Thus the villages of Dankama and Jibiya, which are within a few miles of the border, have more than half their population immigrant from outside the Division. To base a proportion of immigrants on the totality of Intensive Census villages will give too high, while the 40 special villages will give too low a percentage of immigrants from outside Nigeria. The figure of 1·5 per cent for the proportion of Natives enumerated in Nigeria though born outside it, has been adopted, tentatively, for the Northern Provinces.

There is less material for an estimate in the Southern Provinces; the proportion of ½% per cent—that found for Lagos being 1 per cent—has been taken for the foreign-born element among Natives of Nigeria, though it is arguable that even that is too high.[4]

[1] 'A Native of Nigeria means any person whose parents were members of any tribe or tribes indigenous to Nigeria and the descendants of such persons, and includes any person one of whose parents was a member of such a tribe' (*Census of Nigeria, 1931*, vol. ii, p. 1).

[2] 'A Native Foreigner means any person (not being a Native of Nigeria) whose parents were members of a tribe or tribes indigenous to some part of Africa and the descendants of such persons, and includes any person one of whose parents was a member of such a tribe' (ibid.).

[3] See ibid., vol. i, p. 10.   [4] Ibid., p. 24.

TABLE 8. *Natives by Birthplace, Selected Areas, Nigeria, 1931*[1]

Birthplace	Northern Provinces — Katsina Division — 6 Districts Nigerian	6 Districts Foreign	16 villages Nigerian	16 villages Foreign	40 villages[2] Nigerian	40 villages[2] Foreign	Townships Nigerian	Townships Foreign	Form 7[3] Nigerian	Form 7[3] Foreign	Total Nigerian	Total Foreign	Lagos[4] Nigerian	Lagos[4] Foreign
Nigeria, Northern Prov.	242,969	5	55,082	8	95,164	49	16,193	263	3,430	86	412,838	411	11,922	} 1,508
Nigeria, Southern Prov.	25	1	169	—	144	—	8,064	96	1,708	34	10,110	130	99,931	
Gold Coast	26	—	8	3	1	2	11	545	2	215	48	766	166	974
Other Br. W. Afr. Colonies	1	—	2	3	—	—	7	320	3	188	13	511	126	869
Egypt and Sudan	10	—	2	2	5	2	3	10	1	2	21	16	5	7
French Equatorial Africa	57	1	38	1	81	15	312	436	55	78	543	532	19	126
French West Africa	5,091	2	4,209	1	656	7	565	473	104	90	10,625	573	483[5]	} 2,202[6]
French Cameroons	15	1	19	1	300	90	219	91	87	37	640	220		
Other African countries	—	—	5	—	1	3	20	44	2	17	28	65	50	1,189
Africa unspecified	7	—	3	—	2	—	3	—	3	1	8	1	291	34
Asia	—	—	1	—	4	—	4	—	1	—	19	—	2	—
Europe	—	—	—	—	1	—	2	5	2	—	6	5	13	6
America	—	—	—	—	—	—	1	17	1	10	2	27	24	175
Continent unspecified	222	—	62	—	83	—	501	40	306	23	1,174	63		21
Total	248,423	10	59,600	21	96,442	168	25,905	2,340	5,705	781	436,075	3,320[7]	114,193[8]	7,111
Nigeria	242,994	5	55,251	8	95,308	49	24,257	359	5,138	120	422,948	541	113,014	1,508
Outside Nigeria	5,207	5	4,287	13	1,049	119	1,144	1,941	258	637	11,945	2,715	888	5,548
Unspecified	222	—	62	—	85	—	504	40	309	24	1,182	64	291	55

[1] Computed from *Census of Nigeria, 1931*, vol. ii, pp. 99–104; vol. iv, pp. 35–6. Nigerian means 'Native of Nigeria'; Foreign means 'Native Foreigner'.

[2] In one of the 41 villages (Shellen with 2,714 inhabitants) the birthplace was not coded.

[3] Residing outside townships in households of non-Natives and educated Native Foreigners.

[4] Excluding the 3,361 persons enumerated in Waterside Canoes, on Trains, and on Roads.

[5] Other French West African Colonies.

[6] Other French African Colonies.

[7] Of these 3,320 persons, 1,565 were recorded as of British nationality (894 Gold Coast, 671 Sierra Leone), 486 as of French nationality (French Equatorial Africa), and 1,269 as of another nationality; see *Census of Nigeria, 1931*, vol. ii, p. 140.

[8] Including 1,161 born in Nigeria (not specified whether in Northern or Southern Provinces).

This estimate leads to the result that of 19,922,729 Natives 235,967 or 1·2 per cent. were born outside Nigeria.

	Natives of Nigeria			Native Foreigners		
	Total	Immigrants per cent.	Immigrants	Total	Immigrants per cent.	Immigrants
Northern Provinces[1]	11,422,510	1·5	171,338	10,589	80·0	8,471
Southern Provinces[1]	8,473,012	0·5	42,365	16,618	83·0	13,793

[1] Including Mandated Territory.

Sex. Information about the sex ratio among Natives in the Southern Provinces is very scanty. According to *Statistical Tables, Colonial Possessions* there were in 1911 in Southern Nigeria 3,613,307 males and 4,241,709 females[1] or 117·4 females to 100 males. The Census Officer reported:

From the percentages rendered by the District Commissioners, it is to be noted that there is on the average a preponderance of females in the Colony and Protectorate, the ratio overall being 46% males and 54% females, or, say, roughly 9 males to 11 females. In referring to these particular statistics, it should be pointed out that the percentages are in many instances based upon estimates made by the officers up-country and not, as a general rule, upon actual house to house counting. At the same time it is to be observed that the sex returns of the officers concerned are, with a few exceptions, not very dissimilar.

Taking the ports alone, it is found, not unnaturally, that the proportion of males and females are reversed, the former being in a pronounced majority. Thus in the eleven principal ports, where an actual house to house enumeration was made, we find that there were 57·6% males and 42·4% females. This difference between the average for the whole of the Colony and Protectorate and the ports alone may be accounted for by the large numbers of Kroo and other labourers employed on the seaboard by the merchants, steamship owners, and government departments, and also, especially in Lagos, by a very considerable number of up-country male traders in the towns unaccompanied by their wives.[2]

According to the 1921 'census' there were in the Southern Provinces excluding Cameroons Province 3,919,149 males and 4,150,233 females. If the returns were correct, the number of males would have increased by 8·5 per cent. and the number of females would have decreased by 2·2 per cent. But it seems more likely that the disproportion between the sexes was overstated in 1911. Including Cameroons Province there were, in 1921, 4,069,796 males and 4,298,692 females or 105·6 females to 100 males. The corresponding returns at the 1931 'census' showed 4,036,126 males and 4,453,571 females or 110·3 females to 100 males. These figures would suggest a large rise in the preponderance of females since 1921. But the Government Statistician rightly says: 'I fear that neither of the Southern Provinces' counts commands sufficient confidence to lay any stress on this increase.'[3] In any case, there cannot be the slightest doubt that for

[1] See *Statistical Tables 1910*, p. 420. These figures were obtained by allocating 46 per cent. to males and 54 per cent. to females.
[2] *Report on Southern Nigeria Census, 1911*, pp. 3–4.
[3] *Census of Nigeria, 1931*, vol. i, p. 9.

some Provinces the sex ratio was misrepresented in the 1931 returns. Thus the ratio of 147 females to 100 males in Ijebu Province must be wrong because the enormous excess of females does not appear only among the adults where it might have been caused by a (temporary) absence of men but also among the children where no satisfactory explanation seems conceivable.

For the Northern Provinces the available information is much more ample. Separate figures for males and females were given at the earliest population estimates. They may be summarized as follows:[1]

Sex	1904	1905	1906	1909	1910
Males.	3,828,710	3,965,637	3,422,260	3,067,828	3,408,799
Females	5,332,990	4,816,546	3,742,491	3,646,210	4,402,510
F. to 100 M.	139·3	121·5	109·4	118·9	129·2

Sex	1911 (a)	1911 (b)	1912	1913	1921
Males.	3,379,185	4,033,743	4,088,837	3,481,337	4,839,743
Females	4,731,446	5,235,257	5,523,104	5,486,499	5,157,403
F. to 100 M.	140·0	129·8	135·1	157·6	106·6

Most figures, of course, were arrived at by guessing, and it appears that up to the First World War there was, on the whole, a tendency to over-estimate the excess of females. In 1904 the original returns did not show the sex ratio for some Provinces; it was assumed that the ratio in Kano was the same as in Sokoto, and in Bassa and Yola the same as in Muri. Sir Frederick Lugard made the following comment:

This return, rough as it is, furnishes some indication both of the relative density of the population and of the proportion between the sexes. Both bear striking witness to the devastation caused by war and slave raids.[2]

But one gets rather the impression that some District Officers thought that because there had been wars and slave-raids there must be a large excess of females. For Bauchi Province the total population estimated at 920,000 was subdivided into 240,000 males and 680,000 females. However, in the following year, while the total estimate of 920,000 was maintained, the returns showed 460,000 males and 460,000 females, and the ratio of females to 100 males for the whole of Northern Nigeria dropped from 139 to 121. For Nassarawa the 1904 returns showed 550,000 males and 950,000 females, and the 1905 returns 555,000 males and 945,000 females, but it appeared that the population had been grossly over-estimated and the 1906 returns showed 279,285 males and 321,720 females. The ratio of females to 100 males for the whole of Nigeria dropped to 109. Thereafter the ratio increased again. It was shown to be 129 in 1910, 140 according to the 1911 census returns, and 130 according to the revised

---

[1] See for 1904–6 Colonial Reports, Northern Nigeria 1904, p. 84, 1905–6, p. 62, 1906–7, p. 99; 1909–10 Northern Nigeria, Blue Book 1909 R, p. 1, 1910 R, p. 1; 1911 (a) Original Census returns Northern Nigeria, Census 1911; 1911 (b) Revised Census returns Blue Book 1911 R, p. 1; 1912–13; ibid. 1912 R, p. 1, 1913 R, p. 2; 1921 Census, Meek, vol. ii, p. 180.

[2] Colonial Reports, Northern Nigeria 1904, p. 84.

census data. But the figures for the various Provinces were quite erratic. Kano and Yola may serve as examples:

| Province | Estimate 1910 | | Census Returns 1911 | | | |
| | | | Original | | Revised | |
	Males	Females	Males	Females	Males	Females
Kano	1,181,482	1,674,057	1,159,256	2,013,490	1,544,687	1,955,313
Yola	82,052	107,852	79,260	98,490	111,300	188,700

In the following years the ratio increased again and amounted in 1913 to 158. For eight of the thirteen Provinces (Sokoto, Central, Zaria, Kontagora, Nassarawa, Muri, Yola, Ilorin) the number of females was given in each district as twice the number of males. That the ratio for the whole of Northern Nigeria was not higher still than 158 females to 100 males was mainly due to the fact that the revised Kano figures for 1911 were entered unchanged in the 1913 returns.

After the amalgamation of Northern and Southern Nigeria the sex ratio was no longer shown in the annual statistics. According to the 1921 'census' there were 106·6 females to 100 males,[1] the ratio fluctuating between 92·6 in Kontagora and 117·3 in Ilorin. In 1931 there were 106·4 females to 100 males,[2] the ratios varying between 97·5 in Plateau Province and 120·8 in Bornu, but the results of the Intensive Censuses suggest that the excess of females was actually higher than ascertained at the General Census.

Age. The first population estimate made in Southern Nigeria (1905) distinguished men, women, and children. The proportion of children was given as 36 per cent., but the percentage varied enormously in the various Districts. In Ikot-Ekpene it was 57, in Obubra 51, and in Owerri 50. On the other hand, it was only 14 in Forcados and 15 in Eket and in Brass and Akassa. There cannot be any doubt that the proportion was over-stated in the former districts and understated in the latter. The ratio of adult females to 100 adult males was 134. Apart from two small Districts (Okuni and Forcados) women exceeded men everywhere. As stated above, in Ikot-Ekpene women were shown to be exactly twice as numerous as men. In the country as a whole there were about as many children as women but the ratios varied enormously in the various districts.

The 1911 census report gives figures concerning age only for the 11 principal ports. The Census Officer said:

In the ports where an individual count was feasible and accomplished, the percentages . . . worked out at 6·2% Infants [under 3], 21·7% Children [from 3 to marriageable age], 13·6% 'Young Persons' [of marriageable age up to 20], and 58·5% Adults [over 20], but . . . there was a large proportion of adult males unaccompanied by their wives and, of course, children in the coast towns on census day.

In the out-districts, the estimates varied so considerably, and are in many cases so incomplete, that I am not prepared to place on record any figures concerning age which might be considered reliable as an all round average for the whole of Southern Nigeria.[3]

[1] Excluding Northern Cameroons for which the population was not given by sex.
[2] Including Northern Cameroons for which the figures by sex were not given separately.
[3] *Report on Southern Nigeria Census, 1911*, p. 4.

According to the 1921 'census' there were in the Southern Provinces including Cameroons Province 2,410,805 men, 2,574,915 women, and 3,382,768 children. The proportion of children was high; it amounted to 40·4 per cent. In Oyo it was 46·2 per cent., but in Cameroons Province it was only 28·9 per cent. The ratio of women to 100 men was 106·8, and there were 122·8 children to 100 women. In Oyo there were 164 children to 100 women, but in Cameroons Province only 81.

The 1931 'census' showed in the Southern Provinces including Cameroons Province 2,348,579 men, 2,622,820 women, and 3,518,231 children. The proportion of children was 41·4 per cent. In Ijebu it was 51·7 per cent., in Oyo 49·9 per cent. In Abeokuta, on the other hand, it was only 33·4 per cent. The ratio of women to 100 men was 111·7, and there were 134·1 children to 100 women. In Ijebu there were 182 children to 100 women, but in Abeokuta only 88.

The Census Officer for the Southern Provinces, in discussing the 1931 ratios of adult females and non-adults to adult males, says:

> In the present state of statistical knowledge in the Southern Provinces it is impossible to say within what limits these ratios may be accepted as reasonable. However, it may be said that if many of the ratios found in the Returns of this Census are genuine, then the composition of the native population of the Southern Provinces differs very considerably from that of most other peoples in the world. . . . Without valid evidence little credence can be attached to the anomalous values of the ratios reported from the various Provinces.[1]

For the Northern Provinces hardly any figures concerning age seem to have been published before 1921.[2] As to the facts ascertained in that year Mr. Meek reports:

> In the townships it was possible to ascertain with a moderate degree of accuracy the age of each inhabitant, and the results were tabulated in five groups: (1) Up to 3 years; (2) 3–15; (3) 15–30; (4) 30–50; (5) 50 and over.[3]
> In the provinces, as far as the natives and native foreigners were concerned, two age-groups only were used, viz. the adult and non-adult—the non-adult including all persons up to the age of 15, and the adult all persons from the age of 15. . . . It will appear from the various tables that even although these two age-groups only were employed the returns were vitiated by unintentional misstatement, and probably also by intentional misrepresentation.[4]

In the Provinces there were 2,880,009 men, 3,363,152 women, and 3,733,052 children.[5] The proportion of children was 37·4 per cent.

We cannot, however, fail to notice the great disparity shown in the age ratios as between the various provinces. While 48·2 per cent. of the inhabitants of Kontagora Province appear as non-adults, in Nupe and Nasarawa Provinces the proportion is only 25·9 per cent. It would appear that in these two latter provinces either many

---

[1] Census of Nigeria, 1931, vol. iii, p. 6. For the inaccuracy of the age data obtained at the census in Lagos see ibid., vol. iv, pp. 13–14. For Cameroons Province see Kuczynski, pp. 253–61.

[2] As regards the overestimate of the proportion of children by Sir F. Lugard see p. 589 above. For Nassarawa Province the Resident, in a Memorandum dated 31 Dec. 1919, put the number of men at 98,014, the number of women at 94,096, and the number of children at 75,030; see Notes on Nassarawa Province, p. 26.

[3] The seven townships, however, contained altogether only 18,302 Natives, 1,384 Native Foreigners, and 506 non-Natives.   [4] Meek, vol. ii, p. 195.

[5] These figures exclude not only the population of the townships, but also the 1,247 Native Foreigners and the 662 non-Natives living outside townships.

non-adults have been classed as adults, or, more probably, that many parents have, in accordance with the well-known Negro custom, deliberately concealed the true number of their children. In Kontagora Province, on the other hand, many adults have probably been classed as non-adults with a view to the concealment of taxable capacity.[1]

The ratio of women to 100 men was 116·8 for the country as a whole. It exceeded 120 in Ilorin (132·6), Sokoto (128·9), Kano (122·9), and Bornu (120·8).[2] Mr. Meek makes the following comment:

> These provinces are mainly Muslim and the most highly civilized, and it is possible that some portion of the excess female adults may be due to the presence of additional wives from other provinces. . . . It is more probable, however, that the large excess figures should be ascribed to incorrect enumeration. The mortality among adult males cannot be so much greater proportionately than among adult females, that an excess of 82 per thousand in the non-adult group becomes a deficiency of 168 in the adult group.[3]

It is doubtful, it seems to me, whether 'the presence of additional wives from other provinces' in mainly Muslim areas has anything to do with those apparently large excesses of women over men. In Ilorin, which showed the greatest preponderance of women, only 32 per cent. of the population were Muslims.[4] There was, on the other hand, an excess of men over women in Zaria where the proportion of Muslims was 70 per cent. The ratio of females to 100 males was 109·1 in Kano, 108·5 in Bornu, and 108·1 in Sokoto; it differed very little from the ratio for the whole country (106·6). The apparently excessive ratio of women to men in most Provinces was evidently due exclusively to incorrect allocation of females to the two age groups. In the country as a whole the ratio of girls to 100 boys was shown to be 91·8. In Sokoto it was 85·4, in Kano 91·9, in Bornu 85·1. In these and other Provinces evidently many girls were counted as adults at an age where males were considered non-adults. Assuming that there were actually 102 girls to 100 boys, the ratio of women to 100 men appears to be 110 for the country as a whole, 115 in Kano, 114 in Sokoto, and 112 in Bornu.[5]

In any case there is no evidence that women exceeded men more among the Muslims than among the pagans. Mr. Meek, it is true, says:

> If we examine the figures for the various tribes we are confronted with the fact that the predominantly Muslim tribes show a higher proportion of women than the animistic tribes . . . Three explanations of this may be given: (a) The social circumstances are easier for the Muslim woman than for the Animist; (b) many animistic women become the wives or concubines of Muslims; (c) the Muslims may have misstated the number of adult males to a greater extent than the Animists.[6]

Among the Hausa and Fulani, who among them comprised three-quarters of all Muslims,[7] the ratios of women to 100 men were in fact 121·8 and 120·4 respectively. But the ratios of females to 100 males were 108·0 and 106·1,[8] or practically the same as for the whole country (106·6), and if we assume again that there were actually 102 girls to 100 boys the ratios would appear to be 113 for the Hausa and 109 for the Fulani as compared with 110 for the whole native population.

---

[1] Meek, vol. ii, p. 196.   [2] See ibid., p. 203.   [3] Ibid., p. 199.   [4] See ibid., p. 249.
[5] In Ilorin, with only 32 per cent. Muslims, the ratio would appear to be 128, but here either the number of females must have been overstated or the number of males understated.
[6] Ibid., p. 201.   [7] See ibid., p. 250.   [8] See ibid., p. 209.

TABLE 9. Native Population by Sex and Age, Nigeria and Cameroons, 1931

Provinces	Adults		Children		Total		Females to 100 males			Children to 100 women
	Males	Females	Males	Females	Males	Females	Adults	Children	Total	
NORTHERN PROVINCES[1]										
Adamawa[2]	215,760	244,712	97,421	94,468	313,181	339,180	113.4	97.0	108.3	78.4
Bauchi	304,978	357,613	181,414	181,305	486,392	538,918	117.3	99.9	110.8	101.4
Benue	293,323	304,630	197,596	191,809	490,919	496,439	103.9	97.1	101.1	127.8
Bornu[3]	317,495	411,282	189,031	200,552	506,526	611,834	129.5	106.1	120.8	94.7
Ilorin	147,986	186,654	100,411	102,508	248,397	289,162	126.1	102.1	116.4	108.7
Kabba	130,871	158,551	85,533	87,771	216,404	246,322	121.2	102.6	113.8	109.3
Kano	839,416	825,641	388,865	382,922	1,228,281	1,208,563	98.4	98.5	98.4	93.5
Niger	160,210	174,895	68,852	69,110	229,062	244,005	109.2	100.4	106.5	78.9
Plateau	202,695	187,899	85,336	92,808	288,031	280,707	92.7	108.8	97.5	94.8
Sokoto	525,161	613,879	344,466	331,672	869,627	945,551	116.9	96.3	108.7	110.1
Zaria	361,316	432,723	302,312	261,058	663,628	693,781	119.8	86.4	104.5	130.2
Total	3,499,225[4]	3,898,479	2,041,237	1,995,983	5,540,462	5,894,462	111.4	97.8	106.4	103.6
Excl. Northern Cameroons	3,380,609	3,751,860	3,907,494				111.0			104.1
Northern Cameroons	118,616	146,619	129,726				123.6			88.5
SOUTHERN PROVINCES[5]										
Colony	96,406	94,947	64,708	67,502	161,114	162,449	98.5	104.3	100.8	139.2
Abeokuta	125,483	164,030	64,438	80,459	189,921	244,489	130.7	124.9	128.7	88.3
Benin	141,953	148,175	98,988	104,010	240,941	252,185	104.4	105.1	104.7	137.0
Calabar	258,399	273,035	179,278	188,398	437,677	461,433	105.7	105.1	105.4	134.7
Cameroons	118,118	128,601	66,000	61,888	184,118	190,489	108.9	93.8	103.5	99.4
Ijebu	60,603	87,079	63,361	94,825	123,964	181,904	143.7	149.7	146.7	181.7
Ogoja	182,270	206,118	156,193	163,918	338,463	370,036	113.1	104.9	109.3	155.3
Ondo	134,631	151,268	81,818	95,061	216,449	246,329	112.4	116.2	113.8	116.9
Onitsha	350,906	350,571	201,103	204,885	552,069	555,456	99.9	101.9	100.6	115.8
Owerri	459,517	498,520	317,147	324,313	776,664	822,833	108.5	102.3	105.9	128.7
Oyo	299,203	370,731	308,890	357,792	608,093	728,523	123.9	115.8	119.8	179.8
Warri	121,360	149,745	85,563	87,700	206,923	237,445	123.4	102.5	114.8	115.7
Total	2,318,579	2,622,820	1,687,547	1,830,751	4,036,126	4,453,571	111.7	108.5	110.3	134.1
Excl. Cameroons Province	2,230,461	2,494,219	1,621,547	1,768,863	3,852,008	4,263,082	111.8	109.1	110.7	135.9
NIGERIA AND CAMEROONS										
Total	5,849,283	6,521,587	3,728,723	3,826,686	9,578,006	10,318,273	111.5	102.6	108.0	115.9
CAMEROONS[6]										
Total	236,734	275,220	257,614				116.3			93.6

[1] See Census of Nigeria, 1931, vol. ii, pp. 19, 21. The figures include 1,142 male non-Natives (1,418 adults, 24 children) and 383 female non-Natives (365 adults, 18 children); see ibid., p. 35. The figures for Northern Cameroons do not tally with those in Table 7; see explanation p. 596 above. [2] Including 66,392 adult males, 72,928 adult females, 61,268 children in Northern Cameroons. [3] Including 52,224 adult males, 73,691 adult females, and 68,458 children in Northern Cameroons. [4] Including 14 on trains. [5] See Census of Nigeria, 1931, vol. iii, pp. 19-20, 30. The figures include 37 male and 30 female non-Native children; see ibid., vol. i, p. 32. [6] The figures include all non-Natives in Northern Cameroons and the non-Native children in Cameroons Province.

The ratio of children to 100 women was 111·3. It oscillated between 67·4 in Nupe and 190·1 in Kontagora.[1]

According to the 1931 'census' returns there were 3,497,807 men, 3,898,114 women, and 4,037,178 children. The proportion of children was 37·1 per cent. It oscillated between 29·2 per cent. in Niger Province and 41·5 per cent. in Zaria Province. The ratio of women to 100 men was 111·4, varying between 92·7 in Plateau Province and 129·5 in Bornu Province. The ratio of children to 100 women was 103·6, varying between 78·4 in Adamawa and 130·2 in Zaria. Large as these differences between Provinces may seem, the differences between the returns for the various Divisions of one and the same Province are in many cases not less startling. I shall quote a few striking examples:[2]

Province	Division	Men	Women	Children	Children per cent.	Women to 100 men	Children to 100 women
Kabba	Igala	73,096	80,184	72,232	32·0	109·6	90·8
	Igbira	30,217	42,263	76,196	51·2	139·8	180·3
	Kabba	15,219	22,440	19,557	34·2	147·4	87·2
	Koton Karifi	12,339	13,664	5,319	17·0	110·7	37·5
Niger	Abuja	23,634	26,912	23,870	32·1	113·8	88·7
	Agaie-Lapai	20,148	23,915	12,077	21·5	118·6	50·5
	Bida	57,759	66,546	47,653	27·7	115·2	71·6
	Kontagora	22,163	23,046	23,970	34·7	103·9	104·0
	Kuta	23,548	21,300	19,836	30·7	90·4	93·1
	Zungeru	12,958	13,176	10,556	28·8	101·6	80·1
Plateau	Jemaa	22,436	24,103	29,780	39·0	107·4	123·6
	Jos	57,282	41,330	33,685	25·5	72·1	81·5
	Pankshin	58,149	54,375	48,228	30·0	93·5	88·7
	Shendam	35,859	39,632	42,811	36·2	110·5	108·0
	Southern	28,969	28,459	23,640	29·2	98·2	83·1
Zaria	Katsina	219,037	284,457	422,354	45·6	129·8	148·5
	Zaria	142,279	148,266	141,016	32·7	104·2	95·1

The Census Officer makes the following comment:

One knows of no such conditions prevailing in Kabba Province as would account for the enormous disproportions of non-adults shown in the Division of Koton Karifi . . . and Igbira . . . or for the low figure . . . in Agaie-Lapai Division of Niger Province. In Jos Division, however, where there is a large immigrant adult male population to the mining areas, one would expect to find a lower proportion of adult females and non-adults.[3]

As a matter of fact all ratios of sex and age derived from the General Censuses are open to grave doubts, since these 'censuses', also in the Northern Provinces, were based largely on the tax registers and, as regards women and children, on rough estimates or guesses. In some Divisions, such as Katsina, where a large excess of females (30 per cent.) was recorded for adults and a large deficiency of females among children (18 per cent.), this anomaly may be due to the custom of counting even

[1] See Meek, vol. ii, p. 203. The ratio for Kontagora is so high in spite of the fact that apparently many girls were counted as women.
[2] See *Census of Nigeria, 1931*, vol. ii, pp. 33, 52–3. Figures comprise total population.
[3] Ibid., p. 33.

TABLE 10. *Native Population by Sex and Age in six Katsina Districts, Nigeria, 1930–31*[1]

		Durbi	Ingawa	Magajin Gari	Marusa	Mashi	Tsagero	Total
Men	(a)	15,516	12,961	5,910	5,371	8,493	2,930	51,181
	(b)	18,661	15,881	9,794	6,609	9,887	3,758	64,590
Women	(a)	21,558	17,296	8,610	7,080	11,875	4,180	70,599
	(b)	22,075	17,851	10,285	7,255	11,835	4,379	73,680
Boys	(a)	21,085	14,404	7,604	6,366	11,782	3,881	65,122
	(b)	17,219	12,170	6,569	5,194	10,010	3,463	54,625
Girls	(a)	17,691	11,265	5,707	5,290	10,037	3,185	53,175
	(b)	17,991	12,397	6,604	5,080	9,834	3,488	55,394
Total males	(a)	36,601	27,365	13,514	11,737	20,275	6,811	116,303
	(b)[2]	35,895	28,064	16,374	11,806	19,901	7,223	119,263
Total females	(a)	39,249	28,561	14,317	12,370	21,912	7,365	123,774
	(b)[2]	40,084	30,277	16,918	12,339	21,685	7,868	129,171
Total	(a)	75,850	55,926	27,831	24,107	42,187	14,176	240,077
	(b)[2]	75,979	58,341	33,292	24,145	41,586	15,091	248,434
Women to 100	(a)	139	133	146	132	140	143	138
men	(b)	118	112	105	110	120	117	114
Girls to 100	(a)	84	78	75	83	85	82	82
Boys	(b)	104	102	101	98	98	101	101
Females to	(a)	107	104	106	105	108	108	106
100 males	(b)	112	108	103	105	109	109	108
Children to	(a)	180	148	155	165	184	169	168
100 women	(b)	160	138	128	142	168	159	149

(a) Latest Assessment figures.   (b) Intensive Census figures.

[1] See *Census of Nigeria, 1931*, vol. ii, pp. 94, 192–6.
[2] Including unspecified as to age.

TABLE 11. *Native Population by Sex and Age, 200 Villages Northern Provinces, 1931*[1]

Age (years)	Males	Females	Total	Females to 100 males
Under 1	13,173	13,270	26,443	101
1–4	23,587	24,082	47,669	102
5–9	27,203	28,654	55,857	105
10–14	20,923	18,573	39,496	89
15–19	17,421	20,551	37,975	118
20–24	14,941	19,642	34,583	131
25–29	14,455	17,222	31,677	119
30–34	12,788	16,178	28,966	127
35–39	10,045	11,354	21,399	113
40–44	10,417	11,783	22,200	113
45–49	7,489	6,625	14,114	88
50–54	7,467	7,597	15,064	102
55–59	4,084	3,705	7,789	91
60 and over	11,228	12,729	23,957	113
Unspecified	76	125	201	..
Total	195,297	212,093	407,390	109

[1] See *Census of Nigeria, 1931*, vol. ii, p. 94. The figures comprise six complete districts in Katsina Division, 16 villages in other Katsina districts, and 40 villages in other Provinces.

the youngest wives as adults.[1] It is very interesting to compare in this connexion the figures obtained through the Intensive Census in six complete Districts of the Katsina Division with the last preceding assessment figures which were secured in most cases about six months before the census date. While the assessment figures in these Districts show an enormous excess of females among adults (38 per cent.) and a large deficiency of females among children (18 per cent.), the returns of the Intensive Census are quite acceptable, since the excess of women (14 per cent.) is not unbelievably large and since boys and girls were recorded in about equal numbers. The enormous differences between the numbers of men, between the numbers of boys, and between the ratios of children to women recorded, on the one hand, through the assessment, and, on the other hand, through the Intensive Census are due, to be sure, in part to the fact that the age limit for male children was 16 years at the assessment but 15 years at the Intensive Census.[2] However, the differences are so great as to shatter the confidence in the figures of the General Census even in the Northern Provinces.

The Intensive Censuses in the Northern Provinces provide also some insight into the age distribution of children and adults. But it appears that the data obtained were untrustworthy. In 200 villages[3] 26,443 children were recorded as being under one year but only 47,669 between 1 and 5 years. It seems that many children over 1 year must have been counted as infants.[4] Far too few females seem to have been allocated to the age group 10–14 and also to some older groups (45–49 and 55–59). Nor can the apparently small proportion of females between 10 and 15 be attributed to a tendency to count all married women as being over 15, since a considerable number of wives were recorded in the group 10–14.

Conjugal Condition. No data are available for the Southern Provinces.[5]

---

[1] It should be noted, however, that the ratio of children to women was extraordinarily high in Katsina Division, and that if the number of women was swelled by counting girls as adults, the ratio of children to women would have been higher still than shown in the census returns.

[2] See pp. 562–3, 569 above.

[3] The townships present so peculiar conditions that they have been excluded.

[4] It may be mentioned incidentally that the same mis-statements in the number of infants occurred also in the townships, where 604 children under one and only 1,110 children between 1 and 5 were recorded.

[5] It is much to be regretted that even for Lagos the conjugal condition of the population was not ascertained in 1931. The few data on illegitimate births that have been published are quite puzzling. They may be summarized as follows:

Year	Legiti-mate	Illegiti-mate	Year	Legiti-mate	Illegiti-mate	Year	Legiti-mate	Illegiti-mate
1892	483	90	1899	1,687	242	1932	1,733	1,302
1893	854	180	1900	1,723	217	1933	1,762	1,268
1894	990	207	1903	1,829	213	1934	2,142	1,275
1895	1,193	250	1904	2,097	243	1935	2,287	1,240
1896	1,320	225	1928	1,369	1,344	1936	2,015	1,195
1897	1,438	223	1929	1,388	1,406	1937	2,368	880
1898	1,539	234	1930	1,356	1,394	1938	3,026	404

(See *Colonial Reports, Lagos 1892*, p. 3, *1894*, p. 6; Lagos, 'Abstract of Registration 1896', p. 130; Lagos, *Abstract of Registration 1898*, p. 5; Lagos, 'Report of Registrar General 1900', p. 78; Lagos, *Vital Statistics for 1904*, p. 1; Lagos Town Council, *Report of Medical Officer of Health 1928*, p. 17,

According to the Intensive Censuses in the Northern Provinces, the ratio of wives to 100 husbands was 130·8. Though the excess of females in the total population was small, and though very few men never married, polygamy was possible owing to early marriages of women and late marriages of men. While the proportions of husbands in the age groups 10–19, 20–29, and 30–39 were 6·3, 59·6, and 84·4 per cent. respectively, the percentages of wives were 48·4, 94·1, and 92·9. Of the men over 40 only 1·6 per cent. had never married, of the women over 40 only 0·9 per cent.

TABLE 12. *Natives of Nigeria by Sex, Age, and Conjugal Condition, Selected Areas Northern Provinces, 1931*[1]

Age (years)	Males					Females				
	Single	Married	Widowed	Un-speci-fied	Total	Single	Married	Widowed	Un-speci-fied	Total
Under 10	65,540	—	—	—	65,540	67,767	—	—	—	67,767
10–14	21,782	130	9	69	21,990	17,518	1,575	38	58	19,189
15–19	17,017	2,519	269	92	19,897	3,233	18,414	529	22	22,198
20–29	12,205	21,316	2,256	214	35,991	1,098	39,462	1,372	51	41,983
30–39	2,154	23,143	2,124	69	27,490	444	27,600	1,681	27	29,752
40–49	506	18,017	1,331	21	19,875	227	15,776	2,954	15	18,972
50–59	112	11,059	810	3	11,984	77	7,040	4,338	6	11,461
60 and over	79	10,114	1,213	6	11,412	89	3,021	9,667	11	12,788
Unspecified	143	93	8	29	273	53	154	12	8	227
Total	119,538	86,391	8,020	503	214,452	90,506	113,042	20,591	198	224,337

[1] See *Census of Nigeria*, 1931, vol. ii, pp. 158, 160.

In the Dikwa Emirate the assessing officers ascertained in 1924 that, excluding the pagan districts, 25,113 men had one wife, 7,810 two wives, 1,583 three, and 313 four.[1] This would give a total of 34,819 husbands and 46,734 wives or 134 wives to 100 husbands. Since according to the assessment census of 1923 there were in the Emirate, excluding the pagan districts, altogether 35,970 adult males and 49,787 adult females, the excess of women was here so ample that no man needed to remain single owing to the incidence of polygamy.[2]

IV. COMPOSITION OF NON-NATIVE POPULATION

1. *Total Non-Native Population*

Prior to 1911 figures concerning non-Natives covered only Europeans.[3]

1929, p. 16, *1930*, p. 25, *1933*, p. 25, *1935*, p. 21, *1937*, p. 26, *1938*, p 25. All data refer to Lagos Island only. Those for 1892–1904 include still-births. Those for 1932–8 exclude the few non-Native births.)

While the proportion of illegitimate births was 13 per cent. in 1892–1904, it amounted to 50 per cent. in 1928–30, to 39 per cent. in 1932–6, to 27 per cent. in 1937, and to 12 per cent. in 1938. In the earlier period children were deemed to be illegitimate only when their parents were neither married according to native custom nor according to the provisions of the Marriage Ordinance, 1884 (see *Abstract of Registration 1898*, p. 1; 'Report of Registrar General 1899', p. 315).

[1] See *Report on the Cameroons 1924*, p. 55.

[2] Some figures referring to polygamy are also available from Cameroons Province, but these are so small that they cannot be considered as representative. See for details, *Assessment Report on Buea District* (1931), p. 41; Kuczynski, pp. 291–3.

[3] The Lagos census reports for 1881 and 1891 contain in addition a few data regarding Mulattoes, of whom 68 were counted in 1881 (see *Census Report Lagos 1881*, Enclosure No. 2) and 81 in 1891 (see ibid. *1891*, p. 13). But the Superintendent of the 1891 census considered the figures untrustworthy (see ibid., p. 7).

The 1911 census of Southern Nigeria showed 2,940 non-Natives, namely 2,354 Europeans, 99 Asiatics,[1] and 487 'coloured Non-West Africans—chiefly negros born in the Brazils, and West Indies'.[2] The 1911 census of Northern Nigeria showed 5,350 non-Natives, namely 678 Europeans and 4,672 'African non-natives',[3] but the great majority of the 'African non-natives' were natives from other West African colonies (including Southern Nigeria),[4] and no figures were given for people who were neither Africans nor Europeans.

The 1921 census of the Southern Provinces (including Cameroons Province) showed 2,947 non-Natives, namely 2,762 Europeans and 185 Asiatics.[5] Though the figures for Natives are stated to comprise only Natives of West Africa, Africans from other countries were probably allocated to Natives. The 1921 census of the Northern Provinces (including Northern Cameroons) showed 1,174 non-Natives, namely 1,133 Europeans and 41 Asiatics.[6] Coloured persons from such countries as the West Indies, Brazil, and Tripoli were not counted as non-Natives, but as Native Foreigners.[7]

The 1931 census of the Southern Provinces (including Cameroons Province) showed 3,617 non-Natives, namely 3,283 Europeans and 334 Asiatics.[8] The 1931 census of the Northern Provinces (including Northern Cameroons) showed 1,825 non-Natives, namely 1,669 Europeans and 156 Asiatics.[9] Both in the Southern and the Northern Provinces all persons descended from an African tribe (including, for example, Arabs of North Africa) were counted as Natives or Native Foreigners.

I shall now discuss the composition of the non-Native population in the whole of Nigeria (including the Cameroons) as ascertained at the 1921 and 1931 censuses.

The number of non-Natives (non-Africans) in Nigeria and the Cameroons increased from 4,115 in 1921 to 5,442 in 1931.[10] The number of British increased from 3,475 (3,121 males, 354 females) to 4,167 (3,404 males, 763 females), the number of non-British from 640 (489 males, 151 females) to 1,275 (972 males, 303 females). The increase in the number of non-British was due mainly to the increase of Germans from 3 to 264 and of Syrians from 143 to 419.

[1] 90 Syrians, 4 East Indians, 4 Chinese, and 1 Caucasian.

[2] *Report on Southern Nigeria Census, 1911*, p. 1. Of the 412 coloured non-West Africans ('negros, mulattos or quadroons') counted in Lagos Municipal Area 327 were Brazilians, 56 West Indians, 24 Cubans, 2 South Africans, and 3 Americans; see ibid., p. 16.

[3] See Northern Nigeria, *Census 1911*.

[4] The countries of origin were stated as follows: Sierra Leone 73, Gold Coast 255, Lagos 47, Arabia 108, Gambia 1, Southern Nigeria 179, Keffi 1, West African Colonies unknown 3,992.

[5] 117 Syrians, 44 Arabs, 16 Indians, 4 Chinese, 2 from Ceylon, 2 Armenians; see Talbot, vol. iv, pp. 150–1.

[6] 26 from Syria and 15 from Arabia (Aden). See 'Figures taken from the 1921 Census', p. 41; Meek, vol. ii, p. 194.   [7] See ibid., p. 193.

[8] Including 296 Syrians and 31 Indians. See *Census of Nigeria, 1931*, vol. i, p. 32, vol. iii, p. 36.

[9] Including 123 Syrians. See ibid., vol. i, p. 32, vol. ii, pp. 97–8.

[10] The 1921 figure includes 564 'Europeans on ocean boats' (Talbot, vol. iv, p. 20); the 1931 figure includes 312 non-Natives 'enumerated on ships in the Lagos harbour' (*Census of Nigeria, 1931*, vol. iv, p. 11).

TABLE 13. *Non-Native Population by Sex and Age, Nigeria and Cameroons, 1921 and 1931*[1]

Provinces	Males				Females				Total				Total	
	Under 15		15 and over		Under 15		15 and over		Under 15		15 and over			
	(a)	(b)	(a)	(b)	(a)	(b)	(a)	(b)	(a)	(b)	(a)	(b)	(a)	(b)
1921														
Northern	12	4	966	32	9	1	138	6	21	5	1,104	38	1,125	43
Southern	13	30	2,476	77	13	28	260	50	26	58	2,736	127	2,762	185
Total	25	34	3,442	109	22	29	398	56	47	63	3,840	165	3,887	228
1931														
Northern	15	9	1,309	109	12	6	333	32	27	15	1,642	141	1,669	156
Southern	7	30	2,697	200	6	24	573	80	13	54	3,270	280	3,283	334
Total	22	39	4,006	309	18	30	906	112	40	69	4,912	421	4,952	490

(a) Whites.   (b) Asiatics.

[1] Computed from Meek, vol. ii, p. 232; Talbot, vol. iv, Table facing p. 154; *Census of Nigeria, 1931*, vol. i, p. 32.

TABLE 14. *Non-Native Population by Nationality and Sex, Nigeria and Cameroons, 1921 and 1931*[1]

Nationality and country of origin	1921						1931					
	Northern Provinces		Southern Provinces		Total		Northern Provinces		Southern Provinces		Total	
	M.	F.	M.	F.	M.	F.	M.	F.	M.	F.	M.	F.
British (Empire)												
England	628	77	1,551	159	2,179	236	762	177	1,526	282	2,288	459
Ireland	53	8	162	17	215	25	80	8	154	47	234	55
Scotland	121	13	404	40	525	53	180	39	301	79	481	118
Wales	26	—	66	7	92	7	28	9	57	18	85	27
Channel Isles	—	—	—	—	—	—	—	—	5	1	5	1
Australia	47	4	8	3	55	7	38	2	7	8	45	10
Canada, Newfoundland	15	14	9	1	24	15	14	16	2	2	16	18
West Indies	—	—	—	—	—	—	—	—	7	2	7	2
New Zealand	8	3	6	—	14	3	5	—	8	2	13	2
South Africa	9	8	2	—	11	8	18	12	17	5	35	17
Aden	15	—	—	—	15	—	12	—	—	—	12	—
India	1	—	15	1	16	1	2	1	82	12	84	13
Others	1[2]	—	7[3]	—	8	—	1[4]	—	1[5]	—	2	—
Unspecified	—	—	—	—	—	—	37	12	104	29	141	41
Americans (U.S.A.)	11	7	18	24	29	31	39	48	22	11	61	59
Arabs (of Arabia)	—	—	28	16	28	16	6	3	1	—	7	3
Armenians	—	—	2	—	2	—	2	—	4	—	6	—
Belgians	—	—	1	—	1	—	1	1	—	—	1	1
Danes	5	9	33	—	38	9	7	12	3	—	10	12
Dutch	1	—	2	3	3	3	—	—	16	6	16	6
French												
France	16	1	67	12	83	13	33	3	89	17	122	20
Syria	19	7	58	59	77	66	91	31	102	101	283	136
Martinique	—	—	—	—	—	—	1	—	—	—	1	—
Unspecified	—	—	—	—	—	—	6	—	—	—	6	—
Germans	—	—	2	1	2	1	7	—	220	37	227	37
Greeks	6	—	20	—	26	—	15	1	46	5	61	6
Italians	12	2	75	—	87	2	35	1	25	3	60	4
Norwegians	—	—	28	1	28	1	—	—	—	—	—	—
Portuguese	—	—	1	—	1	—	—	—	1	—	1	—
Spaniards	—	—	15	5	15	5	—	—	1	—	1	—
Swedes	—	—	1	—	1	—	1	—	2	—	3	—
Swiss	18	1	13	—	31	1	12	2	28	11	40	13
Turks	1	—	—	—	1	—	5	3	—	—	5	3
Others	1[6]	—	2[7]	2[7]	3	2	2[8]	—	13[9]	2[10]	15	2
Unspecified	—	—	—	—	—	—	2	1	—	—	2	1
Total	1,014	154	2,596	351	3,610	505	1,442	383	2,934	683	4,376	1,066

[1] Computed from Meek, vol. ii, p. 194; Talbot, vol. iv, pp. 150–1; *Census of Nigeria, 1931*, vol. ii, pp. 97–8, vol. iii, p. 40.
[2] Mauritius.   [3] 2 Malta, 3 Cyprus, 2 Ceylon.   [4] Palestine.
[5] Malay.   [6] Russian.   [7] Chinese.   [8] 1 Pole, 1 Yugoslavian.
[9] 2 Austrians, 4 Czechoslovakians, 1 Egyptian, 2 Finlanders, 1 Iraquian, 1 Russian, 2 South Americans.
[10] 1 Austrian, 1 Czechoslovakian.

TABLE 15. *Non-Native Population by Nationality and Age, Nigeria and Cameroons, 1921 and 1931*[1]

Age (years)	Whites									Asiatics				
	British	French	Germans	Greeks	Italians	Swiss	Americans	Others	Total	Arabs[2]	Indians	Syrians	Others	Total
NORTHERN PROVINCES 1921														
Under 15	18	—	—	—	1	—	2	—	21	—	—	5	—	5
15 and over	1,017	17	—	6	13	19	16	16	1,104	15	1	21	1	38
Total	1,035	17	—	6	14	19	18	16	1,125	15	1	26	1	43
SOUTHERN PROVINCES 1921														
Under 15	14	1	—	—	—	—	10	1	26	9	—	48	1	58
15–29	957	22	—	15	34	10	15	49	1,102	17	6	24	5	52
30–49	1,311	49	1	5	36	3	15	31	1,451	17	6	34	1	58
50 and over	158	7	2	—	5	—	2	9	183	1	4	11	1	17
Total	2,440	79	3	20	75	13	42	90	2,762	44	16	117	8	185
NORTHERN PROVINCES 1931														
Under 15	10	—	—	—	—	1	13	3	27	3	—	9	3	15
15–19	1	—	—	—	1	—	—	—	2	1	—	4	—	5
20–9	423	29	4	3	13	1	15	4	492	5	1	57	4	67
30–9	600	9	3	6	11	11	46	8	694	8	—	34	1	43
40–9	307	4	—	5	9	1	11	11	348	2	—	12	2	16
50–9	84	—	—	—	1	—	2	—	87	—	—	6	—	6
60 and over	15	—	—	2	1	—	—	—	18	2	—	1	1	4
Total	1,440	42	7	16	36	14	88[3]	26	1,669[3]	21	1	123	11	156
SOUTHERN PROVINCES 1931														
Under 15	4	—	7	—	—	1	1	—	13	—	—	54	—	54
15–19	24	3	8	2	1	—	1	—	39	—	6	31	—	37
20–9	816	64	110	27	7	14	9	15	1,062	—	16	99	3	118
30–9	1,088	24	71	18	10	19	15	13	1,258	1	6	44	1	52
40–9	574	5	41	4	7	2	7	9	649	—	3	35	2	40
50–9	141	6	17	—	2	2	1	3	172	—	—	18	—	18
60 and over	17	4	3	—	1	1	1	—	27	—	—	7	—	7
Total	2,727[4]	106	257	51	28	39	35	40	3,283[4]	1	31	296[5]	6	334[5]

[1] Computed from Meek, vol. ii, p. 232; Talbot, vol. iv, pp. 150–1; *Census of Nigeria, 1931*, vol. i, p. 32; vol. ii, pp. 97–8, vol. iii, p. 36.
[2] Including Aden.
[3] Including 1 with unspecified age.
[4] Including 63 with unspecified ages.
[5] Including 8 with unspecified ages.

TABLE 16. *Non-Native Population by Birthplace, Nigeria and Cameroons, 1931*[1]

| Birthplace | Northern Provinces | | Southern Provinces | | Total | | |
	Males	Females	Males	Females	Males	Females	Total
Nigeria. . .	20	13	35	32	55	45	100
Brit. Possessions in Africa . .	2	—	24	8	26	8	34
Elsewhere in Africa	41	16	—	2	41	18	59
Total Africa .	63	29	59	42	122	71	193
Arabia . . .	12	1	1	—	13	1	14
Cyprus. . .	4	—	4	1	8	1	9
India . . .	34	5	84	12	118	17	135
Syria . . .	78	26	159	76	237	102	339
Turkey in Asia .	6	2	4	3	10	5	15
Elsewhere in Asia .	16	1	10	2	26	3	29
Total Asia .	150	35	262	94	412	129	541
England . .	734	183	1,526	283	2,260	466	2,726
Ireland . .	61	9	154	47	215	56	271
Scotland . .	154	34	302	80	456	114	570
Wales . . .	34	8	57	18	91	26	117
Channel Isles .	—	—	6	1	6	1	7
Denmark . .	7	10	2	—	9	10	19
France . .	36	2	87	21	123	23	146
Germany . .	7	—	223	35	230	35	265
Greece . . .	14	1	40	1	54	2	56
Italy . . .	30	—	29	2	59	2	61
Portugal . .	—	—	1	—	1	—	1
Russia . . .	3	1	2	1	5	2	7
Spain . . .	—	—	4	—	4	—	4
Switzerland . .	11	1	27	7	38	8	46
Elsewhere in Europe	6[2]	2[3]	38	8	44	10	54
Total Europe .	1,097	251	2,498	504	3,595	755	4,350
Canada, Newfound- land . . .	13	12	6	2	19	14	33
United States .	41	50	23	12	64	62	126
West Indies . .	13	2	20	3	33	5	38
South America ,	7	1	16	5	23	6	29
Total America .	74	65	65	22	139	87	220
Total Australasia .	50	3	17	12	67	15	82
Unspecified . .	8	—	33	9	41	9	50
Total . .	1,442	383	2,934	683	4,376	1,066	5,442

[1] Computed from *Census of Nigeria, 1931*, vol. ii, p. 105; vol. iii, pp. 37–8.
[2] Including 2 not classified as to European country.
[3] Including 1 not classified as to European country.

Strange to say, the number of children did not increase. It was 110 in 1921 and 109 in 1931. The number of British children decreased from 32 to 14; the number of Syrian children increased from 53 to 63. In Lagos with 1,443 non-Natives in 1931 (including 134 Syrians) there were 19 children, all of whom were Syrians.[1] In the Southern Provinces excluding Lagos there were 209 married British women but only 4 children.[2]

In 1931 the non-Natives constituted 0·02 per cent. of the population in the Northern Provinces and 0·04 per cent. of the population in the Southern Provinces. But in Lagos the proportion was 1·14 per cent.

According to the 1931 census 2,843 non-Natives were born in England and Wales, 570 in Scotland, 271 in Ireland, 265 in Germany, 361 elsewhere in Europe; 100 in Nigeria, 93 elsewhere in Africa; 339 in Syria, 135 in India, 67 elsewhere in Asia; 126 in the United States, 100 elsewhere in America; 82 in Australasia; 50 in unspecified countries.

The numbers of non-Native passengers arriving and departing from Lagos by sea or river were as follows:[3]

	1928	1929	1930	1931	1932	1933	1934	1935	1936	1937	1938
Arriving .	4,024	4,508	4,721	3,322	3,252	3,775	3,496	3,474	4,093	4,647	3,954
Departing.	3,015	3,095	3,435	3,750	3,526	3,423	3,356	3,133	3,399	3,904	3,290

The Medical Reports give as total number of non-Natives for 1934–6 5,021, 5,246, and 6,823 respectively[4] but at least the figures for 1934 and 1935 comprise only Europeans. For 31 December 1938 the non-Native population by sex and nationality is given as follows:[5]

Sex	British	Danish	Dutch	French	German	Greek	Italian	Swiss	American	Syrian	Other	Total
Males	3,926	5	75	282	459	149	62	132	129	627	89	5,935
Females	1,661	15	16	62	111	19	6	22	156	191	29	2,288
Total	5,587	20	91	344	570	168	68	154	285	818	118	8,223

Thus the number of non-Natives in Nigeria including the Cameroons increased from 5,442 in April 1931 to 8,223 at the end of 1938, or by 51 per cent. The number of British increased from 4,167 to 5,587, or by 34 per cent., and the number of non-British from 1,275 to 2,636, or by 107 per cent. The increase was particularly large for females. Their total number rose from 1,066 (763 British and 303 non-British) to 2,288 (1,661 British and 627 non-British).

[1] See *Census of Nigeria, 1931*, vol. iv, p. 23.

[2] See ibid., vol. iii, p. 41. No data concerning marital condition were published either for the Northern Provinces or for Lagos.

[3] See *Colonial Reports, Nigeria 1934*, p. 17; *1936*, p. 16; *1937*, p. 16; *1938*, p. 17.

[4] See Nigeria, *Medical Report 1936*, p. 14.

[5] See *Colonial Reports, Nigeria 1938*, p. 16.

2. European Population

The number of Europeans in the Colony and Protectorate of Lagos has been reported as follows:[1]

Date	Lagos Town		Remainder		Total	
	Males	Females	Males	Females	Males	Females
1866	42	—	..	..	..	..
1868	81[1]	6[1]	..	..	..	..
Apr. 1871	77[1]	5[1]	12	—	89	5
Jan. 1874	90		..	..	..	..
Apr. 1881	103	8	6	—	109	8
1881–5	107[2]		..	..	..	..
1886–90	111[2]		..	..	..	..
Apr. 1891	127[3]	16	7	—	134[3]	16
1895	..	..	..	..	200	
1897	..	..	..	..	250[2]	
Apr. 1901	200[4]		108[5]		308[4]	
1905	400[6]		..	..	..	..

[1] Lagos and its vicinity.	[4] Including 31 on ships.
[2] Average number of residents.	[5] Including 33 in Ebute Metta.
[3] Including 19 on ships.	[6] Including Ebute Metta.

In the Niger Coast Protectorate (from 1900 on Protectorate of Southern Nigeria) the European population was as follows:[2]

Date	Males	Females	Date	Males	Females	Officials	Non-Officials
1894–5	214		1900–1	316		101	215
1895–6	215		31 Dec. 1901	353	44	121	276
1896–7	198	16	31 Dec. 1902	377	27	125	279
1897–8	206		31 Dec. 1903	423	37	159	301
1898–9	204	23	31 Dec. 1904	467	33	157	343
1899–1900	270		31 Dec. 1905	494	39	199	334
Census 1901	258	32					

For the first years after the amalgamation of the Colony and Protectorate of Lagos with the Protectorate of Southern Nigeria no complete figures were available for the new Colony and Protectorate of Southern Nigeria.

In the Eastern and Central Provinces accurate statistics have been prepared for the European section of the community; it is unfortunate that equally reliable statistics for the Western Province have not been kept, but an estimate of the European population has been made . . . in Lagos and Ebute Metta . . . .[3]

[1] See for 1866–71 Lagos, *Blue Book 1866*, p. 228, *1868*, p. 160, *1871*, p. 228; 1874 *Colonial Possessions Papers 1874*, Part II, p. 118; 1881 Lagos, *Blue Book 1881*, p. 114; 1881–5 and 1886–90 *Colonial Reports, Lagos 1890*, p. 13; 1891 Lagos, *Census Report 1891*, pp. 33–5; 1895 *Colonial Office List 1896*, p. 143; 1897 *Colonial Reports, Lagos 1897*, p. 8; 1901 Lagos, *Census Report 1901*, pp. 2–3; 1905 *Colonial Reports, Southern Nigeria (Lagos) 1905*, p. 33.

[2] See *Report on the Niger Coast Protectorate 1896–7*, p. 7; *Colonial Reports, Niger Coast Protectorate 1898–9*, p. 10; *Statistical Tables, Colonial Possessions 1901*, p. 767; *1902*, p. 856; *1904*, p. 489; *1905*, p. 452; *Colonial Reports, Southern Nigeria 1902*, p. 46; Southern Nigeria, *Medical Report 1905*, p. 5. The figures for 1894–5 to 1900–1 represent the average resident population.

[3] *Colonial Reports, Southern Nigeria 1906*, p. 56.

For 1906 the number of Europeans in Lagos and Ebute Metta was estimated again at 400.[1] In the Eastern and Central Provinces the European population on 31 December 1906 was given as follows: 193 male and 5 female Officials, 67 male and 55 female Missionaries, and 300 male and 2 female Traders.[2] The returns for 1907–10 from Lagos and Ebute Metta on the one hand, and the Eastern and Central Provinces on the other hand, may be summarized as follows:[3]

| Date | Area | Males | | | Females | | | Total |
		Officials	Mission-aries	Traders, &c.	Officials	Mission-aries	No occu-pation	
31 Dec. 1907	(a)	184	14	203	3	16	20	440
	(b)	207	68	292	4	43	—	614
31 Dec. 1908	(a)	271	28	240	3	36	13	591
	(b)	210	68	336	5	67	5	691
31 Dec. 1909	(a)	229	17	228	3	20	17	514
	(b)	259	86	367	13	55	7	787
31 Dec. 1910	(a)	221	11	264	3	17	19	535
	(b)	230	61	432	9	39	6	777

At the 1911 census the European population was enumerated in the whole of Southern Nigeria. The results may be summarized as follows:[4]

Provinces	Officials	Mission-aries	Traders, &c.	Wives excl. of mission-aries	Chil-dren	Total	Males	Females
Western	355	80	335	19	1	790[1]	725	65
Eastern and Central	275	111	463	9	—	858[2]	801	57
Total	630	191	798	28	1	1,648[3]	1,526	122

[1] Excluding 72 on ocean steamers.
[2] Excluding 634 on ocean steamers.
[3] Excluding 706 on ocean steamers.

For 1912 the total European population was given as 1,840 (760 officials and 1,080 non-officials),[5] and the Colonial Report for 1913 stated:

The average number of Europeans in the country may be placed at, roughly, 1,800, of whom about 40 per cent. are officials. The climatic conditions of the country make long periods of residence by Europeans impossible and the white population is therefore continually changing.[6]

[1] See Colonial Reports, Southern Nigeria 1906, p. 58.
[2] See Southern Nigeria, Blue Book 1906 R, p. 2.
[3] See Southern Nigeria, Blue Book 1907 R, p. 2; 1908 R, p. 2; 1909 R, p. 3; 1910 R, pp. 3–4. (a) means Lagos and Ebute Metta, (b) means Eastern and Central Provinces. According to Southern Nigeria, Medical Report 1910, p. 22, there were in the Western Province outside Lagos and Ebute Metta on 31 Dec. 1909, 50 Railway Officials, 59 Missionaries, and 40 Merchants, and on 31 Dec. 1910, 65 Railway Officials, 53 Missionaries, and 47 Merchants.
[4] See Report on Southern Nigeria Census, 1911, pp. 2, 7.
[5] See Colonial Reports, Southern Nigeria 1912, p. 26.
[6] Ibid., 1913, p. 23.

The latter fact must, of course, be borne in mind in appraising all the above figures.[1]

The average European population in Northern Nigeria[2] was reported as follows:[3]

Period	Total	Year	Officials	Non-officials	Males	Females
Apr. 1898–Mar. 1899	156	1902	260	30	..	..
Apr. 1899–Mar. 1900	163	1903	274	35	..	..
Apr. 1900–Mar. 1901	165	1904	270	52	312	10
Jan. 1901–Dec. 1901	165	1905	277	65	331	11
		1906	282	65	333	14
		1907	338	86	402	22
		1908	399	100	481	18
		1909	438	106	527	17
		1910	424	213[1]	..	..
		1911[2]	369	272	616	25
		1912	325	378	683	20
		1913	326	478	779	25

[1] 'The large increase in the non-official population was due to the extension of the mining industry.'

[2] The 1911 census showed 651 males and 27 females.

---

[1] For 1911 the total number of officials resident was given as 1,372 and the average number resident 595; the corresponding figures for 1912 were 2,068 and 801, for 1913, 2,146 and 843, and for 1914, 1,740 and 822. See Nigeria, *Medical Report 1914*, p. 58.

[2] From 1903 on, the information seems to have been obtained in accordance with the following instructions issued on 8 Nov. 1902 (*The Northern Nigeria Gazette*, 29 Nov. 1902, p. 172):

'Officers and British N.-C. Officers Commanding Military stations will on the last day of every month render through the proper channels for the information of the P.M.O. and compilation of Medical Statistics a return showing the average strength of European members of the Northern Nigeria Regiment in the station during the month.

Residents in charge of provinces will similarly render to the Secretary a return of the average strength in each station of members of the Civil Service.

Business firms, European missionaries, traders and others are also requested to furnish a similar return, addressed to the Secretary to the Administration, Zungeru.'

As regards the difficulty of computing the average European population in earlier years, see the statement of the Acting Principal Medical Officer in his Report for 1900–1: 'The average population has been somewhat difficult to arrive at owing to a fairly large floating population composed of Boundary Commissions, Missionary Expeditions, Ashanti War and various European traders passing to and fro, but 165 is, I think, a fair mean' (Northern Nigeria, 'Medical Report 1900–1', p. 57).

To what extent the official population was depleted by leave of absence and unfilled vacancies may be inferred from a comparison of the average number of officials present in the country and the following figures showing the total strength:

Officials	1900–1	1901–2	1902–3	1903–4	1904–5	1905–6
Civil	104	155	163	231	248	266
Military	200	163	157	186	207	208
Total	304	318	320	417	455	474

See *Colonial Reports, Northern Nigeria 1905–6*, p. 107; see also ibid. *1901*, p. 23.

[3] See ibid., p. 35; *1903*, pp. 20, 34, 39; *1904*, pp. 138, 144; *1905–6*, p. 102; *1906–7*, p. 44; *1907–8*, p. 64; *1908–9*, p. 13; *1909*, p. 16; *1910–11*, p. 21; *1911*, p. 17; *1912*, p. 19; Northern Nigeria, *Blue Book 1911* R, p. 2; *1913* R, p. 3. The figures for 1908–12 exclude the officials engaged on the northern extension of the Lagos Railway, stationed in Northern Nigeria.

The distribution of the European population by occupation was as follows:[1]

Occupation	1912	1913	1914	1915	1916	1917	1918	1919	1920
Government officials	325	326	543	507	350	343	495	354	399
Missions	35	36	38	84	119	107	129	81	158
Trading firms	93	156	165	178	126	149	134	183	695
Mining companies	250	286	223	128	167	180	231	229	205
Total	703	804	969	897	762	779	989	847	1,457

At the beginning of this century the Europeans in the Colony and Protectorate of Lagos, the Protectorate of Southern Nigeria, and the Protectorate of Northern Nigeria, i.e. in the present territory of Nigeria (excluding the Cameroons), aggregated about 760. Ten years later, according to the censuses of 1911, they numbered 2,326. The first Colonial Report for the whole of Nigeria, after having pointed out that the average number of Europeans in the Northern Provinces was 969, said:

In the Southern Provinces the number is estimated at roughly 2,000, of whom about 40 per cent. are officials. The European population of Nigeria may therefore be put in round figures at 3,000, of whom about 1,300 are officials.[2]

Subsequent Colonial Reports convey the following information:[3]

Date	Northern Provinces		Southern Provinces		Nigeria		
	Officials	Non-officials	Officials	Non-officials	Officials	Non-officials	Total
31 Dec. 1915 .	300	400	800	1,200	1,100	1,600	2,700
31 Dec. 1916 .	350	412	1,250	750	1,600	1,162	2,762
31 Dec. 1917 .	343	436	1,250	750	1,593	1,186	2,779
31 Dec. 1918 .	495	494	1,250	750	1,745	1,244	2,989
31 Dec. 1919 .	354	493	1,250	750	1,604	1,243	2,847

But the figures for the non-official population of the Southern Provinces were quite uncertain. The Medical Reports for 1917 and 1918 estimated it at 1,650 and 1,600 respectively.[4] For 1919 and 1920 these reports put the non-official population of the whole of Nigeria at 2,193 and 2,908 respectively.[5] According to the 1921 census there were in Nigeria, excluding the Cameroons, 3,267 Europeans, and including the Cameroons, 3,325. These figures cover both officials and non-officials.

For 1924–7 the Medical Reports published estimates of the official and non-official European population by sex.[6]

[1] See Colonial Reports, Northern Nigeria 1913, p. 13; Nigeria, Medical Report 1915, p. 7; Nigeria, Blue Book 1916 R, p. 2, 1917 R, p. 2, 1918 R, p. 2, 1919 R, p. 2, 1920, Section 15, p. 4.

[2] Colonial Reports, Nigeria 1914, p. 22. The average number of officials in the Northern Provinces was 543 (see above), and in the Southern Provinces (see Medical Report 1914, p. 58) 822.

[3] See Colonial Reports, Nigeria 1915, p. 19; 1916, p. 24; 1917, p. 16; 1918, p. 16; 1919, p. 13.

[4] See Nigeria, Medical Report 1917, p. 12; Southern Nigeria, Medical Report 1918, p. 11.

[5] See Nigeria, Medical Report 1919–21, p. 20.

[6] See ibid. 1925, p. 12; 1927, p. 21.

Year	Average monthly				31 December				
	Officials		Non-officials		Officials		Non-officials		
	Male	Female	Male	Female	Male	Female	Male	Female	Total
1924	..	..	..	..	1,465	18	1,837	510	3,830
1925	1,671	23	1,510	487	1,968	31	1,474	577	4,050
1926	2,156	31	1,506	619	2,377	33	1,715	708	4,833
1927	2,664	34	1,483	724	3,017	40	1,582	854	5,493

For 31 December 1928–31 only totals were published, namely, 5,699, 7,056, 8,249, and 4,882.[1] The Medical Department explained the drop in 1931 as follows:

For previous years the total population was compiled from figures supplied by the Immigration Officer. For 1931 figures were obtained from the Government Statistician.

The census of 1931 had in fact revealed that the preceding estimates had been far too high. It showed that the number of whites[2] in Nigeria, including the Cameroons, had increased only from 3,889 in 1921 to 4,952 in 1931, the males from 3,469 to 4,028, and the females from 420 to 924.[3] The most spectacular increase was that of the Germans from 3 to 264. It was due mainly to the return of the Cameroons plantations to their former owners. The occupational statistics of the 1931 census are very defective. No particulars of occupation were taken in Lagos, and the classification by occupations differs widely for the Northern and the Southern Provinces. It would seem, however, that one-half of the British male adults were Government officials.[4]

For 31 December 1931–5 the Medical Reports give as European population 4,882, 4,375, 4,729, 5,021, and 5,246 respectively.[5] The Medical Report for 1938 says that 'the white population is very small totalling only about 5,500, of whom some 2,000 are officials'.[6] But this was evidently an understatement, as according to the details published in the annual Colonial Report for 1938 the number of Europeans exceeded 7,000.[7] The increase was particularly great in the Cameroons, where the European population developed as follows:[8]

	1931	1932	1933	1934	1935	1936	1937	1938
Adult males . .	213	192	210	213	242	252	281	305
Adult females . .	52	52	72	73	79	98	98	101
Children . . .	13	10	22	30	33	32	29	40
Total . . .	278	254	304	316	354	382	408	446

[1] See *Nigeria, Medical Report 1928*, p. 17; *1929*, p. 21; *1930*, p. 15; *1931*, p. 15.
[2] Europeans, Americans, and persons of European and American extraction, i.e. all non-Natives except Asiatics.   [3] These figures include persons on ocean boats.
[4] See *Census of Nigeria, 1931*, vol. ii, p. 141; vol. iii, pp. 15, 39.
[5] See Nigeria, *Medical Report 1933*, p. 10; *1935*, p. 8. The number of Europeans is given ibid. *1932*, p. 14, as 5,442, but this was the total number of non-Natives ascertained at the 1931 census. According to *Colonial Reports, Nigeria 1933*, p. 15, the number of Europeans in 1933 averaged 4,317 (Males 3,300, Females 1,017).
[6] Nigeria, *Medical Report 1938*, p. 1.   [7] See p. 616 above.
[8] See *Report on the Cameroons 1932*, p. 100; *1933*, p. 84; *1934*, p. 111; *1935*, p. 115; *1936*, p. 135; *1937*, p. 105; *1938*, p. 107.

Of the 446 whites who were in the Cameroons in 1938 no fewer than 285 were Germans, while 86 were British and 75 had another nationality.

The proportion of officials among the European population of Nigeria decreased considerably between 1931 and 1938. It became smaller still in the Cameroons, where in 1938 out of 305 white men only about 40 were officials, while 74 belonged to the missions and 170 were employed by plantation companies.[1]

TABLE 17. *European Officials Resident in Nigeria, 1916–38*[1]

Year	Total	Average	Year	Total	Average	Year	Total	Average	Year	Total	Average
1916	1,708	1,055	1922	2,110	1,406	1928	2,853	1,990	1934	2,107	1,508
1917	1,633	1,120	1923	2,092	1,396	1929	2,914	2,581	1935	2,053	1,473
1918	1,598	1,081	1924	1,921	1,567	1930	2,895	2,649	1936	2,164	1,560
1919	1,931	975	1925	2,221	1,466	1931	2,144	1,581	1937	2,131	1,520
1920	1,874	1,166	1926	2,526	1,776	1932	1,709	1,641	1938	2,197	1,525
1921	2,039	1,302	1927	3,049	1,752	1933	2,095	1,586			

[1] See Nigeria, *Medical Report 1917*, p. 55; *1919–21*, p. 13; *1924*, p. 9; *1927*, p. 22; *1930*, p. 16; *1933*, p. 11; *1936*, p. 15; *1938*, p. 10.

The Colonial Office published for each year from 1930 to 1938 the number of non-Native officials by sex and age. The results are summarized in Table 18. It appears that in 1930, following a very large increase of the staff, no fewer than 70 per cent. of the male officials were under 40. However, with the retrenchment of the establishment the proportion of young officials declined, and in 1938 the proportion of those under 40 was only 61 per cent. But it was still much larger than in the remainder of the British West African possessions where in 1938 it was only 52 per cent.

TABLE 18. *Non-Native Officials by Sex and Age, Nigeria and Cameroons, 1930–38*[1]

Date 1 Jan.	20–24 years M.	F.	25–29 years M.	F.	30–34 years M.	F.	35–39 years M.	F.	40–44 years M.	F.	45–49 years M.	F.	50–54 years M.	F.	55– years M.	F.	Age unknown M.	F.	Total M.	F.
1930	164	3	570	11	627	19	518	18	409	11	257	8	111	—	23	—	16	—	2,695	70
1931	142	2	576	18	629	17	504	22	427	11	281	6	105	3	20	—	5	—	2,689	79
1932	94	1	522	14	560	13	501	23	399	13	268	4	108	5	10	—	2	—	2,464	73
1933	49	—	438	11	525	15	483	23	352	13	206	5	80	3	6	1	—	—	2,139	71
1934	33	—	374	13	504	13	472	19	348	13	215	8	69	4	7	1	—	—	2,022	71
1935	20	—	289	9	480	17	461	16	347	14	212	12	72	1	7	1	—	—	1,888	70
1936	26	—	230	9	463	17	464	11	348	20	229	10	77	1	3	—	—	—	1,840	68
1937	50	1	215	9	466	22	455	9	392	18	252	11	80	1	4	—	—	—	1,914	71
1938	68	—	229	12	453	20	471	9	427	19	262	12	85	1	6	—	—	—	2,001	73

[1] See *West Africa, Vital Statistics of Non-Native Officials 1930*, p. 1, to *1938*, p. 1.

V. BIRTH AND DEATH REGISTRATION

1. *Lagos*

Voluntary registration of births and deaths was introduced in Lagos by the Ordinance of 28 October 1863[2] which was to 'come into effect immediately after the passing thereof'. But registration came into opera-

[1] See *Report on the Cameroons 1938*, pp. 74–5, 129, 133–4, 139–43.   [2] See p. 542 above.

tion only on 1 August 1867.[1] The Ordinance of 1863 was repealed by 'An Ordinance to amend the law relating to the Registration of Births and Deaths and the Regulation of Burials' of 10 July 1889,[2] which made compulsory the registration of births and deaths. The Ordinance was to come into operation on 1 January 1890. But on 30 December 1889 there was passed 'An Ordinance to delay the coming into operation of the Births, Deaths and Burials Ordinance, 1889'[3] which stated that 'it has been found impracticable to bring the said Ordinance into force on the day appointed' and which provided that 'The said Births, Deaths and Burials Ordinance, 1889, shall not come into operation until such day as shall be fixed by proclamation under the hand of the Governor to be published in the Gazette'. The Ordinance, then, came into operation only on 1 July 1892[4] and continued to be in force in Lagos after the amalgamation with the Protectorate of Southern Nigeria. It was finally repealed in 1917 by an Ordinance which consolidated the various birth and death registration acts then in force in Lagos, the rest of Southern Nigeria, and Northern Nigeria.

The Ordinance of 1863 provided for registration in the whole Settlement, but it is doubtful whether any births or deaths occurring outside the Island of Lagos were ever registered. The Ordinance of 1889 provided that the Governor may divide the Colony into Districts or constitute any District or Districts in the Colony and appoint a Registrar of Births and Deaths for each such District. He thereupon by Order of 21 May 1892[5] constituted 'the Town and Island of Lagos a District for the purposes of the said Ordinance' and by Order of 18 June 1892[6] appointed a Registrar for this District. A second District, comprising the Island of Iddo and part of the

[1] See Government Notice of 1 Aug. 1867, reprinted in Payne, *Lagos Almanack and Diary for 1878*, p. 27; see also Nigeria, *Medical Report 1928*, p. 17.

[2] No. 5 of 1889, *Lagos Ordinances 1886–1901*, reprinted in *Ordinances, &c., in Force in the Colony of Lagos 1893*, pp. 532–53. The Ordinance was amended by Ordinance No. 1 of 1890 (28 Jan.), reprinted ibid., pp. 575–6, and by No. 4 of 1905 (9 Mar.), *Government Gazette, Colony of Lagos*, 15 Mar. 1905, pp. 216–18. Orders in Council No. 3 of 1911 (17 Feb.), *Southern Nigeria Government Gazette*, 8 Mar. 1911, pp. 364–6, and No. 9 of 1913 (14 Mar.), ibid., 2 Apr. 1913, pp. 433–4, made under 'The Births, Deaths and Burials Ordinance' for the Colony of Southern Nigeria (formerly the Colony of Lagos), modified the Schedule of Medical Death Certificate. (I do not list here amending Ordinances and Orders in Council dealing merely with graves.) The Ordinance as it stood after the enactment of Ordinance No. 1 of 1890 is reprinted in *Ordinances, &c., in Force in the Colony of Lagos 1901*, vol. ii, pp. 577–96.

In order to obtain a complete picture of the system of registration in that period the reader should consult furthermore 'An Ordinance to provide for the registration and protection in certain other respects of Alien Children in Lagos' of 19 Dec. 1877 (No. 18, reprinted in *Ordinances, &c., in Force in the Colony of Lagos 1893*, pp. 316–23), which was amended on 18 June 1892 (No. 5, reprinted ibid., p. 644), and 'An Ordinance to institute a General Registry and constitute a Registrar General and for kindred purposes' of 19 Nov. 1888 (No. 9, *Lagos Ordinances 1886–1901*), which was supplemented by an Ordinance of 9 Dec. 1895 (No. 9, ibid.), both Ordinances being repealed by 'The Registration Ordinance 1901' of 30 Mar. 1901 (No. 5, *Government Gazette, Colony of Lagos*, 13 Apr. 1901, pp. 230–4, reprinted in *Ordinances, &c., in Force in the Colony of Lagos on April 30th, 1901*, vol. ii, pp. 930–4).

[3] No. 17 of 1889, *Lagos Ordinances 1886–1901*.

[4] See *Ordinances, &c., in Force in the Colony of Lagos 1893*, p. 547; *Statistical Tables, Colonial Possessions 1891–3*, p. 390.

[5] Reprinted in *Ordinances, &c., in Force in the Colony of Lagos 1901*, vol. ii, p. 597.

[6] Reprinted ibid., pp. 597–8.

mainland at Ebute Metta, was constituted by Order of 11 March 1901.[1] Four more Districts, one each for the Towns of Badagry, Ikorodu, Shagamu, and Epe, were constituted by Order of 11 February 1908.[2]

The birth and death statistics were, of course, defective prior to 1 July 1892 when registration became compulsory.

TABLE 19. *Registered Births and Deaths, Town and Island of Lagos, 1867–93*[1]

Year	Births	Deaths	Death-rate	Year	Births	Deaths	Death-rate	Year	Births	Deaths	Death-rate
1867	247	421	..	1876	198	630	20·0	1885	214	1,013	28·9
1868	630	717	..	1877	201	656	20·7	1886	249	866	24·0
1869	640	681	..	1878	197	842	26·2	1887	298	976	26·7
1870	556	705	..	1879	194	840	25·5	1888	253	970	26·4
1871	500	629	20·1	1880	195	682	20·4	1889	265	966	25·5
1872	317	540	17·4	1881	248	688	20·5	1890	268	1,211	31·6
1873	201	625	19·9	1882	227	683	20·3	1891	245	1,536	39·5
1874	182	421	13·3	1883	232	795	23·5	1892	573	1,383	34·9
1875	170	521	16·7	1884	235	956	27·8	1893	1,034	1,387	34·0

[1] For births and deaths see Lagos, *Blue Book 1867*, p. 175; *1868*, p. 161; *1869*, p. 207; *1870*, p. 231; *1871*, p. 229; *1872*, p. 101; *1873*, p. 120; *1874*, p. 119; *1875*, p. 113; *1876*, p. 109; *1877*, p. 113; *1878*, p. 113; *1879*, p. 103; *1880*, p. 107; *1881*, p. 115; *1882*, p. 117; *1883*, p. 130; *1884*, p. 55; *1885*, p. 40; *1886*, p. 36; *1887*, p. 38; *1888*, p. 40; *1889*, p. 42; *1890*, p. 48; *1891*, p. 48; *1892*, p. 52; *1893*, p. 54. The death-rates have been taken from *Census of Nigeria, 1931*, vol. i, p. 129. The death figures apparently include still-births, while the birth figures prior to 1 July 1892 exclude them.

TABLE 20. *Registered Births by Sex, Lagos, 1875–92*[1]

Year	Male	Female	Year	Male	Female	Year	Male	Female
1875	83	87	1881	146	102	1887	..	..
1876	92	106	1882	123	104	1888	132	121
1877	111	90	1883	123	100	1889	148	121
1878	115	82	1884	135	100	1890	162	105
1879	99	95	1885	105	110	1891	133	112
1880	101	94	1886	113	136	1892	293	280

[1] See Payne, *Lagos and West African Almanack and Diary for 1887*, pp. 49–52; *1894*, pp. 57–8. The data are given also by months.

Under the Ordinance which came into operation on 1 August 1867, for some years probably about one-half of the births and deaths that occurred in Lagos Town and Harbour were actually registered. But registration, particularly of births, deteriorated thereafter. When the number of registered births which had decreased from 640 in 1869 to 317 in 1872 dropped to 201 in 1873, the *Blue Book* said:

As registration of Births is not compulsory, the number registered is probably far under the actual number of births.[3]

Registration of births did not improve, and in a report dated 11 October 1880, Lieutenant-Governor Griffith pointed out that to judge from the average number of births and deaths registered in 1875–9 (192 and 698

[1] *Government Gazette, Colony of Lagos*, 16 Mar. 1901, p. 145; reprinted in *Ordinances, &c., in Force in the Colony of Lagos on April 30th, 1901*, part ii, pp. 599–600.

[2] Order No. 3 of 1908, *Southern Nigeria Government Gazette*, 26 Feb. 1908, p. 350.

[3] Lagos, *Blue Book 1873*, p. 120.

TABLE 21. *Registered Deaths of Native and Coloured Population by Sex and Age, Lagos, 1868–92*[1]

	Male					Female				
Year	1 to 7	7 to 14	14 to 21	21 and upwards	Total	1 to 7	7 to 14	14 to 21	21 and upwards	Total
1868	210	28	82	58	378	196	21	67	55	339
1869	204	46	61	43	354	187	44	49	37	317
1870	159	43	113	91	406	134	40	60	63	297
1871	171	24	59	65	319	179	20	43	59	301
1872	141	18	74	74	307	124	16	35	49	224
1873	141	14	15	175	345	117	13	18	105	253
1874	113	9	18	97	237	77	3	15	74	169
1875	122	4	17	108	251	124	5	15	99	243
1876	152	11	12	144	319	141	7	14	136	298
1877	143	9	17	158	327	154	12	9	137	312
1878	205	20	26	205	456	176	19	17	152	364
1879	151	23	19	228	421	159	11	12	227	409
1880	133	14	21	181	349	131	8	6	173	318
1881	168	9	21	153	351	157	13	8	149	327
1882	189	21	22	133	365	147	11	8	169	335
1883	187	15	18	163	383	203	18	7	173	401
1884	264	31	19	179	493	222	36	21	173	452
1885	238	36	24	189	487	235	29	24	230	518
1886	191	19	9	169	388	231	11	24	203	469
1888	210	23	19	226	478	211	14	16	240	481
1889	250	20	21	199	490	222	14	11	218	465
1890	336	32	15	252	635	273	27	19	252	571
1891	380	58	28	322	788	316	52	24	338	730
1892	305	39	13	304	661	291	38	45	340	714

[1] See Payne, *Lagos and West African Almanack and Diary 1881*, pp. 39–40, *1887*, pp. 49–52, *1894*, pp. 57–8. For 1868–74, and possibly also for 1875, the age groups read 1 to 7, 7 to 20, 20 to 40, 40 and upwards.

respectively) 'the population of the Island of Lagos would appear to be decreasing by 506 annually'.

On questioning the Registrar as to this he states that the registration of births is not compulsory, and, such as it is, is confined to Lagos alone. If the births were all registered he thinks the figures would exhibit a different result but by no means such as would show an increase of population; somewhat more control can be exercised in ascertaining deaths, but not unfrequently it happens that natives who die on the Island of Lagos are taken across to the mainland to be buried according to their 'customs', which the sanitary arrangements of the Island do not permit to be exercised in it. Sometimes, however, the deaths of the persons so removed are first registered by their friends.[1] Taking the deaths in the Island of Lagos for five years, that is 1875 to 1879, as shown already at 3,489 and the births at 960, it would appear that the population of the Island has diminished in that space by the deaths of 2,529 persons, and even throwing off 529 for unregistered births there would still remain a net loss of 2,000 of population.[2]

The Registrar evidently assumed that death registration was fairly complete (and that the majority of births were registered). But the Colonial

[1] While the Ordinance of 1863 provided that the father or mother should register the birth (within ten days). it did not state by whom (and how soon) a death should be registered. This, I suppose, explains the registration of deaths by 'friends'.
[2] *Colonial Possessions Reports 1879*, p. 216.

Surgeon and Medical Officer of Health, in his report on the sanitary condition of Lagos for the year 1882, expressed the opinion that death registration was quite defective.

I am aware that the registrar of births and deaths supplies a monthly tabular statement [of births and deaths]; but—and this I have on a former occasion commented on officially—whilst acknowledging his industry in search of correct information on this subject, I am unable to give his reports that credence which they would demand, were he in a position to arrive at true data. But under existing circumstances I should exact an impossibility were I to call for that accuracy, which it is not in his, nor, for the matter of that, in any one else's, power to command.

The evil, however, which is likely to accrue from his reports is this: They may be accepted some day by a statist ignorant of the deadly nature of the climate as a proof of its extraordinary salubrity. And indeed were a stranger to be guided in his estimate of this climate by a study of the registrar's figures, he would naturally conclude that it was more sinned against than sinning. For these reports go to prove that in a population of 40,000 inhabitants, living in a country whose climate is, even to the native, so inimical to life, the rate of mortality from all causes is only 17·32 per 1,000.

This is the rate calculated from the registrar's reports for the year 1882 which is actually *below* the annual death rate of Portsmouth and Brighton, the healthiest towns in England.

From this we must accept one of two facts, either that the registrar's reports are altogether inaccurate and therefore misleading, or that Lagos is as healthy a town as Portsmouth or Brighton. For myself I prefer to incline to the former belief. Yet, as above said, hardly much blame can be attached to that officer; for in his search after correct information, he is met by difficulties which it is not even in his power to control.

Any one who knows how prejudiced the heathen, and therefore the greater, portion of our population is against official inquiry into their domestic concerns, and with what characteristic jealousy they guard against 'the stranger's' intrusion into their traditional, and where sickness or death is concerned, sacred usages, will concur with me that to arrive at true data as regards the vital statistics of this town, is a task not to be accomplished at any rate in our day and generation.[1]

The Medical Officer of Health probably overestimated the population of Lagos Town[2] and, therefore, probably understated the death-rate, but there cannot be any doubt that death registration was all the time quite incomplete[3] and that only a small fraction of the births that actually occurred were registered. The Sanitary Reports for 1885 and 1887 show that the authorities had no illusions about the deficiencies of registration.

1885. It is, and always will be, impossible to obtain reliable data respecting the mortality occurring among the natives, but it must be very high.[4]

1887. This disproportion [between registered births and registered deaths], while it would be strange without explanation, cannot be viewed as attributable to a decreasing population, but rather to insufficiency of data consequent on a condition of the law dating from 1863 and much behind the times.

I may here remark that a Bill for the registration of births and deaths and regula-

[1] *Colonial Possessions Reports 1882*, p. 250.

[2] According to the censuses of 1871 and 1881 the population was 28,518 and 37,452 respectively and it probably was overstated in 1881; see p. 546 above.

[3] In 1871–7 probably less than one-half of all deaths had been registered and in 1878–82 probably not more than one-half.

[4] Report by Dr. Grant, Lagos, 'Gold Coast, Sanitary Reports 1885' (*Colonial Possessions Reports 1884–6*), p. 117.

tion of burials is before the Legislature, which I hope will, when passed into law, meet the peculiar wants of the Colony.[1]

Registration cannot be expected to be effective in the absence of any penalty for its enforcement.[2]

Although the Ordinance of 1889 which made registration compulsory came into force only on 1 July 1892, death registration improved considerably from 1890 on, and birth registration followed suit in the latter part of 1892. The number of recorded deaths increased from 966 in 1889 to 1,211 in 1890, and to 1,536 in 1891. It was somewhat lower again in 1892–4, but rose in 1895 to 1,775 and in 1897 to 1,926. The Registrar-General said concerning the death figures of 1891 and 1892, 'I think these figures may be taken to be accurate'.[3] But the Medical Officer Dr. Turner said 40 years later that 'little reliance can be placed on them until the year 1895, when it was said very few deaths occurred without registration'.[4]

The number of recorded births increased from 245 in 1891 to 573 in 1892 (122 in the first and 451 in the second half-year),[5] and to 1,034 in 1893. The Registrar-General found the figures still very small, but thought that the low birth-rate was due to the absence from Lagos of many mothers at confinement.

In view of the fact that the census return, 1891, gave the population of the district as 32,508, the registration of births cannot be regarded as at all satisfactory. I have made inquiries on this subject with the result that I find that many children of Lagos parents are born away from Lagos. Many are born at farms outside the district, and many at towns in the interior, e.g., Abeokuta, Illorin, Ilesha, Porto Novo, &c. and it is extremely difficult to trace them.[6]

But when the number of recorded births rose in 1895 to 1,443 as against 1,197 in 1894, the Acting Colonial Secretary reported:

This large increase is due, in the opinion of the Registrar-General, rather to a wider recognition of the requirements of the Registration Ordinance than to any sudden wave of philo-progenitiveness on the part of the population.[7]

In the following year the Registrar reported:

Births. The number registered during the year is 1,545 as against 1,443 in 1895. . . . This increase is probably due to an extended knowledge among parents of the requirements of the Registration Ordinance.

The births registered are fewer than the deaths by 157. In 1895 the difference was 332 and in 1894 it was 294. From these figures it may be inferred that a knowledge of the requirement of the Registration Ordinance is being gradually acquired by the

---

[1] Letter of Governor Moloney to Lord Knutsford, dated 15 May 1888, *Sanitary Report on Lagos 1887*, p. 3.

[2] Report by Colonial Surgeon, ibid., p. 7.   [3] *Colonial Reports, Lagos 1892*, p. 30.

[4] *Census of Nigeria, 1931*, vol. i, p. 125. See also ibid., p. 129: 'Registration [of deaths] . . . did not become fully effective until the year 1897, when the then Principal Medical Officer stated that probably very few deaths were not recorded.'

[5] It should be noted, however, that from 1 July 1892 onwards the registered births included still-births (26 in the second half-year 1892).

[6] *Colonial Reports, Lagos 1892*, p. 30. See also the statement of the Medical Officer, Ebute Metta District, in Lagos 'Medical Report 1900–1901', p. 152: '. . . many women from Lagos have given birth here, and returned.'

[7] *Colonial Reports, Lagos 1895*, p. 8. See also the statement of the Government Statistician: 'The Birth Register figures themselves are very unreliable prior to 1895' (*Census of Nigeria, 1931*, vol. i, p. 71).

illiterate residents in Lagos. The returns show an increase in the births registered during the year by Mohammedans and Pagans, of 100: while the number registered by Christians exceeds the return of 1895 by 2 only.[1]

By 1899 the number of registered births had increased to 1,929, but the Registrar still thought that registration was incomplete.

That the registration of births among the Pagan population is almost wholly disregarded is evident from the fact that only 182 births of pagan parents were registered.

The Mohammedans registered 1,321. The Christians 426.[2]

In the following year he repeated his complaint that birth registration 'is disregarded by the Pagan population'.[3] But the Commissioners appointed in January 1901 by the Governor 'to enquire into and report upon the actual extent of Infantile Mortality, past and present, in Lagos and its suburbs' held a different view:

As regards the Registration of Births and deaths we are of opinion that there is not any neglect of registration taking place in Lagos now.

The people, even the most illiterate among them, know that it is the law.

. . . We do not think that the Pagans neglect to register the births of their children to any extent if at all. It must be remembered the Pagans form the smallest section of the community now.[4]

It seems, however, that the Registrar was right in asserting that birth registration was largely disregarded by the pagan population. The numbers of births and deaths registered show for 1891–1904 the following distribution by religion:[5]

Religion	Registered births										
		1892									
	1891	1st half-year	2nd half-year	1895	1896	1897	1898	1899	1900	1903	1904
Pagan . .	23	11	27	150	185	196	182	182	177	188	214
Mohammedan.	84	59	282	947	1,012	1,131	1,188	1,321	1,363	1,440	1,656
Christian .	138	52	142	346	348	334	403	426	400	414	470

Religion	Registered deaths				
	1898	1899	1900	1903	1904
Pagan . . .	484	504	459	529	423
Mohammedan . .	1,066	1,252	1,143	1,059	1,249
Christian . . .	327	400	384	304	313

The Pagans ascertained at the censuses of 1891 and 1901 numbered 9,217 and 8,252, the Mohammedans 14,295 and 21,221, and the Christians 8,996 and 9,881 respectively.[6] The percentages of Pagans, Mohammedans,

[1] 'General Abstract of Registration for the year 1896', p. 125.

[2] 'Report of the Registrar General 1899', p. 315.

[3] Ibid. 1900, p. 76.   [4] 'Report of the Committee', p. 246.

[5] See *Colonial Reports, Lagos 1892*, pp. 31, 34; 'Abstract of Registration 1896', p. 130; *Abstract of Registration 1898*, pp. 5, 7; 'Report of Registrar General 1900', pp. 78, 88; *Vital Statistics 1904*, pp. 1, 9. For some years data have apparently not been published.

[6] See Lagos, *Report of the Census 1901*, p. 8.

and Christians among the total population and among the registered births and deaths were as follows:

Religion	Population		Registered births				Registered deaths	
	1891	1901	Jan. 1891 to June 1892	July 1892 to Dec. 1892	1895 to 1900	1903 to 1904	1898 to 1900	1903 to 1904
Pagan . .	28	21	9	6	10	9	24	25
Mohammedan	44	54	39	62	68	71	58	59
Christian .	28	25	52	32	22	20	18	16

It appears that prior to July 1892 birth registration was incomplete throughout. Even among the Christians less than one-half of the births were then registered. From the second half of 1892 onwards birth registration improved throughout, and it is possible that by 1898 nearly all Christian and Mohammedan births were registered, but as late as 1904 a considerable proportion of Pagan births remained unregistered. As regards deaths, the figures do not indicate that registration was incomplete among any section. The low proportion of registered deaths among Christians may have been due to a lower mortality caused by better living conditions.

The deterioration of registration in the 1870s and the subsequent improvement may be inferred from the following table:[1]

Period	Population	Average yearly registrations		Birth-rate	Death-rate
		Births	Deaths		
1868–70	30,000	609	701	20	23
1871–7	32,000	253	575	8	18
1878–89	35,000	234	856	7	24
1890–1	38,000	257	1,374	7	36
1892	39,000	547	1,383	14	35
1893–4	40,000	1,116	1,437	28	36
1895–1900	42,000	1,601	1,904	38	45

Compulsory registration was extended to Ebute Metta on 1 July 1901. But registration, particularly of births, was here obviously quite defective for some years. When in 1908 compulsory registration had been further extended to the Towns of Badagry, Ikorodu, Shagamu, and Epe, the Principal Medical Officer of the Colony and Protectorate of Southern Nigeria reported:

Efforts are now being made to secure better registration of births and deaths in other towns in the Colony and also in the Protectorate; but it is evident that much time must pass before anything like a fair estimate of the real figures can be formed.

So far as Lagos and Ebute-Metta are concerned, it must be rarely that a death escapes registration, though it is possible that a few births may not be reported to the Registrar. In districts, however, where interment in any place but a cemetery is possible, it is highly probable that many deaths are, and will for a long time be unrecorded.[2]

[1] The population figures are, of course, uncertain. The birth figures exclude still-births except in 1893–4; the death figures include still-births.

[2] Southern Nigeria, *Medical Report 1908*, p. 12.

The numbers of births and deaths registered in 1909 in the four towns were:[1]

Epe		Ikorodu		Shagamu		Badagry	
Births	Deaths	Births	Deaths	Births	Deaths	Births	Deaths
279	253	414	221	783	128	7	32

The Senior Medical Officer of the Western Province (the former Colony and Protectorate of Lagos) made the following comment:

Births and Deaths.—This is the first full year in which Records of these have been sent in by the Sub-Registrars at Epe, Ikorodu, Shagamu and Badagry, and although they may not yet be quite reliable, especially those from the last named District, it is a step in the right direction and each year will bring greater accuracy.

The Senior Medical Officer was certainly right in assuming that the records especially in Badagry, which for this town of about 10,000 people showed 7 births and 32 deaths, were not 'quite reliable', but his expectations that 'each year will bring greater accuracy' were not fulfilled. The year 1909 was the only one for which any figure has been published for any town in the Colony except Lagos and Ebute Metta, the Medical Report for 1910 did not mention registration in any other place, and the Reports for the following years stated merely:

1911. Except at Lagos and Ebute Metta Vital Statistics are unreliable . . . .[2]
1912. . . . reliable statistics are not available from other parts.[3]
1913. With the exception of Lagos and Ebute Metta, Vital Statistics are quite unreliable . . . .[4]

Finally, the Medical Report for 1915 said:

Registration being compulsory in Lagos and Ebute Metta only, statistics are available for these places only . . . .[5]

By this time the Order in Council making registration compulsory in Epe, Ikorodu, Shagamu, and Badagry had evidently fallen into oblivion, and registration was considered compulsory only in the 'Sanitary District of Lagos' which comprised about the same area as 'Lagos Township' to-day. In all vital statistics of this century this area has been subdivided into 'Lagos' (or 'Lagos Island') and 'Ebute Metta' (or 'Mainland'). These terms are somewhat confusing, but the situation may roughly be described as follows: There is a Registrar of Vital Statistics in Lagos with an office serving Lagos Island (i.e. the north-west corner of the island, Victoria Beach, and Ikoyi), and a Deputy Registrar in Ebute Metta with an office serving Iddo Island and the mainland portion of Lagos Township, comprising Ebute Metta, Apapa, Yaba, Surulure, and neighbouring villages.[6]

As shown above, the birth and death records in 'Lagos' and 'Ebute

[1] See Southern Nigeria, *Medical Report 1909*, p. 24.   [2] Ibid. *1911*, p. 5.
[3] Ibid. *1912*, p. 7.   [4] Ibid. *1913*, p. 7.
[5] Nigeria, *Medical Report 1915*, p. 42.
[6] See Lagos, *Medical Report 1930*, p. 26; *1931*, p. 19; *1933*, p. 23; *1934*, pp. 26–7.

Metta' were considered reliable in the Medical Report for 1911. Some later comments read as follows:

1913. In Lagos and Ebute Metta registration is compulsory, and the statistics are given, though they cannot be considered as very reliable.[1]

. . . the actual number of deaths shewn is accurate. The number or births recorded is, for various reasons, probably slightly under the real figure for Lagos.[2]

1915. In Lagos at least (if not in Ebute-Metta) it is probable that nearly all births and deaths are registered.[3]

1918. . . . registration of both non-natives and natives for Lagos and Ebute Metta has now long been accurately maintained . . . .[4]

1919–21. Too much reliance must not be placed upon the somewhat alarming figures as regards Infantile Mortality [in Lagos and Ebute Metta].

It must be borne in mind that whilst approximately all the deaths are registered, it is by no means probable that such is the case as regards births.

The illiterate African has not yet arrived at the stage of realising the need of registration from the point of view of legality ; still less is he interested in its statistical aspect.

He cannot bury his dead until he has obtained a burial permit, which is only issued after the death has been registered; but no formalities impede the process of birth.[5]

1922. All deaths are registered, otherwise it would not be possible to bury. The same does not hold good as far as the births are concerned.[6]

1923. The statistics for Lagos may be taken to be as accurate as those of many European towns. No burial can take place without a burial certificate. With regard to births, a few may escape registration but it is believed not in sufficient number to affect the value of the statistics seriously.[7]

1927. While it is possible that there may be evasion of registration of births and infantile deaths, generally speaking it would be extremely difficult to evade registration of a death.[8]

In his report on the 1931 census of Nigeria the Government Statistician made the following statements concerning the completeness of registration in the township of Lagos:

. . . we have here a record of births and deaths which, in recent years, is probably not more than 5 per cent in error.[9]

. . . the Birth Registration data, which are probably less than 5 per cent in defect during the last decade, and during the last few years, are regarded by Dr. Cauchi, the Medical Officer of Health, as even more accurate.[10]

As to death registration, although it was begun in Lagos in 1867, it was clearly very incomplete until the decade 1891–1901. From that time onwards the omission of deaths has been probably not greater than 10 per cent. At the present time it is claimed that very few deaths escaped registration,[11] but the exact extent of omission to register is unknown.

. . . in calculating rates of mortality for all Males for the decade 1921–1930, I have assumed . . . that an additive correction . . . of 5 per cent to the registered number of deaths should be made.[12]

---

[1] Southern Nigeria, *Medical Report 1913*, p. 12.   [2] Ibid., p. 51.
[3] *Report on the Lagos Municipal Board of Health 1915*, p. 19.
[4] Southern Provinces, *Medical Report 1918*, p. 36.   [5] Nigeria, *Medical Report 1919–21*, p. 23.
[6] Ibid. *1922*, p. 19.   [7] Ibid. *1923*, p. 21.   [8] Ibid. *1927*, p. 21.
[9] *Census of Nigeria, 1931*, vol. i, p. 3.   [10] Ibid., p. 68.
[11] This claim, however, was made as far back as 1897; see p. 627 above.
[12] *Census of Nigeria, 1931*, vol. i, p. 76. In computing death-rates for males and females in 1932 he assumed 'that five per cent of the deaths escape registration' (see Lagos Town Council, *Report of Medical Officer of Health 1932*, p. 26) which, if he meant what he said, means that he added 5·26 per cent. to the registered number of deaths.

Since the number of deaths registered in Lagos Township was 2,016 in 1930 and 1,789 in 1931 he apparently assumed that about 100 deaths had not been registered in each of those years. But he certainly would not have taken so favourable a view of the completeness of death registration if he had studied the separate figures for the mainland section of the township, the population of which he estimated at 37,000 for 1930 and at 39,000 in 1931. The deaths registered there numbered 345 in 1930 and 327 in 1931. An estimate which would put the omissions in this section alone at 300 a year would certainly be quite conservative. But omissions were not confined to the mainland. Referring to visits made in 1933 to the Island the Medical Officer of Health Dr. Cauchi said:

> There is reason to believe that the provisions of the Births and Deaths Ordinance are not always observed in the outlying parts of the township. The Assistant Medical Officer of Health visited fifteen such outlying villages during the year and asked the villagers to register all deaths, bury dead bodies in the approved cemeteries and to register all births.[1]

This is the first intimation that even within Lagos Township the provisions concerning burial permits were disregarded, and while Dr. Cauchi in this report said that the provisions concerning registrations were 'not always observed' in the outlying villages, he said in the following year that 'many births and deaths remained unregistered' in those villages.

> It has been felt for some time that many births and deaths remained unregistered when they occurred in outlying villages of the township in spite of the law that enforces such registration. Many such villages are too far off motor roads for the desirable amount of supervision and frequency of inspection to be exercised with the staff available. Dr. Oluwole, Assistant Medical Officer of Health, has now visited most of these villages and explained to the accredited head of each village and to the residents present that the law required them to register their births and deaths and that cemeteries have been declared outside which burials are not allowed. The Registrar of Vital Statistics, Lagos, or the Deputy Registrar, Ebute Metta, accompanied Dr. Oluwole on each of these visits.[2]

> The plea of ignorance on this point, therefore, cannot be accepted from these villages in future.[3]

Of the villages thus visited in 1933 and 1934, 21 were in Lagos and 61 on the mainland. The argument that many of these villages were too far off motor-roads for the desirable amount of supervision and frequency of inspection to be exercised with the staff available is not convincing. Compulsory registration had been in force in Lagos for over 40 years and the registration area of Lagos is 9 square miles; compulsory registration had been in force on the mainland for over 30 years and the registration area there is 15 square miles. The staff of the Medical Officer of Health consisted of about 70 persons, including about 50 Sanitary Inspectors. It is difficult to understand why the staff available was not sufficient to exercise the desirable amount of supervision and frequency of inspection so as to prevent many people in the outlying villages being buried without registration of their deaths. On the other hand, it would be a mistake to believe that omissions in the outlying villages may have reduced essentially the total

---

[1] See Lagos Town Council, *Report of Medical Officer of Health 1933*, p. 22.
[2] Ibid. *1934*, pp. 26–7.   [3] Ibid., p. 27.

number of registered births and deaths. This is out of the question since these villages comprised only about 5 per cent. of the population on the mainland and rather less on the island. The Medical Department does not seem to have been aware of this fact. In his report for 1934 Dr. Cauchi, calling attention to the low death-rate on the mainland, said:

Death-rates have been strikingly lower for the mainland portion than for the rest of the township for many years. Most of the mainland houses and streets are constructed according to a proper lay-out, and congestion of buildings is less, and insanitary buildings are fewer, than on Lagos island. These are factors favourable to public health and may be expected favourably to affect death-rates on the mainland portion of Lagos township.

The relatively larger population living in outlying villages on the mainland, as compared with Lagos island must account for more deaths going unregistered and undetected and a correspondingly lower (apparent) death-rate.

The presence of the large African Hospital on Lagos island, to which patients come from all over the township and from which deaths are registered at the Registry for Lagos island favour an apparently higher death-rate for the latter.[1]

In the following year he said:

The mortality rates for deaths registered in Ebute Metta are again considerably lower than for those registered in Lagos. The fact that a similarly considerable difference is also shown in the birth-rates makes one suspect that failure to register, presumably on the part of outlying villages, is an important, though possibly only partial, explanation of the discrepancy.[2]

His successor, Dr. Oluwole, said in his report for 1936:

For several years now reference has been made in each annual report to the failure to register all the births and deaths which occur on the mainland portion of the Township, 'presumably on the part of outlying villages.' There is reason to believe that there was a slight improvement in registration during the year, and this increased registration of deaths may be partly responsible for the infant mortality rate showing an increase for the Township as a whole. But at 139·9 per 1,000 the infant mortality rate is the highest recorded when compared with the previous eight years.[3]

The actual figures, however, do not support this view. The number of registered births decreased in the mainland portion of the Township from 943 in 1935 to 865 in 1936, while the number of registered deaths increased from 432 to 461. This does, it seems to me, not offer reason to believe that there was any improvement in registration. As regards infant mortality in the Township as a whole the number of registered infant deaths decreased apparently from 581 to 571, and the infant mortality rate rose only because the number of registered births showed a suspicious drop from 4,482 to 4,081. It should be noted moreover that the Nigeria Medical Report for 1936, which considered the mainland birth-rate to be very high, said:

. . . it is not improbable that a number of births registered in the Ebute Metta district actually occur in villages situated in the surrounding bush whose inhabitants

---

[1] Ibid., p. 28.
[2] Ibid. *1935*, p. 22. See also in this connexion ibid., p. 20: 'A new cemetery has been declared for the inhabitants of the Abebe Villages on the mainland part of the township. They have been warned that the declaration of such a cemetery does not exempt them from registration of their dead and the necessity of obtaining a burial permit before undertaking an interment.'
[3] Ibid. *1936*, pp. 22–3.

have learnt to appreciate the value of a birth certificate—obtainable after registration—in connection with educational and vocational requirements.[1]

In 1937 the number of registrations on the mainland (births 847, deaths 472) was nearly the same as in 1936, while on the island registered births showed a negligible increase (from 3,216 to 3,258) and registered deaths a considerable increase (from 1,943 to 2,182). Dr. Oluwole made the following comment:

The Registration of deaths continued to improve and this increased registration is believed to be the chief factor for the increase in the general death rate.[2]

But the Annual Colonial Report for the same year said:

The increase in the 1937 death-rate figure reflects an increase in those for deaths due to diseases of the respiratory system.[3]

Actually the number of registered deaths on the island dropped essentially in 1938 (to 2,055). But Dr. Oluwole did not attribute this decrease to more defective registration.

Deaths are now being better registered, and no case of unauthorised burial outside a recognised cemetery was found.[4]

The comments of the Medical Officers are certainly not very helpful. Until 1936 these officers were puzzled by the fact that the official birth- and death-rates of the Mainland lagged considerably behind those of Lagos. While in 1931–5 the birth-rate for Lagos oscillated between 28 and 30 and the death-rate between 15 and 16, the birth-rate for the Mainland oscillated between 18 and 22, and the death-rate between 8 and 9. The officers then suggested that the apparently lower mortality on the mainland was due to better sanitary conditions and the lower birth-rate to defective registration. But when in 1936, owing to the reduction of the population estimate for the mainland from 50,000 to 20,000,[5] the birth-rate there jumped to 43 (and the death-rate to 22) they gave as an explanation that a number of births registered in the mainland district actually occurred in the surrounding bush. That this explanation was not adequate may be inferred from the fact that the total number of Pagan births registered in the mainland district in 1932–7 was 21 while the number of Pagan deaths registered in the same period was 286,[6] and that when in 1938 the births registered but not occurring in the District were excluded from the statistics the number of births considered did not decrease.

[1] Nigeria, *Medical Report 1936*, p. 10. Such births and also all deaths occurring outside Lagos Township have been excluded from the vital statistics since 1937. See Lagos Town Council, *Report of Medical Officer of Health 1938*, p. 23: '. . . in order to make the figures represent the vital statistics of the township proper, "permissible" deaths—that is, those occurring just outside the township but registered in the township to allow of burial in an approved cemetery in the township—have been excluded; "permissible" births have also been excluded; these are births occurring outside the township but registered in the township for the purpose of obtaining birth certificates.' [2] Ibid. *1937*, p. 26.
[3] *Colonial Reports, Nigeria 1937*, p. 13. Deaths from pneumonia were 479 in 1937 as compared with 316 in 1936; see Lagos Town Council, *Report of Medical Officer of Health 1936*, p. 26, *1937*, p. 27. [4] Ibid. *1938*, p. 22. [5] See p. 660 below.
[6] See Lagos Town Council, *Report of Medical Officer of Health 1933*, p. 25; *1935*, p. 21; *1937*, p. 26.

Any doubt that birth registration had been very incomplete all the time not only in the outlying villages on the mainland but also in Lagos must have been dispelled, moreover, by the fact that the number of native births registered in Lagos Township rose gradually from 4,288 in 1938 to 7,240 in 1944. As regards death registration it is more difficult to say something definite. But the fact that the official death-rate in 1938–41 was only 16 makes it probable that the number of deaths which were not registered was considerable even in those years.

2. Southern Nigeria

In the Protectorate of Southern Nigeria, constituted in 1900, compulsory birth and death registration was introduced by 'The Births and Deaths Proclamation, 1901',[1] which was to come into operation on 1 January 1902. The Proclamation was very similar to the Lagos Ordinance of 1889, but was less explicit concerning burials. As regards the registration area and the persons subject to registration the Proclamation provided:

3. The High Commissioner may from time to time by order published in the 'Gazette' divide the Protectorate into districts, or declare any areas, towns, or places in the Protectorate to be districts, and apply all or any of the provisions of this Proclamation to any such districts, and to all persons, or to Natives or non-natives, or to persons of any nationality, or of any class in any such districts, and he may in like manner from time to time amend, alter, suspend, or revoke any order made under this section.

This Proclamation, which apparently was never enforced,[2] was repealed by 'The Births and Deaths Proclamation, 1903'[3] which remained in force in the Protectorate of Southern Nigeria after the amalgamation of the Colony and Protectorate of Lagos with the Protectorate of Southern Nigeria into the Colony and Protectorate of Southern Nigeria (1906). It was finally repealed in 1917 by the Ordinance which consolidated the birth and death registration acts then in force in the various parts of Nigeria.

The Proclamation of 1903 distinguished 'Aliens' and 'Natives'.

'Alien' means any person who is not by native law and custom a member of a Native Community.

[1] No. 17 of 1901 (27 July), *Government Gazette Protectorate of Southern Nigeria*, 29 July 1901, pp. 215–33, reprinted in *Proclamations*, &c., *in Force in Southern Nigeria, 31 Dec. 1901*, pp. 350–70. See also ibid., pp. 219–9. 'The General Registry Proclamation, 1901' (No. 16, 27 July) which came into operation on 1 Sept. 1901.

[2] See 'General Abstract of Registration 1903', p. 288: 'Prior to 1st October [1903], there was no law in force making registration of Births and Deaths incumbent on the inhabitants. Proclamation No. 17 of 1901, "The Births and Deaths Proclamation, 1901," was obsolete.' See also *Colonial Reports, Southern Nigeria 1903*, p. 24: '"The Births and Deaths Proclamation, 1901," was found by experience to be practically inoperative and the returns thereunder to be useless for statistical purposes.'

[3] No. 8 of 1903 (10 Jan.), Southern Nigeria, *Proclamations*, &c., *1903*, Part I, pp. 33–46. The Proclamation was amended by Proclamation No. 12 of 1904 (23 Nov.), ibid. *1904*, pp. 31–2. Order in Council No. 4 of 1911 (17 Feb.), *Southern Nigeria Government Gazette*, 8 Mar. 1911, pp. 367–9, modified the Form of Medical Death Certificate. The Ordinance as it stood after the enactment of Proclamation No. 12 of 1904 is reprinted in *Laws of the Colony of Southern Nigeria 1908*, vol. ii, pp. 1089–1103 (chapter 97).

'The Births and Deaths Proclamation, 1903' was supplemented by 'The Burial Proclamation, 1903' (No. 27, 15 Oct., Southern Nigeria, *Proclamations*, &c., *1903*, Part I, pp. 115–20, reprinted in *Laws of the Colony of Southern Nigeria 1908*, vol. ii, pp. 1104–9, chapter 98).

'Native' includes any person who by native law and custom is a member of a Native Community.

Many provisions of the Proclamation applied to both alien and native registration and did not differ essentially from those in other British Dependencies. Some peculiarities of the registration of native births and deaths as it was then envisaged may perhaps best be illustrated by quoting some sections from 'The Births and Deaths Registration Rules'.[1]

2. Every Head of a House or other Chief who is appointed to be a Native Registrar of Births and Deaths shall order the members of the native community over which he has control to give to him or in his absence to the Deputy Native Registrar of Births and Deaths of such community, as soon as possible after every birth or death in the community, information of the particulars required to be registered under the Ordinance in respect of such birth or death.

3. When a Native Registrar of Births and Deaths or a Deputy Native Registrar of Births and Deaths has received the necessary information, he shall enter in the Community Register of Births or Deaths, as the case may be, the particulars required to be registered. If the Native Registrar of Births and Deaths or the Deputy Native Registrar of Births and Deaths requires assistance in entering such particulars, he shall, after obtaining the necessary information, go to the Clerk of the nearest Native Court of the District and shall, with the assistance of such Clerk, enter the required particulars, and place his signature or mark opposite the entry.

4. It shall be the duty of such Clerk to render every assistance to such Native Registrar of Births and Deaths and Deputy Native Registrar of Births and Deaths, so as to ensure that the entries in the Native Community Registers are duly and properly made.

5. It shall be the duty of every Native Registrar of Births and Deaths, or in his absence of the Deputy Native Registrar of Births and Deaths, to inform the mother of every child, whose birth has been duly registered, as soon as possible after such registration, that she and her child are entitled under the provisions of the Ordinance for a period of two years from the date of such birth to medical attendance and medicine free of charge at the Government Dispensary in the district.

6. The Native Registrar of Births and Deaths, or in his absence the Deputy Native Registrar of Births and Deaths, shall give the mother of every child, whose birth has been duly registered, a printed certificate addressed to the Medical Officer in Charge of the nearest Government Dispensary of the district, certifying that she and her child are entitled under the provisions of the Ordinance to medical attendance and medicine free of charge, and such Medical Officer shall give such medical attendance and medicine accordingly.

The Proclamation defined the registration area as follows:

3. This Proclamation shall apply (1) to all births and deaths occurring among aliens in the Protectorate, and (2) to all births and deaths occurring in any Native Community to which this Proclamation by any rule made by any Native Council under the provisions of 'The Native Courts Proclamation, 1901,' may, subject to the approval of the High Commissioner, be applied.

The first 'Native Council Rule relating to Registration of Births and Deaths' was made on 16 June 1903 by the Native Council of Warri.[2] It read as follows:

WHEREAS by Section 36 of 'The Native Courts Proclamation, 1901,' (No. 25 of 1901) the Native Council of Warri has power to make, subject to the approval of

---

[1] Rule No. 9 of 1903 (1 Oct.), Southern Nigeria, *Proclamations*, &c., *1903*, Part III, pp. 53–5, reprinted in *Laws of the Colony of Southern Nigeria 1908*, vol. ii, pp. 1101–3.

[2] Warri, Native Council Rule No. 1 of 1903, Southern Nigeria, *Proclamations*, &c., *1903*, Part V.

the High Commissioner, Rule embodying the native law with such modifications and additions as may be expedient, and also Rules for the welfare of the natives:

AND WHEREAS by Native Law the birth and death of every native must be reported to the Chief of the House of which such native is a member:

AND WHEREAS the said Native Council are of opinion that advantage should be taken of the privileges to be granted by Section 38 of 'The Births and Deaths Proclamation, No. 8 of 1903' whereby every child whose birth is registered in accordance with that law and the mother of every such child become entitled, subject to certain conditions, to medical attendance and medicine free of charge for the period of two years succeeding such birth:

AND WHEREAS the said Council are further of opinion that every birth and death should in addition to being reported to the Chief of the House concerned be also registered:—

The Native Council of Warri do hereby make the following rules subject to the approval of the High Commissioner:

1. 'The Births and Deaths Proclamation, of 1903,' (No. 8 of 1903) shall from the time when the said law is brought into operation, apply to all Native Communities over whom the Native Council has jurisdiction.

2. Every Head of a House or Chief who is appointed to be Native Registrar shall order the members of the Native Community over whom he has control to give him as soon as possible after any birth or death in that community the information necessary to fill in the Register.

When such Head or Chief receives information of a birth or death he shall come to the next meeting of the Council or Minor Court or shall send a representative, who has all the necessary information concerning the birth or death, to such meeting. The Head or Chief or such representative shall bring the proper Register to such meeting and shall enter into the Register with the assistance of the clerk of the Council or Court all the required information concerning such birth or death.

It shall be the duty of such clerk to render all assistance to every such Native Registrar to ensure that the Registers shall be correctly entered up.

3. It shall be the duty of every Head of a House or Chief being a Registrar to inform the mother as soon as possible after she has given birth that she is entitled to free medical attendance and free medicine for the next two years provided she attends Government Dispensary.

Such Head or Chief shall give such mother a printed authority addressed to the District Medical Officer stating that the mother is so entitled. The printed authority shall be taken from a counterfoil book numbered consecutively and such book shall be sent with the Register to the next meeting of the Council or Court in order that the identity of the woman who has obtained medical attendance and medicine with the mother of the child whose birth has been registered may be verified and recorded. After such record has been made such book shall be handed back by the clerk to the Chief or Head or representative aforesaid.

Passed by the Native Council of Warri this 16th day of June, 1903. In witness whereof we hereunto make our marks.

Further Rules were made in 1903 for the Districts of New Calabar and Brass, and in 1904 for the Districts of Sapele, Benin River, and Okrika.[1] The Rules for these five Districts were practically identical. The Rule for New Calabar read as follows:

WHEREAS it is expedient that for the peace, good order and welfare of the Natives in the District of New Calabar that all the provisions of 'The Births and Deaths Proclamation, 1903,' should so far as the same relate to members of Native

---

[1] New Calabar, Native Council Rule No. 2 of 1903 (8 Aug.); Nembe, N.C.R. No. 3 of 1903 (1 Sept.); Sapele, N.C.R. No. 1 of 1904 (29 Dec. 1903); Benin River, N.C.R. No. 2 of 1904 (9 Jan.); Okrika, N.C.R. No. 1 of 1904 (10 Mar.). All these rules are reprinted ibid. *1903*, Part V, and *1904*, Part V.

Communities apply in the said District to the Native Communities, known as Houses or otherwise, hereinafter mentioned:

Now, THEREFORE, the Native Council of New Calabar do hereby in pursuance of the powers vested in them by 'The Native Courts Proclamation, 1901,' make the following rule:—

All the provisions of 'The Births and Deaths Proclamation, 1903' (No. 8 of 1903) shall so far as the same relate to members of Native Communities apply in the district of New Calabar to the following Native Communities, namely— . . .

Thus compulsory registration was established for non-natives in the whole Protectorate and for natives in six districts.

'The Births and Deaths Proclamation, 1903', which after the amalgamation of Lagos and Southern Nigeria was called 'The Births and Deaths Registration (Protectorate) Ordinance', provided that a copy of the records of the Native Registrars (appointed by the Governor[1]) should be transmitted through the District Registrar (District Commissioner) to the Principal Registrar (Principal Medical Officer).

9. Every Native Registrar shall on or before the fifth day of every month, or on or before such day of the month as the Governor may prescribe, produce the Community Births Register and the Community Deaths Register kept by him to the District Registrar of his District, who shall forthwith enter the particulars to be transcribed therefrom in the Native Births Register and the Native Deaths Register respectively kept by him.

10. Every District Registrar shall on or before the tenth day of every month, or on or before such day of the month as the Governor may prescribe, make and deliver to the Principal Registrar a true copy certified under the hand of such District Registrar of all entries made during the preceding month in the Registers kept by him.

But registrations were very scanty. In 1903 the total number of registered births was 34 (including 11 native) and the total number of registered deaths 177.[2] In 1904–7 the numbers of births registered were 153 (including 129 native), 98, 89 (68), and 74 (57), and the numbers of deaths registered 211 (including 144 native), 121 (81), 81 (62), and 115 (80).[3] The Southern Nigeria Medical Reports for 1905–9 do not mention the subject. The Report for 1910 contains the following statement by the Provincial Senior Medical Officer, Eastern Province:

The total number of Native deaths registered in Calabar was 54.

The District Medical Officer's Returns however show 284. It is impossible to get anything approaching the real figures, but the system of registration introduced into the Districts may be expected to give a more accurate estimate next year.[4]

Since he says that 'the Population of Calabar is estimated to be 129,969' the actual number of native deaths must have amounted to several thousands, of which only 50 male and 4 female were registered. The number of registered native births was 12.[5] No further report mentions native registration in the Protectorate and death registration was considered incomplete even among the (non-official) European population.[6]

---

[1] I am now using the terminology of Laws of the Colony of Southern Nigeria 1908.

[2] See Southern Nigeria, 'General Abstract of Registration 1903', p. 288.

[3] See Colonial Reports, Southern Nigeria 1904, pp. 37–8, 1905, pp. 35–6; 'General Abstract of Registration in Southern Nigeria (Eastern and Central Provinces) 1906', pp. 26–7, '1907', pp. 134–5.   [4] Southern Nigeria, Medical Report 1910, p. 44.   [5] See ibid., p. 45.

[6] See ibid. 1913, pp. 12, 14; Nigeria, Medical Report 1914, pp. 54, 59; 1915, p. 42; 1917, p. 12; Nigeria, Southern Provinces, Medical Report 1916, p. 8; 1918, p. 11.

For registration in Southern Nigeria since 1917, see 4. *Nigeria and Cameroons*.

3. *Northern Nigeria*

In the Protectorate of Northern Nigeria, constituted in 1900, compulsory death registration for non-natives was introduced by the 'Notification and Registration of Deaths Proclamation 1901',[1] which came into operation on 4 June 1901. It was repealed in 1917 by the Ordinance consolidating the birth and death registration acts in the various parts of Nigeria.

Compulsory death registration for all persons dying in a Cantonment was introduced by 'The Cantonment Proclamation 1904'[2] which came into operation on 30 September 1904.[3] It provided:

3. (1) The High Commissioner by Government Notice in the *Gazette* may order that the provisions of this Proclamation, or of any regulation made thereunder, or such of them as shall be specified in the order, shall apply to any town or village or land adjacent to a Cantonment or to any Government Station in any Province.

20. Whenever any death shall take place in a Cantonment, the same shall be reported forthwith by the holder of the permit [of residence] if the death took place within the premises of such holder, failing him by any relatives of the deceased residing in the Cantonment, and failing such relatives, by the persons living nearest to the deceased or by any person who may well know of such death and that it has not been reported to the Cantonment Magistrate, under a penalty not exceeding £2, or, in default, to 7 days imprisonment.

A High Commissioner's Order of 20 April 1906[4] stipulated that the section providing for death registration in cantonments 'shall be applied to all Government Stations throughout the Protectorate'. Notice had to be given to the 'Resident or Assistant Resident'.

Compulsory birth registration was introduced in 1911 in the Cantonment of Zungeru under 'The Infectious Diseases Proclamation 1908'.[5] The respective Order and Rules, issued on 26 October 1911[6] by the Governor, read as follows:

Order under Section 17.

From the 1st day of December 1911 and until further order all children found in the Cantonment of Zungeru who have not been previously inoculated or vaccinated successfully or already had small pox shall be vaccinated.

[1] No. 5 of 1901 (28 Feb.), *The Northern Nigeria Gazette*, 28 Feb. 1901, pp. 24–7. The Proclamation was amended in 1904 (see No. 30 of 1904, 28 Sept., Ibid. *Extraordinary*, 30 Sept. 1904, pp. 100–1). The Proclamation in its amended form is reprinted in *Orders in Council and Proclamations, in Force in Northern Nigeria 1 Oct. 1904*, pp. 106–9, and in *Laws of the Protectorate of Northern Nigeria 1910*, pp. 557–9 (chapter 48).

[2] No. 28 of 1904 (27 Sept.), *The Northern Nigeria Gazette, Extraordinary*, 30 Sept. 1904, pp. 83–94, reprinted in *Orders in Council and Proclamations in Force in Northern Nigeria 1 Oct. 1904*, pp. 687–704.

[3] *Abstract of Arrangements respecting Registration in the British Dominions beyond the Seas*, published in 1904, did not mention the 'Notification and Registration of Deaths Proclamation 1901', but said (p. 16): 'Deaths of all persons occurring in cantonments are . . . registered by the cantonment magistrate under the Cantonment Proclamation of 1900.' However, this Proclamation which was repealed by the Proclamation of 1904 did not provide for death registration.

[4] *The Northern Nigeria Gazette, Extraordinary*, 20 Apr. 1906, p. 48.

[5] No. 12 of 1908 (13 Aug.), *The Northern Nigeria Gazette, Extraordinary*, 13 Aug. 1908, pp. 71–9, reprinted in *Laws of the Protectorate of Northern Nigeria 1910*, pp. 505–10 (chapter 38).

[6] *The Northern Nigeria Gazette, Extraordinary*, 26 Oct. 1911, p. 69.

Rules under Section 24.

With a view to carrying out the above order the following rules are hereby made under the provisions of section 24.

Registration of Births.

1. When a child is born alive in the Cantonment of Zungeru, the parent of the child, and in default of such parent, every person present at the birth, and, in default of such person, if the birth took place in a house to the knowledge of the occupier thereof, then such occupier shall within 21 days next after the birth, give personally notice of such birth together with such particulars as may be required for the purposes of identification to the Cantonment Magistrate.

2. The Cantonment Magistrate shall make an entry thereof in a book to be kept for the purpose and shall if required give a certificate of such entry without fee or reward.

3. Any person who neglects to comply with the provisions of the above rules shall be liable on conviction to a penalty not exceeding forty shillings or to imprisonment not exceeding one month.

Thus compulsory birth registration for natives and non-natives was confined to the cantonment of Zungeru with 5,000 or 6,000 inhabitants, while compulsory death registration for non-natives covered the whole Protectorate and compulsory death registration for natives a number of places besides Zungeru. The Medical Report for 1911 mentioned a plan of recording native births and deaths in all the large cities.

Arrangements are now being made by the authorities to supply birth and death rate returns from all the large cities to this department for registration. Registration has not, so far, been compulsory in the Protectorate.[1]

But this plan was never put into operation. The Medical Report for 1912 suggests at one place[2] that native deaths were registered (inadequately) under the Cantonment Proclamation ('. . . the registration of deaths is as yet necessarily unreliable for statistical purposes'), but says at another place[3] that 'figures regarding births and deaths . . . are as yet unobtainable'. The report for 1913 says that 'no reliable statistics of births and deaths are obtainable',[4] but the reports for 1916 and 1917 state more definitely:

1916. No statistics as to [native] births and deaths are available, the only records kept are those relating to deaths of Europeans and non-European aliens.[5]

1917. Records of Births and Deaths among the Europeans and non-European Aliens only are kept.[6]

4. Nigeria and Cameroons

Legislation. After the amalgamation of the Protectorate of Northern Nigeria with the Colony and Protectorate of Southern Nigeria (1914) the position of registration in Nigeria was as follows:

(1) Colony. Registration was compulsory for all births and deaths occurring in the 'Town and Island of Lagos' and in the Island of Iddo and part of the mainland at Ebute Metta. The Order in Council of 1908

---

[1] Northern Nigeria, *Medical Report 1911*, p. 5.　　　　[2] Ibid. *1912*, p. 6.
[3] Ibid., p. 8.
[4] Ibid. *1913*, p. 7. See also Nigeria, *Medical Report 1914*, p. 8; *1915*, p. 7.
[5] Nigeria Northern Provinces, *Medical Report 1916*, p. 7.
[6] Nigeria, *Medical Report 1917*, p. 115.

making registration compulsory in the towns of Epe, Ikorodu, Shagamu, and Badagry had fallen into oblivion.

(2) Southern Provinces. Registration was compulsory (*a*) for all alien births and deaths, and (*b*) for all births and deaths occurring in a Native Community for which a Native Council had introduced registration through a Rule approved by the Governor. Such Rules had been made in 1903–4 for six districts but they were apparently never enforced and probably became obsolete after a few years.

(3) Northern Provinces. Registration was compulsory (*a*) for all non-native births and deaths, (*b*) for all deaths occurring in Government Stations, and (*c*) for all births occurring in the Cantonment of Zungeru. But by the time the amalgamation took place native births or deaths were apparently no longer registered.

On 30 August 1917 there was enacted 'An Ordinance to provide for Registration of Births and Deaths, and to regulate Burials'[1] which repealed and consolidated all registration Ordinances then in force in the various parts of the Colony and Protectorate of Nigeria.[2] It came into operation on 1 April 1918[3] and was amended five times.[4]

Section 50 of the Births, Deaths and Burials Ordinance provided that the Governor in Council may make Regulations, and the first Regulations were made on 4 October 1917.[5] They have been amended twice.[6] The main provisions referring to registration as they stand to-day[7] are as follows:

1. Every registrar shall at the beginning of each month forward to the Principal Registrar a true copy, certified under the hand of such registrar of all entries made during the preceding month in the registers kept by him.

[1] No. 48 of 1917, *The Nigeria Gazette*, 30 Aug. 1917, Supplement; reprinted in Nigeria, *Ordinances 1917*, pp. 523–50.

[2] The Acts repealed were: No. 5 of 1889 of the Colony of Lagos, 'The Births, Deaths and Burials Ordinance'; No. 8 of 1903, Southern Nigeria, 'The Births and Deaths Registration (Protectorate) Ordinance'; No. 27 of 1903, Southern Nigeria, 'The Burials Ordinance'; and No. 5 of 1901, Northern Nigeria, 'Notification and Registration of Deaths Proclamation'.

[3] See Government Notice No. 129, *The Nigeria Gazette*, 15 Nov. 1917, p. 470.

[4] Ordinance No. 24 of 1922 (8 Nov.), 'Interpretation (Amendment) (No. 2) Ordinance, 1922', reprinted in Nigeria, *Ordinances 1922*, pp. 73–6; No. 34 of 1938 (9 Dec.), 'Births, Deaths and Burials (Amendment) Ordinance, 1938', reprinted in *Laws of Nigeria 1938*, Part A, pp. 167–8; No. 18 of 1943 (24 Apr.), 'Native Authority (Substitution for Native Administration) Ordinance, 1943', reprinted ibid. *1943*, Part A, pp. 105–9; No. 34 of 1944 (27 Apr.), 'Births, Deaths and Burials (Amendment) Ordinance, 1944', *Supplement to Nigeria Gazette*, 27 Apr. 1944, pp. 543–5; No. 11 of 1945 (16 Apr.), 'Births, Deaths and Burials (Amendment) Ordinance, 1945', *Supplement to Nigeria Gazette*, 19 Apr. 1945, pp. 963–4. The Ordinance as it stood after the enactment of the Ordinance of 1922 is reprinted in *Laws of Nigeria in Force 1923*, vol. i, pp. 571–93 (cap. 47).

[5] No. 41 of 1917, *The Nigeria Gazette*, 11 Oct. 1917, Supplement; reprinted in *Orders in Council, Regulations, &c., under Ordinances of Nigeria in Force 1918*, pp. 457–9.

[6] No. 2 of 1920 (20 Jan.), *The Nigeria Gazette*, 5 Feb. 1920, Supplement; No. 1 of 1941 (7 Jan.), *Nigeria Gazette*, 9 Jan. 1941, Supplement.

[7] Reprinted in *Laws of Nigeria in Force 1923*, vol. iii, pp. 330–1. Two supplementary Regulations made under Section 50 on 4 Mar. 1918 and 23 Nov. 1936 (No. 18 of 1918, reprinted in *Orders in Council, Regulations, &c., 1918*, Part II, p. 59; No. 43 of 1936, reprinted in *Laws of Nigeria 1936*, Part C, pp. 131–3) modified the registration forms for native births and deaths.

Apart from these general Regulations special Regulations concerning fees were made by the Governor in Council for various areas. See No. 25 of 1942 (10 Mar.), reprinted in *Laws of Nigeria 1942*, Part D, p. 44; No. 25 of 1943 (20 Apr.), reprinted ibid. *1943*, Part D, pp. 72–3; No. 62 of 1943 (7 Sept.), reprinted ibid., p. 162.

2. Every registrar shall keep alphabetical indexes showing all births and deaths respectively registered in his office. Separate indexes shall be kept for non-natives and native registrations.

4. The entries in the registers shall be made in order, and shall be numbered progressively from the beginning to the end of each year, the entries for each year beginning with number 1. Every entry shall be divided from the preceding one by a line.

5. In cases in which no certificate of a medical officer is produced, registrars shall ascertain as accurately as possible from the person registering a death the cause of such death.

The Births, Deaths and Burials Ordinance was followed by 'An Ordinance to make provision for the custody of registers and records relating to births, deaths, and marriages'.[1] It stipulated among other things:

3. (1) The Principal Registrar shall at the commencement of each year cause to be prepared alphabetical indexes showing all births, deaths and marriages registered during the preceding year.

Such indexes shall be in such form and shall contain such particulars as the Governor may require, and shall be preserved as records in the office of the Principal Registrar.

4. The Principal Registrar shall at the commencement of each year furnish to the Chief Secretary to the Government a general abstract of the number of births, deaths and marriages registered during the preceding year, in such form as the Governor may require.

5. All registers, records, indexes and other documents relating to the registration of births, deaths and marriages which are at the commencement of this Ordinance deposited elsewhere, and all registers and records in the custody and control of registrars which now are, or hereafter shall be, disused or filled shall be deposited in the custody of the Principal Registrar, either in his office or in such place as the Governor may direct.

6. On the payment of the prescribed fees and subject to regulations under this Ordinance, every person shall be entitled at all reasonable times to search all registers and indexes deposited or kept in any place in pursuance of this Ordinance, and to obtain a certified copy of any entry in any such register or index.

9. The Governor in Council may make regulations prescribing the fees to be paid and generally for the purpose of giving effect to the provisions and purposes of this Ordinance.[2]

The main provisions of the Births, Deaths and Burials Ordinance, ensuring the registration of births and deaths are as follows:

Principal Registrar, Registrars, and Registry Offices

4. The Governor may by notice in the Gazette:—

(a) appoint registry offices and direct for what areas and in relation to what class of persons each such office shall be the proper office for the registration of births and deaths under this Ordinance;

(b) appoint a Principal Registrar, and

(c) appoint such registrars and deputy registrars as he may think proper.

---

[1] No. 55 of 1917 (25 Oct.), *The Nigeria Gazette*, 25 Oct. 1917, Supplement; reprinted in Nigeria, *Ordinances 1917*, pp. 573–6, and in *Laws of Nigeria in Force 1923*, vol. i, pp. 594–5 (cap. 48).
[2] Regulations under this Ordinance, prescribing the fees, were made on 13 Nov. 1917 (No. 48), *The Nigeria Gazette*, 29 Nov. 1917, Supplement; reprinted in *Orders in Council, Regulations, &c., under Ordinances of Nigeria in Force 1918*, p. 460, and in *Laws of Nigeria in Force 1923*, vol. iii, pp. 331–2.

Birth and Death Registration

3. (1) Births and deaths are registrable under this Ordinance in the cases following:—

(*a*) All births and deaths occurring amongst non-natives in Nigeria or in the territorial waters of Nigeria.

(*b*) All births and deaths occurring amongst natives in any area or territorial waters of Nigeria defined in an Order in Council made under sub-section (2).

(2) The Governor may by Order in Council direct that all births and deaths occurring amongst natives in an area defined in such order shall be registered.

(3) The birth of a child still-born is not registrable under this Ordinance.

48. A native authority may, with the approval of the Governor,

(*a*) make rules providing for the registration of births and deaths occurring amongst natives in any area in which such births and deaths are not registrable under this Ordinance and for the imposition of fees in respect of such registration, and

(*b*) appoint registration offices and registrars for the purposes of any such registration.

A registrar shall keep himself informed of all births and deaths occurring and registrable in his office.

When a registrable birth occurs (1) the parent, (2) the person having charge of the child, (3) the occupier of the house in which the birth occurred, shall within 21 days register the birth or shall be liable to a fine of £2.

When a registrable death occurs (1) the relatives of the deceased present at the death or in attendance during the last illness of the deceased, (2) every person present at the death, (3) the occupier of the house in which the death occurred, (4) the person causing the body of the deceased to be buried, shall within 48 hours register the death or shall be liable to a fine of £2.

When a birth or death occurs which is not registrable any person desiring that it shall be registered may register it.

Burials

Unless a magistrate or medical officer of health shall order otherwise, no body of a deceased person whose death is registrable shall be buried or otherwise disposed of until a certificate shall have been granted by the registrar or an order shall have been made by the coroner. Penalty: a fine of £20.

Headings of Registers

Non-Native Birth (Form A): No.; Date of Birth; Place of Birth; Sex of child; Name (if any); Name and nationality or country of Father; Maiden name and nationality or country of Mother; Rank or occupation, and address of Father (or, in default, of Mother); Signature, description and address of informant; Date of Registration; Signature of Registrar; Name if added after Registration of birth.

Native Birth (Form B): No.; Date of birth; Place of birth; Sex of child; Full name (if any); Full name and tribe of father; Full maiden name and tribe of mother; Age of mother; Rank or occupation and address of father (or, in default, of mother); Signature, relationship, if any, and

address of informant; Date of registration; Signature of registrar; Name if added after registration of birth.

Non-Native Death (Form C): No.; Date of Death; Place of Death; Name; Sex; Age; Rank or occupation; Nationality or country; Abode; Cause of Death; Name of certifying Medical Practitioner (if any); Duration of illness; Place of Burial; Signature, description and address of informant; Date of Registration; Signature of Registrar.

Native Death (Form D): No.; Date of death; Place of death; Full name; Sex; Age; Nationality or tribe; Place of birth; Rank or occupation; Usual place of residence; Period of continuous residence in registration area; Last place of residence before arrival in registration area; Cause of death; Name of certifying medical practitioner (if any); Duration of illness; Place of burial; Signature, description and address of informant; Date of registration; Signature of registrar.

The Principal Registrar receives no salary for his services in this capacity; the Registrar of Vital Statistics and two Deputy Registrars of Vital Statistics receive a salary; the officer performing the duties of Deputy Registrar of Vital Statistics at Ebute Metta receives a yearly allowance (£20).[1] Registration of a death is free of charge. The same is true of registration of a birth in due time. But a fee has to be paid for a delayed registration of birth (when the child is more than 3 but not more than 12 months old, 2s. 6d., when the child is more than 12 months old, 5s.), for entering the name of a child after registration of birth (1s.), for correcting an error of fact in a register (2s. 6d.), for each search of the index to, and inspection of an entry in, a register (1s.), for each certified copy of an entry in a register (2s. 6d.).[2]

Receipts from birth and death registration in 1927–40 were as follows:[3]

Year	£	s.	d.	Year	£	s.	d.	Year	£	s.	d.	Year	£	s.	d.
1927	30	0	0	1931	11	18	0	1935	15	15	0	1939	35	18	0
1928	12	16	0	1932	13	1	2	1936	17	4	6	1940	22	0	0
1929	12	6	0	1933	11	2	0	1937	19	6	0				
1930	13	12	0	1934	11	10	0	1938	25	9	6				

Registration Area. All births and deaths occurring in Nigeria (and the Cameroons) among non-natives are compulsorily registrable.[4] Births and deaths of natives are compulsorily registrable only in so far as they occur

[1] See Nigeria, *Estimates 1939–40*, p. 49; *1944–5*, p. 54.

[2] According to Regulations No. 48 of 1917 made under the Registration Ordinance, there are furthermore to be paid for every general search of the registers and indexes in the custody of a Principal Registrar £1, for every particular search in such registers and indexes 10s., for every certified copy of an entry in any such register or index 2s. 6d.

[3] See Nigeria, *Medical Report 1927*, p. 53; *1928*, p. 49; *1929*, p. 55; *1930*, p. 44; *1931*, p. 56; *1932*, p. 5; *1933*, p. 5; *1934*, p. 5; *1935*, p. 3; *1936*, p. 3; *1937*, p. 37; *1938*, p. 33; *1939*, p. 1; *1940*, p. 2.

[4] See, however, Nigeria, *Medical Report 1919–21*, p. 64: 'The registration of births and deaths of non-natives is compulsory throughout the Northern and Southern Provinces, but, over large regions, the term "non-native", is so loosely applied, and excludes so many of those who ought to be so designated, that the resulting figures are far from reliable and are not to be taken seriously.'

in an area for which a special order has been made by the Governor in Council under section 3 (2). The following Orders in Council have been issued so far:

All Births and Deaths occurring amongst Natives in the Township of Lagos shall be registered.[1]

All births and deaths occurring amongst natives in the township of Kano on and after the 1st January, 1926, shall be registered.[2]

All births and deaths occurring amongst natives in the township of Calabar on and after the 1st day of September, 1926, shall be registered.[3]

All births and deaths occurring amongst natives in the township of Port Harcourt on and after the 1st April, 1932, shall be registered.[4]

All births and deaths occurring amongst natives in the township of Enugu on and after the 1st January, 1937, shall be registered.[5]

All births and deaths occurring among natives in the township of Aba on and after the 1st January, 1937, shall be registered.[6]

All births and deaths occurring amongst natives in the area comprised within a circle having a radius of two miles of the Alkali's Court, Minna, on and after the 1st day of January, 1938, shall be registered.[7]

All births and deaths occurring amongst natives in the areas specified in the Schedule hereto, on and after the 1st day of July, 1939, shall be registered.

SCHEDULE

ABUJA.—The area comprised within a circle having a radius of two miles of the Native Administration Dispensary, Abuja,

BIDA.—The area comprised within a circle having a radius of three miles of the Zukoko cross roads, Bida,

KONTAGORA.—The area comprised within a circle having a radius of three miles of the Native Administration Central Office, Kontagora.[8]

All births and deaths occurring amongst natives in the area known as the Kano Sabon Gari . . . shall be registered.[9]

All births and deaths occurring amongst natives in Jos Township on and after the 1st of January, 1944, shall be registered.[10]

Thus, registration of native births and deaths until 1926 remained confined to the Township of Lagos. This was not what had been expected when the Ordinance was enacted.

1917. From the Sanitary point of view the Ordinance is of value in affording a good basis on which to compile the Vital Statistics of Townships . . . .[11]

[1] No. 10 of 1918 (28 Mar.), reprinted in *Orders in Council, &c., 1918*, Part I, p. 45.

[2] No. 16 of 1925 (28 July), *The Nigeria Gazette*, 6 Aug. 1925, Supplement, reprinted in *1933 Supplement to the Laws of Nigeria*, p. 685.

[3] No. 22 of 1926 (28 June), *The Nigeria Gazette*, 8 July 1926, Supplement, reprinted in *1933 Supplement to the Laws of Nigeria*, p. 685.

[4] No. 57 of 1931 (28 Dec.), *The Nigeria Gazette*, 7 Jan. 1932, Supplement, reprinted in *1933 Supplement to the Laws of Nigeria*, p. 685.

[5] No. 78 of 1936 (15 Dec.), reprinted in *Laws of Nigeria 1936*, Part B, p. 131.

[6] No. 6 of 1937 (22 Feb.), reprinted ibid. *1937*, Part C, p. 7.

[7] No. 1 of 1938 (28 Dec. 1937), reprinted ibid. *1938*, Part C, p. 1.

[8] No. 16 of 1939 (17 July), 'Births, Deaths and Burials (Abuja, Bida, Kontagora) Order, 1939', reprinted ibid. *1939*, Part C, p. 19.

[9] No. 38 of 1940 (12 Nov.), reprinted ibid. *1940*, Part C, p. 95. This Order in Council was revoked by Order in Council No. 33 of 1941 (13 Sept.), reprinted ibid. *1941*, Part C, p. 44, which substituted 'Kano African Town (Sabon Gari)' for 'Kano Sabon Gari'.

[10] No. 30 of 1943 (16 Dec.), reprinted ibid. *1943*, Part C, p. 51. See also No. 19 of 1944 (23 May), *Supplement to Nigeria Gazette*, 1 June 1944, p. 641.

[11] Senior Sanitary Officer, Northern Provinces, in Nigeria, *Medical Report 1917*, p. 134.

1918. The sphere of influence of his [Principal Registrar] duties . . . will be very considerably increased still further when the Births and Deaths of natives become registrable in townships in both the Southern and Northern Provinces, involving an increase in the work of the staff also.[1]

1923. Registration of births and deaths of Natives should be made compulsory in all townships.[2]

1924. Some advance is expected to be made as regards the registration of Births and Deaths of Natives in some of the townships other than Lagos.[3]

From 1926 onwards the statements in the Medical Reports became confusing. The report for 1925 had stated correctly:

Registration of births and deaths of non-Natives is compulsory throughout Nigeria but in the case of Natives is only so in Lagos Township. It comes into force in Kano Township in January, 1926.[4]

The Report for 1926 listed under 'Legislation' the Order in Council ordering the registration of all births and deaths in the Township of Calabar from 1 September 1926,[5] but stated a few pages later that 'registration is only compulsory in Lagos and Ebute Metta',[6] and this statement was repeated literally in subsequent reports.[7] Finally the report for 1931 said:

Registration of births and deaths amongst the African population is at present compulsory only in Lagos and Ebute Metta. It is hoped next year to obtain figures also from Port Harcourt . . . .[8]

But this hope was apparently not fulfilled, and the Medical Reports for 1932, 1933, and 1934 stated again:

Registration of births and deaths is compulsory only in the Lagos area . . . .[9]

The following report, however, said:

Vital statistics for the Lagos area of the Colony are summarised below ; compulsory registration is also in force at Port Harcourt, Calabar and Kano Township but the figures are not yet sufficiently reliable for publication.[10]

But a year later the Medical Report contained those very figures. The returns available for 1935 and subsequent years are as follows:[11]

	Calabar				Kano		
	1935	1936	1937	1938	1935	1936	1937
Population .	17,169[1]	17,291[1]	18,000	. .	8,907	9,204	8,710
Births . .	246	303	514	632	138	133	. .
Deaths . .	358	338	365	324	100	116	. .
Birth-rate .	14·3	17·6	27·2	. .	15·5	14·5	12·8
Death-rate .	20·8	19·5	20·2	. .	11·2	12·6	25·0

[1] Mid-year.

[1] Senior Sanitary Officer, Southern Provinces (Principal Registrar of Vital Statistics, Nigeria), in Southern Provinces, *Medical Report 1918*, p. 36.

[2] Nigeria, *Medical Report 1923*, p. 29. See also ibid. *1924*, p. 55.

[3] Ibid., pp. 53–4.   [4] Ibid. *1925*, p. 12.

[5] See ibid. *1926*, p. 9.   [6] Ibid., p. 16.

[7] See ibid. *1927*, p. 20; *1928*, p. 16; *1929*, p. 21; *1930*, p. 15.   [8] Ibid. *1931*, p. 14.

[9] Ibid. *1932*, p. 10; *1933*, p. 10; *1934*, p. 9.   [10] Ibid. *1935*, p. 7.

[11] See ibid. *1936*, pp. 9–10; *1937*, p. 9; *1938*, p. 9. No figures have been published for 1939 and later years.

| | Port Harcourt | | | Aba | Enugu |
	1935	1936	1937	1937	1937
Population . .	18,608	19,409	20,000	9,152	14,541
Births . . .	279	229	..	..	..
Deaths . . .	217	194	..	..	..
Birth-rate . .	15·0	11·8	10·6	31·5	26·0
Death-rate . .	11·7	10·0	9·9	18·9	19·7

The Medical Department made the following comments:

1936. Vital Statistics. In considering the data furnished in this section of the Report certain factors should be borne in mind. First, although non-native births and deaths occurring throughout the Colony, the Protectorate and the Mandated Territory are registrable, those affecting natives are only registrable when taking place in the five registration areas of Lagos and Ebute Metta in the Colony, Calabar and Port Harcourt in the Southern Provinces and Kano Township in the Northern Provinces.

Secondly, and arising out of the above, the areas included in the five registration districts form a very small portion of Nigeria as a whole, and the sum of the population of such districts amounts to little more than one per centum of the estimated population of the Colony and its dependencies.[1]

For this reason it would be unwise to draw any firm inferences from the available statistics and due regard should be paid to this in evaluating such data as have been collected. To quote but one instance, seven deaths were registered as being due to smallpox in 1936, whereas 611 deaths from this disease were notified from areas to which the system of death registration has not yet been applied.

It might, perhaps, be well to mention that representations were made to the local Administrations during the year under review which will result in data being collected in 1937 from several additional areas which will be brought within the scope of the 'Births, Deaths and Burials Ordinance' during the year. In course of time, it is to be hoped that registration will be extended to all the major townships in Nigeria.[2]

Birth registration depends to a great extent on the interest taken by the local Health Authorities in this aspect of public health work, since the general public still require a stimulus to persuade them to register the births of their children.[3]

The marked discrepancy in the figure for, say Port Harcourt, with a [death] rate of 11·8 for 1936 and that of 43·4 for Ebute Metta cannot be accounted for altogether by the differences in the age-sex constitution of the population. A more likely solution is afforded by the fact that Ebute Metta with its suburb of Yaba is growing rapidly and that its estimated population, as based on the 1921–1931 census figures, is far smaller than its actual population. In addition, it is not improbable that a number of births registered in the Ebute Metta district actually occur in villages situated in the surrounding bush . . . .

The very much smaller differences in death-rates as compared with birth-rates in the five registration districts, seems to support the thesis that the completeness of birth registration depends to some extent upon the amount of time the local Health Authorities can spend in suasion.

Death registration, is of course, a preliminary to burial; consequently it is likely to be much less dependent upon the factors influencing the registration of births.[4]

1938. The statistics obtained even from towns where compulsory registration is in force cannot be regarded as reliable, except in the case of Lagos, which is the only area in which the proportion of deaths certified by Medical Practitioners is at all

[1] The total population of the registration area was given for mid-year 1935 as 202,314, for mid-year 1936 as 206,621, and for 1937 as 226,303. See Nigeria, Medical Report 1936, p. 9; 1937, p. 9.
[2] Ibid. 1936, pp. 7–8.   [3] Ibid., p. 9.   [4] Ibid., p. 10.

high. The table showing comparative death and birth rates in the various registration areas is therefore omitted in this year's report. It should, however, be added
that greater accuracy is steadily being attained in townships other than Lagos. At
Calabar for instance investigation has led to considerable improvement . . . particularly in so far as registration of births is concerned . . . .[1]

Native Authorities. Apart from registration established directly by the
British Administration, steps in the same direction have been taken by
Native Authorities. The earliest attempt of the kind was apparently
made in the Protectorate of Lagos.

1900. During the year, 699 Deaths and 490 Births were registered at the Basho-
run's Court. These figures are, of course, utterly unreliable and as a guide completely fallacious.
The credulity of the native is such that the compliance with a simple innovation
is fraught with suspicion and fear.
But although these figures are useless, the registration of them serves to familiarize
the people with the act and in time, no doubt, something approaching the true state
of affairs will be returnable.[2]

In 1903–4, as shown above, some Native Councils in Southern Nigeria
introduced birth and death registration in accordance with 'The Births
and Deaths Proclamation, 1903'. In 1911 the Emir of Katsina (Northern
Nigeria) introduced birth and death registration in Katsina Town.[3]

The Nigeria Births, Deaths and Burials Ordinance of 1917 provided
that a native administration may, with the approval of the Governor,
make rules providing for the registration of births and deaths occurring
amongst natives of Nigeria in any area in which such births and deaths
were not registrable under this Ordinance. Native birth and death registration was thereupon introduced in Kano City (Kano Province) in 1918,
in Biu Town (Bornu Province) in 1921, and in Ilorin Town (Ilorin Province) in 1924.[4] At about this time the Medical Department became
interested in the expansion of such schemes.

1923. Native Administrations should be invited to initiate registration of births
and deaths in all their principal towns.[5]
1925. The question of establishing a simple form of registration of births and
deaths which could be applied to all towns including Native Administration towns
was discussed at the Medical Conference held at Accra and it was considered that
even if [only] the numbers of births and deaths could be registered it would be an
advance of value and wherever possible further details as to whether male or
female, adult, child or infant should be added. Proposals on these lines are being
made.[6]

[1] Nigeria, *Medical Report 1938*, p. 9.
[2] 'Report for the Year 1900 on that Portion of the Lagos Hinterland under the Control of the
Resident of Ibadan', p. 26.
[3] See *Census of Nigeria, 1931*, vol. i, p. 35. In Zaria Town registration was apparently introduced a year earlier, but not upon the initiative of a Native Authority. See Northern Nigeria,
'Medical Report 1910', p. 136: 'A beginning was made at Zaria, during the year, in the direction
of compiling the vital statistics of native towns. The Resident inaugurated a scheme of monthly
record of the births and deaths occurring in the Native town, on which he and the Medical Officer
are very keen. This is a most interesting experiment—the Emir has taken kindly to it—and if
successful, will be gradually extended.'
[4] *Census of Nigeria, 1931*, vol. ii, pp. 31, 186.
[5] Nigeria, *Medical Report 1923*, p. 30. See also ibid. *1924*, p. 55.
[6] Ibid. *1925*, p. 12.

In the meantime the Emirs concerned had introduced native birth and death registration in the remainder of Kano Emirate in 1925 (deaths) and in 1926 (births) and in the remainder of Katsina Emirate in 1926. But everywhere births and deaths were apparently merely 'recorded' and not registered.

No registers are kept, but the procedure is that the village headmen or Ward Heads in the City, inform the District Heads every month of the births and deaths which occurred within their units, and the District Heads forward the combined figures to the Emir. A return is then made out, the Emir's office showing the total for each district. In Kano there is a gap in the records for births from January, 1925, to March, 1926, and of deaths for June, 1925. The figures were inaccurate and were regarded as of use more from an educational than a statistical point of view.[1]

The Director of Medical and Sanitary Service was now anxious to develop a procedure for such registration throughout the Northern Provinces. The matter was discussed at a Residents' Conference held at Kaduna in September 1926, 'and it was decided that, for the present, it was not practicable for Native Administrations to furnish more than a monthly return of births and deaths in the chief towns, and a monthly return of deaths in the districts'.[2]

The 1931 census report for the Northern Provinces contains some more details concerning this scheme and its functioning.

In 1926 the possibility of introducing machinery for the collection of vital statistics was considered, and an attempt was made to develop a procedure for the registration of births and deaths of natives throughout the Northern Provinces, and a specimen form prepared by the Director of Medical and Sanitary Service was circulated with a view to some method of registration being introduced when it was considered that the Native Administrations were in a position to undertake the task. In general, it was not thought possible to provide for more than a monthly return of births and deaths for chief towns, and for a monthly return of deaths from Emirates. A system of registration had been in operation for some time in Ilorin City, and separate weekly returns are now being rendered for Kano City, but though attempts were being made in the districts, and little difficulty had been experienced, the statistics were generally thought to be unreliable. Returns were sent in irregularly, and after considerable delay, so that they were of no value from the point of view of watching epidemics.[3]

From 1926 to 1930 registration was extended to many other places in the Northern Provinces.

Returns were in 1931 being sent to the Health Office, Kaduna, for Kano City and Emirate, Plateau Province, Katagum Division of Bauchi Province, Zaria, Sokoto, and Niger Province, and in other Provinces and Divisions they were sent to the local Medical Officer and retained by him.[4]

An interesting attempt to use all the available records from the Northern Provinces was made in connexion with the 1931 census.

For the purpose of the Census, Residents were asked to supply figures of births and deaths for the decade 1921–1930, for the Towns and Townships for which any

---

[1] *Census of Nigeria, 1931*, vol. ii, p. 31.
[2] *Report on the Northern Provinces 1926*, p. 50.
[3] *Census of Nigeria, 1931*, vol. ii, p. 32.   [4] Ibid.

vital statistics for any whole year or years were available. . . . The figures are not reliable, and some of them on the face of it clearly inaccurate, but they seem to be improving, and their recording and critical examination, without the danger of their being misleading, will only serve to show the present position, and to bring about a further improvement in the returns.[1]

The census report shows for Kano Province the numbers of male and female births and the numbers of male and female deaths of infants, children, and adults.[2] The results may be summarized as follows:[3]

Year	Total births	Total deaths	Infant deaths	Year	Total births	Total deaths	Infant deaths
KANO CITY				KANO EMIRATE			
1918	1,141	2,445	..	1925	..	55,887[2]	..
1919	1,253	1,525	..	1926	33,566	37,239	11,630
1920	1,364	1,465	..	1927	40,997	41,143	16,518
1921	932	1,181	..	1928[3]	35,310	30,473	10,536
1922	1,168	1,691	..	1929	43,796	39,964	15,462
1923	1,249	2,372	..	1930	42,488	39,041	14,228
1924	2,956	6,240	..	KANO TOWNSHIP			
1925	156[1]	2,602	..				
1926	2,873	3,270	790	1926	51	175	..
1927	4,223	4,586	1,358	1927	36	204	..
1928	1,858	1,649	399	1928	68	91	..
1929	2,469	2,289	680	1929	45	60	..
1930	3,164	2,656	865	1930	46	206	..
HADEJIA EMIRATE				DAURA EMIRATE			
1926[4]	5,357	3,077	1,136	1926[5]	2,119	653	187
1927	5,004	5,049	1,579	1927	3,051	1,999	683
1928	4,919	4,522	1,368	1928	3,446	1,333	443
1929	5,339	6,066	1,863	1929	3,608	1,627	555
1930	5,891	5,832	1,860	1930	3,585	1,715	504
GUMEL EMIRATE				KAZAURE EMIRATE			
1926[4]	1,607	780	369	1926[5]	2,277	717	255
1927	1,381	1,732	913	1927	2,497	1,157	431
1928	3,004	2,045	1,108	1928	2,135	885	375
1929	3,457	2,175	1,044	1929	1,982	1,034	464
1930	1,889	1,307	530	1930	1,447	675	231

[1] Figures for February only available.
[2] Figures for January missing.
[3] Figures for July missing.
[4] Figures for Jan. to Mar. not available.
[5] Figures for Jan. to May not available.

It is evident that the early returns from Kano City and the returns from Kano Township were quite inadequate.[4] The data from Gumel and Kazaure Emirates also inspire little confidence. But in the two most

[1] *Census of Nigeria, 1931*, vol. ii, p. 32.   [2] See ibid., pp. 187–90.
[3] For population see the next table (native population of Kano Township was 7,371). The deaths figures given for Kano City in Nigeria, *Medical Report 1924*, p. 46, differ for some years considerably from those shown in the Census Report. The statements concerning figures missing in Kano Emirate differ also (see *Census of Nigeria, 1931*, vol. ii, pp. 31, 188).
[4] It is noteworthy that the most incomplete birth returns are those from Kano Township, the only place in the Province where registration was under the direct control of the British administration.

populous Emirates, Kano and Hadejia, registration was apparently more regular, though there cannot be any doubt that, particularly in parts of Kano Emirate, registration must have been incomplete.

Apart from these basic figures for Kano Province the following birth- and death-rates were given in the census report:[1]

Province	Area	Population 1931	Year	Birth-rate	Death-rate
Adamawa	Adamawa Emirate	433,121	1930	5	6
	Muri Division	171,241	1930	3	2
	Numan Division	47,441	..	4	3
	Gashaka[1]	8,566	1927	1	16
Bauchi	Bauchi Town	10,629	1929	16	15
			1930	16	15
	Gombe Town	3,243	1928	17	34
			1929	25	29
			1930	21	18
Benue	Abinsi Town	1,339	1928	117	36
			1929	33	24
			1930	73	35
	Makurdi	7,655	1928	8	16
			1929	9	16
			1930	12	12
	Lafia	6,594	1929	36	19
			1930	51	29
	Doma	4,953	1929	37	29
			1930	52	42
	Keana	1,773	1929	57	37
			1930	109	66
	Ibi	4,990	1928	34	37
			1930	26	21
Bornu	Bornu Emirate	714,335	1930	14	15
	Dikwa Division	194,364	1930	1	8
	Potiskum	99,074	1930	..	26
	Biu	110,284	1927	..	23
	Biu Town	4,127	1921	16	13
			1922	16	9
			1923	14	7
			1924	13	10
			1925	13	14
Kabba	Lokoja Native Town	5,963	1928	99	82
			1929	106	90
			1930	108	89
Kano	Kano City	89,162	1930	35	30
	Kano Emirate	1,903,137	1930	22	21
	Hadejia Emirate	198,168	1930	30	29
	Gumel Emirate	72,551	1930	26	18
	Daura Emirate	99,442	1930	36	17
	Kazaure Emirate	66,148	1930	22	10
Niger	Kuta Division	64,177	1930	21	20
	Bida Town	25,231	1929	12	10
	Agaie Town	4,814	1928	30	16
			1929	36	15
			1930	36	15
	Lapai Town	2,843	1928	21	13
			1929	20	28
			1930	27	14

[1] Since 1928 merged in Adamawa Division.

[1] See *Census of Nigeria, 1931*, vol. i, p. 35; vol. ii, pp. 186, 191.

Province	Area	Population 1931	Year	Birth-rate	Death-rate
Niger (cont.)	Kontagora Division	69,154	1927	24	16
			1928	23	12
			1929	24	15
			1930	26	17
	Abuja Emirate	74,405	1929	24	18
			1930	16	13
Plateau	Jos Hausa Settlement	5,681	1928	37	66
			1929	31	62
			1930	34	52
Zaria	Katsina Town	22,347	1923	27	..
	Katsina Division	925,360	1928	46	23
	Zaria City	21,953	1928	38	39

Further birth- and death-rates derived from native records were given in the Medical Report for 1932.[1]

Area	Estimated population	Birth-rate	Death-rate
Sokoto (Town)	20,075	12·9	8·2
Birnin Kebbi (Gwandu District) . . .	285,886	36·7	11·7
Zuru (Dabai, Kontagora and Yauri Emirates)	162,035	38·1	22·0
Katsina (whole Emirate)	905,475	40·9	15·5
Katsina (Town)	28,362	20·4	10·2
Bornu (Province)	1,114,368	18·2	13·6
Bauchi (Town)	10,646	25·4	16·1
Azare (Katagum Emirate)	342,807	40·3	19·1
Minna (District of Niger Province) . .	166,436	19·9	18·9
Wukari (District)	213,099	15·7	8·1

It is obvious that many of the rates were based on records which were absolutely untrustworthy, and no new data have been published since 1932. This is very much to be regretted as Native Authorities apparently went on sending returns to the Administration. The Colonial Reports say year in year out:[2]

The Emir of Katsina introduced registration in Katsina Town in 1911 and later certain other native administrations in the Northern Provinces have followed suit; at the present time returns are received from various northern areas, while data are also available for several individual towns, since 1928 or 1929. Except in a few special areas registration is imperfect, but some of the resultant crude birth and death-rates probably provide an indication of the facts. The following are the figures for 1930 in the more reliable areas of the Northern Provinces:—

Province	Place	Population 1931	Crude Rates per Mille	
			Birth	Death
Benue .	Abinsi Town . .	1,339	73	35
,, .	Doma ,, . .	4,953	52	42
Kano .	Kano City . . .	89,162	35	30
,, .	Hadejia Emirate .	198,168	30	29
Plateau .	Jos Hausa Settlement .	5,681	34	52

[1] See *Nigeria, Medical Report 1932*, p. 11.

[2] See *Colonial Reports, Nigeria 1933*, p. 11; *1934*, p. 12; *1935*, pp. 10–11; *1936*, p. 11; *1937*, p. 12; *1938*, pp. 12–13. (The wording is not always literally the same; I quote from the 1938 Report.)

It is difficult to see why these should be 'the more reliable areas of the Northern Provinces'. The birth- and death-rates of Abinsi Town, Doma Town, and Jos Hausa Settlement may 'provide an indication of the facts' in those places in 1930, but those facts are of no interest, as the number of inhabitants is far too small to permit the drawing of conclusions. In any case it is regrettable that if actually 'at the present time returns are received from various northern areas' the Colonial Reports go on quoting merely those results for 1930. It may well be that if the Administration had taken the trouble to study more closely, for example, the returns from the various areas of Kano Emirate, vital statistics similar to those from certain districts of Uganda might have been developed.

In the Southern Provinces very little has been done towards registration of native births and deaths outside the few districts where it is carried on in accordance with the Orders-in-Council quoted above, and the few efforts that have been made were due to the initiative of individual British administration officers rather than of Native Authorities. The first attempt of the kind was apparently made in Cameroons Province. The 1925 Report to the Council of the League of Nations said:

> In order to study the causes which make for an increase or decrease in the population an attempt will be made in 1926 to compile regular statistics of births and deaths in a portion of the Victoria Division, but the former will present great difficulties.[1]

The report for 1926 showed the results of the first attempts to introduce birth and death registration:

> A commencement has been made in recording the births and deaths in certain selected areas. In the Victoria Division, with educated chiefs in charge of both Victoria and Buea Districts, it may be hoped that in a few years' time the returns may possess some value and accuracy. For this first year it is not claimed that the returns are full or exact. For a period of nine months the Buea District, with a population of 9,261, recorded 100 births and 109 deaths. . . . The Victoria District, with a population of 6,970, recorded in 11 months 132 births and 196 deaths. . . .
>
> Similar registrations have been begun in selected areas of Mamfe and Kumba Divisions, but for a shorter period of time, and the results are not yet worth recording.

In Bamenda Division registration of births and deaths was commenced in August in the two Districts of Bali and Bandop, with the following results:—

Bali District
Total Population, 7,621.

	Births	Deaths
August–September . .	26	32
October–November . .	43	48

Bandop District
Total Population, 15,104.

	Births	Deaths
August–November . .	643	328[2]

It is necessary to go slowly, as the native has to be convinced that no sinister motives underlie European curiosity.[3]

[1] *Report 1925*, p. 96.   [2] Ibid. *1926*, p. 101.   [3] Ibid., p. 82.

The reports for 1927 and 1928 did not give any figures, but related merely the inadequacy of the results.

1927. Registrations of births and deaths have been continued in selected areas, the Buea and Victoria Districts of the Victoria Division and five Districts of Bamenda Division, but the results cannot yet be considered of any value for statistical purposes.[1]

1928. Registration of births and deaths has been continued in selected areas, but the results have proved no more satisfactory than those of previous years and figures are still so patently inaccurate as to be of no statistical value.[2]

Attempts in other Provinces are reported as follows:

1927. Ijebu Province. The Ijebus have now become accustomed to report deaths and little difficulty is experienced from their concealment. Figures given by the Resident in his annual report, show that as the result of careful calculation, the death rate per 1,000 of the population is estimated at fourteen which is remarkably low considering the high rate of infantile mortality prevalent throughout the country.[3]

Onitsha Province. The compilation of more reliable vital statistics than hitherto at Onitsha revealed that out of a population estimated at 12,000 there were 418 deaths during the year.[4]

1928. Ijebu Province. Under the Native Authority's Plague Regulations the registration of deaths is compulsory, and, although all deaths are not registered, the vast majority are and it appears that the death rate for the year was about twenty-four per thousand. The difference between this figure and that of fourteen given last year is thought to be due mainly to the greater insistence on registration but partly to a large number of deaths from pneumonia at the end of the year when the harmattan was very severe.[5]

1929. Abeokuta Province. The scheme for the voluntary registration of births, deaths and marriages has been in operation for fifteen months and just over 2,000 certificates of each kind have been taken out.[6]

Another legislative step towards introducing registration of native births and deaths was taken in the 'Native Authority Ordinance, 1933'[7] which came into force on 1 April 1934. It stipulated:

8. Subject to the provisions of any Ordinance or other law for the time being in force, a native authority may, subject to the general or specific directions of the native authority, if any, to whom it is subordinate, issue orders, to be obeyed by such persons within its area as may be subject to its jurisdiction and to whom the orders relate, for all or any of the following purposes:—

(j) requiring the birth or death of any persons subject to its jurisdiction to be reported to it or to such person as it may direct.

This Ordinance applied to the whole Protectorate,[8] and a similar Ordinance was enacted in 1937 for the Native Authorities in the Colony other than in the Township of Lagos.[9] But only few Native Authorities seem so far to have issued such orders concerning registration.[10]

[1] *Report 1927*, p. 90.   [2] Ibid. *1928*, p. 105.
[3] *Report on Southern Provinces 1927*, p. 39.   [4] Ibid., p. 58.
[5] Ibid. *1928*, p. 30. A birth-rate of 36·0 and a death-rate of 27·0 are given for Ijebu Province, 1937, in Nigeria, *Medical Report 1937*, p. 9.   [6] *Report on Southern Provinces 1929*, p. 8.
[7] No. 43 of 1933 (23 Nov.), reprinted in *Laws of Nigeria 1933*, Part A, pp. 161–73.
[8] It was repealed by Ordinance No. 17 of 1943 (3 May), reprinted in *Laws of Nigeria 1943*, Part A, pp. 61–104. The new Ordinance contained literally the same provisions as those quoted above but inserted after the word 'requiring' the words 'the marriage'.
[9] No. 39 of 1937 (20 Dec.), 'Native Authority (Colony) Ordinance, 1937', reprinted in *Laws of Nigeria 1937*, Part A, pp. 149–60.
[10] Such orders have been issued according to Nigeria, *Blue Book 1938*, Section 1, p. 46, in the Egba Division of Oyo Province and in Oyo Town; according to Nigeria, *Medical Report 1938*, p. 9,

Conclusion. The situation regarding native birth and death registration may be summarized as follows:

(1) Registration was introduced by the British Administration in Lagos in 1867 and has been carried on uninterruptedly, with varying success. It became fairly effective towards the end of the nineteenth century, but it is doubtful whether any improvement in completeness has been achieved since. Registration was extended in 1926 to the townships of Kano and Calabar, and in 1932–44 to a few more places. The scanty data published indicate that registration outside Lagos has been quite incomplete.

(2) Northern Provinces. Registration was introduced in a few places by Native Authorities in the first quarter of this century. From 1925 to 1930 praiseworthy efforts were made to expand registration over large parts of the country. Statistics prepared in 1931–2 suggest that many records were quite inadequate, but that registration was by no means a failure everywhere. It is regrettable that the Administration has not published any more recent data.

Southern Provinces. Some kind of registration was introduced in some places by the Administration in collaboration with the Native Authorities in 1925–9. But it seems that these efforts were given up very soon. In recent years a few Native Authorities have issued orders concerning registration of births and deaths, but results have so far not been reported.

Surveys. One important reason for the unsatisfactory state of native registration (and still more so of native vital statistics) is that the Administration, apart from a short period (1923–32), took evidently very little interest in the matter. This can also be inferred from the fact that special inquiries about fertility and mortality have been extremely scanty.

(1) In 1913, a Political Officer in the Sokoto Province made inquiries in 'a small unit of population (20,000)' about the number of boys and girls 'born during the last 12 months' and the number of boys and girls 'born during the last 12 months who have died'.[1] He apparently secured these data in connexion with tax assessment, but it has not been reported from whom he obtained the information.

(2) In the Mamfe and Bamenda Divisions of Cameroons Province the assessing officers, at the annual tax censuses of 1925–6, asked a number of women how many children they had borne and how many of these children had died at various ages.[2]

(3) In connexion with the 1931 census two Medical Officers of Health made a thorough examination of selected villages comprising in all 20,514 inhabitants. Since these inquiries covered only one-thousandth of the total population, the results cannot be considered as representative for

---

in Abeokuta, Oyo, and Makurdi; according to *Laws of Nigeria 1942*, Part D, p. 44, in Ikorodu; according to ibid. *1943*, Part D, pp. 72, 162, in Badagri Town and in Onitsha Town. See also *Medical Report 1943*, p. 8: 'Native Authority have made rules for, and adopted, the registration of births and deaths in Makurdi and Onitsha towns, in the Egba Division of Abeokuta Province, in the Oyo Division and the Ife-Ilesha District of Oyo Province, in the Lagos Colony towns of Badagri and Ikorodu.'

[1] See Northern Nigeria, *Medical Report 1913*, p. 8.
[2] See *Report on the Cameroons 1925*, pp. 93–4; *1926*, pp. 82–3.

the whole area, but they constitute an important source of information for certain districts.[1] The Medical Officer of Health who conducted the Medical Census in the Southern Provinces wrote:[2]

The mode of conducting the census was as follows. The administrative officers of the chosen areas were approached, the nature of the examination explained and their consent and promise of help obtained. Meetings were then arranged to explain the nature and object to the native rulers and these in all cases signified their assent and promised to help as far as possible. To increase the popularity of the census, medical treatment was given for minor degrees of sickness and in some areas free yaws treatment was given. The area concerned was divided roughly into units of about 100 individuals and these were notified well in advance to appear for examination on a specified date at convenient centres.[3] This procedure was carried out throughout the census, except at Arogbo, where the nature of the country made it impossible for the observer to travel to the numerous hamlets scattered over difficult swamp country.

The average time allowed for each individual examination was three minutes and a clerk recorded the observations made by the Medical Officer.

The difficulties encountered in carrying through the census were described as follows:

Southern Provinces.[4] The main difficulty was to see the people. In Abeokuta, which is the mother town of the Egbas, many had gone to their farms and their town houses were closed or only a few members of the family were resident. Many deliberately evaded the census, and the percentage seen was estimated to be only about 30 per cent. of the possible in the area. In Arogbo, where the main occupation is fishing, the observer's visit coincided with the departure to the fishing grounds, some of which were several days' journey distant. Many of the people also live in hamlets of two or three families scattered over an area of about 400 square miles and amongst these evasion was very high, only a few representatives coming from each hamlet and promising to send the others later. Some of the larger hamlets deliberately refused to come as the visit coincided with the annual tax collection. Not more than 50 per cent. of the whole population were seen in the Arogbo area. In the Cameroons the percentage seen varied from 50 to 70 per cent., and the greatest shortage was in adult males, who evaded for tax reasons, or had emigrated to the coast or to the plantations in search of work.[5] In all areas it was found that the people suspected some association between the census and counting for tax purposes.

Northern Provinces.[6] With the exception of one or two, the obstacles encountered were surmountable by the exhibition of tact, persuasion and patience. Thus, in one village (Zangan Aya) a large number of the inhabitants fled to neighbouring villages two days before the arrival of the Medical Census Staff, and for a fortnight the village was semi-deserted except for the sick and the aged. It was by the free medical treatment of these sick persons that the confidence of the fugitives was gradually regained, and a month later all the inhabitants had returned. The heads of households were eventually persuaded by argument and demonstration that there was

[1] Thus, the Medical Census of the Southern Provinces, which covered 11,023 persons, included 4,122, or 6 per cent., of the inhabitants of the Mamfe Division of Cameroons Province.

[2] *Census of Nigeria, 1931*, vol. vi, p. 2.

[3] For the Medical Census in the Northern Provinces see ibid. vol. v, p. 4: 'Arrangements were made for the examination of the inhabitants in batches of 60 or 80 each day, two empty huts being used as waiting-rooms (one for adult males and one for women and children).'

[4] Ibid., vol. vi, p. 2.

[5] At ages 15 to 29 there were counted in Cameroons Forest Zone 198 males and 568 females; see ibid., pp. 34–5.

[6] Ibid., vol. v, p. 3.

nothing to fear in the investigation, and that they and their families would be subjected to the minimum amount of inconvenience.

The demographic information obtained for each person was: Sex, age, tribe, birthplace, occupation (in the Southern Provinces also married or single). In the case of women the additional information required in the Southern Provinces was: Total pregnancies, children alive, children dead under 1 year, children dead over 1 year, miscarriages. In the Northern Provinces females 10 years of age and over were asked: Total pregnancies, children alive, children dead under 1 year and stillbirths, children dead 1 year and over, premature births, miscarriages, numbers and types of multiple births, number of months pregnant.[1]

Special difficulties were met in ascertaining fertility.

Southern Provinces.[2] The information on fertility was given by the women concerned and the statement was checked as far as possible by reference to the husband or to the chief. Many lies were told to cover the absence of children who were left behind to look after homes and farms, or because of the difficulty of carrying them. A greater difficulty lay in the fact that some tribes object to giving the number of their children. It is considered unlucky and a truthful answer might entail the death of one. In the Cameroons forest some women excluded the number of children conceived with any former husband, so that an appreciable error may occur with the older women.

Northern Provinces.[3] From the outset a difficulty arose in connection with the questioning of adult females as to the numbers and results of their pregnancies. For reasons which are easily understandable, a large number of the women could not be induced to give the correct number of their total pregnancies, with their subsequent histories. Conspiracies arose amongst the women in each village, their aim being deliberately to mislead the Medical Census Officer. For example, in Kaita there was a 'No birth' conspiracy, and a large number of women between the ages of 20 and 40 years stated that they had never been pregnant. Similarly in Laminga, there was a 'Two birth' conspiracy. Out of 60 women examined in one day, 40 stated that they had had two children and that one was alive and the other dead.

To defeat these conspiracies it was necessary to examine the women a second and a third time (the second time the husbands were present and were asked to confirm their wives' statements, and the third time the village chiefs were present). At each questioning totally different results were obtained in a large percentage of the cases. Several women were questioned on as many as six different occasions (at intervals of a week) and on each occasion gave different answers.[4]

The results of the special investigations will be discussed in the following section.

VI. Native Fertility, Mortality, and Population Growth

1. Lagos

Introduction. Birth and death data from Lagos are now available for more than 70 years. But quite apart from incompleteness of registration the official vital statistics present defects which make it necessary to use them with great caution.

(1) Very often the same figure is given in some documents for deaths of

---

[1] See ibid., vol. v, p. 2; vol. vi, p. 1.　　[2] Ibid., vol. vi, p. 2.　　[3] Ibid., vol. v, p. 4.
[4] See also ibid.: 'The average native woman cannot be induced even to refer to her first-born, and as often as not excludes it from the number she gives as her total pregnancies.'

Africans, in others for deaths of non-Europeans, and in still others for deaths of the total population.[1]

(2) The treatment of still-births in the official reports is somewhat confusing. They seem to have been included in the numbers of deaths (and also in the numbers of infant deaths) from the outset[2] until 1909. But since at first still-births were not registered as births, but merely recorded in connexion with burials, they were not included in the numbers of births prior to 1 July 1892,[3] from when on they were included in the numbers of births until 1909. From 1909 on still-births have been excluded from both the numbers of births and deaths. The Administration and Medical Officers very often seem not to have been aware of the actual position. For the years prior to 1892 the excess of deaths over births has been computed by deducting the number of births, excluding still-births, from the number of deaths including still-births. The official birth, death, and infant mortality rates which since 1909 excluded still-births have been compared indiscriminately with the rates of the preceding years which included still-births.

(3) The value of the official birth- and death-rates is greatly impaired by the fact that the population figures ascertained at the censuses, and still more so the intercensal population estimates, have been uncertain.

Prior to 1905 the numbers of births and deaths were related, as a rule, to the population ascertained at the preceding census. In his Memorandum of 29 October 1909, mentioned above, the Governor stated:

In 1905 I discovered that throughout the decade 1891–1900 the vital statistics of Lagos were calculated on the census figures for 1891 without any allowance for increase in population. Also that since 1901 the figures had been calculated on the results of that census without any addition. The population of the town has been steadily increasing. The death rate—as given in the reports—had steadily increased during the decade 1891–1900, presumably owing to increase in population not being allowed for. The same tendency was evident in statistics from 1901 to 1904.

As a matter of fact the official death-rate for Lagos Town dropped from 61 in 1900 to 46 in 1901[4] (although the number of deaths decreased only from 1,986 to 1,835) because the deaths of 1900 were related to the population ascertained at the 1891 census (32,508) while the deaths of 1901 were related to the population ascertained at the 1901 census (39,387). In 1904 the official death-rate was still computed on the basis of the 1901 census results,[5] but for 1905 it was calculated, according to the instructions of the Governor, by assuming that the yearly increase of Lagos Town since the census of 1901 had been equal to the average yearly increase between 1891 and 1901, i.e. 687. The number of deaths in Lagos Town 1905,

[1] As the published data do not make it possible to exclude consistently non-natives, I shall use in this section, unless otherwise stated, figures referring to the total population.

[2] See, for example, *Colonial Possessions Reports 1879–81*, p. 303, where it appears that the 667 registered native deaths include 10 still-births. (The 130 deaths of Europeans registered from 1868 to 1879 included 2 still-births.)

[3] The birth statistics show for 1891 and the first half of 1892 no still-births and for the second half of 1892, 26 still-births. The death statistics show for 1891. 25 still-births and for 1892. 44 still-births. See *Colonial Reports, Lagos 1892*, pp. 31–6.

[4] See Lagos, *Blue Book 1900*, p. 67; *1901*, p. 77.   [5] See ibid. *1904*, p. 78.

therefore, was related to a population of 42,135, but in computing the birth-rate for Lagos Town and the birth- and death-rates for Ebute Metta the census figures (39,387 and 2,460) were still used:[1]

	Births	Deaths	Birth-rate	Death-rate
Lagos . . .	2,370	2,172	60·1	51·6
Ebute Metta . .	165	286	67·0	116·2

But the Vaccination census taken in 1905 suggested that the population increase since 1901 had been much greater than assumed by the Governor, and for 1906–8 the Medical Reports published death-rates based (a) on the assumptions of the Governor, and (b) on the Vaccination census. For 1909 and 1910 only rates (b) were published, but the 1911 census showed that even these rates had been too high. The results for Lagos and Ebute Metta may be summarized as follows:[2]

Year	Population		Births	Deaths	Birth-rate		Death-rate	
	(a)	(b)			(a)	(b)	(a)	(b)
LAGOS								
1906	42,822	48,467	2,240	1,908	52·4	46·2	44·9	39·4
1907	43,509	50.551	2,272	1,946	52·2	44·9	44·7	38·4
1908	44,196	52,612	2,281	1,978	51·6	43·3	44·7	37·5
1909	—	53,299	2,312	1,975	—	43·3	—	37
1910	—	53,986	2,389	1.937	—	44·2	—	35·8
1911	61,000		2,430	1,873	39·8		30·7	
EBUTE METTA								
1909	—	7,417	264	284	—	35·5	—	38·2
1910	—	8,104	262	325	—	32·3	—	40·1
1911	—	12.000	288	317	24		26·4	

The comparability of the official rates for 1920 and 1921 was again impaired considerably by an underestimate of the population. The results for Lagos and Ebute Metta combined were as follows:[3]

Year	Population	Births	Deaths	Birth-rate	Death-rate
1920	84,694	2,845	2,443	33·5	28·8
1921	98,625	3,002	2,472	30·4	25·1

The population estimates for the late 1920s agreed well with the 1931 census returns, but the erratic estimates made in subsequent years created an absolutely chaotic condition in the official birth- and death-rates. I shall confine myself to reproducing here the rates for Lagos Township from the Reports of the Lagos Medical Officer of Health.[4]

[1] See ibid. *1905*, p. 82.
[2] See Southern Nigeria, 'Medical Report 1906', pp. 287–8; *1907*, pp. 14, 16; *1908*, pp. 12, 15; *1909*, pp. 38. 41; *1910*, pp. 11, 13; *1911*, p. 9.
[3] See Nigeria. *Medical Report 1919–21*, p. 23. The results were not shown separately.
[4] For (a) see Lagos Town Council. *Report of Medical Officer of Health* 1928, p. 15, *1929*, p. 14, *1930*, p. 25, *1936*, p. 24; for (b) see ibid. *1931*, p. 19. *1935*. p. 21; for (c) see ibid. *1937*, pp. 25–6.

Year	Population			Births	Deaths	Birth-rate			Death-rate		
	(a)	(b)	(c)			(a)	(b)	(c)	(a)	(b)	(c)
1927	114,500	126,000	—	3,310	2,322	28·9	26	—	20·2	18	—
1928	118,500	129,000	—	3,333	2,454	28·1	26	—	20·7	19	—
1929	122,000	132,000	—	3,457	2,151	28·3	26	—	17·6	16	—
1930	122,000	135,000	—	3,494	2,016	28·6	26	—	16·5	15	—
1931	(126,767)	138,000	139,800	3,458	1,789	—	25	24·7	—	13	12·7
1932	(129,409)	140,000	142,500	3,869	1,832	—	27·6	27·1	—	13·1	12·8
1933	(132,051)	156,000	145,300	3,893	2,171	—	24·9	26·7	—	13·9	14·8
1934	(134,693)	160,000	148,200	4,475	2,097	—	27·9	30·1	—	13·1	14·1
1935	137,335	170,000	150,700	4,482	2,372	32·6	26·3	29·7	17·3	13·9	15·7
1936	139,977	—	153,300	4,081	2,404	29·2	—	26·6	17·2	—	15·7
1937	—	—	155,900	4,105	2,654	—	—	26·3	—	—	17·0

How unsafe it would be to draw any conclusions from the official rates can perhaps best be illustrated by showing the 1935 rates separately for the two sections of Lagos Township, the figures being taken from the Nigeria Medical Report for 1935 (a) and 1936 (b) respectively.[1]

District	Population		Births	Deaths	Birth-rate		Death-rate	
	(a)	(b)			(a)	(b)	(a)	(b)
Lagos . .	120,000	137,336	3,527	1,932	29·4	25·7	16·1	14·1
Ebute Metta .	50,000	20,294	943	432	18·8	46·5	8·6	21·3

Fertility. In his 'Notes on the Medical History of Lagos' the Medical Officer Dr. Turner said:

The birth-rate has fallen continuously throughout the period for which accurate data are available. The following figures show the decline:—

1897	.	.	.	51 per 1,000.	1920	.	.	.	33 per 1,000.
1902	.	.	.	52 ,, 1,000.	1921	.	.	.	30 ,, 1,000.
1909	.	.	.	43 ,, 1,000.	1929	.	.	.	28·3 ,, 1,000.
1910	.	.	.	44 ,, 1,000.	1930	.	.	.	28·6 ,, 1,000.

The reasons for this fall are manifold: but probably the most important is the sterility which has resulted from the widespread infection with gonorrhoea, and less so, of syphilis. The average pregnancies per woman in former days was probably about six, it is now only between three and four. I am informed by the Medical Officers in charge of the African Hospital that 80 per cent of the attendances of women are for sterility. Corrected birth-rates would show even lower figures (correction factor 0·9).[2]

The above birth-rates, to be sure, are not strictly comparable with one another. The rates for 1897 and 1902 refer to Lagos Town only and include still-births, while those from 1909 cover also the mainland and exclude still-births. Moreover, all rates prior to 1921 were swelled by relating the number of births to an underestimated number of inhabitants. The average number of registered live-born in Lagos Town rose from 1,595 in 1897–8 to 1,804 in 1899–1900, 1,933 in 1903, and 2,250 in 1904. There is no reason to assume that the birth-rate decreased in this period, and it probably

[1] See Nigeria, *Medical Report 1935*, p. 7; *1936*, pp. 9–10.
[2] *Census of Nigeria, 1931*, vol. i, p. 126. The Government Statistician had made a computation according to which the crude birth-rate for Lagos must be multiplied by the factor 0·89 in order to bring it to the basis of a standard population (see ibid., pp. 89–90).

exceeded 45 in 1904.[1] But the number of registered live-births oscillated in 1907–19 between 2,156 and 2,483 without showing a definite trend, and as the population no doubt increased very much it is safe to say that the birth-rate decreased considerably. Between 1919 and 1923 the number of births registered in Lagos Township[2] increased from 2,517 to 3,423, and it is likely that the birth-rate increased again in those years, but from 1924 to 1931 the number of registered births changed very little, oscillating

TABLE 22. *Registered Births and Deaths in Lagos Town, 1892–1901*[1]

Year	Live-born	Still-born	Total deaths excl. still-born	Total deaths incl. still-born	Deaths under 1 excl. still-born	Deaths under 1 incl. still-born
1892	547	44	1,339	1,383	328	372
1893	1,034		..	1,387	..	399
1894	1,197		..	1,487	..	537
1895	1,342	101	1,674	1,775	541	642
1896	1,469	76	1,626	1,702	547	623
1897	1,535	126	1,800	1,926	626	752
1898	1,655	118	1,759	1,877	614	732
1899	1,811	118	2,038	2,156	746	864
1900	1,796	144	1,842	1,986	698	842
1901	2,055		..	1,835	..	..

[1] See *Colonial Reports, Lagos 1892*, pp. 34–6; Lagos, 'Abstract of Registration 1896', pp. 130–1, *Abstract of Registration 1898*, p. 5, 'Report of Registrar General 1899', p. 317, '1900', p. 78; Lagos, 'Report by Commissioners appointed to enquire into Infantile Mortality', pp. 251–2; Lagos, *Blue Book 1901*, p. 77.

merely between 3,261 and 3,494. Birth registration and census returns were incomplete. But assuming that the proportion of omissions was the same in both records, the birth-rate would have been about 28 in 1928–31 as well as in 1918–20. From 1932 on the situation is somewhat obscure. The number of registered births rose from 3,458 in 1931 to 3,869 in 1932, 4,475 in 1934, 4,980 in 1939, 5,341 in 1940, 5,929 in 1942, and 7,240 in 1944.[3] The population estimates in this period, as shown above, were quite erratic. If the figure for 1944 (172,000) could be trusted, the birth-rate in that year would have been 42; but the population was probably much larger. The only conclusions which can be derived from the available data, therefore, seem to be: (1) the birth-rate declined considerably in the first two decades of this century; (2) there is no evidence that the birth-rate is lower now than 20 years ago.

The proportion of still-births registered in Lagos Town dropped from 6·6 per cent. in 1895–1900 to 5·1 per cent. in 1907–18, and to 3·2 per cent. in 1924–38. In Lagos Township the percentage declined from 4·9 in 1908–26 to 3·1 in 1927–44.

The decline in the number of still-births was probably due to the

[1] Even if registration had been complete the birth-rate would have exceeded 45, provided the results of the 1905 Vaccination census (48,467) can be trusted.

[2] No separate data are available for Lagos Town.

[3] From 1939 on the figures exclude non-native births.

TABLE 23. *Registered Births and Deaths in Lagos Township, 1902–44*[1]

Year	Lagos Town					Ebute Metta				Lagos Township				
	Live-born	Still-born	Total deaths	Deaths under 1	Infant mortality rate	Live-born	Still-born	Total deaths	Deaths under 1	Live-born	Still-born	Total deaths	Deaths under 1	Infant mortality rate
1902	1,997		1,783	660	…	124	11	173[2]	…	2,057	120	1,959	…	…
1903	1,933	109	1,895	774	…	134	16	176	…	2,384	106	2,112	…	…
1904[1]	2,250	90	2,172	951[1]	341			217	22	2,535		2,458[2]	796	334
1905	2,370		1,908²	763[1]	344	165		286[2]	89[2]		111	2,080[2]	1,040[1]	…
1906[2]	2,240		1,830	683	…	192		283[2]	86[1]	2,486		2,230[2]	738[2]	318
1907	2,156	116	1,857	759	317	214	10	284[2]	78[1]	2,321	131	2,162	877[2]	352
1908	2,160	121	1,975	729	351	234	21	305	84	2,394	176	2,259	843	315
1909	2,312	155	1,937	774	315	264	17	284	83	2,576	140	2,262	812	323
1910	2,389	123	1,873	692	324	262	22	325	83	2,651	154	2,190	857	288
1911	2,430	132	1,820	670	285	288	28	317	91	2,718	146	2,178	783	274
1912	2,391	118	1,867	643	280	315	25	346	71	2,706	154	2,175	741	263
1913	2,437	129	1,735	610	264	327	17	311	83	2,764	128	2,043	726	272
1914	2,261	111	1,712	625	270	337	24	308	96	2,598	140	1,960	706	261
1915	2,342	116	1,848	644	267	362	21	248	81	2,704	135	2,102	700	272
1916	2,332	114	1,892	684	276	329	27	254	81	2,661	151	2,167	725	279
1917	2,483	144	2,838	723	275	363	27	275	111	2,846	171	3,254	795	330
1918	2,220	124			326	300		416	108	2,520	125	3,256	831	296
1919										2,517	151	2,443	746	305
1920										2,845	116	2,472	869	285
1921	2,887	122	2,144			532	36	328		3,000	168	2,628	855	291
1922	2,711	109	2,231			550	26	397		3,263	163	2,510	948	264
1923	2,735	111	2,092			598	33	418		3,423	172	3,265	904	236
1924	2,739	81	2,867	524	230	571	26	398	138	3,419	158	3,748	806	238
1925	2,713	90	2,366	419	244	620	33	382	160	3,261	135	3,054	777	199
1926	2,794	70	2,574	364	192	663	26	480	97	3,310	144	2,322	662	175
1927	2,758	90	1,836	345	153	744	33	483	118	3,333	107	2,454	579	138
1928	3,041	66	2,021	368	134	700	35	433	83	3,457	123	2,151	461	134
1929		107	1,708	298	123	828	38	443	88	3,494	105	2,016	463	129
1930		99	1,671		134	852	13	345		3,458	128	1,789	451	112
1931		95	1,462		108	1,046	29	327		3,869	79	1,832	386	129
1932		116	1,473		144	943	19	350		3,893	136	2,097	393	137
1933	3,041	110	1,794		124	865	20	377		4,475	118	2,171	533	119
1934	3,429	119	1,712		139	847	21	385		4,482	115	2,372		130
1935	3,539	148	1,940		147	858	16	432		4,081	137	2,404		140
1936	3,216		1,943		140		9	461		4,105	131	2,654	553	135
1937	3,238		2,182		140			472		4,304	135	2,525	545	127
1938	3,446		2,055		129			470		4,980	157	2,669	631	132
1939[4]										5,341	167	2,623	706	114
1940[2]										5,272	154	3,098	601	124
1941[3]										5,929	164	3,734	733	140
1942[3]										6,653	194	3,674	934	116
1943[3]										7,240	236		837	
1944[3]											252			

[1] See Lagos, *Blue Book 1902*, p. 76, *1905*, p. 82; Lagos, *Medical Report 1904*, p. 12; Lagos, *Vital Statistics for 1904*, pp. 1, 11, 13, 16; Southern Nigeria, 'Medical Report 1906', pp. 287–8, 290; Southern Nigeria, *Medical Report 1907*, pp. 14, 16, *1908*, pp. 12, 15, *1909*, p. 38; Nigeria, *Medical Report 1914*, p. 61; *Report of the Lagos Municipal Board of Health 1915*, pp. 17–19, *1916*, p. 15; *Report of the Lagos Town Council 1917*, p. 12, *1918*, p. 15; Nigeria, *Medical Report 1919–21*, p. 23, *1922*, p. 19, *1923*, p. 18, *1924*, p. 66 (and Graph), *1925*, p. 12, *1926*, p. 17, *1927*, p. 20; Lagos Town Council, *Report of Medical Officer of Health 1928*, pp. 15–17, *1929*, pp. 25–6, *1931*, pp. 15, 19, *1933*, p. 15, *1937*, pp. 25–6, 28, *1938*, pp. 24–5; Nigeria, *Medical Report 1939*, p. 6, *1940*, p. 7, *1941*, p. 6, *1942*, p. 6, *1943*, pp. 8–9, *1944*, p. 8; *Census of Nigeria, 1931*, vol. iv, p. 8.
[2] Including still-births.
[3] Excluding non-natives.

extension of medical care.[1] But it is very difficult to explain the trend of the live-birth rate. There cannot, to be sure, be any doubt that the heavy drop in the first two decades of this century was due, at least in part, to the spread of gonorrhoea. Dr. Turner in his 'Notes on the Medical History of Lagos' says:

The most important single disease is gonorrhoea, with its manifold sequelae and its important bearing on the fertility of the race. Some years ago a medical practitioner in close touch with conditions in Lagos stated that, before many generations had passed, the Yoruba native population would markedly diminish. This has not yet happened, but fertility data show that the event is not unlikely. Accurate information is urgently needed to throw light on this matter.[2]

Venereal Disease. (a) Gonorrhoea. Little or no exact information is available, but all Medical Officers are unanimous in stating that it is widespread. The social habits of the people tend to cause a rapid spread and conservative estimates state that at least 50 per cent of adult males are infected. The effect on the birth-rate is already noticeable and widespread sterility is the result. It is difficult to decide when the disease was first introduced, but there is little doubt that it was very early, as natives from the hinterland had many remedies as early as 1897. The more rapid spread in recent years may be due to the more lax moral condition of the people in the transition state of civilization.

(b) Syphilis. The information concerning syphilis is even more vague than that concerning gonorrhoea, as the only reliable test is also positive for Yaws, which is endemic over the greater part of Southern Nigeria. Aneurism and aortic heart lesions are becoming more common, or patients are coming forward for treatment more readily.

In general, all that can be stated is that both diseases are present, and to a dangerous extent, and that a great deal of further information is required.[3]

But when Dr. Turner wrote his 'Notes' the fall in the birth-rate had stopped many years ago, and there is no evidence that sterility was widespread.[4] Further information concerning the incidence of venereal diseases has not been forthcoming, and it is not impossible that the apparent stability of the birth-rate in the last 20 years may have been due to a check in the spread of venereal disease.

General Mortality. Lagos Island, 'originally a mudbank covered by mangrove',[5] had for a very long time the reputation of being a most unhealthy place. The Acting Colonial Surgeon in a report to the Administrator, dated 25 August 1870, said that 'Lagos still possesses the unenviable distinction of a sanitary position almost as bad as could be'.[6] Ten years later, on 11 October 1880, Lieutenant-Governor Griffith wrote:

... in order to remove from Lagos the reproach of being a most unhealthy settlement drainage and filling up of pestilential swamps will have to be attended to far beyond what is authorised by the present allotment of funds for such work.[7]

---

[1] The Commission appointed in January 1901 to inquire into the extent of Infantile Mortality was 'appalled' to find such a large number of still-births (see 'Report', p. 247). 'We are of opinion that the large number of still-births are due to these native medicine men as they appear to know nothing about artificial respiration and other means for making the apparently lifeless new born infant live' (ibid., p. 249).

[2] Census of Nigeria, 1931, vol. i, p. 126.   [3] Ibid., p. 128.

[4] The only fact cited by Dr. Turner is that of all the pregnancies of 124 women over 40 questioned in Lagos 15·6 per cent. had ended in miscarriages and that 6·5 per cent. of the 124 women (i.e. 8) had never been pregnant; see ibid., vol. vi, p. 9.   [5] Ibid., vol. i, p. 125.

[6] State of Colonial Possessions 1869, Part II, p. 24.   [7] Colonial Possessions Reports 1879, p. 210.

After another ten years the Colonial Secretary reported:

Much has been and is being done to improve the sanitary condition of the town: the swamps in its immediate vicinity are being gradually filled up and a better system of scavenging has been introduced. A large number of wells has been sunk by the Government, from which fairly good water is obtained. . . . But when all is said and done the fact remains that it is almost impossible to conquer by sanitary measures and precautions so bad a climate as is unfortunately to be found in Lagos.[1]

Opinions about the effects of the slight sanitary improvements upon mortality were influenced by the official death-rates,[2] which owing to the incompleteness of registration were quite misleading, and it is perhaps no accident that only when death registration in the 1890s became fairly complete the urgency of fundamental sanitary reforms became generally recognized. But it took some time before action was taken.

1897. Discussion is still going on as to a feasible scheme for the sanitary reform of Lagos town in connection with water supply and drainage that can be carried out reasonably within the means of the Colony. It will be easily comprehensible that on a malarial island a mile or two long by half a mile broad, with a population of 50,000 souls living on it, and a much larger number of bodies dead and buried in it for many years past, disturbance of the soil is to be avoided by every possible means. No scheme has yet been approved.[3]

1898. The question of improving the sanitary condition of Lagos has engaged the attention of the Government for some years past, but, so far, it has not been found possible to devise a scheme likely to give satisfactory results which the Colony is able to afford. There are hardly any drains, and what there are are only to carry off the surface water in wet weather. There are both land latrines and latrines over the water, and all Government buildings and some private houses are supplied with earth closets.[4]

1899. The sanitary condition of the Island of Lagos has been considerably improved during the last few years. New latrines have been erected in several quarters of the town in the course of the year. There is, however, no underground drainage, and no water supply has yet been provided.[5]

Early in the month of May the new Governor of the Colony, Sir William MacGregor, arrived. The question of improved sanitation and a water supply at once occupied his attention. The original scheme for obtaining water from Ikoyi, unfortunately, has so far failed, and it is difficult to see what can be done in a place situated as Lagos is to ensure an adequate and continual supply of water without very great expenditure. . . . Lagos itself is practically nothing more than a sandbank, and there appears to be little left to hope for except that before many years are past it may be found possible to remove the Government to an inland position, where proper sanitary conditions may be instituted.[6]

1901. The sanitary state of the town has greatly improved within the past ten years, but there is room for still greater improvement.[7]

We are fully aware that there is in this town an appalling amount of sickness, which is attended by a frightful rate of mortality. Two thousand two hundred persons die in this small town every year.[8]

---

[1] *Colonial Reports, Lagos 1890*, p. 13. See also *Colonial Possessions Reports 1882*, pp. 252–3, *1884–6*, p. 118; *Colonial Reports, Lagos 1894*, p. 6.

[2] See, for example, *Colonial Possessions Reports 1879–81*, pp. 302, 304.

[3] *Colonial Reports, Lagos 1897*, p. 10.   [4] Ibid. *1898*, p. 15.

[5] Ibid. *1899*, pp. 21–2.   [6] Ibid., p. 27.   [7] Ibid. *1900–1*, p. 10.

[8] Speech of Governor Sir William MacGregor at the foundation of the 'Lagos Ladies' League' (25 Jan. 1901), ibid. At the same time the Governor in a Message to the Legislative Council complained about the inefficiency of the Sanitary Inspectors: 'The staff provided should if well

As to general sanitation, schemes for the removal of sewage of the Colony of Lagos into the sea have been proposed, but, as they involve considerable capital expenditure, and, what is more serious, a large annual expenditure, it has been decided to defer action for the present, and until the Colony is in a better position to afford expenditure on this improvement.[1]

1902. During the past five or six years there has been marked improvement in the sanitary condition of the town, though there is a very great deal yet to be accomplished in the direction of sanitary improvement—notably the institution of an adequate method of sewage disposal, and of surface drainage.[2]

The construction of the town, where some 40,000 persons are collected mainly in native huts, the over-crowding of these latter, the absence of any proper method of disposing of household slop water, of surface drainage, and of sewage disposal—all constitute obstacles to the attainment of even a moderately high standard of sanitation; but that improvement under new and scientific methods has, as before remarked, been markedly in evidence during the past six years, is a fact beyond dispute.[3]

1903. There can be no reasonable doubt that Lagos can be made a fairly healthy town within a few years from this, if the hygienic measures in use there now are persevered in; and if these are supplemented by the execution of the scheme submitted to you, with the full approval of the consulting engineers, for furnishing the inhabitants with a sufficient supply of good water.[4]

1905. Reclamation of Swamps, &c. This work was actively continued in various parts of Lagos Island, and over 50,000 cubic yards of soil were used in filling in the areas reclaimed. The appearance of the northern and southern points of the Island has in consequence of these operations undergone a complete change as compared with, say, four years ago, and the prospects of good health in these parts of the town have been greatly enhanced—this apart from the throwing open of considerable space excellently adapted for business premises on the north, and dwelling houses on the south, in a town which had already become very congested.[5]

In his report for the year 1909, the Acting Medical Officer said:

In conclusion I am very glad to be able to state that Lagos is at present in a fairly good sanitary condition, when one realises that a large portion of the Town has been reclaimed, only a small portion laid out properly, houses packed too closely together, Streets too narrow and not in alignment, very few open spaces, therefore ventilation defective, and the highest part of the Town only 20 feet over sea-level and the difficulty of getting a fall for drains—taking all these things into consideration, I think that on the whole, the condition of the Town is satisfactory.[6]

There can in fact be no doubt that mortality in Lagos had begun to decline. In spite of a large increase in population the number of deaths registered in 1897–1917 did not rise. The average death-rate which in the

administered be sufficient to effect a very great improvement in the sanitary condition of Lagos. It is impossible to say that sanitary inspection is carried out in a manner that could be considered satisfactory to the most casual observer; but that is not the fault of this Council which has generously provided the necessary salaries, but is to be imputed to the inefficiency of the men to whom the salaries are paid. There need be no doubt that efficient inspectors can be obtained on the basis of the vote as submitted to you. The question is of far greater importance than is represented by the small sums of money involved, and the Council may rest assured it will receive particular attention and that efficiency will be insisted on either from the present inspectors or from their successors' (Government Gazette, Colony of Lagos, 23 Mar. 1901, p. 163). It should be noted, however, that the whole sanitary staff of Lagos consisted in 1900 of 1 part-time Medical Officer of Health and 2 African Sanitary Inspectors (see Census of Nigeria, 1931, vol. i, p. 130).

[1] Colonial Reports, Lagos 1900–1, p. 11.   [2] Ibid. 1902, p. 22.   [3] Ibid., p. 23.
[4] Sir William MacGregor to Mr. Lyttelton, ibid. 1903, p. 3.   [5] Ibid. 1905, p. 36.
[6] Report on the Municipal Board of Health 1909, p. 12.

second half of the 1890s must have exceeded 40 was probably less than
30 in 1911–17. It exceeded 30 again in 1918 and 1924, but since 1928 it has
been below 20 probably in every year. Not much more can be said, I think,
about mortality in general. The Government Statistician, it is true,
computed several life tables for Lagos[1] showing as mean expectation of
life at birth for males in 1921–30 36·4 years, for male Yoruba in 1931
40·1 years, for males in 1932 46·7 years, for females in 1932 52·8 years,
for males in 1933 46·8 years, and for females in 1933 51·7 years, but the
basic data used in computing these tables—population by age, births, and
deaths by age—are all so inadequate that the results are by no means
conclusive. Nor do they seem plausible. It may well be, to be sure, that
according to mortality in 1931 the mean expectation of life at birth was
40 years for males (and, say, something like 45 years for females), but the
number of deaths registered in Lagos Township was lower in 1931 than
in any other year from 1899 to 1944, and all the available evidence suggests
that mortality has not decreased since 1931.[2]

There remains, however, the incontrovertible fact that mortality in
Lagos in the last 35 years was considerably less than in the first 40 years
of British occupation. Important factors were swamp reclamation and
the introduction of a piped water-supply which reduced very much
the incidence of malaria and dysentery[3] and eliminated guinea-worm.[4]
Another factor was vaccination against smallpox. Dr. Turner described
the progress achieved as follows:

No figures are available for the years prior to 1896, but comment was made on the
endemicity of smallpox and the fact that outbreaks were of frequent occurrence.
The period 1896–1905 gave an average annual incidence of about 100 cases per
annum. Vaccination up to this time had been inadequate, and in the years 1904 and
1905 a vaccination census was made which, on completion, showed that the majority
of Lagos residents had been vaccinated. It is to be regretted that the detailed report
has been lost. Since 1910 the average annual incidence has been 12 cases per annum.
Outbreaks in this period have been due to importation of cases from ships and the
mainland, where vaccination is less complete, and not a few have been traced to the
efforts of Shopona priests to maintain their cult. In 1904 a survey of persons met at
random in the street showed that of 208 adults 16 per cent had had smallpox. In
the same year 10 per cent of 1,390 school children showed evidence of past smallpox.
No recent data are available on the incidence in various age-groups, but figures are
available for some groups of school children.

In 1930, of 227 boys aged 14–19, 7·5 per cent had had smallpox. Of 285 girls of
all ages 2 per cent had had smallpox. A probable average for all school children is
about 4 per cent. This does not represent the Lagos incidence as many of the children
are immigrant. A rough estimate for Lagos in the early days prior to vaccination
would show an average annual incidence of at least 0·5 per cent and probably nearer
1 per cent of the gross population.[5]

[1] See *Census of Nigeria, 1931*, vol. i, pp. 80–5; Lagos Town Council, *Report of Medical Officer
of Health 1932*, p. 26; *Report of Lagos Town Council 1933*, p. 45.

[2] Some official reports give as an explanation that 'clearly longevity cannot be increased
indefinitely' (*Colonial Reports, Nigeria 1933*, p. 13; *1934*, p. 13; *1935*, p. 12; *1936*, p. 12).

[3] Dr. Turner suggests that before 1900 malaria and dysentery 'killed many hundreds of people
annually' (*Census of Nigeria, 1931*, vol. i, p. 129).

[4] 'This disease disappeared since the introduction of a piped water supply, e.g. in 1914 there
were 234 cases treated at the African Hospital and in recent years, none' (ibid., p. 127).

[5] Ibid., pp. 126–7.

Thus, according to Dr. Turner, the average annual incidence was about 200 or 300 in the early days prior to vaccination, about 100 in 1896–1905, and 12 in 1911–31. With regard to the period prior to 1896 Dr. Turner reports:

Smallpox was said to be epidemic every other year and to be the main scourge of the island and the hinterland.[1]

But this was possibly an exaggeration, and Dr. Turner's statement that no figures are available for the years prior to 1896 is also not correct. According to Payne's *Lagos and West African Almanack and Diary for 1882* the 'Registrar's Return of Deaths Caused by Small Pox in Lagos' for 1868–79 was as follows:[2]

1868	1869	1870	1871	1872	1873	1874	1875	1876	1877	1878	1879
—	1	6	22	44	187	53	11	7	29	112	25

A perusal of the annual administration reports yields the following results:[3]

1876. The population 'scarcely suffered at all from smallpox'.[4]

1877. 41 cases, 16 deaths.[5]

1878. 201 cases, 74 deaths. '. . . a severe epidemic of small-pox raged at the early part of the year, followed up by the most unhealthy season for years previous in the recollection of some of the old native inhabitants of the place.'[6]

1882. 'Small pox being endemic in this country occasional cases appear now and then. . . .'[7]

1885. 'The epidemic of small-pox which raged last year has disappeared.'[8]

1887. 'There were but few cases of small-pox during the year.'[9] No deaths.[10]

1891. 129 deaths.[11]

1892. 23 deaths.[12]

1895. 50 deaths.[13]

In 1896–1905 the average number of cases, according to Dr. Turner, was about 100. The number of deaths in 1896–1900 has been given as 32, 16, 30, 22, and 10 respectively.[14] The Colonial Report for 1902 said:

. . . smallpox—endemic in this country—has almost vanished from Lagos town. There is, however, a constant influx of infected persons from outlying districts, and so cases must be expected, every now and then, to occur in the town of Lagos itself.[15]

---

[1] Ibid., p. 129.

[2] See Payne 1882, p. 41. The deaths from smallpox are given there by sex for each month.

[3] The death figures for 1877 and 1878 in the Administration reports are lower than those shown by Payne.

[4] *Colonial Possessions Reports 1876*, p. 119.   [5] Ibid. *1876–8*, p. 164.

[6] Ibid. See also ibid., pp. 153, 158.   [7] Ibid. *1882*, p. 251.

[8] Ibid. *1884–6*, p. 117.   [9] *Sanitary Report on Lagos 1887*, p. 3.

[10] See ibid., p. 5.   [11] See *Colonial Reports, Lagos 1892*, p. 30.

[12] See ibid.   [13] 'General Abstract of Registration 1896', p. 126.

[14] See ibid.; *General Abstract of Registration 1898*, p. 2; 'Report of Registrar General 1899', p. 315, 1900, p. 76.   [15] *Colonial Reports, Lagos 1902*, p. 23.

The Medical Report for 1904 stated:

Only 56 cases of Small-pox were treated in the Small-pox Hospital this year with 7 deaths, as against 120 with 17 deaths last year.[1]

The total number of cases reported in 1906–18 was only 116. But in 1919–20 there was an epidemic which was more serious than the preceding one of 1903, and cases were numerous also in 1933–4. Thus the average number of cases rose from 9 in 1906–18 to 34 in 1919–38.[2] On the whole, the available data suggest that smallpox in the nineteenth century claimed possibly less victims than is usually believed and that, on the other hand, the fight against this disease has not been quite as successful as had been expected a generation ago.

TABLE 24. *Cases of Smallpox, Lagos, 1906–38*[1]

Year	Cases	Year	Cases	Year	Cases	Deaths	Year	Cases	Deaths	Year	Cases	Deaths
1906	3	1913	5	1920	238	90	1927	34	6	1934	122	20
1907	2	1914	3	1921	22	4	1928	6	3	1935	13	1
1908	4	1915	2	1922	4	1	1929	15	4	1936	7	2
1909	13	1916	4	1923	6	3	1930	18	7	1937	4	—
1910	20	1917	15	1924	4	—	1931	3	1	1938	34	10
1911	37	1918	1	1925	14	5	1932	10	3			
1912	7	1919	61	1926	11	3	1933	59	10			

[1] See Southern Nigeria, *Medical Report 1907*, p. 2, *1908*, p. 2; *Report on The Lagos Municipal Board of Health 1915*, p. 2, *1916*, p. 4; Lagos Town Council, *Report of Medical Officer of Health 1917*, p. 1, *1918*, p. 1, *1938*, p. 10.

A disease which in the 1920s proved at least as disastrous in Lagos as smallpox in the earlier period was plague. It was introduced in June 1924[3] and the deaths reported in 1924–31 numbered 349, 88, 476, 151, 509, 176, 66, and 5 respectively.[4] The main reason why this disease gained so much ground was apparently overcrowding. The Deputy Director, Sanitary Service, of Nigeria, in his report for 1926, said:

The sanitary problems presented in Lagos are the most difficult in West Africa, and they all arise from one cause namely gross human congestion.[5] Excluding Ikoyi and the southern Marina the western half of that part of the Island of Lagos between the MacGregor Canal and Carter Bridge is in reality one huge market, and in that market seventy to eighty thousand African people live. Sanitary effort as ordinarily applied, is quite helpless in face of the difficulties presented. Lagos, without doubt, could be made safe against plague if all rats could be destroyed but this is quite impossible under the conditions existing in the greater part of Lagos Island.[6]

However, no case of plague has been reported from Lagos since April 1931. Nor has there been any other serious epidemic in the 1930s. It is, therefore, the more noteworthy that mortality as a whole has apparently not decreased in the course of the last 15 years. The principal reason probably are the deplorable housing conditions.

[1] Lagos, *Medical Report 1904*, p. 8.
[2] The average number of cases in 1911–31 was not 12 as stated by Dr. Turner but 24.
[3] See Nigeria, *Medical Report 1924*, p. 42.
[4] See Lagos Town Council, *Report of Medical Officer of Health 1931*, p. 7.
[5] As far back as 1885 the Medical Officer, Lagos, had written: 'Overcrowding of houses is a prolific source of disease' (*Colonial Possessions Reports 1884–6*, p. 118).
[6] Nigeria, *Medical Report 1926*, p. 25.

The general housing conditions of the Township may be gauged from the fact that it is estimated of the 14,949 recorded premises approximately 50 per cent are unfit for human habitation. It is not practicable to eradicate these insanitary premises by ordering their demolition under the Public Health Ordinance. The most that can be accomplished is to improve the light and ventilation of such premises, and reduce excessive overcrowding, a policy which has been in practice for some years.

Such a policy, by itself, cannot bring about a radical change for the betterment of the general housing conditions; moreover, for as long as this policy is carried on so long will the housing position remain at a very low level.

The progress made by the Lagos Executive Development Board is, of necessity, slow, and where progress has been made there still remains the out-of-date method of collection and disposal of nightsoil by the conservancy system and its consequent evils.

There are so many deplorable insanitary premises in the township that it is almost impossible to decide why any particular house should be selected for demolition on the grounds of it being unfit for human habitation. Further, the structural condition of many of these insanitary premises is such that wholesale harbourage for rodents exists therein, and many are actually rodent infested. . . .[1]

Infant Mortality. The number of deaths under one year seems to have been ascertained for the first time in 1891, and until 1909 the official figures included still-births. The infant deaths thus recorded in 1891–1900 were 384, 372, 399, 537, 642, 623, 752, 732, 864, and 842 respectively. The proportion of infant deaths among all deaths rose in this period from 25 to 42 per cent., the increase evidently being due to more complete and more accurate registration. But by 1896 the number of recorded infant deaths began to cause concern. The Colonial Report for that year said:

Infant mortality was especially heavy, 623 deaths of children under one year of age being registered.[2]

In his report for 1899 the Registrar-General stated:

The number of deaths of infants under one year of age was 864, this is undoubtedly a very high rate. Compared with the rate of infantile mortality in England the excess is about 300. Again the total number of births registered is 1,929, giving a death rate of 447·9 per 1000 under one year of age, or in other words barely half the children born live to be 12 months old. This matter would certainly seem to call for attention at the earliest possible opportunity.[3]

The Governor thereupon, in January 1901, appointed a Committee 'to enquire into and report upon the actual extent of Infantile Mortality, past and present, in Lagos and its suburbs', and, furthermore, created the 'Lagos Ladies' League'. He told the ladies whom he had invited for this occasion:

It appears from official returns that about one-half of our children die within the first year. Now that is not a matter for us to sit by and look at with our hands folded. The great question is: Can we do anything to improve it? I believe that we can do a great deal, and if it is true that we can do so, it is my duty and yours to do what is in our power.[4]

[1] Lagos Town Council, *Report of Medical Officer of Health 1938*, p. 7. See also *Speech and Address by Governor Sir Arthur Richards to the Legislative Council 18th March, 1946*, p. v.

[2] *Colonial Reports, Lagos 1896*, p. 8. See also Lagos, 'General Abstract of Registration 1896', p. 126; Lagos, *Abstract of Registration 1898*, pp. 2–3.

[3] 'Report of Registrar General 1899', p. 315. See also ibid. '1900', p. 76; 'Medical Report 1900–1', p. 130; *Colonial Reports, Lagos 1900–1*, p. 12.   [4] Ibid., p. 10.

The main conclusions of the Committee were:

We are of opinion that the Infantile Mortality in Lagos is not any greater than in former years and that it has always existed.[1]

When we compared the deaths of infants under one year of age with the births for the last nine years we found the highest percentage of mortality to have occurred in the year 1892, namely 64·92.

The lowest percentage of mortality was in the next year 1893, namely 38·59.

The high percentage in the year 1892 can be accounted for by the fact that all or nearly all the deaths of infants were registered on account of extra vigilance on the part of the Government to stop intra-mural burials, whereas many births were neglected to be registered.

This explanation we consider to be correct and therefore there is very little difference really between death-rate of infants under one year of age now and for the past nine years.[2]

As to the specific disease to which the alleged infantile mortality is due we have found that the diseases to which infants under one year of age chiefly succumb are Diseases of the Respiratory System, Digestive System, Fevers, Dysentery and Convulsions, the latter not being really a disease but rather a symptom.

We were unable to obtain any direct evidence as to the prevalence of Malarial Fever as the word Fever is used in a loose way on this Coast.

Fever accounted for 321 deaths amongst infants in the year 1899; that is more than half the deaths from Fever in that year occurred in infants under one year of age.[3]

(Direct Causes of the prevalent Infantile diseases) 1. Want of proper management of the infants at births and of the mothers in the puerperal state . . . .

2. Ignorance on the part of the parents of the most elementary laws of health for themselves and infants. Bad and irregular feeding. . . .

3. Exposure of the infants to variations of temperature both at the time of birth and also afterwards. This accounts for the number of deaths from Diseases of the Respiratory Organs.

4. . . . the indiscriminate use of Agbo, which is a decoction of leaves and roots. It is thought by many to be the most important food for infants and is given in preference to the natural food—the mother's milk.

5. A total lack of actual responsibility on the part of the male parent for the care of the infant and mother.

The Indirect Causes we have found to be:—

1. General bad sanitary surroundings.
   (a) Due to local conditions such as, certain parts of this Town.
   (b) Total disregard for cleanliness in their houses and compounds.
   (c) Over-crowding in their houses.
   (d) Living in small ill-ventilated badly lighted houses and rooms.
   (e) Over-heating of their houses by day and by night through the use of corrugated iron alone for the roofs.
   (f) Crowding together of a lot of small houses preventing any ventilation.

2. Superstition which gives free scope for the practices of the medicine man. . . .

3. Parents do not seem now to have as much control over their sons and daughters and this leads to a lowering of the moral tone and a looser way of living amongst the young people.

Native marriage laws are not respected. Children are born out of wedlock nearly always of too young parents with the result they are weakly from the start and the mothers are unable to nurse them properly.

This lower moral tone and loose way of living we have found applies to all classes of the community.

4. A general unhealthiness prevails in the town.

---

[1] 'Report of the Committee', p. 245.   [2] Ibid., p. 246.   [3] Ibid., p. 247.

5. We have found that the native medicine men do a lot of harm in the town and contribute to a very great extent to the high Infantile Mortality. . . .

6. We have found that a great many people consult these so-called Druggists in cases of sickness in their children. . . .[1]

In 1894–1900 the ratio of infant deaths (including still-births) to 1,000 births (including still-births) had oscillated between 403 and 453. In 1902 it was apparently somewhat lower. The Colonial Report stated:

Infant mortality is very high, but has sunk during the past six years from 45 to 37 per cent. (during the first year of life), since the attention of the natives has been directed to the taking of precautions against malaria, and to the proper feeding and care of infants—for it is chiefly to malaria and improper feeding that the fearful mortality among infants and children is due.[2]

In 1903–10 the ratio oscillated between 341 and 401. Excluding still-births, the infant mortality rate had decreased from 392 in 1895–1900 to 327 in 1907–10. Thereafter the rate has exceeded 300 only in 1918 and 1920. Apart from these two years, the rate oscillated (in Lagos and Ebute Metta) in 1911–23 between 261 and 296. In 1924 and 1925 it was 236 and 238 respectively; it dropped to 199 in 1926, 175 in 1927, 138 in 1928, and gradually to 102 in 1932. From 1933 to 1944 it oscillated between 114 and 140 without showing any definite trend.

It is not easy to explain the development of infant mortality in Lagos. Dr. Turner in his 'Notes on the Medical History of Lagos' says:

. . . the data show a very marked and sustained improvement. The rate for the period 1898 to 1900 was about 450 per 1,000 births. From 1900 to 1910 it had fallen to about 350 per 1,000, in the period 1910 to 1920 it averaged 280[3] and remained steady about that figure until the commencement of infant welfare work in 1924, since when it has fallen rapidly to the present figure of about 130.[4]

But infant welfare work did not commence in 1924. The Medical Report for 1924 said:

Maternity and Child Welfare. No advance has been made so far as regards promoting these two important matters. Hopes are entertained that 1925 will show a beginning in this respect and that some organisation will be brought into being in a big centre such as Lagos.[5]

It took in fact some years more until effective infant welfare work commenced. The first African woman Health Visitor was appointed in

[1] Ibid., pp. 247–9.

[2] Colonial Reports, Lagos 1902, p. 23. Some Medical Officers, to be sure, had strange ideas about what constitutes 'proper feeding'. See, for example, the following statement of the Acting Senior Sanitary Officer (Southern Nigeria, Medical Report 1913, p. 51): 'The causes of the high infantile mortality [in Lagos] are the same as those found elsewhere, together with a prejudice on the part of native mothers against artificial feeding, and a liking for dosing the infants with various harmful concoctions which are forced into the stomach by hydraulic pressure. The gradual educating of mothers in the care of their infants and the introduction of artificial feeding would go far to reduce the present high mortality.'

[3] Dr. Turner was apparently not aware that the official rates until 1909 included still-births while from 1909 on still-births were excluded. The infant mortality rate, including still-births, was 432 in 1898–1900, 357 in 1910, and 323 in 1910–20. Excluding still-births it was 391 in 1898–1900, 324 in 1910, and 288 in 1910–20. (To what extent the decrease from 1898–1900 to 1910–20 was due to improvement in birth registration it is impossible to tell.)

[4] Census of Nigeria 1931, vol. i, p. 126.   [5] Nigeria, Medical Report 1924, p. 54.

November 1925 and by the end of 1927 the Visitors numbered eight; a Dispensary with a women and children's section in charge of a Lady Medical Officer was opened on 1 November 1926, and 'Infant Welfare Clinics were started on 30th April, 1928' and were 'held three times weekly' at the new Dispensary.[1] In the meantime the number of infant deaths had dropped from 904 in 1923 to 806 in 1924, 777 in 1925, 662 in 1926, and 579 in 1927. It is obvious that the enormous drop from 1923 to 1926 was not due to (non-existing) infant welfare work. It is possible but unlikely that the further improvement in 1927 was caused by the efforts of the Health Visitors.[2] It is probable that the continuation of the decline in 1928 (to 461) was mainly the result of the newly opened Infant Welfare Clinics.

The great reduction in infant mortality started about 3 years before infant welfare work became effective, it went on during the first years of these activities, but no progress has been made since. There are, I suggest, three reasons why infant welfare work apparently had not a decisive effect on mortality.

(1) Those diseases which such work usually fights most successfully had lost their importance in Lagos when infant welfare work began. According to the report of the Lady Medical Officer for 1928 only 5 per cent. of the deaths of infants were due to gastro-intestinal complaints, but 31 per cent. to broncho-pneumonia and other allied pulmonary complaints.

Statistics of the year show that thirty-one per cent. of deaths are due to these diseases. This is not to be wondered at, when the condition of the houses of the poor during the rainy season is considered. To the over-crowding, dirt and darkness is now added damp, from leaky roofs and unpaved mud floors. In order to make the room dryer, usually a pot of glowing charcoal is placed near the newly-born infant, who lies on a thin mat on the floor. Can any further encouragement to the disease be added ? Indeed, the resistance of these infants is truly almost incredible.[3]

(2) Of the deaths of infants in 1928, 9 per cent. were due to prematurity and 30 per cent. to congenital debility. Many of these deaths could probably have been prevented if infant welfare work had been supplemented by antenatal care. An Antenatal Clinic, it is true, is held in conjunction with and simultaneously with the Infant Welfare Clinic,[4] but the numbers of women who attended for advice were only 11 in 1928, 8 in 1929, 12 in 1930,[5] and apparently remained negligible.

(3) 'The Registrars of Vital Statistics submit lists of births as registered daily. Every address where a birth is thus known to have occurred is visited by Health Visitors.'[6] But many children are dead before their

---

[1] See Nigeria, *Medical Report 1926*, p. 37; *1927*, p. 35; *1928*, p. 29.

[2] See in this connexion 'Annual Report of the Lady Medical Officer for the Year 1928', *Report of the Lagos Town Council 1928*, p. 28: 'On the whole, the work of the Health Visitor has been found to be satisfactory, and an effort is being made to raise their standard from being almost entirely record keepers, and to encourage a greater sense of responsibility. . . . The Health Visitors were found to have practically no knowledge of the physiology and care of infants.'

[3] Ibid., p. 29.   [4] See Nigeria, *Medical Report 1928*, p. 29.

[5] See *Report of Lagos Town Council 1928*, p. 28 ; *1929*, p. 28; Lagos Town Council, *Report of Medical Officer of Health 1930*, p. 19.   [6] Ibid. *1932*, p. 15.

births are registered. In her report for 1929 the Lady Medical Officer stated:

Notification of births within thirty-six hours, or registration within seven days, would enable more preventive work to be done than is done at present.[1]

But her recommendation had no success and the Nigeria Medical Report for 1940 says:

Concerning infantile and maternal mortality, the Medical Officer of Health, Lagos, reports that 209 babies and seventeen mothers had died before the Health Visitors could visit the houses and remarks that many lives could be saved if the period allowed between births and their notification was considerably less than the twenty-one days permitted at present.[2]

Population Growth. In his report on the 1931 census the Government Statistician said:

All the estimates and counts, with the exception of that of 1891, indicate an increasing population during the last 100 years, which accords with our knowledge of the increase of trade, of the opening-up of communications both sea-wards and towards the hinterland, with improvement in sanitation, the reclamation of swamps and the diminution of the death-rate, which, as in other parts of the world, has only been partially off-set by the fall in the birth-rate.

There is, thus, good evidence that the economic and biological conditions in Lagos during the last seventy years have been, apart from the appearance of relatively minor epidemics, uniformly progressive, so that there is good reason to apply to the population the same 'logistic' law of growth that has been used with success by Raymond Pearl and Udny Yule to describe the population growth in the United States, England and Wales, Sweden, France and elsewhere.[3]

However, in discussing the population growth of Lagos in the hundred years preceding the 1931 census it seems advisable to consider separately three periods.

(1) Until 1871. In 1855 the Rev. J. T. Bowen estimated the population of Lagos as 20,000. 'In 1861, Lagos Town was said to contain 30,000.'[4] The official estimate for 1864 was 40,000. The census of 1866 showed a population of 25,083. The official estimate for 1867 gave 35,000. The census of 1871 showed a population of 28,518. The only safe conclusion to be drawn, I think, is that we know nothing about the population trend in this period. But there is some evidence that a considerable proportion of people found at the 1871 census in Lagos were not born there.[5]

(2) 1871–1901. The population ascertained in the town at the censuses of 1871, 1881, 1891, and 1901 was 28,518, 37,452, 32,508, and 39,387. The census returns were not accurate, but I see no reason to assume that there was a gradual population increase. Deaths were at least as numerous as

---

[1] *Report on Lagos Town Council 1929*, p. 31.   [2] Nigeria, *Medical Report 1940*, p. 7.
[3] *Census of Nigeria, 1931*, vol. i, p. 63.   [4] Ibid.
[5] See statement by Acting Administrator, *Colonial Possessions Reports 1873*, Part II, 2nd Division, p. 41: 'Next to the natives of the place and the interior, the Brazilian Emancipados are the most numerous, they are constantly arriving by every opportunity at Lagos, I presume in consequence of the late Emancipation Law in Brazil; their number is estimated by some from 4,000 to 6,000. They are principally Roman Catholics, and are very poor; then come the Sierra Leonians, Kroomen, and Fantees.' As regards the influx of visitors and settlers in the years preceding the census see *State of Colonial Possessions 1867*, Part II, p. 22; *1868*, Part II, p. 26; *1869*, Part II, p. 19.

births, and periods in which immigration exceeded emigration may have alternated with periods in which more people left than arrived.[1]

(3) From 1901 to 1931 the population increased as follows:[2]

| | Lagos Town | | | Suburbs | | | Lagos Township | | |
| | Popula-tion | Increase | | Popula-tion | Increase | | Popula-tion | Increase | |
Year		Number	per cent.		Number	per cent.		Number	per cent.
1901	39,387	..	..	2,460	..	..	41,847	..	..
1911	56,653	17,266	44	17,113	14,653	596	73,766	31,919	76
1921	77,561	20,908	36	22,129	5,016	29	99,690	25,924	35
1931	90,193	12,632	16	35,915	13,786	62	126,108	26,418	27

These figures suggest that the population of Lagos Town increased from 1901 to 1931 by about 130 per cent. as compared with hardly 40 per cent. in 1871–1901. The increase was much larger still in the suburbs. The population of Lagos Township in 1931 was apparently three times as large as in 1901. The decennial increase was about 75 per cent. in 1901–11, about 35 per cent. in 1911–21, and about 25 per cent. in 1921–31. While the excess of births over deaths was negligible in the first decade it may have accounted for one-third of the total rise in the third decade. Immigration which must have been enormous in the first decade declined considerably thereafter. Very many immigrants went to the suburbs both in 1901–11 and 1921–31, but in 1911–21 the bulk came to Lagos Town.

According to the 1931 census only 42 per cent. of the total population of Lagos Township were born there. Of the 114,193 natives of Nigeria 50,618 were born in Lagos Township, 3,604 elsewhere in the Colony, 32,083 in Abeokuta, Ijebu, and Oyo Provinces, 13,626 elsewhere in the Southern Provinces, 11,922 in the Northern Provinces, 1,161 in Nigeria 'unclassified', and 1,179 elsewhere.[3] The scanty data published for earlier censuses[4] indicate likewise that the bulk of the immigration to Lagos Township came from the neighbouring districts.

2. Nigeria and Cameroons

Fertility. Statistics bearing on fertility are scanty outside Lagos.

(1) In 1913 a Political Officer in Sokoto Province showed in his Assessment Report that among a population of 20,444 the number of children

---

[1] Between 1871 and 1881 the population of Lagos and the adjoining districts was said to have increased from 60,000 to 75,000. Lieutenant-Governor Griffith, in his report on the 1881 census, stated (pp. 14–15): 'Consulting with the Registrar upon the question, he told me he thought that large additions were annually made to the population of the Settlement by the influx of Slaves who make their escape from their owners in the Countries whose people come to trade at Lagos, and he considered a large portion of the excess of 15,049 has arisen in this way, as well as by means of the Alien Children's Ordinance.' But the Lieutenant-Governor himself was 'inclined to think that the population of the Settlement was larger in 1871 than was represented by the counting of that year. And therefore that the excess of 15,049 persons in 1881 as against 1871 is apparent rather than real' (ibid., pp. 13–14; see also *Colonial Possessions Reports 1879–81*, p. 301). In 1889 Governor Moloney reported that the population 'is augmented to no inconsiderable extent by the number of escaped slaves who succeed from time to time in reaching the Colony, and in thus securing their natural liberty' (Lagos, *Report on Blue Book 1887*, p. 27). No other information concerning immigration seems to have been published.   [2] See *Census of Nigeria, 1931*, vol. iv, p. 1.

[3] See ibid., pp. 35–7.   [4] See *Report on Southern Nigeria Census 1911*, p. 16; Talbot, vol. iv, p. 181.

'born during the last 12 months' was 1,320. This would indicate an extra-ordinarily high birth-rate, but it may well be that the count of the population was incomplete and (or) that a number of children born more than 12 months ago were included.

(2) Birth records are available from Kano City for 1918–30, from many places and from some large districts for 1926–32, and from a few towns for 1935–7. I have summarized the results in the preceding section. They vary enormously, but as a rule suggest low birth-rates. It is, however, quite likely that many births escaped registration.

(3) In 1925–6 inquiries concerning fertility were made by assessing officers in Cameroons Province. The results may be summarized as follows:

Locality	Year	Women questioned	Children born	Births per woman
MAMFE DIVISION				
Assumbo . .	1925	571	1,018	1·8
Anyang . .	1925	198	567	2·9
Bangwa . .	1925	1,000	2,137	2·1
Nkongwa . .	1925	850	1,641	1·9
Mangew . .	1925	427	797	1·9
BAMENDA DIVISION				
Bali . . .	1925	13	54	4·2
Mogamaw area .	1926	. .	. .	4·4
Ngemba area .	1926	. .	. .	4·6
Chingang . .	1926	100	180	1·8
Kawle . . .	1926	46	63	1·4
Tschati . .	1926	66	110	1·7

Since nothing is said about the age of the women questioned no con-clusions about fertility can be drawn from these figures.

A similar inquiry was made in 1929 by the Assistant District Officer of Buea District. He found that 309 women had borne 1,036 children or 3·35 on an average.

(4) At the 1931 Intensive Census in the Northern Provinces a question as to the number of children alive was asked of both parents. The Government Statistician reported:

There was, however, some difficulty in obtaining a double entry in respect of each child, that is, once for each parent. Some doubt arises, therefore, as to the validity of the figures for paternal fertility.[1]

The Census Officer, Northern Provinces, however, says that a table 'showing the nett fertility for males was abandoned in the interests of economy'.[2] In any case, such a table was published only for females. Table 25 shows the results for all tribes. The data were published also separately for each tribe.[3] The Government Statistician uses these data for showing 'the tribal order of nett fertility', giving (a) the 'children alive per mother', (b) the 'percentage of sterile women in the 30–39 age-group'.

	Fulani	Tuareg	Kanuri	Gwari	Hausa	Munshi	Idoma	Sura	Yoruba	Nupe	Total
(a)	2·8	2·8	2·7	2·7	2·6	2·4	2·4	2·3	1·8	1·8	2·6
(b)	17·6	13·6	20·8	21·1	25·0	18·5	20·9	8·6	27·1	58·0	22·7

[1] *Census of Nigeria, 1931*, vol. i, p. 53.   [2] Ibid., vol. ii, p. 49.   [3] See ibid., pp. 150–7.

TABLE 25. *Females over Ten Years by Age and Number of Children Alive, Intensive Census, Northern Provinces, Nigeria, 1930–1*[1]

Age (years)	Number of children alive																		Total	Average
	0	1	2	3	4	5	6	7	8	9	10	11	12	13	15	16	20	21		
10–14	18,961	126	16	8	—	—	—	—	—	—	—	—	—	—	—	—	—	—	19,111	0·01
15–19	12,764	7,254	1,727	226	50	8	1	2	1	—	—	—	—	—	—	—	—	—	22,033	0·53
20–29	11,524	10,579	10,288	5,733	2,447	769	172	34	9	2	—	—	—	—	—	—	—	—	41,557	1·52
30–39	6,697	4,757	4,774	4,592	3,852	2,615	1,401	531	189	36	14	4	1	—	—	—	—	—	29,463	2·40
40–49	4,341	2,976	2,801	2,425	2,146	1,754	1,180	674	343	127	35	7	2	1	—	1	1	—	18,814	2·63
50–59	2,919	2,032	1,695	1,400	1,236	934	535	334	188	59	26	10	4	1	1	—	—	1	11,375	2·40
60 and over	3,716	2,469	2,024	1,577	1,182	782	496	250	97	55	16	4	3	1	1	—	1	—	12,674	2·06
Not stated	155	29	9	17	9	—	1	—	—	—	—	—	—	—	—	—	—	—	220	..
Total	61,077	30,222	23,334	15,978	10,922	6,862	3,786	1,825	827	279	91	25	10	3	2	1	2	1	155,247	..

[1] See *Census of Nigeria, 1931*, vol. ii, pp. 150–1. The table excludes 276 females for whom neither age nor number of children were stated.

The percentage of sterile women between the ages of 30 to 40 seems to be a fair index of infecundity. In most cases, as shown in both Intensive and Medical Census data, the proportion of women who have not borne children increases from 40 years of age onwards, suggesting that fertility to the extent common in Nigeria is inimical to longevity.[1]

But 'sterile' women, as the term is used in this connexion, comprise all women who had no child alive at the time of the census. They include, therefore, the women who have lost all their children. Thus, the percentage of 'sterile' women between the ages of 30 to 40 cannot represent 'a fair index of infecundity'. That the proportion of 'sterile' women increases from 40 years of age onwards does, therefore, also not suggest that 'fertility to the extent common in Nigeria is inimical to longevity'. It suggests merely that the proportion of women who have lost all their children increases from 40 years of age onwards, and this is what was to be expected, since the women over 40 years bear no children while they lose more and more children with increasing age.

(5) A little more light was thrown on fertility by the Medical Censuses taken in 1930–2. The main results are summarized in Table 26. It appears that the 2,277 females over 40 years covered by the investigations had had on an average 4·6 pregnancies, of which 0·3 resulted in miscarriages and 4·3 in births. The average number of pregnancies varied between 3·3 (Zangan Aya) and 8·4 (Creek Zone), the average number of miscarriages between 0·1 (Kaita) and 1·0 (Creek Zone), and the average number of births between 3 (Laminga) and 7·5 (Creek Zone). The number of miscarriages recorded for all females amounted to 7·3 per cent. of the pregnancies, varying between 1·9 per cent. (Kaita) and 12·5 per cent. (Cameroons Forest Zone). The results for the various areas vary enormously. Some of the greatest differences may be due to inaccurate answers by the women questioned. It is hard to believe, for example, that of the 520 females over 20 questioned in the Creek Zone actually not more than 7 should never have been pregnant. Omitting the Creek Zone, the average number of pregnancies of women over 40 varied between 3·3 and 5·8, the average number of miscarriages between 0·1 and 0·6, and the average number of births between 3 and 5·4. These figures would suggest a rather low fertility. But it seems impossible to draw any final conclusions from the data of the Medical Censuses[2] as the number of pregnancies, particularly of older women, may have been understated. All that can be safely said, I think, is that the Medical Censuses afford no evidence that fertility, on the whole, was high.

[1] *Census of Nigeria, 1931*, vol. i, p. 55.
[2] On the basis of the Medical Censuses the Government Statistician computed the following past birth-rates (see ibid., p. 58):

Kaita	Zangan Aya	Bakori	Laminga	Cameroons Forest	Cameroons Hill	Creek
40	30	25	29	32	42	57

The Government Statistician did not compute such a rate for Abeokuta because he considered the data for this district too inaccurate. For Cameroons and Creek it is possible furthermore to

The Medical Census for the Southern Provinces paid special attention to the Cameroons Province, and the Reports to the League of Nations and the Minutes of the Permanent Mandates Commission contain some additional information on fertility in this area. The 1922 report, which took a low fertility for granted, stated:

The fact that the birth-rate is low does not appear to be due to venereal disease, few cases of which are seen except in the stations, where they appear to be imported and do not go with a system of professional prostitution. Promiscuous relations seem generally due to the inability of the man to pay the dower asked for a girl, who may thereupon decide to live with her 'friend' for a period, depending on his whim or means. As such union gives her no claim on the children, the discarded woman has to find another refuge, having no independent means. The practice of holding the children of a marriage in bond to the woman's parent until the whole dower is paid has also an adverse effect on the increase of families; and as the man in a position to afford several wives is usually elderly, there are few children in proportion born to him, with the added disadvantage that the offspring of the young and healthy women of a village may be nearly related by blood.[1]

In a Memorandum on 'The Economic Development of Mandated Territories in its Relation to the Well-Being of the Natives',[2] Sir F. Lugard suggested that 'the sudden introduction of an industrial civilization' entailing in some cases too heavy a burden on a population not yet accustomed to the new conditions and to European methods may be one cause for the decrease of native populations. The 1925 report to the League contained some 'Observations' on this Memorandum, in which the population decline of the Bakweri was attributed mainly to a decline of fertility caused by the wage labour introduced by Europeans.

The statistics of population that have so far been collected by the administrative staff, though more than usually elaborate for so undeveloped a territory, are not yet sufficiently exhaustive or continuous to enable final conclusions to be formed regarding the increase or decrease of the population of the Cameroons Province or any of its divisions. But if exact data are lacking, in the opinion of those natives and

relate the number of children under one year to the total population (see for basic data ibid., vol. vi, pp. 34–5).

	Cameroons Forest	Cameroons Hill	Creek
Population . . .	2,594	1,528	2,215
Under one . . .	132	85	134
Under one per 1,000 . .	51	56	60

Taking account of infant mortality the birth-rates in each of these Districts would appear to have been enormous. But it may well be that many children over one were recorded as being under one. On the other hand, the rates computed by the Government Statistician may be wide of the mark, as the formula which he used for the calculation was necessarily quite arbitrary.

It is obvious, furthermore, that the figures concerning numbers of pregnancies and ages of mothers ascertained at the Medical Censuses are too unreliable to permit the computing of any specific fertility rates. Yet the Annual Colonial Reports state, year in, year out (see, for example, Colonial Reports, Nigeria 1938, p. 15): 'Fertility diminishes rapidly with age over the whole reproductive period, particularly among the Ijaw [Creek Zone], among whom a woman of thirty-six has a potential fertility of less than one-sixth of a woman of seventeen years of age. The general trend of fertility and age follows that found for women in Northern India, where, however, the decrease of reproductive capacity with age is somewhat smaller than it is in Nigeria.'

[1] *Report on the Cameroons 1922*, p. 46.
[2] See Permanent Mandates Commission, *Minutes*, 7th Session, pp. 194–7.

others best qualified to judge, the Bakweri tribe in the Victoria Division, which more than any other is affected by wage labour, is on the decline. The chief reason for this seems to be the moral laxity of the women occasioned by the presence of a large number of bachelor wage-labourers freed from tribal restraints and in constant receipt of ready money. In pre-European days the chastity of the women was in large measure safe-guarded by the severity of the punishments awarded for adultery, it being common for a man to be sold as a slave for this offence. But the relaxation of these harsh forms of punishment coupled with the constant exposure to temptation has changed the moral character of the Bakweri woman, so that she has now earned a reputation for sexual licence. This does not take the form so much of promiscuous prostitution as of temporary unions, and there are now many young women who ought to be married and the mothers of several children, but who prefer illicit intimacy. This sexual freedom has undoubtedly increased the spread of venereal disease and caused a decline in the birth-rate. In the 1923 Report it was said that syphilis and gonorrhœa were very prevalent in the southern parts of the Cameroons Province on the plantations and the seaboard, a statement based on the number of cases treated in the hospitals. And this number was by no means exhaustive, as there are many persons suffering from the disease who from shame and other reasons do not come to the notice of the medical authorities. In these cases the disease is not eradicated from their systems with consequent dire effects on the fertility of the women and hereditary taint in the few children that are born of them. It is roughly estimated that not more than ten per cent. of the Bakweri women nowadays have five or six children, whereas in pre-European days such a number for a woman was common.[1]

. . . if the concentration of a large number of wage-labourers in a comparatively small area such as the Victoria Division has been prejudicial to the health and fertility of the Bakweri women owing to the resulting sexual licence, the reaction on the labourers themselves will also be injurious, and the ill effects sooner or later will be communicated to those inland tribes from which the labourers for the most part emanate. It may be added that the owners of the larger plantations give encouragement to wage-labourers to bring their wives and children and supply free rations for them, and this policy, if persisted in, should do something to alleviate the evils of large bachelor wage-labourer camps.[2]

But conditions in Cameroons Province, the only area in British West Africa with European plantations, are, of course, peculiar, and should not be generalized.

Unfortunately, the reports from Nigeria proper throw very little light on this problem. In the first decades of British administration the official documents refer hardly at all to fertility. The 1910 Medical Report for Northern Nigeria said:

Syphilis causes an enormous amount of abortion, still-birth, and infantile mortality; and it is no exaggeration to say that, outside of the Pagan country, one half of the women of child-bearing age are barren on account of early Gonorrhœa.[3]

---

[1] *Report 1925*, pp. 91–2.

[2] Ibid., p. 93. See also ibid. *1931*, pp. 46–7. See finally *Assessment Report on Buea District* (1931): 'The growing tendency of their women to consort with strangers is a great trouble to the Bakweri, but they do not seem to be able to prevent it. The chief complaint is that the strangers give these women drugs to prevent conception and love philtres to tempt them from their husbands, and so make them barren. By taking aphrodisiacs to increase their own sexual powers, they are able to satisfy the women more than their own husbands can.' (p. 17.) 'The birth rate appears low and the principal causes for this comparative sterility are inter-breeding, venereal disease and the preference of the women for strangers' (p. 40).

[3] Northern Nigeria, 'Medical Report 1910', p. 135. See also Nigeria, *Medical Report 1917*, p. 140.

TABLE 26. *Average Number of Pregnancies, Births, and Miscarriages by Age of Women in Nigeria, Medical Census, 1930–2*[1]

Age in years	Females			Pregnancies	Births	Miscarriages	Average number per female			Average number per fertile female		
	Total	Sterile	Fertile				Pregnancies	Births	Miscarriages	Pregnancies	Births	Miscarriages
NORTHERN PROVINCES												
Kaita												
15–19	95	36	59	78	74	4	0·8	0·8	0·0	1·3	1·3	0·1
20–4	132	11	121	278	273	5	2·1	2·1	0·0	2·3	2·3	0·0
25–9	125	8	117	398	393	5	3·2	3·1	0·0	3·4	3·4	0·0
30–4	93	1	92	362	357	5	3·9	3·8	0·1	3·9	3·9	0·1
35–9	94	6	88	452	446	6	4·8	4·7	0·1	5·1	5·1	0·1
40 and over	251	22	229	1,241	1,212	29	4·9	4·8	0·1	5·4	5·3	0·1
Total	790	84	706	2,809	2,755	54	3·6	3·5	0·1	4·0	3·9	0·1
Zangan Aya												
15–19	91	34	57	76	73	3	0·8	0·8	0·0	1·3	1·3	0·1
20–4	155	18	137	314	294	20	2·0	1·9	0·1	2·3	2·1	0·1
25–9	100	10	90	289	284	5	2·9	2·8	0·1	3·2	3·2	0·1
30–4	105	14	91	346	334	12	3·3	3·2	0·1	3·8	3·7	0·1
35–9	70	7	63	291	281	10	4·2	4·0	0·1	4·6	4·5	0·2
40 and over	431	57	374	1,440	1,371	69	3·3	3·2	0·2	3·9	3·7	0·2
Total	952	140	812	2,756	2,637	119	2·9	2·8	0·1	3·4	3·2	0·1
Bakori												
15–19	80	35	45	62	58	4	0·8	0·7	0·1	1·4	1·3	0·1
20–4	169	32	137	288	270	18	1·7	1·6	0·1	2·1	2·0	0·1
25–9	134	9	125	381	362	19	2·8	2·7	0·1	3·0	2·9	0·2
30–4	118	14	104	385	364	21	3·3	3·1	0·2	3·7	3·5	0·2
35–9	109	11	98	388	361	27	3·6	3·3	0·2	4·0	3·7	0·3
40 and over	379	50	329	1,520	1,377	143	4·0	3·6	0·4	4·6	4·2	0·4
Total	989	151	838	3,024	2,792	232	3·1	2·8	0·2	3·6	3·3	0·3
Laminga												
15–19	37	17	20	31	28	3	0·8	0·8	0·1	1·6	1·4	0·2
20–4	85	18	67	142	135	7	1·7	1·6	0·1	2·1	2·0	0·1
25–9	59	8	51	137	132	5	2·3	2·2	0·1	2·7	2·6	0·1
30–4	64	12	52	227	208	19	3·5	3·2	0·3	4·4	4	0·4
35–9	56	12	44	201	182	19	3·6	3·3	0·3	4·6	4·1	0·4
40 and over	202	35	167	679	606	73	3·4	3	0·4	4·1	3·6	0·4
Total	503	102	401	1,417	1,291	126	2·8	2·6	0·3	3·5	3·2	0·3
Total												
15–19	303	122	181	247	233	14	0·8	0·8	0·0	1·4	1·3	0·1
20–4	541	79	462	1,022	972	50	1·9	1·8	0·1	2·2	2·1	0·1
25–9	418	35	383	1,205	1,171	34	2·9	2·8	0·1	3·1	3·1	0·1
30–4	380	41	339	1,320	1,263	57	3·5	3·3	0·2	3·9	3·7	0·2
35–9	329	36	293	1,332	1,270	62	4·0	3·9	0·2	4·5	4·3	0·2
40 and over	1,263	164	1,099	4,880	4,566	314	3·9	3·6	0·2	4·4	4·2	0·3
Total	3,234	477	2,757	10,006	9,475	531	3·1	2·9	0·2	3·6	3·4	0·2

[1] See *Census of Nigeria, 1931*, vol. v, pp. 39–43; vol. vi, pp. 46–9. Births include still-births; infertile females comprise all those who were never pregnant; women under 15 are omitted. The meaning of the figures for the Northern Provinces is not quite clear; I have interpreted them as best I could.

Age in years	Females			Pregnancies	Births	Miscarriages	Average number per female			Average number per fertile female		
	Total	Sterile	Fertile	Pregnancies	Births	Miscarriages	Pregnancies	Births	Miscarriages	Pregnancies	Births	Miscarriages

SOUTHERN PROVINCES

Abeokuta Zone

Age in years	Total	Sterile	Fertile	Pregnancies	Births	Miscarriages	Pregnancies	Births	Miscarriages	Pregnancies	Births	Miscarriages
15–19	255	244	11	13	10	3	0·1	0·0	0·0	1·2	0·9	0·3
20–4	323	97	226	292	275	17	0·9	0·9	0·1	1·3	1·2	0·1
25–9	296	16	280	671	636	35	2·3	2·1	0·1	2·4	2·3	0·1
30–4	250	8	242	811	767	44	3·2	3·1	0·2	3·4	3·2	0·2
35–9	214	2	212	901	840	61	4·2	3·9	0·3	4·3	4·0	0·3
40 and over	614	5	609	3,188	3,022	166	5·2	4·9	0·3	5·2	5·0	0·3
Total	1,952	372	1,580	5,876	5,550	326	3·0	2·8	0·2	3·7	3·5	0·2

Cameroons Forest Zone

Age in years	Total	Sterile	Fertile	Pregnancies	Births	Miscarriages	Pregnancies	Births	Miscarriages	Pregnancies	Births	Miscarriages
15–19	213	75	138	233	189	44	1·1	0·9	0·2	1·7	1·4	0·3
20–4	191	29	162	379	342	37	2·0	1·8	0·2	2·3	2·1	0·2
25–9	164	13	151	503	439	64	3·1	2·7	0·4	3·3	2·9	0·4
30–4	133	22	111	417	374	43	3·1	2·8	0·3	3·8	3·4	0·4
35–9	122	18	104	436	372	64	3·6	3·0	0·5	4·2	3·6	0·6
40 and over	164	10	154	735	640	95	4·5	3·9	0·6	4·8	4·2	0·6
Total	987	167	820	2,703	2,356	347	2·7	2·4	0·4	3·3	2·9	0·4

Cameroons Hill Zone

Age in years	Total	Sterile	Fertile	Pregnancies	Births	Miscarriages	Pregnancies	Births	Miscarriages	Pregnancies	Births	Miscarriages
15–19	114	45	69	98	88	10	0·9	0·8	0·1	1·4	1·3	0·1
20–4	76	2	74	185	175	10	2·4	2·3	0·1	2·5	2·4	0·1
25–9	64	—	64	264	246	18	4·1	3·8	0·3	4·1	3·8	0·3
30–4	62	9	53	255	235	20	4·1	3·8	0·3	4·8	4·4	0·4
35–9	49	1	48	290	272	18	5·9	5·6	0·4	6·0	5·7	0·4
40 and over	96	2	94	552	520	32	5·8	5·4	0·3	5·9	5·5	0·3
Total	461	59	402	1,644	1,536	108	3·6	3·3	0·2	4·1	3·8	0·3

Creek Zone

Age in years	Total	Sterile	Fertile	Pregnancies	Births	Miscarriages	Pregnancies	Births	Miscarriages	Pregnancies	Births	Miscarriages
15–19	150	29	121	211	191	20	1·4	1·3	0·1	1·7	1·6	0·2
20–4	131	2	129	523	460	63	4·0	3·5	0·5	4·1	3·6	0·5
25–9	99	—	99	603	548	55	6·1	5·5	0·6	6·1	5·5	0·6
30–4	77	1	76	592	532	60	7·7	6·9	0·8	7·8	7	0·8
35–9	73	2	71	661	567	94	9·1	7·8	1·3	9·3	8·0	1·3
40 and over	140	2	138	1,181	1,044	137	8·4	7·5	1·0	8·6	7·6	1·0
Total	670	36	634	3,771	3,342	429	5·6	5·0	0·6	5·9	5·3	0·7

Total

Age in years	Total	Sterile	Fertile	Pregnancies	Births	Miscarriages	Pregnancies	Births	Miscarriages	Pregnancies	Births	Miscarriages
15–10	732	393	339	555	478	77	0·8	0·7	0·1	1·6	1·4	0·2
20–4	721	130	591	1,379	1,252	127	1·9	1·7	0·2	2·3	2·1	0·2
25–9	623	29	594	2,041	1,869	172	3·3	3	0·3	3·4	3·2	0·3
30–4	522	40	482	2,075	1,908	167	4·0	3·7	0·3	4·3	4·0	0·3
35–9	458	23	435	2,288	2,051	237	5·0	4·5	0·5	5·3	4·7	0·5
40 and over	1,014	19	995	5,656	5,226	430	5·6	5·2	0·4	5·7	5·3	0·4
Total	4,070	634	3,436	13,994	12,784	1,210	3·4	3·1	0·3	4·1	3·7	0·4

GRAND TOTAL

Age in years	Total	Sterile	Fertile	Pregnancies	Births	Miscarriages	Pregnancies	Births	Miscarriages	Pregnancies	Births	Miscarriages
15–19	1,035	515	520	802	711	91	0·8	0·7	0·1	1·5	1·4	0·2
20–4	1,262	209	1,053	2,401	2,224	177	1·9	1·8	0·1	2·3	2·1	0·2
25–9	1,041	64	977	3,246	3,040	206	3·1	2·9	0·2	3·3	3·1	0·2
30–4	902	81	821	3,395	3,171	224	3·8	3·5	0·2	4·1	3·9	0·3
35–9	787	59	728	3,620	3,321	299	4·6	4·2	0·4	5·0	4·6	0·4
40 and over	2,277	183	2,094	10,536	9,792	744	4·6	4·3	0·3	5·0	4·7	0·4
Total	7,304	1,111	6,193	24,000	22,259	1,741	3·3	3·0	0·2	3·9	3·6	0·3

The Medical Report for 1912 stated:

Kwongoma Division (Southern Portion) of Niger Province. In many of the villages, until recently, the men were more numerous than the women; because, in the slave raiding days not long over, more females than males were captured; but now, the female members of the population are increasing steadily, both actually and relatively, and the birth-rate shows a welcome tendency to go up.[1]

It was only in the 1930s that a little more attention was paid to fertility. For the Southern Provinces the discussion started with the comments of Dr. Turner in his report on the Medical Census. Dr. Turner stated:

Puberty is variable in its onset, but is usually about the thirteenth or fourteenth year. It has been noted as early as eleven years and as late as 16 years. The menopause also varies, but it appears on the average to occur about the 37th to the 38th year. Pregnancies usually commence about the age of 15 years and continue more or less regularly up to the onset of the menopause.[2] Most tribes attempt to have a three-year spacing of their pregnancies, and this is followed by the Yoruba and the Cameroon peoples. The Ijaws on the other hand allow no interval and many families were seen with only a year spacing the children. The former policy is adopted to allow the women more freedom to follow their occupation and also because of the long period of suckling. Women often refuse to cohabit with their husbands during the interval, and unless he has other wives, he frequently patronises harlots. This tends to spread gonorrhœa.[3]

Referring to the great differences in the average number of pregnancies per woman in the various districts he said:

It is difficult to explain the varying fertility on the basis of disease alone, as Abeokuta, Cameroons Forest and Arogbo have probably a high and comparable incidence of gonorrhœa. In the Cameroon Hill area venereal disease is practically unknown. A possible explanation is on the basis of diet, those places with a higher protein diet having a higher fertility, e.g., the people in Arogbo eat large quantities of fish, the Cameroons hill people have good hunting grounds, and Abeokuta has ample meat for sale in the markets. Probably both disease and diet play their parts.[4]

As regards miscarriages he stated:

European estimates state that roughly 12 per cent. of pregnancies result in miscarriage.

The extent of infection with syphilis is unknown, but it is believed not to be great. Other causes of miscarriage are probably over-indulgence in sexual intercourse, continuous hard work without proper food, chronic malarial infection and intercurrent epidemic disease.[5]

Finally he said in his Summary:

Fertility would appear to be more closely determined by an adequate diet rich in animal protein than by disease. The general impression is that fertility in most areas is declining, and this is supported by the evidence given by village elders; but until wider and more exact information is available, no definite assertion can be made.[6]

Some evidence is given that gonorrhœa is playing an important role in lessening fertility. Exact figures are not obtainable and this subject deserves further study.[7]

---

[1] Northern Nigeria, *Medical Report 1912*, p. 48.
[2] This startling statement is not confirmed by the pregnancy figures obtained at the Medical Census.
[3] *Census of Nigeria, 1931*, vol. vi, p. 8.   [4] Ibid., pp. 8–9.
[5] Ibid., p. 9.   [6] Ibid., p. 30.   [7] Ibid., p. 31.

The Medical Report for 1931 explained the differences in the incidence of sterility and miscarriages between the Hill Tribes and the Forest Tribes of Southern Cameroons as follows:

> In the former venereal diseases and yaws are almost absent and in the latter yaws is universal and gonorrhœa is extremely prevalent.[1]

A Memorandum on 'General Condition of the Hausa People' prepared by Dr. McCulloch for the information of a newly formed dietetics committee contained the following passage:

> There is . . . a poor fertility rate. The slightest consideration would make this extremely probable. The house servants of Europeans have a steady income, must keep themselves clean, and they marry under better conditions than the average of their class. It is very rare to find a Hausa servant who has several children and I believe that the majority are childless. This is partly because polygamy is not encouraged in the household of Europeans, and so the man has not as many chances of proving his fertility as he would in his own proper environment. But there is experimental proof of the lack of fertility. . . . The millets and milk (the vast bulk of the Hausa food) are thus clearly shown to be deficient in Vitamin E, the fertility vitamin. There is evidence that mineral deficiency also plays a part in the low Hausa fertility rate but this is not yet proven. One extremely interesting observation is this. Bakori is a town which is famous for its fertile women. Many women have as many as nine children, and it is a matter of pride to them. Bakori is built in a grove of kuka trees and the people certainly have more kuka leaves to eat per head than any other town which I know. The kuka leaf is one of the richest leaves in calcium which I have yet analysed. On the basis of the edible portion, just as put in the stew, it contains over 2·0 per cent. calcium. This result is consistent for leaf from all over Northern Nigeria. As mineral deficiency can most certainly prohibit fertility this observation is being followed up by experimental feeding.[2]

Subsequent reports stated:

> 1934. From a station in the Southern Provinces a Medical Officer . . . writes as follows:—
>
> . . . Towards the end of pregnancy native medicine is given in increasingly large doses and is responsible for the high abortion, miscarriage and still-birth rate. The large quantities of this medicine given during delayed labour, is a serious menace to delivery and is only too frequently the cause of death of both mother and child.[3]
>
> Northern Provinces. Fertility is high on the Plateau ten to fifteen pregnancies being normal. . . . Goitres are very frequent amongst Rukuba females (sixty per cent of females over puberty) and relatively rare among men. It would seem that the goitres are associated with excessive sexual activity as the Rukuba until recently had as many as five or six miscarriages before marriage and as many normal pregnancies afterwards.[4]
>
> 1935. The notoriously prodigal habits of the Tiv farmer combined with abnormal fecundity in the clans occupying the area have resulted in the farming of every inch of land, so that it is hardly surprising that the area is now almost entirely bare of trees.[5]

Venereal Diseases. The official reports do not say much about the influence of venereal diseases upon fertility, but for several decades they have left no doubt that in vast areas such diseases have greatly impaired

---

[1] Nigeria, *Medical Report 1931*, p. 12.   [2] Ibid. *1932*, pp. 109–10.
[3] Ibid. *1934*, p. 29.   [4] Ibid., p. 99.
[5] *Report on Northern Provinces 1935*, p. 18.

the health of the natives. In his first annual report on Northern Nigeria Sir Frederick Lugard said:

I am also considering with the Principal Medical Officer means of checking the prevalence of venereal disease.[1]

The Medical Reports from Northern Nigeria for 1904–18 contain the following passages:

1904. Venereal diseases have been very prevalent amongst natives, syphilis being widely distributed throughout the northern and eastern parts of the Protectorate.[2]

1905. Venereal disease is still very prevalent.[3]

1906. Venereal diseases are very prevalent in the Northern Provinces [of Northern Nigeria]—gonorrhœa is commoner near the coast, but syphilis is met with much more frequently in Bornu and the Provinces along the Northern border.[4]

1907. Syphilis. The Northern States returns give a constantly increasing number of cases of this disease which is said to be principally imported through the Arab traders and their caravans.[5]

1908. Syphilis. As in former years the north eastern part of the Protectorate has furnished the greatest amount of sickness from this disease.[6]

1910. Mosquito-borne, fly-borne and tick-borne diseases, water-borne diseases and leprosy need to have constant war waged against them: as is the case throughout West Africa. But, in the Mahommedan part of Northern Nigeria—by far the most important area of the country—I can say, without the slightest fear of contradiction, that venereal diseases work more havoc than do all the diseases, mentioned above, put together. In the Sudan, venereal diseases have always followed the track of the trader particularly the track of the Arab trader. The European has been familiar with them at home, and, consequently, they do not appeal to his imagination so dramatically as do the so-called tropical diseases; but they are all the more dangerous on this account.

Syphilis and Gonorrhœa account for a larger number of the numerous cases of blindness—generally ascribed by the Natives and non-medical Europeans to Small-pox . . . .

Our advent has stopped slave-raiding and internecine wars, which, formerly, were the great hindrances to increase of population; but it has made practically the entire country safe for the trader, and he carries venereal disease wherever he goes.

So far as we know, the Pagans, in their hitherto isolated communities, are practically free from venereal diseases . . . . Our advent has brought security to the Pagan, as well as to the Mahommedan trader. The Pagan does not altogether realise this yet; but, when he does, he will emerge from his ancient seclusion and will mingle with other races. The inevitable result of this will be the spread of venereal diseases among the Pagan . . . .[7]

1911. Syphilis. The cases treated were 531, of which 8 were fatal.

Gonorrhœa. Of this disease 1,452 were treated. The cases of those two diseases which come under treatment are but as a drop in a bucketful of water. Knowledge, together with private conduct and public action—which must neither be fussy nor meddlesome—based thereon, affords the only means of effectually dealing with this scourge.[8]

1912. Venereal Diseases. The figures are slightly in advance of last year. I am of opinion that through the aid of the repeated efforts of the Medical and Sanitary Officers, who are continually pointing out to the native community simple measures

[1] *Colonial Reports, Northern Nigeria 1900–1*, p. 27.   [2] Ibid. *1904*, p. 143.
[3] Ibid. *1905–6*, p. 105.   [4] Ibid. *1906–7*, p. 49.
[5] 'Report on the Public Health of Northern Nigeria 1907', p. 93.
[6] 'Northern Nigeria Medical Report for 1908', p. 99.
[7] Senior Sanitary Officer in Northern Nigeria, 'Medical Report 1910', p. 135.
[8] Idem, *Medical Report 1911*, p. 44.

for the prevention of such diseases, a diminution in the incidence may be anticipated in the near future.[1]

Kwongoma Division (Southern Portion) of Niger Province. The Pagans . . . are free from venereal diseases; and although they are taking to trading freely, they remain jealous of the sanctity of their women, so far as outsiders are concerned.[2]

As reported before, venereal diseases, Pagan areas excepted, are deplorably common everywhere, and there are places where the people who do not suffer from some form of venereal disease are in the minority.[3]

1913. Venereal Diseases. To judge from statistics this class of affection is increasing, but, as in the case of smallpox, figures are misleading. That this nature of disease is widespread we recognise, but I do not consider it possible to offer an opinion as to its decrease or otherwise; nor can any perceptible change be reported with accuracy for a considerable time yet to come.

It is satisfactory to know that the subject of venereal disease is receiving every attention in the Provinces, and that natives, outside those in Government employ, receive the most careful treatment, when presenting themselves at the hospitals or dispensaries.

Although both Medical and Political Officers are continually urging upon the various chiefs the common rudimentary measures for preventing the spread of this disease, progress on a large scale can scarcely be hoped for under existing laws, which do not admit of compulsory notification with forcible isolation.[4]

1914. Several instances were recorded of headmen having refused the entry to their towns of strangers known to be suffering from venereal disease.[5]

1915. Syphilis and gonorrhœa are common diseases all over Nigeria except in the pagan districts of the North, where the natives are reputed not to intermarry with those of other tribes.[6]

Venereal Diseases. This section continues to receive constant attention. The principle of having the market and the caravansary outside of each new town is steadily followed, and in various regions the Natives of old-established towns are making the change voluntarily.

Most of the pagan Natives remain free from these diseases, and they are always encouraged to preserve their aloofness from the non-pagan peoples, so far as everything but trade is concerned. Educational efforts against the spread of venereal diseases are in constant practice.

It may be that, when the normal routine shall have been completely re-established after the war, it may be possible to render many syphilitics non-infective by greatly extending the use of salvarsan; but too much must not be expected from this, for there will be a perpetual stream of imported infection from without the Nigerian borders.[7]

1916. Venereal diseases . . . are very prevalent and unfortunately are frequently regarded by the patients themselves as of no consequence.[8]

---

[1] Acting Principal Medical Officer, ibid. *1912*, p. 13.
[2] Ibid., p. 48.   [3] Senior Sanitary Officer, ibid., p. 59
[4] Principal Medical Officer, ibid. *1913*, p. 15. See also ibid., p. 12: 'For certain reasons I considered it desirable, in the early part of the year, to call the attention of Medical Officers to the necessity of reporting, confidentially, cases of this nature occurring among Europeans (whether Government Officials or others), and that patients themselves should be led to understand that the confidential nature of any such reports would be strictly respected. I adopted this method with a view to minimising, if possible, instances of concealment of the diseases. To this may be assigned the difference in the figures shown in the accompanying tables as compared with previous returns. For obvious reasons I do not use the term "increase" over previous years. Nor do I think there is an increased incidence among Europeans in the Northern Provinces; but I certainly consider that the above arrangement, whilst affording statistics of perhaps greater value, tends to more satisfactory results as regards treatment.' The total number of Europeans treated for gonorrhœa increased from 2 in 1912 to 32 in 1913 and the total number treated for syphilis from 1 to 10; see ibid. *1912*, pp. 28–9, *1913*, p. 26.
[5] Nigeria, *Medical Report 1914*, p. 17.   [6] *Colonial Reports, Nigeria 1915*, p. 20.
[7] Nigeria, *Medical Report 1915*, p. 17.   [8] Northern Provinces, *Medical Report 1916*, p. 5.

After the termination of the war, the venereal diseases will have to be tackled after a radically new fashion, if any extensively effective, racial result be aimed at.[1]

1917. Venereal Diseases constitute a subject which leaves little or nothing of new to be said. To wipe them off curtly is not to belittle their significance; for, in the opinion of the present reporter, they constitute by far the gravest problem of the country, whether regarded from the general medical, or the more restricted sanitary, point of view. Little progress is being, or can be, made in fighting against them under existing conditions. The mortality from small-pox is great; but that from Venereal Diseases is probably greater still, if, as they ought to be, abortions, still-births, infantile mortality and barrenness directly traceable to them be counted as mortality. . . .

The plague is too general for the Medical Officers, posted to Stations or Districts, to hope to make much impression on it: although, of course, their work in their own Stations and the educative influence which they are able to diffuse around them do a certain amount of good. But the Medical Officers are tied too securely to their own Stations by their statutory duties to be able to chase the venereal diseases so widely disseminated among the indigenous natives.

Although nothing which is stated in this report and which has been written in former reports, touching the prevalence of this disease, is exaggerated, it must not be forgotten that their incidence is along the trade routes and in the towns thereon: the rural people are just about as simple and pure in their lives as are the rural people at home. . . .

It is to be hoped that, after the war, a considerable number of medical officers may be seconded for duty away from recognised stations: at great indigenous Native centres exclusively. This is absolutely necessary, if solid and enduring progress be aimed at: and it ought to be; for the indigenous races concerned constitute, on the whole, a fine people and a people eminently worth preserving.[2]

1918. Venereal Diseases maintained their prominence among the diseases of the country.[3]

During the same period it was reported from Southern Nigeria:

1908. Syphilis is, as always, rare in the Western Province, which has been protected to a very considerable extent, in my opinion, by the Lagos Bar. In the other two Provinces—especially the Eastern—where the Ports permit the entry of ocean steamers, the disease is as usual in evidence.[4]

1909. I am afraid Syphilis and Gonorrhœa are on the increase although the figures in the Tables do not indicate it.

So many cases are treated privately that no reliable statistics can be obtained about either of these diseases.

Practising privately as I do I can form a very good opinion.[5]

1912. Venereal diseases appear, unfortunately, to be making headway. More patients present themselves for treatment but they do not sufficiently realize, in spite of instructions given, the serious consequences which may result both to themselves and others of the community from not continuing that treatment to its proper termination, and as a result the disease is propagated.[6]

1915. Venereal Disease is extremely common. The returns do not in any way represent the true incidence of syphilis and gonorrhœa in the community.[7] If the

---

[1] Northern Provinces, *Medical Report 1916*, p. 18.

[2] Senior Sanitary Officer, Northern Provinces, in Nigeria, *Medical Report 1917*, pp. 140–1. See also ibid., p. 135.

[3] Northern Provinces, *Medical Report 1918*, p. 21. See also ibid., p. 9; Nigeria, *Medical Report 1917*, p. 113.   [4] Principal Medical Officer in Southern Nigeria, *Medical Report 1908*, p. 3.

[5] Acting Principal Medical Officer, ibid. *1909*, p. 4. See also ibid. *1911*, p. 18.

[6] Ibid. *1912*, p. 24.

[7] See also ibid. *1913*, pp. 9, 39; Nigeria, *Medical Report 1914*, p. 76; Southern Provinces, *Medical Report 1916*, p. 18; Nigeria, *Medical Report 1917*, p. 23; Southern Provinces, *Medical Report 1918*, p. 22.

truth were known it would probably cause a very unpleasant surprise. An investigation into the extent to which these diseases are responsible for the high infant mortality, their effect on the birth rate, etc., would make an interesting study.[1]

There is no doubt that gonorrhœa is very prevalent indeed, and is the primary cause of a considerable proportion of other affections, for which relief is sought. Syphilis, from all one can gather, is distinctly spreading.

. . . At Calabar syphilis is said to be very prevalent, and not only there but in all the Cross River Districts.[2]

1916. Venereal disease is very common, especially in the open ports.[3]

From 1919 on the Reports often discuss at the same time the prevalence of venereal diseases in the whole of Nigeria and in the Cameroons.

1919–21. There can be no question but that these are the scourge of West Africa. . . .

The paucity of our Medical Staff, coupled with the ineradicable customs of the people, inasmuch as the relations of the sexes are concerned, mitigates against their eradication.

A Medical Officer practising in the Niger Delta writes:—

'Gonorrhoea amongst the native population, together with all its innumerable and remote effects, constitutes the curse of this part of the coast and urgently calls for drastic and far-reaching measures of attack.

'Compared with this disease, especially in its bearing on women and on the race, other diseases constitute but the trivial round, the daily task of medical practice. . . .'[4]

The Venereal Diseases.—These constitute the gravest medical and sanitary problem of Nigeria. But it is not necessary to deal with them at length here, so fully has the state of affairs been set forth in former reports. It is necessary, however, to remind all the authorities concerned of the very strict limitations to which anti-venereal workers are restricted in Nigeria. The first limitation is the small staff of workers, the percentage of medical men to population, compared with the same proportion in England, is something like what a micro-organism is to an average insect, and all know how inadequate is anti-venereal machinery even in England. Furthermore, the anti-venereal worker in England is working among his own people, and he is, in this respect, in an altogether different world from that occupied by his fellow worker in Nigeria, who is lost in the multitude, and confused in his understanding by the congeries of divergent races, tongues, manners and customs and religions, which faces him. His problem does not consist in the acquisition of greater knowledge of the venereal diseases, especially in their more obscure manifestations: his difficulty is to get at the mass of gross material which hits him in the eye everywhere. Were the necessary funds available—it is hopeless to waste time dreaming about the possibility of this under existing conditions—a systematic course of action could be planned forthwith; for it is inconceivable that any medical man in Nigeria does not know perfectly well what the work done ought to be for the next century to come. For all really practical purposes, the only genuine prospect (so far as Syphilis is concerned anyhow) is the probability of gradual attenuation to extinction taking place: it has taken place in the world before.[5]

1922. Venereal diseases . . . appear to be as widely disseminated in the southern section of the British Mandatory Territory of Cameroons as they are in Nigeria. Much of the labour on the Plantations, e.g., is rendered ineffective for prolonged periods by chronic sores and ulcers which will not heal. . . .[6]

1923. Cameroons. Syphilis. This disease is very prevalent in the southern part of the territory, in the plantations, and on the seaboard. The northern districts appear to be fairly free and cases recorded leave room for doubt as to whether there may not be confusion with yaws and even perhaps with lupus. . . .

[1] Nigeria, *Medical Report 1915*, p. 39. [2] Ibid., p. 50.
[3] Southern Provinces, *Medical Report 1916*, p. 7. [4] Nigeria, *Medical Report 1919–21*, p. 11.
[5] Ibid., p. 63. [6] Ibid. *1922*, p. 53.

In Bamenda the medical officer comments on the incidence of recorded cases being mainly females . . . .

The infection has probably been introduced by the trade routes and by three classes, viz., traders, labourers, and, in the northern part, African troops.

Gonorrhœa is very prevalent in Victoria, Buea, Kumba and Mamfe and to a less extent is found in Bamenda. . . . The sources of the spread of this disease are very similar to syphilis, viz.: Victoria as a seaport: Buea and Kumba from imported labour: Bamenda by troops and traders and Mamfe mainly by extension from Akunakuna on the Cross River. As contributory causes of the spread of venereal diseases may be mentioned:—

(a) The high price of wives.

(b) The transfer of wives from one purchaser to another owing to failure in paying the instalments of the purchase price.

(c) Desertion of wives brought into the country by traders and others.

(d) Unattached women traders, and

(e) Wandering prostitutes.[1]

1924. Venereal Diseases.—The actual number of cases coming under treatment represents but a small fraction of the actual prevalence. One can only guess at the latter but it is a fairly reliable guess to say that both Syphilis and Gonorrhœa are widespread throughout the country.[2]

1925. Syphilis. This disease is very prevalent especially in the coast towns in the south, along rivers and is reported to be widely distributed and very prevalent in the Northern Provinces in the Mohammedan areas. . . .[3]

1926. Syphilis is reported to be increasing in parts of the Northern Provinces but not in the Southern Provinces. . . .

In the minds of a certain proportion of the lay community all large ulcers, which are very common, are syphilitic and this gives rise to reports of the prevalence of syphilis which are incorrect.[4]

Cameroons Province. There is considerable divergence of opinion as to the prevalence of venereal diseases. The Medical Officer, one plantation manager, and the District Head, Victoria, are of opinion that venereal diseases are common. On the other hand the majority of the plantation managers state that these diseases are not common. It is quite likely that many cases are never reported and labourers endeavour to cure themselves with native medicines.[5]

1927. Venereal Diseases.—These diseases still remain common throughout both the Northern and Southern Provinces. The consensus of opinion of the medical officers is that gonorrhœa is more common than is usually realised, while the incidence of syphilis has been exaggerated. Under present conditions it is impossible to do more than guess.[6]

1928. Venereal Diseases.—These diseases are very common throughout the colonies, particularly so in the Northern Provinces; gonorrhœa is the most prevalent but syphilis is also widespread, cases being only seen in the advanced stages as the African does not appreciate the seriousness of either disease.[7]

1929. Generally speaking, the gonorrhœal infection rate is high in the Southern Provinces and the syphilis rate is low whereas in the Northern Provinces the syphilis rate is high. The actual gonorrhœa rate is, however, difficult to obtain. The African regards this disease as trivial and seldom comes voluntarily to the European Medical Officer for treatment except in case of complications. Native remedies are universal and, consisting as they do of decoctions containing essential oils together with instructions to imbibe large quantities of fluid, are reasonably effective. The attitude

---

[1] 'Medical Report on Mandated Territory of British Cameroons', *Report on the Cameroons 1923*, p. 80.

[2] Nigeria, *Medical Report 1924*, p. 8. See also ibid., p. 48; *1923*, p. 25. According to ibid. *1924*, p. 7, syphilis appeared to be on the increase.

[3] Ibid. *1925*, p. 23.   [4] Ibid. *1926*, p. 15.   [5] *Report on the Cameroons 1926*, p. 47.

[6] Nigeria, *Medical Report 1927*, p. 19.   [7] Ibid. *1928*, p. 15.

of the African towards gonococcal infection is illustrated by a belief which is common among uneducated classes of the Yoruba people that a man cannot propagate his species until he has suffered from this disease.[1]

1930. An interesting situation exists in Bauchi Emirate of Bauchi Province where the Mohammedan Hausa-Fulani town is heavily infected with syphilis whereas the surrounding pagan population suffers greatly from yaws.[2]

1931. A similar instance to that reported from Bauchi in the report for 1930 has been recorded from Adamawa Province where syphilis and gonorrhoea are common diseases in the Fulani towns, whereas they are rare amongst the surrounding pagan tribes. Yaws is common amongst these pagans and is known by the Fulani as 'pagan syphilis'.[3]

In the Cameroons an interesting comparison is made in that report [on the Medical Census] between the hill people and the forest people. In the former venereal diseases and yaws are almost absent and in the latter yaws is universal and gonorrhœa is extremely prevalent.[4]

Southern Provinces (Medical Census). Gonorrhœa.—No exact information is available owing to the nature of the examination.[5] In various places during the census adult males were questioned on this point and after confidence was gained roughly 50 per cent. admitted having or having had the disease. Hospital statistics and experience amply demonstrate that the disease is widespread. The possibility of the existence of Schistosoma hæmatobium infection must be guarded against.

The indirect evidence in favour of widespread gonorrhœa is not satisfactory owing to the lack of any standards. So far as could be learned, gonorrhœa is almost non-existent in three villages in the Cameroons hill area. These villages are comparatively isolated in a secluded valley and have comparatively little communication with trade centres. In addition, these people are not allowed by tribal law to cohabit with any other of the near-by clans of the Assumbo where V.D. does exist.[6]

No case of gonorrhœal ophthalmia was seen in any area, and in Lagos, where the incidence of gonorrhœa is known to be high, ophthalmia is represented by a few cases annually in about 3,000 births. Iritis is not common, only five cases being seen. A possible explanation of the low incidence of ophthalmia may be the comparatively rapid deliveries, labour normally lasting not longer than 5–6 hours.

Gonorrhœa is an old disease and was known long before the European occupation of Nigeria. The Yoruba have many remedies for it, most of which aim at being either diuretic or purgative. It is doubtful if any permanent cures are effected, although the immediate symptoms are improved. In many places there is an objection to irrigation treatment on the grounds that it impairs virility.

Syphilis.—Information on this disease is even more vague than on gonorrhœa, but it is believed that it is not so prevalent. Serum tests are useless owing to the association with yaws in most areas and diagnosis is made on clinical grounds. The figures obtained seem to indicate that syphilis is more common in Yoruba country than elsewhere. This is partly to be expected owing to closer and longer contact with Europeans at the seaports and to the large number of Hausa traders who are found all over Yorubaland. The Hausa is believed to be generally infected. Experienced practitioners in Lagos seaport state that aortic lesions are becoming more frequent.

Parasyphilitic lesions are very rare and true G.P.I. or locomotor ataxia are never seen. Crude cerebral syphilis is occasionally seen.[7]

1935. Little progress can be said to have been made in the elimination of syphilis which is rampant through, particularly, the northern Emirates of the Northern Provinces. Funds and staff have not permitted an intensive campaign which is much required in Bornu and almost equally in Sokoto.[8]

[1] Ibid. 1929, p. 18.　　[2] Ibid. 1930, p. 13.　　[3] Ibid. 1931, p. 12.　　[4] Ibid.
[5] See Census of Nigeria, 1931, vol. vi, p. 2: 'With regard to disease condition the examination included the head, the upper part of the trunk and the extremities. No examination was made of the genital area.'
[6] Ibid., p. 22.　　[7] Ibid., p. 23.　　[8] Nigeria, Medical Report 1935, p. 5.

1936. Venereal disease is very common throughout the whole country. The incidence of gonorrhœa is excessive everywhere, but syphilis is most prevalent in the north where yaws is comparatively rare. Apart from improvement in the hospital and dispensary facilities for the treatment of gonorrhœa and syphilis, little progress has been made in dealing with the venereal diseases problem.[1]

. . . venereal diseases, especially gonorrhœa, are a common cause of ill-health in the Cameroons. . . . An effort is being made to persuade managers of plantations to encourage labourers to bring their families with them. This is a very desirable stabilising factor since facilities for early and continuous effective treatment of individual cases will have little effect in reducing this social evil unaided by improvement in social conditions.[2]

1937. Were it not for the very widespread incidence of venereal disease it could be said that the health of the population (apart from epidemics) is good. We can at present only guess at the number of persons suffering from venereal disease and from leprosy but there are indications that the number is very great.[3]

1939. Among African in-patients the commonest group was that of venereal diseases . . . . This is a deplorable fact and one which calls for a mass attack on this scourge.[4]

1940. Among African in-patients we must again note the pre-eminent place taken by venereal disease with a percentage of 11·9. This is more than double the number of cases of malaria.[5]

We contemplate at the end of hostilities putting into force massed organised attacks on the more prevalent diseases on lines analogous to the Sleeping Sickness Campaign. Yaws and venereal diseases call for concentrated action. The Senior Medical Officer, Kano Division, points out that of all cases diagnosed in that division during the year 27·5 per cent were cases of venereal disease,—and he draws attention to the steady increase: e.g., in Kano Station itself the percentage of venereal cases was 8·1 per cent in 1930, 16·6 per cent in 1935 and 22·1 per cent in 1940. It is obvious from these figures that only mass treatment on a thoroughly organised basis can hope to succeed.[6]

1941. A study of the reports from the Medical Divisions and an examination of the African Hospital statistics both of in-patients and out-patients reveals the great seriousness of the venereal disease problem in Nigeria. Of all admissions to African hospitals in the north over 6,800 were the result of venereal disease, a figure thrice as high as that for malaria which was 2,200. The figures for malaria and venereal disease in the south are approximately equal—2,218 and 2,128. Cases treated as out-patients totalled 56,000.

When it is remembered that the hospitals are used by only a fragment of the population it is realized that these numbers give no indication of the full extent of these diseases, but do show that the problem is a vast one and one that must be tackled on a big scale.

As in certain areas there is only one Government Medical Officer to a million people it is obvious that the hospitals can never adequately handle this problem.

Added to this is the fact of re-infection—probably the most serious aspect of the problem.

As soon, therefore, as the present crisis passes, a mass attack on venereal disease must take precedence over many other problems.[7]

1942. Of all cases treated in hospitals in the north 16·3 per cent were cases of venereal disease. In the south the same group only accounts for 4·7 per cent.[8]

The work of the hospitals alone will never stamp out this curse and only by mass attack can any lasting results be obtained.[9]

---

[1] Nigeria, *Medical Report 1936*, p. 6.   [2] *Report on the Cameroons 1936*, p. 118.
[3] *Report on Northern Provinces 1937*, p. 4.   [4] Nigeria, *Medical Report 1939*, p. 4.
[5] Ibid. *1940*, p. 6.   [6] Ibid., p. 4.
[7] Ibid. *1941*, p. 3.
[8] Ibid. *1942*, p. 3.   [9] Ibid., p. 5.

1943. Venereal Disease. This problem remains one of the most serious in the country. In the Hospitals in the Kano Division the number of cases is 18 per cent of total cases of disease, and more than double that of Malaria. Of mines selected labour examined in the Kano Division 7 per cent were found to be suffering from syphilis and 9 per cent from gonorrhoea. In the Zaria area, it is reported that many fewer than was expected were infected. The Senior Medical Officer, Victoria, writes 'The rate of dissemination of venereal diseases especially of gonorrhoea is becoming increasingly difficult to discern owing to the acquisition and sale of private stocks of sulphapyridine and similar compounds by unlicensed dealers. Police and Customs confiscations point to an alarming increase in home-medication. If cures were being maintained by this method of treatment the number requiring hospital treatment would show a corresponding decline—but this is far from being the case.'

Only mass treatment will eradicate these diseases. Hospital cases seldom remain long enough to assure cure.[1]

1944. Venereal Disease. This problem remains as serious as ever, particularly in the Northern Provinces. Hospital statistics show an increase in the number of syphilitics treated. Cases of gonorrhoea remained about the same. In the more northerly parts of the country particularly those adjacent to the great trade and pilgrim routes to the Sudan, the incidence of venereal disease is very high among all sections of the population. At Maiduguri hospital, Bornu, 43 per cent of all African patients were infected. In Hadeija and Kano Province, nearly 50 per cent of all hospital cases had venereal disease. The Senior Medical Officer, Kano, reported that this was an hospital general index of the high incidence of venereal diseases all over the Province. The problem is complicated by the fact that patients in the North only attend for treatment when their lesions are severe. Troop movements during the war years have aggravated the risk of spread of infection.

Inadequate treatment and resistance to sulphapyridine through illicit sale of this drug especially in the South is leading to dissemination of resistant strains of gonorrhoea. Mass treatment, particularly in rural areas, would be the only satisfactory solution of the problem.[2]

General Mortality. Data concerning general mortality are more scanty still (outside Lagos) than those concerning fertility, as the special investigations (Medical Censuses, &c.), while covering births and child deaths, did not inquire into mortality of adults. The only available figures, therefore, are those obtained through the, very imperfect, current registration in a few areas. These registration returns have been shown in the preceding section. They are valuable inasmuch as they indicate the enormous fluctuations in mortality.[3] But they are far too unreliable to convey a correct picture of the general level of mortality. The Government Statistician drew the following conclusions from the birth and death-rates ascertained for 1930:

It is clear that unless the birth- and death-rates among the rural are less than among the urban population, to an extent which is hardly credible, there must be a considerable failure to report births and deaths in the rural areas. The higher crude birth- and death-rates are, therefore, more convincing than the lower, and I am inclined to regard a crude death-rate of about 40–50 per 1,000 per annum as a rough guide to mortality in the Northern Provinces in non-epidemic years.* The

* 'There is, assuredly, some failure to report births and deaths even in towns. This failure is partially offset, so far as birth- and death-rates are concerned, by the omissions in the Census counts, so that the crude rates in towns may be fairly close to the truth.'

---

[1] Ibid. *1943*, p. 6.   [2] Ibid. *1944*, p. 5.
[3] See, for example, the effects of the epidemics of influenza (1918), cerebrospinal meningitis (1923–4), and relapsing fever (1924) in Kano City.

figure of 30 per 1,000 for the 1930 death-rate in Kano City may reflect improved sanitary conditions, or immigration, or both.[1]

As a rough figure . . . the expectation of life in the Northern Provinces may be regarded as about 20 to 25 years.[2]

The Government Statistician was certainly right in distrusting the death-rates of the rural districts. But his treatment of the fourteen urban areas for which data are available is somewhat arbitrary. He rejected the death-rates of the eight towns where the rate was below 30; he attributed the rate of 30 of Kano City with 89,162 inhabitants to exceptional conditions and based his conclusions for the Northern Provinces as a whole (with 11·4 million inhabitants) on the 1930 death-rates of five towns with 19,709 inhabitants. His opinion that the death-rate in the Northern Provinces was about 40–50 per 1,000 in non-epidemic years would seem unacceptable under any circumstances.[3] But it is particularly difficult to see how it could possibly be reconciled with his statement that the population of the Northern Provinces had increased in the period from October 1926 to April 1931 by 25 per 1,000 per year.[4]

[1] *Census of Nigeria, 1931*, vol. i, pp. 35-6.

[2] Ibid., p. 36. He estimates the expectation of life of males in the villages of the Katsina Emirate covered by the Intensive Census at 22 years; see ibid., pp. 37, 40.

[3] He gives the following explanation for the amazing fact that according to his computations the mean expectation of life at birth in the Northern Provinces is only about half as long as in the unhealthy overcrowded town of Lagos:

'If there is anything in the comparative estimates of the death-rates in Lagos and in the Northern Provinces countryside, the latter is greater than the former by about 80 per cent. Has this always been so, and is the difference racial, the Yoruba being essentially longer-lived than the Hausa, Fulani, Munshi and Nupe, or is the lower death-rate a simple consequence of the improved sanitation of Lagos ? Dr. J. G. S. Turner's review of the Medical history of Lagos . . . shows that prior to the vaccination campaign in 1905, and the introduction of a piped water supply in 1915, death-rates of 35 and 40 were common. The death-rates in Lagos 20 or 30 years ago were, in fact, similar to those obtaining at the present time in the Northern Provinces. It is true that 20 to 30 years ago they may have been even higher in the Northern Provinces than they are now. In other words, there may have been a universal fall in the death-rate of a secular kind, unrelated to environmental changes. The evidence however, seems to show that the lower mortality of the Yoruba Male in Lagos is due in part to his better environment and in part to the continued recruitment of the Lagos population from the healthier young men and women of the rural areas. Whether the Yoruba has a greater racial longevity in addition, might be tested by analysing separately the deaths of Hausas in Lagos. As, however, the total Hausa population of Lagos in 1931 was only 3,693 (2,032 Males, 1,561 Females), even the deaths in a period of three years would give only a rough estimate of mortality.' (Ibid., pp. 40-1. The total Hausa population was actually 3,593; see ibid., vol. iv, p. 21.)

It should be noted in this connexion that the Government Statistician computed for 1932 a mean expectation of life of 46·7 years for all males of Lagos as compared with 40·1 years for the Yoruba males of Lagos in 1931!

Recent official reports have even gone so far as to say that 'the evidence provided by the Intensive Census in the Katsina Emirate and by the Medical Censuses indicates that the expectation of life at birth is from 22 to 25 years for persons living in the rural areas in Nigeria' (*Colonial Reports, Nigeria 1932*, p. 10; *1933*, p. 13; *1934*, p. 14; *1935*, p. 12; *1936*, p. 12; *1937*, p. 13; *1938*, p. 14). It evidently has been forgotten (1) that the estimate of the expectation of life in the Katsina Emirate, owing to the lack of birth and death figures, was necessarily based on quite arbitrary assumptions, (2) that the expectation of life for the rural areas of the Northern Provinces was not based on the Medical censuses but on the 1930 death rates for five towns with 20,000 inhabitants, and (3) that the Government Statistician never suggested that his figures should represent conditions outside *Northern* Nigeria.

[4] Since he considers immigration as negligible, the birth-rate should have been about 65-75, even if epidemic years are left out of consideration.

In other cases death records have led to an underestimate of mortality. Thus, when in Ijebu Province in 1927 the death-rate appeared to be 14, it was accepted as genuine since registration was considered to be complete.[1] But, on the whole, opinions concerning the death-rate were based on impressions rather than on facts. This must certainly have been true of the following statement in the Northern Nigeria Blue Book for 1908:

The native death rate varied but little throughout the year, and owing to the absence of any serious epidemics was much lower than in any year since the Protectorate was established.[2]

As a matter of fact, until the late 1920s most official reports stated that 'the general health of the natives' was 'good'[3] or 'satisfactory'[4] or 'normal'[5] or 'much as in recent years',[6] while in a few exceptional cases it was said that the general health of the natives compares unfavourably with previous years.[7] Some Medical Officers, of course, were aware that their contacts with an utterly heterogeneous population of many millions spread over an enormous area were far too scanty to permit the making of any such sweeping statements, but the satisfaction about the general health of the natives vanished only when the officials began to realize the spread of sleeping-sickness and the deficiencies in the diet.

An interesting general statement concerning European influence upon the vitality of the natives was made by Governor H. Hesketh Bell in his annual report on Northern Nigeria for 1909:

It is the object of the Government to maintain the prestige and increase the authority of the native rulers in every legitimate direction, and there is reason to believe that many of them feel a genuine appreciation of our methods and policy. On the other hand, it must never be forgotten that we are 'protecting' a people in spite of themselves, and that almost every improvement and development initiated by us is absolutely opposed to all their instincts and traditions. Though we have relieved the Hausa peasant from the grinding tyranny of his Fulani oppressor, and have freed the primitive pagan from the fear of a ruthless slave-master, it should be remembered that we are imposing on all these people a monotony of existence that stifles their spirit of adventure, and that we are forcing on them a wearisome sense of security that is taking all the sport and variety out of their lives.[8]

Some official reports on Southern Nigeria deal with the health conditions of individual tribes.[9] The 1910 Colonial Report for Southern Nigeria says with regard to the Yoruba that 'excellent eugenic marriage laws have

---

[1] See p. 654 above.   [2] Northern Nigeria, *Blue Book 1908* R, p. 2.

[3] See, for example, *Colonial Reports, Northern Nigeria 1904*, p. 143, *1906–7*, p. 48; Northern Nigeria, *Blue Book 1909* R, p. 2; *Colonial Reports, Nigeria 1921*, p. 8, *1922*, p. 9; Nigeria, *Medical Report 1923*, p. 19.

[4] See, for example, Northern Nigeria, *Blue Book 1910* R, p. 2, *1911* R, p. 2, *1912* R, p. 3, *1913* R, p. 4; Nigeria, *Medical Report 1922*, p. 7, *1926*, p. 13.

[5] See, for example, *Colonial Reports, Nigeria 1915*, p. 19.

[6] See, for example, Southern Provinces, *Medical Report 1916*, p. 6.

[7] See, for example, Nigeria, *Medical Report 1917*, Southern Provinces, p. 10.

[8] *Colonial Reports, Northern Nigeria 1909*, p. 3.

[9] References to the health of native tribes in Northern Nigeria are extremely scanty. The Colonial Report for 1903 says (p. 7) that 'the Jogwadawa Fulanis are credited with being the healthiest people in the country'. The 1918 Medical Report for the Northern Provinces discusses (p. 13) 'a progressive deterioration of physique and loss of stamina during the last three generations' in the town of Yola.

helped him to keep down disease and maintain unimpaired the physique of his race'.[1]

Dr. E. J. Wyler, on the other hand, two years later discussed the poor physique of the Ibo in the Udi District of the Central Province:

An observer of the Ibo people of this district cannot fail to be struck by their general poor standard of physique, their incapacity as carriers and workers, and their obvious disinclination for bodily exertion.

As testimony to their indolence and poor physique, I cite the following remarks of Mr. G. H. Fleming, Chief Surveyor, Onitsha–Udi Railway Survey, whose wide experience of West African negroes lends additional emphasis to his views. In a letter to me, from which he kindly allows me to quote, he says:—

'I have had the following different tribes working for me during the past 12 years: Timinies and Mendies (Sierra Leone); Kroo, Waussa and Tantis (Gold Coast); Yoruba, Haussa, and Ibo (Southern Nigeria). Out of the whole lot I find that the Ibo is the most indolent.

'The Mendies are the best workers as labourers; a man will do double the amount of work in one day that an Ibo will do. The Ibo is also a poor carrier.'

It would be of no small interest to know precisely to what extent the tribes mentioned by Mr. Fleming are infected by the hook-worm, for it seems not improbable that the saturation of the inhabitants of this district with Ankylostoma infection, bringing in its train grave systematic changes, probably produced by actual toxic absorption . . . and other minor changes, such as digestive troubles, which, though transient, are none the less productive of considerable disability, is largely responsible for some of the tribal characteristics of Ibos in these parts, and that these features are not ascribable either to Malaria or bad food *per se*.[2]

A more recent report spoke unfavourably about the health of the Hausa.

The Hausa are not a healthy race. Parasitism is widespread, the most important parasites being malignant malaria, intestinal amoebæ, intestinal worms, schistosomes, and trypanosomes. It is difficult to imagine a native entirely free from all five of these parasites and the result is that there is a high morbidity rate. That the high rate of ill-health is only beginning to be realised is shown by the great numbers of the ailing who attend the 'bush dispensaries' from the moment that they are opened.[3]

The Medical Census report, speaking of the Cameroons Forest Zone, points to 'the poor physical condition of the people, defective feeding, and poor sanitary conditions',[4] and says of the Southern Provinces in general:

The life of the native is such that only the fittest survive, and many are injured in the fight against disease. From birth he is assailed by epidemic and endemic disease, and unless he succeeds in building up immunity with speed his ultimate fate is certain. It is clear that his immunity to most infections is high and one is repeatedly amazed at his recovery from serious pyogenic infection.[5]

[1] *Colonial Reports, Southern Nigeria 1910*, p. 35. The Government Statistician also suggested that the Yoruba may have 'a greater racial longevity' than some other tribes; see *Census of Nigeria, 1931*, vol. i, p. 41.

[2] Southern Nigeria, *Medical Report 1912*, p. 44. See also Nigeria, *Medical Report 1923*, p. 28 (quoted below).

[3] Ibid. *1932*, p. 109.

[4] *Census of Nigeria, 1931*, vol. vi, p. 17; see also ibid., p. 14. The 1928 Report on the Southern Provinces (p. 23) had said with regard to Cameroons Province as a whole: 'Medical reports do not speak favourably of the health of Africans of this province.' For details concerning the health of the plantation labourers in Cameroons Province see Kuczynski, *Cameroons and Togoland*, pp. 300–32.

[5] *Census of Nigeria, 1931*, vol. vi, p. 16.

The war demands revealed many defects in the physique of young men. The reports on the Western Provinces (formerly part of the Southern Provinces) said:

1940. The high percentage of recruits who have been rejected on medical grounds[1] is an indication of the amount of work required to be done in the medical and health field. Better water supplies, better living conditions, a more scientifically balanced diet, and, perhaps above all, child welfare work, are among the first essentials.[2]

1943. It became increasingly difficult to find recruits of the required standards of literacy and physique but our record improved in the latter part of the year when these standards were lowered and the Military opened a 'conditioning school' where by proper feeding, Health and Beauty exercises and medical treatment men who would otherwise have been rejected were brought up to standard. A 'circus' of tradesmen trained in the Army toured the Western Provinces in order to demonstrate the value of such training and popularise recruiting.[3]

The 1943 report on the Northern Provinces stated:

Recruiting for the Army and the Minesfield has revealed a far higher percentage of medically unfit males than was thought even by the pessimistic to exist. True, men were rejected on account of 'tissue paper' scars on their limbs: but remembering the most frequent cause of these scars and the large numbers of farmers incapacitated year after year by guinea-worm a line of post-war development is clear: the provision of good water supplies all over the north is the first great need to be met.[4]

The 1944 report on the Labour Department said with regard to the 'men selected under the Compulsory National Service Regulations for service in the mines':

. . . it may have come as a surprise to the authorities that when selected men were medically examined in their own districts with a view to conscription about 50 per cent of the so-called able-bodied men were rejected as unfit for heavy manual labour through one physical disability or another.[5]

---

[1] See also *Report on Western Provinces 1942*, p. 1.

[2] *Reports for the Northern, Western, Eastern Provinces and Colony 1940*, p. 16.

[3] *Report on Western Provinces 1943*, p. 2.

[4] *Report on Northern Provinces 1943*, p. 2. The need for improved rural water-supplies was emphasized, for example, also in *A Ten-Year Plan of Development and Welfare for Nigeria 1946*, p. 43:
'The present position regarding Rural Water Supplies is most unsatisfactory. In the drier districts of the north there is always an extreme water shortage. It is not unusual during more than half the year for people there to have to walk 12 miles each way in order to obtain a gallon or two of water of very inferior quality, which is almost always heavily contaminated with guinea worm and other water-borne diseases and pests. At certain times of the year the amount of water available is so small and of such bad quality that water consumption per head is seriously below the proper minimum. There are places where guinea-worm infection is as high as 75 per cent of the population. The consequent loss of productive effort is enormous.
'The water shortage in the North is, perhaps more apparent than in the South, because in the southern districts there is a very much heavier rainfall. Nevertheless, the source of potable water in these areas is usually just as unsatisfactory, and during the dry season the quality and quantity are acutely bad.
'From the existing records of population (now estimated at something over 22,000,000) it is considered that not less than 18,000,000 of the rural population have inadequate and mostly unsatisfactory water supplies.'

[5] *Report on Department of Labour 1944*, pp. 3–4. Even those who were not rejected showed a high morbidity and mortality. See ibid.; see also Nigeria, *Medical Report 1943*, p. 21: 'The sickness rate among selected labour proved to be even higher than was expected. In the dry season there was much pneumonia and epidemics of bacillary dysentery, cerebro-spinal meningitis and smallpox. At the height of the wet season conditions were even worse.' As regards venereal disease among selected labour, see p. 691 above.

Deficiencies in diet, as stated above, have attracted attention only in recent years. But food shortages have, of course, been discussed also in former times. Famines seem to have been very severe in Northern Nigeria in 1902–4 with great loss of life.[1] In 1907 it was stated concerning Yola Province:

The famine which devastated the country so terribly in 1904 still continues among some of the pagan tribes, but has been alleviated very largely by the abundant crops of the Fulani, and assistance, in the shape of corn, rendered by the Government. It is estimated that fully 50 per cent. of the riverain pagan tribes in the Gongola Valley have died from starvation, and numbers more are still scattered over the country in search of food. To quote two cases: The towns of Banjeran and Shillem originally contained 8,000 and 4,000 apiece, but now only 336 and 676 respectively; such is the effect of a bad famine caused by the destruction of the grain crops by aphis.[2]

Famines in Northern Nigeria were also reported on for 1914 and 1927,[3] but until about 1923 the European officials saw no food problem for the natives of Nigeria in normal years. The Deputy Director of Sanitary Service, in describing the slump period after the First World War, said:

In most regions, the people are well nourished; they are well clad, and increasingly well clad; the professional beggar is as flourishing as he ever was, and knows nothing about any slump; and the appearance of the happy children simply inspires the observer with regret that there are not more of them; for any idea of adequate provision for them not being available, does not enter his mind. . . . Nigeria is one of those happy countries in which none need starve who is willing to work: those genuinely unable to work need not starve either; so habitually charitable are, as a whole, the people of most races in the country. The only thing which causes starvation is famine due to drought, or some other natural cause of failure of the crops: and then people are liable to starve whether they be industrious or not. Were this not the case, the equivalent of the British soup-kitchen (run by Government) would be in evidence everywhere at present; whereas it has been quite unnecessary to contemplate even the probability of the necessity for any such expedients. Even as things are, the number of well-fed idlers going about, who are manifestly not earning their own living, yields ample evidence of the fact that the slump does not mean local scarcity. . . . here we have no problem equivalent to that of feeding and clothing school children at home; . . . a 'Class III' physical standard is seldom or never traceable to food deficiency; and . . . in tackling the local public health everywhere outside of the Government Gaols, the question of the public food supplies, may be completely and safely ignored; for there is no considerable section of the community habitually hovering over, or just under 'Subsistence Level'.[4]

The Medical Report for 1923 was apparently the first one to mention the regular recurrence of food shortage in certain regions.

Over a considerable area of the country there is usually a food shortage between January and July. This is more noticeable in the populous areas east of the Niger inhabited by the Ibo and Ibibio tribes and deficiency œdema can be found amongst them before the new crops are available. The physique of these peoples is also inferior to that of the Yoruba for example. The storage of yams is a much more difficult problem than with maize, guinea corn or rice. Encouragement might be given in

---

[1] See *Colonial Reports, Northern Nigeria 1904*, pp. 6–7, 48, 52, 79; *1905–6*, p. 61.

[2] Ibid. *1906–7*, p. 23.

[3] See Nigeria, *Medical Report 1914*, pp. 11, 12, 20, 28; *Report on Northern Provinces 1927*, pp. 16, 41, 43–4.

[4] Nigeria, *Medical Report 1919–21*, pp. 54–5.

suitable areas where the yam is the staple article of food for the introduction of cereal crops as has been tried in the case of rice at Ogoja in the Southern Provinces.[1]

But the report for 1929 was apparently the first which referred to 'the important questions of dietetic deficiencies in African races'.

These are almost certainly of the utmost importance in leading to a lowered resistance to all forms of infection. The work of Dr. McCulloch has proved that the grain-eating people of the Northern Provinces suffer from a serious deficiency of protein and of salts, and also probably of vitamins. Plans have been made to enable research into dietetic deficiencies to be carried out. Work has been commenced at Kaduna, in the gaol, and will be continued at Katsina.[2]

The 1931 Medical Census report for the Southern Provinces said:

Over most of Southern Nigeria the food taken is largely carbohydrate and fat with as much protein as the individual can obtain. In the creek region the position is reversed, and protein is available in excess of requirements in the form of fish. In general it may be said that the adult native makes the fullest possible use of local foodstuffs and that his diet is not well-balanced owing to the shortage of animal protein. All available sources are tapped for protein, e.g., bush meat, fish (fresh or dried), crabs (land and sea), shrimps, flying ants, locusts when available, crocodile, dogs, cats and even rats. Since the widespread introduction of firearms a good deal of the wild game has been indiscriminately slaughtered and in most places in the Southern Provinces it is now difficult to obtain. There is no restriction as to season, and any meat, irrespective of size or condition, is taken.

Domestic cattle cannot be secured in the south owing to trypanosomiasis, and the fact that grazing grounds are not available.[3]

Subsequent Medical Reports said:

1931. Cases of various forms of deficiency diseases are reported from time to time and it is probable that much ill-health must be caused by a lowered resistance to infections caused by unbalanced diets.[4]

1934. The school population of Katsina were examined . . . . The results of the examination indicate that approximately fifty per cent of pupils attending the schools in Katsina are below normal in nutrition and physique. This percentage was fairly constant from the elementary school to the higher college. It was noted that there was some improvement in the middle school in those who had been resident for more than one year.

A tour was made amongst some of the pagan tribes in the Plateau and the percentage of boys and girls reaching normality was from seventy to eighty per cent. The pupils in the school examined showed the lowest percentage of normals (seventy per cent) and the highest percentage of well below normals. It is probable that there is some selection of children of poor physique in the schools.

It is difficult to attribute the difference in nutrition between the two groups to any other cause than diet. Venereal disease is not an important factor until adult life and sanitary conditions and worm infestation are similar in the two groups. It seems that the pagan superiority is due to their lack of scruple as to their source of protein and also to the fact that beniseed forms part of the daily diet. Beniseed contains a good protein and it is interesting to note that this is one of the few areas where red palm oil is available and appreciated.[5]

---

[1] Ibid. 1923; p. 28. See also ibid. 1925, p. 28.   [2] Ibid. 1929, p. 14.

[3] Census of Nigeria, 1931, vol. vi, p. 12. For details in the areas covered by the Medical Census, see ibid., pp. 12–14, 29, 54–5, 84. See also ibid., vol. v (Medical Census Northern Provinces), pp. 10, 44–8, 50–1.

[4] Nigeria, Medical Report 1931, p. 6. See also 1932, p. 7, and ibid., p. 110 (quoted p. 683 above).

[5] Ibid. 1934, p. 99.

1937. Conditions indicating various degrees of avitaminosis and of lack of balance in the constituents of the local dietary continue to be observed in many areas . . . .[1]

1938. Avitaminosis, particularly among members of the labouring class and in poorer school children, is common, and the signs usually observed are geographical tongue, perleche, phrynoderma and, in more advanced cases, retrobulbar neuritis. The common dietary deficiencies are in the south, protein, and in rural areas in the Northern Provinces protein and green fresh food.[2]

1939. Gross avitaminosis is not frequent, but varying partial deficiencies in dietaries are common in different parts of Nigeria and no doubt have an influence on the incidence and course of such endemic conditions as ulcers, leprosy, etc.[3]

In a pamphlet *Food in Relation to Health* the Government stated:

The examination of Nigerian diets shows that the main shortage is in good quality protein, in mineral salts and in vitamins. Generally speaking there is enough food except after years of deficient rainfall. In the north at the end of the long dry season there may be an actual shortage of the staple foods. . . . Wherever ample protein food is available one finds good physique, as amongst the Fulani and the Ijaws; where protein foods are scarce one finds poor physique as amongst the Cameroon Forest region tribes. The remedy for this state of affairs is difficult as it involves raising the economic standard of the people, educating them in the proper use of foods, and inducing them to grow new and improved crops. . . . The poor peasant and the labourer in towns get on the average less than half of the protein recommended by the League of Nations Experts. It is by no means certain that European standards apply to the tropics, but, even with greatly modified standards, their consumption is still deficient.[4]

The high mortality in children in Nigeria is partly due to the lack of an adequate diet and all experts agree that milk is absolutely essential. The value of milk in the north is realised, but the supply is so poor and the yield per cow so low that only small quantities are available. The adult members of families usually take the major part of the supply available and do not subscribe to the belief that children and women come first.[5]

The Committee on Nutrition in the Colonial Empire reported:

In normal years there are no marked signs of deficiency disease; but in the north in famine years beriberi is commonly found. There is a patchy distribution of goitre especially among women in whom the incidence may be as high as 60 per cent. Dental disease is exceedingly common; and there is a generally low resistance to anaemia, pneumonia, tuberculosis and leprosy. Anxiety is being caused by a pellagroid condition, described as optic neuritis, occurring among the boarding-school population and unemployed labourers of the cassava-eating people in the Southern Provinces (Lagos). . . . The vital capacity of the Nigerian native is much below European standards. In growth rate and sports record he lags about 10 per cent. behind.[6]

On the whole, town dwellers are better fed than the ordinary village peasants; but the bush Fulani, a nomadic cattle-owning people, have better physique than the settled Hausa whose diet is known to be deficient.[7]

But the war may have affected the nutrition of the town dwellers more than that of the village peasants. The Medical Report for 1940 states:

The Medical Officer of Health, Lagos, reports that cases of avitaminosis have been more commonly found than usual among day scholars especially in elementary

---

[1] Nigeria, *Medical Report 1937*, p. 22. See also ibid. *1936*, p. 37. See, furthermore, *Report on Southern Provinces 1937*, p. 70 (Warri Province): 'Malnutrition is widespread, particularly in the Isoko District, where proper food is difficult to obtain.'   [2] Nigeria, *Medical Report 1938*, p. 19.
[3] Ibid. *1939*, p. 9.   [4] Nigeria, *Food in Relation to Health*, pp. 3–4.
[5] Ibid., p. 4.   [6] *First Report*, Part II, p. 40.   [7] Ibid., p. 39.

schools. This may possibly be due to the rise in price of local foodstuffs consequent on greater demands for available supplies. There are indications in other reports that in some places the price of essential foodstuffs may go beyond the reach of the poorer classes. Though no gross examples of food deficiency diseases have been reported, there is abundant evidence in the way of perleche, etc., of the general poor quality of living.[1]

The 1943 report on the Northern Provinces said:

It is probable that the requisitioning of grain from the harvests of 1942 and 1943 has stimulated the farmers to increase their farms. There are, indeed, evident signs that in the latter half of the year people in the North had more to eat than they had had for some years. If they can be persuaded to keep up this standard of effort when there is no more need for corn to be requisitioned and will apply the extra production of grain to improving their own diets much good will result indirectly from this operation, as distasteful now to the chiefs as it is distressing often to the peasant.[2]

But the Medical Report for the same year was less favourable.

In the Northern Provinces, the late rains caused a food shortage which affected the health of the population. In Katsina province this was regarded as the responsible factor for an increase in the death rate and a decline in the birth rate.

Eighty tons of iodised salt were distributed in the Tiv Division where goitre is very prevalent, but larger quantities are required.[3] . . . Meat has been very scarce and expensive in most areas, and the cost of essential foodstuffs has increased.[4]

The 1944 report on the Northern Provinces found the current position likewise unsatisfactory.

It is [by] the improvement of farming methods and consequently the production of more nutritious food that post-war planning can confer the greatest benefit upon the predominantly agricultural population of the Northern Provinces, after the essential better supplies of water have been provided. The improvement of methods of irrigation to enable a greater amount of the man-power that is available during the long dry season to be usefully employed will be specially valuable and will provide means for introducing variety into what appear in varying degrees in different localities to be monotonous and probably deficient diets. It is disturbing to think that on a survey of school children in a native administration elementary school in Ilorin Province, which is regarded as particularly well supplied with foodstuffs, only nine out of seventy could be classed as 'healthy'.[5]

I shall now supplement these notes on mortality and health in general by a brief historical survey of the incidence of some specific diseases.

Smallpox. No other disease among natives has been discussed so much in the early official documents from Nigeria as has smallpox, and epidemics of smallpox still take much space in the reports of recent years.

The reports on the Niger Coast Protectorate which cover the period 1891–9 tell of the erection of many smallpox hospitals[6] and of many more or less severe outbreaks of smallpox.[7] A few quotations may illustrate the position.

---

[1] Nigeria, *Medical Report 1940*, p. 10.   [2] *Report on Northern Provinces 1943*, p. 2.
[3] See also Nigeria, *Medical Report 1944*, p. 13.
[4] Ibid. *1943*, p. 13. See also *Report on the Department of Labour 1944*, p. 4.
[5] *Reports for Northern, Western, Eastern Provinces and Colony 1944*, pp. 2–3.
[6] See *Report on the Niger Coast Protectorate 1891–4*, p. 6; *1894–5*, pp. 15–17.
[7] See ibid. *1894–5*, pp. 14, 17, *1895–6*, p. 109, *1896–7*, pp. 7, 12, *1897–8*, p. 6; *Colonial Reports, Niger Coast Protectorate 1898–9*, p. 11.

1896. Owing to the prevalence of small-pox, which is endemic throughout the Protectorate, it would be advisable to erect permanent contagious diseases hospitals in each district to replace the temporary ones (built of mud and wattle) now in use, and which require constant repairing to keep them habitable.[1]

1897. The only European hospital in the Protectorate is situated at Old Calabar. At out stations there are only native contagious hospitals, all of them being principally for the reception of cases of small-pox, a disease, I regret to say, very prevalent throughout the entire territories . . . .

Of course, the small-pox throughout the territories is to a great extent due to the extremely dirty and insanitary condition in which the towns and villages in the interior are kept. It is, however, very uphill work to attempt to remedy this, but all the officers of the Protectorate do what they can to effect improvement in this direction.[2]

1899. This disease is a most terrible scourge throughout the territories; and when epidemics occur inland the natives die by thousands, all general intercourse among the tribes is stopped, civilizing influences make a retrograde movement, and trade suffers very considerably.[3]

The Governor of Lagos Sir William MacGregor, in a Memorandum on Vaccination read on 16 November 1903 before the Board of Health, said as regards the Ekiti people:

Formerly they were harassed, and plundered, and their population was devastated and sold into slavery, by Ilorin and Ibadan. Their great towns are more than half empty. Now they have and enjoy peace, which they appreciate, but they suffer terribly from the dreaded scourge of small pox. Some of the chiefs of that district informed me that their towns are afflicted by small pox about once in four years. That would seem as regards frequency to be above the average. It is, however, only too clear that every now and then some town is decimated by this dire disease. No wonder that the helpless people try to propitiate it as if it were a destroying demon. Far and wide this country is covered by altars of some kind or other, erected by a people deeply imbued with religious sentiment, at which they try, in a way that is, in these days of scientific sanitation, most pitiful to see, to appease this deadly monster that is eating into the heart of the population.[4]

References to outbreaks of smallpox in the last 40 years and to progress of vaccination are to be found in hundreds of official reports. I must confine myself to quoting here some statements which, taken together, may convey a picture of the situation.

1903. Southern Nigeria. The number of cases of small-pox throughout the Protectorate has, in the opinion of the medical authorities, decreased considerably within recent years.[5]

Northern Nigeria. Systematic vaccination in Northern Nigeria has been commenced during the year. . . .

The native population is at present (with the exception of 174 cases successfully vaccinated during the last three months, and those who have already suffered from the disease), entirely unprotected from small-pox. On account of the enormous size of the Protectorate, and the relatively small staff available for these duties, it will be many years before much can be done to vaccinate even a small proportion of the inhabitants, but in view of the frequency of outbreaks of this disease, it is of the

[1] *Report on the Niger Coast Protectorate 1895-6*, p. 117.
[2] Statement by R. Moor, Commissioner and Consul-General, ibid. *1896-7*, p. 12. See also ibid. *1897-8*, p. 6.
[3] *Colonial Reports, Niger Coast Protectorate 1898-9*, p. 12.
[4] *Government Gazette Colony of Lagos*, 28 Nov. 1903, p. 593.
[5] *Colonial Reports, Southern Nigeria 1903*, p. 27.

utmost importance that active measures should be taken to protect, at any rate, those natives who live in the vicinity of European stations.[1]

1906. Northern Nigeria. The Fulani herdsmen are said to practise a form of inoculation with cow-pox virus, having discovered that this renders them immune from small-pox. Other natives inoculate with small-pox virus.[2]

Southern Nigeria, Central Province. . . . smallpox has again proved a terrible scourge chiefly in the Benin and Kwale Districts. Natives, however, are beginning to appreciate the benefits of vaccination, and of isolation of infected cases.[3]

1910. Northern Nigeria. Small-Pox is endemic; but takes the Epidemic form, somewhere, every year.

Only a small proportion of the cases comes under medical observation. This is not surprising, when one remembers that the Medical Officers, actually in residence, work out at one to an area twice the size of the Crown Colony of Jamaica.[4]

In some places it is very difficult to get cases to vaccinate: as the people have religious or other prejudices against it. In others, many more vaccinations could easily be done, were it not that, Syphilis being so common, the Medical Officers were afraid to practise arm-to-arm vaccination.[5]

1911. Southern Nigeria. Small Pox occurs sporadically in most of the places here and occasionally, in Towns in out-lying Districts, takes on an epidemic character, partly, in some cases it is to be feared, by artificial means on the part of the Small Pox Juju Priests. The Prohibition of the Worship of the Small Pox Juju in 1907 has been of considerable effect in the main towns, many Priests have been compelled to remove, the places of worship have been closed and in some instances the Priests themselves have been heavily fined.[6]

Northern Nigeria. This endemic disease, which assumes the epidemic form annually, is very prevalent throughout the Protectorate; but, as things are at present, it is impossible to compile accurate statistics of it. It generally begins to show itself in the second half of the dry season and, as a rule, dies down when the rainy season has seriously set in.

Constant efforts are directed towards the breaking down of the prejudice against vaccination which is harboured by many natives.[7]

1912. Southern Nigeria. As in last year, no large epidemic of Small Pox occurred. It is hoped that this may be a permanent result of the greatly increased number of vaccinations performed during the year.[8]

Northern Nigeria. Vaccination is steadily appealing to an ever increasing number of the people.[9]

1914. Southern Provinces. Small-pox, like many other diseases known in this country, does not seem to produce such ravages among the people as it did some years ago, and is no doubt being partially prevented from doing so by the general but very gradual improvement in sanitation throughout the land.[10]

Northern Provinces. Until what time it shall have become possible to get several Medical Officers apart for vaccination and sleeping sickness investigation exclusively, little permanent progress can be hoped for in the direction of stamping out small-pox.

That this time may come soon is the earnest hope of every enlightened friend of this country, for there can be little doubt that small-pox effects as much havoc among the natives now as war and slave-raiding used to.

The reason for this is not far to seek; the ending of slave-raiding and internecine wars has rendered intercommunication safe and has encouraged the spread of communicable disease.[11]

[1] *Colonial Reports, Northern Nigeria 1903*, p. 38.   [2] Ibid. *1905–6*, p. 105.
[3] 'Report, Central Province 1906', p. 331.
[4] Northern Nigeria, 'Medical Report 1910', p. 137.   [5] Ibid., p. 138.
[6] Southern Nigeria, *Medical Report 1911*, p. 18.
[7] Northern Nigeria, *Medical Report 1911*, p. 42.
[8] Southern Nigeria, *Medical Report 1912*, p. 8.
[9] Northern Nigeria, *Medical Report 1912*, p. 55.
[10] Nigeria, *Medical Report 1914*, p. 75.   [11] Ibid., pp. 19–20.

1915. Northern Provinces. The effect of the attenuation of the Medical Staff was marked in the case of vaccinations . . . .[1]

1916. Southern Provinces. There was . . . an increase in the number of cases of small-pox, although no actual epidemic occurred; shortage of staff and the consequent impossibility of prosecuting vaccination with the usual vigour probably accounts for the increase.[2]

Northern Provinces. . . . the actual number of vaccinations performed and the number of successful vaccinations had diminished as compared with the previous year.

The reason is not far to seek: during the greater part of the year, some of the stations to which Medical Officers are normally posted had no medical service at all; whilst others only enjoyed the services of Medical Officers intermittently.[3]

1917. Northern Provinces. There has been a very great increase in the number of cases of this affection, reports of outbreaks, which have resulted in a considerable mortality, having been received from almost every part of the country.[4]

1918. Southern Provinces. With the close of the war and the increase of staff every effort will be made to advance vaccination, which is one of the most potent means at our disposal for preservation of child life and population.[5]

Northern Provinces. The limitations incidental to the state of war persisted throughout the year: and the wide incidence of small-pox, which had been feared, was experienced in many regions.[6]

To get at this disease by vaccination has become progressively more difficult since the outbreak of War. . . .

The problem, now, is not how to induce the people to submit to vaccination: it is how to meet the earnest desire of the people to be vaccinated.[7]

1919-21. [A] notable event in the history of the public health of the period was a severe epidemic of Small-pox in the Southern Provinces: an epidemic which filled a large part of the Sanitary stage from the end of 1919 until well into the Spring of 1920. This epidemic was a very general one throughout the Southern Provinces; but it excited most anxiety around the Enugu district on the Eastern Railway System: the Enugu district being the centre of the coal-mining industry; a going concern of pronounced public importance, the integrity of which stood to be gravely threatened by an epidemic visitation calculated to hamper the recruiting of labour and the production of food-stuffs.[8]

---

[1] Nigeria, *Medical Report 1915*, p. 16.   [2] Southern Provinces, *Medical Report 1916*, p. 6.
[3] Northern Provinces, *Medical Report 1916*, p. 18. It is interesting to note in this connexion the changes in the numbers of vaccinations (see Southern Nigeria, *Medical Report 1909*, p. 3; Southern Provinces, *Medical Report 1918*, p. 21; Northern Nigeria, *Medical Report 1912*, pp. 55-6, *1913*, p. 13; Nigeria, *Medical Report 1915*, p. 16, *1917*, p. 139; Northern Provinces, *Medical Report 1918*, p. 21):

Provinces	1908	1909	1910	1911	1912	1913
Southern .	114,524	121,867	135,647	166,394	243,316	168,491
Northern .	..	..	..	5,494	10,112	13,916

Provinces	1914	1915	1916	1917	1918
Southern .	149,273	101,467	136,279	152,803	133,706
Northern .	17,504	10,612	9,314	9,147	11,035

The decrease in the number of vaccinations in the Southern Provinces in 1913 was 'possibly due to the fact that there has been no epidemic of small-pox during the year' (Southern Nigeria, *Medical Report 1913*, p. 9).
[4] Nigeria, *Medical Report 1917*, p. 113; see also ibid., pp. 117, 139. For extensive outbreaks in Southern Provinces see ibid., p. 22.
[5] Southern Provinces, *Medical Report 1918*, p. 21.   [6] *Colonial Reports, Nigeria 1918*, p. 19.
[7] Northern Provinces, *Medical Report 1918*, p. 20.   [8] Nigeria, *Medical Report 1919-21*, pp. 49-50.

1922. The usual outbreaks of Small-pox in epidemic form were experienced in numerous parts of the country.[1]

1925. Smallpox frequently occurs in small outbreaks in all parts of Nigeria, but the extent of such outbreaks is becoming noticeably less year by year.[2]

1926. Smallpox is becoming less common in the Southern Provinces where vaccination is compulsory and is constantly carried out.[3]

. . . in the Northern Provinces vaccination is not compulsory except in areas which, when necessary, have been declared 'Prescribed Areas' under Section 6 of the Vaccination Ordinance. In remote parts of the country where Europeans seldom visit, smallpox may be kept alive by the native practice of inoculation. The inoculation is ordinarily made on the back of the wrist from vesicle content from an actual case of smallpox which has occurred in the village. The mortality from inoculated smallpox is low, and in many cases the illness is not so severe as to keep sufferers at home, and in this way the disease is rapidly spread over considerable areas.

Inoculation is prohibited under the Vaccination Ordinance but it is extremely difficult to enforce this in remote parts of the country.[4]

1927. Smallpox is endemic in Nigeria, particularly in the Northern Provinces. During the early months of the year it was epidemic in the Plateau, Bauchi and Kano Provinces, and was particularly severe among the pagan tribes in these provinces. Smaller but considerable outbreaks occurred in Yola, Zaria, Bornu, Ilorin, Kabba and other provinces.

In the Southern Provinces small outbreaks were reported in the provinces of Abeokuta and Oyo, and at Ossidinge and Buea in the Cameroon Mandated Territory.

Nowhere in the Southern Provinces did the smallpox outbreaks become so extensive as they did in the Northern Provinces.

The principal reasons for this are delayed notification of early cases, particularly in the larger towns under Native Administration, and in consequence the disease has usually got well spread in the community before action can be taken. Vaccination is not compulsory in the Northern Provinces and except in the presence of a severe outbreak the people do not readily come up for vaccination.[5]

1928. Outbreaks of smallpox have been reported from many areas both in Southern and Northern Provinces, but as in previous years epidemics in the North have been much more severe than those in the South.[6]

1929. Smallpox has been prevalent especially in the Southern Provinces but the mortality rate has been low. . . . The Northern Provinces have been comparatively free.[7]

1930. Outbreaks of smallpox of varying severity were reported from various parts of Nigeria throughout the year.[8]

1931. Southern Provinces. Generally speaking smallpox cases are concealed in most areas until the outbreak reaches sufficient dimensions to frighten the people. This is done owing to the dislike of interference and of the vaccination campaign which usually follows. In some areas it is believed that inoculation is done by the medicine men to ensure a milder attack. The death-rate varies in different outbreaks, but in an attack of average severity, it is usually about 30 per cent. of all cases attacked. Some natives are believed to be skilled in treatment, but as the evidence is entirely given by natives it is unreliable. Native treatment usually consists in smearing the body with palm oil and local herbs ground to a powder.

It is difficult to suggest any safe figure for the extent of vaccination necessary to rid the country of its epidemics, but it is believed that with almost 60 per cent. of people protected little spread occurs.[9]

[1] Ibid. *1922*, p. 40.   [2] *Colonial Reports, Nigeria 1925*, p. 12.
[3] Nigeria, *Medical Report 1926*, p. 15.   [4] Ibid., p. 25.
[5] Ibid. *1927*, p. 28.   [6] *Colonial Reports, Nigeria 1928*, p. 34.
[7] Ibid. *1929*, p. 31.   [8] Nigeria, *Medical Report 1930*, p. 22.
[9] *Census of Nigeria, 1931*, vol. vi (Medical Census Southern Provinces), p. 20.

1932. The Northern Provinces suffered from an unusually severe and widespread visitation of smallpox, which reached epidemic form in many districts . . . .[1]

This recrudescence differed from the one in 1926–27 in that it was in the villages and rural districts that the disease was most prevalent, the large towns being practically unaffected. As the percentage of vaccination in the people of the towns is still low it is difficult to attribute this immunity to vaccination alone, and it is more likely to be the effect of past epidemics. For example, a rough count at Jos indicated that approximately fifty-five per cent. of the population examined had already had smallpox.

It is useless to anticipate that smallpox will be brought under control in the Northern Provinces until, by a process of education, the Native Administrations have been brought to realise that the remedy is in their own hands.

The obvious remedy is, of course, compulsory infant vaccination and it is hoped that the Native Administrations will eventually be willing to introduce this measure.[2]

There were no really extensive outbreaks of smallpox in the Southern Provinces . . . .[3]

1933. Smallpox continues to prove the most serious of the epidemic diseases affecting Nigeria as a whole.[4]

1936. Smallpox afflicted the country, chiefly Northern Nigeria, in a severe form during 1936. Apart from the regrettable loss of life, ulceration of the cornea with impaired vision or actual blindness is a common sequela of this disease.[5]

1937. Smallpox was again prevalent throughout the year and was again particularly severe in the Northern Provinces . . . .[6]

1938. This disease was again prevalent throughout the year and, while it was very severe in the Northern Provinces, the increase in cases in the Southern Provinces was even more marked . . . .[7]

The incidence of smallpox in the Northern Provinces is high and accounts for many deaths and much disablement. The efficacy of vaccination is generally realised and it is rare that a prejudice against it persists.[8]

1940. Northern Provinces. Smallpox is endemic and antipathy to vaccination is still general though weakening in some areas . . . .[9]

1941. Northern Provinces. Smallpox is still prominent but the results of vaccination have improved the situation. Fewer cases were reported from the Northern Provinces than in the Southern Provinces.[10]

1942. Northern Provinces. There was an increase in the number of smallpox and cerebro spinal fever cases: but as the result of continuous vaccination and special campaigns it is hoped that the number will fall.[11]

Nigeria. Extensive movements of population resulting from war requirements, e.g., military recruitment, and abnormal labour recruiting for increased mineral production, are no doubt largely responsible for the increased incidence of this disease.[12]

1943. Northern Provinces. There has been a great increase in the number of cases of smallpox in all areas of the Northern Provinces.[13]

Lagos. The Council's Health Department reports an unusually large number of cases of smallpox, some among soldiers and others from outside the Township.[14]

1944. The incidence of smallpox in Nigeria is still much too high and it is hoped that the plans made for epidemic teams will result in better control of this disease.[15]

---

[1] Nigeria, *Medical Report 1932*, p. 6.
[2] Ibid., p. 22. [3] Ibid., p. 21. [4] Ibid. *1933*, p. 17.
[5] Ibid. *1936*, p. 22. [6] Ibid. *1937*, p. 15. [7] Ibid. *1938*, p. 7.
[8] *Report on Northern Provinces 1938*, p. 3.
[9] *Reports for Northern, Western, Eastern Provinces and Colony 1940*, p. 3.
[10] *Report on Northern Provinces 1941*, p. 3. [11] Ibid. *1942*, p. 5.
[12] Nigeria, *Medical Report 1942*, p. 8. See also ibid. *1943*, p. 21.
[13] *Report on Northern Provinces 1943*, p. 4. [14] *Report on the Colony 1943*, p. 3.
[15] Nigeria, *Medical Report 1944*, p. 10.

1945. Epidemics of smallpox have continued to occur throughout the year and the incidence was highest in Katsina, Calabar, Plateau, Oyo and Bauchi Provinces.[1] Extensive outbreaks of smallpox . . . still ravage the country every year.[2]

Twenty-five years ago Dr. Blair said that 'although, in the Northern Provinces, endemic small-pox assumes the epidemic form at some places every year, those epidemics do not appear to be any more severe, or relatively larger, than those to which the Southern Provinces are accustomed'.[3] This may seem surprising as by that time several million vaccinations had been performed in the Southern Provinces as against about 100,000 in the Northern Provinces. But it must be realized that even in Southern Nigeria the minority that had been vaccinated was probably too small to hinder effectively the spread of the disease. The number of vaccinations in Northern Nigeria continued to be negligible for some years and became more extensive only in recent years.[4] This is probably the main reason why the prevalence of smallpox in the Northern Provinces has apparently not decreased in the course of time. The reduction of the incidence of smallpox in the Southern Provinces, on the other hand, may be due mainly to a quite satisfactory increase in the number of vaccinations.

As regards the mortality from smallpox, it is impossible to estimate it. The numbers of deaths notified in 1936–44 were 611, 527, 1,593, 653, 422, 210, 502, 1,234, and 816 respectively,[5] but it is obvious that these figures cover a very small percentage of all deaths from this disease.[6]

Sleeping-sickness. The menace of sleeping-sickness seems to have caused concern in Nigeria for the first time in 1906. In that year the Resident W. F. Gowers wrote to the Governor of Northern Nigeria Sir F. D. Lugard:

On my recent journey from Sokoto to Lokoja while proceeding on leave, I paid especial attention to the distribution of the tsetse fly along the route traversed, and I ventured to bring before Your Excellency's notice the facts observed by me.

The fly was found at three points on the road from Sokoto, within the Kontagora Province . . . .

[1] *Speech and Address by Governor Sir Arthur Richards to the Legislative Council 18th March, 1946*, p. 41.   [2] *A Ten-Year Plan of Development and Welfare for Nigeria 1946*, p. 69.
[3] Nigeria, *Medical Report 1919–21*, p. 61.
[4] The numbers of vaccinations in 1932–44 were as follows (see ibid. *1932*, pp. 21–2; *1933*, p. 17; *1934*, pp. 17–18; *1936*, p. 23; *1937*, p. 15; *1939*, p. 7; *1940*, p. 7; *1942*, p. 8; *1943*, p. 10; *1944*, p. 10):

	1932	*1933*	*1934*	*1935*	*1936*	*1937*
Southern Provinces	537,245	489,845	1,005,835	508,870	477,876	433,660
Northern Provinces	172,675	195,951	232,453	247,897	754,331	477,862

	1939	*1940*	*1941*	*1942*	*1943*	*1944*
Southern Provinces	} 1,226,268	} over 1,000,000	} 916,000	1,169,000	} about 1,500,000	} 1,137,212
Northern Provinces						

[5] See ibid. *1938*, p. 7; *1939*, p. 7; *1940*, p. 7; *1941*, p. 7; *1942*, p. 8; *1943*, p. 10; *1944*, p. 9.
[6] In 1932, 666 deaths from smallpox were recorded in the pagan hill districts in the Dikwa Emirate with a population of approximately 55,000 (see *Report on the Cameroons 1932*, p. 91). But it probably seldom occurs that in one year more than 1 per cent. of the population of a district die of smallpox.

If sleeping sickness should be introduced into Northern Nigeria it seems probable that it would spread over part of the country with the same disastrous rapidity as in Uganda, the means of its transmission being ready to hand. It seems to me, therefore, that an exact knowledge of the distribution of this species of tsetse is of considerable importance, and it is for this reason that I now take the earliest opportunity of laying before you the facts which I have observed. I would beg to suggest that officials should be warned that by omitting to take all possible precautions against being bitten by this fly they are exposing themselves to the possible risk of an infection far graver than that which is conveyed by the mosquito.[1]

The Principal Medical Officer of Northern Nigeria stated in his report for 1906:

Three cases of sleeping sickness were treated among the native troops, and it has been discovered that trypanosomiasis is fairly common in certain parts of the Protectorate, several cases having been diagnosed by gland puncture—the banks of the Benue and the Bassa Province being the parts of the country where most of the cases have been found. Unfortunately the particular district from which it is reported is not yet opened up, and it is only possible to pursue investigations in the immediate vicinity of the station. From enquiries made, it would appear, however, that sleeping sickness is well known to the natives, and has apparently always existed, without spreading to any considerable extent, but as the *glossina palpalis* has been found to be widely distributed along the Niger Valley, there is danger of it extending at any time. A native hospital, established by a native for the treatment of this disease by native remedies, has been discovered near Loko, and several cures are reported to have been effected.[2]

The official reports from Northern Nigeria for 1906–18 contain much information about the few cases of sleeping-sickness discovered each year and about the measures taken by the Administration to check the incidence of the infection.[3] I shall confine myself to quoting a few passages which show the opinions on the prevalence of this disease.

1907. Generally speaking, the natives say that sleeping sickness is nearly always fatal and is infectious. We have no evidence to prove the occurrence of epidemics such as occur in Uganda and Central Africa. The valley of the Benue is the most likely starting point of an epidemic if it does come. Specimens of Glossina palpalis and *G. Tachinoides* have been collected in this area.[4]

1908. There is ... considerable evidence to show that this disease is not uncommon on the Benue, but the portion of the Protectorate where it is said to occur has not yet been thoroughly examined. It is apparently confined to small areas and has never assumed the form of epidemics such as have occurred in East Africa.[5]

1909. From the reports from the various provinces, sleeping sickness—though only sporadic cases are now found—was responsible in the past for many deaths,

---

[1] *The Northern Nigeria Gazette*, 29 Sept. 1906, p. 114. See also *Colonial Reports, Northern Nigeria 1905–6*, p. 93.

[2] Ibid. *1906–7*, pp. 48–9.

[3] See *The Northern Nigeria Gazette*, 31 Oct. 1906, p. 124, 31 Dec. 1906, p. 145; 'Report on Public Health of Northern Nigeria 1907', p. 92; 'Northern Nigeria Medical Report 1908', p. 99, '1909', p. iii, '1910', pp. 134, 137; Northern Nigeria, *Medical Report 1911*, pp. 26, 31, 37, 40–1, *1912*, pp. 12–13, 37–8, 42, 44–7, 54–5, *1913*, pp. 8, 48–9; Nigeria, *Medical Report 1914*, pp. 11, 16–18, 27–8, *1915*, pp. 9, 12, 14–15; Northern Provinces, *Medical Report 1916*, pp. 5, 8, 16–17; Nigeria, *Medical Report 1917*, pp. 113, 137, 142; Northern Provinces, *Medical Report 1918*, pp. 8, 12–13, 18, 28, 48–9; *Colonial Reports, Northern Nigeria 1907–8*, p. 54, *1910–11*, p. 22, *1911*, pp. 19, 27, *1913*, p. 15; *Colonial Reports, Nigeria 1914*, p. 26, *1915*, pp. 20–21, *1916*, p. 27.

[4] 'Report on Public Health of Northern Nigeria 1907', p. 93. See also *Colonial Reports, Northern Nigeria 1907–8*, pp. 54, 65.

[5] 'Northern Nigeria Medical Report 1908', p. 99.

and, although native evidence as to the nature of epidemics is not always reliable, there is no doubt that the disease has existed for many years in Kabba, Bassa, Bautshi, Katagum, and Sokoto.[1]

1911. The alleged foci of Sleeping Sickness are not confined to one region, on the contrary, they are dotted all over the country in different and widely separated provinces . . . . The majority of Sleeping Sickness foci, actual or suspected, are in Pagan districts.[2]

From the point of view of public health, Sleeping Sickness is probably the most difficult problem in the country. All the intelligence collected up to date leads to the conclusion that the disease has always been endemic. Most intelligent natives in all parts of the country—many of them who have never been near an alleged Sleeping Sickness locality—know the disease well by reputation, and can, roughly, retail the symptoms of it; cases are often reported; and, more often than not, when a Medical Officer goes to investigate, he cannot diagnose a single case. Often, for example, old cases of paralysis, together with any case of debility which may be attended by lethargy, are apt to be mistaken for Sleeping Sickness and reported as such, chiefly because the reporters—in many cases quite honest and straightforward —have heard about the disease, without ever having seen a case.

Again, more frequently than is suspected by most, a certain village, having a grudge against another one, will spread a report that the people in the other village are dying of Sleeping Sickness, simply in order that those people may be stirred up by the white man.

Lastly, where Sleeping Sickness has been in existence once—no matter how long ago—the people retain a traditional and wholesome dread of it, and they go on ascribing any obscure malady to that disease for generations after it has died out.

Nevertheless, as Sleeping Sickness undoubtedly does exist in different parts of the country, it is impossible to discount any rumour of its appearance, however nebulous; but the nursery cry of 'wolf' being so frequently repeated, and human nature being what it is, there is always the possibility of a genuine outbreak being ignored some day.[3]

1912. In some parts of the country—the forest country in the south—many cases probably occur in villages concealed in dense kurumis, the existence of the villages themselves being unknown to all but their own inhabitants.[4]

1913. The true incidence of the infection will not be even approximately known until what time the Pagan regions shall have been effectively opened up and their inhabitants induced to invoke medical aid.[5]

1914. Nothing approaching a just estimate of the amount of human trypanosomiasis present in the country has ever been made; the data necessary for such an estimate have never been obtainable by the investigators available.[6]

1915. . . . it must be remembered that operations against trypanosomiasis are a constant war, in which the enemy is apt, unexpectedly, to change his venue from time to time; and, in this war, surprise attacks of trypanosomiasis will probably always be as unpreventable as are Zeppelin raids over Britain now.[7]

1917. During the year, two Europeans and seven Natives were treated for this disease. Probably every European case comes to light sooner or later: it can hardly be otherwise; considering the careful attention which Europeans receive, both in Nigeria and at home. But the number—seven—given for Natives is not of the slightest use for statistical purposes. Taking the safely conservative hypothesis that the incidence of Trypanosomiasis is twice as great among Native as it is among European communities, 16,000 is much liker the probable truth. Of course, it has to be remembered that, as a general rule, it may be taken as true that Trypanosomiasis is a disease

[1] Ibid. '1909', p. iii.
[2] Northern Nigeria, *Medical Report 1911*, p. 37. See also Northern Nigeria, 'Medical Report 1910', p. 135.
[3] Northern Nigeria, *Medical Report 1911*, pp. 40–1. [4] Ibid. *1912*, p. 54.
[5] Ibid. *1913*, p. 48. [6] Nigeria, *Medical Report 1914*, p. 18. [7] Ibid. *1915*, p. 15.

of remote backward tribes, that, in contact with such tribes, the proportion of Europeans to Natives is much less than it is in the case of the more highly civilised races among which the disease is rare, and that consequently, given the true inci- dence among Europeans, the incidence among Natives cannot be calculated by a simple rule of three; but, bearing in mind the cautious supposition on which it is based, the probability stated above is not likely to be very wide of the mark.[1]

1918. Trypanosomiasis is endemic in various regions and previously unknown centres are reported from time to time.[2]

Sleeping-sickness began to be discussed in Southern Nigeria at about the same time as in Northern Nigeria.[3] The Principal Medical Officer, Dr. Strachan, in his report for 1907, said:

Tse-tse flies abound in various parts of the Colony and Protectorate, in the usual habitat, along course of streams.

It is noteworthy that in spite of the occurrence in the Lagos Province of occasional cases of Sleeping Sickness furnishing the parasite causing it, and the prevalence of Tse-tse flies available to spread the disease, the latter is, actually, so rarely seen. Nearly all the cases which have occurred in the past have been persons who came from other territories or who had left Lagos (Western Province) and resided for a time in other Colonies or Provinces. It is said that cases have occurred in the past in the Hinterland but they have not been reported to Medical Officers.

In the Central Province a few cases have been reported, chiefly in and near Aboh, where I have captured Tse-tse flies. . . .[4]

Though so few cases of Sleeping Sickness have been seen, (five—one of which appears to be a very doubtful case—with three deaths), one must remember that, in the Eastern and Central Provinces, there must be many thousands of natives who have not been seen by any European—certainly not by a Doctor—and it may be, as the territory is more and more opened up, that it will be found that there is more Sleeping Sickness in the Eastern and Central Provinces of Southern Nigeria than at present seems to be the case.[5]

He wrote in his next report:

No case of Sleeping Sickness occurred in the Western Province. Two (one of which was doubtful) are reported from the Central Province, and one from the Eastern Province.

I may once again say that it is as satisfactory, as it is strange, that with the number of Glossinas existing in the Western Province, Sleeping Sickness is still so great a rarity there. As to the other Provinces I may repeat what I wrote in the last Annual Report—it is quite possible that there may be many cases of which we know nothing, and can know nothing until the country is more and more explored and opened up.[6]

Subsequent Medical Reports for Southern Nigeria said:

1909. No case of Sleeping Sickness was reported in the Western Province, one only, Agbor-Ishan District, in the Central and none in the Eastern.

[1] Nigeria, *Medical Report 1917*, p. 137. Thus, the basis of the first, and so far the only estimate of the number of natives suffering from sleeping-sickness in Northern Nigeria was as follows: Two Europeans were treated in 1917 for this disease; as the natives are 4,000 times as numerous as the Europeans and as the incidence of sleeping-sickness is at least twice as great among the natives, there are at least 16,000 natives suffering from the disease.

[2] Northern Provinces, *Medical Report 1918*, p. 18.

[3] 'It was in the year 1906 that the first case of Sleeping Sickness was met with by Mr. W. C. W. Eakin, of Qua Ibo Mission' (Southern Nigeria, *Medical Report 1913*, p. 62).

[4] See also 'Report on Central Province 1907', p. 290: 'Only one Station in the Province (Aboh) sends a return of cases of Sleeping Sickness . . . .'

[5] Southern Nigeria, *Medical Report 1907*, pp. 7–8.

[6] Ibid. *1908*, p. 5. See also ibid., pp. 26, 32.

This is a satisfactory state of affairs seeing how numerous Glossinae are.[1]

Glossina (in most cases palpalis) are reported from Ogoja, Obudu, Ikom, Afikpo, Opobo, Bende, Arochuku, Owerri, Degema, Calabar, Bonny.

There is serious cause for apprehension here. Up-country something may be done by clearing to diminish the danger of Sleeping Sickness establishing itself. But the presence of Glossina in the Mangrove swamps of the whole seaboard of the Eastern Province is a grave menace.

Let the fly but become infested and the spread of Sleeping Sickness will probably be rapid along the whole seaboard. Fortunately Sleeping Sickness is a very rare disease. We probably do not hear of all the cases but undoubtedly it is a rare disease at present.[2]

1910. The Glossina Palpalis is found everywhere in abundance.

The limits of the belt have not been found.

All the country is sleeping-sickness free; a doubtful case occurred in a native of Northern Nigeria. It was lost sight of unfortunately.[3]

1911. Although Trypanosomiasis is probably endemic in the Niger Delta only five cases have come under observation during the year and two of these were certainly imported from Fernando Po.[4]

1912. Western Province. There were no cases of . . . Trypanosomiasis.[5]

Central Province. Trypanosomiasis is, from the returns, rare; yet one cannot but be anxious as to the future, having in view the roads and railways which are being made and the increasing traffic from province to province, from administration to administration.[6]

Eastern Province. During the year 152 cases were reported, as against 1 in 1911. . . . In the Eket district 149 cases were found and three cases in the Ikotekpene district. . . . The mortality is said to be about 5 per cent. Dr. Foran informs us that the disease is reported to have existed in the district for perhaps centuries. From the evidence collected it appears to have been in those days more common and more fatal. In olden times, the natives, recognising it to be of an infective nature and very fatal, with the object in view of preventing its spread, passed certain 'laws' compelling those infected to isolate and segregate themselves. Nowadays this segregation is not enforced, the inhabitants recognising its lower mortality. Dr. Foran attributes this to the parasite being much reduced in virulence, having passed from one to another of the same tribe during a very long period of years; he is of opinion that the great majority of cases undergo spontaneous cure.[7]

1913. One case of this disease was reported in the Western Province, but none was found in the Central Province.

In the Eastern Province in the Eket District 376[8] cases were discovered, and one was reported from Calabar.[9]

From 1919 on, the Medical Reports, as a rule, deal simultaneously with sleeping-sickness in the Northern and Southern Provinces. Until 1927

[1] Acting Principal Medical Officer, ibid. *1909*, p. 7. See also ibid., pp. 22, 25, 37.

[2] Senior Medical Officer Eastern Province, ibid., p. 34. See also ibid. *1910*, p. 42.

[3] Senior Medical Officer Western Province, ibid. *1910*, p. 31. See also ibid., pp. 6, 22.

[4] Ibid. *1911*, p. 5. See also ibid., pp. 16, 28, 30–1.

[5] Ibid. *1912*, p. 32.

[6] Ibid., p. 33. The Senior Sanitary Officer of Northern Nigeria held the opposite view: 'The new Eastern Railway from Port Harcourt, the construction of which has now begun, will probably on the whole tend to the decrease of Sleeping Sickness' (Northern Nigeria, *Medical Report 1913*, p. 49).

[7] Southern Nigeria, *Medical Report 1912*, p. 35. See also ibid., pp. 7, 21–2, 39, 45, 128.

[8] The figure 736 in *Colonial Reports, Southern Nigeria 1913*, p. 24, is evidently a misprint.

[9] Southern Nigeria, *Medical Report 1913*, p. 27. See also ibid., pp. 7, 56–71, 138, 146–7; Nigeria, *Medical Report 1914*, pp. 55, 71, 94, 130, 144–55, *1915*, pp. 39, 47, 62; Southern Provinces, *Medical Report 1916*, p. 16; Nigeria, *Medical Report 1917*, pp. 10, 21; Southern Provinces, *Medical Report 1918*, p. 20.

the number of newly discovered cases which, except in 1912–13 in the Eket District, had always been negligible remained small.

1919–21. During the period 1919–1921, seventy-three cases of this disease came under treatment, three of whom were Europeans.[1]

The figures given for Natives cannot be taken seriously; for they represent such a minute fraction of the whole.[2]

1927. There were 602 cases during the year as compared with 298 cases in 1926, but this gives no indication as to the prevalence of the disease. Unfortunately there seems to be little doubt but that trypanosomiasis is spreading in parts of the Northern Provinces.[3]

Sleeping sickness showed an increase of cases and it was found in districts hitherto unsuspected.[4]

1928. There were 2,273 cases of this disease reported during the year. . . . In addition to the cases quoted above 723 were also treated by the Sleeping Sickness Officers on tour, making a total of 3,012 cases of the disease seen and treated in the Northern Provinces . . . .[5]

The appointment of the four Sleeping Sickness Officers to the Tsetse Investigation has been fully justified, their work having made apparent hitherto unsuspected foci of the disease which are of such extent as to constitute a serious menace to the population of considerable tracts of the country.[6]

1929. In the Northern Provinces this disease is causing anxiety. 3,629 new cases were treated during the year by the Sleeping Sickness Officers attached to the Investigation and 1,748 cases were treated at other hospitals, twelve cases occurring in Europeans.[7]

Of the 3,629 new cases treated by the Sleeping Sickness Officers, 1,515 were found in the Ganawuri District of the Plateau Province.[8]

The district was first visited by a Sleeping Sickness Officer in November, 1928, and in three months over two thousand sleeping sickness cases were diagnosed and treated. At the end of this period new cases were coming in just as rapidly as at the beginning. At another visit in November, 568 cases were diagnosed and treated in the first six weeks. It is probable that over 50% of the total population are infected with the disease. Many of the cases found in the second visit were patients who had relapsed through having had insufficient treatment previously. The disease has increased in virulence and the depopulation of some of the villages is a striking testimony to its ravages.[9]

1930. Apart from isolated imported cases trypanosomiasis is not met with to any great extent in the Southern Provinces, but it is a very prominent disease in the Southern Cameroons at and around the port of Tiko. . . .

Out of a total of 6,988 persons examined by the Medical Officer, Buea, 234 cases of infection were discovered, a percentage rate of 3·3.[10]

---

[1] Nigeria, *Medical Report 1919–21*, p. 9. See also ibid., pp. 30–2, 52–3; *1922*, pp. 9, 50, 63; *1923*, p. 7, Appendix, pp. 42–5; *1924*, pp. 7, 40; *1925*, p. 8, Appendix, pp. 101–6; *1926*, pp. 13, 21, Appendix, pp. 179–84.

[2] Ibid. *1919–21*, pp. 62–3.　　　　　　　　[3] Ibid. *1927*, p. 17. See also ibid., p. 26.

[4] *Report on Northern Provinces 1927*, p. 50. See also ibid., p. 30.

[5] Nigeria, *Medical Report 1928*, p. 14; see also *Report on Northern Provinces 1928*, pp. 12, 29. It is often difficult to tell which were the actual figures. *Medical Report 1928*, p. 22, says: 'Most of the cases of trypanosomiasis reported have occurred in the Northern Provinces, 2,628 cases having been reported during 1928 . . . .'

[6] *Colonial Reports, Nigeria 1928*, p. 35. See also Nigeria, *Medical Report 1928*, Appendix, pp. 47–64. (The work of the Sleeping Sickness Service until 1939 is described in great detail in Appendices to the Medical Reports.)

[7] Ibid. *1929*, p. 16. See also *Report on Northern Provinces 1929*, pp. 42–3.

[8] See Nigeria, *Medical Report 1929*, Appendix, p. 46.　　　　[9] Ibid., Appendix, p. 48.

[10] For details see *Report on Cameroons 1930*, pp. 93–5.

In the Northern Provinces 4,954 cases with sixty-nine deaths were reported.[1]

During the year 5,234 cases of sleeping sickness have been treated, 2,891 by the travelling Sleeping Sickness Medical Officers and 2,343 at hospitals and dispensaries, including the dispensary at the Tsetse Investigation Headquarters. . . .

An experiment in intensive sleeping sickness surveys of infected areas was undertaken in the Jaba district of the Jemaa division, Plateau Province, with satisfactory results. The population of the district was found by the survey team to be 14,842. Of these ninety-eight per cent. were inspected and 2·6 per cent. found to be infected and given a full treatment.[2]

1931. Some 5,000 cases were treated by the sleeping sickness staff and 3,000 cases were diagnosed by the survey parties and were awaiting treatment at the end of the year. In addition, 3,466 cases were treated at hospitals and dispensaries during the year, of which 62 cases were treated in the Southern Cameroons by the medical officer detailed for sleeping sickness duty at Buea and 92 at Victoria.[3]

It should be mentioned that the number of cases treated has depended largely upon the staff available and bears little relation to the real amount of sleeping sickness in the country. . . .

Work done has shown that the position with regard to sleeping sickness is very much more serious than we had previously imagined. Large parts of Southern Zaria are known to be infected, we believe that there are thousands of cases in that part of the country and the infected area extends well down into Niger Province. To the north of us there is a serious epidemic involving the Galadima and Gamawa districts of Katagum Emirate, the Serikin Dawaki, Chiroma, and parts of Auyo and Wambai districts of Hadejia Emirate and the Bedde Emirate. The position here is very serious as this epidemic appears to be of a recent origin, is spreading rapidly and is of a very virulent type, killing off patients in under one year.[4]

1932. This disease is seldom reported in the Southern Provinces except in part of the Victoria division of the Cameroons Province. . . .[5]

There has been a considerable extension of the system of mass examination and treatment. At the beginning of the year the investigation had two teams working but in September we were able to put a third team into the field. Some 150,808 persons have been examined and 13,514 cases of sleeping sickness diagnosed.[6] . . .

The position with regard to sleeping sickness in this country is very disquieting and we feel that we are still only touching the fringe of the matter. This year we found about 7,000 cases in the comparatively small area of the Katagum and Hadejia survey. When the size of this area is compared with the whole extent of the country which is known to be infected, the magnitude of the problem will be realised. In the Plateau Province new surveys were made in the Kaleri district of Pankshin division,[7] the Doka areas of Shendam division and the Miango and Kwall areas of Jos division, these gave total infection rates of 15·2 per cent., 11·6 per cent. and 11·6 per cent. respectively. In Lafia division of Benue Province the total infection of the districts surveyed was found to be 11·9 per cent. while Lafia, Keana and Awe

[1] Nigeria, *Medical Report 1930*, p. 21.

[2] Ibid. *1930*, p. 108. See also *Report on Northern Provinces 1930*, pp. 13, 32.

[3] Nigeria, *Medical Report 1931*, p. 10. See also *Report on Northern Provinces 1931*, pp. 6, 12, 44.

[4] Nigeria, *Medical Report 1931*, p. 94.

[5] Ibid. *1932*, p. 17.

[6] 'In addition, 3,255 cases were diagnosed and treated at the Tsetse Investigation Laboratory and at hospitals throughout the country' (ibid., p. 7).

[7] See also *Report on Northern Provinces 1932*, p. 35: 'An unfortunate error in the preparation of Tryparsamide injections in the Kamwai District of Pankshin Division resulted in the deaths of twenty-four patients and the total blindness of thirty-five others—a tragedy which not only led to the immediate abandonment of the anti-sleeping sickness campaign in the vicinity but has proved to be a severe blow to the prestige of our administrative and medical services.' 'The cause is thought to be that the solution of tryparsamide was made with hot water instead of cold water' (Nigeria, *Medical Report 1932*, p. 94). A similar incident occurred in 1931 in the French Cameroons when 500 or 600 patients became blind (see Kuczynski, p. 183).

towns gave infection rates of 20·3 per cent., 24·3 per cent. and 30·8 per cent. respectively.[1]

A preliminary survey was made in the Abuja and Kuta divisions of Niger Province and sleeping sickness was found to be wide spread in both these divisions. Reports from District Officers throughout the north show that the disease is prevalent in many areas which have never been visited by our staff.[2]

1933. . . . the survey teams examined 228,925 persons in the Northern Provinces during the year and diagnosed 22,583 cases of trypanosomiasis and . . . 16,101 persons were examined in the Ahoada district [Southern Provinces], the disease being diagnosed in 4,713 cases. In addition, 4,210 cases of the disease were treated at the tsetse investigation laboratory at Gadau and at hospitals and dispensaries elsewhere in the country.[3]

The infection rates which have been found give some indication of the magnitude of the problem with which we have to deal. The infection rate in Bedde Emirate of Bornu Province was twenty per cent, and it was the same in two of the districts in Hadeija Emirate of Kano Province. In Zaria Emirate two districts had infection rates of twenty per cent and sixteen per cent respectively. Gwagwa district of Abuja Division had an infection rate of twenty-four per cent. While in the Southern Provinces in the Abua district of the Ahoada Division of Owerri Province twenty-nine per cent of the population were found to be infected. There is a good deal of indirect evidence to show that the disease has spread rapidly during the last few years. Areas previously known to be endemic are now epidemic. For instance, in 1931 the east and north-easterly areas of S. Auyo and Wambai districts of Hadeija Emirate were surveyed. The combined survey and treatment was not a success owing to the hostility of the people, and not more than fifty per cent of the population could be examined. In 1933 two years later these areas were re-examined and the survey was almost a hundred per cent successful. Whereas in 1931 the infection rate in that portion of the population examined was four per cent, two years later it had increased to nineteen per cent.

In many areas the death rate has been high and there has been a definite decrease in population. This has been particularly noticeable in Zaria Emirate where the shrinkage in population has been alarming. In Soba district according to the Native Administration census the population has decreased from about 32,000 to 22,000 in the last ten years. The recent survey showed sixteen per cent of the remaining population to be infected with sleeping sickness. The causes of this decrease in population are (a) deaths and (b) the reduction in fertility. Deaths due to sleeping sickness seem to occur (1) among the toxic cases which never reach the stage of showing severe nervous manifestations, (2) as the terminal phase of the 'sleeping' cases, and (3) among the numerous very chronic cases in which the disease may lie latent for many years. In this class patients die of intercurrent diseases owing to the diminished resistance caused by their trypanosomal infection.[4]

1934. In the Southern Provinces, the Southern Cameroons around Tiko and the Ahoada Division of the Owerri Province are the only known epidemic centres of sleeping sickness, but isolated cases are not infrequently reported from other areas, chiefly east of the Niger.[5]

---

[1] See also *Report on Northern Provinces 1932*, p. 16: 'A Sleeping Sickness Survey of Lafia Town and Keana District unfortunately failed owing to a variety of causes, of which the principal was fear of blindness as a consequence of treatment. The night before the survey was to be begun in Lafia Town practically the entire population decamped; confidence was quickly restored, but the survey was very incomplete and attendances for treatment very poor.'

[2] Nigeria, *Medical Report 1932*, pp. 91–2. See also *Report on Northern Provinces 1932*, p. 10.

[3] Nigeria, *Medical Report 1933*, p. 8. There were apparently 'a further 3,000 cases which have been diagnosed but not treated' (ibid., p. 79). For 201 cases in Cameroons Province which possibly are not included in the above figures see *Report on Cameroons 1933*, pp. 76–7.

[4] Nigeria, *Medical Report 1933*, pp. 79–80. See also *Report on Northern Provinces 1933*, pp. 38–9, 48, 63.

[5] Nigeria, *Medical Report 1934*, pp. 15–16.

During the year 381,712 people have been examined and 43,017 cases of sleeping sickness diagnosed by the Tsetse Investigation staff. Of these less than 600 cases had been treated previously. Altogether 47,187 cases have been treated this year. This figure includes about 9,000 cases whose treatment had been started in 1933 but does not include about 5,000 cases diagnosed towards the end of 1934.[1]

The majority of mining leases are in Wamba district quite close to the border of Mama. An examination of the permanent mines employees showed that out of 377 of them at the various camps 171 were infected an infection rate of 45·4%. As these permanent employees work anywhere and everywhere on the leases, helping to supervise the pagan casual labour, they serve as a constant source of infection for tsetse, and it is hardly to be wondered at that large numbers of pagan labourers become infected while at work. A survey of the villages from which the greater part of the pagan labour is drawn showed that 400 out of 2,806 villagers were infected a rate of 14·3%. If people who had worked on the mines had been excluded the rate would have been nearer 2%. The position is serious. Here is an epidemic almost entirely due to conditions of labour on the tin mines. Local history relates that in this area sleeping sickness started at the first tin mining camp and that this had to be closed owing to the disease which has spread far and near in the last few years.[2]

1935. The spread of sleeping sickness in the Northern Provinces has become alarming and is a serious menace to the country.[3]

It is clear that, in spite of intensive campaigns of mass treatment and the establishment of sleeping sickness dispensaries the disease is not yet under control. There is evidence to show that new areas are becoming infected and that the type of disease in some of the older epidemics is becoming worse.[4]

During the year 407,203 people were examined at the surveys in the field and 84,364 were found to be infected with sleeping sickness. Altogether 87,369 cases were treated by the teams; this number included some 4,000 patients who were diagnosed at the end of 1934. As no resurveys were carried out during the year practically all these patients were new cases. A further 4,358 patients were treated at field dispensaries, and 4,825 patients at general medical stations, making a grand total of 96,552 cases of sleeping sickness treated during the year.[5]

In Agaie Emirate [Niger Province] the incidence of infection was found to be 43·2 per cent, higher than that found so far in any part of Nigeria.[6]

1936. During 1936, 417,495 people have been examined by the sleeping sickness teams and 47,550 were found to be infected. Of these 40,897 had completed treatment by the end of the year. A further 10,450 cases were diagnosed and treated at field dispensaries and 4,021 at general medical stations. This brings the total for the year to 62,021 cases.[7]

Prospects for the control of the disease in the Northern Provinces are now very much brighter. In the past it has been felt that in spite of all efforts sleeping sickness has been spreading, and has been causing increasing mortality and depopulation in certain areas.[8]

1937. The advance of sleeping sickness into new areas and the depopulation which has resulted from the disease in parts of the Northern Provinces has for some years been causing much anxiety. Treatment alone or treatment combined with minor

[1] Ibid., p. 78. See also *Report on Northern Provinces 1934*, pp. 40, 48.

[2] Nigeria, *Medical Report 1934*, pp. 83–4. See also ibid. *1935*, p. 75; *Report on Northern Provinces 1934*, pp. 2, 43.

[3] Nigeria, *Medical Report 1935*, p. 5. See also *Report on Northern Provinces 1935*, p. 2.

[4] Nigeria, *Medical Report 1935*, p. 71.

[5] Ibid., p. 72. See also *Report on Northern Provinces 1935*, pp. 17, 52.   [6] Ibid., p. 43.

[7] Nigeria, *Medical Report 1936*, p. 97. '. . . the year's figures bring the total number of cases diagnosed and treated by the Sleeping Sickness Service since the survey system was started in 1931 to 240,900 patients. During the same period 24,033 patients have been treated at general medical stations.' (Ibid., p. 93.) See also *Report on Northern Provinces 1936*, pp. 7, 44.

[8] Nigeria, *Medical Report 1936*, p. 93.

measures of tsetse control have proved inadequate and the Deputy Director of the Sleeping Sickness Service prepared a comprehensive plan to deal with the problem. His proposals involve among other things, the removal of hamlets from heavily infected sleeping sickness belts and the re-settlement of the people in newly established villages in 'clean' or 'protected' areas, where seed, farming land, wells and other necessities will be provided for the settlers.[1]

During the year 447,358 people have been examined by the sleeping sickness teams and 29,011 were found to be infected. Of these 28,426 had completed treatment at the end of the year. A further 8,187 cases were diagnosed and treated at field dispensaries and 4,460 at general medical stations. This brings the total for the year to 41,658.[2]

At the survey of the Eastern districts of Zaria Emirate infection rates of 20%–40% were found and there was ample evidence that the disease was doing very serious damage.[3]

1938. During the year 378,109 people have been examined by the Sleeping Sickness teams and 21,073 of them were found to be infected. Of these 20,995 had completed treatment at the end of the year. A further 9,661 cases were diagnosed and treated at field dispensaries and 4,272 at general medical stations. This brings the total cases for the year to 35,006.

In addition to the above, 9,016 persons were examined in connection with the scheme for the control of Mines Labour in the Southern Division of Plateau Province. 127 cases of sleeping sickness discovered among these labourers were treated at the Sleeping Sickness Dispensary at Wamba.[4]

. . . an average infection rate of approximately 5·6% was found among the persons examined. During the previous year 447,358 people were examined with an average infection rate of 6·3%. The reason for the smaller numbers for this year is due partly to the fact that in some instances we have been working in areas where the service has never operated before. As the people in these areas are often rather frightened at the idea of a mass survey and treatment, a considerable amount of time has had to be spent in carrying out propaganda among them. The results of this propaganda have been most gratifying and the time spent on it has certainly not been wasted. The chief reason, however, for the fall in the figures is that re-examinations in areas surveyed some years earlier have been carried out to a much greater extent than formerly. Three out of six teams have in fact been chiefly engaged in carrying out these re-examinations.

The difference between the findings of surveys in new areas and the resurveys is very marked. During the new surveys some 208,611 people were examined of whom 19,037 were found to be infected, the average infection rate being about 9·1%. In the course of the resurveys 169,498 people were examined, of whom only 2,036 were found to be infected, the average rate of infection thus being only 1·2%.

It is noteworthy however that high infection rates, ranging from ten per cent to forty per cent, are still being obtained in the Nasarawa Emirate of Benue Province, an Emirate in which no mass treatments had ever been carried out before this year.[5]

1939. The success of the sleeping sickness campaign has shown what can be accomplished by a well organised mass attack on a particular disease . . . .[6]

[1] Nigeria, *Medical Report 1937*, p. 5.

[2] Ibid., p. 69. According to *Report on Northern Provinces 1937*, p. 4, the decrease was 'due partly to a shortage of medical officers and partly to the fact that the teams have been working on the periphery of the main epidemic areas and so infection rates have been less'.

[3] Nigeria, *Medical Report 1937*, p. 72. See also *Report on Northern Provinces 1937*, p. 5: 'In Anchau District of Zaria Emirate, the infection rate was so high and the population so scattered that concentration of population will be necessary. In the new settlements every effort is to be made to ensure that by careful rural planning there is as much room for development as possible.' For other Provinces see ibid., pp. 9, 18, 35–6, 38, 43, 52.

[4] Nigeria, *Medical Report 1938*, pp. 57–8. See also ibid., pp. 7, 60–1; *Report on Northern Provinces 1938*, pp. 3–4, 14–15, 18, 34, 51–2, 57–8.

[5] Nigeria, *Medical Report 1938*, pp. 59–60.   [6] Ibid. *1939*, p. 2.

The onset of war led to changes which otherwise might not have been necessary for some time. Gadau has been closed. Research will be limited to testing new drugs. Re-surveys have shown that the incidence of infection in the main central epidemic belt is now only about a ninth of the old figure. This made it possible to reduce the number of teams to three, setting free both European and African trained staff for the Field Ambulance.[1] . . .

During the year 494,428 people were examined by the teams and 20,054 cases found, an average of 4·0 per cent. The progressive fall in the average infection rate, has been maintained. A further 8,035 cases were treated at sleeping sickness dispensaries and 2,001 at general medical stations, giving a total for the year of 30,090.

Among people examined in new areas there were 18,105 cases an infection rate of 6·7 per cent. The majority were found in Benue Province where little work had been done prior to 1938. The rates there are comparable with the old high figures of the earlier years of the mass treatment system. At re-surveys 1,946 cases were found, an infection rate of 0·88 per cent. This compares favourably with the average of 8·1 per cent found at the first surveys of the same areas.

An indication of what has been accomplished in recent years is given by the population figures of Zaria Emirate. During 1933–1937 some 78,000 cases were treated in mass campaigns, started because of the high incidence of the disease and progressive depopulation. During 1923–1933 the number of adult males had fallen by 12 per cent. There is evidence that this decrease was correlated directly with the incidence of sleeping sickness. In 1933 the total population was 373,195. By 1937 it had increased to 402,257 and to 418,037 in 1939. There is now only a fraction of the old amount of sleeping sickness.

The system of control of mining labour in parts of Plateau Province continued to give good results. The incidence of the disease among labourers on the Kabba-Ilorin goldfields is causing concern. Whereas the infection among the general population is only 1·3 per cent and is of a mild type, it is about 40 per cent among the mining labourers. As the disease is of a more virulent type and mining only started in 1938, it seems clear that it was brought into the district by labourers from further North.[2]

1940. During the latter half of the year there were further reductions in the Sleeping Sickness Service's activities partly as a war economy and partly so as to release staff for military service. Only one sleeping sickness team is being kept at work; in Benue Province. The reduction in the infection rate in a great part of the Northern Provinces has made it possible to stop surveys and mass treatment and to rely on the permanent treatment facilities provided by chains of sleeping sickness dispensaries. The dispensary system is being still further expanded and improved.

During the year 278,611 people were examined and 19,596 cases were found. These together with about 10,000 cases treated at sleeping sickness dispensaries and about 3,000 at general medical stations give a total of about 33,000 cases treated for the year. The majority of the new surveys were done in Benue Province, the average infection rate being 9·7%. The re-survey of areas previously treated gave an average infection rate of 1·7%.[3]

1941. The service is now on a maintenance basis as regards mass survey and settlement work, but the dispensary system and the control of mines labour have been expanded.

The survey team, examining 200,000 people in Tiv Division, treated 3,700 of trypanosomiasis . . . . In re-surveys in the Zaria, Niger and Plateau Provinces, the examination of 12,000 people revealed 280 infected with sleeping sickness. Hospitals,

[1] The Field Ambulance proceeded overseas about mid-year 1940.

[2] Ibid., pp. 15–16. See also *Reports for Northern, Western, Eastern Provinces and Colony 1939*, pp. 4–5, 22, 51.

[3] Nigeria, *Medical Report 1940*, p. 15. See also *Reports for Northern, Western, Eastern Provinces and Colony 1940*, p. 3.

dispensaries and the mines staff were responsible for the treatment of approximately 1,900, 9,000 and 900 cases respectively, making a total for the year of 15,700.

Rigid control has greatly reduced the epidemic proportions of trypanosomiasis in the Kabba and Ilorin gold mines. In Niger Province the staff available has been insufficient to ensure a similar reduction of the severe type of endemic disease encountered. Infection rates in the Southern Division of Plateau Province remain low, but improvement in the Jemaa Division is slow. The general effect of the extended control is shown in the finding of only 885 cases from 38,000 examinations, as compared with the 1940 figures of 1,300 and 22,000 respectively.

Full scale activities in the Anchau tsetse-free corridor finished temporarily in March after the transfer of 1,700 people to new villages.[1]

1942. In 1942 the sleeping sickness service remained on a maintenance basis. Only one sleeping sickness team was at work. The control service was carried on by a skeleton staff.

In spite of this, progress has been satisfactory. Most new surveys were done in the lightly infected central part of Tiv division of Benue Province. In new areas some 168,658 people were examined and 2,200 cases found, an average infection rate of 1·3 per cent. Another 34,456 people were examined at re-surveys and 793 cases found, an average of 2·3 per cent. It is noteworthy that of 11,000 people re-examined, in what used to be a more heavily infected part of Tiv, the infection rate was 1·2 per cent. It was 9·8 per cent in 1939. The other re-surveys were done in areas which used to be very heavily infected and these also showed a proportionate reduction.

Including control of mines labour, over a quarter of a million examinations were carried out during the year, with an average infection rate of less than 2 per cent. This compares favourably with the position a few years ago. In the period 1931–1938 over two million people were examined and 250,000 cases found, an average of 11·2 per cent. From 1939 onwards, another million people were examined at new surveys and about 50,000 cases found, an infection rate of about 5 per cent. In the same period, over half a million people were examined at re-surveys and 6,534 cases found, an average of only 1·2 per cent.

Since the survey system was first started in 1931, some 307,456 cases have been diagnosed and treated by the teams. A further 68,680 cases have been treated at dispensaries during the last seven years. These together with about 43,000 cases treated at general hospitals and missions give a total of about 420,000 cases of sleeping sickness treated during the last twelve years. Of these 30,000 to 50,000 were relapsed cases.

The success of the policy of surveys and mass treatment followed by the establishment of dispensaries as permanent treatment centres is shown by the general reduction which has occurred in infection rates. There is probably only a fifth or sixth of the amounts of the disease that there used to be.

This year 11,313 cases were treated at dispensaries. This increase over last year, in spite of a gradual falling off in cases at some of the older established dispensaries, was largely due to new treatment centres in Benue Province. Treatment is already available at nineteen centres there and six new sleeping sickness dispensaries are being built.

The control of mines labour in the sleeping sickness restricted areas of Plateau, Niger, Kabba and Ilorin Provinces continued. Progress was satisfactory on the whole. Over 51,289 examinations were carried out and 1,042 cases found, the average infection rate being 2 per cent, compared with 4·3 per cent in 1941 and 6 per cent in 1940. This was partly due to a recent decrease in gold mining in some of the more heavily infected areas. Even there the present infection rates are only small fractions of the old figures. With the increased war time need for tin, work in Southern Division and Jemaa is increasing in importance.

Approximately 17,350 cases were treated altogether, allowing for about 2,000 cases at general hospitals and missions.[2]

[1] Nigeria, *Medical Report 1941*, pp. 14–15.   [2] Ibid. *1942*, pp. 15–16.

1943. In 1943 the Sleeping Sickness Service treated about 19,000 cases. Of these 5,321 were found at mass surveys, about 13,100 at dispensaries and 540 at the periodic examination of mines labour. With 830 treated at Mission stations and about 1,500 at general medical stations the year's total was approximately 21,300. This increase over the previous year's figure was due to concentrating survey work on the re-examination of bad areas which have always been adversely affected by mining and to the increase in the number of dispensaries established as permanent treatment centres. There was no evidence of any general increase of the disease.

Owing to War-time shortage of staff most re-surveys were done by the Sanitary Superintendents in charge of the sleeping sickness control of mines labour in Plateau and Niger Provinces. In the worst area of Jemaa Division of Plateau Province, 39,534 people were examined and 1,434 cases found: an average infection rate of 3·8%. This high figure was partly due to the fact that much of the casual pagan labour had been evading the sleeping sickness restrictions. This situation has now been put right.[1]

In Niger Province the position was reasonably satisfactory. Some 96,803 people were examined and 2,619 cases found, an average incidence of 2·6 per cent. Among 21,686 people examined in the worst areas of Benue Province the average infection rate was 1·0 per cent, less than a tenth of the old figure.

In Zaria, spot re-surveys were carried out both inside and outside the tsetse-free corridor. Altogether 35,709 people were examined and 503 cases were found, an average of 1·3 per cent. In and near the present area of the corridor infection rates were 0·2 to 0·5 per cent. Altogether 197,307 people were examined at re-surveys and 4,877 cases found, an infection rate of 2·4 per cent. Some 19,616 were examined in a new area in Bauchi Province where the average infection rate was 2·1 per cent.[2]

The policy of establishing permanent treatment centres in areas where surveys have been made is gradually being implemented. Eight new sleeping sickness dressing stations were completed in the Benue Province and work has been started on nine more. In all there are now 43 sleeping sickness dispensaries and dressing stations together with 29 Native Administration dispensaries at which attendants specially trained in sleeping sickness work have been posted. Over 13,100 cases of sleeping sickness were treated at these centres during the year. The sleeping sickness dispensaries also treated about 75,000 general cases.

In the tin areas in the south-west of the Plateau Province and the gold areas of the Niger and Kabba Provinces the systematic control of mines labour has been continued. The whole labour force numbering about 6,000 was examined every six weeks. It was found that an average of 1·4% of the labourers contracted sleeping sickness every six weeks.[3]

1944. The sleeping sickness service is on a maintenance basis. Including a wells foreman there are usually from eight to ten officers in the field. They are equally divided between the treatment and control services.

Mass examination and treatment were confined to re-surveys by one full team and several temporarily constituted sub-teams. In Zaria Province, village re-surveys are also made by dispensary staff. Various forces of mines labour totalling over 6,000 men are examined and re-examined at six-weekly intervals. Apart from routine inspection of all patients attending dispensaries 183,000 examinations were made. Infection rates averaged 2 per cent.

Seven new dispensaries have been opened. Treatment facilities are available at 50 Sleeping Sickness and 37 Native Administration dispensaries, 26 hospitals and a variable number of temporary posts in the restricted minesfield areas. 15,629 cases of trypanosomiasis were treated by the teams and at these centres during the year. . . .

Control of mines labour is satisfactory in Niger Province and in the Southern

[1] *Report on Northern Provinces 1943*, p. 5.
[2] Nigeria, *Medical Report 1943*, p. 20.
[3] *Report on Northern Provinces 1943*, pp. 5–6.

Division of Plateau Province, less satisfactory in Jemaa. There is now only a very small labour force in the Kabba-Ilorin restricted area.[1]

Governor Sir Arthur Richards in his Address to the Legislative Council on 18 March 1946 said:

The Sleeping Sickness Service is controlling human trypanosomiasis by drug treatment and by reduction of contact between man and the tse-tse fly. About 18,000 cases of sleeping sickness are treated annually. Much of this work is in the Northern Provinces, but a recently completed survey in the Obudu Division of Ogoja Province has shown a moderate incidence of a rather severe form of the disease. . . .

Permanent control of sleeping sickness by complete eradication of tse-tse fly from 700 square miles of country, together with concentration of population and rural development, are the objects of the Anchau Settlement Scheme. Allied with this is the protection of villages over a wide area by communal clearances at points where contact with tse-tse fly is greatest. To date some 400,000 people have benefited by these measures. . . .[2]

The expenditure for the Sleeping Sickness Service decreased from £44,124 in 1939–40 to £36,711 in 1940–1, and to £21,931 in 1941–2; it amounted to £30,498 in 1942–3, to £36,679 in 1943–4, and to £37,938 in 1944–5.[3]

The situation with which we are confronted is, therefore, as follows: Prior to the establishment of the special Sleeping Sickness Service the number of cases discovered was very small; the number of cases diagnosed by this Service rose from a few thousand in 1928–9 to 84,364 in 1935 and dropped thereafter to 2,993 in 1942; the total number of cases treated increased from 298 in 1926 to about 8,500 in 1931 and to 96,552 in 1935, and decreased thereafter to approximately 17,350 in 1942. Two questions, therefore, arise: (1) was the actual incidence of sleeping-sickness much greater in 1935 than in 1931 or in 1926? (2) has the spread of the disease been checked?

(1) The difficulties of appraising correctly the increase in the incidence of sleeping-sickness can perhaps best be illustrated by giving the details for a specific area. I shall select the Mandated Territory of Cameroons because the available material is here more ample than for Nigeria proper. In the Cameroons Province one case of sleeping-sickness had been reported in 1922, none in 1923, and one in 1924.[4] The report for 1925 said:

There have been only three cases of this disease, all being reported from Tiko. . . .

In the Mamfe Division, although *Glossina Palpalis* is common, no case of sleeping sickness has been reported, and the Medical Officer in charge thinks it probable that none exists. . . .

In the Bamenda Division, there was no case of Trypanosomiasis reported. On the whole it seems improbable that the disease exists to any great extent in the Cameroon province, as the mortality of untreated cases is so great that it would be impossible to conceal it.

Both in this and previous years in most of the cases of trypanosomiasis which have occurred, the infection has been traced to Fernando Po.[5]

[1] *Report on Northern Provinces 1944*, p. 21.   [2] *Speech and Address*, p. 8.
[3] See Nigeria, *Medical Report 1941*, p. 2, *1942*, p. 3, *1943*, p. 5, *1944*, p. 3; Nigeria, *Estimates 1946–7*, p. 18.
[4] See *Report on Cameroons 1922*, p. 54; *1923*, p. 79; *1924*, p. 40.   [5] Ibid. *1925*, pp. 76–7.

A few more cases were reported from Tiko in 1926–8.[1] Of those reported in 1928 four were European employees of German plantations.[2] Thereupon, a specialist Government Medical Officer was detailed to investigate. He diagnosed, in 1929, 67 cases (apart from 35 native and 7 European cases reported from hospital centres). A 'Medical Officer experienced in sleeping sickness work' was then sent to the infected area.[3] As shown above, he examined in 1930 6,988 persons and discovered 234 cases. He continued his work in 1931 and examined 3,592 more persons among whom he found 62 cases.[4] In 1932 apparently very few cases were reported from Tiko area. The reports for 1932–5 said:

1932. There is no sign of any spread outside the Victoria-Tiko area. There has in fact been a definite improvement at Tiko, which is probably due to systematic treatment of all known cases, together with the large amount of bush clearing associated with the rapid extension of banana cultivation.[5]

1933. It is intended that a unit of the Tsetse Investigation section of the Medical Department should be detailed in 1934 to make a survey in the neighbourhood of Tiko, Victoria Division, where sleeping sickness is now considered to be endemic. In 1933, 190 cases (of which 17 were fatal) were reported in the Victoria-Tiko area, 7 at Mamfe and 4 at Kumba.[6]

1934. It was not found possible during the year to detail a unit of the Tsetse Investigation section to make a survey in the neighbourhood of Tiko, Victoria Division; but arrangements were complete for this survey to be undertaken in January, 1935. There were 156 cases with 12 deaths reported in the Victoria-Tiko area; 11 from Kumba Division with no deaths, and two cases with no deaths from Bamenda.[7]

In regard to the increase in these diseases [sleeping sickness, leprosy, and smallpox] shown by the statistics, it must be remembered that the number of cases brought to light each year by the natives on account of their increasing sense and confidence and the improvement of communications, is growing rapidly year by year. No organized survey of the diseases of the country is possible and an increase in cases treated does not necessarily imply a spread of the disease. In the views of Medical Officers there is no noticeable spread of leprosy, smallpox or sleeping sickness among the native population.[8]

1935. Between January and June, a unit of the Tsetse Investigation Section made a survey in the neighbourhood of Tiko, Victoria Division; the area surveyed was 350 square miles in extent and included seven plantations and twenty-one villages, the latter situated on the banks of the Mungo River. Men, women, and children to the number of 8,758 were examined, 1,150 were found to be infected and 919 came under treatment. The percentage of those infected to the number examined was 13·13.[9]

The events, I think, prove beyond any doubt that prior to .the 1935 survey by the Tsetse Investigation Section the Medical Officers had misjudged the situation and that the results of their investigations had been misleading. They thought in 1926 that the six cases which had been reported in Cameroons Province in 1922–5 covered more or less the cases that actually occurred and that it could hardly be otherwise. The

---

[1] See ibid. *1926*, p. 79; *1927*, p. 73; *1928*, p. 92.   [2] See Nigeria, *Medical Report 1928*, p. 14.
[3] See *Report on Cameroons 1929*, p. 88. See also Nigeria, *Medical Report 1929*, p. 16, Appendix, p. 47.
[4] See *Report on Cameroons 1930*, pp. 93–5, *1931*, pp. 78–9; Nigeria, *Medical Report 1931*, p. 10.
[5] *Report on Cameroons 1932*, p. 91.   [6] Ibid. *1933*, pp. 76–7.
[7] Ibid. *1934*, pp. 97–8.   [8] Ibid., p. 99.   [9] Ibid. *1935*, p. 100.

'specialist Government Medical Officer' who in 1929 made an examination of the Tiko area (Victoria Division) diagnosed not more than 67 cases. The 'Medical Officer experienced in sleeping sickness work', who came to the country for two years (1930–1) with the sole purpose of ascertaining the spread of the disease in the infected area and who examined 10,580 people, found only an incidence of 2·8 per cent. (296 cases). For 1932 the Administration reported 'a definite improvement at Tiko'. The cases reported from this area numbered 190 in 1933 and only 156 in 1934, and the increase in cases treated as compared with early years was attributed to a more frequent use of medical facilities by the natives. In the views of Medical Officers there was no noticeable spread of sleeping-sickness. In the meantime, however, a unit of the Tsetse Investigation Section of the Medical Department had started a survey which covered 8,758 people and revealed an incidence of 13·1 per cent. (1,150 cases). The survey was on a very small scale; it comprised only 7 plantations and 21 villages, and it is impossible to tell how many thousands of cases would have been found if the examinations had been expanded. But no further examinations were made. The number of new cases treated in this area was only 242 in 1936 and it dropped to 147 in 1937.

1937. There is evidence that the incidence of trypanosomiasis is decreasing at Tiko and on the plantations in the Victoria Division . . . .[1]

1938. Further evidence has confirmed the belief expressed in the 1937 Report that the incidence of trypanosomiasis is decreasing in the Victoria Division . . . .[2]

The Victoria Division is a small coastal territory of 1,166 square miles with about 45,000 inhabitants of whom (until the outbreak of the war) at least one-half lived on European plantations. The interest of the Europeans in the health of the natives was here, for obvious reasons, greater than elsewhere and the ratio of Medical Officers to total population was exceptionally high. Yet no one apparently had noticed prior to 1935 the considerable incidence of sleeping-sickness; no one can tell whether the incidence in 1935 was equal to or rather a hundred times as high as in 1925, and no one who has not an ineradicable faith in the belief of Medical Officers (confirmed by unspecified evidence) can say for certain whether the incidence has increased or decreased in the Victoria Division since 1935.

The situation is more obscure still in the three other Divisions of Cameroons Province, which cover 15,415 square miles with about 400,000 inhabitants. As shown above, hardly any cases had been discovered there until 1937. The report for that year said that 'the disease is thought to be gaining ground at Kumba'.[3] The next report stated that 'considerable numbers of cases were reported in 1938 from the Kumba, Mamfe and Bamenda Divisions',[4] and it listed sleeping-sickness among the four 'principal diseases to be countered by those responsible for public health in the Cameroons Province'.[5]

(2) It is obvious that the spread of the disease has not been checked in

[1] *Report on Cameroons 1937*, p. 96.   [2] Ibid. *1938*, p. 87.
[3] Ibid. *1937*, p. 96.   [4] Ibid. *1938*, p. 87.   [5] Ibid., p. 86.

Cameroons Province. But this Province comprises only 4 or 5 per cent. of the area and only 2 per cent. of the population of Nigeria. It would be wrong, therefore, to generalize the results here obtained. Although a survey was made by a unit of the Tsetse Investigation Section in part of the Province, it was made only once. It may well be, therefore, that in the areas continually covered by the Section the situation up to 1940 was fairly in hand. But it would be wrong again to generalize the results here obtained, and in view of the damage done in other countries by over-estimating local successes in the fight against sleeping-sickness the optimism expressed in the most recent Medical Reports of Nigeria is by no means reassuring. It should be borne in mind, moreover, that the restrictions of the activities of the Sleeping Sickness Service, due not only to the release of staff for military service but also to 'war economy', may cause a recrudescence in the areas formerly under adequate control.

Malaria. By the end of the nineteenth century adult people had already gained a certain immunity against malaria, while the number of infants and children affected was apparently extremely high.[1] Whether the incidence of malaria has increased or decreased in the course of the last 40 years, it is difficult to tell. Complaints about a high incidence have been numerous throughout. A few quotations may serve as illustrations:

1911. Malaria is widespread throughout the whole of Southern Nigeria . . . .[2]

1926. Malaria is still the most prevalent of the tropical infections. It is responsible for a considerable number of infant and child deaths amongst Africans.[3]

1936. Malaria continues to be one of the major public health problems met with in Nigeria, breeding places for both *Anopheles gambiæ* and *A. funestus* being commonly found throughout Nigeria.[4]

1938. The amount of malaria in Nigeria varies little from year to year[5] . . . . While epidemic waves of the disease are rare there appears to be a small seasonal wave reaching its peak about October but observations over a number of years are required to confirm this statement.[6]

1940. In Lagos, through post-mortems the Pathologist found that malaria was the cause of deaths of seventy-two out of 520 children aged three years and under. In twenty-five instances the malaria was of the cerebral type. As Lagos is more fortunate in its medical facilities than the vast extent of the country, malaria must take a much heavier toll of young life all over, and will continue catastrophic to infancy till education—especially female education—is general enough to make simple protective measures against mosquitoes in the homes a common precaution.[7]

1942. This disease remains one of the leading causes of mortality in infants and young children and a common cause of sickness and invaliding in the adult non native. This endemic disease is probably of minor importance in native adults who have a considerable degree of resistance to such infection. There is no doubt, however, of the extreme usefulness of suppressive drugs for the native infant and young child, while they are building up their natural resistance . . . .[8]

Cerebrospinal Meningitis. The first general epidemic witnessed by Europeans in Northern Nigeria occurred in 1905. The official reports about the

---

[1] See Strachan, *Health Conditions of West Africa*, p. 10.

[2] Southern Nigeria, *Medical Report 1911*, p. 5.

[3] Nigeria, *Medical Report 1926*, p. 21.   [4] Ibid. *1936*, p. 18.

[5] But see ibid. *1939*, p. 6: 'The Senior Health Officer reports unusually high prevalence of malaria owing to heavy rains in the Northern Provinces in 1939.'

[6] Ibid. *1938*, p. 6.   [7] Ibid. *1940*, p. 7.   [8] Ibid. *1942*, p. 6.

spread and the incidence of the disease are somewhat contradictory. The annual Colonial Report contained the following summary:[1]

During the first three months of 1905 a very severe epidemic of cerebro-spinal fever broke out in all the provinces except Sokoto,[2] Borgu, Kontagora, and Bornu.[3] The mortality was very great indeed, and is said to have been over 100 a day in Kano.[4] The case mortality is estimated at 50 per cent.; 132 died in Zungeru cantonment. . . . The natives say that this disease occurs periodically in an epidemic form;[5] it is entirely a dry weather disease—the germs being probably carried by dust storms— and ceases with the rains. At Zaria the Resident reports that the natives, apparently from some superstitious fear, would not allow themselves to be seen by a doctor. 'At the commencement of the epidemic the case mortality was appalling, many of those attacked practically falling dead at their work; later, however, its violence became attenuated.'

In 1906 'an epidemic of cerebro-spinal meningitis occurred in March when a large body of natives were congregated in Sokoto',[6] but elsewhere 'only the usual number of sporadic cases' was seen.[7] 'In the dry season, 1906–1907, an epidemic of Cerebro-Spinal Meningitis of the limited variety took place at Zungeru', but apparently 'did not spread beyond that station'.[8] Few cases only were reported in the following decade.[9] But this, according to Dr. Blair, was no proof that cases were actually few.

Outbreaks of this disease have always been patchy in their incidence.

But the patchiness of its incidence makes it a fair inference that numerous isolated outbreaks occur beyond the ken of the European; for Medical Officers are few and far between in those regions where the disease is most likely to occur; and prolonged acquaintance with the Natives, and consequent increasing information elicited from them, makes the observer incline to believe that this inference is a correct one.[10]

Very little is known about the prevalence of cerebrospinal meningitis during the influenza pandemic of 1918.[11] But there is ample evidence that

[1] *Colonial Reports, Northern Nigeria 1905–6*, pp. 104–5.

[2] But see the report on Sokoto Province ibid., p. 11: 'There was an outbreak of small-pox, but the epidemic of cerebro-spinal meningitis was much more serious, and accounted for some 50 deaths daily for a short time . . . .' See also, for example, Northern Provinces, *Medical Report 1918*, p. 19: 'There was a general epidemic of Cerebro-Spinal Meningitis—observed first at Sokoto —in 1905.'

[3] For the outbreaks in Zaria, Bauchi, Ilorin, and Yola Provinces see *Colonial Reports, Northern Nigeria 1905–6*, pp. 36, 40, 51, 54.

[4] But see also ibid., p. 29: '. . . there was a terrible epidemic in February and March, and hundreds of natives died in the city [Kano]'.

[5] Dr. M. Cameron Blair, who joined the West African Medical Service in 1901, thought that the disease has been endemic 'in the northern peripheral group of the Northern Provinces' for a very long time. See Nigeria, *Medical Report 1919–21*, p. 58.

[6] *Colonial Reports, Northern Nigeria 1906–7*, p. 8.   [7] Ibid., p. 48. See also ibid., p. 45.

[8] Northern Provinces, *Medical Report 1918*, p. 19.

[9] See 'Report on Public Health of Northern Nigeria 1907', p. 92; 'Northern Nigeria Medical Report 1908', p. 99, '1909', p. iii, '1910', p. 137; Northern Nigeria, *Medical Report 1911*, p. 42.

[10] Nigeria, *Medical Report 1915*, p. 15. See also Northern Provinces, *Medical Report 1916*, p. 17; Nigeria, *Medical Report 1917*, p. 138; Northern Provinces, *Medical Report 1918*, p. 19.

[11] See ibid. *1918*, p. 19: '. . . during the invasion of the country by pandemic Influenza, some of the cases were, in their clinical manifestations, inseparable from Cerebro-Spinal Meningitis . . . and in the absence of an acknowledged epidemic of Influenza, the cases showing cerebro-spinal symptoms would undoubtedly have been returned as Cerebro-Spinal Meningitis. . . . It would have been most interesting, had it been possible, to have had an analysis of the cases in the dry North, showing particularly the proportion assuming the cerebro-spinal form; but this was impossible; as the scanty medical personnel available was overwhelmed with work; whilst only a very small proportion of the cases was seen by medical men at all.'

the Northern Provinces suffered very much from cerebrospinal meningitis in 1921–5. The first epidemic started late in 1920[1] and by January 1921 it had 'assumed alarming proportions'.

Fortunately, however, the ravages of the disease were confined to the western half of the Sokoto Province, and to that Northern strip of the Kontagora Province marching therewith.[2] The case mortality was very high: as usually is the case with this disease, it took its heaviest toll from among the poorer, and therefore more overcrowded, classes; and from among the young rather than the old. It raged during the height of the cold, dusty Harmattan (the cold dry wind which sweeps over the Sahara from the North-East or North of East, during the centre of the dry season), when the people tend to close up all ventilative openings even more than they usually do, when every market-place is covered by a cloud of germ-laden dust, and when every movement of men or of animals raises still more dust.[3]

Dr. Moiser, the Provincial Medical Officer at Sokoto, who 'obtained statistics as near as possible from Political Officers', gave the population of Sokoto Province as 1,361,000, the number of deaths from cerebrospinal meningitis 'as 45,900 and a mortality rate of 33 per 1,000 population'.[4] The epidemic of 1905 'had covered a wider area' but whether it had caused more deaths it is impossible to tell.[5]

'The advent of the rains in May completely closed down the epidemic.'[6] But early in 1922 there was a recrudescence of the disease in the north-eastern region of Kontagora Province, i.e. immediately south of the eastern limit of the epidemic of the previous year.[7] 'The victims received no individual medical treatment as it was impossible (on account of the limited personnel of the Medical Staff), to detail medical officers for the purpose. But . . . the ring-fencing of the affected region was overtaken after a highly successful fashion, and the advent of the rains did the rest.'[8] Dr. Blair thought that without the isolation of the affected region 'the long odds are that the visitation would have taken in all of the northern peripheral provinces', but he had no illusions as to the value of such a localization of outbreaks.

The number of healthy carriers of the infection in those northern provinces must be enormous; accumulations are bound to reach explosive point periodically; and (in the absence of some effective means of mass treatment) highly fatal epidemics must be expected at intervals for many decades to come.[9]

The Medical Report for 1929 said:

Cerebro-spinal fever which prevailed in the Kontagora (now Nupe) Province during 1922 again appeared in the same Province in February to a limited extent. A few cases were reported in March and April at Katsina, Daura, Kano, Zaria and Jebba; the epidemic died down in the rainy season but there was a recrudescence towards the end of the year when a few cases occurred at Jos and Kaduna.[10]

[1] See Colonial Reports, Nigeria 1920, p. 7.
[2] 'The extent of country affected was in area about equal to that of Scotland' (ibid. 1921, pp. 8–9).
[3] Nigeria, Medical Report 1919–21, p. 50.   [4] Ibid. 1924, p. 45.
[5] See ibid. 1919–21, p. 59.   [6] Ibid., p. 50.
[7] See Colonial Reports, Nigeria 1922, p. 9; Nigeria, Medical Report 1922, p. 39, 1924, p. 44.
[8] Ibid., p. 50.   [9] Ibid., p. 51.
[10] Ibid. 1923, p. 19. See also ibid., p. 7, and Colonial Reports, Nigeria 1923, p. 12.

170 cases with 154 deaths were notified in the Northern Provinces. 150 of these occurred in the months of February, March and April . . . .[1]

It may well be that only a few cases were reported to the Medical Department in March and April from Katsina, Daura, Kano, Zaria, and Jebba and that only 20 cases were reported from the whole country between May and December. But it seems that many hundred people died from the disease in Kano City alone,[2] and in the last quarter of the year the disease was 'spreading far and wide beyond all previous limits'.

By January, 1924, it had spread from the Province of Sokoto east-ward through-out the Province of Kano; the Katsina Emirate suffered very severely and 1,000 deaths are recorded as having occurred in Katsina and the district around. Further east-ward the disease spread through the Province of Bornu. At the same time its spread took place in a southerly direction: on the east towards the southern boundary of the Nupe Province threatening an advance further south into Ilorin; on the west the disease spread south-ward into the Yola Province and Muri Province with cases reported from Ibi south of the River Benue and its advance now threat-ened the northern borders of the Southern Provinces.

Down the centre of the Northern Provinces the disease invaded Zaria Province, Bauchi Province and Nassarawa Province. The end of the year still saw cases occurring amongst labourers employed on the Eastern Railway Construction.[3]

No figures concerning cases or deaths have been published. But there is no doubt that the numbers for the total of the nine Provinces affected must have been very great.[4]

In 1925 'the outbreaks of this disease in the Northern Provinces were extensive and as usual were attended with high mortality',[5] but the number of victims was probably much smaller than in 1924.[6] It was apparently smaller still in 1926[7] but the reports for this year are somewhat contradictory. The Acting Director Medical and Sanitary Service said: 'There was an epidemic in Kontagora from January–March, but only sporadic cases were reported from the other Provinces.'[8] Yet the Deputy Director, Sanitary Service, stated:

The actual number of cases of this disease during the year is not known but 673 deaths were reported from the Northern Provinces. The provinces chiefly affected were Niger, Munshi and Yola Provinces. Sporadic cases occurred in Sokoto, Kaba, Ilorin Provinces. Ten deaths were reported from Kaduna [Zaria Province].[9]

The Medical and Sanitary Department of the Northern Provinces re-ported:

Only thirty-nine cases . . . were treated and in no places did it reach epidemic proportions, except in Kontagora and Kuta Divisions, both units of the Niger Province. A considerable number of deaths also occurred in Adamawa Province.[10]

---

[1] Nigeria, *Medical Report 1923*, p. 22. [2] See ibid. *1924*, p. 46. [3] Ibid., p. 45.

[4] See ibid., pp. 8, 38, 45. In Kano City the average monthly number of registered deaths (from all causes) was 128 in 1919–22, 189 in 1923, and 640 in the first half of 1924. In February and March the figures reached 1,340 and 820 respectively. The rise in 1923 was due to cerebrospinal fever, the rise in the first half of 1924 partly to this disease and partly to relapsing fever. See ibid., p. 46.

[5] Ibid. *1925*, p. 8; see also *Colonial Reports, Nigeria 1925*, p. 11.

[6] See Nigeria, *Medical Report 1925*, p. 18. [7] See *Colonial Reports, Nigeria 1926*, p. 9.

[8] Nigeria, *Medical Report 1926*, p. 14. [9] Ibid., p. 27.

[10] *Report on Northern Provinces 1926*, p. 50.

The number of deaths in Adamawa (Yola) Province (with 550,000 inhabitants) seems to have been considerable indeed. The Resident reported:

Outbreaks of cerebro-spinal meningitis occurred in three of the four Divisions in the Province. Accurate figures were not obtainable but approximately 3,500 deaths took place.[1]

In his report for 1926 the Acting Director Medical and Sanitary Service had said:

The decrease in cases is more probably due to the cycle of the disease than to precautionary measures which can only be small in the large areas in which the disease appears in epidemic form.[2]

This statement proved to be correct. Only local outbreaks of apparently not a very severe kind were reported in the following decade,[3] but in 1936 the turning-point was reached again.[4] The Medical Report for 1937 said:[5]

The cases of cerebro-spinal fever reported as occurring in the Northern Provinces towards the close of the year 1936 proved to be forerunners of a very severe epidemic which during the year was responsible for 2,823 deaths in a total of known cases of 3,452. This was the first serious invasion since the period 1920 to 1924 when a most devastating epidemic occurred affecting Northern Provinces.

The disease first appeared in dimensions of severity in Benue Province in the month of February, but strangely enough, this outbreak very quickly subsided. In March and April it became more widespread in the more northerly areas, the provinces most seriously affected being Adamawa[6] and Bauchi. In the former of these two areas the disease almost completely disappeared within the space of two months, but in Bauchi it continued with great severity, the peak of the epidemic being reached in the month of May when no fewer than 1,188 cases with 1,185 deaths were reported.[7] The late advent of the rains accounted for the persistence of the disease in epidemic proportions until July, after which the number of cases very rapidly diminished. A fair number of cases also occurred in Plateau, Bornu and Kano Provinces, although outbreaks in these areas were never so large as in Bauchi or Adamawa.

From the figures reported it is certainly of great doubt whether all cases were reported, while on the other hand deaths due to other causes may have been erroneously attributed to this disease.

The Medical Report for 1938 stated:[8]

The epidemic of cerebro-spinal meningitis which caused great havoc in 1937 and disappeared at the onset of the rainy season, reappeared at the end of that year, and continued with even greater severity in 1938 during which period it was responsible for more than 6,000 known deaths. This number refers to cases reported by Medical Officers, but there is every reason to believe that the toll was very much greater, as reports from outlying areas not yet reached by the medical organisation indicate a very considerable increase in the general mortality rate, which may reasonably be attributed to extension of the epidemic. The brunt of the attack fell

---

[1] Ibid., p. 9.   [2] Nigeria, *Medical Report 1926*, p. 14.
[3] The epidemics in pagan areas of Adamawa Province in 1932–3 possibly constituted an exception; see ibid. *1932*, p. 23; *1933*, p. 17.
[4] See ibid. *1936*, p. 24.   [5] Ibid. *1937*, pp. 15–16; see also ibid., p. 7.
[6] Concerning Adamawa Province see also *Report on Northern Provinces 1937*, p. 8: 'Once again an epidemic of Cerebro-Spinal Meningitis took heavy toll of the population, probably accounting in five months for nearly a thousand deaths.'
[7] See also ibid., p. 13.   [8] Nigeria, *Medical Report 1938*, p. 7.

on Sokoto,[1] Katsina[2] and Zaria[3] Provinces;[4] the case mortality rate was approximately sixty per cent and more than half of the cases occurred in children.

As regards the incidence in 1938, the Report on the Northern Provinces says:

Various estimates are given of the numbers affected, one estimate being as high as approximately 80,000 cases with a sixty per cent mortality. More than half of the cases occurred in children.[5]

In 1939 only 276 cases were notified with 236 deaths,[6] and no serious outbreak has been reported. In 1940 the position was not so good, but the available information is very scanty. The Report on the Northern Provinces, after having discussed smallpox, said:

Cerebro-spinal fever, the other great scourge of the people, has been somewhat more evident than in the previous year and is said to have caused 2,000 deaths in Adamawa Province.[7]

The Medical Report for 1940, on the other hand, stated:

130 cases and 57 deaths were notified, but, as with other infectious diseases, dilatoriness in notification or no notification at all by Native Authorities leads to many preventable deaths, e.g., the Medical Officer, Yola, in his Annual Report for 1940, the first intimation of the occurrence, mentions an epidemic of cerebro-spinal fever at Zinna 'with a total of some 2,000 deaths.' Such post-event reports emanating from backward areas must be treated with considerable reserve, as normally they are most inaccurate and grossly exaggerate the true course of events.[8]

In 1941 notifications were also few but they became again more numerous in 1942, and there was apparently no improvement in 1943.

1942. There were 828 cases with 180 deaths giving a case mortality rate of under 22 per cent. In 1941, the corresponding figures were 139 cases with forty-eight deaths, equivalent to a case mortality rate of nearly 35 per cent. It is anticipated that increased successful use of sulphonamides in the treatment of this scourge will steadily become more widely known: a factor which should lead to earlier notification of outbreaks.[9]

Better housing, and education to improve ventilation and prevent overcrowding, are necessary before the incidence of cerebro spinal fever can be much reduced.[10]

1943. Cerebro-spinal fever has carried on throughout the dry season for the last two years though usually it dies down or dies out after one season. The focus of infection has been the Plateau during the dry season. This is to be expected when there is an imported population doing unfamiliar work in strange surroundings under a different climate and conditions of living. The early reporting of cases with prompt treatment by M & B and Sulphanilamide by Epidemic Teams has reduced the mortality rate from about 20% to 11%.[11]

2,389 cases with 558 deaths are known to have occurred. The increased movement of people in connection with increased minesfield labour and with army requirements, and the very overcrowded conditions on trains, no doubt contributed to spread of the disease. A proportion of the cases would doubtless have escaped notice by the medical authorities were it not for improved organisation of epidemic

[1] See also *Report on Northern Provinces 1938*, pp. 4, 52.
[2] See also ibid., pp. 37–8.　　　　　　　[3] See also ibid., p. 58.
[4] Serious outbreaks occurred also in Bauchi Province, and epidemics were likewise reported from Kano and Plateau Provinces. See ibid., pp. 14, 34, 52.
[5] Ibid., p. 2.　　　　　　　　　　[6] See Nigeria, *Medical Report 1939*, p. 7.
[7] *Reports for Northern, Western, Eastern Provinces and Colony 1940*, p. 3.
[8] Nigeria, *Medical Report 1940*, p. 8.　　　[9] Ibid. *1942*, p. 8. See also ibid. *1941*, p. 7.
[10] *Report on Northern Provinces 1942*, p. 5.　[11] Ibid. *1943*, p. 4.

staff. The efficacy of the sulphanamide drugs against this disease must also encourage reporting by communities who were inclined to conceal cases before the coming of these chemotherapeutic agents, when the measures available in the presence of an outbreak were more or less limited to the isolation of cases and contacts.[1]

1944. There has been a significant increase in the number of hospital cases of cerebro-spinal meningitis. There were 574 in 1942, 1,273 in 1943 and 2,060 in 1944.[2]

The outbreak of cerebro-spinal meningitis was more severe during 1944 than in the previous year, most provinces being affected. 7,800 cases reported with 1,079 deaths as compared with 2,389 cases with 558 deaths in 1943, but the efficacy of the sulphonamide drugs against the disease is reflected in the drop in mortality rates—23·48 per cent in 1943 and 13·8 per cent in 1944. Epidemic control by the establishment of treatment centres has proved popular and communities are now willing and eager to bring cases for treatment in earlier stages of the disease. The increased movement of people due to war conditions has contributed to the spread of the disease. A disquieting development is the extension of the epidemic season into the rains particularly in the Southern Provinces. Benue, Owerri and Plateau Provinces were the most heavily affected.[3]

1945. There has, regrettably, been little reduction in cerebro-spinal Meningitis during the year, and there was a heavy incidence in many provinces. The provinces most affected were Bornu, Katsina, Sokoto, Onitsha, Bauchi, Adamawa and Plateau. This showed a considerable difference in distribution from the previous year. Owing to the outbreak of typhus fever at Jos mobile epidemic staff who would normally have dealt with cerebro-spinal Meningitis had to be posted to typhus control.[4]

Our lack of more precise information on the mortality caused by the epidemic of 1905 has been explained by the fact that 'at that time the country had hardly been effectively occupied by the British Administration'.[5] The Medical Report for 1940 does not suggest that a notable improvement has been achieved in this respect in the last 40 years. It is, therefore, extremely difficult to appraise the demographic effects of the disease in Nigeria. 'In the Southern Provinces, cerebro-spinal meningitis has never been epidemic, sporadic cases only occur and these are generally imported from the north.'[6] But in the Northern Provinces the number of deaths may have exceeded in some years 100,000.

Relapsing Fever. This disease seems to have affected general mortality conspicuously only in 1924–5, but in these two years claimed an enormous number of victims. The appearance of relapsing fever in 1923 was described as follows:

An outbreak of an obscure disease previously quite unknown to the inhabitants was reported as prevalent in Kontagora (now Nupe) Province during the last quarter of 1923. A Medical Officer was deputed to investigate the disease which was eventually diagnosed as relapsing fever. In all thirty-six cases were reported with a case mortality of 41·7%. Six cases also occurred in Lagos mainly during the month of September in the native town. One case was reported from Kaduna also.[7]

[1] Nigeria, *Medical Report 1943*, p. 10.   [2] Ibid. *1944*, p. 4.

[3] Ibid., p. 10. The increasing incidence in the Southern Provinces may be inferred from the following statement referring to the Northern Provinces: 'Recorded cases of cerebro-spinal fever amounted to 5,092, with 770 deaths, compared with 1,957 cases in 1943 when there were 466 deaths' (*Reports for Northern, Western, Eastern Provinces and Colony 1944*, p. 4).

[4] *Speech and Address by Governor Sir Arthur Richards to the Legislative Council 18th March, 1946*, p. 40.

[5] Nigeria, *Medical Report 1919–21*, p. 59.   [6] Ibid. *1925*, p. 18.

[7] Ibid. *1923*, p. 20.

This is the first record of an outbreak of relapsing fever in Nigeria and since the end of the year a considerable epidemic with a high mortality has developed.[1]

In 1924 the epidemic covered a wide area and became quite severe.

In the Northern Provinces both Cerebro-spinal Fever and Relapsing Fever prevailed in most parts of the country causing a very great mortality, the true extent of which cannot be stated even approximately.[2] Cerebro-spinal Fever prevailed mainly from January to April and Relapsing Fever from September to December.[3]

The spread of infection from Kontagora Province radiated southward into the Ilorin Province and northward into the Provinces of Katsina, Sokoto, Kano and then into Bauchi and Bornu where at Maiduguri it assumed a severe outbreak. . . .

By the month of December the disease was attaining its maximum intensity in the Provinces already mentioned.

In Kano and Katsina, where records of deaths are maintained by the Native Administrations, the mortality can be stated to have been appalling. On the plateau in Jos Township alone, eighty cases were treated by the Medical Officer in the Hospital. Later the disease spread into Nassarawa Province . . . .

In these southern reaches of the Northern Provinces, viz: Ilorin, Nupe, Nassarawa, and Muri, the end of the year saw them invaded by Relapsing Fever but the subsequent history of its prevalence in these areas and of spread of the disease further south will be reserved for the 1925 report.[4]

In Kano City the monthly average number of deaths was 640 from January to June and 424 from July to December as compared with 128 in 1919–22. 'In the first quarter of the year the two diseases Cerebro-Spinal Fever and Relapsing Fever were running concurrently.' But in the second half of the year 'the main cause of this high mortality was Relapsing Fever which attained its worst in December occasioning 558 deaths. The intensity of the disease continued high with somewhere near 400 deaths per month during the first quarter of 1925 but this will form a chapter in 1925 report.'[5]

Unfortunately, there is no trace of such a chapter in the 1925 report. This report gives a number of details concerning a small outbreak of relapsing fever in the Ondo Province,[6] but says with regard to the Northern Provinces merely:

Relapsing Fever. This disease appeared in epidemic form throughout all the districts of the Northern Provinces.[7]

There has been a great reduction in the prevalence of this disease also [as in the case of cerebro-spinal fever]. The epidemic of 1924 was continued on into the early months of the year; Sokoto (Birnin Kebbi), Yelwa, Kano, Katsina, Maidugari, Bauchi, Gwando and Wase districts producing 90% of the cases reported in the Northern Provinces.[8]

But the Colonial Report for 1925 suggests that the epidemic was quite severe, at least in the early part of the year.

---

[1] Nigeria, Medical Report 1923, p. 23. See also ibid., Appendix, p. 9.

[2] See also ibid. 1924, p. 44, where it is said that cerebrospinal fever and relapsing fever 'have been widespread throughout the Northern Provinces causing a very heavy mortality that cannot be stated in figures even approximately but is estimated to run into deaths amounting to hundreds of thousands'.

[3] Ibid. 1924, p. 38. See also ibid., pp. 7–8; Colonial Reports, Nigeria 1924, pp. 11–12.

[4] Nigeria, Medical Report 1924, p. 46.   [5] Ibid., pp. 46–7.

[6] See ibid. 1925, pp. 8, 19.   [7] Ibid., p. 8.   [8] Ibid., p. 18.

The violence of the epidemics of relapsing fever and cerebro-spinal meningitis in the Northern Provinces was devastating in its effects in several areas, and the death roll has been enormous. Relapsing fever had been severe in the north in 1924 and fears were then expressed that, owing to its method of propagation, extension would take place; these fears were fully justified.[1]

For 1926 the position is less clear still. The Medical Report for the year states first:

There has been a notable absence of epidemics of relapsing fever . . . with the exception of a moderate outbreak of relapsing fever in the Ondo Province . . . .[2]

It then states:

There were 814 cases with 107 deaths treated among Africans. The cases treated represent only a small proportion of the cases which occur. Sporadic cases occurred in all the Northern Provinces except Bornu. It was epidemic in Sokoto in the first quarter of the year and 450 deaths were reported from the Benue Province in September. No cases were reported from the Eastern Province. The Central Province[3] was infected with relapsing fever from the North in 1925, and it again appeared in epidemic form in Ado-Ekiti and Owo, towns in the Ondo Province. The Medical Officer in charge reported 615 cases with eighty-six deaths and the epidemic was finally stamped out.[4]

It says finally:

There was no very serious outbreak of this disease during the year. The outbreak which occurred in Arigidi in Ondo Province, Southern Provinces, Nigeria, last year has since spread to Ado-Ekiti and many other villages in that area. . . . Towards the end of the year the cases reported from Ondo Province showed a steady decline.[5]

The Colonial Report contains the following two statements:

There have been no serious outbreaks of epidemic disease during the year. . . . Relapsing fever has also [as cerebro-spinal meningitis] subsided to a great extent, though there was a heavy outbreak at Keana in the Lafia Emirate of the Benue Province. This has now been subdued.[6]

There has been a notable absence of epidemics of relapsing fever . . . the only exception being Ondo Province and Keana in Benin Province, where moderate outbreaks of relapsing fever occurred during the year.[7]

The Report on the Northern Provinces says with regard to this territory as a whole:[8]

The year has been singularly free from the scourges of cerebro-spinal meningitis and relapsing fever. . . . Sporadic cases of relapsing fever were reported from every province except Bornu;[9] it was endemic in the first quarter at Sokoto, and 480 deaths were reported at Keana in the Benue Province in September.

The report tells furthermore that in Bauchi Province the yield of the General Tax 'was considerably less than that of the previous year, a

[1] Colonial Reports, Nigeria 1925, p. 11. See also ibid., p. 8.

[2] Nigeria, Medical Report 1926, p. 13.

[3] The terms Eastern and Central Province probably refer to the administrative subdivision prior to 1914.

[4] Statements by Acting Director Medical and Sanitary Service, ibid. 1926, p. 14.

[5] Statement by Deputy Director, Sanitary Service, ibid., pp. 26–7.

[6] Colonial Reports, Nigeria 1926, p. 9.

[7] Ibid., p. 12. Keana is situated in Benue (Northern Provinces) not in Benin (Southern Provinces).

[8] Report on Northern Provinces 1926, p. 50.

[9] See for Adamawa Province ibid., p. 9, for Kano Province p. 31, for Sokoto Province p. 41.

decrease principally due to the ravages of the relapsing fever epidemic and emigration'[1] and says of Ilorin Province:

> Relapsing fever was again prevalent, causing more deaths during the year than any other single disease. It is impossible however to estimate the death roll as nearly all the patients were carefully hidden by their friends.[2]

For 1927 and 1928 only small outbreaks were reported.

> 1927. Small outbreaks of relapsing fever were reported in various districts in the Northern Provinces, and in the Ondo province in the South. All the outbreaks were mild in type. No cases were reported among Europeans, but amongst Africans 303 cases were treated in Government hospitals and dispensaries, with six deaths.[3]

> There was no very serious outbreak of relapsing fever during the year. A total of 264 cases, with forty-three deaths, were reported; 205 of these cases occurred in Northern Provinces and were reported mainly from Makurdi area, Bornu and Plateau Provinces.[4] All the cases (fifty-nine) reported from Southern Provinces occurred in Ondo Province. This is the province in which a considerable outbreak occurred in 1925 and continued into 1926.[5]

> 1928. Small outbreaks of this disease occurred from time to time in both the Northern and Southern Provinces, chiefly in the Ondo area in the latter. The total number of cases reported being 265 with nineteen deaths;[6] all the outbreaks were mild in type . . . .[7]

> No serious outbreak of this disease occurred during the year.

> 161 cases with seventeen deaths were reported from the Northern Provinces of which 158 cases occurred in the Bornu Province prior to the final termination of an outbreak which commenced there during the latter months of 1927.

> No cases were reported in the Southern Provinces.[8]

It is extremely difficult to estimate the total number of deaths from relapsing fever. The Medical Report for 1924 says:

> Kano City with a population of 50,000 . . . in normal years had an average number of deaths at 1,536 with an average death rate of 30 per 1,000 per annum but during 1924 the total deaths came to 6,384 with an average death rate of 130 per 1,000 population per annum.

> What has been said of the mortality in Kano can be said with safety of the rest of the towns and villages not only in the Kano Emirate and the Emirate of Katsina but also of Sokoto and Bornu in which Provinces the disease first inflicted such loss of human life and then later spread southward . . . .[9]

If we assume that in Kano City 5 per cent. of the population died in 1924 of relapsing fever and that the proportion was the same in the rest of the Kano Emirate, in the Katsina Emirate, and in Sokoto and Bornu Provinces the total number of deaths would have exceeded 250,000 in these areas. But the epidemic also affected other Provinces and the number of deaths must have been still considerable in 1925. For the whole

---

[1] *Report on Northern Provinces 1926*, p. 11.   [2] Ibid., p. 22.

[3] Nigeria, *Medical Report 1927*, p. 17.

[4] *Colonial Reports, Nigeria 1927*, say (p. 31) that 'a further outbreak has been reported from Abinsi in the Benue Province'.

[5] Nigeria, *Medical Report 1927*, p. 30. The 264 'reported' cases, mentioned here, are evidently not included in the 303 cases treated in Government hospitals and dispensaries.

[6] This is a mistake. The figure of 265 does not refer to the cases reported but to the number of new patients treated in Government hospitals and dispensaries. (There were at the beginning of the year 10 in-patients; 165 were admitted during the year; of the total 175 in-patients 19 died; there were in addition 100 out-patients. See ibid. *1928*, p. 61.)

[7] Ibid., p. 14.   [8] Ibid., p. 25.   [9] Ibid. *1924*, p. 47.

of Nigeria the number of deaths from relapsing fever in 1924–5 may have been greater even than the number of deaths from influenza in 1918.

Plague. The outbreak of plague which began in Lagos in July 1924, and remained confined to Lagos and Iddo Islands during that year, appeared in 1925 on the mainland in the village of Agege, the infection having apparently spread by railway from Iddo. The first cases were recognized in March, and a total of 12 cases with 9 deaths were reported. In August 1925 a considerable outbreak was reported from the Remo District of the Ijebu-Ode Province about 30 miles from the railway. It involved a group of four villages with approximately 12,400 inhabitants, and 521 cases with 381 deaths were reported. In November 1925 an outbreak was reported in an outlying section of the large town of Abeokuta with 44 cases and 44 deaths.[1]

A fresh and more severe outbreak made its appearance in March 1926 in the town of Ijebu-Ode and gradually spread to sixteen neighbouring villages. In Ijebu-Ode with 21,950 inhabitants, 442 cases were reported with 393 deaths; in the sixteen villages with 76,831 inhabitants 391 cases with 334 deaths. Nine cases were reported from Abeokuta.[2]

In 1927 the only outbreak of importance on the mainland was confined to the village of Ogere near Ijebu-Ode with 2,900 inhabitants; there were 209 cases and 160 deaths. Elsewhere only 33 cases with 30 deaths were reported.[3]

In 1928 only 15 cases, all fatal, were recorded.[4] No case seems to have been reported from the mainland in subsequent years.

Thus, the incidence of plague has been very slight outside Lagos.

Pneumonia and Influenza. The early official reports mention only occasionally that the Natives suffer in the dry season from respiratory diseases 'brought on by the cold nights'.[5] But from 1910 on the information becomes more explicit.

1910. Northern Nigeria. Pneumonia ... often appears to assume Epidemic form, when, during the cold weather, the natives huddle together in ill-ventilated huts for mutual warmth.[6]

1911. Northern Nigeria. There is very little doubt that Pneumonia, as seen here, is generally epidemic.[7]

1912. Northern Nigeria. Early in the year, two outbreaks of disease had been reported from the Province of Kabba—one of Small Pox, the other an obscure disease attended by fever, cough and extensive mortality. . . .

The other epidemic, which had almost died out when the Province was visited, was undoubtedly one of Pneumonia. An apparently identical outbreak had been alleged to have decimated the same part of the Province about seven years before.

The centre of the outbreak was a Pagan town called Omjiami; it was stated by the natives that during the previous six months 122 persons out of a population of about 700 had died of the disease, and the place, together with the people and their

---

[1] See ibid., p. 43; *1925*, pp. 19–20; *1926*, p. 191.
[2] See ibid., pp. 24, 200–1.
[3] See ibid. *1927*, p. 18, Appendix, p. 101.
[4] See ibid. *1928*, p. 23, Appendix, pp. 113–15.
[5] *Colonial Reports, Northern Nigeria 1905–6*, p. 103.
[6] Northern Nigeria, 'Medical Report 1910', p. 138.
[7] Northern Nigeria, *Medical Report 1911*, p. 43.

habits, afforded a classical example of how epidemic Pneumonia becomes such a fatal disease in this country. The town occupies a bare wind-swept site. The situation is often damp and cold. The people wear practically no clothing, and they go to sleep on the bare earthen floors of their huts.[1]

1914. Southern Provinces. Pneumonia is one of the most serious acute diseases from which the native suffers. It is most common during the cold harmattan season.[2]

1917. Northern Provinces. Pneumonia and Influenza are exceedingly common everywhere and may be numbered with the endemic diseases which account for vague reports of 'outbreaks of sickness' forthcoming from lay sources. Were it not for the very brief course so often run by Pneumonia, many more cases of the disease would be admitted to the Native Hospitals. A large proportion of the cases which are admitted comes from among the Soldiery and Police; for with them, a very brief prostration means failure to appear on parade and consequent reporting sick.[3]

The pandemic of influenza in 1918 caused probably many more deaths in Southern Nigeria than any other catastrophe that has ever befallen that country. A report transmitted to the Secretary of State described the events as follows:

Lagos was infected on the 14th September; generally the Epidemic spread northward and eastward: the river Niger in the Southern Provinces being reached during the middle of October, the Eastern Railway at the end of the month, the Cross River early in November, and the Cameroons about the middle of November.

The disease spread chiefly along the railway, and by river and road along the trade routes.

The onset and decline in each place were remarkably rapid: there was a period of about a fortnight during which the disease reached its maximum followed by a fortnight when the disease was at its maximum, then a third fortnight of rapid decline.

Practically all prophylactic measures were useless.

The Epidemic was too overwhelming for treatment to have much effect—except in a few places where Medical Officers are stationed. Matters had necessarily to be left to themselves. Excluding the Cameroons, the population of the Southern Provinces of Nigeria is about nine million, the area about 78,600 square miles, and the Medical Officers about 32.

More than half the population suffered from the disease in a more or less acute form.

More than 5% of those attacked in a more or less acute form died.

Nearly 3% of the population of the Southern Provinces of Nigeria, that is at least 250,000 individuals, died from Influenza during the Epidemic.[4]

For Northern Nigeria the published information is very scanty. The Medical Report for 1918 said:

. . . the native population was universally affected and a very large number of deaths occurred.[5]

Among the native population the mortality has been very high, but an estimate of its amount, even approaching accuracy, is practically impossible.[6]

---

[1] Northern Nigeria, *Medical Report 1912*, p. 36. See also ibid., pp. 13, 57, *1913*, p. 50; Nigeria, *Medical Report 1914*, p. 20, *1915*, p. 15.

[2] *Colonial Reports, Nigeria 1914*, p. 24. See also Southern Nigeria, *Medical Report 1913*, p. 9; Nigeria, *Medical Report 1914*, p. 77, *1915*, p. 38.

[3] Ibid. *1917*, p. 138.

[4] Southern Provinces, *Medical Report 1918*, p. 27.

[5] Northern Provinces, *Medical Report 1918*, p. 5.

[6] Ibid., p. 6. For some other comments on the epidemic, see ibid., pp. 8, 11, 12, 18–19, 51–3.

Though probably much less severe than in the Southern Provinces[1] the epidemic in the Northern Provinces apparently lasted longer.

Northern Provinces.—The influenza epidemic which caused such a high death and sick rate ceased practically as an epidemic about February though a few sporadic cases were reported from the various stations for some months after, the severer forms of this disease being amongst the native population.[2]

Finally the Medical Report for 1919–21, covering the whole of Nigeria, stated:

Influenza and Pneumonia.—With the subsidence of the great pandemic of 1918, these two closely allied (if not identical, for Nigerian purposes) diseases seem to have shot their bolt for the time being. Strictly localised epidemics of them recur at some one district or another annually: during the triennium they followed what may be called their normal endemic routine.[3]

Medical Reports for subsequent years said:

1922. Pneumonia and Influenza.—These infections were very prevalent in various parts of both sets of Provinces towards the end of the year.[4]

1923. Influenza of an extremely mild type appeared, but never assumed epidemic form. The cases occurred mainly in the Northern Provinces.[5]

1924. Influenza shows a much higher figure than formerly but did not appear in epidemic form.[6]

1925. Influenza. This disease has been reported as being epidemic in many places e.g. Port Harcourt, Ibadan and Onitsha in the Southern Provinces and Zaria, Minna, Kaduna and Jos in the Northern Provinces. These epidemics were of a mild type and the mortality was small.[7]

1928. In the harmattan season and during the height of the rains pneumonia is very common and the death rate heavy . . . .[8]

1934. The pneumonias, especially broncho-pneumonia, continue to take a heavy toll of life, especially of infants.[9]

1935. Pneumonia infections are exceedingly common and account for a very large percentage of deaths.[10]

1937. . . . pneumonia . . . may be roughly calculated to account for twenty-five to thirty-three per cent of all native deaths.[11]

1940. Pneumonias. 2,410 cases with 805 deaths were reported during the year. Broncho-pneumonia was found by autopsies to have caused 277 (55·4%) of the deaths of 500 children of three years and under who died in Lagos in 1940. Lobar pneumonia was responsible for twenty-six of their deaths (5·2%), so the pneumonias were responsible for almost two-thirds of these infant deaths.

[1] Some areas in the Northern Provinces, of course, also suffered enormously. While in Lagos, the primary focus of infection, 'at least' 1,200 people are said to have died from influenza (see Southern Provinces, *Medical Report 1918*, p. 28), the number of deaths in Kano City with only half the population of Lagos may have been almost 1,000 (see the table p. 650 above).

[2] Colonial Reports, *Nigeria 1919*, p. 14.   [3] Nigeria, *Medical Report 1919–21*, p. 59.

[4] Ibid. *1922*, p. 51. See also *Report on Cameroons 1922*, p. 46: 'A large number of cases of acute broncho-pneumonia occurs at the "change of season" from the dry to the wet, and vice versa; the natives themselves attribute this to the effects of the influenza epidemic of 1918. It is probable that the infection of that epidemic will linger for some time, especially in the areas of overcrowding and heaviest rainfall.'

[5] Nigeria, *Medical Report 1923*, p. 7.   [6] Ibid. *1924*, p. 7.

[7] Ibid. *1925*, p. 22. See also ibid. *1926*, p. 14.

[8] Ibid. *1928*, p. 13. See also ibid. *1927*, p. 16. In 1927 there was a serious epidemic of pneumonia in Adamawa Province (see *Report on Northern Provinces 1927*, p. 9).

[9] Nigeria, *Medical Report 1934*, p. 19.

[10] Ibid. *1935*, p. 13. 'There was a severe influenza epidemic in Yola early in the year with a death-roll of 135' (*Report on Northern Provinces 1935*, p. 6).

[11] Nigeria, *Medical Report 1937*, p. 17.

If such can occur in Lagos, infantile mortality from respiratory diseases throughout the country must be very heavy. The sulphonamides render great service at points where patients can be admitted to hospital, but these are mere 'islands' in the expanse of disease, so here, as in all other cases, the real 'cure' is prevention through social uplift.[1]

1941. Where hospital treatment is sought, the pneumonias, like cerebro-spinal fever, have gained a vastly improved prospect of recovery through the introduction of sulphonamide medication. A very large proportion of the cases, however, never come under medical notice.[2]

1942. A comparison of diseases treated in the Northern and Southern Provinces yields interesting details. . . . Respiratory diseases are percentagely roughly equal in north and south and in both over 50 per cent of the cases were pneumonias, but while in the North the mortality was 9·9 per cent in the South it was 18·6.[3]

In Lagos, deaths from all forms of pneumonia amounted to 500, or 16 per cent of total deaths, . . . showing no appreciable change from the corresponding rate in 1941.[4]

1943. Pneumonia. 4,274 cases with 898 deaths were notified but it is certain that very many cases occurred about which nothing was heard.[5]

1944. Pneumonia. 3,602 cases were notified with 795 deaths, but these figures give no real idea of the prevalence of the disease as there is no doubt that many cases are never notified.[6]

Tuberculosis. This disease, just as pneumonia, was apparently not discussed in official reports before 1910 and its incidence, unlike that of pneumonia, was at first considered to be small. But opinion changed soon. I shall first quote some passages referring to Northern Nigeria.

1910. Tuberculosis is an exceedingly rare disease among the natives; but it is not at all uncommon among African non-natives from the Coast.[7]

1912. It is a source of thankfulness that Tuberculosis cannot really be called an endemic disease in the Protectorate; and it is probable that, in the cases now mentioned, either the patients themselves were importations or the infection was imported from without.

Were the disease to obtain a real footing in the country it would assume epidemic proportions on account of the conditions which have been mentioned in referring to Pneumonia.[8]

1913. It is rather distressing to note that the infection shows signs of obtaining a footing. Beyond isolating natives who appear with it in hospital or gaol, little can be done to stamp it out.[9]

1915. With the end of the year, it had become necessary to recognise enteric fever and tuberculosis as naturalised members of the endemic community, for it was no longer either truthful or possible to regard examples of them as isolated importations.[10]

1917. Tuberculosis although not very widely disseminated, obtrudes itself on the observer with painful regularity. It is showing its ugly presence amongst the Arabs of the North, in whom it was unknown until quite recently, so far as the present reporter [Dr. Blair] has been able to discover.[11]

The 1911 Medical Report for Southern Nigeria[12] merely stated that 'more cases of Tubercular Disease have come under notice in Lagos

---

[1] Nigeria, *Medical Report 1940*, p. 8.   [2] Ibid. *1941*, p. 8.   [3] Ibid. *1942*, p. 3.
[4] Ibid., p. 9.   [5] Ibid. *1943*, p. 11.   [6] Ibid. *1944*, p. 10.
[7] Northern Nigeria, 'Medical Report 1910', p. 138.
[8] Northern Nigeria, *Medical Report 1912*, p. 59.
[9] Ibid. *1913*, p. 51. See also Nigeria, *Medical Report 1914*, p. 21.
[10] Ibid. *1915*, p. 9. See also Northern Provinces, *Medical Report 1916*, p. 8; *Colonial Reports, Nigeria 1916*, p. 27.   [11] Nigeria, *Medical Report 1917*, p. 138.
[12] See Southern Nigeria, *Medical Report 1911*, pp. 5, 18.

(Municipal Area) than elsewhere'. Since only '92 cases were treated in that town' the number of cases ascertained elsewhere was evidently negligible.

The 1912 Report contained two somewhat contradictory statements. The Principal Medical Officer said:

Tuberculosis is a disease attended with high mortality among negro races. The known incidence has not been great in past years in Southern Nigeria, but it is a danger which will, it is hoped, be lessened with the gradual advance of improved sanitation. The following shows the percentage of Tuberculosis to total cases treated during the last six years, and indicates that no marked increase has occurred.

1907	1908	1909	1910	1911	1912
0·17	0·17	0·18	0·15	0·19	0·15[1]

The Senior Sanitary Officer, however, reported:

More patients suffering from Tubercular disease are now seen than used to be the case but there are no statistics available to show whether it is simply that more of the sufferers are coming for treatment or that the affection is really increasing; some Medical Officers appear to hold the opinion that the latter is the correct view.[2]

In his report for 1913 the Acting Senior Sanitary Officer said:

That there has been a marked increase in tuberculous patients is alarming, but it is just possible that with the more careful diagnostic methods in use at present a large number of cases formerly relegated to bronchitis and other allied diseases are now included under this heading. The increase, which is very marked, is six times that of 1912, and was confined entirely to the Central Province.[3]

In his next report he said under 'Aids to increase of tuberculosis':

The insanitary conditions under which most natives live, their inherent love of small, stuffy rooms, and their disregard for the rudiments of sanitation with respect to the food they eat and the water they drink, are important factors in predisposing them to tuberculous disease.[4]

According to the sanitary reports for the following years tuberculosis was on the increase.[5]

I shall now quote some passages referring to the whole of Nigeria.

1915. Cases of pulmonary tuberculosis were observed more frequently than in former years. Although confined for the most part to the humid Southern Provinces a few cases have also been seen amongst the natives in the drier Northern Provinces. In the opinion of the medical and sanitary officers, this disease is on the increase and often assumes a very virulent form.[6]

Enteric fever and tuberculosis are much more difficult to stamp out than is yellow fever; and the advent of all three is one of the penalties which have to be paid for easier communication with the outer world.[7]

1919-21. The fact that they [influenza and pneumonia] are endemic probably accounts, partly at least, for the slow but steady advance of imported pulmonary tuberculosis.[8]

This invasion makes slow but steady progress: it is much more prevalent in the

[1] Ibid. *1912*, p. 8.   [2] Ibid., p. 24.   [3] Ibid. *1913*, p. 39.
[4] Nigeria, *Medical Report 1914*, p. 76. See also ibid. *1917*, p. 23; Southern Provinces, *Medical Report 1918*, pp. 23–5.
[5] See Nigeria, *Medical Report 1915*, pp. 49–50; Southern Provinces, *Medical Report 1916*, p. 18.
[6] *Colonial Reports, Nigeria* 1915, p. 20.   [7] Ibid., p. 21.
[8] Nigeria, *Medical Report 1919–21*, p. 59.

Southern, than it is in the Northern Provinces; in the Southern Provinces, it is more common on the coast than it is inland, and it appears to be more prevalent in Lagos than it is at any other point on the coast, but statistics are less unreliable at Lagos than they are anywhere else in Nigeria: as a matter of fact, the figures of the last few years, taken superficially, would seem to indicate a relative decrease in its prevalence in Lagos.[1]

1922. Leaving out the more or less anglicised classes of the Coast, it is not a disease which has so far obtained a footing among the upper classes: this is not surprising for they lead comparatively hygienic lives vis-à-vis this infection.[2]

1923. Statistics are not available except for Lagos, the disease however is widely spread throughout Nigeria. . . .

The total deaths registered in Lagos during 1923 were 2,492 and since out of 1,081 certified deaths there were 91 deaths from tuberculosis it may be assumed that a proportionate number occurred amongst the uncertified which would mean that possibly over 200 deaths from tuberculosis occurred. Lagos is grossly overcrowded, however, and the tuberculosis rate cannot be taken as an index of the extent of the disease generally.[3]

1924. Tuberculosis and syphilis appear to be on the increase.[4]

1925. Very little accurate information is available as to the prevalence of tuberculosis in Nigeria. Cases occur in widely separated places. As a rule infection is of the pulmonary type and so far as is known invariably ends fatally.[5]

1926. Tuberculosis, chiefly pulmonary, is increasing throughout Nigeria.[6]

1927. The number of cases treated does not give a reliable idea of the incidence amongst Africans, as many cases not recorded in the returns are seen in the villages on tour and the natives do not seek treatment readily for this disease.[7]

1930. Tuberculosis must be considerably more common in the Southern Provinces than hospital and dispensary returns would indicate. In the Northern Provinces it does not appear to be a very common disease and only a few cases were reported during the year.[8]

1932. Except in Lagos exact information about the prevalence of tuberculosis is lacking, but it is clear from the hospital returns that in its pulmonary form it is a disease of great importance throughout Nigeria. . . .

The chief hope for the future lies in the gradual improvement in housing conditions that is taking place in many parts of the country and in bringing home to the mass of the people by education and propaganda the practical measures necessary to prevent the spread of the disease.[9]

1936. Although there is no direct evidence of a rapid increase in the loss of life from tuberculosis in Nigeria—principally pulmonary in origin—there is little doubt in the minds of various persons who have investigated the subject that the disease constitutes a very real menace. This is particularly the case owing to the fact that the type encountered is usually the acute, exudative or infantile variety with rapid dissemination and a fatal issue within a year or so.

In order that an effort might be made to stem the tide of this disease (which was responsible for over nine *per centum* of deaths from all causes in Lagos in 1936) it was added to the list of diseases, which are compulsorily notifiable and against which certain administrative measures can be taken.[10]

1937. Plans have been prepared for the erection of a small tuberculosis ward at

[1] Nigeria, *Medical Report 1919–21*, p. 60. See also *Colonial Reports, Nigeria 1919*, p. 16.
[2] Nigeria, *Medical Report 1922*, p. 51.
[3] Ibid. *1923*, p. 26. See also ibid. *1925*, pp. 22–3.
[4] Ibid. *1924*, p. 7.   [5] Ibid. *1925*, p. 22.   [6] Ibid. *1926*, p. 16.
[7] Ibid. *1927*, p. 19. See also ibid. *1928*, pp. 16, 24–5; *1929*, p. 29.
[8] Ibid. *1930*, p. 23. See also Medical Census Southern Provinces (*Census of Nigeria, 1931*, vol. vi), p. 24: 'There is little doubt that the disease is becoming more frequent and that it will spread amongst the interior tribes. As a general rule native cases run a rapid course and death occurs in from six months to one year.'
[9] Nigeria, *Medical Report 1932*, p. 23.   [10] Ibid. *1936*, pp. 24–5.

Yaba—a suburb of Lagos—where a few of the most infectious cases of the disease would be treated. With so many other urgent claims on the country's revenue, more ambitious anti-tuberculosis measures of a specific nature cannot be considered yet. Prevention of this disease, however, is closely connected with the improvement of housing and other general sanitary conditions.[1]

1940. One disturbing feature is the large death rate from pulmonary tuberculosis. Of those admitted to hospital suffering from this complaint thirty per cent died. The majority of cases are seen in a very advanced condition, but it is also very evident that immunity to this disease has not been acquired.[2]

1941. 992 cases with 304 deaths of tuberculosis of all types came to the notice of the medical authorities. These two figures cannot be taken as in any way a true measure of case-mortality: with a hopeless disease such as tuberculosis often proves to be in the non-resistant African, most cases leave hospital or dispensary attendance to return to, and almost certainly succumb in, their native village or town. For Lagos, the corresponding figures were 340 cases with 226 deaths and the latter represented 8·6 per cent of all deaths in the township.[3]

1942. Another matter of serious import is the rise in incidence of tuberculosis. 25 per cent of all invalidings of African officials during the year were due to this disease. The high mortality, the ease of spread in the overcrowded areas and the lack of immunity among the people of this country produce a situation of extreme gravity. A small tuberculosis hospital has been erected at Yaba, but it is the early curable cases we must endeavour to control. The whole subject is receiving earnest consideration.[4]

In Lagos, where notification is more frequent than anywhere else in Nigeria, there were 265 deaths notified from tuberculosis of all types, representing a crude death-rate of 1·58 per thousand of population. . . . Deaths from tuberculosis amongst the native population represented 8·6 per cent of all deaths in Lagos township, during 1942: this percentage shows no change from 1941.

In other medical stations of Nigeria, outside Lagos, an increasing number of cases of tuberculosis are being seen by Medical Officers, who notified a total of 1,111 cases. The disease is known to be rapidly fatal in the majority of cases, though only a proportion of the deaths come to the notice of the medical authorities owing to the vast scattered population and the limited number of medical practitioners available outside a few large towns.[5]

1943. Tuberculosis still appears to be on the increase and 1,218 cases were notified, of which 407 were fatal. . . . 481 cases of which 304 proved fatal, occurred in Lagos township during the year. 134 cases were reported in the Western Provinces but it is stated that only those in the last stages attend the hospitals.[6]

Invaliding figures of African officials from this disease are disquieting e.g. in the Police Department 39 per cent of all invalidings of officials was due to Tuberculosis. In the Railway the figure was 29 per cent, Public Works Department 21 per cent, Medical Department 17 per cent.[7]

1944. 1,200 cases of tuberculosis of which 393 terminated fatally, were notified; figures which show little difference from last year. . . . 373 cases were notified in Lagos Township, of which 304 died, 584 cases with 113 deaths were notified from the Northern Provinces. The disease is believed to be on the increase in Port Harcourt. Poor housing and overcrowding amongst the population with a low degree of resistance to this disease, are no doubt leading factors in spread. War conditions have brought in large additional numbers of people into the urban areas [and] at the same time interfered with the necessary additional provision and improvement of housing.[8]

Invaliding figures of African Staff for this disease remain high, 23·6 per cent of the total.[9]

[1] Ibid. *1937*, p. 17. [2] Ibid. *1940*, p. 6. [3] Ibid. *1941*, p. 8.
[4] Ibid. *1942*, p. 3. [5] Ibid., p. 9. [6] Ibid. *1943*, p. 11.
[7] Ibid., p. 6. [8] Ibid. *1944*, p. 10. [9] Ibid., p. 4.

The position has been recently summarized as follows:

Tuberculosis is a problem causing much concern as the African is very susceptible to the disease, which as a rule is rapidly fatal. The conditions of poor housing and over-crowding, in which he lives, provide a fertile soil for its spread. In Lagos, the only area for which accurate vital statistics are available, tuberculosis is responsible for 9 per cent of all deaths. . . . A specialized enquiry will be required before large work or expenditure on tuberculosis can be justified, and a close study of the incidence of the disease in different parts of the country is needed, while the conditions under which natural recovery occurs will have to be known before suitable preventive measures can be devised.[1]

Leprosy. On 30 November 1910 *The Northern Nigeria Gazette* published Notes 'compiled from Reports by Residents and other Officers on the subject of Leprosy among the natives of the Protectorate'.[2] They stated with regard to the prevalence of the disease and to segregation:

Prevalence of the Disease. Leprosy seems to be found throughout the Protectorate, though the disease appears to be much more prevalent in the Northern than in the more Southern parts of the country.

The number of lepers in Sokoto Province is returned as 6,595.[3] In the Kano Emirate alone there is an estimated number of 5,000, and in the other three divisions of the [Kano] province about half that number. In Bornu the number is estimated at 4,000.

In Bassa the acting Resident, Mr. Maynard, writes 'Leprosy is not at all prevalent in this province taken as a whole'.

The Resident of Yola reports the same. In Muri, Capt. Ruxton considers that an average of 2 cases might be found in every village along the main trade routes.

From Ilorin, Mr. Dwyer reports that the disease is not very prevalent. . . .

Several reports state that the disease is more common among Mahommedans than among the Pagan tribes.

Segregation of Lepers. In this, native custom differs widely in the various districts and speaking generally the Pagans seem to enforce far more rigid segregation than the Mohammedans; thus among the Pagans of the hill division of Bautchi, Lepers are given separate houses. The Resident Niger reports that amongst the Gwaris and Nupes all contact with lepers or their belongings is avoided. Mr. Maynard reports from Bassa that the Igara people drive lepers from the towns, while the other tribes give the leper a separate house in which he is forced to live, although, as a rule, he is within hail of his family who supply his wants. Mr. Withers Gill writes that among the Zaria pagans, lepers live on their own farms and receive assistance from the outside at seed time and harvest.

The acting Resident of Kabba, Mr. Sciortino, reports that the Egbiras and Kukurukus enforce segregation to the extent of separate huts, but husband and wife are not separated.

Among the Aworo the custom is stricter; Lepers are isolated in the bush, and husband and wife are separated.

In the Mahommedan states on the other hand, there is hardly ever any attempt at segregation, and that, when attempted, is of the slightest.

Mr. Arnett, acting Resident Kano, reports that two years ago an attempt was made to confine lepers to separate compounds; the only result was to drive many out of the town into the outlying districts and the scheme failed: a similar attempt at Katsena met with the same fate.

---

[1] *A Ten-Year Plan of Development and Welfare for Nigeria 1946*, p. 73.

[2] 'Notes on Leprosy in Northern Nigeria', *Gazette*, 30 Nov. 1910, pp. 265–6.

[3] 'The Emir of Sokoto has caused a census to be made of all the lepers in his territory', 'Abstracts from the report by the Resident of the Sokoto Province for the quarter ending 30th September 1910', ibid., 31 May 1911, p. 122.

In the provinces of Sokoto and Bornu no attempt at segregation appears to have been made by the native authorities.

In Zaria province, in the capital alone, there is a leper quarter. Mr. Withers Gill, acting Resident, writes that this quarter contains about 200 men, women, and children, and that many of the latter are not lepers.

In Sokoto Division with a population of about 1,000,000 the number of lepers was 5,381. But the incidence of leprosy varied enormously from district to district.

. . . no less than 16 districts out of 46 show a proportion of over 100 per 10,000 of population, and of these 3 districts have over 200 per 10,000 (Kwarre, 236·4 Dinawa, 224 and Zurmi 203) whereas in only two districts does the figure fall below 20 per 10,000 (Gummi 17·6 and Sokoto town and district 17·7).[1]

The figures stated are I consider very alarming even if they should prove to be over-estimated, which is improbable since doubtless many of the less obviously affected have not been included.[2]

The total number of lepers in the province is so large (nearly 6,600) that it is obviously beyond the powers of the native administration to deal with them satis-factorily, and short of such large measures of effective segregation and treatment as can be afforded by Government institutions it is doubtful whether much is to be expected.[3]

While the figures for lepers in Sokoto Division may have been approxi-mately correct the statistical position in the Protectorate as a whole was quite obscure. The Medical Officer had stated:

The average for the whole of Sokoto Division is 53·2 per 10,000, and I doubt if this figure is exceeded in any part of Africa in a similar area.[4]

But if the estimate of 4,000 lepers for Bornu Province with about 700,000 inhabitants was exact the proportion of lepers would have been higher there than in Sokoto Division. Governor Bell in his report for 1910–11 said:

Leprosy . . . has been found to be terribly rife among the natives of the Moslem States. It is estimated that, in the Sokoto Emirate alone, there are more than 6,000 lepers, and that in the whole Protectorate there are probably some 80,000. The problem is one that requires vigorous action, due consideration being at the same time paid to native susceptibilities.[5]

If there were actually 80,000 lepers in the whole Protectorate, the proportion of lepers in Sokoto Emirate would have been considerably below the average. The Senior Sanitary Officer realized the necessity of securing more accurate figures for the other Provinces.

Steps are being taken . . . to establish Segregation Camps: and the Medical and Political Officers all over the country are collecting statistics of Lepers; but the evidence, upon which the statistics, compiled up to date, rest, is so largely only hear-say that they cannot be regarded as reliable.[6]

But nothing seems to have been done to obtain more reliable data.

The number of lepers is very large, but the day for an accurate leper census is not yet.[7]

[1] Statement by the Medical Officer, Sokoto, Dr. Dalziel, Northern Nigeria, 'Medical Report 1910', p. 151.   [2] Ibid., p. 153.   [3] Ibid., p.151.   [4] Ibid., p. 153.
[5] *Colonial Reports, Northern Nigeria 1910–11*, pp. 5–6.
[6] Northern Nigeria, 'Medical Report 1910', p. 138.
[7] Northern Nigeria, *Medical Report 1911*, p. 44.

Some segregation was carried out in the following years[1] but it was realized that the figures of admissions were 'trifling having regard to the great prevalence of Leprosy in the country'.[2] Moreover 'the progress in leper segregation was greatly curtailed by the outbreak of war; in more than one region there was actual retrogression'.[3] The fluctuations in the number of cases treated in Northern Nigeria were as follows:[4]

Year	Remaining at end of previous year	Admissions	Total cases treated	Deaths	Year	Remaining at end of previous year	Admissions	Total cases treated	Deaths of in-patients
1911	1[1]	83	84	..	1915	666	..	..	..
1912	61	744	805	66	1916	636	45	686[2]	63
1913	708	243	951	113	1917	538	108	661[3]	62
1914	784	185	969	124	1918	534	47	611[4]	92

[1] Total cases treated in 1910, 37; see Northern Nigeria, 'Medical Report 1910', p. 138.
[2] Including 5 out-patients.   [3] Including 15 out-patients.   [4] Including 30 out-patients.

The number of lepers ascertained at the 1921 'census' in the Northern Provinces was as follows:[5]

Bauchi	Bornu	Ilorin	Kano	Konta-gora	Mun-shi	Muri	Nasa-rawa	Nupe	Sokoto	Yola	Zaria	Total
4,605	837	1,189	10,653	886	1,970	897	1,708	1,604	5,068	1,034	2,321	32,772

The average for the country was 33 lepers for each 10,000 inhabitants. The proportion was highest in Zaria (61) and lowest in Bornu (11). In Sokoto Province (30) it was somewhat below the average. Mr. Meek makes the following comment:

The number of lepers in Nigeria is thus proportionately very much higher than in India. But in India care was taken to exclude from the statistics all diseases such as leucoderma which have the outward appearance of leprosy, and are believed by the natives to be such. On the other hand, it is probable that numbers of genuine lepers were concealed in the Nigerian census.[6]

In Southern Nigeria leprosy likewise began to cause concern a few years before the First World War.

There can be no doubt that the disease is far more prevalent in the Central Province, and probably other parts of Southern Nigeria, than available returns indicate . . . .
The matter is one which has already occupied the attention of the Government and presents a problem which will demand earnest consideration in the future. It is

[1] See Northern Nigeria, *Medical Report 1911*, p. 44; *1912*, pp. 12, 58; *1913*, pp. 14, 51; *Colonial Reports, Northern Nigeria 1911*, p. 19; *1912*, p. 32; *1913*, p. 15.
[2] Northern Nigeria, *Medical Report 1912*, p. 58.
[3] Nigeria, *Medical Report 1914*, p. 11. See also ibid., p. 28; *1915*, p. 10; Northern Provinces, *Medical Report 1916*, p. 18; Nigeria, *Medical Report 1917*, p. 138; Northern Provinces, *Medical Report 1918*, pp. 9, 20.
[4] See Northern Nigeria, *Medical Report 1911*, p. 21, *1912*, p. 28, *1913*, p. 26; Nigeria, *Medical Report 1914*, p. 40; Northern Provinces, *Medical Report 1916*, p. 35; Nigeria, *Medical Report 1917*, p. 158; Northern Provinces, *Medical Report 1918*, p. 42.
[5] See Meek, vol. ii, p. 238.   [6] Ibid., p. 216.

possible that it may best be dealt with in connection with similar steps in Northern Nigeria.[1]

At that time there existed two small leper asylums at Yaba (Lagos) and Onitsha (Central Province), and a larger settlement at Ibusa (Central Province) which had been started in 1908 in an endemic centre of the disease.[2]

The Medical Reports for the following years said:

1913. In the Western and Eastern Provinces leprosy is comparatively a rare disease. The principal foci appear to be at certain stations in the Central Province on the left bank of the Niger, viz.:— Onitsha, Asaba, Aboh, Awka and Idah. A scheme for the segregation of lepers in villages is at present under consideration by Government.[3]

1914. Nearly 90 per cent. of the cases of leprosy occur on the river Niger in the neighbourhood of Onitsha, while the Eastern Provinces appear to be almost free from the disease.[4]

A scheme was introduced during the year for a modified system of segregation and isolation in those parts of the country where leprosy is most common, namely, the establishment of leper settlements or 'villages,' principally in the neighbourhood of the larger towns.[5]

But here again the war made an end to promising efforts.

1917. The present time does not afford facilities for the enforcement of extensive segregation measures.[6]

The total number of cases treated was as follows:[7]

1911	1912	1913	1914	1915	1916	1917	1918
41	124	137	248	81	80	114	106

In connexion with the census of 1921 an attempt was made to ascertain the number of lepers also in the Southern Provinces. But no figures were obtained from some Divisions and from the Colony. The total found was 7,444. Mr. Talbot made the following comment:

The table . . . of the number of lepers in the Southern Provinces is not of much value for two reasons. First no expert knowledge was available and it is probable that many people afflicted with cellulitis and other forms of skin disease have been included in the return. Secondly, it is apparent that in many Divisions the census officials could not find time to go into the matter at all thoroughly, and it is certain that in most even of those Divisions, where some time and trouble were devoted to the question, only a comparatively small proportion of lepers would be enumerated. How far these two points neutralise one another it is difficult to say, but it is probable that leprosy exists to a larger extent than would be concluded from the numbers in the table.[8]

[1] Southern Nigeria, *Medical Report 1912*, p. 8. See also ibid., p. 33.
[2] See ibid., p. 8. For the activities of these institutions in the preceding years see ibid., *1908*, pp. 10, 27; *1909*, pp. 12–13, 28; *1910*, pp. 5, 26–7. See also, for example 'Report on the Yaba Leper Asylum 1900–1'.
[3] Southern Nigeria, *Medical Report 1913*, p. 8.
[4] See also Nigeria, *Medical Report 1915*, p. 62: '. . . leprosy is almost exclusively found in the region of the Niger River . . . .'
[5] Ibid. *1914*, p. 56. See also ibid., pp. 77, 92; *1915*, pp. 50–1; Southern Provinces, *Medical Report 1916*, p. 18; *1918*, pp. 22–3.
[6] Nigeria, *Medical Report 1917*, p. 23. See also Southern Provinces, *Medical Report 1918*, p. 22.
[7] See ibid., p. 54.   [8] Talbot, vol. iv, p. 171.

Neither in Northern nor in Southern Nigeria did the end of the war lead to an intensification of the fight against leprosy. The Nigeria Medical Report for 1919–21 says:

A number of the Native Administrations maintain isolation villages for the segregation of these unfortunates, but owing to the depletion of the Medical Staff, it has hitherto not been found possible to attempt much in the way of treatment.[1]

No fresh departure in the tackling of this disease has been made for years—certainly not during the triennium now under review. The reasons for this lack of progress in later years are too well known to call for mention.

So far as the Northern Provinces—especially the Northern two-thirds of them—are concerned, Leprosy fills much the same place as Tuberculosis does in Europe: this may not be true of the Southern Provinces, where, however, the infection is widely prevalent.[2]

Subsequent reports said:

1922. Leprosy.—The long contemplated movement against this widespread indigenous infection has not yet been materialised and there is little immediate prospect of any change. As stated in former reports,[3] in Nigeria it largely takes the place occupied by Tuberculosis at home, and the systematic tackling of it presents much greater difficulty than does the tackling of Tuberculosis in England, where the existing machinery, although transcending anything of the sort conceivable in Nigeria within the life-time of any now living, does not accomplish everything expected of it.[4]

1923. There is no progress to record in the control of this disease beyond that mentioned in previous reports.[5]

The numbers of cases treated in the whole of Nigeria were given as follows:[6]

| Year | In-patients | | | | Out-patients |
	Remaining at end of previous year	Admissions	Total cases treated	Deaths	
1919	511	62	573	48	17
1920	502	525	1,027	48	32
1921	35	524	559	26	49
1922	446	59	505	55	58
1923	401	839	1,240	36	118
1924	382	436	818	25	220
1925	336	225	561	32	756
1926	135[1]	353	488	15	1,150
1927	202	414	616	32	1,430

[1] According to Nigeria, *Medical Report 1925*, p. 49: 390.

In 1925 both the number of patients presenting themselves for treatment in Hospitals and Dispensaries[7] and the interest of the Administration in the suppression of the disease increased.

---

[1] Nigeria, *Medical Report 1919–21*, p. 10.   [2] Ibid., p. 60.

[3] See Northern Provinces, *Medical Report 1916*, p. 18; *1918*, p. 20; Nigeria, *Medical Report 1919–21*, p. 60.

[4] Ibid. *1922*, p. 51.   [5] Ibid. *1923*, p. 26. See also ibid. *1924*, p. 8.

[6] See ibid. *1919–21*, p. 79; *1922*, p. 70; *1923*, p. 55; *1924*, p. 18; *1925*, p. 49; *1926*, p. 55; *1927*, p. 65.

[7] See ibid. *1925*, p. 8.

Interest in the suppression of this disease has been awakened by the visit of Mr. F. Oldrieve, the Secretary of the British Empire Leprosy Relief Association, to Nigeria, and it is proposed to form a branch in Nigeria. At present, knowledge of the extent of leprosy in Nigeria is very defective. A few leper camps exist wherever the local chiefs and people have favoured the segregation of lepers in their area; such segregation camps exist at Zaria, Yola, Maidugari and Keffi in the Northern Provinces and at Onitsha and Ogwashi in the Southern Provinces. There is no compulsion with regard to these and the inmates go out and in as they choose, public opinion being the controlling factor although the hope of treatment is also a powerful inducement.

There is a leper Asylum at Lagos but here there is compulsory detention.

At large Medical Stations where treatment of lepers has been carried on lepers come from distant parts of the country for treatment.[1]

The Medical Reports for 1926 and 1927 said:

1926. Leprosy is very prevalent particularly in the Benin, Kwale, Asaba and Onitsha Districts. It is gratifying to observe that patients in the early stages have begun to attend for treatment voluntarily. Voluntary segregation settlements have been opened in several of the Northern Provinces and the patients get regular treatment.[2]

1927. The problem of leprosy in Nigeria is a very large and a very difficult one. There are a number of voluntary settlements, but most of these are of doubtful value and such provision as they afford affects only a few hundred lepers in an advanced state of the disease. It has been estimated that there are 32,000 lepers in the Northern Provinces[3] and the number in the Southern Provinces, though not known, is probably greater.[4]

The 1928 report contained 'A Study of Leprosy in Southern Nigeria' which said among other things:

It has repeatedly [been] observed by medical and political officers that leprosy is a very common disease in the Southern Provinces of Nigeria. No accurate figures have been obtained but some observers have estimated that in certain districts there is an incidence of more than thirty lepers *per mille*. The parts of the country in which the disease is most prevalent are very densely populated, and the actual number of cases must therefore be enormous. In the Northern Provinces the natives live in towns and walled cities, and the number of lepers can be fairly accurately assessed. This is not so in the Southern Provinces where the people exist on countless small farms. These farms are sometimes grouped together and constitute a village, but generally they are scattered throughout almost impenetrable bush. It is therefore obvious that we cannot form any accurate idea of the number of lepers in these parts. Whether leprosy is more common in the north than in the south is a question open to dispute, but the salient fact remains, that leprosy is rife throughout Nigeria and constitutes a serious menace to the native population of some eighteen million persons.

For a number of years the problem of how to deal with [this] scourge has exercised the mind of the Nigerian government, but until recently no reasonable solution has been found. Legislation with the object of enforcing the segregation of all lepers has been considered impracticable because it would entail an enormous expenditure and might defeat its own object by making lepers hide themselves, rather than be taken forcibly from their families and virtually imprisoned for an indefinite period.[5]

---

[1] Ibid., p. 23.   [2] Ibid. *1926*, pp. 15–16.
[3] This was the 1921 'census' figure.
[4] Ibid., *1927*, p. 19. Rogers and Muir had still said in 1925: 'In British Nigeria leprosy is . . . more common in the northern than in the southern portion . . . ' (*Leprosy*, 1st ed., p. 27).
[5] Nigeria, *Medical Report 1928*, Appendix, p. 89.

The 1930 report which expressed the belief that the number of cases treated had increased considerably[1] said:

It must not be concluded from this that leprosy is on the increase; there is no reason whatsoever to think so, it is only a question of better facilities for treatment.[2]

In 1931 the number of lepers was ascertained at the General and the Intensive Censuses in the Northern Provinces.[3] The results of the General Census were as follows:[4]

Adamawa	Bauchi	Benue	Bornu	Ilorin	Kabba	Kano	Niger	Plateau	Sokoto	Zaria	Total
3,959	3,172	3,358	2,125	837	835	7,367	2,429	1,666	5,104	4,536	35,388

The total result was about the same as in 1921; there were returned 31 lepers for each 10,000 inhabitants. The proportion was highest in Adamawa (61) and lowest in Ilorin (16). In Sokoto Province (28) it was again somewhat below the average.

In the six complete Districts in Katsina Emirate covered by the Intensive Census 863 lepers were counted in a population of 248,434 or 35 per 10,000. In 16 villages in the rest of Katsina 310 lepers were counted in a population of 59,628 or 52 per 10,000, and it is interesting to note that in these 16 villages only 236 lepers were enumerated at the General Census. In 40 villages in the other Northern Provinces 370 lepers were counted in a population of 99,328 or 37 per 10,000.[5]

The Medical Report for 1932 showed a very high incidence of leprosy in an area in the Southern Provinces.

A leprosy survey undertaken in the Kwale Division of Warri Province at the end of the year by Dr. R. C. Jones, Medical Officer of Health, showed 3,181 lepers amongst 29,782 persons examined in seven villages—i.e., 10·68 per cent. of the population are suffering from leprosy. These figures were obtained by clinical examination only and it is possible that certain conditions simulating leprosy were included, but it is also likely that many early cases were missed. Enough has been said to indicate the magnitude of the problem. The solution appears to be mainly in propaganda and general education in hygiene, aided by the establishment of farm colonies in which *early* cases of the disease will be encouraged to reside. Treatment campaigns within the limits of possible expenditure by the country at present are not likely to give results commensurate with the cost until a general improvement of rural hygiene occurs. It is unfortunate that in spite of the adoption of modern methods of treatment by doctors especially expert in the treatment of the disease results generally are disappointing. Many cases, especially young adults, in whom the disease has apparently been arrested by treatment, return to the camps with recrudescence of the disease some time after they have been discharged.[6]

Other investigations showed likewise a high incidence in certain areas.

1937. A number of leprosy surveys were made by the Superintendents of certain settlements and by the British Empire Leprosy Relief Association doctors in heavily infected areas in the South-Eastern provinces and infection rates as high as seven per cent were recorded.[7]

[1] See p. 747 below.   [2] Nigeria, *Medical Report 1930*, p. 14.
[3] The Medical Censuses covered too few people to yield useful results.
[4] See *Census of Nigeria, 1931*, vol. ii, p. 38.   [5] See ibid., pp. 39, 106.
[6] Nigeria, *Medical Report 1932*, pp. 9–10.   [7] Ibid. *1937*, p. 8.

The Colonial Report for 1938 said:

It is estimated that there are some 200,000 lepers in Nigeria—about 1 per cent of the total population—and that of these nearly 6,000 are in voluntary segregation. Government maintains two leper colonies, but the bulk of the work done to control the disease is in the hands of the Native Administrations. The present policy is for these to encourage segregation by providing farm settlements for lepers, who are there subject to care and treatment by staff belonging to the medical missions which have undertaken the management of the settlements on behalf of the Native Administrations. Management is being organised on a provincial basis . . . .[1]

The Medical Report for that year showed the results of a special survey:

A valuable survey of twenty-four representative villages of the Ibiono Clan in the Calabar Province was made by the Medical Superintendent of the Itu Settlement. Among 4,626 persons examined he found 352 affected with leprosy, a rate of seventy-six per 1,000. The rate varied from 17·5 to 215 in different villages. This area is considered to be one of the most heavily infected in the Southern Provinces.[2]

For Cameroons Province the Report on the Administration of the Cameroons contains the following table which 'is based on figures supplied by the Native Authorities over a considerable period in the Victoria, Mamfe and Bamenda Divisions, and in the case of the Kumba Division embodies the result of a census of lepers taken by them in 1938':[3]

Division	Population	Lepers	Rate per Mille
Victoria . .	46,788	105	2·25
Kumba . .	70,404	511	7·26
Mamfe . .	68,139	700	10·28
Bamenda . .	260,422	500	1·92
Total . .	445,753	1,816	4·07

The Report makes the following comment:

The true incidence is believed to be considerably higher than that derived from these figures; the estimate for Bamenda is certainly too low, and the Medical Officer at Banso considers that the disease is on the increase in the Division. . . .

For the Province as a whole it may be assumed that the average incidence of leprosy is not less than 6 per mille . . . .

The Medical Report for 1939 stated:

The most encouraging work of the year has been accomplished in the sphere of leprosy control. This work is yet in its early stages in Nigeria, but a number of settlements under Mission management are now actively engaged in it. Their activities are no longer limited merely to the treatment and care of their resident patients, but their help has been extended to the surrounding villages where, with the co-operation of the people, they have established clinics and treatment centres and undertaken surveys and propaganda work.[4]

The success of the voluntary system of segregation as practised in Nigeria has been evidenced by the increasing demand for admission to the settlements. The number of inmates has risen from 2,500 ten years ago to approximately 7,000 to-day.[5]

This, however, does not imply that the total number of lepers treated has increased in the same proportion. The statistics up to 1927 have been

[1] *Colonial Reports, Nigeria 1938*, p. 24. The same figures were given ibid. *1937*, p. 23. See also Rogers and Muir, *Leprosy* (3rd ed., 1946), p. 29: 'E. Muir, as the result of a tour in Nigeria in 1936, estimated the number of leprosy cases at 200,000, 10·5 per mille.'

[2] Nigeria, *Medical Report 1938*, p. 8.   [3] *Report on Cameroons 1938*, p. 88.

[4] Nigeria, *Medical Report 1939*, p. 4.   [5] Ibid., p. 5.

summarized above.[1] For 1928–44 the general returns of diseases and deaths reveal the following figures for lepers:[2]

Year	In-patients			Deaths	Out-patients
	Remaining at end of previous year	Admissions	Total cases treated		
1928	244	447	691	31	2,109
1929	297	539	836	40	3,440
1930	547	758	1,305	55	2,849
1931	539	103	642	12	2,251
1932	6	305	311	15	2,359
1933	79	296	375	8	2,593
1934	66	314	380	23	2,493
1935	180	479	659	12	1,978
1936	142	458	600	18	1,910
1937	270	641	911	16	1,397
1938	88	428	516	10	1,051
1939	144	(393)	537	12	803
1940	..	..	333	5	972
1941	..	..	300	7	817
1942	..	..	243	2	592
1943	..	..	253	6	1,273
1944	..	..	289	12	547

The Nigerian Branch, British Empire Leprosy Relief Association, gave the following figures for the numbers of lepers under treatment in Government Leper Colonies and Mission Stations at the end of 1928 and 1929:[3]

Year	Northern Provinces			Southern Provinces			Nigeria		
	In-patients	Out-patients	Total	In-patients	Out-patients	Total	In-patients	Out-patients	Total
1928	389	204	593	1,723	673	2,396	2,112	877	2,989
1929	697	340	1,037	1,661	932	2,593	2,358	1,272	3,630

Finally, the Medical Reports show for 1931–5 the average leper population under treatment at leper settlements, for 1936–8 the approximate number of patients resident in such settlements, and for 1931–6 the cases of leprosy which received treatment at Native Administration Dispensaries:[4]

Year	Leper settlements			Dispensaries		
	Northern Provinces	Southern Provinces	Total	Northern Provinces	Southern Provinces	Total
1931	1,341	1,663	3,004	438	230	668
1932	1,529	2,032	3,561	912	1,298	2,210
1933	1,584	3,276	4,860	586	1,241	1,827
1934	1,758	2,909	4,767[1]	891	930	1,821
1935	1,869	3,247	5,116	1,705	677	2,382
1936	1,674	3,625	5,299	1,331	1,495	2,826
1937	1,750	3,923	5,673	..	..	..
1938	2,085	4,707	6,792	..	..	..

[1] Total does not tally with sum of items.

[For notes 1–4 see opposite

It is difficult to interpret the combined results of these various statistics. The Medical Report for 1930 said:

Absolutely accurate figures of lepers under treatment are difficult to obtain but Government Medical Officers had under treatment 4,124 cases during the year to which must be added, although not included in the statistics of this report, 1,326 cases under treatment in the Southern Provinces by Missions and 719 in the Northern Provinces, a total of 6,169 cases treated during the year which shows a great advance on previous years.[1]

Whether the figure of 6,169 really showed a great advance on previous years seems doubtful. The number of cases treated by Government Medical Officers decreased from 4,276 in 1929 to 4,154 (or 4,124) in 1930, and if the number of cases treated by Missions during 1930 was 2,045 it was probably not very much larger than in 1929 since according to the report of the Nigeria Branch, British Empire Leprosy Relief Association, the number of lepers treated in the Mission Stations was 1,644 at the end of 1929. But from 1931 on, the number of cases, no doubt, increased, owing mainly to the opening in that year of standard Native Administration Dispensaries. In 1936 the total number of cases treated may have exceeded 10,000. Moreover, the proportion of out-patients had decreased somewhat. It should be realized, however, that even so only a tiny fraction of all lepers were under treatment.

The Second World War interfered again with the prosecution of anti-leprosy work. The Medical Report for 1940 said:

Leprosy.—The year has on the whole been one of steady advancement, although lack of money and increased cost as a result of the war have had a hampering effect. . . .

The leprosy problem of Nigeria is of the very greatest importance, but a firm foundation already exists on which we can build later when adequate funds become available.[2]

The supply of adequate funds is, of course, decisive. The Medical Report for 1937 said:

Expenditure on leprosy was approximately £4,600 by Government, £7,600 by the Native Administrations of the Northern Provinces and £6,000 by those of the Southern Provinces; a total of more than £18,000. The missions in most cases met the salaries and other expenses of their European staff and the British Empire Leprosy Relief Association provided two doctors and ten Toc H. lay workers.[3]

[1] Nigeria, *Medical Report 1930*, p. 14.
[2] Ibid. *1940*, p. 6. See also ibid. *1942*, p. 5; *Report on Western Provinces 1943*, p. 7; *Report on Eastern Provinces 1943*, p. 5; *Speech and Address by Governor Sir Arthur Richards to the Legislative Council 18th March, 1946*, p. 43.
[3] Nigeria, *Medical Report 1937*, pp. 7-8.

Notes to opposite page]

[1] See p. 742.
[2] See Nigeria, *Medical Report 1928*, p. 61; *1929*, p. 68; *1930*, p. 57; *1931*, p. 67; *1932*, p. 63; *1933*, p. 53; *1934*, p. 53; *1935*, p. 51; *1936*, p. 71; *1937*, p. 48; *1938*, p. 44; *1939*, p. 11; *1940*, p. 11; *1941*, p. 11; *1942*, p. 12; *1943*, p. 14; *1944*, p. 15.
[3] See ibid. *1928*, Appendix, p. 156; *1929*, Appendix, p. 99.
[4] See ibid. *1931*, pp. 13, 41, 43; *1932*, pp. 9, 42; *1933*, pp. 9, 33; *1934*, pp. 8-9, 34; *1935*, pp. 6-7, 28; *1936*, pp. 7, 47; *1937*, p. 8; *1938*, pp. 8-9. The Reports for 1936-8 say that the figures do 'not include six or seven small leper camps of less than twenty patients each'.

The contribution by the Native Administrations meant certainly a great effort and it may be that not much more could be expected from them, but the expenditure by Government appears very small. However, large sums were recently granted from the Colonial Development and Welfare Fund.[1]

The problem of leprosy in Nigeria is an immense one. It is generally admitted that there are at least 400,000 lepers in the country.[2] The incidence of leprosy in large areas which have been carefully surveyed is as high as fifty to sixty per thousand of the population. Of these only about 6,000 are receiving treatment in leper colonies or asylums.[3]

Regarding the incidence of leprosy it may be said in conclusion: There is no evidence that in the Northern Provinces the disease is much more prevalent now than it was a generation ago. But the position is different in the South. Unless the incidence was greatly underestimated in former times leprosy must have spread there enormously. The policy which the Government has pursued so far and which consisted mainly in providing for those natives who presented themselves voluntarily for segregation, did not presuppose a knowledge of the actual spread of the disease. But a policy which aims at a large-scale reduction of leprosy is impossible without a careful count of the total number of lepers in the country.

Medical and Sanitary Staff. In his first report on Northern Nigeria, Sir Frederick Lugard stated:

Among the flood of literature which has lately been poured out on tropical diseases, the diseases of the natives seem to have been lost sight of.[4]

A year later he reported:

Up to the present very few natives have attended the hospitals and dispensaries [other] than Government employés.[5]

After another year he said:

I hope next year to establish dispensaries for the free treatment of natives at all centres of the administration. The small sum required for the building of such dispensaries at Lokoja and Zungeru has been provided. The result will, I hope, be to confer a great benefit on the people, to popularise our rule, and to check the present mortality.[6]

The situation was very different when on 1 January 1914 Sir F. Lugard became Governor of the amalgamated territories of Nigeria. The medical

---

[1] See *Speech and Address by Governor Sir Arthur Richards to the Legislative Council 18th March, 1946*, pp. 42–3.

[2] Dr. Muir, who in 1936 had estimated the number of lepers at 200,000 (see p. 745 above), put it in 1940 at 400,000 (see Rogers and Muir, *Leprosy*, 3rd ed., 1946, pp. 14, 48). On 26 June 1945 he said at the annual meeting of the British Empire Leprosy Relief Association: 'In Nigeria, with its calculated 400,000–500,000 lepers, at least 100,000 of whom must be of the infectious type, there is room in institutions for only some 6,000–7,000' (see 'Leprosy', *The Lancet*, 7 July 1945, p. 24). In a more recent paper Sir Leonard Rogers estimated the total number of lepers in British Africa at 750,000 and said that 'about three-fourths of the total estimated cases are in Nigeria' ('Progress in the Control of Leprosy in the British Empire', *British Medical Journal*, 1 June 1946, p. 825). Dr. Haden Guest, on 9 July 1946, said in the House of Commons: 'The headquarters of leprosy in the world is Nigeria and when I was there just before the war began I calculated that there were about one million cases, affecting some 5 per cent. of the population' (*Parliamentary Debates*, vol. ccccxxv, No. 172, col. 280).

[3] *A Ten-Year Plan of Development and Welfare for Nigeria 1946*, p. 80.

[4] *Colonial Reports, Northern Nigeria 1900–1*, p. 27.

[5] Ibid. *1901*, p. 32.　　　　　　　　　　[6] Ibid. *1902*, p. 80.

and sanitary progress achieved in the preceding decade was quite conspicuous, particularly in Southern Nigeria,[1] and there were good reasons to expect that in the course of another generation mortality in Nigeria would be considerably reduced. That these hopes were not fulfilled was, I think, due mainly to the fact that the medical and sanitary staff was depleted during the First World War and has not been adequately replenished and supplemented since. I shall first quote a few passages from the Medical Reports on Northern Nigeria for 1914–18:[2]

1914. The year opened with an ambitious programme, so far as the amount of work in contemplation was concerned, and, for seven months, the work was conducted with the requisite swing; but, thereafter, the war having broken out, sanitary activity, beyond the usual maintenance of established routine, had necessarily to give place to affairs of more pressing importance.

Many medical stations had to be closed down, to release the Medical Officers, normally posted thereto, for military service; while many Political Officers, accustomed to the helping on of sanitary activity, had their attention monopolised otherwise. Likewise, various persons, whose collaboration was necessary for the adequate carrying out of specific pieces of sanitary work, ceased to be able to co-operate with the Sanitary Officers.

The consequence of this was that, during the last five months of the year, the activities of the Sanitary Officers were directed, to a considerable extent, either to work of secondary importance from their point of view, or to strictly Medical duties.[3]

The investigation of various Entozoal affections was effectually carried out by the Medical Officers throughout the Northern Provinces, but, for obvious reasons, was practically suspended after the month of August, as the stations where most work of this nature is undertaken were either without Medical Officers altogether, or, in those in which two Officers were usually employed, the one man remaining had not the time at his disposal.[4]

It would be hollow and pretentious to table recommendations for future work when so much desirable work is actually in view, which, for the time, cannot be got at.

Last year's programme was not completed, and much of the work indicated in the Report for 1913 remains to be done.

The obvious policy is to keep up with routine work and to overtake arrears as soon as possible.[5]

1915. The attenuated Medical Staff, naturally, failed to maintain progress in vaccination[6] and in leper segregation.[7] This attenuation of the Staff also rendered it necessary to postpone, until the advent of better times, the carrying out of the *ante bellum* scheme of extending the dispensaries financed by various Native Administrations.[8]

Unfortunately, during the year under review, the worst foci of the disease [Ankylostomiasis] happened to be in those regions in which the endemic activities of Medical and Sanitary Officers had to be suspended. The advent of war found, and very

[1] 'The sanitation of the Southern improved more rapidly than did that of the Northern settlements: this was at least one good point about the liquor traffic; for the South, where trade liquor was permitted, enjoyed a larger revenue than did the North where it was not, and being richer could afford to spend more on sanitation' (Nigeria, *Medical Report 1922*, p. 45).

[2] For similar, but not quite as bad, conditions in the Southern Provinces see ibid. *1915*, pp. 43, 63; Southern Provinces, *Medical Report 1916*, p. 10; Nigeria, *Medical Report 1917*, pp. 13, 31; Southern Provinces, *Medical Report 1918*, pp. 12–13.

[3] Nigeria, *Medical Report 1914*, p. 10. See also ibid., p. 16.

[4] Ibid., p. 29. See also Northern Provinces, *Medical Report 1916*, p. 28.

[5] Nigeria, *Medical Report 1914*, p. 24.

[6] See also ibid., *1915*, p. 16; Northern Provinces, *Medical Report 1916*, p. 18.

[7] See also Nigeria, *Medical Report 1915*, p. 20.   [8] Ibid., p. 10.

materially crippled, an effective crusade against the disease; a crusade which shall be resumed as soon as possible.[1]

. . . much of what was formerly called arrears must now be numbered with problems of the future, to be tackled when the times will permit.[2]

1916. The amount of touring accomplished by the Sanitary Officers was unavoidably meagre. Such a state of affairs is particularly unfortunate in the Northern Provinces where the most important form of sanitary activity is—and must be, for years to come—a constant crusade.[3]

Water supply. . . . no new departure was made: the *res angusta domi*, incidental to the war, precluded this. Several ambitious schemes are in view; but to advocate them now would be a case of: 'Nero fiddling while Rome was burning.'[4]

Lectures are not delivered: under existing conditions, they could serve no useful purpose.[5]

1917. During 1917, the world-wide war continued to dominate and heavily hamper sanitary activity. The Sanitary Officer was divorced from the normal duties of his office throughout the year; the Senior Sanitary Officer was able to devote only about one half of his time to his own proper sphere exclusively; and depletions in the personnel of the Medical Staff inevitably involved sudden and arbitrary changes and consequent breaches of continuity.[6]

For obvious reasons, tours made by the Sanitary Officers were more restricted than they had ever been before. This, although unavoidable, was very unfortunate . . . .[7]

Some of the smaller landward stations were only occupied intermittently during the year, or were not occupied at all.

. . . the purely Native towns received much less attention than was their due.[8]

1918. Since the outbreak of the great War, the Sanitary Branch of the Medical Department has been, steadily and with increasing rapidity, taking a back seat. This has been the fault of nobody—the ex-Kaiser alone excepted—for, when it is a case of 'all hands to the pumps,' in the presence of the exigencies of a great war, the civilian who asserts his claim to being allowed to stick to his own job is merely understudying 'Nero fiddling whilst Rome was burning.' During the war, 'business as usual' has not been the rule in the Northern Provinces: the attenuated personnel of the Medical Department has been subjected to chronically progressive shrinkage; and, naturally, the Sanitary Officers have been morally bound to fill gaps of pressing importance left by their medical colleagues called off for military service.[9]

. . . the hands of the sanitary clock have been put back and back, until now zero has been reached: *i.e.* . . . . the Sanitary Branch now stands pretty well where it did, what time it had been created in the Spring of 1910. In other words, it behoves the Sanitary Branch to begin again from the beginning: *i.e.*, the Sanitary Branch, practically, will have to be reorganised, if not actually recreated.[10]

The chief feature of the Sanitary Branch at present is its morbidity and the symptoms of this morbidity are accumulated arrears, together with the absence of plans for work which ought, not only to have been planned but, to have been effected long ago.

There are numerous centres of alleged sleeping sickness and of other diseases which ought to have been inspected and systematically dealt with long ere now, but which have not, so far, even been visited. . . .

The necessity for reconstruction seems to be the paramount one over most parts of the Empire; but, if it be permissible to compare small things with great, nowhere is reconstruction more urgently called for than it is in the Sanitary Branch of the Medical Department of the Northern Provinces of Nigeria.[11]

[1] Nigeria, *Medical Report 1915*, p. 17. See also Northern Provinces, *Medical Report 1916*, p. 19.
[2] Nigeria, *Medical Report 1915*, p. 20.
[3] Northern Provinces, *Medical Report 1916*, p. 8.   [4] Ibid., p. 21.   [5] Ibid., p. 22.
[6] Nigeria, *Medical Report 1917*, p. 116.   [7] Ibid., p. 117.   [8] Ibid., p. 118.
[9] Northern Provinces, *Medical Report 1918*, p. 23.   [10] Ibid., p. 24.   [11] Ibid., p. 28.

The chances for a speedy reconstruction seemed then (spring 1919) particularly great as the post-war period started 'with prosperity reigning everywhere'.

The boom raised high hopes in the sanitary worker, who fancied he could foresee the achievement, at an early date, of much necessary work which had hung fire for years . . . . But . . . the medical and sanitary personnel was attenuated; the difficulty in obtaining sanitary labour at many places was exceedingly great . . . and many imported materials reached prices which were practically prohibitive.

At the end of 1920 came the slump.

[It] made labour for sanitary purposes much more easily procurable, but full advantage could not be taken of this, on account of the falling revenue. Sanitary activity had necessarily to be restricted to matters of routine, and even those were not always effected satisfactorily; for at many places, sanitary arrears accumulated, just as cumulative poisons do in the animal economy.[1]

In 1924, when plague raged in Lagos and the most severe epidemics of cerebrospinal meningitis and relapsing fever killed many hundreds of thousands of natives, 34 of the 92 posts for Medical Officers were vacant,[2] and economy was apparently stricter still in sanitary matters.

Shortage of Staff, with the needs of the Medical branch to be met first, and the necessity of having to exercise the strictest financial economy for four to five years after the close of the War in November, 1918, were the main causes of the set back of Sanitation, so that improvement schemes had to be held in abeyance and revival has proved slow during the succeeding two years.[3]

The later development may be illustrated again by a few quotations from the Medical Reports.

1927. The problem . . . , in the towns at any rate, is not how to encourage the African to take advantage of European medicine, but how to cope with the amount of work which goes on increasing steadily and will continue to do so. The extreme shortage of qualified medical staff has been a serious hindrance to the much needed extension of medical and sanitary work. The establishment has never yet been up to pre-war strength. There remain stations unopened since the war and medical officers in some cases are still working under the strained conditions which were brought about by the war . . . It is unfortunate that at the very time when expansion is so very necessary in all branches of the work, recruitment should fail to produce an adequate supply of officers. Provision of medical officers for camps of exercise and for patrols has only been possible by the shutting down temporarily of other medical work, which, needless to add, is a very unsatisfactory arrangement.[4]

1928. As pointed out in my report for 1927, the European establishment has never yet been up to pre-war standard . . . .[5]

1929. During 1929 the shortage of European staff which has so crippled the Medical Department since the war has been made good to a considerable extent. At the beginning of the year extreme difficulty was experienced owing to the depleted staff, but twenty new Medical Officers were appointed during the year. This more than made good loss by retirements and at the end of the year the Medical branch of the service showed only eleven vacancies. The staff of the Health branch was also brought up to strength and the full number of thirteen Medical Officers of Health will have been appointed by March 1930 . . . .[6]

1930. It was hoped that in 1930 the staff of the Medical Service would be brought

---

[1] Nigeria, *Medical Report 1919–21*, pp. 53–4. See also ibid., pp. 49, 52; *1922*, pp. 35, 62.
[2] See ibid. *1924*, p. 5.   [3] Ibid., p. 33.   [4] Ibid. *1927*, p. 11.
[5] Ibid. *1928*, p. 11.   [6] Ibid. *1929*, p. 11.

up to authorised strength but owing to financial stringency six vacancies in the medical branch could not be filled, and the vacancy caused by the invaliding of one Medical Officer of Health could not be filled. This is unfortunate at a time when extension of Medical Service to the African population, largely through the Native Administrations, is occurring.[1]

1931. Owing to the depressed financial position of the Colony it was necessary during the year to reduce European personnel. This was effected by retrenchment and by keeping vacancies unfilled. . . . The reduction of European personnel which had occurred or was impending at the end of the year was as follows:—

Administrative staff .	.	. reduced from	10 to 5
Pathological and research staff .	,,	,,	16 to 10
Various specialist appointments.	,,	,,	8 to 5
Clinical medical staff	. . ,,	,,	104 to 98
Health officers	. . . ,,	,,	15 to 14
Matrons .	. . . . ,,	,,	2 to 1[2]

1937. The increase in the establishment of Medical Officers of Health and Sanitary Superintendents restored the strength of the Health Service to approximately what it was in 1931.[3]

1938. The drastic reduction in the number of administrative posts during the years of depression 1931–35 resulted in a serious deterioration in the organisation of the Department. Provincial Medical Administration disappeared and the mass of detail which had thus to be dealt with direct by the staff at Headquarters left little time for inspection of outstations and for the study of major problems.

The continued prosperity up to the end of 1937 was reflected in an increase of £33,293 in the expenditure Estimates for 1938–39 as compared with 1937–38. Extra equipment and diets, necessitated by the ever-expanding work of hospitals and dispensaries, and the higher standard of treatment aimed at in recent years, accounted for some £15,000 of the increase.

Unfortunately by April it was clear that the period of prosperity was at an end, and to meet the falling revenues of Government, the estimates of expenditure under 'Other Charges'[4] were cut by seven and a half per cent.[5]

1939. That the present curative facilities are woefully inadequate is well realised, but if real advance is to be made the spectacular curative side must not be allowed to eclipse the more essential preventive aspect.[6]

The outbreak of war had its effect on the Medical Department as on all other departments.

. . . the department is now carrying on its usual duties with a depleted staff.[7]

1940. About mid-year the First Field Ambulance proceeded overseas and later a second was formed, all qualified personnel being supplied from the department. In all, thirty members of the qualified staff have been seconded for military service and these comprise:—

1 Assistant Director of Medical Service
1 Senior Health Officer
1 Senior Medical Officer
1 African Surgical Specialist
2 Pathologists
3 Medical Officers of Health
and 21 Medical Officers.

[1] Nigeria, *Medical Report 1930*, p. 10.
[2] Ibid. *1931*, p. 5. The 'Approved Expenditure 1931–32' was originally £523,118. It was 'reduced owing to financial stringency' to £485,416.
[3] Ibid. *1937*, p. 4.
[4] The two main items of expenditure are 'Personal Emoluments' and 'Other Charges'.
[5] Ibid. *1938*, p. 3.   [6] Ibid. *1939*, p. 2.   [7] Ibid., p. 1.

This depletion of staff has made the work of those remaining very much more arduous, but with the introduction of longer tours and shorter leave it has been possible to maintain services at normal level.[1]

What the effect on general health will be as a result of the extended tours now operative it is difficult to predict. It is a necessity in these abnormal times, but West Africa is not yet a suitable country for prolonged residence without leave.[2]

1941. The shortage of staff as a result of military commitments continues[3] while the work has materially increased, but this extra work has been cheerfully undertaken by all.[4]

Neurasthenia and General Debility account for more than half of the total invalidings. It has been noted that leave spent in South Africa has not the same tonic effect as might have been expected and that several people on return have suffered from sickness in the early months of their succeeding tour and do not appear to be in good physical condition or to react in a satisfactory manner.[5]

1942. The number of invalidings of European officials rose from 74 per cent in 1941 to 103 per cent in 1942 and of these half were due to debility and neurasthenia— a sign of the effect of the prolonged tours and family separation brought about by war conditions. We do not have the figures for European unofficials but the same circumstances apply in both cases. As was pointed out in last year's report leave spent in South Africa does not have the same beneficial effect as leave in the United Kingdom.[6]

1945. The serious shortage of staff in the Medical Services continues to hamper effort and it has regrettably been found necessary to close down one Medical Station during the year, while a further one has been without a Medical Officer for several months. This shortage of qualified doctors and Nursing Sisters seems likely to continue for some time, but it is hoped that the numbers of applications for new appointments among discharged Services personnel will shortly increase and relieve the situation. It seems almost inevitable, however, that slowing up of the development programme will occur.[7]

Since 1930 there has been a large increase of out-patient attendance and clinical work at the hospitals, but owing to pre-war financial stringency, followed by the war-time difficulties of obtaining Medical Officers and Nursing Sisters in replacement of those absorbed into the Army, the whole time of the Medical Officers has been absorbed in hospital work, and they have been unable to provide adequate supervision of clinical work at rural dispensaries.[8]

Nigeria is four times the size of Great Britain . . . .

To serve such a country there is a small Government Medical Service, supplemented by voluntary bodies and a few private practitioners in the bigger cities in the South. There are one hundred and sixty-five Government Medical Officers. Owing to the diversity of the duties of the Medical Department only about one hundred of these doctors are available for ordinary clinical work at any one time. There are thirty-five mission doctors and thirty-one private practitioners. A total of fifty-three Government and Native Administration hospitals provides about 4,275 beds (less than 1 to 5,000 of the population). In addition there are twenty-five Mission institutions, including maternity centres, which provide about 1,500 beds.[9]

[1] Ibid. *1940*, p. 1.   [2] Ibid., p. 4.
[3] See also, for example, *Report on Northern Provinces 1941*, p. 3: 'The Sanitary Staff (Medical Officers of Health as well as Sanitary Superintendents) has been still further decreased.'
[4] *Medical Report 1941*, p. 1.   [5] Ibid., p. 5.
[6] Ibid. *1942*, p. 5. See also ibid. *1944*, p. 4.
[7] *Speech and Address by Governor Sir Arthur Richards to the Legislative Council 18th March, 1946*, p. 40.
[8] *A Ten-Year Plan of Development and Welfare for Nigeria 1946*, p. 75.
[9] Ibid., p. 67. See also ibid., p. 74: 'At present there are only two Government dentists and six private practitioners in Nigeria. There is a wide field for development in this field particularly in private practice. The popular idea that the African is invariably blessed with sound teeth is incorrect.'

The existing medical and health services have been built up in little more than one generation from small beginnings. Until now the limiting factor has been finance, which has always had to take precedence over the real needs of the people. Annual expenditure on medical services has been about sixpence per head of the population, probably the lowest in the Colonial Empire. In the circumstances the results that have been obtained are a credit to all who have shared in their creation and maintenance. This does not alter the fact that present services are completely inadequate for a country of this size.[1]

The expenditure by Government on Medical Services for 1930–1 to 1944–5 has been as follows:[2]

1930–1	1931–2	1932–3	1933–4	1934–5	1935–6	1936–7	1937–8
£	£	£	£	£	£	£	£
485,940	441,590	384,743	391,340	384,722	377,671	387,600	462,629

1938–9	1939–40	1940–1	1941–2	1942–3	1943–4	1944–5
£	£	£	£	£	£	£
458,385	442,403	450,378	445,676	522,188	642,131	676,636

The expenditure per head was about 5d. per year, as compared with about 2s. in the Gold Coast.

Infant Mortality. I shall first summarize the few data available.

(1) In 1913 a Political Officer in the Sokoto Province showed in his Assessment Report that among a population of 20,444 the number of children 'born during the last 12 months' was 1,320 and the number of children 'born during the last 12 months who have died' 266.

The figures given are for only one year, and are for only a small unit of population (20,000), and consequently they cannot be taken as standard values. They may be much above or much below the average. I asked if there had been any noticeably large or small numbers of deaths among the babies, and was told that, as far as they were aware, they were much as usual; at any rate there had been no epidemic among them.[3]

The Political Officer, or the Principal Medical Officer who published these figures, computed therefrom an infantile mortality percentage of 20·15. But it must be realized that some of the 1,054 infants who survived died in the next year before having reached the age of one, and these deaths were not included in the above figures.

(2) According to the birth and death records kept in Kano Province in 1927–30 the infant mortality rates were as follows:[4]

	Kano City	Kano Emirate	Hadejia Emirate	Gumel Emirate	Daura Emirate	Kazaure Emirate
Births . .	11,714	162,591	21,153	9,731	13,690	8,061
Infant deaths .	3,302	56,744	6,670	3,595	2,185	1,501
Rate . . .	282	349	315	369	160	186

[1] *A Ten-Year Plan of Development and Welfare for Nigeria 1946*, p. 68.
[2] See Nigeria, *Medical Report 1938*, p. 4; *1939*, p. 2; *1940*, p. 3; *1941*, p. 2; *1942*, p. 3; *1943*, p. 5; *1944*, p. 3; Nigeria, *Estimates 1946–7*, p. 18.
[3] Northern Nigeria, *Medical Report 1913*, p. 8.
[4] See *Census of Nigeria, 1931*, vol. ii, pp. 187–90.

Some of the rates are very high, but it may well be that in these cases birth records were less complete than death records.

(3) In 1925 and 1926 the assessing officers asked a number of women in Cameroons Province how many children they had borne and how many of these children had died. The results concerning infant mortality may be summarized as follows:[1]

	Mamfe Division				Bamenda Division				
	As-sumbo	An-yang	Bang-wa	Man-gew	Moga-maw area	Ngemba area	Chin-gang	Kawle	Tschati
Births . .	1,018	567	2,137	797	..	..	180	63	110
Infant deaths .	367	..	551	352	..	..	51	14	26
Per cent. . .	36	40	26	44	29	27	28	22	24

The infant mortality rates, according to these inquiries, varied between 22 and 44 per 100 births.

Another inquiry was made in Cameroons Province in 1929 among Bakweri women from ten villages situated in different parts of the Buea District. It appeared that of 1,036 children 356 or 34·4 per cent. had died under one year and 87 or 8·4 per cent. 'under puberty'.[2] The enormous preponderance of deaths 'under one year' suggests that a number of older children were counted as infants.

(4) The same questions were asked at the Medical Censuses of 1930–2. The Government Statistician summarized the results as follows:[3]

Date of observations	Area	Number of mothers	Total live births	Children dying below one year	Infantile mortality rate per 1,000 live births
Southern Provinces 1930–1–2	Abeokuta, Urban and Rural . . .	1,580	5,550	499	90
	Cameroons, Forest .	820	2,356	680	289
	Cameroons, Hill. .	402	1,536	385	251
	Creek . . .	634	3,342	778	233
Northern Provinces 1930–1	Kaita . . .	650	2,701	48	18
	Zangan Aya . .	752	2,579	337	131
	Bakori . . .	766	2,721	496	182
	Laminga . . .	374	1,266	319	252

He made the following comment:

The infantile mortality rates given above for Abeokuta and Kaita especially, are clearly below the true figures. In Lagos, in 1900, the rate was 430 per 1,000,[4] and even in 1924 was 236. The Abeokuta rural rate found by Dr. Turner is 330 per 1,000. The Abeokuta urban data are, like the fertility data, quite unreliable.

[1] See Report on Cameroons 1925, pp. 93–4; 1926, pp. 82–3.
[2] See Assessment Report on Buea District, p. 40.
[3] See Census of Nigeria, 1931, vol. i, p. 59.
[4] Excluding still-births the rate was actually 389, and it was probably swelled by incomplete birth registration.

Dr. Turner himself (who does not give the rate for urban Abeokuta) says:

The figures obtained were as follows:—

Abeokuta (Rural)	330/1,000
Cameroons—Forest	288/1,000
,, Hill	250/1,000
Arogbo	233/1,000

The Abeokuta figure is probably too high owing to the tendency of the women to understate the number of pregnancies. The Cameroons data for the several villages gave rates varying from 250–350 per thousand.[1]

In some areas the inquiry proved in fact to be a complete failure. Of the 539 women under 40 in Kaita one was reported to have lost 3 children in infancy, one woman 2, and all others none.[2] It is obvious that the officials who conducted the inquiry did not succeed in asking the question in the proper form and that they did not realize their mistake in time. As regards the Cameroons, Dr. Turner's comment is not quite clear. He says that the rates for the several villages varied between 250 and 350, but if the rate for the Hill area, which comprised four villages, was 250, the rate must have been lower than 250 in at least one village unless the rate was 250 in each of the four villages. The explanation of the rate for rural Abeokuta is also not plausible, as it suggests that understatements of surviving children were more frequent than understatements of deceased infants. The rate for rural Abeokuta may appear very high at first sight, but it must be realized that the 'infant deaths' ascertained at the Medical Censuses included not only children born alive and deceased under one but also still-births[3] and some children deceased over one.

In the enquiry it was found to be impossible to separate stillbirths from infant deaths, and as the term 'year' is vague to the native, all deaths of viable children up to the period at which the child walks were included.[4]

The fact that in the Cameroons the women of 30 to 40 reported 388 'infant deaths' and only 253 deaths of older children—although many of their children must have been exposed to death for more than ten years—suggests that a considerable number of deceased 'infants' were over one year old. It may well be, therefore, that if still-births and deaths of children over one had been excluded, an infant mortality rate of 330 would have been reduced to 250 or less. On the other hand, it is not unlikely that quite a few deceased infants were omitted in the mothers' statements.[5]

Thus, all the available facts about infant mortality in Nigeria (outside Lagos) consist of (1) an incomplete inquiry of infant deaths occurring in 1913 among a population of 20,000, (2) records of infant deaths in Kano Province in the second half of the 1920s which are not conclusive, as birth

---

[1] *Census of Nigeria, 1931*, vol. vi, p. 10.　　[2] See ibid., vol. v, p. 40.
[3] See ibid., vol. v, pp. 2, 44–8; vol. vi, pp. 50–3.
[4] Ibid., p. 9.
[5] In the Cameroons, where the inquiry was apparently carried out with more success than elsewhere, the 'infant mortality rate' among the children of women over 40 was 216 as compared with 298 for the women under 40. This suggests that the older women in particular did not report all their children who died as infants.

records may have been more incomplete than death records, (3) a few sample surveys made in the Cameroons Province in 1925, 1926, and 1929 which did not distinguish between recent deaths and deaths in a remote past, and (4) figures collected at the Medical Censuses which were all more or less unreliable and which moreover included still-births and a number of children over one. We know nothing about infant mortality in any area since 1930, and none of the earlier figures permit the drawing of definite conclusions concerning the past.

I shall now give a brief survey of the opinions and estimates to be found in official reports.

In December 1900 the Chief Medical Officer, Lagos, in an address to the African Trade Section of the Liverpool Chamber of Commerce, stated:

That impaired health and a very high death-rate prevail on the West Coast of Africa among European residents is so notorious that it is not necessary for me to dilate on the point. . . . But it is not so well known, perhaps, that there is a fearfully high mortality among native infants and children—the future population, on which the working of these colonies, governed by European nations, mainly depends, and whose sanitary salvation must of necessity devolve on their European rulers.[1]

Two years later Sir Frederick Lugard said:

Investigations into the causes of the great mortality among native infants, estimated by Dr. Miller, C.M.S., at 50 per cent., will, I hope, result in a diminution of this evil. My own opinion is that the main cause is the horribly insanitary condition of the native cities, which Residents are already doing what they can to improve.[2]

Subsequent reports related:

1903. Northern Nigeria. Gando and Argungu. Major Burdon made a tour through these western districts bordering on the Niger and on French territory, and reports as follows:—

'. . . the Jogwadawa Fulanis are credited with being the healthiest people in the country. I made particular enquiries about child mortality, and was assured that it was less amongst them and the nomad herdsmen than amongst any other people. The reason assigned was their milk diet.'[3]

1905. Northern Nigeria. . . . I regard the improvement of sanitation in native cities as a matter of very great importance, in order to decrease the infant mortality (which is appalling), and so aid the increase of the population.[4]

1906. Southern Nigeria, Central Province. The infant mortality is still as terrible a factor as ever in the Vital Statistics.[5]

In the next quarter of a century infant mortality was apparently discussed only twice in Nigerian medical reports.

1916. The problem of infantile mortality received considerable attention from the administration. It is a serious problem here, as it is in many other parts of the

---

[1] Strachan, *Health Conditions of West Africa*, p. 3. See also ibid., p. 10: 'Another point of much importance is the fact that native infants and children are affected by Malaria to a very large extent, the number per cent. of the infant population attacked is extremely high, and the death-rate correspondingly so; thus the malarialised infant population forms one of the constant sources of infection.'

[2] *Colonial Reports, Northern Nigeria 1902*, p. 80.   [3] Ibid. *1903*, p. 7.

[4] Statement by Principal Medical Officer quoted ibid. *1905–6*, pp. 103–4. See also ibid., pp. 11, 61; *1906–7*, p. 17.

[5] Southern Nigeria, 'Medical Report 1906', p. 284. See also Southern Nigeria, *Medical Report 1907*, p. 11.

world; but, for obvious reasons, it's extent cannot be accurately estimated from the data which are available. Although—which is all to the good—more than one fallacy touching it was exposed, no systematic plan of tackling the problem was decided upon; but an useful train of inquiry was started, which it is hoped will afford a fruitful field for medical activity, what time the termination of the war shall have restored to the staff it's normal dimensions. Infantile mortality is almost certainly greater among the Mohammedan than it is among the pagan divisions of the population: and, remembering the conditions of mohammedan domestic life, it hardly seems necessary to labour the point, how much more difficult this fact renders the problem.[1]

1926. At Ilorin the Medical Officer registered 438 births during the last nine months of the year, 202 were again examined by the Medical Officer at six months old and all were vaccinated.

Taking into consideration the children who were lost sight of the Medical Officer is of opinion that the infant mortality was about 378 per 1,000.[2]

In his report on the Medical Census taken in the Southern Provinces in 1930–2 Dr. Turner, after having shown the rates for some areas,[3] said:

A fair estimate for Southern Nigeria would appear to be about 300 per thousand, and data from the Ibibio country and from Lagos, prior to an infant welfare scheme, give similar figures. Results in Lagos, where the mortality has been reduced to 134 per 1,000, shew that a great deal of the mortality is preventable. . . .

The principal causes of the high mortality are probably congenital debility, incorrect feeding of the infant, broncho-pneumonia from exposure and living in a smoky atmosphere, bad housing conditions, infantile diarrhœas from impure water, the agbo given to the Yoruba infant, lack of care on the part of the mother because of her occupation, the neglect of minor ailments, and the poor advice or lack of it by the native doctor, and epidemic disease. Tetanus plays an important rôle in early infant deaths, and is due to faulty methods in cutting the cord.[4]

The 1932 Report on the Administration of the Cameroons, after having quoted Dr. Turner's estimate of infant mortality in Southern Nigeria, said:

There is no reason to suppose that infant mortality is any greater in the mandated territory than in Nigeria or any other tropical country where the climatic and other conditions are similar.[5]

In his Memorandum on the Hausa People, dated 11 November 1932, the Dietetics Pathologist Dr. McCulloch said:

We cannot arrive at the infantile death rate at present but it is undoubtedly very high. In Katsina Town, where there is a system of recording, the average for four years was the appalling total of 412 per thousand infants. This figure was raised by the presence of epidemic disease, but I feel confident that the normal infantile death rate is not less than 300 per thousand.

There is an extremely high infantile mortality rate conditioned by inherited disease, chiefly venereal, inherited poor physique, and terrible environmental conditions.[6]

The statement concerning Katsina Town is evidently incorrect. Mr. Brooke, who in his Report on the Census of the Northern Provinces

[1] Northern Provinces, *Medical Report 1916*, p. 10.
[2] Nigeria, *Medical Report 1926*, p. 37. [3] See p. 756 above.
[4] *Census of Nigeria, 1931*, vol. vi, p. 10. Dr. Turner does not say which of these 12 principal causes were the most important. The reports on the Administration of the Cameroons which contain many complaints about high infant mortality suggest repeatedly that the economic condition of the people and overworking of the mothers were the main causes (see Kuczynski, pp. 299–300). [5] *Report 1932*, p. 94. [6] Nigeria, *Medical Report 1932*, p. 109.

collected all the records available, was not in a position to give the numbers
of births and deaths for Katsina Town and said: 'In 1927 the infantile
death rate for Katsina City was estimated at 412 per 1,000 births.'[1] This
was an estimate for one year and not an average for four years computed
from records. It is, moreover, quite unlikely that 'the presence of epidemic
disease' should raise a 'normal infantile death rate' of 300 to an average
rate of 412 for four consecutive years.

Other reports say:

1933. (Ilorin Province.) No reliable figures are available, but there can be no
doubt that among the Yorubas and Nupes of this Province child mortality is
appalling. Local methods of treatment are crude in the extreme, and it is necessary
to contend with the combined forces of ignorance and superstition. The parents
are devoted to their children, and no doubt in time they will accept new methods,
but meanwhile public opinion and the conservative instinct of the mother-in-law
has to be overcome.[2]

1934. (Pagan tribes in the Plateau.) There is . . . an exceedingly high infantile
mortality which varies from 400–800 per 1,000.[3]

1938. (Plateau Province.) . . . attempts have . . . been made to examine the question of infantile mortality, which appears to be very heavy indeed, and to obtain
more accurate statistics of population.[4]

The incidence of infant mortality in Nigeria is now as much as ever
anybody's guess.

Population Growth. When Sir F. Lugard, in January 1900, took over
the administration from the Royal Niger Company he was convinced that
Northern Nigeria was a country depopulated by slave-raids, and that
slave-raids still had a devastating effect.

There is, probably, no part of the 'Dark Continent' in which the worst forms of
slave raiding still exist to so terrible an extent, and are prosecuted on so large and
systematic a scale as in the British Protectorate of Northern Nigeria.[5] Each year,
as the grass dries up, armies take the field to collect slaves. Nor are they even
provident of their hunting grounds, for those who are useless as slaves are killed
in large numbers, the villages burnt, and the fugitives left to starve in the bush. The
first great step to check this evil was taken by the Royal Niger Company in 1897,
when, after the defeat of Bida, they severed from the rule of that emir all the
territories south of the Niger (Kabba province). The relief came almost too late,
for the country is depopulated, and hundreds of ruins attest the former existence
of a population and a prosperity which have gone.[6]

I have found that there is a considerable export of slave children.[7]

[1] *Census of Nigeria, 1931*, vol. ii, p. 191.   [2] *Report on Northern Provinces 1933*, p. 29.
[3] Nigeria, *Medical Report 1934*, p. 99.
[4] *Report on Northern Provinces 1938*, p. 48. For Kabba Province see ibid., p. 30; for Niger Province see *Reports for Northern, Western, Eastern Provinces, and Colony 1939*, p. 44. Finally, see
the passage from Nigeria, *Medical Report 1940*, p. 7, quoted p. 721 above.
[5] He emphasized in particular 'the necessity of checking the rapid depopulation by organised
slave-raiding in the eastern states' (*Colonial Reports, Northern Nigeria 1900–1*, p. 10). *Colonial
Office Lists 1901*, p. 245, *1902*, p. 255, *1903*, p. 272, said that 'large areas are frequently devastated
by slave-raids'.
[6] *Colonial Reports, Northern Nigeria 1900–1*, pp. 12–13. See also *ColonialReports, Nigeria 1914*,
p. 37: 'Slave-raiding had assumed gigantic proportions, and the armies of the Emirs had depopulated vast areas which had previously been inhabited by a dense and industrious pagan popula
tion.'
[7] *Colonial Reports, Northern Nigeria 1900–1*, p. 15. See also ibid. *1904*, p. 79: 'The famine
which prompted the people to sell their children caused a great increase in the slave trade.'

When a few years later he presented a table showing the population per square mile and the proportion of males to females he pointed out that 'both bear striking witness to the devastation caused by war and slave raids'.[1] But as he says that the returns are largely guess-work it may well be that in many cases the sex ratio—in Bauchi Province 1 male to 2·83 females—was wrongly guessed.[2]

Finally, in 1919, he stated:

> The population of the North—described 60 years ago by Barth as the densest in all Africa—had by 1900 dwindled to some 9 millions, owing to inter-tribal war, and, above all, to the slave raids of the Fulani. But these dreaded horsemen could not penetrate the forests of the South, where a population estimated at 7¾ millions (probably an over-estimate) found refuge.[3]

Northern Nigeria had suffered in fact very much from slave-raids. But since most of the slaves captured by the Fulani remained in the country, their raids caused probably less depopulation than the raids which, before 1860, had furnished slaves for the export to America. Even so Northern Nigeria was about as densely settled in 1900 as Sweden is to-day, and the Colonial Office apparently shared the then prevailing opinion that Northern Nigeria had the densest population of any country in the whole African Continent.[4] This opinion was based on a gross overestimate of the population and was not quite correct, since density was greater in Southern Nigeria. But I doubt whether in any earlier period the population of Northern Nigeria had been very much greater than in 1900.

Since Sir F. Lugard estimated the population in 1919 at approximately 9,000,000 he evidently did not think that it had increased between 1900 and 1919,[5] and it certainly did not increase between 1919 and 1926, as the

---

[1] *Colonial Reports, Northern Nigeria 1904*, p. 84.

[2] It is interesting to note in this respect the estimates for Kontagora Province. Sir F. Lugard said in his report for 1902 (p. 46): 'The province is under Major Sharpe, C.M.G., and will, I hope, gradually recover its population and prosperity. Major Sharpe states that at present its condition is lamentable. There are few children and no girls, and everywhere are to be seen the ruins of burnt villages. He estimates the population of the province at 9,500 men, 6,000 women, and 5,000 children.' This indicates an enormous preponderance of males. Two years later, Sir F. Lugard accepted an estimate by the Assistant Resident showing 34,350 males and 44,650 females. The population was now put four times as high as two years earlier, and the enormous excess of males had changed into a huge surplus of females. After another year the population was given as 45,269 males and 44,409 females (see *Colonial Reports, Northern Nigeria 1905–6*, p. 128), suggesting an increase of nearly 10,000 for males and a slight decrease for females. 'The meagre population of this devastated province is reported to have increased by about 10,000 during the year, owing to the return of people to their former districts and the influx of ex-slaves' (ibid., p. 56). For 1909, on the other hand, the population was given as only 36,489 males and 40,286 females (see *Blue Book 1909* R, p. 1).

Slave-raids, of course, may just as well reduce the number of females as of males. As shown above it was stated in 1913 concerning the Kwongoma Division of Niger Province that 'in many of the villages, until recently, the men were more numerous than the women; because in the slave raiding days not long over, more females than males were captured'.

[3] *Report on the Amalgamation of Northern and Southern Nigeria*, p. 5.

[4] See *Colonial Office List 1900*, p. 195, quoted p. 587 above.

[5] In earlier years he apparently had expected an increase. See his statement in *Colonial Reports, Northern Nigeria 1905–6*, p. 61: 'I should imagine the population of the Protectorate to be about 8½ millions. It is no doubt increasing rapidly, both by immigration and by natural causes; but, on the other hand, the epidemics of cerebral fever and small-pox, and the severe famines of 1902–04, together with the terribly high rate of infant mortality, have counteracted the increase which might otherwise have been expected.'

Northern Provinces in this period suffered enormously from cerebrospinal meningitis and relapsing fever. The estimate for 1926 based on tax assessment showed, it is true, a native population of 10,233,000 (including Northern Cameroons), but this does not necessarily imply that the population was larger than in 1919. The official reports in the first quarter of this century discussed frequently conditions in various provinces, but they did not suggest that the population of the Protectorate as a whole increased in this period, and I suppose there is a consensus of opinion that the population in 1926 did not differ essentially from that in 1900.

From 1926 on, the question becomes controversial. The 'census' of 1931 showed a native population of 11,433,000, and the Government Statistician concluded therefrom that the population had increased by 1,200,000 or 11·7 per cent. in $4\frac{1}{2}$ years. I have shown above[1] that the apparent large increases in some Provinces were due to closer counting and that also the smaller increases in some other Provinces were due to this cause. A comparison of the 1921 and 1931 census returns for various tribes conveys a similar picture.[2]

	Tuareg	Manga	Munshi	Kanuri, Kanembu	Yoruba	Hausa	Fulani	Nupe
Increase . .	68,502	51,467	127,958	197,405	98,219	212,292	73,899	−22,991
Per cent. . .	155	89	29	27	24	6	4	−7

The Fulani and Hausa who in 1931 comprised about half the population of the Northern Provinces showed only a small increase since 1921. As regards tribes which showed a very large increase the Census Officer, Northern Provinces, reported:

A striking feature of this Census has been the large increase in number of Tuareg from 44,000 to 112,650 mainly as a result of closer enumeration.[3]

. . . the Kanuri, who are found in large numbers in Kano, Bauchi, Zaria, and Sokoto Provinces, have been more closely enumerated. . . . The increase in the Manga (the figures for the tribe are doubled) is also due to a closer enumeration.[4]

The Munshi and Yoruba increases seem to be due to a large extent to closer enumeration.[5]

As regards the Nupe, who showed a decrease, the Census Officer said:

The Nupe including their sub-divisions, show a decrease of 23,500 or 7 per cent. This decrease coincides with a low net fertility rate, with high per mille figures for blindness (10·5) and a low proportion of non-adults (895) per 1,000 adult males.[6]

[1] See pp. 593, 595.

[2] See Meek, vol. ii, pp. 185–92; Census of Nigeria, 1931, vol. ii, pp. 26–9, 68–74.

[3] Ibid., p. 26. The Government Statistician said (ibid., vol. i, p. 55): 'The very remarkable increase in the number of Tuareg in the last decade from 44,000 to 112,650 is, at least, partially explained by the high fertility of their mothers, and the low sterility among their women of reproductive age.' But he shows on the same page that fertility (children alive per mother) was exactly the same (2·8) among the Fulani with an increase of 4 per cent. as among the Tuareg with an increase of 155 per cent., and the differences in sterility (actually percentage of women 30–39, who have no children alive) were not very considerable (Tuareg 13·6, Fulani 17·6). See also p. 675 above.   [4] Ibid., vol. ii, p. 28.   [5] Ibid., p. 29.

[6] Ibid. It should be noted, however, that the net fertility rate of the Nupe (1·8 children alive per mother) was exactly the same as that of the Yoruba. As regards blindness, the proportion of 10·5 per mille was that ascertained at the General Census for the whole of the Niger Province (see ibid., p. 38). According to the Intensive Census which gave figures by tribes, the proportion for the Nupe was 5·9 per mille as compared with 6·8 per mille for all natives (see ibid., p. 110).

Thus, there is a great deal of evidence that the increase appearing from a comparison of the 1931 and 1926 population figures was more or less fictitious. It was wholly fictitious if the Government Statistician's estimate of a death-rate of 40–50 per 1,000 in the Northern Provinces in non-epidemic years was correct. But this, I think, was a gross overestimate,[1] and it may well be that the population had actually increased somewhat between 1926 and 1931.

The population estimate for 1942 suggests an increase of 1,000,000 or 8·7 per cent. since the census of 1931. I see no reason whatsoever for assuming that the increase was larger than that. However, all figures are so uncertain that it is impossible to say anything definite. The population may have increased between 1926 and 1940 by something like 10 per cent., but one cannot rule out the possibility that it has not increased at all.

The situation in the Southern Provinces is more obscure still. The data on which population estimates were based have been all the time quite inadequate and prior to 1931 the official reports paid very little attention to population growth. When the census of 1921 showed a native population of 8,369,000 as compared with 7,856,000 in 1911, Dr. Talbot said:

> Despite the immense mortality among children the West African negro is probably even more prolific than the native of South Africa. The increase, however, in the last ten years has perhaps been more than counterbalanced by the large number of deaths due to the influenza epidemic of 1918. It is difficult to estimate the effect of this disease on the mortality, but in Lagos, where registration is compulsory, there was a case incidence of at least 50%, while it was estimated that quite 15% of the population died from this cause. Among the 418 Europeans who were treated, the deaths amounted to 35%. On the other hand small-pox, which is endemic in the country, has been brought, to a certain extent, under control through the larger number of people now vaccinated when the disease breaks out in a neighbourhood. On the whole, therefore, it is probable that the population is about the same as in 1911.[2]

But this argument is not at all convincing. There is no evidence that the natives of Southern Nigeria were particularly prolific or that child mortality was immense or that the number of people dying from smallpox (outside Lagos) had decreased considerably. As regards the influenza epidemic, mortality in Lagos had been estimated at 1·5 per cent. (not 15 per cent.) and in the whole of Southern Nigeria at nearly 3 per cent. But it may well be that Dr. Talbot's suggestion that the population in 1921 was about the same as in 1911 was correct.

The 'census' returns for 1931 and the estimate for 1942 show a native population of 8,490,000 and 8,828,000 respectively and, therefore, indicate a very slight increase since 1921. I have discussed above[3] at great length the value of these figures. At this place it will suffice to note that the increase since 1921 has been possibly much larger.

It is hardly necessary to add anything concerning Nigeria as a whole. I am inclined to think that the population increased very little, if at all, in the first quarter of this century, and that it increased somewhat but probably less than 10 per cent. in the following 15 years.

[1] See p. 692 above.   [2] Talbot, vol. iv, pp. 5–7.   [3] See pp. 554–60.

VII. Non-Native Mortality[1]

1. *Lagos*

Until the beginning of this century mortality among Europeans was excessive. It was very much higher than among natives and was frequently discussed in official reports.

1873. Amongst the European population, which at the beginning of the year numbered 90, there were 13 deaths, showing a mortality at the rate of 14·4 per cent. per annum.[2]

1868–79. . . . dysentery and fever, the chief diseases of hot climates, have been productive of the greatest mortality among Europeans in Lagos.[3]

1880. The deaths among Europeans, which were 10 in 1879, rose to 15 in 1880, but only 10 of these can be attributed to climatic causes. People who come here from abroad are now more careful of themselves than were many of their predecessors.[4]

1885. Eight deaths in 1885; of these six were due to climatic causes, 23 were invalided, one died shortly after leaving port. The Europeans at Lagos usually number 100, hence the death rate in 1885 was 9 per cent., or 90 per 1,000, a figure which well represents the deadly nature of this climate.[5]

1887. . . . there was a large mortality amongst the European population in the town. Ten deaths were registered. In addition two persons who were invalided died at sea. This, out of a resident population of almost 100, is a large per-centage, and gives a fair idea of the amount of sickness. It also points out the urgency for sanitary works, as most of the deaths were due to malaria.[6]

1890. The average annual number of residents from 1881 to 1885 was 107; the average number of deaths for the same period was 8¾ per annum; the death rate was therefore as nearly as possible 8 per cent. Calculations on a similar basis show that from 1886 to 1890, inclusive, the average number of Europeans and Americans was 110⅗; there were in all 44 deaths for the five years, giving an average of 8⅘ per annum; the death rate, therefore, for the second period was much the same as for the first, viz., nearly 8 per cent.

. . . Rain-water tanks have been provided for all officers' quarters and public institutions, and the planting out of eucalyptus in considerable quantities has been resorted to in the hope that in this way the malarious character of the climate may be to some extent counteracted.[7]

1893. . . . there was no epidemic disease, but the number of deaths amongst the European population amounted to 17, which is the highest death-rate recorded for the last 10 years, the lowest being 5 in 1890, and the highest 11 in the years 1883, 1884, 1888, and 1889.[8]

1894. The death rate among Europeans during the year is by far the heaviest

[1] Data concerning non-native births are extremely scanty for the early times. In a report showing that 130 Europeans died in Lagos from 1868 to 1879 still-birth is given in two cases as the cause of death (see *Colonial Possessions Reports 1879*, p. 217). A report for 1882 says that no European birth occurred in that year in Lagos (see ibid. *1882*, p. 243). In 1883 one European child was born in Lagos (see Lagos, *Blue Book 1883*, p. 130). For 1928–30 the numbers of non-native live-born in Lagos have been given as 3, 6, and 6 respectively, and for 1932–8 as 6, 11, 12, 6, 10, and 16 respectively (see Lagos Town Council, *Report of the Medical Officer of Health 1928*, p. 15; *1929*, p. 14; *1930*, p. 25; *1933*, p. 25; *1935*, p. 21; *1937*, p. 26; *1938*, p. 25).
In the whole of Nigeria the numbers of non-native live-born in 1931–4 were 18, 25, 42, and 36 respectively (see Nigeria, *Medical Report 1931*, p. 19; *1932*, p. 14; *1933*, p. 14; *1934*, p. 13). No data seem to have been published for any earlier or any more recent year.
[2] *Colonial Possessions Reports 1874*, Part II, p. 118.
[3] Ibid. *1879*, p. 218.   [4] Ibid. *1879–81*, p. 304.
[5] Ibid. *1884–6*, p. 117.   [6] *Sanitary Report on Lagos for 1887*, p. 7.
[7] *Colonial Reports, Lagos 1890*, p. 13.   [8] Ibid. *1893*, p. 7.

on record, viz. 23 . . . this, out of an estimated population of 150, being nearly 16 per cent . . . can only be termed appalling, and clearly shows that this part of Africa is still unfortunately entitled to be termed 'the white man's grave.'[1]

1895. Among Europeans the deaths numbered 16, in a community of about 150, seven of them appearing in the returns as due to fever. This though better than in 1894, when nearly 16 per cent. died, is still sufficiently appalling.[2]

1896. The year was very fatal to Europeans, there being no less than 28 deaths out of an estimated population of 150. From these figures it will be seen that the European death rate reached 190 per thousand. Six Government officials died during the year in Lagos . . .[3] [in addition] Major Edward Stanley, who was invalided home and expired at Accra some few hours after leaving Lagos.

This is a very heavy record, especially when it is remembered that all the persons named were in the prime of life and had been medically examined before they were appointed.

In 1895 there were sixteen deaths amongst the European section of the community . . . . In 1894 . . . the total number of deaths amongst Europeans [was] 23.

From these figures it does not look as if the conditions of life in Lagos have become more healthy as the Colony has developed. It may, of course, be said that 1896 was an exceptionally bad year and this is undoubtedly true, but I regret to say 1897 shows no improvement, as up to the present date (10th September) no less than 18 Europeans have died, of whom six were in the service of the Government.[4]

TABLE 27. *Registered European Deaths in Lagos 1868–96*[1]

Year	Deaths	Year	Deaths	Year	Deaths	Year	Deaths	Year	Deaths	Year	Deaths
1868	4	1873	11	1878	22	1883	11	1888	11	1893	17
1869	10	1874	15	1879	10	1884	11	1889	11	1894	23
1870	2	1875	8	1880	15	1885	8	1890	5	1895	16
1871	9	1876	13	1881	10	1886	9	1891	8	1896	28
1872	9	1877	17	1882	4	1887	10	1892	8		

[1] See *Colonial Possessions Reports 1879*, p. 217, *1879–81*, p. 302; *Colonial Reports, Lagos 1892*, p. 37; Lagos, *Abstract of Registration 1898*, p. 4. The 130 deaths in 1868–79 include 2 stillbirths. Visitors included were 1881–92: 3, 1, 3, 1, 3, 2, 4, 0, 0, 1, 4, 3; 1895–6 ('Abstract 1896', p. 132): 3, 2. In Payne's *Almanack* the deaths are shown by sex for 1868–86 and 1888–92. The totals agree with those given above. The numbers of female deaths were 3 in 1874, 2 in 1875, 1877, 1878, 1889, and 1891, 1 in 1879, 1880, 1888, and 1890, and 0 in all other years (see *Almanack 1878*, pp. 28–9; *1887*, pp. 49–52; *1894*, pp. 57–8).

1897. The resident European population averages about 250. . . . Twenty-three Europeans died during the year . . . .[5]

1898. The health of Lagos Island was, as far as Europeans were concerned, undoubtedly more satisfactory in 1898 than for some years previous.[6]

1899. During the last year or two the health of Europeans has been exceptionally good . . . .[7]

There is no doubt that the climate of Lagos, like that of most places on the West Coast of Africa, remains very unhealthy to Europeans in spite of all the advances that there have been in hygienic matters.[8]

1900. Among the Europeans the deaths rose from 18 in the year 1899 to 21.

[1] *Colonial Reports, Lagos 1894*, p. 6.   [2] Ibid. *1895*, p. 9.
[3] See also Lagos, 'General Abstract of Registration 1896', p. 126: 'Of the 28 deaths 17 are set down to Merchants and Mercantile Clerks. The names of six Government Officials appear on the death roll, 1 Missionary and 3 Mercantile marine.'
[4] Statement by Colonial Secretary, *Colonial Reports, Lagos 1896*, p. 9.
[5] Ibid. *1897*, p. 8. As regards total mortality of officials in 1881–97 see 'Vital Statistics respecting Europeans employed by the Governments of the Gold Coast and Lagos, 1881–97', quoted in chapter 'Gold Coast', p. 536 above.
[6] *Colonial Reports, Lagos 1898*, p. 15.   [7] Ibid. *1899*, p. 21.   [8] Ibid., p. 22.

The character of the climate is well known to be unhealthy and depressing, the more pronounced periods of unhealthiness being at the change of the two seasons of the year, the 'rains' and the 'dries.'

Lagos Island, the seat of Government, could never be made a truly healthy town, and it is proposed to erect residences for Europeans and natives at Oloke Meji hills, on the railway line.

Oloke Meji is situate about ninety miles from Lagos.[1]

Of the 21 deaths occurring in 1900 among the 270 or 280 Europeans in Lagos 17 were due to malaria or blackwater fever. But this was the last year in which these diseases claimed so many victims. The explanation given in 1907 by the Principal Medical Officer was: 'Anti-Mosquito work started, and Quinine Prophylaxis more emphasized during latter part of 1900.'[2] In spite of a very great increase in the European population of the town the average yearly number of European deaths from malaria and blackwater fever dropped from 12 in 1897–1900 to 6 in 1901–10.

TABLE 28. *Registered Non-Native Deaths in Lagos Township, 1897–1910*[1]

Year	Europeans							Asiatics[2]
	Lagos						Ebute Metta	Lagos
	Malaria		Blackwater fever		Other causes	Total		
	Officials	Others	Officials	Others				
1897	2	9	—	2	10	23	..	..
1898	2	2	—	—	4	8	..	..
1899	4	8	—	3	3	18	..	..
1900	5	5	—	7	4	21	..	..
1901	1	5	—	4	5	15³	1	..
1902	—	3	1	4	..	..	..	..
1903	—	5	1	1	3	10	—	1
1904	1	6	—	2	3	12	—	3
1905	1	5	2	—	7	15	2	..
1906	—	5	1	3	4	13⁴	..	..
1907	—	1	—	—	3	4	1	3
1908	—	2	1	1	5	9	—	—
1909	—	1	—	—	4	5	1	1
1910	1	2	—	2	7	12	1	—

[1] See Lagos, *Abstract of Registration 1898*, p. 8, '1900', p. 77; Lagos, *Blue Book 1901*, p. 77; Lagos, *Medical Report 1904*, p. 13; *Colonial Reports, Lagos 1905*, p. 90, Southern Nigeria, 'Medical Report 1906', p. 290; Southern Nigeria, *Medical Report 1907*, pp. 15, 17, *1908*, p. 14, *1909*, p. 40, *1910*, p. 12. In the years 1907–9 there died in addition 'on the two railway extensions' from malaria 1, 4, and 3 Europeans and from blackwater fever 0, 3, and 1.

[2] The Asiatics were nearly all Syrians (the Asiatic deceased in 1909 was said to be an East Indian).   [3] Including Asiatics.   [4] Including Ebute Metta.

From 1911 to 1927 the data concerning non-native deaths in Lagos are extremely scanty.[3] For 1928–38 figures have been published by various Departments, but it is not easy to interpret them.[4] As far as I can make

[1] Ibid. *1900–1*, p. 12.   [2] Southern Nigeria, 'Medical Report 1906', p. 286.
[3] The only year for which I found a figure is 1918, when 25 non-native deaths were reported from Lagos (and 1 from Ebute Metta). See *Report on the Lagos Town Council 1918*, p. 15.
[4] See pp. 657–8 above.

out the non-native deaths in Lagos Township in those 11 years numbered 15, 10, 13, 13, 13, 15, 9, 8, 11, 10, and 12 respectively.[1] These figures suggest a very low mortality.

2. Southern Nigeria

No death records are available for the earliest years of British Administration. The first report on the Niger Coast Protectorate, covering the period from August 1891 to 1894, merely says:

> It is a noteworthy fact that up to the present time no single death or serious case of illness has taken place on the Consulate hill, although on an average there are from fifteen to twenty officials resident thereon, while in the factories which are situated on the river, four Government officials, not counting many members of the mercantile community, have died during the same period; this marked difference is without doubt due to the houses on the hill being situated to a great extent above the malaria of the swamps and also to the clearing of the surrounding bush, which always has a beneficial effect.[2]

In subsequent years the numbers of European deaths in the Niger Coast Protectorate (from 1900 on Southern Nigeria) were as follows:[3]

Year	Total	Year	Officials	Others	Year	Officials	Others
1894–5	16	1900	7	13	1906[2]	9	9
1895–6	19	1901	4	14	1907	4	14
1896–7	21	1902	3	9	1908	14[3]	
1897–8	15[1]	1903	2	10	1909	8	20
1898–9	14	1904	7	12	1910	8	13
1899–1900	20	1905	5	7			

[1] In addition 1 European officer in Benin City.
[2] In addition 5 Europeans died on steamers and were buried in Southern Nigeria.
[3] Including 2 non-residents on ships in harbour.

These figures exclude the Western Province (former Colony and Protectorate of Lagos). Including the Western Province the deaths were given as follows:[4]

	1906	1907	1910	1911	1912	1913	1914	1915	1916	1917	1918
Officials.	33	21	37	9	9	7	5	4	9	15	16
Others .				..	26	37	17	8	8	12	29

[1] See Lagos Town Council, *Report of the Medical Officer of Health 1928*, p. 15, *1929*, p. 14, *1930*, p. 25, *1933*, p. 25, *1935*, p. 21, *1937*, p. 26, *1938*, p. 25; Nigeria, *Medical Report 1931*, p. 20, *1932*, p. 14, *1933*, p. 14, *1934*, p. 13, *1935*, p. 7.

[2] *Report on the Niger Coast Protectorate 1891–4*, p. 6.

[3] See ibid. *1894–5*, p. 18, *1895–6*, p. 116, *1896–7*, p. 7, *1897–8*, p. 5; *Colonial Reports, Niger Coast Protectorate 1898–9*, p. 10; *Colonial Reports, Southern Nigeria 1899–1900*, p. 17, *1900*, p. 17, *1901*, p. 14, *1902*, p. 34, *1905*, p. 34, *1906*, p. 59, *1907*, p. 22, *1908*, pp. 29–30, *1909*, p. 22, *1910*, p. 26; 'General Abstract of Registration in Southern Nigeria 1906', p. 26; Southern Nigeria, *Blue Book 1906* R, p. 2, *1907* R, p. 2, *1908* R, p. 2, *1909* R, p. 3, *1910* R, pp. 3–4.

[4] See *Colonial Reports, Southern Nigeria 1907*, p. 22, *1910*, p. 26; Southern Nigeria, *Blue Book 1907* R, p. 2; Southern Nigeria, *Medical Report 1911*, p. 8, *1912*, pp. 12, 14, *1913*, p. 14; Nigeria, *Medical Report 1914*, p. 60, *1915*, pp. 40, 42, *1917*, pp. 10, 12; Southern Provinces, *Medical Report 1916*, pp. 7–8, *1918*, pp. 10–11.

From 1919 on, no separate statistics have been published for Southern Nigeria.

In the period 1894–1900 mortality among Europeans was excessive. With a population averaging about 225 the yearly deaths averaged 18. But such a mortality at that time did not appear extraordinarily high. The report for 1894–5 said:

> Population of Protectorate, 214; total cases treated, 1,398; deaths, 16; invalided, 33; death-rate, 7·47 per cent. of population, 74·70 per thousand; invalided, 33, 15·4 per cent. of population.
>
> These returns may be considered fairly satisfactory, and if one only had the records of years gone by to compare with these figures it would undoubtedly show that the health of the European residents had materially improved since greater attention has been paid to habits of life and sanitation.[1]

The reports for 1895–6 and 1897–8 emphasize the high mortality among employees of trading firms:

> It is interesting to note that nearly all the deaths which took place in the Protectorate during the period occurred amongst the young assistants of the commercial trading factories. This mortality is in a great measure due to the fact that the majority of assistants sent out to the coast are much too young and inexperienced to contend with the risks of this wretched climate.[2]
>
> The Acting Principal Medical Officer in his report as regards the death-rate of Europeans, makes the following remarks: 'I would like to point out here that the mortality has always been the highest among those of long service (traders' assistants doing three years), and should recommend that something should be done in the matter towards having the excessive service of non-officials shortened.'
>
> These remarks need no comment, and there is no doubt about it that young assistants sent out, of the ages of 19 to 21, who are at work all day, which work is not at all congenial, being the tallying of casks and sacks, should not be sent out for more than eighteen months or two years, whereas the rule is to send them out for three years.[3]

When in 1898–9 the death-rate was still 62 the Governor Sir Ralph Moor said:

> The decrease in the death rate may be attributed to a great extent to the improvement of the conditions under which the Europeans now live, the greater attention given to general sanitation, and (probably) to the general improvement in the methods of treatment of tropical diseases, judging by the statistical returns. Among the stations of the Protectorate, Sapele still maintains its unenviable eminence as being the most unhealthy. With a European population averaging 14, there have been 119 cases of sickness, which would allow each European at the station to have been in the hands of the medical officers between eight and nine times during the year. There have been five deaths and eight cases of invaliding, which totalled would appear effectually to dispose of all but one of the average European population within a year. The death rate shows 214·2 per thousand, which it is satisfactory to note is a decrease on that of last year which was 226 per thousand. This gives ground for slight satisfaction, and I anticipate that in next year's report much better results will be shown, as improvements have been made which it is hoped will appreciably affect the general health at the station.[4]

In the following year the death-rate rose to 74, and the differences at the various stations were again enormous.

---

[1] *Report on the Niger Coast Protectorate 1894–5*, p. 18.   [2] Ibid. *1895–6*, p. 117.
[3] Ibid. *1897–8*, p. 5.   [4] *Colonial Reports, Niger Coast Protectorate 1898–9*, p. 11.

As the majority of the European inhabitants only stay in the Protectorate for one or two years at a time, there is a constant change going on, and consequently a percentage of deaths estimated on a fixed population cannot be quite accurate for purposes of comparison with former years. This system is, however, followed, and is, I think, sufficient for general information. Calculated on this basis, the total European death-rate for the year under review was 7·40 per cent., and shows an increase of 1·24 per cent. over that of the preceding year. . . .

Taking the death percentage in certain details, the death-rate in Old Calabar district was 2·04 per cent., showing a decrease of 5·25 per cent. on that of the previous year. On the other hand, Opobo, Warri, and Benin River districts, which were considered the most healthy in the Protectorate, show for the year under review an increase in the mortality of 14·5 for Opobo, 13·15 for Warri, and 40 per cent. for Benin River. Sapele, which for the last five years has been notoriously unhealthy, compares favourably with the most healthy districts, and shows a decrease in the death-rate of 14·28 per cent. on that of the previous year, which decrease was anticipated by Sir Ralph Moor in his report for 1898–1899.[1]

Mortality decreased conspicuously in the first years of this century. The Resident of the Central Province, in his report for 1906, made the following interesting comment:

Considering . . . the great change which has come over the habits of the majority of the official population in Nigeria, I should imagine that by reason of medical science, sanitation, bush clearing and the knowledge of how and when to take proper precautions, West Africa, especially Southern Nigeria, is nothing like as unhealthy as it used to be.

I can remember when not ⅛ of the work done now in one day was regarded as a day's work, when a march of ten miles was regarded as a most wonderful under-taking, whereas now twenty, thirty or forty miles are often done on a bicycle and a good half day's work as well; when an official no more dreamt of going out in the afternoon sun than he did of flying; when, in fact, anything that might require exercise of either brain or body was recommended to be avoided in deference to the climate.[2]

In 1906–10, with an average population (in the Eastern and Central Provinces) of 675, deaths averaged 19. Some further improvement was apparently achieved in 1911–17, but in this period the death data for the non-official population are too incomplete to permit the drawing of final conclusions. It is furthermore impossible to state anything definite about the comparative mortality of officials and non-officials. The Colonial Report for 1906 said:

It will be noticed that the death and invaliding rates among officials are consider-ably higher than among non-officials. This is no doubt because the officials undergo more exposure than the non-officials, who carry on their business generally at well-

[1] *Colonial Reports, Southern Nigeria 1899–1900*, p. 17.

[2] 'Report, Central Province, 1906', p. 331. But railway and road extension and the increas-ing employment of motor transport apparently changed habits again. In his report for 1922 Dr. Blair said: 'This progress is nearly all to the good; but not entirely so. It is little if any exaggera-tion, to state that with some, walking is becoming a lost art; new-comers are apt to feel ill-used when they have to walk five or ten miles where their predecessors habitually walked twenty or twenty-five, without thinking or saying anything about it; and many clerks and artizans habitually put on the martyr's crown so soon as they find themselves obliged to walk half so far to their work as average London clerks and artizans habitually walk to theirs. While all this increase in the general use of mechanical transport is good for trade, and saving time and economising energy, it is undoubtedly introducing an element of softness which is not good for the public health' (Nigeria, *Medical Report 1922*, p. 48).

established centres, except those employed in the timber industry, whereas the officials are in many cases engaged in opening up new country and improving the methods of Government in up-country districts where the conditions of life are more difficult owing to lack of proper housing accommodation, sanitation, and to the necessity of living to a great extent on tinned food.[1]

But when an investigation of blackwater fever showed that the incidence was apparently higher among officials than among non-officials it was argued:

This fact is difficult to explain, for the official is, on the average, better housed, better segregated, better paid, enjoys better medical treatment, has shorter hours of work, and is usually considerably older than the non-official, and his tour of service is rarely extended over twelve months.[2]

Finally, the Medical Report for 1914 said that the then higher death-rate among the non-official population was 'due probably to longer tour of service, poor housing and lack of strict medical supervision'.[3]

3. Northern Nigeria

The official death statistics start here on 1 April 1898, twenty-one months before the British flag was hoisted in the territory then adminis-tered by the Royal Niger Company. They appear quite adequate until 1919; population data have been published regularly for this period, and official comments on mortality are ample. The death figures for 1898–1902 may be summarized as follows:[4]

Apr. 1898 to Mar. 1899	Apr. 1899 to Mar. 1900	Apr. 1900 to Mar. 1901	Year 1901	Year 1902
32	14	14[1]	9	9

[1] Including 4 deaths at sea from disease contracted in the Protectorate.

Mortality in 1898 was excessive.[5] In the last nine months of that year there were 27 deaths, exactly as many as in the following twenty-four months. Yet mortality was very high still both in the last year of the administration by the Royal Niger Company (1899) and in the first year of the British administration (1900). Both in 1899–1900 and in 1900–1 the deaths constituted about 8·5 per cent. of the average population. It is interesting to see how various medical and administration officers viewed the situation. In a report dated 29 December 1900 the Medical Officer, West African Frontier Force, said:

January 1st, saw the inauguration of the Protectorate, and up to the present little has been or could be done to remedy the insanitary condition of the large towns.[6]

[1] Colonial Reports, Southern Nigeria 1906, p. 59.
[2] Report on Blackwater Fever in Southern Nigeria 1899–1911, p. 26.
[3] Nigeria, Medical Report 1914, p. 59.
[4] See Colonial Reports, Northern Nigeria 1901, p. 35, 1905–6, p. 103. According to Northern Nigeria, 'Medical Report 1 Jan. to 31 Mar. 1900', p. 60, there were 5 deaths in the first quarter of 1899 and 5 deaths in the first quarter of 1900. According to 'Report on the Public Health of Northern Nigeria 1907', p. 91, there were 13 deaths in the calendar year 1900.
[5] See also Colonial Reports, Niger, West African Frontier Force 1897–8, pp. 18–19, 22.
[6] Northern Nigeria, 'Medical Report 1 Jan. to 31 Mar. 1900', p. 60.

A few months later, the Acting Principal Medical Officer, in his report on the year 1900-1 dated 1 April 1901, wrote:

The general health of the Europeans during this period shows an improvement on former periods, but the death rate is still abnormally high. There is no doubt that more suitable houses, healthier modes of living, and improved hygiene are having their due effect, but I do not anticipate that the death rate will reach its normal level for several years yet.[1]

Sir Frederick Lugard, in a report dated London, 1 May 1901, said:

I have the greatest pleasure in recording the fact that the past year has witnessed a most satisfactory diminution of mortality among Europeans in Government service. The steady diminution of deaths and serious illness which has been notice-able since the beginning of 1898 (when the West African Frontier Force was raised) is due largely to the introduction of polo and tennis, which provide the active exercise so vitally necessary in a climate like West Africa. It has become a byeword in the country that no one who plays these games is ever invalided.[2]

From 1901 on, mortality became much more favourable. The Medical Officer, in his reports for the calendar years 1901 and 1902, made the following comments:

The general health of Europeans during the above period [1901] has greatly improved in comparison with the previous years. This is mainly due, in my opinion, to (1) the better housing of Europeans; (2) the improved water supply at Jebba and Lokoja; and (3) great improvement in the sanitation at the different stations. The average strength of Europeans in the Protectorate for the year has been 165. There were six deaths during the year as compared with fourteen, fourteen, and thirty-two, respectively, in the three previous years.[3]

The marked improvement in the health of the Europeans, to which I called attention in my last report, has been well maintained.[4]

But when in 1903 deaths were twice as numerous as in 1902[5] the Medical Officer said:

Comparisons made between statistics of mortality based on such a relatively small population as that of Northern Nigeria, which has been occupied by Europeans for so short a time, are, however, obviously fallacious, and until records of a number of years are available it cannot be stated that the death-rate of one year is above or below the normal rate.[6]

---

[1] Northern Nigeria, 'Medical Report 1900-1', p. 57. He said furthermore (ibid., p. 58): 'There has been a very marked diminution in the number of cases of Blackwater Fever, from 23 in 1899, to 8 in the year 1st April 1900, to 31st March 1901. This is due to the fact that there has been no clearing and digging of ground on a large scale, and also that the conditions of living are much improved.' However, according to Northern Nigeria, *Medical Report 1913*, Chart A, the cases of blackwater fever in 1898–1902 were 21, 22, 12, 12, and 20 respectively.

[2] *Colonial Reports, Northern Nigeria, 1 Jan. 1900 to 31 Mar. 1901*, p. 26. The number of people invalided in 1900-1 was actually 32 as compared with 26 in 1899–1900. See ibid. *1901*, p. 35.

[3] Ibid. *1901*, p. 31. Actually deaths in 1901 seem to have numbered 9.

[4] Ibid. *1902*, p. 80.   [5] The official death-rate rose from 31 to 58.

[6] Ibid. *1903*, p. 34. When the number of deaths in 1905 was very low, the Medical Officer laid great emphasis on the decrease. 'The general health of Europeans has been better than in any year on record. The average death rate for the last five years is 49·56 per thousand, and was this year only 29·23. The average invaliding rate for five years is 144·6, and was this year 143·27 per 1,000' (ibid. *1905–6*, p. 105). But when in the following year the official death-rate rose to 49 and the invaliding rate to 159, the Medical Officer said once more: 'The figures, however, dealt with, are so small that conclusions based on comparisons of one year with another are largely fallacious' (ibid. *1906–7*, p. 44). The same argument was used when the death-rate rose in 1908 (see ibid. *1908–9*, p. 13) while the decrease in the numbers of deaths in 1907 had been considered quite significant (see ibid. *1907–8*, pp. 64, 67).

From 1903 to 1918 the deaths were as follows:[1]

Year	Offi-cials	Others	Year	Offi-cials	Others	Year	Offi-cials	Others	Year	Offi-cials	Others
1903	12[1]	6	1907	4[2]	3	1911	7[4]	6	1915	7	7
1904	8	5	1908	10[3]	—	1912	6	16	1916	7	10
1905	7	3	1909	8[4]	5	1913	4	9	1917	7	12
1906	10[1]	7	1910	7	6	1914	20[5]	7	1918	16[6]	20[7]

[1] Including 3 killed in action.
[2] There were in addition 'four deaths amongst officials on leave in England, two of which were due to blackwater fever'.
[3] Excluding 6 deaths which occurred on the Northern Extension of the Lagos Railway. There were in addition 5 deaths amongst officials on leave.
[4] Excluding one death on the Northern Extension of the Lagos Railway.
[5] Including 9 killed in action.
[6] Including 9 from influenza.
[7] Including 10 from influenza.

Until 1910 non-officials constituted only a small fraction of the European population—increasing from 13 per cent. in 1903 to 24 per cent. in 1909—but one-third of all deaths in 1903–9 occurred among non-officials. The Principal Medical Officer gave the following explanation:

1904. This difference is brought about almost entirely by the more careful selection of candidates for employment in Government service, and by their shorter tour of residence—many of the men sent out by the trading firms being obviously physically unfit for tropical service.[2]

A considerable proportion of the European deaths were due to blackwater fever. The importance of this disease appears from the summary overleaf.[3]

In 1898–9 the incidence of blackwater fever among the average European population was about 13 per cent.; from 1909 to 1918 it was below 3 per cent. in every year without showing any definite trend.

[1] See ibid. 1903, p. 34, 1904, p. 144, 1905–6, pp. 102–3, 1906–7, p. 44, 1907–8, p. 64, 1908–9, p. 13, 1909, p. 16, 1910–11, p. 21, 1911, p. 17, 1912, p. 19; Northern Nigeria, Blue Book 1913 R, p. 3; Nigeria, Medical Report 1914, pp. 6–7, 1915, pp. 7–8, 1917, p. 112; Northern Provinces, Medical Report 1916, p. 4, 1918, p. 6.
[2] Colonial Reports, Northern Nigeria 1904, p. 138. But see also the statement by the administration ibid., p. 113: 'This [difference] is due, no doubt, as the Principal Medical Officer says, to the longer period of service of the non-officials and to the greater care in selection of officials, but also to the better housing and sanitary measures adopted by Government.' See, finally, in this connexion the comment by the Senior Sanitary Officer, Northern Provinces, on the 'Townships Ordinance, 1917' which prescribed that 'the European Reservation shall be separated from the Non-European Reservation by a Neutral Zone having a minimum breadth of 440 yards, or two furlongs': 'It is good that the principle should be the law of the land; it is the only defence which the young commercial European has against his firm, if the latter call upon him to reside against a native slum; and the present writer is thankful, for the sake of his countrymen's reputation, that it is never likely to be his lot to give evidence before a Commission enquiring into past casualties directly traceable to the fashion in which Merchants have quartered their European employees—in the comparatively recent past' (Nigeria, Medical Report 1917, p. 131).
[3] See Northern Nigeria, Medical Report 1913, Chart A; Northern Provinces, Medical Report 1918, p. 8. The Medical Reports show also the percentage of fatal cases but these figures are misleading, as only deaths that occurred in Northern Nigeria were included. Thus while no death was recorded for 1907, two officials on leave in England in that year died from blackwater fever.

Year	Blackwater fever		All other deaths	Year	Blackwater fever		All other deaths	Year	Blackwater fever		All other deaths
	Cases	Deaths			Cases	Deaths			Cases	Deaths	
1898	21	5	22[1]	1905	18	4	6	1912	14	4	17[8]
1899	22	3	11	1906	27	5	9[3]	1913	17	6	7
1900	12	3	6[2]	1907	12	—	6[4]	1914	22	6	12[9]
1901	12	1	8	1908	16	7	1[5]	1915	22	4	10
1902	20	5	4	1909	14	3	6[6]	1916	22	8	9
1903	17	8	7[3]	1910	10	3	10	1917	19	4	15
1904	35	6	6[4]	1911	12	6[7]	7[8]	1918	27	7	29[10]

[1] From April to December.   [2] Excluding 4 on voyage to England.
[3] Excluding 3 in action.   [4] Excluding 1 from accident.
[5] Excluding 2 from wounds.   [6] Excluding 4 from accident.
[7] Including 1 on the Northern Extension of the Lagos Railway.
[8] Excluding 1 from drowning.   [9] Excluding 9 in action.
[10] Including 19 from influenza.

The following quotations may serve to throw additional light on European mortality in Northern Nigeria.

1904. With regard to the probable effect of the meteorological conditions on the health of the community, it may be stated, generally, that Europeans have the best health in the dry season, and natives in the rains. Europeans, by taking proper precautions, avoid in great part the diseases that affect the native in the dry season when water is scarce and polluted, and the native being less affected by the great cause of the excessive mortality amongst Europeans—malaria—a disease more especially of the wet season.[1]

1907. A fact to be remembered is that all the Europeans serving in this country, whether official or non-official, have to be pronounced fit for service before leaving England.[2]

Although the health improves, the climate remains the same. The precautions necessary to attain for one year a tolerable condition of health are irksome, and can only be enforced by constant reiteration.[3]

1908. The greatest amount of sickness among Europeans has been due as in former years to malaria. The total number of admissions from this disease (black-water fever being classified separately) was 307, compared with 318 admissions during last year, and 370 in 1906, 445 in 1905, and 515 in 1904, a progressive diminution in the number of cases notwithstanding the increase of the European population.[4]

The general sanitary condition of the European stations is very satisfactory, and is being improved year by year. The systematic measures taken for the prevention of malaria—segregation of Europeans, drainage, and the general use of quinine as a prophylactic—continue to give most gratifying results . . . .[5]

1910. In spite of a considerable influx of Europeans, mostly in connection with the mines and many of whom have had no previous experience of the tropics, the proportion of deaths and the invaliding rate show a most satisfactory improvement. Greater care in matters affecting health, and better precautions as regards exposure and manner of life generally, are having a marked effect on medical statistics, and the death-rate of 15·35 per 1,000 among the resident European population is the lowest on record since the Government assumed the administration of the territory.[6]

[1] Colonial Reports, Northern Nigeria 1904, p. 140. See also ibid. 1905–6, p. 103.
[2] Ibid. 1907–8, p. 64.   [3] Ibid., p. 67.
[4] Ibid. 1908–9, p. 14.   [5] Ibid.
[6] Ibid. 1910–11, p. 5. Actually, however, the death-rate was 20·4 (see ibid., p. 21) and was somewhat higher than in 1907 and 1908.

1912. Malaria continues to be the most prevalent cause of ill-health. The total number of European patients admitted into the hospitals at Zungeru, Lokoja, and Baro was 219, and of that number 80 were certified as suffering from malaria; the only other complaint that affected more than ten patients was gastritis, which accounted for 13.

Amongst out-patients malaria was responsible for 225 cases of sickness out of a total number of 958 out-patients treated. These figures show an increase of 101 cases of malaria.[1] The increase was principally amongst employees of trading and mining companies, many of whom during the year were compelled to live under unfavourable conditions with regard to both sites and living accommodation.

It has been pointed out by the medical and sanitary authorities that the steadily increasing mining and commercial activities of the country have been responsible for the introduction of an ever-increasing number of Europeans who have never previously served in the tropics . . . .[2]

1917. It remains true that the more experienced members of the European Community are infinitely less affected by Malaria than was the case formerly: it takes toll chiefly of the younger and less experienced. But their lack of experience and possible carelessness do not account entirely for its heavier incidence among the young: as a rule, the younger members of the community endure most exposure; for they do most of the travelling and, consequently, pass most time in undesirable situations which are but rarely visited and not constantly dealt with.[3]

1918. The return of the Nigerian troops, together with their numerous special service officers and non-commissioned officers, from overseas resulted in a very material increase of the official European community; and this led to a heavy incidence of European sickness, for many of the Europeans alluded to lacked the personal experience necessary to safeguard their health adequately in this country.[4]

4. Nigeria and Cameroons

The numbers of European deaths in Nigeria and the Cameroons in 1919–38 are summarized in Table 29. The figures for officials suggest a very low mortality for recent years. Mortality of non-officials has been higher, but it is difficult to appraise it correctly as the numbers of non-officials living in the country are uncertain.[5] There is, however, not the least doubt that mortality of non-officials has also decreased considerably in the course of time.[6]

[1] The numbers of cases treated in 1911–18 were 207, 309, 370, 400, 298, 270, 361, and 545 respectively, and the numbers of deaths 1, 2, 1, 1, 1, 0, 3, and 2 respectively. See Northern Nigeria, *Medical Report 1911*, p. 4, *1912*, p. 6; Nigeria, *Medical Report 1914*, p. 8, *1915*, pp. 7, 23; Northern Provinces, *Medical Report 1916*, pp. 4, 30; Nigeria, *Medical Report 1917*, pp. 112, 153; Northern Provinces, *Medical Report 1918*, pp. 6, 37.

[2] *Colonial Reports, Northern Nigeria 1912*, p. 20. See also Northern Nigeria, *Medical Report 1911*, pp. 39–40, *1912*, p. 12, *1913*, p. 48; Nigeria, *Medical Report 1914*, pp. 18, 26–7, *1915*, p. 13; Northern Provinces, *Medical Report 1916*, p. 15.

[3] Nigeria, *Medical Report 1917*, p. 135.

[4] *Colonial Reports, Nigeria 1918*, p. 19.

[5] Some of the official death-rates for the European population are evidently wrong. Thus, *Medical Report 1932*, p. 14, gives for 'Europeans and Whites' as population 5,442, as number of deaths 27, and as death-rate 4·96. But the figure of 5,442 represents the total number of non-natives ascertained at the 1931 census, including Asiatics. *Medical Report 1937*, p. 11, on the other hand, assumed that 'the average non-native population' was 'in the neighbourhood of 2,500', and as 29 deaths were recorded concluded that 'the death rate is 11·6 or three times the official death rate' which was 3·9. Actually the average non-native population must have exceeded 4,000 in 1937.

[6] During the Second World War health conditions among Europeans deteriorated considerably. There was in particular a great prevalence of malaria. See ibid. *1941*, pp. 2, 4, 6; *1942*, pp. 3, 5; *1943*, p. 5.

TABLE 29. *Deaths of Europeans, Nigeria, 1919–38*[1]

Year	Officials		Non-officials		Total	
	Number	Deaths	Number	Deaths	Number	Deaths
1919	975	19	2,193	26	3,168	45
1920	1,166	23	2,908	23	4,074	46
1921	1,302	11	1,784	23	3,086	34
1922	1,406	7	..	31	..	38
1923	1,396	16	..	13	..	29
1924	1,567	16	(2,347)	23	..	39
1925	1,466	18	1,997	31	3,463	49
1926	1,776	15	2,125	27	3,901	42
1927	1,752	14	2,207	26	3,959	40
1928	1,990	14	..	24	(5,699)	38
1929	2,581	15	..	18	(7,056)	33
1930	2,649	13	..	17	(8,249)	30
1931	1,581	17	..	21	(4,882)	38
1932	1,641	5	..	16	(4,375)	21
1933	1,586	5	2,731	25	4,317	30
1934	1,508	8	..	22	(5,021)	30
1935	1,473	7	..	21	(5,246)	28
1936	1,560	11	..	26[2]	..	37[2]
1937	1,520	6	..	29[2]	..	35[2]
1938	1,525	11	..	27[2]	..	38[2]

[1] See Nigeria, *Medical Report 1919–21*, pp. 13, 20; *1923*, p. 17; *1924*, pp. 9, 11; *1927*, pp. 21–2; *1928*, p. 18; *1929*, p. 22; *1930*, pp. 15–16; *1933*, pp. 10–11; *1935*, p. 8; *1936*, p. 14; *1937*, p. 11; *1938*, pp. 10–11. The population figures in parentheses refer to 31 Dec.

[2] Non-native deaths.

COUNT IN THE PROTECTORATE OF THE GAMBIA, 1945[1]

THE Senior Commissioner, Protectorate Administration, Mr. Neil Weir, describes the method used at this count as follows:

As no decennial census of the Protectorate was taken in 1941, His Excellency the Governor has expressed a wish that I should amplify the information given by the figures contained in the usual returns attached to the Annual Reports which are submitted by the Commissioner of each Division.

Certain changes were made in the forms forwarded with the Annual Reports in 1945. For the purposes of the assessment and annual census two appendices were found to be necessary. The first (D.A.R. Appendix 1) now contains particulars showing the numbers in each District of yards, huts, lodgers, African adult males and females, African non-adult males and females, strange farmers and their followers, literates in English and Arabic, different types of sickness, livestock and lastly non-natives. The second (D.A.R. Appendix 2) shows the areas of each District and the numbers of persons of every prominent tribe within those areas.

Figures are now readily available to provide data for a number of departmental activities which concern particular areas in which these departments are interested, although it should be appreciated that such figures may be far from accurate owing to the fact that the revised forms were in use for the first time last year.

The figures relating to the Protectorate in the official Census Reports of 1911, 1921 and 1931 were obtained in much the same manner as the annual census is taken nowadays when the assessment for payment of tax for the forthcoming year is made. This assessment usually takes place between July and October at a time when the 'Strange Farmers' or seasonal immigrants are in residence for groundnut farming prior to the trade season from November to April.

Scribes are employed temporarily for this assessment, which consists of counting the number of yards in each village in addition to any extra houses over four in number in each yard as well as the lodgers (or persons unrelated to the Yard owner) who reside therein. The Yard owner also declares the number of 'Strange Farmers' working on his land.

Each yard pays a tax or rate of 8/- per annum with an additional 2/- for every extra house over four within the yard. Lodgers pay 4/- and Strange Farmers pay 8/- per annum.

At the conclusion of their count, the enumerators return to Divisional Headquarters where the particulars obtained are entered by Districts on two forms—the Assessment for Tax summary and the Census summary. The latter summaries are consolidated into Divisional Census summaries which are forwarded as Appendix No. 1 with the Annual Report. The tribal statistics are entered separately as Appendix No. 2. It is from all these that the 1945 figures shown herein have been obtained.[2]

The report shows the African residents in the Protectorate ('obtained from Annual Census Summary') in 1939–45 and the Strange Farmers in 1912–45.[3]

---

[1] The first copies of the report on this count, dated 13 March 1946, reached London in June, by which time it was no longer possible to deal with it in the chapter on the Gambia.

[2] *Report of the Senior Commissioner on the Annual Census of the Protectorate of the Gambia, 1945*, pp. 1–2.

[3] See ibid., pp. 5, 10. The figures for Strange Farmers, 1912–31, are identical with those shown p. 334 above, except 1915 (32,330). The figures for 1932–8 read: 16,513, 14,573, 8,332, 13,341, 9,754, 13,497, and 9,195.

Year	Residents			Strange farmers
	Males	Females	Total	
1939	88,665	88,181	176,846	4,643
1940	91,328	87,345	178,673	4,890
1941	89,228	86,795	176,023	3,741
1942	93,573	91,422	184,995	2,585
1943	96,825	96,927	193,752	5,995
1944	105,196	94,161	199,357	10,793
1945	112,524	103,583	216,107	19,979

The number of African residents which was reported to have decreased between 1921 and 1931 from 201,303 to 185,150 and to have oscillated in 1935–42 between 170,255 and 184,995 rose to 199,357 in 1944 and to 216,107 in 1945. Emigration and immigration seem to have fluctuated all the time in the same direction as seasonal migration. Economic factors which attracted Strange Farmers attracted also settlers. But the apparently enormous increase in the number of residents from 1944 to 1945 was probably due in a large measure to more accurate counting.[1]

The 1945 report contains some interesting details about the composition of the population. They may be summarized as follows:[2]

Divisions	Local population (including 3,955 lodgers[1])					Strange farmers and their followers				Non-Natives	
	Men	Women	Boys	Girls	Total	Gambian	French	Portuguese	Total	Male	Female
North Bank	15,215	14,096	8,471	7,797	45,579	737	2,344	137	3,218	17	15
Upper River	15,243	15,352	9,290	8,446	48,331	917	3,982	92	4,991	13	6
MacCarthy Island	18,368	15,193	7,079	7,226	47,866	1,290	6,296	290	7,876	24	13
South Bank	18,167	18,223	10,996	10,931	58,317	722	2,138	434	3,294	4	1
Kombo North and St. Mary	8,067	4,672	1,628	1,647	16,014	176	321	103	600	32	12
Total	75,060	67,536	37,464	36,047	216,107	3,842	15,081	1,056	19,979	90	47

[1] The lodgers in the various Divisions numbered 202, 168, 403, 1,254, and 1,928 respectively.

The report gives also a comparison of the sex and age composition of the African resident population at various dates.[3]

Year	Men	Women	Boys	Girls	Total
1911	42,417	43,575	27,288	25,121	138,401
1921	63,511	60,145	42,256	35,391	201,303
1931	62,142	54,887	34,786	33,335	185,150
1945	75,060	67,536	37,464	36,047	216,107

[1] It seems in particular that the number of females was understated in 1944. The Annual Census Summaries show between 1943 and 1944 an increase of 8,371 males and a decrease of 2,766 females, and between 1944 and 1945 an increase of 7,328 males and an increase of 9,422 females.

It should be noted, furthermore, that, quite apart from inaccuracies, the numbers of residents shown in the various statistics are not strictly comparable. The Senior Commissioner, it is true, assumes that the figures given in the Census Reports for 1901–31 and in the Annual Census Summaries for 1939–45 'include Lodgers, but exclude Strange Farmers'. It is doubtful, however, whether the Annual Census Summaries always included lodgers (see pp. 337–8 above), and while they exclude Gambians temporarily absent working as strange farmers within the Protectorate, such persons were included in the decennial counts.

[2] See *Report*, Table 12.   [3] See ibid., p. 6.

The Senior Commissioner makes the following comment:

In the 1911, 1921 and 1931 Census Reports, adults were considered to be over 15 years, whereas in the year 1945 they were classed as such if 17 years or over which may account for the difference in percentages.

Throughout the period, non-adults represented 37% of the population whereas in 1945 they were 34% only. Boys are shown as 4% more than girls.[1]

But the raising of the age limit between non-adults and adults from 15 to 17 years cannot account for the *increase* in the percentage of adults. To what extent the large rise in the number of adults between 1931 and 1945 was due to the influx of foreign settlers it is impossible to tell. As regards non-adults the figures suggest that the number of children (under 15) decreased enormously between 1921 and 1931 and that there was also a slight decline thereafter. The data are too uncertain to permit the drawing of final conclusions, but they raise grave doubts as to the validity of the opinion 'The bulk of the races forming the population of the Gambia are sufficiently virile and their numbers are definitely on the increase'.[2]

While the census reports for 1921 and 1931 did not mention any non-Africans outside Bathurst and while the annual Blue Books state explicitly that there are no whites in the Protectorate,[3] the report on the 1945 count showed 137 Non-Natives.

[1] Ibid.   [2] See p. 383 above; see also p. 361.   [3] See pp. 340–1 above.

SOURCES QUOTED

GENERAL[1]

Report of the Commissioners of Inquiry into the State of the Colony of Sierra Leone (Parliamentary Papers England 1826–7, vol. vii, pp. 267–410).

Papers relating to the Colony of Sierra Leone (P.P. 1830, vol. xxi, pp. 225–319).

Report from the Select Committee on the West Coast of Africa; Together with the Minutes of Evidence, Appendix, and Index (P.P. 1842, vols. xi and xii).

Report of Colonel Ord, the Commissioner appointed to Inquire into the Condition of the British Settlements on the West Coast of Africa (P.P. 1865, vol. xxxvii, pp. 287–350).

Correspondence relating to the recent Expedition to the Upper Gambia under Administrator V. S. Gouldsbury. C. 3065 (P.P. 1881, vol. lxv, pp. 395–441).

Tables of the Revenue, Population, Commerce, &c. of the United Kingdom and its Dependencies, Part I, from 1820 to 1831, both inclusive; Supplement to Part III, Colonies 1832 to Supplement to Part VIII, Colonies 1837 to 1839; Part IX, Colonies 1839; Part XII, 1842 to Part XXII, 1852. London, 1833–54.

Statistical Tables relating to the Colonial and other Possessions of the United Kingdom, Part I, 1854 to Part XXVI, 1901. London, 1856–1903.

Statistical Tables relating to British Colonies, Possessions and Protectorates, Part XXVII, 1902 to Part XXXII, 1907. London, 1904–9.

Statistical Tables relating to British Self-Governing Dominions, Crown Colonies, Possessions and Protectorates, Part XXXIII, 1908 to Part XXXVII, 1912. London, 1910–14.

Statistical Abstract for the British Empire in each Year from 1889 to 1903 to 1928 to 1937. London, 1905–38.

The Reports Made for the Year 1845 to the Secretary of State having the Department of the Colonies: in continuation of the Reports annually made by the Governors of the British Colonies, with a view to exhibit generally The Past and Present State of Her Majesty's Colonial Possessions, Transmitted with the Blue Books for the Year 1845. Same for 1846 to 1863. London, 1846–65.

Reports Showing the Present State of Her Majesty's Colonial Possessions, Transmitted with the Blue Books for the Year 1864 to 1870. London, 1866–72.

Papers relating to Her Majesty's Colonial Possessions 1873 to 1876. London, 1873–6.

Papers relating to Her Majesty's Colonial Possessions, Reports for 1875–6 and 1877 to 1889. London, 1877–90.

Annual Colonial Reports, The Gambia 1890 to 1938; Gold Coast 1892 to 1921, 1922–3 to 1938–9; Northern Territories of the Gold Coast 1901 to 1921, 1922–3 to 1925–6; Ashanti 1905 to 1921, 1922–3 to 1925–6; Lagos 1889 to 1899, 1900–1, 1902 to 1905; Niger Coast Protectorate 1898–9; Southern Nigeria 1899–1900, 1900 to 1913; Niger, West African Frontier Force 1897–8; Northern Nigeria 1 Jan. 1900 to 31 Mar. 1901, 1901 to 1903, 1904–5 to 1908–9, 1909, 1910–11, 1911 to 1913; Nigeria 1914 to 1938; Sierra Leone 1890 to 1938.

[1] Sources quoted only in the Introduction or in more than one Chapter.

The Colonial Office List for 1862 to *1925*. London.

The Dominions Office and Colonial Office List for 1926 to *1940*. London.

An Economic Survey of the Colonial Empire (*1936*); (*1937*). Colonial Nos. 149, 179. London, 1938, 1940.

Colonial Office, *Vital Statistics respecting Europeans employed by the Governments of the Gold Coast and Lagos, 1881–97*, reprinted in *The Northern Nigeria Gazette*, 30 Sept. 1903, pp. 102–3.

Colonial Office, *West Africa, Vital Statistics of Non-Native Officials, Returns for 1921* to *1938*. London, 1922–39.

Papers relating to the Health and Progress of Native Populations in Certain Parts of the Empire. Colonial No. 65. London, 1931.

West Africa, Report on Certain Outbreaks of Yellow Fever in 1910 and 1911. London, 1913.

Report by The Hon. W. G. A. Ormsby-Gore, M.P. (Parliamentary Under-Secretary of State for the Colonies), on his Visit to West-Africa during the Year 1926. Cmd. 2744. London, 1926.

Economic Advisory Council, Committee on Nutrition in the Colonial Empire, *First Report*, Parts I and II. Cmd. 6050, 6051. London, 1939.

Gold Coast, *Census 1883* (MS. Colonial Office Library).

Development and Welfare in the Gambia, June, 1943. Bathurst.

Parliamentary Debates (Hansard) House of Commons, Official Report, London.

Sixth Report of the Directors of the African Institution, Read at the Annual General Meeting on the 25th of March, 1812 ; Seventh Report, 24th of March, 1813; Eighth Report, 23rd of March, 1814 ; Ninth Report, 12th of April, 1815 ; Tenth Report, 27th Day of March, 1816 ; Eleventh Report, 26th Day of March, 1817 ; Twelfth Report, 9th Day of April, 1818 ; Fourteenth Report, 17th Day of May, 1820 ; Eighteenth Report, 11th Day of May, 1824. London, 1812–24.

Statistical Year-Book of the League of Nations 1942/44. Geneva, 1945.

JAMES EDWARD ALEXANDER, *Narrative of a Voyage of Observation among the Colonies of Western Africa, in the Flag-Ship Thalia,* &c. 2 vols. London, 1837.

J. M. GRAY, *A History of The Gambia*. Cambridge, 1940.

LORD HAILEY, *An African Survey, A Study of Problems arising in Africa South of the Sahara*. Oxford, 1938.

PRINCE HOARE, *Memoirs of Granville Sharp, Esq.*, Composed from his own Manuscripts, and other Authentic Documents in the Possession of his Family and of the African Institution. London, 1820.

DR. JAMES AFRICANUS B. HORTON, *Physical and Medical Climate and Meteorology of the West Coast of Africa, &c.* London, 1867

— —, *West African Countries and Peoples, British and Native*, &c. London, 1868.

ROBERT R. KUCZYNSKI, *The Cameroons and Togoland, A Demographic Study*. Oxford, 1939.

SIR F. D. LUGARD, 'Northern Nigeria', Paper read at the Royal Geographical Society, 4 Nov. 1903, *The Geographical Journal*, vol. xxiii, pp. 1–27.

— —, *The Dual Mandate in British Tropical Africa*. 4th ed. London, 1929.

— —, 'Economic Development of Mandated Territories in its Relation to the Well-Being of the Natives', League of Nations, Permanent Mandates Commission, *Minutes* 7th Session, Oct. 1925, pp. 194–7.

JAMES MACQUEEN, *The Colonial Controversy*, &c.; *fully considered, in a Series of Letters, addressed to The Earl of Liverpool; with a Supplementary Letter to Mr. Macaulay*. Glasgow, 1825.

ROBERT MONTGOMERY MARTIN, *History of the Colonies of the British Empire in the West Indies, South America, North America, Asia, Austral-Asia, Africa, and Europe.* London, 1843.

PAYNE, *Lagos Almanack and Diary for 1878.* London.

— —, *Lagos and West African Almanack and Diary for 1879; 1881 to 1888; 1893; 1894.* London.

SIR LEONARD ROGERS, M.D., and ERNEST MUIR, M.D., *Leprosy.* 1st ed., Bristol, 1925 ; 2nd ed., Bristol, 1940 ; 3rd ed., Bristol, 1946.

DR. HENRY STRACHAN, Chief Medical Officer for Lagos, *Paper on the Health Conditions of West Africa*, prepared for the African Trade Section of the Incorporated Chamber of Commerce of Liverpool. Liverpool, 1901.

SIERRA LEONE

The Royal Gazette and Sierra Leone Advertiser.

The Sierra Leone Royal Gazette.

Sierra Leone, *Acts of Governor and Council from 1800 to 1827.* N. W. M. Scripsit, Anno 1830 (MS. Colonial Office Library).

Sierra Leone Acts 1811–48 (ibid.).

Acts of Governor and Council, Sierra Leone 1829–40 (MS. ibid.).

The Ordinances of the Colony of Sierra Leone (Now in Force), Commencing 12th October 1811, and ending 5th October 1857, compiled by A. Montagu. London, 1857.

Ordinances of the Colony of Sierra Leone, Passed in the Years 1858, 1859, and 1860; Ordinances Repealed, but of Occasional Reference; Royal Charters; Treaties of the Government of Sierra Leone with the Native Chiefs, &c. &c., compiled by Algernon Montagu. London, 1861.

Sierra Leone Ordinances 1879–92; 1893–8; 1899–1903; 1904–6 (C.O. Library).

Ordinances, Orders-in-Council, Governor's Orders, Rules of Court, Regulations and Proclamations of the Colony of Sierra Leone passed during the year 1907; 1908; 1909; 1910; 1913; 1920; 1924; 1931; 1935; 1942. Freetown, 1907–10, 1914, 1920, 1924, 1931, 1936, 1942.

A Revised Edition of the Ordinances of the Colony of Sierra Leone, with an Appendix containing Governor's Orders, Orders-in-Council and Rules made under Ordinances, &c. 1811–1908, prepared under the Provisions of Section 15 of the Interpretation Ordinance, 1906, by Donald Fortescue Wilbraham. 4 vols. London, 1908–9.

A Revised Edition of the Ordinances of the Colony of Sierra Leone, containing all Ordinances, &c. passed 1909–1913, prepared under the Provisions of the Statute Law Revision Ordinance, 1913, by Donald Fortescue Wilbraham. London, 1914.

The Laws of the Colony and Protectorate of Sierra Leone, containing the Ordinances thereof, the Orders in Council, Governor's Orders, Rules, Bye-Laws and Proclamations made thereunder, in Force on the 1st Day of January, 1925. Revised Edition, prepared by Michael Francis Joseph McDonnell. 3 vols. London, 1925.

Supplement to The Laws of the Colony and Protectorate of Sierra Leone, containing the Ordinances of Sierra Leone enacted between the 2nd January, 1925 and the 31st December, 1930. London, 1932.

'Population of the Colony of Sierra Leone (exclusive of the Military) 1818', *The Royal Gazette and Sierra Leone Advertiser*, 27 Feb. 1819, p. 168.

General Census of Persons inhabiting the Colony of Sierra Leone, exclusive of the Military (Europeans or Natives) and their Families, on the 8th Day of July, 1820, ibid., 8 July 1820.

'Census of the Colony of Sierra Leone, exclusive of the Military (European or Native) and their Families, taken on the 1st day of January, 1822', ibid., 10 Aug. 1822, p. 126.

Sierra Leone, *Census of Population and of Liberated Africans 1831* (Public Record Office, Colonial Office 267, vol. cxi).

Sierra Leone, *Censuses of Liberated Africans, &c. 1832–3* (C.O. 267, vol. cxxvii).

Report on the Census of Sierra Leone and its Dependencies, taken in 1881. Freetown, July 1881.

Sierra Leone, *Report and General Statistics of the Census of 1891.* Freetown, 1891.

Colony of Sierra Leone, *Census 1901,* from the Registrar-General to The Hon. The Colonial Secretary. London, 1902.

Preliminary Report on the Census of 1911, from the Compiler of Census to The Honourable The Colonial Secretary. (Typescript.)

Colony of Sierra Leone, *Report and Summary of the Census of 1911.* London, 1912.

Colony of Sierra Leone, *Report and Summary of the Census of 1921.* London, 1922.

Sierra Leone, *Report of Census for the Year 1931.* Freetown (1931).

Colony of Sierra Leone, *Report on the Labour Department 1941–2; 1943.* Freetown, 1944.

Sanitary Reports on the City of Freetown 1897 and 1898.

Sierra Leone, *Annual Reports on the Medical Department, for the Year ending 31st December, 1900, and Year ending 31st December, 1901.* London, 1902.

Sierra Leone, *Annual Report on the Medical Department, for the Year ending 31st December, 1902; 1905 to 1918.* London, 1903, 1906–(1919).

Sierra Leone, *Annual Report on the Medical and Sanitary Department for the Year ended 31st December, 1919.* London (1920).

Sierra Leone, *Annual Medical and Sanitary Report for the Year ending 31st December, 1920 to 1928.* London (1921); Freetown, 1922–30.

Sierra Leone, *Annual Report of the Medical and Sanitary Department for the Year 1929 to 1936.* Freetown, 1931–7.

Sierra Leone, *Annual Report on the Medical Services 1937; 1938.* Freetown, 1938–(1939).

Sierra Leone, *Annual Report, 1939, Medical and Health Services.* (Typescript.)

Sierra Leone, *Annual Medical Report for the Year 1940.* (Typescript.)

Sierra Leone, *Medical Report for the Year 1941.* Freetown, 1942.

Colony of Sierra Leone, *Report of the Medical and Health Services 1942.* Freetown, 1944.

Sierra Leone, *Annual Report of the Medical and Health Services for the Year 1943.* Freetown, 1945.

Report of the Registrar General for the Year 1923; 1924; 1926; 1928. (Partly MS., partly typescript.)

Annual Report of the Northern Province for the Year 1924; 1933; 1934. (1933 and 1934 typescript.)

Annual Report of the Provincial Administration for the Year 1928; 1937.

The Sierra Leone Almanac, for the Year of Our Lord 1822, &c. Published by Authority. Freetown (1822).

Sierra Leone, *Blue Book 1824* to *1942*. (1824–93 MS.; 1939–42 partly MS., partly typescript.)

Sierra Leone, *Report on the Medical Department for 1887, Colonial Possessions Reports* (1887), No. 26. London, 1888.

Sierra Leone, *Report on the Blue Book for 1887* to *1889*, ibid. (1887–9), Nos. 42, 75, 115. London, 1889–90.

The Handbook of Sierra Leone by T. N. Goddard, Assistant Colonial Secretary, Sierra Leone, compiled and published by authority of the Government of Sierra Leone. London, 1925.

Sierra Leone, *Report of the Committee appointed by His Excellency the Governor to advise on the Amendment of the Births and Deaths Registration Ordinance, 1924 (Cap. 16), with a view to placing the Registration of Births and Deaths under the Control of the Deputy Director, Sanitary Service* (Sessional Paper No. 2 of 1927).

Sierra Leone, *Correspondence relating to a General Survey of Disease in the Protectorate of Sierra Leone* (No. 4 of 1927).

Sierra Leone, *Review of Present Knowledge of Human Nutrition with remarks on Practical Measures taken by the Medical Department in the past to its improvement in Sierra Leone* (No. 5 of 1938).

Sierra Leone, *Report of the Slum Clearance Committee, 1939* (No. 9 of 1939).

Sierra Leone, *Preliminary Report on the Freetown Water Supply* by G. Howard Humphreys (No. 3 of 1945).

Colony of Sierra Leone, *An Outline of the Ten-Year Plan for the Development of Sierra Leone*. Freetown, 1946.

Appendix to Address delivered by His Excellency Sir H. C. Stevenson, on opening the Eighteenth Session of the Sierra Leone Legislative Council, 4th November, 1941.

Legislative Council of Sierra Leone, *Minutes of Meeting held at the Council Chamber, Freetown, Sierra Leone, on Tuesday, the 12th of May, 1942*; on *Tuesday, 19th of May, 1942.*

Address delivered by His Excellency Sir H. C. Stevenson, on opening the Nineteenth Session of the Sierra Leone Legislative Council, 3rd November, 1942; Appendix to Address.

Minutes of Council Sierra Leone, 14 Feb. 1792 to 9 July 1794 (C.O. 270, vol. ii).

Copies, Letters from Governor & Council to the Court of Directors, and Officers in the service of the Sierra Leone Company, 15 Dec. 1794 to 5 June 1798 (C.O. 268, vol. v).

Sierra Leone, *Despatches from Governor MacCarthy*, 1819, 1823 (C.O. 267, vols. xlix, lviii).

Report of the Commissioners of Inquiry into the State of the Colony of Sierra Leone (1827), First Part, Appendix A, B, C (C.O. 267, vols. xci, xcii).

Sierra Leone, *Despatches from Secretary of State*, 8 Sept. 1827 to 22 Dec. 1834 (C.O. 268, vols. xxviii, xxx).

Sierra Leone, *Despatches from Ricketts, Fraser, and Lewis*, 1830 (C.O. 267, vol. cii).

Sierra Leone, *Despatches from Lieutenant Governor Findlay*, Apr. to Dec. 1830 (C.O. 267, vols. ciii, civ).

Sierra Leone, *Despatches Slave Trade*, 1830 (C.O. 267, vol. cv).

The Parliamentary Register, &c., containing an Account of the most interesting Speeches and Motions, &c., vols. xxix and xxx. London, 1791.

Minutes of the Evidence taken before a Committee of the House of Commons, being a Select Committee, appointed on the 23rd Day of April 1790, to take the Examination of Witnesses respecting the African Slave Trade, 1790; 1791.

Report from the Committee on the Petition of the Court of Directors of the Sierra Leone Company, Ordered to be printed 25th May 1802 (*Parliamentary Papers England* 1801–2, vol. ii, pp. 339–73).

Report from the Committee on the Petition of the Court of Directors of the Sierra Leone Company, Ordered to be printed 27th February 1804 (*P.P.* 1803–4, vol. v, pp. 81–209).

Report from The Committee to whom the Petition of the Court of Directors of the Sierra Leone Company was referred, Ordered to be printed 3rd February 1807 (*P.P.* 1806–7, vol. ii, pp. 61–70).

Extracts from the Report of the Commissioners appointed for investigating the State of the Settlements and Governments on the Coast of Africa (*P.P.* 1812, vol. x, pp. 277–96).

Papers relating to a Recruiting Depôt on the Coast of Africa, for the West India Regiments (ibid., pp. 301–10).

A Return of all Ships or Vessels, brought into any Port in the Colonies of Great Britain, and Condemned therein, under any of the Acts for the Abolition of The Slave Trade 1808–1812 (*P.P.* 1813–14, vol. xii, pp. 321–4).

Further Papers relating to Captured Negroes Enlisted, and to the Recruiting of Negro Soldiers in Africa, for the West India Regiments (ibid., pp. 345–64).

Report from the Select Committee on Papers relating to the African Forts 1816 (*P.P.* 1816, vol. vii B).

Papers relating to the Slave Trade (*P.P.* 1817, vol. xvii, pp. 205–16; 1819, vol. xviii, pp. 427–532).

An Account of the Number of Slaves Captured and Condemned at Sierra Leone, from 5th January 1814 to 21st April 1823; showing The Number seized in each Year, how disposed of, &c. (*P.P.* 1824, vol. xxiv, pp. 21–2).

An Account of the Number of Slaves Captured and Condemned at Sierra Leone, from 5th January 1814 to 5th January 1824, &c. stating the Disposal of the Slaves, &c. (*P.P.* 1825, vol. xxv, pp. 913–18).

Accounts relating to the Duties, Exports, Imports; Population; Schools, Churches, Marriages; &c. of the Colony of Sierra Leone (ibid., pp. 919–59).

Papers relating to the Slave Trade: Correspondence between the Admiralty and Naval Officers, &c. November 1825–July 1827 (*P.P.* 1828, vol. xxvi, pp. 87–122).

Correspondence with Foreign Powers, relating to the Slave Trade 1826–1827 (*P.P.* 1826–7, vol. xxvi, pp. 301–482); *1828* (*P.P.* 1829, vol. xxvi, pp. 327–461).

A Return of the Number of the Population in Sierra Leone, by the latest Returns; distinguishing the Number of each Class, and the Liberated Africans, from the other African Residents (*P.P.* 1829, vol. xxv, pp. 23–4).

Returns of the Number of Slaves Captured, and brought into Sierra Leone, and Emancipated there, in each Year, since the 1st of January 1808; stating the Vessels of the respective Countries in which they were captured; also, the Number of Slaves received into the Colony from 1808 to 1819, prior to the Establishment of the Court of Mixed Commission (ibid., pp. 25–8).

Report from the Select Committee on the Settlements of Sierra Leone and Fernando Po (*P.P.* 1830, vol. x, pp. 405–546).

Charge delivered by Mr. Chief Justice Jeffcott to the Grand Jury of Sierra Leone, on the Subject of the Slave Trade, with Correspondence thereon (P.P. 1831–2, vol. xlvii, pp. 489–530).

Report from the Select Committee on Aborigines (British Settlements); with the Minutes of Evidence, Appendix and Index (P.P. 1837, vol. vii, pp. 1–304).

Report from the Select Committee on the Accounts of Colonial Receipt and Expenditure; with the Minutes of Evidence, Appendix and Index (ibid., pp. 305–543).

Accounts of all Vessels Captured and Condemned for Violating the Treaties and Acts for the Suppression of the Slave Trade, from 1831 to 1837 (House of Lords, Sessional Papers 1837–8, vol. xvi, pp. 1–16).

Returns of the Number of Slaves on Board the Slave Ships captured during the last Ten Years, and the Number landed at Sierra Leone or elsewhere, &c. (ibid., pp. 31–2).

Statistical Reports on the Sickness, Mortality, & Invaliding, among the troops in Western Africa, St. Helena, the Cape of Good Hope, and the Mauritius; prepared from the records of the Army Medical Department and War-Office Returns [by Major Alex. M. Tulloch] (P.P. 1840, vol. xxx, pp. 135–252).

Papers relative to the West Indies, 1841, Part II, Jamaica (P.P. 1841, 2nd Section, vol. iii, pp. 325–733).

Papers relative to the West Indies: Antigua, Trinidad, St. Lucia, Grenada, 1841–2 (P.P. 1842, vol. xxix, pp. 351–530).

Report from the Select Committee on West India Colonies; together with the Minutes of Evidence, Appendix, and Index (P.P. 1842, vol. xiii).

Extracts of any Correspondence relative to Emigration, &c. (P.P. 1842, vol. xxxi, pp. 49–608).

Returns of Vessels which have been adjudicated in the Courts of Mixed Commission at Sierra Leone, from 1830 to 1841, &c. (P.P. 1842, vol. xliv, pp. 513–30).

Return of the Number of Vessels Employed on the West African Station since 1828; —also Return of Slave Vessels Captured by Her Majesty's Cruisers since 1831, and the Disposal of the Slaves (ibid., pp. 531–42).

Further Return of Slave Vessels brought before the Courts of Mixed Commission for Adjudication, &c., between 1 January 1840 and 31 December 1841, &c. (ibid., pp. 551–60).

Return of the Number of Patients received into Kissy Hospital, Sierra Leone, (the Hospital attached to the Liberated African Department), with the Nature of the Diseases as far as reported; together with the Number discharged Cured, and the Number of Deaths there, for the Years 1835 to 1842 inclusive (P.P. 1844, vol. xxxiv, pp. 257–60).

Correspondence relative to Emigration of Labourers to the West Indies and the Mauritius, from the West Coast of Africa, the East Indies, and China (P.P. 1844, vol. xxxv, pp. 297–597).

Returns of Cases adjudged under Slave Trade Treaties, and Number of Slaves Emancipated in consequence, &c. (P.P. 1845, vol. xlix, pp. 589–634).

Returns, showing the Number of Free Emigrants into Jamaica, British Guiana, Trinidad and the Mauritius, since the Abolition of Slavery in 1834; the Number of Liberated Africans, and their Destination; and the Number of Emigrant Labourers now ordered by the above Colonies (P.P. 1847, vol. xxxix, pp. 15–18).

Reports made in 1844 and 1845, by Mr. R. G. Butts and Mr. Robert Guppy, as Commissioners of Inquiry into the Subject of Emigration from Sierra Leone to the West Indies (P.P. 1847–8, vol. xliv, pp. 23–170).

Return of the Number of Slaves captured in each Year since January 1810, &c. (*P.P.* 1847–8, vol. lxiv, pp. 1–2).

Returns of the Number of Vessels Captured, &c. *during the Years 1846 and 1847 respectively; And of the Number of Slaves Landed at Sierra Leone*, &c., *and then Liberated, in each of the Years from 1832 to 1847, both inclusive* (ibid., p. 3).

[Four] *Reports from the Select Committee on the Slave Trade; together with the Minutes of Evidence and Appendix* (*P.P.* 1847–8, vol. xxii).

Report from the Select Committee of the House of Lords, on the African Slave Trade, with Minutes of Evidence, Appendix and Index, Session 1849 (*P.P.* 1850, vol. ix, pp. 1–584).

Extracts of any Correspondence with the Secretary of State for the Colonies, relative to the Emigration of Labourers from Sierra Leone and St. Helena to the West Indies (*P.P.* 1850, vol. xl, pp. 271–697).

A Return of all Vessels, their Names and Tonnage, captured (on suspicion of being engaged in Slave Trade), from 1840 to 1848 (*P.P.* 1850, vol. lv, pp. 89–110).

Correspondence with the British Commissioners, at Sierra Leone, The Havannah, Rio de Janeiro, and Surinam, relating to the Slave Trade 1822, 1823 (*P.P.* 1823, vol. xix, pp. 311–468); *1823, 1824* (*P.P.* 1824, vol. xxiv, pp. 215–426); *1824–5* (*P.P.* 1825, vol. xxvii, pp. 281–461), *1825–6* (*P.P.* 1826, vol. xxix, pp. 299–393); *1826–7* (*P.P.* 1826–7, vol. xxvi, pp. 127–300); *1827* (*P.P.* 1828, vol. xxvi, pp. 281–448); *1828* (*P.P.* 1829, vol. xxvi, pp. 131–325); *1829* (*P.P.* 1830, vol. xxxiii, pp. 23–174); *1830* (*P.P.* 1831, vol. xix, pp. 321–462); *1831* (*P.P.* 1831–2, vol. xlvii, pp. 533–679); *1832* (*P.P.* 1833, vol. xliii, pp. 1–104); *1833* (*P.P.* 1834, vol. xliv, pp. 573–644); *1834* (*P.P.* 1835, vol. li, pp. 1–168); *1835* (*P.P.* 1836, vol. l, pp. 1–372); *1836* (*P.P.* 1837, vol. liv, pp. 1–375); *1837* (*P.P.* 1837–8, vol. l, pp. 1–180, Further Series, pp. 181–285); *1838–9* (*P.P.* 1839, vol. xlviii, pp. 1–212, vol. xlix, pp. 99–263); *1839–40* (*P.P.* 1840, vol. xlvi, pp. 9–315, 317–414, 1841, vol. xxx, pp. 1–371); *1841* (*P.P.* 1842, vol. xlii); *1842* (*P.P.* 1843, vol. lviii, pp. 17–345).

Correspondence with the British Commissioners at Sierra Leone, Havana, Rio de Janeiro, Surinam, Cape of Good Hope, Jamaica, Loanda, and Boa Vista, relating to the Slave Trade 1843 (*P.P.* 1844, vol. xlviii, pp. 1–496); *1844* (*P.P.* 1845, vol. xlix, pp. 1–403); *1845* (*P.P.* 1846, vol. l, pp. 5–818).

Correspondence with the British Commissioners at Sierra Leone, Havana, Rio de Janeiro, Surinam, Cape of Good Hope, Jamaica, Loanda, and Boa Vista, and Proceedings of British Vice-Admiralty Courts, relating to the Slave Trade 1846 (*P.P.* 1847, vol. lxvii, pp. 85–493).

Correspondence with the British Commissioners at Sierra Leone, Havana, Rio de Janeiro, Surinam, Cape of Good Hope, Jamaica, Loanda, and Boa Vista, Proceedings of British Vice-Admiralty Courts, and Reports of Naval Officers relating to the Slave Trade, 1 Jan. 1847 to 31 Mar. 1848 (*P.P.* 1847–8, vol. lxiv, pp. 133–485).

Correspondence with the British Commissioners at Sierra Leone, Havana, the Cape of Good Hope, Jamaica, Loanda, and the Cape Verd Islands; and Reports from British Vice-Admiralty Courts, and from British Naval Officers, relating to the Slave Trade, 1 Apr. 1848 to 31 Mar. 1849 (*P.P.* 1849, vol. lv, pp. 1–315); *1 Apr. 1849 to 31 Mar. 1850* (*P.P.* 1850, vol. lv, pp. 111–426); *1 Apr. 1850 to 31 Mar. 1851* (*P.P.* 1851, vol. lvi, Part I, pp. 163–600); *1 Apr. 1851 to 31 Mar. 1852* (*P.P.* 1852–3, vol. ciii, Part I, pp. 17–396).

Correspondence with the British Commissioners at Sierra Leone, Havana, the Cape of Good Hope, and Loanda; and Reports from British Vice-Admiralty Courts, and from British Naval Officers, relating to the Slave Trade, 1 Apr. 1852 to 31 Mar. 1853 (*P.P.* 1852–3, vol. ciii, Part III, pp. 1–199); *1 Apr. 1853 to 31 Mar. 1854* (*P.P.* 1854, vol. lxxiii, pp. 1–222); *1 Apr. 1854 to 31 Mar. 1855* (*P.P.* 1854–5, vol. lvi, pp. 1–177); *1 Apr. 1855 to 31 Mar. 1856* (*P.P.* 1856, vol. lxii, pp. 1–165).

Abstract of the Acts of Parliament for abolishing the Slave Trade, and of the Orders in Council founded on them. London, 1810.

Colonial Land and Emigration Commission, *First General Report 1840* to *Fifteenth General Report 1855.* London, 1843–55.

Emigration Commission, *Sixteenth General Report 1856* to *Thirty-third General Report 1873.* London, 1856–73.

British and Foreign State Papers 1872–3, vol. lxiii. London, 1879.

Selections from Colonial Medical Reports for 1898 and 1899, Colonial Reports, Miscellaneous, No. 16. Cd. 614. London, 1901.

Substance of the Report of the Courts of Directors of the Sierra Leone Company to the General Court, held at London on Wednesday the 19th of October, 1791. London, 1791.

The same (2nd ed.), abbreviated but *to which is added a Postscript.* London, 1792.

Substance of the Report Delivered by the Court of Directors of the Sierra Leone Company, to the General Court of Proprietors, On Thursday the 27th March, 1794. London, 1794.

Substance of the Report of the Court of Directors of the Sierra Leone Company, Delivered to the General Court of Proprietors, On Thursday the 26th February, 1795. London, 1795.

Substance of the Report of the Court of Directors of the Sierra Leone Company, Delivered to the Court of Proprietors, On Wednesday the 30th March, 1796. London, 1796.

Substance of the Report, Delivered by the Court of Directors of the Sierra Leone Company, to the General Court of Proprietors, On Thursday, the 29th March, 1798, With an Index to this, and all the preceding Reports. London, 1798.

Substance of the Report Delivered by the Court of Directors of the Sierra Leone Company, to the General Court of Proprietors, On Thursday the 26th March, 1801, With which is Incorporated the Substance of the Reports for the two preceding Years. London, 1801.

Substance of the Report Delivered by the Court of Directors of the Sierra Leone Company, to the General Court of Proprietors, On Thursday the 29th March, 1804. London, 1804.

Substance of the Report Delivered by the Court of Directors of the Sierra Leone Company, to the General Court of Proprietors, On Thursday the 24th of March, 1808. London, 1808.

Special Report of the Directors of the African Institution, made at the Annual General Meeting, on the 12th of April, 1815, respecting the Allegations contained in a Pamphlet entitled 'A Letter to William Wilberforce, Esq. &c. by R. Thorpe, Esq. &c.' London, 1815.

Continuation of the Appendix to the Second Report of the Committee on African Instruction. London, 1824.

Proceedings of the General Anti-Slavery Convention, called by the Committee of the British and Foreign Anti-Slavery Society, and held in London, from Friday, June 12th, to Tuesday, June 23rd, 1840. London, 1841.

Yellow Fever Commission (West Africa), *Second Report*. London, 1914.

ARCHIBALD, Ex-Governor, 'Story of Deportation of Negroes from Nova Scotia to Sierra Leone', read 12 Mar. 1885, *Collections of the Nova Scotia Historical Society, for the Years 1889–91*, vol. vii, pp. 129–54. Halifax, 1891.

GEORGE AUGUSTIN, *History of Yellow Fever*. New Orleans, 1909.

JAMES BANDINEL, Foreign Office, *Some Account of the Trade in Slaves from Africa as connected with Europe and America*, &c. London, 1842.

CAPTAIN PHILIP BEAVER, R.N., *African Memoranda: Relative to an Attempt to Establish a British Settlement on the Island of Bulama, on the Western Coast of Africa, in the year 1792*, &c. London, 1805.

CHARLES BOOTH, *Zachary Macaulay, His Part in the Movement for the Abolition of the Slave Trade and of Slavery*. London, 1934.

JAMES BOYLE, Colonial Surgeon to Sierra Leone, Surgeon R.N., *A Practical Medico-Historical Account of the Western Coast of Africa*. London, 1831.

D. BRYMNER, Dominion Archivist, 'The Jamaica Maroons, How they came to Nova Scotia—How they left it', *Transactions of the Royal Society of Canada*, Second Series, 1895–6, vol. i, Section II, pp. 81–90.

ALEXANDER BRYSON, M.D., *Report on the Climate and Principal Diseases of the African Station*; Compiled from Documents in the Office of the Director-General of the Medical Department, and from other Sources, in Compliance with the Directions of the Right Honorable the Lords Commissioners of the Admiralty, under the immediate Direction of Sir William Burnett, M.D. London, 1847.

CAPTAIN F. W. BUTT-THOMPSON, *Sierra Leone in History and Tradition*. London, 1926.

THOMAS FOWELL BUXTON, *The African Slave Trade and its Remedy*. London, 1840.

(CAMPBEL), *Reasons against giving a Territorial Grant to a Company of Merchants, to Colonize and Cultivate the Peninsula of Sierra Leona, on the Coast of Africa*. London, 1791.

COLONEL J. E. CAULFEILD, *One Hundred Years' History of the 2nd Batt. West India Regiment from Date of Raising 1795 to 1898*. London, 1899.

DR. ROBERT CLARKE, Senior Assistant Surgeon to the Colony of Sierra Leone, *Sierra Leone, A Description of the Manners and Customs of the Liberated Africans*, &c. London (1843).

Diary of Lieutenant J. Clarkson, R.N. (Governor, 1792), *Sierra Leone Studies*, No. VIII, Mar. 1927.

THOMAS CLARKSON, *The History of the Rise, Progress, and Accomplishment of the Abolition of the African Slave-Trade by the British Parliament*. 2 vols. London, 1808.

R. COUPLAND, 'The Abolition of the Slave Trade', *The Cambridge History of the British Empire*, vol. ii, pp. 188–216. London, 1940.

J. J. CROOKS (Major), Late Colonial Secretary, Sierra Leone, *A Short History of Sierra Leone*. Dublin, 1900.

— —, *A History of the Colony of Sierra Leone, Western Africa*. Dublin, 1903.

— —, *Historical Records of the Royal African Corps*. Dublin, 1925.

R. C. DALLAS, *The History of the Maroons, from their Origin to the Establishment of their chief Tribe at Sierra Leone,* &c. 2 vols. London, 1803.

BRYAN EDWARDS, *The History, Civil and Commercial, of the British Colonies in the West Indies.* 1st ed., 2 vols., London, 1793; 3rd ed., 3 vols. London, 1801.

MAJOR A. B. ELLIS, *The History of the First West India Regiment.* London, 1885.

L. E. C. EVANS, 'An Early Constitution of Sierra Leone, With an Introduction', *Sierra Leone Studies,* No. XVIII, Nov. 1932, pp. 26–77.

ANNA MARIA FALCONBRIDGE, *Two Voyages to Sierra Leone, during the Years 1791–2–3, In a Series of Letters,* &c. London, 1794.

LIEUTENANT FORBES, R.N., *Six Months' Service in the African Blockade, from April to October, 1848, in Command of H.M.S. Bonetta.* London, 1849.

WILLIAM FOX, *The Western Coast of Africa: Comprising Suggestions on the Best Means of Exterminating the Slave Trade;* &c. London, 1851.

CLAUDE GEORGE, *The Rise of British West Africa, comprising the Early History of the Colony of Sierra Leone, the Gambia, Lagos, Gold Coast etc. etc.* London, 1904.

JOHN GRANT, Late Member of the Council in the Colony of Sierra Leone, *An Account of some recent Transactions in the Colony of Sierra Leone,* &c. London, 1810.

EARL LESLIE GRIGGS, *Thomas Clarkson, The Friend of Slaves.* London, 1936.

DR. JAMES AFRICANUS B. HORTON, Staff Assistant-Surgeon of H.M. Forces in West Africa, *Political Economy of British Western Africa,* &c. London (1865).

E. G. INGHAM, Bishop of Sierra Leone, *Sierra Leone after a Hundred Years.* London, 1894.

DR. R. H. KENNAN, Senior Medical Officer, Sierra Leone, *Freetown 1800 to 1870, From a Sanitarian Point of View,* read before the Dublin University Biological Association, 13 Jan. 1910. Dublin, 1910.

— —, 'Street and Place Names in and around Freetown', *Sierra Leone Studies,* No. IX, Aug. 1927, pp. 9–34.

VISCOUNTESS KNUTSFORD, *Life and Letters of Zachary Macaulay.* London, 1900.

J. J. LAMPREY, Surgeon Army Medical Staff, 'Outbreak of Yellow Fever in Sierra Leone, 1884', *The British Medical Journal* 1885, vol. ii, pp. 594–7.

E. C. P. LASCELLES, *Granville Sharp and the Freedom of Slaves in England.* London, 1928.

PETER LEONARD, Surgeon, R.N., *Records of a Voyage to the Western Coast of Africa, in His Majesty's Ship Dryad, and of the Service on that Station for the Suppression of the Slave Trade, in the Years 1830, 1831, and 1832.* Edinburgh, 1833.

SAMUEL LEWIS, *The Agricultural Position of Sierra Leone.* Liverpool, 1881.

EDWARD LONG, *The History of Jamaica, or General Survey of the Antient and Modern State of that Island,* &c. 3 vols. London, 1774.

T. C. LUKE, 'Some Notes on the Creoles and their Land', *Sierra Leone Studies,* No. XXI, Jan. 1939, pp. 53–66.

KENNETH MACAULAY, Member of Council at Sierra Leone, *The Colony of Sierra Leone Vindicated from the Misrepresentations of Mr. Macqueen of Glasgow.* London, 1827.

ZACHARY MACAULAY, *A Letter to His Royal Highness the Duke of Gloucester, President of the African Institution, occasioned by a Pamphlet lately published*

by Dr. Thorpe, late Judge of the Colony of Sierra Leone, entitled 'A Letter to William Wilberforce, Esq.' &c. &c. 2nd ed., enlarged. London, 1815.

(ZACHARY MACAULAY), *An Exposure of some of the Numerous Misstatements and Misrepresentations contained in a Pamphlet commonly known by the Name of Mr. Marryatt's Pamphlet, entitled 'Thoughts on the Abolition of the Slave Trade [&c.]'.* London, 1816.

DAVID MACPHERSON, *Annals of Commerce, &c., from the earliest Accounts to the Meeting of the Union Parliament in January 1801.* 4 vols. London, 1805.

JAMES M'QUEEN, *A Fourth Letter to R. W. Hay, Esq. &c. &c. in Reply to Mr. Kenneth Macaulay's 'Sierra Leone Vindicated'.* Glasgow, 1827.

— —, *A Geographical Survey of Africa, &c., to which is prefixed, A Letter to Lord John Russell, regarding the Slave Trade, and the Improvement of Africa.* London, 1840.

(JOSEPH MARRYATT), *Thoughts on the Abolition of the Slave Trade, and Civilization of Africa; with Remarks on the African Institution, &c.* London, 1816.

JOSEPH MARRYATT, M.P., Agent for Grenada, *More Thoughts, occasioned by Two Publications which the Authors call 'An Exposure [see Zachary Macaulay above]' and 'A Defence of the Bill for the Registration of Slaves'.* 2nd ed. London, 1816.

P. H. MARTEROY, 'Freetown 1899–1938', *Sierra Leone Studies*, No. XXI, Jan. 1939, pp. 81–7.

EVELINE C. MARTIN, *The British West African Settlements 1750–1821, A Study in Local Administration.* London, 1927.

R. MONTGOMERY MARTIN, *History of the British Possessions in the Indian & Atlantic Oceans, &c., The British Colonial Library,* vol. x. London, 1837.

— —, *The British Colonies; Their History, Extent, Condition, and Resources,* Vol. IV: *Africa and the West Indies.* London (1852).

WILLIAM LAW MATHIESON, *Great Britain and the Slave Trade 1839–1865.* London, 1929.

LESLIE PROBYN, Governor of Sierra Leone, 'Sierra Leone and the Natives of West Africa', *Journal of the African Society 1907*, pp. 250–8.

F. HARRISON RANKIN, *The White Man's Grave: A Visit to Sierra Leone, in 1834.* 2 vols. London, 1836.

GRANVILLE SHARP, *Short Sketch of Temporary Regulations (until better shall be proposed) for the Intended Settlement on the Grain Coast of Africa, near Sierra Leona.* London, 1786.

— —, *Free English Territory in Africa.* (1790.)

WILLIAM WHITAKER SHREEVE, *Sierra Leone: The Principal British Colony on the Western Coast of Africa.* London, 1847.

HENRY SMEATHMAN, *Plan of a Settlement to be made near Sierra Leona, on the Grain Coast of Africa, &c.* London, 1786.

ROBERT THORPE, Chief Justice of Sierra Leone, and Judge of the Vice Admiralty Court in that Colony, *A Letter to William Wilberforce, Esq. M.P. Vice President of the African Institution, containing Remarks on the Reports of the Sierra Leone Company, and African Institution, &c.* 3rd ed. London, 1815.

— —, *A Reply 'Point by Point' to the Special Report of the Directors of the African Institution.* London, 1815.

— —, *Postscript to the Reply 'Point by Point;' containing an Exposure of the Misrepresentation of the Treatment of the Captured Negroes at Sierra Leone; and other Matters arising from the Ninth Report of the African Institution.* London, 1815.

George Otto Trevelyan, *Life and Letters of Lord Macaulay*. 2 vols. London, 1913.

F. A. J. Utting, formerly Normal Master and Lecturer in History at Fourah Bay College, Sierra Leone, *The Story of Sierra Leone*. London, 1931.

C. B. Wadstrom, *An Essay on Colonization, particularly applied to the Western Coast of Africa, with some Free Thoughts on Cultivation and Commerce; also Brief Descriptions of the Colonies already formed, or attempted, in Africa, including those of Sierra Leone and Bulama*. 2 vols. London, 1794-5.

Rev. Samuel Abraham Walker, *Missions in Western Africa, among the Soosoos, Bulloms, &c. being the first undertaken by the Church Missionary Society for Africa and the East*. Dublin, 1845.

— —, *The Church of England Mission in Sierra Leone; including an Introductory Account of that Colony and a Comprehensive Sketch of the Niger Expedition in the Year 1841*. London, 1847.

West-African Sketches: Compiled from the Reports of Sir G. R. Collier, Sir Charles Maccarthy, and other Official Sources. London, 1824.

Thomas Winterbottom, M.D., Physician to the Colony of Sierra Leone, *An Account of the Native Africans in the Neighbourhood of Sierra Leone; to which is added, An Account of the Present State of Medicine among them*. 2 vols. London, 1803.

The Gentleman's Magazine: And Historical Chronicle, for the Year MDCCLXXXVI, vol. lvi. London, 1786.

The Annual Register, or a View of the History, Politics, and Literature, for the Year 1792; 1793. London.

The Missionary Register for 1816 to 1827, containing the Principal Transactions of the Various Institutions for Propagating the Gospel, &c. London, 1816-27.

'Memoir of Z. Macaulay, Esq.', *The Christian Observer* 1839, pp. 756-68, 796-817. London, 1839.

GAMBIA

Government Gazette, Colony of the Gambia.

Gambia Government Gazette.

Laws and Ordinances of the British Settlements in the Gambia and their Dependencies. London, 1852.

Gambia Ordinances 1867-88; 1889-1904; 1905-15; 1916-26 (Colonial Office Library).

Ordinances of the Settlement on the Gambia, Passed in the Years between the 10th August 1818 and 15th February 1879, compiled by Algernon Montague. London, 1882.

Ordinances of the Settlement on the River Gambia from the 15th day of September 1879 to the 24th day of October 1882, compiled by Francis Smith. London, 1886.

Ordinances of the Settlement on the River Gambia from the 6th March 1883 to 30th December 1885, &c., compiled by Francis Smith. London, 1887.

Ordinances of the Colony of the Gambia, in Force 31st July, 1900, &c., by Alexander David Russell. 2 vols. London, 1900.

Colony of the Gambia, *Ordinances, Rules, Regulations, Proclamations, &c., 1920; 1930; 1933; 1937; 1940*.

A Revised Edition of the Ordinances of the Colony of the Gambia, including Governor's Orders, &c., by Sidney Spencer Sawrey-Cookson. 2 vols. London, 1926.

A Revised Edition of the Ordinances of the Colony of the Gambia, including Governor's Orders, &c., by John Milner Gray. 3 vols. Bathurst, 1942.

Detailed account of the Census of the Population of the British Settlement on the River Gambia, taken on the 4th April 1881.
Abstract of the Census Statistics 1891.
Colony of the Gambia, *Census, 1901, Report of the Superintendent.* London, 1902.
Report and Summary of the Census of the Gambia, 1911. London.
Report and Summary of the Census of the Gambia 1921. Bathurst, 1921.
Report and Summary of the Census of the Gambia 1931. Bathurst, 1932.
Report of the Census Commissioner for Bathurst 1944. Bathurst, 1945.
The Gambia, *Report of the Senior Commissioner on the Annual Census of the Protectorate of the Gambia, 1945.* Bathurst, 1946.

Colony of the Gambia, *Report of the Department of Agriculture for the Year ended March 31st, 1931; March 31st, 1932; 31st March, 1933; for the Period 1st April, 1933 to 31st May, 1934; for the Year ending 31st May, 1935 to 31st May, 1945.* London, 1931; Bathurst, 1932–45.
Gambia, *Annual Report of Labour Department 1942; 1943.* Bathurst 1943, 1944.
Colony of the Gambia, *Annual Report on the Medical Department for the Year Ended 31st December, 1907.* (Typescript.)
Gambia, *Medical and Sanitary Report on the Colony and Medical Report on the Protectorate 1908.*
Colony of the Gambia, *Annual Report of the Medical Department for the Year 1909 to 1913.* London, 1910–14.
Colony of the Gambia, *Annual Medical and Sanitary Report for the Year 1914 to 1919.* London, 1915–20.
Colony of the Gambia, *Annual Medical Report for the Year 1920; 1921.* London.
Colony of the Gambia, *Annual Medical and Sanitary Report for the Year 1922 to 1942.* London (1923)–1931; Bathurst (1932)–1943.
The Gambia, *Report on the Medical and Health Services for the Year 1944.* Bathurst, 1945.
Annual Report on the North Bank Province, 1934 to 1939. (Typescript.)
Annual Report on the South Bank Province, 1934 to 1939. (Typescript.)
Annual Report on MacCarthy Island Province, 1934 to 1939. (Typescript.)
Annual Report of the Upper River Province 1923; 1934 to 1939. (Typescript.)

Colony of the Gambia, *Blue Book 1828 to 1941.* (1828–97, 1939–41 MS.)
Report on the Gambia Blue Book 1884; 1885. London, 1885–7.
Gambia, *Report on the Blue Book for 1886 to 1889, Colonial Possessions Reports* (1887–9), Nos. 3, 41, 61, 99. London, 1888–90.
Annual Report on the Social and Economic Progress of the People of the Gambia, 1939. Bathurst, 1940.
Second Report on the Animal Diseases of the Gambia to Colonial Office by Captain A. G. Todd, reprint from *Government Gazette, Colony of the Gambia,* 27 Apr. 1907, pp. 139–44.
Sanitary Report on Bathurst, Gambia, November 22nd to December 5th, 1910 by R. H. Kennan, Senior Sanitary Officer.
Legislative Council, *Meeting held in the Council Chamber on Tuesday, the 16th November, 1943; on Tuesday, the 25th January, 1944; on Tuesday, the 6th November, 1945.*

Sierra Leone, *Despatches from Governor McCarthy 1818* (Public Record Office, Colonial Office 267, vol. xlvii).

Extracts of Papers relating to the recent Outbreak of Cholera in the Settlement of the Gambia (*Parliamentary Papers England* 1868–9, vol. xliii, pp. 767–846).

Francis Bisset Archer, Treasurer of the Colony, *The Gambia Colony and Protectorate, An Official Handbook*. London (1905).

F.R.G.S. [Sir Richard Francis Burton], *Wanderings in West Africa from Liverpool to Fernando Po*. 2 vols. London, 1863.

William Fox, *A Brief History of the Wesleyan Missions on the Western Coast of Africa*, &c. London, 1851.

Major William Gray and the Late Staff Surgeon Dochard, *Travels in Western Africa in the Years 1818, 19, 20, and 21*, &c. London, 1825.

Earl Grey, *The Colonial Policy of Lord John Russell's Administration*. 2 vols. London, 1853.

Captain J. F. Napier Hewett, *European Settlements on the West Coast of Africa; with Remarks on the Slave-Trade and the Supply of Cotton*. London, 1862.

Sir C. P. Lucas, *A Historical Geography of the British Colonies*, Vol. III: *West Africa*. Oxford, 1913.

R. Maxwell Macbrair, *Sketches of a Missionary's Travels in Egypt, Syria, Western Africa*, &c., &c. London, 1839.

William Moister, *Memorials of Missionary Labours in Western Africa and the West Indies; with Historical and Descriptive Observations*. London, 1850.

Thomas Eyre Poole, *Life, Scenery, and Customs in Sierra Leone and the Gambia*. 2 vols. London, 1850.

Dr. John L. Todd and Dr. S. B. Wolbach, 'The Diagnosis and Distribution of Human Trypanosomiasis in the Colony and Protectorate of the Gambia, First Report of the Expedition of the Liverpool School of Tropical Medicine to the Gambia, 1911', *Annals of Tropical Medicine and Parasitology*, vol. v, pp. 245–86. Liverpool.

GOLD COAST AND TOGOLAND

Gold Coast, *Government Gazette*.

Gold Coast Gazette.

Ordinances, &c. relating to Her Majesty's Forts and Settlements on the Gold Coast. London, 1860.

Ordinances of the Settlement of the Gold Coast; Royal Charters; Acts of Parliament; Orders of Council; Treaties of the Government of the Gold Coast with the Native Chiefs, &c. &c. &c., compiled by Algernon Montagu. Published by Authority. London, 1874.

Ordinances of the Gold Coast Colony in Force June, 1898, with an Appendix containing Rules under Ordinances, Orders in Council, etc., prepared under the Authority of 'The Reprint of Statutes Ordinance, 1896,' by Sir William Brandford Griffith. 2 vols. London, 1898.

The Ordinances of the Gold Coast Colony with the Rules and Orders made thereunder in Force on the 31st Day of December, 1909. Revised Edition, prepared under the Authority of 'The Reprint of Statutes Ordinance, 1909,' by Frederick Harrison Gough. 3 vols. London, 1910.

The Ordinances of Ashanti with the Rules and Orders made thereunder in Force on the 31st Day of December, 1909. Revised Edition, prepared under the

Authority of 'The Reprint of Statutes Ordinance, 1909,' by Frederic Harrison Gough.   London, 1910.

The Laws of the Gold Coast Colony, containing the Ordinances of the Gold Coast Colony and the Orders, Proclamations, Rules, Regulations and Bye-Laws made thereunder in Force on the 31st Day of December, 1919. Revised Edition, prepared under the Authority of The Revised Edition of the Laws Ordinance, 1920, by Donald Kingdon. 3 vols. London, 1920.

The Laws of Ashanti containing the Ordinances of Ashanti and the Orders, Proclamations, Rules, Regulations and Bye-Laws made thereunder in Force on the 31st Day of December, 1919. Revised Edition, prepared under the Authority of The Revised Edition of the Laws Ordinance, 1920, by Donald Kingdon. London, 1920.

Gold Coast Ordinances 1879–92 (Colonial Office Library).

Gold Coast Colony, Ashanti and Northern Territories, *Proclamations, Orders-in-Council, Miscellaneous Orders, Rules and Orders of the Governor for the Year 1929* to *1935.* Accra.

Ordinances of the Gold Coast, Ashanti, Northern Territories, and Togoland under British Mandate 1926 to 1936. Accra.

Annual Volume of the Laws of the Gold Coast containing all Legislation enacted during the Year 1939; 1942; 1944. Accra, 1940, 1943, 1945.

The Laws of the Gold Coast Colony, containing the Ordinances of the Colony and the Orders, Proclamations, Regulations, Rules and Bye-Laws made thereunder in Force on the 1st Day of January, 1928. Revised Edition, prepared under the Authority of The Revised Edition of the Laws Ordinance, 1928, by Ernest Gardiner Smith. 3 vols. London, 1928.

The Laws of Ashanti, the British Sphere of Togoland and the Northern Territories of the Gold Coast, containing the Ordinances and the Rules, Orders, &c., made thereunder in force on the 1st Day of January, 1928. Revised Edition, prepared under the Authority of The Revised Edition of the Laws Ordinance, 1928, of Ashanti, &c. by Ernest Gardiner Smith. 2 vols. London, 1928.

The Laws of the Gold Coast (including Togoland under British Mandate), containing the Ordinances of the Gold Coast, the Gold Coast Colony, Ashanti, the Northern Territories, and Togoland under British Mandate, and Subsidiary Legislation thereunder Enacted on or before the 1st Day of September, 1936. Revised Edition, prepared under Statutory Authority by Leslie Ernest Vivian M'Carthy. 4 vols. Accra, 1937.

Report on the Census of the Gold Coast Colony for the Year 1891.

Colony of the Gold Coast, *Report on the Census for the Year 1901.* London, 1902.

Gold Coast Colony, *Census of the Population, 1911.* Accra.

Census Report 1921 for the Gold Coast Colony, Ashanti, the Northern Territories and the Mandated Area of Togoland. Accra, 1923.

The Gold Coast, 1931, Vol. I: *A Review of conditions in the Gold Coast in 1931 as compared with those of 1921, based on figures and facts collected by the Chief Census Officer of 1931, together with a Historical, Ethnographical and Sociological Survey of the People of that Country* by A. W. Cardinall, Chief Census Officer; Vol. II: *Appendices containing Comparative Returns and General Statistics of the 1931 Census.* Accra, 1932.

Gold Coast Colony, *Report on the Labour Department for the Year 1938–9* to *1944–5.* Accra 1939–45.

Sanitary and Medical Report on the Gold Coast Colony for the Year Ended 31st December, 1895. London, 1897.

Medical Report of the Gold Coast Colony for the Year Ended 31st December, 1896. London, 1897.

'Sanitary and Medical Report of the Gold Coast Colony for the Year Ended 31st December 1897' (Enclosure 15 in Gold Coast No. 318 of 25th July, 1898, pp. 171–206).

'Medical Report on the Gold Coast Colony for the Year Ended 31st December, 1898' (Enclosure 16 in Gold Coast No. 257 of 8th July, 1899, pp. 315–29).

Medical and Sanitary Report on the Gold Coast Colony for the Year Ending 31st December, 1899.

Government of the Gold Coast, *Report of the Principal Medical Officer for the Year 1900.* London, 1901.

'Medical Report on the health and sanitary condition of the Gold Coast Colony for the year 1901' (Enclosure 1 in Gold Coast No. 103 of 11th March, 1902, pp. 1–35).

Government of the Gold Coast, *Medical and Sanitary Report for the Year 1902* to *1918.* London, 1903–19.

Government of the Gold Coast, *Report on the Medical and Sanitary Departments for the Year 1919.* Accra, 1920.

Government of the Gold Coast, *Report on the Medical Department for the Year 1920; 1921; Jan. 1922–Mar. 1923; Apr. 1923–Mar. 1924.* Accra, 1921–(1924).

Government of the Gold Coast, *Report on the Medical and Sanitary Department for the Period Apr. 1924–Mar. 1925* to *Apr. 1927–Mar. 1928.* Accra.

Gold Coast Colony, *Report on the Medical and Sanitary Department for the Financial Year 1928–9; 1929–30.* Accra, 1929–30.

Gold Coast Colony, *Report on the Medical Department for the Year 1930–1* to *1933–4; 1934* to *1944.* Accra, 1931–45.

Report of the Accra Laboratory for the Year 1915. London.

Government of the Gold Coast, *Report on the Kumasi Public Health Board for the Year ended 31st March, 1927.* Accra.

Government of the Gold Coast, *Report on the Mines Department for the Year 1903–4; 1904.*

Government of the Gold Coast, *Report on the Mining Industry for the Year 1905.* London, 1906.

Government of the Gold Coast, *Report on the Gold Mining Industry for the Year 1906* to *1909.* London, 1907; Accra, 1908–10.

Government of the Gold Coast, *Report on the Mining Industry for the Year 1910* to *1918.* Accra, 1911–19.

Government of the Gold Coast, *Report on the Mining Department for the Year 1919; 1920.* Accra, 1920, 1922.

Government of the Gold Coast, *Report on the Mining Industry for the Year 1921; Jan. 1922–Mar. 1923.* Accra, 1922, 1924.

Government of the Gold Coast, *Report on the Mines Department for the Period Apr. 1923–Mar. 1924* to *1938–9.* Accra (1924)–1939.

Government of the Gold Coast, *Report on the Eastern Province* [of the Colony] *for the Year 1912; 1921.* Accra, 1913, 1922.

Gold Coast Colony, *Reports on the Eastern and Western Provinces of Ashanti for the Year 1930–1.* Accra, 1931.

Government of the Gold Coast, *Report on Registration of Births and Deaths for the Year 1919* to *1921.* Accra, 1921–2.

Government of the Gold Coast, *Report on the Births and Deaths for the Period Jan. 1922–Mar. 1923; Apr. 1923–Mar. 1924; Apr. 1924–Mar. 1925; Apr. 1925–Mar. 1926; 1926; 1927.* Accra, 1924–(1928).

Annual Summary and Report of the Principal Registrar of Births, Deaths and Burials of the Gold Coast for the Year 1928 to 1938. Accra, 1929–39.

Gold Coast Colony, *Blue Book for the Year 1846 to 1861; 1867 to 1872; 1875 to 1944.* Accra (1846–82 MS., 1939–44 typescript.)

Gold Coast, *Sanitary and Medical Reports for 1886 and 1887, Colonial Possessions Reports* (1887), No. 12. London, 1888.

Gold Coast, *Report on the Blue Book for 1888*, ibid. (1888), No. 74. London, 1889.

Gold Coast, *Sanitary and Medical Reports for 1887 and 1888*, ibid. No. 76. London, 1889.

Gold Coast, *Report on Yellow Fever in Accra March–June, 1927.* Accra, 1928.

Gold Coast Colony, *Legislative Council Debates, Session 1926–7, 22nd February, 1926.* Accra (1926).

The Gold Coast, A Review of the Events of 1920–6 and the Prospects of 1927–8 by Sir Frederick Gordon Guggisberg, Governor and Commander-in-Chief of the Gold Coast Colony and its Dependencies, Accra, 3rd March, 1927.

Address Delivered by His Excellency the Governor, Sir Alan Burns, on the occasion of the Opening of the 1943 Session of the Legislative Council 23rd February, 1943; on the occasion of the Opening of the 1944 Session of the Legislative Council 13th March, 1944. Accra.

Gold Coast Colony, *General Plan for Development in the Gold Coast* (Dispatch from Governor Sir Alan Burns to the Secretary of State for the Colonies, 26 July 1944, *Sessional Papers*, No. II of 1944). Accra, 1944.

Gold Coast Government, *The Gold Coast Handbook 1937.* London.

Statistical Abstract for the Several Colonial and other Possessions of the United Kingdom in each Year from 1850 to 1863 to 1888 to 1902. London, 1865–1903.

Colonial Office, *Reports on the Administration of Togoland under British Mandate 1920–1 to 1938.*[1] London, 1922–39.

Report by Professor W. J. Simpson on Sanitary Matters in various West African Colonies and the Outbreak of Plague in the Gold Coast. Cd. 4718 (*Parliamentary Papers England* 1909, vol. lxi, pp. 553–713).

Kolonial-Abtheilung des Auswärtigen Amts, *Medizinal-Berichte über die Deutschen Schutzgebiete für das Jahr 1903/4.* Berlin, 1905.

S. DEUTSCHMAN, 'Geographical Distribution of Human Trypanosomiasis in Africa', League of Nations, *Epidemiological Report of the Health Section of the Secretariat*, Oct.–Dec. 1936, pp. 201–18. Geneva.

G. SAUNDERS, Senior Medical Officer, Kintampo, Gold Coast, 'Public Health Conditions in Wartime: Northern Gold Coast', *The Journal of Tropical Medicine and Hygiene*, Dec. 1945–Jan. 1946, p. 157.

NIGERIA AND CAMEROONS

Government Gazette, Colony of Lagos.

Government Gazette, Protectorate of Southern Nigeria.

Southern Nigeria Government Gazette.

The Northern Nigeria Gazette.

The Nigeria Gazette.

---

[1] For varying titles see Kuczynski, *Cameroons and Togoland*, p. 554.

Ordinances of The Settlement of Lagos; Royal Charters; Acts of Parliament; Orders of Council; Treaties of the Government of Lagos with the Native Chiefs, &c. &c., compiled by Algernon Montagu. London, 1874.

Lagos Ordinances 1886–1901 (Colonial Office Library).

Ordinances, and Orders and Rules thereunder, in Force in the Colony of Lagos on December 31st, 1893. London, 1894.

Ordinances, and Orders and Rules thereunder, in Force in the Colony of Lagos on April 30th, 1901, compiled by Edwin Arney Speed. 2 vols. London, 1902.

Proclamations, Orders and Rules, Enacted during the Years 1900 and 1901, in Force in Southern Nigeria on the 31st December, 1901. London, 1902.

Southern Nigeria, *Proclamations, Orders, Rules, Gazette Notices, and Native Council Rules, 1903 ; 1904.*

Laws of the Colony of Southern Nigeria, being the Schedule to the Statute Laws Revision Ordinance, 1908, edited by Edwin Arney Speed. 2 vols. London, 1908.

Southern Nigeria, *Ordinances 1911.*

Orders in Council and Proclamations, and Rules, Regulations, Government Notices, and Orders thereunder, in Force in the Protectorate of Northern Nigeria on thè 1st Day of October, 1904, compiled under the Authority of 'The Reprint of Statutes Proclamation, 1904,' by Henry Cowper Gollan. London, 1905.

Laws of the Protectorate of Northern Nigeria, being the Schedule to the Statute Laws Revision Proclamation, 1910, edited by Edwin Arney Speed. London, 1910.

Nigeria, *Ordinances 1917; 1922.* Lagos, 1918, 1923.

Orders in Council, Regulations, Rules, Bye-laws & Notices under Ordinances of the Colony and Protectorate of Nigeria in Force on the Second Day of May, 1918, compiled by Ralph Molyneux Combe. Lagos, 1918.

Orders in Council, Regulations, Rules, and Bye-laws 1918. Lagos, 1918.

The Laws of Nigeria containing the Ordinances of Nigeria in Force on the 1st Day of January, 1923, and the Orders, Proclamations, Rules, Regulations and Bye-Laws made thereunder in Force on the 1st Day of May, 1923, and the Principal Imperial Statutes, Orders in Council, Letters Patent and Royal Instructions relating to Nigeria. Revised Edition, prepared by Donald Kingdon. 4 vols. Lagos, 1923.

1933 Supplement to the Laws of Nigeria containing the Ordinances of Nigeria enacted between the 2nd January, 1923, and the 31st December, 1932, and Subsidiary Legislation published since the 1st May, 1923, and in Force on the 1st January, 1933, prepared by the Attorney-General of Nigeria. Lagos, 1933.

Annual Volume of the Laws of Nigeria containing all Legislation enacted during the Year 1933 to 1943. Lagos, 1934–44.

Census of the Settlement of Lagos and its Dependencies for 1881 (MS.).

Colony of Lagos, *Report of the Superintendent of the Census for the Year 1891.* London, 1892.

Colony of Lagos, *Report of the Superintendent of the Census for the Year, 1901.*

Southern Nigeria, *Census Report, 1911.* Lagos 1912 (also published as 'Report on the Southern Nigeria Census, 1911', *Annual Reports of the Colony of Southern Nigeria for the Year 1910,* pp. 629–56).

Northern Nigeria, *Census Returns, 1911.* (Typescript.)

'Figures taken from the 1921 Census', *The Nigeria Gazette,* 31 Jan. 1924, pp. 41–2.

P. AMAURY TALBOT, Resident, *The Peoples of Southern Nigeria; A Sketch of their History, Ethnology and Languages, with an Abstract of the 1921 Census.* 4 vols. Oxford, 1926.

C. K. MEEK, District Officer and Census Commissioner, Nigeria, *The Northern Tribes of Nigeria; An Ethnographical Account of the Northern Provinces of Nigeria together with a Report on the 1921 Decennial Census.* 2 vols. Oxford, 1925.

Census of Nigeria, 1931. 6 vols. London, 1932–3.

Vol. I. *Nigeria.* By S. M. Jacob, Government Statistician.

Vol. II. *Census of the Northern Provinces.* By N. J. Brooke, District Officer.

Vol. III. *Census of the Southern Provinces.* By H. B. Cox, Acting Assistant District Officer.

Vol. IV. *Census of Lagos.* By H. N. G. Thompson, Acting Assistant District Officer.

Vol. V. *Medical Census Northern Provinces.* By Dr. R. C. Jones, M.O.H.

Vol. VI. *Medical Census Southern Provinces.* By Dr. J. G. S. Turner, M.O.H.

Lagos, *Sanitary Report for 1887, Colonial Possessions Reports* (1887), No. 20. London, 1888.

Lagos, *Reports on the Resources and Condition of the Western District,* ibid., No. 40. London, 1888.

Lagos, *Report on the Blue Book for 1887, 1888,* ibid. (1887, 1888) Nos. 68, 80. London, 1889, 1890.

Colony of Lagos, 'General Abstract of Registration for the year 1896', *Government Gazette, Colony of Lagos,* 31 Mar. 1897, pp. 125–34.

'Report for the Year 1900 on that Portion of the Lagos Hinterland under the Control of the Resident of Ibadan (Ibadan, Awyaw and Ife territories)', Lagos, *Annual Reports for the year 1900–1,* pp. 19–29.

Colony of Lagos, *General Abstract of Registration for the Year 1898, made under The General Registry Ordinance No. 9 of 1888.*

'Annual Report of the Registrar General of Births, Deaths, and Marriages in Lagos, 1899', *Government Gazette, Colony of Lagos,* 1 Sept. 1900, pp. 315–30.

'Annual Report of the Registrar General of Births, Marriages and Deaths in Lagos, 1900', Lagos, *Annual Reports for the year 1900–1,* pp. 76–93.

'Report on the Yaba Leper Asylum for the Financial year 1900–1, (first nine months)', ibid., pp. 149–51.

Colony of Lagos, 'Report by the Commissioners appointed to enquire into and report upon the actual extent of Infantile Mortality, past and present, in Lagos and its suburbs', *Government Gazette, Colony of Lagos,* 20 Apr. 1901, pp. 245–54.

Colony of Lagos, *Annual Report on the Medical Department for the year 1904,* ibid., 18 Oct. 1905, Supplement.

Colony of Lagos, *Vital Statistics for the year 1904,* ibid., 31 Jan. 1906, Supplement.

Southern Nigeria, *Annual Report on the Municipal Board of Health for the year 1909.* Lagos, 1910.

'Annual Report of the Lagos Municipal Board of Health, for the Year 1910' to '1912', *Annual Reports of the Colony of Southern Nigeria for the Year 1910,* pp. 83–93; *1911,* pp. 95–109; *1912,* pp. 93–114. Lagos, 1912–14.

Nigeria, *Annual Report of the Lagos Municipal Board of Health for the year 1914 to 1916.* Lagos.

Nigeria, *Annual Report of the Lagos Town Council 1917, 1918, 1928 to 1938.* Lagos 1918, 1919, 1929–39.

Nigeria, Lagos Town Council, *Annual Report of the Medical Officer of Health for the Year 1917, 1918, 1928 to 1938* (reprinted from Annual Reports of the Lagos Town Council).

Report on the Administration of the Niger Coast Protectorate, August 1891 to August 1894, Africa No. 1 (1895). C. 7596 (*Parliamentary Papers England* 1895, vol. lxxi, pp. 1–46).

Report on the Administration of the Niger Coast Protectorate, 1894–5, Africa No. 9 (1895). C. 7916 (ibid., pp. 47–68).

Report for the Year 1895–6 of the Administration of the Niger Coast Protectorate (Diplomatic and Consular Reports, Annual Series, No. 1834–*P.P.* 1897, vol. lxxxix, pp. 7–138).

Annual Report on the Niger Coast Protectorate for the Year 1896–7, Africa No. 3 (1898). C. 8775 (*P.P.* 1898, vol. lx, pp. 345–60).

Annual Report on the Niger Coast Protectorate for the Year 1897–8, Africa No. 2 (1899). C. 9124 (*P.P.* 1899, vol. lxiii, pp. 367–94).

Southern Nigeria, 'General Abstract of Registration for the Year 1903', *Government Gazette, Protectorate of Southern Nigeria*, 23 Sept. 1904, pp. 288–9.

'General Abstract of Registration in the Protectorate of Southern Nigeria (Eastern and Central Provinces) for the Year 1906', *Annual Reports of the Colony of Southern Nigeria 1906*, pp. 25–8. Lagos, 1908.

'Annual Report, Central Province, Southern Nigeria, 1906', ibid., pp. 313–51.

Southern Nigeria, 'Annual Report on the Eastern Province for the Year 1907', ibid. *1907*, pp. 19–48. Lagos, 1909.

'General Abstract of Registration in the Protectorate of Southern Nigeria for the Year 1907', ibid., pp. 133–6.

Southern Nigeria, 'Annual Report on Central Province, for the Year 1907', ibid., pp. 270–308.

Southern Nigeria, 'Annual Report on the Eastern Province for the Year ended 31st December, 1911', ibid. *1911*, pp. 121–34. Lagos, 1913.

Southern Nigeria, *Annual Medical Report for 1905* (reprinted from *Government Gazette, Protectorate of Southern Nigeria*, 13 Apr. 1906, Supplement, pp. i–x). Calabar, 1906.

Southern Nigeria, 'Annual Reports on the Medical Department, for the Year 1906', *Annual Reports of the Colony of Southern Nigeria 1906*, pp. 283–312. Lagos, 1908.

Southern Nigeria, *Annual Report on the Medical Department for the Year 1907 to 1911*. Lagos, 1909–12.

Southern Nigeria, *Annual Medical Report for the Year ending December 31st, 1912; 1913*. London, 1913, 1915.

'Medical Report for the Protectorate of Northern Nigeria from 1st January, 1900, to 31st March, 1900', 'Medical Report 1st April, 1900, to 31st March, 1901', *The Northern Nigeria Gazette*, 31 May 1901, pp. 57–61 (reprinted in *Selections from Colonial Medical Reports for 1900 and 1901*, pp. 239–46).[1]

'Annual Report on the Public Health of Northern Nigeria, with Meteorological Report for the year 1907', *The Northern Nigeria Gazette*, 30 May 1908, pp. 91–9.

'The Northern Nigeria Medical Report for 1908', ibid., 31 May 1909, pp. 98–107.

---

[1] The Medical Reports for 1903, 1904, and 1906 are printed in *Colonial Reports, Northern Nigeria 1903* (pp. 34–41), *1904* (pp. 138–47), and *1906–7* (pp. 44–9).

'The Northern Nigeria Medical Report for 1909', ibid., 31 May 1910, Supplement, pp. i–xiv.

Northern Nigeria, 'Annual Medical Report for the Year ending 31st December, 1910', ibid., 31 May 1911, pp. 127–54.

Northern Nigeria, *Annual Medical and Sanitary Report for the Year ending 31st December, 1911.* London, 1912.

Northern Nigeria, *Annual Medical Report for Year ending 31st December, 1912; 1913.* London, 1913, 1914.

Nigeria, *Annual Report on the Department of Labour, Nigeria, for the year 1944.* Lagos, 1945.

Nigeria, *Annual Medical and Sanitary Reports of the Northern and Southern Provinces for the Year ended 31st December, 1914; 1915.* London, 1915, 1916.

Nigeria, Northern Provinces, *Annual Medical and Sanitary Report for the year ending 31st December, 1916; 1918.*

Nigeria, Southern Provinces, *Annual Medical and Sanitary Report for the Year ending 31st December, 1916.*

Nigeria, *Annual Medical and Sanitary Reports for the Northern and Southern Provinces for the Year ended 31st December 1917.* London, 1918.

Nigeria, Colony and Southern Provinces, *Annual Medical and Sanitary Report for the year ending 31st December, 1918.*

Nigeria, *Annual Medical and Sanitary Report for the period 1919–21.*

Nigeria, *Annual Medical and Sanitary Report for the Year 1922 to 1929.* Lagos, 1923–(1930).

Nigeria, *Annual Medical and Health Report for the Year 1930.* Lagos (1931).

Colony and Protectorate of Nigeria, *Report on the Medical and Health Department for the Year 1931.* Lagos, 1932.

Colony and Protectorate of Nigeria, *Report on the Medical and Health Services for the Year 1932 to 1934.* Lagos, 1933–5.

Nigeria, *Annual Report on the Medical Services 1935 to 1940.* Lagos, 1936–41.

Nigeria, *Report on the Medical Services for the Year 1941 to 1944.* Lagos, 1942–6.

Annual Report on the Southern Provinces and Colony of Nigeria for the year 1926. (Lagos 1928.)

Annual Report on the Southern Provinces of Nigeria for the year 1927 to 1929; 1932 to 1938. Lagos (1928)–1940.

Nigeria, *Annual Report on the Colony for the year 1927 to 1938.* Lagos (1928)–1939.

Annual Report on the Northern Provinces of Nigeria for the year 1926 to 1938; 1941 to 1943. Lagos 1927–(1930); Kaduna (1931)–1939. (1941 to 1043 typescript.)

Nigeria, *Annual Reports for the Northern, Western, Eastern Provinces, and the Colony 1939; 1940; 1944.* Lagos, 1940, 1941, 1945.

Annual Report on the Western Provinces, 1941 to 1943. (Typescript.)

Annual Report on the Colony for the Year 1941 to 1943. (Typescript.)

Memorandum on the Taxation of Natives in Northern Nigeria by Sir F. D. Lugard, *Miscellaneous Colonial Reports* No. 40. Cd. 3309. London, 1907.

Report on Blackwater Fever in Southern Nigeria 1899–1911 by W. M. Graham. London, 1912.

Report by Sir F. D. Lugard on the Amalgamation of Northern and Southern Nigeria, and Administration, 1912–19. Cmd. 468. London, 1920.

Notes on Nassarawa Province, Nigeria, by J. C. Sciortino, Resident. London, 1920.

Report of the Commission of Inquiry appointed to Inquire into the Disturbances in the Calabar and Owerri Provinces, December, 1929. Lagos, 1930.

Aba Commission of Inquiry, *Notes of Evidence taken by the Commission of Inquiry appointed to Inquire into the Disturbances in the Calabar and Owerri Provinces, December, 1929.*

Nigeria, *Assessment Report on Buea District* by B. G. Stone, Assistant District Officer. Lagos, 1931.

Colony and Protectorate of Nigeria, *Reassessment Report on Dan Zomo District* by M. V. Backhouse, Assistant District Officer. Lagos, 1932.

Report of the Committee appointed by His Excellency the Governor to examine the methods of Direct Taxation in force in Lagos and the Colony. Lagos, 1936.

Nigeria, *Food in Relation to Health.* Lagos, 1938.

Lagos, *Blue Book for the Year 1863; 1866 to 1905.* (1863–83 MS.)

Colony and Protectorate of Southern Nigeria, *Blue Book 1906 to 1913.* Lagos, 1908–14.

Protectorate of Northern Nigeria, *Blue Book for the Year 1903 to 1906, 1908 to 1913.*

Colony and Protectorate of Nigeria, *Blue Book 1914 to 1942.* Lagos 1915–39. (1939–42 typescript.)

Nigeria, *A Ten-Year Plan of Development and Welfare for Nigeria 1946, as amended by the Select Committee of the Council and approved by the Legislative Council on 7th February 1946.* Lagos, 1946.

Nigeria, *Speech and Address by His Excellency the Governor Sir Arthur Richards to the Legislative Council 18th March, 1946.* Lagos, 1946.

Nigeria, *Estimates 1939–40 (Excluding Nigerian Railway)*; same *1946–7.* Lagos, 1939, 1946.

'Abstract of Arrangements respecting Registration of Births, Deaths, and Marriages in the British Dominions beyond the Seas', Appendix to *Sixty-Fifth Annual Report of the Registrar-General of Births, Deaths, and Marriages in England and Wales (1902).* Cd. 2003. London, 1904.

Colonial Office, *Reports on the Administration of the Cameroons under British Mandate 1921 to 1938.*[1] London, 1922–39.

League of Nations, Permanent Mandates Commission, *Minutes*, 7th Session. Geneva, 1925.

'Leprosy', *The Lancet*, 7 July 1945, pp. 24–5.

MARGERY PERHAM, *Native Administration in Nigeria.* Oxford, 1937.

SIR LEONARD ROGERS, M.D., 'Progress in the Control of Leprosy in the British Empire', *British Medical Journal*, 1 June 1946, pp. 825–8.

[1] For varying titles see Kuczynski, *Cameroons and Togoland*, pp. 553–4.

INDEX [1]

Aberdeen, Earl of, 106.

Abortions:
Deliberate *G.* 361; *G.C.* 468; *S.L.* 230, 265, 286.
FACTORS CAUSING OR PROMOTING:
Hookworm *S.L.* 230.
Malaria *G.* 364; *G.C.* 469; *N.* 682; *S.L.* 230.
Malnutrition *N.* 682.
Native medicine *N.* 683.
Over-indulgence in sexual intercourse *N.* 682.
Suckling, extended, *G.C.* 468.
Venereal diseases *G.C.* 474; *N.* 679, 682–3, 686; *S.L.* 230.
Incidence *G.* 361, 364; *G.C.* 467–9; *N.* 657, 663, 677, 679–83; *S.L.* 230, 265, 286.

Accra (*G.C.*) 136, 297, 390, 393, 395, 397, 400, 402, 407, 411, 413–14, 420, 422, 427, 430, 448–9, 452–5, 458, 461, 463, 465, 471, 474, 476–8, 480, 486, 488, 490, 493–5, 498, 500, 508, 511, 522–7, 533, 648, 794–5.

Ada (*G.C.*) 393, 395, 398, 413–14, 430, 448–9, 452, 454, 461–4, 471, 476–7, 529.

Aden, born in, *N.* 612–13.

African Institution, 19, 73–4, 76, 79, 81, 90–1, 97, 113–15, 133, 150, 154, 779, 786, 788–9.

Afzelius, Adam, 58, 69.

Age-composition *G.* 317, 324, 333, 343–5, 776–7; *G.C.* 396, 416, 429, 434–7, 441–2, 529; *N.* 555–9, 568–9, 583, 586, 589, 591, 596, 604–11, 614, 621, 760–1; *S.L.* 33–5, 70, 81, 84–5, 92, 117–18, 171–6, 185, 190, 192, 196, 237, 279. *See also under* Asiatics, Children, Europeans, Non-Africans.

Age, difficulty of determining, *G.* 312; *G.C.* 434, 451; *N.* 561; *S.L.* 173–4, 176. *See also under* Children, Infants.

Aitkin, Dr., 239, 248, 256.

Aku *S.L.* 121, 136–7, 158.

Albreda (*G.*) 308, 317, 327, 356, 363, 370.

Alcoholism *G.* 377; *G.C.* 13, 475–6, 528; *S.L.* 43–5; *W.A.* 14. *See also under* Europeans.

Alexander, James Edward, 131, 317, 364, 779.

Andrews, Edward Bullock, 407, 489.

Ankylostomiasis, *see under* Helminthic diseases.

Ante-natal care, *see under* Infant Mortality.

Arabia, born in, *N.* 612, 615; *S.L.* 196.

Arabs *G.C.* 441–2, 541; *N.* 612–14, 734; *S.L.* 192–3, 196.

Arbuckle, Dr. H. E., 249, 265.

Archer, Francis Bisset, 311, 325, 327, 368, 382, 385, 792.

Archibald, Adams G., 54–7, 61, 66, 68, 95, 787.

D'Arcy, G. A. K., 326, 328, 382, 385.

Area *G.* 330–1, 337–8; *G.C.* 404–6, 408–9, 412, 415–16, 420–1; *N.* 542, 573–7, 584, 590–1, 594, 598–9, 732; *S.L.* 33, 44, 47, 75–6, 95–6, 158–61; *W.A.* 14.

Arnett, E. J., 738.

Arthur, George, 151–2.

Asamangkese (*G.C.*), Yellow fever epidemic, 480, 493–6.

Ascension, Liberated Africans sent from *S.L.*, 116, 126.

Ashantees, *see under* Ashanti.

Ashanti, 11, 182, 389–90, 394–402, 405–6, 411, 415–37, 439–43, 455–8, 461–2, 468–9, 473–4, 485, 489, 492–3, 495, 498–510, 528, 530–1, 778, 792–4.

ASIATICS:
Age-composition *N.* 614; *S.L.* 196.
Birthplace *N.* 5; *S.L.* 4, 167, 192, 196, 286.
Census, special provisions for, *G.C.* 396–7, 400, 403.
Children *G.C.* 5; *N.* 5, 614; *S.L.* 5, 192; *W.A.* 5.
Conjugal condition *S.L.* 192, 196.
Deaths *N.* 765; *S.L.* 307.
Nationality *G.C.* 441–2; *N.* 614; *S.L.* 192–4.
Number *G.* 3; *G.C.* 3; *N.* 3, 612, 614; *S.L.* 3, 167, 171, 191–4, 196, 276; *W.A.* 2–3.
Sex *G.C.* 4, 441; *N.* 4; *S.L.* 4, 171, 192, 194, 196; *W.A.* 4–5. *See also under* Arabs, Indians, Non-Africans, Syrians.

Athy, 532.

Augustin, George, 300, 301, 787.

Australia, born in, *S.L.* 195; *N.* 613.

Australians *S.L.* 193–4.

Axim (*G.C.*) 392–3, 395, 397, 400, 411, 413–14, 420, 427, 430, 447–8, 452, 454–5, 461, 471, 489.

Babatu, 428–9, 431.

[1] *G.* = Gambia; *G.C.* = Gold Coast and Togoland; *N.* = Nigeria and Cameroons; *S.L.* = Sierra Leone; *W.A.* = West Africa.

Maxwell, Dr., 232, 242, 265.
Maynard, H. C., 738.
Maynard, Jane, 55.
Medical and Sanitary Services:
Cost *G.* 373; *G.C.* 10, 485, 503–4, 754;
N. 10, 687, 689, 718, 748, 751–2,
754; *S.L.* 250–2, 258–60; *W.A.* 10.
INADEQUATE:
for Africans in particular *G.* 375–6;
G.C. 10, 479–80, 490, 521; *N.* 686,
700–1, 748, 753; *S.L.* 239, 248–50,
252–3, 260, 304; *W.A.* 9.
for fight against special diseases *G.*
364, 373–4; *G.C.* 475, 480, 489–90,
502–3, 506–7, 512–13, 521; *N.* 685–7,
689–91, 700–2, 705, 711, 713, 715–17,
721, 749–50; *S.L.* 239, 249–50, 257–
60; *W.A.* 9–10, 12.
Hospitals *G.* 375–6; *G.C.* 479; *N.* 690,
700, 753; *S.L.* 108–9, 249–52.
in general *G.C.* 10–11, 479–80; *N.* 10,
664–5, 702, 748–54; *S.L.* 239, 248–
53; *W.A.* 10.
Medical Officers, numerically, *G.* 368;
G.C. 479–80, 489–90, 503–4, 512–13;
N. 10, 686–7, 689–90, 700–2, 711,
715–17, 721, 732, 737, 742, 749–54;
S.L. 60, 65, 68, 239, 248–53, 257,
260; *W.A.* 10.
Medical Officers, qualitatively, *G.C.*
479; *S.L.* 61–3, 248.
See also under Diseases, Knowledge of
Incidence.
Increasing need *N.* 751; *S.L.* 251–3;
W.A. 10.
VARIATIONS:
Expansion before the First World War
G.C. 479; *N.* 742, 748–9; *S.L.* 249–
50; *W.A.* 9.
Fluctuations between World Wars
G.C. 10–11, 479; *N.* 10, 751–2; *S.L.*
250–2, 258–9; *W.A.* 10.
Reductions in First World War *N.* 687,
702, 749–50, 758; *S.L.* 250, 257–8;
W.A. 9–10.
Reductions in Second World War *N.*
715, 717, 721, 752; *S.L.* 253; *W.A.*
10, 12.
Medical 'census' *N.* 8, 572, 655–7, 677–8,
680–2, 689, 691–2, 703, 744, 755–7,
797.
Meek, Charles Kingsley, 561–2, 567, 591,
597, 603, 605–6, 608, 612–14, 740,
761, 797.
Mendi *G.C.* 425; *S.L.* 38–9, 163, 172,
256, 280, 694.
Metcalfe, Charles Theophilus, 93.
Midwives *G.* 358, 380; *G.C.* 465, 522;
S.L. 265–70, 289.
Migrant Labourers *G.* 321–3, 334, 336,
366–7, 379; *G.C.* 8–9, 392, 424–9,
431–2, 434, 474–5, 481–6, 488, 506,

Migrant Labourers (*cont.*)
515–20; *N.* 656; *S.L.* 76–9, 82, 85,
95, 137, 237, 244, 246–8, 275–6, 279,
283; *W.A.* 10, 14. *See also under*
'Kroomen', Migration, internal.
Migration, internal *G.* 313–14, 316–29,
332, 336–8; *G.C.* 395, 415, 422–9,
431–3, 474–5, 483–6, 504, 515, 528;
N. 567, 606, 608, 656, 708, 730, 760;
S.L. 25, 76–9, 82, 84–6, 137, 162–4,
246–7, 255, 274–83; *W.A.* 10. *See
also under* Bathurst, Birthplace,
Freetown, Lagos, Migrant Labourers, 'Strange Farmers'.
Military:
AFRICAN:
Mortality *G.C.* 491; *S.L.* 110, 121–2,
125; *W.A.* 376.
Pensioners *G.* 325, 327–8; *S.L.* 122–5,
142, 156, 162.
Present *G.* 318, 320, 324–7, 329, 367,
373, 384; *G.C.* 411–12, 473, *N.* 548,
706, 773; *S.L.* 99, 110, 114–23, 125,
140, 142, 144–5, 147, 157, 163,
166–7, 181–2, 184.
World War, Second, *G.* 322–3, 367,
373; *N.* 704.
European *G.* 317–19, 324–7, 340, 367,
373, 384–5; *G.C.* 430, 443–4; *N.* 548,
619, 773; *S.L.* 57–60, 63, 65, 88,
117–23, 154–5, 157, 159, 178–90,
199, 247, 255, 275, 283, 286–8, 290–3,
298–9, 302–6; *W.A.* 15–16. *See also
under* Europeans.
Hospitals *G.* 375; *S.L.* 292, 298–9.
Miller, Dr., 757.
Mine labourers *G.C.* 395, 424–9, 431–2,
443, 475, 482, 486, 506, 514–21; *N.*
608, 713–17; *S.L.* 251; *W.A.* 10.
Miscarriages, *see under* Abortions.
Missionaries *G.* 324–5, 327–8, 347, 376;
G.C. 391, 397, 403–4, 410, 412, 438,
443–6, 477–8, 534–40; *N.* 561, 618–
20, 622, 708, 716–17, 745, 747, 753,
764; *S.L.* 109, 113, 127, 129, 153–6,
186, 190–1, 199, 254, 287, 294–8,
305; *W.A.* 16.
Mohammedans *G.* 355, 381–3; *G.C.* 403,
478; *N.* 562, 565, 606, 628–9, 684,
688, 738–9, 758; *S.L.* 33, 80, 120,
176–8, 229, 301. *See also under*
Fulani, Hausa, Mandingoes.
Moiser, Dr. B., 723.
Moister, William, 324, 792.
Moloney, C. Alfred, 409–10, 627, 674.
Moor, Ralph, 700, 767–8.
Morris, A. H., 416.
Morris, K. S., 502, 504, 506.
Mortality:
CAUSES:
Accidents *G.* 386, 388; *G.C.* 481–2,
515; *N.* 772; *S.L.* 121, 297.